PIETY AND PROFESSION

PIETY AND PROFESSION

American Protestant Theological Education, 1870-1970

GLENN T. MILLER

William B. Eerdmans Publishing Company
Grand Rapids, Michigan / Cambridge, U.K.

Published 2007 by
Wm. B. Eerdmans Publishing Co.
2140 Oak Industrial Drive N.E., Grand Rapids, Michigan 49505 /
P.O. Box 163, Cambridge CB3 9PU U.K.

Printed in the United States of America

12 11 10 09 08 07 7 6 5 4 3 2 1

Library of Congress Cataloging-in-Publication Data

Miller, Glenn T., 1942-
Piety and profession: American Protestant theological education, 1870-1970 /
Glenn T. Miller.
p. cm.
Includes bibliographical references.
ISBN 978-0-8028-2946-7 (pbk.: alk. paper)
1. Theology — Study and teaching — United States — History — 19th century.
2. Theology — Study and teaching — United States — History — 20th century.
3. Protestant theological seminaries — United States — History — 19th century.
4. Protestant theological seminaries — United States — History — 20th century.
I. Title.

BV4030.M55 2007
230.071′173 — dc22

2006039451

www.eerdmans.com

For Frankie

Contents

Preface

When I began work in the 1970s on the history of Protestant theological education, I was conscious of living near the end of an era. Trends in theological education that began at the end of the Civil War were coming to their end as schools, faculties, and churches began to come to terms with a new world that spoke a very different theological and ecclesiastical language. Something was in the wind, although I was not sure at the time (and am still not sure) what all of that meant. But it seemed to me that the basic chronological scheme was fixed.

Protestant theological education in the colonial period and the early nineteenth century struggled with the question of how the creeds and confessions of the churches could be reexpressed in the Enlightenment and post-Enlightenment worlds. In a profound sense this was "confessional" education, as Presbyterians, Lutherans, Episcopalians, Baptists, Methodists, and a host of emigrant churches struggled with the twin issues of theological integrity and intellectual clarity. The greatest voices of this period were, hence, theologians like the Presbyterian Charles Hodge and the energetic Baptist James P. Boyce, whose skilled, logical eye could spot a poorly constructed syllogism at a mile's distance. Emigration and religion is a vast topic, one that American religious historians have only begun to mine, but, in theological education, the perceived victory of rationalism sent thousands across the sea to establish new "cities on a hill" that might send light abroad. Both the Missouri Synod and the Christian Reformed Church represented this deep spiritual impulse. The still wide-open spaces of the new nation made it possible for many of these groups to live in comparative intellectual and social isolation from each other. As I indicated in *Piety and Intellect,* ethnicity allowed some religious groups to continue this pattern of theological education into the early twentieth century, and, not surprisingly, the memory of the earlier confessional homogeneity often influenced discussions much later. In the 1970s, for example, some Lutheran theologians anxiously debated what made Lutheran theological education Lutheran.[1] At the same time, Episcopal seminaries often continued to follow, often at considerable cost, the formation models implicit in the earlier Anglo-Catholic movement and to resist the tendency toward distance education and part-time study. The past takes a long time to die, and when custom is enshrined in social structures and human activities, its dying may take generations or even centuries.

In talking about the passing of the confessional period of theological education, we are not talking about the disappearance of older alternatives or influences. History is too fluid for that, and despite the advantages of generational analysis, humanity renews itself year by year and not decade by decade. Rather, what happens is that the points of reference for the larger discussion and, more slowly, for institutional practice shift from one set of issues to another.

Historians are used to analyzing the ways the shifting sands of context change the meanings of words, ideas, and practices. Slavery provides a graphic example. Although the ancient Roman social philosophers used many of the same words and ideas to discuss the Roman slave system that American proslavery advocates used later, the fact that the American discussion took place in a world in which the rights of humanity were better understood than in former ages gave the American discussion a repressive edge that the earlier discussion lacked. Context has even more impact on understanding theological and religious argumentation. Christianity provides its adherents with a finite number of symbols, ideas, and religious possibilities that must be reinterpreted continually. In this world the same words and phrases do not have the same meaning. To give one obvious example, the work of Thomas Aquinas in his time was a freeing and liberating opening to the new world disclosed by Islamic philosophy and the newly recovered works of Aristotle. Despite Thomas's scholastic mode of presentation, only the most intellectually insensitive could fail to feel viscerally the excitement of his formulations. To be with Thomas is to be

1. The very fact that thoughtful people feel that they need to discuss an issue indicates that the solution to the dilemma is not self-evident. In the case of "Lutheranism," this observation is particularly important. Although Lutheran scholarship had much influence on early nineteenth-century American theology and played a crucial role in the early history of the biblical guild, its influence was to grow exponentially from 1880 to 1960. During that period it was difficult, if not impossible, to find a reputable theologian who was not in dialogue, pro or con, with Continental sources. A reading knowledge of German was a presumed qualification for the doctoral degree. Perhaps the more interesting questions, at least from a historian's point of view, might have been what parts of American theological education were not touched by Lutheran precedent and how did American Lutherans respond to those elements.

with a master theologian and to enjoy the artistry of his arguments. The neo-Thomism that followed the nineteenth-century papal pronouncement that Thomas was the perpetual theologian of the church, however, was another matter. Even when the neo-Thomists used Thomas's words and methods, they often did so woodenly and artificially, and one sensed that these theologians were often defending the walls rather than launching a new intellectual offensive. Not surprisingly, the most brilliant advocates of neo-Thomism, such as Karl Rahner, could not resist studying the transcendental philosophy of Kant as well!

In short, the contention of this volume is that theological education in the century from 1870 to 1970 underwent an important shift in the points of reference that determined the discussion. These points of reference included the new specialized university with its highly developed academic guilds, the biological and physical sciences and new engineering, the historical critical approach to the Bible, the new sociology and psychology, and the dynamics of industrial capitalist society with its concomitant large cities, mass transportation systems, and mass population shifts. This new context was one in which peacetime prosperity became more glorious and wartime distress more horrible. History had no precedent for the increasingly high standards of living that many Americans experienced, and no precedent for the destruction of the two great world wars. Organization was another feature of this society. The railroad, the telegraph, and later the telephone and radio made possible levels of human cooperation that would have seemed utopian in the early nineteenth century. The master of this new America, "the professional," was the person who could blend the various elements of this new modern world into an effective and efficient presence in the world.

This is the larger matrix in which American Protestant theological educators found themselves. They wanted both the symbols and the trappings of this brave new world. The doctorate, for example, became a sine qua non for teaching at the better seminaries, and theologians were anxious to establish the "scholarly" character of their now-diverse crafts. Seminaries were passionately concerned about how to relate the faith to the new dynamic capitalist order. Whether the proposed solution was a new theological ethic, such as the social gospel, evangelistic crusades, or social service, a common passion united those who thought seriously about such things. The dominant image of the Protestant minister during the period — the religious professional — itself suggested the schools' and their denominational sponsors' embrace of this world. This was a world in which those who were educated to the highest degree possible were able to unlock its mysteries and lead the faith into difficult waters. If the schools were not always clear about what they meant by such terms as "professional," "well-educated," or "trained," they were unanimous in their embrace of the idea that schooling was the key that would unlock the future of the church. Even evangelism and counseling had their appropriate method, their appropriate subject matter, and their distinctive ethos. Above all, the schools wanted for their graduates and for themselves the high status that Americans gave to the expert, to the person who knew what needed to be done and how to do it. The minister should be at least as skilled in the cure of souls as the modern physician, who had received similar professional training, was in the cure of bodies.

Social and cultural forms are rarely directly reflected in the thought of specific individuals or groups. The human mind serves as both a sponge and a filter for ideas, and this was particularly true in an America that revered the right and capacity of individuals to think and choose for themselves. While it is overly simple, one might say that the ancient Christian value of believing what the church believes, whether implicitly or explicitly, gave way to the belief that individuals, groups, and parties had the right to interpret the faith for themselves and by their own canons. One mark of this was that conservatives often saw themselves not simply as defenders of the faith once delivered, but as people who represented an important theological option!

The idea that certain aspects of American life were points of reference for theological education allows us to deal with two paradoxical results of our study: the often confusing response of various theological schools and movements to modernity, and the way certain theological ideas both lost and gained content as they were expressed in differing contexts.

First, whatever might be true of religion on the world stage, few American religious groups have been able to be consistently antimodern. In fact, at least as seen in their theological institutions, American religious groups have helped themselves to the smorgasbord of modern life in ways that often seem inconsistent or even contradictory. Very conservative Bible schools and seminaries, for example, have often been remarkably open to modern educational theories and techniques, and they have often innovated, in some cases radically, with new methods of education. American conservatives have often had more media savvy than their liberal opponents and have been willing to use whatever media were available, ranging from the mail to the radio and later television, to educate religious leaders. Similarly, liberal schools have often clung to dated understandings of the minister and his or her role in society long after that role had declined or even disappeared. Only a handful of churches wanted the modern version of the scholarly minister — a teacher of religion as thoroughly at home in technical scholarship as in the social world of the congregation — to be their pastor. Most wanted someone who could make religion relevant, not to the abstractions of the academy, but to the ordinary lives of men and women. Consequently, one has the paradox that some theological seminaries that took the contemporary intellectual world with an almost deadly earnestness were also experienced by some of their graduates as almost hopelessly "irrelevant." In contrast, the graduates of those schools that intentionally ignored contemporary intellectual issues often saw their alma maters as "practical," "rooted in experience," and "up-to-date."

Second, modern experience changed the meaning of core theological ideas and affirmations. In the 1920s the question of the historicity of the virgin birth was at the center of many debates about the ordination of particular people or the theological orientation of certain seminaries. The church historian, aware of the centrality of this teaching to the early church parents and the great medieval doctrinal syntheses, expects to find a profound discussion of the relationship of flesh and logos or, at least, of the meaning and possibility of incarnation. Instead, the discussion appears to have been part of an elaborate theological code that was as much about the possibility of direct divine intervention in nature as it was about Mary or Jesus. In this context the seemingly historical character of the debate was less important than the implications of affirming or not affirming the teaching itself.[2] But this understanding of the role of the virgin birth in the liberal-fundamentalist battle of the 1920s and 1930s points to the depth of the common understanding of the issues that united both parties. The issue was whether biblical supernaturalism was a necessary part of faith, and every discussion sooner or later returned to this core disagreement.

Points of reference, further, are those things that one must discuss even if one wishes to disagree with the current theological consensus. H. Richard Niebuhr, arguably the most adept American theologian of the period, was always careful to separate his decision to take a different course from most "liberal" theology from his equally serious determination to take the modern world with utmost seriousness. Similarly, Carl F. H. Henry, the most notable American conservative after Machen, felt that he had to write about the "uneasy conscience" of modern fundamentalism and that he had to participate as fully as possible in the current theological discussion. Even many radical fundamentalists insisted on the harmony of their position with science "rightly understood." In a similar vein, it is no accident that the liberal theologian William Adams Brown was also a sensitive and perceptive participant in the ecumenical movement, seeking to understand those, including the fundamentalists, with whom

2. Both Harnack and Machen reached similar conclusions about the age of the passages that related the stories of the virgin birth, and both located these stories in the Palestinian strata of the New Testament.

he most vigorously disagreed. What is interesting to the historian is that one cannot find any serious theological thinkers, even those most apparently opposed to the modern constellation of ideas, that did not feel that they had to discuss these issues, pro or con.

The emphasis on the importance of these points of reference reflects my own conviction that Protestant theological education from 1870 to 1970 formed a somewhat coherent and understandable whole. Indeed, one of the most remarkable marks of the period is what and who is not present in the story. In simple terms, seminaries and Bible schools were ***largely white, male*** institutions that taught an understanding of ministry that was directly and easily related to the standards of success or failure in contemporary American culture. While there were some African American theological institutions, these schools often appeared next to their white counterparts in much the same relationship as the "Negro" leagues in baseball had with their big-league counterparts. And the walls between these institutions were maintained with a determination that should cause deep embarrassment even today. Both Benjamin E. Mays and Howard Thurman, who deserve inclusion on any list of the most able American religious leaders of the early twentieth century, were rejected by Newton Seminary, and both experienced discrimination at the schools that finally accepted them, Mays at the University of Chicago and Thurman at Colgate Rochester. Women, if admitted at all, were often confined to a "pink ghetto" that assumed they would not become ordained religious leaders. Georgia Harkness, a woman theologian of great heart and intellectual and personal strength, was never ordained by her denomination, despite her importance as an exponent of Methodist spirituality. Liberal did not mean accepting!

I have not attempted in this manuscript to tell the history of parallel ways of preparing religious leaders. It is possible to argue that every religious institution has ways of preparing leaders and that a good history of "theological" education would include these. I have not written such a history for several reasons. First, I do not have sufficient knowledge of all the various ins and outs of differing religious institutions in America to write such a book. American religion, even in the so-called period of the Protestant establishment, is a Joseph's coat of many colors and of multiple convictions and institutions. Like many historians, I have had to specialize within my discipline and my subdiscipline in order to get some control over the sources. I hope others may use what I have written and what they learn from their own researches to more thoroughly investigate all the ways in which churches and religious societies prepare their leaders.

Second, and perhaps equally important, I am not sure the popular (and for seminaries profitable) identification of theological education and ministerial preparation is necessarily cogent. My own understanding of ***Protestant*** theological education is that it involves at least an attempt at a careful and detailed study, including critique, of the Christian faith, or, to use fellow Baptist E. Y. Mullins's cogent phrase, the "Christian religion in its doctrinal expression."[3] While I firmly believe in theological education as part of the life of the ministry, I can conceive of forms of ordained and lay Protestant leadership that require little more than a superficial knowledge of the Bible, some awareness of how to conduct a meeting, and a good heart. Further, American history provides example after example of "spirit-filled" people who, armed with their own passionate experience and a sense of love and compassion for others, spread vital religion. Theologically, I am confident that many have been brought to a saving knowledge of Jesus Christ by just such a ministry. Further, I know from experience that often someone ministering in the rural American South has more need of "street smarts" about how Southerners "do business" than of any intellectual skill. I do not depreciate such street smarts or the ways such knowledge is acquired, but I do tend to separate them from theological education. Nor is it true that all who have attended seminaries have had ministries blessed by that experience. In some cases the critics of theological education who charged that seminaries might "ruin" the young men and women whose evident piety promised much may have had a point. Not everyone emerges from theological study with a religious life that matches his or her intellectual development, and not everyone who attends seminary has a richer ministry because of the experience.

Third, this book is also written from a deep sense that theological education as practiced in theological schools, including Bible schools and colleges, is part of the history of the American "middle class." The more I study theological education, the more I am convinced that whatever else the schools accomplish, they enable their graduates to hold their heads high in middle-class society. To exclude people from theological education, thus, is to exclude them, often deliberately, from substantial economic and cultural benefits. Even if the local African American Pentecostal preacher had deeper religious insights than any credentialed counterpart, this preacher suffered serious discrimination at every step of the way: the number of denominations where one could serve was limited, one would not be invited to participate in larger cultural and social events, and one could not become a chaplain in the military. In simple terms, the local

3. The modifier "Protestant" must be taken seriously here. There are many forms of theological education, such as the *lectio divina* of the Benedictines, that produce deep spiritual and intellectual insight and do not necessarily share the Protestant passion for clarity and critique. The importance of this reservation is even more important outside of Christian circles where one has to consider radically different methods of study and religious tradition. My only claim is that Protestant theological education is linked to these two goals.

Presbyterian elder with his degree would be invited to pray at graduation; the local Pentecostal or Independent Baptist would not. Even in African American and poorer white denominations, education was often the ticket to the larger and, if not larger, better-paying congregations. Even among the most dispossessed, education often marked people for leadership and for prized positions as writers in denominational presses or speakers on the platform of the annual meeting. The only real alternative to theological education would be one that produced not only religious leaders but also people with the equivalent status and power within and without their own denomination. The history of American pluralism leads through the deliberate or unconscious prejudices and pains of a society caught between exclusion and inclusion.

Why stop in 1970? Clearly, some of the stories continue past that date, and I have, with sovereign disregard of my own title, carried several tales further in history. What is the point of writing a book if one cannot break one's own rules? I am also acutely aware that the period after 1970 is the period of my own active ministry in theological education and that the issues in that period are still very much part of my theological map. As he or she gets closer to his or her own experience, even the most skilled historian begins to write the story of his or her life and experience and to lose the larger picture. At some time I will take up this task, perhaps after retirement, but I hope to be able to label those reflections accurately as reflections on the recent past of American Protestant education.

But the terminal date is also a self-conscious historical judgment. By 1967 the season of Protestant expansion that began in the post-Revolutionary era had come to what appears, in retrospect, to be its high point. Thereafter Protestant church growth began to decline. The social location of Protestantism also changed dramatically. The full social effects of the Second World War were now evident. Whatever its status among America's elite, Protestantism was no longer central to the American middle class. One might argue that Protestantism, the predominant religion among the nation's poorest, had been displaced by a highly educated (as a result of the GI Bill) urban Catholicism[4] and Judaism. In many ways Protestantism had come to resemble a Third World country with solid representation among the privileged, including many in Congress and the courts, but also among the not privileged, including many in rural slums, urban ghettos, and barrios. The old adage, beloved of mystery writers, that one should follow the money is as valid in religion as in murder. If nothing else had happened after 1967, the erosion of Protestantism's social basis

4. I am aware that heavy Catholic immigration from Latin America has created a new immigrant Catholicism that is making that church more socially varied than it was between 1960 and 1990.

as the religion of America's middle classes would have dramatically changed its forms of theological education, especially since that education was closely and intimately tied to such middle-class concepts as competence and professional status.

The 1960s were the beginning of a season of change in America that has been far-sweeping. In simple terms, America has gone from a white European nation that deliberately kept the reins of power in its own hands to a much more racially and religiously pluralistic society. At the same time, inherited pictures of what it means to be male or female also changed. By the end of the millennium, no one was shocked when a conservative president appointed an African American as secretary of state, or that this person followed a woman in that same strategic position. The implications of these social and political changes for theological education have been staggering as schools have struggled to include others, to find different theological and religious perspectives, and to maintain a measure of religious and spiritual stability. These changes, moreover, support the periodization that I have adopted. The story after 1970 is very different from the story before 1970. To use the analogy of points of reference that I used earlier, the racial and gender changes also marked the coming of new points of reference for theological education.

Protestantism has changed institutionally as well as socially. In 1970 it was assumed that fundamentalism and evangelicalism were rearguard maneuvers destined to be absorbed into the Protestant mainstream. Forty years later this is not a self-evident proposition, as evangelical and conservative Protestantism has continued to more than hold its own against the acids of modernity. But this has also changed American theological education. Not only are such schools as Fuller Seminary now among the most wealthy and successful of American seminaries, but evangelical scholars are also on the faculties of more mainstream institutions. Many mainstream Protestant leaders and theologians yearn to find ways to dialogue with a "generous orthodoxy."

For all the theological attractiveness of "generous orthodoxy," the period after 1967 was one of violent and divisive theological controversy. The Missouri Synod Lutherans and the Southern Baptists, to cite only two examples, almost came to physical blows. In both cases the careers of able Christian scholars were cut short or redirected, and both denominations have suffered from the loss of the dialectical strength that they had as more comprehensive institutions. If not as bloody, similar battles have raged under the surface in most Protestant denominations. The churches are not walking in one accord.

If some of the intellectual challenges of the earlier period, especially science and biblical criticism, continue to pose important issues for Christian theology, the larger intellectual frame of reference has also shifted. Whatever postmodernism might be — and the term may be as difficult to define as "romanticism" — the intellectual world changed from one in which science and rigorous humanistic study set the intellectual standard that all other forms of inquiry must meet to a world that at least formally acknowledges a multiplicity of perspectives, methods, and subject matters. The various scholarly guilds often appear more to be loose alliances of related specialists than groups of people that share a common set of commitments or subject matters. Again the distance from the pre-1960 period is striking. The early period had a canon, even if its meaning was disputed, and the formal curriculum of a school was an attempt to enshrine the various normative studies in a course of study that would give the student, subject by subject, an exposure to the whole theological realm. But theological educators have been forced to think in new, less precise ways. Again the distance from the pre-1960s period is great. A 1950s faculty would lack even the formal tools needed to evaluate the more innovative of present-day curricula.

In short, the volume ends in 1967 because I believe that year marks a natural divide in the history of American Protestant education. If I am wrong about this, the story I tell of the period from 1870 to 1970 may still be of value; if I am right, the reader may come to share my sense that the material covered in this volume concerns a world far, far away in a time very different from our own.

Every author has intellectual presuppositions that color his or her work. I hope mine are clear. This is a history of ***Protestant*** theological education. By that I mean the various ways Protestant churches have carried out the study of Protestant thought and practice. The study is clearly biased toward those institutions and movements that have stressed the need for clear, critical thought about both the intellectual and practical implications of Protestant faith.

The study also reflects my own somewhat jagged theological course. When I reread the narrative, I was struck by how much Ernst Troeltsch's understanding of history permeated my own work. Almost from page 1, I see reflected Troeltsch's belief that historical meaning is dependent on the context of past events, ideas, and persons. I was also impressed by how deep and abiding the influence of H. Richard Niebuhr was on my thought. In many ways Niebuhr was the American theologian who gathered up the concerns and interests of the early twentieth century and pointed to ways to consider them constructively. Niebuhr, an intellectual as well as a theological monotheist, was willing to let all final answers ultimately lie in the hands of God while insisting that human beings had to struggle with those questions.

The text also reflects my own evangelical faith. Aside from a brief period in my twenties when I flirted with neoorthodoxy, my theological thinking has been a continuation of my evangelical Baptist heritage. I recognize that the word "evangelical" has been damaged by overuse and that anyone who uses it needs to offer some explanations. For me, evangelicalism represents a deep commitment to the Bible *as* the revelation of God, and an emphasis on personal religious experience, especially conversion. While I believe that American religious liberty watered and nurtured this style of faith, I do not feel that it is an American theology. A deep evangelical thread runs throughout the history of the church and often has provided the whole church with the leaven that leavens the lump. My own personal goal has been for my faith to be a "generous orthodoxy" that could find the strength and wisdom in other points of view while holding firm to the evangelical core. I know that I have not completely succeeded in this aim, and I am sure that critics will point out places where my love of polemic defeated my hope for quiet, thoughtful consideration.

Acknowledgments

Books are communal products. This is certainly true of this one. Reaching back to the Auburn Project in the History of Theological Education, this book has evolved in dialogue with such valued friends as Robert Lynn, Virginia Brereton, James Frazer, and Barbara Wheeler. In particular, Robert W. Lynn has been my trusted teacher, friend, and confidant over the almost thirty years that I have spent thinking and writing about theological education.

Libraries are also particularly important to any scholar. Without the libraries of Bangor Theological Seminary, Southeastern Baptist Theological School, Southern Baptist Theological Seminary, Duke Divinity School, Harvard University, Andover-Newton Theological School, Hartford Theological Seminary, and others, I would not have been able to do the research in this volume. In addition, I want to thank all the various libraries that I have encountered on my journeys. The Internet is great, and I have used it to check the accuracy of some of my citations, but there is nothing like the feel of a book or a journal in the hand or the close relationship that one can establish with a text.

Over the years the Lilly Endowment has been financially and personally supportive of my work. Both Robert Lynn and Craig Dykstra were more than Endowment officers. They worked and worked hard at encouraging me to continue at the task. I am deeply appreciative.

The trustees of two theological schools, Southeastern Baptist Theological Seminary and Bangor Theological School, contributed academic leaves that enabled this project to be completed. And a special word of thanks to my colleagues at Bangor who have been very understanding of my need for time to think and to write and who have been willing to go the second mile to give me the time that I needed to study.

Again, thanks to all who helped, encouraged, argued, and supported.

Glenn T. Miller

Introduction

My first foray into the history of American Protestant theological education was an examination of the colonial and national periods. What I found in that volume, *Piety and Intellect,* was a world in which theological considerations trumped all other approaches to the education of Protestant ministers. Even the rise of cosmopolitan ideals during the Enlightenment did not substantially modify the basic paradigm. Indeed, such skilled dialecticians of the soul as Charles Hodge were able to incorporate the new science and the new outlook on the world into their more traditional confessional worlds. Theology, not as some vague term describing a multitude of disciplined intellectual pursuits but as good old-fashioned, hard-nosed dogmatic theology, was the mark of a learned minister. With the irony often evident in religious history, two of the greatest explosions of emotional religion — the First and Second Great Awakenings — fed this passion for theological precision. The rush of emotion released in conversion seemed to demand the counterbalance of the rigorous restraints and careful logic of the Protestant schoolmen.

This first volume also noted, in a tentative way, the beginnings of American biblical criticism and the early nineteenth-century fascination with the precision and art of German scholarship. The newer biblical criticism — far more historical and textually based than the pale denials of Enlightenment scholars — promised to turn the theological world upside down. But, to use a biblical analogy, it was a cloud only the size of a man's hand against the theological horizon, and only the most prophetic foresaw the storm that was coming.

The current volume, *Piety and Profession,* begins where *Piety and Intellect* ends: with the dogmatic model of theological education more or less intact and housed in a new and apparently successful type of school, the theological seminary. The new institution, designed for college graduates, was most often a freestanding school, complete with its own library and student residences, that provided a complete environment where students could receive the theological formation demanded by their learned profession. I selected Princeton, both one of the oldest and definitely one of the most successful implementations of this model, as my beginning point. Princeton was not great because it was creative; the school was great because it was the best and fullest manifestation of this nineteenth-century understanding of the seminary. They did seminary well, and no one did it better or with more grace and skill. Little wonder that the theological schools of many seemingly very different denominations found in Princeton an inspiring teacher of the arts of theological education.

Everyone writes out of his or her background. As an evangelical, devoted to a believing stance toward Scripture, I remember the long nights of anguished thought when I first encountered the new biblical studies in the 1960s. Like all manifestations that ring the holy, they held me with both a deep fear and a deep fascination. The new studies were, for me, a gateway to exciting and important discoveries, discoveries that greatly enriched my appreciation of the literary character of the Bible, and a gateway to doubts about the historical framework of redemption. Did it make a difference if Moses did not receive the Ten Commandments on Sinai or if the Ten Commandments that the historical Moses taught were, in fact, mere ritual prohibitions? From then on, those questions whirled in my mind as I grew and matured spiritually and theologically.

By analogy, which Ernst Troeltsch reminded us is an essential part of historical logic, I believe that I am able to interpret the shock waves that followed the spread of the new biblical studies in the 1880s and 1890s. For many, liberal and conservative, the new biblical criticism redrew the theological landscape. Old landmarks were upset and moved miles from their original locations, and familiar truths were spread over an unmarked plain. Not all reacted in the same way, but the power of the new ideas was such that everyone had to react in some way. New theologies, often called liberal or modernist, came into being, and the advocates of old orthodoxies found themselves the voices of different movements, often called fundamentalism, that sought to retain the most important historical markers from the past. The living questions of the early part of the century had become matters of merely historical interest. Old questions that had dominated the theologian's speculations, such as the almost infinite dissection of the will by New England theologians, seemed foreign, almost quaint, and definitely not modern.

If the changes in the understanding of the Bible broke the back of the older understanding of the seminary, they came in a season of intellectual and educational change. The old comfortable pattern of a scant elementary education for most people followed by a language-based academy and college for the elite was almost completely replaced by the turn of the century. In its place, at least in the urban areas, was a dynamic system of education that included elementary schools, high schools, and a new form of higher education, the graduate university. This new education had its pundits and teachers, such as the great William James, but it had certain hallmarks that were more important than any of its parts: the use of modern pedagogy, psychology, and sociology; the shift in the curriculum from Latin and Greek to a program that featured modern mathematics, the principal sciences, social science, and the humanities. Professional education also changed. Not only were there many new professions, ranging from teaching to social work, but these professions were modeled on the idea of the "applied sciences." And the new education apparently went from triumph to triumph as it churned out the clerks, teachers, lawyers, engineers, physicians, and civil servants needed by a dynamic and growing economy. By the end of the Second World War, the GI Bill gave this system yet another major influx of capital and students. The GI Bill promoted social mobility, especially among former ethnic minorities (not including African Americans) and white Southerners. Whatever its contribution to the postwar economic miracle, neither the popularity of the new education nor the growth of the new economy could be understood independently of each other.

The education of ministers could not stand still in this new educational and economic world. The question was not whether seminaries would change. That much was obvious, and even those that resisted change found themselves slowly forced by events to do things differently. More interesting was the question of the nature of that change. Should the seminaries or new institutions that would compete with them become Bible schools that would quickly provide Christian workers for a host of parochial, denominational, and interdenominational agencies? Should they follow the pathway of the medical schools and become institutions of applied science? If they followed that pathway, how should they honor their past as centers for the study of theology and Scripture?

Much of the twentieth-century debate was taken up with this question. Theological educators wrote articles, founded an accreditation agency, and experimented with new theologies and new theological understandings of their task. I have tried to tell the story of these discussions and events. In the process I have highlighted the stories of some of the most important people and institutions. But the theme has been the development of a characteristic way of thinking about theological education and its practices. No one could write a comprehensive one-volume history of theological education. Unfortunately, I have had to omit many interesting stories, either because they simply repeated what I had seen elsewhere or because of space considerations or because they did not contribute to the larger theme. With few exceptions, especially the story of the Methodists and their fascination with the new universities, I did not tell this story along denominational lines.

I ended the story of this understanding of the seminary with events in 1970. There were several reasons for ending at this point, not the least of which was the sheer length of the manuscript. But the most important historical consideration was my conviction that the professional understanding of theological education had begun to recede in the 1960s. As I see the period from the 1960s to the first decade of the new millennium, this view of the seminary has undergone significant modification as the seminaries have acquired new clienteles, have experimented with new pedagogies, and have faced new regulatory challenges. But that is a matter for another book.

Just as I ended *Piety and Intellect* by talking about the new biblical studies that were just emerging, so I felt that the appropriate climax for *Piety and Profession* would be the story of the rise of the new religion departments. The new religion departments, bright and brash, represented a fundamental challenge to the seminary's traditional role in religious scholarship and, through their domination of the education of future teachers, became the de facto determiner of the academic standards of the seminary professoriate. I believe that seminaries are extraordinarily sensitive to changes in the intellectual landscape, and this strikes me as the most important agent of change in the post-1960s world.

I do not plan to close my historical reflections on theological education with this volume. But my next study, dealing largely with the period from 1960 to the present, will be written from another perspective. I finished Union Seminary in the early 1970s, and I will be retired from active teaching and administration before the next study can be completed. By necessity it will be a reflection on my own time in this fascinating world of theological education, and like all reflections on one's own times, it will both benefit and suffer from being written by an eyewitness.

No book is ever written alone. Special thanks should be given to Craig Dykstra, Robert Lynn, and the Lilly Endowment. Without their generous financial and personal support, this project would never have been completed. In addition, I would like to thank Robert Lynn for his countless hours of reading various versions of the manuscript and the earlier *Piety and Learning.* The long discussions that he and I have had on the subject of theological education and its history have shaped my thinking in fundamental ways. Perhaps most important, Bob has been a good friend and faithful companion who has supported me personally and professionally. And, of course, I would like to thank my wife, Frankie, for the many sacrifices that she made as I researched and wrote this volume. Her many sacrifices made this book possible.

Glenn T. Miller
Bangor Theological Seminary

PART I

A New Understanding Forms

CHAPTER ONE

The Compleat Seminary

When the Old School and New School Presbyterians merged in 1869, Princeton Seminary was among the richest and most influential American theological schools.[1] The school's power and position came from its close relationship with the increasingly wealthy Presbyterian Church. American Presbyterians were a people on the move. Although still impressed by ministers with a Scottish brogue — witness the election of the Scottish philosopher McCosh as president of Princeton College — Presbyterians were leaving their Scottish and Irish immigrant roots behind them. Like the Lutherans, the Presbyterians had experi-

1. Princeton has been one of the most studied American theological schools. William K. Selden, *Princeton Theological Seminary: A Narrative History, 1812-1992* (Princeton: Princeton University Press, 1992); David Calhoun, *Princeton Theological Seminary: Faith and Learning, 1812-1868* (Edinburgh: Banner of Truth Trust, 1994); David Calhoun, *Princeton Theological Seminary: The Majestic Testimony, 1869-1929* (London: Banner of Truth Trust, 1996) are excellent examples of the level of these studies. Selden's account is more of a classical institutional history, while Calhoun's is an intellectual "biography." What makes this later study so important is that it recognizes that, perhaps more than other American institutions, the people who made Princeton Seminary were children of the mind and denizens of libraries who passionately believed that sound theology was the greatest need of their time. Few American seminaries have maintained such an unqualified love of learning and study over such a significant period of time. Other crucial studies include W. Andrew Hoffecker, *Piety and the Princeton Theologians — Archibald Alexander, Charles Hodge, and Benjamin Warfield* (Grand Rapids: Baker, 1981); Hugh Kerr, ed., *Sons of the Prophets: Leaders in Protestantism from Princeton Seminary* (Princeton: Princeton University Press, 1963); Mark A. Noll, *The Princeton Theology, 1812-1921 — Scripture, Science, and Theological Method from Archibald Alexander to Benjamin Breckinridge Warfield* (Grand Rapids: Baker, 1983); Mark A. Noll, *The Princeton Defense of Plenary Verbal Inspiration* (New York: Garland Press, 1988); also very useful, although not exclusively on Princeton, Mark Noll, *Between Faith and Criticism: Evangelicalism, Scholarship, and the Bible in America* (San Francisco: Harper and Row, 1986).

enced two periods of Americanization. In the eighteenth century the New Side Presbyterians, closely allied with the prorevival party among the Congregationalists, had led the church into a close relationship with American culture. Princeton College was the symbol of this Americanized Presbyterianism. In the next century the new wave of Scotch-Irish settlers contributed to the strength of the Old School party. Although the wave of national feeling that followed the Civil War weakened the power of inherited ideas and practices, at least in the victorious North, the conflicts between those who looked back to Scotland and Ireland and those who looked forward to a newborn American church were not over.

The signs of Presbyterian prosperity were visible everywhere. Presbyterians were rising in the world, often becoming wealthy, and they were willing to give to support the causes they believed in. An educated ministry was one of those causes. In part this was because of the nature of the church. Reformed Christianity was more than a religious tradition; it was an intellectual tradition that provided its members with a comprehensive understanding of the world, art, and civil government. Although Presbyterians claimed to be passionate biblicists, their theology rested on an artful synthesis between philosophy, modern science, and scriptural teaching.

Presbyterian prosperity did not mitigate the militancy that the American denomination shared with other Reformed churches. In many ways those churches that traced their intellectual legacy to Zwingli and Calvin were the Protestant equivalent of the Jesuit Order. In the sixteenth and seventeenth centuries they stood in the forefront of the struggle against the Catholic Reformation. This same determination had been occasionally directed against those Protestant rulers who failed to adhere to the full Reformed faith. In Scotland, for example, Presbyterians had resisted all efforts by the monarchs to cast their church in an Anglican mode under the Stuarts, and Reformed Christianity had straightened the backs of the Dutch opponents of Spanish rule.

As modernity swept over Europe, nineteenth-century Reformed conservatives directed much of their traditional hostility against the Enlightenment and its alternative understandings of human life. In Scotland these struggles contributed to a schism that resulted in the creation of a free (non–governmentally supported) church and the new University of Edinburgh. Holland, closely related theologically to Scotland, experienced a similar division. There the Dutch Christian Reformed Church and its Free University of Amsterdam acquired considerable influence, even electing a prime minister. The seeds of later Presbyterian fundamentalism were sown deep in the soil of a tradition that saw itself standing at Armageddon and battling for the Lord.

Given the tensions within the worldwide Reformed family, American

Presbyterians entered the post–Civil War period in an irenic mood. The Civil War had dissipated much of the nation's energy for conflict, and many Americans, including the bulk of the middle classes, were ready for peace. The new industrial order, marked by cutthroat competition and violent swings of the business cycle, provided excitement enough. But perhaps equally important was the Presbyterian acceptance of, almost veneration for, the American relationship between church and state.

More than anything else, this separated American Presbyterians from their European counterparts. Although they had founded free churches in extremis, European Reformed leaders shared the common belief in a unified Christendom. For them the ideal situation was one in which church and state together worked to coordinate life, sacred and profane. In contrast, American Presbyterians had accepted the voluntary principle. Presbyterians were confident that they and other Protestants could shape the new nation and its institutions indirectly. In their view faith was more powerful in a society where its advocates were passionately on mission for their God and righteousness. This did not imply that the Presbyterian pastor would directly address public affairs. With the exception of the few remaining New School zealots, most Presbyterians believed that the clergy should stick with preaching and let the membership of the church draw its own political and social conclusions from the message. In fact, Presbyterian clergy could not afford to be too far ahead of their congregations. America had no parish system, and the dissatisfied might either stop financially supporting a disagreeable minister or withdraw from one congregation and join another. The correlation between prophecy and unemployment was close.

A cynical observer might note that American denominational life reflected the lifestyle of secular capitalism, and the captains of piety who directed American religious organizations behaved remarkably like their counterparts in seeking economies of scale, growth, and market share. Presbyterians realized, perhaps before many other American Protestants, that denominational life required ministers who could present the message in a winsome and attractive way. Equally important, they realized that their clergy had to be able to speak to the middle classes that dominated the country politically and economically. Princeton Seminary was a major asset in the denomination's drive to claim its place at the center of American life. This alone would have been enough to make it a prize in Presbyterian politics.

Princeton Seminary had provided leadership to American Presbyterians as they adjusted their churches and aspirations to life in the new republic. Working as an agency of the General Assembly, the school had developed both a theological and a ministerial understanding that was adequate to the antebellum period. The primary task of a Presbyterian pastor, as Princeton envisioned that vocation, was to be a learned interpreter of the Christian faith. The curriculum of the seminary was directed toward this goal: the young theologian mastered the Bible in the original languages, studied the traditions and government of the church, and learned a comprehensive and, hopefully, defensible understanding of the faith. As funds became available, the board and faculty carefully expanded the curriculum around this traditional core.

Missions formed part of the school's formal and informal curriculum, and the school prided itself on the number of missionaries it dispatched around the world. Personal piety was encouraged through prayers, private conversations and spiritual counsel, and regular community worship. Equally important, the faculty saw themselves as on the front lines of scholarship, and under such skilled linguists as Charles Hodge and Joseph Archibald Alexander, the seminary had become a center for the study of the languages of the ancient Near East. Learning was not confined to languages. The seminary's journal, the *Biblical Repertory,* published reviews of the latest European books almost as soon as they left the press. Long before it became the norm, many of Princeton's teachers, including Hodge himself, trained in German universities. Princeton's faculty had a thorough grasp of the newer ideas about specialized learning and research that drove the late nineteenth-century American educational revolution.

In short, the Princeton of 1870 was the compleat American seminary, a symbol of American theological education at its best. Closely related to its church, to a theological tradition, to its social location, and to churches of like faith and order around the world, Princeton set the standard for much of contemporary American theological education. Yet, in little more than fifty years the school would find itself at the center of a titanic battle in which one side wished to bring the school closer to the center of its sponsoring denomination and the other wanted to maintain the school's fidelity to its past. To tell the story of these fifty years is to introduce many of the trends that remade American theological education and created the present-day seminary. It is also to begin the story of the deep and often contested divisions in church and theological education that have fractured and continue to fracture the fragile unity of various American Protestant communities.

I. Foundations: Charles Hodge, Joseph Addison Alexander, and William Henry Green

The foundations of the Princeton theology were laid primarily by Charles Hodge and his brilliant if somewhat quixotic protégés Joseph Addison Alexander and William Henry Green. If nothing else, their longevity contributed to their influence. Although Alexander died young, Hodge and Green each served extraordinarily long professorships of more than fifty years. Taken together, their service to the school covered the entire nineteenth century. But their influence was even greater than their longevity suggests. They were the primary creators of the Princeton style of theological education.

All three men were capable Hebraists who had mastered the rapidly evolving field of Semitic studies. This area of specialization is important for understanding their approach to the Bible and to seminary education. From the time of the Renaissance, European scholars had not known where to place the study of the Hebrew language. Like the study of Greek, the study of Hebrew seemed to be part of the work of the preparatory school and the faculty of arts. Indeed, in the eighteenth-century German university the faculties of theology customarily taught the Old Testament from the Latin text. Consequently, Old Testament theology was often seen primarily as preparation for the greater revelation to come in the New Testament. In other words, classical Old Testament criticism was a combination of the literary traditions of the arts faculties and the predominately historical interests of the theologians.

Although the three Princeton professors were profoundly theological men, their understanding of the Bible was rooted more in the tradition of the study of Hebrew than in the theological study of the Old Testament. In other words, their academic past stressed the literary exposition of the Scriptures. Princeton's scholars paid close attention to the details of the text, to the Bible's use of literary forms and formulas, and to the meaning of the language. Further, Princeton's biblical tradition was predisposed to treat the biblical stories as a whole. The biblical stories, hence, could appear as wheels within wheels that spun out the story of redemption. The stories as stories were central to the meaning and authority of the Old Testament, and Princeton's literary tradition led its primary voices to refuse any attempt to separate the truth of the stories from the truths they supposedly contained or illustrated.

Academic life tends to move among scholars with similar interests. The natural dialogue partners of Princeton scholars were those engaged in the recovery of the literature of the ancient New East. Hence, Hodge and Green were fascinated by the rediscovery of the cognate Semitic languages of the East, just being deciphered at the time, and by the new fields of biblical archaeology and geography.[2]

2. Marion Ann Taylor, "The Old Testament in the Princeton School" (Ph.D. diss., Yale University, 1988), has demonstrated the importance of Semitic studies for Princeton's self-understanding and for the school's biblical style.

The theological implications of this beginning point were profound. From Hodge onward the Princeton biblical scholars advocated "progressive revelation": the belief that God had gradually exposed God's truth to Israel and the church. Consequently, it was not surprising that the prophets, for instance, had a nobler and more developed understanding of God's righteousness than the patriarchs or that Jesus' understanding of God's gracious character superseded all the Old Testament intimations of forgiveness and acceptance. This meant that those parts of the Bible that did not seem to be in harmony with other parts were not related as primitive to advanced or as false to true but as parts to the larger whole. In 1891 Princeton established a chair of biblical theology — the study of how revelation had unfolded historically, as distinct from systematic theology, which viewed revelation as a rationally coherent whole.[3]

Biblical theology filled an important place in Princeton's understanding of the theological curriculum. The Princeton theologians, like other American theological educators, were interested in the efforts of theological encyclopedists to arrange the theological disciplines in a consistent way. They understood "theological encyclopedia" as a number of perspectives on the body of revelation. B. B. Warfield, who followed A. A. Hodge as professor of theology, described Princeton's understanding of curriculum:

> In this outline it is required of every student whose preparation for the ministry shall be made in this seminary, that he shall engage in the thorough study of Biblical Criticism, Apologetics, Dogmatic, Church History, and the various branches of Practical Theology. These five departments of study, it will be at once perceived, constitute the essential divisions of what is called "Theological Encyclopedia," and when arranged in scientific order

3. Nineteenth-century Princeton's use of the term "biblical theology" should not be confused with the later, neoorthodox biblical theology movement. The neoorthodox movement was concerned with showing how the theologian could speak of "the acts of God" in the context of an essentially naturalistic understanding of the biblical text. During its strong neoorthodoxy period under Presidents Mackay and McCord, Princeton was a center for this type of biblical theology. In his inaugural address, May 15, 1934, Donald MacKenzie said: "It is well-known that the modern separation of biblical theology as a distinct branch of theological study was due to a certain dissatisfaction with what . . . was regarded as the unwarranted extensions and elaborations of certain dogmatic theologians, either in the form of Roman Catholic or Protestant Scholasticism. . . . This was what happened at the Reformation when Scholasticism departed by subtlety from the simplicity of Scripture. The Bible always calls us back to reality and so Biblical theology is ever necessary. It is not the immediate duty of the Biblical theologian to start with credal statements and find their verification in Scripture." Quoted in George Lamar Haines, "The Princeton Theological Seminary, 1925-1960" (Ph.D. diss., New York University, School of Education, 1966), p. 79.

> will be recognized as a scientifically complete theological curriculum. Every one who would obtain a comprehensive knowledge of theological science, in other words, must give adequate attention to these five disciplines: Apologetics, Exegesis, Histories, Systematic, and Practics; and in these five disciplines the circle of theological sciences is complete.[4]

Biblical theology was another point on the circle that stood equidistant from the center.

Progressive revelation did not originate with Princeton. The Princeton theologians had inherited a strong doctrine of scriptural authority from the Westminster divines and from such theologians as Turretin. In its simplest form it could sound like a simple fideism. At the fiftieth anniversary of his appointment to the faculty, Charles Hodge described his predecessors and, by implication, himself: "Their theological method was very simple: The Bible is the word of God. That is to be assumed or proved. If granted, it follows, that what the Bible says, God says. That ends the matter."[5] In the more heated theological situation of the 1880s and 1890s, Warfield often sounded the same note. At times Warfield could speak almost as if the Word of God were somehow inscriptured into the human words of the Bible, much as the divine Logos was incarnate in Christ. Thus, he maintained, "justice is done to neither factor of inspiration and to neither element in the Bible except that which conceives of it as a divine-human book, in which every word is at once divine and human." Every page of the Scriptures, every word, was divine and human, "both of which penetrate them [the biblical words] at every point, working together harmoniously to the production of a writing which is not divine here and human there, but at once divine and human in every part, every word and every particular."[6]

We should not discount the importance of this type of theological bravado for Princeton Seminary. Princeton was proud that, unlike other seminaries, it refused to compromise its principles for popularity, enrollment, or endowments. The Princeton theologians exhibited an almost Kierkegaardian

4. Quoted in Ronald Clutter, "The Reorganization of Princeton Theological Seminary Reconsidered," *Grace Theological Journal* 7, no. 2 (1986): 179-201. Clutter's article argues that issues involving the curriculum and its organization were at the heart of much of the disagreement at the school in the 1920s. His work clearly indicates the importance of curricular issues for Princeton, and most important, the extent to which Princeton regarded the theological curriculum as an organic whole.

5. *Proceedings Connected with the Semi-centennial Commemoration of the Professorship of Rev. Charles Hodge, D.D., LL.D.: in the Theological Seminary at Princeton, N.J., April 24, 1872* (New York: A. D. F. Randolph and Co., 1872), p. 52.

6. Quoted in Calhoun, *Princeton Theological Seminary: The Majestic Testimony, 1869-1929*, p. 141.

willingness to suspend themselves over forty thousand fathoms and dare the sea to engulf them. They acted almost as if strong belief itself was evidence of theological masculinity, and any sign of weakness would cost them their theological manhood.

At first glance, progressive revelation would seem to weaken this radical biblicism. After all, why should not the eternal God reveal Godself all at once? Mere human sinfulness would not explain the divine reluctance, since saving faith, in any event, required God to act in the life of the believer. But, in fact, Princeton's biblical scholars were not as biblicistic as they appeared. Both Charles Hodge and even more directly Joseph Addison Alexander were indebted to the German theologian Ernst Wilhelm Hengstenberg. Hengstenberg, whose *Christology of the Old Testament* was a popular text in American seminaries,[7] was one of the influential leaders of the German *Erweckungsbewegung*, or awakening. His salon in Berlin, almost a Christian imitation of the French Enlightenment salons, was an influential gathering place for young Christian intellectuals anxious to promote biblical Christianity in the wake of the Napoleonic Wars. Other leaders of the awakening movement, including the church historian Johann August Neander, were frequent visitors. J. A. Alexander was only one of many young Americans who found themselves charmed by Hengstenberg's immaculate manners, well-stocked larder, and sharp wit.

J. A. Alexander had met Hengstenberg not only when the Prussian theologian was at the top of his powers, but also as the biblical issue was just beginning to be publicly debated in Germany. The great scandal of the 1830s was of course the publication of D. F. Strauss's *Life of Jesus* (1835-36), but that was only the tip of an iceberg that included the Tübingen school of F. C. Baur and the seemingly relentless development of Old Testament criticism. Although the debate over these new methods and how much believing Christians could use or not use them raged until the First World War, it was at its most polemical during this period.[8]

7. Reuel Keith, a professor at Virginia's Episcopal Seminary and a student of Moses Stuart, translated the Christology. Ernst Wilhelm Hengstenberg, *The Christology of the Old Testament*, trans. Reuel Keith (Alexandria, Va.: W. M. Morrison, 1836-39). J. A. Alexander translated Hengstenberg's influential Psalms commentary. Ernst Wilhelm Hengstenberg, *The Psalms Translated and Explained*, trans. J. A. Alexander (New York: Baker and Scribner, 1850). There were also British editions of this work.

8. It is useful to see the biblical debate moving somewhat as a wave from Germany west. The decades from 1830 to 1860 can be seen as the German period; the period from 1850 to 1880 as the English phase; and the period from 1880 to 1920 as the American phase. Yet one has to be careful. The movement of the wave westward was a matter more of the public's apprehensions of the issues than of the general knowledge of the questions themselves. From the time of Moses

II. Inerrant and Progressive

Hengstenberg's defense of orthodoxy had three characteristics. First, his interpretation tended to stress the supernatural elements in the biblical story. Christian faith was about God's intervention in history; it was about miracle; it was about matters beyond ordinary comprehension. The interpreter's attention was thus directed to the events of the Bible as the place where God's power and influence were most evident. There was of course nothing new about this view of faith, and Hodge, among others, had a similar view apart from Hengstenberg's influence. What was different in Hengstenberg's teaching was the way the supernatural was accented. Second, Hengstenberg tended to stress the more traditional modes of literary interpretation, including typology and prophecy, that could be used to knit the various stories in the Bible together as a whole. In terms of defending the faith against its enemies, real or apparent, this emphasis made it difficult to be selective in one's reading of the biblical accounts. Since everything was related to everything else, to challenge one part of the picture was to challenge the whole, kind of like removing a brick from a stack without disturbing its neighbors. Third, Hengstenberg shifted the emphasis from plenary verbal inspiration, the old scholastic doctrine, to his own interpretation of inerrancy.

The belief that the Bible told the truth about God and humankind was by no means new. Both the decrees of the Council of Trent and the elaborate discussions of the Bible in the Reformed confessional documents had stressed the divine authorship of the Bible and had implicitly or explicitly taught that the biblical history was an accurate account. Particularly among Reformed Protestants, it was common to further elaborate the doctrine as plenary, verbal inspiration: the claim that the Bible was inspired in the very words it used, both in whole and in part.[9] What Hengstenberg did was to say that inspiration secured the truth of the text that we have before us by the ordinary means of provi-

---

Stuart, American theologians had followed German developments avidly, just as they routinely followed the British discussions. This tended to create a greater gap between American public opinion and American scholarly opinion than was common in either England or Germany.

9. Protestant scholasticism often moved like a snowball roaring downhill at high speed. An idea would be proposed and incorporated into the discussion, and would pick up other ideas as it moved from thinker to thinker. The most famous example of this is the doctrine of election, which began with the mystery of God's choice of the Israelites and grew to the point where one of the most important tasks of Reformed theology was sorting out the various decrees of God, determining which were before and which after the fall, and placing the work of Christ in this context. By the time the idea finally stopped, it had acquired so much mass that its heart and core, the gracious love of an all-powerful God, was almost completely hidden from sight.

dence. The biblical books could be understood as any other literature was understood. Thus the biblical authors could write in their own style, use various sources for their accounts, and be limited by their own times in their knowledge of science, history, and, to some extent, theology. Further, Scripture could and did make statements that seemed wrong, if not outrageous, to later generations, but which were thoroughly understandable in the historical context of the author or the sources the author was using. God's contribution, so to speak, was to protect the authors from making mistakes of fact (errors) or substance. If, as Hodge often said, one heard God when one heard the Bible, one heard God speaking in very human accents.

This stance permitted William Henry Green and his companions to engage fully in the biblical studies of their day, and yet to maintain their distance from their more radical conclusions. The answers to genuine historical questions were not predetermined in advance, at least not in principle, and hence Green could impartially examine such issues as the nature of the sources of the Pentateuch or the authorship of the Psalms. An almost grim realism was part of the position. The most natural reading of such biblical narratives as the exodus is that a significant number of people left Egypt and moved, together with most of their possessions, into first the wilderness and then the Promised Land. Much of the criticism of the period, particularly after Wellhausen, moved away from this plain reading of the text. The doctrine of inerrancy meant that Princetonians could legitimately ask questions about aspects of the story, such as the number of those involved, without losing the event itself. As Green noted, "Here is no question merely of the strict inerrancy of Scripture, of absolute accuracy in unimportant minutiae, of precision in matters of science. . . . The truth and evidence of the entire Mosaic history are at stake. And with this stands or falls the reality of God's revelation to Moses and the divine origin of the Old Testament."[10]

Inerrancy and progressive revelation also solved a number of theological embarrassments. Traditionally these problems had been handled by harmonizations, elaborate arguments designed to show that the Bible possessed, when interpreted correctly, a coherent message. The Princetonians never completely abandoned this method, of course, perhaps because it had some apologetic value. But they did move beyond it. Even the most difficult-to-understand biblical books could be allowed to stand in all their critical and theological complexity. The book of Ecclesiastes, for example, presents an understanding of life that is almost epicurean. While one might feel that most of this book is less apt theologically than more elevated passages in the canon, the doctrine of inerrancy allows the material to stand as a report of what the king (possibly Solo-

10. Quoted in Taylor, "The Old Testament," p. 465.

mon) had learned from his own experience. Much the same can be done with the openly erotic poetry of the Song of Songs or with the Old Testament's apparent endorsement of polygamy.

In some ways Darwinism tested the ability of the doctrine to handle the rougher cases. Charles Hodge published his *What Is Darwinism?* in 1871. To Hodge, Darwinism cut the throat of the argument from design, one of the most popular apologetic arguments of the time, and seemed to leave chance enthroned as the ultimate principle of creation.[11] But he was the last of the Princetonians to stand on that mountain. Instead, the tradition in both the college and the seminary followed the lead of James McCosh. Francis Patton, far from the most left-leaning leader of the school, noted: "Darwinism was a matter of controversy when McCosh first came to the country. He was a defender of the faith but he knew that truth has often more to fear from its friends than from its foes. He undertook to show that evolution can do some things and that there are some things it cannot do and that so far as it is claimed to be a theory explanatory of the origin of species it was a mistake to regard it as atheistic or in irreconcilable hostility to the Bible."[12] In other words, Genesis could be interpreted in much the same way as the biblical references to a three-storied universe. Whatever the biblical writers might have believed those passages implied, as the passages stood they were effective literary means of communicating divine revelation.

One of the problems in interpreting Princeton's biblicism is that the advocates of the position talked about the inerrancy of the original writings and refused to attribute inerrancy to later versions. Despite the conservatism of Princeton's textual criticism,[13] even they admitted that the original autographs

11. David Livingston, *Darwin's Forgotten Defenders: The Encounter between Evangelical Theology and Evolutionary Thought* (Grand Rapids: Eerdmans, 1987), summarizes the reception of Darwinism among conservative American theologians at the end of the century. By 1900 the debate was essentially over on the theological level. Among the most important of Princeton's allies abroad, this was also true. James Orr of Scotland, for instance, perhaps the leading British critic of Ritschlian theology and a major contributor to the Fundamentals, was firmly in the evolutionary camp, as were such staunch conservatives as E. Y. Mullins and Augustus Strong. The one exception that I know of is Abraham Kuyper, the founder of the Free University of Amsterdam, who believed that evolution was inherently atheistic. The anti-evolutionary crusade of the 1920s seems to have caught many of these conservatives by surprise.

12. Quoted in Joseph E. Illick III, "The Reception of Darwinism at the Theological Seminary and the College at Princeton, New Jersey," *Journal of the Presbyterian Historical Society* 38 (1960): 152-65, 234-43, here p. 241.

13. Green had been chair of the committee that prepared the Old Testament for the American Revised Version of the Bible. Many contemporary biblical critics, including Charles Briggs of Union, felt that the revision was too conservative, especially in not highlighting rejected readings in the notes.

were beyond recovery. Critics of the doctrine, both then and now, use this undeniable fact as a reductio ad absurdum of the whole position.[14] After all, the fact that a book of mathematical tables contained accurate computations of the value of the trigonometric functions when the tables were compiled is little comfort to a ship of adventurers lost at sea who have a flawed copy of that original work. Sailors need accuracy, precision, and reliability to set their course. But both Princeton and its critics may have gone overboard on this aspect of the teaching. The Princeton theologians knew that "the present controversy concerns something more vital than the bare 'inerrancy' of the Scriptures, whether in the copies or the autographs,"[15] and many who argued against Princeton knew, or at least suspected, that the assumptions behind many critical arguments presupposed a world in which orthodox faith was difficult, if not impossible, to maintain. Both knew that the real issue was whether the biblical histories were reliable and whether one could build a theology on those accounts.[16]

III. The Heart of the Matter

Princeton's passionate defense of biblical authority was a fence protecting the school's fascination with biblical studies and with the Bible. Although Princeton's curriculum contained much doctrinal theology and some church government, the course of study was overwhelmingly concentrated on the Bible. Within this concentration, Princeton's curricular development — allowing for the idiosyncrasies that particular faculty interests introduce in almost any specific course of study — followed many of the newer ideas about theological education current at the time. For instance, the elective program was comparatively well developed. B. B. Warfield described the variety of offerings available in 1895:

> In the seminary itself we propose as large a supplementary body of special classes — seminars if you will — as proves each year to be possible with the

14. See Jack B. Rogers and Donald K. McKim, *The Authority and Interpretation of the Bible: An Historical Approach* (San Francisco: Harper and Row, 1979).

15. B. B. Warfield, in Calhoun, *Princeton Theological Seminary: The Majestic Testimony, 1869-1929*, p. 145.

16. One wonders whether inerrancy was not for both Princeton and its critics a safe diversion from the more serious theological issues of the later part of the nineteenth century. The liberals believed that the choice they were making was the only one that preserved any faith at all; in other words, that the church had to change or lose credibility. The Princetonians believed that if the church changed it would lose connection with its past and perhaps with its message. Neither alternative was very attractive. The liberals ran the risk of infidelity in order to preserve religion; the Princetonians ran the risk of irrelevance in order to preserve continuity.

> force of teachers at our disposal. The last year, for example, there were sixteen of these courses in actual operation: and as they are purposively varied from year to year, a student who stays with us the three years course out, will have some forty-eight of these special courses brought to his attention. It will give some idea of the topic treated in them to enumerate the list for the year just closed. They included classes in advanced Hebrew, New Testament Greek, Arabic, Early Aramaic Inscriptions, Old Testament contemporary history, the Higher Criticism of the Hexateuch, the Hebrew Feasts, exegesis of Job, and of Zechariah, New Testament Introduction, Exegesis of James, Justin Martyr, History of Doctrine, Philosophical Apologetics, the Person and Work of Christ, Analysis of Texts.[17]

In addition to these courses, the seminary had an agreement with the college — which became a university in 1896 — that allowed students to select courses in line with the seminary's special interests.

Another mark of the seriousness of the biblical focus was Princeton's approach to the bachelor of divinity degree. As professionals became more important in the United States, both economically and socially, following the Civil War, seminaries and other professional schools moved to become degree-granting institutions. Until accreditation encouraged some uniformity in the degree standards, what a school required for its degree provides some insight into the institution's self-understanding. At Princeton, those who completed the course were granted a diploma. To qualify for the degree a student needed to invest a fourth year in serious, supervised study. Given the nature of the elective offerings, this meant that almost all who received a degree had the present-day equivalent of a graduate degree in biblical studies.

IV. The Minister's Work

The curricular focus on the Bible reflected Princeton's understanding of the minister's work. For Princeton, whatever else a modern minister might need to be, a minister was first and foremost a servant of the Word of God whose weekly exposition of the Bible provided the congregation with a point of contact with revelation. While the Princetonians never said the sermon was a form of the Word of God, they did see it as the means by which that Word was faithfully transmitted from generation to generation. Understandings of the word of

17. B. B. Warfield, "The Improvement of Our Theological Seminaries," *Independent,* June 20, 1895, p. 828.

the minister that downplayed this distinctive role were, consequently, to be rejected or even ridiculed. Warfield, Princeton's spokesperson on this as well as on other matters, wrote:

> If the functions of the ministry come to be conceived lowly; if the minister comes to be thought of, for example, fundamentally as merely the head of a social organization from whom may be demanded pleasant manners and executive ability; or as little more than a zealous "promoter" who knows how to seek out and attach men to his enterprise[,] a multitude of men; or as merely an entertaining lecturer who can be counted upon to charm away an hour or two or dull Sabbaths; or even — for we have, of course, an infinitely higher conception — as merely an enthusiastic Christian eager to do work for Christ . . . we might as well close our theological seminaries.[18]

In the constellation of American professions then forming, the minister's work was more like that of a college or university teacher than that of a social worker or businessperson. The minister was the resident Christian intellectual, equipped to teach in either pulpit or classroom.

The equation of ministry and scholarship was by no means unusual. Many Americans, especially those in Reformation traditions, held to a similar concept, and, as at Princeton, this belief inspired prospective theological teachers to go to Germany and to a lesser extent Scotland to learn their craft. What is interesting about Princeton is the consistency with which the late nineteenth-century faculty built their institution on this foundation.

V. A Matter of Conscience

The Reformers were far more radical than they intended. Luther seems to have initially believed that once the truth was made known, people would accept it joyfully. A new Catholicism, thus, would rise phoenixlike from the old. But it did not work that way. Even within Luther's own circle of friends and supporters, people insisted on applying their own criteria to theological and ecclesiastical affirmations and practices. To meet the threat of doctrinal chaos the Reformers devised summary statements of faith — confessions and catechisms — and required their ministers to swear that these documents either faithfully reflected the teachings of Scripture, understood as the final authority, or reflected their own faith. In Europe these affirmations were guaranteed by the state that

18. B. B. Warfield, "Our Seminary Curriculum," in Warfield, *Selected Shorter Writings*, ed. J. E. Mercer (Philadelphia: Presbyterian and Reformed, 1970), p. 369.

had the right to punish perjury. By the eighteenth century, however, many Protestant governments were increasingly unwilling to enforce confessional adherence. The responsibility for a minister's personal orthodoxy, thus, was increasingly dependent on the minister's professional judgment about the truth (or lack of truth) of his church's official teachings.

Most American seminaries were founded with a requirement that the faculty subscribe or swear to a specific statement of faith. Often this act was both solemn and public with the newly elected professor signing a book before an assembly of trustees, fellow faculty members, and students. At some schools subscription took place only once in a person's teaching career; at others it was repeated every year.

The theory behind subscription was simple. The founders of seminaries believed that the public and solemn taking of an oath would commit the prospective teacher to fidelity to the foundational teachings of the school. If a faculty member departed from that declaration, then that teacher ought to resign or, if need be, could be removed from office by the board. The system rarely worked as intended. Most professors' theological positions slowly evolved over the course of their careers; they were rarely aware when they had crossed a confessional line, although their mature position might be some distance from where they began. Moreover, in the midst of thinking seriously about faith, many were honestly convinced that they had only reinterpreted a traditional teaching, even when they had moved considerably beyond it. Theological adjustment to the modern world added yet another wrinkle to an already confused and confusing situation. Heresy trials or even hearings, hence, were messy affairs that always seemed to leave those that questioned a teacher's specific teachings looking like persecutors. Princeton, or at least ecclesiastical leaders closely identified with the seminary, played a prominent role in the trials of David Swing and Charles Briggs. Although both Swing and Briggs left the Presbyterian Church as a result of the trials, the victories were hollow. The prosecution won the battle in the church courts; the defendants won in the court of public opinion.

Princeton and other seminaries in the Old School tradition were more shaped by their confessions of faith than were other schools. Not only had they inherited strong confessional traditions from Scotland and Ireland, but the American battles over revivalism had reinforced their commitment to a straightforward reading of the school's confessional documents. Further, in both Germany and Holland vibrant confessional theologies were involved in struggles against rationalism in the national churches.[19] Yet one must be careful

19. Walter H. Conser, *Church and Confession: Conservative Theologians in Germany, England, and America, 1815-1866* (Atlanta: Mercer University Press, 1984).

not to overemphasize the role of precedent. Princetonian theologians were aware that the type of doctrinal hairsplitting that had separated the two wings of Presbyterianism was no longer proper. The 1892 Portland Deliverance (affirmed many times thereafter, most notably in the 1910 Five Points Deliverance) was primarily concerned with the doctrine of Scripture, and the assembly's 1910 action affirmed Scripture, along with a handful of christological statements. If Princeton expected its own faculty to affirm all of traditional Calvinism, it had made peace with the reluctance of the whole church to do so.

In line with this style of traditionalism, the Westminster Confession and Westminster Catechisms penetrated the school at every point. At the school's centennial celebration Francis Landry Patton declared: "The theological attitude of Princeton Theological Seminary is, I think, pretty well understood: . . . I do not for a moment deny that there may be a place in the world for an institution the professors of which work in the unhampered exercise of their judgment in the search for theological truth; but in the nature of the case the seminary which is ecclesiastical in its origins and relationships and which does its work under the rubrics of confessional obligations cannot have that sort of freedom."[20]

Princeton's experience of its confession of faith was positive. Where many outside the Princeton tradition tended to see the confession as restrictive, as a document that said no to where people might have otherwise gone intellectually, those within the institution tended to see it more like a fence. Within the area enclosed by the confession, one had considerable space to explore ideas, to investigate historical and biblical problems, or to form alternative understandings of the church and ministry. Unless one wanted to wander beyond the boundaries set by the confession, one had no more reason to feel hemmed in by that statement than by any other set of affirmations or expectations.

Princeton's confessionalism had another benefit. The intense piety that had fired much of the controversy around the First and Second Great Awakenings had begun to die down. Dwight L. Moody, for example, did not expect his converts to break down emotionally as part of their conversion, and most revivalists had made similar adjustments. People were to accept Christ and resolve to live a moral life. The family altar, so characteristic of high Victorian culture, had begun to disappear along with the overstuffed furniture and the outdoor privies. In this new world the belief that Christianity did not depend on an emotional experience or a felt-change of status from sinner to saint was com-

20. Francis Landry Patton, "Princeton Seminary and the Faith," in *The Centennial Celebration of the Theological Seminary of the Presbyterian Church in the United States of America at Princeton, New Jersey* (n.p.: The Seminary, 1912), pp. 341-42.

forting. Like other seminaries, Princeton struggled with how to maintain the outward trappings of piety in a more secular age, but it did not have the additional burden of forcing people toward an experience or experiences that were no longer as culturally normative as they once had been.

VI. The Influence of Commonsense Philosophy

Princeton Seminary has been known for its distinctive style of theology. The Scottish commonsense philosophy dominated much of early nineteenth-century American life. Although it had some fruitful variations, Scottish commonsense philosophy was essentially an inductive empiricism that believed that human beings arrived at truth by amassing as many facts about something as possible and then attempting by induction to derive a theory that would explain the data. Such theories were, in principle, always subject to revision. An investigator might discover additional information that the theory could not explain, or some of the data might prove to have been inaccurate or flawed. Ideally, theories were supported when they were able to predict future data. If the system could not explain how scientists came to their fundamental insights, it did reflect the way science presented its arguments for or against certain positions.

Commonsense philosophy was a potent weapon against the type of romantic theology associated with Henry B. Smith or Edwards Amasa Park at midcentury. These theologians tended to stress the role of intuition in theology and to see theology as an interpretation of human consciousness or feeling. Such theologians as Hodge could and did appeal to the facts of Scripture as providing an alternative to a theology of apprehension, and Hodge in particular was willing to argue that the theologian, like other scientists, arranged the facts of his discipline into larger scientific formulations. In other words, Scripture provided the data that justified theological teaching.

Scottish commonsense philosophy served primarily to reinforce certain presuppositions held by the Princeton theologians. The most important of these was an assumption about language. If our knowledge of the world comes from the human attempt to explain the world around us, then it is possible, in principle, to understand other humans who are struggling with the same or similar situations. Hence, while the New Testament authors, for instance, did not know as much about the world as we do, they were struggling with the same spiritual and material world as we are. It is an error to see the supernatural as something they were able to believe because they lived in a prescientific age and thus had another consciousness. The New Testament writers might have been wrong. Many of those who claimed the direct intervention of God in the Middle Ages were wrong, and modern people do not hesitate to say so. But we can understand the testimony of both the New Testament writers and the medieval chroniclers.[21]

Commonsense philosophy also reinforced the interest of such Princetonians as Warfield in apologetics. Much of late nineteenth-century theology was apologetic, of course, as theologians tried to persuade people to maintain faith in the face of newer discoveries in biology or historical study. One popular liberal approach was to try to distinguish religious faith from other types of human experience. Given this separation, a theologian could argue that religious faith remained solid despite the surrender of much of the traditional historical information that had sustained such faith. In contrast to this approach, Princetonian apologetics attempted to argue from what humans knew about the world that faith in God was still the most rational choice.

Princeton's emphasis on the hard data of history was not unusual in the late nineteenth century. Since the days of Herodotus, with his claim to have examined the sources impartially, historiography has had two foci: the verification of information about the past and the interpretation of that information. Leopold von Ranke, a near contemporary of Green, had placed much of the emphasis of "scientific" history on the problem of verification. For von Ranke the historian's explorations were to be so thorough that the result would be "as it actually happened." This was a high standard, rarely attained, but an important one. Further, nineteenth-century society also placed a high premium on factual knowledge. Whatever might be the philosophical fashion, scientists continued to use an empirical model to verify their conclusions, and this model yielded new and more precise understandings of nature. Even experimental physics, the area where a more theoretical model might be seen as evolving, found itself waiting for verification before it would validate the conclusions of its more venturesome mathematical practitioners. And this interest extended to religious claims. One thinks, for instance, of such people as Arthur Conan Doyle visiting mediums to see whether their claims of visitation from another sphere were credible or not. Frank Clifford, the famed British agnostic, was not alone in demanding that religious bodies make good their claims about empirical reality or abandon those claims altogether. It was, as he said, a matter of the morality of knowledge.

21. Darryl Hart, "The Princeton Mind in the Modern World and the Common Sense of J. Gresham Machen," *Westminster Theological Journal* 46, no. 1 (Spring 1984): 8-9, makes this point about the impact of common sense. It goes a long way to explain the Princetonian passion for exegesis. Once we understand the linguistic forms used in a text, we should be able to respond to its truth claims.

In short, the tendency of the Princeton theologians to insist on an examination of the factual basis of faith was not only a matter of precedent. Many of the technical distinctions in Scottish commonsense theology tended to become less obvious in the Princeton theology after Charles Hodge. What remained was an attitude toward the data of history and religion that, while becoming less common among academic theologians, was very much part of the intellectual world of the time.

VII. Challenges of a New Day

In 1912 Princeton rolled out the red carpet and celebrated its centennial. One sister school's greeting noted simply that Princeton was "the mother of us all" and the school "that set high standards for all similar institutions."[22] The occasion came at the end of a half-century of fairly steady advance. During the previous half-century the school had raised its endowment, created one of the finest theological libraries in the United States, added electives to its programs, and added faculty who made major contributions to the school's academic and ecclesiastical reputation. Archibald Alexander and B. B. Warfield were massive bookends for a century of solid intellectual work, and the newest appointment to the faculty, J. Gresham Machen, was a person of solid academic promise. Unlike many of Princeton's most noted biblical teachers, who were Old Testament specialists, Machen was a New Testament scholar with an advanced knowledge of Greek, a thorough historical background, and an effective writing style.

The representations and greetings sent to the school indicated its position in world Christianity. Robert Speer, the energetic lay secretary of the Presbyterian Board of Foreign Missions and one of the nation's premier church administrators, noted with pride that through Princeton "have passed between five and six thousand men, one-half as many as have gone out from any other theological seminary in the land; and one out of thirteen of these men has gone into the foreign field."[23] The percentage over the last twenty-five years had climbed to one in nine. With the possible exception of Union, New York, no other American school was in such close contact with Christians around the world or enjoyed such widespread respect.

The prosperity of the school was evident in its buildings. "In the 1920s,

22. The phrase is in the greeting from the Presbyterian Theological Seminary of Louisville, Ky.

23. Robert Elliot Speer, "Princeton on the Mission Field," in *The Centennial Celebration of the Theological Seminary of the Presbyterian Church in the United States of America at Princeton, New Jersey*, p. 420.

there were ten buildings on the campus: chapel, recitation Hall, gymnasium, three dormitories, power plant, and two libraries plus 11 houses nearby."[24] Further, the seminary shared some facilities with the university. Campus visitors might have supposed themselves at a prosperous college rather than a theological seminary. These material blessings had been gifts of a devoted body of Presbyterian lay leaders such as John Green, James Lenox, Alexander Stuart, Robert Stuart, and oilman Calvin Payne and his wife. Slowly but surely the school was building an adequate endowment. The school's enrollment — the one area where people might have criticized it — had in fact remained steady, despite a shift of seminary enrollment toward the west.[25]

Yet, although Princeton was not above celebrating its glories, the centennial meeting did not sound the high notes that the school's achievements would seem to have warranted. The mood of many of the speakers — and not only those from more liberal institutions — was that they were visiting a living anachronism. Charles Beatty Alexander spoke these ominous words: "One does not have to be a professional theologian to be aware that the kind of thought for which Princeton Seminary has always stood more firmly is now attacked from many quarters. Voices come to us from across the sea and are raised here at home telling us that the sun is fast setting upon the old faith, and that the doctrines taught here will pass away like those of the Athenian and Roman schools. It may be said that in our own country, the seminary stands in a somewhat isolated position."[26] The sense that the times had changed and left Princeton stranded on a far shore was also sounded by Russell Cecil, moderator of the Presbyterian Church, US, and pastor of Second Presbyterian Church, Richmond, Virginia. After the expected praises, he observed pointedly: "There are different departments of church work for which men should be specially prepared; and experience shows that, for the attainment of this end. The course of study in the seminary has not been happily arranged[;] it has been too much of a procrustean bed upon which all classes of students, if they desire a degree, are compelled to lie. The law of adaptation of mean to end has not been wisely ap-

24. Selden, *Princeton Theological Seminary,* p. 117. See also H. L. McGill Wilson, "On the Buildings of the Theological Seminary of the Presbyterian Church in the United States of America, 1817-1950," *Princeton Theological Seminary Bulletin* 43 (Winter 1950): 24-27.

25. Princeton was doing comparatively well here. Some schools that were strong in the early part of the century, such as Andover, declined by more than 50 percent between the Civil War and the First World War, and the University of Chicago Divinity School, one of the few institutions to rival Princeton in size and prestige, experienced many losses in the wake of the debate over George Burman Foster.

26. Charles Beatty Alexander, "Princeton in Its Early Environment and Work," in *The Centennial Celebration,* p. 466.

plied."[27] Even the address by Francis Landry Patton, the president of the seminary and former president of the university, sounded a note midway between affirmation and defense. In effect, Patton said Princeton had become the representative of a party rather than of the whole. He ended his oration with this uncertain exhortation: "My friends, that is what this Seminary is for. Will you help us? Will you give us books? Will you give us men with special learning and peculiar aptitude to enlist in the greatest work that the world can do? Will you do it? Will the great, rich Presbyterian Church say 'No' to Princeton Seminary, which is ready to do what needs to be done, and withhold from her the sinews of war?"[28] It was a good question.

But it was also a question that might have led a casual observer to pause and reflect on why it was being asked in that way. Successful armies focus their attention on the prize to be won; they do not cast backward glances to see if the rear echelons are in place or whether there are sufficient supplies for the campaign. Victory generates its own momentum. But one might wonder whether Patton, an old man ready to retire to the Bahamas, was at a place in his career where he could have issued a more definite call to arms. The trustees and directors of the seminary may have thought so, for two years later they selected J. Ross Stevenson, an energetic Baltimore pastor, as Patton's successor, and there were high hopes that Stevenson would prove a more effective leader and administrator than his predecessor. But that was not the real problem. William Hallock Johnston, president of Lincoln University, a Presbyterian school for African Americans, offered a remarkable list of the challenges before theological schools at the time:

> The wonderful development and ever extending boundaries of the sciences, the obvious utility of scientific study as a preparation for many vocations in life, the relative depreciation of the classics, the demands of a not infallible, but very human student body, seeking the line of least resistance, the development of elective courses, the application of candidates for the ministry without classical training, the marked popular interest in sociological questions growing out of our industrial organization and the progress of democracy, all of these causes have had their effect upon the theory and the actual arrangement of our theological curricula.[29]

27. Russell Cecil, "The Making of a Minister," in *The Centennial Celebration,* p. 398.

28. Francis Landry Patton, "Princeton Seminary and the Faith," in *The Centennial Celebration,* p. 346.

29. William Hallock Johnston, "Princeton in Theological Education and Religious Thought," in *The Centennial Celebration,* p. 420.

Johnston's list was an impressive summary of the challenges of the last half-century. When the list is viewed as a whole, one has a sense of the forces that were encouraging American theological schools to find new ways to define themselves.

The task of new self-definition was not an easy one. Unlike Europe, the United States did not have the fixed lodestars of inherited class and culture to guide its educational development. Instead, the country was a vast free market of institutions, operating on different educational and professional levels, that served selective clienteles, each of which was somehow identified as the public. Each of these institutions was in competition with the others. Schools and educational styles would flourish for a season and then decline, occasionally close, or redefine themselves with a different set of values, goals, or objectives. In 1912 Princeton was near such a moment of redefinition, a task made paradoxically more difficult by its past successes.

The problem for the seminaries was not that no one knew what a seminary was; the problem was that everyone knew what a seminary was, and everyone was talking at the same time. What those concerned about theological schools had to do was find an orderly way to manage the discussion — to select some elements to emphasize and place less stress on others.

The task was one of definition and of order. What they wanted to accomplish was to establish definitions and standards that provided a common Protestant understanding of theological education. Not even the most sanguine, however, believed they would be able to establish more than a relative consensus. American Protestantism was a constantly changing Joseph's coat of many colors that generated new movements, new religious understandings, and new forms of ministry. No one could tame that whirlwind, although many feared that the winds it generated would swamp the entire enterprise or, de facto, make more organized Catholicism the dominant national religion. It was a complex quest that involved intellectual, institutional, religious, and professional issues. If, in retrospect, those who stood in the midst of this process did not succeed as well as they hoped, the story of their efforts still illumines the problems and potential of American theological schools.

CHAPTER TWO

Seminaries Face a Reordered World

If Princeton had fulfilled its destiny so well, why did the school find itself increasingly isolated at century's end? To a casual observer, the situation might have seemed like something out of Greek tragedy. All things were done well, but success brought its own punishment. And this interpretation contains much truth. Princeton had become almost an archetype of what its founders (and the founders of similar schools) hoped a theological school might be: intellectually vigorous, denominationally central, and theologically loyal.

These very attainments, however, were the things that put the school most at risk. History identifies the period between the Civil War and the First World War as one of rapid social and economic change wherein the older rural America was replaced with a new modern urban nation. Like all generalizations, this one has its weaknesses, and the exceptions to this thesis seem to render it less than compelling. After all, much of the South and West was still agrarian, and many of the inhabitants of the cities, including the waves of immigrants from eastern Europe, were more displaced rural people than sophisticated urbanites. Yet, all these qualifications notwithstanding, change happened. Not surprisingly these changes were felt most acutely in educational institutions. Schools straddle generations: they transmit to the coming generation the wisdom of the past and prepare the new generation to take leadership. Schools are charged with preparing a new generation to enter not the present world of their parents' culture, but the coming world that current movers and shakers have seen only at a distance.

I. A New Land, Yet More New

The half-century separating the Civil War from the First World War saw the transformation of almost all areas of American life.[1] Few events in history have a clean beginning or ending point, and this was as true of this half-century as of any other epoch. Two of the most important agents of social change, the railroad and industrialization, began before the War between the States, and both were important factors in the North's eventual victory in that contest. Yet the Civil War does mark the beginning of a period of rapid and sustained change in American life. The war was both catalyst and cause of the increased pace of modernization that followed Lee's surrender.

The war acted as a catalyst by generating a seemingly unlimited demand for goods and services. The growth of this demand was almost exponential. Despite Lincoln's initial confidence that the struggle might last only a few months, his constant calls for more and more men led the nation inexorably to construct one of the largest military machines ever assembled. This machine required everything: guns and butter, petroleum and whale oil, uniforms and bandages, food and medicine, horses and railroads. Those who sold these goods profited mightily, and in turn purchased more goods and services. In short, the war was like a giant money pump, watering the economy. For those young Americans fortunate enough or wealthy enough not to serve, there were fortunes to be made, and some made them. Many of these new capitalists were born around 1839, including John D. Rockefeller, J. P. Morgan, Andrew Carnegie, and Jay Gould. Some of these new fortunes would help finance American philanthropy, including schools. In turn, the new money is a cause of prosperity in that money,

1. For the theme of transformation, see Thomas J. Schlereth, *Victorian America: Transformations in Everyday Life* (New York: HarperCollins, 1991); Robert Wiebe, *The Search for Order, 1877-1920* (New York: Hill and Wang, 1967); Samuel Hayes, *The Response to Industrialism, 1885-1914* (Chicago: University of Chicago Press, 1957; rev. ed., 1995); Howard Mumford Jones, *The Age of Energy: Varieties of American Experience, 1865-1915* (New York: Viking Press, 1971); and Alan Trachtenberg, *The Incorporation of America: Culture and Society in the Gilded Age* (New York: Hill and Wang, 1982). Warren Susman, *Culture as History: The Transformation of American Society in the Twentieth Century* (New York: Pantheon Books, 1984), is a very important contribution to cultural and social historiography. The word "revolution" and its various cognates have become somewhat hackneyed in describing rapid cultural and social change and make it difficult to identify the dynamics of change. In contrast, a transformation suggests that the material substance of a thing is given another form or shape. Thus the transformation of agriculture includes the introduction of new forms of machinery, such as the harvester; the development of the steam and gasoline tractors; the introduction of hybrid seeds; and the new experimental farming of the state agricultural universities. When all these were applied to traditional agriculture, one of the world's most stable vocations became something quite different from what it had been.

wisely invested, contributes to further economic growth. Equally important, the existence of large capital stocks contributes to people's willingness to lend more money for more new enterprises. The United States was a debtor country until World War I, but one reason it could be such was that it had enough capital on its own to encourage foreign investors to put up their capital.

What was happening in America (and for that matter, throughout western and much of central Europe) was what might be called the end of scarcity. The new industrialization, particularly in transportation and communications, was making possible an unprecedented level of production and consumption. In part, this was the result of technical and scientific advance. Once Americans and Europeans, for instance, learned more about the germ theory of disease and, in particular, about the relationship between sanitation and health, they were able to move the privy inside the house and connect it to a sewer line, and clean up the neighborhood. Such transformations of everyday life took place at almost blinding speed. A new innovation would be discovered, often in a German laboratory, and there would be a limited commercial application in or near the largest cities. Within a short time the innovation would spread to smaller cities, then to towns, and finally to those rural areas closest to urban centers. In fact, the presence or absence of certain material comforts provided Americans of that time with their symbols of the culturally backward. The outdoor privy or outhouse, itself a response to new sanitation measures, was used in many cartoons to mark the boundaries between the sophisticated readers and those whose lifestyles were now open to mockery.

The flow of goods and services meant that scarcity, at least as people had traditionally understood that term, was becoming a thing of the past. What was produced in one region could be carried by rail through the nation in a matter of days. Meat, slaughtered in Chicago, could be served in New York, and was as fresh or fresher than meat locally prepared. The same was true of almost all agricultural and manufactured goods. In the not-so-distant past, only coastal ports or cities on deep rivers could enjoy access to such largesse. What the railroad did was make America a vast inland sea with almost every town enjoying the economic privileges of a port.

Changes in transportation deeply affected how the residents of American cities lived their everyday lives.[2] The traditional American (and European) city was defined by a dense core population that had access to the rest of the city by

2. Two of the most important studies of this transformation, Kenneth T. Jackson, *Crabgrass Frontier: The Suburbanization of the United States* (New York and Oxford: Oxford University Press, 1985), and Sam Bass Warner, *Streetcar Suburbs: The Process of Growth in Boston* (Cambridge: Harvard University Press, 1978), give detailed pictures of this process and its relation first to the horsecars and then to the electric trolleys.

foot. Beginning with the horsecar and railroad and accelerating with the electric streetcar, it became possible for people to live a greater distance from the center, particularly if they had enough money to use the emerging transportation system. Those comfortably well-off could live a substantial distance from their place of employment, although an hour's commute was about all that most were willing to invest. The benefits for this sacrifice of time and treasure were great. The cities were traditionally scenes of contagion, and both human and animal filth lay scattered on the few open spaces. Further, the density of population enabled microbes to spread quickly from one person to another, giving cities a consistently high mortality rate. Add to this the other advantages of new areas of settlement, including the greater privacy of a detached or semidetached house, the beauty of a lawn and garden, places for children to play, and the often-lower price of real estate, and flight to the suburbs was a very rational decision.

Immigration was closely related to the growth of transportation and the transformation of the cities. On the one hand, the development of both the railroads and the ocean steamer meant that ordinary people could travel relatively cheaply from one area to another. Throughout Europe, the United States, and Canada cheap transportation contributed to the beginning of a massive population shift as rural dwellers deserted the countryside for the nation's cities. The railroad remade the world as metropolis, whether that world was Berlin, New York, or Toronto. The cheap ocean steamer, itself a development of the same technology that created the railroads, enabled people to cross the ocean, especially in steerage, for a relatively low fare. To the poor peasant, New York was not much more distant, measured in financial costs, than London, and many believed it more hospitable. Further, news of employment in the Pennsylvania coalfields did not take long to reach Poland or the Ukraine. Culture, particularly ideas, crossed the seas with similar ease. The "latest" German opera, Parisian fashion, or English novel was available in New York shortly after its introduction abroad.

The very fact of such a material cornucopia raised the question of why everyone did not share, at least to some extent, in the new wealth. The question was most acute in the South and the West. The new system of production added value to raw materials at each stage of their manufacture. As the processing became more sophisticated and elaborate, the value added was proportionally greater. Both the South and the West were primarily producers of raw materials and simple manufactures based on extractive industries. As such they were at the bottom of the economic ladder, receiving comparatively little for products that were labor-extensive. Resentment of the industrial East was always high and occasionally led to political unrest. The working classes (the plural is important) also felt a similar relative deprivation. Craft workers, for instance, saw themselves as almost entering the broad middle ranks of American society. Many were able to purchase small homes in the "streetcar" suburbs of the cities, often their children went to high school or beyond, and later, along with the farmers, they would be part of the "mass market" that created the American automobile industry. But the "almost" was a key word, and falling just short was as painful in the city as in the countryside. The less skilled and the unskilled found their position one step closer to desperate, but they were less able to organize, in part, because their numbers were swollen by large numbers of immigrants whose cultural isolation made effective protest more difficult. Protest was also dampened by the fact that many of these immigrants found life in America much more financially stable than their old life in Europe. Even if America was not the land of milk and honey they had been promised, it was much better than what they had previously or perhaps better than what the more sober-minded had expected when they sailed for the new world. The new communications and transportation system kept the immigrant well acquainted with conditions back home.

The war did more than provide a new source of capital. Although we usually view the struggle in the framework provided by military history, the war was also an important chapter in the development of American management. To put that large an army into the field, to supply it, to take measures to protect the physical health of the troops, and even to supply it with religious services was a tremendous undertaking that required creativity and imagination beyond anything that Americans had attempted earlier.

After the war American entrepreneurs continued to experiment with larger and more integrated patterns of organization. The achievement of the new industrialists did not lay in their ability to either create or recognize technical innovation. Only two of the nation's greatest tycoons, Thomas Edison and Henry Ford, were inventors with hands-on knowledge of their businesses. The others — the Vanderbilts, the Hills, the Carnegies — were essentially organizers who were able to envision how large numbers of men, complex and expensive machinery, and widely dispersed markets could be brought under control. They were people of order in yet another sense as well. None of them were laissez-faire capitalists. The most striking business innovations of the period were such legal fictions as the trust, which attempted to place certain enterprises, such as railroads, coal, oil, and steel, outside the routine business cycle. The logic of this, at least in retrospect, is obvious. The large American market was subject to periods of intense boom and bust in which the fortunate few, whether bears or bulls, profited, and many fine enterprises collapsed beneath the weight of fair and unfair competition. Price was a major factor in this struggle for existence. To maintain market share and to keep very expensive machinery busy, producers had to cut prices to increase sales in depressed times, and thus drive those firms that could not sustain the losses to the wall. Once prosperity returned, of course, prices would rise again. It is better, the captains of industry reasoned, to find ways of controlling prices, production, and entry into the marketplace. Large corporations, trusts, holding companies, large-scale commercial banking, etc., were attempts at a solution.

Perhaps the greatest triumph of the new management was the organization of the nation's railroads.[3] The railroads had to run on a tight schedule that enabled them to make maximum use of very large but finite resources. In simple terms, the more people and freight they could move on their lines, the higher their profits. Telegraph wires that paralleled the tracks kept track of the various trains' arrival and departure times from particular points along the way, and conductors, whose authority was symbolized by their oversized and very accurate watches, did all they could to insure that the schedule was met. Also, Pullman cars or sleepers, which were actually owned by the Pullman Company, had to be added or subtracted from the train and such routine tasks as refueling and provisioning had to be carried out. The organizational needs of the railroad, further, provoked one of the most radical transformations of everyday life. Americans had been in the habit of setting local time by the position of the sun; hence, the time varied from city to city, not to mention from state to state or from region to region. In an action of great boldness, the railroads divided the nation into four time zones — significantly based more on business needs than on geography — and persuaded the nation to accept them. Meanwhile Frederick Taylor (b. 1856) monitored the movements of factory workers in an effort to find the most efficient way to accomplish a variety of management tasks.

II. An Organizational Movement of Their Own

America's churches began their own participation in the organizational revolution during the Civil War. To be sure, both armies needed chaplains, and both were more or less successful in recruiting able people for those positions. But even more important was the discovery that such sacramental ministry was not sufficient. Under the leadership of the Young Men's Christian Association (YMCA), Protestant evangelicals organized the Christian Commission to help

3. The growth of the railroads throughout this period was extraordinary. In 1865 the nation had 35,000 miles of track; in 1880, 93,000 miles; in 1890, 164,000; and in 1916, 254,000. The railroads influenced every area of American life. One of the best introductions to railroad history remains John Stover, *American Railroads* (Chicago: University of Chicago Press, 1961; new ed., 1997).

meet the spiritual needs of the troops.[4] The commission was no minor undertaking. Over five thousand people, both ministers and laypeople, took time to be with the army, talking to the wounded, reading Scripture, helping young men write letters home, reading letters from home, working with medical supplies, and providing some amateur nursing.[5]

The YMCA, sponsor of the Christian Commission, was perhaps the most important large-scale Protestant undertaking between the Civil War and the First World War.[6] George Williams had founded the Y in 1844 as a way of helping young immigrants from the countryside find their way in the city. The Y's structure evolved in a way similar to the bureaucracies of many influential businesses. In its earliest days the Y's structure was largely based on finding volunteers who could get the work done. But as time passed people with special skills needed in different aspects of the work became more and more competent in those areas. Naturally, they began to recruit others with those same skills and to provide those people with more training and education. By World War I the Y's organizational structure was as complex as that of any worldwide business enterprise.

The YMCA initially stressed Bible study groups and evangelism. As its leaders learned more about late nineteenth-century young men, they began to expand their services. By the 1870s the Y was constructing buildings that combined places for meetings, gymnasiums, and other recreational facilities. This expanded understanding of the organization's mission was expressed in its familiar triangle logo that stood for the union of body, mind, and spirit.

The Y's leaders were also among the advocates of a new understanding of Christian manhood or masculinity.[7] This new understanding saw sports and

4. J. Moorhead, *American Apocalypse: Yankee Protestants and the Civil War, 1860-1869* (New Haven: Yale University Press, 1978).

5. Harry S. Scott and D. Scott Cormode, "Institutions and the Story of American Religion: A Sketch of a Synthesis" (unpublished), p. 17, offer a similar view of the importance of the organizational experience of the Civil War. "For example, Peter Dobkin Hall argues that the centralized hierarchies we associate with bureaucratization actually began with ministers theologizing about the role of voluntary associations in the 1840s and 1850s. The organizational link between antebellum religion and postbellum business, he argues, is the relief effort of the Civil War. Parallel organizations arose under the pressure of war, separated compassionate charity from efficient philanthropy."

6. The standard history of the YMCA is Charles Howard Hopkins, *History of the YMCA in North America* (New York: Association Press, 1951). Hopkins is particularly useful in detailing the complicated organizational changes in this period.

7. One of the most useful histories of the changing understanding of masculinity in this period is Anthony Rotundo, *American Manhood: Transformations in Masculinity from the Revolution to the Modern Era* (New York: Basic Books, 1993).

physical competition as a substitute for such traditionally masculine rites of passage as war and the duel. Above all, it saw the Christian knight as one who was devoted to Christian action of all kinds: evangelism, Sunday schools, missions and youth work, and eventually social and political reform. Eventually the Y was involved in almost every cooperative Christian activity, including serving as an important recruiting agent for the ministry.

The Y was a serious attempt to deal with one of the crises of late nineteenth-century faith: the growing alienation of men from the churches. The churches' difficulties reaching men had many different dimensions. Not only were women and children approximately two-thirds of those attending services, but much contemporary religious language with its emphasis on "trust and obey" was in direct conflict with the average young man's need for striving and personal success and with society's expectation that men would triumph on the urban frontier.

Another way to look at the Y is to see it as one of the earliest and most successful Protestant parachurch bodies. Essentially, a parachurch body undertakes a ministry, often evangelistic or missionary, on behalf of Christians but without formal ties of ecclesiastical financial support or control. These groups are thus nests of activists, held together by minimum theological commitments. The combination of a commitment to action and a tendency to travel light theologically enables parachurch bodies to adjust quickly to changing conditions that will later on impact congregations. In other words, parachurch bodies provide American religious entrepreneurs with a religious and socially acceptable way to provide services without waiting for the permission of ecclesiastical authorities who do not see the same opportunities. These "Captains of Faith" often had the same skills and abilities as the "Captains of Industry" that dominated the secular economy.

Dwight L. Moody (1837-99) was a Christian organizational artist, perhaps the faith's version of a Rockefeller or a Carnegie. Moody learned the art of organization during the Civil War as a member of the U.S. Christian Commission and perfected it while serving as the energetic secretary of the Chicago Y. His passion for Christian outreach led him to continually try new experiments. For instance, becoming aware of the plight of poor children in the slums, he went into one of the darkest corners of Chicago, rented a saloon for Sundays, and invited the children to come in. Work with the children led him to work with their parents, and he established a church for those without social position. The same organizational skill led him, after the initial destruction of his work in the Great Chicago Fire of 1871, to develop a new style of evangelism that rested on the thorough organization of a city's Christians before the revival began and the skillful use of advertising and the press to popularize his meetings. Almost everyone who founded a significant parachurch body between the 1880s and 1920 was deeply influenced by his spirit and his work.

The Student Volunteer Movement (SVM), a youth movement devoted to the "evangelization of the world in this generation" that came to have representatives on the vast majority of the nation's campuses, was founded during Moody's 1886 student conference at Mount Hermon, Massachusetts. The group's youthful advocates, Robert E. Speer and John R. Mott, carefully divided the nation's campuses between them and set out to visit many of them with word of the new organization. The success of the SVM was a major factor in the church's development of newer means of fund-raising, since the movement had produced more people willing to serve than the traditional missionary collections could support. It, incidentally, also led many into the theological seminaries, causing those institutions to experience a minor boom in class size and to dream again of restricting admission to college graduates.

At the same time Moody and the Y made the parachurch movement more prominent, the denominations were undergoing an organizational revolution.[8] With the partial exception of the Methodists, antebellum American Protestantism had been organizationally light. The various denominations had just enough organization to provide a measure of discipline over the clergy, although even this modicum of control was lacking among some congregationally based churches. Extras, such as a denominational press or home missions or Sunday schools, had often been handled by individual initiative. For instance, *Bibliotheca Sacra,* perhaps the premier antebellum theological journal, was privately owned. We see some important exceptions to this pre–Civil War pattern. Methodists early established a national press, and Old and New School Presbyterians came to place their missions under General Assembly patronage. After the Civil War, however, American churches organized themselves more closely, following modern business methods, and the phenomenon of the church headquarters came into being. In some denominations, such as the Congregationalists, this was painful. It was not until 1871 that this denomination had its National Council to coordinate its work, and even then the council's mandate was very restricted. Only in 1913 did the churches grant it some more clearly administrative functions. By 1908, when thirty-three American denominations founded the Federal Council of Churches, the churches had de-

8. For the organizational changes in the churches, see Ben Primer, *Protestants and American Business Methods* ([Ann Arbor]: UMI Research Press, 1979). Although he deals in more detail with some of the later changes, James Moorhead, "Engineering the Millennium: Kingdom Building in American Protestantism," *Princeton Seminary Bulletin* 15 (1994): 104-28, is a useful source.

veloped an able, competent corps of administrators and others with organizational skills.[9]

Part of the history of late nineteenth-century Protestantism was the jockeying for position between organizations that were primarily tied to the parachurch world and those that were more related to the various denominational structures. The Sunday school was one of those contested areas. During the fifty years that followed the Civil War, the various denominations struggled with ways to include the Sunday school in the larger church organization. Partially for theological and partially for financial reasons, various denominations became major producers of Sunday school materials and most had a national "board" charged with oversight of the work. Yet, much of the real excitement in the Sunday school movement was interdenominational. The large Sunday school parades in such cities as Washington, D.C., and Brooklyn were interdenominational in character, and the Chautauqua Assembly, founded by Methodists Lewis Miller and John Vincent as a "Sunday school" university, was never incorporated into any denominational structure. This aspect of the Sunday school encouraged denominational leaders, in fact, to resolve to work together in various conferences, conventions, and other organizations to try to bring order into this area of Protestant life.

Missions were both the core of the new denominational bureaucracies and an area that the new church leadership could never completely organize. Once the mission became the world, the work was beyond the organizational capacities of any one denomination or of all the denominations taken together. The massive size of the task, to be sure, inspired some church managers to enter into comity agreements that assigned certain areas to certain boards. In time this would be one of the inspirations of the ecumenical movement and of such meetings as Edinburgh 1910 that gathered missionary leaders from around the world. Nonetheless, there was always work to be done. The founders of the China Inland Mission, for instance, were appalled by the way denominationally financed boards hugged the coasts. With much bravado Hudson Taylor launched a movement in faith to reach all of that fabled land. The persistence of many independent missionary organizations was of course not peculiarly American. In Europe, such organizations were customarily separate from the official church government.

Youth work was another contested area. In 1881 Congregationalist Francis E. Clark of Portland, Maine, gathered the young people of his church together with a covenant of service, worship, and study. As Clark's work became

9. For the institutional changes in Congregationalism, see John von Rohr, *The Shaping of American Congregationalism, 1620-1957* (Cleveland: Pilgrim Press, 1992), p. 346.

known, other congregations established similar groups, and by 1887 Clark had gathered these into a national organization with its own magazine. Although Christian Endeavor, true to its Congregational roots, permitted some local variations, the societies came to be very similar to one another with committees devoted to service, to Bible study, and to missions. The national literature encouraged other uniformities as well. The success of Christian Endeavor inspired the various denominations to organize their own youth-training programs.

What, then, of the seminaries? Where did they fit in the emerging worlds of church organization? The answer is by no means clear. Almost all seminaries were private bodies, managed by boards of trustees that had fiduciary responsibility for the institutions. In many ways these boards were similar to the governing boards of other "charities" — in our twentieth-century parlance, nonprofits — and, like other charities, were related to the various denominations in different ways. Both Presbyterians and Methodists tended to claim the right to appoint the trustees for their schools, although this right often was pro forma. In Tennessee, when Methodists tried to use their privilege to select new members of the board of Vanderbilt University who were different from those desired by the board itself, the court ruled with the trustees. While Southern Methodists continued to claim that privilege at Emory and Duke, both established in reaction to the Vanderbilt case, they were careful not to conflict with those boards' wishes. The reunion of the Old and New School Presbyterians in the North in 1870 established an elaborate system of review of board and faculty appointments by the General Assembly. However, when the extent of this control was tested, for instance, by the decision of Union Seminary in New York to leave the denomination, the law sided with the school's trustees. The only case where the Presbyterian Church's authority over its seminaries was affirmed was when the General Assembly voted to place the authority for governing Princeton solely in the hands of its board, a decision in line with the general tendency in seminary organization.

In other words, the organizational revolutions of the late nineteenth century left the seminaries in a difficult position. On the one hand, they were clearly related to the various denominations that received reports from them and often debated their policies and finances in their various assemblies. Further, their graduates tied them to their sponsoring denominations. In the better-educated churches, the graduates of a particular school were at least a potential block of support for the seminaries in their church's councils. Moreover, the seminaries were closely related to the missionary movement. From the beginning, the mission boards had insisted on the highest level of education possible for male missionaries, and in turn the seminaries had actively supported the missionary effort. In most cases the leaders of the various new church bureaucracies were also graduates of the seminaries. The same was true of the pastorates of the larger and more influential churches.

Yet the lack of integration meant that the seminaries always had some distance from their denominations as well. James P. Boyce, the founder of Southern Baptist Theological Seminary, had the instincts of a fox when he devised the governance of his school. He wanted the school clearly identified with the Southern Baptist Convention, and yet he had the planter's fear of the populace. Hence, he very carefully worded the school's charter to allow the denomination to nominate new trustees for the school's board, while leaving election to the board clearly in the hands of its existing authorities.

One of the common elements in the confusion of seminary governance in this period was the tendency to rely on the confessional tradition to tether the schools to their sponsoring bodies. Protestants had relied heavily on confessions of faith in the Reformation and post-Reformation period to maintain a consensus in their often-contentious movements. While the confessions had different origins, they all represented political processes that enabled the new Protestant churches to stay on a more or less even course theologically. At times the nature of these compromises was subtly hidden from view. Melanchthon, for instance, wrote the Augsburg Confession with one eye on his contentious colleague Luther, who was carefully kept away from the diet in a semi-imprisoned residence at the Coburg, and the other on the various princes, who wanted to disturb the religious peace as little as possible. In contrast, other documents in the *Book of Concord,* the most authoritative collection of Lutheran confessions, were written in the heat of theological battle and afterward compiled in a single volume. The records of the debates in the Westminster Assembly also reflect both intense theological debate and artful compromise.

The basic idea was that a faculty member would affirm the confession of faith of the denomination in the same or similar language to that used by a minister of the church at ordination. For most faculty members this represented a second oath to teach in accord with the same basic documents and was, in that sense, not something added to their basic ministerial credentials. There were, of course, exceptions to this rule. Andover Seminary remained burdened by the so-called Associate's Creed, a long, detailed summary of early nineteenth-century Edwardsianism that was almost incomprehensible two generations later. But that exception affirms the more general rule that subscription was usually to a denomination's standard documents. After all, no other Congregational seminary, including the very Edwardsian Bangor or the proponent of older orthodoxy, Hartford, followed Andover's cribbed lead.

The exact meaning of subscription was (and in some schools, still is) a difficult matter to determine. For many people subscription was intended to be a clear statement of a professor's principles, a summary of what the teacher believed the Bible said, so to speak. Particularly outside the seminaries, people tended to view subscription in this manner. Others were not sure that subscription was that precise. They saw the various creeds more as symbols of a common faith than as summaries of biblical faith. Such folk wanted to affirm them in outline rather than in detail. In that sense subscription was a controversy waiting to happen, and almost every controversy in the later part of the nineteenth century included angry charges by conservatives that a professor had violated his oath and equally angry assertions of the integrity of the person under attack.

Despite the apparently legal quality of subscription, the separation of church and state may have in fact changed the meaning of the practice. Like many ties binding the seminaries to their denominations, confessional subscription was essentially voluntary; that is, it was primarily binding on the consciences of a school's teachers. It could hardly be otherwise. If for no other reason, the confessions spoke so definitely to so many different questions that agreement was often more to the spirit than to the letter of particular confessions. Even Charles Hodge, an intellectually and religiously committed confessionalist, had some reservations about such matters as infant damnation that were clearly taught in Westminster. However, there were more serious problems on the horizon than a professor's quibbles. Such collections as Philip Schaff's *Creeds of Christendom* revealed, at least for those with eyes to see, the variety and complexity of the Protestant confessional tradition.[10] It was difficult to read such collections without asking how much these documents could be binding on people who neither shared their context nor debated the issues that were central to them. For intellectually decisive souls, such issues were serious enough to raise the problem of what exactly professors affirmed when they swore that they held to a particular system of doctrine. However the confessions and creeds were understood, clearly their status as part of a school's legal governance was questionable. By 1880, it would be everywhere questioned.

In the looseness of their ties with their sponsoring bodies, seminaries had some affinities with the various parachurch bodies; there remained significant differences between them and such organizations as the YMCA, however. More than the cords of memory bound the schools to their denominations. Seminary graduates tended to hold the most influential pulpits, and the new bureaucracies tended to be recruited from the ranks of those who had completed advanced training. Further, seminary professors often served as church intellectu-

10. Philip Schaff, *The Creeds of Christendom* (New York and London: Harper and Brothers, 1919).

als for their denominations, producing the literature that enabled the churches to think through issues of faith and practice. There was also a reflective quality to the seminary that separated it from the more active realm of the parachurch organizations. In short, the seminary was part of neither of the great organizational movements in the late nineteenth-century church: they were not parachurch or missionary bodies, nor were they denominational agencies. Only a handful would be able to become national institutions or to penetrate effectively the larger religious and educational market.

Since the precise meaning of this outsider status was difficult to communicate, both within and without the schools, seminaries invited controversy and misunderstanding. Church people and ministers felt free to demand certain actions from what they believed were their schools, only to find that in most cases the existing structures resisted their demands. The seminaries were not part of the bureaucratic system of the churches. With few exceptions, the churches could not dictate such matters as curriculum, faculty members, or budget. Nor did they control the administration of the schools. On the other hand, seminary leaders, finding themselves chronically short of funds, appealed to the churches as though their ministry was a fully integrated part of the organization. They were frequently shocked that the churches did not usually respond favorably to their pleas.

Who then owned and governed the seminaries? One is tempted to say that those who paid the piper called the tune, and every seminary had its own lineup of supporters, whether contributors of funds or recruiters of students, that had some influence over the school's direction. But that statement is too simple. By 1914 seminaries had developed complex and often hidden systems of accountability that included other scholarly institutions; their own boards of trustees; their own internal bureaucratic structures, particularly the faculty meeting and the president's office; and that evasive presence, public opinion. At least before the First World War, their marginal participation in the managerial revolution of their times established some distance between the schools and their surrounding culture. In a time in which basic theological and moral issues would be contested, the ambiguity of this position may have been a blessing.

III. Of Money, Rails, and Locations

The new post–Civil War economy was crucial for the development of the American seminary. The nineteenth century was everywhere a great paradox. As Kenneth Scott Latourette has stated, this was the great century for Protestant missions, the period in which Protestants came to take seriously their responsibility for the evangelization of the world.[11] The same could be said of Protestant initiatives in home and urban missions. But despite the great revivals in America and such movements as the awakening movement *(Erweckungsbewegung)* in Germany, the Protestant churches seemed to be losing popular support. The resolution of this anomaly is that the increase of wealth as a result of industrialization permitted the churches to raise more money from a comparatively smaller base.

Unlike European universities or even the emerging American state universities, the government did not support American theological schools. In concrete terms, this meant that they depended on gifts for their financial lifeblood. When capital was readily available, as it was in times of financial boom, the schools could raise enough money to make some advances. Perhaps a wealthy person would be willing to make a substantial gift and endow a professorship or be persuaded to give substantial funds toward the construction of a new building. In times of depression, seminaries had to rely more on their investments and endowments and on smaller contributions from supporting churches.

Clearly, finances determined much of a school's life. A school's faculty and board, for instance, could clearly see the need for a professorship in a new area of study and not be able to secure the funds for that position. In such a case the school might wait for years before an enterprising president found a donor willing to underwrite the new discipline. More than any other factor, the need to increase funding produced gaps between a seminary's best thinking and its actual program. There was also a significant correlation between substantial endowments and a school's willingness to innovate theologically. By 1914 many of the better-endowed theological schools had lined up behind the new liberal theology and were actively engaged in implementing it in their curricula. These included Union (New York), Pacific School of Religion, Garrett Biblical Institute, Rochester, and Newton.

Finances were a major factor in a school's location. The other was availability to students and to churches. Both of these combined to make location in a city well served by the railroads an essential element in a seminary's success. Southern Baptist Seminary, located in Greenville, South Carolina, for instance, was unable to raise enough to pay for its operation, although the school's enrollment was substantial. This convinced President Boyce that he had to relocate. After many conversations with people in different areas, he decided to move the school to Louisville. Louisville, like most of Kentucky, had been

11. Kenneth Scott Latourette, *A History of the Expansion of Christianity* (New York: Harper, 1937-45).

spared the economic devastation that plagued the defeated South, and yet it contained many wealthy families with Southern and Baptist connections.

The motives for the move to Louisville were of course not only financial. Like other American enterprises, James Boyce, the school's professor of theology and first president, wanted to locate his school where it could be used to maximum effect. "With its extensive railroad facilities we are put in immediate connection with all portions of the South. . . . Beginning with Maryland on the northeast, and extending to Missouri on the southwest . . . in connection with the Southern Baptist Convention there are one million one hundred thousand church-members, and five million five hundred thousand persons associated with Baptist congregations, seven thousand Baptist ministers, and 13,000 churches."[12] Students came to the old "downtown" campus via the railroad, whose passenger station was conveniently nearby, and they went out from that campus on weekends to preach or otherwise attend to nearby churches on those same rails. In the 1920s the seminary moved out the trolley lines to a more suburban, parklike campus that offered all the advantages of the country with all the conveniences of the city. The trolleys were again at the base of the students' ministry.

Other schools also moved toward the nodes of the new transportation system.[13] McCormick Theological Seminary, for instance, moved to Chicago where it was both near rail transportation and significantly closer to its wealthy backers in the Fourth Presbyterian Church of that city.[14] Similar motives inspired Baptists to establish the "Old" University of Chicago and the Morgan Park Seminary in the Windy City, and they appear to have played a role in convincing Rockefeller to locate his new superuniversity in that city. Likewise, the Methodist decision to locate major schools in Evanston, Illinois, a Chicago streetcar suburb, and in Boston reflected the need for prime locations where wealth and the railroads intersected.

While some seminaries in the North had rural or semirural locations, such as Baptist Colgate, they were few. Where they existed, fellow members of

12. James P. Boyce, quoted in William Mueller, *A History of Southern Baptist Theological Seminary* (Nashville: Broadman, 1959), p. 45.

13. I have extended the thesis of John Stilgoe, *Metropolitan Corridor: Railroads and the American Scene* (New Haven: Yale University Press, 1983), to include seminaries. Stilgoe argues that the location of the railroads and their associated industries shaped the American industrial corridors.

14. William Cronon, *Nature's Metropolis: Chicago and the Great West* (New York: Norton, 1991), indicates that Chicago was almost a natural magnet for the resources of the Middle West and West and that goods and services tended to flow to this great inland port and railhead. The seminaries seem to follow the same pattern as other commodities.

their denominations often established rival schools nearby on the rails. Thus, by the 1850s Colgate found itself competing with urban and urbane Rochester, which, located in an expanding node of the New York rail system with close ties to the upper Midwest, offered many advantages not available to its more rural counterpart. Ironically, these advantages included access to more small, rural churches that students could serve while studying at the seminary. Despite the distance between Rochester and much of the countryside, rail transportation made it easier to travel from Rochester to a larger hinterland than was possible from Colgate. Distance was measured more in time than in miles. Similarly, Bangor Seminary, located in the heart of Maine's extractive industries, was able to send students out into the countryside on weekends because of its convenient location on the rails.[15]

Other rural schools were overtaken by events. Newton had been something of a small city in the Boston orb, but the coming of the streetcar made it part of the Boston system. Likewise, Cambridge, another small semi-urban enclave, was connected to the New England railroads via the trolley lines. In the South, progressive president Walter Moore of Union Seminary determined to move his school from rural Hampden-Sydney to Richmond. His motives were partially cultural. He was convinced that the cities were the future of the South. But finances and location also played into his decision. In addition to its place as a financial center, Richmond was the railhead that united Baltimore and Washington to the north, the Great Valley and Charlottesville to the west, Norfolk to the east, and Carolina to the south. In short, it was one place from which the three synods that supported the school could all be served.

Perhaps the best evidence of the power of the rails to influence seminary development in the post–Civil War years is that the new schools founded in the South and West to serve those areas tended to be established in cities located on or near the main trunk lines. Chicago was of course the great city of seminaries with almost twenty schools located in or near its limits by 1920. In the West, Iliff was located in Denver, the mountain railroad hub, and San Francisco and Los Angeles, the upstart city to the south, received their share of new foundations. In the San Francisco area the drawing power of transportation was so great that the schools were located near one another, like a string of academic pearls. At least part of the reason for the movement of the new Southwestern Baptist

15. For a discussion of the opportunities and limitations of Bangor's location, see Calvin Montague Clark, *History of Bangor Theological Seminary* (Boston: Pilgrim Press, 1916). The "urban legend" that grew up at Bangor was that farmers, noting the number of students on the Monday milk run returning to the seminary, compared them to "empties being returned to be filled." I have heard the same legend told about other schools.

Seminary from its original home in Waco, Texas, to Fort Worth was the latter city's key location on the Texas rail system.

The same pattern continued until the 1950s when the new interstate road system changed American transportation and resident patterns yet again. But the early impact of the railroads was to shape the seminary system for many years. In the 1960s, when financial needs and ecumenical commitments encouraged seminary consolidation or cooperation, the American Association of Theological Schools identified twenty-five potential clusters that could unite the vast bulk of the nation's seminaries. Despite the new prominence of the interstates, these were still the cities that the railroads had created. The interstates connected those cities that earlier had been railheads.

CHAPTER THREE

The Birth of the Classical Disciplines

The technological and transportation revolutions of the late nineteenth century had important indirect effects on the seminaries. Perhaps the most important of these was the acceleration of scholarship. Technological advance had often sparked intellectual exchange. The development of the printing press at the end of the medieval period is the most obvious example.[1] By increasing the production of books and insuring the delivery of more accurate texts, the printing press had made it possible for scholars to resurrect much of Europe's classical literature. Further, the printed text offered some possibilities for study that had not been previously used or understood. Since the texts were published and both students and others had ready access to them, it was possible for scholars in various locations to study them at the same time. "Footnotes" and other references insured that everyone was "on the same page."

Yet the dissemination of knowledge was still slow. Books moved, as did other commodities, primarily on the sea. Despite book fairs and other means of dissemination, many editions were easily obtained only in the city of their initial publication. To keep track of the most significant literature, scholars formed a "republic of letters" in which the learned used various informal means of communication to keep each other posted of the latest editions and scholarly conclusions. Although the academic system made some small improvements earlier, substantial change came in the nineteenth century. Many different elements served to make scholarly materials more available: government control of the mails; better shipping of printed materials; the expansion

1. Elizabeth L. Eisenstein, *The Printing Press as an Agent of Change: Communications and Cultural Transformations in Early Modern Europe* (Cambridge and New York: Cambridge University Press, 1979).

of libraries, public and private; and, especially after the establishment of rail lines and ocean liners, the easy and relatively inexpensive movement of people. Scholars could thus easily order the newer works in their area, and if they needed ancient or rare materials, travel to the libraries where those were stored. Further, the development of new forms of the press and of cheap paper ensured a steady stream of monographs and other scholarly productions. By 1870 a knowledge explosion was beginning that would, despite some slowing in times of war, affect the whole world.

The expansion of knowledge and the steady growth in resources fueled interest in scholarship and in scholarly specialization. Many current university disciplines, for example, were born in this period as learned people explored the new territories that lay outside of the traditional liberal arts. Throughout Europe the learned amateur in such areas as history and literary criticism was gradually replaced by the professional scholar who had a detailed knowledge of the literature and research methods appropriate to a particular field of inquiry.

American theological educators, whose schools had begun with rudimentary specialization in such areas as Bible, were avid supporters of the new specialization, even if their funds did not permit them to implement it fully. Chester Hartranft, shortly before he became president of Hartford Seminary, gave his fellow Dutch Reformed ministers his vision of the scholarly future:

> Why shall we relinquish the idea of being leaders in theological science? Let us look to the immediate expansion of the Faculty; there should be an early petition of labors, for there is not much future for any theological school which persists in saddling one man with four or five different subjects, any one of which is comprehensive enough to occupy his entire time. It is only the very lowest view of a Seminary as catechetical school, as a sort of manufactory for turning out ministers, that can refuse to lend a hand or give the dollar toward broadening the studies and toward making the Seminary a representative and stronghold of theological science. But you say, "Would you have six or eight professors to fifty students?" Yes, I would have a dozen professors to one student, because the function of a Seminary is not only to teach but to investigate; in five years these professors would have a hundred to listen to them; they would repeat the history of Leyden, Utrecht, Leipzig, and Berlin.

Hartranft knew this meant that the seminary had to shift its values from teaching to research and that this change would be both expensive and perhaps controversial. "Nor let us envy our professors their leisure. It is the leisure, other things being equal, which will make the investigators; it is the leisure which will produce the works. So glad was Leyden to have famous scholars in her halls, that she sometimes extracted no teaching service at all, that they have all their hours for research and authorship."[2] The drive to organize the seminaries around the emerging ideals of scholarship was one of the strongest factors shaping the seminary after the Civil War. Even those seminary leaders who wondered whether this goal was adequate to their institutions paid it some lip service and listed the works produced by the faculty with the same apparent pride as they did the students sent to foreign fields.

I. Specialized Knowledge

One way to describe this change is to say that the republic of letters came to be replaced by a system based on scholarly or scientific disciplines. We can view the new disciplines from a variety of perspectives. In one sense they were, like so much of late nineteenth-century American and European life, an attempt to impose order on a system of production. As the sheer amount of material available to scholars increased, they naturally began to divide up the subject matter among themselves. Although ideas move more rapidly than institutions, this process was slow. At the University of Berlin, the original theological faculty assigned its teachers to multiple fields. When funds became available, the school gradually allowed its teachers to work in more restricted areas. Apparently, the Old Testament was the first area to require a specialized instructor, and the New Testament, considered the common possession of all members of the theological faculty, the last. Faculties in America would follow a similar pattern. After listing all the areas the professor of Old Testament should discuss, William Rainey Harper declared: "First, no one man can be expected to do all this work. No one man can do it, and do it well. The Old Testament department must be doubly manned. Already this has been done in many seminaries; let all seminaries, that would rank high, see to it that there are two professors in the department of Hebrew and the Old Testament."[3]

Perhaps one reason for the early independence of Old Testament studies was that nineteenth-century scholars were rapidly mastering other Semitic languages, drawing parallels between them and Hebrew, and expanding their

2. C. D. Hartranft, *The Aims of a Theological Seminary: An Address Delivered Before the Alumni Association of the Theological Seminary, New Brunswick, NJ* (New York: Board of Publication of the Reformed Church in America, 1878), pp. 50-51.

3. William Rainey Harper, "The Department of the Old Testament in the Seminary," *Old Testament Student* 4 (1884-85): 136-38.

knowledge of the history of the Near East. To participate in that linguistic feast, however, a scholar had to set aside other concerns.

Interestingly, the German theological faculties, like their American counterparts, began a period of expansion in the 1860s.[4] The newly established German Empire of Wilhelm I was committed to education as part of its program of national renewal. While Wilhelm's government was clearly more interested in such matters as scientific and technical advance,[5] theology also benefited from the new appreciation for scientific and professional studies.

One can get a sense of the increasing complexity of American theological schools by looking at representative faculties from the early 1870s. At that time, for instance, the faculty of Andover Seminary was composed of a professor of theology, two professors in biblical studies, a professor in sacred rhetoric, a professor of speech, and a professor of church history.[6] All but one faculty member occupied a chair named for a specific individual. At the same time, Boston University School of Theology had five members, including William Warren, the vice president of the university, who were divided into systematic, historical, exegetical, and practical theology.[7] Boston, however, announced proudly in its catalogue that these teachers were supplemented by lecturers in ministerial office, character, and work; science and religion; missions and missionary work; and Sunday school management. Boston, a newer institution, did not have any named chairs at this time. Auburn Seminary could boast only five faculty members at this time — in Christian theology, sacred rhetoric and pastoral theology, ecclesiastical history and polity, biblical exegesis, and Hebrew language and lit-

4. George Anderson, "Challenge and Change within German Protestant Theological Education during the Nineteenth Century," *Church History*, Mar. 1970, pp. 33ff. This essay has been very influential in shaping my understanding of the relationship between American and German theological education in this period.

5. Much to the horror of academic traditionalists, Wilhelm II changed the entrance requirements for Prussian universities, reducing the requirements in the classical languages for all areas except theology and philology. He, like his father, was an active supporter of various advanced schools for scientific research.

6. Edwards A. Park, Abbot Professor of Sacred Theology; John L. Taylor, Smith Professor of Theology and Homiletics and Lecturer on Practical Theology; Austin Phelps, Barlett Professor of Sacred Rhetoric; Egbert C. Smyth, Brown Professor of Ecclesiastical History; J. Henry Thayer, Associate Professor of Sacred Literature; Charles M. Mead, Hitchcock Professor of the Hebrew Language and Literature; J. Wesley Churchill, Jones Professor of Elocution.

7. William F. Warren, vice president; John Lindsey, professor of exegetical theology; Luther T. Townsend, adjunct professor of historical theology; William F. Warren, professor of systematic theology; David Patten, professor of practical theology; lecturers: Bishop Davis W. Clark, ministerial office, character, and work; D. D. Lore, missions and missionary life; K. Ames M'Cosh, religion and the sciences; and John H. Vincent, Sunday school management and teaching.

erature.[8] The two Bible chairs, as elsewhere, mark the beginning of the separation of Old and New Testament studies. While some chairs were named for specific donors, others were named for heroes of the New School Theology, such as Edwards and Taylor. In contrast, Augustana Seminary, an immigrant school, had a faculty of four who were scattered over different disciplines. The same teacher was responsible for church history, symbolics, and isagogics, while another covered such diverse fields as Hebrew, Greek, and exegesis. Interestingly, some members of the faculty are designated as general professors.[9]

The expansion of faculties and subjects in both Germany and America led to an attempt to find the proper ordering of theological studies. In a sense, that search began with Friedrich Schleiermacher's *Brief Outline of the Study of Theology,* published in conjunction with the organization of the University of Berlin. In this masterful short treatise Schleiermacher attempted to demonstrate that the theological student should begin with such humanist studies as the philosophy of religion and work steadily through various historical studies until ready for practical theology. Most important to Schleiermacher's understanding of theological study was his recognition that theological study was always the combination of diverse academic or scientific disciplines in the service of the church.

> Christian theology, accordingly, is the collective embodiment of those branches of scientific knowledge and those rules of art, without the possession and application of which a harmonious guidance of the Christian Church, that is a Christian Church Government is not possible. The said branches of knowledge when they are acquired and possessed without reference to the government of the church cease to have a theological character, and become assignable to those sciences [to] which, according to the nature of their contents, they respectively belong.[10]

In other words, theology was not a simple science that had an easily defined object or a single method. Part of what made theology theological was its capacity

8. Edwin Hall, Richards Professor of Christian Theology; J. B. Condit, Belamy Edwards Professor of Scared Rhetoric and Pastoral Theology; Samuel M. Hopkins, Hyde Professor of Ecclesiastical History and Church Polity; E. A. Huntington, Taylor Professor of Biblical Criticism; Willis H. Beecher, Professor Elect of Hebrew Language and Literature.

9. General faculty: O. Olsson, A. W. Williamson. Special faculties: Olof Olsson, president, professor of catechetics, homiletics, and pastoral theology; Nils Forsander, professor of church history, symbolics, and isagogics; Conrad Emil Lindberg, professor of dogmatics, liturgics, church polity, etc.; Carl Elofson, acting professor of Hebrew, Greek, and exegesis.

10. Friedrich Schleiermacher, *Brief Outline,* trans. William Farrer (reprint, Lexington, Ky.: American Theological Library, 1963).

to use materials from other sciences for ecclesiastical purposes. To give an example, if the study of ancient Babylonian enriched the study of the Old Testament, Babylonian had some claim to a place in theological studies.[11] And the converse was also true. It was possible to study the Old Testament apart from the service of the church. In that case, Old Testament studies would not be theological but philosophical.[12]

Schleiermacher's explication of theology as a professional or practical discipline was in line with German educational theory. Two specific points need to be noted. First, German governments early took control over the qualifications and education of professionals in their lands. In part, this was accomplished by moving the right to certify professionals from the universities to the government. Whatever students might want to get from their university study, they had to stand for a series of rigorous examinations that would determine their professional future. In addition, ministers were expected to stand for two church examinations in theological subjects. Second, unlike England or the United States, the German governments themselves were the primary employers of the middle classes. Beginning with such rulers as Frederick the Great and Joseph of Austria, German governments were acutely conscious that Germany was behind the Western states in scientific and economic development. The ease with which Napoleon had defeated the two most professional German armies, those of Prussia and Austria, made this same point even more forcibly. Once the strong post-Napoleonic reaction passed, German governments became the sponsors of universities, research institutes, mining and technical schools, and in fact anything that might contribute to the military and economic development of their country. The Krupp steelworks and the University of Berlin were both beneficiaries of this policy.

Schleiermacher's *Brief Outline* is important, primarily because it is so well

11. Schleiermacher's interpretation of theology could easily have been used in its outlines for law, the civil service, or medicine. All these fields borrow extensively from many disciplines to enable professionals to do their job effectively. Indeed, it was the flexibility of medicine that permitted it to move from the study of selected classical texts to an approach that used both chemistry and biology. Likewise, the good lawyer had a grasp both of the history of society and of government as well as a knowledge of specific legal practices. One misunderstands Schleiermacher if one assumes that his work was somehow developing a theology of ministry that was different from the theory that underlay other professions.

12. While Schleiermacher was primarily concerned with theology, his basic understanding of the nature of professional studies can be applied to any professional faculty. Sociology, for instance, taught in the school of social work, differs primarily in its goal, the informing of those who work caring for people, from sociology as taught in a faculty of arts and sciences. The same is true of anatomy taught in a medical school and anatomy taught as part of a biology program in the school of arts and sciences.

done. But the rapid increase of theological knowledge led many other nineteenth-century theologians to draw their own road maps of the study of theology. Whereas Schleiermacher's *Brief Outline* was primarily directed toward fellow teachers and the bureaucrats in the department of culture, most of these latter were written for beginning students who were planning their studies with an eye to the inevitable state examinations. Most apparently began as a series of university lectures. Perhaps the most important of these, at least judging by the number of English and American editions, was that of Karl Rudolf Hagenbach, *Encyclopaedie und Methodologie der theologischen Wissenschaften.*[13] Hagenbach divided theological studies into the now familiar fourfold pattern of biblical, historical, theological, and practical and suggested ways for students to concentrate their study. Each of the four areas of theology was then carefully divided into subdisciplines.

Apparently, American theologians took over from their German counterparts the practice of lecturing on theological encyclopedia. Although the work of August Tholuck circulated widely at midcentury,[14] the most important American version of the theological encyclopedia was that of George Richard Crooks and John Hurst, *Theological Encyclopaedia and Methodology: On the Basis of Hagenbach.*[15] Philip Schaff, who bore the title of professor of theological encyclopedia at one point, also published an influential encyclopedia.[16]

By 1900, while interest in the unity of the various theological disciplines continued,[17] the passion for theological encyclopedias began to abate. Although many reasons might be offered for this decline, the most important was the continued growth of the theological curriculum. Both the academic study of Christianity and the development of important insights into the church's

13. K. R. Hagenbach, *Encyclopaedie und Methodologie der theologischen Wissenschaften* (Leipzig: Weidmann'sche Buchhandlung, 1833).

14. August Tholuck, *Theological Encyclopaedia and Methodology* ([Andover, Mass.]: [Allen, Morrill, and Wardwell], 1844).

15. George Richard Crooks and John Hurst, *Theological Encyclopaedia and Methodology: On the Basis of Hagenbach* (New York: Phillips and Hunt; Cincinnati: Walden and Stowe, 1884). Bibliography and other materials in Hagenbach needed to be revised in the light of further research and Anglo-American practice. The practice of updating reference works was common in the nineteenth century. At times, the alterations in such texts were extensive. A person wanting a feeling for the transformation of such texts can examine the century-long tradition of the revision of Williston Walker.

16. Philip Schaff, *Theological Propaedeutic: A General Introduction to the Study of Theology, Exegetical, Historical, Systematic, and Practical, Including Encyclopaedia, Methodology, and Bibliography; A Manual for Students* (New York: Scribner, 1892-93).

17. In the 1930s William Adams Brown and Mark May would offer an important interpretation of theology based on the different tasks performed by the professional ministry.

place in contemporary culture continued, as did the attempt to systematize ministerial practice. Seminary catalogues and curricula increasingly contained long lists of courses, more or less organized under departments that were occasionally related to larger fields. More and more continued to be known, thought, and done. Knowledge of the whole was rapidly losing place to knowledge of the parts.

II. The Disciplines

The most important figure in the evolution of American theological scholarship was German-born Philip Schaff. Schaff began his career at tiny Mercersburg Seminary, a school maintained by the German Reformed Church; he used that platform to introduce Americans to German thinking about the church and sacraments. In 1863 he went to teach at Union Theological Seminary (New York), just as that school was beginning to assemble the premier theological library in nineteenth-century America. Surrounded by his beloved texts and supportive colleagues, Schaff became a theological cottage industry. Among his works were three volumes of *Creeds of Christendom,* an eight-volume *History of the Christian Church,* and a thirteen-volume translation of the Nicene and post-Nicene Fathers.

One can sense the strength of the new American critical community by examining some of the projects that required the cooperation of scholars. The first major cooperative work of scholarship was the translation of J. P. Lange's *Bibelwork,* a multivolume commentary published in Germany between 1858 and 1877. The *Bibelwork* represented the broad middle party in German theology that was very responsive to the new studies, especially in philology, but that also rejected the historical skepticism associated with some advanced critical positions.[18] Schaff, who had been interested in these commentaries from the appearance of their first volume, secured a contract from Scribner for the publication of the translations in 1862, and began the project in 1864. Lange's text separated the analysis of the text from its application, and Schaff enlisted prominent American preachers as well as scholars to work on different volumes. Schaff clearly saw the project in terms of the formation of an American biblical

18. In 1880 the Edinburgh firm of T. &. T. Clark, which published many German theological works, including Hagenbach's *Theological Encyclopedia,* elected to publish the commentaries of Franz Delitzsch, an influential German conservative. To get a sense of the speed with which German scholarship was moving, it was Delitzsch's son, a famous Orientalist, whose studies of Babylonian raised the intense "Bibel oder Babel" debate in the 1890s.

tradition. He urged his translators to update the research where appropriate and to translate the materials freely.[19]

The team Schaff enlisted for the Lange translation was crucial for several other early cooperative projects, the most important of which may have been the production of the Revised Version of the Bible (1881-85). In 1870 Bishop Samuel Wilberforce made a motion to the upper house of the Convocation of Canterbury that a revision of the Authorized Version be undertaken. The reasons for the revision were as important as the work itself. During the nineteenth century the gap between the text on which the King James translation had been based and the most probable readings of the manuscript tradition had widened. In his motion the bishop noted that the new version should indicate "by marginal notes or otherwise, . . . all those passages where [there were] plain and clear errors, whether in the Hebrew or Greek text originally adopted by the translators or in the translation made from the same."[20] With a few minor revisions the motion was passed, and two committees, one on the Old Testament and one on the New, were established. The archbishop of Canterbury, however, was aware that the Church of England only partially represented English Christian opinion. At his insistence representatives of the Scottish churches and of English dissent were invited to participate. Interestingly, the noted Unitarian scholar G. Vance Smith and John Henry Newman were both invited, although Newman was unable to participate. It was in line with this ecumenical approach to translation that the archbishop also invited the Americans to form an ecumenical committee that would work side by side with the English revisers.[21]

The project was not as easy as it sounded. Although the committees had been charged with changing as little as possible, once the work began it became clear that substantial changes would have to be made. The reasons were more scholarly than aesthetic. A century of intensive research had changed the understanding of the biblical languages themselves. Hebrew was now understood in terms of cognate languages that were unknown to the earlier translators, and the Greek of the New Testament, when viewed in historical perspective, was believed to be a koine, or common, Greek that substantially varied from the classical paradigms of the language. Translators had other important insights to

19. For Schaff's role in the Lange project, see George H. Shriver, *Philip Schaff: Christian Scholar and Ecumenical Prophet; Centennial Biography for the American Society of Church History* (Macon, Ga.: Mercer University Press, 1987), p. 50.

20. Quoted in F. F. Bruce, *The English Bible: A History of Translations* (London: Lutterworth, 1961), p. 135.

21. Philip Schaff wrote two accounts of the work of the revisers. *A Companion to the Greek New Testament and the English Version* (New York, 1883) and *A Documentary History of the American Committee on Bible Revision* (New York, 1885).

work with as well. Hebrew poetry, unlike the poetry of the West, tended to repeat images and concepts in different poetic lines. Thus the first line of a passage might refer to the starry heavens and the second line to the diamonds of the night. Knowing this, the revisers were able to break with tradition and publish their version with the poetic passages set in lines and stanzas.

Perhaps more than anything else, the complexity of the task may explain why the American and British revisers failed to agree on a number of points. By 1876 Schaff was engaged in anxious negotiations with his British counterparts. It was finally agreed that the initial publication of the revision would follow the British emendations but the American reservations would be published in an appendix.[22] After fourteen years the Americans secured permission to publish their own version. When the time came, they did so. The American committee continued to work on the problems in the interim. In effect, the revision of the Bible provided America's most advanced biblical scholars with a twenty-five-year seminar on textual and critical problems.

The revision itself inspired further scholarship. Alvah Hovey, the energetic president of Baptist Newton Seminary, believed that it provided a chance for Baptist scholars to demonstrate their wares. Using his extensive contacts among Baptist professors, he edited *An American Commentary on the New Testament.* The series placed the Authorized Version and the revision near each other so that the reader could see the nature of the changes. Of course, the notes made clear the reasons for those emendations and their scholarly support.

While Hovey's series was an important indicator that Baptist scholarship had acquired equality with that of the wealthier denominations, it was also important for indicating the growth of an American biblical discipline. To be sure, many of the contributions were not original in their thought or research, but all of them reflected a mastery of the contemporary exegetical literature. A major intellectual task could be assumed and completed.

Another example of intensive American scholarship, inspired in part by the revision, was James Strong's *Exhaustive Concordance,* published from 1890 to 1894. The work was much more than a list of where key words could be found in the Bible. In addition to listing the English words in both the King James Bible and the Revised Version, Strong traced each word back to its Hebrew or Greek original and indicated where that basic word occurred in the text. With knowledge of the languages, a scholar or minister could use this concordance as a valuable check on the English translation and revision. Yet, even if one's knowledge of these languages was poor or limited, the work made possible a much more careful understanding of the English than might have been

22. For these negotiations, see Shriver, *Philip Schaff,* p. 77.

otherwise possible. When Brown, Driver, and Briggs produced their updated version of Gesenius's *Hebrew Dictionary*,[23] they were careful to note that they had cross-referenced their entries to Strong's work.

The earliest American society related to theological studies was the American Oriental Society, founded in 1842 to promote the study of the new materials from the Near East. Interestingly, the society maintained its own library as well as its own journal. The Society of Biblical Literature and Exegesis was formed in 1880, and the American Society of Church History shortly thereafter in 1888. Not surprisingly, Philip Schaff played a major role in the formation of these two societies. Frederic Gardiner, a professor at Berkeley, an Episcopalian school in Connecticut, suggested that a society be formed devoted to "the promotion of study in biblical literature and exegesis."[24] An organizational meeting was held at Schaff's New York apartment that brought together Charles Briggs, Daniel R. Goodwin, Jacob I. Mombert, Charles Short, James Strong, and E. A. Washburn. They agreed "to form a Society of Biblical literature and exegesis for the purpose of promoting a thorough study of the Scriptures by the reading and writing of original papers."[25] Thirty-five scholars attended the first meeting. For the first ten years the papers published by the society were primarily exegetical in nature.[26]

The phrase "Biblical Literature and Exegesis" may have had a deeper meaning as well. In ancient Athens the exegete was the person appointed to read the laws annually to the people. The most common use of the verbal root of the word means to narrate. Hence the word came by extension to refer to interpretation. Throughout the late nineteenth century Western scholars tended

23. New editions of Gesenius appeared about every ten years. The reason was not only the love of revision. Knowledge of Hebrew and its cognates was growing very rapidly.

24. Ernest W. Saunders, "A Century of Service to American Biblical Scholarship," *Council on the Study of Religion* 11, no. 3 (June 1980): 69.

25. Saunders, "A Century of Service," p. 70.

26. The reasons for this concentration are not evident at this time. Saunders cites the opinion of T. H. Olbricht, "The SBL: The Founding Fathers," a paper read at the SBL meeting in 1978, that this may have been because many members of the society were moderates. While plausible, this explanation is not completely convincing. Many of the leaders, including Union's Francis Brown, were convinced higher critics. My own supposition is based more on what was done in the classroom. American biblical teaching was still overwhelmingly exegetical in character with only the most advanced schools moving toward something like the introductory or "bread courses" given in the German universities. Although the society removed the words "and exegesis" from its name in 1962, exegesis was very much what it meant to do biblical studies on an advanced level. The publication of the International Critical Commentary would later confirm the place of higher criticism in biblical study for many serious scholars by demonstrating that the new method's results could be confirmed exegetically.

to name their rapidly expanding academic disciplines after Greek precedents. Thus there were psychology, poimenics, and pedagogy. These new names served to set the scientific or scholarly study of a subject apart from its earlier antecedents in philosophy or the arts. Thus, many people replaced the older idea of natural philosophy or naturalism with such sophisticated coinages as zoology. For exegesis the older term had been "exposition," a word that included both the more rigorous type of study characteristic of the schools and the churches' attempt to repristinate that meaning in its contemporary message. Interestingly, Lange's commentary, which was so vital to the development of the discipline, separated the exegesis from the exposition, as would the later *Interpreter's Bible.* The much more technically precise International Critical Commentary omitted exposition altogether.[27]

Although church history had long been part of the American seminary curriculum, it was not as central as biblical studies and developed more slowly. Ironically, its development might have been slowed by the significant number of works by such European masters of the craft as Neander and by such major European projects as Migne's *Patrologia.* The *Patrologia* was a collection of the writings of the Latin and Greek Fathers that eventually included 162 volumes of Greek text and 221 volumes of Latin. While Migne's texts had many misprints and critical errors, they made it possible for the most provincial library to acquire the tools for serious research.[28]

Like American biblical studies, American church history developed through the publication of significant works and collections. Schaff's translation of the Nicene and post-Nicene Fathers, which was reprinted as recently as 1976, provided American readers with important texts and, equally importantly, with sufficient historical and grammatical notes to make them intelligible.[29] Schaff was also a leader in the production of significant reference volumes. The great German encyclopedia by Herzog, Plitt, and Hauck had an American edition as early as 1858,[30] and Schaff's three-volume edition was a late

27. See *OED* articles, "exegesis" and "exposition." The German *Schriftsauslegung* and the English "exposition" are linguistic parallels. Another such pair of words is "interpretation" and "hermeneutics." "Interpretation" is customarily used for the more popular attempts to understand a text, while "hermeneutics" tends to be used for those interpretations done in a more scholarly or systematic fashion.

28. See R. H. Bloch, *God's Plagiarist: Being an Account of the Fabulous Industry and Irregular Commerce of the Abbé Migne* (Chicago and London: University of Chicago Press, 1994).

29. Schaff's work on the texts apparently stopped with the second volume. After that, the work was continued by an associate.

30. *The Protestant Theological and Ecclesiastical Encyclopedia: Being a Condensed Translation of Herzog's Real-Enzyklopädie* (Philadelphia: Lindsay and Blakiston, 1858).

nineteenth-century standard reference. The various editions of this classic illustrate the rapid growth of American scholarship. The 1900 edition, now sold as the Schaff-Herzog *Encyclopedia of Religious Knowledge,* had thirteen volumes. The able S. M. Jackson supervised much of the expansion. A similar project, and one that also retained its value, was John McClintock and James Strong's *Cyclopaedia of Biblical, Theological, and Ecclesiastical Literature.*[31]

These great reference works were, of course, valuable for the sheer mass of information they assembled. If a person wanted to know the basic outline of what scholars had learned about such topics as the history of the canon, the beginnings of Christianity in Russia, or the development of theology in Germany, they gave a succinct and well-researched outline. Many articles, further, had a short list of the basic literature available on the topic. In this sense the encyclopedias were a way of organizing the massive amount of information that was becoming available in monographs and journal articles. While they were not intended to provide original research, the better articles were such accurate summaries of the current research as to make the often-halting steps of investigators seem to follow a logical path through complex material. But what is interesting about these volumes is that American scholarship had matured enough to provide authors, editors, and, equally important, a market for such undertakings. Despite the expense of purchasing such reference works, most American seminaries had one or more editions of them in their libraries. While these references were not a substitute for the many volumes and articles they summarized, they did have the practical effect of making information readily available to students and teachers.

The American Society of Church History had inauspicious beginnings. The American Social Science Association was the oldest society working in a similar area, having been founded in 1865. As specialization advanced in universities and colleges, historians formed their own professional body, the American Historical Association, in 1885, the same year the American Economic Association was formed. As was true for the Society of Biblical Literature, the organizational meeting was held in the home of Philip Schaff, who selected the participants. The first meeting was held in Washington, D.C., that year. Perhaps the most interesting aspect of the early history of this society was its difficulty in deciding whether it was a section or branch of the American Historical Association or whether it was an independent body. From 1897 to 1906 it was part of the larger organization, and it has continued to hold its meetings at the same time as the larger group.[32]

31. John McClintock and James Strong, *Cyclopaedia of Biblical, Theological, and Ecclesiastical Literature* (New York: Harper, 1869-80).

32. Henry Warner Bowden, "The First Century: Institutional Development and Ideas

These societies performed two services for the emerging disciplines. First, their journals provided a way for interested scholars to keep up with the developments in their own fields. Far more books were published than any particular scholar could hope to read, and the reviews were important for separating important from less important studies and for their overview of current research. Second, the societies provided an opportunity for some scholars in the disciplines to meet together. This provided a way to exchange information and promote the careers of younger colleagues whose work was not yet known.

Perhaps the most interesting failure to form a discipline was in systematic theology. Despite the formation of the American Theological Society, systematic or dogmatic theologians did not come to a similar technical understanding of their craft. The reasons for this are complicated. In part, it was the difficulty of establishing any consensus on the method that should be employed in doing systematic theology. Theologians did not have (and still do not have) any ready analogue to the methodological consensus found among biblical scholars and historians, and much of the material they use, including biblical and historical materials, is treated by the historical disciplines. But the reason may be more than the ability to develop a place in a larger scheme of scholarly investigation. Particularly in America, systematic theologians have been charged with more than the orderly study and development of the church's teachings. They are the ones in the seminary community charged with maintaining a measure of coherence in the midst of the rapidly changing modern intellectual world. In many cases this meant that the theologian was much more of a public Christian intellectual than his or her faculty counterparts. This task did not involve determining what a text said or meant in its own context, but what faith might mean in the modern world.

III. Scholarly Skills

American theologians began traveling to Germany in the 1820s for advanced study. The numbers seeking such training increased steadily throughout the middle decades of the nineteenth century and apparently began to decline after that. During that crucial half-century, most of the acknowledged leaders in

---

about the Profession," in *A Century of Church History,* ed. Henry Warner Bowden (Carbondale and Edwardsville: Southern Illinois University Press, 1988), pp. 294-97, suggests several reasons for this organization's struggles over its identity. Although Bowden did not stress it, the most important reason for the group's indecisiveness may have been that there were few real differences between the two groups of historians, other than subject matter. In that sense church history was one of many historical specialties. Since 1907, other historical specialties have formed their own societies: American historians, western historians, women historians, etc.

American theological education spent time studying in Germany. These included scholars as diverse as Methodists William Warren White and Hinckley Mitchel, Baptists Crawford Toy and William Whitsitt, and Presbyterians B. B. Warfield and William Adams Brown. In 1890 the majority of the faculties of Princeton and Union had some German training, and even schools less noted for scholarship had some teachers who had studied abroad. Theological schools were not alone in relying on Germany for an understanding of the basic disciplines. Particularly in such areas as physics and chemistry, German-trained scholars made up the bulk of the American professorate.

What did Americans find when they went to Germany? Although both nineteenth- and twentieth-century Americans have tended to see German theology and scholarship as homogeneous, Southern theologian Robert Dabney accurately warned his readers: "Men speak of 'German theology' . . . often as though it were something single and unique, and separated from all other schools of theology by uniform traits. Whereas there are as many German theologies, at least, as there are British or American, differing as widely from each other in merit and opinions."[33] Throughout the century the German schools were marked by intense theological and scholarly debate. In some states these debates were sufficiently divisive for various state ministries of culture (or other appropriate governmental bodies) to insist that the faculties appoint certain candidates to balance the views of one or another party.[34]

What did American theologians see when they went to Germany, and what did they learn? We must remember that most Americans who went to Germany to study did not take a degree, nor did they plan to. The purpose of their trip was often to learn the language, to meet the most important scholars, and to collect books for their own institution's libraries. Like their contemporaries who founded museums, large public libraries, opera houses, and orchestras, Americans visiting Europe were in search of a culture that could give luster to an American culture that many saw as somewhat rude and materialistic. As

33. Robert L. Dabney, "The Influence of the German University upon Theological Literature," *Southern Presbyterian Review*, Apr. 1881, pp. 440-65.

34. Anderson, "Challenge and Change," p. 33. I am deeply indebted to Anderson throughout this section. Other principal works that inform my understanding are Daniel Fallon, *The German University: A Heroic Ideal in Conflict with the Modern World* (Boulder, Colo.: Associated University Press, 1980); Charles E. McClelland, *State, Society, and University in Germany, 1700 to 1914* (Cambridge and New York: Cambridge University Press, 1980). In addition, two "midlevel" sources were extremely important. Friedrich Paulsen, *The German Universities and University Study* (New York: Scribner, 1906), which was originally prepared as part of the German exposition at the Chicago World's Fair, and Abraham Flexner, *Universities: American, German, English* (New York: Oxford University Press, 1930).

pilgrims, they were convinced that the Holy Grail was at the end of their quest, and hence they were not surprised when they found it. Perhaps most important, most of them were not "students" in the ordinary sense of the word. Almost all had completed a full seminary course from one of the stronger seminaries, such as Andover, Union, or Princeton, and most had been thoroughly drilled in linguistic studies before they traveled. Further, these were students who had been already marked, either by inclination, temperament, or performance, as potential candidates for the professorate or were actively engaged in teaching before they went. Hence they were highly selective in how they used the university. In a letter back home to William Rainey Harper in 1894, a man named Burton wrote with some pride that he both registered for and attended Harnack's lectures.[35] Their selective view probably made them more oblivious than usual to parts of the German system. Only a handful, like Shailer Mathews, for example, noted that German students tended to receive their academic training in the university and then, between their first and second theological examination, their practical training in the church.[36]

In one sense Americans visiting Germany were involved in a great circle of expectations. As students in American seminaries, they had been introduced to German scholarship of a high quality. They expected to find such intellectual attainments when they arrived, and to no one's surprise they discovered what they had been primed to expect. But this argument should not be carried too far. Particularly in such areas as biblical studies and church history, both American and British scholars recognized that Germany had established a clear lead, much as Germany also had in such areas as chemistry and electrical manufacturing. In going to Germany they were seeking to find a way to meet or (perhaps in their secret dreams) to exceed this real standard in their own work.[37]

35. Burton to Harper, 1894, University of Chicago Archives.

36. "Most of the American theological students were planning to become teachers, and inevitably carried into American theological education this attitude of the German university. Different results might have followed had they attended the German institutions devoted to the practical aspects of ministry." Shailer Mathews, *New Faith for Old: An Autobiography* (New York: Macmillan, 1936). American Lutherans, in contrast, were actively aware of this feature of European education, and while they generally did not adopt the two-examination system, they did retain the idea of a vicar year in which the student supplemented formal academic training with practical experience and some peer seminars.

37. The British also envied the Germans, but unlike the Americans, they did not have as deep a sense of inferiority. Hence, they were often more selective in what they took from their study of German scholarship. But Britain had its own clearly defined educational system that was rapidly modernizing. Not only were dissenters to be admitted to the schools, but a system of examinations was instituted that, if not quite as detailed as the German state exams, served a similar purpose.

The American theologians who visited Germany were deeply impressed by three aspects of their experience. First, they were impressed with the academic freedom that German professors claimed for their own work. While there were in fact many restrictions on what a German professor could say, the Americans saw the German university as allowing the mind free rein.

Second, the social and political standing of academic people in Germany impressed them. German professors were professional people who were treated with respect by their society. Germany seemed a country that placed culture on a similar level to business and commerce. The system also seemed to reward scholarship. German professors taught comparatively few hours in a week and did not have the administrative and religious duties of their American counterparts. Hence, they had the time to do the research needed to master a field thoroughly. The German academic also had the chance to teach at a higher level. Recitation, that dreary academic exercise where students repeated verbatim the words of a textbook or engaged in endless examination of small points of grammar, was confined to the gymnasium. University professors held lectures that bravely attempted to summarize the field of inquiry to date, and what was perhaps even more creative, their most advanced students gathered in seminars to pursue research under a professor's guidance. To many the German system with its well-lined libraries, comparatively high salaries, and seemingly well prepared students[38] seemed to be almost an academic's nirvana. American faculty abroad caught a glimpse of what the professionalization of scholarship might mean, and they wanted something similar for themselves when they returned home.

Third, they were impressed by the universities themselves. Americans traveled to Germany toward the end of a major academic revolution. France had abolished its universities during the French Revolution in favor of a system of state-supported institutes tied to French culture and to the Enlightenment. Many German intellectuals apparently thought something similar might be useful in their country. But as the movement toward national regeneration gathered momentum, the university itself became a source of German pride. The new University of Berlin, made necessary by the fall of Halle to the French, redesigned the German university around such modern ideas as research and scientific study, pioneered at such schools as Göttingen. Unlike many reforms, these became permanent. The research university became an important part of nineteenth-century German professional culture.

38. German students may not have been any more scholarly in the main than American students preparing for a professional career. Although some Americans did attend the lectures, especially those in biblical introduction, most confined their classroom to the seminar.

German scholarship had resources beyond American dreams. Andover's Edwards Amasa Park, visiting the German conservative theologian Hengstenberg, was overawed by his library. "I saw his library, in two large rooms, and it contains 21,000 volumes, only 200 less than our whole Seminary Library. No wonder these men know something."[39] Further, the schools worked together. Education in America, even in its higher branches, was ill organized and poorly defined. Lines between academy and college, for instance, were not clear, and before 1876 the United States had no institution devoted to academic and professional research. In contrast, the German system moved students from gymnasium to university and from university to profession in what seemed neatly measured stages. Alvah Hovey's son wrote that his father traveled to Germany "not to study a subject. He could do that by means of German as well as English books and periodicals. But it was to study the methods of management and of teaching practiced at the best universities and by the most famous professors."[40]

What did these traveling professors learn from their foreign experience? It is hard to make generalizations. Different individuals received different things from their journeys. For some the trip to Germany was only a busman's holiday that enabled them to get some needed rest while reading some important works. For others it was a chance to make scholarly contacts in an increasingly international scientific community. For others still, the trip was an opportunity to lay up treasures, both for their own libraries and for those of their institutions, that would make possible a life's work. A handful, like Shailer Mathews and Walter Rauschenbusch, stepped into new understandings of history and historical research that were to have important implications for their subsequent work. The one thing, however, that all seemed to receive from their journey was a new sense of self-confidence and of their own place in the modern world. Men left New York thinking of themselves primarily as teachers of young men; they returned, as often as not, conscious of themselves as researchers, scientists, who worked near the border of the known and the unknown. American seminary professors abroad were socialized into their profession, just as they struggled to create an academic profession at home.

39. Frank Hugh Foster, *The Life of Edwards Amasa Park* (New York: Fleming H. Revell, 1936), p. 190.

40. G. R. Hovey, *Alvah Hovey* (Philadelphia: Judson, 1861-62). Bernas Sears, Hovey's teacher, had also studied in Germany. While there Sears helped found the first modern Baptist church in that country.

IV. Professional Scholars

The steady professionalization of American theological scholarship was not of course an isolated event. In almost all areas of knowledge, scholars were building larger and stronger departments, establishing scholarly societies, and traveling abroad for learning and inspiration. While some of the smaller and more economically marginal schools may have lagged behind, the instructors from better and more economically viable seminaries seem to have more or less kept pace with other academic professionals, such as professors of English and history.[41]

From one perspective the new theological guilds did not stand out in the larger academic world. The aspirations of seminary faculties for larger libraries, for an identity that stressed scholarship over teaching, and for publishing their findings were coming to be widely shared by most people engaged in American higher education. Nor was their growing demand for academic freedom in itself unusual. On a sociological level, one mark of a profession is its claim to judge professional practice by standards set by other professionals. Only a practicing physician, aware of the options for treatment, can evaluate the work of another physician. By analogy, the only person with the knowledge and expertise to judge technical biblical study is another person who has studied the field in some detail.[42] Academic freedom was of course more easily granted when the issue was the proper form of a Hebrew verb or the comparative age of manuscripts. By the mid-1880s, however, the issues raised by higher criticism would challenge the newly formed biblical and historical disciplines at their very core. Yet, as we shall see, the fact that the formation of these academic disciplines was already well advanced gave the more adventurous critics the self-confidence to fight their battles without flinching.

As important as this sense of self-confidence was, the more significant result of the early professionalization of biblical and historical studies may have been the tendency to view these studies as "classical fields" or disciplines. "Classical" is a complex word that reflects the traditional standing of Greek and Latin literature in Western culture. When used outside of literary circles, "classical" implies the continuation of an older but still valid standard. In this sense the early evolution of the biblical and historical guilds shaped one definition of a theological school: a place where scholars who have specialized in those fields study historical and biblical questions. Since even the largest seminaries and di-

41. Louise Stevenson, *Scholarly Means to Evangelical Ends: The New Haven Scholars and the Transformation of Higher Education in America, 1830-1890* (Baltimore: Johns Hopkins University Press, 1986).

42. Thus the question is not whether Professor X is an atheist, Communist, or Republican, but whether his or her work meets acceptable standards of scholarly depth and precision.

vinity schools are comparatively small enterprises, biblical and historical professors have had sufficient institutional power to see that this understanding of the seminary is always a part of their school's self-definition as well as part of the popular understanding of what a seminary ought to be. This does not mean that others have not challenged this understanding. Since the 1880s, challenges to this understanding have come from Christian activists, from missionary-minded women, from those who wanted a more "professional" understanding of ministry, and particularly from those who wanted the ministry more grounded in sociology and psychology than philology. But, despite these challenges, the classical fields have been strong enough to maintain the redoubt against all comers.[43]

43. The curious phrase that occurs so often in seminary literature, "a graduate professional school," may illustrate this process. On the one hand, "graduate" can simply mean a school open to those who have completed their general or basic education. And it is occasionally used in this sense in the literature. On the other hand, "graduate" can imply a place where investigation and teaching are conducted at a high level. Despite the fact that much seminary teaching is in fact on an introductory or beginning level, this meaning of "graduate" is also found in the literature. Particularly for professors in the classical fields, the best analogue to the seminary is the graduate school of arts and sciences, the American equivalent of the philosophical faculty.

CHAPTER FOUR

Spiritual Crisis and the New Science

In 1874 a casual observer might have pronounced the health of American Protestantism as good to excellent. Although the heated idealism of the Civil War period had cooled considerably, American Protestant churches were flourishing. A new, less judgmental style of evangelism was "winning" people to Christ daily,[1] and many of them were joining the more democratic churches. Further, the home mission movement and, more particularly, the desire of folk for churches had penetrated the Old West and were beginning to enter newer areas of settlement. Although clerical salaries remained low, new wealth was flowing into Christian enterprises. The foreign missionary enterprise was growing, church bureaucracies were expanding, and the so-called Princes of the Pulpit — men such as Henry Ward Beecher and Phillips Brooks — were speaking to large, enthusiastic urban audiences. Yet, two books published in 1874, James William Draper's *The Warfare between Science and Religion* and Charles Hodge's *What Is Darwinism?* pointed to tensions, perhaps even contradictions, between the churches and the emerging scientific culture of the nation. A sense of spiritual uneasiness, a hidden but real spiritual crisis, particularly among the educated, reflected a widespread skepticism about inherited theological positions. Individuals differed in their experience of this malaise. Some went through agonizing periods of uncertainty and left the church altogether or stayed within it without recovering conviction; others spent hours worrying about religious issues and ended by deciding to live as right as they could; oth-

1. See Paul Carter, *The Spiritual Crisis of the Gilded Age* (De Kalb: Northern Illinois University Press, 1971). One result of the individualism made possible by the new industrial prosperity was that people experienced their society and culture differently, in part, depending on choices they made about such matters as reading, education, style of life, etc. Comparative wealth allows many responses to matters that are public.

ers still experienced uneasiness around issues of faith. The English preacher Frederick Robertson, who died in 1853, spoke for many when he said:

> It is an awful moment when the soul begins to find that the props on which it has blindly rested so long are many of them rotten, and begins to suspect them all; when it begins to feel the nothingness of many of the traditional opinions which have been received with implicit confidence, and in that horrible insecurity begins . . . to doubt whether there be anything to believe at all. It is an awful hour — let him who has passed through it say how awful — when this life has lost its meaning and seems shriveled to a span; when the grace appears to be the end of all, human goodness nothing but a name, and the sky above this universe a dead expanse, black with the void from which God himself has disappeared.[2]

Such deep-seated anxieties did not have a single cause.[3] It was an age of anxiety and neurosis in which men retreated to the countryside for their "nerves" and women suffered from "hysteria."[4] Urbanization may have also complicated spiritual life for many people as the "plausibility" structures of a village or small town that earlier maintained their childhood faith were no longer present. Yet, when all these have been considered, the intellectual questions, doubts and fears, still seem to have provoked much contemporary soul-searching.

While a person aware of the structure of theological argument might maintain that the "higher criticism" of the Bible was more theologically significant, evolution was the issue that caught many people's eye. The power of Darwinism came from two sources: its own intrinsic merits and the use that other people made of the evolutionary hypothesis.

The intrinsic merits of Darwin's theory lie close to the surface of his writ-

2. Frederick Robertson, *Life and Letters,* quoted in Howard Macquery, *The Evolution of Man and of Christianity,* new ed. (New York: D. Appleton and Co., 1891), pp. 9-10. Macquery was one of the few tried for his views on science and religion and convicted of heresy. He was an Episcopalian who later became a Unitarian.

3. Frank Turner, "The Victorian Crisis of Faith and the Faith That Was Lost," in *Victorian Faith in Crisis: Essays on Continuity and Change in Nineteenth Century Religious Belief,* ed. Richard J. Helmstadter and Bernard Lightman (New York: Macmillan; Palo Alto, Calif.: Stanford University Press, 1990), offers the interesting observation about England that this crisis occurred most often among adolescent males who came from strongly evangelical families. He argues that the dynamics of family life were a crucial part of the situation. Urbanization may have also complicated spiritual life for many people as the "plausibility" structures that maintained their childhood faith in a village or small town were not as present.

4. For gender and masculinity questions as they relate to nervousness and hysteria, see Anthony Rotundo, *American Manhood: Transformations in Masculinity from the Revolution to the Modern Era* (New York: Basic Books, 1993), especially pp. 192ff.

ings. Although he claimed that he had rushed the *Origin of Species* into print to establish scientific priority over his fellow biologist Wallace, the book reflected more than twenty years of close observation and data gathering. From this mass of material Darwin set forth a very lean argument, one that was almost beautiful in its simplicity, and embedded it in a mass of detail. As Gertrude Himmelfarb remarked: "the theory of natural selection is in many respects almost the ideal scientific theory; it is eminently naturalistic, mechanical, objective, impersonal and economic." The theory can be stated simply:

> Organic nature tends to almost exuberant variety of individual living things that differ, either slightly or significantly, from their parents. No two cats, no two people, no two lobsters, are exactly identical. At the same time, animals and plants reproduce themselves profusely, producing more off-spring and/or potential off-spring (seeds) than the available resources will support. Although it is almost a tautology, these two observations lead to the common sense statement that those individuals who could best use the available resources and/or avoid the obvious dangers would most often survive and, in turn, reproduce again. Some of the variations among individual members of a species help the individual survive and reproduce, some hinder these two activities, and most have no effect on the individual's capacity either for survival or reproduction.[5]

Given enough time — always the crucial element in Darwin's theory — the slow, steady transmission of variations that tend to promote survival and reproduction will lead to those variations becoming dominant. In time, this process might proceed to the point where a new species, closely related to the older form, would emerge. Darwin called the observed relationship between variations and the formation of species "modification through natural selection," which was less ambiguous than the term "evolution."

To support his position Darwin marshaled considerable evidence, ranging from the human experience with domestic animals to the fossil record to contemporary observations of animals and plants. While Darwin knew that "many and grave objections may be advanced against the theory of descent with modification through natural selection," he felt he had made his case. As in other scientific matters, the real decision about the new theory would come through the sifting of further evidence. If the theory continued to best explain the observed facts about the world, it would be sustained and accepted; if not, it would be modified and eventually discarded.

5. Gertrude Himmelfarb, *Darwin and the Darwinian Revolution,* quoted in James Moore, *The Post-Darwinian Controversies* (Cambridge: Cambridge University Press, 1979), p. 299.

At least for the scientific community, that verification was not long in coming. Although a small rear guard, including noted Harvard naturalist Jean Louis Agassiz, initially questioned the theory, Darwin's understanding was too important to many scientific questions to be allowed to sit on the shelf. "By 1869 the Darwinian theory was clearly in the ascendant in the learned societies — accepted, not as demonstrated truth, but as a view for which there was now enough factual data to permit its being used with confidence as a working hypothesis. This applied particularly to the general theory of descent."[6] In that same year Charles Eliot became president of Harvard. Eliot was thoroughly committed to the new science and to a new role for science in American education. He used his position as president of the nation's most prestigious college to promote both.

The second reason for the power of Darwin's theory was its apparent usefulness outside the biological realm. Evolution proved to be an evocative explanation for many human phenomena, such as history, society, and government, that had earlier seemed beyond scientific treatment. Like the human race itself, human institutions could begin in a distant past, be modified as they struggled with their environment, and eventually die and give way to new forms. This sea change in understanding human experience rocked the careful synthesis of Greek and Hebrew thought that had seen nature as an essential harmony, apart from human sin, and a reflection of the divine nature.[7] The sustaining logos had given way to change and chance.

Clearly, the use of Darwin and evolution in the intellectual life of the late nineteenth century did not spring suddenly from the *Origin of Species* as Athena did from the head of Zeus. One can find the antecedents of these arguments in Hegel and others. Yet by rooting the idea of development in the natural order, Darwinism gave such arguments added intellectual force and power. Darwinism played a similar role in the development of the "social sciences." The raw materials of many of the early insights of social science were clearly at hand in historicism and other sources, and many of those who advocated the new studies may have been as influenced by Herbert Spencer and John Fiske as by Darwin's writings.[8] Nonetheless, Darwinism seemed to provide the new so-

6. Frederick Burkhardt, "England and Scotland: Learned Societies," in *The Comparative Reception of Darwinism*, ed. Glick Thomas (Chicago: University of Chicago Press, 1988), pp. 32-74, here p. 59.

7. John Greene, *The Death of Adam* (Ames: Iowa State University Press, 1959), makes the point about worldview convincingly. I have tried to be careful, as Greene is, to nuance this observation. See also Moore, *The Post-Darwinian Controversies.*

8. See Jim Moore, "Herbert Spencer's Henchmen: The Evolution of Protestant Liberals in Late Nineteenth Century America," in *Darwinism and Divinity: Essays on Evolution and Religious Belief*, ed. John Durant (Oxford: Basil Blackwell, 1985), especially pp. 80-81.

ciologists (and Spencer, for that matter) with the needed scientific foundations to move from social philosophy to social science. As in many other intellectual areas, Darwin made many interpretations of reality that had earlier seemed only "possible" now seem plausible.[9]

Darwin's theory also seemed to offer some answers to the moral and ethical dilemmas that bedeviled the late Victorian era. In part, as such thinkers as Spencer and Fiske illustrate, it could be used to buttress the Victorian confidence in "progress." But its influence was indirect. Most late Victorians assumed progress to be true, and the doctrine of progress may have made Darwinism more acceptable than the reverse.[10] Equally often, the idea of natural selection (often expressed as the survival of the fittest) was used to support nationalism, racism, and imperialism. In such interpretations the power of the economically and politically dominant western European nations was, at least in part, a reflection of their superior biological and mental makeup. This made them the natural conquerors of others and, at best, imposed on them a "white man's burden" for the elevation of lesser breeds without the law.[11] At worst, it could justify passive or active genocide. Interestingly, by the end of the century evolutionary thinking was incorporated into a reinterpretation of masculinity that stressed the importance of physical activity, bodybuilding, and various types of male violence, ranging from war to football. The death of some men in those activities was just part of the price for the biological future. Finally, in the multiracial United States evolution was used to buttress segregation in the South and to justify discrimination in the North.

The ubiquity of Darwinism in the cultural life of the late nineteenth cen-

9. The truth of a proposition does not depend on its antecedents or its context. But the human ability to understand and affirm an intellectual position is not nearly as independent of circumstances. Without some supporting structures, even the most evident positions seem improbable and disemboweled. I use the term "plausibility" to describe those factors that make an intellectual position seem more or less right to those who learn of it.

10. The doctrine of progress was confirmed for many people not because of any ideological affinity with the position, but because of their own experience of the world. The nineteenth century saw the discovery and popularization of a cornucopia of material goods that substantially improved the standard of living for many people, especially the middle classes. No one needed Spencer or Darwin to tell them that a world in which human life had been extended, machines did some of the labor that had earlier worn people out with toil by their forties, and vast new markets were opened for a host of new products — ranging from aspirin to stainless steel to cheap cotton — was an improvement on eighteenth-century conditions. Nor, even at the heights of pessimism about human progress in the 1920s or 1930s, were there many people who wished to stop further technological and economic advance.

11. For a discussion of social Darwinism in America, see Richard Hofstadter, *Social Darwinism in America* (Philadelphia: University of Pennsylvania Press, 1944).

tury and beyond makes it difficult to draw neat temporal boundaries around the discussion. Historians of American religion are aware that the debate over evolution has had a continuous history from the 1860s to the present and has been more publicly visible at some times than at others. For instance, evolution was a crucial element in the fundamentalist controversies of the 1920s and in the creation science controversies of the 1980s. During such periods significant numbers of Americans have expressed their views publicly and attempted to install them, whether pro or con, as the teaching enforced by law. Equally important, long after the opposition to evolutionary thinking was able to secure the dismissal or trial of a faculty member, leaders of explicitly Christian institutions faced questions about evolution and how it was taught (whether as fact or theory) in their schools. The underlying tensions were one factor, among many, that led to the secularization of many Christian colleges. Yet the discussion of evolution from 1860 to 1900 was more than the first and highest mountain in this range. It was part of a major intellectual revolution in how Americans understood religion and, by implication, theological education.

I. The Late Nineteenth-Century Theological Debate

Although no one drew them all, the number of possible theological implications of the new science was staggering. That Darwinism and the Bible appeared to teach a different understanding of the beginnings of life was a given. The most natural reading of the biblical saga is that God intentionally created the world as a place for humankind. In the Bible's view, God created the plants and other animals to further God's central project in the creation of human beings, and the fall of humanity naturally had consequences for all living things. Darwinism challenged almost every element of this understanding. A very complex network of chance had allowed those most adaptable to their environment to reproduce living things, including humans, linked to one another. Human beings were a relatively late product of this process.

For many American Protestants, who had been raised to consider the Bible a ready sourcebook on every issue from anatomy to Zerubbabel, this conflict was not a minor matter. If the Bible was wrong on how human life had originated, what other serious mistakes lurked in the text? The problem was how to deal with the Bible's fallibility and to determine how far that fallibility extended. Was it just a matter of ancient ideas that God had used, knowing that humankind would outgrow them, or were these ancient ideas part of the warp and woof of biblical teaching?

That question was not trivial. For classical Christian theology, the doctrine of creation was not only an account of the beginnings of the human race. From the apologists to the Reformers, creation had been the keystone that held together an elaborate intellectual edifice that included the sinfulness of humankind, redemption, and heaven and hell. "In Adam's fall, we sinned all," and this sin could be removed only by Christ, the second Adam. Different churches ritualized this experience in different ways. Lutherans, many Episcopalians, and Roman Catholics saw baptism as effecting regeneration, while Baptists, Methodists, Congregationalists, and Presbyterians tended to stress personal conviction or, in many cases, emotional conversion. Traditionally, Adam's sin had disrupted creation, leading to human death, and served as a partial explanation for the disasters that overtook humankind. Further, while Darwinism did not necessarily imply that the process of natural selection was progressive, most people saw it in that light.[12] Did this mean that humankind "fell upward"? In short, the explanation of why Christ had come and died had been removed, and the task of reformulating Christology without this anchor was not an academic puzzle; in effect, all the laws and prophets rested on an answer.

Darwin also called into serious question the Christian apologetic tradition. Almost from the beginning of the church, Christian leaders had developed a variety of arguments designed to show that the existence of the world was not self-explanatory. These arguments ranged from the so-called proofs of the existence of God, classically stated by Saint Thomas, to the elaborate physical theologies of the eighteenth century. Whatever the philosophical or logical weaknesses of these positions,[13] many people accepted them. Perhaps most important, they were integrated into popular Christian writing and into sermons, albeit in an often sentimentalized form. The most important of these in the nineteenth century was the argument from design.[14] William Paley, a pro-

12. That a cockroach, one of the most indestructible of life-forms, may be more "fit" for survival and, hence, better able to reproduce is not an idea easily entertained by the mind.

13. In his *Critique of Pure Reason* (1781), Kant demonstrated, at least to his satisfaction, that these arguments were necessarily inconclusive. But few people outside the academy studied Kant, and many who did reached less radical conclusions. Darwinism did more in the popular mind to make these arguments suspect than the more formally logical arguments of German philosophy.

14. Jonathan Wells, *Charles Hodge's Critique of Darwinism: An Historical-Critical Analysis of Concepts Basic to the Nineteenth Century Debate* (Lewiston, N.Y.: Edwin Mellen Press, 1988), has been formative for my understanding of the issues around design. As Wells notes, the issue is not simply one of apologetics. If it had been, theologians would simply have given up the argument from design and moved to another statement of their case. This was in fact the overall response to the arguments in Kant's *Critique of Pure Reason* against the traditional theistic proofs. But what bothered Hodge was more fundamental. If God were the god of traditional theism, a god who creates and orders all that is, we ought to be able to see some vestiges of his

lific writer of textbooks, enshrined this argument in his *View of the Evidences of Christianity* (London, 1794). For much of the nineteenth century, English and American college students read Paley as part of their intellectual training.

The most serious challenge of Darwinism to the apologetic tradition was the fact that evolution enthroned chance. While scientists could discern patterns in nature, these patterns did not necessarily reflect the imposition of an order from outside or even from inside the system. To use an overly simple metaphor, the new biology offered explanations but it did not offer reasons. At best, the regularities observed were statistical, and more easily discussed under the rules of probability than with the methods of geometry. In fact, Darwin's theory rested on the belief that most variations led nowhere; they were just part of the continual shuffling of the biological cards.[15] Darwin conceded the power of this argument. In his conclusion to *Origin of Species* he noted that while it was difficult to believe that the complexities of the world "should have been perfected not by means superior to, though analogous with, human reason, but by the accumulation of innumerable slight variations, each good for the individual possessor,"[16] the difficulty did not invalidate the argument. The apparent wisdom of the ages was simply wrong.

Death was another serious problem. In the Darwinian view, death was as essential to evolution as sexual reproduction. In this sense, while one might mourn one's own death or the death of a friend, death itself was not the "last enemy"; it was an evolutionary friend and ally. Like sexual reproduction, death fed the cycle of variation and adaptation. The theory also cut at the vitals of much American middle-class morality. In a world where the ultimate role of every being is to pass on its own variations to its offspring, arguments for sexual restraint seemed strangely out of place, as did such traditional Christian values as kindness, gentleness, meekness, etc. Further, the theory implied a re-evaluation of sexual morality. The traditional Christian belief in sexual restraint seemed to be almost counterproductive.[17] The biological future be-

---

nature in the things he has made. Yet, if Darwin is right, there are no such vestiges. Hence, Hodge's stark conclusion that Darwinism was atheism.

15. Those who emphasized the role of chance in Darwin's theory were, in the long run, correct. Genetics, which were not even on the horizon when Darwin published his work, later demonstrated that sexual reproduction followed the lines of probability mathematics.

16. Charles Darwin, *The Origin of Species*, conclusion, at http://www.talkorigins.org/faqs/origin/chapter14.html.

17. This is not to say that all these conclusions were drawn by any particular thinker, but they were all possible implications of Darwin's position. Although later Americans would poke fun at such anti-evolutionists as Billy Sunday or William Jennings Bryan, there were sound reasons for questioning the social consequences of Darwin's arguments. The entire faculty at Con-

longed not to those who limited their desires, but to those able to populate the earth with the most offspring. Whether the meek might inherit the earth was a moot point — their children would not.

In short, Darwin and his teachings were a serious challenge to Christian theology and Christian practice. While few people read or understood Darwin, his influence was a primary source of the spiritual crisis that enveloped much of Anglo-American life after 1860. To be sure, this uneasiness took many different forms. For some it did little more than weaken their confidence in faith, while for others the spiritual crisis took the form of full-blown unbelief. In most thinking people, apparently, the spiritual crisis was more the cumulative effect of many factors, of which Darwinism was one, that made them religiously uncomfortable. For America's theological establishment, however, it was a call to action and reflection.

From 1870 to 1900 Darwinism was vigorously discussed by American religious and scientific leaders. Newman Smyth, perhaps the most able evolutionary theologian, noted three stages in the debate: (1) a stage in which people anxiously asked whether they could accept the new science, (2) a stage in which people attempted to reconcile evolution and faith, and (3) a stage in which people asked, "How are we to use the help of both — the light of science, and of the spirit — in the rational interpretation of the universe?" This latter period, Smyth insisted, was "the age of critical review and of judicial reconstruction."[18] Smyth's narrative outline provides a useful way to systematize the debate, especially if one remembers that the discussion moved less smoothly than his analysis implied. Some were always still debating the issues raised in the first stage while much of the discussion — its cutting edge — had moved substantially elsewhere.

The first stage of the discussion is perhaps best associated with some scientists who were also convinced Christians: Asa Gray (Harvard), Joseph LeConte (University of California), George Frederick Wright (Andover), and Alexander Winchell (Syracuse, Vanderbilt, and Michigan).[19] What these teachers

cordia, apparently, made this choice: Carl S. Meyer, *Log Cabin to Luther Tower* (St. Louis: Concordia, 1965), p. 91.

18. Newman Smyth, *Old Faiths in a New Light* (New York: Scribner, 1887).

19. Many of the people that Moore identifies as Christian Darwinists, as distinct from Darwinianists, were professional scientists with little theological training. The notable exception was, of course, George Frederick Wright, an enthusiastic graduate of Oberlin, close friend of many members of the Andover faculty, and biblical scholar as well as a noted amateur geologist. They were, hence, as Moore notes, more likely to be accurate in discussing the scientific character of Darwinism than they might have been in discussing its theological views. See Moore, *The Post-Darwinian Controversies,* especially chap. 12. In contrast, many of those in

were able to bring to the discussion was a sharp eye for the scientific claims of Darwinism and, hence, the ability to clarify the scholarly issues. Since all were blessed with able literary styles, they were able to do this in a clear manner that communicated to people the necessity of thinking about the issues posed by the new science. Perhaps the most important of these works was Asa Gray and George Wright's *Darwiniana* (1876). They were joined by some of America's most influential college presidents, including James McCosh of Princeton and Paul A. Chadbourne of Williams, who were able to use the prestige of their positions to advance the discussion. There was something both reassuring and challenging in McCosh's words: "It is no use denying in our day the doctrine of evolution in the name of religion, or any other good cause. . . . The time is at hand when all intelligent people, religious or irreligious, will perceive there is nothing impious in development considered in itself, though it may be carried to excess and turned to atheistic purposes."[20] Such arguments influenced people in subtle ways. William Lawrence, reflecting on his more than fifty years in the ministry, remembered Andover's Edwards Amasa Park assuring him that a man "could not believe in evolution and remain a Christian," and that Asa Gray and others had introduced a radical change that "took years" to seep into the thinking of the country.[21] Others, such as George Coe, the noted religious educator, took a little while to think about it, and resolved to let science handle the matter.

The second stage in the discussion went in two directions. To be sure, there were some superficial reconcilers who argued that the outline of Genesis 1 and the outline of evolution were similar and that, in that sense, Genesis taught science. But most of the reconcilers took a different tack. Changes that were taking place in Protestant thought at midcentury are crucial for understanding their arguments.

Horace Bushnell, the most creative American theologian at mid–nineteenth century, made two primary contributions to American theology. First, his thought removed many of the rougher edges from theological doctrine. For instance, in his analysis of language, attached to his christological

---

Smyth's later stages were professional theologians, often trained in Germany, who had a finer eye for some of the theological implications of Darwinism than for its scientific details. Moore's belief that these Christian Darwinists' understanding of original sin may leave them more open to some of the disagreeable parts of Darwinism appears somewhat overdrawn, as does his belief that a more rigorous trinitarian doctrine might have made the discussion more profound.

20. James McCosh, quoted in Joseph E. Illick III, "The Reception of Darwinism at the Theological Seminary and the College at Princeton, New Jersey," *Journal of the Presbyterian Historical Society* 38 (1960): 152-65, 234-43, here p. 240.

21. William Lawrence, *Memories of a Happy Life* (Boston and New York: Houghton Mifflin, 1926).

treatise *God in Christ,* Bushnell argued that the nature of human language was such that the more abstract words became, the less they identified their referent. Human language was better at describing a dog or a cat than the human soul or God. Consequently, people would almost inevitably use different words and creedal expressions for the same religious realities. Further, Bushnell refused to draw sharp lines between the natural and the supernatural. Although human will was part of the natural order, human will was "supernatural" in its capacity to affect the world. Likewise, God could be totally immanent in nature and still be able to direct its course. Bushnell also favored organic metaphors that stressed growth and development.

Second, and perhaps equally important, Bushnell was an early example of the public Christian intellectual. The Christian intellectual was not the traditional pastor-theologian, although there were some obvious similarities. Rather, the Christian intellectual was someone whose literary productions were directed at the expanding world of information and media. Even before the Civil War, improvements in printing and in the distribution of books and magazines had encouraged some Americans to make their living commenting on the ideas and events of the day. Ralph Waldo Emerson, who toured the country giving popular talks on self-reliance, was one such person, as were the large number of people who staffed the various lyceums and who contributed materials to the press and, especially, to the increasingly popular magazines. The business of these entrepreneurs of the spirit was to form an opinion on the issues of the day and communicate that opinion to others. What made an intellectual a Christian intellectual was that his or her works were directed toward the Christian public and its specific needs.[22]

After leaving his Hartford pulpit in 1859, Bushnell devoted much of his energy to his work as a Christian intellectual. Since he wrote easily and well, he was able to comment on ideas as diverse as the new passion for recreation, the need of education, and the business potential of California. His thoughtful essays were an important precedent for American Protestants. Although they lacked the popular character of the writings of Henry Ward Beecher, his near contemporary, the middle-level theological discourse they provided permitted a consideration of important issues that was thoughtful and relevant but, equally importantly, lacked the often technical and occasionally pedantic ornamentations of professional theologians.

Bushnell's most noted disciples continued his habit of publishing per-

22. The most-noted twentieth-century Christian intellectual was Reinhold Niebuhr, whose occasional writings had as much or more influence than his more formal theological studies. Later, Martin E. Marty assumed a similar role to a somewhat reduced Protestant audience.

sonal thoughts on public issues. Theodore Munger and Washington Gladden, for instance, wrote popular accounts of new ideas that combined solid thought, a popular style, and a sense for the issues that were "hot." Other people joined the Bushnellians in this role. The winsome Scottish writer and professor Henry Drummond, a friend of Dwight L. Moody, was a noted author, popular speaker, and commentator. Perhaps the most successful, at least financially, were two pastors of Plymouth Church in Brooklyn: Henry Ward Beecher and Lyman Abbott. Beecher, who loved the limelight and saw himself almost as a performer, founded the *Christian Union*, a weekly newspaper of opinion. His successor at the church, Lyman Abbott, a former editor of the "Literary Record" in *Harper's Magazine*, took over the journal in 1876 and renamed it the *Outlook* in 1893. Like Bushnell, whom he resembled in many ways, Abbott found his work as an intellectual more rewarding than his pastoral labors. He resigned from Plymouth Church in 1898 to devote full time to his literary work.

American Protestants were fortunate that the Christian intellectuals provided much of the first response to the new science. The Christian intellectuals, who were not bound by the confessional restrictions of the seminaries, had the freedom to confront issues that their more scholarly colleagues lacked. In part, this freedom was the freedom of the American marketplace. While Beecher's reputation as a "Christian evolutionist" did little to improve his reputation with his fellow Congregational clergy, the same tag made his journal all the more attractive. But the freedom also came from the role itself. People expected those who discussed current events and ideas to address the important issues, whether controversial or not. In effect, they had permission to think aloud.

The basic thrust of the argument of the Christian intellectuals was to ignore the role of chance in Darwin's theory and to consider evolution as a synonym or metaphor for development.[23] Human life was marked by a natural movement from one stage to another. Thus, human experience provided the basic metaphor for the natural process. Abbott wrote that the evolutionist "can trace the process by which reason is developed out of instinct, and patience out of passivity, and sympathy out of imagining the troubles of others, and carefulness out of parental instinct, and conscience out of approbativeness, and honesty and honor out of self-interest."[24] Since one was dealing with a process that continued here and now, it was "immaterial" whether Adam fell "six thousand years ago." We can treat that story as "a beautiful fable" and "ask what truth is in

23. See John Durant, "Darwin and Divinity: A Century of Debate," in *Darwinism and Divinity*, especially pp. 19-22.

24. Lyman Abbott, *The Theology of an Evolutionist* (Boston and New York: Houghton Mifflin, 1897), p. 41.

that fable."[25] What finally counted was the way the natural experience of nature was recapitulated in the life of every person: "Innocence, temptation, fall, sin — this is the biography of every man. . . . Every man when he yields to temptation and sins falls from a higher to a lower, from a spiritual to an animal condition. He falls back from that state from which he had begun to emerge. It is true that the animal man is worse in his animalism than the animal from which he has emerged or is emerged."[26] Granted this perspective, the public intellectuals argued, we can make a minor leap of faith and see ourselves as evolving toward spiritual life and hope that the process will be continued after our deaths.[27]

Abbott's contrast between the animal and the spiritual was of course an attempt to restate the classical Western Christian understanding of humankind as the midpoint on the great chain of being. For Augustine and other thinkers in this tradition, sin gives persons a weight that pushes them down the chain toward the animal, the material, and the ultimately mysterious world of nonbeing. In contrast, obedience to God lightens the soul's burden, allowing it to rise to God. What Abbott and the other popularizers, particularly Henry Drummond, did was to attempt to transfer that Neoplatonic understanding of religion from ontology to nature. "So the spiritual man at the apex of the pyramid of life finds in the vaster range of his environment a provision, as much higher, it is true, as he is higher, but as delicately adjusted to his varying needs. . . . It is not a strange thing, then, for the soul to find its life in God. This is its native air."[28]

The third stage in the discussion, the critical appropriation and exploration of evolution, had, understandably, fewer representatives. Perhaps the most able was Newman Smyth, pastor of Center Church in New Haven. After graduating from Andover, where he studied under Edwards Amasa Park, he went to Germany for advanced study at Halle and Berlin. While there he began to study the three key figures in his theological development: the dogmatician Isaak Dorner, the biblical scholar Heinrich Ewald, and the philosopher Hermann Lotze.[29] Each gave the young American the gift of a particular insight into how theological thinking could be done in the modern world. From Dorner he received a conviction of continuities. Nature and grace, the material and the spir-

25. Abbott, *Theology of an Evolutionist,* p. 43.

26. Abbott, *Theology of an Evolutionist,* p. 45.

27. This was, of course, a major mixing of categories. It would be one thing to say that human life was evolving in a spiritual direction or that human beings might give way to a more spiritual species, but quite another to argue that each individual was so evolving.

28. Henry Drummond, *Natural Law in the Spiritual World,* at http://henrydrummond.wwwhubs.com/law17.htm.

29. Smyth, *Old Faiths,* p. xxx.

itual, were not opposites but different aspects or parts of a larger whole. Faith provided humankind with a way to move within this larger sphere and not a way to transcend its limitations. Ewald communicated to Smyth a very sophisticated understanding of the history of Israel, based on sound philology, that saw Israel's religious history as the continual development of monotheistic faith. For Ewald (and even more for his American disciple) God purified Israel's faith through that nation's historical experience.[30] In effect, Israel was always learning what its faith meant as it moved from the monaltry of Moses to the high monotheism of the prophets and Jesus. Lotze's contribution was equally formative. Lotze originally studied in the faculty of medicine,[31] and he had a deep respect for the type of meticulous observation that was characteristic of that study. Throughout his philosophic career Lotze believed that the scientific method provided the key to the problems of epistemology and metaphysics. Hence, he avoided such easy solutions to the metaphysical problems of his time as the popular belief in vitalism, the conviction that life has a quality — later philosophers would call it an élan vital — that sets it apart from all nonlife. Lotze maintained that, however comforting such beliefs might be, they were part of what was questioned, not part of what was known. Instead, he urged his followers to follow science wherever it led. What distinguished Lotze's thought from that of such contemporaries as his fellow physician Ernst Haeckel[32] was his conviction that human beings were naturally inclined to metaphysical thought and speculation. Although a scientifically trained person might not accept the truth of this or that metaphysical assertion, metaphysical statements nonetheless reflect the complex ways in which human beings value their world and understand their place in it. This insight was particularly important for liberalizing Protestants since it encouraged the philosopher or theologian not to reject an outmoded doctrine out of hand but to analyze that doctrine until its human meaning (value) was clearly understood. To use the title of Smyth's classic work, Lotze encouraged theologians not to form new faiths, but to see "old faiths in a new light."

30. While Ewald lacked the technical brilliance of Julius Wellhausen, his younger contemporary, his system did not require as many gaps; Wellhausen maintained that we knew virtually nothing about Israelite history or faith before the exile.

31. American medicine was much further behind European medicine than American theology was behind European theology. Even in the later nineteenth century, many American practitioners received only a brief "empirical" introduction to their craft. At the same time, their European counterparts were thoroughly enmeshed in the more scientific understanding of the body and of disease.

32. Haeckel was a noted biologist and evolutionist who argued that science necessitated a philosophical materialism. Similar views were popularized in England by Huxley and Clifford.

Newman Smyth was similar both in his antecedents and in his conclusions to the European Ritschlians. In many ways he was the American equivalent to the scholarly and yet warmly pious Wilhelm Hermann,[33] whose seminar influenced such diverse thinkers as Karl Barth and Paul Tillich. Yet there was one obvious difference between the two contemporaries: Smyth was not permitted to enter a classroom.[34] Edwards Amasa Park dominated Andover Seminary throughout much of the 1860s and 1870s. Park had begun his theological career as a fresh voice in New England theology, deeply interested in the classical Edwardsian question of how the religious emotions or feelings influenced personal faith. But under the impact of a world that was changing more rapidly than he could, Park became more and more an antiquarian, concerned with preserving what he called "the New England Theology" against all attacks. Indeed, his later work was the construction of an academic shrine to his predecessors. He and his disciples explored each step in the development of the Edwardsian school in ever increasing detail. Perhaps the most abiding monument to their combination of filial piety and scholarly precision was Frank Hugh Foster's masterful *A Generic History of the New England Theology.*[35] But this orderly development was disrupted in 1881 when Park retired from his post. The faculty, which had been moving in other directions, refused to nominate Foster, Park's handpicked successor, and turned to Newman Smyth, the brother of Egbert Smyth, Andover's German-trained church historian and a leading advocate of the new disciplinary approach to church history. The choice, however, was not due to nepotism. Smyth had already published three widely discussed volumes, *The Religious Feeling, Old Faiths in a New Light* (first edition, 1879), and *The Orthodox Theology of Today* (first edition, 1881). By any objective standard the thirty-eight-year-old pastor of Bangor's First Congregational Church (today, All Souls Congregational Church) was among America's most promising young theologians.

The filling of the Abbott professorship would have been controversial at any time, especially if the new appointee differed radically from his predecessors. What was deceptive was that this appointment went so smoothly at first. Smyth was the unanimous and enthusiastic choice of the faculty and of eleven

33. Despite his own personal piety, Hermann and the other Ritschlians tended not to have the confidence in religious experience that Smyth, a product of New England evangelicalism, inherited from Edwards and other New England thinkers.

34. For an excellent account of the struggles over the Smyth appointment, see David Kling, "Newman Smyth," in *Dictionary of Heresy Trials in American Christianity,* ed. George H. Shriver (Westport, Conn.: Greenwood Press, 1997).

35. See Joseph Conforti, *Jonathan Edwards: Religious Tradition and American Culture* (Chapel Hill: University of North Carolina Press, 1982).

of the trustees, and the appointment appeared to be secure. Then disaster hit. The Board of Visitors, a legal body of three members originally established to guard the funds left to maintain the Hopkinsian theology, vetoed the appointment. In their view, Smyth did not clearly affirm the Andover Creed, one of the documents on which the school had been founded. It is hard to fault the visitors. They were charged with protecting a heritage, and the existence of the board was a testimony to the fears of some of the initial contributors that this heritage might eventually be questioned or denied. In both the wording of the documents and the historical situation that had informed their composition, the need to reject the nomination of someone like Smyth was the reason for the elaborate system. Smyth was personable, intellectually able, and precocious. But by no stretch of the imagination was the young teacher a representative of the Edwardsian-Hopkinsian theology,[36] and no one seriously believed he held such views.

The visitors originally asked the trustees to withdraw their nomination of Smyth on the grounds that his theology was more "poetic" than doctrinal or speculative. This was of course an evasion of the issue of whether Smyth should or could hold the office, and perhaps an attempt to avoid charging Smyth's supporters, many of whom had subscribed to the Andover Creed, with perjury. When the trustees refused this suggestion, the visitors bit the bullet and decided to enforce the clearly defined will of the founders and rejected Smyth.[37]

The irony was that the actual discussion was not that straightforward. The issue that dominated the controversy was the vexing question of "second probation." Basically this position, advanced earlier by Dorner, held that the Bible was not as clear on the fate of those who had not heard of Christ as the received theological tradition taught. According to Dorner, no specific biblical teaching compelled the church to teach that all those who died without faith would spend eternity cut off from God or perhaps annihilated. If faith was the sole condition of salvation, perhaps those who had never heard of Christ during their lifetimes might be given an opportunity to believe in the afterlife. In other words, both those who had heard of Christ and those who had not would

36. At the time, this and subsequent battles over the Andover Creed were fought in terms of the legal exegesis of the documents in the light of the fact that the supreme court of Massachusetts was the ultimate guarantor of the various trusts. My own reading, above, is a more general one. Whether this or that detail in the creed could be interpreted in terms of Smyth's theology or not, he clearly was concerned with different problems and conclusions than the Edwardsian tradition. To appoint him was in fact to set theology at Andover on a different course.

37. In that sense Smyth was technically rejected not for heresy but for incompetence. Given the logical rigor of his thought, it was a classic case of blaming the victim.

be on the same footing and responsible for the same choice. Smyth had affirmed this position in a public address, and he later published Dorner's eschatology so that others could evaluate it for themselves. But Smyth did not apparently consider second probation an important theological issue. He was more interested in such problems as science and biblical criticism.

Second probation, however, was especially attractive to New England Congregationalists. New England had poured human and financial resources into the Christian world mission, and most missionary enthusiasts were aware that many people from other cultures found the Christian teaching that their ancestors were in hell a hindrance to conversion. As Smyth argued, the fact that the position was not excluded from Scripture gave Christians the right to hope in the "merciful obscurities" of revelation. Such a hope might remove one of the bars to the foreign reception of Christ. The same missionary interest made second probation repugnant to others. They were convinced that the once-and-for-all-time character of a decision for Christ had to be preserved at all cost. Second probation seemed to offer an easy way to avoid the agony of deciding for or against faith and a possible motive for putting that decision off into the indefinite future.

Both the trustees and the faculty wanted to fight the Board of Visitors after Smyth's rejection. Smyth was urged to accept a position at Andover that did not require subscription to the associate founders' creed, or to accept the position offered by the board and force the visitors to take the issue to court. Smyth, however, was unwilling to live his life under those conditions and refused any appointment that would distract him from his life's work. Accepting the pulpit of New Haven's famous Center Church, a position that primarily required him to preach to a very intellectual audience, he turned his full energies to a study of evolution. Perhaps because of the influence of Lotze on his thought, he did not make this a purely literary study. Since the pastor of Center Church was considered a part of the Yale community, he requested and received permission to use the Yale laboratories and museums to study Darwin's theories.

One way Smyth contributed to the discussion of evolution was by clarifying the issues. His own study of the scientific data convinced him more than even before that evolution was the main means that God had employed in the creation of life. In that sense Smyth concluded that the question of the truth of the hypothesis had been put beyond debate. To dispute whether evolution had occurred was obscurantist. But he also rejected the theory that the Bible somehow taught evolution before the evolutionists. In a sharp aside, he notes: "We are not anxious, then, from our educational view of the scientific side and tendency of the Bible, to enter into a particular comparison of the Mosaic account and the last geological table. Many who are curious to learn the latest discrepancies and coincidences between geology and Genesis can find the subject treated in detail in Principal Dawson's recent book on the 'Origins of the World.'" What Smyth meant by the educational understanding of the Bible was that the Bible had laid the foundations of modern science in its teachings about such matters as creation, nature, and the nature of humankind. For him, "the whole vexed question, then, of the scientific truthfulness to the Bible seems to us to reduce itself to simple inquiries like these: 'Is the scientific alphabet of the Bible good? Do the Scriptures teach the few first principles of nature so well that man has not been compelled to unlearn them in order to acquire the language of nature?'"[38] In contrast, Smyth wanted to affirm that biblical religion was, so to speak, the seedbed from which Western science and history grew.

> Let us gather up, then, the separate threads of our reasoning in one conclusion: the Biblical account of the creation meets the necessities of the elementary instruction of a race chosen from idolatrous surroundings to become the bearer of a divine gospel to mankind. The teaching of the Bible, on its scientific side, is so free from superstition, so correct in its understanding of the alphabet of nature, so retentive in its grasp of the elementary truths of the creation — its spiritual origin, its unity, continuity, and divine order — that, altogether, it presents a unique literary phenomenon, — one which must have a cause, but whose cause does not appear in the conditions of the times, of the historical environment of the Bible. The simplest explanation of this literary wonder of antiquity, if upon other philosophical grounds we are not prevented from giving it, is that some special divine providence was at the source of this marvelous life in Israel; that, in some manner provided for in his own laws, the God of history gave to the children of Adam these greatly needed rudimentary lessons; himself, in some of his many open ways of suggestion to the soul of man, taught the human reason these elementary truths of the creation.[39]

In short, although Newman Smyth was vitally concerned with the metaphysical implications of evolution for Christian theology,[40] he was more concerned with understanding the relationship between faith and scientific culture. Smyth believed that science was the language of the future and that believing people had to recognize science's Christian past and contemplate science's Christian future.

38. Smyth, *Old Faiths,* p. 280.

39. Smyth, *Old Faiths,* p. 183.

40. He was one of the few theologians to tackle head-on the question of the role of death in evolutionary thought. See Newman Smyth, *The Place of Death in Evolution* (New York: Scribner, 1897). See also Newman Smyth, *Through Science to Faith* (New York: Scribner, 1902).

The larger issue posed by evolution was, consequently, more important than the specific issues at stake in the immediate debate.

Smyth himself never appears to have regretted the abortion of his teaching career. Ironically, the trustees' decision freed him from a small school, located some distance from a major center of learning, to work near a college that was rapidly becoming a leading American university. Few places in America offered a serious thinker the resources and stimulation of New Haven.[41] Since his church took pride in his intellectual achievements, he had more freedom to study and write than he would have had tending to the intellectual and spiritual needs of young Andover students. Yet the strange case of Newman Smyth does point to several structural problems in American theological education. Smyth was among the most able and best-trained theologians of his generation, a careful scholar who possessed both an understanding of modern intellectual methods and substantial literary gifts. What type of seminary system left such a person on the academic sidelines? Further, Smyth's later intellectual success at Yale raised a more fundamental question: Was the seminary the place for serious theological study at all? Did not the modern world demand more? Informed people would increasingly ask those two questions as the century wore to its close.

II. Trials and Tribulations

Newman Smyth was not formally charged with teaching evolution in the informal hearings that surrounded his nomination and election at Andover. The same could not be said for two others: Alexander Winchell of Vanderbilt University and James Woodrow of Columbia Seminary. Both victims were unlikely choices. Winchell was a nationally known scholar and scientist who had resigned from a prestigious position as chancellor of Syracuse University to take up duties at newly established Vanderbilt University. He was a deeply committed Methodist whose scholarly output often dealt with the interface between science and religion. While not America's leading scientist, Winchell was both prominent and respected in his field of geology. Woodrow was an almost equally prominent scientist. He had studied at Jefferson College and at Harvard's Lawrence Scientific School, and he had received a doctorate in chemistry from the University of Heidelberg. There were few Americans who had as extensive scientific knowledge or contacts.

The case of Winchell demonstrates the power of uninformed church

41. Perhaps Cambridge, Mass., with Harvard; Baltimore with Johns Hopkins; Chicago with the University of Chicago; and Berkeley, Calif.

opinion to affect events at a school legally owned by a denomination. Methodism, North and South, emerged from the Civil War running at full steam. Supported by its own laity and by a significant number of the new capitalists, Methodism became a major participant in American education. Among those new foundations was Vanderbilt University in Nashville, Tennessee. The energy for this new school was generated in part by Bishop Holland McTyeire, who persuaded a reluctant Southern Methodism to establish Central University in Nashville. The impoverished conferences that established the new university could hardly have hoped to support it, but McTyeire was fortunate in his relatives. Commodore Vanderbilt, the wealthy owner of the Erie Railway, among other properties, had recently taken a second wife, Frank Crawford, considerably younger than himself, and he doted on her. Using his relationship as nephew by marriage to the new Mrs. Vanderbilt, and the commodore's recently awakened awareness of himself as a philanthropist, McTyeire persuaded the shipping magnate to invest heavily in the new Methodist school. As a boon to Vanderbilt's pride, the school was to bear his name. The substantial funds available in this way enabled McTyeire to assemble an unusually fine faculty, including geologist Winchell, and thus to move Vanderbilt into the front rank of Southern schools from the time of its opening in 1875.

Winchell's open advocacy of evolution provoked the suspicions of Thomas O. Summers, dean of the theological department of the school.[42] Summers was an able enough scholar, who had prepared an edition of Wesley's sermons and of Richard Watson's theological institutes. Further, most Southern Methodists had confidence in Summers, and his ecclesiastical popularity was one reason he was appointed. Summers was convinced that Southern Methodism was in danger of losing its doctrinal orthodoxy and, consequently, its hard-won popularity in the South. Winchell, with his Northern accent and evident openness to newer ideas, was a natural target of Summers's wrath.

When Winchell was charged with teaching heresy in the *Nashville Christian Advocate,* the situation rapidly deteriorated. McTyeire apparently informed his professor of the charges just before Winchell was to deliver a lecture, and shortly thereafter the bishop asked Winchell to decline reappointment to his position. When Winchell refused, McTyeire told him the funding for his position had been withdrawn. Winchell was left to find something new for himself, and he quickly located another teaching position at the University of Michigan, where he had taught previously.

42. For Summers, see Frederick V. Mills, Sr., "Alexander Winchell," in *Dictionary of Heresy Trials in American Christianity,* p. 461. I have relied heavily on Mills's account throughout this section.

McTyeire, one of the best ecclesiastical politicians of his time, apparently believed that Methodists did not want to be publicly identified with the teaching of evolution, and the supporting conferences agreed with him on this. In an excess of condemnation, the Tennessee Conference was to say later that Winchell's dismissal was "a blow, the force of which scientific atheism will find it exceeding difficult to break."[43]

Had Winchell kept silent, the event would have been a private humiliation to be passed around at scholarly meetings to academic colleagues. Such petty tyrannies, more than the more publicized trials and firings, convinced many academic people to work for legal protections of their freedom to teach as they believed their disciplines demanded and to work behind the scenes for the secularization of American education.[44] While Winchell could not save his job, he could protest what he felt was an injustice. On June 16, 1878, his story was featured in the *Nashville Daily American* under the headline "Science Gagged at Vanderbilt." A bitter press war followed that included articles for and against Winchell in both the secular and religious press. Equally important, Edward L. Youman, the editor of *Popular Science Monthly,* then one of the leading magazines concerned with scientific and technical questions, took up the professor's cause.

Events surrounding James Woodrow at Columbia Seminary were equally dramatic. Woodrow was one of a handful of church leaders who, following Lee's surrender, went to work to marshal the resources to keep the Southern churches afloat. Woodrow served as the editor and proprietor of the prestigious *Southern Presbyterian Review* from 1861 to 1885.[45] He also served the church as treasurer of its foreign missions program from 1861 to 1872. His careful stewardship of this undertaking during the difficult years of the war and early Reconstruction was a major contribution to the survival of the denomination. In short, Woodrow was as prominent and dedicated a church leader as the Southern church produced in this period. He was also devoted to Columbia Semi-

43. Quoted in Mills, "Alexander Winchell," p. 463.

44. Books like White's noted *History of the Warfare of Science with Theology in Christendom* need to be read against the background of individual professors being attacked and, subsequently, pressured by their administrations to change how they taught or even what they taught. These minor indignities, extended over a long enough period, could limit academic freedom as much as more dramatic firings and dismissals. Conservative Christian pressures on the public schools in the 1980s, to cite a more recent example, may not have resulted in the dismissal of many high school teachers, but they apparently resulted in the trimming of many topics from textbooks and considerable pressure on some faculty.

45. Many religious journals, although they bore denominational or institutional names, were in fact the private property of their editor-owners.

nary, holding a position there, throughout the reconstruction years, when the school was on the verge of bankruptcy. At the same time, Woodrow also served as a teacher of science at South Carolina College. He would end his career as president of that institution.

Despite an earlier dispute over his work as treasurer of his denomination's foreign missions work, Woodrow must have been surprised when his teachings became the center of a passionate debate that led to his dismissal from Columbia Seminary. The course of events was simple enough.[46] Woodrow held the Professorship of the Relationship between Natural Science and Religion that had been established in 1859 by a Mississippi judge, James Perkins. The chair was initially intended to teach the then popular apologetic arguments from nature, in Perkins's words, "to evince the harmony of science with the records of our faith, and to refute the objections of infidel scientists."[47] Although the trustees, in turning to a practicing scientist, may have realized that science was about to become more contentious, they shared Judge Perkins's intellectual commitments.

Woodrow had a naturally adventurous mind, and he followed developments in English and German science as avidly as he could. His sharp mind and extensive knowledge, combined with the excitement that science was generating in the period, made his classes exciting and popular. Soon Woodrow had moved well beyond traditional apologetics and was beginning, on an academic level, to take up the more difficult issues of the meaning of new scientific discoveries and theories. Naturally, Genesis, geology, and evolution came to occupy a prominent place in these classes.

Woodrow's theological style was not in vogue in post–Civil War Southern Presbyterianism. The most powerful theologian in the denomination at that time was Robert Lewis Dabney, who taught first at Union Seminary, Richmond, and then helped to found Austin Seminary. In his essay "Theological Education," Dabney argued that theological seminaries should confine themselves strictly to teaching those doctrines that were explicitly taught in the Westminster Confession of Faith. While Dabney was particularly concerned with speculations that might call into question Southern racial orthodoxy, he was also concerned with what he called "anti-Christian" science. Just as Dabney hoped to build a political fence around the church with his doctrine of the spirituality of the church, a belief that the church should not become involved in political

46. In researching Woodrow, I have found Robert K. Gustafson, *James Woodrow (1828-1907): Scientist, Theologian, Intellectual Leader* (Lewiston, N.Y.: E. Mellen Press, 1995), an invaluable resource. Gustafson summarized his conclusions in "James Woodrow," in *Dictionary of Heresy Trials in American Christianity*, pp. 475-83.

47. Cited in Gustafson, *James Woodrow (1828-1907)*, p. 58.

affairs, so he hoped to build a wall around the church's intellectual life with his strict confessionalism.[48] John Girardeau, Woodrow's colleague at Columbia, largely shared Dabney's narrow perspective.

Like the Winchell case, the Woodrow incident escaped those who wanted to contain the controversy. Woodrow's enemies do not appear to have wanted to try him or to remove him from the ministry. Rather, their goal was to remove him from his seminary professorship and replace him with someone closer to their position. The method they chose was ingenious. In 1883 the board of trustees asked Woodrow to prepare a series of lectures on evolution. Woodrow did so and presented his arguments to a meeting of the seminary's alumni association in May 1884. The argument was far from that of a convinced advocate of evolution. Although Woodrow had apparently come to accept evolution as a probable account of the development of human life, his primary concern was to show that nothing in the Scriptures, properly understood, prevented a person from accepting the new science. The Bible and science had very different purposes, and each had to be interpreted in the light of its own goal. In some ways this position was similar to that of Augustus Strong of Rochester and other Northern conservatives who wanted to continue to use Scripture theologically, while allowing room for disagreement on whether evolutionary doctrine was true.[49] One could maintain Woodrow's position and still hold to a strict doctrine of biblical inspiration. Having stated his position that clearly, Woodrow did want people to know that he personally accepted the evolutionary hypothesis. "The more fully I become acquainted with the facts of which I have given a faint outline, the more I am inclined to believe that it pleased God, the Almighty Creator, to create present and intermediate past organic forms not immediately but mediately, in accordance with the general plan involved in the hypothesis which I have been illustrating."[50] Although Woodrow generally avoided exegetical issues in his presentation — his case did not need them, and such arguments only muddied the discussion — he could not resist arguing that the dust from which Adam was created in Genesis 2 was "organic" matter or that the story of Eve was historical.

It was enough. Despite Woodrow's claims that while he personally accepted evolution he was careful not to teach it as proven, but to leave that question to his classes, the trustees requested his resignation. In the normal course of seminary life at the time, Woodrow would have, however unhappily, submit-

48. In some ways, Dabney's theology was an extension of the Southern belief in the strict interpretation of the constitution to religious and political matters.

49. This position has a long history among American conservative Christians, even those with some relationship to classical fundamentalism.

50. Quoted in Gustafson, *James Woodrow (1828-1907)*, pp. 160-62.

ted. But these were not ordinary times. As professors at South Carolina College, Woodrow and his colleagues were participants in the general movement toward professionalism taking place among American academics. But more important, Woodrow was Presbyterian. He demanded that he be tried for heresy, the only grounds for dismissal under the seminary's charter. Subsequent events resembled the proverbial three-ring circus. Woodrow's own presbytery in Augusta initially refused to conduct the trial, and when the General Assembly ordered it to do so, presbytery members found their highly respected colleague innocent. The sponsoring synods of the seminary, however, urged the trustees to remove Woodrow, which they did officially in 1886. In one of those curious twists of such affairs, the General Assembly in 1888 officially overturned Woodrow's acquittal by the Augusta Presbytery but failed to order a new trial or to try the issues itself. Consequently, Woodrow remained a minister in good standing in the Presbyterian Church and continued to hold leadership positions in both church and seminary. Woodrow was not a heretic, nor was he orthodox.

The paradox of the Woodrow decision may have been the clearest statement of the meaning of the Darwinian debate for Southern Presbyterians. Like many individual Southern Presbyterians, neither Columbia Seminary nor the church was quite sure what to do with evolution. They had to discuss it, and despite Dabney, there was no demand that the Perkins chair be eliminated. At the same time, there was a deep uneasiness about any attempt to square the Darwinian circle. This uneasiness continued to lie just beneath the surface of Southern religious and theological civility. It would erupt again periodically among Presbyterians and Baptists in the South in demands for the removal of seminary teachers or the division of denominations along theological lines.

III. The New Responsibility of Theology

Perhaps the most important outcome of the evolutionary debate had to do not with the actual doctrines taught in the schools but in the effects of the controversies on the theological schools' self-understanding. The most important of these shifts was a subtle redefinition of theology that came to be accepted on all sides of the issue. This new understanding was: no matter how important it is to transmit a particular confessional tradition — and different schools and denominations had very different understandings on this point — it was crucial that those that taught theology take up the questions before the church at the present time. In other words, the debate over Darwin shifted the focus of American theology from the exposition of traditional theological loci to the discussion of the contemporary questions before the church. In effect, the theologians moved toward the type of theologizing associated with such public Christian intellectuals as Beecher and Abbott. A Jonathan Edwards had discussed theology on behalf of the public, as part of his role as a teacher of religion; an Egbert or Newman Smyth discussed public issues as part of his role as a theologian.

CHAPTER FIVE

The New Biblical Studies: Round One

A passionate American debate over the interpretation of the Bible began in the 1880s and, despite ebbs and flows, continues until the present.[1] At the center of the controversy was "higher criticism." While the phrase may have gone back to the eighteenth-century German scholar Eichhorn, it was popularized by William Robertson Smith, a controversial Scottish professor, who was dismissed from the Free University of Aberdeen. In many ways the term clouded the discussion. In 1924 Dr. Harry Emerson Fosdick noted that were a search undertaken for words more "suggestive of superciliousness, condescension, and destructiveness," even skilled wordsmiths would have difficulty finding them.[2] Many Americans, both ministers and laypeople, responded to the emotional tone of the phrase and believed the phrase implied a negative judgment on the Scriptures. In the popular mind a critic was a person constantly engaged in finding fault with something or someone, and hence a "higher critic" was someone who approached Scripture determined to tear it apart. Supporters of the new methods therefore found themselves in the unenviable position of having to apologize for their use of technical language before they discussed more substantial matters.

To the advocates of the newer approaches, higher criticism was just another name for the historical study of the Bible and, in particular, for those questions particularly associated with "introduction": authorship, place of composition, date, etc. In that sense, anyone who sought to interpret the Bible was a higher critic: conservatives were those whose conclusions supported tra-

1. Ira V. Brown, "The Higher Criticism Comes to America, 1880-1900," *Journal of Presbyterian History* 38, no. 4 (Dec. 1960): 193-212.

2. Harry E. Fosdick, *The Modern Use of the Bible* (New York, 1924), cited in Brown, "The Higher Criticism Comes to America, 1880-1900."

dition, liberals were those whose conclusions called for the revision of the common wisdom. Whether a particular scholar believed that the conclusions of the new biblical scholarship should be widely published or not, this point of view stressed the sole competence of professional scholars to decide the truth or falsity of any particular opinion.

This scholarly interpretation of the issues — favored by the new guild of biblical scholars — did not convince everyone. Many who opposed higher criticism were not convinced that the debates over the Bible were as objective as the language implied. Applying what later scholars would call a "hermeneutic of suspicion," opponents maintained that the new method's results were given within its philosophical and historical assumptions. If so, "higher criticism" was only another name for the by-then commonplace rationalist objections to Scripture.[3] Religious populists carried the critique further and associated higher criticism with the new elites that were dominating the nation's economy and politics. This interpretation was particularly convincing to those who, like many rural Americans, had suffered from the consequences of the new social order. Having one's faith run over by university scholars felt very much like having one's farm run over by the railroads.

I. Americans Welcome the Critical Tradition

Although Theodore Parker published an English translation of Wilhelm de Wette's *Introduction to the Old Testament* in 1843,[4] resources for serious study were rarely found in American libraries. Consequently, many of those most serious about biblical studies went to Germany. In the middle decades of the nineteenth century, these Americans abroad tended to study with one of the more conservative scholars. Franz Delitzsch and Ernst Hengstenberg were popular teachers. Those who studied around midcentury would also have witnessed the end of the debate over David Friedrich Strauss's *Life of Jesus.* At least politically, this debate apparently led to the rout of the more extreme biblical scholars, including the Tübingen school, and their exclusion from the German and Swiss university system.

3. The charge of rationalism and its denial are commonplace in the sources. By and large, the issue was never engaged at a sophisticated level. Many of the questions raised by the higher critics, in fact, had earlier been raised by Deists in England and in Germany, although without the sophistication that nineteenth-century scholarship would bring to the task.

4. John W. Rogerson, *W. M. L. de Wette, Founder of Modern Biblical Criticism: An Intellectual Biography* (Sheffield: JSOT Press, 1992), is the best English discussion of de Wette and his work.

Two English debates may also have had great influence. In 1860 *Essays and Reviews* appeared. The book, written by seven liberal churchmen, argued for broader latitude in the interpretation of Scripture and of religious questions in general. More than eleven thousand clergy rallied to protest its conclusions, and almost all the popular journals joined the hue and cry. More directly to the point was the controversy over Bishop John William Colenso of Natal. The bishop's *The Pentateuch and the Book of Joshua Critically Examined* appeared in installments from 1862 to 1879. While the book was not as carefully researched as many German volumes, it made important contributions to the larger discussion, including its emphasis on the work of the Priestly writer in the Pentateuch. Perhaps it is indicative of the close literary relationship between the United States and England that William Green of Princeton published a refutation of Colenso, *The Pentateuch Vindicated from the Aspirations of Bishop Colenso,* in 1863, only a year after its English appearance.

The apparent defeat of radicalism abroad served to hide the steady advance of critical views in both Continental and, to a lesser extent, English universities. Although the newer ideas were discussed in the classroom, American biblical scholarship from 1860 to 1880 was primarily concerned with the publication and republication of scholarly resources. John Hurst's *A Select and Classified Bibliography of Theology and General Religious Literature* was typical of this work.[5] Publicly, at least, American theologians kept the newer discussions at a distance.

What happened in the classrooms may have been another matter. Professors at Andover Theological Seminary, the nation's oldest graduate school of theology, had monitored the German discussion since the days of Moses Stuart, and many of the school's brighter students stayed for an extra year of biblical study once they had finished the regular curriculum.[6] Further, in the 1860s such students as G. Stanley Hall, who attended New York's Union Seminary, later remembered that they had been convinced of the truth of the new perspective during their student years.[7] Indeed, it would have been almost impossible for students at the nation's better seminaries to avoid hearing and discussing the questions. Even where a scholar disagreed with a particular conclusion, the dis-

5. John Hurst, *A Select and Classified Bibliography of Theology and General Religious Literature* (New York: Scribner, 1853).

6. Jerry Wayne Brown, *The Rise of Biblical Criticism in America, 1800-1870: The New England Scholars* (Middletown, Conn.: Wesleyan University Press, 1969). See also Glenn T. Miller, *Piety and Intellect: The Aims and Purposes of Ante-bellum Theological Education* (Atlanta: Scholars, 1990).

7. George Marsden, *The Soul of the American University: From Protestant Establishment to Established Nonbelief* (Oxford and New York: Oxford University Press, 1994), p. 161.

puted position needed to be presented in class, discussed, and debated before it could be rejected.

Of course, this process did not occur everywhere. The teaching methods in many American classrooms obscured the issue as much as they informed students about biblical questions. Benjamin Bacon of Yale, a noted New Testament scholar and expert on the Gospel of John, observed: "It was a deliberate matter of policy to limit instruction in Biblical science to the safe but (for beginners) unrewarding fields of textual criticism and grammatico-lexical exegesis. Partly this policy was due to a dread of superficiality, leading in college and divinity school alike to severe standards of scholarly exactitude, but partly it was adopted in the expectation that the storm-clouds of enquiry into the validity of the tradition regarding the origin of the canonical books would 'blow over.'"[8] Bacon was not always so generous. He referred to his two biblical teachers at Yale as having used the pedagogy to carry out a "policy of suppression" toward the newer conclusions.

Bacon's picture of the possible negative consequences of the teaching methods of his student years was accurate. Students would meet with the instructor in small groups with the text open between them, and the instructor would call on them to translate or to give the grammatical forms of particular words. Since competence in Greek and Hebrew was limited, an instructor could take up each class with an almost endless round of recitation and correction. Such tactics did not of course keep determined students from exploring the material on their own. Bacon, an inveterate reader and scholar, studied the higher criticism on his own while serving as a parish minister. Although his first book, *The Genesis of Genesis,* was on the Old Testament, he specialized in New Testament studies, in part because of his limited linguistic skills.

Bacon's self-education in the new scholarship was not unusual. Despite the popularity of study in Germany, the primary way many professors learned their craft was by preparing for class. Hinckley Mitchell of Boston University described his own conversion to more radical studies: "the more deeply I went into the new views, the more strongly they appealed to me. I did not, however, adopt them wholesale, or any of them without thorough examination."[9] Union's Charles Briggs apparently had a similar experience, as did William Rainey Harper, though he experienced a little more Sturm und Drang over his eventual decision.

The process was implicit in the normal academic pattern of classroom

8. B. W. Bacon, "Enter the Higher Criticism," in Vergilius Ferm, *Contemporary American Theology* (New York: Round Table Press, 1932-33), 1:11.

9. Hinckley Mitchell, *For the Benefit of My Creditors* (Boston: Beacon Press, 1922).

preparation. Since no class could cover the whole Old or New Testament, Bible teachers had to deal frequently with those passages that were Rosetta stones for the new criticism: Genesis 1–2, the Ten Commandments, the messianic passages of Isaiah, and John.[10] The close link between teaching and scholarship may also explain the apparently quick conversions of many scholars to the new methods. Scholars may have read the materials for years as part of their classroom preparation, but nothing forced them to decide one way or the other on the merits of a particular argument. When confronted with a particular situation, such as a public controversy or their desire to publish a book, they had already assembled the materials they needed to make up their minds. A long process of study, consequently, might resolve itself in a moment of reflection or writing.

II. A Defining Moment at Southern Baptist Seminary

The interplay between learning and teaching provided the context for the dismissal of Professor Crawford Toy of Southern Seminary in Louisville. James P. Boyce, the founder of Southern Baptist Theological Seminary, attended Brown College where he was deeply influenced by Francis Wayland, one of the premier antebellum Baptist leaders. However, as Northern Baptist sentiment drifted toward a more antislavery position, Boyce decided to do his advanced theological study at Princeton Seminary, considered safe on the slavery issue, a vital issue for the scion of one of South Carolina's largest slaveholding families. It was a significant choice. While at Princeton Boyce became a disciple of Charles Hodge. After graduation Boyce returned home and became the leading advocate of a Southern Baptist theological school. In his "Three Reforms in Theological Education," Boyce's plan for a South-wide institution, he insisted that the faculty of the proposed school sign a confession of faith — the Abstract of Principles — as a condition of employment.

Boyce had two reasons for this requirement. First, he had witnessed the disruption caused by the well-educated and articulate Alexander Campbell and worried about what might happen to the churches were such a person to teach prospective ministers. His other worry was more distant. Boyce believed that the influence of Germany on Anglo-American scholarship was potentially harmful. Since he hoped Southern Seminary might eventually provide prospective teachers with advanced instruction and contribute to the production of

10. Bacon saw John as analogous in New Testament criticism to the Pentateuch in the Old Testament. It was even more important for the teacher-scholar since its Greek, like that of the letters of John, is easy to read and translate.

needed theological literature, he wanted to protect the South's theology from contamination at its source.

Despite Boyce's personal conservatism, Southern's Abstract of Principles was a moderate document that set forth the central affirmations of the modified Calvinism common among Southern Baptists. The statement on the Bible was particularly mild: "The Scriptures of the Old and New Testaments were given by inspiration of God, and are the only sufficient, certain and authoritative rule of all saving knowledge, faith and obedience."[11] There were sound Baptist reasons why the magisterial reformation's insistence that it was the Bible in Greek and Hebrew that had authority was not affirmed. Throughout their history, Baptists had relied on ministers who had little formal education and whose understanding of the Bible, by necessity, came from the English version. They had maintained that, however much might remain mysterious in Scripture, the central biblical message — "saving knowledge, faith and obedience" — was evident to any person who would trust Christ. This audacious hermeneutic was also enshrined in Southern's educational program that later was a model for many other Baptist schools, North and South. The school ad-

11. The Abstract was actually written by Basil Manly, another Princeton graduate. "The Baptist Faith and Message," adopted first during the evolution crisis of the 1920s, contains a much fuller doctrine of Scripture:

> The Holy Bible was written by men divinely inspired and is the record of God's revelation of Himself to man. It is a perfect treasure of divine instruction. It has God for its author, salvation for its end, and truth, without any mixture of error, for its matter. It reveals the principles by which God judges us; and therefore is, and will remain to the end of the world, the true center of Christian union, and the supreme standard by which all human conduct, creeds, and religious opinions should be tried. The criterion by which the Bible is to be interpreted is Jesus Christ. (1963 version)

Like the Abstract, "The Baptist Faith and Message" carefully avoids mention of any special authority in the original languages or the original text. Westminster, chapter 1, for instance, reads:

> The Old Testament in Hebrew (which was the native language of the people of God of old), and the New Testament in Greek (which, at the time of the writing of it, was most generally known to the nations), being immediately inspired by God, and, by His singular care and providence, kept pure in all ages, are therefore authentical; so as, in all controversies of religion, the Church is finally to appeal unto them. But, because these original tongues are not known to all the people of God, who have right unto, and interest in the Scriptures, and are commanded, in the fear of God, to read and search them, therefore they are to be translated in to the vulgar language of every nation unto which they come, that, the Word of God dwelling plentifully in all, they may worship Him in an acceptable manner; and, through patience and comfort of the Scriptures, may have hope.

Nor did the Baptist confessions, unlike the confessions of the magisterial Reformed churches, ever list the biblical books.

mitted college graduates and nongraduates and shaped many of its educational practices around those who did not know Hebrew, Greek, or Latin. Elementary biblical study was based on the English text. The "elective system" allowed those with more education to use their linguistic skills in advanced courses.[12]

The struggle to keep Southern open in the years after the Civil War exhausted Boyce, who was one of the better administrators in American theological education, and left him little time for reflective theology or writing. In some ways, that fiscal battle appears to have mellowed him, theologically and personally, as the theological idealism of his youth was replaced, in part, by the pragmatic values needed to save an endangered but large institution. In any event, the two faculty appointments made during the 1870s were both German-trained scholars, the Hebraist Crawford Toy and church historian William Whitsitt. Toy and Whitsitt were both committed to the research ideals they had learned in Germany. When their talents were combined with those of Virginia-trained John A. Broadus, a leading New Testament textual critic, Southern had one of the most advanced faculties in the nation, far ahead of its closest Baptist rival, Newton.

Southern seemed destined to be a national leader in religious and theological thought, perhaps the equal of Union or Princeton. But it was poorly financed and forced to scramble for every penny needed to educate a large student body. Often its financial agents were only a few whistle-stops ahead of its creditors. Baptist democracy may have served well the students and inspired an excellent faculty, but that same democracy had trouble providing the money needed to maintain a major educational enterprise.

Crawford Toy was Southern Seminary's child of promise. As a child, Toy was a member of Professor Broadus's Virginia church. A natural linguist, he was fascinated by languages from his earliest days, and he studied Greek and Latin with his pastor and with his father, a druggist and amateur linguist. Toy made substantial progress in biblical languages during his study at the University of Virginia and at Southern Baptist Seminary, but his scholarly development was interrupted by service in the Confederate army. Following his capture at the Battle of Gettysburg and parole by the Union army, Toy resumed his studies. After teaching briefly at the Universities of Alabama and Virginia, the young scholar went to Germany in 1868 where he specialized in Semitics, work-

12. Southern's elective system antedated Charles Eliot's introduction of his elective system at Harvard. It was based on the elective system at the University of Virginia, where students received separate certificates for each course they completed. As at Virginia, when students had enough certificates, if they were in the right subjects, they might receive a degree. But both systems were designed to permit a student to use the school without seeking the type of social certification suggested by the classical degree.

ing with Roediger and Dieterici. In 1870 he became professor of Old Testament interpretation and Oriental languages at Southern Seminary.

Toy was a popular teacher, a master of the recitation style then favored at Southern, who involved his students deeply in discussions of current scholarly issues. In his hands recitation became something like the seminar classes he had attended abroad. Toy's colleague Whitsitt was also known for his seminar-like approach to teaching. As his classes exegeted the classical loci, students raised many questions about how the texts related to the present intellectual climate. Naturally, these issues included evolution and Genesis and the disputed authorship of many biblical books. Toy was reading avidly on these topics, and he apparently shared his new discoveries with his classes as he made them, often jumping from one new construct to another without much worry about their intellectual consistency. More than once or twice[13] Broadus warned his younger protégé that he was in danger of causing controversy. Each time Toy promised to stay closer to his assigned tasks, only to fall back into old habits again. Questions posed by his students tempted him to sally forth again into disputed territory, and each extemporaneous session inspired new questions and new investigations. Toy's excursuses took place around the edges of assigned translation assignments and were part of a student's training in scriptural exegesis. The informal quality of those remarks may have hid from Toy himself how far he was moving away from the Baptist consensus.[14]

Toy's habit of advancing his personal scholarship through teaching might have continued indefinitely, but in 1879 he wrote a series of articles for the *Sunday School Times* on the suffering servant prophecies of Isaiah. The essays, although written in a popular style, indicated that Toy adopted many contemporary conclusions about ancient prophecy. He argued, for instance, that the suffering servant was properly identified with Israel, not with Christ, and that the focus of the passages was on the Israel of the exile. Only after the passage of time, he argued, had these prophecies found their higher fulfillment in Christ's

13. Since the articles were popular pieces, Toy did not list the bibliographical resources he had used to formulate his opinions. My guess is that he was working with Abraham Kuenen's *The Prophets and Prophecy in Ancient Israel* (1877). Although less well-known than Wellhausen's 1878 history, Kuenen's understanding of prophecy developed many of the major themes of later prophetic studies, including the belief that the great prophets were more preachers than predictors of the future and that the meaning of their message was to be found in their contemporary situations, that is, the situations the prophecies addressed.

14. See Pope A. Duncan, "Crawford Howell Toy," in *Dictionary of Heresy Trials in American Christianity*, ed. George H. Shriver (Westport, Conn.: Greenwood Press, 1997), p. 432. If Duncan's dating is accurate, Toy must have accepted Wellhausen's views shortly after the appearance of the latter's history of Israel. In his earlier years, Toy may have been more influenced by Ewald, Kuenen, and de Wette than by Wellhausen.

suffering and death. To Toy's surprise, controversy broke out over these views. He sent a communication on his views to the seminary's board, meeting in Atlanta, in which he defended his position. If his defense was not adequate, he offered to resign his professorship. In this letter Toy labored to show that his views on prophecy were only part of his understanding of the development of Hebrew literature. "The early history of Israel was for a long time not committed to writing but handed down by oral tradition, under which process it was subject to a more or less free expansion. In the expanded form it was received at a comparatively late time by the Prophets and Priests who put it into shape, and made it the vehicle of religious truth."[15] Toy admitted that his position, which he believed conformed to the seminary's confessional statements, was not held by many contemporary Baptists.

The board was not sure what to do with the communication. A committee was appointed to confer with Toy. Few believed, or were willing to say they believed, that Toy had violated the Abstract, but the committee did agree with Toy that his views were not those of the Baptist majority. The committee and Toy knew what this meant for the struggling institution. Although it was unsaid, the committee worried that Toy's employment at the school might endanger the school's already limited ability to raise funds. Hence, the board decided to accept Toy's resignation, although they did not convict him of a teaching contrary to the seminary's Abstract of Principles. Indeed, the story is told that both Broadus and Boyce accompanied Toy to the train station at Louisville when he left the seminary for the last time, to see him off and wish him well. Putting his arm around Toy's neck and lifting his other arm in the air, Boyce exclaimed, "Oh Toy, I would freely give that arm to be cut off if you would be where you were five years ago and stay there."[16]

After leaving Southern Seminary, Crawford Toy spent a year in New York as an editor before accepting an appointment in Charles Eliot's nondenominational Harvard Divinity School. While he continued to be interested in Old Testament studies and contributed to the International Critical Commentary, his academic interests centered on Semitic languages and literature. George Foote Moore described his work:

> Toy, at first single-handed, offered courses not only in the Hebrew language and the interpretation of the Old Testament, introduction, and the history of the Hebrew religion with comparison with other semitic religions, but in Arabic, and in Mohammedan history (the Caliphates); and from time to

15. Quoted in Duncan, "Crawford Howell Toy," p. 434.
16. Quoted in Duncan, "Crawford Howell Toy," p. 436.

> time, as students offered themselves, in Ethiopic, the Phoenician inscriptions, and other subjects. In 1882, David Gordon Lyon, a pupil of Toy's at Greenville and Louisville, who, since leaving the seminary in the summer of 1879, had been pursuing his studies in Germany, particularly in Assyrian, was appointed Hollis Professor of Divinity, and became Professor Toy's colleague in the Semitic field, taking part of the instruction in Hebrew and Aramaic, as well as Assyrian, and Old Testament history.[17]

In this sense Toy was one of the principal creators of the modern field of Near East studies, and his work in that area was perhaps to have far greater academic significance than his contributions to the study of the Old Testament. If the Baptist seminary world lost a promising young scholar, the larger academic community gained a valuable new discipline.

Toy's dismissal had lasting effects on Southern. The most difficult question before a seminary in a democratic denomination was whether its primary task was to reflect the best opinion in the church or to reflect the best of its own scholarship. To many Southern Baptist laypeople, the answer was obvious. Southern Baptist Seminary was their school; they would hire its graduates, and they should set its course and direction. While they wanted the school to raise the educational level of the ministry, they did not want it to challenge the theological understanding of the churches. The financial plight of the school made it difficult, if not impossible, for the seminary to resist this argument. Later, Toy's German-trained colleague William Whitsitt would also be forced to resign following a challenge to Baptist public opinion.

The events in Louisville, however, did not spark a national debate. Toy was not a contentious person, and he had little interest in engaging his former colleagues or employers in a heated public debate over his conclusions or his research. Toy went quietly, content with his own integrity. Scholarly questions were to be settled by scholarly means, and the public opinion that supported him had no more value than the public opinion that had demanded his removal. But other scholars were less willing to rest content at the center of the storm. Such scholars suspected that the time had come for a fundamental debate over the newer scholarship. All that was needed was an event that would capture the attention of the scholarly community in such a way as to force serious discussion.

17. George Moore, "An Appreciation of Professor Toy," *American Journal of Semitic Languages and Literatures* 34 (Oct. 1919): 6-7.

III. Wellhausen and His Kin

There was such an event. In 1878 Julius Wellhausen published his masterful *History of Israel.*[18] Like many great works of science and scholarship, this history came at the end of a long and often confusing discussion among scholars.[19] Since the eighteenth century, many investigators had believed that much of the Pentateuch was a compound document, that there were serious problems with the traditional attribution of the Psalms to David, and that some of the prophetic books may have been written over many years. Further, the traditional attribution of Daniel to the Babylonian period seemed inaccurate. Yet no one had found a historical framework that made sense of these difficulties. As a result, advanced biblical studies often appeared to be chaotic. What Wellhausen did was to introduce order into the discussion. Agreeing with such earlier scholars as de Wette that the Old Testament was not a historical study, he cut the Gordian knot and assumed that the first real history encountered in the Old Testament was in the books of Samuel and Kings. This meant that those books, rather than the Pentateuch, should be used to reconstruct the framework in which Hebrew literature had developed. Within this broad framework Wellhausen argued that the development of the Israelite cult, as reflected in the books of Kings, provided the key to many controversial issues.

Wellhausen's decision to center on the cult was fruitful. In his view the various ancient Israelite festivals did not begin as commemorations of historical events. Rather, those festivals were reinterpreted later by the authors of the Pentateuch in monotheistic terms that obscured their primitive Semitic origins. Following this clue, Passover was an agricultural feast, perhaps connected with the birth of lambs, that was reinterpreted much later in terms of the "escape" from Egypt. Likewise, the centralized worship envisioned in Deuteronomy dated from after the separation of the two kingdoms, since Samuel and Kings continued to reflect the observation of local feasts and festivals well after David's conquest of Jerusalem and Solomon's construction of the temple. Once such arguments were accepted, the other pieces of the puzzle fell rapidly into place. Israel's religion had developed from a typical western Semitic folk religion into a system that stressed first the worship of one God and eventually the existence of only one God. On this basis Wellhausen demonstrated how the

18. The second edition was renamed *Prolegomena to the History of Israel.* For an account of Wellhausen, see John William Rogerson, *Old Testament Criticism in the Nineteenth Century* (Philadelphia: Fortress, 1985).

19. For a similar point about Darwin, see above, chap. 4. In many ways the science and scholarship of the late nineteenth century involved as much organizing what was known as it did striking new discoveries.

various "sources" of the Pentateuch were finally edited into one story by a redactor who, Wellhausen assumed, may have authored some of the material.

Even more than one hundred years later, the boldness of Wellhausen's scholarship is striking. In the details of his often pedantic arguments, Wellhausen rendered many commonplace assumptions about the Old Testament questionable. Moses, for example, was not the great prophet of monotheism nor did he formulate (or transcribe) most of the Israelite law, including the Ten Commandments. Perhaps most interesting, the great struggle between Israel and the Philistines was stripped of its religious overlays, and the messianic hope was a comparatively late development. Most of David's psalms reflected the religious life of the Second Temple. Many people, including Wellhausen himself, wondered whether the Old Testament retained any value for contemporary religion.

Whatever the theological implications of the position, Wellhausen's argument changed Old Testament studies. Professional scholars almost immediately recognized the brilliance of his bold synthesis.[20] In Scotland, W. Robertson Smith became quickly convinced of the basic accuracy of his approach and outlined the German scholar's work in the ninth edition of the *Encyclopedia Britannica.*[21] The *Britannica* was then near the height of its reputation as a summary of contemporary scientific and scholarly knowledge. Each article was written by a noted scholar and carefully edited for content and references. Like other articles in the encyclopedia, Smith's essays were presumed to set forth the status of the question and the consensus among the most able Old Testament scholars. In other words, the encyclopedia's editors gave Wellhausen's analysis of the Pentateuch a normative status or legitimacy that it had not yet earned in scholarly circles.

Smith's articles had less scholarly repercussions. Despite Smith's personal reputation for piety and for lively faith, he was accused of heresy and removed from his chair in 1881. The Pentateuchal question, consequently, became entwined with the discussion of academic freedom in theological education. Smith and his ideas became a cause of scholars everywhere.

Among those who became involved was Charles Briggs of Union Seminary. Briggs had been one of the more conservative members of the American biblical fraternity, but his review of the Smith case for the *Presbyterian Review* convinced him that the issues had to be decided "free from the complications

20. This was true even of scholars, such as Greene, who disagreed with Wellhausen.

21. Warner M. Bailey, "William Robertson Smith and American Biblical Studies," *Journal of Presbyterian History* 51 (Fall 1973): 285-308; Ronald Nelson, "Higher Criticism and the Westminster Confession: The Case of William Robertson Smith," *Christian Scholar's Review* 1 (1970): 5-18.

and technicalities of ecclesiastical proceedings, by competent scholars on both sides." The entry of Briggs into this arena had two foci: his own private study and his sponsorship of a scholarly debate.

Briggs apparently had not accepted the Wellhausen hypothesis when he entered the debate over Smith's orthodoxy.[22] However, he was already hard at work on his *Biblical Study,* a book written to encourage biblical scholarship in America that he published in 1883. Whether he accepted Wellhausen's solution at this time is not clear, but he had become convinced that Wellhausen's focus, the nature and dating of the Pentateuchal sources on the basis of the development of Hebrew religion, was the central issue before the biblical fraternity. He urged them to their duty with a militant exhortation:

> We have thus far been, at the best, spectators of the battle that has raged on the continent of Europe over the Biblical books. The Providence of God now calls us to take part in the conflict. Our Anglo-American scholars are but poorly equipped for the struggle. We should prepare ourselves at once. We should give our immediate attention to the history of this great movement, the stadia through which it has passed, and the present state of the question, in order that as soon as possible our scholars may attain the highest marks reached by our foreign brethren and advance to still greater achievements.[23]

Briggs, for one, was willing to pay whatever it cost in time, effort, and treasure to determine where the truth lay.

The *Presbyterian Review* gave Briggs the chance to have the issues around Smith publicly aired. Since the journal was jointly published by the faculties of Princeton and Union, with Briggs the Union editor and A. A. Hodge the Princeton editor, Briggs was able to use the journal to orchestrate one of the great debates in American theological history. A list of the articles gives a sense of the scope of the discussion: "Inspiration," B. B. Warfield and A. A. Hodge; "Critical Theologies of the Sacred Scriptures in Relation to Their Inspiration," Charles A. Briggs; "Professor W. Robertson Smith on the Pentateuch," William Green; "Delitzsch on the Origin and Composition of the Pentateuch," S. Ives Curtiss; "The Logical Methods of Prof. Kuenen," William J. Beecher; "A Critical Study of

22. Although Briggs could often be militant and even rash in his debates with others, he was extremely cautious as an Old Testament scholar. My reading of the material at this point is that while Briggs was not ready to publicly identify himself in the Smith-Wellhausen camp, he had already moved a considerable distance in that direction. Other scholars, including William Rainey Harper, showed a similar reticence.

23. Quoted in Ira Brown, "The Higher Criticism," p. 199.

the Higher Criticism with the Special Reference to the Pentateuch," Charles Briggs; and "Dogmatic Aspect of the Pentateuchal Criticism," Francis Patton.[24]

In one sense the debate was deceptive. Despite the fine article by Green on Smith's views of the Pentateuch and Beecher's careful analysis of Kuenen's contributions, the articles do not really present the pros and cons of Smith's or Wellhausen's theory. It is as though all parties recognized that those discussions would have to be conducted in the more specialized journal literature, already primarily read by specialists. But they did come down hard on the question of the nature of biblical study. For Hodge, Green, Patton, and Warfield, biblical study was part and parcel of theological study and affirmation. Hence, it was perfectly reasonable to expect biblical scholars, especially those employed by the church, to stay within the confessional boundaries set by the church. In this, biblical studies share with other theological studies a primary accountability to the Christian community. In principle, this accountability is the same for those who teach the Bible as for those who teach dogmatics.

In this debate the crucial question is exactly what the confession of faith teaches about the Bible and whether a particular scholar teaches in accord with that position. In particular, the issue boils down to whether ecclesiastical doctrine attributes inspiration to statements the Bible makes about science and history as well as about faith, or to frame the question differently, whether the doctrinal statements made by the biblical authors are separable from their place in the biblical narrative.

The answer to this question is not self-evident. The biblical account of the Passover appears to be integral to theological teachings about the Passover. The instructions for the festival see the Passover as a commemoration of the Israelites' escape from Egypt that dated back to the original participants in that event. In observing the festival from Moses' time onward, the ancient Israelites had a graphic picture of God's continued presence with them. On the other hand, if the Passover was an ancient agricultural observance adopted by later Jews to serve their own purposes, the festival is an all-too-human part of Israel's history. The theophany that supposedly launched the original observance is at least mythical and perhaps even fraudulent.[25] The Ten Commandments

24. For a thorough discussion see Max Rogers, "Charles Augustus Briggs: Conservative Heretic" (Ph.D. diss., Columbia University, 1964); Mark Stephen Massa, *Charles Augustus Briggs and the Crisis of Historical Criticism* (Minneapolis: Fortress, 1990); Carl E. Hatch, *The Charles A. Briggs Heresy Trial: Prologue to Twentieth-Century Liberal Protestantism* (New York: Exposition Press, 1969).

25. Ironically, Wellhausen agreed with the Princetonians on this point. He withdrew from the church and taught Semitics because he believed that his conclusions were foreign to the Lutheran Confessions.

suffer a similar fate when separated from their supposed origins. What does it mean to say that God spoke these words when it appears that they were composed by Israel's religious leaders much later, perhaps as a means of holding the nation together after the disaster of the fall of Jerusalem?

Briggs, Henry Preserved Smith, and Beecher,[26] however, were not looking at the issue as systematic theologians. They had already begun to see the Old Testament as a series of documents that could be best understood by ordinary historical means. As Briggs said: "It simply will not do to antagonize the critical theories of the Bible with alternative theories, for the critic appeals to history against tradition, to an array of facts against so-called inferences. History, facts, and truth are all Divine products, and must prevail."[27] In a later article, published in the *Independent* in 1899, Briggs reiterated his belief that biblical study was scientific. "What we must insist upon over and against radical and conservative alike is a scientific study of the Holy Scripture. We are aiming at what the Bible gives us, no more, no less. We are not as Biblical scholars studying the Bible in the interest of any theory or dogma, or any party or any system. We study the Bible with the same openmindedness with which the astronomer studies the heavens, the geologist the rocks, and the physician the science of medicine."[28] In other words, the questions raised by criticism could be discussed only in terms of professional historical criteria, and not on other grounds, however compelling those arguments might seem to be. Hence, the importance of the article by Professor Curtiss on Delitzsch. For despite the conservative trust in his scholarship, Delitzsch had admitted that there were critical questions about the Pentateuch that could be answered only by historical research. The difference between Delitzsch and Wellhausen, thus, was not in their approach but in their conclusions. Further, the critical party believed that it had sound theological reasons for proceeding as it did. In line with the basic Protestant approach to theology, they believed that theological questions ought to be resolved on the basis of exegetical study and not vice versa. To follow another procedure was to deny *sola Scriptura,* the basic insight of the Reformation that the Bible stood superior to any other source of truth. If this meant the surrender of some beloved opinions and symbols, so be it.

The theological questions posed by the new study were serious for all Christian denominations. But these issues were particularly pressing for Presbyterians. The covenant theology, enshrined in the Westminster Confes-

26. Beecher was by far the most conservative of the three on critical questions.

27. Briggs, "Biblical Authority," quoted in Massa, *Charles Augustus Briggs,* p. 63.

28. Charles Briggs, "The Scientific Study of Holy Scripture," *Independent,* Nov. 30, 1899, p. 3208.

sion and catechisms, placed its emphasis on God's acts in history as much as on the Bible's abstract teachings about God. For covenant theology, history was part of the substance of the message, not merely an occasion for teaching doctrinal truth. Each covenant was related to the previous covenant by a chain of events that, so to speak, provided the plot for the whole narrative of salvation. The sequence of covenants from Adam to Christ was as much a part of official Presbyterian teaching as the doctrine of justification or ecclesiology.

In this sense the debate over biblical criticism was almost an intrinsic part of the debate over the revision of the Westminster Standards that occupied the Presbyterian Church in the 1880s and 1890s.[29] Briggs's first contribution to that discussion was his *American Presbyterianism* (1885), a book researched in the newly acquired McAlpin Collection of the Union Library. In this study Briggs contended that the Puritan foundations of the Presbyterian Church had been corrupted by a scholasticism that all but obscured the teachings of the Westminster documents. Using a popular genre among people advocating change, Briggs argued that the best way forward was to return to the church's foundations and leave the innovations behind.[30] Ironically, Briggs's sensitivity to the scholastic elements in American Presbyterianism may have been sharpened by his own study under Hengstenberg in Berlin, one of the most important European advocates of biblical inerrancy.

When the General Assembly formally opened the question of revision in 1889, Briggs was prepared. Although his initial response was to urge looser terms of subscription, the logic of his earlier writing led to revision. In *Whither: A Theological Question for the Times,* published in 1889, he restated his belief that the Presbyterian Church needed to reclaim its earlier freedom. The centerpiece of his argument was a discussion of chapter 4, creation, which seemed to imply a literal reading of Genesis. Briggs (together with many other Presbyterians) believed that science had proved that the creation account could not be historical. But if this was so, Briggs reasoned, then the church needed to recognize that other apparently historical claims might not rest on demonstrable fact. The difference between Briggs and his critics, hence, was a matter of degree.

29. Although the assembly did not begin to debate the issue until 1889, the question had been around since the trial of David Swing in Chicago for teaching liberal theology.

30. Briggs had a clear view of his opponents. The Princeton theology did rely heavily on the theology of the scholastic Calvinist Francis Turretin. It also relied heavily on the popular commonsense realist philosophy of science. Where Briggs may have overstepped his bounds was in the use of the jeremiad formula that saw the present as a step down from an earlier, higher truth. One could argue, as Princeton theologians were wont to do, that Princeton Calvinism was a modern expression of an ancient faith and an improvement on the past. Historically, Briggs perhaps overdrew the distance between Westminster and the Protestant scholastics.

IV. The Briggs Trial and Its Aftermath

Meanwhile, in 1890 Charles Briggs was transferred from the Davenport chair of Hebrew to the newly endowed Edward Robinson professorship in biblical theology. To celebrate his new position, Briggs, at the urging of Charles Butler — the donor of the chair — took up the question of biblical authority. The lecture was a tour de force. Speaking with both passion and precision, Briggs rang the chimes on the issues that separated the biblical critics from their opponents. He began by tackling the vexing question of religious authority in general. Here, whether Briggs was influenced by Wesley or not, he advocated a position remarkably like the Methodist Quadrilateral. Real authority, Briggs asserted, came from the working together of reason, Scripture, and the church. And when the Bible is viewed in the light of these three criteria, we can see where human beings have erected barriers to its understanding and to its power. There were six such barriers: superstition, verbal inspiration, authenticity, inerrancy, miracles (as violations of the laws of nature), and minute prediction. With the exception of superstition, all the items in the list were part of the standard doctrine of Scripture. Both verbal inspiration and inerrancy were held to be characteristic of the text, and authenticity (apostolic and prophetic authorship), miracles, and particular prediction were evidence of its divine character. Seen from the perspective of tradition, the address was a sweeping attack on what most informed Presbyterians considered biblical authority to mean. The address also dealt with the primary areas in which the newer studies were reinterpreting the tradition. Despite disagreement among biblical scholars on specific issues, the new biblical criticism had raised substantial questions about the authorship of the Pentateuch, Isaiah, and John. Further, Kuenen's studies of biblical prophecy, published in English translation in 1877, indicated that most biblical prophecies were not predictions of the future. If accurate, Kuenen's analysis rendered untenable the traditional argument that the coming of Christ had been predicted in the Old Testament. Miracles, at least as supernatural interventions in the course of nature, had long been disputed.

The constructive section of the address was, as might be expected, the weakest. While Briggs had clearly identified the "stumbling blocks" to the understanding of the text, he had much more difficulty explaining how the authority of the Bible ought to function in the church. In part, he was limited by his own professionalism. Like many seminary teachers in the new classical disciplines, he devoted the bulk of his intellectual efforts to mastering the tools and techniques of his guild. When it came to the implications of those methods, his own lack of experience as a systematic theologian was evident. The best he could do was argue that the Christology of Isaak Dorner and of Henry B.

Smith with its emphasis on Christ as divinely fulfilled humanity would suffice for the crisis. Ironically, the much more directly relevant reflections of the Ritschlian school, then dominant in Germany, were not used by him or his defenders.[31] "Briggs was a rigorous writer whose words often sounded like a call to battle: Criticism is at work with knife and fire. Let us cut down everything that is dead and harmful, every kind of dead orthodoxy, every species of effete ecclesiasticism, all those dry and brittle fences that constitute denominationalism are the barriers of Church Unity. Let us remove every encumbrance out of the way for a new life; the life of God is moving throughout Christendom, and the springtime of a new age is about to come upon us."[32] Conservatives who feared that their most precious beliefs were under assault could find little comfort in such language. Briggs had, whether consciously or not, called for a holy war on the question.[33] Briggs was Luther at the Wittenberg door: "We stand on the heights of the last of the great movement of Christendom. . . . It must be evident to every thinking man that the traditional dogma has been battling against philosophy and science, history, and every form of human learning. . . . There can be little doubt but that the traditional dogma is doomed. Shall it be allowed to drag down into perdition with it the Bible and the Creeds?"[34] Perhaps, like Luther earlier, Briggs did not completely anticipate the reaction to his words. Or, as with Luther and the Ninety-five Theses, the implications of the address were perhaps greater than Briggs yet understood. In any event, his op-

31. Part of the irony was that Harnack's understanding of Christianity as "corrupted" reinterpretation of its Hebrew foundations by Greek thought and ecclesiastical authority was similar to Briggs's understanding of contemporary Presbyterianism as a "scholastic" reinterpretation of the more biblical theology found in the Westminster standards. It should be noted that Harnack had problems of his own at this point. He was engaged in a titanic struggle over the Apostles' Creed that ended with his exclusion from the ordination examinations of the Church of the Old Prussian Union.

32. Quoted in Massa, *Charles Augustus Briggs,* p. 89.

33. Then and now sympathetic observers have thought that Briggs's remarks obscured his meaning. Robert Handy, for instance, noted: "When he had dealt with these themes before, he had set them more carefully in the context of his own evangelical views, and with greater clarification and qualification. This time some of his points were not carefully stated; for example, one could interpret his remarks about the three sources of divine authority to mean that they were coordinate or even mutually independent." *A History of Union Theological Seminary in New York* (New York: Columbia University Press, 1987), p. 73. Clearly, Briggs did have an evangelical, even conservative, side. For instance, he would later have much difficulty with A. C. McGiffert's belief that the virgin birth was not historical. But Briggs was also a crusader for the new scholarship that he believed was liberating the church from superstition and folly. The deliberate choice of such words as "stumbling blocks" that had clear biblical references to unbelief was not incidental to Briggs's message: he meant them.

34. Briggs, "Biblical Authority," quoted in Massa, *Charles Augustus Briggs,* p. 91.

ponents were ready to draw some of those implications. The 1891 General Assembly heard a motion that Briggs's transfer to his new position be vetoed, and that motion, brought by its standing committee on theological seminaries, passed. The Briggs affair now involved more than charges against an errant faculty member; it now involved the relationship between the Presbyterian Church and its largest and richest seminary.

At almost the same time, the Presbytery of New York began a heresy process against Briggs. The initial two charges were vague. The first only alleged that Briggs had taught doctrines contrary to the confession of faith, and the second contended that he taught progressive sanctification after death. After vigorous debate the presbytery voted to dismiss the charges, and Briggs's opponents immediately appealed the decision. Despite the apparent requirement that the appeal go to the Synod of New York, the case was brought before the 1892 General Assembly in Portland, Oregon, and returned to the presbytery. This time Briggs's opponents redrew the charges and took pains to see that they were specific. Again, Briggs was not convicted, and the long process of appeal continued. After more wrangling the assembly agreed to hear the case. The trial began on May 29, 1893. After passionate speeches on all sides and considerable discussion of the evidence, the General Assembly voted to suspend Charles Briggs from its ministry. In 1899 he became a priest in the Episcopal Church.

Although the Briggs case has significance as part of the struggle of seminary professors for academic freedom, its implications for the history of American theological education were perhaps even more significant. Union's decision to support Briggs and to withdraw from the Compact of 1870 with the Presbyterian Church was more than a shift in governance. In effect, Union was claiming that theological study could be best conducted in an atmosphere in which institutions were primarily responsible to their own boards and, more important, to the academic standards maintained by their faculties. Since one mark of a profession is that only competent professionals or peers can judge the work of other professionals, this was a major step. Most members of seminary faculties might continue to be ministers, but their primary professional responsibility, Union suggested, was to their academic colleagues and not to their denominations. In short, a seminary professor was more like a university teacher than like a church official. As the universities became more powerful in American education, this model became progressively more attractive. At the time, however, although many schools would later adopt a similar understanding of their faculties, Union's position was a distinctly minority opinion. Union action also implied other shifts in what a seminary might be. Both the board of trustees and the stronger financial supporters of Union gained influence as the Presbyterian role declined.

In the short run, Briggs and Union lost. The 1892 Assembly passed the Portland Deliverance that declared "that it is a fundamental doctrine of this church that the Old and the New Testaments are the inspired and infallible Word of God. Our church holds that the inspired Word, as it comes from God, is without error, and the assertion to the contrary cannot but shake the confidence of the people." In 1899 the Deliverance was expanded to include four "essential and necessary" doctrines, and the version adopted in 1910, 1916, and 1923 expanded that number to five. While such declarations did not produce uniformity, they did help to align the Presbyterian seminaries, with the exception of Union and Auburn, primarily with the more conservative position.

At the same time, the trials continued. Henry Preserved Smith, a friend and later coworker of Briggs who taught at Cincinnati's Lane Seminary, was accused of heresy in 1893 for his vigorous defense of his friend. The actual charges against Smith were less specific than those against Briggs, and primarily were that he had taught that the Scriptures were not inerrant. Smith, consequently, made his trial a test of the Portland Deliverance, arguing that the doctrine of inerrancy was not a necessary teaching of the Confession of Faith or a logical implication of it. That doctrine, he stated, was inconsistent with the facts, since we do not have the original autographs, and further, inerrancy was not taught in any of the Reformed Confessions. Smith maintained that biblical authority referred to Scripture's truth for "faith and life," and not to the factual details in the text. These details should be left to the scholar to decide. "As an exegete it is my duty to deal with the facts of Scripture, and state them. It is the duty of the theologians to make their theory accord with those facts, and if the theory is not in accord with the facts, the fault does not lie with the facts."[35] The presbytery did not accept the argument. Smith was convicted, and the General Assembly refused to hear his appeal. He was suspended from the ministry and resigned his professorship. In protest, George Foote Moore, arguably the best-informed American student of Semitic cultures, resigned from the Presbyterian ministry.

Smith's younger fellow scholar, Arthur C. McGiffert, who moved to Union Seminary in 1893 to take up Philip Schaff's former position, was also forced to resign his standing. After McGiffert published in 1897 *A History of Christianity in the Apostolic Age,* the 1898 General Assembly asked him to conform to the church's standards or to resign. Neither side wanted a trial. The trials of Briggs and Smith had left behind enough of a bad taste, and the various Presbyterian bodies that heard the case, while agreeing that McGiffert taught

35. Quoted in Roger R. Keller, "Henry Preserved Smith," in *Dictionary of Heresy Trials in American Christianity,* p. 355.

contrary to the standards, did not want the publicity that a formal trial might bring. But when a trial began to look inevitable, McGiffert realized that he had no chance for acquittal, since the General Assembly had already expressed itself on the various items alleged against him. Consequently McGiffert resigned in 1900 and joined the Congregational Churches.

The effect of these trials was, as Lefferts A. Loetscher noted, to make "the Presbyterian Church . . . a decidedly conservative voice in theological education." Princeton and all the Old School seminaries, except McCormick, continued to reject the newer criticism on theological grounds and to mount strong arguments for the truth of that tradition. Tiny Lane Seminary moved in the same direction, especially after the resignations of Smith and McGiffert. McCormick Seminary (the Presbyterian Theological Seminary of the Northwest) took a slightly different course. In part because of the long and effective tenure of Andrew Constantine Zenos, the school steered more toward the middle. Auburn, a former New School seminary, also continued to have faculty who supported a moderate critical position. In this conservative atmosphere, Union continued to be the subject of attack, often in the form of questions about the fitness of its graduates for ordination.

Yet, although the conservatives apparently won a major victory, they were also changed by the season of controversy initiated by the Briggs trial. Beneath the surface, conservative Presbyterians were becoming identified not with the advocacy of biblical truth, but with opposition to the newer critical methods. In that process the theological commonplaces of the Portland Deliverance in its various incarnations underwent transformation. In the 1890s those statements were the "essential" doctrines of Christianity, sustained by a broad consensus of American Presbyterians and, beyond that denomination, by most American Protestants. By 1920 the same affirmations were one version of the "five fundamentals," the banner of a militant army all too ready to rend the churches with controversy.

V. Heresy Trial, Methodist-Style

Conservatives did not always win the victory. By and large the Methodist Church in the North embraced the new studies in their theological schools. The reason for this openness to the new scholarship was due, at least in part, to the aftermath of the "trial" of Hinckley Mitchell of Boston University, who was removed from his position by the church's bishops.

From the time of his appointment at Boston University, Mitchell was a controversial teacher. Although Mitchell attended the University of Leipzig from 1876 to 1878, just as Wellhausen's theories were becoming well known, he does not seem to have adopted them then. While in Germany he elected to study under the conservative, Delitzsch, and to concentrate on Hebrew. His motives were, in part, career oriented. The Methodist Church needed Hebraists, who were hard to find, and Mitchell wanted to teach. It was this passion for teaching, in fact, that led him to ever more radical positions. Like many other teachers, he apparently came to accept those views in part as the result of his own research and in part because they enabled him to explain things more clearly to his classes.

Complaints about Mitchell's classes emerged early in his career. Mitchell was a skilled wordsmith and logician whose careful questioning often led students to see the implications of their positions. Many students found this painful but exciting. They would match wits with Mitchell, retreat to their rooms, revise their position, and come back for more. Others found it personally threatening. In part, this was because they were unwilling or unable to join in the spirit of the academic debate, but perhaps equally important, they may have felt that Mitchell used his superior learning and position to humiliate them. Yet, many of the students who most vocally complained about his theological teachings said Mitchell was unfailingly polite in class and always treated them personally with respect. This agrees with Mitchell's own understanding of his classroom work. He believed he was intellectually and theologically aggressive, while remaining deeply concerned with his students as individuals and as Christians.

What may have happened was that Mitchell's pedagogy was too effective. Whereas students might have ignored materials that were dictated to them, Mitchell's methods made them face the implications of both his and their position. Hence, the student reports that said they were honestly troubled by Mitchell's conclusions may have been an honest appraisal of their experience. This is not to say, of course, that the students completely understood Mitchell or that Mitchell always nuanced his position. Since Mitchell's most offending statements were not made in lecture classes, where he might have been forced to pay more attention to details than in a discussion session, Mitchell may well have argued points far in advance of what he might have maintained in a more structured genre. The students may also have heard his remarks as more radical than they were.

In 1895 a group of thirty-eight students presented a petition to the trustees of Boston University requesting that the school not renew Mitchell's contract. The board investigated the charges and found that Mitchell had been unwise in his methods of presenting materials in class. After the president, William Warren, secured a promise from Mitchell that he would be more circumspect, the board renewed the contract. The same ritual was repeated in 1900 with the student complaints becoming more specific. They charged that Mitchell had argued that the prophets never mentioned Jesus Christ, that Mitchell doubted the historicity of Noah and Isaac, and that he taught Wellhausen's views of the Pentateuch. Although Mitchell probably would not have disagreed with these statements, he equally probably would not have stated them as baldly as the students remembered. One of the essential parts of Mitchell's self-understanding as a scholar was that all conclusions were tentative. As he told the board: "The methods that I employ are the best and most successful that I have been able to invent; but I am not wedded to them; and I shall change them as soon as I can get as good or better results without offending anybody. . . . I am willing to make any concession that will not abridge my right as a scholar to think as I must."[36] President Warren defended Mitchell again, and the board renewed his contract for another five years.[37]

In 1901, however, Mitchell published his controversial *The World Before Abraham.* Although scholarly, the book clearly set forth Mitchell's belief that the early chapters of Genesis were not historical accounts but legendary materials that the ancient Israelites had used to interpret their relationship with God. Mitchell's conclusions were not unusual among biblical critics at the time. But they were not as widely known by the general public. When Mitchell's renewal came up again in 1905, the Methodist bishops, who had been given a veto over appointments to Methodist theological faculties in 1901, decided to exercise their prerogative. Despite another board investigation, the bishops refused to reopen their discussion of the appointment. Mitchell's contract was not renewed.

Mitchell, like Toy earlier, was not formally charged with anything. He believed he had a right to be charged with his specific violations of Methodist teaching and to be tried by the procedures outlined in the book of discipline. He demanded a trial, a demand that was also raised by Francis McConnell, but the Methodist hierarchy had no taste for an event that could involve the whole church in a battle that would be widely reported in the press. The conclusion they had reached — "that some of his statements . . . seem to be unwarranted and objectionable" — was allowed to stand. It was a flagrant violation of due process and of Methodism's internal system of checks and balances.

36. Mitchell, *For the Benefit,* p. 243.

37. Mitchell was deeply offended by the student remarks and cited the documents in his autobiography, *For the Benefit of My Creditors.* I have used Mitchell's account in researching this section. See also Robert Chiles, *Theological Transition in Methodism* (New York: Abingdon, 1965), and Frederick Mills, "Hinckley Gilbert Mitchell," in *Dictionary of Heresy Trials in American Christianity.*

In any event, Mitchell was the last biblical scholar fired by a Methodist school for using higher criticism. Mitchell's views were not unusual among Methodist scholars at the time. Milton Terry of Garrett Biblical Institute, for instance, while not an innovative scholar, supported most of the Kuenen-Wellhausen position in class and in print, and the same perspectives were common at Drew. Mitchell's dismissal may have come at an unfortunate conjunction of events. Mitchell, after all, retained the confidence of both his colleagues and the Boston University board. Appointments at Boston, unlike most Methodist schools, were subject to five-year renewals. This enabled the bishops to step into the process at the height of a controversy and settle it to their satisfaction. The dismissal also reflected the internal development of Methodism. Like most American denominations, Methodism was becoming more organized, especially on the national level, and this meant that the bishops' power in the structure was increasing. Their entry into the world of scholarship may have been nothing more than a step too far. In 1908 the conference stripped the bishops of the right to review the theological positions of faculty members, and in 1928 they lost the right to approve or disapprove initial appointments.

The bishops looked vaguely ridiculous to many contemporaries, and they may have come to look so to themselves. After all, Boston University was not a theological seminary, and the school, under Warren's leadership, had grown in both size and reputation. The school's faculty was thoroughly professionalized, and it judged academic competence by academic standards. Further, the broader public expected the school to operate according to professional scholarly criteria. If these considerations were not enough to save Mitchell's position, they were enough to deter the bishops from similar actions in the future. Given Methodism's history as a popular evangelical denomination, it is perhaps fitting that Methodist institutions were able to lead in the study of the Bible in the twentieth century.[38]

Where the new biblical criticism won its triumphs was, over the long haul, as significant as the victories themselves. During much of the nineteenth century the seminary was at the apex of American theological education. Although many of those who taught in the latter half of the century went to Germany or Scotland for further training, the seminary degree itself was sufficient to certify a person as a college or seminary instructor. However, by 1880 American theo-

38. The situation was not as open in the South, where Andrew Warren Sledd, Wyatt Aiken Smart, William Arthur Shelton, John A. Rice, and James H. Stevenson were all under a cloud for their advocacy of the new biblical studies. The union of Northern and Southern Methodism meant that the more liberal attitudes of the Northern church on scriptural interpretation would tend to become normative among Southern Methodists as well.

logical education was adding another tier. Increasingly, those who wanted to teach or to engage in advanced scholarship, especially in the so-called classical disciplines, were expected to spend time in a university in addition to the seminary and, preferably, to earn an advanced degree. The new biblical studies triumphed in many of the schools that would dominate this new level of theological study, especially Yale, Harvard, Union, and the University of Chicago. When these schools were added to the English and European universities, where the new biblical criticism was also victorious, it was hard for a person with scholarly aspirations to escape the newer interpretations. In effect, the new biblical criticism was increasingly part of the expected background of a serious scholar and teacher. The new biblical studies were the new scholarly orthodoxy: the starting point even for those who wanted to dissent.

The new biblical studies also triumphed in many seminaries with substantial endowments, including Rochester, Andover, Chicago Theological Seminary, Pacific School of Religion, Newton, Boston University School of Theology, Vanderbilt, and the University of Southern California School of Theology. While the biblical departments of these schools contributed to their institutions' reputation as leading and even elite schools, the equation balanced both ways. The prestige and wealth of these schools contributed substantially to the reputation of the new biblical studies. Even more than endowment, biblical criticism became one of the marks of an elite or want-to-be-elite institution. By 1920 only Princeton, Southern Baptist Theological Seminary, and the smaller Presbyterian seminaries among the richer American schools continued to resist the newer directions in biblical studies. These two conservative schools, incidentally, were the only ones involved in the early Conference of Theological Seminaries that eventually became the American Association of Theological Schools.[39] This organization was to determine which schools would be accredited and which would not.

39. The social location of those who hold certain ideas does not necessarily influence the claim of any particular idea or set of ideas to be true, but that social location may help explain why certain ideas come to seem almost self-evident to those who hold them. A set of ideas taught in the leading graduate schools and held by respected teachers in the best-endowed and most respected seminaries has a presumption of truth it would not have without these social supports. Later American biblical conservatives would mourn the loss of these prestigious institutions and seek to establish new schools with high scholarly standards and substantial resources to make their own position more credible.

CHAPTER SIX

The Changing World of Schools: A New Ecology

In the late nineteenth century Americans adopted changes in their approach to education that reorganized how culture was transmitted.[1] These changes involved every level of schooling from elementary schools to postcollegiate education. While this reorganization did not produce a fully rational national system of schools, the changes provided American education with an internal logic that enabled people to relate different components of the system to each other. Many different factors fueled these changes, but the most important was the widespread acceptance of the belief that education was the key both to personal economic success and to social betterment. Education was a mirror of the progressive hope for national reformation. Apologists for education claimed that schools produced gradual social change and inculcated a genuine democratic character in their students. In short, schools were the place where science, expertise, organization, and optimism combined to make a difference in human life.

Seminaries, of course, benefited from the growth and expansion of American schooling. Whatever opposition had existed to formal education for ministers gradually weakened and disappeared in the period, and many prospective clergy sought to get all the schooling they could afford. Of equal importance, theological schools found themselves without a clear place in the

1. Education was, of course, much more than schooling, the focus of this volume. Most Americans participated in varying educational configurations that included churches, work, service in the army, and such obvious educators as the mass media that rapidly expanded after 1870 as newer styles of magazines and newspapers came to be mass-produced and mass-mailed to Americans. See Lawrence A. Cremin, *Traditions of American Education* (New York: Basic Books, 1976), "The Metropolitan Experience: 1876-1976," pp. 89-164. I have relied heavily on Cremin in this analysis.

emerging educational order. Few found it self-evident where the schools, their curricula, or their faculties fit into the larger picture. Much of the history of the thought about seminaries from 1900 to the present has revolved around the questions of what theological education is and how it ought to relate to the larger educational scene. In other words, the late nineteenth-century educational revolution raised issues around academic standards and standing that have remained with theological schools ever since. Another way to put this is: the schools were marginal to the larger national efforts in education and had to find ways to relate their location on the margins to the center.[2]

I. The Old Order of Schools

The seminary fit comfortably into the antebellum educational world. While we must be careful not to read the idea of a system into this period, education had a rough order that can be discerned through the chaos. While science was attaining a foothold, particularly in the new state universities, the old-time college stood firmly in an intellectual tradition that reached back to the Renaissance and, beyond that, to late antiquity. Basically, the schools existed to transmit a literary culture, based on the ability to read Latin and Greek easily. This was supplemented by some instruction in science and mathematics. Significantly, both Harvard and Yale found it advisable early on to establish "scientific schools" that paralleled their liberal arts work and, for a season, kept the sciences in their place. In this world the academy existed to prepare young men for college, and many young men elected to stay longer in their academies knowing that they could acquire the equivalent of the first or second collegiate year there. In theory, the academies were more places for drill in the basics of the languages while the colleges were designed for those who had already acquired basic linguistic skills. Many colleges, especially in the South and West, developed their own preparatory departments. Although some of the more prominent physicians and lawyers attended colleges, most did not. Most physicians learned their occupation working with an established practitioner who would then sign that person's medical "license." In a similar way, lawyers most often read the law while serving as a clerk in an office. When ready to practice

2. Bruce Kuklick, *A History of Philosophy in America, 1720-2000* (Oxford: Clarendon, 2001), chap. 6, pp. 95-110, sees the defeat of the theologians in American higher education as almost total. The new world of the university was a place where philosophy and natural science took the cultural place that theology had traditionally occupied. Kuklick's argument interestingly enough also notes that the cultural position of the person of letters, the master of the lyceum, also shifted at this time. In other words, Emerson was as dated as his divinity school critics.

before a court, they were "admitted to the bar" by symbolically moving within the barrier that separated those with business before the court from the general public.

In this educational world the seminary represented the highest rung on the ladder. While economics (and the comparatively small number of college graduates) often led seminaries to experiment with English programs, their stock-in-trade was a thorough study of the Christian faith, based on the Greek and Hebrew text of the Bible. In theory, the student's mastery of Latin and Greek letters in college prepared the student for the arduous tasks of reading the Bible in the original and of studying church history and theology from sources that were, in part, in Latin. In the process of acquiring this basic training, a student might receive some instruction in preaching or liturgics, but these were secondary parts of the curriculum. The person who finished the course (and most did not) was among the most educated people in many American towns or villages, and even in the cities had some claim to intellectual preeminence.

Many Americans were dissatisfied with this educational system. Such people as Francis Wayland of the College of Rhode Island believed that the schools needed to stress the sciences more, and democratic leaders wondered whether the system did more than train men in aristocratic manners and arts. Women were largely excluded from the world of the academy and college before the 1850s, and the institutions were in fact based on certain masculine values. The "feminization of culture" in the 1850s was to offer an alternative understanding of the arts that could be used to support women's academies and colleges.[3] The one place where the system apparently had cash value was in the development of linguistic skills. Even among the Methodists, college-trained people took the lead in such areas as publications. Further, almost all denominations needed some ministers who were educated sufficiently in the manners and mores of the upper class to serve their more prosperous pulpits. Colleges also provided churches with a measure of social prestige.

II. Education at the Base

Perhaps the most important aspect of the transformation of education was its changing relationship to the society. In the early nineteenth century, education was often seen as essentially elitist. The pioneer and the yeoman farmer did not

3. See Alan Trachtenberg, *The Incorporation of America: Culture and Society in the Gilded Age* (New York: Hill and Wang, 1982), pp. 145-47.

need "book learning" to get ahead. But in the half-century between the Civil War and the First World War, education came to be seen as essential to economic success. A person needed basic skills — social, intellectual, and physical — to participate in the good life promised by the industrial cornucopia. This mania for education affected all classes. The Lynds noted the way education had become engrafted into American life: "If education is oftentimes taken for granted by the business community, it is no exaggeration to say that it evokes the fervor of a religion, a means of salvation, among a large section of the working class."[4] American Catholics shared this mania for schooling, and for many of the same social reasons. Like other Americans, they believed that education marked the way forward in American economic life, and they did not want to fall behind. The Catholic sisters, like their public school counterparts, were passionate advocates of social advancement, good manners and morals, and personal discipline.

The educational revival had its first and most dramatic effects on the base of the educational ladder. Beginning in the Northern cities, post–Civil War America rapidly adopted the eight-grade elementary program as a standard. The goals of this program were to develop basic literacy, including the ability to write grammatically correct English, to do basic arithmetic, and, above all, to practice good morals and American values. To secure these goals, education was organized into a hierarchy with superintendents, principals, and teachers; curriculum was organized throughout the system and carefully graded by age group and attainments; and order and efficiency were stressed. Attendance was carefully taken and punctuality was prized. The administration of city or county schools early became a profession in its own right with the good administrator mindful of statistics and costs. State and federal bureaus of education were formed, and both compiled volumes of statistical and other information useful to those who had to make educational decisions. Education was also directed toward the social habits that were needed in the industrial age. The schools became one of the first American institutions to "go by the clock."

Although the administrators and many leading educators were male, the classroom teachers in American elementary education were overwhelmingly female. Many were recruited from earlier classes or from the new high schools that were becoming increasingly popular. But the new style of education was bureaucratic and professional. Many prospective teachers, consequently, went to normal schools where they were not only drilled in academic subjects but also taught such practical matters as the theory and practice of teaching. The

4. Robert S. Lynd and Helen Merrell Lynd, *Middletown: A Study in Modern American Culture* (1929; reprint, New York: Harcourt Brace, 1957), p. 187.

normal school was thus something new in American education: it offered education on an advanced or collegiate level and, at the same time, offered very practical work that related directly to the job at hand. If for no other reason than the availability of teaching positions, education courses early entered into women's colleges, coeducational schools, and the new land-grant institutions. Education often lagged behind in the more conservative eastern universities that continued to admit only men or admitted women only to coordinate colleges. Teachers College, one of the most prestigious eastern schools of education, has never been fully incorporated into Columbia University.

The gender pattern in elementary education reflected a larger pattern among the American professions. Just as new occupations were opened for women, these occupations came to reside on one side of a gender barrier that was common to American professions.[5] In general, positions of leadership and responsibility were confined to males while women occupied lower positions. Thus, business came to have managers and secretaries, medicine to have doctors and nurses, social work to have managers of charities and social workers. In religion, while the lower ranks were never as gender-specific as in other occupations, a similar separation existed between ordained pastors and unordained "Christian workers," many of whom, especially abroad, were women.

Urban America was deeply worried about the behavior of its teenage children. While working-class young people often went to work as children or immediately following elementary school, middle-class children faced a period in which they were not ready to take up their adult tasks but were no longer schoolchildren. The high school provided a solution. High schools continued the early work of the academies by preparing young people for college, usually by teaching Latin, but they quickly expanded into other areas. There was a tendency for subjects to migrate down from the colleges. Thus basic mathematics, including algebra and trigonometry, came to be taught in the better high schools. Introductions to the various sciences also migrated and became available early on. The most striking success of the high school, however, was its commercial programs. High school programs provided young women, who were entering the workplace in large numbers as clerks, secretaries, and salespeople, with the basic training they needed to be employed. Likewise, men found the commercial programs to be their gateway into the work of bookkeeping, sales, and other newly important positions in large companies.

5. The gender bar in the church was also reinforced by theological and exegetical considerations, but it is important to note that the restriction of the upper level of ministry to men had social and cultural analogies in other professions that could not appeal to Scripture for the justification of their practices. Significantly, that line ran at roughly the same place in all professional hierarchies.

Partly because of costs, the public high schools gradually replaced the academies as the place of preparation for college. Many middle-class parents appear to have reasoned that they could save substantially by having their children live at home and attend tuition-free schools, thus freeing their savings to finance college education. Private preparatory schools, consequently, became the preserve of the very wealthy or those whose children needed either additional work or, often, more structured discipline than was available at home. Equally important, high schools contributed to a growing interest in education beyond high school. In Middletown the Lynds noted that almost a third of those who completed high school went on to do some college work. The statistics told the tale: "Between 1890 and 1924, while the population of the state (Indiana) increased only 25%, the number of students enrolled in the state university increased nearly 700%, and the number of those graduating nearly 800 per cent. During the same period the number of students enrolled in the state engineering and agricultural college increased 600 per cent, and the number of those graduating over 1000 per cent."[6] In a similar way, Lawrence Cremin noted that the total enrollment in American colleges of those between eighteen and twenty-four rose from 1.8 percent in 1890 to 31 percent in 1990.[7]

The success of the high school also pressured the colleges to make changes in their admission and other standards. Dartmouth, for instance, early introduced a more selective admission policy so that it could choose qualified students from a national pool, and Harvard and other schools experimented with standardized testing. But most colleges were not selective. And when, for example, the pool of candidates with Latin declined, the college standards changed to place less emphasis on that language, either allowing some candidates to begin Latin in college or to substitute a modern language for the classics. Other areas of the collegiate curriculum became dependent on the high schools as well.

The high schools, thus, carved out a position for themselves at the heart of industrial America. Their graduates held the more bureaucratic or routine positions needed to organize and manage the newer businesses. Every large store, whether a Wanamaker's in Philadelphia or a more modest shop in a smaller town, needed a number of clerks to make the sales and a number of skilled bookkeepers to measure the profit and loss. Although there were some professional engineering schools, many American engineers were trained on the job, and these men found the mathematical training offered by the high schools foundational for their profession. In the eighteenth century the ability

6. Lynd and Lynd, *Middletown,* p. 185.

7. Cremin, *Traditions of American Education,* p. 101.

to do surveying was a mark of an educated gentleman; by the beginning of the twentieth century, it was routinely done by a high school graduate.

The high school rapidly became a norm for America's middle and lower middle classes, and the diploma became a standard qualification for many semiprofessional occupations. In 1890 there were 202,963 students in high schools; in 1920 there were 1,851,965. The ratio of graduates to total population became significantly smaller. The Lynds noted that most of the children in Middletown, a classic American community, "now extended their education past the elementary school into grades nine to twelve. In 1882, five graduated from high school, one for each 1,000 persons in the community; in 1890 fourteen graduated from high school, one for each 1,110 persons in the community; in 1899 thirty-four graduated, one for each 810 persons; in 1899 thirty-four graduated . . . making one for each 588 persons; in 1920 114 graduated, or one for each 320 persons; and in 1924, 236 graduated, or one for each 161."[8] For America's popular denominations — the Baptists, Methodists, and Disciples — the high school replaced elementary education as the basic credential for ministry and, perhaps equally important, increased the pool of candidates available for denominational colleges.

High school also raised the level of lay education in many churches. A minister who addressed a congregation where many, if not all, were high school graduates had to have more education to be socially and intellectually respected. The minister needed to be one step above the congregation educationally to secure the respect that had traditionally been given to the clerical office. Thus, a minister addressing a congregation of high school graduates needed a college degree; a congregation with a substantial number of college graduates demanded a seminary-trained leader; and the most prestigious congregations were rarely satisfied with less than a doctor of divinity or, as time passed, an earned doctorate.

Moreover, high school graduates formed much of the market for popular magazines. This meant that many congregations had one or more members who had heard of Darwin, knew something about the increasing interest in the humanity of Jesus, or were aware of the various heresy trials. The link between high school and popular culture forced ministers to adjust to a dynamic and much better informed popular opinion. At a minimum, preachers needed to be more up-to-date and in touch with common concerns.

The high school was only one institution among many that served those anxious to get ahead in the new industrial America. Most cities, particularly in the North, had a number of schools that provided a level of training somewhere

8. Lynd and Lynd, *Middletown,* p. 183.

between elementary education, now almost universal among white Northerners, and the college or land-grant school. These included business colleges, vocational schools, night schools, citizenship and English classes for immigrants, and courses for homemakers. Such schools served both those who had no high school and those who had completed high school, and their level tended to vary with the students they were able to enlist. The better such schools, especially in areas that were moving toward becoming professions, such as dentistry, later became parts of universities.

Just as high school or other postelementary education was emerging as a standard, America's evangelical churches were entering into a period of expansion and growth that would last through the First World War. While this revival had many components — the urban revivalism of D. L. Moody, the expansion of city and rescue missions, the growth of the Sunday school, the continued growth and development of foreign missionary work — one of its features was an increased role for semiprofessional religious leaders. There was a wide variety of such positions, even in the more highly educated churches, and they included various city workers, charity administrators, church secretaries, Sunday school leaders, choirmasters, music directors, YMCA workers, and various staff positions abroad. Many of these positions were open to women. On the foreign field, for instance, women workers came to greatly outnumber male missionaries as the missions increasingly emphasized social services and education.

Such missionary enthusiasts as A. J. Gordon, Moody, and A. B. Simpson set out to found such schools that could train such "gap men" for the new work. At the same time, energetic women such as Lucy Meyers established what they called Trained Schools to prepare women for their missionary labors. Simpson offered this definition: "institutions less technical and elaborate than the ordinary theological seminary, and designed to offer some specific preparation for direct missionary work, and to meet the wants of that large class, both men and women, who do not wish formal ministerial preparation, but an immediate equipage as lay workers."[9] Baptists were particularly active in this type of education, establishing women's training schools in Boston, Chicago, Philadelphia, Louisville, and Fort Worth. These schools emphasized the development of usable skills as well as a firm grasp of the English Bible.[10]

While the Bible and training schools insisted they were not substitutes for the colleges and seminaries, some of them came to train pastors for a variety of

9. Quoted in Virginia Lieson Brereton, *Training God's Army: The American Bible School, 1880-1940* (Bloomington and Indianapolis: Indiana University Press, 1990), p. 55.

10. See Brereton, *Training God's Army,* especially chap. 5, for details on the place of these schools in the American ecology. Also see below, chap. 10.

churches. There were many reasons for this. Many students, looking at the seven-year course, found that they needed something quicker, if only for financial reasons. Older students especially found this feature of the schools compelling. Others simply were not convinced that either college or seminary would materially improve their performance in the ministry. Rather than spend years drilling in the languages and learning painfully to read them, they felt they could learn as much or more with a style of education that stressed a thorough practical knowledge of the biblical text and some hands-on experience in religious work. And some, an increasing number as time passed, found that these schools tended to reflect their own theology more than the more abstract and, increasingly, liberal theological seminaries. These schools were part of the general education revolution and the general rise in standards. In most cases the new schools competed not so much with the seminary as with the idea that "no special training" was needed for the ministry. Fewer congregations and ministers wanted the young man who went immediately from plow to desk without some stopover in the groves of academe.

III. A New College Model

The most important changes were in the colleges. When the Civil War ended, most American colleges looked much as they had in 1800. Classical literature remained the core of the program, sciences remained on the fringes of the program, and professional training was largely ignored. Many of their students were destined for the ministry of one of the more educated denominations. Up until the Civil War these churches provided the largest and most significant market for learned men. Afterward, however, the market for educated people expanded. Although such self-made men as John D. Rockefeller and Andrew Carnegie founded many of America's largest businesses, the organizations they established to administer those businesses were hungry for expertise. Some of this hunger was technological. Rockefeller hired experts to help him sweeten the smell of oil from his Ohio fields, and Edison, although an amateur scientist, hired technically educated men to carry his inventions further. But even more than this, the new organizations required people with intellectual skills who could read, write, and solve problems. Often these new managers also had to meet the public and serve as spokespeople for their enterprises. At the same time, the need for bureaucrats grew at all levels of government.[11] The expan-

11. Frederick Rudolph, *Curriculum: A History of the American Undergraduate Course of Study* (San Francisco: Jossey-Bass, 1977).

sion of publishing, in the form of both newspapers and magazines, also provided a significant market for those with advanced intellectual skills. The colleges adapted their programs to these social and economic changes. As Bledsoe put it, the schools became part of the American "culture of professionalism."[12]

Since the establishment of the University of Virginia, the states had been establishing state colleges. In almost all cases the legislature mandated that the schools provide a program that included useful studies in addition to the classical programs. Thus, the University of Wisconsin (Madison) had to include departments of education, law, science, and medicine as well as liberal arts subjects.[13] Such public-spirited education caught the fancy of the nation's small-town and urban business elites who also supported tax-supported elementary and high schools. The Civil War provided this class with an opportunity to get federal support for their program. When Southern Democrats — who had generally opposed federal programs of all sorts — withdrew from Congress, the new Republican Party had a majority in both houses that permitted it to enact many of its constituents' hopes into law. Among these was a proposal for an expansion of public education that had been before the House of Representatives since 1857. Called the Morrill Act, after its sponsor, Congressman Justin Morrill of Vermont, the 1862 law provided for "The endowment, support, and maintenance of at least one college where the leading object shall be, without excluding other scientific and classical studies, and including military tactics, to teach such branches of learning as are related to agriculture and mechanic arts . . . in order to promote the liberal and practical education of the industrial classes in the several pursuits and professions in life." Almost by definition, such schools were founded on a different basis than the older colleges. The goal of the land-grant schools was to provide education that served a clear social and economic purpose. While hardly dealing a deathblow to the college devoted to classical studies, the land-grant schools, like the state universities, indicated that much of the market was interested in a different educational style.

Economics were not the only factor making for changes in collegiate studies. Although some schools may have had some intellectual excitement,

12. Burton Bledsoe, *The Culture of Professionalism* (New York: Norton, 1976). Bledsoe's use of culture is almost anthropological. For him the culture of professionalism was a set of assumptions about the social and economic order that was largely invisible and that nonetheless functioned as a maze through the routines of ordinary life. "The culture of professionalism has been so basic to middle class habits of thought and action that a majority of twentieth century Americans have taken for granted that all intelligent modern persons organize their behavior, both public and private, according to it" (p. 1).

13. By the progressive period, this concept would ripen into the idea that the state university should be the nursery of an active civil service.

most of them appear to have been as dull as their formal curricula implied. Languages were most often taught by drill, and the recitation method whereby a student would study a textbook and recite it to the teacher in class was followed in too many classes. Discussion appears to have been rare, and Augustus Strong noted: "Never was it suggested to us that a subject might have light thrown upon it by side reading; never were we referred to books for illustration; never was the history of a science spoken of."[14] Strong, president of Rochester Seminary and a strong advocate of educational change, may have exaggerated the sterility of the antebellum college, but he was a graduate of Yale, one of the better schools, and had experienced the system at its best. The growing insistence on a more relevant education outside the colleges corresponded to an equally strong demand within higher education that the colleges be brought into line with modern intellectual life. Similar forces were at work in English education, likewise based on the classical college that would lead to similar changes. Science and modern history, for instance, would migrate from such upstart schools as the University of London to Oxford and Cambridge, and examinations would be established to gauge, however imperfectly, a student's academic progress.

Over the next fifty years American higher education tended to follow aspects of the land-grant and state university model. While each school transformed itself differently, schools generally passed through an orderly succession of steps. At first they expanded their offerings in science, history, and other areas. This tended to crowd the curriculum so that at a certain point schools adopted a system that made all or some of their studies elective. In turn, this provoked the growth of yet more new areas of study and the division of the college into either schools or departments. The modern college catalogue with its long list of the options offered by the institution dates from about this time. As the school shifted to a system based on courses, the percentage of work required in the learned languages declined, and by 1900 most colleges had reduced their Latin requirement to two years and some had replaced it entirely with a modern language requirement. At about this time Greek disappeared from the list of required courses in many schools.

The decline of classical studies was a crisis for seminary curricula. The traditional seminary program was an extension of the collegiate study of classical literature and was, in effect, advanced study of the Bible in Greek and Hebrew as well as some theology and church history. Undergraduate study more or less merged into seminary study with seminary instructors urging colleges to

14. Quoted in Garth M. Rosell, "Finney's Contribution to Higher Education," *Fides et Historia* 25, no. 2 (Summer 1993): 59.

add introductory Hebrew to their programs; most colleges, however, knowing this would not suit those of their students not headed for the ministry, resisted passively and actively. But whatever the status of Hebrew studies, most students arrived at the seminary well drilled in language skills, often able to read Greek with little difficulty, and primed to learn Hebrew. By 1900 that type of student was a rare bird. Fewer colleges were requiring Greek, even for a bachelor of arts degree, and even Latin was in decline. Equally important, significant numbers of students lacked the grammatical skills that had aided the learning of Hebrew (or increasingly elementary Greek). Further, if a seminary continued to require Greek for admission, that seminary could not recruit from among all college graduates — a small enough number of potential students to begin with — but its admission pool was restricted to those who had elected a certain program almost from the beginning of their undergraduate program. Despite the prosperity of Protestant churches from 1865 to 1920, they had difficulty attracting first-rate candidates into their service. If the ministry had been financially and economically rewarding, it could have insisted on its own lists of prerequisites. Contemporary German theologians, for instance, were able to retain the classical prerequisites for their faculties at a time when other faculties had moved to more open admissions requirements. But if the ministry ever had such power in America, it was in the distant past.

In place of the older fixed curriculum, the new model college introduced a system of majors and minors. This added another complication to the overall picture of American theological education. Many colleges added departments of religion or Bible to their programs. While these programs were clearly undergraduate, they often followed the program of the seminaries, offering serious work in Bible, theology, philosophy, and occasionally the pastoral arts. Particularly in the South, many college departments of religion became larger than many seminaries. Richmond, Mercer, Furman, and Wake Forest were the principal educators of the Baptist ministry in their states, despite the success of Southern Seminary, and Colby had a similar position in Maine.

Unlike the biblical schools, the new departments of religion were a genuine alternative to the seminary. There were two reasons for this: The first and perhaps more important was that a student could get many of the educational and social advantages of college and seminary from the college alone. Part of the problem was that while the first two years of college might be considered preparatory work, it was hard to make this case for the whole four-year program.[15] Why should a person become a historian or a psychologist before be-

15. Thus Ernest Cadman Colwell, "Toward Better Theological Education," *Journal of Religion* 20, no. 2 (Apr. 1940): 109-23. The first step to be taken in turning away from the "graduate"

coming a minister? What was the theological and religious payoff of the popular English major? Economics reinforced such considerations. Many candidates, facing the cost of a full seven years, may well have reasoned that they received almost the same training with a sound general educational program followed by two or three years in a strong religion major. Secondly, seminary was still an option for students who later changed their minds, and the undergraduate major might provide an edge in finding a student pastorate or other religious work to help support advanced studies. In any event, the college major in Bible or religion did not close out any options while it opened others.

One seminary response to the expansion of the collegiate program was the Th.B. (bachelor of theology) degree, popular until the 1960s. Almost inevitably the Th.B. required two years of liberal arts, usually taken in the seminary, followed by three years of theological study. In their heyday, Th.B. programs had the further advantage of closely paralleling the "best practices" of medical and law schools that customarily admitted students after their second or third year of undergraduate education. The more progressive colleges allowed the first year of professional training to complete the undergraduate course, further contributing to the prestige of this approach. Tiny Bangor Seminary in Maine, as early as the 1890s, experimented with a version of this approach that allowed students to do two years of undergraduate work that they could apply to a college degree after completing their theological studies. The close relationship between the seminary and the host of small New England colleges initially made this possible.

In the midst of this confusion, the only thing that seemed certain was that, no matter how often they violated their own ideal, usually by admitting nongraduates, most seminary educators saw their schools as postcollegiate institutions. This meant that they presupposed the college without necessarily building on any of the specific studies (aside from classical languages) that students undertook there. The more the college modernized, the more distant it became from the seminary. Did this mean that the seminary was primarily a vocational school, only tangentially related to the intellectual streams of America's higher culture? If so, what did that say about the power of religion, particularly Protestantism, to shape or even influence cultural development?

---

conception of the curriculum to a truly professional pattern is to begin the seminary program at the end of the junior college course. The graduates of a first-rate junior college have as good a general education as their fathers had received from the older four-year college. In the organization of higher education in America today, the third year of the college course is the natural point for the beginning of specialized programs — either for the various professions or for graduate study. If the program of the seminary began at this point, all the values of the present curriculum could be conserved in a four-year course of study (p. 119).

IV. The Rise of the Universities

The most important "new" element in American education after the Civil War was the rise of the university. The word "new" must be heavily qualified. Many of the institutions chartered before the Civil War proudly bore the name university, even though they were in fact small liberal arts colleges. But some schools took genuine steps toward real university status. The University of Virginia, for instance, began with an elective system that stressed the sciences and allowed (even encouraged) students to bypass classical studies. New York University, established in 1831, was established to promote professional and scientific studies and was self-consciously modeled on the University of London, the first of the "redbrick" schools established as rivals to Oxford and Cambridge. While the ethos of the school was Protestant, New York University was self-consciously nonsectarian and practical. Francis Wayland of the College of Rhode Island hoped his school might develop in a similar direction.

One of the most intellectually successful of the early universities was Henry Tappan's University of Michigan. Tappan was an admirer of the Prussian university system with its emphasis on a professional faculty and large and substantial libraries. Like his German counterparts, Tappan saw the state as the ultimate guarantor of religious and academic freedom, and he believed his university's link to the state of Michigan might protect it from what seemed to him and others the militant sectarianism of much American religion. This hope was unfortunately ill placed. In the rough world of antebellum Michigan politics, Tappan's program seemed elitist and foreign to the state's social and religious character. Tappan was dismissed in 1863 by his board and retired to Europe.

But politics was not the primary problem for those who wanted true American universities — money was. Federal and state governments had comparatively small budgets, and there were few large fortunes to be tapped for educational purposes. Consequently, there was little surplus capital available for such niceties as buildings, endowments, and faculty salaries. Many schools appear to have lived almost from day to day, with only the larger and more prosperous able to afford courses in chemistry or the law. And the older program had been inexpensive. Almost any college-trained clergyman could teach the classics. Similarly, most ministers could teach the elementary mathematics required for the degree. For all their talk about such values as "mental discipline," most schools appear to have been marking their time, awaiting the development of future funding. Once that funding became available after the Civil War, those that could attract funds changed with breathtaking rapidity.

The Civil War and the subsequent development of American industry generated the needed funds. In 1863 Cornell was founded, followed rapidly by

Vanderbilt in 1873, Johns Hopkins and Stanford in 1876, Clark in 1889, and the University of Chicago in 1892.[16] These were new schools that did not have a body of precedents that limited their present course of action. Freedom permitted experimentation at a time when many educators were searching for new approaches.

In some cases the wealthy founders of schools set the agenda for the institutions they financed. In effect, they used their money to make changes they considered desirable. Thus Cornell, following the somewhat sharp dictates of Ezra Cornell, a former Quaker and Unitarian, stressed the breadth and utility of its program. The school was to be comprehensive and the newer studies, such as the sciences, were to be equal to more traditional disciplines.[17] Clark was devoted to the development of the sciences because Jonas Clark, its patron, was impressed by the relationship between German educational methods and the growth of knowledge. He sought Hall to be president because, he believed, Hall shared his values. Likewise, the railroad magnate Leland Stanford had strong interests in technical education and tried to shape his new university around technical advance.[18]

Other founders allowed their leaders to follow their own course. Johns Hopkins was the principal stockholder in the Baltimore and Ohio Railway and an investor in Baltimore's banks. Like Ezra Cornell, he had a passionate dislike of sectarianism and bore a calm confidence in the capacity of human reason to solve the world's problems. His will directed the trustees to follow a nonsectarian approach to education and to place the trust above all religious controversies.[19] But

16. My own reading tends to stress the role of the newer institutions and their comparative freedom from precedent. Many of these new presidents were extraordinary men whose writings were as influential as the institutions they helped establish. But the process may have been less driven by personalities. Cremin writes: "At the same time that undergraduate education became popularized, graduate and professional education proliferated to embrace more occupations and coalesced to form the comprehensive American universities of the twentieth century. Medicine, law, and theology came into their own, along with graduate training in the arts and sciences; but so did education, business, engineering, nursing, librarianship, social work, public administration, police science, and hotel management. And they coalesced, as Laurence R. Veysey has made abundantly clear, into a variety of different sorts of universities. Ranging from Cornell, with its explicit commitment to utilitarianism, to Princeton, with its explicit commitment to liberal culture, to the University of Wisconsin, with its explicit commitment to social service" (*Traditions of American Education,* p. 102).

17. Laurence Veysey, *The Emergence of the American University* (Chicago: University of Chicago Press, 1965), p. 63.

18. Stanford may have succeeded in the long run better than he knew. Stanford was to be the research center that sparked the development of California's Silicon Valley.

19. See "Death of Johns Hopkins," *Sun,* Thursday morning, Dec. 25, 1873; reprinted on the Web pages of Johns Hopkins University, visited July 27, 1997.

aside from a few such mandates in his will, Hopkins, who died three years before the school opened in 1876, had little input in his creation. Daniel Coit Gilman, a Yale graduate and former president of the University of California, was called to be its first president. Gilman believed that the best way to realize the founder's goals was to devote the school primarily to research in the sciences and humanities. Until the 1890s Hopkins was the leading research-oriented school in America. Like the city of Baltimore, Hopkins faced south and had its primary influence on the emerging state universities of that region. Although Rockefeller and Vanderbilt established their respective universities before they died, they also allowed the presidents to set the schools' direction. Both were, however, instrumental in the selection of the first presidents.

At the same time, other schools were able to harness the wealth of local business and religious communities and, thus, join the list of elite institutions. Boston University, for instance, was able to draw on the resources of a rapidly growing metropolitan area as well as New England's socially advancing Methodists, while Northwestern in Evanston (suburban Chicago) developed significant ties to the Chicago business community. Some of the old-time colleges also did well in the race for funds and status. Harvard, always the best endowed of the private colleges, had sufficient wealth to claim university status under Charles Eliot, and both Yale and Princeton quickly followed. All three schools had access to rapidly developing financial and industrial wealth.

What were the marks of the new universities? Perhaps the most important was the development of graduate education. German scholarly production was one inspiration for the new programs. Americans studying in Germany were deeply impressed by the work of their mentors in such areas as philology, science, and history. This research was marked by a thoroughness and completeness that were rarely attained by British and American scholars. When Americans visited Germany, they were impressed by the orderly development of German intellectual life. Foundational lectures that covered a whole field of knowledge were followed by research seminars that provided young scholars with hands-on experience in investigating scholarly issues. The program was, of course, capped by the doctor of philosophy dissertation, an independent, publishable study produced by an apprentice scholar under the guidance of a doctor-father.

Academic scholarship was not the only emphasis in a German university. Like the Scottish universities, the German schools trained people for a variety of professions needed by the state and civil society. In addition to university professors, German universities also trained doctors, ministers, and Protestant clergy. Although the law schools (faculties) had little direct influence on American education,[20] the philosophy, theology, and medical schools (faculties) were to have considerable influence. Well before the American Civil War, German medicine had adopted a scientific paradigm and led the world in the study of the human body. University-related medical schools tended to follow this model and to avoid the sharp debates between the various "sects" of American healers, such as homeopaths.

In a sense, different American schools borrowed parts of the German paradigm and used them for their own purposes. With the exception of Johns Hopkins in its earliest years, American universities retained some version of the bachelor of arts degree or the newer bachelor of science degree as a four-year preparatory program. This program remained the schools' bread-and-butter degree. Not only did it attract the children of the wealthy, who supported the school by tuition and gifts, but its graduates also formed a pool of supporters for the institution. Since the bachelor's degree had an important place in the American economic hierarchy, it also attracted to the school many who were seeking advancement. It was indeed the economic value of the bachelor's degree that sparked its popularity. In turn, those who received it were the primary market for the professional schools maintained by the universities. In the long run, not even as well endowed a school as Hopkins could neglect the potential income and graduate students that a bachelor's program provided.

To the base provided by the bachelor's programs, different schools gradually added different emphases. Yale, which had already added a scientific school, a theological department, and a law school, added a Ph.D. program in 1861. Yale grew from a college to a university almost by indirection, as each addition to its mission paved the way for the next. Harvard moved into university status in much the same way. Unlike Yale, America's oldest college was fortunate in having one of the nation's true "captains of erudition,"[21] Charles Eliot, one of the creators of modern university administration.[22] Lawrence Cremin called Eliot

20. The German historical interpretation of law, however, was to influence American social reformers. Both Richard Ely and Walter Rauschenbusch, although not lawyers, used these studies as a significant part of their plans for social reform.

21. This evocative term goes back to Thorstein Veblen, *The Higher Education in America: A Memorandum on the Conduct of Universities by Business Men* (New York: Huebsch, 1918). There is a sense in which Veblen's term is inaccurate. University administrators were much more like the successful heads of large state and federal bureaucracies or the second-generation managers of large enterprises than they were like entrepreneurs. The basic skills in building a great university required patient teamwork, close attention to budgets and other details, and the capacity to mobilize voluntarily donated resources. In other words, more "experts" than "inventors."

22. Charles Eliot, *University Administration* (Boston and New York: Houghton Mifflin, 1908).

"the foremost member of the generation that built the American University,"[23] and Eliot's career paralleled the growth of the new institution. Significantly, Eliot was not part of the classical fraternity. He began his teaching career as a chemist at Harvard in 1854, and he retained a passion for science throughout his career. As an instructor, Eliot was remembered for replacing recitation with written examinations. In 1865 he became president of the Massachusetts Institute of Technology, one of the nation's earliest and best technical colleges, and in 1869 he assumed the presidency of Harvard College. Eliot was determined to make Harvard a national university, and he strengthened the school's law, medicine, and theology schools and added schools of arts and sciences, applied sciences, and business administration. Whereas other schools did some of these things as well as Harvard, no other school in America did them all as well.

Harvard and the other universities used their position as educators of teachers to extend their influence throughout the country. George Santayana noted: "These graduates came to form a sort of normal school for future professors, stamped as in Germany with a Ph.D.; and the teachers in each subject became a committee charged with something of the functions of a registry office, to find places for their nurslings. The university could thus acquire a national and even an international function, drawing in distinguished talent and youthful ambition from everywhere, and sending forth in various directions its apostles of light and learning."[24] Other schools found graduate education appealing for similar reasons. Although all college and university teachers were not Ph.D.s, a Ph.D. from a good school was increasingly important for a sound initial appointment. The thirteen institutions in the Association of American Universities (founded in 1908) were, in part, interested in providing a place where presidents and deans could discuss the problems of graduate education and, despite the presence of three state universities, protect their market against the rising state universities, almost all of whom had added doctoral programs.

Where did the seminary fit in the university world? The answer was not self-evident. Although few of the new universities were secular in today's sense of the word, many were militantly nonsectarian. They believed that education was best done in a religious environment that stressed the commonly held religious assumptions of American life. Often such schools believed in an explicit or implicit identification of Christianity and civilization. To advance the one was almost necessarily to advance the other. Yet, Protestant theological educa-

23. Lawrence A. Cremin, *American Education: The Metropolitan Experience* (New York: Harper and Row, 1988).

24. Quoted in Bruce Kuklick, *The Rise of American Philosophy: Cambridge, Massachusetts, 1860-1930* (New Haven and London: Yale University Press, 1977).

tion was almost inevitably sectarian. Ministers were called to preach to people who had committed themselves to membership in specific denominations with public theological standards. Further, in the state universities constitutional considerations seemed to keep the seminaries outside the gate. To provide funding for the training of Protestant clergy would seem to violate the separation of church and state. True divinity schools, consequently, were possible only in a handful of institutions: the New England private universities, Temple University, the new Methodist schools, and the University of Chicago. Some schools that might have developed divinity schools in the normal course of affairs, such as Columbia and Princeton, had close relationships with nearby schools that retained their independence.

But this left most seminaries in limbo. Theological schools had little in common with the large number of private for-profit schools that were founded to teach everything from bartending to law and medicine. The seminaries' peers were the professional schools that were moving toward university affiliation and not the vocational schools that struggled to maintain themselves outside of such affiliations. The seminary became the only major professional school that is not part of a larger university world. The result was isolation from both the best of theory and the most able reflection on "best practices." The difference was a matter of standards. In other fields, especially law and medicine, there was often no comparison between those schools that either joined universities or were founded by them and those that remained outside. The university schools were deeply interested in enabling students to think seriously and rigorously about their experience and to purify their own practices through such reflection. Those that remained outside the university often had a "this has worked in the past" type of expertise. Further, those schools that joined the university were concerned with the future development of the profession and, hence, with the expansion of knowledge. Even the business schools had a research element.

The problem was also complicated by the seminary's task. As the Princeton theologians repeatedly affirmed, Christianity is a doctrinal religion. As a religion of teaching, the seminaries had the task of transmitting their tradition to the next generation. But they had to transmit it in teachable form. They were involved in theological and religious research from their beginning, and they had an obligation to pass on the specific skills needed for high-level religious study. But this was the area where the university clearly had the edge. The new schools had extensive libraries, well-administered doctoral degree programs, and larger faculties. In time the universities also had the prestige that comes with long periods of successful and innovative study. Should seminaries see themselves essentially as university faculties that had been cut administratively from the rest of the university by the separation of church and state? Should they abandon their research interests and concentrate on educating local church leaders and pastors? Or should they interpret themselves as mini-universities concerned with providing the churches with a wide variety of leaders and professional services?

V. Education on the Margins

The development of twentieth-century theological education was deeply influenced by the nineteenth century's marginalization of theology. If nothing else, the schools, most of which are about the size of a university professional school, had to take responsibility for all areas of their life: buildings and grounds, fund-raising, recruitment, and other functions, including libraries, that seemingly are better shared with other parts of a larger institution. Few seminaries have benefited from economies of scale, and most have had to struggle financially. It could hardly be otherwise. The schools have had to provide many of the same services for a student body of between 50 and 200 that universities and colleges have provided for student bodies in the thousands.

Far more serious has been the problem of academic and professional standards. While all professions have their own criteria for admission to practice, university professional schools have been responsible to their sponsoring universities as well. In the long haul, no university can afford to let, for instance, its school of social work or school of education fall too far beneath the general level maintained by the university. In that sense, even the modern multiversity is much more than a parking lot and a heating system shared by diverse people. As in the case of basic educational services, the seminaries have had to do much of the work of determining and setting standards for themselves that reflect their own unique place in the educational order.

The marginality of the seminary has also had serious intellectual consequences. While the best of American theology has often been very good indeed, American theologians have often suffered from their comparative isolation from the larger cultural world. Other disciplines have also maintained a splendid isolation from the larger cultural realm, to be sure, and the distance between the scientific and the literary departments of many universities is as great or greater than either one's distance from the seminary. One advantage of the university is that it permits and even encourages the development of the novel and the esoteric, and some schools have benefited from the advocacy of heterodox positions by some of their departments. But theological study always involves a serious cultural component. Even in the more sectarian traditions, theologians are called upon to offer an understanding of how faith fits into both the moral and intellectual culture of the times. Talk about God always includes talk about what society considers the good, the true, and the beautiful; in other words, the idea of the ultimate implies that something lies behind a very concrete penultimate. The failure of the seminaries to find a place in the larger organization of American knowledge complicates this task.

In theory, the seminaries' location on the margins should have enabled them to trade relevance for purity; that is, the schools should have been able to maintain their denomination's particular teachings. But, as we shall see, marginality is not the same as isolation. The seminaries have struggled with the same broad cultural issues as American culture as a whole; their marginal character has only forced them to do this at a distance rather than face-to-face.

CHAPTER SEVEN

The Case of Andover Theological Seminary

From 1880 to 1931 Andover Theological Seminary, the nation's first seminary, was racked by controversies that wrecked its endowment, contributed to a decline in its enrollment, and finally led the school to seek "merger" with first Harvard and then Newton. Seldom has an institution suffered so long and so hard at the hands of its supposed friends and supporters. The story is filled with irony. During the period of its greatest travail, Andover Seminary had a pace-setting curriculum that provoked the envy of many of its rivals. By 1920, many of Andover's innovations had become commonplace among the nation's better seminaries and might even be interpreted as the standards that separated institutions into "better" and "less effective" seminaries. Further, the seminary's faculty, while perhaps not as able as that of Union in New York or the new University of Chicago, was distinguished academically and ecclesiastically. Andover graduates were frequently called upon to serve as presidents of colleges, and the advanced training Andover provided enabled them to transform their schools into modern institutions. George Peterson notes: "The student of the twentieth century must reckon the liberal takeover of the Andover Theological Seminary, and through it the traditional New England Colleges, a fortunate event. The standards of scholarship now prized by the New England colleges could not have been attained so long as the colleges were under the command of creeds."[1] Of course, the Andover-trained educational leaders had learned more from their alma mater than a dislike of creedal Christianity. They had absorbed a respect for science, for the scholarly study of society, and for modern educational methods in general.

1. George E. Peterson, *The New England College in the Age of the University* (Amherst, Mass.: Amherst College Press, 1964).

Andover Seminary was intellectually active to an unusual degree from 1880 to 1920. New ideas, European and American, were quickly absorbed. The *Andover Review,* published by the faculty, recorded their wrestling with intellectual innovation. The most important books were reviewed, thoughtful essays were provided, and challenging (perhaps too challenging) editorials were written. It was among the first and certainly among the best of the new seminary "scholarly" journals that were the nation's earliest forms of continuing education. Unlike the journals published by academic guilds, these journals were intended for readers who had received a thorough theological education but were not specialists in any particular theological discipline.[2] Andover continued to be on the cutting edge of such dynamic Protestant movements as missions, settlement-house work, and applied or social Christianity.

A cynic might suggest that Andover was a demonstration of the old adage that no good deed goes unpunished, and perhaps, given the perversity of human nature, that quip contains some truth. But much more was involved in the Andover case than sheer meanness. Almost all the issues that impacted seminaries in the 1880-1920 period, including whether they needed cooperative relations with universities, entered into the Andover debate. In that sense the debates and court cases were symbolic of issues that many schools faced then and later. Like an iceberg, the Andover case represented the top third of a discussion that capped the bulk of the arguments that were hidden from public view. The public squabble over Andover reflected many battles that occurred in other schools in more hidden and less open forums, such as faculty and trustee meetings. Perhaps most significant, Andover's trials raised the most basic question about the role of the seminary in the age of the university: How can a small, self-standing institution secure sufficient freedom to lead intellectually? Or to put it in another way, had intellectual and theological leadership passed, consciously or unconsciously, to the universities, to the handful of divinity schools related to them, and to the better and more prosperous colleges? But at its deepest level the question was how far such private ends, such as the maintenance of a certain perspective, can be secured by public means.

2. Such journals still are important gauges of a seminary's intellectual strength and commitment. In recent years, rapidly rising printing costs have forced some schools to cut back or to eliminate their journals. The seminary journals were middle-level publications that stood between the religious journals, such as the *Outlook,* and the specialized, disciplinary publications.

I. Progressive Orthodoxy

In general, Congregational seminaries were not disrupted by the national debates over evolution and biblical criticism. Although the church had been noted for its cantankerous theological life in the early nineteenth century, the theological temperature cooled considerably after 1840. The reasons for this were multiple.

Socially, New England Congregationalism had changed. The Congregational churches had grudgingly accepted disestablishment, and while they retained considerable social prestige, they were no longer the most numerous Protestant denomination in the region. Further, significant numbers of New Englanders had begun a massive trek westward that would continue almost to the present. If the advocates of home missions are to be believed, these migrants often left the religion of their childhood behind them. Given the dynamics of midcentury life, the social and economic places vacated by these migrating New Englanders were quickly taken by the new waves of Irish and French-Canadian immigrants that poured into the area after 1840. Congregationalists had much to do besides battle each other for control of their shrinking empire.

Intellectually, New England was also very different than it had been in the heyday of Edwardsian theology. New England, which remained the heartland of the denomination, was the home of American romanticism. The romantics stressed feeling and intuition over strict logical reasoning, and tended to see religion more as a response to the presence of the eternal in the temporal than as the acceptance of a supernatural revelation. Many New Englanders, orthodox and unitarian, believed that it was their duty to form their own response to the ultimate instead of meekly accepting the spiritual styles of the past. Ralph Waldo Emerson, Henry David Thoreau, and Theodore Parker suggested that traditional rational theology had grown "corpse cold" and that only a religion of the feelings was adequate to Victorian sensibility. Among the orthodox, Horace Bushnell, a Hartford pastor, demonstrated that such romantic intuitions might enable thoughtful people to reinterpret (and retain) traditional faith. In *God in Christ* (1849), Bushnell argued that the nature of religious language meant that such talk could not express sharply drawn distinctions. Language, he insisted, became less precise and more evocative as it moved further from immediate descriptions of things and actions. Hence, religious language pointed to its object (God) only indirectly and inferentially. Seemingly contradictory statements could simply be different ways of affirming the same spiritual realities. Bushnell also modified the traditional hyper-supernaturalism of much New England theology by describing God's providential work as a matter of agency rather than of ontology. Like humankind, God worked within the natural order to attain God's own intentions. God's intentions were, thus, beyond nature, while God's being and actions could be understood as within nature. It was a bold theological gambit.

While such romantic views were never universal among Congregationalists, they were pervasive. Even those who did not accept them were familiar with them, and often recognized their value. Other factors were also loosening Congregational doctrine, including an increasing emphasis on the freedom of the will, even at Hartford and Andover Seminaries, and a general openness to the findings of science. In 1883 the Congregational churches adopted a new confession of faith that sharply curtailed their inherited Calvinism.

Most Congregational battles over liberalism, consequently, were short-lived. A. C. McGiffert observed: "The alleged and martyred heretic serves as a kind of substitutionary atonement for the denomination at large. Once he has been punished for his theological sin, others could commit the same offense without the same penalty. So it was in the case of the Seminary [Chicago Theological]. The theological methods and assumptions which got [George Holley] Gilbert into deep trouble came shortly to be taken for granted by the Seminary Faculty and Board alike."[3]

The Gilbert case was, as McGiffert suggested, an excellent example of this process. Gilbert had been a student of Charles Briggs at Union, graduating in 1883. He joined the Chicago faculty in 1886, after further training in Leipzig, and signed that seminary's creed. As he matured, Gilbert became even more convinced that the historical method was essential to an understanding of the Bible. Further, he had accepted the important corollary of this position: the belief that theological tradition had no right to veto any conclusion reached on historical grounds. After he said Jesus' death should be understood in the context of Christ's life, and not in the context of dogmatic theology, demands arose that he be disciplined or removed. The board resisted those demands on the grounds that the seminary recognized the right of a professor to follow his own investigations, and Gilbert was granted an academic leave to work on his new book, *The First Interpreters of Jesus.* The first sheets from this volume created a stir on the board, and Gilbert, to avoid the embarrassment of a dismissal, resigned in 1901.

The Gilbert case interrupted the steady growth of academic freedom at the school. Before this controversy Samuel Curtiss, professor of Old Testament, taught unimpeded, despite his belief that Isaiah 53 referred to Israel and not to Christ and his well-known acceptance of Wellhausen's dating of the Old Testa-

3. A. C. McGiffert, Jr., *No Ivory Tower: The Story of the Chicago Theological Seminary* (Chicago: Chicago Theological Seminary, 1965), p. 116.

ment books. Further, W. Douglas Mackenzie, later to be president of Hartford Seminary, had objected to subscribing to the creed in 1901 and had been exempted from the subscription ceremony. Mackenzie, however, did state that he agreed with the substance of the creed, and Gilbert affirmed it vigorously. However, in 1905, further, the board elected Clarence Beckwith, a noted theological liberal, as its professor of theology. Gilbert was an interlude.

Other Congregational seminaries had even fewer problems with the new theology. At Bangor Seminary the gentle Lewis Stearns introduced the newer theological themes in his classes almost from his appointment in 1883. After his premature death, he was followed by Clarence Beckwith, who was even more outspoken in his advocacy of the new theology. Calvin Clark noted: "It was . . . not difficult for them [the board of trustees] in the early part of this present century to accord to the newer members of the Faculty the same individual freedom of faith which Congregationalists everywhere accord to their active pastors."[4] The experience of Hartford was similar.

In contrast to these incidents, the Andover case was intertwined with the school's goals and purposes. The seminary had formed in the midst of a three-cornered theological battle between two types of New England Calvinists and the new Unitarian movement. When Harvard College became Unitarian, the two orthodox parties united to establish Andover Seminary. Each of the parties was anxious to put its own theological standards into the school's governing documents. The founders, as the trustees of Phillips Academy in Andover were called, insisted that the faculty supported by their endowment be responsible to the Westminster Catechisms; the associate founders, who were primarily followers of Samuel Hopkins of Newport, wrote an elaborate creed to which those supported by their donation had to subscribe every five years. To ensure that this subscription would not become merely pro forma, the associate founders established a three-member Board of Visitors to watch over the seminary. While the trustees of Phillips Academy retained full-fiduciary authority, including the right to hire faculty, the visitors claimed the right to veto appointments on their own foundation and to bring charges of heresy.

Setting aside the elaborate arguments about this or whether a particular teacher's specific affirmation contradicted or did not contradict a specific article of the creed, the founders' intention was plain: they wanted to establish a school that clearly taught a certain understanding of the Christian faith, and they wanted only teachers who accepted this purpose to be part of the faculty. In that sense the associate founders were not interested in only orthodox theol-

4. Calvin M. Clark, *History of Bangor Theological Seminary* (Boston: Pilgrim Press, 1916), p. 387.

ogy or in the general task of the preparation of ministers; they knew what they wanted, and they thought they had found a way to secure what they wanted in perpetuity.

The Andover Creed was not analogous to the confessional documents of any of the American denominations. The various Reformed confessions of faith were hammered out in the midst of intense theological debate. While intended to provide a fence around correct teaching, they were also meant to be as broad and comprehensive as possible. They were, thus, inclusive documents that sought to define the catholic faith in a particular locale and at a particular time.[5] In contrast, the Andover Creed was never the expression of a church or religious community. It represented a private or personal vision that the associate founders wanted to maintain through public and legal means. To use Ernst Troeltsch's famous distinction, the Andover Creed was sectarian, not ecclesiastical, and more than the various denominational seminaries, it represented the spirit and purposes of a movement within a church. In the challenges to the Andover Creed and in the various court battles over it, the issue was how far sectarian or movement goals could determine the future course of an institution, especially after the issues that animated that movement had become somewhat shopworn over time.[6]

The struggle began with the decision of the Board of Visitors to reject the nomination of Newman Smyth as Edwards Amasa Park's successor on the Andover faculty.[7] But Smyth's decision not to fight the visitors' decision had postponed the issue. Initially, it seemed that this incident ended the conflict.

5. Reformed confessions of faith were different from either the Augsburg Confession or the *Book of Concord* in that they were seen as revisable. There were first and second Helvetic Confessions, for example, and when the Puritans temporarily secured control of England in the 1640s, they produced a new confession, the Westminster Confession, to summarize their theological position at that time. Congregational and Baptist Christians were both very generous producers of creeds. See Williston Walker, *The Creeds and Platforms of Congregationalism,* introduction by Elizabeth Nordbeck (New York: Pilgrim Press, 1991).

6. This same issue tends to arise in the second and third generation of any school that has been deeply influenced by a movement in its early days. Thus, in the 1960s Fuller Seminary had to consider its relationship to dispensationalism, a key part of the thought of many of its founders, just as its teachers were stepping out into a broader intellectual world.

7. See above, chapter 4. In 1880 William J. Tucker, one of the most able of the Andover faculty, prefaced his subscription to the creed with the statement: "I fully accept [the creed] as setting forth the truth against the errors which [it] was designed to meet. No confession so elaborate and with such intent may assume to be the final expression of truth or an expression equally fitted in language or tone to all times." However, Tucker's reservations did nor provoke a public crisis. Tucker may have remembered his reservations out of chronological order. Cited in Daniel Day Williams, *The Andover Liberals: A Study in American Theology* (New York: Octagon Books, 1970), p. 29.

The new appointment, George Harris, although lacking Smyth's brilliance, occupied much the same theological position. In subscribing to the creed, he stated bluntly that *"I accept this creed as expressing substantially the system of truth taught in Holy Scripture."* His inaugural address, "The Relational and Spiritual Verification of Christian Doctrine" (Andover, 1883), offered no concessions to the visitors' perspective. Daniel Day Williams noted a significant difference between Harris's position and the older Andover tradition. Whereas the earlier Andover theologians had preferred such terms as "Calvinism" or "Hopkinsianism" to describe their position, Harris consistently used the broader terms "Christianity" and "religion" to describe his own faith.[8] This subtle terminological change summed up the challenge in a nutshell. Whatever else "religion" and "Christianity" might mean, both terms were significantly broader than "Calvinism," "Hopkinsianism," or the "New Divinity." And both "religion" and "Christianity" made an explicit appeal to a broader understanding of human faith than the traditional language.

The retired Park recognized the nature of the challenge immediately. He published a ninety-three-page refutation of Harris's inaugural, and then a scholarly study of the associate creed that argued that no one could both accept the new theology and sign the creed with integrity. Park's argument was not a narrow repristination of the Edwardsian tradition. He believed there were four points on which Harris and his fellow teachers had left the faith of their fathers: the reliability and trustworthiness of the biblical text, the governmental doctrine of the atonement, the sinfulness of man, and the certainty of future punishments.[9] Park was clearly right historically. With the exception of the governmental theory of the atonement, it was hard to imagine any of the earlier New England theologians disagreeing with this list of necessary theological orthodoxies.

But Park was not the only one feeling the sting. In 1882 Professors Charles M. Mead and Joseph Thayer both resigned rather than resubscribe to the creed, and the faculty established the *Andover Review* in 1884 to present its side of the argument. Unlike most American theological journals, the *Andover Review* did not intend to be open to all theological opinions. Its goal was to advocate what the Andover faculty called "Progressive Orthodoxy." As they understood their position, they represented a middle party in American Protestantism, somewhat similar to the German mediating tradition that ran from Schleiermacher through Dorner and later to Ritschl. This tradition rejected ra-

8. Williams, *The Andover Liberals,* p. 29.

9. Henry Rowe, *History of Andover Theological Seminary* (Newton Mass.: [Andover-Newton Theological School?], 1933), p. 175.

tionalism on the one hand and rigid orthodoxy on the other. When asked whether they would accept articles by Unitarian James Freeman Clark or conservative William G. T. Shedd, they answered no to both.[10] The Andover liberals' conviction that they occupied the middle ground perhaps made it harder for them to hear their critics. In their own minds, their position represented a compromise, something like a synthesis of the options, and further compromise would destroy the fine balance they had established between competing positions.

The issues were obscured by the concurrent debate over second probation.[11] Isaak Dorner, a German mediating theologian, argued that those who did not accept Christ in this life would have a future opportunity to do so. Although Dorner and his American followers were careful to say that each individual had only one opportunity to decide for or against Christ, the popular misinterpretation of the position was that there were two chances to accept or reject him, one in this life and one in the life to come. Hence the term "second probation." In a period in which many thoughtful people had rejected the idea of damnation or any type of hell torments,[12] this was a middle path between that radical position and the hellfire and brimstone preaching of much traditional New England religion.

H. M. Dexter, the influential editor of the *Congregationalist,* put his journal in the service of the older doctrine and kept up a running attack. The debate over second probation raged until the 1890s, and in good Congregational fashion tended to be fought out in local ordination councils and in the yearly anniversary meetings of the American Board of Commissioners for Foreign Missions. The American Board was at the peak of its influence. It was still the largest American missionary agency, and its leaders were among the best-regarded experts on missionary work. Two Andover graduates, William A. Noyes and Daniel Torrey, were rejected by the board in 1887 for believing that the heathen would be given a chance to accept Christ after death. Andover graduate Robert Hume was denied reappointment for the same reason.

If in one sense the debate over second probation was less central to the theological argument, it was central to the public relations dimension of the

10. William J. Tucker, *My Generation: An Autobiographical Interpretation* (Boston: Houghton Mifflin, 1919).

11. Tucker drew a distinction between the battle over second probation and the larger battle for a freer theology that I have found useful. See *My Generation,* p. 126.

12. This trend was much more advanced in England and on the Continent than in the United States. For the American development, see James H. Moorhead, *World without End: Mainstream American Protestant Visions of the Last Things, 1880-1925* (Bloomington: Indiana University Press, 1999).

case. Andover Seminary had represented more of a movement than a denomination, and the missions had often provided the glue that held that movement together. In a sense the seminary won the dispute in the American Board when the national society agreed that local Congregational associations, which examined candidates for ordination, should judge the orthodoxy of prospective missionaries. This allowed candidates to seek ordination in those associations where their views would not be as controversial. But in another sense the school lost the dispute. Many of Andover's students had come with foreign missions as a career already in mind, and these students began to seek safer, or at least less controversial, posts.

In 1886 the Board of Visitors charged five faculty members with heresy. The five were: Egbert Smyth, William J. Tucker, J. W. Churchill, George Harris, and E. V. Hincks. There were sixteen total specifications. These should be quoted in full:

1. That the Bible is not the only perfect rule of faith and practice, but is fallible and untrustworthy even in some of its religious teachings.
2. That Christ in the days of His humiliation, was merely a finite being — limited in all His attributes, capacities, and attainments.
3. That no man has power, or capacity, to repent, without knowledge of the historic Christ.
4. That mankind, save as instructed in a knowledge of the historic Christ, are not sinners, or if they are, are not of such sinfulness as to be in danger of being lost.
5. That no man can be lost without having had knowledge of Christ.
6. That the Atonement of Christ consists essential and chiefly in His becoming identified with the human race through His incarnation; in order that, by His union with men, He might endow them with the power to repent, and thus impart to them an augmented value in view of God, and so propitiate God to men, and men to God.
7. That the Trinity is modal, and not personal.
8. That the work of the Holy Spirit is mainly limited to natural methods, and within historic Christianity.
9. That without the knowledge of the historic Christ, men do not deserve the punishment of the law, and that therefore their salvation is not wholly of grace.
10. That faith ought to be rational and scientific, rather than Scriptural.
11. That there is and will be probation after death, for all men who have not in this [life] had knowledge of the historic Christ.
12. That this hypothetical belief in probation after death should be brought

to the front, exalted, and made central in the theology, and in the beliefs of men.

13. That Christian Missions are not to be supported and conducted on the ground that men who know not Christ are in danger of perishing forever, and must perish forever unless saved in this life.
14. That a system of physical and metaphysical philosophy is true which by fair interference neutralized the Christian doctrine as taught in the creed of the seminary.
15. That there is a new theology better than the old which we apprehend is not in harmony with the Creed, but fatally opposed to the same.
16. That the said Professors hold and teach many things which cannot be reconciled with that orthodox and consistent Calvinism which the Statutes require of them, and to which they stand publicly committed, and that in repeated instances these professors have broken substantial promises when they subscribed the creed.[13]

The conservatives had clearly overstepped the bounds on some of the charges. For instance, the charge that the Andover faculty taught that missions should not be supported was clearly an attempt to paint the accused with a distant — and not necessary — implication of their own position. In fact, they believed that "as never before, the world is prepared for the gospel."[14] But other charges were closer to the mark. Perhaps the most graphic of these was metaphysical. The Andover theologians, following Dorner and Schleiermacher, had adopted immanence instead of transcendence as the most important attribute of God; hence, God was seen primarily as working in and through nature and human experience. There was also less room or need for radical gaps in religious or personal development. Conversion, for example, could in most cases be seen as nurture.

The visitors clearly were not sure what to do with the case — they were apparently divided in their decision. Julius Steelye wanted to acquit all the faculty; Joshua Newell Marshall wanted to convict them all; and William T. Eustus, who had not been at the trial, refused to convict those he had not heard. The charges against all the faculty, with the exception of Smyth, were dropped, and those against Smyth reduced to three: the denial of biblical infallibility, probation after death, and maintaining that people could repent without knowledge of the historic Christ. At the time and since, this outcome seemed strange. Since all five faculty members edited the journal, all were equally responsible for its

13. Tucker, *My Generation,* p. 190.
14. *Andover Review,* cited in Williams.

contents. But there were sound reasons to limit the case. The charter allowed for appeals to the Massachusetts Supreme Court, and it was clear that whoever lost the case would appeal. Smyth, the most prominent, was a test case.

The battle before the supreme court was not edifying nor necessarily germane to the issues raised in the heresy trials. Smyth and the board claimed the visitors had acted without hearing the trustees, who had to be considered original parties to the case, and that the decision violated the trustees' rights and made it difficult for them to discharge their duties. In 1891 the supreme court agreed with this argument and sent the case back to the visitors, who had the right to renew the trial. But by this time new visitors were in place, and the charges were dropped.

William Tucker noted correctly that the trial did not touch the real issue: the power of the visitors or the influence of the creed on the school's future development. In that sense the battle had not touched the real issue. Perhaps the court had hoped that by returning the case to the visitors and the board, a decision could be found that the seminary could live with in the future. Litigation was of course very expensive. At a time when Andover was rapidly expanding its program, the total cost ($36,779.35, or over $650,000.00 in 1998 dollars) may have substantially weakened its treasury. While it is hard to judge, it is probable that the human cost exceeded the cash cost. The trials weakened the faculty's morale and sapped some of its creativity.

II. Educational Creativity

American religious liberalism was educationally as well as intellectually creative. We can sum up this creativity with three important affirmations: (1) The liberals believed firmly in the immanence of God in history and nature. (2) The liberals had confidence in the future. (3) Liberalism, in general, was open to insights from many sources.[15] While all these had their own educational dynamic, when they worked together, as they did at Andover, they contributed to significant modifications of the inherited models of theological education.

The Andover theology was emphatically theological and not dependent on the popular Kantian and Hegelian idealism that dominated contemporary academic philosophy. Schleiermacher and Dorner had argued that theological affirmations had their origins in religious consciousness and not in any partic-

15. For the varieties of religious liberalism, see K. Cauthen, *The Impact of American Religious Liberalism* (New York: Harper and Row, 1962). Cauthen tends to stress the difference between the later modernist liberals and the earlier evangelical liberals more than I would.

ular system of philosophy, no matter how cogent. This rejection of the philosophical a priori for theology was perhaps the most obvious place that the Andover theologians differed from their New Divinity ancestors whose thought was often a tangled web of philosophical distinctions drawn ever more precisely as the debate forced this or that theologian to reexamine his position. It also freed the Andover theologians to follow an independent course in adapting their educational program to the perceived needs of the times.

The Andover liberals insisted that the curriculum was not closed philosophically or theologically.[16] In the heated discussion of theological encyclopedia, they insisted that the curriculum was a work in progress that had few, if any, fixed points. While they honored the traditional program, they wanted to supplement it with new and different studies. These included science and religion, biblical theology, biblical archaeology, sociology, and social conditions (social ethics), and they used their location near Boston to attract lecturers on other areas of contemporary religious concern. In addition to their confidence that theology itself could provide sufficient norms for their work, the basic premises behind an open curriculum were the belief in the future and in the immanence of God. Since God was at work within the search for knowledge, all knowledge had theological implications that might cast light on God's being and character. The Andover liberals did not want to merely give a theological interpretation of knowledge or, as in the older apologetics, to show that knowledge had Christian implications. God was not a deduction from the real. Rather, the real itself mediated and presented the presence of God to the human mind. In this they applied the Pauline principle that we see through a glass darkly as a serious guide to the work of theology. What the theologian did, in effect, was to unmask the presence of God in human experience.

The open curriculum was closely related to Andover's belief in progress. In the aftermath of the two world wars, neoorthodox theologians were often hard on the earlier liberal confidence that human life might be improving in more than a material sense. But the Andover belief in progress was thoroughly theological. God is at work within the world and within human history. While

16. I use "open" rather than "elective" to describe the Andover understanding of theological education. One could offer, as such encyclopedias as Hagenbach's suggested, a number of electives that were bound to a priori theological judgments. Many theological curricula, including some of the most conservative, have been built on this style of elective system. The Andover liberals believed that the theological curriculum was as potentially broad as human experience. If its center in biblical and doctrinal studies was somewhat fixed, it had no discernible outer limit. The theologian needed to follow God where God led, not to confine God to a particular place or time. Since the work of God was so vast, the Andover liberals did not want to use the professional work of the ministry as a guide to curricula.

God's work may be slow and arduous, it is certainly real and purposeful. For the believer, then, the task is to be willing to accompany God on God's way. When seen from this theological perspective, the liberal belief in progress is only another version of the perennial Christian search for a holy life. Like all theories of holiness, this theory demanded that the believer "love God with the whole mind," and this meant close attention to knowledge as one way that God's work was revealed historically. To be open to God is to be open to God's light wherever found.

The same confidence in the power of knowledge led them to strive for absolute honesty about the biblical books. In an 1886 editorial, "The Bible as a Theme for the Pulpit," the editors of the *Andover Review* talked about the need laypeople had for honest discussion of biblical issues.

> They have enough scientific culture to know that neither history nor geology gives acceptance to all the statements found in the Biblical narrative. Moreover, they find on the face of Scripture blemishes apparently inconsistent with a verbal inspiration. The introduction of the Revised Version has very likely set them questioning as to the original perfection of a book which must become imperfect in transmission to future ages and foreign peoples. They wish fairly to face the questions thus raised, and to decide in view of the answers obtained what Christianity claims for the Bible as regards sanctity and separateness from other literature.[17]

The editors believed that the pastoral way to do this was not to "preach a series of sermons" to show that popular understandings of the Bible were incorrect. The Andover theologians recognized that such a series might end a ministry. Instead they argued that the minister needed to enter into "an examination of facts . . . an historical inquiry into the genesis of Scriptures" that will show that "Christian faith is not necessarily committed to the infallibility of the Bible."[18] The Andover curriculum with its increasing emphasis on such studies as biblical introduction, English Bible, biblical archaeology, and the like was shaped around this concern for a new style of biblical teaching. Although Andover remained a center for the study of biblical languages, the school shifted its focus from linguistics to historical research.

As Daniel Day Williams noted in *The Andover Liberals,* Andover's embrace of biblical criticism was limited. The Andover theologians, like many early liberals, wanted to maintain a strongly incarnational theology that emphasized the centrality of the person of Jesus. But Williams is also right in not-

17. "The Bible as a Theme for the Pulpit," *Andover Review* 5 (Apr.-June 1886): 408.
18. "Bible as a Theme," p. 409.

ing that by 1891 a different spirit had entered Andover's New Testament studies. The certainty that one could read the Gospels as a historical reflection of Jesus' life receded, and the Andover liberals moved from talking about Jesus to describing Jesus' "impression on men that He gave them such a revelation of truth and such an inspiration of life as no other man has ever given."[19] Since much of the Andover liberals' early theology was an attempt to restate Dorner's Christology with its incarnational emphasis, this was a radical step away from their own position. But this step does illustrate the educational dynamics of their theology. Having decided that the historical study of the Bible was an intrinsic good, they had to follow that good wherever it led.

Although the school was located in semirural Andover, the system of trains and trolleys shortened the time needed to go into the city, and the seminary knew that "the field had become a spiritual and social laboratory."[20] Perhaps the most important sign of this curricular experimentation was the beginning of a program of supervised work at the Berkeley Temple under the supervision of Charles Dickerson. The Berkeley Temple was an institutional church that offered a variety of ministries to its community, and the seminary offered a stipend of $100 for ten students to engage in "evangelistic" work at the school. Robert Woods, an Andover graduate, founded Andover House, a social settlement, to provide further laboratory work for students. Woods traveled to England to study the settlements there and to learn about the best methods and approaches. Students were expected to live at the house while ministering to human conditions nearby.

The term "laboratory," used of these innovations, should be taken seriously. Obviously it was meant to call to mind science and its careful observation of nature. But it was not only human nature that was being observed. The Andover liberals believed that God was at home in the movement of social forces, and hence the students who were working with social conditions were potentially watching God at work.[21] In studying social change one was studying God, so to speak, in the raw, and gathering data about the divine. Social service, thus, confirmed liberal theology's belief in a God who redeems humankind in the midst of historical forces and change. "The good society itself becomes a worthy object of human desire, and one of the central goals of God's creative purposes."[22] This was the earlier form of American social theology. Later, liber-

19. Williams, *The Andover Liberals*, p. 105.

20. Earl Thompson, "The Andover Liberals as Theological Educators," *Andover-Newton Quarterly* 8, no. 4 (1968): 219. I have followed Thompson in much of this section.

21. Later modernists, such as D. C. Macintosh, would have a similar interest in observing God through the medium of personal and corporate religious experience.

22. Williams, *The Andover Liberals*, p. 165.

als, more deeply influenced by Ritschl and his school, would modify this sense of religious immediacy by stressing the mediated character of the kingdom and the role of human judgments in history.[23] Nonetheless, the less theologically refined, but emotionally more powerful, response of the Andover liberals has continued as one religious dimension of American religious social reform.

III. The Story Concludes

The decline of Andover Seminary in numbers and influence at the turn of the century remains one of the great mysteries in the history of American theology. The school, which had been among the nation's largest and best endowed, failed to hold its position among American schools. Many forces seem to have been at work. The school's rural location was clearly a factor. Colgate Seminary, the oldest Baptist school in New York and one of the best-known American schools, was forced to unite with Rochester partially for this reason. But other things were also involved. The long, drawn-out heresy trial had cost the school a substantial amount, and the newer style of education favored by the faculty required a more substantial budget. Yet, as these financial needs climbed, the school had less support from traditionally friendly congregations, pastors, and donors. At the same time, despite the excellence of its program, enrollment declined. This decline apparently affected all the liberal schools to a lesser or greater extent and, in retrospect, may have reflected some of the shifts in American higher education. Many of the smaller colleges that had served as "feeder schools" to the seminaries grew in numbers, wealth, and sophistication. The liberal seminaries thus no longer appealed to the "poor but pious" young men who had previously attended them on their way to a ministerial or educational career. But whatever the cause, the decline was real.

The trustees decided to move the school. To do this the legal arrangements that governed the institution had to be changed. The trustees of Phillips Academy, consequently, asked the Massachusetts legislature to establish a new corporation: the Trustees of Andover Seminary. This corporation then received all the funds and endowments held by Phillips Academy on behalf of the theological institution.[24] The next step was to negotiate with Harvard for a location near that university, construct a new building, and reopen the school. The rea-

23. Walter Rauschenbusch, for instance, began with the earlier sense of social revelation and, later, primarily in his *Theology of the Social Gospel,* provided a more Ritschlian and reflective social theology.

24. *Dates and Data* (n.p.: Trustees of Andover Seminary, 1926), p. 20.

sons for location in Cambridge were given in the 1908 trustee action: the location was in Massachusetts and in the same general area of the state as the bulk of the school's supporters; Cambridge was near the center of "the largest metropolitan district in New England"; and "no where is there a larger number of students from the families and the churches the Seminary was designed to serve than in Harvard University."[25]

But these reasons were less important than the possibility of an alliance with Harvard University. Like many other Americans, Harvard President Charles Eliot was impressed by Thomas Jefferson's proposal that theological schools be grouped around a major university. Consequently, he had worked to locate the Episcopal Theological School near Harvard and to secure privileges for its faculty and students. At about the same time, William Rainey Harper was encouraging such schools as Chicago Theological Seminary to move near, and share some privileges with, the new University of Chicago. The Disciples Divinity House was an extension of the same idea. In effect, the Disciples provided room and board for their students and some denominational guidance, while using the resources of the larger institution. Such affiliations seemed to be working well and appeared to be the wave of the future.

The Harvard affiliation was particularly attractive. Harvard's department of Semitic languages was one of the largest and best in the country, and the divinity school was prospering. The trustee action noted: "In its allied departments Harvard University is unsurpassed by any institution in the country in the number of courses of interest and value to candidates for the ministry, all of which the Seminary may employ at its discretion in the enrichment of the instruction it offers."[26] At the same time, they believed that the opportunity to work with Harvard students, both those in the divinity school and those in other programs, would make Andover more attractive to faculty as a place to teach. There were two other aspects of the vision. First, "Establishing Andover Theological Seminary, with its influence and facilities at Cambridge, will strengthen the religious forces, and enhance the credit and efficiency of theological instruction, in a great university center." Secondly, "the effect of this would be to render the calling of the minister more honorable and attractive in the eyes of educated young men and draw a larger proportion of them into the profession. And thereby indirectly, as well as by the opportunity of giving instruction to more students in its classes, the Seminary will be enabled to increase the number of learned and able Ministers of the Gospel."[27]

25. *Dates and Data,* p. 21.
26. *Dates and Data,* p. 21.
27. *Dates and Data,* p. 22.

The union between the two schools proceeded slowly. The next step was the establishment through a 1910 agreement of the Andover-Harvard library to merge the divinity collections of the two schools. Both the books and the library endowment of Andover were maintained separately. On May 24, 1922, the Andover trustees adopted the Plan for Closer Affiliation that would have virtually merged the two schools. Under this agreement "The President and Fellows of Harvard College and Trustees of Andover Theological School shall join to form a non-denominational theological school." The new school was to have a single faculty, roll of students, administration, and catalogue. The former Andover faculty were to be listed in Harvard publications as "the Andover Foundation." Interestingly, the Andover trustees reserved the right to grant Andover degrees to Andover students. The plan was too much for the visitors, who declared "that said plan is inconsistent with the Associate Foundation Statutes"; they therefore declared "void the plan for closer affiliation." Both the trustees and the visitors appealed to the supreme judicial court. In the process of the case the visitors amended their action to include theological complaints as well, including that the faculty had not vowed "to maintain the Christian faith, as expressed in the creed and in opposition not only to Atheists and Infidels, but to Jews, Papists, Mahometans, Arians, Pelagians, Antinomians, Arminians, Socinians, Sabellians, Unitarians, and Universalists." They also noted "that the teaching in the Andover Theological Seminary since the year 1908, has not been and is not in accordance with or consistent with the Westminster Assembly's Shorter Catechism or with the creed described and set forth in the Constitution."[28]

In its ruling on September 19, 1925, the court agreed with the visitors, ruling that "an undenominational theological school was foreign to their purpose and alien to their declarations." With historical accuracy, the court contended that "doctrine and creedal requirements were of the essence of the purpose of the founders of the Andover Seminary."[29] On this ground the court laid aside the argument of the trustees that the teachers were the heirs of historical Congregationalism: "The question presented is quite different from what it would be if the seminary had been founded simply or in substance for the training of orthodox Trinitarian congregational ministers. Doubtless if that had been the foundation, the seminary rightly could be administered according to the beliefs of those in the historical succession of New England Trinitarian congregationalism."[30] On this ground the visitors' action declaring the Plan for Close Affilia-

28. *Dates and Data,* p. 22.

29. *Dates and Data,* p. 31. For a detailed discussion, see Richard D. Pierce, "The Legal Aspects of the Andover Creed," *Church History* 15 (1946): 28-47.

30. *Dates and Data,* p. 32.

tion void was allowed to stand. Further, the Andover Creed was declared to be still in effect. The decision caused the most serious crisis in the school's history. Classes were suspended for the next academic year, and the trustees were forced to decide how to carry out their mandate without buildings or library. The dilemma was also theological. Richard D. Pierce noted:

> The decision resulted in the immediate resignation of the entire faculty and the suspension of the activities of the Seminary. The Trustees saw no relief for the dilemma of the Institution — how could its primary purpose be fulfilled and the creed maintained? Its primary purpose was "the providing of learned, able and devout ministers for the Trinitarian Congregational Churches," particularly of New England. To indoctrinate students with the Calvinism of the Andover Creed would defeat this end, for there were not half a dozen Trinitarian Congregational churches in New England that would call a minister who held such doctrines.[31]

In a sense the issue had come to an impasse. The private purposes of the original associate founders no longer had a public interested in the realization of their goals.

Acknowledging the impasse, however, does highlight the difficult question posed by the history of Andover: To what extent is theological education a private matter that ought to be determined by the whims of the donors? While institutions can be founded to perpetuate any set of beliefs, popular or unpopular, part of the idea of a theological school is that such schools prepare leaders for religious organizations. If this purpose is part of their nature, how does it rank in their hierarchy of goals and objectives of a theological school? In particular, it would seem that the public purpose of training leaders for churches would outweigh the purpose of maintaining a more private religious doctrine.

The court eventually accepted this argument. Newton Theological Seminary in nearby Newton Centre, the nation's oldest Baptist seminary, was, like Andover, searching for a partner. At least since 1900, with the election of George Horr as president, Newton had moved in a more liberal direction, and like many other contemporary schools, its newer theological commitments had strained its resources. After considerable negotiation the two schools devised a plan of affiliation that allowed both to remain legally separate while sharing a president, a faculty, common buildings and grounds, and a common academic schedule. Students were to receive their degrees from either Andover or Newton, depending on their denominational affiliation. There was one catch. The trustees of Newton refused to consummate the agreement until the Massachu-

31. Pierce, "The Legal Aspects of the Andover Creed."

setts Supreme Court set aside the requirement of subscription to the Andover Creed. The court did so, paradoxically, by affirming the public character of the Andover trust: "The creedal requirements are hereafter to be enforced only to the extent of seeing to it that the theological views held by the professors, the students, and by the members of Board of Visitors are in conformity with those obtaining among Trinitarian Congregationalists generally . . . and that instruction given in the seminary by such professors is not hereafter to be called into question because of inconsistency with the creedal requirements of the Constitution and Statutes."[32] Andover and Newton cooperated under this plan until 1965 when the two boards of trustees voted to legally combine the two foundations as the Andover-Newton Theological School. One of the reasons for the final measure was the increasingly ecumenical (undenominational) character of the school's students and faculty.

Andover Seminary, the nation's first graduate theological school, was founded in the midst of intense theological and religious controversy. Its founders, particularly those on the Associate Foundation (the Hopkinsians), wanted to tie the school down so tightly with legal restrictions that it could never follow the example of Harvard and defect to a theological enemy. At the time of the school's founding, its theological position, while not universal in New England, was also not unusual. Andover was supported by numerous churches, by enthusiasts for missions, and by many "feeder" colleges. In many ways the school expressed the hopes and aspirations of a movement. But movements tend to die down. And as their ardor cools, they tend to become more sectarian than ecclesiastical or denominational; the passage of more time tends to reduce even sectarianism to more of a trifle, to something quaint or unusual, but hardly to be taken with public seriousness. From its early liberalization after the retirement of Edwards Amasa Park, Andover's faculty and trustees resisted forces that would have turned them in a sectarian direction. However, they were unable to win a decisive battle over those forces. The sectarian understanding of the school continued through the persistence of the Board of Visitors and the Andover Creed. At any moment these relics from its past could be resurrected and stand in judgment over the school's future. And that is what happened. Just as the school seemed prepared to find a new identity as part of Harvard University, its debt to the past came due. And with justice, the court ordered that debt honored. The Andover trustees' contention that union with Harvard was a natural evolution of the thought of the associate founders was historically and legally unconvincing. The union with Harvard was precisely

32. Supreme Judicial Court, Equity Case, no. 544469, final decree cited in Pierce, "Legal Aspects," p. 47.

the type of thing the associate founders had hoped their money and institution would resist to the death. But having paid that piper, the problem of the sectarian character of a public institution still remained. When the Andover and Newton trustees appealed to the court for "relief" from the ancient mandates, they asked the court to set aside a provision in a trust that time had rendered inexpedient. To grant this petition did not require the court to declare that black was white or to rule on the intentions of the founders or their documents. The court could rule that the trustees were allowed to administer the funds they had received as a public trust that belonged, in some sense, to the trinitarian Congregationalists of New England.

Andover was the clearest example of a school established for private theological ends, but other such "independent" or "movement" schools were established in the nineteenth and twentieth centuries. Although few have had as elaborate a legal structure as Andover, many have been bound to a confession of faith rather than to a living ecclesiastical body. Although no one can predict the future, it is possible they will pass through a similar process at some time.[33] If so, the courts may have to determine again how private and public interest intersect in American theological education.

33. The battles over dispensational and biblical inerrancy among conservative evangelicals have had some of the character of the earlier Andover debates.

CHAPTER EIGHT

The Impact of the Social Awakening

When Congregationalist Home Missionary advocate Josiah Strong published his ringing call to arms, *Our Country,* in 1885, he did not intend to write about theological education. His concern was with the nation and with what he felt was a critical moment in its history. Like the contemporary progressive historian Frederick Turner, Strong's purpose was to highlight what he considered a major change in American life. As Strong understood the situation, the older western frontier, which had been evangelized largely by the Second Great Awakening, had disappeared. The American nation was supreme from New England to the desert southwest, and as population entered an area, the church responded to the needs of new settlements by supplying evangelists and church builders. In a sense the older American Home Missionary movement had accomplished its purposes. But only in a sense. Strong believed that the frontier had moved: it was now located in the new urban centers that were the new magnets, drawing people from rural areas, both at home and abroad. These large cities were the new wild west where "each of the dangers we have discussed is enhanced and all are focalized." Most strikingly: "It is the city where wealth is massed; and here are the tangible evidences of it piled many stories high. Here the sway of Mammon is widest, and his worship the most constant and eager. Here, also, is the congestion of wealth the severest. Dives and Lazarus are brought face to face; here, in sharp contrast, are the ennui of surfeit and the desperation of starvation. The rich are richer, and the poor are poorer, in the city than elsewhere; and, as a rule, the greater the city, the greater are the riches of the rich and the poverty of the poor."[1] Strong's argument was not just jere-

1. Josiah Strong, *Our Country,* extract in Ronald C. White and C. Howard Hopkins, *The Social Gospel* (Philadelphia: Temple University Press, 1976), p. 56.

miad. Like the "experts" called to testify before the British House of Commons and later before the American Congress, he buttressed his arguments with statistics detailing such matters as the number of saloons and the number of evangelical churches for every hundred thousand people.

Strong's book captured the strange mood of the late nineteenth century. The rapid industrialization of the nation following the Civil War upset many people's equilibrium. As immigrants flooded into America's cities, the small town and village of the early part of the century became an idyllic real America in the minds of many, almost an American golden age. The present, in contrast, seemed fraught with peril. Massive strikes, such as the Homestead strike of 1892 and the Pullman strike of 1894; continuing tensions over immigration; and the declining quality of city life suggested a nation that was living on the edge. The pattern of people's personal economies was also shifting. Few Americans lived or worked as independent farmers or businessmen. Most were employed by someone else and subject to the apparent whims of that employer. "Nerves" became a common medical diagnosis. Yet, many Americans remained hopeful, even confident. Problems were meant to be solved; obstacles were, like temptations in an earlier period, present primarily to be overcome.

If Strong's book was about the sense of national crisis, not about theological education, many theological educators were thinking along similar lines. *Our Country* is an early example of a style of theological thinking that was to be influential in the progressive period. In many ways the book can be seen as the agenda for many theological educators, especially among Congregationalists, Baptists, Methodists, and Disciples.[2] The book makes three theological and ecclesiastical assumptions that had educational import. First, Strong assumes that Christianity possesses important resources for dealing with the world's problems. In that sense the various religious and theological terms used to describe this way of thinking were apt: the "social gospel," the "new evangelism," the "new home missions." The theological task is to mine the faith — particularly the Bible and the teachings of Jesus — for the religious and moral inspiration needed for the "living of these days." Second, Strong was convinced that it had to deal with problems scientifically. The word "science," then as now, had many notations and connotations. What Strong and other advocates of the new home missions meant by it was the organization of sufficient pertinent information for a reasonable person to make a moral decision about a social issue. In his

2. Social Christianity, of course, affected all major denominations and a number of minor ones to a greater or lesser extent. As such, it deeply affected many schools. It was also very influential among American holiness groups. See Grant Wacker, "In the Beginning Was Finney . . . or Was It Bushnell? The Holy Spirit and the Spirit of the Age in American Protestantism, 1880-1901," Notre Dame Seminar in American Religion, Center for Continuing Education, p. 2.

opinion it was no longer sufficient to point to the town drunk as an example of degradation. The Christian reformer needs to know how many alcoholics live in a town or city, how much their unfortunate habit costs them and their employers, what links exist between alcohol and spousal abuse, and what social factors, including profits from the sale of liquor, promote the problem. The third assumption was that serious social problems required social or mass solutions if vice and evil were to be defeated.

While the particular strategy to be used varied, almost all advocates of the new evangelism favored the "crusade" or mass movement that mobilized people to fight this or that evil. The movement was seen as a particularly democratic form of social action. In a nation where the people ruled, the quickest way to change conditions was to change the people, or enough of them to launch a movement. Movements were not directed toward general or structural changes in society. Almost by definition, a movement had a specific goal or purpose, such as labor reform or women's rights, and focused its energy, especially its publications, on that objective. Activists, consequently, often participated in a variety of movements, some of which espoused very different ideologies or justifications for their work. Thus a person might participate in the urban revivalism of Dwight L. Moody and Billy Sunday as a way to promote sobriety or to restrain sexual vice; in the peace movement to prevent war; in the institutional church movement to promote social service; in the Young Men's Christian Association or Young Women's Christian Association to reach the young; in the Student Volunteer Movement as a way to the "evangelization of the world in our generation"; in the Men and Religion Forward Movement to reach men and boys; and in Laymen's Missionary Movement to improve church finance. Movements rested on the power of persuasion. But if publicity and persuasion failed or, more often, ran afoul of deeply embedded economic interests, as occurred with alcohol and impure food and drugs, the advocates of the new evangelism were willing to write their goals into law.[3]

3. Seen from a later perspective, the progressives in general appear to have been leery of using the government to correct social wrongs. Yet one must be careful not to be anachronistic here. Many progressives greatly admired the German system of social insurance, and many flirted with what they called "socialism" — a very imprecise term in an era given to much fuzzy language. Perhaps more to the historiographical point, present-day observers tend to think of government intervention in social problems more in terms of the level of government activity that followed the two world wars or the almost equally great crisis of the Depression. The progressives lacked those experiences and cannot be faulted for not incorporating their lessons into their worldviews. As it was, they did propose governmental intervention on what many considered a broad front: to stop the manufacture and sale of alcohol, to regulate housing, to secure pure food and drugs, to promote public health, to clean animal wastes from city streets, and to administer an empire abroad. To a nation accustomed to almost total lack of regulation and tax-

I. A New Discipline

Strong's book marked a fresh way of thinking about theological issues. Like much of the Western theological tradition, Strong adopted a method of thinking about religious matters that used a philosophical or scientific framework to interpret the Bible and the Bible to interpret that framework. This is the way Thomas Aquinas used Aristotle and Charles Hodge used Scottish common sense. Where Strong differed from the earlier tradition was that he elected not to use classical metaphysics or ethics as the dialogue partner; rather, he allowed the new science of sociology to provide the material he would interpret from a Christian perspective. Or, if one wanted to stress the authoritative place of religion in this scheme, one might say he applied Christianity to social science. At the time, theologians gave different names to this type of thinking, including sociology, Christian sociology, applied Christianity, and social ethics. Religious education will represent a similar attempt to use a new social science — education or pedagogy — as the basis for a theological discipline.

Part of our difficulty in tracing this important addition to the theological curriculum is the problem of definition. Sociology was a new field of inquiry in late nineteenth-century America. There is no entry "Sociology" in the comprehensive ninth edition of the *Encyclopaedia Britannica.*[4] The original American Association of Social Science was an organization of educators and professional leaders who were concerned with social and particularly educational reforms.[5] The first American groups concerned with social research were bodies like the National Conference of Charities and Correction, founded in 1874, that wanted to collect information that might strengthen the work of its various agencies. For many Americans in this period, sociology was synonymous with social reform. Scott Nearing of the University of Pennsylvania named one of his influential books *Social Religion: An Interpretation of Christianity in Terms of Modern Life* (1913), and Simon N. Patten called one of his contributions *The Social Basis of Religion* (1911).[6] Francis Peabody, Harvard's great advocate of social re-

---

ation, the program was radical enough to upset some. If Theodore Roosevelt was not yet the antichrist that his cousin Franklin became, he was close enough to the hellish pit of big government to be thoroughly hated by many.

4. *Encyclopaedia Britannica: A Dictionary of Arts, Sciences, and General Literature,* 9th ed. (New York: Samuel L. Hall, 1878-95).

5. Thomas L. Haskell, *The Emergence of Professional Social Science: The American Social Science Association and the Nineteenth Century Crisis of Authority* (Urbana: University of Illinois Press, 1977).

6. Scott Nearing, *Social Religion: An Interpretation of Christianity in Terms of Modern Life* (New York: Macmillan, 1913); Simon N. Patten, *The Social Basis of Religion* (New York: Macmillan, 1911). Selections are cited in White and Hopkins, *The Social Gospel.*

form, saw social reform as a subject that ought to concern every educated man: "The problems of social reform are no longer subjects which the educated can ignore. A few years ago they were questions of specialists in philosophy and political economy. . . . They are not questions of administration or economy; but broad, moral problems, demanding the special attention of educated men."[7] Andover's William J. Tucker noted: "The venture . . . into the field of sociological studies was an innovation in a theological school. Few colleges had then entered the field; there was lack of a proper scientific background for the more practical professional uses of the new science."[8]

Two of the leading seminary pioneers were Graham Taylor of Hartford and Chicago and Francis Peabody of Harvard. The two represented different approaches to the subject. Taylor, who began his career as a rural Reformed pastor, changed denominations when he moved to Hartford to become pastor of the Fourth Congregational Church.[9] The Fourth Church had earlier been the primary supporter of the abolition movement in the city. This was a fortunate connection. Many progressive reformers came from abolitionist families, and there was a tendency for people with that background to transform their parents' passion for the liberation of the slaves into support for a wide range of causes. Taylor's congregation followed this pattern. He was soon involved in a number of causes as he and his fellow Congregationalists mounted a campaign to provide social services to an increasingly diverse city.[10] He was already known when the president of Hartford Seminary, Chester Hartranft, invited him to teach at that school. Using some of the new techniques being pioneered by sociologists at the time, especially the survey, Taylor put together a program of what later theological educators called "field education" that enabled him to track his students as they worked in city charities. His most impressive project at Hartford was directing a survey of the city's population and religious forces commissioned by the Connecticut Bible Society. Most of the work was done by Hartford Seminary students, who received a first-rate sociological education by participating in the project. Taylor's reward was an invitation to teach at the Chicago Theological Seminary, one of the most prestigious Congregational schools.

7. Francis Peabody, "Social Reforms as Subjects of University Study," *Independent,* Jan. 14, 1887, p. 563.

8. William J. Tucker, *My Generation: An Autobiographical Interpretation* (Boston: Houghton Mifflin, 1919), p. 272.

9. The standard bibliography of Taylor is Louise Wade, *Graham Taylor: Pioneer for Social Justice, 1851-1938* (Chicago: University of Chicago Press, 1964).

10. Andrew Harold Walsh, "For Our City's Welfare: Building a Protestant Establishment in Late Nineteenth Century Hartford" (Ph.D. diss., Harvard University, 1996).

Taylor threw himself into his professorship in earnest. In addition to founding Chicago Commons, a settlement house, to help train his students, he developed courses in religious sociology. This was no mean undertaking. In addition to the usual labors of teaching, Taylor had to develop his own list of books and other educational resources. In an 1894 article, "Sociological Training of the Ministry," he admitted that the literary resources available to him were slight: "Small though the beginnings of a distinctively Christian sociological literature may be, they indicate the rise of a mighty social movement within the churches, which, while quite unrecognized, and hardly conscious of its own existence as yet, is deep, pervasive, intensely practical, eager to learn, and destined to prevail. It is already ordaining the ministry to new service."[11] Taylor was by no means an ordinary pedagogue. His classes were marked by his and his students' reflections on their experience and by far-reaching discussions that often seemed to follow their own lead. But the freewheeling style did not prevent Taylor from an acute analysis of the problems of teaching his new discipline. In the sociological training of the ministry, he made seven suggestions for the development of a comprehensive program:

1. To establish departments of sociology in seminaries. For Taylor, sociology was the equal of the older theological disciplines and deserved a place in the seminary that was their equal. At the time, this was an audacious claim. The theological curriculum was oriented toward either historical studies or normative studies. In contrast, Taylor's proposal would have focused at least part of the curriculum on the present and its needs.
2. Fieldwork as a social laboratory. For Taylor, this meant far more than supervised experience. He believed that one could learn about society and social issues only by studying, in effect, human documents. Observation and experiment were mandatory.
3. Library equipment for the study. The inadequacy of seminary libraries was a serious problem, particularly when one stepped outside the biblical and historical fields. The need for the proper resources to teach was a constant theme in Taylor's writings.
4. Real expertise. Taylor, like many early teachers of social science, was a largely self-educated person. As an educator, however, he had a deep appreciation for schools and for directed education. Interestingly enough, he believed that teachers needed leaves to conduct the research needed to teach effectively. Like other progressives, he believed in the "expert," the

11. Graham Taylor, "Sociological Training of the Ministry," in *Christianity Practically Applied,* vol. 2 (New York: Barker and Taylor, 1894), p. 401.

person with extraordinary knowledge in an area, who could advise others. The expert was an increasingly important figure in legislative halls, and the new magazines often featured articles by experts on this or that aspect of contemporary life.[12]

5. Cooperation between seminaries and colleges in the preparation of sociologically sensitive ministers. Like other seminary educators at the time, Taylor was deeply concerned with the place of the college and of general education. Before 1870 the college had largely been concerned with the transmission of the classics, but that educational world had passed. The study of Greek and even of Latin was in decline, and the present-day liberal arts curriculum was being formed. Taylor hoped that social science would have a place in that emerging curriculum so that a student could use the advanced faculties of the seminary to build on earlier social training.[13]
6. "The use of the church as the center of social unity and the agency of the broadest social service." Taylor believed that the church was the central organization in human life, and he never departed from his confidence that the church was the best way to approach social problems and their solutions.
7. "Use of university extension methods." The late nineteenth century saw a variety of experiments in the delivery of educational materials, which were often described under the rubric of university extension. These included classes in nontraditional locations, such as churches or rural public schools, and forms, such as correspondence courses and public lectures on various subjects. Taylor, like many other progressives, saw such programs as a democratization of education that made learning more available to average people.

Taylor's suggestions were an application of progressivism to education. The key to his thinking about his new discipline can be found in three central educational ideals. First, Taylor accepted the educational and professional gains made by the new scholarly disciplines. From one perspective the new disci-

12. The word "expert" comes from the same root as "experience." The expert was the person who had experience in an area. Expertise and experience-centered learning were two sides of a single coin for Taylor.

13. The nature of undergraduate study has remained very fluid through the twentieth century with the B.A.–B.S. program being capable of many interpretations and emphases. Taylor's hope that the seminary could be a graduate school of social science as it had earlier been a graduate school for classical religious literature was not adopted, even by the most modernistic institutions.

plines were an effective way to secure human and intellectual resources for teaching and learning, and Christian sociology needed those resources to make an impact on the ministry. Just as the most creative work in the older theological disciplines was inspired by their teachers' participation in larger scholarly communities, so Christian sociology needed to create its own community of expert scholars. This community needed to be open to those outside the discipline, such as those with special knowledge of settlement houses, and to develop and make available an extensive literature on the subject. One of the marks of an established discipline was its possession of its own "canon" of works that the informed scholars in an area acknowledged as exemplary. In 1900 Taylor published *A Syllabus in Biblical Sociology,* which outlined both the methods and basic works in the field. Second, the teaching of Christian sociology had to take place outside the classroom as well as in it. Taylor believed that students could learn about social reform and social involvement only by actually becoming involved in the task. His use of the term "laboratory" was not an unconscious imitation of the physical sciences. Taylor believed that one could learn about social processes only by a combination of observation and analysis similar to that in a scientific laboratory. Fieldwork, as a means of acquiring both knowledge and skill, was essential. Both colleges and churches had an important role to play in this training, as did experts with their own specialties. The use of university extension methods was of course another way of expanding the community.

Taylor knew that his proposed program was visionary. But he had seen sociology become an increasingly important part of the curriculum. In the 1880s it was usually taught in seminaries by a lecturer who was invited to campus for a specific purpose. The next stage, first taken at schools like Andover and Yale, was to offer elective courses that individual students might find helpful in their personal preparation for ministry. Although a few schools followed a different order, such as Hartford where sociology was required in 1881, the next stage for most schools was the development of a required course and the appointment of a regular faculty member to teach the discipline. In 1894 there were full professors, for instance, at both Yale and Chicago. In 1896 *Lend-a-Hand* magazine listed the following programs:

Chicago had thirteen sociological electives.
Hartford had a department of sociology.
Harvard Divinity School had one course on ethics and the social question.
Union had ten courses.
Yale had two courses.
Andover, Newton, Meadville, and Bangor had lectureships.

Perhaps more important, Taylor and other advocates of the social sciences seem to have won their larger point that social training was essential to a modern understanding of the ministry. In 1907 George Foote Moore, one of the most thoughtful advocates of change in theological education, told his fellow Congregational ministers: "The education of the modern minister must therefore include not merely the knowledge of man in his state of sin and need of salvation, but of the world which is to be saved; sociology, social psychology and social ethics must have their place beside anthropology and individual psychology and ethics, in the plan of study."[14] Indeed, the use of social science as part of a theological method would continue as a feature of many seminaries into the 1930s, and even thereafter such influential movements within theological education as the rural church movement often relied heavily on sociological methods of study. The seminaries themselves would use the survey as a way of examining their own work and proposing constructive reforms of theological education itself.

The advocates of Christian sociology had an almost touching confidence in facts and scientific reasoning. As David Danborn commented, many Christian social leaders mixed Christian and scientific reform concepts rather promiscuously, and they "integrated concepts of empiricism and efficiency into the messages with little difficulty."[15] Like other progressives, Christian sociologists assumed that once people knew the truth about social conditions, they would be willing to make the changes needed to correct those evils. This model was not as utopian as it might seem to some present-day Americans. After all, the discovery of the germ theory of disease had resulted in new standards of urban cleanliness, and some traditional American plagues, such as yellow fever, were almost eradicated. The public dung heaps were gradually removed, at least from urban areas, and piped water replaced the hodgepodge of wells, springs, and fountains that had supplied the cities. Whatever their faults, such muckraking works as *The Jungle* did create climates of opinion that supported pure food and drug laws. In our own day, a strong public education program on the transmission of HIV has contributed to a substantial slowing of the rate of infection.

Further, the understanding of Christian sociology as the presentation of the facts to an essentially moral public fit neatly into the American understanding of Christian witness. In a nation where church and state are separate, the

14. George Foote Moore, "The Training of the Modern Minister: Address before the National Congregational Council," Hartford Seminary Record, 1907, p. 37.

15. David B. Danborn, *"The World of Hope": Progressives and the Struggle for an Ethical Public Life* (Philadelphia: Temple University Press, 1987), cited in Robert T. Handy, *Undermined Establishment: Church-State Relations in America, 1880-1920* (Princeton: Princeton University Press, 1991), p. 140.

primary way that religious organizations can affect society is through persuasion. The Federal Council of Churches was able to intervene in many labor crises, in part because people trusted the council to provide them with the facts of the case.

II. Social Settlements

Although Taylor did not organize his social settlement, Chicago Commons, until comparatively late in his career, the social settlement provides an excellent example of his approach to theological education. Basically, the settlement house was a large residence (although some, such as Jane Addams's famed Hull House, were substantial buildings) located in a poor section of town. Middle-class people, especially students, would live for a period in a settlement, observing social conditions, and often providing some social services for the community. Settlement houses were sponsored by many different types of institutions, although the majority were affiliated with colleges, universities, or missionary training schools. Between 1886 and 1911, 17,500 students spent time in a social settlement. Although some of the schools establishing settlement houses, such as Louisville's Southern Baptist Theological Seminary, were all-male or virtually so, many settlement houses primarily attracted women residents and directed much of their work toward women. The settlement houses maintained by Andover, Union, and Southern Baptist seminaries, for instance, had a majority of women residents throughout their history. Interestingly, the women at the Women's Missionary Union Training School in Louisville did not spend the night at the Southern Baptist Theological Seminary settlement there but commuted to the settlement by trolley each day.[16]

The settlement house was designed to serve two functions. First, it provided, more or less successfully, a number of social services for the poor. These ranged from the provision of pure milk (an important service at a time when not all cattle were inspected for TB) and some clothing, to classes on everything from sewing and citizenship to child raising, nursing, and hygiene.[17] While

16. For women's interpretation of the social gospel, see below, pp. 176-78. Women were deeply involved in the social movement and avidly followed the writings of such men as Shailer Mathews, Walter Rauschenbusch, and others. In many denominations women's temperance and missionary organizations were perhaps more open to elements of the social gospel than their male counterparts.

17. What was called "domestic science" or, later, "home economics" was an important part of the progressive movement as it influenced the American home and the lives of many women. Women were, of course, the primary caregivers for most minor health emergencies,

some today might fault the settlement house for its determination to Americanize the immigrant, often at the expense of the inherited culture, we must remember that this same approach to the problem of the immigrants was followed by the very successful parochial school movement as well as numerous charities supported by assimilated German (Reform) Jews. It is also important to notice that many of these services were in fact teaching survival skills to people in a harsh and often unforgiving environment. Other aspects of the programs, such as musical evenings, were part of America's own newly discovered interest in music and art and an attempt to share pleasures that middle-class America was discovering at the turn of the century.[18]

But as valuable as the social services they provided might have been, settlement houses were also educational institutions. Young men and young women were to move into an immigrant or poor section of a city and experience firsthand the actual social situation. To use the language of later anthropology, they were to be "participant observers," who learned both by acute observation of the situation and by sharing some of the experiences of their subjects. The founders of influential settlements, such as Taylor (Chicago Commons), Jane Addams (Hull House), or Robert Woods and William J. Tucker (Andover House), saw them as centers for the social training of the ministry. Indeed, they could serve as graduate schools for people concerned with social ministries. When Scarritt, a Methodist Episcopal missionary training program for women, invited Mabel Howell to teach sociology in 1900, she visited prominent settlement houses to prepare for her work.

> During this year allotted for investigation and study, time was taken to visit theological seminaries to discover what they were attempting along the line of sociological instruction. This was a very depressing experience. I did not find one of these major theological schools which included Sociology in the scope of their teaching program, or indeed thought it essential. More help-

---

and their work as homemakers made them the primary people responsible for such important aspects of life as healthy food and sanitation. The new scientific approach to housekeeping was taught in a variety of ways: in high school classes, in some women's colleges (which often had domestic chores as part of their programs!), and through advertisements and magazine articles. In this sense the settlement house did not attempt to substitute American customs for European ones. In fact, the traditional homemaking patterns of both were, not surprisingly, almost identical. Rather, it tried to introduce "reforms" into immigrant life that were just taking root in the urban home and only gradually spreading to the American countryside.

18. Present-day Americans, who have come to expect a considerable democratization of culture, need to remember how class-stratified art and music were at the turn of the century. Nor was this stratification a merely American phenomenon. Concerts and operas were upper middle-class and aristocratic entertainment in Europe as well as America.

> ful was the time spent in visiting such social institutions as were then arising. In Chicago, I visited Hull House and the Chicago Commons, and caught a glimpse of the creative Christian spirits of Jane Addams and Graham Taylor. In New York, I visited the Jacob Riis settlement in the Hebrew section of that city. I lived for a short time on the East Side of New York in the Jewish quarter. I saw the beginnings of St. George's Institutional church in New York. By this time, the new teacher of sociology was "rearing to go." Four courses were outlined for the new department: Problems of American Society, Poverty and charities; Crime and its Punishment; and the Church and Social Service.[19]

Social settlements also had another educational mission. They were designed to educate the emotions and personal commitment of their residents. If young people learned nothing else from their time in a settlement, they learned to identify with the poor in new ways, and thus were incorporated into the larger movement. Thus, the settlements could provide an intense personal experience, not altogether different from the Wesleyan belief in an emotional call to the ministry, that might inform a person's life course.

Walter Rauschenbusch did not have his experience of social awakening in a settlement house, but his experience was typical of what the settlement house hoped might happen to its residents. Rauschenbusch was the son of a successful seminary teacher who had played a major role in the creation of the German department of Rochester Seminary. After flirting with foreign missions, Rauschenbusch accepted a call to a small German Baptist church in Hell's Kitchen. Rauschenbusch entered his ministry a convinced evangelical. He spent part of a summer, for instance, in one of Moody's summer meetings at Northfield, and he was noted as the translator of Ira Sankey's hymns into German. He remained disappointed that the churches did not demonstrate the "glow of spiritual fervor" that ought to set the Christian apart from the world.[20] As a result of his experiences as a pastor, however, he realized that "when I began to apply my ideas to the conditions that I found, I discovered that they didn't fit." The young pastor's inner turmoil was ended by a religious experience of great power.

19. Mabel Katherine Howell, *Women and the Kingdom: Fifty Years of Kingdom Building by the Women of the Methodist Episcopal Church, South, 1878-1928* (Nashville: Cokesbury Press, 1928), p. 105. See also John Patrick McDowell, *The Social Gospel in the South: The Women's Home Missionary Movement in the Protestant Episcopal Church, South, 1886-1939* (Baton Rouge: Louisiana State University Press, 1982).

20. Walter Rauschenbusch, "The New Evangelism," in Robert T. Handy, *The Social Gospel* (New York: Oxford University Press, 1966), p. 327.

> So Christ's conception of the kingdom of God came to me as a new revelation. Here was the idea and purpose that had dominated the mind of the master himself. All his teachings center about it. His life was given up to it. His death was suffered for it. . . .
>
> When the Kingdom of God dominated our landscape, the perspective of life shifted into a new alignment, I felt a new security in my social impulses. The spiritual authority of Jesus Christ would have been sufficient to offset the weight of all the doctors, and now I knew that I had history on my side. But in addition I found this new conception of the purpose of Christianity was strangely satisfying. It responded to all the old and all the new elements of my religious life. The saving of the lost, the teaching of the young, the pastoral care of the poor and frail, the quickening of starved intellects, the study of the Bible, church union, political reform, the reorganization of the industrial system, international peace — it was all covered by the one aim of the reign of God on earth.[21]

Such experiences were very important for many involved in social Christianity. The social and psychological conditions that had contributed to the intense spiritual experiences of the First and Second Great Awakenings had passed, but the yearning for such experiences of personal integration and wholeness was as intense, if not more intense, than ever. Moody, for instance, never had a classical conversion experience, and, like Rauschenbusch, his most intense experience of faith was through Christian activism. The type of sanctification common in Keswick circles — a sense of being sustained by God — likewise was a similar experience of being sustained by Christ through an active style of life.

The comparison between the social awakening and the Holiness movement has another advantage. For both holiness advocates and social gospel advocates, there was a sense in which their social awakening was something added to a deep personal faith. In one of the most moving passages in turn-of-the-century theological literature, Rauschenbusch wrote:

> Personal religion has a supreme value for its own sake, not merely as a feeder of social morality, but as the highest unfolding of life itself, as the blossoming of our spiritual nature. Spiritual regeneration is the most important fact in any life history. A living experience of God is the crowning knowledge attributable to a human mind. Each one of us needs the redemptive power of religion for his own sake, for on the tiny stage of the human soul all the vast world tragedy of good and evil is reenacted. In the best

21. Walter Rauschenbusch, quoted in "Walter Rauschenbusch," in Handy, *The Social Gospel*, p. 256.

> social order that is conceivable men will still smolder with lust and ambition, and be lashed by hate and jealousy as with the whip of a slave driver.[22]

The Christian settlement houses hoped for a "conversion" of "conversion." People who had been to the mountaintop were to come back, like Moses, with a reborn vision of what needed to be thought and done. Rauschenbusch, in fact, used the language of revival to describe the movement: "We are having a revival of religion. There is a big camp meeting going on from Maine to Oregon, and if anyone has not come out on the Lord's side, I invite him to come and get salvation. It would be a spiritual disaster to be left unsaved while others are moving up to a new level of religion, moral insight, and manhood. This is true of denominations as well as individuals. . . . God is today writing a flaming message of social righteousness, and you and I must learn to read it."[23]

One of the limits of the settlement house was that the student had to live there in order to reap its benefits. Many theological students were financially pressed and supported their advanced study through various combinations of outside employment — usually but not exclusively church work — loans, scholarships, and the like. There was little time for settlement work, and in fact, even those settlement houses administered by seminaries were often primarily staffed by women from nearby colleges or universities. Nicholas Paine Gilman of Meadville Theological Seminary tried another pattern. He invited students to join him on a two-week trip to New York City over the Christmas holiday. During this journey students visited the most important social agencies, Ellis Island, and the University Settlement. If the trip provided less data than the settlement, it had a similar impact as a spur to social awakening.[24]

The settlement houses were largely but not exclusively an upper middle-class phenomenon. But the type of educational experience they supported often cut across social and denominational lines. Missionary enthusiast A. J. Gordon deliberately located his Missionary Training School in the Fenway area

22. Walter Rauschenbusch, *Christianizing the Social Order* (New York: Macmillan, 1912), p. 104. In my opinion, this volume is the best and clearest of Rauschenbusch's works. It was published before the tragedy of the world war, which loomed so large in his *Theology for the Social Gospel.* His sense of the link between liberty and faith, an old American theme, is much stronger here than elsewhere. In particular, the book makes clear the distinction between the kingdom of God and a Christianized social order. It is noted that a Christianized social order encourages bad people to do good things while an unchristianized social order encourages good people to do bad things.

23. Quoted in Donald K. Gorrell, *The Age of Social Responsibility: The Social Gospel in the Progressive Era, 1900-1920* (Macon, Ga.: Mercer University Press, 1988), p. 194.

24. See Charles Howard Hopkins, *The Rise of the Social Gospel in American Protestantism* (New Haven: Yale University Press; London: Oxford University Press, H. Milford, 1940), p. 169.

of Boston so that his students could learn to conduct city missions and become aware of urban conditions. The original program involved significant field education that forced prospective students to use the neighborhood as a laboratory. In a similar way, Moody Bible Institute sought an inner-city location so that its students would be immersed in the problems of the metropolis and learn their work under less than ideal conditions. One of the more interesting variations on this theme was the "homes" maintained by such holiness churches as the Church of God. Their New York missionary home described its work in these words: "This home offers an excellent place for the training and instruction of workers whom God has called. No prescribed course of lessons is given, but . . . a number of established ministers and missionaries are always here, ready to give the young worker the benefit of their varied experiences in gospel work, expound the Scriptures, and present the best methods for the study of the Bible, how to win souls and conduct meetings in the most effectual way."[25] Holiness homes characteristically featured healing as one of their ministries and sought to promote the physical as well as the moral and spiritual health of their communities.

The settlement house ideal of combining residence, study, and experience was an influential expression of progressive American Christianity. Little wonder that variations on this theme were found across the emerging theological spectrum that separated (to some extent) liberal and conservative Christians. For some, the changing context of ministry in the new urban areas demanded some such way to combine the study of the new conditions, the practice of ministry and Christian service, and lived experience. For others that same combination seemed the best way to ensure an effective evangelism that met people where they were and brought them to Christ in that context. Both were anchored to the city as a place of learning.

III. Another Tradition of Christian Social Thought

At the same time that Christian sociology was beginning, another approach to Christianity and the social order was also arising. At the time few people would have distinguished the two, and any attempt to make them too separate would be historically distorting. The two converged in their common interest in the cities, in their confidence that reform was both necessary and possible, and in the advocate's identification of social issues as the spearhead for the home mis-

25. Quoted in Barry L. Callen, *Guide of Body and Mind: The Story of Anderson University* (Anderson, Ind.: Anderson University and Warner Press, 1992), p. 23.

sionary work of the day. Yet they also differed in their emphasis. Although a present-day observer might marvel at the amount of theology in the sociology of Taylor or Henry Holt of Chicago, much of their work clearly was entered on the social scientific side of the ledger. In contrast, the type of thinking we find in Francis Greenwood Peabody and Walter Rauschenbusch represents the attempt to do a social theology more in conjunction with the classical aims of Christian theology.

Francis Greenwood Peabody, although an ordained Unitarian minister, was a person whose life and thought were shaped by his participation in the emerging university. Charles Eliot appointed him to teach at Harvard as part of his program to modernize the divinity school. Like many contemporary university intellectuals, Peabody had studied in Germany, interestingly enough under the more evangelical August Tolluck, and had returned home with a passion for study. He began lecturing in the divinity school at Harvard in 1880, offering one of the first courses in social ethics, and Eliot promoted him to Parkman Professor of Christian Theology the next year. In 1886 Eliot moved him into the university department of philosophy and appointed him Plummer Professor of Christian Morals. In his new position he clearly had the whole university community under his care, and his classes were as popular with undergraduates as with divinity students. In 1900 he became dean of the divinity school and served in that capacity until 1906 when he became professor of social ethics in Harvard University in one of the nation's few endowed departments of social ethics. By 1903 he had begun to collect materials for a social museum that eventually housed one of the largest American collections of materials on social reform.[26]

What made Peabody's position distinctive was his belief that the social issue was not simply a contemporary question. Hence, he wanted to go beyond a bare recital of social conditions and the resources needed to work with those problems to a systematic exposition that "philosophically [provided] illustrations of the principles which control and interpret human life." His use of the case study method was an inductive way of illuminating the larger human condition, much as traditional Christian casuistry had struggled with the larger questions of Christian existence by the careful examination of particulars. This belief that the particulars bore the general would also mark the work of his successor, Richard Cabot, who was fascinated by the possibilities of clinical work as a source of insight about the human condition.

26. For the larger context of Peabody's work, see David B. Potts, "Social Ethics at Harvard, 1881-1931: A Study in Academic Activism," in *Social Sciences at Harvard, 1860-1920*, ed. Paul Buck (Cambridge: Harvard University Press, 1965).

The theologian who best exemplified this approach, however, was the very different Walter Rauschenbusch.[27] Rauschenbusch began his career at the Second German Baptist Church in the Hell's Kitchen area of New York City, and he remained deeply affected by that experience throughout his life. The son of a seminary professor, Rauschenbusch had an active mind that was always searching for new perspectives on the world. Although many Americans studied in Germany, Rauschenbusch, the son of an immigrant, was thoroughly at home in both cultures. His first experience of Germany had been as a young gymnasium student at Gütersloh in Westphalia. He returned for a period of university study in the 1890s, in the midst of his Hell's Kitchen pastorate. His loss of hearing forced him to change vocations, and after a brief period in the German department of Rochester Seminary, President Augustus Strong invited him to become professor of church history. Although he taught a course on social issues, this was never his field. The vast bulk of his teaching comprised a more or less standard survey of church history, a course that forced him to pay close attention to the way change had been effected in the past.

It also brought Rauschenbusch into intellectual contact with the influential Ritschlian school. Albrecht Ritschl (1822-89), the school's founder, began as a historian concerned with the problems of the New Testament and early church, and throughout his career maintained an active interest in history. His *History of Pietism,* for instance, remains one of the classical studies of a post-Reformation movement. His successors, particularly Adolf von Harnack, continued this tradition. Harnack was of course one of the seminal thinkers of the age. Harnack was very conservative on questions of biblical criticism, and he developed his perspective in his *History of Dogma* in seven volumes. This work did not merely summarize the facts about the development of Christian thinking about the Trinity and Christology — after all, much of the factual material had been known for some time — but offered a historically credible account of how those doctrines evolved. To oversimplify a very complex discussion, Harnack argued that Christian theology developed in tandem with the larger Christian mission. Thus, Christianity entered into new territories and was accepted by people with different cultural traditions, theologians progressively modifying its message to meet the current missionary challenge. Over nearly half a millennium, Christianity had absorbed so much of the culture of the Hellenistic world that its essence was almost obscured by the material that its leaders had pressed into service to make its message intelligible to the Hellenis-

27. For a more detailed comparison, see Jacob H. Dorn, "The Social Gospel and Socialism: A Comparison of the Thought of Francis Greenwood Peabody, Washington Gladden, and Walter Rauschenbusch," *Church History* 62 (Mar. 1993): 82-100.

tic world. Equally important, the account was smooth and seamless. Harnack had no need for a "Constantinian revolution" or any other specific event to explain the course of events.

Rauschenbusch, like many other historians, found Harnack's account compelling.[28] But even more than the content of Harnack's argument, Rauschenbusch was fascinated by its morphology. If past forms of Christian orthodoxy were understood as responses to the Christian mission, then present forms of Christian orthodoxy should also be responses to the contemporary mission of the church. A theology that began with the mission to the poor, the immigrant, and the lost of the cities would be very different from one that began with the assumption that past theology was a perfect treasure to be handed down from generation to generation.

The model of a theology shaped by cultural forces was important to Rauschenbusch in two ways. First, it enabled him to point to theological change as a normative part of Christian experience. Naturally, as the world changed, the church's proclamation had to change. Secondly, it enabled him to cut away elements of the Christian tradition that were no longer useful by comparing the tradition with Jesus' own proclamation of the kingdom of God. A sound understanding of the situation, thus, was the key to significant movement forward. At the beginning of *A Theology for the Social Gospel,* Rauschenbusch puts his theological presupposition in a pithy aphorism: "We have a social gospel. We need a systematic theology large enough to match it and vital enough to back it."[29] The affirmation of the social gospel in this famed passage has two foci. (1) It points to the proclamation of the kingdom of God by Christ. In that sense the affirmation is one of the continuing power and validity of the earliest Christian message. This is the critical edge. (2) The world of contemporary Christian experience indicates the cultural and theologically shaping power of the social question. In that sense the social gospel, like the early Christian expansion into the world of Hellenism, is part of the church's natural accommodation to its environment. As Rauschenbusch was fond of saying, the social gospel represented the "new evangelism," the new missionary imperative of the day. The Men and Religion Forward Movement demonstrated the power of this approach:

28. One of the most difficult tasks in interpreting Rauschenbusch is that while his personal faith was deeply influenced by biblical criticism, historical research, and such contemporary scientific movements as evolution, his writings (and one presumes much of his teaching) were far less visibly liberal. His passion for preaching, thus, often hid some of his theological presuppositions.

29. Walter Rauschenbusch, *A Theology for the Social Gospel* (1917; reprint, New York: Abingdon, 1960).

> The Men and Religion Forward Movement of 1911 and 1912 is another evidence of the ascendancy of social Christianity. It was the most comprehensive evangelistic movement ever undertaken in this country and was planned with consummate care and ability. . . . All the varied departments of the movement found their spiritual center and unity in the idea of the Kingdom of God on earth, which is the doctrine of social Christianity. When the movement began to be tried out, it grew increasingly plain that it was the trumpet call of the social gospel which rallied the audiences and brought men under moral and religious conviction.[30]

In a similar way the Methodist church, perhaps the most evangelistic of the major denominations, adopted its social creed in 1908. For many Methodists the social creed was a continuation of the church's quest for the spread of practical holiness as a means of evangelism.[31] The most successful ecumenical organization to date, the Federal Council of Churches, was organized around the principles of social Christianity.

It was this very success that suggested the need for thorough reformation of the church's proclamation. When exposed to the contemporary interest in social change, traditional Christian affirmations often seemed "puny and inadequate."[32] The way forward was to examine theology from the perspective of the social gospel. For Rauschenbusch this involved above all a recognition of the social nature of sin and of salvation. His analysis of sinfulness provides an excellent understanding of his approach. Rauschenbusch has no doubt that the doctrine of original sin has much to teach the contemporary church. But he notes that the doctrine of the biological transmission of sin fails the test of our knowledge of the world. Science had gone far toward demystifying the process of reproduction, and evolution had shown that human sexuality was part of a larger pattern of human development. For us, the universality of sin is best expressed in the social transmission of sinfulness from one generation to another. For Rauschenbusch, as for most progressive Christians before the Great De-

30. Rauschenbusch, quoted in Gorrell, *Age of Social Responsibility*, p. 154. The evangelistic success of the social gospel was very important to Rauschenbusch and other advocates of the social gospel. In this case the social gospel succeeded where traditional evangelism had failed: it helped to reverse, at least partially, the retreat of males from the churches that was so evident in Victorian America and in contemporary Europe.

31. The Methodist decision to adopt the social creed significantly was not a product of the influence of the seminaries on the church. Less than a fourth of the ministers of the church were seminary graduates at the time. Since the Methodist seminaries became leaders in Christian sociology and religious education, it is more likely that the influence flowed from the churches to the seminaries.

32. Rauschenbusch, *A Theology*, p. 6.

pression, alcohol was among the best illustrations of evil, and he noted that what had sustained the use of alcohol was social habit. "In the wine-drinking countries wine is praised in poetry and song. The most charming social usages are connected with its use. It is the chief reliance for entertainment and pleasure. Laughter is attached to mild intoxication provided a gentleman carries his drink well and continues to behave politely. Families take more pride in their wine cellars than in the tombs of their ancestors. Young men are proud of the amount of wine and beer they can imbibe and of the learning which they refuse to imbibe."[33] In other words, alcoholism was transmitted by a culture, not by a fault in human nature. In principle, then, it could be changed as other aspects of culture had been changed. Other great evils, such as war — which was raging in 1917 — were also embedded in human culture. Because sin is transmitted culturally, those forces that pervert social institutions form a kingdom of evil that stands over and against the kingdom of God. The corruption of culture happens perversely, almost ironically. A trust is formed to "steady prices and to get away from antiquated competition" and ends by "evading or purchasing legislation."[34] The church begins in the teachings of Jesus and, yet, "the most disastrous backsliding in history was the deterioration of the Church. Long before the Reformation the condition of the Church had become the most serious social question of the age."[35] Again sin has a dual quality: it is given and reinforced culturally; it can be limited also by the intelligent use of cultural forces.

This brings us to an important distinction in Rauschenbusch's theology. He believed it was possible to Christianize the social order. What he meant by this was not utopian. "Even a Christian social order cannot mean perfection. As long as men are flesh and blood the world can be neither sinless nor painless."[36] In fact, "every child is born a kicking little egotist" who has to be socialized into each society he or she enters later in life. Rather, Christianization was a high but attainable good: "An unchristian social order can be known by the fact that it makes good men do bad things. It tempts, defeats, drains, and degrades, and leaves men stunned, cowed, and shamed in their manhood. A Christian social order makes bad men do good things. It sets high aims, steadies the vagrant impulses of the weak, trains the powers of the young, and is felt by all as an uplifting force."[37] By these criteria marriage was a Christianization of sexual relationships; sound business laws were a Christianization of economic life; and democracy — almost a manifestation of the Holy for Rauschenbusch and other

33. Rauschenbusch, *A Theology*, p. 63.
34. Rauschenbusch, *A Theology*, p. 72.
35. Rauschenbusch, *A Theology*, p. 73.
36. Rauschenbusch, *Christianizing the Social Order*, p. 126.
37. Rauschenbusch, *Christianizing the Social Order*, p. 127.

progressives — was a Christianization of government. The family provided Rauschenbusch with a potent example. Families had always contained some social good in that they provided protection for the young, but slavery and exploitation marked the earliest families. Not one of the families in the Old Testament "shows us a good home from the modern point of view." In fact, the Old Testament patriarchs were so primitive that "no self-respecting church could retain them as members if they did the same today." What had happened was a progressive development of the family to a higher level.

> The history of the family tells of a slow decrease of despotism and exploitation. Gradually wives were no longer bought outright. The right of divorce was hedged about. The wife gained an assured legal status and some property rights. When polygamy ceased and adultery was considered a crime in man as well as in woman, the basis was laid for equality between man and wife. But only within the last hundred years has woman risen toward acknowledged equality with swift and decisive steps. Most other countries are still far from conceding what our American women have now learned to take as a matter of course. The present agitation for woman's suffrage is one of the final steps of this ascent. The suffrage will abolish one of the last remnants of patriarchal autocracy by giving woman a direct relation to the political organism of society, instead of allowing man to exercise her political rights for her.[38]

In other words, the purpose of Christianization is not the same as "building the kingdom of God." Even were humankind to complete the work of Christianization, evil and vice would remain, and humankind would still stand in need of redemption by Christ. The kingdom is, thus, always a transcendent ideal — something is present, yet not completely, that stands over and against our present situation and calls us to something higher and nobler. But this redemption will not be a rescue from hell: much of traditional evangelism had rested on "self-interest on a higher level," and the very appeal to come to Christ had been marked by selfishness and sin.[39] Instead, redemption led people to a Christlike vision of God.

38. Rauschenbusch, *Christianizing the Social Order,* p. 131.

39. Rauschenbusch, *A Theology,* p. 108. Rauschenbusch's observation of the degree to which much of the evangelism of his day had become corrupted into a somewhat crude "offer that you cannot refuse" from a heavenly tyrant was acute. Much of nineteenth-century American theology had revolved around the question of how much free will people had in order to accept or reject God's "offer" of salvation, and the controversy over second probation was almost completely consumed by this anthropological argument. The Calvinist sense of unholy man before a God of infinite holiness had almost completely receded from American thought.

Walter Rauschenbusch's work had a twofold impact on theological education. First, his work set a standard for future reflection on the theological meaning of social life. More than any of his fellow social gospelers, Rauschenbusch demonstrated that the contemporary situation had rich implications for Christian thought itself. It was not only that the church was challenged by these new developments — and Rauschenbusch was painfully aware that many good people had left Christianity for an alternative social faith — but that this very modernity made possible a new apprehension of the gospel that could deservingly hold its head up among the theologies of the past. Rauschenbusch remains one of the few theologians from that period that can still be read with profit. But Rauschenbusch understood his project also as the Christianization of theology and of theological education. In *A Theology for the Social Gospel* he wrote:

> Can theology expand to meet the growth of faith? The biblical studies have responded to the spiritual hunger aroused by the social gospel. The historical interpretation of the Bible has put the religious personalities, their spiritual struggles, their growth, and their utterances into social connection with the community life of which they were part. This method of interpretation has given back the Bible to men of modernized intelligence and has made it the feeder of faith in the social gospel. The studies of "practical theology" are all in a process of rejuvenation and expansion in order to create competent leadership for the Church, and most of these changes are due to the rise of new ideals created by the social gospel.[40]

His proposal that theology itself be rethought, of course, was neither new nor original. His suggestion that the social needs of the hour might provide its inspiration was. In this enterprise his successors have been legion. In addition to the Niebuhrs, neither of whom ever escaped his influence, feminist, African American, and liberation theologians have joined him in a quest for a theology and theological education equal to their own confidence in the rightness of their cause.

IV. A Gendered Theology?

In many ways the social gospel was the progressive movement at prayer, and it enjoyed all the benefits and suffered from all the defects of that larger social and political movement. Theodore Roosevelt, for instance, was a friend of many so-

40. Rauschenbusch, *A Theology,* p. 6.

cial gospel advocates who found his confidence in reform and his aggressive masculinity attractive.[41] At least part of the new evangelism was the determination of its leaders to reverse the Victorian tendency of identifying religion with femininity and the passive and to enlist men in a faith that stressed action and social change. Those who advocated the social gospel tended to advocate the emphasis on masculine Christianity, and vice versa. The YMCA, perhaps the most important single Protestant institution at the time, exemplified the commitment to both the new evangelism and muscular Christianity.[42] Perhaps the best example of the link between progressivism, the new masculinity, and the social gospel was the Men and Religion Forward Movement, a national attempt to enlist men in religious causes that used the social gospel as the bait to attract them to its meetings. Billy Sunday, at least before the 1920s, was fond of making his invitations in terms of a willingness to do right, to avoid alcohol, and to be a man. There were clear parallels between the renewed Protestant emphasis on foreign missions and the new imperialism advocated by Roosevelt and others. And while the social gospel did not disappear with the decline of the progressive movement after the defeat of Woodrow Wilson's League of Nations, Paul Carter was correct in observing: "For while the older social gospel had been in harmony with its secular milieu, Progressivism, the newer Social Gospel was in the deepest disharmony with its setting, normalcy. And it is a stubborn fact that even the most wholehearted opposition to a social environment necessitates some adaptation to it."[43]

One would make a serious mistake in the interpretation of the social gospel and women were one to confine the discussion to the handful of women, such as Vida Scudder or, later, Georgia Harkness, who wrote social theology. The social gospel was always broader in its appeal and influence than social theology

41. Gail Bederman, *Manhood and Civilization: A Cultural History of Gender and Race in the United States, 1880-1917* (Chicago and London: University of Chicago Press, 1995), p. 183, has highlighted Roosevelt's relationship with various social gospel leaders.

42. See "The Son of Man and God the Father: The Social Gospel and Victorian Masculinity," in *Meanings for Masculinity*, ed. Mark C. Carnes and Clyde Griffen (Chicago: University of Chicago Press, 1990), p. 67: "Some of the young men who helped redefine masculinity were also the authors of a restatement of Protestantism: the social gospel. Social gospelers reacted against the norms of individual responsibility and self-control because as young men, they had failed to live up to these ideals themselves. By the 1880s and 1890s they recognized that it was as difficult to save oneself spiritually and morally as to make a success of oneself in the economy. The feminized version of Protestantism available to them offered some comfort as they struggled to succeed, but it did not satisfy their longing to emulate and surpass their fathers."

43. Paul A. Carter, *The Decline and Revival of the Social Gospel: Social and Political Liberalism in American Protestant Churches, 1920-1940* (Ithaca, N.Y.: Cornell University Press, 1954), p. 30.

was, and part of the excitement of the movement was the number of places it appeared outside of formal theological circles, including the new magazines and the increasingly influential literature produced by the denominations.

If the social gospel often reflected the progressive interest in a new masculinity, it also resonated with some important women's interests. Perhaps the most important of these was prohibition. Women were involved in the prohibition movement for the simple reason that many of the victims of strong drink were women and children who suffered physical, mental, and economic abuse from alcoholic men. Further, these women (and their friends) were aware that traditional moral suasion had not solved the problem: they (or at least their friends) had prayed for the offender, practiced nonresistance, urged faith, and done everything that church and society recommended, and still the beatings did not stop. Prohibition offered one way, at least hopefully, to deal with the problem. But as Emma Willard and other temperance leaders pointed out, prohibition was not the only concern of women. In the large cities prostitution was both common and, whatever the law stated, apparently protected by an unholy coalition of politicians, wealthy people who owned the properties used by prostitutes, and the police. Each of these vested interests profited from the degradation of others, often while piously praising "law and order" or the "family."[44]

Many women were also concerned with the social gospel because of their own experience as urban workers. In the 1880s and 1890s women swarmed into the workplace. New office technology, for instance, encouraged them to become office workers, and the high school's "commercial" programs prepared them for these occupations. Department stores and the public schools were also hiring significant numbers of women. In the South, large numbers of Protestant women and children worked in the textile mills that moved south from New England, and immigrant women in the North were often involved in manufacturing and various kinds of "sweated" and "piecework" employment.

A less obvious but equally important tie between women and the social gospel was the missionary movement, both at home and abroad. Long before religious education became a "women's ghetto" in the churches, missionary work provided women important places of employment and service. Abroad, women served as teachers, as directors of "women's work with women," and as

44. There is a tendency to see the antiprostitution crusades as almost side issues for the social gospel and to confuse them with Victorian prudery about sexual matters. However, this ignores the fact that prostitution, like alcohol, was a business from which many people profited. The antiprostitution crusades were also related to the fear of venereal diseases, especially syphilis, which were epidemic in many American cities. Just as adequate public health laws could require indoor privies, the inspection of restaurants, and the packaging of healthy meat, so public health seemed to demand that prostitution be suppressed as far as possible.

nurses and caregivers. As the foreign missionary movement became more service oriented and less concerned with preaching and conversion, the importance of these women workers grew. Indeed, the rising social interest abroad increased the demand for trained women missionaries to handle the new ministries. The same was true at home. The settlement house, although it did not originate abroad, resembled a late nineteenth-century missionary compound with its various agencies for education, uplift, and evangelism. Although men were involved in the settlement house movement, as they were in foreign missions, both movements had a majority of female workers. Such women as Jane Addams, whose literary talent matched her social concern, kept the concerns of these women workers in the public eye. The deaconess movement, imported from Germany, offered women a structured approach to Christian service, but women also found real employment in the various city missions and other ministries that grew up around urban needs.

If the social gospel represented to some extent a reemphasizing of some of the masculine elements in religion, it was equally important for many women who were seeking church-related vocations outside the home. Unlike preaching and pastoral ministry, which many churches still confined to males, many of the new social ministries at home and abroad were open to both, and some — especially the influential work with women at home and abroad — almost demanded trained women workers.

CHAPTER NINE

Before Fundamentalism: The Educational Dynamics of Dispensationalism

In 1909 former Confederate general Cyrus I. Scofield published the *Scofield Reference Bible.* It was an audacious undertaking. The book itself is an annotated version of the Bible with the notes skillfully located at those places where a reader might naturally have questions. The appendices of the book are likewise filled with the type of information ordinary Bible readers might want at their

---

Since Ernest Sandeen published his almost classic *Roots of Fundamentalism* (Ernest Robert Sandeen, *The Roots of Fundamentalism: British and American Millenarianism, 1800-1930* [Chicago: University of Chicago Press, 1970]), there has been an understandable tendency to interpret dispensational theology from the perspective of one of its consequences, fundamentalism, and to see the early dispensationalists, so to speak, as fundamentalists in the making. While George Marsden, *Fundamentalism and American Culture: The Shaping of Twentieth Century Evangelicalism, 1870-1925* (New York: Oxford University Press, 1980), offered some important correctives to this position, the primary role of dispensationalism remained as a precursor to fundamentalism. The overall point of this interpretation remains useful. Clearly, many, probably the majority, of premillennial dispensationalists migrated toward post–World War I fundamentalism, and many (but not all) fundamentalists in the 1930s and 1940s would have identified themselves with that movement. Yet I am not altogether convinced that the fundamentalist crusade of the 1920s did not change American dispensationalism as much as affirm it. In part, the difference was between dispensationalism as a protest movement and dispensationalism as the theology of protest, but I want to be careful not to overdraw that concept.

Both dispensationalists and fundamentalists have been stereotyped as intolerant crusaders. This is another interpretation I want to bracket, at least for this chapter. Clearly, both dispensationalists and fundamentalists were people of strong views who were not afraid of standing for what they believed, but this has long been characteristic of American religion. If one were to ask, for instance, whether Charles A. Briggs or Reuben Torrey was less tolerant of those with other positions, it would have been a toss-up. Neither man tolerated fools gladly, and Lyman Steward, the oilman who founded the Bible Institute of Los Angeles and contributed

fingertips: lists of the Hebrew kings, a biblical chronology, and a short concordance. Also added are vivid charts interpreting the more difficult prophetic passages. All in all, it is the type of book Sunday school teachers or Christian youth leaders might find a useful addition to their library and a valued aid in Christian witnessing.

Scofield's Bible was, ironically, not really by Scofield at all. Scofield, a friend of Dwight L. Moody, served at various posts in the evangelical movement of the late nineteenth century. He was an effective YMCA secretary, the popular pastor of Hyde Park Congregational Church of Dallas, Texas, and the founder of several Bible schools and missionary organizations. In 1895 he became pastor of the Congregational church in Northfield, Massachusetts, where Moody was a member. Naturally, he was active in the Northfield conferences that Moody held with young people and Christian workers. Further, Scofield was an inveterate attendee at the various Bible and prophecy conferences held throughout the later part of the nineteenth century. Beginning with the Niagara conference in 1875 and continuing both there and, occasionally, in major American cities until the First World War, the Bible and prophecy conferences brought together significant numbers of American evangelicals for Bible study and prayer. The staple of these conferences was the dispensational system of biblical study that provided a holistic interpretation that was easily taught and easily learned.[1] Scofield had demonstrated his mastery of this system in his 1888 *Rightly Dividing the Word of Truth,* but he continued to develop it throughout

heavily to the publication of the *Fundamentals,* was hardly more determined to keep his views before the public than the two Rockefellers, John Sr. and John Jr., who spent massive amounts on first Baptist and then liberal Protestant causes.

It is the intention of this chapter to treat dispensationalism with real respect. I was raised in conservative American Protestantism where this position was common (not dominant), and many of those who influenced my own spiritual development were from this tradition. My reasons for not being dispensational have to do with my own reading of Scripture. In college, as I studied the Bible under some excellent teachers, I reached the conclusion that the dispensationalist position was not taught in Scripture, and my subsequent study has not changed that basic conclusion. In my mind statements about whether dispensationalism is optimistic or pessimistic or what have you are beside the intellectual point. The question is whether it is true: I have concluded that it is not. But I do not for that reason think those who hold this position are necessarily anti-intellectual or unusually intolerant, although I know that some dispensationalists (as well as some antidispensationalists) are both of those. I feel that they were and are wrong. But being wrong is, as Hegel affirmed, a key element in the human discovery of truth.

1. Virginia Lieson Brereton, *Training God's Army: The American Bible School, 1880-1940* (Bloomington and Indianapolis: Indiana University Press, 1990), p. 88. This chapter is deeply indebted to Dr. Brereton and her studies of the Bible school movement. I worked with her earlier on the Auburn history project, and some of that earlier work is reflected in this text.

his ministry. In preparing his reference Bible, Scofield consolidated his notes from those meetings, which were often written in the margins of his copies of Scripture, into a single volume. To secure accuracy he invited a team of editors to work with him in the preparation of the final text. This team included people as diverse as the Methodist Milton Terry, a biblical critic, and James Gray, president of Moody Bible Institute. Relying on the advice he received from his advisory committee and his own further study, Scofield revised his reference Bible in 1917. Since its publication, the Scofield Bible has been a religious best seller, with one of the longest and largest runs of any edition of the Bible.

The Scofield Bible reflected much of the educational foment at the turn of the century. Scofield and his friends designed the book to be read by ordinary people who needed help in understanding the Bible. The target of the book was not the lower classes nor rural America. The hoped-for audience was the person with a strong common or high school education who had become active in Christian work, either as a volunteer, a Christian worker, or a pastor. Most, like Scofield himself, had their ministries in more urban contexts.[2] Such people did not fit easily into classic theological education. While later surveys indicated that only about one-fourth of the pastors among such learned denominations as the Presbyterians and Congregationalists had completed college and seminary, the proportion was much lower among Baptists, Methodists, Disciples, and of course, among the new holiness and Pentecostal churches. The Bible fit the needs of members of these denominations.

Above all, the Scofield Bible was directed toward the new Christian activists who were so prominent a part of the late nineteenth-century American religious scene. From 1880 to 1920, American Christians were in an activist mode. Missionary work abroad increased geometrically. In 1886 students, led by John R. Mott and Robert Speer, organized the Student Volunteer Movement (SVM). The movement was so successful in inspiring missionary candidates that the larger Protestant denominations had to experiment with new forms of fundraising, including the duplex envelope and the "stewardship" campaign. The success of the denominations and the SVM, in turn, inspired the Laymen's Missionary Movement to raise substantial funds for American missions. The faith mission movement, begun by Hudson Taylor's establishment of the China Inland Mission, expanded and came to include the Christian and Missionary Alliance, the Evangelical Alliance Mission, the Central American Mission, the Sudan Inland Mission, and the Africa Inland Mission. The neo-Wesleyan holiness churches and movements, which included the early Church of the Nazarene and

2. The Bible colleges founded by Scofield were located in New York and Philadelphia. His stay in Northfield was his longest adult residence in a small town.

the Church of God (Cleveland, Tennessee), established new congregations. The Holiness movement was often more mission centered than denominationally centered. Holiness leaders were active in establishing various forms of home missionary work, including rescue missions, and often enlisted people from different denominational traditions in their work. Among mainstream Protestants, the YMCA and YWCA were the largest single agencies and were found in almost all American cities and on most American college campuses. But perhaps the largest component of the new Protestant army was the Sunday school movement, found in virtually every American Protestant congregation. The Sunday school enlisted women and men for a wide variety of teaching and administrative tasks. Many of these volunteers, like the earnest but very busy John D. Rockefeller, set aside substantial blocks of time to prepare for their classes.[3]

Scofield's Bible represented an important approach to the education of this rising army of the Lord, but Scofield and others knew that Christian literature would not be enough to get the job done. In part, this was the result of their personal experience. Many who enlisted in the great Christian crusades felt inadequate to the task they were called to perform. They needed, not surprisingly, for someone to tell them the best way to witness to Christ, conduct a meeting, or organize a Y. Others, watching the work of well-intentioned but inadequate workers, recognized the need for more intensive training. Moody, attempting to raise money for his Bible institute, summarized these needs:

> I believe that we have got to have gap-men — men who are trained to do city mission work. Every city mission in this country and Europe has been almost a failure . . . because the men are not trained. If a man fails at anything, put him in city mission work. We need the men that have the most character to go into the shops and meet these hardhearted infidels and skeptics. They have got to know the people and what we want is men who . . . go right into the shop and talk to men. Never mind the Greek and Hebrew, give them plain English and good Scripture. It is the sword of the Lord that cuts deep. If you have men trained for that kind of work, there is no trouble about reaching the men who do not go into the church.[4]

3. William Strauss and Neil Howe, *Generations: The History of America's Future, 1584 to 2069* (New York: Morrow, 1991), call the two generations that were most active from 1880 to 1910 the progressive and the missionary generations. Their names for these cohorts are apt: the progressives, who followed the materialistic Gilded Age cohort, were deeply interested in the transformation of American institutions. Their keynote was reform. The missionary generation was determined to bear the good news, to lead crusades, about many aspects of life. The period when these two generations interacted was one of intense social and religious activism.

4. Quoted in Brereton, *Training God's Army,* p. 51.

Others who worked with the growing number of volunteer, semivolunteer, and semiprofessional Christian leaders felt the same need. To be effective was to be trained. This conviction sparked many of the educational changes of the period.

Yet, one must admit that Moody's other point, almost identical to what such leaders of the social awakening as Graham Taylor were making, was equally important. The current college and seminary programs, which revolved around classical and biblical literature in the original languages, seemed far from the world of real Christian work. Not only did those programs demand a substantial block of a person's time — seven years[5] — but they did not deal with the work that Christian workers had to do. What was needed was a type of school that took less time, was quicker, and dealt with essential matters. In later educational language, the need was for a school somewhere between the last two years of high school and the first two years of college. While the candidates for such education were often referred to as "poor" or "humble" — an old convention in seminary and college fund-raising — those that made up the army of the Lord, whether in seminaries or other educational institutions, tended to be from the lower and middle classes with many (at least into the 1930s) coming from what the denominations called "town and country" churches. Perhaps the most discernible difference between those who wanted training and those who wanted the seminary course is the age at which they decided on Christian work. Many who entered seminary had resolved on the ministry from their early teens. In contrast, many who were part of Moody's army of Christian workers, like Moody and Scofield themselves, had some prior experience in the world, as clerks, salesmen, shopkeepers, and the like, before experiencing their calls to Christian service. Although many were still young by late twentieth-century standards, they had "aged" out of the late adolescent college.[6]

Was Moody's appeal to find a way around the college and seminary "anti-intellectual"? One must avoid oversimplifications here. In general, dispensationalism had a highly intellectual understanding of salvation. One became a Christian by accepting the truth of the biblical teaching about Christ for oneself. Conversion was, in that sense, as much the result of changing one's mind as it was of changing one's heart, as earlier evangelicals had maintained. This may account in part for the deep yearning that many dispensationalists had for a deep personal experience and the reason why so many of them were attracted

5. At a time when most white American males had a life expectancy of around forty-nine years, this represented a seventh of a person's life. It was particularly hard for males to sacrifice the years in their late twenties and early thirties when they established their life pattern.

6. One of the significant later changes in the Bible institutes was when they began to attract students without prior employment experience, often students just out of high school.

to the Keswick holiness movement: a movement that encouraged the personal experiences of being "upheld by Christ."

I. Dispensationalism as an Educational Philosophy

Dispensationalism offered a way, although not the only way,[7] to meet the educational needs that Moody had noted. The dispensational movement can be traced back to John Nelson Darby, a priest in the Anglican Church of Ireland. Like many other ethically and theologically sensitive ministers, Darby was upset by a church that had the marks of catholicity but that, at its best, was an Erastian extension of the government in Whitehall. The basic theological questions raised by the scandal of the Irish church revolved around ecclesiology and authority. John Keble, for instance, began the Anglo-Catholic movement in the Church of Ireland with his 1833 sermon "National Apostasy." The theme of the sermon was the authority of the church, as a body founded and sustained by Christ, to sustain its own affairs. First the Tractarian movement and then the broader Anglo-Catholic movement debated these questions intensely, with some of their more brilliant members, including John Henry Newman, finally despairing of the Church of England altogether and joining Rome. Darby represented a similar reaction in the opposite direction. Whereas the Anglo-Catholics turned toward medieval Christianity and the Church of Rome, Darby turned to the Plymouth Brethren, a restorationist sect that stressed the capacity of individuals to read the Bible for themselves. Like many other restoration movements, the Plymouth Brethren did not have a formal clergy, saw sacraments as only symbolic, and stressed salvation by belief in the truth about Jesus Christ.

How much of the dispensational theology was generated by Darby and how much by other members of the movement or such alternative sources as

7. Other ways included the various English programs — seminary training without prior college — that were offered at almost all seminaries, such innovative combined plans as the Bangor Plan, the Th.B.s that would become popular in the 1920s, and religion majors in colleges. The closely related women's missionary training movement, treated below in chapter 10, used much of the same rhetoric and many of the same techniques, but these schools seem to me to have a quite different spirit. Most of them became part of the seminaries in the 1920s and 1930s. While most of the dispensationalist Bible colleges either admitted women from the outset or came to admit women before the Great War, these schools were neither as gender related or, equally significant, as controlled by women as the training schools. Despite the similarity in rhetoric, the difference in ethos and "gender friendliness" strikes me as reason enough to treat them separately.

Edward Irving or the Scottish prophet Margaret Macdonald may never be answered to everyone's satisfaction.[8] Restorationist movements tend to be characterized by much discussion among the membership, by small Bible study groups, and by each member's personal biblical study. The one essential element in such movements is that all share their perspective on the biblical text with other members of the group. In their congregations American dispensationalists frequently used the "Bible reading" as a form of preaching and group study. The leader of the congregation would take a word or phrase, look up that word or phrase in a concordance, and then read each passage where the word or phrase appeared. One can get the flavor of this style of biblical study by looking at the "chain references" in such contemporary dispensational reference Bibles as the *Thompson Chain Reference Bible.* When the reading was complete, people were held to have the biblical teaching on the subject. The interpretation was of course reserved to the hearers. This type of environment does not make tracing intellectual dependency an easy matter.[9] It also makes for many potential and, unfortunately, actual battles among people holding similar views. Without a real central authority, the right to set the limits of a movement or a church belongs to those who can solicit enough support to either persuade or, in some cases, exclude others. Later, many dispensational schools would establish both creeds and hiring procedures that supported one side or another in these debates.

In any event, Darby was a passionate evangelist. He spread his understanding of the Bible throughout Europe and North America in a series of evangelistic tours that converted many influential people to his views. In turn, such people as James Brookes, Moody,[10] Scofield, A. J. Gordon, Reuben Torrey, and William Blackstone passed the teaching on to their friends, students, and fellow church members. Moody's summer meetings at Northfield were particularly important to the process. Judging from the number of former YMCA secretaries who were prominent in the movement, that organization was also a primary means of transmission.

8. See Timothy P. Weber, *Living in the Shadow of the Second Coming: American Premillennialism, 1875-1982* (Chicago: University of Chicago Press, 1987), p. 21; also p. 248 nn. 21-23.

9. One of the problems for the student of dispensationalism or the early Holiness and Pentecostal movements, all of which were influenced by some versions of restorationism, is the combination of the charismatic authority of some people with a heavy emphasis on the right of individual interpretation and, in many cases, the practice of individual interpretation. The outside interpreter tends to see more of the influence of the leader or leaders, while the person within the movement is more apt to see the diversity of individual perspectives.

10. Martin E. Marty, *Modern American Religion,* vol. 1, *The Irony of It All, 1893-1919* (Chicago: University of Chicago Press, 1986), calls Moody "its most effective carrier" (p. 223).

The dispensational system of biblical interpretation is an intriguing mixture of simplicity and complexity. It exists on two levels. On one level it is a system of biblical interpretation with a firm christological basis. According to Scofield, a dispensation is a period of time during which man "is tested in respect of obedience to some specific revelation of the will of God." Significantly, each such dispensation is marked by "man's utter failure in every dispensation."[11] Thus, in the garden God offered humankind salvation on occasion of their obedience to the command not to eat of the fruit; likewise, under Moses God offered salvation if people would only live under the law. Each failure is, so to speak, more culpable than the one before. But even in the midst of that record of failure and discord, God has kept alive the reality of grace through the prophecies of Christ. And just as the ancient people of God were able to keep alive their faith in the midst of their failures by this blessed assurance, so modern people can hold to the same sure faith. The coming of Jesus is the centerpiece of this scenario. In him salvation is offered once and for all. This is, of course, evangelical Protestantism, perhaps stated more starkly than some evangelicals would prefer, but hardly different in kind from most other expressions of evangelical faith. For those shaped by the faith of the nineteenth-century revivals, this was the "old-time religion" they had heard since childhood.

What made dispensationalism unique was the question of what to do with the large number of unfulfilled prophecies in Scripture. Many of these refer to Israel and promise such matters as the earthly rule of the Messiah and the restoration of the temple. Although these promises appear, at least on their face, to be as messianic as the prophecies more often cited as referring to Christ, they have not yet been fulfilled. In a similar way, the most natural reading of Revelation is that the various prophecies of the end time are at hand and that Christ will soon return in glory with his saints to rule. And, as the dispensationalists were fond of saying, the same was true of the teachings of Jesus himself. Taken at face value, many of Jesus' words seem to refer to the supernatural establishment of the kingdom either in his lifetime or shortly after his death.

It must be stressed that there is nothing unusual in any of these conclusions. Critical biblical study reached similar conclusions about much of Old Testament prophecy at about the same time. Clearly, many passages traditionally read as referring to the church or that ecclesiastical interpreters had spiritualized referred to the Jewish people. Further, Jesus had not fulfilled in his earthly life many of the messianic hopes held by earlier Jewish prophets. As Albert Schweitzer noted, if the Synoptics are regarded as basically historical, Jesus

11. Cited in Weber, *Living in the Shadow*, p. 17.

himself appears as an apocalyptic prophet who goes to his death fully confident that his sacrifice will initiate the rule and reign of God.

But there is another point of confluence between dispensationalism and the new biblical studies that is equally important: both are obsessed with the question of history. The new critics wanted to know when the various parts of the Bible were written and, equally important, how they fit into the development of Israelite and Christian religion. The divergence came in the question of what to do with the results of such inquiries. For the biblical critics, who were in the main liberal Protestants, their more embarrassing discoveries could simply be discarded. In an unusually candid article, "American Theological Scene: Fifty Years in Retrospect," Carl S. Patton wrote: "The transition from a Bible alike and equally valuable in all parts, which you had to believe whether it seemed reasonable to you or not, to a Bible which requires not to be defended but to be understood, of which you may believe what you will, but the rejection of any part of which carries no moral blame, is a tremendous step. The Bible has ceased to be an authority and has become a source book."[12] Another way of saying much the same thing is to note that biblical criticism is a form of deconstruction. To know the history of something — its place in a larger pattern of development and its relationship to its own time — was also to confine that thing to its own period. Dispensationalism refused this step. Exegetical conclusions and theological convictions had to match.

Both dispensationalists and their critics have frequently identified biblical literalism as a mark of the movement. Caution, however, is needed in interpreting this observation. Although some dispensationalists clearly believed "the Bible from cover to cover, including the statement that it was bound in genuine leather," most dispensationalists avoided such populist excesses. Moody, Sunday, Torrey, and Gray were all aware that the Bible contained metaphor and poetry as well as much Oriental hyperbole. One of the foci of dispensational biblical interpretation was the attempt to "decode" the various symbols used in apocalyptic literature. So what did "literal" mean? For most it meant that where an event was presented as historical in the Bible, it should be interpreted as a historical event. Thus, when the Bible says Moses brought the Ten Commandments from Sinai, the Bible meant that a historical person, Moses, brought the tablets that God had inscribed down the mountain. It happened in ordinary history and time. In contrast, Briggs and Driver were equally convinced that the Sinai story, at least as it related to what contemporary Christians called the Ten Commandments, was a comparatively late development of

12. Carl S. Patton, "American Theological Scene: Fifty Years in Retrospect," *Journal of Religion* 16 (Oct. 1936): 456.

the Moses legend. The earliest "commandments" were largely ritualistic and probably originated among those Palestinian tribes that had not participated in the exodus. Briggs and Driver, in short, agreed that the story claimed to describe an event, but they also believed that the event had not happened. They left it to the theologians to debate "how much was left of the old doctrines."[13]

The solution was to redefine traditional or historical premillennialism.[14] From the earliest period of church history, some Christians believed that Christ would return to earth prior to the millennium predicted in Revelation. The most obvious problem with the position was that interpreters failed to accurately identify the prophetic events leading to the end. More Antichrists were available than needed. What the dispensationalists did was cut the Gordian knot that required them to identify those key events and persons. The argument moved around the christological focus. Since the promises said they would be fulfilled in Jesus, this must have happened. But, at least in empirical history, it apparently had not. The kingdom had not been restored and Messiah was not recognized as King. So something else must have happened to separate Christ and the prophecies that spoke of his coming. That something else, the dispensationalists argued, was that God had inserted parentheses into the fulfillment of prophecy. These parentheses set apart a period of time beginning shortly after Christ's death and resurrection during which the fulfillment of prophecy was suspended. Dispensationalists believed that this period would end with Christ's rapture, the return of Jesus to gather his saints to himself.[15] After the rapture the prophetic calendar would move quickly through the remaining events until, at the second coming, Christ would reestablish the kingdom of David as a worldwide monarchy and rule triumphantly with his saints for a thousand years.

The doctrine of the rapture, thus, enabled the dispensationalist to speak of the return of Christ *for* his saints as an imminent event. Christ could return at any moment! By interposing this event into the calculations, some of the most serious interpretative problems in the Bible appeared to be solved. One could live in the "shadow of the second coming" without the embarrassment of

13. This was the title of an influential lecture series by Gladden.

14. I have found Millard J. Erickson, *A Basic Guide to Eschatology: Making Sense of the Millennium* (Grand Rapids: Baker, 1998), a reprint of *Contemporary Options in Eschatology: A Study of the Millennium* (1977), to be a very useful guide to the nuances between eschatological positions.

15. The rapture is based on 1 Thess. 4:16-17: "For the Lord himself shall descend from heaven with a shout, with the voice of the archangel, and the trump of God; and the dead in Christ shall rise first, then we which are alive and remain shall be caught up together with them in the clouds, to meet the Lord in the air; and so shall we ever be with the Lord."

predicting too closely which events had to precede Christ's appearance. Further, the dispensationalist was able to escape another minor cul-de-sac. Much of traditional preaching had stressed heaven as the reward of faith. But heaven's glow had dimmed in the late nineteenth century.[16] Victorian sentimentality had turned the concrete images of earlier eschatology into wisps, almost ghosts, and much contemporary theology had replaced heaven with a general immortality. The believing unbelief of Tennyson's *In Memoriam* was characteristic. In contrast, the dispensational millennium was real, earthy, and easily visualized. If some aspects of prophecy were unpleasant or frightening, they were followed by a heroic period in which the saints were called to arms and overcame their foes. Perhaps equally important for the period from 1890 to 1910, the images had a rough masculine sound. Americans, particularly American men, were searching for an opportunity to stand at Armageddon and battle for the Lord. Like the social gospel, dispensationalism called on men to stand firm, to be men, and to win the battles of life. Every revivalist from Moody to Sunday held men's meetings where the new masculinity was exalted.[17]

At the same time, the place of death in human experience changed. In preindustrial societies death visited almost all human cohorts equally, with the largest number of deaths occurring in childhood and adolescence. Revivalists like Solomon Stoddard and Jonathan Edwards had reaped many a rich harvest after the death of a young person made the other youth more serious and more disposed to religion. But by 1900 the more common end of life came after maturity, to people in their fifties, sixties, or seventies. Revivalists found it hard to use death as an event to call people to salvation. The rapture solved this problem by making the return of Christ the spark for both conversion and service. Time was short.

Although dispensationalism could have been read as simply a call to action, the system had elements that almost demanded schools. Part of that logic was, of course, the very urgency of the task. As in any war, it was important to get men and materials to the front, and the struggle with the powers of darkness required no less. But, to continue the military analogy, more was needed than raw recruits. What the church needed were trained workers who could accomplish the needed task in the time remaining before Christ came. The two — urgency and training — are the themes of early Bible institute history. The term "training" provides an important clue to the workings of this philosophy. Ordi-

16. See James Moorhead, *World without End: Mainstream American Protestant Visions of the Last Things, 1880-1925* (Bloomington: Indiana University Press, 1999).

17. For dispensationalism and gender roles, see Margaret Bendroth, *Fundamentalism and Gender, 1885 to the Present* (New Haven: Yale University Press, 1993), and Beth DeBerg, *Ungodly Women: Gender and the First Wave of American Fundamentalism* (Minneapolis: Fortress, 1990).

narily "training" refers to the more physical or routine tasks. We train athletes, for instance, so that they run faster or jump higher; we train soldiers to fire weapons; we train salesmen to deliver a pitch to a client. The goal of training is not reflection or critical self-examination: training's goal is the performance of a given task. Another way of looking at "training" is to note that it is usually connected with efficiency or improvement rather than innovation.

Like many other Protestants, dispensationalists believed that the truth about God and humankind was in the Bible. In the late nineteenth century, American Protestants were at the height of a popular interest in biblical study. The Bible was studied in Sunday school, where it almost completely replaced the older catechetical tradition. The Chautauqua assembly in New York State, designed by its founder, John Vincent, as a Sunday school university, had a large map of Palestine that people could explore on foot as they learned the names of the biblical places. For years Chautauqua classes included Hebrew lessons, taught by William Rainey Harper, who later became president of the University of Chicago. Wilbert White, founder of the Bible Teacher's Training School that became New York's Biblical Seminary, was in great demand as a teacher of his inductive or literary method of Bible study. The Sunday school expanded to include classes for adult men and women as well as children, and the YMCA featured Bible study in its meetings, especially on college campuses. Almost all Protestants carried their Bibles to church with them. Memorizing biblical passages was a common act of devotion as well as education.

American[18] dispensationalism fit easily into this world. The leaders saw themselves primarily as Bible teachers and as evangelists. They wanted to make the Bible available to anyone who would take the time and effort to read it. But they knew, often at first hand, how daunting that task could be. Not only did most Americans study the Bible in the Authorized Version, although many had difficulty with the seventeenth-century English, but the Bible itself was an ancient book, filled with references to long-dead kings, to nations that had vanished from the earth, to exotic temples and unfamiliar rituals. To learn the Bible, thus, one needed aids. The Scofield Bible was of course one of the most successful and most easily used. But dispensationalists produced other aids as well, including guides to the uniform lessons, tracts, and other handy volumes. Moody Press was as much a part of the educational mission of Moody Bible Institute as the formal classes.

One other educational aspect of dispensationalism deserves mention.

18. The "American" here is self-conscious. European and English dispensationalists were far less involved in the popular biblical culture of their countries, at least as far as I can see, than the Americans.

Dispensationalism shared with many other Protestants a strong doctrine of the "fall of the church." In dispensationalism this common Protestant perspective was reinforced by the doctrine of the parenthesis and by explicit teachings on the apostasy of the church as a sign of the approaching end. Among the Plymouth Brethren, these teachings reinforced a strict sectarianism, and the later practice among some fundamentalists of first- and second-degree separation reflected a similar interpretation of the doctrine.[19] Yet this was not the only reading of the teaching. Many dispensationalists, including Moody, never felt called to separate from their denominations. Aside from the natural inconsistencies that accompany all but the most systematic theologians, there were intellectual and doctrinal reasons within dispensationalism itself that counterbalanced the more extreme interpretation of the doctrine. One might argue, for instance, that what was decisive — both for the Christian mission and for personal salvation — was a passionate commitment to the cause of Christ. If this is so, then denominational distinctives become, so to speak, relative to a person's willingness to participate in the larger cause. Thus, the Niagara Bible Conference in 1878 adopted a stripped-down creed that stressed only those doctrines essential to their own understanding and practice of evangelism.[20] Many American evangelicals have found that position congenial, particularly in those denominations, such as the Northern (American) Baptists, whose pastors often attended Bible schools. However one decided issues of merely denominational

19. First-degree separation is to leave churches that are modernist in their doctrine; second-degree separation is to deny Christian fellowship to any who remain in churches that tolerate modernism.

20. Timothy Weber, *Living in the Shadow of the Second Coming*, saw the real reference in the Niagara creed as liberalism. He writes: "Though such a statement obviously ignored vast areas which had been important to Christians in the past, such as the sacraments and church government, it did express what many believed were essentials in light of the liberal restatement of traditional beliefs. It would be easy to show the Christian gospel has at times meant much more than the contents of the Niagara Creed, but it would be difficult to show that it had ever meant much less — as far as American evangelicals were concerned" (p. 27). One problem is, of course, that there were few liberals openly at work in 1878, unless one wants to point to Henry Ward Beecher and perhaps some of the disciples of Bushnell. More striking to me is the fact that the creed contains all of what evangelicals used to call the "Roman Road" or the "Way of Salvation." This was a short collection of biblical passages and doctrines that could be used to witness to a person about Christ. Campus Crusade's Four Spiritual Laws is a more recent expression of this same tradition. Ironically, given Weber's understanding of Niagara, William Newton Clarke's *Outlines of Christian Theology*, the basic evangelical-liberal textbook, omitted sacraments and the church also. As nearly as I can determine, the ecumenical movement, particularly in the 1930s, was the primary spark for serious reflection on the church by thinkers in the liberal tradition, although some more Ritschlian liberals, such as William Adams Brown, had a stronger ecclesiology, rooted in the theology of their German teachers.

import, what counted lay elsewhere. One could travel light with much of traditional doctrine.

The irony here is that American liberal Christians had reached much the same position. Pressed by the intellectual issues raised by modern science and history and challenged by their awareness of the social crisis, more liberal believers were also willing to travel light theologically. Such historically central denominational and confessional teachings as Chalcedonian Christology, the Nicene Trinity,[21] and the atonement were either deemphasized, reinterpreted, or set aside altogether. For good or ill, the central act of liberal faith was commitment to faith itself, or perhaps more accurately, commitment to the Christian cause.

Was dispensationalism anti-intellectual? In *The Scandal of the Evangelical Mind,* Professor Mark Noll argued:

> For the purposes of Christian thinking, the major indictment of the fundamentalist movement, and especially of the dispensationalism that provided the most systematic interpretation of the Bible for fundamentalists and many later evangelicals, was its intellectual sterility. Under its midwifery, the evangelical community gave birth to virtually no insights into how, under God, the natural world proceeded, how human societies worked, why human nature acted the way that it did, or what constituted the blessings and perils of culture.[22]

In some respects Professor Noll's criticisms are accurate. Although deeply interested in knowing, dispensationalists were not deeply interested in speculative or scholarly issues. Most wanted information rather than insight, answers rather than questions, and techniques rather than sociological analysis. But these preferences were also the preferences of many people in their communities. Although many occupations were beginning the slow rise to professional

21. Many evangelical liberals continued to use the terms "Father," "Son," and "Holy Spirit," particularly in liturgy, but they had moved substantially away from the theology of persons and incarnation of classical doctrine. Again, 1930s modernist Carl Patton called the shot: "How much real trinitarianism is there left? Of a kind, I should say, considerable. All of us [?] use the trinitarian formulas. All of us [?] would feel quite at sea without them. All of us [?] still naturally think of God first as the creator or ground of all things, second as revealed in Christ, and third as active in the human process generally. This is trinitarianism of a sort. To those who perceive that the newer theism cuts the ground alike from under the old trinitarianism and the old unitarianism, it is quite enough" ("American Theological Scene," p. 448). My own reading of the liberal tradition from William Newton Clarke through the Niebuhrs indicates that this "trinitarianism of a sort" was the main line of development and that Nicene doctrine was primarily of interest in ecumenical and later Barthian circles.

22. Mark A. Noll, *The Scandal of the Evangelical Mind* (Grand Rapids: Eerdmans, 1994), p. 137.

status, at the end of the nineteenth century, many who worked at these jobs came to them either from a training school or from practical experience. The vast bulk of young bookkeepers were trained in high schools and business "colleges" that stressed the mastery of good technique, carefully entered numbers, accurate addition, and the complete ledger. Only a handful went to such institutions as the Harvard Business School where the underlying principles of accounting were part of the bill of fare. But it is not fair to fault the high schools and commercial colleges for not generating new ideas about business; that was not their goal or their purpose.[23]

The dispensationalists tended to reflect the can-do type of thinking that was a very important part of American culture at the turn of the century and that has continued to influence our society. In many ways the dispensationalist Bible colleges were similar to the large number of sectarian medical schools that dotted the medical landscape before the Flexner report made the university medical school with its attendant teaching hospitals and clinics the norm. These schools often dogmatically adhered to a specific type of medical doctrine, such as homeopathy, that they transmitted to their students along with a considerable body of empirical medical knowledge — some good, some bad — that the aspiring physician could use to treat a very high percentage of the cases that came into his office. Like dispensationalism (or many denominational institutions), these schools attracted people who had made certain commitments. Neither did they produce scholars or philosophers.

Perhaps the more interesting question about the dispensationalist schools is not whether they sparked advanced scholarship or not, but why they have remained for more than a century an important component of American ministerial education. Despite numerous attempts by Protestant leaders to define theological education in ways that exclude Bible colleges and schools, including a depreciation of training, the schools — with many upgrades and updates — continue to be an important option for training pastors and other Christians, the most long-lasting and abiding "alternative" to the seminary.

II. Structuring the Vision

The dispensationalists found an outlet for their educational vision ready at hand. One of the revolutions in European missionary activity in the nineteenth

23. During the fundamentalist controversy, dispensationalists were able to establish one school on the seminary level, present-day Dallas Theological Seminary. In general, the genius of the movement has been in the establishment of lower-level institutions.

century was the shift of the responsibility for missions from governments to private voluntary organizations. In part, this reflected the increasing pluralism of European governments, particularly those in central Europe. While a strong consensus continued for state-supported churches, there was much less interest — from both political and religious leaders — in religion as an instrument of state. This was especially true of those who advocated the "new imperialism" of the period. The British East India Company, for instance, was not long in learning the same lesson that the earlier Muslim conquerors of India had learned: they had to rule in conjunction with the existing religious majority or not rule at all. The company, in fact, resisted the entry of missionaries into India until the government, inspired by the evangelical Clapham sect, forced a change in policy. The separation of missions from the structure of the state churches gave European missionary movements — from foreign missions to the German Innere Mission and the closely allied deaconess movements — a decidedly lay character. In turn, this meant that these movements were not necessarily related to the formal theological education given by the universities maintained by the state. Part of the significance of David Livingstone, for instance, was that his work inspired many young university men to take up missionary work. The various missionary societies, as well as some independent pastors and educators, established schools to provide some training for those going abroad.[24]

Perhaps even more important were the various institutes for the training of deaconesses. Deaconesses were unordained women religious workers who performed various "home missionary" and charitable works, including nursing. The deaconess training school at Kaiserswerth was a worldwide example of this type of training, and Baptists and Methodists in particular organized similar schools for women missions volunteers. The first missionary training school in the United States was the Baptist Missionary Training School in Chicago, organized and supported by Northern Baptist women. Many of these schools were established to enable women, who were often kept at arm's length by the seminaries, to enter into ministries for which they were ecclesiastically and socially acceptable. The Southern Baptist Woman's Missionary Union Training School in Louisville, for instance, prepared many women for work abroad.

Both the missionary and the women's training schools had elements that were very important to dispensationalist educators. Both shared a sense that

24. See Brereton, *Training God's Army,* pp. 55-59. She cites an influential article by A. B. Simpson, the founder of the Christian and Missionary Alliance, "Missionary Training Colleges," *Christian Alliance* 1 (May 1888), as evidence of American familiarity with these schools and their methods. American missionaries would have also learned much about these and other forms of training from their work abroad. After the initial push, much missionary work was ecumenical, at least in spirit.

the harvest was vast and the laborers were few, and that the signs of the times required the enlistment of all who had heard a call. The belief that the task before the church was too large for the cumbersome institutions that Protestants had established was, incidentally, held not only by dispensationalists and missionary enthusiasts. Charles Briggs of Union Seminary, New York, wrote: "The evangelization of our cities, of our outlying populations, and of the heathen world is the greatest religious problem of our time. We need an enormous army of evangelists for this task. It is impossible to train them all in theological courses of our seminaries. We must have either new institutions for that purpose, or our theological seminaries should have sufficient elasticity to adapt themselves to the work."[25] For dispensationalist educators, this meant a willingness to reach down and try to educate and train many who would not have qualified for the more established colleges and seminaries.

Although social class has always influenced American religion in both open and hidden ways, it was not the only line that divided college from Bible institute. Age was, of course, a factor. The Bible schools were notably open to what later educators called "second career" students. Another prominent issue was dissatisfaction with the idea that a college was a necessary prerequisite for theological study. By 1900 both colleges and seminaries were moving away from programs that were predominantly based on the mastery of the learned languages, and many were unwilling to invest the time or money in an elongated program. Even with free tuition at most seminaries, the substantial investment required by the college/seminary paradigm offered a far from adequate return. Too many dollars, too little benefits.

The somewhat quixotic figure of Wilbert White is important in this story. Although White went on to found Biblical Seminary in New York, a school that was initially midway between a missionary training school and a seminary, he was also a popular biblical teacher. White was a graduate of Xenia Seminary who went from that school to Yale, where he studied Old Testament with William Rainey Harper. Like many young Bible enthusiasts, White was deeply impressed by Harper's string of adult Hebrew classes, his various journals, and his popular style of teaching. While a graduate student, he conducted a survey of 1,000 ministers for his mentor that disclosed that many of them were deeply dissatisfied with the biblical training they had received. Although some of the dissatisfaction may have been traceable to higher criticism, much of it had to do with the widespread seminary dependence on the exegetical method. Teachers would take specific passages in Hebrew or Greek and exhaustively examine every word or phrase for its last scintilla of meaning. Students, conse-

25. Quoted in Brereton, *Training God's Army*, p. 61.

quently, felt that they knew very much about very little. But White was also troubled by the higher criticism. Like the exegetical studies on which it claimed to be based, higher criticism was an analytical method that separated different parts of the text from other, apparently related, sections. Johns Hopkins professor Paul Haupt's Polychrome Bible printed different "sources" in different colors. This type of cutting the text apart is an illustration of the type of study that bothered White. After leaving Yale, White developed both spiritually and intellectually. In place of the analytical methods favored by traditional exegetes and higher critics, he favored a more literary approach that dealt with the Bible and individual biblical books as coherent wholes. The student, hence, should examine the way the Bible characterized different personalities, how different themes were continued through the same and different books, and how different literary genres worked together. In some ways he was advocating something similar to late twentieth-century canonical criticism.[26]

Although White did lecture at Moody Bible Institute, he was more an example than a mentor. The heart of the new Bible institutes would be in adapting such popular methods of teaching to the problem of teaching Scripture. Since Bible institutes were, as their name implies, places where the Bible was studied, each institute became known for the style of biblical teaching associated with its primary teacher. Like seminary teachers, Bible institute instructors used various methods: a system of pointed questions and answers that forced students to examine the text (Torrey) and a system of reading the books all the way through at a single sitting (Gray) were popular alternatives, as were other ways of encouraging the student to search the text for information and inspiration. Torrey, who was educated at Yale and in Germany, constructed his instruction on a more systematic format, moving from biblical introduction, exegetical study in sections and books, biblical doctrines, and study of the best methods of communicating the Bible, through to practical work with the student, the text, and people outside the school. White, at least while at Moody, followed an outline that proceeded from introduction through historical and biographical study, through chapter studies to word studies,[27] and special topics. James Gray, perhaps the most influential of the early Bible teachers, developed his method around the reading of an entire book of the Bible at one sitting. Students were to continue to read a book until its meaning became clear. Gray had six rules for biblical study: begin at the beginning, read the book

26. A. R. Wentz, "A New Strategy for Theological Education," *Christian Education,* Apr. 1937, p. 18, gives an account of White's life and intellectual methods. Wentz, a Lutheran professor, was impressed by White's methods and saw them as a way forward.

27. Word studies were particularly important in many conservative schools at the time.

through, read the book continuously, read the book independently, read the book repeatedly, and read the book prayerfully.[28] Although each Bible institute promised its own "methods of study," even within the same school there were considerable pedagogical variations. Bible schools would use everything from "programmed" learning to correspondence education to enable the student to master the contents of the Scriptures. Results, not pedagogy, were what counted.

This was in line with the activist nature of the biblical institute movement. In contrast to the seminaries, Bible institutes tended to originate in individual ministries. A common pattern was for an effective evangelist, who had numerous requests for training in his perspectives and methods, to establish an informal school. Thus A. J. Gordon, an active Northern Baptist missionary advocate, encountered many people who were qualified for missionary service in his work as a pastor and as a denominational official. It was a short step to invite them to attend some classes in his church, and as the ministry prospered, to expand the operation by adding teachers and, finally, buildings and libraries. A. B. Simpson's school, the later Nyack College, began in his own active ministry as the organizer of the Christian Alliance and the Missionary Alliance, two parachurch organizations that later became one. The Bible Institute of Los Angeles (BIOLA), historically one of the strongest of the dispensationalist schools, was formed out of a series of classes for young men and women in the business section of Los Angeles. The active support of oilman Lyman Steward turned this relatively small ministry into a school by enlisting teachers and building a building. BIOLA early had a campus in China that served both as a center for training and as a mission in its own right.

The relationship between the founding ministry and the school could be close or more distant. Moody, for instance, was more of a distant figure. He had originally been interested in a school for women workers, and his partnership with Emma Dyer, an energetic and able advocate of the women's missionary movement, may have reflected this concern. But by the late 1880s his interests and rhetoric had changed. Although he still relied on Ms. Dyer for raising money, he was far less interested in a women's training school.[29] The Chicago Evangelization Society began its work in 1887-88 with a series of traditional evangelistic crusades in churches and tents throughout the city and invested only a small amount of time and money in its 1888 "Bible Institute," a three-

28. William A. Runyan, *Dr. Gray at Moody Bible Institute* (New York: Oxford University Press, 1935), p. 73.

29. For the Farwell Hall meeting, see James Findlay, "Moody, Gapmen, and the Gospel: The Early Days of Moody Bible Institute," *Church History* 31 (Sept. 1962): 322-25.

month program for women workers. The 1889 inauguration of the training school was clearly a continuation of Moody's basic work. In his announcement, Moody wrote:

> On the fourth day of April, 1889, I will begin holding in Chicago a Convention of Christian workers, similar to those held in the summer at Northfield.
>
> These meetings will continue from 30 to 60 days, and instruction will be given by well-known leaders of Christian thought and action. As this is the beginning of a movement which it is hoped will culminate in a permanent school, to fit men and women for work among the neglected masses of Chicago and other cities, the instruction will from the first, take a practical turn. The mornings will be devoted to study of, and lectures upon the Bible and its application to the wants of this age; and to these meetings the public will be invited.
>
> The afternoons and evenings will be given to "Applied Christianity." And no pains will be spared to bring the workers face to face with the masses who have renounced or are ignorant of the gospel.[30]

The meetings were successful, and Moody and his board of trustees opened their training school officially in September 1889. The process was remarkably similar to the one that brought other Moody-sponsored enterprises into being, including the Student Volunteer Movement. Interestingly, Moody, like some university founders, would establish an organization and then allow others to bring it to successful completion.

The story of BIOLA is even more interesting. Los Angeles was a city in formation at the time. Such key industries as oil and the production of movies were just beginning, and the city had yet to acquire the system of freeways and connecting highways that would make it the nation's prime example of urban sprawl. Many of those who came to Los Angeles came from the South and upper Midwest, while the area around San Francisco attracted a more eastern and northern Midwestern type of immigrant. This pattern was reflected in the educational patterns of the two Californias. Early on, northern California had established theological institutions in the Berkeley area similar to those in the East. Indeed, Berkeley was in many ways a "second Cambridge," with seminaries and other schools ringed around the University of California in much the way Charles Eliot of Harvard had hoped might happen to his beloved city and university. Southern California was more open territory. The University of South-

30. Quoted in Gene Getz, *MBI: The Story of Moody Bible Institute* (Chicago: Moody Press, 1969), p. 1.

ern California, under nominal Methodist influence, had its own theological school, but there were fewer institutions to serve the population than in the north. In this context two evangelistic clubs, the Fishermen's Club for men and the Lyceum Club, began active ministries. Immanuel Presbyterian Church sponsored these clubs, which were an extension of the ministry of its pastor, T. C. Horton, and which had the important financial support of oilman Lyman Steward. Steward, somewhat like his contemporary and rival John D. Rockefeller, was a deeply devoted Protestant who was active, financially and personally, in the Presbyterian Church. He had been an active financial contributor to Occidental College until that school turned more to liberalism. Interestingly, despite Steward's own passionate dispensationalism, dispensationalism was not part of the confessional requirements of the Bible institute. The same was true of Steward's other, better-known ministry, the 1913 publication of the *Fundamentals*.[31]

Not all biblical institutes outlasted their founders' initial ministries. Survival for Bible institutions was as much a financial issue as anything. Schools like Moody, BIOLA, and Gordon with their corps of teachers — increasingly professionalized as time passed — and substantial investments in buildings and other educational equipment were able to flourish because they had strong financial support. Moody Bible Institute, for instance, had the firm support of the McCormicks and other prominent members of the Chicago business community, and BIOLA, of course, had access to the Union Oil fortune. Those who could not find such funding often disappeared.

Part of the problem for the historian is that there was no organization of dispensationalist educators that maintained an authoritative list of such schools or established standards for their operation. But, although many of the Bible school founders were friends and often converts of Dwight L. Moody, this did not mean that the movement was confined to them. Initially, the Bible institute arena was, like much of American religion, a vast free market in which the capacity to attract students, supporters, and contributors was essential to success. But one of the rules of a free market is the obvious one: the market knows no real restraints. But it also had other, very important consequences. First of all, it created a predilection toward controversy. The schools were, after all, in competition with each other. These controversies could be minor and more a difference of brand or style, such as the long-standing competition between Moody and BIOLA, or they could be much more severe, such as the later battle over "separation."

31. The best source on Lyman Steward is Robert Martin Krivoshey, "Going through the Eye of the Needle: The Life of Oilman Fundamentalist, Lyman Steward, 1840-1923" (Ph.D. diss., University of Chicago, 1973).

Competition and the lack of standards also created a climate that could be religiously creative. On January 1, 1901, Agnes N. Ozman received the gift of tongues at the Bethel Bible College, a school maintained by Charles Parham, a prominent holiness evangelist. The movement then spread to the other students at the school and, through them, influenced the Azusa Street Revival that marked the beginning of the Pentecostal movement in America. At first glance, the relationship between this development and the Bible institute movement seems somewhat distant. Edith Blumhofer writes:

> Dispensationalism, as articulated by Scofield, understood the gifts of the spirit to have been withdrawn from the Church. Rejecting the latter rain views by which Pentecostals legitimated their place in God's plan, dispensationalists effectively eliminated the biblical bases for Pentecostal theology; and although Pentecostals embraced most of Scofield's ideas (and enthusiastically promoted the Scofield reference bible in their periodicals), they remained irrevocably distanced from fundamentalists by their teaching on the place of spiritual gifts in the contemporary church.[32]

Yet, neither the shift nor the teaching is that surprising. Many dispensationalists were restorationists who were predisposed to various holiness teachings. This position is faithfully reflected in the Scofield Bible and in the literature of the Bible schools. In fact, on the issues that separated Calvinists and Wesleyans, the Bible institutes were self-consciously nondenominational and wanted to serve both positions. What the holiness people who became Pentecostal did was to modify what they had received from the dispensationalists slightly. In typical dispensationalist fashion, they did this by addressing a question to the text and receiving back an answer. The question was: What are the characteristics of the period before the rapture? The answer is that it is a period in which God's gifts are renewed to strengthen God's people for their final mission. Not all dispensationalists liked the answer or the question, and many strongly and emphatically rejected the Pentecostal answer, but their reaction to Pentecostalism does not mean that Pentecostalism was not part of the spiritual and religious creativity of the dispensational movement. It was a split from it; certainly in the eyes of some it was heretical; but it was nonetheless intertwined with it. Pentecostals and holiness people later developed their own form of the Bible institute, a denominational version, that represented a logical development of the earlier dispensationalist institution.

32. Edith Blumhofer, *The Assemblies of God* (Springfield, Mo.: Gospel Publishing House, 1989), p. 193.

CHAPTER TEN

Training Women for Mission

A casual observer of American Protestantism anytime from 1880 to 1920 might have noticed the high level of interest and participation in missions. On the world stage, American missionaries had created a virtual empire, and they were actively engaged in exporting the ministries that succeeded in their own evangelization efforts at home. In addition to churches, American missionaries were active apostles of education, creating schools, colleges, and eventually universities abroad. They also transported much of the new urban missionary movement with them. The YMCA, for example, was an international movement with thriving chapters in India, China, Latin America, and Japan, and its leaders often were unofficial Protestant ambassadors.

Missions captured the popular Protestant mind to an extraordinary extent. Americans, like their counterparts in England, avidly followed the adventures of David Livingstone, the missionary physician, whose search for the headwaters of the Nile provided the international press with special editions and increased sales. The missionary movement likewise energized the life of the sending churches. For instance, the excitement generated by the Student Volunteer Movement and the Laymen's Missionary Movement inspired Protestant leaders to revise their approach to giving and to develop new methods, such as the duplex envelopes, to help finance the work. Most church organizations claimed some relationship to the missionary movement, and the best way to introduce a new ministry, a new school, or a new movement was to link it to the larger missionary enterprise.

I. Missions and a Women's Social Gospel

Missionary work provided women with their most significant early entry into Protestant church leadership.[1] The work abroad, and later, the work in the big cities, was different from that in a classical parish, and both home and foreign missionaries had to innovate to meet the new demands. Robert Speer, the popular and effective leader of Presbyterian foreign missions, noted in 1902 that Western churches had 7,319 stations, 14,364 churches, 94 colleges and universities, 20,458 schools, 379 hospitals, 782 dispensaries, and 152 publishing houses.[2] From the beginnings of this movement, the needs encountered by the missionaries were greater than what the number of male volunteers could fulfill.

The wives of missionaries were among the first to reflect on the missionary vocation of women. Ann Judson, the spouse of Adoniram Judson, was noted for her understanding of what it meant to be a missionary wife. From the beginning she insisted that she was called to her own work abroad, and her letters to mission enthusiasts at home, replete with details of her own labors, did much to make Baptists strong supporters of the work in Burma. These letters stressed her entry into situations where males would not be welcome or effective. A popular antebellum engraving depicted Ann Judson pleading with the authorities in Burma to spare her imprisoned husband's life. The Burmese, not without cause, suspected that Judson was an agent of British imperialism.

By the end of the Civil War, single women, including Methodist Isabella Thoburn and Baptist Charlotte (Lottie) Moon, went abroad with their own ministries. Although Western gender roles often influenced what women were allowed to do on the field, the ministries of both single women and missionary wives varied. Some taught, some did office work, some served as nurses and occasionally doctors in medical missions, and many — perhaps more than the missions reported back to headquarters — exhorted and preached. "Women's work with women" was a crucial part of this outreach. Since many cultures strictly regulated face-to-face conversations across gender lines, women missionaries provided the only access that the missionaries had to women and their children. Dr. Ida Scudder, for instance, found her personal vocation when a family in India refused the services of her missionary physician father because

1. R. Pierce Beaver, *All Loves Excelling: American Protestant Women in World Mission; A History of the First Feminist Movement in North America,* rev. ed. (Grand Rapids: Eerdmans, 1980), provides a clear narrative of women's involvement in foreign missions.

2. Robert Speer, cited in William Hutchison, *Errand to the World: American Protestant Thought and World Missions* (Chicago: University of Chicago Press, 1987), p. 100.

Muslim tradition prohibited intimate contact between the sexes. Scudder wrote in her diary:

> I could not sleep that night — it was too terrible. Within the very touch of my hand were three young girls dying because there was no woman to help them. I spent much of the night in prayer. I did not want to spend my life in India. My friends were begging me to return to the joyous opportunities of a young girl in America. Early in the morning I heard the "tom tom" beating in the village and it struck terror in my heart, for it was a death message. I sent our servant, and he came back saying all of them had died during the night. . . . after much thought and prayer, I went to my father and mother and told them I must go home and study medicine, and come back to India to help such women.[3]

Scudder did as her conscience directed. Returning to America, she earned a medical degree from Cornell Medical School, one of the most rigorous and scientific of American schools, and returned to India where she established the Vellore Medical Center. The Vellore Center was the leading women's hospital in Asia.

Ida Scudder's concern for the plight of women abroad was widely shared by other women missionaries. Women's missionary magazines told story after story of life in the zenana, of child marriage, the binding of feet, child brides, suttee, and other issues that particularly affected women and children. Whether these women saw themselves as "Westernizers" or not, they were determined to do what they could to end the evils they encountered.

Much the same was true of their sisters at home, who were equally concerned with issues that were impacting women's lives. The rise of the great "world cities," such as Chicago, London, and Berlin, caused an intensification of traditional social problems.[4] There were three areas of special concern to women.[5] First were questions connected with health, particularly children's

3. Quoted in Ruth A. Tucker and Walter Liefeld, *Daughters of the Church* (Grand Rapids: Zondervan, 1987), p. 320.

4. I borrowed the term "world city" from Giles MacDonough, *Berlin: A Portrait of Its History, Politics, Architecture, and Society* (New York: St. Martin's Press, 1997). MacDonough points out that all European and American large cities at this time had a vast immigrant population that was attracted by the promise of work in the factories. Similar points are made by Peter Hall, *Cities in Civilization* (New York: Pantheon Books, 1998); see especially chaps. 12, 13, and 25.

5. Given the nature of late nineteenth-century society, women social gospel advocates did less writing than their male counterparts, and those that did write had little time to produce the types of monographs we associate with the "social gospel." The writings of such historians as Mary Agnes Dougherty have helped me to realize that there are many ways to discover the con-

health. Cities were of course historically centers of disease and infection, in part because of the lack of sanitation, and children, in particular, frequently died from these diseases. Moreover, as time passed, many of these diseases became preventable. As the traditional homemaker and healer in families, women often avidly followed the new medical discoveries, and many were determined that this knowledge be communicated to other women and used by them. Other women's missionary organizations, such as settlement houses, saw health education as a major part of their mission.

Second, while the late nineteenth century did not invent alcoholism or alcohol abuse, urban Protestants were deeply aware of the dangers of alcohol. Many women believed that alcohol was a major cause of the abuse of women and children, and they were struck, as were many male progressives, by the way the profits from alcohol lined many an already well-lined pocket. No longer content with preaching individual repentance or the denunciation of the evil from the pulpit, such women as Frances Willard and the Woman's Christian Temperance Union resolved to end the curse once and for all by forcing alcohol off the market. Joining with the more masculine Anti-Saloon League, they helped launch one of America's great moral crusades, one that led eventually both to one constitutional amendment ending the legal manufacture of alcohol and another guaranteeing women the right to vote.

Third, the apparent increase in prostitution awakened women's concerns. While it is difficult to determine whether the total number of sex workers increased or decreased in world cities such as Chicago, the existence of the oldest profession was a sign of women's economic and social vulnerability. Many lower-end female vocations did not pay enough to sustain life without additional income, and single women, alone and unsupported, were caught between morality and necessity. As with alcohol, many women found the traditional moralizing about the issue hollow. The problem lay in the social structures that encouraged such evil.

> The deaconess movement also perceived prostitution as primarily a social problem, rather than a question of individual depravity, and sought to combat it through prevention — the solution favored by the progressives. Deaconesses did not establish homes for fallen women as gospel welfare workers had done in the past. Instead they stationed themselves in railroad

---

tent of the "social gospel" that informed women's missionary efforts. The three items above as well as the concern for cultural deprivation were almost universally present in deaconess work, in settlement houses, and in institutional churches. For that reason they seem to me to form a women's "social gospel." The writings of Rauschenbusch and Mathews were very popular in the training schools.

> depots, where they kept a watchful eye for young women who appeared new to the city and none too sure of themselves, approached them, and directed them to a respectable boarding house if they did not have friends or relatives in the city.[6]

Perhaps not incidentally, the late nineteenth century also saw a syphilis epidemic that threatened the lives of married women as well as their single counterparts.

There were other gender-related issues that were, if not unique to the period, at least evident to many at the time. Access to information about modern life was often related to social class. The new domestic science that sought to apply modern principles to homemaking, for instance, was widely known among middle-class American women. The privileged had access to programs in women's colleges and in the more progressive high schools, and perhaps above all, to the large number of women's magazines. The latter were important not only for their articles, but also for their advertisements that contributed to a woman's education as a consumer and manager of domestic affairs. Such sources were less readily available to poorer women. Educational deprivation nurtured female poverty. Many poorer women lacked marketable skills, whether the new secretarial and clerical skills that provided employment for the rising middle classes or the more traditional women's trades of sewing and piecework. To further complicate matters, the new "world cities" were often cold and hostile places where the comforts of conversation and visiting were often lacking. At times issues of cultural deprivation were also important. Americans, in general, had only begun to discover the role of beauty and art. But the pleasures of this new aesthetics were often confined to those with money. All settlement houses and institutional churches had some programs designed to make the world brighter.

This cluster of women's issues at home and abroad constituted a woman's social gospel that many women believed demanded action. Because women were comparatively powerless — unable to vote in secular elections and excluded from many governing structures of Protestant churches — they had to find appropriate organizational structures to express their concerns. Thus, in order to appoint single women missionaries (and to ensure that women's issues were addressed), women formed their own missionary societies that worked with their denominations while maintaining some independence from them. By 1894 there were thirty-three women's foreign mission boards. At much the

6. Mary Agnes Dougherty, "The Social Gospel according to Phoebe," in *Women in New Worlds: Historical Perspectives on the Wesleyan Tradition*, ed. Hilah F. Thomas and Rosemary Skinner Keller (Nashville: Abingdon, 1981).

same time, women formed home missionary societies to support their sisters in urban ministry. In addition, the various city societies often had substantial female membership. The most important urban agencies for women missionaries, however, were the settlement houses, the institutional churches, and missionary homes. The programs of these agencies revolved around the issues of the women's social gospel, as their directors sought to find ways to meet women's needs. They were a domestic counterpart to the "women's work with women" so influential abroad. What was perhaps most distinctive about these agencies, compared with more masculine forms of outreach, was their concern with a ministry that might alleviate such burdens as loneliness and the general drab quality of urban life. The "visitor" — a woman who might or might not have nursing training — was an important bearer of this type of social service.[7] Visitors had a ready ear for domestic problems, good advice about issues of health and domestic economy, and often a working knowledge of their city's charities.

To some extent the women's social gospel was an extension of the popular understanding of women's and men's spheres. Historian Michael Kimmel writes: "There had always been, of course, a division of labor between the sexes, from hunting and gathering to agricultural to early industrial societies on both sides of the Atlantic. What was new — and distinctly American — were the strictness and the degree to which men and women were now seen as having a separate sphere. The home became entirely the domain of wives; husbands were even less involved than before. Men ceded both responsibility and authority over household management."[8] Seen from this perspective, what women missionaries were doing was extending their role as family nurturers to the larger social order. Lucy Rider Meyer, one of the most articulate women leaders, provided some evidence for this view: "The real origin of the work in America was, in the mother instinct of woman herself, and in that wider conception of woman's family duties that compels her to include in her loving care the great

7. The visitors were often willing to do the messy things that more secular charity workers avoided, such as attending the poor when they were dying and washing and dressing the corpse and even providing funds for a "religiously" proper burial. See Mary Agnes Theresa Dougherty, "The Methodist Deaconess, 1885-1919: A Study in Religious Feminism" (Ph.D. diss., University of California, Davis, 1979).

8. Michael Kimmel, *Manhood in America: A Cultural History* (New York: Free Press, 1996), p. 53. Kimmel's claim that the doctrine of separate spheres was uniquely American seems questionable, either as a construct or in terms of strictness and degree. The middle classes in all Western countries seem to have passed through a similar stage in their development in which the woman becomes, so to speak, the captain of the domestic ship and her husband, away during the day on business in the city, steps away from direct family leadership.

needy world-family as well as the blessed little domestic circle."[9] People like Meyer and her more secular friend, Jane Addams, were in effect "mothers," or at least maiden aunts, to industrial America.

Yet perhaps this interpretation should not be stretched too much. Part of what was happening as society specialized was that specialists now did work previously left to generalists. Something like this was happening to home keeping as the middle-class woman increasingly became a "specialist" in everything from family health and sanitation to child raising and the proper management of the domestic economy. The value of these skills, or many of them, to those both outside and within the family was evident to many women who took legitimate pride in their achievements. One can see something similar happening in farming. The traditional work of the peasant was drudgery that required little thought, planning, or training. However, as the various agricultural revolutions took place, the knowledge needed to operate a successful farm — in the modern style — grew. Agricultural colleges taught agriculture in the same way that some women's colleges taught "domestic science." As in agriculture, women's work could lead to further and more creative specializations. Thus, it was a short step from women's newly acquired task of family health manager to nursing, or from general family care to social work and personal counseling. What is important is that the new understanding of domesticity also involved the creation of real, socially valuable skills that could be used elsewhere.[10] The "mother instinct" that Meyer prized so much was in fact a highly complex social and cultural construct capable of creating additional cultural values.

II. Turning toward Training

Like the dispensationalists, women's missionary activists turned to the concept of training as best suited to their educational aims and goals. Not surprisingly, this ensured many points of similarity between the two groups of schools in curriculum and in the use of some educational style. Even at the time, some people believed that these similarities made them expressions of the same

9. Quoted in Dougherty, "The Methodist Deaconess, 1885-1919," p. 131.

10. Another way to put this argument is to say that the new understanding of the work of middle-class women created "social capital" that could be invested elsewhere. The term "social capital" is taken from Robert Putnam, "Bowling Alone: America's Declining Social Capital," *Journal of Democracy* 6 (Jan. 1995): 65-78. Like economic capital, social capital can be converted to another form and put to a different use. Thus, just as one can convert one's share in a factory into cash and in turn invest that cash in a new technological company, so one can convert "social capital" into "skills and knowledge" that have "cash value in another context."

movement. Yet, one needs to be cautious. The idea of training for various vocations has a long history outside of theological education, and some elements of training programs, including the strong emphasis on learning through experience, were common to preparation for a number of jobs. People often do similar or occasionally the same things for very different reasons throughout higher education. A professor at a liberal theological seminary, for instance, may believe in requiring the biblical languages as a way of securing the next generation of scholars, while a professor at a dispensationalist school may believe that the languages are necessary for a literal or plain reading of the text. Both may use the same textbook, and perhaps the same exercises, but the classes, as experienced and as taught, will be substantially different.

Writing in 1914, William Adams Brown called attention to gender as the distinguishing mark of a number of schools. "Apart from the ordinary means of theological training open to men and women alike provision is made for the religious training of women in a group of institutions specially designed for them, such as the training schools for deaconesses conducted by the Episcopal church and the training school of the Young Women's Christian Association."[11] Some of these schools were very small and, like some early Bible schools, flourished for a season under a charismatic leader or leaders and then passed from the scene. In 1915, at the height of the movement, one surveyor of the schools located 36 training schools exclusively devoted to training women for missionary service with 17 training schools devoted to both men and women. Many of the latter appear to have been Bible schools.[12] One distinguishing mark of the women's training schools was their denominational affiliation. The denominations with such schools included: American Baptist (4), Southern Baptist (2), Congregationalist (2), Canadian Methodist (1), Disciples of Christ (1), Evangelical Lutheran (1), Methodist Episcopal (16), Methodist Episcopal South (2), Presbyterian (6). In most cases the training schools were related directly or indirectly to the women's missionary societies, although particularly among Methodists, some were more closely affiliated with the deaconess movement. Among the better-known schools were the Chicago Baptist Missionary Training School, the Chicago Training School and Deaconess School, the National Training School of the Young Women's Christian Association (New York City), and Scarritt Training School (Kansas City and later Nashville).

11. William Adams Brown, "Theological Education," in *A Cyclopedia of Education*, ed. Paul Monroe, 5 vols. (New York: Macmillan, 1914), 5:598.

12. John T. McFarland, Benjamin Winchester, R. Douglas Fraser, and James Williams Butcher, *The Encyclopedia of Sunday Schools and Religious Education: Giving a World-Wide View of the History and Progress of the Sunday School and the Development of Religious Education Complete in Three Royal Octavo Volumes* (New York: Thomas Nelson and Sons, 1915), p. 916.

As schools for women directed by women, they had to deal with the actual conditions of their students. Since few women were college or even high school graduates, for instance, it was impractical to use graduation as an admission standard. Moreover, gender determined how much a family might contribute to their children's education. If funds were tight — as they often were in the rural families that fed the training schools — families often devoted the money to educate their sons. Many (but not all) training school women had watched enviously as brothers had left the farm or village for college and perhaps seminary, knowing that the world of learning and adventure that awaited their siblings was not available to them. The training schools with their low costs and high sense of morality and purpose, like the foreign and home missionary movements, offered a way for adventure, personal growth, and development. But they met another need as well. Those women able to finish college — and this included many of the founders of training schools — found their way to a religious vocation blocked at that point. Most Protestant churches at the time believed that women should not be ordained, and the seminaries tended to have admission policies that either prohibited women from attending or discouraged them. And where women were admitted, their reception was less than enthusiastic. The training schools provided a place, both as leaders and as students, for some highly educated women to find fulfillment outside the seminary orb.

Once the larger Bible schools were excluded from the list, the average size of the training school was between 13 and 26 students, although the Southern Baptist Women's Missionary Training School reached 142 students in 1922. In many ways the schools were defined by their size. Most were able to meet in large homes that served as dormitories, classrooms, and student life centers. Following a popular model from women's colleges, the residents had assigned domestic responsibilities as well as instruction in domestic science. The chores also enabled the training schools to keep their costs to a minimum. At a time when women's colleges generally charged $325 dollars a year for tuition alone, for instance, many training schools charged only $3 or $4 a week for board, with room and tuition free.[13] The same economic conditions affected teaching. Lacking endowments, the schools were often dependent on volunteer teachers. At times the volunteers provided a high quality of instruction. The University of Chicago Divinity School faculty frequently lectured at the Baptist Chicago Training School, and the faculty of Garrett Theological Institute served the Methodist school in the same way.

13. T. Laine Scales, "All That Befits a Woman: The Education of Southern Baptist Women for Missions and Social Service at the Women's Missionary Union Training School, 1907-1926" (Ph.D. diss., University of Kentucky, 1994), p. 110. Male seminaries likewise charged no tuition.

An even closer relationship characterized the Woman's Missionary Union (WMU) Training School and Southern Baptist Theological Seminary. While the school provided the instructors for such courses as music and domestic science, the seminary provided the biblical and theological instruction. Ironically, some of the instruction at the training school was better than the teaching at the seminary. Southern Seminary continued the older pattern of recitation longer than many other institutions, while teachers at the training school used such newer methods as lecture and discussion. Further, the WMU school attracted the more socially progressive members of the Southern faculty, such as Charles Spurgeon Gardiner and, later, W. O. Carver.[14] Not surprisingly, these faculty members introduced their students to the work of the more progressive social gospel advocates in the North, especially Walter Rauschenbusch and Shailer Mathews. In this sense the women's social gospel appears to have been significantly less bound by regional loyalties and styles than the male-dominated Southern church.[15]

Unlike teachers in dispensationalist schools, women's training school teachers presented a cross section of American Protestant theological opinion,[16] including advocacy of critical views of the Bible. And they may have been more than simply abreast of the seminaries on this issue. Since the training schools were not teaching critical exegesis, lecturers could use a developmental approach to introducing the biblical text that emphasized the growth of the biblical tradition over the analytical examination of any particular passage.[17] But ahead or behind, the content of instruction at the women's training schools was more like the teaching at the seminaries than like the teaching at the Bible schools.

The training schools were educationally creative in their use of practical

14. Gardiner was the instructor of choice for such young Baptist liberals as Herbert Gezork, the later president of Andover-Newton, and Carver was one of the leading Southern Baptist advocates of participation in the ecumenical movement.

15. See Paul Patrick McDowell, *The Social Gospel in the South: The Woman's Home Mission Movement in the Methodist Episcopal Church, South, 1886-1939* (Baton Rouge: Louisiana State University Press, 1982).

16. William Vance Trollinger, *God's Empire: William Bell Riley and American Fundamentalism* (Madison: University of Wisconsin Press, 1990), notes that Riley throughout his ministry demonstrated a loyalty to many of the earlier progressive causes, including prohibition, but did not accept the new progressivism of Franklin Roosevelt. The same apparently can be said of many theological conservative leaders who were educated before the First World War. This seems to have been particularly true of those Baptist conservatives who elected to stay within the Northern Baptist Convention after the fundamentalist/modernist battles of the 1920s.

17. For a popular text with this approach, see Washington Gladden, *Who Wrote the Bible? A Book for the People* (Boston and New York: Houghton Mifflin, 1891).

missionary work as part of their curriculum. Many of the duties Protestant church employees had to perform were (and perhaps still are) best learned through on-the-job experience, preferably with the help of a supervisor or mentor. Such tasks include the administration of charity, personal visiting, Sunday school teaching and management, and youth work. The training schools, which occasionally functioned as missions in their own right, provided ample opportunity for mentored experience. Almost as soon as their bags were unpacked, women students were put to work at one or another ministry. Like all forms of supervised learning, the quality of these placements varied. At its best, such training was excellent. A student at Lucy Rider Meyer's Chicago Training School and Deaconess Home, for instance, who worked in the school's hospital, received excellent hands-on training in nursing under the supervision of physicians with impressive credentials.[18] Whether this level of training was available in many other schools, however, is doubtful. Like seminary field education, the quality of on-the-job training often depended on who was available to work with a student and how much a supervisor had to invest in the student's work. Not all successful or creative practitioners of an art or skill are effective teachers.

The training schools also pioneered courses on "methods." Then, as now, "method" was a loaded term in education and philosophy. Part of what gave the term such power was its association with science. Popular writing about science (and even some more sophisticated treatments) assumed that science was not so much a body of knowledge as a way of approaching the world or a method of investigation. In this view, modern advances in science, particularly in technology, came about because of the application of such tools of learning as experiment to an ever widening number of physical phenomena. The scientific emphasis on method had another, less obvious, intellectual advantage. Then, as now, scientific conclusions changed rapidly as new knowledge was gathered and assimilated. To be a scientist was to recognize the roots of this revisionism in science itself. Further, "methods" was also used in such emerging fields as advertising and sales to describe various "tried and true" ways of increasing production. When applied to religious work, the term could mean anything from a list of practical pointers to a fairly sophisticated analysis of how certain situations could be handled. In religious education, one of the practical concerns shared by the training schools and the seminaries, the term often suggested the application of educational research to religious teaching.

18. Meyer had attended medical school and had visited the famous school for nurses at Kaiserswerth in Germany.

III. Lucy Rider Meyer and the Deaconess Movement

In Romans 16:1 Paul mentions Phoebe, a deacon of the church at Cenchreae, near Corinth. For many women in the nineteenth century, Phoebe and her ministry became the symbol of a new office in the Protestant churches, the deaconess. In Germany Theodore Fliedner, an activistic young pastor with connections to those who founded the Innere Mission, noted the new style of ministry that was becoming common among Catholic sisters, especially those in orders inspired by the seventeenth-century Vincent de Paul. Catholic authorities had historically advocated the enclosure of religious women and had attempted to restrict their work to the teaching of girls and to such holy feminine arts as the embroidery of vestments. Vincent had taken his Sisters of Mercy (who originally did not take binding vows) out of the convent and assigned them social and charitable work in Louis XIV's Paris. Although the work of the Sisters of Mercy was criticized in the seventeenth and eighteenth centuries, the Vincentian understanding of the work of holy women flourished in the nineteenth. The church, everywhere pressed by the new forces of urbanization and secularism, needed far more workers than the male priesthood and religious orders could provide. Various orders of Vincentian nuns rushed in to meet those needs, helping to create such institutions as the parochial school systems in Germany and, later, the United States. Like other Protestants, Fliedner was impressed by the sisters' dedication and effectiveness. To do similar work among Protestants, he created a new Protestant order of deaconesses who wore distinctive garb and whose work was supposed to be primarily service. Like Catholic sisters, these women were initially unpaid, receiving only enough for room and board. In 1836 Fliedner established his famous school for sisters at Kaiserswerth. This institution was the first professional school for nurses, and it attracted many visitors and students from other countries. Although American imitators of Fliedner's sisters appeared before the Civil War among Episcopalians and Lutherans, the deaconesses did not become a significant movement among American Protestants until the 1880s.

Lucy Rider Meyer was among those inspired by the new movement. Lucy Rider was born into a Vermont farm family, and she early developed strong religious views. Meyer was passionately interested in education. She graduated from Oberlin College and attended the Philadelphia Women's College of Medicine. Subsequently, she studied chemistry at the Boston Institute of Technology and completed her medical training at Northwestern University, where she received the doctor of medicine. Rider was scientifically sophisticated enough to write one of the period's better-selling chemistry textbooks. She became active in the Sunday school and served for a season as a Sunday school worker in Illinois. As a Sunday school leader and writer, she traveled to London for the 1876 world conference of Sunday school managers and advocates. While there she met most of the important leaders in American Christianity, including Dwight L. Moody, John Wanamaker, and John Vincent, all of whom were enthusiastic about the expansion of Christian schooling. During her tour of the Continent, she met others with a similar passion. She began to dream about establishing a school, and by 1882 was agitating for a training school by writing in the Methodist press and hounding anyone who would listen to her plans or read her letters. Finally, in 1885, she secured a tentative authorization for such a school when a sudden storm ensured that people would stay for an after-meeting where she received tentative "authorization."[19] The response was far from enthusiastic, but it was enough. Armed with that authorization and a new husband with real financial and administrative skills, she opened her school with three students. While at Oberlin, Meyer had flirted with the Holiness movement, and her decision to start and continue the school was similar to that of other founders of "faith" enterprises. In the absence of formal church financing, she had to trust God and her friends for support.

The new deaconess movement fit Meyer's plans well. She became an enthusiastic supporter of it, designed the distinctive garb worn by the Methodist deaconesses, and worked hard to secure the recognition of the deaconess order and of her school by the national church. This latter goal was attained in 1887. The deaconess movement added to the spirit of sacrifice that surrounded the school. Deaconesses were to be unmarried; they were to receive no salary apart from a place to live, and board; and they were to be willing to do whatever work was needed to alleviate suffering. The genius of the new movement was the flexibility provided by its evangelical poverty. As with the Catholic Sisters of Mercy, evangelical poverty provided the deaconess with flexibility. The decision to found the deaconess hospital in Chicago came out of an experience where a deaconess acted to meet an immediate crisis.

> With warmth and food she was soon able to give an account of herself, an account aptly verified. She was the widow of a man who had been a wealthy merchant in an eastern city. Both were influential members of a Methodist church. A dissipated son squandered the father's fortune, and dragged his widowed mother down to the direst poverty. At last he had pawned her gold-bowed spectacles for drink, leaving her half-blind and helpless. The visitor had found her at first in a cold room with no fire, and nothing to eat.

19. The facts about Meyer are drawn from Isabelle Horton, *High Adventure Life of Lucy Rider Meyer* (New York: Methodist Book Concern, 1928).

> She refused to be moved, for she was looking for the return of her son with "something to eat." Going again, the deaconess found her about to be turned out of that poor lodging and brought her to the only shelter she knew aside from the county home.[20]

Since the Deaconess Home did not have sufficient room to meet the needs of such cases, Meyer moved to establish a small hospital. Her contacts in the Chicago medical community volunteered their services (most medicine, at that time, was practiced in the home), and the deaconesses provided the necessary labor.

Methodist resistance to Meyer and her movement was substantial. The school was never strongly supported by the denomination, and student recruitment was always a problem. At times the school and its leader were forcibly put in their place. In 1908, for instance, Meyer was ordered by the Conference Committee not to wear the distinctive garb of a deaconess, because she was a married woman and, hence, technically not entitled to such an honor! At another point Jane Addams, the founder of Hull House and a frequent lecturer at the training school, joined the school's board of trustees. Conservative Methodists violently objected to the appointment on the grounds that Addams did not include evangelism in the program of her settlement and was not connected with the work of any church. Meyer was forced to ask her friend to step down from the board. Such battles had their effect. Meyer's health was often poor, and she had to frequently retreat to California to recuperate.

By 1914 Meyer's health had declined to the point where the question of the future of the school needed to be faced. In that year her husband, who had served as the financial manager of both the school and the *Deaconess Advocate*, a journal that told the story of the movement, decided it was time for the *Advocate* to cease publication. In some ways the discontinuation of the paper marked the beginning of the end. The question was no longer whether Meyer would step down, but when and under what conditions. With that strange irony that history often contains, the last two years of Meyer's stewardship were marked by the larger conflicts that were shaping American Protestantism. Josiah Meyer had serious reservations about the historical critical approach to the Bible. To him, as to many other activist Christians, it seemed to cut the nerve of missions and to replace certainty with doubt. In contrast, his wife was an unabashed supporter of the new scholarship: "I can never consent that the historic method of Bible teaching should be given up. It is reasonable and sensible. I could no more go back to the old way than I could put myself in the little

20. Horton, *High Adventure Life*, p. 155.

calico dresses I used to wear when I was ten years old."[21] At the same time, the Meyers also disagreed about the future leadership of the school. Lucy Rider Meyer wanted her place as principal taken by a woman, preferably one who had come up through the ranks and could continue her spirit of service and innovation. Her husband, perhaps because he had grown weary keeping track of the business affairs of a constantly changing constellation of enterprises, wanted the new principal to be a man with substantial training in educational administration.

The battle over the succession was fateful. Josiah Meyer won the battle in the board, and a male successor was appointed. As is so often the case, the choice of a new leader was also the choice of a different future. In part inspired by the promise of support from the centenary fund of the Methodist church, the Chicago Training School underwent a series of reorganizations that carried it far from its initial sense of mission. For example, a graduate program was initiated, men were admitted, and in the 1920s a pastoral training program began that eventually evolved into a three-year program. The new funds never materialized. The Methodist drive, like other fund-raising drives at the end of the First World War, failed to attain its goals. Even worse, the new programs were hardly adequate, much less innovative.

Perhaps even more critical, the training school leaders continued to be unclear about their goals. If the principal aim was now to produce ministers, could the Chicago Training School claim to do this better than well-financed Garrett? If on the other hand its major objective continued to be the training of men and women as Christian lay workers, could it adequately certify them as "professionals" for the various fields of Christian work? Or could other institutions, such as seminaries and schools of social work, do this better?[22]

To state the question in those terms is already to answer it in the negative. The Chicago Training School, for all its strengths, was no substitute for Garrett or for the schools of social work at Northwestern and the University of Chicago. In that world it was clearly a "country cousin," condemned by the circumstances of its birth and youth to lag behind its "big city" rivals. Perhaps the most remarkable part of the story is not that the school finally merged with Garrett but that it lasted as an independent institution until 1935. Other such schools, including the very similar New England Deaconess Training School, died more quickly.

21. Horton, *High Adventure Life,* p. 322.

22. Virginia Lieson Brereton, "Preparing Women for the Lord's Work," in *Women in New Worlds,* p. 196.

IV. Edinburgh 1910

The future of Protestant missions appeared almost unlimited in 1910 when enthusiastic missionary leaders met for the third World Missionary Conference. The title of the meeting was, like so many other uses of the word "world" before the Great War, pretentious and misleading. In fact, most of the delegates were either from the United States, Britain, or the "white" dominions with only a smattering from the Continent and even fewer from the newer churches established by the missionaries.[23] Yet, for all its limitations, the conference marked the beginning of some important reexaminations of the missionary enterprise. Perhaps the most important was done by Commission V, headed by W. Douglas Mackenzie, president of Hartford Seminary. This commission was given the loaded task of evaluating the education of missionaries and making recommendations for its improvement.

While more restrained than the later Hocking report,[24] the report issued by this commission was clear enough about basic problems. The most important was a change in the nature of missionary work: "[W]e have worked too much upon the assumption that a missionary's work consists in the first place in doing some evangelistic preaching, and then gathering little groups of people to whom you give elementary Christian instructions. [It] may have been so in the earlier days of missions, and it may be so still in some of the fields where you are working among ruder races."[25] To put this conclusion in other words, the task of the missionary had changed from the work of the pioneer and the creator of new institutions to the much more difficult work of building permanent structures for Christian life abroad. Despite both pre- and postmillennialist hoopla about the evangelization of the world in this generation, the crusade against paganism had become a war of attrition that would require the presence of missionaries and of missionary workers for some years to come. But if this assumption was correct, then the implications for the training of mission-

23. Hutchison notes that 1,000 delegates were British or North American, 170 were from the European continent, and only 17 were from the newer churches.

24. William Ernest Hocking, *Rethinking Missions: A Layman's Inquiry after One Hundred Years* (New York: Harper and Brothers, 1932). This report, commissioned by the Rockefeller-financed Institute for Social and Religious Research, was a hard-hitting attack on much contemporary American Protestant thinking about missions based on an examination of the work actually done abroad. Although it was strongly opposed by many missionary leaders at the time, many of its conclusions have subsequently been accepted.

25. Dr. Campbell Gilson, in *The Preparation of Missionaries: The World Missionary Conference; The Report of Commission V; The Training of Teachers* (London and Edinburgh: Oliphant, Anderson and Ferrier; New York, Chicago, and Toronto: Fleming H. Revell Co., 1910), p. 159.

aries followed with the force of a mathematical demonstration. It was no longer enough for missionaries to receive the traditional education given to Protestant clergymen. What was needed was a professional curriculum that included five areas of study: the science and history of missions, the religions of the world, sociology, pedagogy, and the science of language. In other words, the prospective missionary needed to be trained in what later missiologists would call the art of cross-cultural communication. This was a demanding task that called for a thorough mastery of both the missionary's own culture and the culture that would receive the missionary.

As often appears to have been the case, the raising of professional standards had profound implications for women and the institutions that trained them. In effect, as soon as women were able to clear the bar, those guarding the gates raised the bar one or two more notches, making victory less attainable. The commission did not wait to draw those conclusions. The problem with the women's training schools was that they attracted comparatively few college graduates or others educated to a sufficiently high standard to meet the new demands of work abroad.[26] The schools that trained women missionaries, hence, needed to raise their standards and to focus the education of their students. In concrete terms this meant that the deaconess sister needed to be replaced by the professional nurse, the missionary teacher by the normal- or university-trained educator, the visitor and charity worker by the social worker. And all these professionals needed advanced training in comparative religion and social science.

Were the men on Commission V trying to exclude women from the foreign field? Probably not. Mackenzie, after all, was president of one of a handful of seminaries that had admitted women on almost the same basis as men,[27] and he appears to have believed that women had a vital place in the church's leadership. Rather, the commission appears to have done its work with little reference to the actual value of what women were accomplishing on the field. The evangelistic work of women, "women's mission to women," was breaking down some of the most ancient and socially repressive structures by demonstrating that alternatives existed,[28] and the women they trained in the Bible were important role and personal models for other women abroad. As was often the case, too, male missionary leaders seemed oblivious to some of the real evils, at home and abroad, that affected women's lives. Suttee, forced child marriage, and other practices may have been part of cultures that Westerners only dimly

26. *The Preparation of Missionaries,* p. 59.

27. Women were not eligible for funds under the beneficiary system that financed much male theological study at the time.

28. Women Peace Corps workers often achieve much the same result by living independent lives and participating in women's activities.

understood, but they were also part of women's nightmares, of the realm of things too horrible to contemplate sociologically or anthropologically.

Commission V, or to be more precise, the line of thinking it represented, marked the beginning of the end for many women's training schools. There were increasing demands that the schools meet new and higher standards,[29] but there was rarely the money available to do so. The drive in the 1920s toward greater church efficiency also diminished the resources available to the training schools. During that period many of the women's home and foreign mission societies were folded into the larger missionary societies of the churches as such innovations as the unified budget and the national church budget took hold. In effect, the women's schools became orphans, losing the needed voice in the church's councils to make their case effectively for financial support. The church's fiscal crises, beginning in the 1920s and 1930s, often provided the coup de grâce that ended a school's life or caused the fatal wounds that drained its lifeblood.

V. Two Schools That Survived: The Woman's Missionary Union Training School and Scarritt

Two of the women's training schools that survived long into the twentieth century were the Woman's Missionary Union (WMU) Training School at Louisville and the Scarritt Training School for Christian Workers in Nashville. The WMU school survived as a special school for women until 1945 when it began to admit men and changed its name to the Carver School of Missions. In 1957 the school was incorporated into Southern Seminary as the Carver School of Missions and Social Work. The Carver school was unusual in that it granted an accredited social work degree that was nationally respected. Scarritt's story was similar. It began to admit men in the 1920s and survived as a school for Christian workers until 1988, when the Women's Division reclaimed the property of what was then the Scarritt Graduate School for a retreat center. In 1964 Scarritt absorbed the National College, formerly the National Training School. National had specialized in the training of missionaries.

At first glance, there was little unique in the story of these institutions. The WMU school had been begun by missionary activists more or less independent of the parent organization. In 1907, at the end of Fannie Heck's presi-

29. For instance, a 1916 survey of training schools by Warren Palmer Behand, of the Baptist missionary training school in Chicago, "An Introductory Survey of the Lay Training School Field," *Religious Education* 11 (1916): 52, called for standardization and the raising of standards.

dency of that organization, the WMU officially took charge of the school. This was a fateful decision. Unlike other women's missionary organizations, the WMU had experienced considerable opposition in the larger convention, and for years its president had to recruit a man to read its report to the convention, lest any might think Southern Baptists were encouraging women exhorters.[30] In large measure, the strong prejudice against women's leadership among Southern Baptists enabled the WMU to escape the type of incorporation of women's missionary organizations that was common in the 1920s. Although Protestant leaders rarely delivered on their promises, such unions were usually accompanied by promises that women would be given more influence in the management of missionary affairs. Southern Baptist men were unwilling to make such an accommodation, even verbally, and the women retained their independence.

Meanwhile the WMU Training School became part of the highly complex subculture of the Woman's Missionary Union. In part because of their isolation from the convention and occasionally from the local churches, Southern Baptist women constructed their own world of meaning and service. Perhaps the best symbol of this world was the set of rituals that might accompany a young Southern Baptist woman as she moved toward maturity. Each girl was enrolled in the GA, or Girls' Auxiliary, at an early age. GAs underwent a thorough program of missionary training that involved increasingly detailed knowledge of Baptist work abroad, of foreign cultures, and of their own history as Baptist women. The program was climaxed by a ceremony in which the girl, now a radiant young woman, marched to the front of the church or, in some congregations, the WMU wearing a white dress. At which point she was invested with a crown and scepter and recognized as a queen. By this point she was also thoroughly socialized into the work of the WMU.

The power of this culture became manifest twice a year when the WMU collected the Lottie Moon and the Annie Armstrong offerings for foreign and home missions. During the difficult financial years of the 1920s and 1930s, when the Cooperative Program was unable to collect sufficient funds to support the convention's programs, these WMU collections provided the sinews for strong programs at home and abroad. Graduates of the training school were not incidental to these funding activities. The national and state leaders of the WMU, people on whom the convention ultimately depended from the 1920s to the 1960s, were often drawn from among WMU Training School graduates. Their active contributions to the denominational cause magnified the importance of

30. For information on women in Southern Baptist life, see Leon McBeth, *Women in Baptist Life* (Nashville: Broadman, 1979).

their alma mater. Further, many graduates of the WMU school married men destined for the mission field, and they used their training to become very effective missionaries in their own right, if not with their own salary.[31] Their tours of the South, while home on furlough, were often festive affairs as they brought with them all the paraphernalia of women's life in exotic places, including dolls and native dress, and stories of the plight of women abroad. The ideal of "women's work with women" was continually kept before Southern Baptist women.

The WMU school in Louisville survived, thus, because it continued to have a vital place in a women's subculture that the larger Baptist community in the South had to take seriously, if only for financial reasons. When that culture began to slowly unravel in the 1950s, those who earlier would have attended the WMU school either shifted to Southern Seminary's School of Religious Education or found another niche in the structure. Yet, the Carver school continued to play an important role in the life of Southern Baptist women, even as a coeducational school, until the fundamentalist leadership of the SBC closed the school in the 1990s. While the significance of this event was lost to many Americans, those within Southern Baptist life recognized it as part of the conservative determination to encourage a "biblical" understanding of women's ministries in the churches.

The Southern Methodist women who supported Scarritt did not inhabit as tight a women's subculture as their Baptist sisters. Although there was considerable resistance to women's participation in the conference and to women's ordination, Methodism provided women with a more open atmosphere and with more places of leadership in the general church. Partly for these reasons, Scarritt seemed on the same path as the Chicago Training School and Deaconess Home and the New England Deaconess Home and Training School toward finding a home in a nearby university or seminary. But this did not happen. Why?

Founded in Kansas City, largely as a result of the work of Belle Harris Bennett, the school was provided a small endowment by Nathan Scarritt, a local Methodist pastor, and his wife. The school had pioneered in the study of religious sociology and religious pedagogy or education, drawing on the professional help of women trained at the Hartford School of Religious Pedagogy. However, by 1921 Scarritt had grown a bit long in the tooth. The school's physi-

31. I knew many such graduates of the WMU Training School personally and know from my own experience how determined they were for the work abroad to be successful. Many continued the older traditions of "women's mission to women" as well as a host of other tasks in the missions.

cal plant badly needed replacement and the financial situation was bleak. Like the Chicago Training School, it tried initially to solve its problems by electing a male leader, Jesse Cunniggim, a noted Methodist educator and advocate of correspondence training for ministers.[32] Cunniggim, a graduate of the University of North Carolina, Vanderbilt, and the University of Chicago, was as aware of the demand for more professional missionary leaders as the other training school administrators, but his educational past suggested different courses of action. William Rainey Harper, the educational entrepreneur who built the University of Chicago, believed theological institutions should cluster around universities while retaining their own ecclesiastical identity. A similar idea was being tried at Vanderbilt, which had been separated (almost expelled) from the Methodist Episcopal Church, South, after an extended brawl over issues of theology and control. Cunniggim decided to seize the day. In 1924 he moved the school to Nashville, where he could use some of Vanderbilt's superior resources, especially teachers and the library, for his work. The choice also protected the school since Southern Methodists, still bitter over the "loss" of their university, were not likely to propose merger with that institution as they might have done had Cunniggim moved nearby the Methodist schools in Atlanta, Dallas, or Durham.

But Cunniggim also had the good sense to protect the school's mission. While he admitted men to the school, he refused to follow the popular training school route of beginning a shortened course for ministers. Perhaps he realized that the seminaries would sooner or later, if only because of superior wealth and prestige, win that competition. In the 1920s seminaries were beginning to organize their own accrediting body that was designed, in part, to define seminary training in ways that self-consciously did not include training or Bible schools.[33] Consequently, Cunniggim shifted the school's stance just a bit. Again he followed in Harper's train. Harper had believed that the first two years of college were general education that prepared students for professional or true university work in their last two years. This model was popular among some seminaries, especially Baptist schools, which issued the bachelor of theology as their basic degrees. In a similar way, Cunniggim made two years of college the requirement for admission to Scarritt's programs that could now be defined as professional work in Christian social work and education. At the time, it was a creative solution to a complex problem, and it did enable Scarritt to meet the

32. For the masculinization of the training schools, see Richard E. Tappan, "The Dominance of Men in the Domain of Woman: The History of Four Protestant Church Training Schools, 1880-1918" (Ed.D. diss., Temple University, 1979).

33. See below, chap. 19.

objections to training schools raised by Edinburgh 1910. The women and men trained at Scarritt were professionals, but they were not seminary-trained.

The eventual disappearance of the women's training schools tells us something about the history of gender in the United States. Such schools flourished at a time when women were rapidly entering the secular and religious workplace but it was also still acceptable for women to appeal to feminine virtues, especially nurturing, as part of their mandate for service. The schools, thus, represented a combination of the feminist demand that women be included in religious leadership and the renewed appreciation of women's unique contribution to society. It is no accident that many training schools, including Louisville's WMU school, often looked to a balance between domestic concerns and academic concerns, typical of schools like Mount Holyoke, as an ideal model. The schools, thus, represented two sides of a complicated turn-of-the-century women's world. On the one hand they were part of the rising demand for professional education for women. Such women as Lucy Rider Meyer were professionals in their own right, and, in her case, in several professions, including medicine and science. But they were also part of a movement to professionalize women's work. Like those who taught domestic science in high schools and colleges or wrote for or read the newly popular "women's" magazines, they wanted to apply modern knowledge to the traditional work of women as homemakers, nurturers, and counselors. The *Epworth Herald* stated the matter simply: "The deaconess Girl, who is none of these, is mixed of them all. She has borrowed from her Sister her devotion, and from the social expert her modernity. . . . I have seen her act like Lady Bountiful without condescension, and like the janitor's wife without embarrassment. . . . I have discovered that she can be judge and advocate, housekeeper and hostess, investigator and friend, saint and woman, and count it all in a day's work."[34]

Did the women's training schools have an impact on the larger world of Protestant education at the turn of the century? Clearly their existence, along with that of the Bible schools, helped convince many seminary leaders to band together in an accrediting association. But to some prophetic leaders they suggested more than merely competition. While we often think of a university, for instance, primarily as a research institution, turn-of-the-century Americans saw much of the university's promise in its work as a federation of professional schools that maintained the highest standards of knowing and of practice. The new practical fields were essential to this understanding of theological education, as was some type of theological clinic or field experience. Whether these

34. Cited in Dougherty, "The Methodist Deaconess, 1885-1919," p. 134.

new disciplines and educational techniques originated in the training schools or not — and I do not think they did — the training schools made significant contributions to their development and, hence, to theological education as a whole. And, although lines of transmission are always difficult to document, the training schools, along with such organizations as the YMCA, the councils of churches, and the home mission movement, may have been one of the important ways in which social Christianity became part of American Protestantism's religious fabric.[35]

35. Although it is only a conjecture, it is interesting that two important progressive leaders, Theodore Roosevelt and John D. Rockefeller II, first became deeply socially concerned after struggling with the issue of prostitution in New York City. Rockefeller was an important financier of progressive Protestant institutions.

CHAPTER ELEVEN

Doing It Right: The Early Years of the University of Chicago Divinity School

By the 1890s many American theological educators yearned for a chance to do it right. Since the 1870s they had been exploring new ideas about their work, ranging from faculties composed of professional scholars to the need for a social exploration of faith, but natural institutional inertia held institutional innovation to a minimum. Some schools had taken significant steps. Union Theological Seminary in New York had made itself the unofficial capital of American theological scholarship,[1] and Harvard and Yale had taken tentative steps toward transforming their schools into true university divinity schools. At Harvard, President Charles Eliot applied many of the same strategies he had pioneered in other areas of professional education, especially the graduate and medical schools, to transforming the divinity school. Under his prodding the once Unitarian denominational seminary dropped its formal affiliation, began to explore non-Christian religions, built a superior program in Semitic languages, and developed one of the first departments of social ethics. Further, Harvard divinity faculty was integrated into the larger university. Yale moved more slowly in the same direction. President Timothy Dwight III had improved the scholarly credentials of the faculty, and the school attracted students of different denominations from many areas of the country.[2] While Harvard's nondenominational sta-

1. Kim Younglae, *Broken Knowledge: The Sway of the Scientific and Scholarly Ideal at Union Theological Seminary in New York, 1887-1926* (Lanham, Md.: University Press of America, 1997), tells the story of Union's centrality in American scholarship in the two decades around the turn of the century.

2. For Yale, see George Wilson Pierson, *Yale College: An Educational History, 1871-1921* (New Haven: Yale University Press, 1952), and Roland Bainton, *Yale and the Ministry: A History of Education at Yale for the Ministry from the Founding in 1701* (New York: Harper and Brothers, 1957).

tus was primarily based on scholarship, Yale's tended toward a coalition of the centrist positions in many denominations. Despite intense controversy, Andover had demonstrated what a curriculum based on the newer liberal theology might include and had begun to explore more modern approaches to its task. But its freedom to innovate was limited by its inability to generate support. But, as significant as all these changes were, in many ways they were only baby steps. What was needed was a school that could bring together all the suggestions for change into a single institution and show that they were viable. Almost by definition, the only place where that was possible was a new school.

The Divinity School of the University of Chicago was that new — or to be precise, almost new — institution. From its founding until sometime in the 1940s, when the school's focus turned more toward scholarship, the Divinity School was a central (perhaps *the* central) institution for those who believed that Protestant ministers should receive training analogous to that received by other modern professionals.[3] Like other professional schools, the divinity school was expected to operate according to the larger academic and educational standards of the university. Divinity professors were not allowed to segregate themselves. They were expected to serve on university-wide committees and to teach in a variety of university programs. At the same time, the divinity school was to have access to the skills and learning of other members of the faculty. Yet it was also to draw its standards from the actual practice of ministry. Theological science was not to be practiced for its own sake but to improve the capacity of ministers to communicate their message to the present world. As in schools of medicine, law, and social work, ministerial training was to be a public enterprise, directed to the good of church and commonwealth.[4]

The University of Chicago was, like Princeton Seminary, also the home of a particular way of thinking about theology, the so-called Chicago School or Chicago modernism. In many ways Chicago School modernism held a place in the history of American theology similar to the place the divinity school held in

3. By the 1940s the divinity school at the University of Chicago had moved more in the direction of training an academic elite for the American university. Neither the university nor the divinity school was completely happy with this development, and repeated efforts have been made since then to steer a slightly different course. One motive behind the Federated Faculty experiment — one of the most creative attempts to fuse the research university and the seminary — was the university's desire to recover its role as a center for ministerial training. A similar motive lay behind Chicago's early development of a professional doctorate in ministry. Yet, while the university has continued to be a center for theology and for the study of the history of religion, it has lost its early lead as a center for issues around ministerial preparation.

4. Robert Wood Lynn, "The Harper Legacy: An Appreciation of Joseph Kitagawa," *Criterion* 24, no. 3 (1985): 6.

the history of American theological education. Early American theological liberalism of the type associated with such classical exponents as Lyman Abbott, Washington Gladden, William Newton Clarke, and Charles A. Briggs was often formulated, so to speak, on the fly. Such issues as evolution, biblical criticism, and the social crisis demanded theological treatment now. Many implications of the new theology were not clear, perhaps even to those who formulated them, and were left for later liberal theologians to ferret out. The question of God was one such issue. The early liberals believed that it was important to talk about God as immanent in natural and historical process and to erase the distinction between the natural and the supernatural. But, having reached such conclusions, they seldom asked whether such formulations made it necessary to conceive of God in impersonal terms or explored the implications of their position for personal piety. Further, early liberals assumed the truth of Jesus' teachings about the Fatherhood of God much as their conservative counterparts accepted his warnings about hellfire. The second generation could not rest long with such unexamined pieties. If the modernists often seemed radical, it was because they had to clean out the corners of the liberal house where their predecessors had left the less pleasant implications of their own position. In short, the Chicago School was essentially the second and third generation of American liberal theological thought, and like all second- and third-generation work, it was a scholasticism that used philosophical technique to make sense of the work of earlier reformers.[5]

I. Harper's Vision

In the 1890s Chicago was near the center of America's new urban and industrial development. In part, the city's significance came from its location at a key

5. For the development of American liberal theology, see William R. Hutchison, *The Modernist Impulse in American Protestantism* (Cambridge: Harvard University Press, 1976); Kenneth Cauthen, *The Impact of American Religious Liberalism* (New York: Harper and Row, 1962). Cauthen developed a useful typology that distinguished between various shades of liberal opinion, based largely on their distance from traditional evangelical Protestantism. Cauthen's typology, however, does not explain why liberalism developed as it did. In my opinion, the transitions often reflected different intellectual generations as much as they did abstract theological decisions. Since "theological generations" often overlap in the same institution, the generational character of the distinctions is often obscured. My own model for understanding the transitions is an application of Weber's well-known idea of the routinization of the charisma. The first generation of any theological or religious movement is too busy dealing with the world and its needs to stop and consider all the implications of its position. Subsequent generations, so to speak, not having to reinvent the wheel, have to try to understand the legacy they have been given.

transportation intersection. The Great Lakes and the Erie Canal united Chicago with the East and much of the Old Northwest, but more important, Chicago was the railroad hub of the Midwest. The railroads had, in effect, transformed the region into a vast inland sea whose business leaders shipped goods, people, and raw materials with the ease and economy traditionally associated with coastal areas.[6] This expanding economy required a large army of professionals, and Chicago was home to many independent professional schools.

Religion, likewise, flourished in this new city as the various Protestant churches established congregations and schools. Even before the University of Chicago was established, the city promised to be the "city of seminaries": the Presbyterians established Lake Forest College and moved McCormick to the area; the Congregationalists, Chicago Theological Seminary; and the Baptists, Baptist Union Seminary (Morgan Park). The Methodists elected to put their institutions, Northwestern University and Garrett Biblical Institute, in nearby Evanston. In addition, Baptists and Methodists maintained training schools for women in the city, and the independent conservatives located their flagship school, Moody Bible Institute, there as well.[7]

William Rainey Harper, the future president of the university, was an early convert to the city and its advantages. In 1879 he was called to teach Hebrew at the Baptist Union Seminary at Morgan Park, then a nearby suburb, and he taught at that school until 1886. In that year Harper left to teach in the graduate school at Yale where Dwight hoped his reputation as a linguist and teacher would make his school more competitive with Harvard. Given the intensity of that competition, Yale was willing to invest much in keeping its "star" in its constellation. But Harper had remained in touch with those who wanted to find ways to re-create the financially defunct Old University of Chicago, including Henry Morehouse, Thomas Goodspeed, and Frederick Gates.[8]

Harper promised them he would consider the presidency of a new uni-

6. William Cronon, *Nature's Metropolis: Chicago and the Great West* (New York: Norton, 1991), especially chap. 1.

7. Interestingly, a similar concentration of seminaries took place in San Francisco and developed at about the same time.

8. The whole question of how committed Harper was to the Yale position has not been clarified by time. While working closely with the group that wanted to re-create the University of Chicago, he also engaged in continual negotiations with Yale for more money and privileges. At one point he persuaded Timothy Dwight III to raise $2,000,000 for a new language department with Harper at its head. Dwight was so angered at Harper's later resignation that he told his former academic star that he wished that "he had never come to Yale at all." Thomas Wakefield Goodspeed, *A History of the University of Chicago: The First Quarter Century* (Chicago: University of Chicago Press, 1916).

versity in that city. The reason he was willing to be held, so to speak, in reserve was John D. Rockefeller, whom the Chicago advocates hoped to enlist in their plans. Rockefeller was America's premier businessman. Under his occasionally ruthless leadership, the oil industry, which had been subject to violent price fluctuations as more or less crude oil came to market, had been organized into a virtual monopoly. Rockefeller saw his consolidation of this chaotic industry as a public service. He had ensured that Americans would have a continual supply of a clean burning product at an affordable and constant price. In contrast, his opponents saw him as the villain of a melodrama who had risen to the pinnacle of wealth and influence by swindling widows out of their inheritance and driving competitors to bankruptcy. But whether an angel or a devil, Rockefeller was a convinced Baptist and one of the most generous supporters of denominational enterprises. He had already given substantial amounts to Rochester Seminary, the Baptist Union Seminary, and Southern Baptist Theological Seminary and was rumored to be interested in new ways to support his denomination's causes.

The most important of these was a Baptist university. Augustus Strong, president of Rochester Seminary and a Rockefeller relation by marriage, was one of the most vocal advocates of the plan: "We need an institution which shall be truly a university, where, as at Johns Hopkins, there shall be a large number of fellowships, where research shall be endowed, where the brightest men shall be attracted and helped through their studies, where the institution itself shall furnish a real society of people distinguished in science and art."[9] Strong had two clearly denominational objectives. Although Baptists had established many small colleges, few Baptist schools were distinguished. Strong hoped for a strong Baptist university that would be the equal of Unitarian Harvard or Congregationalist Yale. Such a school, Strong hoped, would attract the brightest and best graduates of Baptist colleges and academies and provide these students with advanced intellectual training. In turn, this would contribute to the formation of a national Baptist elite. Second, Strong hoped the school could have a "theological school" at the "center, giving aim and character to the whole."[10] But such an institution was expensive. Strong knew from firsthand

9. Cited in W. Carson Ryan, *Studies in Early Graduate Education: The Johns Hopkins, Clark University, the University of Chicago* (New York: Carnegie Foundation for the Advancement of Teaching, 1939). See also Conrad Henry Moehman, "How the Baptist University Planned for New York Was Built for Chicago," *Colgate Rochester Divinity School Bulletin* 9 (Feb. 1939): 119-34, and Leonard Sweet, "The University of Chicago Revisited: The Modernization of Theology, 1890-1940," *Foundations* 22 (1979): 324-51.

10. Ryan, *Studies*, p. 96. Strong had struggled to make Rochester a center for Baptist theology, and he had done much to make the school an important center of Baptist thought. For an

experience how budget-intensive university education was, and as a practical administrator, he knew that theological education was equally costly, especially as the newer standards for ministerial education required more faculty and staff.

Strong's wooing of Rockefeller ran into many difficulties. The president of Rochester was not a person who knew when to speak and when to be quiet, and he wearied Rockefeller by arguing for his proposals almost incessantly during a trip to Europe. But, considerations of personality aside, Strong also leveled with Rockefeller about the cost of his dream: $22 million. At that time Rockefeller did not have the money for such a major investment, and the backers of a Chicago school were able to woo him with the promise of a far more modest undertaking. They were willing to leave "what present need there may be, if any, for technical or professional schools in Chicago under Baptist control . . . to the natural growth of time."[11] To be sure, by the time Rockefeller was finished with Harper, he would give the president of Chicago more than $26 million, but those gifts, given over a number of years, came after the automobile raised Rockefeller's massive fortune to obscene levels. When Rockefeller expressed interest in the proposed college, Harper insisted that at least one professional school — a divinity school — had to be included. This was not a serious change in the proposal. Unlike the Old University of Chicago, the Morgan Park seminary, of which Rockefeller had been a trustee, was a successful school that could contribute many assets to the new venture. These included an established reputation, experienced teachers, and a relatively strong endowment. Although the Morgan Park school remained legally independent, it was part of the projected school almost from the beginning.

How much of the university existed in Harper's mind when the project started? Was the school, as hostile critics charged, "Harper's Bazaar," a somewhat incoherent institution that grew haphazardly? Or was it the working out of a master plan, known only to Harper, that he gradually revealed as he persuaded Rockefeller to give ever more money? Or perhaps the plan for the school partook of elements of both of these interpretations. While Harper was always ahead of Rockefeller in his dreams for the school, he was in fact learning as he went. When Harper became president, he was after all a comparatively young man, born in 1856, with no experience in college or university administration. He had all the problems of the eager amateur on the way to becoming a profes-

---

account of Strong's work at Rochester, see LeRoy Moore, Jr., "The Rise of Theological Liberalism at the Rochester Theological Seminary, 1872-1928" (Ph.D. diss., Claremont Graduate Schools, 1966).

11. Thomas Goodspeed, *A History,* p. 60.

sional: he underestimated costs, saw more promise in certain ventures than they may have possessed,[12] and occasionally failed to recognize the true value of a contentious professor, such as the brilliant John Dewey. Yet, more often than not, Harper's instincts were right on target. Harper was willing to invest heavily in good faculty members, often calling the best available people from other schools, and he had an especially good eye for theological teachers. Perhaps more than many of his competitors, Harper had a sense of the zeitgeist, of the spirit of the present, and he was a master of contemporary jargon. His writings sparkle with such words as "efficiently," "scientific," "democratic," "popular," and "active." Few university presidents have had such command of popular culture or of the American love affair with schools, degrees, and social advancement. Unlike at the stuffy intellectual factories of the East, Harper was willing to try any innovation at Chicago — a university press, numerous scholarly and popular journals, a quarter system, summer schools, coeducation, correspondence schools, junior as well as senior colleges, support for emerging professions and education for their pioneers, creative academic disciplines, and patterns of cooperation among institutions. In two decades Harper made the University of Chicago into one of America's premier schools and helped it attain a worldwide reputation.

II. Bold Proposals

Harper's genius was that he was profoundly unoriginal. While he was perhaps the best Hebrew teacher of his generation, his own scholarly contributions, such as his *International Critical Commentary on Amos and Hosea* (1905), largely reflected the consensus of contemporary scholarship. The same was true of his famous literary debate with William Green over the authorship of the Pentateuch. What made Harper devastating in that argument was his capacity to summarize the arguments of others, to fill the many lacunae of logic left by more creative minds, and to direct the result at the weaknesses of his opponent's case.[13]

Harper's essay "Shall the Theological Curriculum Be Modified, and

12. He tried, for example, to sponsor his own training school in competition with the two Chicago training schools and with Moody Bible Institute. Not surprisingly, the enterprise failed and had to be reborn as a school of social work.

13. Green, a master logician, would have made quick work of a more creative mind, as he did on many occasions, and his erudition would have carried the day against a traditional exegete, but Green had far more difficulty with Harper's capacity to put "what everybody" knows into effective prose.

How?"[14] likewise contained few ideas that others had not pioneered. What made the essay exciting was its scope, its capacity to name the problem clearly and to propose solutions to existing dilemmas. The essay began with an appraisal of what Harper felt was the problem of theological education:

> Many intelligent laymen in the churches have the feeling that the training provided for the students in theological seminary does not meet the requirements of modern times. These men base their judgment upon what they see in connection with the work of the minister who has been trained in the seminary. Nor is this dissatisfaction restricted to the laity. Ministers who, after receiving this training, have entered upon the work of the ministry, and who ought to be competent judges, are frequently those who speak most strongly against the adequacy and the adaptation of the present methods in the seminary. So prevalent is this feeling that students for the ministry often ask the question, "Is there not some way of making preparation other than through the seminary?"[15]

The keywords in this succinct statement stand out: "requirements of modern times," "the work of the ministry," and "present methods." These phrases were almost a shorthand version of Harper's understanding of his divinity school.

The sense that religion and the ministry were out of touch was a commonplace at the turn of the century. Although some might believe that the world was entering "the Christian century," many others wondered what the church had to say to a world that was increasingly dominated by science, technology, and industry. Modernity was not simply a matter of new intellectual challenges to faith, but modern people appeared almost different in kind than their predecessors. Although Harper was aware that many theologians and biblical scholars had completely changed their approach to religion, he believed that many American theological schools were hidebound, tied to forms of education that were as dated as many dogmatic textbooks. What the schools needed to do was adjust their approach to education to the insights of their best teachers.

14. W. Clark Gilpin, *Preface to Theology* (Chicago: University of Chicago Press, 1996), p. 86, notes the close relationship between Harper's essay and the essay by Charles Eliot, "On the Education of Ministers," *Princeton Review,* May 1883, pp. 340-56. Many of the themes are in fact parallel. Both Harper and Eliot, for example, shared a deep conviction that the university was the best place to train ministers, and both were deeply committed to the elective system. For Harper, electives are a democratization of education that exalted the place of the individual. Yet, Eliot is only one of a number of sources that might have influenced Harper, whose reading and thought were encyclopedic.

15. W. R. Harper, "Shall the Theological Curriculum Be Modified, and How?" *American Journal of Theology* 3 (1899): 46.

In an urban world, for instance, the seminary remained resolutely rural.[16] Unlike the countryside, seen as narrow and parochial, cities were naturally intellectually broadening; urbanites had to live with people of diverse perspectives and had to adjust their thought to these differences. For Harper, location was more than physical place; location was a metaphor for the context in which people lived and thought. In a time of cosmopolitanism, the ministry had become parochial.

Harper believed, apparently correctly, that many ministers did not know either the methods or the conclusions of modern science and that their preparation kept them from any serious encounter with one of the principal intellectual forces shaping the world. The requirement of a liberal arts degree in the better theological schools was a step in the right direction, but Harper knew that the small, often poverty-stricken colleges that many prospective ministers attended were part of the problem.[17] Such schools often lacked modern innovations like laboratories, and new disciplines were only slowly added to their programs. The churches were caught in a similar trap. Much Protestant church life, even in large cities, had changed little since the early nineteenth century. But the failure to change served to highlight the church's distance from the surrounding culture. Over the last century, the way people did things — their methods — had changed in almost every area, from housekeeping to printing to engineering. The churches were almost alone in their proud isolation. For Harper, the only way out of this morass for seminary and church was to link the work of ministry with modern and up-to-date methods.

Harper hoped that the churches would turn to the universities for guidance in meeting this crisis. He saw three aspects of the professional education offered by universities as crucial elements in producing an up-to-date ministry: an elective curriculum, the use of research-oriented seminars, and the critical examination of practical experience. All of these involved an increasing role for individuals in determining the pattern of their learning: "First of all, and if I mistake not, most fundamental of all, is the principle of individualism — a principle capable of application alike to students, instructors, and institutions. Every man born into the world comes into it with the limitations of his work

16. Harper, like other turn-of-the-century advocates of changes in theological education, exaggerated the rural and small-town character of American theological education. Few important schools — Hamilton and Auburn come to mind — were located in rural areas, and many of these would either move to the cities or merge with urban schools over the next few decades.

17. Both the Kelly and the Brown-May studies of theological education indicated that most theological students attended small denominational schools. The number of students that entered the ministry from the more prestigious schools, such as Harvard, Yale, and Williams, had been in continual decline since the Civil War.

clearly defined by nature. The man who succeeds in life is simply the man who is fortunate enough to discover the thing that nature intended him to do."[18] The principle of individualism was remaking the other professions, Harper noted, as physicians, lawyers, scientists, and university professors increasingly devoted their time to the study of narrower topics or problems.

> To put the whole matter in a single proposition: The day has come for a broadening of the meaning of the word, minister, and for the cultivation of specialism in the ministry, as well as in medicine, law, and in teaching. In the village and small town, a single man can do all the Christian ministry, as well as in law and medicine. There is evidently no room here for the specialist in any field. But in the small cities, as well as in the large cities, the time has come when specialism in the ministry is as necessary as specialism in any other profession.[19]

At the time of his essay, Harper identified four specialized areas: the preaching ministry, education, missions, and administration, although he did not intend for the list to be comprehensive.

From these premises, certain conclusions followed with the inevitability of a syllogism. The seminaries had to reshape their work around a more modern, professional understanding of the ministry. In some ways this principle worked like Occam's famous razor — "it is vain to do with more what can be done with less." For example, biblical studies had long been dominated by the ideal that all ministers should be their own exegetes. But this ideal was increasingly dated. The average practitioner did not have the time to attain this ideal. Modern biblical studies simply required too much time and too many expensive resources for an isolated individual to do serious research. Hence, while a university-related school would offer the courses and languages necessary to become a skilled biblical scholar, it would provide those with other special interests with a general overview of the Scriptures and biblical studies. Naturally, one approach to such general studies was to center basic instruction on the English text.

The emphasis on the English Bible flip-flopped Harper's earlier understanding of biblical studies. Before becoming president of the University of Chicago, Harper had been the nation's best-known and perhaps best teacher of Hebrew. He had established summer schools of Hebrew around the country and had conducted lay courses in it at the Chautauqua institutes. He often

18. William Rainey Harper, "Ideals of Educational Work," *Proceedings of the National Educational Association* 34 (1895): 990.

19. Harper, "Shall the Theological Curriculum?" p. 59.

seemed to believe that, armed with his inductive method, he could teach anyone the rudiments of the language in a fortnight. In 1881 he had stated: "Hebrew will never generally be made an elective. That is, for full graduation from a theological seminary there will be demanded in the future, as the past, some knowledge of the language."[20] But by 1899, after struggling with the issue for almost two decades, he had come to realize that this was no longer an attainable goal.[21] Most students would do better to invest their limited time in other studies. Hebrew, he reluctantly concluded, should be an elective in a truly professional curriculum.

The new style of theological education also required the application of "the assured results of modern psychology and pedagogy." The later fascination with the social context of the New Testament and of Christian teaching that was so characteristic of Shirley Jackson Case and Shailer Mathews was an example of the application of this axiom. Harper was also concerned that ministers receive instruction in those disciplines. To lead human beings to God, the minister had to have a thorough understanding of humankind. Closely related to this was Harper's demand that theological schools increasingly use "clinics" or various forms of supervised experience as part of their teaching methods. There was no way to learn to do something without actually doing it, and the best way to do it was with a more experienced expert at one's side. The good clinical course was not just experience; it was evaluated experience that allowed one to see and learn from one's worst practices and to work toward establishing better practices. The clinic differentiated the divinity school from a graduate school of religion. "Without its clinics the medical school is a school for the study of certain facts of science; it would not be a school for the training of physicians. Without its clinics the theological school is a school for the study of history and philosophy, and is not a place for the training of preachers or Christian workers."[22] The clinic was also a scientific way of approaching humankind. Only by observing religious people closely could the prospective minister learn how religion actually functioned in human life.

Harper was a prophet in yet another sense. He knew that the type of pro-

20. William Rainey Harper, "Bible Study in the Pastorate: Facts and Figures," *Old Testament Student* 6 (1881): 131-35.

21. Part of the reason was his own survey of the teaching of the language in seminaries that revealed that the amount students were learning was minimal. See William Rainey Harper, "The Teaching of the Old Testament," *Old Testament Student*, Mar. 1888, especially p. 291. Equally important, the standard for what constituted a useful knowledge of Hebrew kept rising. And as it did, the time needed to clear the bar kept increasing. See William Rainey Harper, "The Department of the Old Testament in the Seminary," *Old Testament Student* 4 (1884-85): 136-38.

22. Harper, "Shall the Theological Curriculum?" p. 6.

fessional training that the modern ministry needed was expensive; he proposed that, as each seminary could not make provision for all specialties in Christian work, an agreement be reached among seminaries located in a given district by which the students of all institutions in that district that wished to work in a given specialty be advised to go to the seminary in which the specialty was cultivated.

In practice, Harper believed that the concentration of resources in a university made possible an even more audacious plan of cooperation. Just as the divinity school remained a legally separate body from the University of Chicago while being thoroughly incorporated into the larger mission of the university,[23] so several seminaries could cluster themselves around the university and use its resources, as well as those of its divinity school, freely.

The idea was not original. Harvard's Eliot had made a similar proposal and had attracted the Episcopal Theological School to an adjacent site, and began negotiations with Andover, either for a move or a union, that continued until the two schools merged.[24] The fact that Chicago was still relatively virgin territory would make the cluster idea more viable there. The first school to join in a cooperative plan with the university was the Disciples' Divinity House. Later Meadville Seminary, a small Pennsylvania Unitarian school, began exchanging students during the university's summer session and, pleased with the results, relocated in Chicago. In 1926 Congregationalist Chicago Theological Seminary, which had been located on the West Side of Chicago, moved to Hyde Park in order to cooperate more fully with the university.

Harper's proposals were the most consistent alternative to the traditional seminary curriculum yet offered, and he invited five other theological educators to respond to them in a number of the *American Journal of Theology* published later that year.[25] Like many artificial debates, some of those who responded answered more off the top of their heads than from the depths of their experience. And some, like Augustus Strong, who believed that Harper was calling for a form of education modeled on the Ph.D., missed the point almost

23. This curious arrangement continues today with the divinity school technically owned by the Baptist Educational Society. Harper did not want to endanger the whole university in the theological battles among Baptists and wanted the freedom to jettison the divinity school if need be.

24. Similar ideas were common in California at this time. The University of California was, at least by common repute, Harvard West, and a number of seminaries clustered around the university's Berkeley campus. This would become the core of the later Graduate Theological Union.

25. George Harris et al., "Modifications in the Theological Curriculum," *American Journal of Theology* 3 (1899): 46.

completely. Nonetheless, Harper's skillful summary of the thinking of a generation set the stage for many of the debates that would occupy American theological education for almost a century.

III. The Empirical Reality of an Empirical School

The divinity school was committed to a twofold understanding of its mission: "the interest of the university is distinctly in a school of theology which shall partake exclusively of a scientific character, while it is also within the scope of the university to develop a school of theology which shall emphasize the practical side of the work."[26] During the first years of its history, the divinity school attempted to be a scholarly center and a research center, and a place for scientific professional preparation.

Before becoming president of the university, Harper had been a successful and popular teacher of Old Testament and Hebrew, and the school he created was a center of both popular and professional biblical study. Many journals that Harper had published before becoming president as a means of uniting those interested in biblical studies were continued by the University of Chicago Press, although often under other names. The *Hebrew Student,* for example, became the *Biblical World.* But more important, the university in its early years continued to popularize biblical studies. Bernard Meland observed: "Under William Rainey Harper and Ernest DeWitt Burton, and later J. M. P. Smith and Edgar Goodspeed, the study of the Bible took on the romance of a popular movement among the people of the churches of the Midwest, not unlike the Great Books movement of the Thirties."[27] In addition to these instructors, Dean Shailer Mathews almost lived on the rails as he traveled to colleges and churches spreading the good news about contemporary scholarship and theology. He also served as president of the Northern Baptist Convention and worked closely with the Conference of Theological Schools, the precursor of the Association of Theological Schools. Divinity faculty were very active in the life of local churches. Harper and his fellow teachers almost adopted the Sunday school at the Hyde Park Baptist Church as a part of the university and worked to make its work among the most efficient and up-to-date in the city. This hands-on experience encouraged Harper to organize the Religious Educa-

26. Quoted in Martin E. Marty, "Joseph Kitagawa, the Harper Tradition, and the Divinity School," *Criterion* 24 (1985): 12.

27. Bernard Meland, "A Long Look at the Divinity School and Its Present Crisis," *Criterion* 1 (Summer 1962): 21-30.

tion Association to promote advance in religious and biblical instruction. Chicago's faculty played major roles in the International Sunday School Lesson Committee and in other popular biblical enterprises.

For Harper, the historical study of the Bible was a practical part of the church's outreach: "The cry of our times is for the application of scientific methods in the study of the Bible. . . . If the methods of the last century continue to hold exclusive sway, the time will come when intelligent men of all classes will say, 'If this is your Bible we will have none of it.'"[28] The university went to great lengths to protect the scientific character of its biblical study. Although the same person frequently held both positions, the school established chairs of Old and New Testament languages in both the divinity school and the university. This arrangement protected teachers from the controversy over the Bible that was taking place among Baptists, and anchored biblical study in a larger academic community. Perhaps most exciting, at least from a student's perspective, was that the number of teachers available in Bible was approximately twice that available at the old Morgan Park seminary. And these instructors were not alone. Students had access to such university teachers as Robert Harper in Assyriology and James Breasted in Egyptology. Biblical study, particularly Old Testament studies, was part of a much larger and growing academic world.

Edgar J. Goodspeed's experience with papyrology illustrates how this larger biblical community worked. He gave this account of his first exposure to the new discipline: "I heard of it one night at the New Testament club, when Dr. Clyde W. Votaw said there was a papyrus in Dr. Breasted's office. Next morning I called on my own friend James Henry Breasted and asked about it. He got it right out and in five minutes there I was, well started on the downward path to papyrology."[29] The experience with the papyrus was typical. Chicago avidly collected the resources needed for original biblical research. Among the collections that the school acquired were the library of Ernst Wilhelm Hengstenberg, a noted German Old Testament scholar; the collection of the American Bible Union; the stock of Heinrich Simon, a Berlin bookseller; and numerous papyri. The faculty searched for treasures while they were abroad, and eagerly reported their finds to Harper or one of his successors. Although the money was not always available, it usually was. In less than a decade the divinity school accumulated the resources to carry out its scientific work, surely one of the great stories of library building in American history. As Thomas Goodspeed said, "rarely has

28. Maria Freeman, *Pursuing the Higher Criticism: New Testament Collections at the University of Chicago* (Chicago: University of Chicago Press, 1993), p. 1.

29. Edgar J. Goodspeed, *As I Remember* (New York: Harper and Brothers, 1953), p. 98.

any faculty possessed so large a proportion of editorial and journalistic writers and producers of books."[30] The University of Chicago Press made sure that these writings, whether in the form of books or as contributions to the *American Journal of Theology* (after 1920 the *Journal of Religion*) or the *American Journal of Semitic Languages and Literature*, were made available to other scholars.

The study of sociology in the university enriched the biblical studies of the divinity school. One of Harper's first choices for the university faculty was the sociologist Albion Small, and he favored the hiring of teachers with a social cast. In the 1890s, further, Harper called Shailer Mathews to teach New Testament at the divinity school. Mathews was a graduate of Colby and Newton, but his graduate education in Germany was in secular history. From the beginning, Mathews was deeply interested in how religious ideas related to the larger social culture, and this correlation was the theme of his later studies. In 1908, after Mathews was transferred to the department of theology, Shirley Jackson Case was appointed in New Testament. Case was convinced that social analysis provided the interpreter with the clearest picture of how the New Testament and its characteristic theology evolved. Sociological study provided Chicago's theologians with their characteristic form of liberalism. Essentially, the social and historical study of doctrine indicated that Christian (and other religious) teaching arose in a social milieu to help faithful people understand the needs of their own time.

The understanding of the milieu in which ideas originated was crucial. The natural inertia of culture meant that religious teachings, like philosophical abstractions, often outlived their original context. Such worn-out ideas might continue until they became "an enemy of progress . . . fastened on society." Historical study helped thoughtful people discern when that had occurred. In that sense, critical study was the first step in liberating people from teachings that had became instruments of injustice. In other words, historical study was the preparation for the more constructive work of the theological school as a whole: to weigh the church's teachings, to see which ones were still useful and discard the rest. If, as Mathews argued, "the history of Christianity is one of successive applications of a religious inheritance to new needs," then the present had the obligation to do for its generation what earlier theologians had done for theirs.[31] The historicism of this position lay in the fact that it assumed that each generation had the task of reformulating its religious heritage into symbols and teachings that spoke to its own generation in its own generation's words. To a casual observer, a vast distance separated Edgar Goodspeed's collection of papyri from the speculations of the systematic theologians, but Chi-

30. Thomas Goodspeed, *A History,* p. 364.

31. Shailer Mathews, *The Faith of Modernism* (New York: Macmillan, 1924).

cago's professors saw them connected by a close and intricately woven world of inference.

From the beginning this approach to biblical studies and to theology was controversial. The tension between the school and the Baptist constituency was so great that Harper had to resort to extraordinary means. Shailer Mathews told the tale:

> Some of the religious newspapers of the country were unqualified in their demand that certain members of our faculty, including the President himself, should be disciplined, if not dropped. It was President Harper's policy never to get into controversy. And attacks made upon himself personally he let go unanswered. But he took the bold step of asking the Baptist Conventions of the Central States to appoint members of a committee to come and investigate the Divinity School and to decide as to what the policies should be. . . . The body had no authority, but it gave an opportunity for President Harper to offer an alternative as to whether the Divinity School should have academic freedom or to cancel the contract existing between the Baptist Theological Union . . . thus, giving the University an opportunity to organize its own independent theological school.[32]

The committee met for several years and gave the divinity school needed support at a crucial time in its history.

The case of theologian George Burman Foster was more difficult. Foster joined the divinity school in 1895 and was promoted to full professor two years later. In many ways he was among the last of the Victorians to cry at the "funeral of God."[33] Unlike most liberals, Foster was not sure whether the turn-of-the-century fascination with missions was "the blush of health or the last flush of fever on the cheeks of the dying."[34] Foster was too much a child of the modern world to take comfort in the old verities and far too honest to believe that nonsupernatural versions of Christianity could take their place. "For myself, the biggest loss in the modern view of the world is the loss of comfort. Young

32. Shailer Mathews, *New Faith for Old: An Autobiography* (New York: Macmillan, 1936), p. 67.

33. The term is from a poem by Thomas Hardy. Cited in A. N. Wilson, *God's Funeral* (New York: Norton, 1999).

34. George Burman Foster, "Concerning the Religious Basis of Ethics," *American Journal of Theology* 12 (1908): 219. See also Harvey Arnold, "The Death of God: George Burman Foster and the Impact of Modernity," *Foundations* 10 (1967): 331-53; see p. 337. See also Alan Gragg, "George Burman Foster (1858-1918)," in *Dictionary of Heresy Trials in American Christianity*, ed. George H. Shriver (Westport, Conn.: Greenwood Press, 1997), pp. 142-49, and Edgar Towne, "A Single Minded Theologian: George Burman Foster," *Foundations* 20 (1977): 367-79.

people who have not been battered by life do not appreciate this. But by and by, when your children have died and your life is almost gone, and you seem to have done nothing, is there anything that can give you heart and hope?"[35] Foster was among the first Americans to read Friedrich Nietzsche and to understand that much of Nietzsche's optimism about the Overman was an ironic overlay that masked the philosopher's profound despair at the eternal reoccurrence of all things.

Part of the problem was that Foster had clearly moved beyond traditional theism. He was not alone in believing that the traditional affirmations about God were no longer credible. Many liberal theologians had so emphasized the immanence of God in the natural process that they made such traditional theistic constructs as belief in a personal God almost beside the point. What made Foster unusual was that he drew his conclusions without looking to the left or to the right. If what was believed about God in the past was not believable, then it was not believable, and all honest people should admit this. As Harry Emerson Fosdick had stated, liberalism offered "a generation of earnest youth the only chance they had to be honest while remaining Christian."[36] Foster did not even see such a connection with the past as necessary. Religion in the future might not use Christian language or the language of any set religious tradition. Foster had no interest in rescuing religious language or traditions from the acids of criticism. Nor was he interested in a version of faith that dealt primarily with "appliances, money, and organization."[37] Even if humankind could be saved from "poverty, dirt, and disease," the problem of "spiritual destitution" would remain. And it was here that he felt that the church had few answers.

> Is there no help for lost souls any more? The minister who cannot cope with this deepest need of the modern man may organize spiritual and often impertinent reforms, but he cannot give the bread of life. He may minister to bodily wants — good enough in its way — but he leaves the soul in its bewilderment and forsakenness. . . . It would be the minister's sin against the Holy Ghost, which had never forgiveness, were he to so truncate or abridge the nature and need of man so that our institutionalized religion of scientific efficiency could sustain an easy correlation therein.[38]

35. Quoted in Robert L. Harvey, "Baptists and the University of Chicago," *Foundations* 14 (1971): 347.

36. Harry Emerson Fosdick, *The Living of These Days: An Autobiography* (New York: Harper and Brothers, 1956), p. 178.

37. George Burman Foster, "The Contribution of Critical Scholarship to Ministerial Efficiency," *American Journal of Theology* 20 (1916): 161.

38. Foster, "The Contribution," p. 170.

Foster developed some of the implications of his perspectives in two books, *The Finality of the Christian Religion* (1906) and *The Function of Religion in Man's Struggle for Existence* (1909).

Although Harper yielded to Baptist anger about Foster and transferred him to the department of philosophy, Foster remained near the center of controversy. Many Illinois Baptist churches withdrew from the Northern Baptist Convention and joined the Southern Baptists, while others revolted against the university and established their own seminary, Northern, in Chicago. In that sense Foster reinforced the growing conviction that advanced theological education needed academic freedom, but, like one untimely born, his case came after liberal Protestants had largely settled that issue. The real significance of Foster lay in the theological question that he raised so passionately. Although Christianity has a certain status as the dominant faith of Western culture, is this status enough to privilege Christianity in the university or in daily life? For such liberals as William Adams Brown, it was.[39] For Foster it was not, or at least not necessarily, and if the divinity school never completely accepted his answer, it has equally never been able to abandon his question. The history and philosophy of religion have often been closer to the divinity school's heart than Christian theology, whether liberal or conservative.

IV. Efficiency

From its founding, the University of Chicago was interested in the question of efficiency. Efficiency was, in some sense, the quintessential question of modernity: How can someone arrange things to minimize the use of resources and time and to maximize the final product? Modern industrial production was one example of efficiency. The individual oil producers, for instance, that Rockefeller had driven out of business often used labor- or capital-intensive means of production. In contrast, Standard Oil was able to improve the quality of its product, while lowering the cost, by using more efficient technologies, such as the pipeline and newer methods of "sweetening" or removing sulfur from crude, and by concentrating its production in a few central refineries. Similar points could be made about other successful enterprises. Harper himself had tried to make education more efficient by, for example, convincing

39. William Adams Brown, "The Responsibility of the University for the Teaching of Theology," *Yale Divinity School Quarterly* 16, no. 4 (June 1920): 139-57; William Adams Brown, *The Case for Theology in the University* (Chicago: University of Chicago Press, 1938). In both of these essays, Brown recognized the problem but came down strongly on the side of a predominantly Christian approach to the study of religion.

many of the smaller Baptist colleges to use his university as a center for professional and graduate study. His plan to coordinate junior and senior college work, never completely realized, would have similar effects. And the divinity school itself, among the largest Protestant seminaries in the North, represented another approach to economies of scale.

Frederick Turner's *Principles of Scientific Management* (1911), based on his noted experiments with time/motion studies, was a paean to the use of organization to increase production and quality. Turner's book was a catalyst for much of the divinity school faculty's thoughts about theological education. In 1912 Dean Shailer Mathews published *Scientific Management in the Churches.*[40] The dean's thinking was as practical as the book's title. During the 1920s Baptists reorganized much of their charitable and missionary work around ideas pioneered by Mathews, who advocated greater centralization of giving and budgeting procedures.[41] Mathews also believed that efficiency could serve as the leitmotif for the curriculum.

1. The vocational curriculum should be of such a sort as will lead men to specializations and efficiency in various types of religious work. In general these types are (1) the pastorate; (2) religious education in connection with the churches; (3) work as missionaries; (4) social service; (5) special teaching in some particular discipline.
2. Such vocational curriculum should be organized in the interests of efficiency in the particular vocation, allowing (a) a full opportunity for general introduction to the underlying disciplines, and (b) an opportunity for specialization.[42]

It was an ambitious proposal. Although Mathews's proposals were adopted by the faculty in principle, they were not implemented until the deanship of Shirley Jackson Case. Although rarely in the form that Mathews put them, his principles were to be widely used in other theological schools during the 1920s and 1930s, and they deeply influenced the Brown-May study of theological education.

Other members of the Chicago community took up the theme of efficiency in a series of articles published between 1910 and 1920. Two of these es-

40. Shailer Mathews, *Scientific Management in the Churches* (Chicago: University of Chicago Press, 1912).

41. For the changes in denominations, see James Moorhead, "Presbyterians and the Cult of Organizational Efficiency, 1870-1936," in *Reimagining Denominationalism: Interpretative Essays,* ed. Russell Richie and Bruce Mullin (New York: Oxford University Press, 1994). The Presbyterian experience was typical of the transformations occurring in other religious bodies.

42. Cited in Thomas Goodspeed, *A History,* p. 362.

says were particularly well focused. Samuel Dike, a Congregational pastor in Auburndale, Massachusetts, wrote "Shall Churches Increase Their Efficiency by Scientific Methods?" Dike's point was that the time had come to apply the scientific method to church work in the same way it had "been at work in biblical study and theology."[43] Most churches, he noted, were "a heterogeneous collection of institutions" that operated "without much regard . . . to each other or to the whole." The time had come for a "preliminary scientific study" that would enable the churches to clarify what they were trying to achieve and the methods they needed to adopt to attain those goals. Dike believed that this approach would meet "the demands of businessmen who feel keenly the lack of efficiency in the present chaotic character of church organization."[44]

The divinity school's Theodore Soares took up the theme in his essay "Practical Theology and Ministerial Efficiency." In some ways his essay was an attempt to discuss the muddle of courses, disciplines, and clinics that had grown up around the practical work of the churches. For Soares, too many ministers had to learn how to do their work after being placed in a congregation. While the more capable clergy survived this ecclesiastical baptism of fire, many ministers were overcome by it, and others never mastered the skills needed to do the task well. There were three particular skills that Soares believed seminaries ought to insist on:

1. effectively presenting a spiritual message suited to the needs of the people and of the times,
2. organizing and administrating the church, and
3. leading the church as an educational enterprise.[45]

For Soares, this meant that the seminaries had to take seriously the psychological "questions of mood, the nature of attention, of the emotions, of the will, the whole matter of apperception, the psychology of suggestion."[46] Such attention to how religion was received might enable the preacher to understand how his words were received and to act accordingly. Only slightly less pressing was finding a way to organize the "thousand activities, employment bureaus, organized

43. Samuel Dike, "Shall Churches Increase Their Efficiency by Scientific Methods?" *American Journal of Theology* 16, no. 1 (Jan. 1912): 20-22.

44. Dike, "Shall Churches?" p. 30. Dike's essay makes a point that is often neglected in histories of Protestantism: the churches were losing their grasp on the business community as well as on labor.

45. Theodore Soares, "Practical Theology and Ministerial Efficiency," *American Journal of Theology* 16, no. 3 (July 1912): 427-28.

46. Soares, "Practical Theology," p. 428.

parochial visitations, literary societies, singing classes, choral clubs, recreations, picnics, and . . . more" that filled the life of an urban congregation.[47] Much of this could be learned in a hands-on situation under a qualified teacher-supervisor.

Soares devoted much attention to the new discipline of religious education. He believed that only a handful of people in the country were prepared to teach this new discipline,[48] but that did not make it less important. In part, Soares's emphasis on religious education was a response to the popularity of the Sunday school and to the widespread conviction that the revival was no longer the most effective way to gather a congregation. Yet, it was also related to specific commitments made by the divinity school. Since "religion is not an impartation from above," it is the result of "social interaction." If so, then the church should consciously direct the social interactions that enable "immature persons" to reach their highest "social self-realization."[49] To understand this task, Soares affirmed, the student required interdisciplinary study, including work in "biology, anthropology, sociology, comparative religions, Christian ethics, psychology, education," and practical theology. As Soares realized, religious education was becoming indispensable to a modern theological education. Although his close colleague Frank G. Ward of Chicago Theological Seminary noted that religious education "is not finding it easy to get its own regular chair around the already crowded theological table," it was doing so.[50] By 1920 religious education was an established profession in its own right with its own titles, requirements, and eventually degrees.

Between 1895 and 1920 the divinity school of the University of Chicago managed to square an important circle. Almost every issue that had impinged on theological education in the immediate past was taken up and acted upon. In that sense Chicago carried out the agenda that had been less perfectly put forth by such "advanced schools" as Andover and Union. It was scholarly, free, and well financed. At the same time, the divinity school turned itself toward the issues that would dominate the coming century in theological education: the importance of professionalism, the need for supervised experiences, finding alternatives to the fourfold curriculum, and the relationship between the study of religion and the education of ministers. Simply balancing itself on the thin line separating the ages was itself an achievement, much like an acrobat dancing on

47. Soares, "Practical Theology," p. 433.

48. Soares, "Practical Theology," p. 441.

49. Soares, "Practical Theology," p. 440.

50. Frank G. Ward, "Religious Education in the Theological Seminaries," *Religious Education*, 1915, p. 278.

a high wire. If the spectators note that the high-wire act lacks some of the finesse of the ballet, it makes little difference. The fact that anyone can dance at such a height is enough to amaze.

Almost by definition, any modernism is intimately related to its own "now," to its own place in history, and if the divinity school's work from 1890 to 1920 seems dated, it is because the school pursued not the truth of the ages, but the truth for its own time. Few other institutions have so fully embodied the best thought and practices of their own generation of theological educators, and the combination of a fresh start, strong leadership, and adequate financing that made early Chicago possible was a rarity and perhaps a singularity.

CHAPTER TWELVE

Methodism and the University

By 1860 America had entered the "Methodist age."[1] The phrase is both useful and descriptive. It is useful because it points to the deep, often unconscious relationship between Methodism and American popular religious culture. More than any of their competitors, the Methodists forged a working partnership with ordinary Americans. Like all partnerships, this one involved an exchange of values. To the "common person," to use a phrase beloved in the nineteenth century, Methodism gave a deep sense of religious life and mission. By enlisting under the Methodist banner, the average believer began a faithful quest for holiness of life and singleness of purpose. Under the watchful eye of bishops, circuit riders, class leaders, and other leaders, each Methodist was urged to perfection. At the same time, Methodism absorbed many American and democratic values and attitudes. Methodism was proud of its American heritage and its American ideals. While this meant Methodists were often in danger of confusing the nation with the kingdom, it equally meant they were always striving to make the nation conform to the kingdom. Methodism was inherently social and reformist.[2]

1. Winthrop Hudson, "Methodist Age in America," *Methodist History* 12 (1974): 2-15. Perhaps the classic treatment of Methodism as a popular movement is William Warren Sweet, *Methodism in American History* (New York and Cincinnati: Methodist Book Concern, 1938). More recently, John H. Wigger, *Taking Heaven by Storm: Methodism and the Rise of Popular Christianity in America* (New York: Oxford University Press, 1998). Wigger deals with only the earliest period.

2. One of the most difficult problems for the historian of American religion is the relationship between the Wesleyan impulse and the various Methodist, Holiness, Wesleyan, and Pentecostal churches. These religious groups are often separated as much by style and social status as by theological affiliation, and one often notes that they will tend to follow a similar course

I. Schools and the Modern

The close relationship between Methodism and American life was nowhere more evident than in the Methodist attitude toward education. Like most nineteenth-century Americans, Methodists had a love affair with schools. For them, schools were part of the "culture of aspiration";[3] that is, they offered one of the primary ways Americans could better themselves culturally and economically. Daniel Marsh of Boston University spoke for the denomination when he defined his work as follows: "I am not a beggar; I am an opener of the doors of opportunity."[4]

The close, nurturing relationship between Methodism, schooling, and social aspiration had been part of the movement from the beginning. Wesley had organized his converts into classes, set forth clear educational goals for his preachers and people, and urged people to adopt such habits as cleanliness that promoted social mobility.[5] Moreover, Wesley had been an avid writer and publisher, and the book rack was as characteristic of Methodism as the central pulpit. In America these same Methodist features encouraged Methodists to ally themselves with the drive for compulsory public education and, later, with the high school movement. Schools, like other Methodist-sponsored reforms, promoted religion and morality. The Methodists adopted the Sunday school as a natural supplement to these state-sponsored initiatives, and they were among

---

at different times in their history. Thus, many Wesleyan bodies share a deep loyalty to the college tradition for the training of their church and tend, as did the main branch of the tradition, to want to unite theological education with colleges and universities when they are ready to take that step.

3. I am indebted to David O. Levine, *The American College and the Culture of Aspiration, 1915-1940* (Ithaca, N.Y.: Cornell University Press, 1986), and to Burton Bledsoe, *The Culture of Professionalism* (New York: Norton, 1976), for many of the ideas in this chapter. I am, of course, completely responsible for the attempt to use their ideas to explain American theological education.

4. Gerald O. McCulloh, *Ministerial Education in the Methodist Movement* (Nashville: United Methodist Board of Higher Education and Ministry, Division of Ordained Ministry, 1980), p. 128.

5. Wesley did not plan for the people named Methodist to rise socially, but his theology and church organization here, as in so many other places, had implications that he did not anticipate. Bernard Semmel, *The Methodist Revolution* (New York: Basic Books, 1973); Anthony Armstrong, *The Church of England, the Methodists and Society, 1700-1850* (London: University of London Press, 1973). For a discussion of the impact of local studies to Halévy's hypothesis, see David Hempton, *Methodism and People in British Society* (Stanford: Stanford University Press, 1984). I see Wesley's teachings, where taken seriously as they often were, inspiring his followers to take certain actions that were socially useful in the modernizing societies of the eighteenth and nineteenth centuries.

the earliest and most vocal advocates of this institution. Bishop John Vincent, the founder of the Chautauqua, believed that the Sunday school had replaced the revival, at least in part, and that the schools would be the key to future Methodist growth. Hence, Vincent was tireless in his advocacy of Sunday schools and relentless in his search for new and more efficient ways to organize them. Many of the earliest American professional religious educators, such as George Coe, reflected this Methodist ethos.

William Warren Sweet noted that the reason American higher education was democratic rather than aristocratic was largely due to the evangelical churches.[6] The distinction he drew was an important one. Traditionally, European education had been directed toward an elite that, at least in theory, had the time and resources to study the classical texts. In some respects this tradition was similar to the Confucian tradition in China where young mandarins mastered certain set texts as part of their preparation for public service. Although Methodists participated in the rage for liberal arts colleges in the first part of the nineteenth century, they were never completely at home with the elitism of those institutions or with the more pronounced elitism of the antebellum seminary. They wanted educational institutions that could "square the circle" by providing their graduates with socially respectable credentials and, above all, with the skills they needed to prosper in their society. In the preparation of ministers, or at least of a ministerial leadership, they wanted a type of theological education that would not break the close relationship between the preachers and their people. In other words, they wanted a theological education that was efficient and democratic rather than classical and aristocratic.

The city was liberating for many Methodists, as it was for many other Americans. Although some Methodist churches had located in cities from the beginning, the late nineteenth century saw a shift from the rural to the urban in the focus of Methodist life. Before 1860 Methodists riveted their attention on the hamlets, villages, and small towns of rural America, and the circuit riders evangelized these places thoroughly as they wandered from place to place. But as the nation became more urbanized, Methodism followed suit. Methodists moved to America's larger cities where they were economically and socially challenged by newer styles of life. As Sweet notes, "No longer were Methodists drawn from the lower and humble social and economic groups, but rather represented the great American middle class."[7]

While urban Methodists, like other groups that immigrated into the cit-

6. W. W. Sweet, *Revivalism in America: Its Origin, Growth, and Decline* (New York: Scribner, 1944; Gloucester, Mass.: P. Smith, 1965), p. 150.

7. Sweet, *Methodism in American History*, p. 337.

ies, wanted to keep some of the features of their rural past in their churches, they were also aggressive urbanites who prized the city's get-up-and-go and saw cities as places where they could find fresh opportunities. Thus, when Chicago became the hub of much that was happening in the Midwest, the city's Old Clark Church and the suburb of Evanston became the hub of Midwestern Methodist activity.[8] But if the energy of the new America was attractive, Methodists feared that the "great population within [her] bosom" would be lost unless measures were taken to "prevent this population from being withdrawn from under her care."[9] The *Nashville Christian Advocate* put it as follows: "Not a physician can be educated under Methodist auspices, not a lawyer, nor a theologian, nor a savant. The men who fashion society must acquire their professional lure and skill in places where Methodism is perchance a byword and reproach."[10] Education was, thus, the place where Methodist hopes and fears for the modern world barnacled themselves. Methodism wanted all that the new America had to offer for its people and for its ministers: the prestige, the skills, the sense of leadership in a new urban world, and yet Methodists held back at the same time. The city was the traditional home of vice, of strong drink and loose living, and only if the city might be converted, might the Methodists be at home with the urban world's increasingly high educational standards. Schooling was, as earlier, the heart of the Methodist social gospel.

In its struggle to minister to the new urban America, Methodism had an educational advantage that is easily overlooked. The historic basis for admission to a Methodist Conference in full connection was the Course of Study. The program consisted of a series of readings, including Wesley's sermons and the *Discipline,* that provided the prospective elder with a sound foundation in Christian theology. When this foundation was completed by the on-the-job training mandated by the *Discipline,* the circuit rider was among the most thoroughly trained of American clergy.[11]

While the Course of Study secured a measure of doctrinal uniformity, it

8. For Old Clark Church and Evanston, see Harold Williamson and Payton Wild, *Northwestern University: A History* (Evanston, Ill.: Northwestern University, 1975), chap. 1, especially pp. 2ff.

9. 1848 General Conference, cited in Richard Cameron, *Methodism and Society in Historical Perspective,* Methodism and Society, vol. 1 (New York and Nashville: Abingdon, 1961).

10. Quoted in Hunter Dickenson Farish, *The Circuit Rider Dismounts* (New York: De Capo Press, 1969), p. 269.

11. In some ways the Methodist may have had a better working knowledge of theology and the Bible than his seminary-trained counterpart. Whereas the seminary graduate had to labor long over the biblical languages, often to the exclusion of other studies, the young Methodist spent his time reading materials that were immediately useful in his work.

was also flexible. The standard did not state how candidates were to secure the needed knowledge of the assigned materials or how they were to study those materials. A prospective minister might read the Course of Study privately, work with another, more experienced pastor, or attend a Methodist college or seminary where the materials were covered in the regular curriculum. The Course of Study was thus compatible with a variety of institutions and educational backgrounds and approaches. Methodist bishops made good use of this flexibility. A bishop might assign a college-educated pastor to an urban church with a largely professional membership, and a minister with less formal credentials to a rural church.[12] Even after moving toward a bachelor of divinity/master of divinity standard for full connection in the 1960s, the Course of Study continued to provide this type of flexibility for local pastors.[13]

Methodism's encounter with modernity took a different course than either the Reformed or the Lutheran struggles. The battles over the Bible that so troubled the classical Reformation churches were much less present. This is not to say that Methodism experienced no controversies. George A. Coe, one of the most creative of the early theological educators, moved to Union in New York following an epic battle at Northwestern, and the story of Hinckley Mitchell is well-known.[14] However, the most-pitched battles among Wesleyans were over issues related to holiness and to religious experience. These struggles, which often reflected class conflicts as well, split the once united Methodists into a plethora of sects, holiness associations, and camp meetings. Such debates, however, were over issues internal to the movement and not over larger cultural questions. The debate over holiness, paradoxically, may have provided space for a more liberal Methodism to develop by encouraging those with deeply seated conservative beliefs to establish their own denominations. In any event, the mainstream Methodist church moved steadily and quietly toward a liberal Protestant position at the same time it was debating the holiness question. In 1912 the Course of Study in the North reflected a thoroughly liberal under-

12. The classic study of the Course of Study is Elmer Guy Cutshall, "The Doctrinal Training of the Traveling Ministry of the Methodist Episcopal Church" (Ph.D. diss., University of Chicago, 1922).

13. Since my central emphasis is on the development of the goals and objectives of theological schools and other institutions concerned with ministerial training, I have not approached the Course of Study as a bearer of a unique Methodist theological tradition. And, of course, one of the more difficult questions is how many of those credited with completing the Course of Study actually did so and how many learned more of their craft on the job. My own sense is that Methodist leaders were increasingly inclined, particularly after the Civil War, to judge their churches on the basis of ministerial efficiency and growth rather than theological conformity.

14. See chap. 5.

standing of faith with "one book exclusively literary, three teaching a modern view of the Bible, three psychological and three homiletical, and eight dealing with some phase of the social gospel."[15] Gary Scott Smith notes:

> In the years from 1890 to 1920 Methodist theology underwent much more of a transition than did Presbyterian theology. During the 1890s, evangelical Arminianism and liberal evangelicalism gave way to the evangelical liberalism of Milton Terry, Olin Curtis, Henry Sheldon, Harris Rall, and Albert Knudsen. Professors in Methodist seminaries increasingly studied in European (especially German) universities where they were heavily influenced by rationalism, philosophical idealism, and biblical criticism. The rise of the Social Gospel, with its emphasis on the teachings of Jesus, the kingdom of God, and reformation of American society, also profoundly affected Methodist theology.[16]

While the 1890s generation was key, the liberal movement was also the working out of the deep affinities between Methodism and the modern. Robert Chiles argued, for example, that Methodism moved along a continuum between its earlier emphasis on free grace and an emphasis on free will.[17] This allowed many traditional Wesleyan emphases to be restated in more modern dress. Both classical and liberal Methodism, for instance, believed strongly that the human will could choose either good or evil and that, in this sense, the effects of original sin were limited. Equally important, both emphasized religious experience over creedal formulations and both stressed the importance of the active, moral life as the supreme mark of grace. Both were also temperamentally predisposed to an ecumenical outlook that saw religious truth in a variety of perspectives. Thomas Langford's designation of Methodist theology as "practical divinity" is a useful characterization of a tradition that had historically moved easily around the theological landscape, while retaining a sense of its own identity and mission.[18] Methodism eased into the new liberalism, often with individual Methodists hardly aware that a change had been made.

In short, American Methodism was ready to take some new directions in schooling. Both socially and theologically the university or at least seminaries

15. Cutshall, "Doctrinal Training," p. 82.

16. Gary Scott Smith, "Presbyterian and Methodist Education," in *Theological Education in the Evangelical Tradition*, ed. D. G. Hart and R. Albert Mohler, Jr. (Grand Rapids: Baker, 1996), p. 98.

17. Robert Chiles, *Theological Transition in American Methodism* (New York and Nashville: Abingdon, 1963), pp. 178ff.

18. Thomas A. Langford, *Practical Divinity: Theology in the Wesleyan Tradition* (Nashville: Abingdon, 1963).

closely related to universities were one direction that was in harmony with Methodism's social and intellectual development. Methodism was fortunate, as it entered into its university-building phase, to have William Warren at the helm of Boston University. Warren, who had earned a Ph.D. while serving as a missionary to Germany, was one of the most vocal American exponents of the new university ideal, and with the possible exception of William Rainey Harper, the American educational leader who most recognized the democratic implications of the new educational form. Boston University early had both a school of theology and a school of religious education. And his ministerial students were busy learning their new occupations by working in the field, including street preaching and work in local congregations.

One of Warren's prime catches as president was Bordon Parker Bowne, a graduate of the new City College of New York (bachelor of arts; master of arts) who had attended various German universities.[19] Bowne's theology was idealistic in both of the normal senses of that word. Technically, Bowne was a neo-Kantian idealist who amended Kant's idealism in the light of the work of Wilhelm Lotze. But to recite Bowne's intellectual pedigree perhaps is already to misinterpret a very creative mind. What fascinated Bowne was the way that the mind, always active in its search for meaning and truth, interpreted experience. In religious terms, Bowne was asking how one moved from the religious experiences so prized by Methodists to statements about God; in more scientific terms he was asking how and why the mind shaped its own understanding of the world it experienced. Neither task was neutral. Both intellect and personality were closely connected, and it was beside the point to ask what personality contributes to every area of human learning. Unlike Kant, who had largely confined reason to science, Bowne offered a way of seeing both science and religion, theology and philosophy, ethics (practical reason) and the new human sciences as stemming from one source. At the heart of Bowne's position was a belief that the transcendental aspect of human apprehension was not confined to logic and science.

Instead, Bowne reasoned that the whole of human personality was part of the transcendental realm. This meant that "knowing" was a passionate engagement with existence and not a dispassionate standing back from the world. To investigate any truth was to involve the whole person in the attempt to understand the world. Religion could, consequently, infuse and inform the knowledge of the world at every point without becoming itself knowledge. In concrete terms, Bowne's system encouraged his followers to believe that any and all

19. See Gary Dorrien, *The Making of American Liberal Theology,* vol. 1, *Imagining Progressive Religion, 1805-1900* (Louisville: Westminster John Knox, 2001), pp. 381ff.

knowledge of the world was potentially part of humankind's religious experience. Bowne's personalism was a religious philosophy, not a philosophy of religion, that was attuned to a university tradition that was self-consciously both Christian and scientific.

Bowne's system was also idealistic in the popular sense of the word. People became most human, he believed, when their aspirations exceeded their grasp. One value of belief in God was that it encouraged people to throw themselves headfirst into the future and grasp from that future something not given in current circumstances. Humanity was always on the frontiers of its own experience, and the university was the place that equipped these new frontier men for their journey.

Sometimes the achievements of a thinker are overshadowed by his or her accomplishments. Bowne was one of a handful of America thinkers to father a school of philosophy that spanned several generations. The "personalist" school he inspired had much influence over the half-century following his death in 1910. Almost despite itself, Boston personalism retained its essentially democratic roots, inspiring such divergent thinkers as the woman theologian Georgia Harkness, the conservative Carl F. H. Henry, and the black theologian Martin Luther King, Jr. The school, likewise, contributed much to making Boston University an exciting, urban university that often led in professional education.

Yet Bowne's accomplishment was broader than his influence. More than any other person, Bowne demonstrated, both to his followers and to those who doubted his conclusions, that Methodism could hold its own in the rough-and-tumble intellectual world of the university. Whether later Methodist theologians rejected or accepted the specifics of his intellectual program, they assumed that the link between an active, democratic faith, sound scholarship, and personal faith that Bowne established was valid. While many reasons existed for Methodism's love affair with the university, Bowne's work indicated that, whatever else was said, it was an appropriate match.

Historians have learned to be aware of the influence of what is not there as well as what is. Methodism largely lacked the traditional Reformed and Lutheran tradition of minute biblical scholarship. Wesley's *Notes on the New Testament* had drawn heavily from German critical study, and despite the attempt of some Methodists to formulate a theology based on proof texts, the synthetic approach to biblical study never caught on. The *Discipline*, for example, continued to require the reading of Wesley's notes.

Methodism was open to the newer directions in biblical studies that were becoming known in post–Civil War America. The *Methodist Quarterly Review*, of course, had carried glowing reports of the state of European scholarship, and the establishment of a successful Methodist mission in Germany had exposed some young Methodists to the newer theologies. Warren had served as a missionary in Germany, and he was thoroughly at home with the language and with many newer theological ideas. Similarly, John McClintock had served as pastor of the American church in Paris and had traveled widely. McClintock's knowledge of European thought was almost encyclopedic. And Drew's James Strong, the author of a best-selling nineteenth-century concordance, had done research in Palestine. Charles Bennett of Garrett, one of the founders of biblical archaeology, was also a graduate of a German school.

Perhaps the most important early biblical critic among Methodists was Milton S. Terry of Garrett. In 1883 he published *Biblical Hermeneutics: A Treatise on the Interpretation of the Old and New Testaments.*[20] Like Charles Briggs's *Biblical Study,* published in the same year, Terry's book was written primarily for those who taught the Bible and wanted to be in dialogue with the best of contemporary scholarship. In the midst of the debate over Hinckley Mitchell,[21] Terry published *Methodism and Biblical Criticism* in 1903. The purpose of this pamphlet was to show that new methods were widely accepted among Northern Methodist scholars. According to Terry, Methodist biblical critics had reached many points of agreement: the variety of literatures in the Bible, the composite character of many biblical books (among others, the Pentateuch, Isaiah, Zechariah), the postexilic dating of many of the Psalms, the historical evolution of the canon, and the belief that the Bible contained "a priceless record of . . . progressive revelation."[22] Terry's summary of the conclusions of Methodist scholarship appears accurate. With the exception of the dismissal of John Rice, an undergraduate instructor at Southern Methodist University, no Methodist biblical scholar was dismissed for heresy in the twentieth century.

Methodist schools drew the logical consequences from their changed understanding of theology and the Bible. Two were particularly important. First, the method of teaching the Bible changed. American theologians had tended to see exegesis from the original languages as the heart of the theological program, and even at the turn of the century many Presbyterian seminaries devoted half or more of their curriculum to this type of study. The new biblical studies, however, suggested that it might be better to teach students the larger context of the Bible in "introductory" courses that surveyed the field. This new type of study allowed biblical scholars to rely on the English text (to be sure, supple-

20. Milton Terry, *Biblical Hermeneutics: A Treatise on the Interpretation of the Old and New Testaments* (New York: Phillips and Hunt; Cincinnati: Cranston and Stowe, 1883).

21. See pp. 108-11.

22. A helpful abridgment of this work can be found in Thomas Langford, *Wesleyan Theology: A Sourcebook* (Durham, N.C.: Labyrinth, 1994), pp. 137-47; the quote is from p. 146.

mented by commentaries and corrections) and to stress its mastery. The Garrett alumni record noted: “Men whose years and lack of training renders the study of ancient languages difficult and of dubious value can now devote themselves to the Scriptures in English. Released from the severe demands of linguistic study, they have time for theology, history, sociology, and practical topics.”[23]

The university connection accelerated this transformation. The universities, in part because of the popularity of the elective system, tended to remove the languages from the list of required courses earlier than the colleges. American professional schools also moved in this direction. At the turn of the century, few law or medical schools required a bachelor of arts degree for admission, and the requirement of the learned languages was also fading. When these schools later moved toward a college degree as a requirement, they did not require the older classical degree. Medical schools, in fact, preferred a candidate with a sound scientific background, and law tended to prefer a candidate with substantial study in history, political science, or English. The same was true of the newer professional schools in such areas as dentistry, social work, education, and business. As these schools came to be centered in the university, they set the standard for professional training, and those theological schools in a university context found it easy to follow. If Methodist schools took the lead in this area, others certainly followed. As the undergraduate schools changed, seminaries had to revise their programs. Some added introductory courses in the languages and reduced the percentage of exegetical study required. In many cases, like the Methodist schools, these institutions discarded the language requirement completely.

In other words, Methodism had largely paid its debts to modernity before it devised its system of university and university-related divinity schools. Although theological change would probably have continued to be slower in the South than the North, the essential changes were well under way as Methodists, North and South, threw themselves passionately into the business of founding academic institutions. The university, especially the American university with its combination of undergraduate work and a variety of graduate professional schools, was made to order for a denomination deeply reformist and deeply committed to America’s possibilities.

23. Quoted in Robert Kelly, *Theological Education in America: A Study of One Hundred Sixty-One Theological Schools in the United States and Canada*, foreword by Rt. Rev. Charles Henry Brent (New York: George H. Duran, 1924), p. 105.

II. Methodist Schools and Their Cultures of Giving

Among other things, the separation of church and state in America meant that theological education was primarily a matter for the private sector, or "civil" society. While this has had many implications for American theological education, one of the most important has been that individual schools exist in a symbiotic relationship with the "cultures of giving" that sustain their economic life. Robert Lynn coined the phrase "culture of giving" to describe patterns of voluntary contributions within communities that sustain institutions. At its simplest level, a culture of giving is the habitual way that a group funds its enterprises. The culture of giving of a voluntary organization, even more than its relationship to its denomination or other entities, is the cornerstone of a school's structure of accountability. He who pays the piper calls the tune.

At the time that Methodist universities were formed, the Methodist culture of giving favored the affiliation of theological schools with universities, or at least their close proximity to them. Methodism was rich in people, growing in popularity, and located in almost every American town and village. But taken as a whole, it was not a rich denomination, nor did it have more than a handful of wealthy people to serve as its patrons. This gave those who had a certain vision of education unusual influence in shaping the new institutions.

In 1866 the Northern wing of the denomination celebrated the centennial of Methodist work in America. Over the past century Methodism had grown from a small religious movement, often identified with the countryside, to the largest American denomination. Abel Stevens noted: "A great occasion grew near; the hundredth year of the cause, which, beginning in such feebleness, had achieved many triumphs, and had now attained national ascendancy in the popular religious faith of the country. Though the republic was still surging with an unparalleled civil war, the Church, which had given to its battlefields a hundred thousand of her children, staggered not with a momentary doubt of the issue of the struggle, or of the destiny of the country. Both had seen a great past. Both expected a great future."[24] A sense of great expectations hung over the celebration. To many Methodists, it seemed that almost every prayer had been answered and that the Methodist combination of faithful life and hard work would continue to triumph. Hence, the question before the church was not the general question of the future — the Methodists believed they owned that — but which future the church wanted to secure first. And the fields before the bishops were white with harvest: Methodist missions were succeeding in places as diverse as Argentina

24. Abel Stevens, *History of American Methodism* (New York and Cincinnati: Methodist Book Concern, n.d.), p. 248.

and Germany, the church was expanding throughout the West, and Methodist authors were successful in the popular press.[25] The bishops assigned the Centenary Committee, which included George Peck, John McClintock, Moses Hill, James Bishop, John Owen, and Edward Sargant, two tasks. The first was to implement the call for "pecuniary contributions from each 'according as God has prospered him.'" The second was to use those contributions to make Methodism "more efficient in the century to come."[26] In other words, the committee was to plan Methodism's first capital campaign.

The leadership of John McClintock on the committee was crucial. McClintock was an unusual figure in pre–Boston University Methodism: he was a genuine scholar and intellectual.[27] As editor of the *Methodist Quarterly Review* from 1848 to 1856, a crucial period in Methodist theological history, he had used the journal to keep Methodists abreast of the latest developments in American and German theology. In 1850 J. L. Jacobi of the University of Berlin agreed to serve as his European correspondent, and Jacobi wrote short pieces on the theological luminaries of the day. McClintock was also among the founders of the Biblical Institute in Bremen, Germany, which was a breeding ground for Methodist scholars. Both William Warren and John Hurst taught at the institute and, like Jacobi, were foreign correspondents with the *Quarterly Review.*

McClintock's vision of Methodism was national. He argued that "ministers educated at Boston or Evanston, in New York or Ohio, or even on the Pacific Coast, are educated for the whole church" and that "young men everywhere . . . should have the opportunity of theological training."[28] If so, then education should be among the national campaign's primary causes. The committee agreed with McClintock and adopted three campaign goals that were directly related to education: (1) to aid young men preparing for a career as missionaries or ministers, (2) to support the Biblical Institutes at Boston and Evanston, and (3) to aid colleges and universities.

25. The nineteenth century saw a revolution in the production of books and magazines. As a result, printed materials became significantly less expensive. Methodists early mastered this transformed media, publishing a number of inexpensive books and pamphlets, and a myriad of *Christian Advocates*. For the revolution in print, see Paul C. Gutjahr, *An American Bible: A History of the Good Book in the United States, 1777-1880* (Stanford: Stanford University Press, 1999).

26. Stevens, *History of American Methodism,* p. 248.

27. Although McClintock had some of the dogmatic interests common at the time, he was more a scholar than a theologian. His intellectual interests ranged across many theological and cultural areas.

28. "Minutes of the Committee," reprinted in Abel Stevens, *The Centenary of American Methodism* (New York: Clinton and Porter, 1865), p. 261.

Was the campaign a success? Although pledges were easier to obtain than actual contributions, an unprecedented five million dollars was pledged for Centenary causes. William Warren, the president of Boston University whose new school (1871) needed every possible dime, reported that the collections had "disappointed just expectations,"[29] and similar comments were made by the leaders of other designated causes. Yet, despite hopes deferred, the Centenary campaign was a moderate success. The denomination collected more than the committee originally projected, and Methodist enterprises received a needed boost. Perhaps most important, the campaign disproved the commonplace that Methodists would not support ministerial education. When Methodists were asked to do so, they were willing to make sacrifices in this area as well as in the more glamorous areas of foreign and home missions. But, having said that, the limited results of the campaign also indicated that Methodist schools needed to find multiple sources of finances to survive.

Since the Centenary campaign was the first of its kind, no one knew what to expect. Subsequent experience, however, indicates that part of the results of a national campaign is the generation of additional support for the cause, and the Centenary campaign did that. When McClintock held a public meeting at Saint Paul's Methodist Church to solicit for the fund, Daniel Drew stepped forward with a promise to build a theological school in New York and to endow it with $250,000. Drew was one of the original "robber barons" who had accumulated a massive amount of money during the Civil War. Like a few other founders of universities, Drew invested much of his own time planning the school, selecting the site, chairing the board of trustees, and managing the endowment he had given. Only when he lost his fortune (and the school's endowment) in 1875, did he step back from active management of the new school's affairs.[30]

Drew was originally a theological school. Its transformation into a university occurred much later when the Baldwin brothers, Leonard and Arthur, two eccentric millionaires, made the school an offer of $1.5 million. The two brothers had done everything together: living in the same house, sharing the same table, serving as business partners, and vacationing together. They wanted the school to commemorate their unique relationship by building a liberal arts college. The trustees of the seminary willingly took that step, and the school became a university.

The university relationship at Garrett was also mediated through fi-

29. Cited in Richard Cameron, *Boston University School of Theology: 1839-1968* (Boston: Boston University School of Theology, 1968), p. 14.

30. John Cunningham, *University in the Forest: The Story of Drew University* (Andover, N.J.: Afton Publishing Co., 1972), p. 95.

nances. Although the primary funding for the school came from a $300,000 bequest by Ms. Eliza Garrett in 1853, the other founders of the school — Grant Goodrich, Orrington Lunt, and John Evans — were also involved in the establishment of Northwestern University. All were active leaders in Chicago's business community. Garrett's husband, Augustus, had been a real estate speculator; Goodrich had an aggressive law practice; Lunt had sold wheat; and Evans had developed Evanston and other suburban properties. Both schools were actively supported by the Chicago business community, and the same people often served as trustees for both schools. Until after the Second World War, the two schools shared many common goals and aspirations. In 1933 Garrett was in such desperate financial straits that a bank had taken title to its buildings, and the university generously provided the money that effected the rescue.[31] But the symbiosis was more than financial. Northwestern established or purchased a number of Chicago professional schools and was one of that city's centers for professional education.[32] Likewise, Garrett was a pioneer in the development of a professional style of curriculum that combined the newer practical courses, particularly religious education, with more traditional theological concerns. The yoke between the two was light.

Iliff was another product of an interlocking local elite. Denver owed its prominence to both the railroads and its location near much of the mineral wealth of the state. John Wesley Iliff himself had moved to Denver to sell cattle to those who were building the railroads, and he stayed to use the rails to market his beef in Chicago. At one point he owned forty thousand head. He married Elizabeth Fraser, a woman who had earned considerable wealth of her own as the local agent of the Singer Sewing Machine company. Like many western women, Fraser used the service industries to earn her living. After her husband's death, she married Henry White Warren, a Methodist bishop. Her first gift was $100,000 to the University of Denver, and after she and her husband decided to establish a theological school, they naturally piggybacked it on the university and located it on university property. Although Iliff received its own board of trustees in 1903, the relationship between the theological school and the university remained close. As in Evanston, the same donors supported both.

The decision of the New England Biblical Institute to become part of Boston University was a result of the workings of Boston's Methodist culture of giving. Boston University was incorporated by Joseph Sleeper, who gave the school $300,000, Lee Chafin, and Isaac Rich. Rich was one of Boston's most col-

31. McCulloh, *Ministerial Education*, p. 132.

32. Frederick A. Norwood, *From Dawn to Midday at Garrett* (Evanston: Garrett Theological Seminary, 1978); Williamson and Wild, *Northwestern University.*

orful millionaires. He began his career selling fish door to door and used his profits to build a fortune of around $1 million in real estate. Earlier the three incorporators had been strong supporters of the Biblical Institute, but they realized they could not support both enterprises from their resources. In the days before national campaigns, giving to educational institutions was largely local, and even Harvard, the most national American institution, sought its financing on State Street.[33] Rich's will made the hopes of all three clear: "I hope and expect that the Boston Theological Seminary and the University will be merged in the said trustees of Boston University and transfer and convey all its . . . estate and become a department only."[34] In many ways Rich was proposing an administrative "trust" in which two institutions would share administrative expenses and donors. Like the formation of other trusts at the time, this was a creative economic act that cut expenses and increased services.[35]

III. Dixie Revisited

The relationship between philanthropy, the university, and Methodist theological education was even closer in the South, perhaps because it had even fewer sources of philanthropic wealth. Every school founded by the Methodist Episcopal Church, South, was at a university. Only one of those universities did not bear the name of a particular founder, Southern Methodist University, and there the divinity school was named after the largest giver to its endowment, Perkins.

Southern Methodism's initial problem in founding theological schools came in part from the South's defeat in the Civil War. With the exception of the Native Americans, no enemy in American history was as thoroughly whipped as the Confederate States. In addition to the loss of millions in slave property, the South's railroads and cities had been systematically destroyed. Such Northern generals as Sherman and Sheridan had followed a "scorched earth" policy, ordering their armies to move through the countryside burning farms, destroy-

33. See Roger Geiger, *To Advance Knowledge: The Growth of American Research Universities, 1900-1940* (New York and Oxford: Oxford University Press, 1986), p. 20; also Merle Curti et al., "Anatomy of Giving: Millionaries in the Late Nineteenth Century," *American Quarterly* 15 (1963): 416-35.

34. Cameron, *Boston University*, p. 156.

35. The contemporary passion for larger business combinations reflects the thinking of those connected with the board of the university. Being businessmen, like the first board of the University of Chicago, they wanted to find an efficient and effective way of training professional people, including ministers and professors, that could serve the community.

ing agricultural implements, and slaughtering livestock. Of course, the defeat of the South made Confederate war bonds, the backbone of many Southern educational endowments, worthless. By the time the smoke cleared, the eleven states of the Confederacy had fallen to the last eleven places in every statistic that mattered, including personal wealth, education, and railroad mileage. The South continued to bring up the rear until well after the Second World War.

In the midst of this destruction, the General Conference of the Methodist Church, South, debated whether it wanted to establish a theological school or schools. Although the education committee's report recommending such a school was adopted, a strong minority report suggested that Southern Methodists would be wiser to invest their funds in colleges: "We shall need the famed energy of Methodism, aided by enlarged Christian liberality, to save the investments and vantage-ground of our literary institutions, and place them upon a basis of collegiate respectability and financial security. We have not a dollar to spare, and no time to lose. We are in far more danger of losing position in the world of letters, caste in society, and human efficiency in preaching the Word of God, from want of first-class colleges, than from any present lack of theological seminaries."[36] Several points in the minority report need to be stressed. First, the report is clear that the future of the church in the South, as in the North, rested upon its ability to enlist the professional classes, especially in the cities. The colleges had a further advantage. The Methodist schools in the South had begun to experiment with Bible chairs (later departments) where all students, not only those interested in the ministry, could study Scripture under Methodist direction. These chairs anticipated the later departments of religion that would be important components of Methodist colleges and that educated many ministers in whole or in part. Both the advocates of a school for ministers and the supporters of colleges agreed on the value of this approach to education. The majority report said: "Not a college belonging to the Church ought at any time to have been without a Chair of Biblical Literature; and no young man should at any time have left its walls without having been taught, in connection with the study of the Bible, the doctrines and usages of the Methodist Church. We should be glad if arrangements were made whereby every student should attend upon the instructions of the Biblical Chair. As a mere literary production, the Bible cannot be ignored by any one pretending to a liberal education."[37] Secondly, the minority report assumed that there was a distinction be-

36. Methodist Episcopal Church, South, Minority Report, Committee on Education, 1870.

37. 1870 Methodist Episcopal Church, South, Report on the Committee on Education, Journal of the General Conference, p. 237.

tween the teaching of culture and the teaching of theology. Methodists were for the former, they maintained, and against the latter.

> Finally, we doubt whether any thing in the history and present circumstances of the Church, or in the world of evil around us, has as yet demonstrated the present necessity or propriety of a theological seminary, even if one could be established. The history of such institutions has little that is favorable to Methodism, and much that is adverse. They have been the fruitful source of heresies innumerable, of a manner of preaching not generally desirable and rarely effectual among us, and of much of that formalism that never favors experimental religion. Methodism in earnest is the best form of religion, and the best religion, we think.[38]

The leader of the opposition to a theological school was significantly Bishop George Pierce, a leading member of the Emory College Board of Trustees and a strong advocate of Christian education. Pierce believed that the churches would do well to conduct schools on all levels, from the most elementary to the most advanced. He was a strong critic of public education, who maintained that Methodists ought to make it possible for faithful people to avoid using the unbelieving public schools.[39]

Holland N. McTyeire, the leading advocate of advanced education for Southern Methodist clergy, responded to the debate over a theological institution by shifting his strategy. McTyeire was a progressive Southerner who listened carefully to what others were saying, particularly Methodists in the North, and had recently founded Boston University. In 1872 he led his fellow Methodists to call an educational convention to consider establishing a central university for the South. The convention was an audacious act. While those who attended it represented the regional conferences, it was not an official body of the Methodist Episcopal Church, South. The convention voted to establish a university on a thoroughly modern model that would include a literary and scientific school, a normal school, a theological school, and a law school. Nashville was chosen as the site for two reasons: its distance from existing Methodist colleges and its location at one of the major Southern railroad hubs. The charter required that $500,000 be raised before the school could open. McTyeire may have already decided where to seek the money. During his

38. 1870 Methodist Episcopal Church, South, Report on the Committee on Education, Journal of the General Conference, p. 242.

39. The bishop was unusual in his opposition to public education. He wanted a system of church schools that could take the young Methodist from elementary grades through college in a morally and religiously protected world.

1875 trip north, he stayed with his wife's kinswoman, Mrs. Frank Crawford Vanderbilt, the young bride of Commodore Vanderbilt. During the visit he persuaded Vanderbilt to give the proposed university the needed funds. Further gifts from the Vanderbilts would bring the family's total contribution to $1,500,000 by 1890.

Although Vanderbilt's gift made possible a theological school, one wonders whether he would have given that much, if anything, to create a theological seminary. Paul Conkin, Vanderbilt's leading historian, believed that the commodore wanted to establish an "educational mission in a benighted land."[40] The university fascinated many of the captains of industry, not because of its learning, but because it represented a form of education that was similar to the business world. In a similar way to corporations, universities brought together under one management many different educational enterprises, including liberal arts colleges and professional schools. This enabled the university to reap the benefits of scale while serving multiple markets. The commodore also made lesser, but substantial, gifts to Yale and Columbia, which were also becoming universities.

Vanderbilt's divinity school was not a traditional seminary constructed around the study of the biblical languages. Instead, it took its initial bearings from the other professional schools of the university. Like them, it did not require college graduation for admission, although it encouraged college graduates to apply. Many students began at Vanderbilt by taking one or two years of arts and then beginning theological study. While Greek and Hebrew exegesis were offered, the school did not require either. From the beginning, then, Vanderbilt stressed the importance of a minister's command of the English text. The school also used the Course of Study of the Methodist Episcopal Church, South, as a guide to its work. At one point the divinity school offered a comprehensive Course of Study program by correspondence. The close relationship with the larger university also bore fruit. As the university developed its own programs of graduate study and raised the standards of its other professional schools, the divinity school followed suit.

Vanderbilt was unfortunately at the center of a series of controversies that lasted until 1914. The final battle was clearly part of a larger struggle over control. Chancellor James Hampton Kirkland had decided to hire as dean a Baptist, Frederick Moore, over the objections of Bishop Warren Candler, who believed that this prestigious office should go to a Methodist. Kirkland, who was facing the chronic financial problems that plagued higher education at the time, could

40. Cited in George Marsden, *The Soul of the American University: From Protestant Establishment to Established Nonbelief* (Oxford and New York: Oxford University Press, 1994), p. 277.

not afford to lose this battle. He was negotiating with the General Education Fund (Rockefeller) for what was essentially Baptist money. At the same time, he was also in a battle royal with the Methodist Episcopal Church, South, over the appointment of trustees. As the school evolved from the initial educational convention, the right to pass on nominations to the board had been transferred from the original sponsoring conferences to the church as a whole. For a season all the bishops of the church had served as ex officio trustees, an arrangement that ended in 1905. The removal of the bishops was probably related to the university's need to meet the conditions of the Carnegie Foundation to participate in its retirement program for educators. The Carnegie Foundation required participating schools to be independent of the control of a specific church. The Tennessee court did not set aside the trustee decision, but allowed the bishops to continue as a board of visitors. Although the powers of the visitors were left unclear, they retained considerable moral and persuasive powers. However, the bishops were not content with this halfway house. In 1910 they nominated their own candidates for the board, the board rejected them, and the issue went back to court. The bishops were naturally elated when the lower court found in their favor, but in 1914 the Tennessee Supreme Court reversed that decision on appeal. Whatever rights the Methodists had, the court reasoned, belonged to the original conferences that had supported the school, and these conferences lacked the legal warrants to transfer those rights to a larger body or to the bishops. But the court's decision also rested on the charter's creation of an independent board of trustees to manage the school's fiduciary trust.[41] All funds had been given to this board, and hence it and not the Methodist church "owned" the school.

The court also noted that the Methodist Episcopal Church, South, did not financially support the school. Indeed, part of the advantage of a university was being able to draw on the resources of a larger community of giving and learning, which were greater than those any denomination could provide. But, the court was saying, access to that broader public came only with a price. The church was only one constituency of the university, even if many of the contributors to the school were its members. This made the church's power indirect. Only insofar as it could influence givers to support or not support the school, could it influence school policy.

What was extraordinary about the Vanderbilt decision was not the court's action, which seems unexceptional, but the reaction of the Methodist leadership. While they might have withdrawn quietly from the battle over control of

41. For a good summary of the legal issues, see Marsden, *The Soul of the American University.*

the university, as the Northern bishops did after the Mitchell case at Boston University,[42] they reacted with anger. Clearly, they felt that the university had betrayed them in seeking the court's decision, and they apparently wanted to show that the school was dependent on them for gifts and students. Consequently, they appointed an education commission to plan the church's educational future. The action had little effect on Vanderbilt. By this time the school's support was broader than the Methodist Episcopal Church, South, and the university continued to prosper. Its divinity school did pass through some lean years, but it emerged from them as a leader in undenominational education.

The education commission did decide to found two new universities, one in the East and one in the West, to replace Vanderbilt. As in establishing Vanderbilt, one reason for choosing a university strategy was the need to sponsor a more efficient institution that could claim the support of a broader community. While the Methodist Episcopal Church, South, boasted that it "owned" these institutions, it did not repeat the Vanderbilt debacle. The church never asserted its "rights" over the new schools' administrations or boards. In effect, they were independent institutions under Methodist auspices from the beginning.

Emory College, located in Oxford, Georgia, might have become a university even without the intervention of the church. By 1914 the school was recommended throughout the South as a sound academic institution and had a notable history as an educator of Methodist pastors. Its primary liability was its location in a very rural area of the state.[43] Many of its active supporters were in Atlanta, including Bishop Warren Akin Candler, who served as president of the school from 1888 to 1898, and his brother Asa Griggs Candler, the Coca-Cola magnate, who was an active trustee and a deep-pocketed giver. When the educational commission met in 1914, Asa Candler was ready with his offer. In a letter to the committee, he pledged $1 million of his own money to establish a center for "sound learning and pure religion" in the city of Atlanta. Further, Candler reported that he had pledges for another $500,000 from local business leaders that could be used to purchase buildings and land. Further, both Candlers were on the board of the Wesley Memorial Hospital, which offered to become the teaching hospital for a new medical school. Since no other city could come close to this offer, the commission began negotiations with Emory College.

Although Candler eventually gave Emory $8 million, his greatest contribu-

42. See pp. 108-11.

43. The school was in a situation very much like Union Seminary in Virginia, which was located deep in the Virginia countryside. In the case of Hampden-Sydney, the theological school, under Walter Moore, moved to the city while the college remained (and still remains) at the original location.

tion may have been his insistence that the school locate in Atlanta. While Emory made a significant contribution to Atlanta's development as the economic capital of the South, Atlanta in turn made Emory successful. It provided Emory with a rich field for fund-raising as well as a broad community of support.

Southern Methodist University was not an existing college, but the school did enlist two of the most effective Methodist fund-raisers in Texas: Robert S. Hyer, president of Southwestern Methodist, and Haram A. Boaz, president of the Polytechnical College of Dallas. Under their leadership the businessmen of Dallas were able to pledge 662.5 acres of land in Hyde Park and $300,000 in financial support. Although the divinity school received its share of these initial gifts, its greatest period of support came after 1945 when J. J. Perkins, a Texas cattle and oil millionaire, gave the school $1.35 million (later increased to $2 million) to build a new campus. Significantly, the Perkinses had been generous givers to the university for some time. Their total gifts to the divinity school eventually totaled over $10 million.

The founding of Duke followed a slightly different pattern. In 1924 James B. Duke, a wealthy tobacco manufacturer and an early investor in electrical utilities, provided the endowment that transformed Trinity College into Duke University.[44] Just as the Candlers had been longtime supporters of Emory, so Duke had been involved with Trinity for some time. Duke was not a passive giver: he supervised the construction of the campus, including the chapel, and took an active role in planning the new school.[45]

Duke appears to have been influenced by William Preston Few (1867-1940), the president of Trinity and a convinced educational reformer. Few received his bachelor of arts degree in 1893 and his doctor of philosophy in 1896, both from Harvard. Although he did not follow all of Charles Eliot's more radical ideas, he did accept much of Eliot's understanding of the university as a place of freedom and learning. Duke and Few wanted a Southern school with national stature. The indenture included these words: "That this institution secure for its officers, trustees, and faculty, men of such outstanding quality, ability, and vision as will insure its attaining and maintaining a place of real leadership in the University world."[46] Duke and Few also shared a commitment to Southern progressivism. Both believed that the South was on the verge of a great step forward, and that the new university was part of that future. As the indenture said, "education, when conducted along sane and practical, as op-

44. The endowment established by Duke included aid for churches, hospitals, and retiring Methodist ministers.

45. The best account of the transformation of Trinity College into Duke University is E. W. Porter, *Trinity and Duke, 1892-1926* (Durham, N.C.: Duke University Press, 1964).

46. Quoted in McCulloh, *Ministerial Education*, p. 201.

posed to dogmatic and theoretical lines, is next to religion, the greatest civilizing influence." In short, Few and Duke held to a classic progressive Protestant educational ideal perhaps best described as the "eternal union of knowledge and religion" — the English translation of the school's motto, *eruditio et religio.*[47]

IV. Two Democratic Cultures

In both North and South, the Methodist culture of giving was distinctive in its representative quality. Like the Methodist church itself, Methodist philanthropy came from the middle of the American cultural and social order. While many of the givers who played major roles in this culture had become wealthy, they had all begun their lives among those of more modest means. Thus, they shared the educational values of those Americans who were in love with schooling while, at the same time, distrusting the elite forms that American educators had inherited from England. The American university with its combination of efficient organization, emphasis on professionalism and expertise, and belief in the discovery of truth was almost tailored to the hopes and aspirations of this group. These givers did not necessarily see the value of long years devoted to the minute study of Greek and Hebrew — some might even have opposed it — but they did believe that people could be educated for the practical work. Ministry was only one of the professions that was needed in a rapidly industrializing culture, and they hoped their religious and secular leaders might benefit from the same educational milieu.

V. Piety, Profession, and Scholarship

The Methodist movement toward the university was not inspired by the research goals of such institutions as Johns Hopkins. Rather, the central inspiration appears to have been an early desire to consider theological education as practical, professional training. In this sense the Methodist schools should be seen as pioneers of the professional model that has had so much influence in the twentieth century. Basically, the professional model has assumed that the best preparation for ordained ministry is a program that takes a careful and thorough look at the contemporary state of the church, including modern

47. Marsden, *Soul,* p. 322. The quote is from the articles of endowment, which are inscribed on a plaque in the center of the campus.

scholarship in such areas as Bible and church history, and provides a number of courses in practical areas to enable a student to become an effective and efficient minister. The goal of such a program is to educate ministers whose knowledge and skill make them at home in the American middle class and who, consequently, are able to lead the church from the center. Harper's proposals in "Shall the Theological Curriculum Be Modified, and How?" present a similar understanding of the structure of theological education.[48]

Methodism's decision to base its seminaries in or near universities was a significant element in the development of this style. Academic freedom in America became a presupposition of academic life in the universities first and then gradually spread to the colleges and seminaries. In part, the commitment to freedom was based on the belief that science was a self-regulating community. If an idea or conclusion was invalid, the process of scholarly and scientific debate would expose the error before harm could be done. If an idea was correct but unpopular, then a free atmosphere could protect it until other researchers had proven its value. Methodist seminaries participated in the general willingness to concede freedom to the universities.

The close relationship between Methodist schools and universities promoted the practical fields. Sunday school pedagogy was taught at Boston University from 1867, and the same school was among the first to establish a School of Religious Education and Social Science. In 1924 Robert Kelly published his study of theological education in which he paid special attention to the Methodist family of schools.[49] His general observation reflects the growing interest among Methodist schools in practical courses: "The expansion of the field of pastoral theology is conspicuous in the Methodist Episcopal group. Their programs propose to relate the church to the present social order. They provide numerous courses in religious education; psychology of religion; practical survey methods, both for church and community; social service; rural church; clinical work, etc. Garrett and Boston are particularly strong in these regards."[50] Kelly also noted that Methodist schools had begun to develop programs for specialists in particular ministries. "This specialization is rarely mentioned in the other groups. Certainly no comparable provision is made for such specialization."[51]

48. See above, chap. 11.
49. Kelly's conclusions are treated in chap. 15.
50. Kelly, *Theological Education in America*, p. 98.
51. Kelly, *Theological Education in America*, p. 100.

VI. Concern for Standards and the Cunning of History

The university context also served to raise the question of academic standards early in the history of Methodist theological education. In 1868 the Methodist Episcopal Church in the North took the first steps toward creating a system of schools by establishing its own board of education to help administer the Centenary Fund. In the 1880s it experimented with a plan devised by C. H. Payne entitled "Basis of Principles for the Federation of Methodist Institutions of Higher Learning" that established a connectional relationship between the different institutions. In 1892 the church created the Methodist University Senate, which was to establish criteria to identify which of the schools established by Methodists ought to be supported by the church and which were too weak to carry the approval of the whole church. While the senate originally did not have jurisdiction over theological schools, it was given the task of approving them in 1924. The Methodist Episcopal Church, South, established its own board of education in 1894.[52]

The Methodist development of an internal accrediting system more closely corresponded to the rise of accrediting agencies among colleges and universities than it did to the separate accreditation of theological schools by the American Association of Theological Schools. This was also part of Methodism's university heritage. In the first decades of the twentieth century, Methodists found it difficult to think about theological education apart from the general problem of higher education. Like the University of Chicago's divinity school, they believed that theological education was best conducted in the general atmosphere of higher learning and not in carefully segregated institutions.

There is something almost ironic in the development of an advanced system of university-related and university-connected schools among Methodists. In many ways the schools were the product more of poverty than of piety. The Methodist community of givers, while large, was comparatively poor, and the church had to lean on the substantial gifts of a few philanthropists to establish schools of any sort. Almost by necessity those schools had to provide both literary and theological education. The university, with its combination of diverse schools and economies of scale, fit this financial situation. The gift of a Vanderbilt could be used more effectively to establish a university than to establish a college and a seminary miles from each other. Further, the universities could combine a number of professional schools at one location and under one administration.

52. Beth Adams Bowser, *Living the Vision: The University Senate of the Methodist Episcopal Church, the Methodist Church, and the United Methodist Church* (Nashville: Board of Higher Education and Ministry of the United Methodist Church, 1992).

There was also something Methodist about the university movement at the end of the nineteenth century. While eastern colleges that developed into universities often retained some of their class consciousness — even when such administrators as Charles Eliot were beating the bushes for students and funds — the newer state and western universities were progressive institutions that were, like their Methodist counterparts, schools of opportunity. As such, they provided a place where the new middle class, based on science and expertise, could claim its place near the more traditional middle class of the Ivy League. At times this put the Methodists ahead of more conservative churches. Methodist schools were important pioneers in the interpretation of theological education as professional education; they early provided a place for free biblical study and creative nondogmatic theology. Their stress on practical efficiency was in harmony with what Americans, particularly those who gave, hoped theological schools might accomplish.

CHAPTER THIRTEEN

The Presidency

At the beginning of the twentieth century, the seminary presidency became unusually important in the life of many theological schools. In part, this was because the office changed. Earlier, a handful of schools had designated a faculty member as president, but the job usually involved little more than serving as the chair of the faculty and occasionally working with the board. The best of these early presidents, such as Bangor's Enoch Pond, Newton's Alvah Hovey, or Southern Baptist's James Boyce, began to expand the scope of the position. Pond, for instance, acquired special influence due to his skill as a fund-raiser; Hovey's power was rooted in his leadership in Northern Baptist life; and Boyce's strength came from his determination to keep his school open. By 1900 a new type of president was becoming more common in theological schools. The trustees of Gettysburg Seminary amended their bylaws with this simple statement: "The Board shall elect from among the professors a president of the seminary, who shall be *ex officio* chairman of the faculty. He shall be the executive officer of the management of the business of the Seminary, and shall represent it before churches and synods, and shall endeavor to advance its interests, financial and otherwise."[1] As at Gettysburg, the new presidents were the public faces of their schools and the chief administrators of their institutions' internal affairs. The office, however, was more than it appeared. Until deans became widespread in the 1950s, the president was often the only senior officer in an institution, the coordinator of all aspects of a school's life. The president hired faculty, oversaw such matters as the seminary commons, planned worship, and often served as the ad-

1. Abdel Ross Wentz, *History of the Gettysburg Seminary of the General Synod of the Evangelical Lutheran Church in the United States and of the Lutheran Church in America, Gettysburg, Pennsylvania, 1826-1926* (Philadelphia, 1927), p. 309.

missions officer. Many schools became the elongated shadows of their presidents. Sometimes this was a blessing, and sometimes a curse.

While the addition of a strong presidency was one of the most significant changes a school could make, not all institutions made it. As late as the Brown-May study in the 1930s, only forty-three of the surveyed schools had a president, apart from a person designated as the chair of the faculty. This is perhaps why this significant change in American theological education was little noted at the time. People interested in seminaries assumed they would acquire leaders more or less like the college administrators. At the turn of the century, college presidents were managing their schools' transition from old-time colleges, essentially devoted to the study of the classics, to modern colleges with an elective program and significant investment in sciences and English. Skillful managers were needed to effect the transition. In a similar way seminaries in the midst of radical academic change — either inspired by a more liberal theology, newer methods of ministry, or both — needed a similar person at the helm.

One of the few early articles on the seminary presidency was by J. L. McLean.[2] McLean was the president of the Pacific Theological Seminary (later, Pacific School of Religion), a small Congregational school located near the University of California at Berkeley. McLean's article, which he wrote in the midst of a very busy presidency, only partially grasped the new importance of the office. He noted a few successful presidents, including Union's Cuthbert Hall and Hartford's Chester Hartranft, and argued from their successes that the position was essential to a school's progress. But what was the new office? The best answer to that question may come from examining the work of some of the most visibly successful turn-of-the-century presidents.

I. Walter Moore Re-creates a Seminary

In 1884 a thin, scholarly young professor, Walter William Moore, arrived at Hampden-Sydney to begin his career as a teacher of biblical languages in the theological seminary. His friend William Rainey Harper called him the "best teacher of Hebrew in the United States," and acted quickly to incorporate the new teacher into his Semitic empire, having him teach in the Summer School of Hebrew that Harper helped establish at the University of Virginia.

Moore's seminary was one of the oldest in the South, and its very name, Union, marked it as one of the earliest cooperative ventures of Presbyterians in

2. J. L. McLean, "The Presidency of Theological Seminaries," *Bibliotheca Sacra* 58 (1901): 314-37. In many ways the same was also true of college and university presidencies, which likewise emerged out of the necessities of the time.

that region. But the school had fallen on hard times. It owned six buildings, all in poor repair, and had an enrollment of forty-eight students and an endowment of only $242,595. When the school was founded, it was located in a prosperous and lush countryside, surrounded by prosperous plantations and related businesses. By the 1880s its wealthier population had left the area, sharecroppers farmed much of the surrounding land, and small on-credit stores had replaced the traditional retail trade businesses. As with many other Southern educational institutions, struggling to make it in the wake of the Civil War, Union's future appeared bleak.

To be sure, the school was sound academically, and perhaps too sound theologically and culturally. Robert Dabney, the leading Southern Presbyterian theologian, had joined the faculty in 1854 and served until 1883, the year before Moore's arrival. Dabney was a thoroughly unreconstructed Southerner whose arguments in *A Defense of Virginia and through Her, of the South*[3] were part of a postwar cult of the lost cause.[4] But what was most important about his political conservatism was the way he entwined Southern regional identity and religious orthodoxy. The new mission of the South, he felt, was to be a theological light to the nation, a center of true religion in the midst of a Calvinism perverted by such heresies as New School Presbyterianism and the Andover theology.[5] For Dabney, this role placed the burden of purity upon the churches of the South. They had to maintain the true faith, the faith once delivered to the saints. Like other Southern church leaders, Dabney believed in the "spirituality of the church," the doctrine that the churches needed to stand above the mundane, particularly the partisan and the political, affairs of their own time. Of course, it was precisely through such an apparent renunciation of worldly power that Dabney believed the churches could acquire the moral and spiritual power to determine the future. Unfortunately, the cement that held Dabney's thought together was a religiously based racism that exalted whites as the bearers of Christian civilization. At one point, for instance, he objected to the location of Union, because the school was in the center of Virginia's black belt. If the school was to stay in Prince Edward County, he hoped it could be the nucleus of a new, white community.

3. Robert Dabney, *A Defense of Virginia and through Her, of the South* (New York: E. J. Hale and Son, 1867).

4. See Charles Reagan Wilson, *Baptized in Blood: The Religion of the Lost Cause* (Athens: University of Georgia Press, 1980).

5. Jerry Robbins, "Robert Dabney: Old Princeton and Fundamentalism" (Ph.D. diss., Florida State University, 1991); see also Merrill Matthews, Jr., "Robert Lewis Dabney and Conservative Thought in the Nineteenth Century South: A Study in the History of Ideas" (Ph.D. diss., University of Texas, Dallas, 1989).

Despite the passions of the Woodrow case,[6] Southern Presbyterians were slowly moving away from their post–Civil War season of reaction. The best sign of this may have been the decision of the synods of Kentucky and Missouri, two border states, to locate a theological school in Louisville. The decision was reached in the wake of the failure of the proposed Central University to establish the full program it had planned. Central University was one of the most ambitious institutions proposed before the establishment of the University of Chicago, and was to have included a College of Philosophy, Literature, and Science; a College of Theology; a College of Law; a College of Medicine; a College of Dentistry; and a preparatory school.[7] The Arts College opened in Richmond, Kentucky, and while efforts to raise funds for the theology school began in 1889, they were not successful. Richmond lacked the urban atmosphere needed for a modern, professional university.

Like the Baptists, the Presbyterians then turned to the most important railhead in the state, Louisville, and located a seminary there in 1893. The school flourished in this urban, commercial, and industrial environment. While clearly a conservative school, it was committed to modern methods of reaching the city, such as urban missions and the Sunday school, and committed itself to educate men for the growing number of positions in such parachurch bodies as the YMCA.[8]

Walter Moore was tempted by an invitation to join the Louisville faculty that seemed on the verge of a new direction in Southern theology. Moore stated his position as "conservatism in doctrines and progressiveness in methods,"[9] and the new seminary promised to live up to both ideals. Perhaps equally important was the more cosmopolitan character of Louisville, a city that faced south and also toward the broad valley of the Ohio. But Louisville was also a counter in any important struggle that Moore was having with his own board.

For years he and others had been saying that Union's location in rural Virginia was a substantial block to any realistic development of the school. In 1892 he had reported to the board that there was widespread dissatisfaction with the "location of the seminary" that discouraged many people from wanting to contribute to the "erection of any more buildings in the wrong place." Moore's

6. See chap. 4. Historically, Southern churches have been more sensitive to the theological challenges of Darwinism than have their Northern counterparts.

7. Ernest Trice Thompson, *Presbyterians in the South,* vol. 3, *1890-1972* (Richmond: John Knox, 1973), p. 198.

8. Rick Nutt, *Many Lamps, One Light: Louisville Presbyterian Seminary; A 150th Anniversary History* (Grand Rapids and Cambridge: Eerdmans, 2002), especially p. 33.

9. J. Gray McAllister, *The Life and Letters of Walter Moore* (Richmond: Union Theological Seminary, 1939), p. 210.

words to his board indicate that he had talked with many of the people who were making such cities as Richmond, Virginia, and Greensboro, North Carolina, into financial centers.[10] The business elite in these cities wanted to leave the Old South behind and to realize the potential of the region for manufacturing, the production of raw materials, and investment. As Moore said, such leaders

> seem to think that the officers of the Seminary have been blind to the changed conditions of the country since the war and have not recognized the vital importance of planting our principal training school for ministers in some center of population and business influence, where its property would accumulate and increase rapidly in value, where its accessibility and metropolitan advantages would commend a much larger patronage, where the best methods of Christian work could be seen in actual operation, and where the contingent of picked men reinforcing the pastors in their Sunday Schools and mission would make Presbyterianism a colossus instead of a pigmy among the Christian denominations of the future.[11]

Moore then went to work finding a business community willing to sponsor the seminary. He found a group of businessmen in Richmond, Virginia, who were engaged in the active development of North Richmond as a streetcar suburb. For financial as well as aesthetic reasons, they were delighted to have the seminary and provided a large parcel of land on Brook Road.

The debate over the new location was bitter. Dabney maintained that the argument that students would be tempted to go to Northern seminaries was invalid, but, even if true, he claimed such students were more concerned with "streetcar conveniences" than with the plain life required by the gospel.[12] While Dabney's language was extreme, his instinctual awareness that an urban location would change the school and, through it, the church was correct. If the medieval adage that "city air makes free" no longer had the same meaning, it was still true. No urban school could ignore the new America.

The most important product of the relocation of the school was the expansion of the curriculum to include such courses as sociology and religious education that were already standard at other seminaries. Moore saw the addition of these courses as necessary:

> [T]he minister is to be the executive head of the church, and as the modern church, especially in the cities, is in many cases an elaborate and compli-

10. Both cities were centers of the new insurance industry and of banking.

11. Quoted in Thompson, *Presbyterians in the South,* 3:202.

12. Cited in Thompson, *Presbyterians in the South,* 3:203.

> cated organization, he should, before undertaking to lead and use it as a force in the community, have some instruction in business methods, in church finance, in the keeping of church records, in the organizing of the membership and the development of its activities, in its relations to the other officers of the church and its various organizations, men's societies, young people's society, and especially to the Sunday School. The seminaries, almost without exception, are now providing instruction in the history of religious education, the principles and methods of teaching, the organization and administration of the Sunday school and the training of its teachers.[13]

In 1915-16 the school added a doctor of divinity degree (later called a doctor of theology) to educate teachers for the South's expanding college system. Union also responded to the demand for more professional training of missionaries, issued by Edinburgh 1910, by establishing a chair of mission and making provision for furloughing missionaries to study at the school. As Moore saw it, the purpose of the seminary curriculum "is not to make accomplished scholars and specialists in the various departments of theological science, but to make good ministers of Jesus Christ, who will serve Him and His church with increasing efficiency year after year."[14]

Moore's most radical step was finding a way to provide theological education for women. In general, Southern churches were more reticent about the expanding place of women in public life than their Northern counterparts. In searching for a model, Moore turned to the Kennedy School of Missions, recently established at Hartford Seminary. Moore wrote: "I am interested to see that the Kennedy School of Missions with its millions has thus far made only a start as we made here at Union in point of attendance, and that the school is organized in precisely the same way that is proposed for our school in Richmond — namely, utilizing the whole force of a well-equipped and well-manned theological seminary. It is perfectly clear to my mind that in this way only can we have a satisfactory training school, one which will do good rather than harm."[15] What Moore was proposing was that Union in effect become two coordinate institutions, sharing resources and personnel. This allowed Moore to serve the Southern proprieties while achieving his larger purpose. Although the school

13. Walter William Moore, "The Preparation of the Modern Minister," in *Opportunities of the Christian Minister,* ed. John R. Mott (New York: YMCA, 1911), p. 77. This article is one of the best summaries of Moore's plans for this school, although it was not intended as a "Union" document.

14. Moore, "Preparation," p. 75.

15. McAllister, *Walter Moore,* p. 456.

later became the Presbyterian School of Christian Education, it was originally a lay training school that had special connection to Southern Presbyterian work in China and Korea.[16]

The theological style of Union reflected Moore's own position. Moore believed passionately in scholarship. Under his leadership the *Union Seminary Magazine* was the only serious theological journal in the Southern Presbyterian church, and the Sprunt Lectures became one of the leading series in the South. On the one hand, Moore believed that the Southern church needed to adopt looser standards of subscription than it had in the past: "We must have more liberty in our church . . . or there is going to be an explosion which will astonish some. . . . It is better not to have that explosion. It is better to profit by the experience of our church in Scotland and [in] the North than to have an experience of our own. . . . In my judgment there is nothing more certain, as to the future of our church than that we must allow a subscription to the 'system of doctrine,' without trying to tie men down to every statement of detail."[17] Clearly, while holding to many conservative views of the Bible, Moore was not an inerrantist who expected the Bible to meet modern criteria of accuracy.[18] Yet, at the same time, Moore invited William Jennings Bryan to give the Sprunt Lectures in 1921. The lectures, published as *In His Image,* went through four editions in their first year. Like Bryan, Moore seemed concerned about the "harmful effects" of evolution, "how it enthrones selfishness and how it embitters the relations of capital and labor."[19]

Moore's biographer called him the "First President and Second Founder" of Union Theological Seminary. This is an apt description of Moore's work. Although Moore had functioned as chief administrator of the school for some years, he was not officially elected president until 1904. Like his original position, his new position was not clearly defined by the board. The seminary badly needed administrative leadership, and Moore was ready and able to provide it. In a sense the needs of the institution dictated the powers of the office. By 1926, the last year of his presidency, his record was impressive. The school now owned property worth $1,260,000 in one of the most prosperous and growing areas of a major commercial and railroad city; it possessed $1,218,672 in endowments, and owned eighteen new buildings. Not counting the training school, its enrollment had reached 158 students, who

16. Over time the lay training school became more independent of the seminary, but this was not Moore's original intention. He wanted to take advantage of the economies of scale.

17. McAllister, *Walter Moore,* p. 208.

18. Balmer Kelly, "No Ism but Biblicism: Biblical Studies at Union Theological Seminary," *American Presbyterianism* 66, no. 2 (1988): 111.

19. Thompson, *Presbyterians in the South,* 3:308.

were now enrolled in five separate programs. In filling an office, Moore had re-created a school.

II. B. H. Carroll and Southwestern

At first glance, B. H. (Benajah Harvey) Carroll of Texas appears to be a character spawned by the myth of the Wild West. Carroll became a Christian when he was challenged at a Methodist revival to test experientially the teachings of the church in his own life, and he agreed to taste and see if the Lord was good. As he sat at the meeting, he had a moment in which, at least in his mind's eye, he saw Christ standing before him and inviting him to come forward. As he said, "in a moment I went, once and forever, casting myself unreservedly and for all time at Christ's feet, and in a moment the rest came, indescribable and unspeakable." Carroll never looked back, and when he returned home, despite his attempts to flee to his room undetected, his mother found him out, pronounced him converted, and they spent the night together, reading Bunyan. "When I came with the pilgrims to the Beulah land, from which Doubting Castle could be seen no more forever, and which was in sight of the heavenly city and within sound of the heavenly music, my soul was filled with such a rapture and such an ecstasy of joy as I had never before experienced." B. H. Carroll advanced rapidly through the Baptist ranks, becoming a licensed preacher, ordained pastor, and finally pastor of the First Baptist Church of Waco. The church was intimately connected with Waco University. Like its sister institution, Baylor University, Waco was a classical liberal arts college with some instruction in theology.[20]

Carroll exemplified the strengths and weaknesses of Texas Baptists at the end of the nineteenth century. On the one hand, he was a superlative pastor and organizer. In addition to his continual success as a preacher of revivals and recruiter of new members, Carroll's church had a modern, well-organized Sunday school, an organized and practiced choir, and a unified budget. The 1883 Southern Baptist Convention met in the congregation's new

20. The early history of Baylor University, originally located at Independence, Tex., and Waco University, a breakaway school located in Waco, is rich in colorful characters and illustrates the competition on the frontier between competing communities, personalities, and theologies. The two schools were united in 1885. Texas Baptists had been divided into two bodies, the Texas Baptist Convention, which sponsored Baylor, and the Baptist General Association, which sponsored Waco. The union of the schools and the union of the competing bodies were essential parts of the same agreement. Much of the information about B. H. Carroll is from Robert A. Baker, *Tell the Generations Following: A History of Southwestern Baptist Theological Seminary, 1908-1983* (Nashville: Broadman, 1983).

building, and the messengers[21] slept and ate in the homes of local people. Carroll's church provided one-third of the total revenue of the Texas State Convention.

Unlike some of his fellow Baptists to the east, Carroll was almost as strong for social and political reform as he was for ecclesiastical purity. At a time when most Southern Baptist churches were moderate on the use of alcohol, for instance, Carroll convinced his church to write prohibition into the Waco Church Covenant. Carroll became a leader in the prohibition and antigambling movements, as well as in other causes for social and moral betterment. But Carroll also represented the less attractive aspects of Texas as well. His sermons often bordered on the bombastic, and he was constitutionally unable to avoid addressing with dogmatic certainty any question disputed by his fellow Baptists. His influence was paramount, for instance, in preventing Texas Baptists from cooperating with the Home Missionary Society of New York and the American Baptist Publications Board. He was also a vocal opponent of evolution.

As a member of the board of Southern Baptist Theological Seminary in Louisville, Carroll was a leader in the controversy over William Whitsitt. Whitsitt, a German-trained historian and president of Southern, studied early Baptist history while on academic leave in England. He concluded that Edward Barber had introduced immersion in 1641, replacing an older Baptist practice of pouring. His findings were first published anonymously in the *Independent*, a popular Congregational journal, and later in an article in Johnson's *Universal Cyclopedia*.[22] When the controversy began, Whitsitt published his conclusions as *A Question in Baptist History*.[23]

Whitsitt knew how controversial his conclusions were to many Baptists. After all, he had published his original article without his signature, a fact that convinced his critics that they had caught him in a compromised position. As Carroll noted: "In the first place Dr. Whitsitt, a teacher of Church History in a Baptist Theological Seminary, writes an editorial for a Pedo-Baptist paper about his own brethren, and writes in the . . . manner and spirit of a Pedo-Baptist. While he writes he stands across the line from us dressed in the uni-

21. In Southern Baptist ecclesiology, the convention is a separate body from the local churches and, hence, receives independent messengers from cooperating churches. These "messengers" are not considered "representatives" of the church, nor are they part of a hierarchical system of church courts.

22. For the Whitsitt controversy, see Rosalie Beck, "The Whitsitt Controversy: A Denomination in Crisis" (Ph.D. diss., Baylor University, 1985); also Rufus Weaver, "Life and Times of William Heth Whitsitt," *Review and Expositor* 37 (Apr. 1912): 159-84.

23. William Whitsitt, *A Question in Baptist History* (Louisville: Charles A. Dearing, 1896).

form . . . of the opposition."[24] Whatever else the anonymity did, it convinced Carroll that Whitsitt was similar to other Protestant theological teachers who had moved away from biblical teachings surreptitiously. "It is a lamentable and appalling fact that every book, doctrine, prophecy, promise or fact in the Holy Scriptures be brought under grave suspicion by some one or another teacher in one or another of the theological seminaries. It is a fact no less alarming that when any one of these teachers conceives it to be his duty to tear down what he was appointed to build up, and paid to build up, there is no practical way to get at him by way or rebuke or removal."[25] Carroll may have had Union Seminary's Charles Briggs in mind when he wrote these words — the Briggs case was well-known in the region. But he may also have been referring to G. B. Foster of the University of Chicago, who seemed to be beyond correction to many Baptists, and whose theology was disliked through much of the Midwest.

One source of the controversy was a popular Southern Baptist theology, Landmarkism, that went back to J. R. Graves. Graves, the fiery editor of the *Tennessee Baptist,* taught three ecclesiological doctrines: (1) that Baptist churches were the only churches that were authentic New Testament churches, (2) that each Baptist congregation was totally separate or independent from all others, and (3) that Baptist churches had existed, although often as an underground movement, since the days of the apostles, and that these churches were related to each other in a historic succession. At this time Baptist journals were often the primary educators of what was essentially an unschooled ministry. Since Graves's publication was the standard Baptist paper from Tennessee to Texas, his ideas had extraordinary impact. Clearly, Whitsitt's researches, if accurate, exposed this theology as unhistorical.

It is not clear whether Carroll accepted the Landmarkist theology or not. While he often used language that suggested the radical independence advocated by the Landmarkists, he was also one of the principal advocates of denominational cooperation in the Southwest, and a sworn opponent of any movement that would weaken the convention. Later, as president of his own seminary, he hired A. H. Newman, a Canadian Baptist with views of Baptist origins similar to Whitsitt's, to teach at his school. Although he later fired Newman in an unrelated squabble, he never restricted Newman's writings or classroom teaching. Part of Carroll's difficulty with Whitsitt may have come from his distrust of the president's supporters among some of his fellow trustees. In a resolution supporting Whitsitt, the trustees had said they "cannot un-

24. Timothy Wade Shirley, "J. P. Boyce and B. H. Carroll: Two Approaches to Baptist Theological Education" (Th.M. thesis, Southern Baptist Theological Seminary, 1987), p. 102.

25. Cited in Shirley, "Two Approaches," p. 51.

dertake to sit in judgment upon questions of Baptist history which do not imperil any of these principles concerning which all Baptists are agreed, but concerning which serious, conscientious, and scholarly students are not agreed. We can, however, leave to continuing research and free discussion the satisfactory solution of these."[26] Carroll believed (correctly) that the trustees were the only body that had the right to formulate an opinion on the direction the seminary was taking. The issue of accountability played a major role in his proposed motion before the Southern Baptist Convention that the churches formally renounce their ties to the seminary and refuse to nominate trustees to its board.

> Resolved that this Convention, without expressing any opinion whatever on the merits of the controversy concerning Seminary matters, about which good brethren among us honestly differ, but in the interest of harmony, particularly with a view to preserve and confirm unity in mission work, does now exercise its evident right to divest itself of responsibility in the Seminary management, by dissolving the slight and remote bond of connection between this body and the Seminary; that is, that this body declines to nominate Trustees for the Seminary or to entertain motions or receive reports relative thereto, leaving the Institution to stand on its own merits and be managed by its own trustees.[27]

However, Carroll never made the motion. After two years of steady debate, Whitsitt resigned from the presidency of Southern Baptist Theological Seminary and accepted a position as professor of philosophy at the Baptist University of Richmond.

If Carroll's real concern in the Whitsitt affair was the theological accountability of the faculties to the churches, it would be consistent with his later actions. As the head of Baylor University's Department of Theology, Carroll moved to separate the school from the university and to place it directly under a board of trustees elected by Texas Baptists and responsible to them. The theme of ecclesiastical accountability is one of the consistent threads in his work as an educator and administrator.

Carroll became initially involved with theological education through his pastoral work. As the pastor of the First Baptist Church of Waco, Carroll came to know many of the young men attending the college, and he and his wife often invited the most promising to share their parsonage. While there, these young men were, in effect, his apprentices, learning their trade from a master.

26. Cited in Baker, *Tell the Generations Following*, p. 92.

27. William Mueller, *A History of the Southern Baptist Theological Seminary* (Nashville: Broadman, 1959), p. 171.

Carroll was also chair of the board of trustees of Baylor University, and one of the school's principal supporters. In the early 1890s, for instance, he and George W. Truett, then a Baylor student, went on a tour of Texas churches to raise money to pay off the school's substantial debts. They did so. By 1893 the university was free of debt. Carroll's interest in the financial problems of Texas Baptist educational institutions was to grow as he aged. After he resigned his pastorate in 1899, he served briefly as the head of the state's educational commission, a body formed to free the state's Baptist colleges from debt. Carroll's interest in teaching, however, was strong. In 1893 Baylor established a Bible Department with Carroll as professor of exegesis and systematic theology, R. C. Burleson as professor of pastoral duties, and J. H. Luther as professor of homiletics. Like similar Bible departments at Mercer in Georgia and Furman in South Carolina, the Baylor department was an undergraduate seminary that offered the traditional seminary courses. In many ways the Baylor department was similar to the divinity school at Vanderbilt, with most students taking a year or two in the regular college program and then electing ministerial and theological courses in the Bible Department. The new system of majors and minors made such study a practical part of a bachelor of arts program. By 1897 the Baylor department added John S. Tanner to the faculty in biblical languages. Tanner was a graduate of Southern Baptist Theological Seminary who had also attended the University of Chicago. At this same time, Baylor established a Summer Bible School to train those Texas Baptist preachers who had no prior college preparation. By 1901 Carroll was able to announce that Baylor had established a full theological department and to attract the services of A. H. Newman, then of McMaster in Canada.

At this point Carroll's school seemed on its way to becoming a divinity school, similar to the schools at Vanderbilt and the University of Chicago. Had it taken that route, it probably would have followed those schools in gradually raising the requirements for admission to college graduation and becoming a more integrated part of its host university. Further, Baylor perhaps held the key to the future development of Southern Baptist theological education. Had the theological department evolved into a divinity school, other strong Southern Baptist colleges might have developed their own Bible departments in the same direction.

But that future was not to be. Carroll moved to separate his school of theology from its host university. Carroll appears never to have wanted to set up a school that was a rival to Southern Baptist Seminary in Louisville, which he saw as an institution that provided the best ministerial preparation for Baptists in the South. On the other hand, he was convinced that Texas needed its own institutions. After all, approximately one-fifteenth of all the Baptists in the world lived in Texas, and the state was "the breeding place of preachers."[28] The Theological Department, as it was now called, enrolled 138 students in 1905, and almost as many attended the summer sessions. The department was thus larger than most American seminaries.

Carroll, ever the financier, hit upon a plan. His first step was to make the theological seminary into a divinity school. To do this, he traveled throughout Texas and raised enough money to pay the expenses of the school for three years. In 1905, in the absence of the president of the university, he introduced a resolution to make the Theological Department a divinity school "teaching all the courses and conferring all the degrees of a regular first class theological seminary."[29] That year the school announced its Th.B., Th.M., and Th.D. programs. The Th.B. was awarded after two years of study; the Th.M. after three; and only the Th.D. required a bachelor of arts degree and prior theological study. The Th.D. degree was a research degree requiring French, German, and a thesis. The new school was called Baylor Theological Seminary. In 1908 the seminary took the next step and separated completely from Baylor. It was reorganized under its own board as Southwestern Baptist Theological Seminary.

Later, Lee Scarborough, the school's second president, would remember that one reason for the separation was the seminary's need to admit ministers who were not college material.[30] Carroll himself stressed the need for preachers to come to the school for one or two years, even without any liberal arts, and receive some training for their task. For that reason the school was deliberately empowered to teach whatever might be useful to ministers or to their work.

There was another reason for the separation. Carroll believed that "School after school all along the line of history, though founded by piety and Christian benevolence has drifted into the infidel column. Over many theological seminaries today infidelity broods and spawns and hatches her slimy, poisonous progeny. No school that is governed by a self-perpetuating board of trustees, or even by a board whose vacancies are virtually filled by the faculty, can be trusted to remain Christian."[31] In many ways Carroll, despite his long association with Baylor, believed that the university itself was a possible corrupter of the church's message. In very strong language, he wrote: "The dominating university spirit will fill them with teachings in many courses that are saturated with the atheistic speculations and universified hypotheses of Epicurean or Darwinian evolution, which theory is applied not only to the natural sciences

28. Cited in Baker, *Tell the Generations Following,* p. 119.

29. Baker, *Tell the Generations Following,* p. 121.

30. Lee R. Scarborough, *A Modern School of the Prophets* (Nashville: Broadman, 1939), p. 52.

31. Quoted in Scarborough, *A Modern School,* p. 39 n. 560.

and to the whole realm of secular historical criticism, but which in a thousand subtle and insistent ways of propaganda demands the role of master in application to the Bible and the whole realm of theology."[32] In other words, Carroll's goal was the opposite of the goal of those like William Rainey Harper or the Methodists who wanted to find a place in the university for theological instruction. Carroll wanted to found an institution that would, over the long haul, be a counterweight to the university and maintain the standards of Jerusalem over against the standards of Athens. In particular, Carroll was deeply concerned that the "death in the pot" — the teaching of evolution — be kept at a distance from theological students.[33]

Unlike Baylor or Southern Baptist Theological Seminary, the new school was to be placed firmly under a board elected by the denomination and accountable to it. Texas Baptists elected its trustees, and the trustees were to remain responsible to the denomination. In addition to his worries about whether the business community at Waco could support both the seminary and the university, Carroll wanted the school to move away from Baylor to protect its orthodoxy. Carroll's fund-raising skills had not declined with time. He recognized that those developing the rapidly growing Texas cities could use the seminary as a keystone in building a pleasant residential community, and he challenged the business community in several Texas cities to make him an offer. Fort Worth's offer of land and money was by far the best, and after convincing the business community there to increase their contribution by $100,000, he moved the seminary to the new location. The land given to the new school was carefully described: "A thirty acre site and one-half interest in 194 acres of the Winston land; ten acres outright and a half interest in ninety-nine acres of land, owned by H. C. McCart; a tract of twenty acres owned by W. D. Reynolds; a ten-acre tract owned by the owners of S. J. Jennings survey and another tract of fourteen acres owned by G. E. Tandy."[34] The value of the land was of course speculative. The site lay some six miles from the heart of the city, and the streetcar system had not been extended to the school. For several years the school was forced to operate its own streetcar, a solution to its isolation that was less than satisfactory. Yet, both the seminary and the businesspeople who had gambled on it were right in the long run. The value of the land and the location grew exponentially as the city expanded. For once, the boosters were right.

Carroll's vision of the seminary was expansive. Like many people who lived on both sides of the passing of the frontier, Carroll was a passionate dem-

32. Quoted in Shirley, "Two Approaches," p. 81.

33. Shirley, "Two Approaches," p. 80.

34. Baker, *Tell the Generations Following,* p. 151.

ocrat. He believed that the English Bible, for instance, ought to be at the heart of the curriculum. Southwestern originally had a program in English Bible in which the candidate read the whole Bible carefully and stood for an examination on every book. It was Carroll's hope that the degree in English Bible would come to have some of the prestige of an earned doctorate. When he lay ill and people feared (prematurely) that he was dying, Carroll received word that A. H. Newman, one of the most able men he had recruited for the seminary, was planning to abolish the work in English Bible after his death. Carroll almost miraculously recovered, and having regained his strength, fired the historian. Some believed that the English Bible had brought the bearded prophet back from the edge of the grave! Carroll's other great passion was the establishment of a chair of evangelism or "A Chair of Fire." The professorship was to deal with theological and historical questions, but Carroll wanted it to be more than that: the occupant of the position would be a practicing evangelist who continued to preach revivals while teaching his courses. Carroll was instrumental in the decision to locate a Woman's Missionary Union Training School at the Southwestern campus, and, unlike Southern Baptist Seminary, he early incorporated the training school into the seminary's degree-granting structure.

How far Carroll would have carried his emphasis on the practical and democratic is unclear. Texas Baptists did not have the funds to finance all his dreams. But we have some idea of where he might have taken the institution. His handpicked successor, Lee Scarborough, was to add schools of gospel music and Christian education that were large enough to be divided into departments in 1921-22. Such movements toward educating people for the expanding ministries of the church were in line with Carroll's own vision of his theological university.

III. Hartranft and Mackenzie

The South and West seemed made to order for vigorous executive leadership. In the South, for instance, the end of the Civil War witnessed a revival of religion in which significant numbers of people joined churches, many for the first time. Likewise, the churches in the middle and far western states were in a period of growth and expansion. In both areas the number of potential candidates was growing, and hence there was an expanding market for ministers. The religious situation was less clear in the East. If anything, the East had more Protestant churches than it apparently needed, and many young men, particularly those from the better or, at least, more prestigious colleges, were finding their careers in other professions. Yet the East also saw the advent of the new presidencies.

At first glance Hartford Seminary seemed to exemplify all the problems of the East. The school was originally founded as a counterweight to the theology of Nathaniel Taylor at Yale, but as theology changed there seemed little reason for the school to continue. Hartford was poorly housed, poorly endowed, and poorly equipped. Two remarkable presidents, Chester David Hartranft and W. Douglas Mackenzie, remade the school, augmented its forces by adding new schools in missions and religious education, and made it a model of a modern seminary, seeking to educate as large a variety of religious professionals as possible.

Chester Hartranft, originally a Dutch Reformed minister and a graduate of New Brunswick Seminary, devoted considerable thought to what a theological seminary ought to be before he was elected to Hartford's faculty. In 1877 he delivered an address, "The Aims of a Theological Seminary," that outlined many of the changes that would take place in the next twenty-five years.[35] For Hartranft, a deeply scholarly historian, the most important of these were in teaching and scholarship. Hartranft believed correctly that he was standing at the beginning of a revolution in academic theology, and he made four suggestions that were to be the heart of his later program as president.[36] Schools, he believed, had to appoint professional scholars, and these scholars had to be more specialized. This meant that the old-style seminary with its three or four faculty members in the principal field of theology had to evolve into a larger-scale institution with a much larger faculty. In turn, this faculty had to be composed of people who were able to do research on their own. The days of the "middle man whose stock of knowledge is made up of superficial scrapings from the works of others" had disappeared. In its place, Hartranft proposed "pioneer(s) and discoverer(s) in the depths and vastness of . . . science."[37] Since it was important that such instructors publish their results periodically, he proposed that each seminary publish its own scholarly journal. Such publications would of course aid research by encouraging the process of discussion and critique, but Hartranft had more than this in mind. He was a firm believer in the Reformed tradition of a learned ministry that made every pastor, in effect, a local theologian. As scholarship moved from its classical roots in the study of

35. Chester David Hartranft, *The Aims of a Theological Seminary: An Address Delivered Before the Alumni Association of the Theological Seminary, New Brunswick, NJ* (New York: Board of Publication of the Reformed Church in America, 1878).

36. Norman Jay Canfield, "Study the Most Approved Authors: The Role of the Seminary Library in Nineteenth-Century American Protestant Ministerial Education" (Ph.D. diss., University of Chicago, 1981).

37. Curtis Manning Geer, *The Hartford Theological Seminary, 1834-1934* (Hartford: Case, Lockwood, and Brainard Co., 1934), p. 126.

Latin, Greek, and Hebrew, Hartranft wanted the ministry to likewise grow in its use and application of newer scholarship.

Hartranft recognized that the key to his vision of a school devoted to the new scholarship lay in his capacity to raise money. Fortunately, Hartford was a thriving community, a pioneer in the insurance business, and he was able to tap the business community there for substantial amounts. When he began at Hartford, there were four members of the faculty; when he left, there were fifteen. Perhaps most important, Hartranft had an eye for people with scholarly potential. During his presidency the school hired such professors as A. C. Zenos in New Testament, Arthur Lincoln Gillett in apologetics, Williston Walker and Edwin Knox Mitchell in church history, Melanchthon Jacobus in Bible, Graham Taylor and later Ross Miriam in Christian sociology, and Louis Bayle Paton in Old Testament.

This acquisition of scholarly talent was at the core of Hartranft's work with the seminary. In 1890 he introduced a modified elective system to allow students to utilize the faculty effectively, and he continually sought new funds for the library, which was headed by the able Charles Snow Thayer. By the end of his presidency the library was among the best theological collections in the United States with more than 80,000 volumes. Academically speaking, Hartranft made Hartford into a school that taught theology from the introductory to the doctoral level. While comparative rankings of seminaries, past or present, are always risky, Hartranft had raised Hartford from a small, somewhat insignificant school to an institution that was almost on par with such theological powerhouses as Union in New York and the new University of Chicago. In effect, he made the school into what his successor, W. Douglas Mackenzie, would call a theological university.

But academics were not all of Hartranft's plans for Hartford. In that same 1877 address he had mentioned the need for specialization. In 1889 he took a very important step in that direction by opening Hartford Seminary to women. In his resolution before the board, he stated that he believed that women should be encouraged to prepare themselves for "Christian teaching," "the missionary field," and "religious work other than the pastorate." A seminary pamphlet, designed to recruit women students, noted: "Country as well as city churches are recognizing that the official ministration which a church owes to the community in which it exists cannot be fulfilled by the pulpit utterances and parish calls of one pastor. There is need for another brain, another heart, another pair of hands. The well-organized home and charitable activities of a church require skilled and trained administration."[38] It is unclear whether any

38. *The Theological Training of Women* (Hartford: Hartford Theological Seminary, 1892).

members of the board resisted Hartranft's suggestion, since the minutes reflected only actions taken. But his motion had two qualifications to his stated ideal that women be admitted "to the regular, special, and advanced courses of the seminary on the same terms as men," and that suggests that some people asked questions. First, women were not to be resident in Hosmer Hall, and second, any scholarship aid needed by them had to come from "special funds." In any event, Hartranft established a special committee of women to raise money for this purpose, and while the total was disappointing, it was one of the first efforts to raise money specifically for female seminarians.[39]

Hartranft had experimented with a short-lived School of Christian Sociology and a School of Church Music, but neither survived more than two years. But the basic idea of multiple institutions that could share expensive resources, especially libraries and faculties, was one that continued to intrigue him. In part, this was because of a shortage of students for the pastorate, at least in New England, and the rise of new forms of church employment.[40] The Springfield School for Christian Workers provided Hartranft with a better opportunity to test this type of organization.

In Springfield, Massachusetts, David Alan Reed, pastor of the New Hope Congregational Church, established a training school for Christian workers in 1885. Reed, an activist pastor, had consulted Dwight L. Moody, George Pentecost, A. J. Gordon, and John Vincent about the types of lay workers that were needed, and he used their input to design his school. The Springfield School for Christian Workers tried to do everything from educating professional YMCA secretaries to training superintendents of Sunday schools. There were four departments: the school for YMCA secretaries, a French Protestant School, a technical school, and a school for religious pedagogy. By 1890 these different institutions had begun to go their own ways. Laurence Doggett, who became head of the YMCA school in that year,[41] saw his school as an independent college that would specialize in work with men and boys, including such new areas of study as physical education. Springfield College was established at a fortunate time in the development of American schooling. By the turn of the century the traditional language-based bachelor of arts degree was no longer normative,

39. For an account of Hartranft's work in this area, see Mary F. Collins, "Hartford's Training of Women," *Hartford Seminary Record* 20 (1910): 293-97.

40. The New England schools all reported declines in enrollment during the period from 1890 to 1905. In part, this was the result of young men, who might have entered the ministry earlier, seeking new vocations. But it was also related to the general growth of theological education elsewhere. New England had too many schools for too few churches.

41. Laurence Locke Doggett, *A Man and a School: Pioneering in Higher Education at Springfield College* (New York: Association Press, 1943).

and in 1905 the school acquired the right to grant degrees, including the first degrees in physical education.

In 1897, that part of the School for Christian Workers devoted to religious education took the name Bible Normal College, and the school clarified its mission by stressing its commitment to the education of children, to the use of modern sociology and pedagogy, and to the use of "the best methods" of Sunday school work.[42] The school also went searching for a more permanent institutional home. After a brief flirtation with Harper's University of Chicago, it agreed to relocate to Hartford Seminary. The two schools were to remain legally and institutionally separate, but they were to share resources. The Bible Normal School thus had access to some of the best biblical instruction in the Northeast and to Hartford's substantial library. Since the seminary charter allowed the school to confer degrees, this opened the way for the Bible Normal School to begin developing a degree structure for religious education. At the same time, the seminary gained five additional instructors, access to some important givers, and the prestige of sponsoring work in a new area. The federated nature of the union between the two institutions gave both time to evaluate the experiment without having to surrender their identities or their hard-earned endowments. Although Hartranft did not intend to set precedent, the model of a federation of institutions as a possible prelude to a more complete merger would be followed by many subsequent institutions, including Andover-Newton and Colgate Rochester.

In 1903 Hartranft retired, to devote the rest of his life to study. His successor was the capable W. Douglas Mackenzie, a South African then teaching at Chicago Theological Seminary. Mackenzie was a theologian and ethicist whose passion was the Christian world mission. Like many missiologists in the first decades of the twentieth century, he was searching for a way to affirm the importance of the Christian mission that would responsibly deal with some of the conclusions of modern historical study. His book *The Final Faith: A Statement of the Nature and Authority of Christianity as the Religion of the World* (1910) tried to steer a middle course between those who saw Christianity as the inherited religion of the West and those who saw it as possessing a supernatural authority.[43] Mackenzie saw Christianity as promoting the highest values, especially science and democracy. Consequently, its expansion was important for secular and religious reasons. As an ethicist, he struggled with the world war

42. Geer, *The Hartford Theological Seminary,* p. 194.

43. W. Douglas Mackenzie, *The Final Faith: A Statement of the Nature and Authority of Christianity as the Religion of the World* (New York: Macmillan, 1910). For an earlier treatment of the same themes, see his *Christianity and the Progress of Man as Illustrated by Modern Missions* (London and Edinburgh: Oliphant Anderson and Ferrier, 1898).

and its implications for Christian faith. Like many theological educators, he was a strong supporter of the League of Nations.[44]

In some ways Mackenzie's task as president of Hartford was typical of those who follow someone who has effected significant change: he had to find ways to regularize and stabilize the gains made by his predecessor. In part, he fulfilled this task by filling out the model of combining schools under one leadership. In 1913 he consolidated Hartford Seminary and the School of Religious Pedagogy into a single corporation, the Hartford Seminary Foundation, which permitted him to raise money for both as a single unit. In 1926 the new campus that he planned for the school opened, bearing witness to Hartford's position of leadership among American seminaries.

Mackenzie's greatest contribution, however, was developing the Kennedy School of Missions. In 1910 he chaired the Commission on Missionary Education at Edinburgh. The conference was highly critical of what was done in missionary education, and suggested that much needed to be done.[45] Part of the way early ecumenical meetings functioned was to establish continuation committees and other bodies to keep the issues uncovered by the meeting alive until another world body could be summoned. Mackenzie continued to research missionary preparation, and in 1912 he presented his report: *Fundamental Qualifications of the Foreign Missionary.*[46] Both at Edinburgh and at New York, Mackenzie stressed the need for foreign missionaries to have the fullest preparation possible, including a college degree, and to have a thorough knowledge of modern social science and of comparative religion. Unfortunately, there were only a few places in the country that could provide such training.[47]

Hartford's president, however, knew where to turn. He had worked on his Edinburgh report with Edward Capen, a missionary specialist, and with his faculty colleague Curtis Geer. Together the three had toured American missions and had interviewed missionaries abroad. Mackenzie also had access to a number of Hartford students who had traveled abroad. Hartford had earlier funded

44. W. Douglas Mackenzie, *The Kingdom of God and the League of Nations* (Hartford: Hartford Seminary Press, 1919).

45. For the effects of the conference on women's training schools, see pp. 216-18.

46. W. Douglas Mackenzie, *Fundamental Qualifications of the Foreign Missionary: Being a Report Presented by President Mackenzie at the Second Annual Meeting of the Board of Missionary Preparation, Held in New York City, Dec. 16, 1912, and Issued in Pamphlet Form by Authority of the Board* (New York, n.d.).

47. The divinity school at Yale was one of these. By using its own resources and the resources of the university, Yale was able to put together an impressive program that combined the history and philosophy of missions, sound theological training, and social sciences. Mackenzie knew this program and may have used it as a model.

a small program that sponsored student travel to the Congregational mission fields in the Near East, and Hartford Seminary already was known for its expertise in Islamic studies. Mackenzie pulled all these things together and made a proposal to Ms. James Kennedy, one of the seminary's wealthy supporters. In 1912 Ms. Kennedy was ready to make a significant gift. She gave $500,000 to found the Kennedy School of Missions and another $500,000 to put the School of Religious Pedagogy on a sound financial basis.

The Kennedy money, in effect, completed Hartranft and Mackenzie's plan for the seminary. Using the device of the Hartford Seminary Foundation, they had created a school that deserved the name of a theological university. At one institution, it was possible for a student to pursue the academic study of theology through the doctoral level, to prepare to serve a Congregational church, to learn how to direct the educational activities of a congregation, and to master those academic subjects needed on the foreign field. In addition to the classical theological areas, Hartford had specialized instruction in the relevant social sciences and a library substantial enough to support its work.

Why did the strong seminary president become important in theological education around the turn of the century? In part, the office was created in response to the times. Higher education had moved away from the classical education that had been the stock-in-trade of the antebellum college and seminary. Things were not yet to the point where Latin and Greek were studied by only a handful who wanted advanced education, but they were studied far less thoroughly and with declining frequency. Someone had to build the bridges that connected the educational past with the future. The new patterns of education were, moreover, much more expensive than the older ones. J. L. McLean, one of the first to comment on the new office, observed:

> The seminary needs money, money continually; needs it, as the college does, "for the proper doing and proper enrichment of its work." In the past it has not, in measure at all commensurate with its necessities, been getting money. It is not doing so at the present time. As a consequence, its work is not being done, properly enlarged, nor properly enriched. For this lack of funds, and therefore for other lacks resultant from this, the seminaries are themselves chiefly responsible. They have not, because they had not — sufficiently and efficiently — sought.

To raise the type of money needed by a Union (Richmond), a Southwestern, or a Hartford required special gifts of persuasion and of vision. McLean noted: "We have called the gaining of benevolent funds an art. It is more than an art, it is a husbandry. This husbandman, too, must be a model of patience, he must wait for the precious fruit of his endeavor, and be patient until it has received the early and the later rain."[48] The new president was, whatever else he might have been, a person able to convince others that his particular vision of the future was the one the church and its schools needed to follow. In other words, fund-raising itself required a special type of person and a special type of vision. Those people who could convince donors had a similar capacity to convince their faculties and their boards of trust. Power followed finances, as it still does.

Yet there were other structural reasons for the strong presidency. As in other areas of higher education, schools had become more complicated. In the early nineteenth century the faculty could meet as a committee of the whole and make the basic decisions about a school's day-by-day operations, and strong members of the boards of trust were likewise able to monitor the comparatively simple affairs of a school closely. By the end of the nineteenth century, this was no longer possible, except in very small institutions, and even these needed closer oversight than before. But, since finances were limited, administrations remained small. Except in the larger schools, the president was often not the chief executive officer; he was the only executive officer. A single person, thus, did the work that later seminaries would divide among recruiters, fund-raisers, deans, and registrars. As Neely McCarter observed: "Likewise in the seminaries, the president who was responsible for almost everything and had few, if any, ecclesiastical or governmental regulations or academic strictures upon his office, could basically run an institution according to his best insights."[49] As administrative offices became more complex, power would diffuse to more people, making the type of close supervision characteristic of the new administrators difficult.

Perhaps the other reason for the rise of strong presidencies in this period lies in the nature of theology itself. Things were changing rapidly in biblical studies, in church history, in doctrinal theology, and in practical theology. Despite the calm of many modernist and liberal theologians, one senses that many people were suffering from cognitive overload as they struggled to find new ways to talk about old faiths or to maintain old ways in the midst of new directions. In that intellectual world, it was easy for the faculty to allow the president of the school considerable power over the school's future direction. There were simply many more important things than directing an institution or recruiting new teachers. The presidents, who had a vision of how things fit together, were ready and able to take over the task.

48. McLean, "Presidency of Theological Seminaries," p. 334.

49. Neely Dixon McCarter, *The President as Educator: A Study of the Seminary Presidency* (Atlanta: Scholars, 1996), p. v.

PART II

Embodying the Dream

CHAPTER FOURTEEN

An Appraisal at the End of the Era of Crusades

From 1890 to 1920 was a rich period in American Protestant history. During this time the churches launched a number of crusades or campaigns to make America a Christian, even a Protestant, nation. Some of these campaigns were continuations of older emphases. Thus, the churches sought to prohibit prostitution and to secure laws that protected the Sabbath from profanation. The voluntary system of church membership, further, imposed on churches a constant need to recruit new members, either through nurture or revival, and both the Sunday school and the revival were heavily promoted means to church growth. As the churches' drive westward established congregations from coast to coast, many Protestant leaders began to see the cities as the new frontier and to advocate aggressive missionary work through such agencies as institutional churches and city missions. Abroad, the foreign missionary enterprise was making what appeared to be exponential gains. Despite the temporary setback of the Boxer Rebellion, for instance, Christian institutions in China, particularly colleges and universities, were growing in popularity.

Some campaigns were new versions of older initiatives. The prohibition crusade is an excellent example of a reborn emphasis. Clearly, alcohol was a more serious problem in the post–Civil War industrial environment than it had been earlier, and then as now, contributed more than its share to the miseries of the poor. Since the days of John Wesley, Protestant Christians had advocated temperance. People would take a pledge either to drink only beer or wine or, in some cases, to abstain totally (hence the word "teetotaler") from drink. Many evangelical churches, especially those in the Wesleyan tradition, adopted rules against members using alcohol socially, and among Baptists and Congregationalists, temperance statements in local church covenants became commonplace. In the 1850s Maine experimented for a season with statewide prohibition. But, as in England, much of Protestant political pressure had focused on regulating the sale of alcohol through licensing, and determining when and where it could be consumed. The new prohibition movement did not oppose these limited goals, but it believed that the nation as a whole should outlaw the use of strong drink. The crusade was as broad as the nation.

Methodism was an important component of these crusades. In part, the reasons were theological. Whatever else the traditional Protestant (and for that matter, Catholic) emphasis on original sin did, it provided a rationale for the persistence of sin in this world. No matter what human beings said or did, personally or collectively, evil was a necessary consequence of human life. While human beings might choose the form of their own depravity, the depravity itself was a given. In contrast, Wesleyans believed that holiness was possible in this life with the help of Christ. If only a handful of saints might find complete sanctification, all human beings could make substantial progress toward perfect love. And, for most Methodists, this growth was progressive. A person took one step at a time until he or she arrived at the goal. Often sanctification involved overcoming different sins at different points. In a sense, the various Protestant crusades fit this pattern almost exactly. An evil — alcohol, disrespect for the Sabbath, poor housing — would be identified and named. People might respond either by remaining with the evil or by moving to its eradication. The various crusades were movements, designed to gain momentum, that would overwhelm the popular indifference to evil and spur an aroused people to democratic action.

One might argue either that progressivism was Methodism in politics or that Methodism was progressivism at prayer. This is of course an overstatement, but it may be a useful one. While many progressive leaders were the children or grandchildren of the antebellum reformers, progressivism was more than a continuation of abolitionism.[1] Its religious core was the belief that evil can be overcome by firm resolution and concerned action. What the future demanded was that people steel their wills to the task, put their shoulders into it, and fight for it. But unlike the previous generation, the progressive generation also felt the sting of modernity. For many, the fervent faith of their childhood was more a still, small voice exhorting to the right than a clear revelation from heaven that rescued them from sin and death.[2] Such believing unbelief enabled them to see the world around them in a different light. Most progressives traveled light theologically.

1. Robert Crunden, *Ministers of Reform: The Progressives' Achievement in American Civilization, 1889-1920* (New York: Basic Books, 1982).

2. James H. Moorhead, *World without End: Mainstream American Protestant Visions of the Last Things, 1880-1925* (Bloomington and Indianapolis: Indiana University Press, 1999).

Much of the power of crusading Protestantism came from an element it shared with other parts of the American economy: the capacity to mobilize both people and resources. Robert Lynn has shown that the period was a crucial one for Protestant finances with churches developing such tools as the unified budget, the pledging system, envelopes, and the theology of stewardship to raise the funds they needed for their ministries.[3] In part, these new funding methods were responses to the crusades. The Student Volunteer Movement for Foreign Missions, founded at Moody's 1886 Northfield student conference, spread rapidly. By 1895 it was part of the World's Student Christian Federation, a group that included students from around the world. The Student Volunteers produced more candidates than the churches could finance, and thus were a goad to the further development of church finance. The Laymen's Missionary Movement illustrates the new dynamic. Founded in 1905, it used an effective fund-raising technique. In each major city, those supporting the movement would organize a banquet that would be addressed by a persuasive missions advocate. Celebrities were invited to address the meetings. Presidents Roosevelt, Taft, and Wilson were among those who made an appeal for more resources for foreign missions. Those present would be urged to make major contributions. Part of the key to the success of the movement was its ability to use the media, especially newspapers, to publicize its events. Whatever else the meetings were, the sponsors made sure they were "news."[4] In large measure because of this crusade, the churches' revenues for foreign missions grew almost 200 percent, with some denominations, including the Presbyterians, experiencing an even larger increase.

In many ways the Men and Religion Forward Movement, the brainchild of Mainer Harry W. Arnold, was the most ambitious of the crusades. Since the colonial period the demographics of American Protestantism had been heavily weighted toward women, and by 1850 many ministers were preaching a feminized gospel that stressed family, feelings, and personal surrender.[5] As male

3. Robert Lynn, "A Documentary History of Protestant Finances" (tentative title), forthcoming.

4. The techniques of the Laymen's Missionary Movement, the Men and Religion Forward Movement, and the revival crusades of Billy Sunday were very similar. All depended on the support of named or known people, on advertising, and above all, on their ability to attract media attention. As time passed, of course, it became more important to make events even more attention grabbing. Aimee Semple McPherson was a logical development of the fund-raising and revival techniques pioneered earlier in the century.

5. Much of the material in this section is dependent on Gail Bederman, "The Women Have Had Charge of the Church Work Long Enough: The Men and Religion Forward Movement of 1911 and the Masculinization of Middle Class Protestantism," in *A Mighty Baptism: Race, Gender, and the Creation of American Protestantism,* ed. Susan Juster and Lisa MacFarlane

life increasingly developed outside the home, the distance between the churches and men increased, both theologically and organizationally. By 1880 the churches were struggling to find ways to present a "muscular Christianity" that might evangelize men, and the YMCA, one of the few Christian groups to be successful with men, was the nation's largest parachurch organization with branches in almost all cities and towns and on many college campuses.

The progressive era was in many ways ideally suited to a religious masculinity. Such progressive heroes as Theodore Roosevelt often pictured themselves as knights-errant struggling against the forces of evil. America's little war against Spain further strengthened the new understanding of religious manhood. Christian men, united by a higher ideal, had liberated Cuba and the Philippines from centuries of ignorance and oppression. The Men and Religion Forward Movement picked up all these themes. Its goal was nothing less than "to unite the churches, the brotherhoods, the Sunday Schools and the Young Men's Christian Associations in a worthy and workable plan of permanent specialized effort for the men and boys." But, suspecting that the traditional revival would not accomplish this task, they preached a vigorous social gospel that sought "to increase the permanent contribution of the Church to the best life of the Continent, socially, politically, commercially, and physically, and to emphasize the modern message of the church in social service and usefulness."[6]

The Men and Religion Forward Movement had a qualified but real success. Together with the other forms of outreach to men, the movement apparently encouraged many men to return to the churches. The importance of this success should not be underestimated. Both theological liberals and social gospel advocates had claimed that theological modifications were the only way the church could retain the loyalty of thinking people, and this movement seemed to demonstrate the basic validity of this position. Walter Rauschenbusch, a strong supporter of the movement, wrote: "This Movement has made the social gospel orthodox in the church. For a long time we had been regarded as heretics. But the social gospel has now come to be one of the dogmas of the Christian faith. A dogma is not necessarily something declared by the church, but is a common conclusion of Christendom; and it has come to be a conviction of Christendom that this world, with all its sin, is to be claimed into the Kingdom of God."[7] In

---

(Ithaca, N.Y., and London: Cornell University Press, 1996); also published in *American Quarterly* 41 (Sept. 1989): 432-65.

6. "Report of the Committee of Ninety-Seven," in *Messages of the Men and Religion Movement,* vol. 1, *Congress Addresses* (New York: Association Press, 1912), pp. 14-15.

7. Walter Rauschenbusch, "The Conservation of the Social Service Message," in *Messages of the Men and Religion Movement,* vol. 2, *Social Service* (New York: Association Press, 1912), p. 121.

this sense the Men and Religion Forward Movement was the capstone of a long development that included the Methodist Social Creed and the formation of the Federal Council of Churches. A new understanding of Christianity had been formulated.[8]

The movement was part of the wave of religious and social excitement that finally enacted prohibition into national law. In retrospect, the new constitutional amendment and the Volstead Act that was passed to enforce it were typical of much progressive legislation. Since the primary enemy was the "money" power or those, like the owners of saloons and breweries, who had profited from the sale and manufacture of alcohol, the law prohibited only those activities — sale and manufacture — that had made the trade profitable. Once the contagion had been cut off at its source, the use of alcohol would gradually disappear. This was the same logic that prohibited impure medicines or required a list of ingredients on prepackaged foods. Without the continual nourishment provided by the profiteers, it was reasoned, alcohol would wither on the vine. Perhaps this is one reason Congress never appropriated sufficient funds for enforcement. After all, once the root dies, it should be easy to remove the plant.[9]

If Prohibition was one clear progressive victory, the First World War was another. In many ways the Great War was an event that had seemed destined never to happen. Few Americans had wanted war before 1917. In 1912 Woodrow Wilson, the first Southerner since Reconstruction to be elected president, won the White House after a tight three-cornered race, defeating Taft and Roosevelt. In 1916 Wilson retained the presidency, because many voters were convinced that he had kept the country out of war.

Concern about international peace was very much part of American life from the Spanish-American War onward. Although the heyday of the peace movement was the 1920s and 1930s, the movement was already gathering steam. More than thirty organizations devoted to world peace existed, and Andrew Carnegie, whose philanthropies often reflected American values, donated more than two million dollars to establish the Church Peace Union and its Carnegie prize. The Fellowship of Reconciliation was founded in 1915, and many of the most vocal social gospel advocates, such as Harry F. Ward, were already sound-

8. Donald K. Gorrell, *The Age of Social Responsibility: The Social Gospel in the Progressive Era, 1900-1920* (Macon, Ga.: Mercer University Press, 1988).

9. In retrospect, such thinking appears to have been almost hopelessly naive. Once the legal suppliers, whose fixed places of business were controllable, left the trade, innumerable illegal suppliers arose to meet the demand who were, by the nature of an illegal business, harder to control. But, naive or not, it was characteristic of the progressive period, and such thinking underlay many progressive laws.

ing the tocsin about the dangers of armed conflict. Anti-imperialist William Jennings Bryan, Wilson's secretary of state until 1916, was a tireless advocate of nonviolent solutions to international problems.[10]

Yet America drifted, almost despite itself, toward participation in the conflict. Whether the ultimate causes of American participation were geopolitical, such as a response to such German "aggressions" as unrestricted submarine warfare and the Zimmermann note, or related to a sense of Anglo-American cultural solidarity can and has been debated. The Great War, whether viewed from the American or the European perspective, remains tantamount to a European death wish, ending five hundred years of political expansion, scientific and intellectual growth, and economic development. But, whatever the causes, Wilson defined the war by harnessing the language of progressive reform and military adventure. The war was to make the world safe for democracy, to be the war that ended all wars, and was to end by securing a just peace on the basis of the Fourteen Points. Christ was meeting Satan on the field of a French Armageddon. The churches responded enthusiastically to this rhetoric that was, after all, their own. Shailer Mathews, for instance, a staunch liberal and social gospel advocate, rang almost all the chimes to identify the war with progressive aims. He believed, firmly, that the war was being fought to keep liberal religion and democracy from potential enslavement, and he accepted Wilson's belief that the war would end with the establishment of a League of Nations.[11] Mathews also took the opportunity to argue that dispensational premillennialism, then at the height of its popularity among Northern Baptists, was inherently unpatriotic, because it rejected the idea that the kingdom could be realized in human history. Needless to say, conservatives disagreed, and a bitter dispute ensued.

After the war George Coe and Henry Sloane Coffin traded appraisals of the clergy's role. For Coe the war was the ultimate sellout of Christian idealism:

> Was there ever a greater spiritual emergency, in fact, than that which the Great War precipitated? Here, surely, were issues sufficient to stimulate to the utmost whatever was of conscience in men. Here were moral confusions to be cleared up; here were temptations as vast as empires to be met; here, if ever, the difference between the Kingdom of God and every other aim in life needed to be brought to the fore in men's thinking concerning the future of society. . . . Yet the ministry in general had nothing distinctively to offer. Here and there a little group — Quakers for instance — bore

10. Bryan was often mocked in the popular press for his devotion to peace and his rejection of American imperialism.

11. See Shailer Mathews, *Patriotism and Religion* (New York: Macmillan, 1918).

testimony by word and deed to something specific that they thought they had received from God.[12]

Coffin's reply admitted that the clergy had made mistakes, but he was not sure that Coe had named these with sufficient clarity.

> I agree with my colleague that much of the preaching during the war was very remotely Christian. Many of the utterances were B.C. rather than A.D. I am not prepared, however, to agree wholly that "the clergy did count, and that splendidly, but it was not their religion that counted." When the clergy counted splendidly, it was not when they voiced on Sunday the same ethical sentiments with which the press was filled throughout the week; but when they faced the ethical perplexities in which Christian consciences found themselves, pointed out that War was not and could never be called a Christian method of solving an international problem, but might under the circumstances be the less un-Christian method of ending an intolerable situation.[13]

Recently, John F. Piper has concluded that most churches officially took a middle position on the war, embracing neither the most extreme crusader language nor pacifism.[14] His judgment is probably accurate. Coffin's observation that the war was the "less un-Christian method" of resolving "an intolerable situation" seems to have been reflected in many churches' official documents.

Did the churches' advocacy of at least the progressive goals of the war contribute to the widespread religious retreat of the 1920s? One must be careful here. Certainly younger Christian intellectuals, such as Karl Barth in Germany and Reinhold Niebuhr in America, were horrified when they looked back on the war years. Viewing it from the perspective of what was learned about war profiteering, about the secret treaties that had led to the war, about Allied war debts, and the rest of what was often a sordid story (both on the Allied and the Central side), one finds it hard not to be revulsed by it. The politically and socially conservative Southern Baptists added a strong statement on war and peace issues to the Baptist Faith and Message, a document designed to check liberalism in the denomination, that warned against the un-

12. George A. Coe, "The Religious Breakdown of the Ministry," *Journal of Religion* 1 (Jan. 1921): 18-29.

13. Henry Sloane Coffin, "Criticism and Queries," *Journal of Religion* 1 (Mar. 1921): 189.

14. John F. Piper, *The American Churches in World War I* (Athens: Ohio University Press, 1985), p. 13. William Hutchison, *The Modernist Impulse in American Protestantism* (Cambridge: Harvard University Press, 1976), p. 243 n. 37, found much ambiguity in the thesis of almost unqualified clerical support for the world war.

christian elements in war, and Christian youth organizations became almost uniformly pacifist.

Yet one wonders whether the moral failure of the churches did not occur much earlier. In 1920 two studies, *Religion among American Men* and *The Army and Religion,* appeared.[15] They were summaries of a series of surveys, interviews, and conversations conducted during the war by military chaplains. The picture could not have been less heartening. Although most American soldiers professed some vague belief in religion, along the line of belief in a higher power, this popular faith had little specific theological content; most demonstrated "widespread ignorance on elementary religious matters." Paul Carter summarized the results in this burning paragraph:

> And the men were found, more often than not, deeply critical of the Church even when they professed loyalty to its ideals. The Christianity "preached by the Church" (as distinguished from an aspired-to, "real" Christianity) was called "primarily a selfish thing — the seeking of a personal reward"; or, alternatively, "mainly a negative, prohibitory thing," administered by "an association of trained killjoys." Church members, said the soldiers, did not live up to their professed standards, and their lives were "often peculiarly colorless or narrow or effeminate." The Church was "a convenient institution for the performance of conventional ceremonies, venerable . . . but not much concerned with the real business of life"; "you go there to be married and buried." Much that it emphasized was "unimportant, uninteresting, and not especially relevant; and the tasks it assigned were often trivial."[16]

The importance of these conclusions should not be overlooked. In the midst of what their elders believed was the climax of almost a half-century of missionary crusading, most American young men did not get the point of it all.[17]

15. *The Army and Religion* (New York: Association Press, 1920); *Religion among American Men* (New York: Association Press, 1920).

16. Paul A. Carter, *The Decline and Renewal of the Social Gospel: Social and Political Liberalism in American Protestant Churches, 1920-1940* (Ithaca, N.Y.: Cornell University Press, 1956), p. 91.

17. Robert T. Handy, *Undermined Establishment: Church-State Relations in America, 1880-1920* (Princeton: Princeton University Press, 1991), argues that the cracks in Protestant America were evident in the last decades of the nineteenth century. In addition to the evidence amassed by Handy, the self-understanding of American theologians needs to be taken into account. Conservative, liberal, and modernist theologians all assumed that apologetics, not dogmatics, was the need of the hour; that is, they assumed that something had to be done to make people aware of their religious heritage. This assumption does not make sense unless serious defections from faith are occurring.

The churches were at their most effective in their attempts to provide religious services to the armed forces. The Federal Council of Churches, which represented most of the Protestant denominations, established a blue-ribbon committee. The General War-Time Commission of the Churches was chaired by Robert Speer and included among its members Harry Emerson Fosdick; Henry Sloane Coffin; John M. Glenn, layman; Fred B. Smith, layman; J. Ross Stevenson, president of Princeton Seminary; William Mackenzie, president of Hartford Seminary; Shailer Mathews, dean of the University of Chicago Divinity School; William Faunce, president of Brown University; Gifford Pinchot, former cabinet member; Carl E. Milliken, former governor of Maine; John R. Mott, representing the YMCA; and Mabel Cratty, representing the YWCA. In addition, there was an Inter-Church Committee on War Work that was chaired by William Adams Brown and enlisted many Union faculty members. Perhaps the most remarkable sign of the vitality of the churches' response to the war was their capacity to raise money for war work. The 1918 United War Work Campaign that brought together Catholic, Jewish, and Protestant agencies (particularly the YMCA and YWCA) raised more than $175 million.[18] The fund-raising techniques by earlier crusades were proving very effective.

The two wartime committees were of course central to many later developments in American theological education. Warfare had changed in the interim between the Civil War and the First World War. Although West Point graduates dominated the high commands of North and South, most American officers were elected by a volunteer unit or chosen because of political influence in Washington. There were no set professional standards for the positions, and the chaplain corps was typical of other officers in this regard. Separate command structures for chaplains were not established until the First World War (army, 1920; navy, 1917), in part in response to pressure from the churches. The major difference, however, was that chaplains were now seen as specialized personnel, somewhat analogous to engineers, physicians, and dentists. As for the other specialized officer positions, the question for the army and navy, who were forced to expand their numbers rapidly, was how to secure people who could do the job with a modicum of further training. The bewildering (at least to outsiders) array of qualifications for the ministry and the almost equally confusing morass of seminary degrees and programs made such needed military judgments all but impossible. War, thus, highlighted a problem that was becoming evident to the leadership of the schools. The Conference of Theolog-

18. Eldon Ernst, *Moment of Truth for Protestant America: Interchurch Campaigns Following World War One* (Missoula, Mont.: American Academy of Religion, 1972), p. 25. I have relied heavily on Ernst's analysis in this section.

ical Schools, which began as a place for seminaries to discuss the impact of the war on their operations, became the nucleus of an accrediting agency as the schools themselves struggled with the issue of standards.

At the same time, the disproportionately large representation of seminary faculty in ecumenical work around the war was a sign of a broadened role for at least some American theological educators. There was a general tendency to tap seminary teachers and administrators, particularly those in the university-related seminaries, to serve as theological consultants and spokespeople for the larger Protestant enterprises. This was particularly true for politically or internationally sensitive issues. It would also be true of representation in the various meetings that led to the formation of the World Council of Churches. On a slightly lower level, the international denominational associations, such as the Baptist World Alliance, would also press seminary teachers into leadership positions. This role was a heady one that cemented the prominence of the university-related faculties among seminaries. But more important, it was the beginning of a shifting understanding of the leadership role of the seminaries. Earlier seminary faculty had seen themselves as leaders of their denominations with only a few becoming well-known Protestant leaders; subsequent leaders would often see themselves as the servants of a coming world-church whose theology and life were just beginning to be shaped by changing circumstances.

The success of the financial campaigns to fight the war, not to mention the successful prosecution of the war itself, suggested another significant possibility as well: that the nation was ripe for further religious and political challenge. The world emerging from the war was clearly different from the prewar world. Much of Europe lay in waste, peoples were awakening in Africa and Asia, and serious evangelistic work needed to be done at home. Most missionary leaders, including Mott and Speer, believed that the changed situation meant that the fields were ripe for harvest, and this belief contributed to a sense of urgency. The hour was now and the challenge was immediate. What was not as clear was whether the American churches would be able to bear the burdens that history had placed on their shoulders. The 1919 Interchurch Emergency Campaign, conducted by fourteen denominations, established Interchurch Sunday, February 19, 1919, as the date for their major drive. To church leaders the success of this postwar drive meant that American Protestants were ready to take up the task of kingdom building in earnest.

Various American denominations were already positioning themselves for major fund-raising drives in the postwar era. Southern Baptists, for instance, had embarked on their $75 Million Campaign that ran from 1919 to 1924; Congregationalists had planned their Pilgrim Memorial Fund for 1920; American Methodists, their Joint Centenary Campaign; the Northern

Presbyterians, their New Era Campaign; and the Disciples of Christ, their Men and Millions programs. These programs, which stressed education and missions, were significant for the seminaries as a whole. The Southern Baptist $75 Million Campaign, for instance, was expected to pay for the new Louisville campus of Southern Seminary and to provide substantial sums for Southwestern. Other seminaries were included in the various proposals. In many ways these campaigns all followed the same approach as the Laymen's Missionary Movement. They were rooted in a series of dinners, widely advertised in the press, where prominent speakers addressed the group, and had fairly clear goals. Like the earlier "movements," they were not designed to be permanent.

The fact that so many different minds believed that the time had come for a major funding push by American Protestants suggested that the denominations might cooperate in this task. The idea is not as far-fetched as it might seem. While each of the denominational drives would include meetings in local congregations to solicit pledges, part of the task of a movement was to generate enthusiasm. The large dinner, the engaging speaker, the whole drama of the pledge could be made even more impressive by including more denominations in the program. A meeting with more than a thousand cheering supporters was much more newsworthy than a meeting with only a few hundred. The experience of both the Laymen's Missionary Movement and the Men and Religion Forward Movement suggested that numbers were an important element in generating and building support for a movement. Since many of those who led the earlier crusades, such as Robert Speer and Henry Sloane Coffin, would be prominent leaders in the new crusade, the importance of past experience cannot be overestimated. The leaders were becoming seasoned funding professionals.

When the Executive Committee of the Presbyterian Church, USA (Southern), called in November 1919 for a joint meeting of missionary leaders to cooperate in raising money for "equipment and support of all their Foreign Mission Work, and to recruit a sufficient force of evangelists, teachers, doctors and nurses to go to the front, that the non-Christian world may be immediately evangelized, and Christian education, medical and sanitary work, and social service may be adequately done in non-Christian lands," the response was enthusiastic.[19] The language of the appeal reminded those with past experience in the Protestant crusades of the very successful Student Volunteer Movement and the Laymen's Missionary Movement. A Committee of Twenty, chaired by S. Earl Taylor, the successful Methodist fund-raiser, met and mapped out an important strategy. The whole of the Protestant mission, at home and abroad, was to be surveyed and the needs determined for at least "the next five years."

19. Quoted in Ernst, *Moment of Truth,* p. 44.

The Committee of Twenty then passed its work on to a general committee. A large meeting of representatives from the various Protestant boards met between April 30 and May 1, 1919, and adopted an official definition of the program. Eldon Ernst summarized their work as:

1. To undertake a scientific survey of the world's needs from the standpoint of the responsibility of Evangelical Christianity.
2. To project a cooperative community and world program to meet the needs as revealed by the survey.
3. To discover and develop the resources of men, money, and power necessary for the accomplishment of the program.[20]

In a real sense the proposed program was a masterful expression of the 1920s' ideal of efficiency. First, the work to be done was identified; then how that work was to be done was determined; and finally the financial requirements of the plan were determined.

The Interchurch World Movement attracted a wide variety of Protestant church leaders. Mott and Speer, the two men whose names were almost synonymous with Protestant missions, were of course high on the list of leaders. Also included were many of the warriors who had made earlier movements successful, such as Fred B. Smith of the Disciples of Christ and S. Earl Taylor, the Methodist fund-raising expert, who had put together many of his denomination's more successful campaigns. William Doughty held a prominent position, as did Daniel Poling. American Baptist Fred B. Haggard was placed in charge of the crucial work of doing the surveys. All these men had held positions of leadership in the Laymen's Missionary Movement and in the Men and Religion Forward Movement.[21] By this time they were an experienced team, used to working together, and able to make arrangements almost effortlessly.

Among the veterans of the Laymen's Missionary Movement was John D. Rockefeller, Jr., who was in charge of the Rockefeller millions. As the plan evolved, Rockefeller's friends from the Laymen's Missionary Movement urged him to take an active role.[22] His father, John D. Rockefeller, had contributed heavily to Baptist causes, including the University of Chicago and Southern

20. Ernst, *Moment of Truth,* p. 55.

21. The importance of the links in personnel between the various "movements" should not be overlooked. In fact, we are dealing with the same people, the same givers, and much the same program repeated several times. *Men and Missions,* the official journal of the Laymen's Missionary Movement, also becomes the official journal of the Interchurch World Movement.

22. Charles E. Harvey, "John D. Rockefeller, Jr., and the Interchurch World Movement of 1919-1920: A Different Angle on the Ecumenical Movement," *Church History* 51 (1982): 198-209.

Baptist Theological Seminary; his son was much more committed to an ecumenical approach. In 1917 the younger Rockefeller published an essay, "The Christian Church: What of Its Future?" in the *Saturday Evening Post.* In the essay Rockefeller made it clear that he believed that churches needed to cooperate with each other in the task of building the kingdom of God.

The *Post* article, however, did not reveal the depths of Rockefeller's theological liberalism. As a young man, his teachers at Brown had decisively influenced the young billionaire, and the foundation they laid was strengthened by his own participation in the Fifth Avenue Baptist Church. Rockefeller was troubled all his life by the militantly anti-Rockefeller rhetoric of much American progressivism and Populism, and this may have led him to embrace a variety of social and philanthropic concerns. Jerry Dean Weber estimated that he gave $97.1 million to various religious charities during his lifetime, in addition to continuing interests in such areas as general education for African Americans, medicine, and the arts.[23]

Rockefeller's general strategy for religious giving is an essential part of the story of much of twentieth-century ecumenical Christianity. First, he would not support any expression of Christianity that was self-consciously sectarian. Like his good friend and adviser John R. Mott, Rockefeller was interested in Christianity rather than the specific work of particular churches. Secondly, the younger Rockefeller continued his father's belief in consolidation rather than competition. He believed that only large-scale enterprises could make a difference in the modern American environment, and he hoped that the churches could find ways to end their often expensive duplication of services. At one point he apparently thought he might spark the formation of a larger church by financing pensions for ministers of all denominations. Those who participated in the retirement plan would have to surrender their doctrinal particularities. Perhaps this utopian proposal reflected more of Rockefeller's own free church heritage than he imagined, and it is difficult, if not impossible, to see any of the confessional churches ever accepting such a plan. But the same guideline did influence Rockefeller's gifts to theological education. He made those gifts in two widely separated periods: the 1920s and the 1950s. In each case his criteria for including or excluding a school was its relationship to his larger ecumenical vision. In practice this meant he was particularly partial to the university divinity schools, such as Union (New York), Yale, and Harvard.

Perhaps, most importantly, it meant the continuation of the basic Rockefeller belief in research and development. Although many reasons can be

23. Jerry Dean Weber, "To Strengthen and Develop Protestant Theological Education: John D. Rockefeller, Jr., and the Seatlantic Fund" (Ph.D. diss., University of Chicago, 1997), p. 10.

given for the success of Standard Oil, Rockefeller's management style made a major contribution.[24] Basically, the older Rockefeller had assembled a management team that knew the business thoroughly, and he had relied on the advice of this team when crucial decisions had to be made. The other aspect of the Rockefeller style was research. Standard Oil prospered because Rockefeller was willing, for instance, to invest significant amounts of money in such new technology as procedures for "sweetening" oil and long-distance pipelines. In many ways the basic strategy of the trust was similar: Rockefeller tried to plan production and distribution in such a way as to even out the cycles of boom and bust that characterized the early days of the oil industry. Such studies of the market made it possible to avoid the disastrous price wars that almost destroyed the nascent industry.

Rockefeller Jr.'s devotion to ecumenism was also a continuation of his father's emphases. Standard Oil was not one company; it was a number of separate corporate entities that had agreed to a common management and marketing strategy. None of the separate corporations could have influenced the larger "market" significantly by varying its own production or pricing, but when these companies were joined together by a trust, they were able to dominate the oil industry. This remained Rockefeller's model for the Christian church. If the various component parts can be convinced to surrender part of their individuality, then they will be able to set the direction for the whole Christian movement and possibly for the nation.[25]

Charles E. Harvey's painstaking research in the Rockefeller archives has demonstrated the full extent of Rockefeller's involvement in the crusade. As a member of the budget review committee, Rockefeller pressed for the Interchurch World Movement to adopt a maximum budget that would exceed

24. At the time, Rockefeller was often seen as almost a demonic figure whose success could be attributed only to a virtual league with the devil. Ida Tarbell, for instance, repeated the story that Rockefeller had cheated a widow out of her refinery, almost a classical example of melodramatic evil. While Rockefeller was a sharp businessman and one who neither asked nor gave quarter in the industrial battles of the late nineteenth century, his success was attributable to more than sharp business practices. After all, many of his competitors, who went bust, were as ruthless or more so than he was.

25. Rockefeller's thinking here is not so much based on the idea of a "New Catholicism" as on American business and on his own Baptist and free church heritage. The latter should not be downplayed. As a Baptist, Rockefeller believed that local churches could both be radically independent and nonetheless give up some of that independence to do such tasks as home and foreign missions or to provide pensions for ministers. Part of the problem Rockefeller faced in dealing with such critics as Robert Speer, who believed that missions inherently belonged to the larger church (the General Assembly instead of local congregations), was thus rooted in Rockefeller's own denominational history, which he never transcended.

the pledges to the general campaign made by the individual participating denominations. To make this more attractive, he personally guaranteed the budget of the movement and became one of its most substantial financial supporters. Beyond a doubt, he had considerable influence behind the scenes in shaping the movement's policies.

The Interchurch World Movement had some notable successes. Its stress on modern promotional techniques enabled religious organizations, including seminaries, to enter into the new media world of the 1920s more easily. The importance of this for American Protestantism should not be underestimated. Protestantism had generally depended on disciplined, discursive speech to communicate its message, but this rhetoric of persuasion was no longer as effective as it had been. The press, for instance, had moved from the careful literary analysis of events to short, easily read accounts that often contained the vital information in a single headline or paragraph. Advertising, which made an art of persuasion, had moved away from texts almost completely. The most effective ads included several banners or headlines, set in large type, a picture, and a snippet of a sentence. Longer discussions were, self-consciously, set in small type for those already hooked by the larger message. The movies were already replacing the stage as the principal form of drama. After Warner Brothers released the first "talkie" — *The Jazz Singer* — in 1927, the stage became even less central. Radio, pioneered before the world war, was ready to begin a phenomenal climb to popularity.[26]

The tie to the newer methods of promotion, however, points to one of the movement's great weaknesses. Unlike earlier Protestant crusades, the size of the Interchurch World Movement meant that its costs rose almost astronomically. By the end of 1919 the movement had spent $2 million, and it would spend another million a month during the first five months of 1920. The leaders justified the expenses by pointing to the greater efficiency the joint campaign offered the churches, but nonetheless there was growing unease. Rockefeller assured his fellow crusaders that their investment was being carefully monitored and conservatively used, but those assurances sounded somewhat hollow.

In fact, the Interchurch World Movement was facing one of the most serious crises before modern American Protestantism: the problem of costs. The American churches had expanded from coast to coast on little more than a wing and a prayer, and the clergy were notoriously underpaid. Paul Carter writes: "If the epigram that 'America has no honors list except the tax list' was true of America in the 1920's, then the honors of the ministry were few indeed.

26. Other voices were also urging Protestants to take heed of these new methods, including that of Bruce Barton, the advertiser.

In 1918, a Literary Digest survey had indicated that a scant 1,671 out of 170,000 ministers paid taxes on incomes of over three thousand dollars. Two years later, the Interchurch World Movement survey of the material state of the Church disclosed an average pastoral income of $937."[27] But clergy were not the only expense. As the churches' mission abroad and at home expanded, the cost of those missions rose dynamically. To maintain a small mission was one thing; to maintain a foreign school system was quite another. The Interchurch World Movement surveys revealed it all, of course, but the movement itself hid the more important point: that raising the money for these increasingly expensive enterprises was itself increasingly expensive.

Expenses were not the only problem plaguing the great campaign. Just as it was getting launched, labor unrest in the steel industry raised a storm of controversy. The Interchurch Movement investigated the problem and published a report mildly critical of U.S. Steel, but like most such reports, this one pleased few. To those who were prolabor, the report seemed too oriented toward management; to those who supported management, it was far too prolabor. But the report did accomplish one purpose: it illustrated graphically the churches' inability to address the public issues of the day from a commonly accepted moral standpoint. When it came to substantial matters, the churches reflected the political and social concerns of their most influential members.

At the same time, the nation as a whole began to move away from progressivism, if it had ever endorsed it. The most dramatic evidence of a changing climate of opinion was the defeat of the League of Nations by the U.S. Senate in 1919 and 1920. The Allies had gutted Wilson's Fourteen Points at Versailles, and Wilson and his progressive allies had swallowed this defeat only because they had secured support for the League of Nations. As they saw it, the League might provide that needed forum for the adjustment of international disputes that would make future wars unnecessary. In short, the League was the practical expression of the pledge to make the First World War the war to end all wars. While the defeat of the League had much to do with domestic politics, it also reflected a changing understanding of public life that would sweep Warren G. Harding into the White House, inspire a revival of the Ku Klux Klan, and contribute to an erosion of civil liberties. The atmosphere was turning against crusades.

In this atmosphere American money stayed close to home. The various denominational fund drives, while not reaching their overall goals — which were perhaps unrealistic from the beginning — raised over $200 million, the largest single gift to the American churches to date. Although much of this

27. Carter, *Decline and Renewal,* p. 72.

money went to the mission fields at home and abroad, some of it went to theological education and to ministerial recruitment. But the Interchurch World Movement itself failed. The "friendly citizen" fund that had been expected to raise $40 million for the movement raised less than $3 million! Since this money was supposed to pay the mounting debts of the campaign, complete the surveys, and provide a nest egg for future ecumenical work, the failure to raise the funds meant that the movement was bankrupt. The initial response was to attempt a second campaign to raise money for the movement itself — without the apparently distracting denominational drives — but this failed even more dramatically than the initial effort. In 1921 the movement officially folded.

The historian must be careful not to overinterpret the failure of the Interchurch World Movement. In one sense the history of the movement confirms the local and denominational character of American Protestantism. From the colonial period onward, American Protestants have somehow balanced the national rhetoric of many of their leaders with a resolute devotion to their local churches and particular denominational relationships. Interestingly enough, although many denominations began as confessional entities, these loyalties have survived even massive theological and ideological change. Even in the ideologically charged 1930s, for example, many ultraconservative Protestants stayed in their local congregations, while contributing to alternative national and international missionary organizations. Given this pattern, one would expect Americans to first support local church funding drives, such as those related to the construction of a new church building or congregational educational center; then denominational funding efforts; and finally national and international agencies. And this, generally speaking, has been the pattern.

What was more important, however, was the residue of the movement. After all the bills had been paid and the movement disbanded, a significant body of social research remained that had to be digested. As part of the negotiations that settled the movement's debts, this material passed to the Rockefeller-controlled Institute of Social and Religious Research, the continuation of the Committee on Religious Surveys. The institute's directorate was composed of close Rockefeller allies John R. Mott, Ernest D. Burton, Raymond Fosdick, James L. Barton, W. H. P. Faunce, and Kenyon Butterfield. The office itself was staffed by a variety of Rockefeller staffers. The managers of the new institute were not necessarily of one mind about its vocation. Richard Fox noted two parties, for instance, within the leadership. One saw sociological study, particularly the survey technique, as primarily a goad for social and religious reform. In other words, the agency was to continue the basic progressive strategy. The other faction believed in a more "scientific" approach that stressed the gathering of facts and the presentation of an objective picture of American religious society.[28] In retrospect, the difference between the two parties was more relative than absolute. Further, Rockefeller, who was after all paying the bills, had his own hopes for the agency. Clearly, he hoped it would further his vision of a liberal, cooperative Protestantism.

Perhaps the most accurate word for the overall work of the Institute of Social and Religious Research is "sobering." Much that was written about American religion in the nineteenth century was written impressionistically. The great Alexis de Tocqueville, for instance, toured the country, and his study, *Democracy in America,* is as much a part of nineteenth-century travel literature as it is of modern social research. The American Church History Series, which appeared at the turn of the century, faced with the almost uncataloguable variety of American Protestants, elected to tell the story of America's churches against the backdrop of the larger national story. Many subsequent American church and religious historians have used this same pattern to help control the data. What made the studies conducted by the Institute of Social and Religious Research so devastating was that they examined the infrastructure of American religion. For more than a decade this infrastructure was probed, examined, and dissected. Despite the almost inevitable flaws, many of the studies were eye-opening. One thinks, for instance, of the Lynds' study of Middletown that revealed a far more secular and class-stratified Midwest than had been supposed, or the Hocking study of foreign missions.[29] Other studies, such as those of rural and city churches, were perhaps less surprising, especially to those who had worked closely with American churches, but they were equally hard-hitting.

What the institute found overall about American religion was that its infrastructure was in terrible shape. There were too many churches, often competing with each other for too few members, with a poorly paid and, often, poorly educated ministry. Despite their rhetoric, these churches did little on a local level to serve any clientele beyond their own membership. Many Anglo-American city churches were chapels of comfort for those who had moved from the countryside to the city, and they were spending much of their time and effort making their newly urban membership feel at home in its new circumstances. Rural religion was in even worse trouble as population and wealth moved to the cities, leaving only a remnant behind in church buildings constructed for twice their number. In words the surveyors would not have used, all American religion — Catholic, Anglo-American, and Lutheran — was

28. Richard Wightman Fox, "Epitaph for Middletown: Robert S. Lynd and the Analysis of Consumer Culture," in *The Culture of Consumption: Critical Essays in American History, 1880-1980,* ed. Richard Wightman Fox and T. J. Jackson Lears (New York: Pantheon Books, 1983), p. 113.

29. See below, pp. 470-73.

more ethnic than one might have suspected. Intellectually, the surveyors found the churches insipid.[30] The general picture painted by the institute's researchers was not of a Protestantism that had gone into a tailspin after the First World War. Rather, it was a picture of a Protestantism that had been in unacknowledged crisis for some time. And the seminaries were no exception to the general rule.

30. A similar set of conclusions was reached by a team of scholars assembled by William Hutchison; see Hutchison, ed., *Between the Times: The Travail of the Protestant Establishment in America, 1900-1960* (Cambridge, U.K., and New York: Cambridge University Press, 1989). Immigrant education is discussed in my *Piety and Intellect.*

CHAPTER FIFTEEN

The Progressive Movement at Its Height: What Kelly Found

The Interchurch World Movement survey of seminaries had been remarkably frank for a fund-raising document. Although its results were printed in a two-column work, complete with color, photographs, pious quotations set in black-rimmed displays, and numerous charts and graphs, the surveyors — Robert Kelly and O. D. Foster — were clearly unhappy with what they found.[1] As expected, they found that the seminaries needed funds, but they also found a lack of coherence among theological schools and a serious need for the schools to cooperate with each other in such areas as defining basic theological degrees and determining adequate preseminary standards. The movement also worried about whether the schools were adequately fulfilling their mandates in some areas, such as providing specialized training or educating people for the new area of teaching religion in undergraduate schools. As at Edinburgh 1910, there was concern about the need for specialized programs for missionaries that took seriously the task of translating Christianity into another culture. The survey also expressed concern about whether the seminaries cooperated sufficiently with each other, with the colleges, and with the churches. Perhaps, the surveyors suggested, the new Conference of Theological Schools would be helpful in working on these problems.[2] The need for continuing education, a constant theme in the literature of twentieth-century seminaries, also appeared. Interestingly enough, the survey noted that a definitive list of seminaries was not available to them.

1. Interchurch World Movement of North America, *World Survey* (New York: Interchurch Press, 1920).

2. Interchurch World Movement, *World Survey,* pp. 226-27.

I. The Fear of Social Science Is the Beginning of Wisdom

The Conference of Theological Schools, meeting at Princeton in 1920, made the Interchurch world survey its principal topic of conversation. The conference was a highly selected body, composed predominately of the better-endowed schools that were very sensitive to criticisms of their work. This was understandable. During the last fifty years, controversies over new directions in theological thinking threatened to swamp the seminaries, and some schools, such as Andover, had been brought to the edge of bankruptcy. Even the University of Chicago, largely insulated from denominational controversies by its large endowment, had to transfer controversial theologian G. P. Foster to the department of philosophy, and the Briggs affair had led to the disciplining or withdrawal of several other scholars. Among Baptists the battle had already begun, and it was only a matter of time before it broke out among Presbyterians. Other cultural battles were on the horizon that had implications for American religious institutions, including the battles over evolution that would be so important in the South. If ever the seminaries needed to take stock, it was at the beginning of this crucial decade.

Further, seminary leaders had read the Flexner Report on Medical Education. The Flexner report was commissioned by the Carnegie Foundation for the Advancement of Teaching at the request of the American Medical Association.[3] If ever proof of the value of the survey method was demanded, the Flexner report would be exhibit A. The report's findings revolutionized medical education. In part, the surveyors did this by highlighting the number of schools that were unacceptable by modern criteria. Of the schools surveyed and visited, for instance, thirty-two were found to be unacceptable and forty-six were seen as marginal. For many of these schools, the survey was the kiss of death. By 1915 the number of medical schools had dropped to ninety-five, and it would continue to drop for another decade. The standards by which Flexner had measured medical education were not arbitrary. Although nineteenth-century medical education had been characterized by passionate debates over the causes and, hence, the cures of disease, the gradual spread of scientific medicine, pioneered in Germany, had ended many of those debates. The goal of medicine was scientific: to understand and, hence, to treat disease with the best available knowledge. The physician was no longer the master of cures, pledged to restore health, but more a scientist who could intervene in natural processes, hopefully for good. By careful observation, laboratory tests, and microscopic

3. Abraham Flexner, *Medical Education in the United States and Canada: A Report to the Carnegie Foundation for the Advancment of Teaching* (New York: Carnegie Foundation, 1910).

analysis physicians had learned more about the etiology of illness. Hence, medical schools needed to educate prospective doctors in schools that provided plentiful opportunities for clinical and laboratory work. Johns Hopkins in Baltimore and Harvard Medical School in Boston pioneered this style of institution, and between them they set the standards that Flexner believed all medical schools needed to follow. For many schools this standard was too high and too expensive. Many independent medical schools, often run by doctors primarily interested in revenues, lacked either the hospital or the laboratory facilities for such education and could not raise the sums needed to provide them. The same was true of many schools affiliated with universities and colleges. Some enterprising presidents had purchased private medical schools hoping to complete their array of professional schools without investing sufficient capital in those schools. In effect, they were as weak as the proprietary schools they had replaced. For other schools the Flexner report highlighted how far they had to go before they attained scientific standing. Clearly, medical education needed substantial funding to improve, and those schools that wanted to meet the new standards had to become effective fund-raisers. Some succeeded in this; others had to close.

Flexner intended for his report to help Carnegie set the standards for future grants to medical schools. However, Carnegie was not interested in an aggressive program to improve medical education. Consequently, Abraham Flexner joined his brother, Simon, at the Rockefeller-controlled General Education Board, where he directed the grant program for medical schools. Interestingly enough, while the board aided some twenty-five schools, the bulk of its funds went to a handful of institutions: Vanderbilt University, $17.5 million; University of Chicago, $14.4 million; Johns Hopkins, $14.4 million; and Cornell, $8.2 million.[4] Many believed that a survey of seminaries might lead Rockefeller, who was the primary financial backer of the Interchurch World Movement, to launch a similar program to improve the seminaries, especially if they reformed themselves.

II. Universities or Freestanding Seminaries

The anxious debate behind the scenes that led to the fuller Kelly report needs to be examined in detail. The issues on the table were similar to those posed by the Flexner report to the medical community: Should seminary education be con-

4. John Ensor Harr and Peter J. Johnson, *The Rockefeller Century* (New York: Scribner, 1988).

ducted at the level of a university professional school, and if so, how could this be accomplished? As in medicine before Flexner, many felt seminaries tended to be isolated from the broader contemporary intellectual debate and to reflect often outmoded forms of pedagogy. The division of the American church into competing denominations, a constant factor in American religious life since the Revolution, made the issue even more complicated as no denomination, no matter how comprehensive, could speak for the whole Protestant religious community.

When the Interchurch World Movement folded and the Institute of Social and Religious Research asked Kelly to expand his study, the Conference of Theological Schools resisted the proposal. Seminary presidents, acutely conscious of financial constraints, believed that the survey might put many schools on the block. Unlike many private school leaders, most seminary presidents and faculties knew their shortcomings. Almost all harbored aspirations for change that exceeded the size of their budgets. Equally important, the presidents feared that a hard-hitting survey might make it difficult for them to raise money. Since many wanted help from Rockefeller, they could not publicly decry his pet project or favorite method (the survey), but that only increased the pressure. Further, all were aware that public confidence was their chief asset. Other reasons for this hesitation existed. Some were suspicious of Robert Kelly. Although Kelly was well connected in Christian higher education, he was not a member of the seminary circle. Kelly was a member of the Society of Friends and a former college president who had clear progressive leanings. The leaders feared, perhaps correctly, that he had little personal sympathy with much of seminary life. Since they could not or would not dissuade the institute from its proposed study, they sought to co-opt and control the report. Even then, as we shall argue, the report was too hard-hitting to be completely satisfactory.

The Continuation Committee of the Conference of Theological Schools adopted a carefully crafted list of criteria for the study that stressed what the seminaries, or at least those represented in the conference, expected the report to include. At its meeting on September 16, 1921, the committee explicitly asked Kelly to include Bible schools "as to their origins, standards, products and general relation to the future welfare of the churches and their ministers."[5] To secure at least a modicum of support for its own position, the committee unofficially assigned W. Douglas Mackenzie to work with Kelly. As it turned out, Mackenzie read every word of Kelly before it was published and annotated his own copy of the typescript liberally. In addition to this personal oversight, Kelly's results were presented to conferences in Chicago, Hartford, New York,

5. Hartford Seminary Foundation Archives (hereafter HSF Archives) document 103796.

Philadelphia, Nashville, Cleveland, Montreal, Toronto, Vancouver, Berkeley, and Minneapolis, and he was expected to include the reactions of these eleven conferences in his final report. Rarely has a report been this censured before it appeared!

The central issue that provoked such careful scrutiny was the nature and role of the small, denominational seminary. Kelly believed, as did Rockefeller and Mott, that denominationalism and denominational competition were the principal force hindering the kingdom of God in America. The seminaries were even more fragmented than the churches, with schools representing not only denominations but also parties, regions, and other divisions within denominations. And few of these schools had the resources to support a modern program of ministerial formation or theological scholarship.

In contrast, Mackenzie was the president of a small seminary that was closely connected to the Congregational Churches of New England. In many ways his school, Hartford Seminary, illustrated the problems that most concerned such financiers as Rockefeller. Hartford had aspirations for theological leadership that far exceeded its financial basis, and the school habitually robbed Peter to pay Paul. Perhaps one reason Mackenzie was selected to bell the cat was that his own aspirations were similar to those of Kelly in some respects. Mackenzie believed in what he called a "theological university." What he meant was an institution equipped to educate Christian leaders, both men and women, for differing types of ministries. Hence, his seminary featured instruction in the pastoral arts, music, missions, and Christian education.

Not surprisingly, Mackenzie believed that Kelly overemphasized the extent to which the denominational seminary reflected the worst characteristics of American religion. In an undated memo to Kelly, he wrote, "I feel that here as well as in chapter I the denominational nature of most seminaries is interpreted in a somewhat hostile spirit." Instead, the action of the churches in establishing seminaries was "part of the raising and training of an adequate ministry" and was "one of the primary functions of Church. It dates back to the Master himself." Seminaries arose because of the need to fulfill this divine mandate, and every "self-conscious section of the Church inherits and must exercise" that role. To condemn the denominational seminaries as if they had not the right to exist, because they must primarily serve their "sect," is to condemn the existence of the denominations as such.[6] In particular, he was stung by Kelly's judgment that the academic level of the denominational schools was lower than that of the university institutions. In a sharp note, he wrote:

6. HSF Archives, no date.

> The denominational seminaries I believe it is only fair to say that they have been usually on a level with the corresponding colleges in their region. Princeton Theological Seminary, with names like those of Hodge and Warfield and others, has produced scholars and teachers equal to any produced by the neighboring university. Some of the best colleges and universities are identified with the Lutheran Church. There they have the tradition of German thoroughness of grounding, even though the range of dogmatic instruction is what we would call narrow.[7]

Mackenzie proposed too much. He was right about Kelly's distrust of denominational schools and their narrowness, but his use of Princeton and the more conservative Lutheran schools as examples of the success of denominationally controlled instruction made Kelly's point: such schools, even when wealthy, were given to a narrow confessional interpretation of the faith.

Kelly was appalled by the educational backwardness of the schools. In one of his replies to Mackenzie, he stated his position bluntly: "At present there is much confusion in this field. Seminaries have all been in a greater or less degree under the spell of certain definite, persistent and too often deadening traditions as to organization, program and method. Many seminaries have the backward look. Only as they break away from these traditions will the various types of tasks which the seminary should perform come clearly into view." The "backward" look meant that most changes in theological education had been piecemeal "additions and subtraction," "new patches on old garments" that lacked "fundamental self-analysis and free experimentation." Only a few seminaries, Kelly observed, had "undertaken radically to overhaul their programs and to reconstruct them in the light of the growing conception of Jesus and the changing social order." Such seminaries were "leaving the a priori methods behind and substituting the social for the individual point of view and are facing the tasks of the present and the future."[8]

Kelly, whose experience had been primarily in higher education, believed that the changes in higher education ought to set the seminaries' agenda. In particular, he looked to the various university-level professional schools for guidance. While these schools varied according to the needs of the different professions, they shared a common commitment to the combination of scientific study and practical efficiency, with the first, ideally, helping to secure excellence in the second. Hence, he was predisposed to see the university-related divinity schools as representing the ideal toward which the schools ought to be aspiring. Like Rockefeller, he was a firm believer in the economics of scale.

7. HSF Archives, no date.

8. HSF Archives, no date.

Many shared Kelly's perspective. An earlier, very brief study, published in *For the Advancement of Teaching,* the sixth annual Carnegie report on teaching, made a similar case more bluntly: "Schools of theology in the United States have no close connection with the universities as have the schools of law and medicine. With a few exceptions, these schools are conducted for the training of men in the service of a particular denomination rather than for the elucidation of theology as a branch of learning. In fact, the teaching of theology as a science fills a relatively small function in the American school of theology."[9] Anson Phelps Stokes, another member of the Rockefeller circle and secretary of the Yale Corporation, had called for a seminary survey immediately after the publication of the Flexner report. Like Kelly, Stokes hoped that a similar report "would show some results almost as startling from the standpoint of efficiency, and would produce important results for the ministry of the future."[10] In other words, Stokes hoped that a survey might produce a thorough cleaning of the seminary barn.

The behind-the-scenes bickering between Kelly and Mackenzie should be seen as reflecting a basic issue that divided the theological community. This debate did not necessarily weaken the historical value of Kelly's survey; one could argue that the clash between two able intellectuals of different perspectives might have made the final product more accurate and perhaps more objective. But it does help explain why that document did not have the impact that one might have expected. The document never spoke with the clear voice of a Flexner, nor did it have the authority of similar studies done in other areas of higher education. The Kelly report was the voice of a reform that never happened.

The debate also illustrates the dilemma of the twentieth-century seminary, particularly after the First World War. Nineteenth-century American higher education had been a predominantly private affair with the strongest schools begun and sustained by private funding. By the end of the First World War, the state universities had assumed a more dominant position. With few exceptions, church and private institutions elected to remain colleges, and the college remained the "entry level" institution for newly prospering universities and professional schools. In this educational world, the establishment of true university-related divinity schools was a difficult task. Those proposing university standards had to struggle with both the American separation of church and state and the increasingly secular character of many private universities and

9. Carnegie Foundation for the Advancement of Teaching, *For the Advancement of Teaching,* Sixth Carnegie Report on Teaching, 1911 (New York, 1912), p. 94.

10. Cited in Jerry Dean Weber, "To Strengthen and Develop Protestant Theological Education: John D. Rockefeller, Jr., and the Seatlantic Fund" (Ph.D. diss., University of Chicago, 1997), p. 97.

colleges. Looking backward, a present-day reader may well conclude that the Stokes-Kelly-Rockefeller party had the best intellectual case and that their proposals would have helped subsequent theological educators with such perennial issues as continually rising costs.[11] In the language of the 1920s, freestanding seminaries were inefficient, expensive, and unscientific. But this judgment must always be conditioned by the equally important caveat that the university-related ideal was becoming part of the heavenly, not the earthly, city of seminary education. Even had Rockefeller and other multimillionaires been able to provide the funding, the structure of American education was against this institutional approach. In the world of the state-supported secular university, much theological education was necessarily marginal.

Perhaps because Kelly's idea could not be realized, the few university schools have had an extraordinary influence on American theological education and, especially, on American theological scholarship. However, we must be careful not to attribute too much of their prominence to their university-related status. American university divinity schools tend to be part of universities with substantial intellectual and economic resources, and the schools have often been the least distinguished components of their respective universities. We also need to remind ourselves that few professional schools (such as dentistry, business, education, etc.) are truly distinguished, despite their relationship to major universities. Most remain militantly average. One may thus wonder: If there had been more university-related schools, would they be, alas, militantly average as well?

III. The Results of the Study

Given the almost paranoid fears of some in the American seminary community, the final version of the seminary survey was hardly controversial. In fact, the published version of Kelly's findings was surprisingly gentle. In many ways the report found most schools better than might have been expected, although the weaker institutions were every bit as bad as their reputations. This basic finding was important. Those who believed that seminaries ought to adopt either accreditation, the newest approach to standards in the secular university and college world, or some other standardization process could count on a significant number of sound institutions to be the heart and core of their enterprise.

Although Kelly found much to praise in American theological education,

11. Universities can spread common costs, such as administration, printing, library, etc., over many schools and departments.

his constant refrain was the contrast between the best and the rest. The best of American theological education was very good, but the very way Kelly highlighted the achievements of the better schools only served to make the weaknesses of the other institutions more evident.

Kelly's evaluation of American theological faculties found the contrast between the best and the rest to be pronounced in the very heart of the academic enterprise. "In so far as higher academic degrees may serve as a measure of scholarship, the seminary faculties compare favorable with other institutions of similar rank."[12] Further, Kelly asserted that the seminaries had unusual numbers of "holders of earned degrees of the higher grade," and many of these came from "European institutions." Membership in professional societies was common. It was not surprising, hence, that Kelly found that "in some seminaries as high a grade of research has been done as in any of the graduate schools of the country" or that the schools "indicated a growing appreciation of the scientific method" (p. 45). Despite the fact that few schools had programs of sabbatical leaves to promote further study, faculty members were unusually prolific in the production of books and denominational literature. Kelly noted that many teachers were in effect teacher-practitioners of ministry who often preached, lectured, or pastored as well as taught. This clearly took time away from research, although Kelly was confident that the schools benefited from having some practitioners on their part-time staffs. What was important about all of Kelly's conclusions about the scholarly quality of the faculty was that many institutions did not fill out these schedules. Best practice set a high standard, but not all reached it.

The theme of the best and the rest continued as Kelly reported on such matters as teaching methods. The older traditions of the textbook or the recitation method and of the lecture were much in evidence. At times, of course, these were done well. But he also noted some spectacular examples of bad teaching: a professor who did both the translation and exegesis of a Greek text, another who spent the hour elaborating his translation with homiletic suggestions, and one who assigned a Hebrew text and told the class to have at it with their dictionaries, while he went from student to student coaching them in their work. He found that "in increasing measure, a small group of institutions is introducing the methods that are usually considered more pedagogical for advanced students — the methods of the seminar, the library, the laboratory,

12. Robert L. Kelly, *Theological Education in America: A Study of One Hundred Sixty-One Theological Schools in the United States and Canada,* foreword by Rt. Rev. Charles Henry Brent (New York: George H. Duran, 1924), p. 42. Further references to Kelly's work are cited in parentheses in the text.

and the field" (p. 57). This made even more serious his observations that most seminary libraries were poorly supported and administered, and that seminaries rarely used students' outside employment effectively (p. 42). In other words, what could be accomplished pedagogically in the best schools was limited by the resources those schools had at their disposal.

Under the watchful eye of Mackenzie, Kelly had to be careful in his criticism of the impact of denominationalism. Kelly noted that denominationalism was a central reality in the life of most theological schools that affected their student bodies, their faculties, and their boards of control. How this reality was expressed, however, varied. Sixty-one schools required faculty members to sign a specified denominational standard, sixteen required church membership, and twenty-eight had some other form of pledge. But even where these formal structures were missing, such as at the University of Chicago, the practice was for "a large majority of the professors" to be Baptists. In one sense Kelly had caught the system just as other factors were becoming more important to a school's identity, such as its location on a larger liberal-conservative spectrum. But in another sense he had located the most persistent truth about American theological education: its intimate relationship to the churches it served.

One of the common problems of seminary life that Kelly located was the spiritual life, an issue that would persist throughout the twentieth century. Despite their rhetoric, most schools made minimal efforts in this area. Chapel services were often provided, and of course, students were exhorted to be faithful in prayer, but in the main, little real instruction was provided. Kelly seemed particularly disappointed that those seminaries "with priestly ideals," where "much prominence apparently is given to the devotional life," did not make much reference "to communion, private and public, to Bible or other devotional reading, and to retreats" (p. 59).[13] In other words, piety, one of the twin supports of the nineteenth-century seminary, was strangely absent from the schools of the twentieth.

Above all, Kelly found that seminaries were essentially conservative institutions. In a masterful understatement, he noted: "The seminaries have not assumed conspicuous leadership in the application of modern educational theory to religion, in interpreting from a Christian standpoint the modern problems of democracy, in working out a metaphysics in the light of the startling developments of the day in the various phases of science" (p. 45). The implications of Kelly's finding are important. During the 1920s, the better seminaries often found themselves in a battle over modernism that stemmed from

13. One wonders why Kelly did not pursue this topic further. Undoubtedly this was a very sensitive issue with members of the conference of theological seminaries who had very different religious expectations for their schools.

their investigation of such new areas as biblical criticism. Kelly suggests that some of the schools were not impacted by the controversy, not because of their virtues, but because they did not understand or study the issues.

Kelly also highlighted one of the great issues among theological seminaries: admission requirements. Andover had innovated by requiring college graduation or its equivalent for admission, and most nineteenth-century seminaries tried to pay at least lip service to the standard. Even the Southern Baptist seminary, which was devoted to serving all Baptists, had its own college graduate program. However, very few had been able to sustain the requirement, and most had adopted various expedients to increase enrollment: English programs, diplomas, etc. By the time of the Kelly report, however, things were looking up. College attendance and, with it, college graduation were rising, and the old ideal began to appear more attainable, at least for the better schools. Kelly came in the middle of this longer process. The schools were still predominately admitting people with varying degrees of preparation. The result was that "most seminaries have in the same classes students who have had a great diversity of academic preparation." Kelly clearly believed that the seminaries had to eliminate the various halfway houses that they had maintained for years: admitting men who were already ordained to "raise the standard of the ministry" or admitting older candidates who did not have all the prerequisites. The denominationalism also had its effects in this area. Baptist and Methodist seminaries, for instance, tended to admit nongraduate students, and the schools awarded the bachelor of theology (Th.B.) to those who completed a combined five-year arts and theology program. At Colgate, only three out of forty-four students were college graduates. But in some ways any such raising of the standard posed problems of its own, the most glaring being which colleges, given the obvious weakness of some schools in languages, science, and history, should be approved. Until accreditation became an established norm, many small church-related colleges functioned at a high school or lower level. But even when this problem was solved, the vexing question of the nature of the preseminary curriculum remained.[14] Which courses or education made college necessary or useful for a seminary education?

Kelly found the same pattern in the exit requirements as in the admission requirements. Many schools, to be sure, confined their degrees to those who had completed college and had studied for three years. The problem was that

14. Medical schools at the time were often requiring only two or three years of college work, and like the seminaries, they had not yet determined which courses constituted a proper preprofessional course. The same was apparently even more true of law schools, which existed in as confusing a pluralism as the seminaries.

this was not uniform. Some granted the degree with two years of college and three years of seminary, others after a year of study beyond the three-year diploma; some required theses, others did not; some had oral examinations, others did not. But what was remarkable was that, with the notable exception of Union (New York), which was experimenting with a four-year bachelor of divinity program, almost all schools fixed the standard program at three years of study, divided into six semesters of sixteen weeks, that included around ninety credit hours of instruction. The few schools on the quarter system followed a similar formula.

IV. The Seminary Curriculum

The Kelly report was the first systematic study of the seminary curriculum to be done after the schools adopted the prevailing college and university practice of dividing their work into separate courses that were evaluated individually. From the beginning Kelly faced a problem common to most people who study seminaries: the lack of a uniform course nomenclature. Depending on local circumstance, the same course may have two different names; electives are often even more difficult to identify accurately. Depending on how one understands certain language, the seminary curriculum taken as a whole reflected either a hearty diversity and constant change or a remarkable uniformity and stability. To thread his way through the thicket, Kelly took three samples. The first was a series of chronological studies that sought to show representative curricula in 1870, 1895, and 1922. These were presented first as individual schools and then as composites. The second was a series of studies of curricula within selected denominational families. These studies indicated that certain emphases were more characteristic of certain theological traditions than of others. The third was an examination of the influence of the size of an institution on its curricular offerings.

The 1870 curricula indicated that the schools had begun a major movement from lists of books, topics, and other such items to a fair presentation of a coherent body of divinity. The heart of the 1870 curriculum was the study of the biblical languages and of exegesis. Thus, at Garrett students took Hebrew and Greek exegesis every year of their program. The same was true of Lutherans in Mount Airy, Pennsylvania; Princeton, with Oberlin and General, offered some English Bible in addition to a strong exegetical program. To this biblical basis were added varying yearlong studies of dogmatics, church history, apologetics, and a large course in either homiletics or pastoral theology. The only curriculum studied that was notable for its particularities was at Oberlin, where students studied biblical geography, history of doctrine, and principles of interpretation for a year each. Kelly's observation was accurate: "The programs of 1870 were essentially the same in all these seven selected seminaries. The chief differences [were] occasioned by the necessity of caring for the denominational peculiarities. . . . The Old and New Testaments in English and in the original languages constituted a large part of the course. In fact, the original languages largely held the field . . . the presentation seems to have been quite uniform. The languages were mastered to discover better the exact shade of meaning the inspired Scriptures meant to convey" (p. 84). In theory, these studies provided the foundation for the study of systematic theology. In all denominations systematic theology (Christian doctrine) was an attempt to correctly order the biblical materials to demonstrate their unity and coherence. To systematic theology was added a modicum of apologetics and church history. Only one seminary of those examined taught ethics, Mount Airy, although some ethical materials must have been taught in the dogmatics classes of the other institutions. Although it was not clear what was taught, there was usually a yearlong course in pastoral theology, sometimes called homiletics.

By 1895 both educational and theological modernization had begun to take effect. The various courses, for instance, had come to be identified by the number of hours devoted to them and were in some sense independent entities, defined by the specialist professor who taught them. Elective systems were beginning to appear at such schools as Oberlin and Union, and whatever unity the pastoral or practical field may have possessed was ending as this area was beginning to proliferate. In general, the practical field was where schools were adding courses at this time. Perhaps the most timely course at a number of schools was one in the relationship between science and religion. Kelly noted that such courses tended to be replaced later by the new field of philosophy of religion that combined traditional apologetics with more modern intellectual concerns.

The 1922 curricula were typical of what would be commonplace until the heyday of neoorthodoxy and the core curriculum. The mark of these curricula is an increase in electives, with many schools cutting back courses required for a degree to only one-third of total classes. Some areas of the former curriculum clearly declined. The heavy emphasis on biblical exegesis, typical of the schools of the previous century, was replaced by programs with far lighter linguistic requirements. The heart of the program was no longer the mastery of revelation or church teaching. Many schools made the work of the ministry the center of the curriculum with new courses in homiletics, religious education, practical theology, sociology, music, and missions (p. 81). Equally impressive was the division of traditional theological fields into a number of courses. Material that had been taught as dogmatics, for instance, was now taught as philosophy of religion, apologetics, psychology of religion, ethics, and even comparative religion. Almost all of these new divisions represented the cross-fertilization of theology by some other academic discipline. Thus, for example, comparative religion, although it retained in some schools much of the older concern with missions, was now drawing on anthropology and sociology as well as theological arguments. In some ways the same was true of dogmatics itself. While systematic theology had always drawn some of its materials from philosophy, many liberal theologians of the 1920s were including studies of religious experience in their work as well as considerable material from both secular and religious sciences. Yale's able D. C. Macintosh, for instance, believed it was possible to make theology an empirical science the conclusions of which might be tested by further research. The number of hours in church history, overall, likewise seemed to have been reduced, although much of that material was also dispersed through a variety of courses that used a variety of methods. Although Kelly did not draw the conclusion, the system of electives in one sense removed all boundaries from the curriculum. Once the required work was completed, faculty members were free to subdivide their fields into as many subspecialties as the size of the school might warrant.

Another way of stating Kelly's conclusion is: the theological curricula of the 1870s reflected a very clear understanding of what theological study entailed. A person with a theological education was able to study the Bible in the original languages, incorporate that study into a consistent explication of the teachings of a particular denomination, and explicate the development of a particular branch of the Christian church. In other words, this person was prepared to be a resident theologian. By 1922 the curriculum had made a major shift. Whereas the earlier curriculum reflected a self-contained discipline, the newer curriculum reflected an intellectual engagement with the larger world. Not only was the historical critical method used in much biblical study and teaching, but the student was expected to use a variety of intellectual resources in understanding his faith. Above all, the curricula in general represented an engagement with the expanding worlds of knowledge.

Kelly then examined the denominational impact. He elected to study three traditions in some depth: the Presbyterian, the Methodist, and the Protestant Episcopal. It was an interesting attempt to establish a typology. As Kelly saw it, other denominations could be understood largely "through combinations of the typical groups cited above" (p. 100). Congregationalists had some of the intense intellectualism of the Presbyterian group, but Kelly felt this had been moderated somewhat by the popularity of Arminianism. In a similar way Baptists often shared the biblical focus of Presbyterianism, but their participation in revivals had introduced many elements from Methodism. Likewise, Lutherans shared many elements with the Episcopalians, especially the emphasis on rituals and priestly life. Like the Episcopalians, they tended to be more interested in their own understanding of church history, for instance, than other denominations (pp. 100-101). Kelly's typology was far from perfect — it did not take account of the importance of confessionalism among Lutherans, for instance — but it had the advantage of highlighting an important point. All American denominations and their schools had to confront the radically new intellectual and moral conditions of the modern world. But the responses to modernity varied greatly.

Presbyterians were among the more reluctant modernists. Both in Scotland and in America, Presbyterianism had been a great intellectual tradition with its own characteristic understanding of the world and of humankind.[15] The seminaries not only wanted to preserve this world of thought; they lived in it, and their teachers thought within its contours. Interestingly, only Auburn Seminary, the school most affected by the nineteenth-century revival, had made Hebrew elective by the time of the Kelly study, and the Presbyterian schools would return to an attenuated Hebrew requirement in the late 1940s and 1950s. Greek was also a high value. In a similar fashion, these schools had retained their heavy emphasis on dogmatic theology and on precision in the formulation of theological ideas. Only McCormick had moved toward the newer emphasis on the philosophy of religion instead of apologetics, and many of the newer elective courses were logical extensions of the older paradigms. The image of the minister as a resident theologian, moreover, was relatively intact. Kelly notes:

> The general subject of religious education receives very little attention in the Presbyterian seminaries. The chief exceptions are Auburn and McCormick. The former has an auxiliary department, whereas the latter offers fourteen hours covering psychology of religion and other subjects having to do with methods and materials of religious education. Princeton announces no course in religious education per se, but has listed a small elective in psychology of religion under the department of apologetics. A chair is to be established in San Francisco Theological Seminary in religious education. (p. 93)

15. John Mulder and Lee Wyatt, "The Predicament of Pluralism: The Study of Theology in Presbyterian Seminaries," in *The Pluralistic Vision: Presbyterians and Mainstream Protestant Education and Leadership,* ed. Milton J. Coalter, John M. Mulder, and Louis B. Weeks (Louisville: Westminster John Knox, 1992), pp. 37-70.

Other areas of practical theology were likewise comparatively undeveloped in these schools, although sacred music received special attention at Auburn, McCormick, and Western.[16]

Kelly's comparative lack of familiarity with immigrant theological education, and especially with Lutheranism, might have led him to overlook a similar division among Lutherans. With the exception of Gettysburg, deep in the "grape juice" belt, most Lutheran seminaries maintained a similar emphasis on exegetical and systematic theology. As with Presbyterianism, the predominant motive for this conservatism was not so much a reaction to modernism — although both Lutheranism and Presbyterianism had significant antimodernist parties — as an attempt to maintain the integrity of a tradition. In that sense confessionalism and the heavily biblical and theological curricula it spawned were as much the product of a way of life — we would say a spirituality — as they were intellectual decisions.

This observation reminds us of an old historical rule: doing the same thing in a different context may have a considerably different meaning. The young scholar mastering the ancient Hebrew text at the University of Chicago might well have been primarily motivated by a desire to master the tools of ancient Near Eastern studies. To be sure, he may have been moved by the beauty of the language and inspired by its moral and intellectual insights, but his goal would have dominated his work. Whereas a young student at McCormick or Princeton might have recognized that Hebrew was an important tool of research — part of the price of admission to the biblical guild — but was primarily moved by the religious meaning of the text. For such a student, the careful study of the Hebrew words of the Bible may have mediated the presence of God in an intellectual but very powerful way. For this student the language had a sacramental quality, bearing the revelation of God in its artful nuance. Of course, every seminary had those who were just going through the motions or earning a "union card" — but the curricula were not designed for those students. They were always constructed with the serious student in mind.

Kelly's second division was the Protestant Episcopal churches. These schools shared many common elements with other schools, although only four of the ten schools required Hebrew in 1922, while all maintained the Greek requirement. What was distinctive about these curricula was their heavier emphasis on church history and their particular stress on liturgics. The same

16. The persistence of the division between Old and New School Presbyterians in theological education is remarkable. For a discussion of this persistent divide, see George M. Marsden, *The Evangelical Mind and the New School Presbyterian Experience: A Case Study of Thought and Theology in Nineteenth-Century America* (New Haven: Yale University Press, 1970).

churchly character was found in courses devoted to such areas as canon law and polity. A high percentage of the total curriculum was set aside for these courses, and hence it is not surprising that "very little time is given to the study of religious education or to the social and industrial problems with which the church has to deal" (p. 94). The same was true of the general pastoral program of these schools: "Apart from the training in actual sermon-building and pastoral care, virtually all the programs of these schools as a group are devoted to subjects theoretical, historical, and speculative. The practical aspect of training here has to do with preparing the student for his ecclesiastical functions" (p. 96). The exception to this general rule, Kelly found, was at those Episcopal seminaries that had cooperative agreements with nearby universities. The Episcopal Theological School in Cambridge, for example, had access to the rich program in social ethics at Harvard; the divinity school of the Protestant Episcopal Church at Philadelphia was related to the University of Pennsylvania, and General students could take courses at Union, Columbia, and New York Universities.

As did the Presbyterian and Lutheran schools, the Episcopal schools represented a powerful intellectual and social tradition. This tradition had considerable resources that had value in the modern world, including its skill in worship and its orderly relationship to inherited authority. As with other old-world traditions, Kelly's findings suggest that these traditions had far more influence on how schools taught than might be apparent at first glance. "Church History is rarely taught in the same way in Episcopal and Baptist Seminaries" (p. 102).

Kelly's third group was the Methodist Episcopal schools. This group was in many ways the antithesis of the other two groups. Kelly noted that "they lay comparatively little stress upon the historical aspect of theological education and put much upon the later developments in the field of religious education and social service" (p. 97). In many ways these schools illustrated the modern trends that were influencing even more conservative institutions. Although, for instance, they continued to have courses in the original languages and exegesis, much of the instruction was in the English Bible and in courses directly related to the newer historical criticism, such as biblical theology, biblical literature, and biblical introduction.[17] While some schools continued to require Hebrew for their degrees, a Hebrew requirement was much more unusual for Methodist students. Where the Methodist schools shined was in two areas: church management and religious education. Kelly noted:

17. "Introduction" has a curious double meaning in Protestant theological education. On the one hand, it refers to those materials traditionally covered in what the Germans styled *Einleitung:* authorship, textual problems, historical and geographical context, the history of research into special questions, etc. On the other hand, it also refers to work on a beginning or nonexpert level.

> In practical theology, so called, are comprehended the various phases of church administration and management, sociology and social applications, including city and rural church. . . . The expansion of the field of pastoral theology is conspicuous in the Methodist Episcopal group. Their programs propose to relate the church to the present social order. They provide numerous courses in religious education; psychology of religion; practical survey methods, both for church and community sociology; social service; city church; rural church; clinical work, etc. . . . Unusual emphasis is placed in the Methodist Episcopal group upon religious education and psychology of religion. (p. 97)

In other words, as Kelly saw it, the Methodists were in fact the vanguard of the changes that were taking place in Protestant theological education. Since many of these changes reflected changes occurring among the American middle class, the home of Methodism, this is not surprising.

Kelly recognized that the Methodists were part of a family of denominations and seminaries that saw the world in similar ways. In a revealing paragraph he wrote:

> The strong Calvinistic leanings in the Congregational group were early influenced by the freedom of Arminianism. There has appeared for this and other reasons an unusual freedom and boldness among them in breaking new fields. . . . This has given them a class of institutions, if one can think of them as a class, somewhere between the Presbyterian and Methodist group. The tendency in the Disciples and Baptist groups is more in accord with the Congregational than with either of the three typical groups discussed here. The tendencies in the more "progressive" Baptist schools are much more in accord with the Methodist than with the Presbyterian leanings. (p. 101)

Kelly did not probe this provocative theological group further. But the meaning of his findings might be clearer if we do so. For instance, what is most interesting about all these churches is their comparative distance from the older European state and confessional churches. None were the descendants of European state churches, and even the Congregationalists, who were established in New England, never developed the elaborate systems of common liturgies, canonical and juridical proceedings, and confessions of faith that the European churches used to maintain national patterns of ecclesiastical conformity. If we add the New School wing of Presbyterianism to the list (as a continuation of Congregationalism), all were deeply influenced by the westward migration of the early nineteenth century and by the urbanization of the East in the later nineteenth century. Both of these larger social movements tended to break down the normative elements in their traditions. Further, all had members among the new industrial elite. If "freedom is just another word for nothing left to lose," these denominations' tendencies to innovate in theological education reflected their own freedom from the positive and negative weight of European tradition.

Kelly's third crosscut was based on types of organization. Kelly recognized the importance of the university-related schools of theology, and he included in his list of such institutions the University of Chicago, Harvard, Yale, Union, Boston, Garrett, Pacific, and Vanderbilt. Although he admitted that there were other schools with such a relationship, he omitted them from this list either because they elected to be considered as denominational schools or because the university to which they were attached was not affiliated with the Association of American Universities, an organization established to protect the integrity of advanced degrees. One of the characteristics of these schools, as Kelly saw them, was that they offered a full range of theological degrees, including the master of arts, the bachelor of divinity, the master of sacred theology, the doctor of theology, and the doctor of philosophy.

But what impressed Kelly most about these schools was their combination of theory and practice. On the one hand, "the scientific attitude toward subjects is maintained, and especial attention is given to methodology. Religious phenomena are subjected to free and frank criticism and scrutiny. This method culminates in many phases of research participated in by many students already possessing theological degrees under conditions not different from those obtaining in the other graduate schools." At the same time, "this scientific spirit is supplemented by the unusual development of phases of practical theology. Practical training and oversight are required for the B.D. degree. Although undenominational, most of them have working relationships with churches in which 'laboratory' work is done" (p. 104). Experiment made possible specialization and professional research. Kelly was impressed by the Yale curriculum, which allowed students to specialize in pastoral work, missions, religious education, social service, or history and philosophy of religion. In addition, Yale had a special course for Christian laymen that was open to YMCA secretaries (p. 105).[18] He also realized that these schools had become "in preeminent degree training centers for seminary teachers" (p. 106). In other words, these schools had a unique place in the future of theological education in America.

18. It should be noted that Yale's student body was predominately composed of the "Congregational" group — Congregationalists, Methodists, and Disciples — with only a few representatives of other denominations.

University status meant that the schools were large enough to be flexible. While all of them, for example, had excellent courses in the languages, only Union required Hebrew for graduation, and neither Harvard nor Chicago required either language. This meant that these schools had been free to concentrate attention on their "introductions" to the Bible and other theological sciences. In the main also, they had access to larger libraries, classes in other departments, etc. In other words, they were not as limited as other schools by the resources they could bring to bear on their task.

In contrast, Kelly noted what he called seminaries of small enrollment, which he defined as schools with fewer than thirty students. These schools often represented smaller denominations, such as the Seventh-Day Baptists, or the various smaller Lutheran ethnic groups, including the Finns, Danes, Swedes, etc. In addition, many of these schools reflected the various accidents of history, such as "peculiarities of environment," the originality of leadership of a founder, or even "mysterious differences of taste and temperament" (p. 107). As a class, these smaller schools shared the general characteristics of American theological education, that is, some were rich, some were poor, some were affiliated with colleges or universities, and the like. The only place where size was significant was when it correlated with the scarcity of resources. In such small institutions the school was continually forced to fit its program to its purse. This meant usually that it chose between "the specialized technique of its own denomination" and "the presentation of present-day problems" (pp. 109-10). It also meant that there was little emphasis on specialization or on the practical side of ministry. The representative curricula Kelly discussed were dominated by the classical theological disciplines, and the presentation of these was limited: "The educational program of this group of seminaries is more likely to be general and extensive; the exegesis does not contain so many intensive courses nor do the other departments contain so many opportunities for intensive courses and seminars; the material as a rule is used in a way more deductive and offers less opportunity in the application of theory or what is known as practical theology. It is also likely to be more technically specialized for a particular denomination" (p. 109).

Perhaps most important for the history of the theological curriculum was Kelly's examination of the courses in city churches, rural churches, and other practical areas. The results show how incomplete the practical revolution was in the early 1920s. Only 15 of 103 seminaries, for instance, had courses in city church work, and only 36 had rural church courses. Many were one- or two-hour courses; only 8 schools offered three-hour courses in the rural church, and only 3 offered six hours. Interestingly enough, 3 seminaries offered ten hours in this area. As with other areas of practical church work, the Methodists and the university-related schools were clearly in the lead in these areas. More surprising, given the prominence of the social gospel, was the comparatively minor attention paid to courses in the "church and industry." Only 19 schools reported courses that Kelly was able to place under this rubric. As in the rural church, this area was dominated by the university-related and Methodist schools (pp. 133-34).

The new discipline that was most widely accepted was religious education, with 80 of the 103 schools reporting work in this area. The courses appear to have developed from earlier work in Sunday school pedagogy or, at least in Lutheran schools, catechetics. "Observation and practice teaching were beginning to appear" (p. 142), and the seminaries were also awakening to the need for such courses as "child development," "theory of education," and "psychology of childhood and adolescence." The same division that Kelly noted elsewhere was also present in this area. Those seminaries related to the confessional denominations, the Presbyterians, the Episcopalians, and the Lutherans, tended to have the least amount of work in this area, while those schools related to the Baptists, Methodists, Congregationalists, and the university had the most number of offerings. The university relationship could produce a very complete program. Kelly described the work of one such program in some detail:

> Indication of recent development in this field is the arrangement projected in 1922-23 between Union Theological Seminary and Teachers College, Columbia University. The departments of religious education in the two institutions are to be treated as one and a joint program of studies is offered from which students in ether institution may elect as they wish. Union considers the work a foundational part of the offering for the B.D. degree, but also provides a vocational diploma for those wishing to engage in religious education as a life's work. Teachers College students specializing in religious education may secure the M.A. and Ph.D. degrees from Columbia University. . . . Union Seminary maintains for laboratory practice the Union School of Religion with an enrollment of 172 pupils for the following purposes: "(1) the religious training and instruction of some of the children and youth of the community; (2) the discovery and demonstration of efficient methods in religious education; (3) the training of teachers and leaders; and (4) the accumulation of a body of experience that shall be at the disposal of other schools." (p. 145)

In retrospect, the most shocking of Kelly's conclusions was that "the seminaries as a class of educational institutions do not offer clinical training (field education) to their students" (p. 145). In most cases students took church work, most often as student pastors, and received no supervision at all. "Inspections are not usually made nor are reports called for." There were a few exceptions to this general rule — Union, Garrett, and Boston University were particularly notable — but the general picture was that the seminaries understood student employment primarily as a means of providing financial support for the student while he was studying at the school, and not as a part of the educational program. Finding creative ways to incorporate student religious employment into the seminary program would be one of the major efforts of twentieth-century theological educators.

In summary, three points stand out from Kelly's survey of theological curricula. First, with the very significant exception of clinical pastoral education, most of the major divisions of the seminary curriculum were already in place by the 1920s. Seminary faculties would rearrange those elements, individual disciplines would develop new electives, and some areas of emphasis, such as the rural church, would decline, but the basic theological encyclopedia had been determined. Second, the distance between the more advanced schools and the rest was particularly important in curriculum development. The larger schools were able to finance very extensive programs, complete with many electives and new disciplines. In contrast, the smaller schools often had to be content with offering more of their courses close to the "core" of the theological curriculum. When all was said and done, theological educators believed they could ignore such courses as religious education in favor of biblical studies where circumstances forced a choice.

Kelly's third observation was the continuing difference between the former European state churches and the Baptists, Methodists, Disciples, and former New School Presbyterians (Union and Auburn). In general, the closer a particular denomination was to its European roots, the more likely its seminaries were to concentrate their teaching on the classical theological disciplines. Kelly did not elaborate on this insight, but tradition must have played an important role. The formerly established churches had a clear picture of the role of the ministry that was inherited from their ancestors, and these churches (including the Presbyterians) often had some ministers from abroad who represented the best of the past. Moreover, there were always important links between the formally established churches and the homeland. As graduate studies developed, for instance, students traveled to England, Scotland, or Germany for more advanced studies. While such students were not the majority, they did help to keep alive the strong sense of standards that characterized European church life.

Kelly's study suggests a link between the modernization of the theological curriculum and the Americanization of particular denominations. The link was of course not absolute, and it probably was not causal in the usual sense of the term. Clearly, as churches and their seminaries moved more in the free church orb, the more need they had of such areas of study as religious education or rural and city church life. In that sense, as ethnicity gave way to churches that had to recruit their membership fresh every generation, the need to train ministers to be successful in the American marketplace became more important. The first generation of Lutherans wanted their children catechized, some of the second and third generations wanted catechetical instruction, but many, if not most, in the fourth and subsequent generations wanted a Sunday school program. The same was true of Presbyterians, many of whose nineteenth-century members were first- or second-generation Irish. So multiple explanations exist for the same phenomenon.

V. Other Findings

Kelly was fascinated by the curriculum, the point at which theological schools most clearly intersect with the larger world of higher education and with academic theology, but he also noted some other facts about the schools of his time. The average theological student, Kelly noted, had completed more education than high school and less than a full college program. Of 7,522 students, 3,313 had a college degree; 2,443 had no college training at all. The percentage that had attended college, however, tended to increase decade by decade, with the 1923 reports indicating that 43 percent had graduated. The remainder fell short of a degree. Most were the sons of farmers or of ministers who believed they had received a unique call to the ministry. In part because of the tendency of theological schools to locate in a few large cities, theological students often had to migrate to attend school. Most students studied in the seminaries of their own denomination (7,000 to 1,700), with Methodists more likely to attend seminaries of other denominations. Interestingly enough, denominational colleges were important "feeders" for Southern Baptists, Methodist Episcopalians North and South, Presbyterians US, and United Lutherans, but were not for Congregationalists, Protestant Episcopalians, American Baptists, and Presbyterians USA. The reasons for this division varied by confessional group. American Baptists, for instance, had fewer colleges than their Southern brethren, and these were not closely tied to the denomination. Many formerly Congregational colleges, to cite another case, had secularized, and the Episcopalians had founded few such institutions. Interestingly, most students would complete their seminary course (pp. 170-72).

Despite the widespread belief that enrollment was declining, Kelly's survey indicated that it was not. There was one student for every 2,600 active church members, or one for every 7,000 or 8,000 in the Protestant constituency. Not surprisingly, enrollment declined during the war and rose immediately after it (p. 173). There was no evidence that any denomination lacked ministers, as one minister was available for every 534 people in the population.[19]

Kelly found many reasons for what appeared to be an oversupply of ministers that ranged from "the general inadequacy between supply and demand of trained people in all fields" to "the denominational tendency which hangs on wherever work has been started." In other words, there were many poorly prepared ministers who served churches that ought to have closed or consolidated. The facts reflected "attitudes, traditions, duties, opportunities for reinterpretation" that called for interpretation and adjustment (p. 186).

Kelly admitted that his study of seminary finances was inadequate. Many schools had failed to report their incomes, and many that had done so presented documents that "contained errors and ambiguities" (p. 195). There was enough data to see that some schools had sufficient resources while others were almost impoverished. The reason for this was that, despite a school's denominational history, its primary source of support was individual contributions and the income from endowments. Kelly's list of the richest schools was instructive: Union Theological Seminary, New York, $5,547,000; Princeton, $3,364,000; General Theological Seminary and McCormick, over $2,000,000; and Crozer, Newton, Rochester, Southern Baptist, Hartford, Garrett, Auburn, and Harvard with more than $1,000,000 each. Unfortunately, libraries followed much the same order.

The cost of educating a theological student, Kelly found, also varied significantly. But what is perhaps most significant was that, at least in the better seminaries, the cost was above the college, university, or professional school average of $466. Thus, Auburn, Andover, General, Hartford, and Oberlin all spent more than $2,000 a student; Harvard almost $1,900; Rochester, Princeton, and Yale an average of $1,300; and McCormick, Drew, Garrett and Boston, and the University of Chicago between $500 and $600. Size was clearly a factor in these calculations. The Episcopal Church, Kelly felt, paid a high price for "the maintenance of her intellectual standards," while the Methodist and Baptist schools were more efficient, educating larger numbers at lower cost per student (p. 208).

19. Even in a very religious country, such as the United States, this proportion seems extraordinary. The most natural reading of Kelly's result is that the nation, as a whole, had more ministers and religious congregations than it could adequately support. The low salaries paid to the average clergyperson in the United States, thus, could reflect the fact that ministers were a "glut" on the market. It also reflected the fact that many rural churches were in decline and unable to afford a full-time minister.

VI. Problems

Both Kelly and his sponsors hoped that the survey's results would spark debate and hopefully change. The most dramatic result of the Flexner report was a rapid decline in the number of medical schools, and Kelly openly faced the question of whether there were too many theological schools:

> The efficient expert would undoubtedly answer this question in the affirmative. . . . There are universities in the United States on each of whose campuses there are in residence more students than in the 161 seminaries under consideration. Each of these universities is conducted as a unit; its various departments are administered as organic parts of that unit; it has a single library and laboratory administration, and operates under a single budget. It undoubtedly is carried on with greater efficiency than 161 separate units can be carried on, each operating alone. (p. 213)

Kelly, perhaps because he was under the watchful eye of Mackenzie and others, carefully qualified his conclusion by noting that ultimately the various denominations would have to consider whether the historical and theological factors that had called the schools into being justified their continuation. Like Rockefeller, he appears to have hoped for a great religious movement that might provide the United States with some sense of cohesion.[20]

But, if the larger dream of a more efficient way of administering theological education was impractical, some of Kelly's other suggestions were more prophetic. He maintained that the schools needed a system of retirement allowances, similar to those prevalent in colleges, and that they ought to stress professional criteria in hiring their faculties. "Modern methods of accounting" needed to be introduced, and the seminaries needed to provide a public accounting of their expenditures (p. 233). Faculty salaries needed to be raised, since many "graduates receive first appointments at salaries considerably in excess of those drawn by the professors with whom they have studied" (p. 232). The schools especially needed to take account of the "recent growth of Bible schools and religious training schools, which in the aggregate now enroll as many students as all the seminaries," and to take account of "the whole problem of training for Christian leadership" (p. 229).

20. Charles E. Harvey, "Speer versus Rockefeller and Mott, 1910-1935," *Journal of Presbyterian History* 60 (Winter 1982): 283-99. Rockefeller's interest in finding an efficient form of Protestantism continued throughout his life. In theological education, it meant support for the university-related schools; in missions, for the Hocking report; and in ecclesiastical affairs, for the National Council of Churches and for Riverside Church. As Harvey has argued, Rockefeller's position was consistent since his earliest involvement with religious philanthropy.

The most important of Kelly's suggestions was that the seminaries pursue standardization. It is important to note that for all the variety Kelly found among the schools, he also found that "the seminaries are now standardized largely by imitation." In other words, the schools were often more alike than they appeared at first glance. What he meant was: "[S]hall the seminaries be subjected to the same type of standardization that is operating in other fields of American education and which is characterized by numerous and powerful standardizing agencies?" (p. 219). That is, could the seminaries establish an accrediting agency to help them find common solutions to the problems they faced? Kelly had found the key question for the next twenty years of seminary history.

CHAPTER SIXTEEN

African American Theological Education: From Emancipation to the Depression

The historian of African American theological education faces many of the same problems as the historian of other aspects of the African American experience. In a famous quotation, W. E. B. Du Bois stated: "It is a peculiar sensation, this double-consciousness, this sense of always looking at one's self through the eyes of others, of measuring one's soul by the tape of a world that looks on in amusing contempt and pity. One ever feels his two-ness, — an American, a Negro; two souls, two thoughts, two unreconciled strivings; two warring ideals in one dark body, whose dogged strength alone keeps it from being torn asunder."[1] In many aspects of the history of education, the American components of African American schools are readily apparent. Rarely have such schools deviated, for instance, from the most commonly accepted curricular patterns or adopted patterns of administrative control of other American institutions.[2] Yet, like other African American institutions, they also have their own character, derived in part from the dynamics of black experience in the United States, that sets them apart from their Euro-American counterparts.

Those interested in the religious and educational life of African Americans also have to consider the implications of this divided character. The most obvious fact about these denominations is their emphatically American character. The largest African American denominations, basically found in three fam-

1. W. E. B. Du Bois, *The Souls of Black Folks* (Chicago: A. C. McClurg and Co., 1903; New York: Johnson Reprint Co., 1968), p. 98, "Of Alexander Crummell."

2. If one did not know, for example, which school was white and which black, one might have real difficulty distinguishing the course offered at Mercer College, a white Georgia Baptist institution, from that offered at Morehouse, a leading African American school in Georgia. The similarity was even more striking from 1890 to 1940, when both Mercer and Morehouse were seriously limited in their offerings by the general poverty of the South.

ilies — Methodist, Baptist, and Pentecostal — originated in the New World, and they developed in tandem with other American religious institutions and movements. The African Methodist Episcopal bishop Daniel Payne, for instance, was very much a child of American Christianity whose Methodism was rooted in the particular experiences of American Methodism. Payne was an "episcopal" Methodist. Many of his achievements occurred almost concurrently with similar achievements by white bishops in the Methodist Episcopal Church, North. The first African Methodist Episcopal college, Wilberforce University, established in the 1850s, was roughly contemporary with white Methodism's aggressive entrance into the American educational market. Similarly, the Colored (later the Christian) Methodist Episcopal Church, a denomination that grew out of the Methodist Episcopal Church, South, planned a Central University in the 1870s, similar to the one projected by their white Methodist counterparts at Vanderbilt.[3] Yet the story of these churches and their schools is not a repeat of the white story with a different cast of characters.[4]

In some ways the analogy between African Americans and European ethnic groups is helpful. Like other ethnic designations, such as Irish American, the term "African American" points to a people with a shared sense of history and culture. Such groups often pursue goals, particularly in religion and education, rooted in their common experiences. For ethnic groups the church is often a "mighty fortress" that provides their cultural identity, already compromised by movement to the New World, with some protections against the new culture. Italian and Polish Catholics, thus, were anxious to build parishes where their own language was spoken and schools were staffed by religious from the home country. Nineteenth-century Princeton College performed many similar functions for Protestant Celtic immigrants, and two of its most successful presidents, James McCosh and Francis Patton, were themselves part of the Celtic diaspora. Similarly, German and Scandinavian immigrants established their own Lutheran denominations, colleges, and seminaries, hoping to strengthen and retain some of their European past. The schools maintained by these ethnic groups, of course, also function as intellectual centers for those cultures. Not only do they transmit language skills, essential to a sense of difference from the

3. The Colored Methodists were unable to raise the money. Their white counterparts probably would have failed as well, but they were rescued by Commodore Vanderbilt, who put up one million dollars to help them with their school.

4. Paul R. Griffin, "Black Founders of Reconstruction Era Methodist Colleges: Daniel A. Payne, Joseph C. Price, and Isaac Lane, 1863-1890" (Ph.D. diss., Emory University, 1983), has convincingly demonstrated that much of Payne's rhetoric about education had its roots in his profoundly Wesleyan theology. Like Martin Luther King later, Payne was a convinced servant of the church whose theological apprehensions formed the foundations of his efforts for his race.

larger culture, but they also are places where the great cultural monuments of the old country are preserved.

In many ways African American churches and schools perform similar functions. The schools have often taken steps to retain and strengthen aspects of the African American cultural heritage. For instance, Atlanta University was early a center for the study of black American life, and many of the contributors to such journals as the *Journal of Negro History* or the *Journal of Negro Education* were instructors in African American colleges and seminaries. Like other ethnic educational institutions, they have mediated the insights of the dominant culture to their students who were, paradoxically, in and out of that cultural milieu.

The analogy with European ethnic groups, however, breaks down at a number of crucial points — most fundamentally in the question of purpose. Although one can argue about the survival of African customs and religions in these churches, neither the churches nor their schools were founded to preserve African culture. Unlike the immigrants, they were not separated from the larger culture so much by ethnic custom as by their race and white Americans' reaction to it. In other words, "racism" has shaped African American history in many decisive ways. The term "racism" is not an ideal one, because for some people it may connote only the passionate dislike of another group of human beings and the various ideological structures that support that hatred. To be sure, African Americans have often been subjected to that type of ideological prejudice. The historian would have little difficulty demonstrating that African American history has been deeply influenced, at times tragically, by such movements as late nineteenth-century social Darwinism or the eugenics movements of the 1920s. These movements directed their ideology against southern and eastern European immigrants as often as they directed it against African Americans. Thus the IQ test results, obtained during the draft for the First World War, form a rainbow of the older culture's prejudices. But racism in America is much more than an opinion or set of opinions about American people of color. Historically, it has also been a pattern of legal and social exclusion that rested only in part on evaluations, however wrongheaded, of the nature of African Americans. Ironically, those patterns of exclusion have often been maintained particularly in the American South, by people who with apparent sincerity wished African Americans well or even enjoyed good relationships with parts of the African American community. American racism was not, however, exclusively Southern. The young black minister and scholar Benjamin Mays might, for instance, find that those patterns of exclusion were temporarily suspended at Bates, a Maine Baptist institution. But when he was nearly graduated, in 1919, he found that the recruiter from Newton, a school that was well represented at one of his earlier alma maters, Virginia Union, did not want him because of his color. Fortunately, the University of Chicago accepted him. He earned two degrees from that institution,[5] while frequently suffering from segregation in the various restaurants and businesses near the school.

To be a "race man" among African Americans, thus, most often has meant something different from leadership in Euro-American ethnic communities. The ethnic leader wanted to preserve his people from the dangerous contamination of the larger culture, to build a colony, to preserve the old world in the new. In contrast, the race man wanted to free his people from the shackles of an oppressive political and economic system. The ethnic leader struggled for the right to keep his or her people out; the race man struggled for the right to let his or her people into the inner sanctum.

One way to describe the effects of racism is to say that it created two cultures, one white, one African American, that often mirrored one another in distorted ways. This image can be very useful in understanding Protestant churches. For instance, white urban Protestant churches tend basically to be middle-class institutions, but the same has also been true of urban African American churches. But racism makes a difference in what middle class means in the two communities. A school principal in the urban white church might be in the middle range of incomes in the congregation, while a black principal might represent the upper class among African Americans. What it means to be educated and highly educated will thus often vary in the two societies. A white Baptist pastor in 1920 with only a high school education, for instance, would have been one of the least well-educated pastors, and his peers would have encouraged him to attend a seminary to earn a Th.B. degree; but an African American pastor with a high school certificate would have been among the better-educated members of his profession and congregation. There would have been little, if any, social pressure for him to secure further schooling. Failure to recognize this mirror relationship between the two cultures can lead to some risky judgments about, for instance, whether black congregations wanted an educated ministry or whether advanced education was a help or hindrance to the African American pastor.[6] The First African Baptist Church of Philadel-

5. Benjamin E. Mays, *Born to Rebel: An Autobiography* (New York: Scribner, 1971), tells this story along with other accounts of his education.

6. African American ministers were among the strongest advocates of education in their communities, and many prominent African Americans remember their passionate advocacy of more schooling as part of their own intellectual formation. Yet, when measured by the dominant society, these ministers often seem to be comparatively unschooled. In fact, within their community they represented a professional and educated elite. The same was often true of white Baptists and Methodists in more working-class areas. Their high school graduation and

phia celebrated its centenary in 1909, proud in the fact that its pastor — Rev. William Abraham Creditt — was a graduate of Lincoln University and Newton Seminary.[7] Before becoming pastor, Rev. Creditt taught Hebrew, using the inductive method popularized by William Rainey Harper. As among whites, then, the more prestigious African American pulpit tended to attract the better-educated clergy, but often the top of the profession among African Americans represented a lower financial and educational level than the equivalent might represent among white Americans.[8]

Racism, as a system of exclusion, also limits a people's options when they struggle with their world. This is particularly true in education. Finances are one important area where this deprivation has been historically experienced. In the post–Civil War South, to cite only one example, very little money was provided by the states for African American education, and very few Southern states constructed African American high schools before the 1920s. In many areas this meant that African Americans had to raise the money for their own primary and secondary education as well as find funding for normal, collegiate, and professional education — in effect, a system of double taxation.[9] African Americans paid their taxes, much of which went to maintain white schools, and then had to provide their own institutions as well. Since schools were scarce, even the best African American colleges had to perform many functions. From

---

touch of college made them the intellectual leaders of their communities and potent advocates of education.

7. Charles H. Brook, *A Brief Historical Review of the First African Baptist Church* [*of Philadelphia*], *Certain Other Interesting Information and the Official Program of the Centennial Anniversary Celebration* (Philadelphia: The Church, 1909).

8. The differential, of course, varies with the situation. My impression, although I admittedly do not have sufficient hard data to prove it, is that the difference has been fairly consistently one educational level. Thus, at the turn of the century, when white Methodists were straining to get high school graduates and a course of study for their average pulpits, the African Methodist Episcopal Church (AME) was insisting on common schooling and their own course of study. Today, white Methodism requires a seminary degree for admission in full connection, while the AME requires college. Among black Lutherans in the 1920s, the denomination required a bachelor of arts, while most white Lutherans were earning a seminary degree (but not all — many Lutherans were graduates of Missouri's practical seminary, a program basically on the level of the African American Lutheran colleges or even slightly below them).

9. James Anderson, *The Education of Blacks in the South, 1860-1935* (Chapel Hill: University of North Carolina Press, 1988), made me aware of the effects of double taxation on the development of higher education for the African American community. In a sense the argument is self-evident. After paying to teach John or Susan to read and then paying for them to attend high school, how much is left either in funds or effort for further education? One gets a sense of the way resources could easily be depleted in Benjamin Mays's autobiography, previously cited, where he talks about the effort needed at every stage of his education.

1865 to 1930, most African American institutions educated people on the elementary, the high school, the college, and the professional levels.[10] Finances are always a crucial element in the development of academic institutions, but "double taxation" means that an economically challenged community has to do more to stay even with the dominant community. Not surprisingly, they often fell off the pace. Further, the effects of "double taxation" gave the handful of white philanthropists who supported African American institutions almost unlimited power over the future of those institutions.

I. Beginnings

Although some African Americans became Christians before the Revolutionary War, the first great missionary outreach to them was the post-Revolutionary evangelical revival in the South. Baptists and Methodists, perhaps because many of their leaders were also socially marginal, preached their hot gospel to any, slave or free, who were willing to give Christ a hearing. While the message of the two popular churches varied theologically, both stressed a faith that called upon the individual to make a bold declaration for the gospel, to step forward from the group, and to live a disciplined life. Further, both churches drew much of their leadership from their converts, some of whom were illiterate or semiliterate, and both stressed the role of exhorters, men and women whose principal ministry was to tell others about their own spiritual experience.

It was a hearty message, and one that African Americans, slave and free, often heard with pleasure. In a world in which they often had no dignity, the message of the evangelists was simple and to the point: in Christ you are somebody, the most precious thing in all creation, and the one for whom Christ died. To hear this message was to be washed in the blood, reborn, and given a new name. This new evangelicalism was a very emotional faith. People were struck dead in the spirit, broke into uncontrollable tears, and on occasion went into deep depressions. African Americans participated in the excitement, and their openness to ecstasy, a part of many African religions, may have contributed to the excitement of the early revival meetings.

The laws of thermodynamics seem to hold as much in the religious as in the physical realm. The fires that burned so intensely on the revivalist forge soon became a smoldering pile of coals with only an occasional finger fire of

10. Such preparatory departments were of course part of many white Southern institutions as well. The aristocrats who ruled the school, like the New England grandees, preferred private schools for their own children.

emotion left of the original passions. But the importance of this first burning should not be overlooked. The Baptist and Methodist churches became the African Americans' churches of choice, as they largely remain today, and they left a threefold legacy. Faith was emotional, it was voluntary, and its leaders were those called by God. But not all African Americans joined these churches. Many — perhaps the majority of African American slaves, like their poor white counterparts — remained technically not members of any church. Some of them may have failed to "get religion" at a revival; others were possibly fearful they could not walk the walk of the rigorous church discipline of the Baptists and Methodists; and still others may not have wanted to join the churches where their masters worshiped. The importance of these semirevived but nonecclesiastically affiliated persons should not be overlooked. When the Civil War ended, both poorer whites and former slaves streamed into the churches in the second great Southern revival. Southern churches, black and white, found themselves struggling with unprecedented numbers.

A significant number of the converted joined churches composed of both white and black members. The freedom allowed African Americans in these churches varied greatly. In some congregations, free Africans had their own deacons, their own place at the services, and were admitted under their own names. And in a handful of churches slaves who were noted for their spirituality were recognized by both whites and blacks as exhorters and as prayer warriors whose words reached heaven itself. In other churches the slaves were almost systematically humiliated, chained to each other during the services and forced to wait until the whites had communed before they were invited to the table. And in many churches, African Americans were confronted with a special "slave theology" that stressed that they were not to steal, be lazy, or break tools.

In the more open of these churches, African Americans received substantial religious instruction. Despite laws prohibiting whites from teaching blacks to read, the love of the Bible among both races inspired some whites to pass their African American friends the Bread of Life secretly. Many free Africans learned the art of reading from their former masters or from other freed Africans who were anxious to teach their fellows the skill or were willing to do so for a price. While it is difficult to determine the exact number of such literate and semiliterate African Americans, they did much to create a biblical culture among the slaves, and they were numerous enough to provide significant leadership in the post–Civil War period. There were always some African Americans with elementary intellectual skills.

Slaves had little choice but to accept their second-class status, although they circumvented it wherever possible by establishing their own secret churches and brush arbor meetings. Free African Americans did not, by and large, accept second-class status. By 1800 there were some independent African Baptist churches, and although laws were often passed demanding that they have "white leadership," those churches continued until emancipation. Such churches existed in the North as well. The First African Baptist Church of Philadelphia, for instance, dated from 1809, although Philadelphia's African Baptists had been meeting together for some time before that. Baptist polity made it easy for people to go their own way, whenever they had the liberty to do so.

If for no other reason than the complexity of its structure, Methodism had more problems adjusting to the needs of African Americans. The founding of the African Methodist Episcopal Church (AME) is a typical story of how American denominations became segregated. Richard Allen (1760-1831), a former slave and Philadelphia businessman, became deeply involved with the Methodist church after his emancipation in 1781. He went on several missionary trips for the new denomination, was an active member of St. George's Methodist Church, and served as a missionary to other free people of color. However, Allen found that the racism of his white coreligionists was more than he could bear. While kneeling in prayer in his own congregation in 1787, he was ordered by an usher to go to the balcony, a space frequently used to segregate African Americans. He asked to finish his prayer, and was ordered again to the segregated section. His heart breaking, Allen and his friends left the building and, shortly thereafter, organized the Free African Society. The society, in turn, gave rise to several independent black congregations, including St. Thomas Episcopal Church and Bethel Methodist Episcopal Church. In 1816 Bethel joined with sixteen other African American churches to form the AME Church. Allen was consecrated as the new denomination's first bishop, and in 1828 Morris Brown became its second. The new denomination spread rapidly among free Africans. Shortly thereafter, other free Africans formed the African Methodist Episcopal Zion Church in response to the same conditions. The same pattern would be repeated after the Civil War in almost every Southern town and city as white and black Methodists went their separate ways.

Although many of the original leaders of the AME Church were unschooled, they were determined to educate their children and their church. Bethel, for instance, had a school for children of color as early as 1795, and Allen was active in forming the Society of People of Color for Promoting the Instruction of the Children of African Descent. Perhaps most important, Bethel's leaders saw the potential of the new Sunday school movement as a place for teaching literacy. The Sunday school would remain one of the basic African American educational institutions until well into the twentieth century, in part because it provided a way to use the one publicly acknowledged day of rest to teach people to read.[11]

II. Daniel Payne

The African Methodist Episcopal Church provided the institutional context for one of the most remarkable figures in the history of American theological education: Bishop Daniel Payne. Payne was born free in Charleston, South Carolina, and initially earned his living in a variety of employments. As a young man, Payne was approached by a white man who wanted to hire him to travel with him. The dialogue between the two changed Payne's life. As he remembered, years later, the man said to him: "If you will go with me, the knowledge that you will acquire of men and things will be of far more value to you than the wages I will pay you. Do you know what makes the difference between the master and the slave? *Nothing but superior knowledge*." Payne continued: "This statement was fatal to his desire to obtain my services, for I instantly said to myself: 'If it is true that there is nothing but superior knowledge between the master and the slave, I will not go with you, but will rather go and obtain that knowledge which constitutes the master.'"[12] Payne's response was to be the essence of his philosophy of education: the only way for African Americans to secure the rights and privileges due them was by achieving sufficient education to be the equal of any master in America. Indeed, for some years he admitted that he believed that emancipation had to wait until the slaves had enough education to function in society.[13]

Payne began an arduous program of self-education that included the classical languages, mathematics, and the sciences. He was so interested in the latter that he did permanent damage to his eyes observing a solar eclipse. By 1829 he was ready to open his first school in Charleston. The school was to provide a place for free Africans and the children of some slaves to come for aca-

11. This was of course the original genius of these schools in England. What was interesting about African American Sunday schools, before and after the Civil War, was their continuation of this original purpose long after many white Sunday schools had become a popular replacement for catechism.

12. Bishop Daniel Alexander Payne, *Recollections of Seventy Years* (New York: Arno Press, 1968), pp. 19-20.

13. This was not an uncommon position at the time, and the gradual emancipation laws in New York and New Jersey both were predicated, at least in part, on the idea that children needed to continue in slavery until they had been educated enough for freedom. Of course, the master was to receive their labor in partial payment for this education.

demic and moral instruction, and Payne was both a good enough teacher to interest his students and a sound enough manager to find ways to support himself. In the America of his day, he might have been well on his way to a career in education, but the racial attitudes of South Carolina intervened. Payne had entered into his new venture in one of the most difficult decades for African Americans. The decade began in 1821 with Denmark Vesey's aborted attempt to seize Charleston, and it ended with Nat Turner's violent uprising in 1831. The period between Vesey and Turner was marked by race riots, such as the one in Cincinnati in 1829, and by the beginning of emigration to Liberia. For free African Americans it was particularly trying, and Payne did not escape his fellows' tribulation. In 1835 the authorities closed Payne's school; despairing of his native city, he set sail for Philadelphia.

Payne's initial experiences in Philadelphia illustrate the small-town character of American urban life at the time. Perhaps with more than a little pride, he remembered encountering Alexander Crummell, the first African American to earn a degree from Oxford University, and making a small contribution to the expenses of Crummell's education.[14] More important, he found that he was in demand as a student. In his words:

> Lastly, I went to Rev. Daniel Strobel, of the Lutheran Church, and presented my letter to him from Dr. Bachman. He read it, and said: "Mr. Payne, I believe you are providentially here, for Dr. Martin has just informed me that the Society of Inquiry on Missions, at Gettysburg, has resolved to educate a talented, pious young man of color for the intellectual, moral, and social elevation of the free colored people in this country, and from what these letters say of you I think you are the very man whom they want. Now, if you will go to Gettysburg, and study theology there, you will be better fitted than you now are for usefulness among your people." I told him that my highest aim was to be an educator, that the sanctities and responsibilities of the ministry were too great and awful for me. But he overcame my objections by showing the enlarged usefulness resulting from such a course, and stating that I would not be obliged to enter the ministry. "And if you should not enter the ministry, your training in theology will make you more useful in the school-room."[15]

After making sure he was not being recruited as part of a colonization scheme, Payne accepted the offer and went to Gettysburg. The next two years, at least

14. Crummell, a lifelong Anglican, had been refused admission to General Seminary in New York.

15. Payne, *Recollections of Seventy Years*, p. 49.

until his eyes weakened too much for the regimen of study, were among the happiest in his life. His command of the classical languages improved, as did his reading knowledge of contemporary European languages. After seminary the Lutherans ordained him, and he served briefly as the pastor of a Presbyterian church, but the white denominations did not offer him sufficient scope for his work. He transferred his ministerial standing to the African Methodist Episcopal Church and rose rapidly through the ranks. In 1852 he was consecrated as bishop.

Payne had entered the AME Church at a crucial moment in its development. Like its white counterpart, the church was becoming more solidly middle class in both ministry and members. African Methodists, for instance, had established their own journal, had begun to work for better education for their race in general, and equally significantly, had adopted a hymnbook to replace (at least in the more established congregations) the traditional ditties and "lined-out" hymns. Some churches were acquiring organs and pianos as well. The younger men entering the ministry were literate and more conscious of themselves as racial leaders.[16] Payne was in the forefront of this reforming second generation: he moved to eliminate the "cornfield ditties" from worship while pastor at Baltimore's influential Bethel AME Church, took an active role in civic affairs, and wrote for the denominational press. Payne found other pastors who shared his interest in serious theological study. Convinced that these younger pastors were the future of the church, Payne began a campaign to introduce a Course of Study into the denomination. The white Methodist Episcopal Church had used such a series of prescribed readings for some time, and Payne's Course of Study was clearly modeled on white precedent. Further, as in contemporary white Methodism, Payne was willing to tie his church's course to an elongated period between when a candidate was admitted on trial and when the candidate was admitted in full connection. Although Payne's proposal was watered down to win support, it was still substantial. The Course of Study included a standard work on English grammar, Paley's *Natural Theology,* Watson's *Institutes,* and two books by Samuel Schmucker. A student mastering the course would be among the best-prepared Methodists, whether in the white or African connection, and much better prepared than the average rural white Methodist local preacher.

When Payne presented his proposal in 1844, the floor indignantly shouted it down. But he had read the situation more correctly than his opponents.

16. For a good account of the development of African Methodists, see Harry V. Richardson, *Dark Salvation: The Story of Methodism as It Developed among Blacks in America,* C. Eric Lincoln Series in Black Religion (Garden City, N.Y.: Doubleday, Anchor Press, 1976). Much of this account is based on my reading of his insightful study.

> The next day, the fifth of the session, as soon as the house was opened, and first of all, Rev. A. D. Lewis, a brother of lofty stature, venerable appearance, dignified mien and delectable countenance, rose to his feet and called for a reconsideration of the rejected proposition. His motion was seconded and stated by the chair. The venerable man then advocated its claims and demonstrated its utility in a speech of uncommon eloquence and power. He addressed the understanding, the conscience, the passions of the audience till it was bathed in tears, and from many a voice was heard the impassioned cry, "Give us the resolution, give us the resolution."[17]

But Payne knew that the resolution was not enough. Returning to his Washington, D.C., charge, he began to write a series of five articles on ministerial education for the denominational press. The result was one of the few true debates over theological training in American history. Payne remembered the battle later:

> These gave much offense to many of the clergy, and produced much excitement among the laity. It was said by one that these "Epistles" were "full of absurdities;" "infidels could do no more." The statements in the fourth of these "Epistles" were branded as "infidelity in its rankest form." Others who could not handle the pen, or had not the courage to appear in the columns of our Church organ, privately called Payne a "devil." One writer charged me with "branding the ministry with infamy" and of "reckless slander on the character of the Connection." So intense was the excitement that the editor of the magazine said: "Great fear is entertained by some that if the measures proposed be adopted by the General Conference discord and dissolution will necessarily take place in the Church between the ignorant and the intelligent portions of it."[18]

Aided by other men his own age, Payne stood his ground. The next year he was elected chairman of the committee on education, and the bishops were obliged to give an address on ministerial education every year.

Payne's appeal was based in part on his sense of the enlightened quality of the nineteenth century. As he saw his own time:

> The fall of ignorance is as certain as the fall of Babylon, and the universal spread of knowledge as the light of the sun; for the Lord hath said, "*Many shall run to and fro, and knowledge will be increased.*" Who does not see that

17. Quoted in Harry Richardson, *Dark Salvation*, p. 108.
18. Payne, *Recollections of Seventy Years*, p. 76.

> this divine declaration is daily fulfilling? The press is pouring forth its millions of publications every year, in every form, and almost every language, so that books and newspapers are becoming as common, as the stones in the streets. Common schools, seminaries and colleges, are being erected in almost every land and nation. Lyceums, literary societies, library companies and historical associations are being instituted among men of all ranks, and all complexions, so that it may be truly said, that the beaming chariot of the *genius of knowledge* is rolling triumphantly on to the conquest of the world.[19]

The church was called upon to convert and consecrate this power to the service of Christ: "Permit me humbly to add, that sanctified knowledge is a power at once beneficent, glorious, and tremendous. It is beneficent, because it is always delighting in good works, and conferring blessings upon mankind — it is glorious, because it shines forth with the brightness of the unclouded sun — it is tremendous, because the man in whom it dwells is like an angel of God, armed with thunderbolts, crushing the strongholds or the empire of Satan."[20] But, above all, Payne believed that an educated ministry was essential to the moral and spiritual well-being of the church.

> [S]ome men imagine themselves called to the work of the ministry, and desirous to engage in it, obtain recommendation from the class, license from the quarterly, and authority from the annual conference, set out booted, spurred and mounted, to do what? I ask again, to do what? You say to preach the Gospel. What Gospel? The Gospel of Christ? Well, do they? No! They preach what is in no Bible under heaven. Not even in the alcoran of Mohomet. Rant, obscene language, rude and vulgar expressions, irreverent exclamations, empty sound nonsense, and the essence of superstition, constitute the gospel they preach. So that by this kind of teaching and this kind of preaching, it has come to pass that some bearing the name of ministers, can be tipplers and drunkards; others can have two living wives, while some laymen can have four, and yet maintain their standing in the pulpit and in the church.[21]

Payne was not only a pulpit advocate of education. He encouraged young preachers to attend Oberlin. In 1856, when some white Methodists in Ohio pro-

19. Payne, *Recollections of Seventy Years,* p. 73.

20. Daniel A. Payne, *Sermons and Addresses, 1853-1891,* ed. Charles Killian, Annual Conference, 1853 (New York: Arno Press, 1972), p. 12.

21. Daniel Payne, "The Christian Ministry: Its Moral and Intellectual Character," in *Sermons and Addresses, 1853-1891,* p. 12. Just as Payne refused to accept excuses for ignorance, so he was very impatient with Methodist ministers whose lives belied their profession.

posed building for African Americans a college, Wilberforce, he was on the board. The college was not initially a success, and the original sponsors wanted to abandon the project. In 1863, however, Payne submitted a bid for the property, to be paid in installments, and secured the college for the AME Church. He left this account of the purchase:

> It had been decided to sell the property [of Wilberforce University], and between the hours of nine and ten P.M. I agreed with them to purchase the property, "in the name of God and the A.M.E. church." The amount required was ten thousand dollars. When I made the bid for the property, I had not a ten dollar bill at my command, but I had faith in God. Within forty-eight hours after that act one hundred dollars was given us by Mrs. James Shorter, wife of Elder Shorter, and by June, 1863, we met the first payment of two thousand five hundred dollars. This sum was pledged and raised entirely by the Baltimore and Ohio Conferences. On the 11th of June, Rev. James Shorter, Prof. John G. Mitchell, and myself consummated the arrangements for the purchase of Wilberforce University, and the title deeds were handed to us as agents of the A.M.E. Church. It was then incorporated, a new charter taken out, and a new board of trustees elected. . . . Within two years from the date on which we made the first payment we had paid the sum of seven thousand five hundred dollars.[22]

Payne served as president of the refounded school, and was also an active bishop. Perhaps his most frustrating experience was his trip to England to raise funds for the school. His visit to Bishop Wilberforce, the son of the great philanthropist, was marked by two tragic revelations. The first was that American Episcopal bishops had assured their English brethren that they had sufficient funds and will to take care of the American black population. Any aid that Wilberforce and his friends might have provided was thus superfluous. Second, in an example of the tragic irony that accompanied so much African American experience, the bishop lectured him that "Wilberforce University was a race school, and he was opposed to any such exclusive schools."[23] Black educators were to hear these two excuses repeatedly over the next century and beyond. But at least Payne had a chance to speak to the bishop; at the meeting of the

22. Payne, *Recollections of Seventy Years,* p. 145.

23. Charles Spencer Smith, *A History of the African Methodist Episcopal Church Being a Volume Supplemental to a History of the African Methodist Episcopal Church by Daniel Alexander Payne, DD, LLD, Late One of Its Bishops, Chronicling the Principal Events in the Advance of the African Methodist Episcopal Church from 1856 to 1922* (Philadelphia: Book Concern of the AME Church, 1922), p. 76. The charge that African American schools and churches were "race" institutions was frequently made.

Evangelical Alliance, which he also attended, he was unable to secure a place on the program.

Wilberforce was far more important than its intellectual achievements might suggest. One could argue for instance that Ashmun Institute, which opened in 1854 and was rechartered as Lincoln University in 1866, was a stronger institution, but Ashmun (Lincoln) remained under white control until well into the twentieth century. Wilberforce was a sign that African Americans were ready and able to take charge of their own educational destiny in America, to do their part in raising up strong leaders. It took sacrificial giving by the church, tireless effort by Payne, and determination by its students, but it worked and produced many of the most significant African American leaders of the pre–civil rights period.

Yet Wilberforce also was an expression of the duality noted by Du Bois and others. Chronologically, the school was established only a few years after the pioneer colleges among white American Methodists. The most natural thing would have been for African Methodism gradually to close the gap between its own schools and the schools of the larger denomination. In other words, the founding of Wilberforce was similar to the founding of many other ethnic seminaries and colleges, and had much the same promise. While Wilberforce's failure to grow as much as might have been expected was due in part to the racism of American society, it was also due to the Civil War. Within four short years the African American churches of the North found themselves confronting one of the greatest missionary and educational opportunities in Christian history. Wilberforce and other African American educational institutions were strained to the maximum as their denominations struggled to provide Christian and secular nurture to the freedmen.

III. The Challenge of the Great War

Although later Americans would think of the Civil War as an "irrepressible" conflict, the appeal to arms appears to have struck most Americans, including those in government, as a surprise. The military was ill prepared for war on a continental scale, and the problems of supply and demand had to be settled almost on the fly, as the nation moved from crisis to crisis, and Lincoln moved from general to general. But if the government was ill prepared for battle, it was even less well prepared for its occasional victories and, in particular, for what should be done with the African American community. From the earliest advances into Virginia and Tennessee, the federal government found itself with large numbers of slaves on its side of the line. Militarily, these slaves could not be returned to their masters. The slaves were, after all, one of the most substantial assets of the Confederacy. Their labor released many Southerners, especially in the planter class, for military service, and the products they produced were the mainstays of the Southern economy. Nor would Northern sentiment permit them to be sold to slaveholders in the still-loyal states of Maryland and Delaware or held as national slaves.

The American Missionary Association (AMA) quickly recognized the opportunities the freedmen represented. The AMA already had a long and distinguished history as a missionary agency concerned with the religious and educational needs of people of color in America and Africa. It began as a response to one of those events that exposed the tensions between the slave and the free states. When the slave ship *Amistad* was captured off Cuba with a large cargo of African slaves, in violation of agreements prohibiting the international slave trade,[24] evangelicals of many different denominations rallied to prevent these slaves from being returned to Cuba. This crusade was successful, and the captives were returned to Africa where some of them, ironically, took up their previous occupations as slavers again. But the men and women who joined the AMA to seek justice for the captives found more than vindication: they found a vocation.[25] In 1846 they united with representatives of three other missionary bodies, the Union Missionary Society, the Committee for West Indian Missions, and the Western Evangelical Missionary Society, to form an organization devoted to the "removal of caste wherever its sins are found." Its missionaries served both in the United States and abroad, and by 1860 it was the second-largest missionary society in the United States, bested only by the American Board of Commissioners for Foreign Missions. Like the American Board, it would later become part of the Congregational national organization.

The AMA was on the field as early as 1861, and by 1862 it had formulated its sense of the needs of the freedmen: "they need education. Few of them can read or write. They need day schools and night schools for children and adults. Every family should at once be supplied with the Bible."[26] The association was as good as its word; as the war progressed, the AMA sent numerous missionar-

24. The Spanish case rested on the assertion that these slaves were only being transported between different points in Cuba, a legal activity, and were not contraband from Africa. Although outlawed, the importation of slaves into Cuba, Brazil, and the American South continued in the nineteenth century. Like some other forms of smuggling, the trade was profitable enough to justify the risk.

25. Joe M. Richardson, *Christian Reconstruction: The American Missionary Association and Southern Blacks, 1861-1890* (Athens: University of Georgia Press, 1986).

26. J. Taylor Stanley, *A History of Black Congregational Christian Churches of the South* (New York: United Church Press, 1978), p. 22.

ies, including the famed Yankee schoolmistresses, to the South, and it continued to do so after the war ended. The most serious problem was the widespread illiteracy of the freedmen.[27] Literacy was both a practical and a religious issue. Without the ability to read contracts, freedmen might be systematically swindled of the fruit of their labors, as many were, or deprived of land or other property. The system of peonage that Southern whites constructed to replace slavery, in fact, often rested on the inability of African American farmers to understand the terms of the contracts that often awarded the white property owner 50 percent or more of the crop. These contracts often charged the tenant outrageous rates of interest for purchases at the plantation store and set high prices for cottonseed and guano or fertilizer.

The religious consequences of illiteracy were equally serious. The evangelical Protestantism that inspired so many Americans was above all a religion of the Book. The Bible was ubiquitous in evangelical culture: it was used to teach reading, to regulate church life, as the object of personal meditation, and as a rich source of simile and metaphor. Under the slave regime, the slaves had experienced some of the power of the Book as they incorporated biblical stories, especially the stories of the Great Liberator, Moses, in their own songs and religious practice. But, as "a deer longs for flowing streams" (Ps. 42:1 NRSV), many longed to drink more deeply in the Scriptures. To do so, however, they had to be able to read the text and perhaps use some of the many popular aids available.

Literacy was, thus, the first step in the religious and theological education of many African Americans. In some ways this was not unique in Southern experience. While Southern white Methodists and Baptists had established some colleges and the Baptists a seminary at Greenville, many of their preachers had learned from their solitary reading of the Blessed Book, perhaps with some readily available aids, but often with no more light than provided by whale or coal oil. For Methodists in the South, basic literacy was the entrance requirement for the denomination's Course of Study, a carefully selected four-year series of readings that gave the minister a well-rounded education. Southern Baptists were less structured, and the denomination provided fewer informal means for such study. The same was true of African Americans. But even a cur-

27. The extent of African American illiteracy is difficult to determine. In part this is because of the problem scholars encounter when they try to define "literacy." Is literacy measured by whether people can write the letters of their name or recognize their name on a contract, by the ability to sound out some words, or by the ability to read simple business documents? Many African Americans may have had rudimentary skills that were not useful in daily life. The New Englanders who came as missionaries had a much higher standard. For them, people could read when they could make out a passage in the Bible. It was a high standard, and one that many whites in the South had not attained.

sory reading of the proceedings of AMA meetings and the church press indicates that self-study and self-improvement were the first steps toward ministerial competency.[28]

The task of teaching literacy to the freedmen was complicated. Southern white slave owners had shown almost Yankee ingenuity in constructing their system. A major part of this oppression was the deliberate deprivation of the use of language among the slaves. Slaves were rarely, if ever, permitted to live on the same plantation with other slaves from the same tribe or linguistic group. This forced them to use their rudimentary knowledge of the white languages to communicate with each other. But they were also deprived of much of the power of their new tongue. They rarely heard it used effectively — churches were one of the few places where they were exposed to rhetoric — and they were, by and large, prohibited from reading. Their linguistic skills, consequently, atrophied. And since the ability to express complicated arguments and abstract ideas is dependent on developed linguistic skills, their horizons were further limited. Linguistic deprivation had the power of a self-fulfilling prophecy. The Southern whites restricted most slaves, especially field servants, to the vocabulary and syntax used by children, and in turn they saw the African Americans as perpetually childlike. Hence, when blacks acquired education, they often understood the experience as finding their voice or, more tellingly, among males, as discovering their manhood.

The appeal of the AMA to teach the freedmen was heard both by other denominations and by the government. In particular, Northern Baptists and Methodists sent significant numbers of missionaries south to work with the freedmen, and both denominations drew on their considerable experience as "popular" educators to aid in their work. Presbyterians and Episcopalians also participated in the effort, with the Presbyterians particularly important in the education of teachers. Where it proved difficult to establish a formal school, for instance, Sunday schools took over much of the task of teaching literacy. And for a season the federal government participated in the work through the Bureau of Refugees, Freedmen, and Abandoned Lands, more popularly called the Freedmen's Bureau. Under the leadership of General Oliver O. Holmes, an active Congregationalist with ties to the AMA, the bureau established more than three thousand schools by 1869.

The African American churches likewise played an important role in

28. Both Southern Baptist Theological Seminary and Vanderbilt University admitted people to the study of theology with only a common school education (basically, demonstrated literacy) until late in the nineteenth century when high schools began to raise the general education level of the South. High school was one of the great revolutions in the training of Baptist and Methodist clergy.

teaching literacy. After the war ended, African American Christians, who had often been members of the same congregations as their white neighbors, began to separate and to be separated from their former congregations. In some churches this separation came about because the African American membership wanted to control their own churches. In other churches African Americans withdrew because their white fellow members insisted on patterns of separation at worship that made them second-class citizens of the kingdom. But the separation was not always that benign or that voluntary. In some churches the white members asked or demanded that their African neighbors leave, at times with some promise of aid toward the construction of their own buildings, but often with simply their church "letters" and a benediction.

Present-day commentators might overlook the financial and emotional costs of these separations. The various church buildings had been built by members of both races with the African Americans frequently contributing their labor to the enterprise. This investment was wiped out almost completely and had to be made good before church life could resume its normal course. Since few of the new congregations could afford buildings as good as those they had lost, this also meant the new buildings lacked the aesthetic qualities of the older meeting houses. The separating African congregations also lost their stake in the string of missionary and charitable organizations that the biracial denominations had built before the war. Since the South had made little investment in public education, many black Christians had to begin the task of institution building from the ground up.

In addition, the resources of African American Christians were strained, as were the resources of their white counterparts, by the religious revivals of the era. Before the Civil War the South was the least-churched section of the nation, with only a minority of whites and African Americans holding formal membership. In part, this was attributable to the rigorous church discipline practiced by the Methodists and Baptists that discouraged those who were not ready to "live a holy and devout life." Among more upper-class Southerners, religion was not considered part of the furnishing of a gentleman. A gentleman might attend church, but only a preternaturally pious man remained for Holy Communion. The war changed these attitudes. Many Southerners, watching the defeat of their armies, found consolation and courage in faith. Others found in religion an escape from the war guilt that the North insisted the South bear for the conflict. But perhaps most important, the place of religion among white Southerners changed. In some obvious and many less obvious ways, the Southern white churches became the bearers of Southern nationalism, the one place where the Southerner could be himself or herself without the domination of the hated Yankees. This transformation was, of course, extremely important for Christian race relations. By and large, Southerners considered their black neighbors to be "smoked Yankees," and they were the only representatives of the hated enemy that were vulnerable to attack. The Ku Klux Klan, whose ritual was permeated by Christian symbols, renewed the warfare against Northern control of the Southern states, not by attacking the Northern troops in their encampments or destroying such Northern investments as the railroads, but by lynching, brutalizing, and terrifying the black population.

African Americans also experienced the post–Civil War revival. In part, the great influx of new members into African American churches came because, as has often been noted, the church was one of the few places where African Americans were firmly in control of their own destiny. In that sense the churches became a vast laboratory for what it meant to be African American and for people to assume the joys and burdens of self-direction.[29] The signs of caring for this place of experimentation and growth were everywhere. Sunday was a day for the best clothes — for women to wear hats and men to wear ties, to ride in a wagon behind the mule, and to feel and be grand.

The churches were, as we have mentioned, crucial as places where schools and Sunday schools could be held. At least at first, there were no other educational facilities available. They were also important for two other reasons. First, the African American ministry served as the encouragers of education among their people. Even if the minister had little or no formal schooling, he wanted his people to rise higher than he had. This was particularly true of those black ministers who laboriously educated themselves by reading whatever they could acquire — as it was of many self-educated Southern white Baptist and Methodist ministers. Second, and more important, the churches were a place where African Americans could learn language. They were temples to the power of words and the Word, and the services there were often almost all-day affairs that combined preaching, exhorting, praying, and public discussion.

Evidence of the African American passion for education and for rhetoric was everywhere. James Anderson, in his excellent *The Education of Blacks in the South,* summarized this data: "Blacks emerged from slavery with a strong belief in the desirability of learning to read and write. This belief was expressed in the pride with which they talked of other ex-slaves who learned to read or write in

29. Most of the classic studies of the black church in America from Du Bois onward noted the relationship between the church as a place where the African American could be somebody and membership in the churches. But often this analysis has been overly caught up in status analysis. The church was not only a place where African Americans could experience a different status order — although this was very important in African American as well as white Baptist and Methodist churches — it was also a place where one could experience a number of different social roles, where the very human desire to be many things could be realized.

slavery and in the esteem in which they held literate blacks. It was expressed in the intensity and the frequency of their anger at slavery for keeping them illiterate. 'There is one sin that slavery committed against me,' professed one ex-slave, 'which I will never forgive. It robbed me of my education.'"[30] Knowledge and power were two sides of the same coin, and the ex-slaves recognized, perhaps even more clearly than their Northern supporters, that it was not possible to maintain freedom without books.

Denominational competition was a countervailing force in the great literacy campaign, as it was wherever Protestant churches wanted to influence public policy. American Baptists and United Methodists wrestled for the souls of black folks much as they had earlier battled for the alliance of white pioneers. There was an irony in this struggle. In the South, where both Baptists and Methodists drew much of their membership from the less advantaged members of society, few evangelical churches maintained rigid doctrinal lines and matters of profound theological difference were often transmitted as slogans, "once saved, always saved," "go on to perfection," and "holiness." If interdenominational strife was debilitating, intradenominational battles were even more discouraging. Baptists did not suffer as much from these as Methodists or Presbyterians, because their churches and associations were loosely connected to each other. And, at least before the Second World War, multiple affiliations of congregations were possible, and some churches might continue to use a Baptist society, particularly the American Baptist Publication Society, long after they had ceased to cooperate on other issues. Methodists, in contrast, wore themselves out in their intradenominational battles. The Methodist Episcopal Church struggled to establish congregations throughout the region and sharply distinguished its work from that of the African Methodist Episcopal Church and the Colored Methodist Church (later the Christian Methodist Church). The latter was a schism from the Methodist Episcopal Church, South, that had some support, officially and unofficially, from that body. The African Methodist Episcopal Zion (AMEZ) Church, a denomination with a history similar to the larger AME Church, was also active in the South.

One of the more ironic events in these intradenominational struggles illustrates the difficulty that white and African American missionaries had hearing one another. Perhaps because of the influence of Bishops Daniel Payne and Henry McNeill Turner, the AME Church was determined to provide leadership in the literacy battles. In his first formal words to the freedmen after the Emancipation Proclamation, Payne had challenged the newly liberated African Americans of the South: "Permit us, also, to advise you to seek every opportu-

30. Anderson, *Education of Blacks,* p. 5.

nity for the cultivation of your minds. To the adults we say, enter the Sunday Schools and the Night Schools, so opportunely opened by Dr. Pierson, in behalf of the American Tract Society. In these latter you can very soon learn to read the precious Word of God, even before you shall have a familiar knowledge of the letters which constitute the alphabet."[31] Further, the AME Church leaders were determined that no one would be received as a deacon or elder who did not have sufficient literacy to use the denomination's Course of Study profitably.[32] When the Methodist Episcopal Church ordained some illiterate African Americans, they faced an angry African American Episcopal hierarchy that suspected the ordinations were motivated as much by racism as by a desire to put religiously effective leaders in the field.[33] The AME Church had expected more from its fellow believers. Bishop J. P. Campbell conveyed their intense disap-

31. Daniel Alexander Payne, "Welcome to the Ransomed," in *Afro-American Religious History: A Documentary Witness*, ed. Milton C. Sernett (Durham, N.C.: Duke University Press, 1985), p. 219. The sermon was preached after Lincoln freed the slaves in the District of Columbia.

32. In discussing Methodists of all denominations and all races, it is important to note that there are many forms of ministry ranging from exhorters to bishops. All Methodist groups used exhorters, for example, whose primary credential was their own experience with Christ. Some of these in all Methodist groups were illiterate. There were also various types of local ministers who were not in full connection whose work was closely supervised. Deacons and elders, however, were in what was called full connection and had wide-ranging responsibilities for both the delivery of religious services and the administration of the church.

33. For the sad effect of intra-Methodist battling, see Clarence Walker, *A Rock in a Weary Land: The African Methodist Episcopal Church during the Civil War and Reconstruction* (Baton Rouge: Louisiana State University Press, 1982), pp. 80-95. Walker's judgment on the motives of white Methodists is more charitable than my own: "To disprove the charge that it was a racist institution, the M.E. Church, North began ordaining blacks and sending them South. Initially the church licensed thirty men to preach to the freedmen. When compared with A.M.E. ministers, they were not well educated; only four could read and none could write. Possessing only the rudest elements of an education, they made up for this difficulty by being spirited evangelists. The message they brought to the ex-slaves was hot and unadorned. In sending out such emissaries, the M.E. Church, North may have been trying to capitalize on the southern black's taste for 'spirit' and not 'larnin' in religious matters. The church may also have been trying to outflank its black competitors by allowing its new communicants to give full vent to their emotions" (p. 91). It seems to me that the white Methodists had a stereotype of the freedmen and selected ministers who fit that stereotype. Only later, it seems to me, did they recognize that their picture of African Americans as emotional children without serious intellectual interests had to be modified. But even then, the history of separate ordination requirements for whites and African Americans continued, at least through the Central Jurisdiction, and in some areas continues today. Among the saddest effects of American racism was the belief, even among whites who otherwise wished the African American well, that emotion always dominated the history of the race. The number of young and able black theologians who were, so to speak, slaughtered in their mother's womb is beyond measure.

pointment: "We . . . did hope that as the mother . . . of Methodism had means without men, and the African A.M.E. Church . . . had men without means . . . our mother would furnish the means, and let us furnish the men."[34] But such dreams were not to become realities.

The successes of the initial drive for black literacy are remarkable. Within a generation the rate of illiteracy went from almost 95 percent to 70 percent, and down to 30 percent by century's end.[35] Among ministers, the rate of decline was even more rapid. By 1900 almost all the black clergy were able to read and to use the many self-help resources available to enterprising people who had to make it in a society without formal credentials or the education that supported those certificates.

It is part of the irony of African American history that African American churches and people were not the prime beneficiaries of the drive to teach the freedmen to read. The Southern planter class had not supported public education before the Civil War, and they continued to question its value even after that conflict. Superior education was, after all, a major element in their social, political, and economic hegemony, and they wished to maintain it as a class prerogative. But the determination of African Americans to secure at least a rudimentary education brought pressure on the former Confederacy to provide some educational advantages for at least their white citizens. African American agitation for schools led to universal free public education — for whites.

IV. From Literacy to Colleges

Literacy cannot be separated from other African American educational goals. While white Southerners often believed that the region was being inundated in Yankee schoolteachers, the facts were otherwise. Even before the passion for reconstruction began to fade, there were never enough young idealists to do the job. African Americans and white missionary leaders both realized that unless significant numbers of African American teachers could be found, most people of color would remain untaught.

Almost from the beginning, there were two strategies for meeting this crying need. The first was through the normal school. Normal schools, or teacher training institutes, had spread through the North as free, compulsory education became a regional norm. Basically, the normal school provided pro-

34. Cited in Walker, *A Rock,* p. 88.

35. Their 95 percent illiteracy rate in 1860 had dropped to 70 percent in 1880 and would drop to 30 percent by 1910. Anderson, *Education of Blacks,* p. 31.

spective teachers with some substantial intellectual training and some practical instruction in how to teach. While many American educators shared a vision of the undergraduate college, at least before the advent of the university, there was less consensus about the nature or level of normal school education. The better schools of education appear to have been almost at college level and, later, at university level, while the weaker schools may not have exceeded a ninth- or tenth-grade level.

The other approach to teaching placed it in the context of the larger liberal arts tradition. A person who had received classical training in Greek and Latin was believed to be well fitted to communicate knowledge to others. Thus, young men in college were often used during their vacation months as rural schoolteachers, and many a young intellectual spent a few years as a tutor to a rich family or as a teacher in a private school before launching a career. The popularity of the English public school model, especially as connected with Thomas Arnold and Rugby School, added an intellectually potent mix of romanticism and enlightenment to this tradition. This tradition, further, had the advantage of linking teaching with other professions based on liberal learning, especially ministry, and as the standards in those professions rose, law and medicine. The liberal arts tradition also provided a breeding ground for intellectuals and for other leaders.

The most famous examples of African American normal schools in the South were Hampton Institute and Tuskegee Institute. Both schools modified a system, manual labor, that was rapidly passing out of fashion among white educators. Basically, manual labor schools claimed that students needed hard work, usually in agriculture, to maintain their health while studying. Manual labor was also believed to be an antidote to the elitism that was an intrinsic part of the liberal arts tradition. Occasionally, the obvious point was made that student labor defrayed a substantial portion of the expenses of maintaining an institution.

Samuel Chapman Armstrong, the founder and primary organizer of Hampton, was a graduate of Williams College who had served as the colonel of a black regiment during the Civil War. As with many whites involved in the earliest days of African American education in the South, Armstrong held a curious mixture of equalitarian and racist beliefs. As an equalitarian, he believed that the African American should be educated and supported the aspirations of many people of color. Yet he also believed that African American horizons were limited and that their future place in America was largely confined to positions in manufacturing and agriculture. He had serious questions about whether African Americans should be allowed to vote and believed that the freedmen's ballots had elected some of the worst governments in American history. Although these beliefs might seem paradoxical to a present-day American,

Armstrong was able to blend them into a successful educational program that provided students with sufficient education to function as educators, while at the same time providing them with much experience in what were believed to be "Negro" positions. Little training was provided in the more skilled trades or in the use of the new machinery that was changing the shape of American life. But, as James Anderson has pointed out, the purpose of Hampton was not to provide industrial workers; it was to provide teachers who would help African American students be content with their lot.

Armstrong's most successful disciple was Booker T. Washington. The Tuskegee Institute, which Washington was later to make famous, was originally established by Lewis Adams in the basement of the Butler Chapel, an AMEZ church. Adams asked Armstrong for a teacher for this one-teacher school, and Armstrong sent Washington, a young Hampton graduate. Although Washington disagreed with some of his former teacher's more racist beliefs — for instance, he believed former slaves should have the ballot — he basically continued the Hampton tradition. Students were expected to learn through hard work and to earn their way through the school. In some cases, such as the night school program, it is hard to see how the students had time or energy enough for substantial study after a day of work in the fields.

Washington was an excellent educational administrator; equally significant, he was also a persuasive speaker and writer who formulated his ideas clearly and concisely. These natural talents made a leader and spokesperson. But he was also cautious. Unfortunately, his early years at Tuskegee corresponded to the period when Southern white reaction to Reconstruction was gathering steam. As the older generation of whites, which had many positive personal experiences with African Americans, died, they were replaced by a new generation that had grown up with the exaggerated racial ideologies of the reaction to Northern rule. These younger whites were determined to complete the tasks their parents and grandparents had left them. Under what were called the Virginia and Mississippi plans, they managed to disenfranchise their black neighbors and to establish a system of legal segregation that went far beyond anything sanctioned by earlier Southern social customs. The federal government blessed the new order directly and indirectly. In 1883 the Supreme Court held in a series of cases that private acts of discrimination were not contrary to the national civil rights law, and in 1896 in *Plessy v. Ferguson,* the Court maintained that as long as the states provided "equal but separate" facilities, segregation met the constitutionally guaranteed test of equal rights.

Perhaps the bitterest pill to swallow was civil service reform. Since African Americans had been the primary supporters of the Grand Old Party in the South, they had benefited from the traditional practice of allowing the party in power to designate the holders of offices. But from Hayes through Roosevelt, public sentiment turned against the "spoils system," especially on the national level, and the number of jobs to be distributed by the victors declined. In many ways the nation did benefit from an increasingly professional and well-credentialed bureaucracy, but throughout the South, civil service reform also meant the purging of African Americans from the federal payroll.[36] By 1890 the Negro was legally and economically at the lowest point since emancipation. Had African American futures been sold on the Chicago Board of Trade, they would have had few takers.

In was in this context that Booker T. Washington advocated the so-called Atlanta Compromise. In a speech at the Atlanta Exposition of 1895, the noted educator in effect offered white Southerners a deal that he felt they could not refuse. The terms of this compromise were that African Americans would accept social and political discrimination, even though Washington himself strongly supported the African American right to vote. In exchange, white Southerners would allow African Americans the right to develop their own economic lives and their own institutions. The combination of education, agriculture, and mechanics taught at Tuskegee was of course well suited to this compromise, as it prepared African Americans for the variety of the positions open to them in the South. Washington's decision to add in 1893 a Bible school, modeled on the training schools in the North, completed the number of occupations available at his institution.

Yet, we must be careful not to attribute too much to the Atlanta Compromise. Unlike most compromises, this one was not accepted by accredited representatives of either race, and neither race felt bound to its terms. If many African Americans in the South did not rebel when they were disenfranchised, it was not because Washington advised them to be content with their lot. With the loss of real support from the national government, the terror tactics adopted by Southern whites were effective. The long arm of "Judge Lynch" and the white supremacists' control of state governments had far more impact than the words of any educator. Nor did white Southerners allow African Americans to develop themselves economically. When jobs were plentiful, some positions were made available to African Americans, but when the economy turned downward, those same jobs were taken by downwardly mobile whites. But that

36. It would have had the same effects, perhaps, upon Irish, Italian, and other Northern ethnic groups, except that their primary power was in city and state government where ethnically based machines continued to have strong influence. Just as there was a hidden, and not so subtly hidden, antiforeign rhetoric among Northern progressives, there was a more open and frank anti-African tinge to national civil service reform. The Pendleton Act (1883) was, after all, passed in Cleveland's term with the support of Southern Democrats.

is not to say that Washington's point of view did not have consequences. As we will argue below, Washington's words helped to tip the direction of black education, including education for the ministry, toward such training schools as Tuskegee and away from the colleges.

The other great by-product of the literacy drive was the development of independent black colleges in the South. The AMA played a significant role in this process. At a prayer meeting at First Congregational Church of Washington, D.C., in 1866, several members, including General Oliver O. Howard, the newly named head of the Freedmen's Bureau, raised the issue of a theological school for African Americans. Perhaps because the Northern victory had made it a season for dreams, these determined reformers kept expanding their proposals until they had advocated a full university. The times were unusually ripe for such a venture. Congress and the president approved the charter of the new institution in 1867, and the national government continued, even after Reconstruction receded, to make financial grants to the school. To avoid unnecessary entanglements between church and state, the AMA funded the theological department, which was self-consciously ecumenical.[37]

Straight University in New Orleans was another AMA school that began with a full-fledged program. When the school opened in 1867, it had full departments of law and medicine as well as normal, preparatory, and arts departments.[38] Although the departments of law and medicine did not survive past 1877, due in large measure to financial problems and a serious fire, their existence set an important precedent. Straight was supported by the African American community of New Orleans, a community that had much in common with other Caribbean mulatto and octoroon communities, including a substantial number of successful professional people and a few individuals with considerable wealth. Although many leading African American families in this community were Roman Catholic, the college had their enthusiastic support as well.

But if such schools as Straight and Howard sprang, so to speak, full-blown from the head of Zeus, this was not true of most of the early colleges established by the AMA or the other white missionary organizations. In retrospect, the thirst for colleges among African Americans was almost impossible to satisfy. Among the schools founded by Northern missionary societies were

37. Howard's establishment of a nondenominational theological school was perhaps the earliest such school in the nation, well ahead of such better-known undenominational schools as Yale, Harvard, or Union. The need for educated teachers and preachers was initially too pressing among African Americans to permit them (or their white supporters) the luxury of denominational exclusivity.

38. For the story of Straight, see Joe Richardson, *Christian Reconstruction*, p. 132.

Talladega College and Tougaloo College (AMA); Bennett College, Clark University, Claflin College, Meharry Medical College, Morgan College, Philander Smith College, Rust College, and Wiley College (Methodist Episcopal Church); Benedict College, Bishop College, Morehouse College, Shaw University, Spelman Seminary, and Virginia Union University (American Baptist Home Mission Society); Biddle University (now Johnson C. Smith), Knoxville College, and Slip-on Seminary (Presbyterian Board of Missions for Freedmen). As soon as they had acquired sufficient financial capacity, the major African American churches also established their own colleges. Many of these church-related schools were established from 1880 to 1900, often on the foundations laid by earlier common schools and academies. Among these institutions were: Morris Brown (1884); Paul Quinn College (1881); Allen University at Columbia, South Carolina (1881); Shorter College (1886); Kettle College (1886); Edwards Waters College (1888); Payne University (1889); Campbell College (1890); Turner College (1890); and Lampton College (1911).

African Americans were determined that these schools would succeed. Early in its history Fisk in Nashville found itself without sufficient funds to sustain its program. The students organized into a chorus, the Jubilee Singers, that toured the North and Europe, singing African American music. Their efforts were sufficient to save the financially embattled school. The costs to the African American denominations of establishing and maintaining these schools was great. The bishops of the AMEZ Church, for instance, each pledged one-fourth of their salaries to help create Livingston College. Joseph Charles Price, Livingston's first president and chief financial agent, was among the most versatile of college fund-raisers, traveling to New York to plead with the Dodges and Carnegies one week, and addressing a conference of impoverished AMEZ pastors the next week.

The early African American colleges were educationally complex institutions. Most often they began slowly as places where basic literacy and perhaps some normal courses were offered. In the early 1870s and 1880s, they began to develop collegiate departments and to encourage their brighter students to complete the full college course. This transition was an important moment, and the schools — and their white supporters — were deeply aware that too serious compromise with standards would make those degrees worthless or, worse, the object of racist jokes. Most such colleges, at least in the early days, had only a handful of students in the more advanced programs, with the bulk of the students in the various preparatory departments. The continuation of preparatory departments was not always a purely voluntary matter. Even after *Plessy v. Ferguson* (1896) mandated "separate but equal" education, many Southern communities refused to recognize the need for African American high schools, and when they did in the 1930s, these schools tended to be seriously substandard. When the Southern states began to establish their own African American agricultural and mechanical colleges in the 1890s, they tended toward the same pattern. When Benjamin Mays attended South Carolina State College, for example, he enrolled in the high school department.

When African American colleges established departments of theology, as many of them did, these departments reflected the complexity of the schools at large. The same class might include students with little more than a common school education, some that were doing college work, and perhaps a handful who had finished college. At the beginning this was not as remarkable as it later became. After all, the two most prominent schools for ministers in the South, Southern Baptist Theological Seminary and Vanderbilt, also enrolled students whose academic preparation ranged from common school to college. Like their African American counterparts, these Baptist and Methodist schools had classes with students that ranged from high school onward under the same instructor. The pattern of combination classes continued until the 1950s in some areas of the South, and it was only gradually ended as government regulation and accreditation forced a rise in standards. African American educators appear to have felt these problems as acutely as their white counterparts, perhaps more so, since they often had to live with an even greater educational gap in the same classroom. They labored hard, as did their white counterparts, to reserve the bachelor of divinity degree or its equivalent for those with college degrees, the bachelor of theology degree for those completing four or five years of primarily college study in theology, and various certificates, diplomas, and the like for other students.

African American colleges elected to follow the most rigorous curricula available for their various programs, and their catalogues sparkle with courses in Latin, Greek, and mathematics. When a new teacher with a new skill joined a faculty, that person immediately taught that skill to others. In this way, most schools came to have fairly comprehensive programs that included the principal sciences, branches of mathematics, and modern European languages. The beginnings of formal African American studies at such places as Atlanta University, where W. E. B. Du Bois introduced them around the turn of the century, represented a significant development in American intellectual life.

The limit was money. The various white denominations that supported African American schools, including the Congregationalists, were themselves strapped. American Protestantism was in perpetual financial crisis and disarray. Few denominations, including the most numerous, had the funds even to provide all their clergy with a living (much less a middle-class) income, and most Protestant wealth was invested in land and buildings. Even such popular missionary enterprises as the institutional church movement, an attempt to reach out to the urban poor with a variety of social and recreational programs, and the even more popular foreign missionary drive were perpetually undersubscribed. Collegiate and seminary education was not at the top of the list of priorities, and African American higher education was a much lower priority. As higher education moved away from relatively inexpensive set curricula toward elective systems, increasingly sophisticated professional specializations, and better-trained faculty, the churches' capacity to meet the new financial requirements lessened. Whatever other factors contributed to the gradual retreat of the churches from the colleges in the twentieth century, the need to cast their nets over an ever wider expanse was among the most important. In other words, most white, non-government-supported schools went through a process of secularization as they struggled with the problems of finances.[39] If philanthropy was not the only force driving private higher education, it was an important factor in the shaping of twentieth-century colleges.

Unfortunately, for the black colleges of the South, the basic strategy of American philanthropy toward African American education in the crucial period from 1901 to the Depression was set comparatively early. In 1901, philanthropist Robert Ogden, a member of the Tuskegee board and a strong supporter of African Americans, persuaded many of his fellow millionaires — including John D. Rockefeller, Jr. — to join him on "the millionaires' special."[40] The destination of the train was the American South, where the millionaires were to examine African American education firsthand at Hampton Institute, Tuskegee Normal and Industrial Institute, and Spelman Seminary. The latter school, in Atlanta, was already a noted Rockefeller charity that was named for John Sr.'s wife and was strongly supported by Ohio Baptists. But they were not the only places or persons on the itinerary. At the turn of the century, some Southern whites, inspired by progressivism and the dream of a "New South," had launched a major campaign to improve Southern white education. Many of these Southern leaders were members of the Southern Edu-

39. For a discussion of some of the impact of fund-raising on Protestant schools, see Dorothy Bass, "The Independent Sector and the Educational Strategies of Mainstream Protestantism," in *Religion, the Independent Sector, and American Culture,* ed. Conrad Cherry and Rowland A. Sherrill (Atlanta: Scholars, 1992). Dr. Bass rightly emphasized the role of the Carnegie Foundation in setting some early secular guidelines that tended to secularize schools. The reason philanthropists were so important was not only that they had money and often ran organizations staffed by dedicated executives. More important was the perpetual financial disarray of American Protestantism.

40. For the story of the train, see John Ensor Harr and Peter J. Johnson, *The Rockefeller Century* (New York: Scribner, 1988), p. 74.

cation Association, a body of philanthropists and college administrators that composed an unofficial lobby for Southern institutions. Among the members of this group were Robert C. Ogden, George Foster Peabody, William H. Baldwin, J. L. M. Curry, Walter Hines Page, Charles Denny, Charles D. MacIver, Edwin A. Alderman, Philander Claxton, and Edgar Gardner Murry. At the almost obligatory meeting of the association attended by the millionaires, Charles Dabney, president of the University of Tennessee, claimed: "Nothing is more ridiculous than the programme of the good religious people from the North who insist on teaching Latin, Greek, and philosophy to the Negro boys who come to their schools."[41] Other members of the association, such as Governor George B. Aycock of North Carolina and legal educator Henry St. George Tucker of Virginia,[42] argued that the millionaires had to consider the claims of white institutions along with the claims of African American institutions. Tucker put the issue in these words: "If it is your idea to educate the Negro you must have the white of the South with you. If the poor white sees the son of a Negro neighbor enjoying through your munificence benefits denied to his boy, it raises in him a feeling that will render futile all your work, you must lift up the poor white and the Negro together if you would ever approach success."[43] The message the philanthropists received was mixed. African Americans needed and wanted education. But the best schools for them were those like Hampton and Tuskegee that stressed manual labor. Perhaps most important, white educational needs, already met largely through taxation, had to be met at the same time as the supposedly more modest needs of African Americans. It was an interesting mix of idealism, racial stereotypes, and firsthand knowledge. But it did inspire action.

When Rockefeller Jr., who was beginning to manage the family's extensive philanthropies, returned home from this junket, he went to work. He enlisted the aid of his father's philanthropic chief of staff, Frederick Gates, and Dr. Wallace Buttrick. Both were former Baptist pastors and graduates of Rochester Seminary. With them he established the General Education Board (GEB) to aid Southern education. The sheer size of Rockefeller's contribution, more than $50 million, would have made the GEB the most significant player on the field of African American education, but the board had more power than its substantial financial muscle would indicate. At one time or another all the

41. Anderson, *Education of Blacks,* p. 86. I am deeply indebted to Anderson's discussion in this section.

42. Tucker believed in the economic aspects of the progressive program but strongly advocated states' rights and segregation.

43. Ron Chernow, *Titan: The Life of John D. Rockefeller, Sr.* (New York: Random House, 1998), chap. 24, especially pp. 481-83.

leading philanthropists, or more important, their advisers on giving to African American institutions, sat on it; the board conducted what was in effect a postgraduate seminar on education in the South. In the main, the other foundations, including the Peabody Fund and Stokes-Phelps, the Jeanes Fund, and the Rosenwald Fund, followed the well-researched and well-presented lead of the GEB.

In concrete terms, this meant that the major American philanthropists and their foundations decided at a crucial point to put the bulk of their money for African American higher education into Hampton, Tuskegee, and similar schools and, in the main, to bypass the black colleges. The emphasis for black education was thus to be on training teachers for common schools, in industrial and agricultural education, and in Bible school–type training for the ministry. To be sure, the GEB could not completely turn the tap on or off. The Rockefellers continued to support Spelman as a family philanthropy, and Carnegie generously provided the AMEZ Church's Livingston College with an excellent library building. But the generalization still holds: the millionaires had gone South, and if they did not return whistling "Dixie," they did come home with a point of view that many white Southern educators supported.

The new direction of philanthropy was not uncontested. The various church missionary societies continued to insist that the African American colleges were of supreme value and to argue for their endowment and support. This direction also contributed to one of the classic confrontations in African American history. W. E. B. Du Bois, a professor at the AMA-sponsored Atlanta University, stepped forward as the advocate of what he called the Talented Tenth. The term "talented tenth" itself was borrowed from Baptist denominational executive Henry Morehouse, a strong advocate of African American higher education. Du Bois, a graduate of Fisk and Harvard who had also studied abroad, wrote with the passion that comes from experience. For him there was no doubt that African Americans needed a black intelligentsia that might inspire the race and make a significant contribution to American culture. With gentle irony he noted in *The Souls of Black Folks:*

> If the Negro was to learn, he must teach himself, and the most effective help that could be given him was the establishment of schools to train Negro teachers. This conclusion was slowly but surely reached by every student of the situation until simultaneously, in widely separated regions, without consultation or systematic plan, there arose a series of institutions designed to furnish teachers for the untaught. Above the sneers of critics at the obvious defects of this procedure must ever stand its one crushing rejoinder: in a single generation they put thirty thousand black teachers in the South;

> they wiped out the illiteracy of the majority of black people of the land, and they made Tuskegee possible.[44]

But this very success, he maintained, should inspire a determination to complete the African American education that "began with higher institutions of training, which threw off as their foliage common schools, and later industrial schools, and at the same time strove to shoot their roots ever deeper toward college and university training."[45] In fact, "no such educational system has ever rested or can rest on any other basis than that of the well-equipped college and university." The discipline of the colleges, he believed, was the essential need of his own times "to maintain the standards of the lower training by giving teachers and leaders the best practicable training; and above all, to furnish the black world with adequate standards of human culture and lofty ideals of life."[46]

The debate with Washington (and really with the philanthropists that were the real target of Du Bois's anger) led him to appraise the work of the missionaries that had established African American colleges and universities. Du Bois, who had been at Fisk when the racism of some administrators was all too evident, was more than willing to admit that the missionaries had their flaws. "They made their mistakes," he wrote, "those who planted Fisk and Howard and Atlanta before the smoke of battle had lifted; they made their mistakes." Yes, but there are mistakes and there are mistakes. These errors "were not the things at which we lately laughed somewhat uproariously," but the foibles of men and women who had the truth firmly in them. In a moving tribute Du Bois wrote:

> That was the gift of New England to the freed Negro: not alms, but a friend; not cash, but character. It was not and is not money these seething millions want, but love and sympathy, the pulse of hearts beating with red blood;— a gift which to-day only their own kindred and race can bring to the masses, but which once saintly souls brought to their children in the crusade of the sixties, that finest thing in American history, and one of the few things untainted by sordid greed and cheap vainglory. The teachers in these institutions came not to keep the Negroes in their place, but to raise them out of the defilement of the places where slavery had wallowed them. The colleges they founded were social settlements; homes where the best of the sons of the freedmen came in close and sympathetic touch with the tradi-

44. Du Bois, *Souls of Black Folks,* p. 96. As Du Bois pointed out again and again, Tuskegee was dependent on people trained in the black colleges for its own staff.

45. Du Bois, *Souls of Black Folks,* p. 98.

46. Du Bois, *Souls of Black Folks,* p. 97.

tions of New England. They lived together, studied and worked, hoped and harkened in the dawning light. In actual formal content their curriculum was doubtless out-fashioned, but in educational power it was supreme, for it was the content of living souls.

The truth that the New England missionaries brought was not of course its local and parochial traditions; that truth was the centrality of the university tradition. In words that call to mind John Henry Newman, Du Bois said:

> Nothing new, no time-saving devices — simply old time-gloried methods of delving for Truth, and searching out the hidden beauties of life, and learning the good of living. The riddle of existence is the college curriculum that was laid before the pharaohs, that was taught in the groves by Plato, that formed the trivium and quadrivium, and is to-day laid before the Freedmen's sons by Atlanta University, and this course of study will not change; its methods will grow more deft and effectual, its content richer by toil of scholar and sight of seer; but the true college will ever have one goal, — not to earn meat, but to know the end and aim of that life which meat nourishes.

In other words, "the roots of the tree, rather than the leaves, are the sources of its life; and from the dawn of history, from academus to Cambridge, the culture of the university has been the broad foundation-stone on which is built the kindergarten's ABC." If the South was to have a future, it lay with those men and women who built schools, not with those who advocated black inferiority or wanted to keep the poor whites from finding the good that their souls needed:

> The Wings of Atalanta are the coming universities of the South. They alone can bear the maiden past the temptation of golden fruit. They will not guide her flying feet away from the cotton and gold; for — ah, thoughtful Hippomenes! — do not the apples live in the very Way of Life? But they will guide her over and beyond them, and leave her kneeling in the Sanctuary of Truth and Freedom and broad Humanity, virgin and undefiled. Sadly did the Old South err in human education, despising the education of the masses, and niggardly in the support of colleges.[47]

Du Bois's clever play on words in this passage should be noted. Atalanta was the maiden in Greek mythology that offered to marry any man who could best her in a footrace; Atlanta, the city of railroads (originally named Terminus), was

47. Du Bois, *Souls of Black Folks*, p. 82.

likewise swift. But Atalanta had been both bested and, paradoxically, fulfilled when she paused in her race with Hippomenes to pick up the Golden Apples that her lover and rival had dropped. Of course, Atlanta — that proud city — should also stoop for the "Truth and Freedom" dropped by her universities.

Du Bois viewed the African American church with the loving eye of a critical historian. He knew that the church had been the first institution to pass into African American control, and he was aware that the African American pastor, like the Negro teacher, was one of the formative figures in his people's history. Du Bois also recognized with a clarity that few of his or our contemporaries have seen that Southern religious culture was not European but "Euro-African."[48] "The Methodists and Baptists of America owe much of their condition to the silent but potent influence of their millions of Negro converts." But he also knew that the days of the "preacher, the music, and the frenzy" were already beginning to pass. Like many other commentators on African American religion, he knew that the black churches "must necessarily be affected more or less directly by all the religious and ethical forces that are to-day moving the United States," and this meant that a new type of African American minister had to emerge.[49] Du Bois, like many other thoughtful people of his time, hoped this new minister would be armed with a new, more social and religious message than the older African American clergy had taught.[50]

V. An Important Report

About the same time Robert Kelly was publishing his survey of theological education, he collaborated with Mr. W. A. Daniel on another survey, *The Education of Negro Ministers.*[51] Like the earlier survey of predominantly white seminaries, this one was sponsored by the Institute of Social and Religious Research. In many

48. I use the word "Euro-African" to distinguish the culture of the American South from other Caribbean cultures, such as that of Cuba or Brazil, where many of the African influences are closer to the surface.

49. Du Bois, cited in C. Eric Lincoln and Lawrence H. Mamiya, *The Black Church in the African-American Experience* (Durham, N.C.: Duke University Press, 1990), p. 6. The need for a better-educated black ministry is consistently cited in the literature of the African American churches from Du Bois through Mays and Nicholson to Mamiya and Lincoln.

50. Du Bois's attitude toward the need for theological reconstruction was similar to that held by other observers of the American scene. His criticism of black religion is similar to the criticisms of generations of white Baptists and Methodists.

51. W. A. Daniel and Robert Kelly, *The Education of Negro Ministers* (New York: George Doran Co., 1925). I used the reprint: New York: Negro Universities Press, 1969.

ways the study reflected the strengths and weaknesses of all the Rockefeller-sponsored religious studies.[52]

The institute's projects tended to have distinguished advisory boards, and this one was no exception. It included, among others: C. H. Parrish, Simmons University (Louisville); James Dillard, GEB; Galen M. Fisher, from the institute; John Hope, president of Morehouse College; George R. Hovey, American Baptist Home Mission Society; Alfred Lawless of the AMA; and Dr. J. W. Perry of the AME Church.

The advisory board and its membership were significant parts of the enterprise. Rockefeller advisory committees tended to be extended seminars that brought together the leaders of a particular Protestant endeavor. In a real sense the meetings of these leaders, although infrequent, were as significant as the books the researchers published. In effect, Rockefeller was sponsoring conversations among those who were able to advocate and make changes in a particular area. Whether the Daniel/Kelly report "caused" or even "contributed" to change is not clear, but it did mark the end of the earlier philanthropic tendency to support industrial education. Both Hampton and Tuskegee, encouraged by Southern laws requiring college graduation for licenses to teach, became degree-granting institutions, and new support for African American colleges was evident in the philanthropic community.[53]

Galen Fisher, the foundation executive who commissioned the study, noted in his introduction that "care was exercised not to impose preconceived standards upon the Negro schools."[54] Like other white philanthropists, he was concerned that African Americans not be embarrassed by the gap between schools they maintained and white institutions. He need not have been as apol-

52. It would be useful to compare this study with the other Rockefeller-sponsored study of the African American church, Benjamin Mays and Joseph Nicholson, *The Negro's Church* (New York: Institute of Social and Religious Research, 1933). If anything, the crisis of the Depression convinced Mays, a University of Chicago–trained black educator, that the theological and other problems of the African American church needed urgent attention. The hidden theme of Mays's doctoral dissertation, *The Negro's God as Reflected in His Literature* (Boston: Chapman and Grimes, 1938; New York: Russell and Russell, 1968), is that African American thinking about God needed to break free from the shackles of tradition and deal with contemporary intellectual and moral problems. Mays and Nicholson, like other pre–civil rights movement commentators on African American religion, were convinced that the church would lose the younger, more urban black population if it did not make substantial theological changes.

53. Far less sympathetic to black hopes for an improved ministry was Thomas Jesse Jones, *Negro Education: A Study of the Private and Higher Schools for Colored People in the United States,* U.S. Bureau of Education Bulletin 1916, no. 38-39 (Washington, 1917). The Jones report basically approved the older Tuskegee model.

54. Daniel and Kelly, *Education of Negro Ministers,* p. vii.

ogetic. African Americans, including Daniel, were deeply aware that their institutions had serious problems. The hard-hitting study of African American religion by Ira De A. Reid in *Divine White Right,* a later Rockefeller production, and the more widely noted study by Mays and Nicholson were as unsparing as any reports on American faith might be.[55] Daniel was among those advocating a realignment of American theological education.

Daniel and Kelly admitted that African American schools had many of the problems of their white counterparts. In that sense the report contained the familiar litany, also found in the Flexner and Kelly reports, of too many schools, too few dollars, and too low academic standards. But many of the particular problems of African American schools could be traced to their particular educational structures. Unlike white schools, most African American schools were part of larger institutions that were already overburdened by the number of tasks imposed on them. Only two of the fifty-two schools studied were independent institutions: Gammon, maintained by the Methodist Episcopal Church, and Bishop Payne, maintained by the Protestant Episcopal Church. Gammon had begun as part of Clark University in Atlanta and maintained a close relationship to that school, somewhat similar to the relationship of Garrett Biblical Institute to Northwestern. Interestingly enough, Gammon was largely supported by an endowment left by Rev. Mrs. Elijah Gammon, initially of $200,000 and later of almost $600,000, given in 1887.[56] Bishop Payne, a very small school in Petersburg, Virginia, was named after the first American Episcopal bishop in Africa. Only two of the surveyed schools would attain Association of Theological Schools accreditation prior to 1960: Howard and Gammon.

The close relationship with the colleges created serious problems. The study noted that these colleges, especially those modeled on Hampton and Tuskegee, were moving toward becoming full-time colleges and that the schools established by state governments were increasingly determining the standards for the private African American institutions.[57] In other words, the African American schools were responding to the same cultural forces that were encouraging the standardization of white colleges. As limited resources had to be allocated to different departments, theological schools found themselves on the tag end of the budget.

55. Ira De A. Reid, "The Church and Education for Negroes," in *Divine White Right: A Study of Race Segregation and Interracial Cooperation in Religious Organizations and Institutions in the United States,* by Trevor Bowen (New York and London: Harper and Brothers, published for the Institute of Social and Religious Research, 1934).

56. For Gammon and finances, see Bowen, *Divine White Right,* p. 276.

57. Daniel and Kelly, *Education of Negro Ministers,* p. 34.

> The rate of improvement of the theological departments in the matters on which standardizing agencies rate institutions of learning, has not been as high as for the college, high-school and teacher-training departments. Thus, although the theological departments are improving, they are, and are considered the tag-ends of the institutions. While the colleges are making every effort to square with the requirements of recognized standardizing agencies, the seminaries benefit only indirectly, and not fully, from this tendency. Some of the leading Negro theological schools have terms from two to six weeks shorter than the best Negro colleges, all of which have school years of thirty-six weeks. In many of the less promising theological departments the length of the year (in hours) is shortened by the omission of Monday or Friday classes, by the virtual suspending of classes during the sessions of some of the denominational conferences or associations, by the press of administrative duties where the president teaches the theological classes, or by the absence of the theological teacher when he is attending to the affairs to a church of which he is pastor or when he is soliciting money for the school.[58]

In other words, the theological schools were as much the victims as the beneficiaries of rising standards in African American education. Not surprisingly, many schools would drift out of the business of training ministers as they focused on the larger task of training African American leaders.

In moving away from ministerial training, African American colleges were basically following a much larger national trend. The Southern white denominational colleges, many of which continued to train ministers in their large Bible and religion departments until the 1960s, were less typical of the nation as a whole. But whereas the withdrawal of the Northern colleges from theological education made the seminaries more important, African Americans did not own or control such a variety of institutions. Changes in college education, thus, did not always contribute substantially to the improvement of African American theological education. Even at Howard, the one black school that was approaching university status, the theological department was comparatively neglected. Only with the coming of Benjamin Mays as dean in the late 1930s did the gap between its work and the work of the other departments begin to close.

The comparative neglect of the collegiate theological departments served to reinforce many of the problems of the ministry. Twentieth-century studies of African American churches indicate that African Americans are only margin-

58. Daniel and Kelly, *Education of Negro Ministers,* p. 44.

ally, if at all, more religious than their white counterparts and that their churches, at least as much as white churches, tend to have a strong majority of female members. From Du Bois onward, the consensus has been that the more educated and urban black population has been less formally religious than their rural predecessors. While the prominence of the black churches (or some of them)[59] in the civil rights movement has partially restored the prestige of the African American churches, these problems have remained. In other words, the situation of African Americans in the twentieth century has tended to shift both wealth and status away from the black ministry and toward other professions, especially such highly prestigious fields as medicine, law, and teaching. The question asked by R. E. Park and cited in Daniel/Kelly and elsewhere was important: "How can a so-called 'profession' gain the full status of a profession when most of its constituents have had no real preparation, and are required to measure up to no standards comparable to other professions in order to enter or continue in its ranks?"[60] The interviews Daniel and Kelly conducted with African American college students supported Park's observation. Most of them rejected, or at least questioned, the prevalent belief that ministers were somehow specially called by God, and most believed that there was a need for higher educational standards for the ministry.[61] At the same time, these same factors pressured African American colleges to neglect or abandon their work in theological education. In other words, declining status meant declining support from educational institutions; in turn, declining support from educational institutions meant a further decline in status.

Daniel and Kelly noted another very important aspect of the African American schools, especially those owned by black denominations: "Of the fifty-two schools included in this survey as having a department or school of theology thirty-four were founded by Negroes. These schools are maintained only at considerable sacrifice. But they are a source of great pride to all who consider themselves a part of this tripartite organization: (1) the supporting and controlling constituency, (2) the administrative and teaching staff, and (3) the students."[62] Interestingly, the same pride was developing in schools established by white denominations that were gradually moving toward African

59. The civil rights movement was a major factor in the split of the National Baptist Convention into two separate denominations.

60. R. E. Park, "Education in Its Relation to the Conflict and Fusion of Cultures: With Special Attention to the Problems of the Immigrant, the Negro, and Missions," *Publications of the American Sociological Society* 8 (1918): 50. The quote is found in Daniel and Kelly, *Education of Negro Ministers,* p. 14.

61. Daniel and Kelly, *Education of Negro Ministers,* pp. 95-96.

62. Daniel and Kelly, *Education of Negro Ministers,* p. 32.

American leadership. In general, this first happened with the appointment of an African American dean or deans and was often completed with the election of a black president. John Hope was a hero for many African Americans wanting power over their own institutions.

Daniel and Kelly noted that racial pride in African American institutions did not imply that these schools differed materially in their aspirations from their white counterparts. "The curricula of the former and of the latter are convincingly alike."[63] Other problems were also much the same as those among white Americans. Interviews with African American college students indicated that they were similar to their white counterparts in rejecting much of the popular Protestant moralism (no drinking, no smoking, no dancing) and in their acceptance of liberal, even modernist, ideas about religious faith.[64] The college students were signs that African Americans were entering the larger culture, and, if so, could their clergy be far behind?

The Daniel/Kelly report was written at a time when both African American expectations were rising and American racial conflict was increasing. A combination of events had propelled African Americans away from their southern homeland: the advent of the tractor and mechanized farming, the First World War and the concurrent decline of immigration, and perhaps above all, the desire for a measure of decency and human respect. African Americans had served honorably and well in the armed forces and had demonstrated their capacity to lead as well as follow.[65] Their reception in the land of Lincoln was not what they had anticipated. Race riots and the Northern revival of the Ku Klux Klan were part of the African American experience of the North in the 1920s. In

63. Daniel and Kelly, *Education of Negro Ministers,* p. 33.

64. Daniel and Kelly, *Education of Negro Ministers,* pp. 60-99. More than any other section of the book, these interviews indicate how far much of the African ministry was from the best of young Negro opinion, perhaps one reason why Daniel and Kelly included the section. Franklin Frazier, himself a product of this younger generation, repeated many of the same criticisms in his critique of the black church. See C. Eric Lincoln, ed., *The Negro Church in America* [by] E. Franklin Frazier; *The Black Church since Frazier* [by] C. Eric Lincoln (New York: Schocken, 1974).

65. Whether Woodrow Wilson, the first Southern-born president after Reconstruction, was more racist than his predecessors or not, he had strong views against the integration of black troops into white units. He worked even against the inclusion of significant numbers of black troops in Pershing's American Expeditionary Forces. Nonetheless, in part because the draft called up significant numbers of African American men, many did serve, and served honorably. The experience increased their pride in themselves and their desire for more status at home. Only at one point did the war impede African American education. Neither African Americans nor the children of immigrants performed well on these culturally biased tests.

addition, the system of residential and religious segregation became, if anything, more rigid. Even in those predominantly white denominations where they had a historic place, including the Methodists and the Congregationalists, African Americans were locked in their own congregations and their own judicatories. But the new black immigrants into the cities had already begun to put down their own roots. They had purchased church buildings from formerly white congregations and established some prestigious pulpits. And for the first time the public schools, including the high schools, were open to them. The Harlem Renaissance and jazz pointed to the general creativity of black culture. The long period of firsts — when the first African American to do this or that was a genuine historical event — seemed to be ending. Both African Americans and to some extent whites were not surprised when a young African American entered a career or was appointed to a position.

But the Depression hit African Americans and their churches hard. The South was in many ways the first area affected as agricultural prices fell hard in the early twenties. The so-called Negro jobs that Booker T. Washington and others had counted on as the foundation of future black prosperity went to displaced whites from the countryside, who organized labor unions to keep the blacks out of the better jobs. As the crisis spread northward, as a cancer might spread first to the lymph nodes and then to the brain, economic disaster followed economic disaster. The churches were among the first African American agencies to feel the pinch. When the whites had sold them in the 1920s, they had sold at the top of the market and the African American purchasers had given notes that they now strained to pay. The funds that might have encouraged more of the Talented Tenth to invest their lives in the churches were always in short supply; now they were not there at all. If one were purchasing "futures" on black clergy, the prices were definitely low.

CHAPTER SEVENTEEN

Troubled Decade, Troubled Churches

As Robert Handy and William Hutchison have argued, the 1920s were a crucial decade for the inherited Protestant establishment. In many ways the bottom fell out as the various Protestant churches suffered serious financial difficulties and had to substantially reduce their expenditures. Many local churches that had borrowed heavily in the religious heyday of the 1900-1920 period found themselves almost bankrupt. Although the church market began to revive in the late 1930s when the nation was preparing for war, the argument can be made that the 1920s marked the end of the Protestant churches as an informal establishment.

Yet the more serious impact of the 1920s, at least in retrospect, was the spectacular decline in the church's intellectual stock. In simple terms, people stopped looking to the churches for answers and began to see Christianity and the churches as part of the problem. While this was not completely unprecedented, it was a somewhat new phenomenon. During the earlier crises over Darwinism and biblical criticism, many people assumed that the churches would provide answers to these vexing problems, and early liberal theologians were convinced they would find a way through the difficulties that confronted faith. Perhaps the best term for this earlier period is "progressive." Its spokesmen believed that much had been done and much would be done. The progressive world was a world of "assured results" in biblical studies, of confident "new theologies," and of steady social, scientific, and technical progress. Under the leadership of an enlightened and inspired American Protestantism, the nation and the world were at the end of the old order and the birthing of the new. What distinguished the 1920s was that this world of progressivism, Protestantism, and privilege died, seemingly overnight.

In many ways the crisis in American church life was less serious and less widespread than the intellectual and cultural crisis in contemporary Europe. In England, Germany, and France the war marked the passing of the older orders of privilege as death and taxation ate away at the material and spiritual supports of the older bourgeois order. The orderly world of the idealists and of historical development was replaced by the disorderly world of Einstein, Nietzsche, Freud, and Jung. The underground culture of sexual experimentation and radical politics, left and right, began to break through into daily life. The world of arts and letters was dominated by experimentation and what was called "modernism." These same forces, although somewhat weaker, also impacted American life and contributed to the sense of crisis.

The twenties were crucial for the evolution of American theological education. The seminaries, faced with mounting losses, had to step back and answer the question of what they did well and what they did poorly. Although generalizations are risky, the overall prestige of the ministry, rarely high in the United States, also fell. Sinclair Lewis knew that many people would recognize Elmer Gantry, his fictional Baptist and later Methodist preacher. Lewis suspected rightly, further, that the irony of the portrayal would not be lost on an America that read and appreciated H. L. Mencken, Walter Lippmann, and John Dewey. Lewis was right. The book was a best seller, and Elmer Gantry became a byword for a type of evangelical minister. After Elmer Gantry, no seminary could avoid the question of the status of the minister in the community. Was the clergyperson the professional leader of an American institution or just another person trying to make a buck in any possible way?

Elmer Gantry was not only about the ministry. Lewis reserved his most subtle ironies for American Protestantism itself. The churches, as he pictured them, were an ironic survival from the past whose present was often a matter of ballyhoo. From revolving electric crosses on the tops of poorly constructed buildings[1] to its dogged determination not to discuss the issues that affected people's lives, the whole edifice was rotten at the foundations.

1. The revolving cross was the hallmark of the Reverend Bill Stidger, a Methodist minister, who had been one of those who had urged Sinclair Lewis to write a novel about the ministry. Stidger was a master of church publicity and of the stunts that clergy were often using to attract crowds. Unlike Gantry, however, no one ever accused Stidger of sexual immorality. See Jack Hyland, *Evangelism's First Modern Media Star: The Life of Reverend Bill Stidger* (New York: Cooper Square Press, 2002). Stridger ended his career as professor of evangelism at Boston University.

I. Seeds of Conflict

Religious conflict was not original with the 1920s. Protestantism is a religion of the Word and of words, and the latter always has produced heated debates, polarizations, schisms, and heresy trials. For all the fundamentalist-modernist rhetoric of the 1920s, the decibel level may not have exceeded that of the Old School–New School Presbyterian division or matched the noxious insults with which frontier Baptists and Methodists consigned each other (as well as Freemasons, Mormons, and advocates of free love) to the bottomless pit. And the rhetoric of the great division over slavery produced its fair share of recriminations and accusations. Perhaps equally important, the period from 1870 to 1920 had not been free of passionate controversy.[2] Many issues in the progressive period were similar to the ones that ignited the battles in the 1920s: the interpretation and authority of Scripture, the nature and goal of the missionary enterprise, the place of scientific reasoning and conclusions in faith, and eschatology. Beneath these questions were issues that were perhaps more abstract, but like all serious theological issues, they were also central to faith: whether God was personal and transcendent or an impersonal force in nature, whether Jesus was "Lord and God" or a moral exemplar (or perhaps only the founder of a religion), and whether Christianity was a final or ultimate revelation or only one of the religions of humankind.[3] These issues produced the noisy public trials of the 1890s and 1900s, and in one form or another divided Protestantism in the 1920s. The environment in the 1920s, however, gave them a particular nastiness. There were five factors that gave old debates new edges: consumerism, the new racism, educational expansion, war weariness, and imperialism. Like multipliers in some economics of the spirit, these large social developments accelerated the intellectual and moral crises of the church.

2. Historians such as Grant Wacker, "The Holy Spirit and the Spirit of the Age in American Protestantism, 1880-1910," *Journal of American History* 72 (June 1985): 45-62, and Donald Dayton, *Discovering an Evangelical Heritage* (New York: Harper and Row, 1976), have performed an important service by pointing out that the bonds of unity remained strong throughout this period. Wacker makes clear that early liberals, especially those concerned with the social gospel, were as concerned with the Spirit as were the most avid attenders at Keswick, and Dwight L. Moody was supported by many on different sides of the issues.

3. Arthur Schlesinger, "A Crucial Period in American Religion," *Massachusetts History Society Proceedings* 64 (Oct. 1930–June 1932): 523-46, is a classic discussion of the extensive intellectual discussion of the late nineteenth century, as is Paul Carter, *The Spiritual Crisis of the Gilded Age* (De Kalb: Northern Illinois University Press, 1971). To be sure, this crisis did not produce as many open secularists in America as in England or Germany, but it was both deep and profound. Indeed, the uneasiness of faith may have been one of the roots of the overheated activism of the period.

A. A Nation of Consumers[4]

Perhaps the strongest leitmotif of the twenties, at least before the Great Crash, was good old-fashioned avarice. Whatever was true militarily, the United States won the world war economically, and the nation was as determined to cash in its chips as any European prime minister was to extract territorial, colonial, or other concessions. For the first time the nation was out of debt to European investors and its businessmen had a more or less clear field at home and abroad. As radios, tractors, automobiles, and home appliances poured from the assembly lines, advertising became a highly respected and paid profession. The only way to keep the machines running was to stimulate the demand side of the economy to make people want more and then more again. The result was a culture of consumerism, symbolized by the rise of General Motors with its flashy yearly model changes, carefully class-targeted vehicles, and showroom glitz. And General Motors was many times a child of the war: its capital was provided by DuPont from munitions profits, its methods of production developed to meet the needs of wartime production, and its advertising applied the techniques of wartime propaganda to the showroom. Similar observations might be made about the other major corporations, such as Radio Corporation of America, that dominated the ticker tape.[5]

Consumerism accentuated the traditional American definition of choice as the deepest meaning of freedom. Every day, or so it seemed, Americans were confronted with a world of proffered choices that seemed almost endless. The automobile, the great contraption, was valued in part because it could promote choice. With an automobile, young people could choose to date far from the prying eyes of parents; with an automobile, one could free up Sunday (and for the middle classes, all of Saturday as well) for a picnic or a jaunt, or if so inclined, one could easily attend a church in a place far from the streetcar lines and neglect the neighborhood places of worship. Churches responded by spending large sums, even if they had to be borrowed, to build splendid new buildings that might attract the now mobile crowd. But cars were only one of the items that poured from the cornucopia; clothing, washing machines, vacuum cleaners, radios, packaged foods, cheap books, watches, paint, lawnmowers, cigarettes, soft drinks, and gadgets of all kinds were plentiful. American productivity and creativity had no end.

4. Hence, Paul Carter's marvelous title, *Another Part of the Twenties* (New York: Columbia University Press, 1977).

5. Warren Susman, *Culture as History: The Transformation of American Society in the Twentieth Century* (New York: Pantheon Books, 1984), and Warren Susman, "Piety, Profits, and Play: The 1920s," in *Men, Women, and Issues in American History,* ed. Howard T. Quint and Milton Candor (Homewood, Ill.: Dorsey Press, 1975).

The message of consumerism was, you are what you consume. The Book-of-the-Month Club, established in 1926, was more than a clever marketing scheme: it was a way for Americans to purchase culture. The purchaser of the monthly selection was told he or she was a person of culture, a member of the elite, who had read the most important books. Interestingly, the Religious Book Club quickly followed the larger company's example, and stressed the importance of ministers and religious works projecting an up-to-date image. The essential message was everywhere. Your choice in cigarettes, your car, your pet, your listening habits on the radio, your clothing — they all identified you as part of a certain group. If these products invited people to live in a world of fantasy, then that was all right. Where else could one enjoy a Walter Mitty Turkish adventure for the price of a pack of smokes?

Advertising fueled this economy. In addition to creating artificial demand, advertising performed the educational task of making Americans aware of the latest products and their virtues. Everywhere one looked, the new ads were present: on the walls of barns, by the side of rural roads, in shop windows, in newspapers and magazines, and of course, on the radio.

Advertising underwrote the growth industries of radio, newspapers, and magazines. The value of the ads, of course, varied directly with the capacity of the particular media to grab and hold the attention of a large number of readers. When events were not dramatic enough — and "real" news was often dull — artificial news had to be created. Dance marathons, flagpole sitting, attempts to capture the world's speed records, sports, and other such activities were sponsored, directly or indirectly, by the media as a way of attracting the public's eyes and ears. By the nature of things, these artificial stimulants had a limited "run" as the spice of one story quickly satisfied the taste and, at the same time, created a yearning for another treat. But this made little difference to either the media or their advertisers; the bottom line was the same whether one dealt with the truly significant or the merely popular. Hype became as American as Mark Twain.

Perhaps most important, radio became part of most Americans' daily lives as both the number of sets and stations multiplied. In America, unlike Europe, the development of this new technology was in private hands, and the new stations had to enlist "sponsors" to pay for increasingly expensive programming. Radio advertisements created demand as slogans and jingles became increasingly well known. Cigarette advertisements, for instance, made Lucky Strike Green a household name and helped to create the idea that cigarette smoking was part of the lifestyle of younger (and more style-conscious) Americans. Radio programs made celebrities overnight as they caught and held popular attention. Although some ministers became noted as radio preachers, including Harry Emerson Fosdick and Samuel Parkes Cadman, few churches used the medium effectively.

Aimee Semple McPherson (1890-1944), a Canadian-born evangelist who founded the Angelus Temple in Los Angeles, mastered the 1920s media as effectively as any American, including those who ran the film industry. Early in her career McPherson learned that she had to create news events for the press, and her publicity stunts provided her crusades with better publicity for free than she could ever have hired. Nor did her use of popular media stop at the press. McPherson's worship services drew upon the traditions of the American stage, particularly vaudeville. She often staged dramatic pageants that illustrated theological and biblical themes and, like the movies, used children wherever possible to increase human interest. Early aware of the power of radio, the Angelus Temple was topped with a large transmitter that carried her voice throughout Southern California.

The conjunction of the media and mass consumption had consequences for the place of religion, especially of Protestantism, in American life. Both radio and the press searched constantly for those stories that might increase their audience, if only by a few points, since the value of advertisements was related to the strength of the medium. Whatever sold papers or airtime was what was featured. Bruce Barton, a noted advertising agency head, argued in *The Man That Nobody Knows* that Christ had used the techniques of modern advertising to further his cause, and countless ministers resorted to various advertising techniques to increase Sunday congregations or to build their Sunday schools. Sermon titles were often slogans and were posted prominently outside the church to catch the eyes of passersby. Advertising-type techniques were used to build church programs, such as Sunday schools and stewardship drives, and independent missionary agencies were often more like advertising concerns than solemn attempts to expand Christ's kingdom. In retrospect, McPherson's offense was not what she did, but the fact that she did it so well.

If radio was the great trendsetter of the 1920s, the movies had a growing impact on the nation's sense of style. Some of the early "silent" films demonstrated the capacity of film to tell stories with a power and immediacy greater than the stage, and *The Jazz Singer* (1927) increased the capacity of film to make an audience feel that they had actually participated in the story. Although some religious films were made, the media had more influence as a mirror of American taste and opinion. Its secularity, thus, reflected the mores of many Americans and suggested a more secular pattern of life to others. The Roman Catholic Church and the various Protestant churches mounted a passionate and intense campaign to keep sexual behavior off the screen and finally established a system of censorship. Censorship bore an ironic testimony to the power of the churches. Clearly, it indicated that they had enough power to get their way; it also indicated that had it been permitted a free choice, the nation might not have elected virtue.

B. Battles over Race

If one set of issues dominated the thinking of many Americans in the 1920s, it was the whole constellation of questions surrounding race and race relations. The world war had created its own hysteria. The teaching of German was banned in many schools, and although many immigrants from the Austro-Hungarian Empire claimed they were fellow battlers against monarchy, these erstwhile children of freedom also suffered. When the war ended, the rhetoric of those who opposed the League of Nations raised the specter of Americans losing their freedom to people of alien races and alien values. In addition, the Russian Revolution of 1917 had its impact. Perhaps the least significant American response was to join Britain and France in an abortive military intervention. In fact, more bullets hit the American soul than penetrated American bodies. Attorney General A. Mitchell Palmer, himself a victim of an anarchist attack in 1919, launched a series of investigations of "Reds" that died down quickly. But the fear of Russian Communism was not as easily banished. The nation would feel its effects for decades.

The war itself had revealed an America that many Anglo-American Protestants did not know existed. The American armies had a significant proportion of men who did not know English or have any ties to the nation or its ideals. In many ways they were similar to those who filled the German or Austrian trenches. The question whether such troops could have sustained a longer conflict was a real one, and political and religious leaders demanded the "Americanization" of America's ethnic communities. Aided by such wartime fears, the push for the restriction of immigration, an old progressive cause, became almost irresistible. In 1924 the Johnson-Reed Act passed, although the nation's overheated economy needed additional supplies of cheap labor. Anti-immigrant feelings were one of the primary inspirations for the Northern Ku Klux Klan.

The historian must be careful not to exaggerate the impact of the antiforeign movement. Anti-immigrant feelings, for example, did not defeat Al Smith in 1928. Smith entered that race with everything against him: he was a wet in a nation that was legally dry, a Catholic in a nation with a large Protestant majority, a big-city candidate in a party dependent on the rural

South, and a man with little cultural or scientific couth in a nation that was in love with experts, education, and efficiency. His candidacy was further complicated by the fact that since the Civil War, the Democrats had been the minority party, having elected only two presidents. Further, he was opposed by a popular American hero, Herbert Hoover, who represented the nation's cultural center. Hoover, widely credited with helping Europe back on its feet, was an engineer, a friend to the big business that most believed made America prosperous, and a dry. Given these impediments, the amazing thing is not that Smith was defeated, but that he did as well as he did. No wonder Smith wanted a rematch four years later, only to see the party nomination fall to another scion of the American nobility, Franklin Roosevelt.

Although much of the anti-immigrant sentiment was specifically directed against Roman Catholics, especially those from eastern and southern Europe, the movement had more than a hint of the anti-Semitism then troubling much of Europe. The American State Department was noted for its anti-Jewish animus, as were a number of the larger American corporations. Henry Ford, who was watching his rivals at General Motors take over much of his traditional market, was obsessed by the perceived Jewish "threat" to American values. Not only did he spread his views through the Dearborn *Independent,* but he also spread them through his willingness to bankroll the publication of such pamphlets as the *Protocols of the Elders of Zion.*

Immigrants were only part of the problem. "Scientific racism" was popular in the 1920s as studies claimed to prove that there were intrinsic differences between the various races. Scientific theories of race were part and parcel of the very popular eugenics movement that hoped to find ways to prevent those with genetic defects from reproducing. Laws were passed, for example, that mandated sterilization after the second illegitimate child. One of the major arguments in the birth control movement was that it would enable society to limit the reproduction of "undesirables."

Scientific racism was part of the climate of opinion that produced the Immigration Act of 1924 that gave the largest quotas to northern and western European countries. The same line of thinking supported American anti-Semitism and its elaborate system of quotas and exclusions. But the most visible targets of the new racism were African Americans who were entering the North in significant numbers. When the world war slowed immigration to a trickle, American business leaders turned to other sources of cheap labor. Semi-skilled African American workers provided an apparently endless pool. These workers had real economic assets: they were familiar with American culture, most were literate, and their religious and ethical values were similar to those of the dominant white culture. The 1920s story was similar to what had happened earlier when African slaves had been introduced as an alternative to white indentured servants or Native American slaves in the seventeenth century. At that time African slaves gradually became dominant, because they brought substantial skills with them from Africa that were better suited to their new environment than other available sources of cheap labor. In much the same way, black immigration in the 1920s included many people who were culturally prepared for life in the new mass manufacturing enterprises of the North and Midwest.[6] In other words, black labor succeeded not because African Americans were inferior, but because they formed an effective, available, and inexpensive workforce.

As often is the case, economic success made possible a cultural flowering. Black writers, musicians, and entertainers created the "Harlem Renaissance," jazz became part of the larger American cultural idiom, and big-city African American churches became religious and cultural institutions with influence beyond the black community.

The new anti-African sentiment was everywhere. Woodrow Wilson, who owed his election in large part to the South, had extended legal segregation to the District of Columbia early in his presidency, and de facto segregation, especially in housing and education, tightened throughout the North. Once the world war ended, a series of race riots racked the nation as angry whites resorted to violence to "protect" their jobs and neighborhoods. Particularly in the North, anti-immigrant feelings merged with antiblack sentiment. Blockbusting was practiced in cities — a real estate technique where a white purchaser would buy a house for top dollar and then transfer the ownership to an African American owner, thus convincing other whites to sell, often for very low prices. Whole subdivisions became black ghettos almost overnight. Since the home was often the only investment that lower middle-class whites enjoyed, the result was widespread loss of capital and social position. Anger was everywhere. The Ku Klux Klan, originally part of the guerilla war that Southern whites waged against Reconstruction, revived and had considerable political power in such Northern states as Pennsylvania and Indiana. *Birth of a Nation,* a film that was as advanced technically as it was racist ideologically, drew large crowds in every American city. The new Klan drew much of its operating mythology, not from the earlier Klan, but from the film. The burning of crosses, for instance, was not a technique of the old Klan, which depended on lynchings. For many white Americans, Harding's promise of normalcy meant a return to antebellum racial practices, and despite the Republican

6. See David Goldberg, *Discontented America: The United States in the 1920s* (Baltimore: Johns Hopkins University Press, 1999).

Party's historic commitment to African Americans, he and his successors were willing to bow to this demand.

If nothing else, the sustained battles over ethnicity and race in the 1920s created a climate of opinion that was angry and cantankerous. People assumed that national unity could be achieved, if at all, only at considerable cost. Equally important, racial and ethnic tensions were ideologically free-floating elements in the national air; hence, they could be (and often were) combined with other grievances or even hidden in them, like leaven in a lump, as a motive force. Further, they posed moral dilemmas that few wanted to face. Thus, the question whether one should side with the white residents who saw the value of their homes, often their only investment, greatly reduced by blockbusters or with the African Americans who desperately needed housing was anxiously debated by ethicists and others. Of course, one could also denounce the real estate agents who often profited from the deal by selling one home at an artificially high price, knowing they would collect commissions both on it and on the subsequent sales, but that did not address the structural issues.

C. Educational Changes

As American business became increasingly concentrated in the larger corporations, the role of education changed. Colleges and universities became part of the American culture of aspiration, to use a term coined by David Levine.[7] Both businesses and young Americans came to see the college as a natural place for a young man with ambitions to begin his career. In part, this was because of the growth of such new professional schools as those of engineering and forestry, but the expansion of vocational education does not explain the phenomenon. Regardless of their major, businesses and government saw college-trained people as the best candidates for the most prestigious positions, and those entry positions with the clearest chances of advancement came to require the "degree." At the same time, there was the hidden, if perhaps more influential, pressure of a more subtle change in the new economy. The traditional beginning places for the young middle-class male had become economically less important. Small businesses were becoming part of larger bodies — witness for instance the rise of the A. & P. supermarket as the rival to the more traditional mom-and-pop local store — and law, perhaps the quintessential American gateway to the upper middle class, reserved its richest rewards for those in corporate practice. During

7. David O. Levine, *The American College and the Culture of Aspiration, 1915-1940* (Ithaca, N.Y.: Cornell University Press, 1986).

the Depression, people saw college training as a strong foundation for a middle-class job that was relatively protected from the worst of the business cycle.

The corporation and the increasingly complex federal bureaucracy fit into American culture at another place: the increasing exaltation of expertise and the expert. Americans had long been fascinated with efficiency and with the best way of doing things, and the 1920s saw this belief become an almost unchallenged cultural axiom. Part of Hoover's appeal was that he was a genuine expert who seemed to have the specific knowledge necessary to make government work, and Franklin Roosevelt, his aristocratic successor, played to this same confidence in the expert with his "brain trust" and various study commissions. While the various American Ph.D. programs were primarily designed to produce scholars and researchers, popular opinion saw them as producing "experts" who had a magisterial command of their subject and its application to daily life. If the difference between experts and scholars was subtle, it was real. Americans distrusted "scholars" with as much intensity as they embraced "experts."

The "culture of aspiration" changed higher education in other subtle ways. To be sure, despite the pipe dreams of academics, young people had always attended college for other reasons than the educational foundation it provided. College and, later, university education was part of the preparation of a gentleman — a finishing experience, if you will — that helped to develop the social graces needed to function in high places in the established order. In other words, nineteenth-century students who went to college did not need college to make a living. Their social location ensured their future. But the shift to a culture of aspiration was a movement away from such aristocratic mores toward a more middle-class ethos of competition, joining together in a common cause, and of course, skill in personal relationships. Much of this education was resolutely noncurricular; it was taught in the YMCAs, the fraternities, the various sports activities, and the dormitories. With the irony of real life, the partial separation of what the faculty taught from what the students came to learn freed the faculty to pursue more of their own interests. Far less time had to be invested in the lives of students.

The progressive incorporation of higher education into the culture of aspiration accelerated some other changes. For one thing, the increased enrollment allowed schools to increase the scope of their operations, especially the very profitable undergraduate departments. Research benefited from the general prosperity. By the 1920s, moreover, the larger colleges and universities were increasingly relying on alumni to financially support their increasingly complex enterprises. This shift was particularly important for the place of Protestantism in American higher education. The churches were rarely as important as sources of support, direct and indirect, for the schools, a fact reflected in the often-noted rapid decline in the number of clergy serving as presidents or as members of governing boards. Presidents were increasingly academic professionals who worked their way up the ranks, while boards came to represent those who paid the bills, a school's real public.

The connection between the culture of aspiration, the students, and finances helps us understand the gradual withdrawal of religion from its apparently central position in the Victorian college and even such "late" Victorian schools as Harper's University of Chicago or Timothy Dwight III's Yale. Kenneth Scott Latourette, the great Baptist church historian and missiologist, noted that secularization had begun from the bottom up.

> Since my student days at Yale I had been concerned with the seemingly inevitable drift from their moorings of colleges and universities begun by earnest Christians. . . . The secularization was first in the student bodies with the enrollment of men who either were not concerned with the faith or opposed it. It then spread to the faculties and finally captured the trustees. I sought to suggest possible ways of reversing the trend. The Board was sympathetic, but took little action. Again and again in a variety of ways I attempted to obtain attention to the problem in more than one denomination, but with little if any success.[8]

The turning point that was reached in the 1920s, in other words, happened when those students who had little formal religious interest matured and became either faculty members or trustees. They were no more committed to the religious character of their schools as faculty members or trustees than they had been as undergraduates. The Christian character of schools, thus, may have decayed as much from the bottom up as from the top down.[9] Indeed, many presidents of colleges may have continued to use the older language long after it was descriptive of their institution or its goals and purposes.

The result was a shift in the atmosphere of higher education. Schools became, if not wholly secular, at least more this-worldly. Gaius Glenn Atkins noted: "When such men as Hyde of Bowdoin, Buckham of Vermont, Tucker of Dartmouth, Dwight of Yale, Carter and Hopkins of Williams, Harris of Amherst and Seely of Smith were succeeded by specialized administrators

8. Kenneth Scott Latourette, *Beyond the Ranges: An Autobiography* (Grand Rapids: Eerdmans, 1967), p. 121.

9. For another view, see George Marsden, *The Soul of the American University: From Protestant Establishment to Established Nonbelief* (New York: Oxford University Press, 1994). Marsden stresses the spread of certain ideas about education as the cause of changes in the system, while I am more inclined to point to social and cultural shifts.

training in the technique of education, something was lost in the age-old relation of religion to education of inestimable worth to religion, to education, and to the integrity of society. Religion had at least lost its intellectual prestige for the undergraduate and became an errant and optional ghost."[10] If the older Victorian rhetoric of an enlightened Christianity did not wholly vanish, it became more a matter for civic and public occasions, a rhetoric that was not necessarily backed by a belief that the truths and unities celebrated were more than a convenient mythology.

Perhaps the most appropriate symbol of this transformation was the changing nature of sociology. Unlike the European sociology of such religious critics as Max Weber and Emil Durkheim, American sociology had its origins in the progressive push to Christianize society. Many early courses in the discipline were taught by clergy or by people, like Chicago's Albion Small, with close ties to the American churches. However, by the 1920s this religious and semireligious approach to the subject was no longer in vogue. The new sociologists wanted to elevate their discipline to a science, and this meant removing the "do-gooders" from positions of power in their departments. Despite the excellent studies being performed by the Institute of Social and Religious Research, a Rockefeller charity, the sociologists of the decade managed to divorce their discipline from religion and from social reform.[11] Similar changes were taking place in philosophy at much the same time.[12]

American Protestant leaders of many different persuasions were troubled by this new world. The YMCA, for instance, experimented with new programs — far less concerned with missions and evangelism — for its college chapters. Perhaps more importantly, informed people, such as Charles Foster Kent of Yale Divinity School, began to search for ways to incorporate the study of religion into the collegiate program. But even Kent's best efforts could not hide the fact that he was seeking a religious appendage to what had become a secular enterprise.

D. The Aftermath of War

The First World War holds an important, if not the premier, place in the history of barbarism. From August 1914 to November 1918 European youth systemati-

10. Gaius Glenn Atkins, *Religion in Our Times* (New York: Round Table Press, 1932), p. 226.

11. S. Reed Myer, Jr., "After the Alliance: The Sociology of Religion in the United States from 1925-1949," *Sociological Analysis*, Fall 1982, pp. 189-204.

12. Bruce Kuklick, *A History of Philosophy in America, 1700-2000* (Oxford: Clarendon, 2001), pp. 199-259.

cally slaughtered each other. The battles were fought over extended fronts that permitted hundreds of thousands of soldiers to be committed to a fight at a single time. Armed with many of the most brutal inventions of a technological society, these almost endless waves of attack and counterattack were fueled by machine guns and, finally, by poison gas, tanks, and airplanes. Artillery remained the king of the hill, and the battles were so laced with explosives that authorities could not identify many bodies once the bombardments ceased. The pieces were too small to have identifying characteristics. The unknown soldiers, entombed in impressive monuments in every nation, might have been individuals, but were more likely a miscellaneous collection of the human debris from a platoon that was totally destroyed. All countries attempted to keep up the illusion that some of the older knightly virtues of courage and bravery were still present — medals were minted and distributed profusely — but the fact was that the war came as close to carnage for carnage's sake as any that humanity ever fought.

As if Satan had a sense of humor to match his cruelty, the war was fought in all countries for the highest ideals. The nature of this war made it essential to enlist the support of the whole population, which would not only have to bear the financial costs but, more importantly, also have to tithe the fruit of their bodies as well. The language of Christian faith and progressive ideals was mined deeply in all combatant countries, and perhaps the United States most of all. The Americans had resisted the war at the onset, preferring to take their profits, and substantial antiwar sentiment remained, even after the declaration. To enlist this people, many of whom were immigrants or the children of immigrants from the countries on the other side, Wilson had to reach deep into the traditional American rhetoric about faith, democracy, and above all, America's moral exceptionalism. Just as McKinley had justified the Spanish-American War by an appeal to American missionary idealism, so Wilson made the war to end all wars the greatest and most significant of all progressive and American crusades. Wilson set himself up for tragedy. Sometime before he left for the Paris Peace Conference, he had come to believe his own rhetoric and to adopt an overly simple understanding of his nation and himself. He went to Paris as a self-appointed messiah. Once there, his allies proved all too willing to use his delusions of moral superiority to manipulate him into a draconian peace. All that was left of his idealism after Paris was the League of Nations, and Henry Cabot Lodge was waiting, like a mountain lion in his lair, to feast on the already-emaciated body of his victim. In the end it was not close. Wilson, his body and mind weakened by stroke and disappointment, served out the last years of his second term only partly conscious of the world around him. American participation in the League died with him.

In many ways the wounded president was an apt symbol of the American progressive spirit. The progressive spirit had a comparatively long run in American political life. Beginning with the fears awakened during the labor unrest of the 1880s, it had matured into an attempt to apply the basic principles of Christian (Protestant) morality to the problems of the nation. Competition was to be protected, even if overly successful competitors had to be restrained; honest labels were to be put on food and drugs; and alcohol — long believed to be one of the causes of poverty and misery — was to be banned. Such ageless evils as prostitution were likewise to be suppressed, and both women and children were to receive legal protection. Women, long denied the rights of public participation, were granted the vote and the right to use it, partly in the hope that their moral purity might lift politics to a higher level.

Although the United States was comparatively untouched by the war — its losses in men and material were minute compared to those of England, Russia, or Germany — it was enough to be the death knell of the progressive movement. In simple terms, what happened was that the pieties of the previous generation were discarded. This was not because of a passionate public debate. Instead, the older progressivism went out of fashion as its ideas became unpersuasive. Many "modern" ideas, in fact, came to look quaint and vaguely old-fashioned, somewhat like the spats that some scions of the old order continued to wear. William Jennings Bryan, perhaps the nation's leading advocate of a genial Midwestern Protestantism, no longer looked like a white knight; rather, he looked like the previous century, despite his courage in opposing Wilson's initial steps toward war.

The effect of this on Protestantism was catastrophic. The link between Protestantism and progressivism was so intimate that one might call the progressive movement Protestantism in politics or Protestantism the progressive movement at prayer. Even in such conservative Southern states as Alabama, where new ideas were often kept at bay by orators stressing the dangers of racial revolution, Baptists and Methodists had accepted much of the progressive rhetoric.[13] E. Y. Mullins, president of Southern Baptist Theological Seminary, was not alone in his near hero worship of Wilson and his ideals. Progressivism also deeply influenced the successors of Dwight L. Moody, whose missions often featured social services for the poor as well as an uncompromising stance on such public evils as drink, prostitution, and gambling. On the foreign field, missionaries had long since incorporated major

13. For a good sense of the impact of progressivism on the South, see Wayne Flynt, *Alabama Baptists: Southern Baptists in the Heart of Dixie* (Tuscaloosa: University of Alabama Press, 1998).

elements of the progressive spirit into their work: they constructed colleges, universities, hospitals, and social service agencies as a way of reaching people with the gospel.[14]

The waning of the progressive spirit left many Protestant institutions in limbo.[15] The churches had constructed large bureaucratic structures to promote efficiency in their work, and local churches had developed a variety of ministries to serve their immediate areas. Many of these large institutional churches, of course, continued to flourish, and some even expanded in the 1920s, but much of the driving vision for this style of church work was gone.[16]

The loss of the progressive impulse was also felt in theology. American liberal theology had gone through a number of permutations. The movement had begun with the evangelical liberalism of the Andover liberals and such American "originals" as William Newton Clarke. By 1900 the best representatives of this tradition, such thinkers as William Adams Brown and Eugene Lyman, were taking their cues from the newer Ritschlian school in Germany. Brown and Lyman saw the Kantian emphasis of this movement as providing space for theological and philosophical speculation, while finding its christocentric emphasis an important bridge to popular American piety. "Jesus" was both a cultural and a religious icon. Although this type of liberalism continued for some years and never completely disappeared from American theology, by the 1920s a more radical form of modernism was becoming popular. Centered at the University of Chicago, this new liberalism had developed out of the work of such men as G. B. Foster. In place of the Ritschlian emphasis on the "essence of Christianity," the new modernists suggested a religious naturalism that could be established on empirical or semi-empirical terms. In time, the advocates of this position would combine its best insights with the new

14. The progressive foundations of much of fundamentalism of the 1920s is well-known. For an account of the progressive antecedents of William Bell Riley, certainly among the most militant of the fundamentalists, see William Vance Trollinger, *God's Empire: William Bell Riley and Midwestern Fundamentalism* (Madison: University of Wisconsin Press, 1990). Frank Norris, his Southern Baptist counterpart, had originally earned his spurs in crusades against vice and gambling.

15. Paul Carter, *The Decline and Revival of the Social Gospel: Social and Political Liberalism in American Protestant Churches, 1920-1940* (Ithaca, N.Y.: Cornell University Press, 1954); see also Donald K. Gorrell, *The Age of Social Responsibility: The Social Gospel in the Progressive Era, 1900-1920* (Macon, Ga.: Mercer University Press, 1988). Gorrell's study is especially valuable in this connection. He demonstrates the ways in which the progressive ethos became part of the very fabric of Protestant institutions, part of their raison d'être.

16. In the latter part of the twentieth century, many evangelicals would create a new form of the institutional church, the megachurch, which, like its predecessor, featured a wide variety of religious and social ministries that were provided seven days a week.

"process theology" introduced with the 1926 publication of *Process and Reality* by Alfred North Whitehead.[17]

What had changed in the movement from the older liberalism to Chicago modernism was not necessarily substance. Almost all liberals questioned or rejected the idea of a transcendent God, who was apart from time and space, and liberalism had tended to emphasize the work of essentially a great teacher whose life revealed the nature of God. The Scriptures were the imperfect record of this revelation. But what was different in the 1920s was that the new liberals or modernists did not speak with the same religious or moral conviction that earlier liberals had inherited from their orthodox ancestors. Nor could they, especially after the world war, speak with the same confidence of the inevitable progress of humankind.

Many younger liberal theologians, especially those closely connected to congregations, recognized the crisis. By middecade these younger theologians were expressing serious reservations about the optimistic core of traditional liberalism and looking for new directions. Harry Emerson Fosdick, for instance, wrote in 1922: "All the progress this world will know waits upon the conquest of sin. Strange as it may seem to the ears of this modern age, long tickled by the amiable idiocies of evolution popularly misinterpreted, this generation's deepest need is not these dithyrambic songs about inevitable progress, but a fresh sense of personal and social sin."[18] Other young American theologians, such as the talented Niebuhr brothers, were learning a similar lesson at the same time. If no American reached quite the heights of Karl Barth's *Epistle to the Romans* — one of the greatest works of theological protest in history — the end of the war found them ill at ease in Zion and ready to think in different ways.

E. A Crisis on the Foreign Fields

The world war marked the beginning of the decline of both the prestige and the power of the West in Asia and Africa. The question was no longer, for example, *would* India become independent, but it was more a question of *when.* Throughout Asia, liberation movements were proliferating as young Asians, newly convinced of the West's moral as well as military weakness, began to

17. For D. C. Macintosh see S. Mark Heim, "The Path of a Liberal Pilgrim: A Theological Biography of Douglas Clyde Macintosh" (parts 1 and 2), *American Baptist Quarterly* 2 (1983): 236-55, and (1985): 300-320.

18. Cited in William Hutchison, *The Modernist Impulse in American Protestantism* (Cambridge: Harvard University Press, 1976), p. 254.

work toward a postcolonial society. Only a handful of non-Western Christians had been present at Edinburgh 1910. By the 1920s their presence was increasingly felt at ecumenical and missionary gatherings.

One did not need Elijah to interpret the cloud the size of a human fist. There was a storm brewing abroad, and the question was more when it would begin than whether it would begin. Missionary leaders reacted to these changes in varied ways. Most wanted to increase their investment abroad while the opportunities were still available. But one major response — albeit on the part of only a minority — was that the church needed to be especially diligent in establishing those civilizing agencies, such as schools, YMCAs, and hospitals, that could help provide the foundations for a modern democracy. Of course, this represented a major shift in missionary strategy from conversion to nation building. The Hocking report, issued at the end of the decade and one of the most controversial documents in American religious history, summarized a decade of insecurity about the goal of American missions and suggested, not too gently, that the churches pursue the more this-worldly interpretation of their work.

II. The Controversies of the Twenties

The social, economic, and political changes of the twenties helped make the clash between the fundamentalists and the modernists into a bare-knuckled barroom brawl that left all the participants wounded. The tendency of historians, especially those blinded by the media accounts of the battles, is to reduce the battle to a bipolar contest in which two clearly defined sides slugged it out. But such interpretations miss, so to speak, the fog of ideological war. At a minimum, the battle involved at least three parties: the modernists or liberals, the conservatives or fundamentalists, and a moderate party. This latter group, in fact, held the balance of power in the influential Presbyterian and Baptist denominations. And the moderates' decision was not for liberalism or conservatism. The moderates wanted, above all, to hold together the denominations and to secure the missionary movement abroad. Robert E. Speer, the great Presbyterian missionary leader, and his YMCA counterpart, John R. Mott, were almost personifications of this central party in the churches.

On closer examination, neither left nor right had more than a modicum of theological coherence. The American liberal tradition, as mentioned above, was in a period of transition. The 1920s saw the beginnings of two significant modifications in that tradition: American realism and process theology. Few serious theologians were happy with what they had been taught, and most believed that the field was in disarray. In a real sense, liberalism was not prepared to speak as clearly in the 1920s as it had twenty years or so earlier.

Ironically, much of the American liberal tradition, particularly in biblical studies, had lost interest in the church. Particularly at Chicago, the study of the Bible had become an extension of general history, and there was a similar trend at such schools as Harvard, Union, and Colgate Rochester.[19] Despite the technical brilliance of much of the work of this period, particularly that of Shirley Jackson Case, Robert Pfeiffer, and Kirsopp Lake, who were deeply influenced by the history-of-religions method, it was often theologically unconcerned. Even allowing for some neoorthodox exaggeration, G. Ernest Wright perhaps accurately described his immediate predecessors:

> Yet the paths which they followed too exclusively so separated them from the work of the churches that in many seminaries during the period between 1920 and 1940 the work of the Old Testament department was looked upon by the students more with amusement than with respect; and the occasional young scholar who majored in the subject was frequently one capable of dealing only with technical details, in all the butt of considerable derision from his fellows in the practical departments or especially in the departments of philosophy and psychology of religion. Consequently, the first great generation of biblical scholarship before the first War was actually unable to reproduce itself, and the decline in quality and quantity of worthwhile output since then has been steady and lamentable.[20]

The great battle over the Bible was thus more a matter for theologians, philosophers, and preachers than for biblical scholars, who saw themselves beyond the fray. The conservative J. Gresham Machen was the biblical scholar most caught up in the struggle, and his interests were often more systematic than historical.

Conservatism was no more unified, and its divisions may have been deeper than those in the liberal camp. Although all conservatives rallied around the war cry "Back to the Bible," it was not always clear what they meant by that slogan. For those most deeply influenced by revivalism, this often meant the "old-time religion" that "was good enough for me." The "old-time" religion emphasized conversion and, above all, salvation through the shed blood of Christ. It was a faith for those "washed in the blood of the Lamb." But other

19. Robert W. Funk, "Watershed of the American Biblical Tradition: The Chicago School, First Phase, 1892-1920," *Journal of Biblical Literature* 95 (1976): 4-22, is very useful in describing these changes.

20. G. E. Wright, "The Study of the Old Testament," in *Protestant Thought in the Twentieth Century,* ed. Arnold Nash (New York: Macmillan, 1951), p. 23.

conservatives, particularly among Presbyterians and Lutherans, centered their theology on the confession of faith and the importance of fidelity to it. Most conservatives accepted biblical inerrancy, but what they meant by this was no longer as clear as it had been. Machen, for instance, accepted evolution as a reasonable interpretation of Genesis 1 and 2, and the Scottish thinker James Orr retained much popularity among conservative believers. Salted throughout the conservative movement were those who advocated premillennial dispensationalism and waited for the rapture.[21] Indeed, part of the reason the fundamentalists did not carry the day was the diversity within their movement. Every fundamentalist majority fell apart at its edges when victory seemed within its grasp.

Our picture of the 1920s is further complicated by the sheer complexity of American Protestant life. The American Protestant experience exists on a variety of levels. On the one hand, American Protestants tend to participate in a number of larger intellectual and social movements. Thus, one can talk about such phenomena as voluntary societies, revivalism, liberalism, fundamentalism, and popular religion. On the other hand, American Protestants tend to organize themselves into denominations and to interpret these larger movements in very denominational terms. To make matters even more complicated, individual congregations within denominations can often sustain their own religious culture, even in the face of considerable opposition from other members and churches in the denomination. These different templates invite debate over such issues as whether the various holiness and Pentecostal bodies were "really" fundamentalists, despite the popularity of the doctrine of biblical inerrancy and the Scofield Bible among them, or whether the Missouri Synod Lutherans were participants in the larger movement or American expressions of European confessionalism.[22] Such questions become even more pressing when dealing

21. Since the publication of Ernest Sandeen's *The Roots of Fundamentalism: British and American Millenarianism, 1800-1930* (Chicago: University of Chicago Press, 1970), most historians have seen premillennialism as part of the essence of fundamentalism. George Marsden has offered an important corrective in his *Fundamentalism and American Culture: The Shaping of Twentieth Century Evangelicalism, 1870-1925* (New York: Oxford University Press, 1980), but he may overemphasize the intellectual side of American conservatism. There were many who "believed the Bible from cover to cover, even when it said it was bound in genuine leather," who could not have parsed "inspire." But Marsden is much more on the mark when he stresses the importance of the intellectual side of fundamentalism for later evangelicalism.

22. Milton H. Rudnick, *Fundamentalism and the Missouri Synod: A Historical Study of the Missouri Synod* (St. Louis: Concordia, 1966). I found this volume useful in understanding the complexity of the debates as the Missouri Synod moved slowly from its first- and second-generation German ethnic ethos to share more of the general American cultural ethos. The larger conservative movement clearly had its appeal as individuals and congregations made this move.

with the conservative Christian Reformed Church that represented a European reaction against modernism. Throughout the 1920s this denomination's official publications stressed themes and doctrines similar to those stressed among fundamentalists, including anti-evolutionism.[23] In addition to the not-surprising articles about religious and moral decline, articles appeared that stressed the behavioral expectations of the later fundamentalist movement.[24] Christian Reformed theologians, such as Cornelius Van Til, came to be widely respected among fundamentalist Christians. Although operating from a more Wesleyan theological basis, the holiness and Pentecostal churches used much of the language of other aggressive conservatives. Wesleyan conservatives denounced modernism in religion with the same passion as they denounced modernism in women's dress or the use of cigarettes. What all these conservative movements had in common was, of course, a willingness to stand and do battle for the Lord.

To further complicate the picture, there was a "secular" fundamentalist movement that, while it shared some leaders with the forces in the churches — especially William Jennings Bryan[25] — had its fountainhead among members of state legislatures from smaller towns and cities who shared the anxieties of their people over America's moral drift. Anxious to do something to please their constituents, these legislators hit upon the idea of banning evolution from the schools. These small-town representatives were not necessarily the hicks that their opponents loved to castigate. They saw, as Bryan did, that evolution seemed to be directed against their fondest hopes and dreams, many of which were progressive in character, not reactionary. For Bryan and his followers, Christianity was a "reform movement." If evolution claimed it could cure human problems in a millennium, Bryan believed, then the doctrine of the new birth could point to their much more rapid eradication. Further, the twenties, like the sixties, were a period in which sexual ethics were anxiously and publicly

23. During his American journey, theologian Abraham Kuyper had surprised Americans — including the faculty at Princeton, which invited him to lecture — with the passion of his rejection of evolution and his confidence that evolution would be the theological issue of the coming century. For a discussion of the 1898 tour, see Peter Heslam, *Creating a Christian Worldview: Abraham Kuyper's Lectures on Calvinism* (Grand Rapids: Eerdmans; Carlisle: Cumbria, 1998).

24. William D. Romanowski, "John Calvin Meets the Creature from the Black Lagoon: The Christian Reformed Church and the Movies, 1928-1966," *Christian Scholar's Review* 25 (Sept. 1967).

25. Bryan was active in the Presbyterian Church and was a candidate for moderator in 1923. In that year he introduced a resolution calling for an end to Presbyterian support of any institution where evolution was taught. It was amended to oppose Presbyterian support of a school that taught a materialistic understanding of life.

debated. In addition to questions around race, the nation saw extended debates over eugenics, birth control, the "new woman," and Freud. Like Darwin, these newer ethical movements saw sex as part of humankind's natural way forward and suggested that a more naturalistic understanding was crucial.

The 1925 Scopes trial, in Dayton, Tennessee, marked the high point of this secular fundamentalist movement. The Butler Act, passed by the Tennessee legislature in 1925, prohibited the teaching of evolution in the schools, colleges, and universities of the state. For many reasons the law seemed ideal for a legal test. Tennessee was a border state with its eastern region historically Republican and its western cotton lands resolutely Southern Democratic. Furthermore, its courts had a strong reputation as upholders of academic freedom. When Methodist-controlled Vanderbilt University fell into a complex battle with its sponsoring church over control of its board of trustees, the state's supreme court had found against the church.[26] When the young biology teacher John Scopes was interested in challenging the law, he had the support of the American Civil Liberties Union (ACLU). In turn, the ACLU procured Clarence Darrow to defend the young teacher. Darrow was no stranger to controversy. He had recently defended Richard Loeb and Nathan Leopold, two young murderers who had kidnapped and murdered a fellow teenager for thrills. Bryan was secured for the prosecution.

Although Bryan technically won the case — Scopes was convicted and, even more important, the Tennessee Supreme Court did not find reversible error or constitutional issues — he lost the battle in the press. This was a result of an almost classical public relations error by Bryan. After successfully excluding the biblical scholars Darrow wanted to call to show that evolution was not necessarily contrary to Christianity, Bryan, a former Sunday school teacher who taught a radio Bible class, was persuaded by Darrow to take the stand as an expert on the Scriptures. It was no contest. Darrow exposed Bryan's biblical ignorance on point after point. The news reporters, who had come to Dayton for a story that would sell papers, had their story. Bryan's failure was trumpeted throughout the country.

The reaction of the popular media to Dayton doomed "secular" fundamentalism to an early grave. Although the movement would pick up a quixotic state legislator here or there, Dayton marked the beginning of its rapid decline. Whatever a particular politician might think about current moral issues, evolution was too hot an issue to pursue in the public forum. If popular opinion and

26. Vanderbilt had been the focus of criticism by some of the Methodist bishops for years, due to the school's willingness to support the historical criticism of the Bible and to make theological accommodations to the teaching of evolution.

sentiment did not likewise simmer down — and the issue resurfaced in the 1980s and 1990s — its cash value for politicians was clearly over. Prohibition, the other hot Protestant topic, died down politically in much the same way. Once Roosevelt demonstrated that being "wet" did not hinder one's ability to get elected, the chorus demanding repeal on the state level as well grew louder and the opponents of demon rum quieter.

The decline of "secular" fundamentalism in the national press, however, did not mark the decline of its religious counterpart in the churches. Although there was a small secession from the Northern Baptist Convention — the General Association of Regular Baptists — the real division of the house did not come until 1948 when the Conservative Baptist Convention was formed. Likewise, the Presbyterian division, long anticipated, did not come until 1936-37. Neither of these divisions was clean-cut. In both cases, almost as many conservatives (and perhaps more) remained in the denominations as left them. After the 1960s, battles between conservatives and liberals became more commonplace within and between denominations. The battle over the Bible has been one that will not die.

CHAPTER EIGHTEEN

The Denominations Impacted, 1917-1930

In 1924 Henry Pitney Van Dusen applied for ordination in the Presbyterian Church. If anyone had the credentials for ministerial success, it was Van Dusen. This scion of a distinguished Philadelphia Presbyterian family and graduate of Princeton and of Union (New York) had already distinguished himself by his wide network of friends that even then included such people as Sherwood Eddy and John R. Mott. Moreover, Van Dusen was poised to make the "right" career moves for someone who hoped to rise in the newly reorganized Protestant hierarchy. Already known for his influence on students — he was the keynote speaker at the 1923 meeting of the Interseminary Movement — Van Dusen was on deck to become the secretary of the Student Division of the YMCA.[1] Yet he was at the center of a maelstrom that threatened both his career and the unity of the Presbyterian Church. Van Dusen was an open supporter of the Auburn Affirmation, a strong statement of support for doctrinal freedom within the Presbyterian Church, who admitted that he questioned the traditional affirmation of the virgin birth of Christ. Although admitted to the New York Presbytery, his admission was appealed to the Synod of New York by the conservative members of that body. John Foster Dulles, an outspoken internationalist, conducted his synodical defense. Dulles was already well known in liberal Presbyterian circles. After Harry Emerson Fosdick's notable (or notorious) sermon "Shall the Fundamentalists Win?" Dulles had defended Fosdick before the New York Presbytery where he served as a lay elder.[2]

1. The Interseminary Movement was a part of the YMCA that brought together seminary students from different campuses to discuss their common aspirations and problems. W. Richey Hogg, "Sixty-five Years in the Seminaries: A History of the Interseminary Movement" (privately published, 1945).

2. Heather A. Warren, *Reinhold Niebuhr and the Christian Realists* (Chicago: University

Since Van Dusen and Dulles won, historians have tended to pass over the case in silence. But much more than the titanic struggles in the General Assembly, the battles in local presbyteries over the ordination of particular candidates were the real marks of the depths of the battles in the twenties (and of much of the thirties and beyond in some areas). In the trenches, so to speak, the issues lost some of their intellectual luster as candidates struggled with whether they could affirm this or that expected affirmation or what it meant to affirm the Westminster Confession. On the other side, many examiners wrestled with whether they should question a candidate too closely, fearing that too much honesty might produce a split or even a negative vote, and candidates struggled with how much they dared say on controversial matters.

Like migratory fowl, young liberals flocked to those presbyteries where they knew they would receive a respectful hearing, planning to transfer later when called. Young conservatives were equally bothered. They wondered whether they would be understood to be "intolerant" or worse, and stories about the fate of those who stood foursquare for the gospel in seminary were legion.[3] Baptists in the North faced a similar situation. Woe to the young University of Chicago graduate who did not know how to find a friendly ordination council.

Even those without clearly marked theological positions, at least in the terms of the competing parties, were uneasy. They had a vague sense that the boat was sinking, and a fear that the life preservers had not been clearly marked. In short, something was seriously wrong in American Protestantism.

Fundamentalism had lasting effects, positive and negative, on many American denominations. Yet the influence of the movement arguably was strongest on four denominations and their seminaries: the Presbyterian Church (US, or Southern), the Presbyterian Church (USA, or Northern), the Northern Baptist Convention, and the Southern Baptist Convention. In these churches the issues were relatively clear-cut and the various parties easily identified. Almost all American churches, however, were affected in some degree, and while one might argue whether the conservative wing in, for example, the Missouri Synod was more or less tinged with American fundamentalism, it shared many characteristics with it. The same was true of aggressively conservative movements among Disciples, Southern Methodists, and other denominations. The media had a way of making one person's battle every person's war.

---

of Chicago Press, 1997). According to Warren, this experience contributed to a lifelong distrust of fundamentalism by Van Dusen and his friends.

3. These stories need not be true to be significant. The important thing was that the climate of opinion encouraged people to believe that they were true.

The four most visibly impacted denominations, consequently, will have to stand in for the rest. Only the Congregationalists appear to have escaped the battle — perhaps because the struggles of the last century had exhausted their appetite for battle.

Part of what makes the controversy in these four denominations so important for our story is that the battles were part of a climate of opinion that led to some substantial changes in how those denominations did and understood theological education. The schools related to these battling bodies changed, both in their ethos and in their programs, and many sought newer theologies that might stand beyond the turmoil of the battles. Neoorthodoxy's later popularity was traceable in part to the fact that it was neither fundamentalist nor modernist in its teachings.

These four denominations had many things in common. All were Reformed in heritage and all were shaped by English Puritanism in significant ways. Although the Northern Presbyterians were more centered in the East and the American Baptists in the "Old" Northwest, when Northern and Southern branches of these churches are considered together, they were national movements that had to take account of the national climate of opinion. All four denominations, further, were "old China hands," with significant missionary work and investments in that country. Perhaps as important, all four had strong theological institutions. Northern Baptist University of Chicago Divinity School was arguably the best theological school in the nation with a distinguished faculty, large endowment, and central location. In addition, Northern Baptists had Newton, Rochester, Colgate (Hamilton), Central, and Northern. Northern Presbyterians were likewise rich in seminaries. In addition to Princeton, one of the best-endowed schools in the country, the church had a string of smaller schools, such as McCormick and San Francisco, that had sound reputations, and Union Theological Seminary, although technically independent, drew many of its students, faculty, and trustees from that denomination. The Southern Presbyterians had Union (Richmond), Austin, and Columbia. The two Presbyterian denominations shared control of Louisville Presbyterian Seminary, formed by a merger of two older seminaries, which served Kentucky and the lower Midwest. Although Southern Baptist institutions did not have the prestige of their Northern cousins, Southern and Southwestern were the largest theological schools in the nation and had notable faculties. In addition, the string of state Baptist colleges in the South played a very important role in the education of ministers with strong faculties at Richmond, Baylor, Wake Forest, Mercer, and elsewhere.

The prominence of these schools was another important shared element in the controversy. The schools were well known within their own denominations. Each school had a core of supporters composed of graduates, interested congregations, and philanthropists.[4] This constituency, incidentally, was disproportionately represented in both the Baptist conventions and the two Presbyterian general assemblies. Seminary-trained pastors tended to be more active in the denomination and in denominational affairs than pastors who were either untrained or had only completed college.[5] In most cases this meant that if the liberals could locate the battle at a high level in the denominational structure, preferably the national or regional judicatory, they had the advantage.

I. Northern Baptist Battles

Although many of the leading conservatives, including the Stewart brothers, were Presbyterians, the fundamentalist controversy may have had Northern Baptist roots. Although some conservatives had viewed the University of Chicago with alarm almost from its founding, the immediate cause of widespread controversy was George Burman Foster (1858-1918). Foster was among the most brilliant of Harper's theological appointments and a man never content with easy answers to complex questions. By 1906, when his *Finality of the Christian Religion* was published,[6] Foster had begun to move toward a thorough religious relativism. His first step was to reject the popular theologically liberal idea of the essence of Christianity. No common marks of Christianity existed throughout its complex history. If there was no cultural or theological essence of Christianity, then theological affirmations, including the Fatherhood of God and the brotherhood of man, were beside the point. When they became worn out or hackneyed, Foster continued, they should be replaced. Foster had a clear picture of what should replace them: human religious experience. Our experience related us directly to the Ultimate and provided us with categories we could use to symbolize that Reality.

4. Philanthropy was already beginning to play a major role in the development and governance of theological schools. The real public for many theological schools, especially such wealthy schools as Rochester and Chicago, was the handful of philanthropists who supported the institution. Union (New York) was similarly protected by an independent board that was supported by many of New York's silk stockings.

5. William Adams Brown and Mark May, *The Education of American Ministers,* vol. 2, *The Profession of the Ministry* (New York: Institute of Social and Religious Research, 1934), studied extensively the relationship between seminary graduation and ministerial efficiency.

6. The question of the "finality of the Christian religion" was much debated at the time. Ernst Troeltsch (1865-1923), perhaps Germany's leading representative of the "history of religions" interpretation of Christianity, published in 1902, just four years before Foster's volume appeared, *Die Absolutheit des Christentums and die Religionsgeschichte,* and shortly before his death, *Der Historismus und seine Probleme* (1922).

At this point Foster was willing to drive home his final point. Even those categories and symbols we considered most adequate to our own experience probably came from our social and cultural context and not from the Ultimate itself. When all was said and done, theologians were more like blind men describing an elephant than scientists describing a natural phenomenon.

Unlike some later modernists with sunnier dispositions, Foster drew the consequences of his position. While he might hope that "our fathers and mothers might enjoy the blessed calm of the evening of life," Foster knew he could not offer them that hope.[7] Experience did not point to a God who was working to bring all things to fruition in a Platonic eternity any more than in an earthly kingdom. Later, Foster would find the works of Nietzsche and other radical European philosophers congenial. Humans had entered a world that had been moving beyond traditional comforts as well as traditional affirmations. Foster was clearly on his way to the more radical affirmation, associated with his disciple Henry Nelson Wieman, that "God" was not nice.

In Foster conservatives had a live, breathing Antichrist, who carried liberal theology to what thoughtful conservatives believed were its logical conclusions. In the Midwest the Foster book set off a series of spectacular debates. At the university's own invitation, a committee was formed to determine whether it was advisable for the divinity school, technically owned by the Baptist Union, to continue as part of the university. While those assembled agreed that the alliance between the schools was still viable, deep unrest continued. Whether Harper agreed or disagreed with Foster or supported Foster's academic freedom, the battle threatened to cut the university's enrollment and funding. Consequently, Harper transferred Foster to the Department of Philosophy.[8]

Harper's capitulation did not end Baptist uneasiness over Foster or modernism. This distrust was not confined to the denomination's conservative wing. In 1907, for instance, moderate Augustus Strong, president of Rochester Seminary and a defender of Rauschenbusch, warned his fellow Baptists against a second "Unitarian Defection."[9] Other Baptist moderates, including Curtis Lee Laws — whose editorials popularized the name "fundamentalists" for conservative pastors — shared these concerns. While they did not want the type of doctrinaire Calvinism associated with some advocates of the Philadelphia Confession, they did want a clear affirmation of the churches' adherence to what they believed were basic affirmations of faith.

7. The quote is from Martin E. Marty, *Modern American Religion,* vol. 1, *The Irony of It All, 1893-1919* (Chicago: University of Chicago Press, 1986).

8. This story is told in more detail above, chap. 11.

9. See George Marsden, *Fundamentalism and American Culture: The Shaping of Twentieth Century Evangelicalism, 1870-1925* (New York: Oxford University Press, 1980), p. 108.

Opposition to the University of Chicago disrupted Midwestern Baptist life almost from the publication of *Finality.* In 1913 more than three hundred churches left the Illinois State Baptist Convention and formed their own convention that, in turn, elected to affiliate with the Southern Baptist Convention. Many of these churches were in the "Egypt" section of Illinois, the southern counties around Cairo that had deep historical and cultural ties with the South. There was a similar culture and history in southern Indiana and in southern Ohio. Baptists in this area often sent their pastors and ministerial students to Southern Baptist Seminary in Louisville, which served both the Southern states and much of the lower Midwest.[10] The next major schism in the denomination would be occasioned by the withdrawal of churches affiliated with the Baptist Bible Union in 1932. Those churches formed the General Association of Regular Baptists.

Moderate conservatives raised cries for an alternative to Chicago after the 1906 publication of Foster's book, and in 1913 Northern Baptist Theological Seminary opened under the presidency of John Dean, pastor of the Second Baptist Church of Chicago.[11] Second Church also provided the meeting space for the new institution. The name, Northern, was intended to reflect adherence to the understanding of theological education at Southern Baptist Seminary. This model stressed the importance of a confession of faith, the education of nongraduates and graduates in the same institution, and the provision of advanced study. Unlike at such moderately liberal schools as Colgate, Rochester, or Chicago, the bachelor of theology degree, awarded for five years of study in both liberal arts and theology, was the heart of the program. Like at Southern, Northern's founders wanted a confession of faith or, to use the Louisville language, an abstract of principles. Initially the school chose the New Hampshire Confession, the most commonly used statement of faith among American Baptists, although it adopted a statement of its own in 1926. Both the New Hampshire Confession and the later Northern statement were broad statements of doctrine that however contained very emphatic statements about biblical authority.

10. The Southern Baptist Convention become much more of a "conservative" alternative in the North in the years after World War II when the denomination was carried north by the migration of Southern workers to Northern factories and offices. These churches would later ally with the neoconservative movement that eventually "took over" the denomination in the 1980s.

11. Warren Cameron Young, *Commit What You Have Heard: A History of Northern Baptist Theological Seminary, 1913-1988* (Wheaton, Ill.: Harold Shaw, 1988), tells the story of Northern with real love and understanding. See also Arthur Bruce Moss, "Something Old — Something New: The First Fifty Years of Northern Baptist Theological Seminary," *Foundations* 8 (Jan. 1965): 26-48.

Another response to the Chicago crisis was the 1911 publication of *The Fundamentals,* a thirteen-volume conservative exposition of the faith, largely written by conservative Baptists and Presbyterians. Oilman Lyman Stewart said in a letter to Amzi Dixon, the editor of the first volumes:

> Now that we are closing up the final details of *The Fundamentals,* my thoughts have reverted to you very frequently, and especially to that Sunday afternoon when, in our [Baptist] Temple Auditorium [in Los Angeles] you were replying to something that one of those infidel professors in Chicago University had published, and during which lecture I was very much impressed to ask for an interview with you. As I have thought about that since, it seems as though the Lord must have given me courage to ask for the interview, as I naturally have a great shrinking from meeting strangers, and this matter which I had to present to you I had never mentioned to a single soul, not even to my own wife. So you were the first that heard it and when you remarked, "It is of the Lord; let us pray," I was deeply impressed.[12]

Stewart put up sufficient funds for the booklets to be distributed to every pastor and YMCA director in the United States.

Theologically, *The Fundamentals* was a very moderate exposition of conservative theology that sought to give a positive picture of what conservative Christians were advocating and not just a polemical picture of what they opposed. The volumes were clearly intended to reflect a conservative consensus and not to raise contentious issues. Where disagreement existed among conservatives, the editors, Amzi Dixon, Louis Meyer, and Reuben A. Torrey, selected authors who represented a variety of current positions. Thus the series included evolutionists and anti-evolutionists. In the same spirit, controversial positions were played down. Although all three editors were dispensationalists, for example, dispensationalism is rarely mentioned in the series. Instead *The Fundamentals* presented a broad conservative theology that stressed the distance between conservative faith and liberalism and modernism. Taken as a whole, *The Fundamentals* did a good job in identifying the principal areas of concern: a supernatural understanding of theism, a Christology that stressed the miraculous nature of Jesus' appearing and ministry, and a strong affirmation of the authority of Scripture.

However, if dispensationalism was not at the heart of Baptist conservatism, it was at the heart of another challenge to Chicago's leadership in the denomination. Baptist ecclesiology allowed local churches to call and ordain any-

12. Lyman Stewart, quoted in Edgar A. Towne, "A Single Minded Theologian: George Burman Foster," *Foundations* 20, pt. 2, p. 171.

one they chose as pastor, and even in 1920 the denomination had many pastors who had gone from plow to pulpit with a minimum of schooling. But just as the increasing prosperity of the nation floated many young Baptists to a social location where they could consider college or seminary, the same rising tide lifted others to the social class where a Bible school education was financially possible. Many Baptist churches had pastors who had been trained at these schools, particularly Chicago's Moody Bible Institute. The student body at Moody always contained numerous Baptists.

Baptists found Bible schools congenial for a variety of reasons. Students, particularly earnest young men who had received the call in their midtwenties, found Moody attractive because it did not require liberal arts training as preparation for theological study, and because its various programs required less time than equivalent seminary programs. Further, many churches were more comfortable with pastors from Moody than with pastors from either the colleges or the seminaries. Bible school graduates came from the same social class as many Baptists, particularly those who moved to the cities from the countryside, and the programs at Moody were very similar to the courses in salesmanship or business that were so popular with the urban Baptist rank and file. Such churches were not always comfortable with seminary graduates, even those who were strongly conservative or premillennial, because of the felt difference in social location. Moreover, Moody Bible graduates had an aggressive can-do approach to evangelism and mission that was in line with the denomination's deepest traditions.[13]

Chicago, especially under William Rainey Harper, was very sensitive to the needs of the average Baptist congregation and its leadership. The school sponsored summer schools, short programs, and correspondence courses. But "Harper's Bazaar" was replaced shortly after the energetic president's death by a university very conscious of its place among the nation's top research institutions. When this happened, the spirit of the divinity school changed, and the social distance between Chicago and many Baptists grew. In simple terms, under Harper the divinity school reflected the broad social base of Baptist churches. But the more the university succeeded in becoming an elite institu-

13. Hugh Hartshorne and M. C. Froyd, *Theological Education in the Northern Baptist Convention* (Philadelphia: Judson, 1945), p. 104, say the great influx of Baptists into Bible colleges came after 1920: "The greatest change has come in the contribution of Bible institutes. Up to 1920, less than 10 per cent of the supply of Baptist ministers were from this source. Since 1935, the proportion has risen to approximately 23 per cent. This amounts to an increase of 136 per cent for the period considered." But these figures need to be put in context. The percentage of Bible school graduates prior to 1920 is probably about the same as the percentage of pastors with both college and seminary degrees.

tion, the more the leadership replaced educational values congenial to Baptists with a value system more representative of the American-educated elite.[14]

To understand why the changes at Chicago aroused such passions, it must be noted that modernism was never the only issue in Baptist politics and that it was often intertwined with other issues. In 1906, when the Foster controversy was just beginning, Northern Baptists were in the midst of an organizational revolution. The old system of societies in which each cause, such as foreign and home missions, was governed by its own financial supporters was antiquated. In its place Northern Baptists adopted a structure more like that of the Southern Baptist Convention. The changes came in stages. In 1896 the Committee on Systematic Benevolence led the three principal Baptist societies — foreign and home missions and publications — to adopt a common appeal to the churches. Beginning in 1901 Northern Baptists held national rallies that brought together the supporters of the various societies in a common meeting. After the 1907 meeting of the Baptist Congress, as these rallies were called, a committee of three — including Shailer Mathews, dean of the divinity school — drafted a plan for closer cooperation. Under these proposals a national convention was to elect the boards of the various societies (which remained legally distinct) at an annual meeting. The system was officially ratified in 1908. Harry Pratt Judson, president of the University of Chicago, served as its first president. The new body, the Northern Baptist Convention, was legally incorporated in 1911 when the Freewill Baptists joined.[15] Although it was not clear that the convention was a "national church," Northern Baptists joined the Federal Council of Churches in 1908 and represented Baptists in many other ecumenical endeavors.[16] While the new denomination shared some structural similarities to the Southern Baptist Convention, it was not as centralized nor did it completely replace the antiquated society system. Perhaps the best comparison would be to the also-new national organizations of the Disciples of Christ (Christian Church) and the Congregationalists.

14. When Baptist colleges became elite institutions, they tended to reflect the elites they served rather than the denomination that spawned them. Harper's Chicago was, in this sense, only the first of many schools that outgrew the Baptist denomination.

15. Freewill Baptists were notably more liberal on many social issues. Bates College in Maine, the principal Freewill Baptist college, was particularly open to African American students. After the merger, Bates closed its small, struggling divinity school in order to concentrate on its work as a liberal arts college. Thereafter, close relationships were maintained between Bates and Newton.

16. This move was always controversial as well. As late as the 1950s, American Baptists felt that they could not set up headquarters at 475 Riverside Drive because that might overly identify the denomination with the council and its work. Instead, a new denominational headquarters was constructed at Valley Forge, Pa.

For Mathews and other denominational enthusiasts, the new system made it possible for Baptists to follow the best models of denominational administration. With the solidarity achieved by the convention system, Baptists could set up "committees on social service and city missions, . . . a pension system, . . . and a Board of Education."[17] Incidentally, the convention could also provide additional support for the seminaries, which had largely been organized in the society era, and it could "recognize" certain schools as worthy of denominational support.

Although the Northern Baptist Convention quickly organized one of the best pension systems in American Protestantism, the new system was not popular with many pastors or with the rank and file. Many Baptist churches continued to designate their giving to the different "societies," and various independent faith missions retained considerable Baptist financial and spiritual support. Compared with the Southern Baptists, Northern Baptists did not identify strongly with the national organization, and pastors tended to see themselves as largely independent of each other. The state conventions, which were also undergoing reorganization at this time, had many of the same problems of support and identification. Local congregations found it easy to drift out of convention membership, and many did so. The most serious schisms among Northern Baptists were not the walkouts that produced the General Baptist Convention and the Conservative Baptist Convention, groups that shared some of the ideas of the parent body, but the hundreds of "independent" Baptist churches that grew up around the fringes of the older churches.

The new organization also meant that the convention could be used to express dissatisfaction with the status quo. Traditionally, Baptist controversies were almost self-limiting. Under the older system of voluntary societies, no one party could capture the denomination. The losers in a dispute need only figuratively go down the street and form a new society while remaining loyal members of those societies with which they agree. In *New Faith for Old*, his autobiography, Mathews noted that the policy had created two parties. "Transformation of the Baptist denomination in the North was in fact a problem of the socialization of democracy. It soon became apparent that the real issue was between those who relied on an educational process and those who relied upon overhead authority. It was natural that the latter policy should have been favored by those who wish conformity. Their devotion to what was then the traditional position of the denomination led them to attempt to formulate denomination orthodoxy en-

17. The board of education was the legal successor of the American Baptist Educational Society. See Shailer Mathews, *New Faith for Old: An Autobiography* (New York: Macmillan, 1936), p. 113.

forced by a central body."[18] Although Mathews claimed many of the value words, such as "democracy," for his side, the new polity almost begged for a division of the house with the convention itself, with its wealth, as the prize for the winner.

An important glitch in the new Baptist convention organization was that it did not really represent the various constituencies of the convention. Although all supporting churches were entitled to representation by the constitution, in fact the members of the convention were from those churches that could afford for their pastor and/or lay leaders to attend the annual meetings. Affordability was a function of church size, to be sure, but the cost of participation was also related to the distance between the meeting place and the local church. Given the vast territory served by the convention, this meant that the same body never met twice. If the convention met in more "liberal" territory, it tended in a liberal direction; if it met in more conservative territory, a more conservative convention resulted. Part of the politics of the body, consequently, was to have the most important votes taken when one side or the other had a geographical advantage. Over the long haul, this worked to the liberals' advantage. The conventions needed to meet in cities that were large enough to provide the needed services for those who came from out of town, and cities tended to be more liberal than the countryside.

As conservatives frequently noted, denominational officials — their expenses paid from the common purse — served as representatives to the convention from their local churches. Since the employees of the various agencies may have constituted as much as a third of each convention, this gave the bureaucracy the decisive voice on many issues. While these denominational officials were never as liberal as the conservatives believed, they knew that the Rockefellers were the major supporters of convention causes and that the Rockefeller family had an "interest" in the success of the divinity school of the University of Chicago. Baptist fundamentalists, such as William Bell Riley, used the same popularist rhetoric in attacking the convention leadership that they directed against big business and big government.

As in so much of American religious life, the world war marked a transition in the continuing Baptist battles over theology. The progressive rhetoric used to justify the war seemed to provide the liberal Baptist with an opportunity to go on the attack. Since the war was fought for progressive principles, to oppose progressive rhetoric was unwise and almost unpatriotic. The dispensationalists were particularly vulnerable. As they read the Bible, the kingdom of God was a radically eschatological event that could occur only after cer-

18. Mathews, *New Faith for Old.*

tain prophetic conditions, including the conversion and return of the Jews to Palestine, had been met. Whether or not the world war was justified — and many conservative American Christians had been deeply influenced by the peace movement — it could not be the war to end all wars or the precursor to God's final purpose for humankind.

In 1917 Shailer Mathews attacked the dispensationalists in his popular pamphlet *Will Christ Come Again?* Shirley Jackson Case, Chicago's brilliant New Testament professor, followed up this salvo with *The Premillennial Hope: A Phase of War Time Thinking* and *The Premillennial Menace.* In essence, Mathews and Case charged that the pessimism of the dispensationalist position stemmed from war weariness and not from Scripture. But more important, they concluded simply that premillennialism was unpatriotic and hinted that it might be sponsored by the Germans as war propaganda.[19]

Although one did not need to be a prophet to identify which dispensationalists were under attack, Mathews and Case carefully avoided naming names. James Gray, president of Moody Bible Institute, however, was convinced — perhaps rightly, given the competition between Chicago and the institute for Midwestern Baptist students — that he was the target. Like others who saw themselves in the Chicago snare, Gray immediately proclaimed his patriotic support of the war, and other dispensationalists followed suit. Not surprisingly, many dispensationalists became hyper-patriots, and this stance has remained part of conservative theology. But defensiveness was not the only response. The conservatives were mindful that many of the liberals were products of German universities. Was there not, they suggested, a clear link between a biblical criticism that weakened moral standards and a German militarism that would stop at nothing to attain its goals?

The attack on premillennialism was of course part of the larger struggle to control Northern Baptist theological education. Mathews's next step was to use the convention structure to rein in such "renegade" institutions as Northern and to try to prevent other conservative schools from securing denominational sanction. The Northern Baptist Convention did not support seminaries, although it did officially recognize theological schools through its board of education.[20] Northern applied for such recognition, but the initial reaction of the board was highly critical. Chaired by Ernest Burton of the University of Chicago, the board attempted to impose six conditions on the new school:

19. Marsden, *Fundamentalism and American Culture,* pp. 146-47, captures the essence of these texts.

20. See Sandford Fleming, "Board of Education and Theological Education, 1911-1963," *Foundations* 8 (Jan. 1965): 3-25.

1. that the school change its name.
2. that its curriculum be constructed around mature students without a college education but with high school.
3. that the curriculum be divided equally between theological subjects and other subjects.
4. that the faculty be recruited with these objectives in mind.
5. that the school not recruit college graduates or offer graduate courses.
6. that a strong board of trustees be established and the advisory committee abolished.[21]

If Northern had followed these directives, the school would have become a preparatory school for the University of Chicago or perhaps a more convention-oriented version of Moody. Most students at Northern before 1960 took the bachelor of theology degree that combined two years of liberal arts study with three years of theological training, including the biblical languages. This was similar to Chicago's program that admitted students to the divinity school after two years of liberal arts study. Northern eventually won the battle by threatening to take the theological issues between itself and Chicago to the convention floor, but the resulting ill will was deep and abiding.

The attacks on dispensationalism and on Northern suggested to the conservatives that they needed to organize, and in 1920 they held a series of meetings that climaxed in a large preconvention rally. Attending this latter meeting were such notable conservatives as J. C. Massee, Curtis Lee Laws, John Roach Straton, Russell Conwell, A. C. Dixon, and Nathan Wood (president of Gordon and former president of Newton). Its target was education, and the group persuaded the Buffalo Convention to appoint a committee to investigate the denomination's secondary schools, colleges, and seminaries. The points to be ascertained were the inspiration of the Scriptures, the deity of Christ, the atonement, the resurrection, Christ's return, the spiritual nature of the church, regenerate church membership, and the missionary imperative.[22] A 1921 pamphlet, *The Denominational Situation: Should Our Schools Be Investigated?* sharpened the issues.

The committee's report on theological schools is hard to understand. The committee concluded that the attacks on the seminaries were unwarranted and that the "charges were largely false."[23] The conclusion seems hardly creditable. Whatever else might be the case, clearly the University of Chicago, Colgate,

21. The list is from Young, *Commit,* p. 45.

22. *NBC Annual,* 1920, p. 48.

23. *Tenth Annual Report, Board of Education of the Northern Baptist Convention,* 1921, p. 7.

Rochester, Newton, and Crozer had faculty members who doubted any verbal doctrine of inspiration, including the modified ones advocated by Augustus Strong and Alvah Hovey, and who found the accounts of the virgin birth to be unconvincing historically. The continuing dispute among Northern Baptists was embittered by such official actions that seemed to fly in the face of such works as Mathews's *The Faith of Modernism* (1924).

The report on the colleges was more straightforward: the denomination did not own any of its colleges or schools. These institutions historically had been founded by individuals or groups that wrote into the bylaws provisions for the election of so many Baptists to the governing board or a regulation that the college must have a Baptist president or a Baptist majority on the faculty. Hence, the colleges were free to act in accord with their formal patterns of governance. Indeed, some of the traditional Baptist colleges had already found it expedient to sever their relations with the denomination. Others made it clear that they believed they honored the denomination more than they were financially supported by it. In effect, no Baptist colleges existed; only colleges that drew some or part of their financial support from members of the denomination. This type of relationship was about as far from control as it was possible to get.

But the collegiate finding was not a liberal victory. The liberals and many moderates had been concerned about the growing influence of the Bible schools in the denomination, and this decision served indirectly to legitimate them. If Baptist college education was Baptist only because of sentiment, then Moody or other Bible schools, also connected to Baptists by ties of love, had a similar right to educate Baptist leaders. The percentage of ministers educated in Bible schools grew steadily until around 1945 when approximately one-third of the Northern Baptist clergy had been educated in such schools. Conservatives also continued to build seminaries to their specification. Curtis Lee Laws and his friends in the Philadelphia area built Eastern Baptist Theological Seminary, largely on the same plan as Northern and Southern, and made it the most scholarly (and the largest) of the conservative Northern Baptist schools in the 1930s and 1940s. Central in Kansas City, another school built on the Southern model, drifted toward a consistently conservative stance as well. This was the natural product of the school's heritage as well as its location. Starting at a different place, Nathan Wood accelerated his plan to transform Gordon into a strong college and seminary in its own right. Like Eastern, Gordon was highly successful. In the 1940s, for instance, the majority of Baptist clergy in the Boston area were trained in the reborn training school.

The question of a confession of faith was part of the fundamentalist-modernist debate among Northern Baptists. The advocates of such a confession believed it would serve as a guide for the various convention agencies in making appointments and in evaluating the theological content of their programs. It is easy to misinterpret this battle. Both the conservatives and the liberals were the children of the progressive movement. As good supporters of the tradition from Roosevelt to Wilson, they wanted Baptists to have a clear national voice that might impact the nation. The debate over a convention-wide confession was a debate over what type of voice that might be. Both believed that the Baptist tradition of social service should be preserved — that, after all, was one reason for the new structure — but after that, they disagreed. Conservatives saw the convention as a positive force for traditional evangelical theology, standing foursquare on the Bible and the need for a decision for Christ. Modernists believed that the churches ought to bring their religious resources to bear on social and economic issues.

When William Bell Riley asked the 1922 convention to recommend the New Hampshire Confession of Faith to the churches, he was opposed by Cornelius Woelfkin — Rockefeller's pastor — who appealed to the frontier Baptist tradition by stating that Baptists affirm that "the New Testament is the all-sufficient ground of our faith and practice."[24] Woelfkin's substitute passed, but the issue remained. The older seminaries continued without a formal confession of faith; the newer evangelical schools adopted one.

Perhaps unfortunately, the failure of Riley's motion served to move the venue of the Baptist debate from the relatively open forum of the convention to the much more private or at least unobserved forum of the various convention boards. Since these represented various constituencies, young candidates could expect to be asked again and again about their position on such issues as the virgin birth, bodily resurrection, and second coming.

The issue that finally divided the denomination, however, was related to foreign missions, in particular China. In many ways the China mission was a natural focal point for dissatisfaction. Missionaries in China tended to live in large missionary compounds, and part of the effect of the Boxer Rebellion of the 1890s was to further concentrate missionaries in these semifortresses. The size of the compounds and the concentration of missionary personnel in them

24. This had been the position of Alexander Campbell, who had led one of the largest defections from the denomination in its nineteenth-century history! In fact, most Baptist associations historically had adopted some confession of faith, and the New Hampshire Confession of Faith was frequently recommended to local churches. Edward Thurston Hiscox, *The Standard Manual for Baptist Churches* (Philadelphia: American Baptist Publication Society, 1890). Baptist "manuals" — which were sometimes published for local churches — included a confession, bylaws and/or a constitution, and a historical sketch.

encouraged the mission to develop a variety of social and educational missions. In turn, these missions attracted missionaries primarily interested in "civilizing" China. The Nationalist Revolution, which had Christians among its leadership, further cemented the alliance between those Chinese who wanted to Westernize and those Westerners willing to do just that. In short, without much discussion the China mission became progressively less interested in traditional evangelism and more committed to social service.

The compound system also encouraged dissension. The missionaries lived closely with each other, attended frequent mission meetings, and voted on disputed questions. No one ever went home to "think about it." The evenings, more likely than not, were occupied by prayer meetings in which winners and losers in mission politics rehearsed their struggles before the Lord. Naturally, the need for allies was not limited to the heavenly allies. Complaints about fellow missioners were frequently featured in letters home, and every visitor from home was assaulted by a recitation of the mission's sins.

The missionary phase of the battle began in 1917. In that year Augustus Strong visited China and returned appalled at what he saw and heard. In *Tour of the Missions: Observations and Conclusions,* Strong detailed the problems he found in China. Many problems were what one might expect, given the volatile character of the mission, but Strong also asserted that the missionaries had lost their theological integrity, that they had failed to minister to the world without losing their own soul. As a theologian he searched for reasons, and came to the conclusion that the missions and the churches had set themselves adrift from the Bible.

> What is the effect of this [the critical] method upon our theological seminaries? It is to deprive the gospel message of all definiteness, and to make professors and students disseminators of doubts. . . . The result of such teaching in our seminaries is that the student, unless he has had a Pauline experience before he came has all his early conceptions of Scripture and Christian doctrine weakened, has no longer any positive message to deliver, loses the ardor of his love for Christ, and at his graduation leaves the seminary, not to become preacher or pastor as he had hoped, but to sow his doubts broadcast, as a teacher in some college, as editor of some religious journal, as secretary of some Young Men's Christian Association, or as agent of some mutual life company. . . . The theological seminaries of almost all denominations are becoming so infected with this grievous error that they are not so much organs for Christ as they are organs of Antichrist. This accounts for the rise, all over the land, of Bible schools, to take the place of seminaries. . . . We are ceasing to be evangelistic as well as

evangelical, and if this down progress continues, we shall in due time cease to exist.[25]

Strong's argument that the new biblical studies were a slippery slope that dulled faith and led, slowly but inevitably, to the decline of any church that embraced them was of course to become a commonplace conservative argument. Variations on the theme have reappeared regularly ever since. But, more immediately, Strong's argument forced conservatives to face the issue of foreign missions. Since this was perhaps the most popular Baptist issue and the primary reason why the conservatives did not leave the denomination, this was a painful confrontation.

Harry E. Fosdick provided confirmation of Strong's observations. He went to China in 1921, like Strong, on a promotional tour of the missions. By this point conservatives had formed the Bible Union of China and were pushing actively for an investigation of the missions. Fosdick was appalled by the conservative theology that he felt dominated the China mission, and his response was his "Shall the Fundamentalists Win?" sermon of 1922. In many ways Fosdick's sermon was the most honest contribution to the debate over China. Instead of arguing whether modernism existed, Fosdick embraced it. If, as some conservatives argued, there were five fundamentals, Dr. Fosdick wanted people to know that he rejected all five. Modern religious and scientific thought, even when it called into question such honored doctrines as inspiration and the virgin birth, was necessary for Christianity's future health.

Unfortunately, Fosdick's candor was not followed. As in the case of the seminaries, it is hard to credit the official denominational response. In one sense the initial response of the convention's officials seemed to be a step in the right direction. The foreign mission board, noting the wide variety of views in the convention, adopted an "inclusive" policy that stated that while they would insist that all appointments be "evangelical," they would not define that term too narrowly. The Beavin Commission report of 1925, however, reverted to the earlier approach. After agreeing with the conservatives that more care had to be taken to ensure that sound candidates were the only ones appointed, the commission turned around and stated that they had found few cases of doctrinal deviation among missionaries! Again, this was a very dubious conclusion.

In point of fact, conservatives did not believe the report (and many liberals probably doubted it as well). The result was a deepening distrust that was much greater than the various votes in the convention might seem to indicate.

25. Strong, *Tour of the Missions: Observations and Conclusions*, pp. 170-74, quoted in Clark H. Pinnock, "Baptists and Biblical Authority," *Journal of the Evangelical Theological Society* 17 (Fall 1974): 193-205, here pp. 201-2.

Convention officials had won the battle, but at a cost they would continue to pay over many years. Many new Baptist congregations in the North were "Independent," and the convention suffered major defections in 1933 and 1948. Neither the liberals nor the conservatives were able to recover the excitement that had called the convention into being or to find ways to sustain earlier patterns of Baptist growth. Like the Disciples of Christ, Northern (later American) Baptists found themselves representing a smaller and smaller percentage of their denominational constituency. Baptists were, ironically, more than ever divided by their common faith.

What of Chicago, whose controversial theologian, Foster, had sparked the initial debate? The 1920s may have been the high-water mark of its influence on Baptist life. The university had become a nondenominational school, and the divinity school, while remaining technically Baptist, became progressively less influenced by Baptists as its students, faculty, and administration were drawn from other denominations. Theologically, it moved in the direction of naturalism. Theologian Shailer Mathews represented the shift. In the 1920s he advocated a form of theological liberalism similar to the evangelical liberalism of such ecumenical stalwarts as William Adams Brown. Indeed, he preferred the term "modernism" to "liberalism" because it allowed him to distance himself and his colleagues from more radical voices. But Mathews's thought was steadily moving in a more radical direction. By the time of his *Creative Christianity* (1935), he had come to see religion primarily as a manifestation of culture.[26] Faith, to be meaningful, had to distance itself from its past cultural forms, not to find a new absolute standard, but to relate to its own time and circumstances. The great champion of modernism, thus, having stirred the hornet's nest, quietly left the field of battle to other, lesser tribes.

26. W. Creighton Peden, "Shailer Mathews," in *Makers of Christian Theology in America*, ed. Mark G. Toulouse and James O. Duke (Nashville: Abingdon, 1997), makes the argument that Mathews has been misinterpreted, largely because he has been read through the eyes of his liberal and fundamentalist critics as a culture Christian (p. 396), but he never indicates where the misreading has taken place. Mathews, like Foster, was early tempted toward a theological naturalism that saw Christianity as one of many religious responses to the human situation. During his early years Mathews saw the contribution of Christianity to its cultural milieu as formative; during his later years he saw the culture as having formed more of Christianity. The natural counterpart to his early theology was an ecclesiastical and Christian activism that sought to change the society by taking religious initiatives. This point of view declines in the 1930s as Mathews moves toward a less applicable understanding of the church/culture dichotomy. At neither stage in his thinking is a transcendent or personal God necessary to the process, nor is Christ a supernatural or redemptive figure. While Mathews may have been right or wrong in these affirmations and right or wrong in his belief that scholars needed to acknowledge the various problems caused by modernity, he clearly held the views attributed to him.

II. The Presbyterian Dispute

Unlike the Northern Baptists, Northern Presbyterians had a long-established connectional system of government that, while modified significantly at different times in the denomination's history, reached back to the Adopting Act of 1729 and, beyond that, to Reformation Scotland. Presbyterianism prided itself on a learned ministry, able to interpret the Bible from the original languages, and holding to a statement of faith, the Westminster Confession. Perhaps most important, the denomination had already had a major debate over theological education in the 1890s. Lefferts Loetscher identified this struggle as having run from 1889 to 1904. This dispute centered around Union Seminary (New York) and certain members of its faculty, especially Henry Preserved Smith, Charles Briggs, and A. C. McGiffert.[27] Perhaps the key document in this early debate was the Portland Deliverance of 1892 that declared the inerrancy of the Bible to be an essential Christian teaching and that required subscription to it by all ministers.

In a sense the conservatives won the first phase of the Presbyterian controversy. While liberal emphases were strong at Union Seminary in New York and at closely related Auburn Seminary, they were not strong elsewhere. Although faculty members at the other Presbyterian seminaries were aware of the critical issues, the schools were solidly conservative in both teaching methods and curriculum.[28] The same point could be made about the expanding Presbyterian bureaucracy, especially the Foreign Mission Board, headed by Robert Speer. Only a few major pulpits, such as New York's prestigious Madison Avenue Presbyterian Church, had liberal pastors, and only a few presbyteries, mostly located in New York State, had liberal majorities. The Baptist battle pitted rebellious conservatives against a new denominational hierarchy, open to more liberal emphasis and deeply influenced by the divinity school and Rockefeller's money. In contrast, the Presbyterian battle was over whether the church was broad enough to give its liberal minority legitimacy and a share of the power. If the rhetoric was often similar, the context was radically different.

27. Lefferts Loetscher, *The Broadening Church: A Study of Theological Issues in the Presbyterian Church Since 1869* (Philadelphia: University of Pennsylvania Press, 1954), p. 94.

28. See John Mulder and Lee Wyatt, "The Predicament of Pluralism: The Study of Theology in Presbyterian Seminaries," in *The Pluralistic Vision: Presbyterians and Mainstream Protestant Education and Leadership*, ed. Milton J. Coalter, John M. Mulder, and Louis B. Weeks (Louisville: Westminster John Knox, 1992), pp. 37-70; pp. 352-53 n. 12 is particularly useful, in which Mulder and Wyatt note that Charles Hodge was used as a textbook at Louisville, Columbia, Princeton, and Western; Augustus Strong at San Francisco and McCormick; while Dabney was used at Austin. Strong was popular at the more conservative Baptist seminaries, including Gordon, Northern, Eastern, and Central.

Part of the battle in the Presbyterian Church in the 1890s had been over the need to revise the Westminster Confession of Faith. This was an old wound. The Adopting Act of 1729, which formed the foundation of Presbyterian polity, stated that all candidates for the ministry had to affirm the "essential and necessary" doctrines of the Westminster Confession, but the act neglected to spell out what those doctrines might be. In both the eighteenth and nineteenth centuries Presbyterians had split over the nature of doctrinal subscription, with strict and loose subscription parties claiming to represent the authentic voice of the Adopting Act and drawing very difficult conclusions about what was "essential and necessary."

In many ways the Presbyterian battle in the 1920s was a revival of the struggle over what was "essential and necessary," that is, over what was fundamental in the Westminster Confession. Interestingly enough, although many conservatives would have preferred strict subscription, most had already moved from that position to one that attempted to identify what was in fact basic to Presbyterianism. In a sense the liberal search for the essence of Christianity was similar in intent, if not in conclusion, to the conservative position. Both agreed that certain clear teachings existed that were necessary to the church; they disagreed over what those teachings might be.

In the years leading up to the 1920s controversy, the General Assembly was clear about what it considered essential teachings. In 1892 the church went on record as supporting the inerrancy of Scripture, and repeatedly affirmed it. In 1910 the assembly affirmed five points as essential: (1) the inspiration and inerrancy of the Scriptures, (2) the birth of Jesus from the virgin Mary, (3) the vicarious atonement, (4) the bodily resurrection, and (5) that Christ performed miracles.[29] The five points were intended to comprehend different interpretations of the Westminster Confession. Hence, a person could hold to the five points while holding to a more New School understanding of salvation and a more Old School understanding of election. The important thing was that people agreed on the grounds of their disagreements.

The most striking point about the five points is what they did not include. Although they appealed to the Princetonian understanding of the inerrancy of the Bible, they did not focus on the Old Testament questions that were so important in the 1890s debates. They made no mention, for instance, of creation in six calendar days or of the universality of the flood or of the historicity of

29. There were some similarities between this list and a similar list of five items adopted by the Niagara Bible Conference to regulate its own faith. However, this does not necessarily prove dependence. Many, if not most, early premillennialists were Presbyterians. It is hard to say whether premillennialists thought these doctrines necessary because they were Presbyterians or whether some Presbyterians thought them necessary because they were premillennialists.

such biblical characters as Jonah and Job. Nor, for that matter, did they mention eschatology. Rather the center of the 1910 action was the four affirmations about Christ. The five points highlight the historical aspects of Christ's life that help identify Christ's work as a supernatural intervention of God into human history. In this sense the fundamentals were an alternative to the liberal idea of the essence of Christianity that had played such an important role in theology from Schleiermacher to Harnack and to the more recent discussions of the "finality of Christianity." The five points also express an abiding Presbyterian belief that theology matters, and matters a great deal. Liberal Presbyterian William Adams Brown wrote:

> Make as much as we will of the differences between the denominations, the fact remains that organized Christianity in all its forms, Protestant and Catholic, stands for certain great convictions about the nature of the world and the meaning of life which are now being taught to children and preached to adults in thousands and tens of thousands of churches. If these convictions are mistaken, they ought to be corrected. If the church is doing harm, it ought to be opposed. But conviction can be fought only by conviction, and a belief that is false must be replaced by a belief that is true. To ignore error is the coward's refuge.[30]

This belief in the importance of theology gave the Presbyterian controversy its own flavor.

As with the Baptists, it is helpful to see the Presbyterian conflict as involving a number of different battles fought over many of the same issues but contested on different fronts. Some were comparatively minor. The 1921 flare-up over the orthodoxy of missionaries, caused by the report of W. H. Griffith-Thomas,[31] was easily contained by Robert Speer and Charles Erdman, who quieted the storm by giving their personal word that the missionaries were orthodox.[32] The missions battle would be fought later and more passionately after the publication of the Hocking report (1932). But its major effect was contributing, albeit indirectly, to the passionate battle over Fosdick's 1922 sermon "Shall the Fundamentalists Win?"

30. William Adams Brown, *Beliefs That Matter: A Theology for Laymen* (New York: Scribner, 1928), p. 10.

31. W. H. Griffith-Thomas, "Modernism in China," *Princeton Theological Review,* Oct. 1921. The article dealt not only with Presbyterian missions but also with the whole of the American presence in China. As in the United States — but with far more effect — there was a move for a unified national church, based on federated principles.

32. Marsden, *Fundamentalism and American Culture,* p. 168. The Briton Griffith-Thomas was a key figure in the founding of Dallas Seminary.

At this time Fosdick was among the rising stars of the American pulpit. He had served as pastor of the wealthy Montclair Baptist Church and had traveled to France as a representative of the churches. Upon his return he became pulpit minister of the First Presbyterian Church of New York, in which position he served until 1925. While there he preached "Shall the Fundamentalists Win?" which was printed in three different journals and published as a pamphlet by Ivy Lee, Rockefeller's publicist. On its face the sermon was a plea for mutual toleration and forbearance. Good Christian people could be found on all sides of the current theological issues, and it would be wrong to exclude any of them from the church. And this was the issue:

> Just now . . . the fundamentalists are giving us one of the worst exhibitions of bitter intolerance that the churches of this country have ever seen. As one watches them and listens to them, one remembers the remark of General Armstrong of Hampton Institute: "Cantankerousness is worse than heterodoxy." There are many opinions in the field of modern controversy concerning which I am not sure whether they are right or wrong, but there is one thing I am sure of: courtesy and kindliness and tolerance and humility and fairness are right. Opinions may be mistaken; love never is.[33]

In short, "the Fundamentalists propose to drive out from the Christian church all the consecrated souls who do not agree with their own theory of inspiration." Such a decision would be, Fosdick declared, "immeasurable folly."[34]

Fosdick's sermon was intended to change the terms of the debate. The issue was not which beliefs, if any, were essential to Christianity or to Presbyterianism; the real issue was tolerance and inclusiveness. In locating the issue there, Fosdick was appealing to the deeply ingrained American habit of friendly disagreement. Just as a Sunday school class could and often did disagree over this or that passage of Scripture, so the whole church could permit a wide variety of opinions among its members and its ministers.

As a rhetorical device, Fosdick's shift of the argument was genius. It was also disingenuous. The New York preacher knew he had been provocative as well as conciliatory. He wrote later in his autobiography: "The trouble was, of course, that in stating the liberal and fundamentalist positions, I had stood in a Presbyterian pulpit and said frankly what the modernist position on some points was — the virgin birth no longer accepted as historic fact, the literal in-

33. Quoted in Harry E. Fosdick, *The Living of These Days: An Autobiography* (New York: Harper and Brothers, 1956), p. 145.

34. William R. Hutchison, *The Modernist Impulse in American Protestantism* (Cambridge: Harvard University Press, 1976), p. 275.

errancy of the Scriptures incredible, the second coming of Christ from the skies an outmoded phrasing of hope."[35] Further, Fosdick knew that contemporary Presbyterianism was very broad. Since the reconciliation of the Old and New Schools, most Presbyterians had conceded the need for a broad toleration of different doctrinal views, and the tent was clearly large enough to include classical Calvinists and many forms of Arminianism. The recent merger with the Cumberland Presbyterian Church, an almost Methodistic body, was a graphic illustration of the point.

Fosdick's argument, further, was intended to make any response from his opponents suspect. It was kind of like trying to answer the question of when you had stopped beating your spouse or when you had left the Communist Party. If you argued that some teachings were not in accord with the Presbyterian position, Fosdick had all the evidence needed to convict you of intolerance. Those caught on the point of this petard were understandably outraged. Fosdick's argument also chose to ignore the frequent statements by fundamentalists that they were not battling for the jots and tittles of correct doctrine but for the broad outlines of orthodox Christianity.

Perhaps most serious, Fosdick avoided the central question raised by the fundamentalists — the question of the uniqueness of Jesus. Had Jesus become our way to God because of his perfect obedience, as Fosdick said in many of his sermons, or was Jesus God incarnate? In their insistence on the virgin birth and the bodily resurrection, the conservatives stood in the classical theological tradition that had rooted Christology in precisely these events.[36]

Fosdick's sermon was an immediate irritant. Clarence Macartney, the pastor of Philadelphia's Second Presbyterian Church and by all accounts one of America's most able preachers, responded with his sermon "Shall Unbelief Win?" Macartney was no rube, and his sermon cut to the issue: Was Christianity a natural product of cultural evolution or a supernatural revealed faith? This was the issue he wanted to debate, not the details of eschatology or even of the Gospels, and he felt it was an essential issue. Bradley Longfield offered this summary:

> Macartney answered Fosdick's sermon point by point. The virgin birth, he maintained, far from being myth or rubbish, was historical fact: the Bible was the inspired and authoritative Word of God; and premillenarians, though mistaken in their exegesis, were at least loyal to the "Person and Claims of Jesus Christ." Liberal preaching, on the other hand, was slowly

35. Fosdick, *Living of These Days*, p. 146.

36. Second-century orthodox theologians, deeply worried about Gnostic inroads into their churches, strongly defended the virgin birth and bodily resurrection as the primary support for Jesus' humanity. These same marks of right belief are found in all the classic creeds.

> secularizing the church. It was a solid, thoughtful response, and years later, Fosdick himself recalled the care with which Macartney had written him to check quotations and to be sure that he understood Fosdick correctly on certain points.[37] Very conscious of proper procedure, Macartney had the Philadelphia Presbytery overture the General Assembly to take action "to direct the Presbytery of New York to take such action as will require the preaching and teaching in the First Presbyterian Church of New York City to conform to the system of doctrine taught in the Confession of Faith."[38]

After two years of political haggling, the General Assembly offered Fosdick the choice of joining the Presbyterian Church and submitting to its discipline or leaving the pulpit of First Church. With great sadness Fosdick resigned the position. For, he wrote, "any subscription made under such circumstances would be generally and, I think, truly interpreted as moral surrender. I am entirely willing that my theology be questioned; I am entirely unwilling to give any occasion for the questioning of my ethics."[39]

In many ways the conclusion of the Fosdick affair was similar to the Dayton trial. Although Fosdick had many capable opponents, such as Macartney, he was blessed by some of his enemies. Many of the attacks on Fosdick lacked credibility or charity, and the media, anxious to sell papers or radio time, paid as much or more attention to these vulgar critics as to the more responsible advocates of the conservative position. Consequently, Fosdick looked like a Daniel set down in the midst of particularly hungry lions who wanted to devour both his body and soul.

The 1924 Auburn Affirmation carried Fosdick's redefinition of the question one step further. While Fosdick's sermon was a thinly disguised appeal for modernism in theology, James Hastings Nichols and the other authors of the Affirmation were careful to avoid any overt or covert reference to the various doctrinal issues involved in the discussion. The document tended to follow the type of theology that Henry Sloane Coffin advocated, and if anything, went out of its way to affirm a very orthodox position as that of its signers.

> Furthermore, this opinion of the General Assembly attempts to commit our church to certain theories concerning the inspiration of the Bible, and

37. For a sympathetic interpretation of Macartney, see C. Allyn Russell, *Voices of American Fundamentalism* (Philadelphia: Westminster, 1976); for Fosdick on Macartney, see *Living of These Days*, p. 147.

38. Quoted in Bradley J. Longfield, *The Presbyterian Controversy: Fundamentalists, Modernists, and Moderates* (New York: Oxford University Press, 1991), p. 11.

39. Fosdick, *Living of These Days*, p. 173.

> the Incarnation, the Atonement, the Resurrection, and the Continuing Life and Supernatural Power of our Lord Jesus Christ. We all hold most earnestly to these great facts and doctrines; we all believe from our hearts that the writers of the Bible were inspired of God; that Jesus Christ was God manifest in the flesh; that God was in Christ, reconciling the world unto Himself, and through Him we have our redemption; that having died for our sins He rose from the dead and is our ever-living Saviour; that in His earthly ministry He wrought many mighty works, and by His vicarious death and unfailing presence He is able to save to the uttermost. Some of us regard the particular theories contained in the deliverance of the General Assembly of 1923 as satisfactory explanations of these facts and doctrines. But we are united in believing that these are not the only theories allowed by the Scriptures.[40]

Instead, the Auburn affirmers turned to an age-old question in American Presbyterianism: loose or strict subscription to the Westminster Confession. According to the Adopting Act (1729) and subsequent legislation, the sole judge of a candidate or minister's subscription was his own presbytery. Hence, for the national church to declare a doctrine essential to the church and, by implication, other doctrines less so was to take the place of the presbytery. If the church wanted to take that route, it had to follow the complicated (and unpopular) task of revising Westminster in such a way as to identify the essential articles. The Auburn Affirmation eventually had the signatures of 1,274 teaching elders. J. Ross Stevenson replied to this argument in the January 1924 *Princeton Review*.[41] On this issue, as on many others, Stevenson advocated traditional Old School positions.

On January 3, 1924, the liberal *Christian Century* ran an article that stated simply that "Two worlds have clashed, the world of tradition and the world of modernism. . . . There is a clash here as profound and as grim as that between Christianity and Confucianism. . . . The God of the fundamentalist is one God; the God of the modernist is another. . . . That the issue is clear and that the inherent incompatibility of the two worlds has passed the stage of mutual tolerance is a fact concerning which there hardly seems room for any one to doubt."[42] In many ways the *Century*'s argument was more emotional than theological. In 1923 the fundamentalists appeared to be winning in the Presbyterian denominations, and the *Century* was preparing its fellow liberals for a crisis of conscience. As horrible as the prospect was, the *Century*'s editors

40. Quoted from http://www.covenantnetwork.org/aubaff.html, accessed Aug. 31, 2006.

41. Loetscher, *The Broadening Church*, p. 120.

42. Loetscher, *The Broadening Church*, p. 120.

believed that the liberals might be forced to walk away from their conservative counterparts.

The idea that conservative and liberal theologies represented two different religions also came naturally to a young assistant professor at Princeton Seminary, J. Gresham Machen. Machen was arguably the most competent American theologian of the 1920s, and one of the few thinkers of that decade whose works still deserve careful study.[43] Since his studies with Wilhelm Hermann in Germany,[44] Machen had struggled with the question of the essence and finality of Christianity. This was the same question that had tormented G. P. Foster and fascinated other American theologians of that generation, including D. C. Macintosh, Henry Nelson Wieman, and Shailer Mathews. In *What Is Christianity?* Adolf von Harnack proposed that Christianity was unique because of its emphasis on a theology — the Fatherhood of God — and on an ethic — the brotherhood of man. While Harnack's position may have satisfied the young university students who heard his lecture series, it had serious intellectual problems, not the least of which was that these two particular teachings are not central to historical Christian theology or ethics. To sense the problem, one need only envision a journal article entitled "The Fatherhood of God and the Brotherhood of Man in Post-Nicene Hermeneutics" or "Aristotelian Transcendence and the Fatherhood of God." In short, as most church histo-

43. For the different interpretations of Machen see D. G. Hart, "Doctor Fundamentalis: An Intellectual Biography of J. Gresham Machen, 1881-1937" (Ph.D. diss., Johns Hopkins University, 1988); revised as *Defending the Faith: J. Gresham Machen and the Crisis of Conservative Protestantism in Modern America* (Baltimore: Johns Hopkins University Press, 1994). This work contains the best discussion of Machen currently in print. I am deeply dependent on Hart for much of what follows, but he in no way is responsible for my errors and idiosyncrasies.

44. Machen wrote about Hermann: "Such an overpowering personality I think I almost never before encountered — overpowering in the sense of religious devotion . . . so much deeper is his devotion to Christ than anything I have known in myself during the past few years. . . . He is a Christian not because he follows Christ as a moral teacher; but because his trust in Christ is (practically, if anything more truly than theoretically) unbounded. It is inspiring to see a man so completely centered in Christ. . . . In New England those who do not believe in the bodily Resurrection of Jesus are, generally speaking, religiously dead; in Germany, Hermann has taught me that is by no means the case. HE believes that Jesus is the one thing in the world that inspires absolute confidence, and an absolutely joyful subjection; that through Jesus we come into communication with the living God and are made free from the world. IT is the faith that is a real experience, a real revelation of God that saves us, not the faith that consists in accepting as true a lot of dogmas on the basis merely of what others have said." Quoted in C. Clair Lewis, "Machen and Liberalism," in *Pressing toward the Mark: Essays Commemorating Fifty Years of the Orthodox Presbyterian Church,* ed. Charles G. Dennison and Richard C. Gamble (Philadelphia: Committee for the Historian of the Orthodox Presbyterian Church, 1986), p. 249.

rians of the time realized, Harnack's attempt to identify the essence of Christianity floundered on the evidence that he himself had so painfully collected. Harnack admitted as much in his *History of Dogma,* where he interpreted the Reformers and Protestant scholastics as the conclusion of the classical Christian quest for clarity in teaching.[45]

By 1921 Machen had reached his mature position on the essence of Christianity. In his James Sprunt Lectures at Union (Richmond), published as the *Origins of Paul's Religion,* he concluded that Paul's faith rested on certain teachings about Christ that were not different in kind from other intellectual convictions. But if this was the case, then arguments about the truth and validity of doctrine were necessary to the further development of Christian truth. Like B. B. Warfield, Machen believed we were still in the infancy of the church as far as the full discovery of Christian truth was concerned, and he hoped for further development of Christian teaching. Machen was not so much committed to a belief that all truth had once been delivered to the saints as he was to the belief that what was committed to the saints was truth! But, as he argued in his 1921 address "Liberalism or Christianity?" — written before the Fosdick controversy — and developed more fully in his *Christianity and Liberalism,* the question posed by the liberals was not this or that expression of Christian teaching. The issue was whether there was any authoritative doctrine or dogma. For the historic church, the answer to that question was an emphatic yes. For modern liberalism, the answer was no. In that sense the central claim of liberalism — that it was a modern expression of Christianity — was false. Noncreedal Christianity was a contradiction in terms.

Machen wrote at a time when the prestige of American science was at a high point.[46] For many Americans, science seemed to offer the best moral and religious guidance into the future available, and the results of science, whether physical or social, were believed to be sound guides for public policy. For many of these Americans the alternatives were not between Machen and Fosdick but between Machen and John Dewey or Walter Lippmann. Fosdick was shocked that he was not supported by the intellectual avant-garde of his time who often, while completely disagreeing with Machen as to the truth of his assertions, found in his position a straightforward alternative to their own.[47]

Ironically, the romantic modernism that Fosdick advocated was already

45. Harnack was, incidentally, excluded from the theological examination of candidates for the ministry in Prussia, because of his views on the historicity of the Apostles' Creed.

46. See James Gilbert, *Redeeming Culture: American Religion in an Age of Science* (Chicago: University of Chicago Press, 1997), chap. 3, "The Republic of Science," pp. 37-62.

47. Fosdick, *Living of These Days,* p. 165. See also Hutchison, *The Modernist Impulse,* pp. 270-74. Significantly, Hutchison picks up on Fosdick's surprise by calling his chapter "The Odd Couple."

passé in many liberal quarters. Contemporary theologians, including such thinkers as D. C. Macintosh, Henry Nelson Wieman, and their younger contemporary Charles Hartshorne, had moved far from Fosdick's romantic understanding of science toward a consistent empiricism. When Whitehead's 1927 Gifford Lectures appeared (published in 1929 as *Process and Reality*), his revision of theism seemed the answer to many contemporaries' deepest intellectual aspirations. For less religious intellectuals, the philosopher John Dewey — who had moved from a Fosdick-like liberalism to a more consistent skepticism — provided the best guide to contemporary life. If Machen was old-fashioned, his words had the advantage of arguing for long-established positions in familiar ways. Hence, while his ideas sounded wrong, dreadfully wrong, they still seemed coherent. In contrast, Fosdick was only a few years out-of-date — a sin that the culturally alienated he hoped to address considered worse than being out-of-date by a millennium.[48]

The other place where Fosdick and the signers of the Auburn Declaration were wrong was in their assumption that people were seeking ways to remain Christian, despite the intellectual winds of change that had swept over Christendom. Again, the assumption seems to be more from their seminary experience, when they had struggled with that question, than it was a vital question in the 1920s. During that decade, an age of secularization and of secularism, many, like H. L. Mencken, passed easily out of the Christian orb and apparently never missed faith.

Machen also represented an uneasiness among his contemporaries that Fosdick, who was at home in the optimistic world of American progressive culture, never understood or appreciated. Machen, like T. S. Eliot — then in exile in England — believed that modern society had become a "waste land" without "great" artists in music, painting, or sculpture.[49] Although Machen's wartime service as a YMCA representative was brief and far from the front, Machen shared the disillusionment of the lost generation. He was not alone in this. Other young theologians were experiencing a similar sense of disjointedness. In Europe, such thinkers as Karl Barth and Emil Brunner, Machen's near contemporaries, shared a similar cultural pessimism.

48. Students of conservative America, such as George Marsden, have rightly called attention to the persistence of the Scottish commonsense philosophy among American conservatives, particularly the Old School. Unfortunately, no one has done a similar study of the relationship of liberalism to the newer scientific thought. I suspect that there was little practical difference between the two sides, although the liberals tended toward a more idealistic and romantic understanding of human learning.

49. See J. Gresham Machen, *Christianity and Liberalism* (New York: Macmillan, 1923; Grand Rapids: Eerdmans, 1946), chap. 1.

In retrospect, one wonders what might have happened had Machen continued to pursue his theological future unimpaired. After all, *The Origins of Paul's Religion, Christianity and Liberalism,* and his later *The Virgin Birth of Christ* (1930) were all essentially programmatic studies, based on research he had done early in his career. He became prominent theologically at about the same time as his fellow student of Hermann, Karl Barth, and many similarities existed between his thought and that of the great Swiss thinker.[50] But the fact of the matter is that the debate over Fosdick was only the prelude to two far more serious battles that occupied all of Machen's time and energy. When they were over, the great conservative theologian had become a sectarian fuming over the peccadilloes of his church.

The first was the reorganization of Princeton Seminary. The issues in this proposal were only partially theological, although the reorganization had profound theological consequences. Like many nineteenth-century seminaries, Princeton had inherited a system of governance that was out of joint with the new models of bureaucratic efficiency that engulfed both churches and theological schools. While the new organizational ideal had many facets, its principal feature was the emphasis on the chief executive officer who, supported by a friendly board, would be able to make decisions about a school's future and implement them. Although Princeton had reluctantly surrendered its traditional faculty-based administration with the election of Francis Patton as president, the school retained much of the character of a faculty-run school. The task of Patton's successor, J. Ross Stevenson, was to make the president's claim to executive power good, and this would have been difficult even in the smoothest of times. At the same time, Princeton's faculty had resisted the new pastoral disciplines, including religious education. To teach the rapidly expanding "classical curriculum" was hard enough to do in three years without adding too many other required and recommended courses. Princeton's retention of a serious language requirement at a time when more and more of the student body lacked college Greek made this even more difficult. Interestingly, Machen's most widely reprinted work, his Greek textbook, was written to help get these students onboard with the heavily exegetical curriculum. Greatly complicating executive action on either of these fronts was the seminary's governance structure that separated doctrinal from fiduciary control.

Stevenson resolved to overcome these two organizational problems. The Princeton president plunged into faculty and denominational politics like a dog on a fresh scent. Charles Erdman, a congenial conservative, premillennial-

50. D. G. Hart, "Machen on Barth" and "J. Gresham Machen, Karl Barth and 'The Theology of Crisis,'" both in *Westminster Theological Journal,* 1991, pp. 189-96 and 197ff.

ist, and expert on teaching the English Bible, headed the president's party. The leadership of those opposed passed to Machen. Even in the best of times, the issues would have become theologized past recognition, and dark questions about motives and the inability of the other side to understand the issues would have filled the faculty lounge and washroom. But these were not ordinary times. The Princeton dispute became a general brawl that, because of the polity of Presbyterian seminaries, was fought out on the national stage. It moved from an almost classic confrontation over seminary governance to a dispute over the future of Princeton and its unique theology itself.

Up to the 1925 assembly at Baltimore, the conservatives in the Presbyterian Church had more or less dominated the discussion, electing William Jennings Bryan and Clarence Macartney as moderators. But in 1925 the conservative majority began to leak. Bryan himself moved in a more conciliatory direction, endorsing William O. Thompson for moderator, and in 1925 Erdman, the leader of the propresidential party, was elected moderator by a coalition that included people as diverse as Billy Sunday and Henry Sloane Coffin. The licensure of Henry Pitney Van Dusen came before this assembly. In many ways this was the least ambiguous of all the cases that could be appealed to that body. The assembly had repeatedly affirmed the importance of the historicity of the virgin birth, and Van Dusen, a protégé of William Adams Brown and of Coffin, had equally emphatically denied that it had ever happened. Since the facts were not in doubt, the only question was what the assembly would do about them. Claiming authority over the Presbytery of New York, the majority said the presbytery had erred and called on it to review the decision. The church was at the edge of schism, and the liberals frankly threatened to take their marbles and go home. It was a desperate ploy, and one that worked. The General Assembly appointed a fifteen-member committee to work toward peace in the church and to report at the next year's meeting. Ironically (considering Machen's own position on evolution) the media fiasco at Dayton may have greatly accelerated the seminary issue. Having moved almost to the point of schism, many Presbyterians did not want to be linked to the populist fundamentalism of barbeque and ballyhoo.

When the 1926 assembly convened in Baltimore, there was a new configuration of people in power. The session began by adopting a statement endorsing "the Christian principle of toleration" in the church. At the same time, the report declared that the early attempts by the General Assembly to declare certain doctrines necessary or essential was illegal. The confession, as it was worded, was the only authority unless and until it was modified constitutionally. In a real sense, during the year following the Van Dusen case, the liberals had carried part of their argument. The assembly then turned to the recommendation of Princeton's board of directors that Machen be elected professor of apologetics. Machen had earned the appointment through his publications, service to the seminary, and hard work on behalf of the church, but the assembly elected not to confirm the appointment. The debate was bitter and acrimonious. Machen's enemies attacked him for his stance on Prohibition and for his "spirit." Formal action was postponed for one year, and a special committee was appointed to investigate the seminary.

The next step was almost predictable. When the commissioners arrived at the seminary, they found a deep difference of opinion. Machen and his party advocated a "Union Seminary" solution in which Princeton would become the voice of conservative Presbyterianism much as Union had become the voice of liberal Presbyterianism. As Machen argued, the church should recognize "the right of thoroughgoing conservatives to have at least one seminary that clearly and unequivocally represented their view."[51] In effect, this would be a de facto recognition of the actual situation. But Erdman and Stevenson rejected that interpretation of the seminary. In their view the school should more nearly reflect the consensus within the church. Whatever the merits of the two arguments, the context determined the situation. The American churches and their seminaries were at the height of their managerial revolution, and the tendency was to affirm strong, central leadership. This the committee did, reporting to the assembly that the root problem at Princeton was the school's governance by two separate boards. The assembly then expanded the committee and instructed it to write a new form of governance for the school. At the same time, it delayed Machen's promotion again.

The sorry spectacle had to end, and it finally did in 1929 when, following the reorganization of the seminary, Machen and three colleagues resigned and founded Westminster Seminary in Philadelphia. The majority of the Princeton faculty, while as conservative as Machen, elected to stay. But starting a new seminary in 1929 was a far more complicated and expensive task than it had been in 1811. Westminster would never gather the resources, power, or prestige of its more favorably endowed parent. Perhaps more important, the Princeton dissenters did not represent a unified conservative party. Most of the moderate conservatives, including the very influential Caspar Hodge, stayed at Princeton, while supporters of Westminster inclined toward dispensationalism, a position that Machen believed was not biblical. In 1937 the fragile unity of this body fell apart as dispensationalists pressed for agreement on their agenda, including the

51. David C. Calhoun, *Princeton Seminary: The Majestic Testimony, 1869-1929* (Edinburgh: Banner of Truth Trust, 1996), p. 380. See J. Gresham Machen, "The Attack on Princeton Seminary: An Appeal for Fair Play" (Philadelphia, 1927).

belief that total abstinence from alcohol was required by the gospel, while the moderate conservatives resolved to maintain their own position. Another seminary schism was inevitable.[52]

The centrality of Princeton Seminary has obscured the fact that other Presbyterian schools were changing as well. Union Seminary in New York, long the bellwether of the New School and liberal parties, was among the first to change to meet the new conditions. The key figure in creating the new Union was Henry Sloane Coffin, who became president of the seminary in 1927. Coffin was a child of privilege, related to many of New York's wealthiest Protestant families. After becoming pastor of the Madison Avenue Presbyterian Church, one of the richest and most influential congregations in the denomination, Coffin became the spokesman for the liberal party in the church. But his leadership was not based solely on his office or even on the fact that, like Clarence Macartney, he was a master of the pulpit. Coffin was at his most effective in personal relationships; he was the type of leader who could look another person in the eye and realize that the two of them shared an understanding that neither necessarily wanted to put into words. Thus, when the Van Dusen matter occupied the assembly, Coffin publicly threatened the assembly with a liberal schism, while working hard behind the scenes to make an alliance with Robert Speer and William Jennings Bryan to forestall any such action.

Coffin's theology had the best marks of liberal evangelicalism: an emphasis on religious experience as the key to faith and theology, a strong sense of social responsibility, and a deep respect for contemporary biblical scholarship. Unlike many of his liberal contemporaries, however, Coffin's own theology was strongly centered on Christ. Christ was not merely a teacher or the founder of a religion. Rather, Christ was the dynamic center of history who effected the redemption he had promised. Christ was God's pattern for what humanity might become. In turn, Coffin's understanding of the church was rooted in his understanding of Christ.[53] Coffin retained much of the older social gospel emphasis on reform and firmly believed that the churches had to take the lead in the construction of a new order. At least part of his interest in ecumenism was rooted in his belief that only a united church would be politically or socially effective.[54] But this was not the only source of his renewed belief in the catholicity of the church. Coffin was an avid participant in both the early international and early national ecumenical movements, including Edinburgh 1910, and like some oth-

52. See George Marsden, "Perspectives on the Division of 1937," in *Pressing toward the Mark,* pp. 295-328.

53. Like Machen, Coffin was a student of Wilhelm Hermann.

54. Longfield, *The Presbyterian Controversy,* pp. 98-100, develops this understanding of Coffin's work.

ers who participated in those movements, his contact with the sheer diversity of Christian life broadened his understanding. In line with many of the younger theologians whose careers he worked to advance, Coffin was coming to see the church as the cradle of redemption as well as an ethical pioneer.

When Coffin became president of Union in 1927, he began almost immediately to move the school away from the modernism of the previous generation. Perhaps the clearest symbol of the shift was Coffin's decision to close the Union School of Religion. The school of religion had been established by George Coe to showcase the ideas of the religious education movement; like Coe, it had drifted toward a consistent modernism that saw religion essentially as the emotive center of ethics. Coffin, noting that the new Riverside Church would establish its own Sunday school, moved to close the experimental school as no longer needed. Harris Parker told, however, another tale:

> The most influential and decisive controversy to gather about the work of the Union School during the Fahs administration developed around a worship service led by Spear Knebel on April 8, 1928. President Coffin was present for this service and was shocked and alarmed by what he heard. Knebel told the stories of the Attis-Cybele resurrection myth and the story of the Resurrection of Jesus as recorded in the twenty-third chapter of Luke. These were Knebel's concluding remarks: "Will we go on living after we die? No one who has died has ever come back to tell us. Many, many people believe that we will, just as they believe that Jesus went on living, as I have read to you. At any rate, we do not need to be afraid, for we can be sure that in some way we will be taken care of after we die."[55]

Coffin was furious. The experimental Sunday school had begun to go beyond Christianity, and Coffin was having none of it. The time had come to close the school, and Coffin knew this act would symbolize to many, liberal and conservative, that a new hand was at the helm.

Coffin's ecumenism was also the clue to his early faculty appointments that included John Bailey, Reinhold Niebuhr, and Henry Pitney Van Dusen. These thinkers did not share a common theology, but their positions did share certain common elements: a willingness to reinterpret the tradition of the church, a belief that the church had to be as much realist as idealist in the political and social order, and a commitment to the ecumenical church. Taking advantage of its links with Columbia University, Coffin's Union was gradually assuming a new role as the educator of teachers for a number of colleges and seminaries influenced by

55. Harris H. Parker, "The Union School of Religion, 1910-1929: Embers from the Fires of Progressivism," *Religious Education* 88 (Fall 1991).

the ecumenical movement. While few other Presbyterian seminaries imitated Union, the new emphasis on ecumenism and the church became central for all Northern Presbyterian schools, including Princeton.

Whether one calls Coffin's emphases at Union "neoorthodox" or "realistic" or "evangelically liberal" is beside the point. What is of interest, at least to the historian of American theological education, is the difference between the way Union and its sister Presbyterian schools ultimately responded to the crisis of the fundamentalist-modernist movement, and the way the Northern Baptist schools responded. Coffin's Union led the way toward a new center that found in ecumenism and the church new and vital ways of expressing Presbyterian connectionism. Although some of the older individualism of early liberalism and fundamentalism remained, the period from the fundamentalist-modernist crisis to the Confession of 1967, including the Life and Work curriculum of 1948, represented the church age among American Presbyterians. In contrast, the Northern Baptists responded by further fragmenting their system of theological schools and continuing to see one of the primary purposes of those institutions as providing a base for different religious, theological, and ecclesiastical points of view.

III. The Southern Story

Fundamentalism is often associated with the South in the popular mind. Yet in many ways the fundamentalist movement, at least as it developed in the North, was foreign to the Southern soul and style of life. The primary event in modern Southern history was the defeat in the War between the States. This humiliation was followed by what appeared to white Southerners as a titanic struggle against great odds to restore "white" rule to the South. The three largest white churches, the Baptist, the Presbyterian, and the Methodist, took the ideological lead in the struggles, developing a Southern "civil theology" that, while never uniform, helped to sustain the region's peculiar identity until the early 1960s. Part of this civil theology was the belief that the churches should not be active in partisan politics but should provide the general cultural and moral foundations of society. Another key part was the belief in Southern religious exceptionalism.[56] Unlike the North, seen as the home of a secularizing liberalism, the South retained the purity of its religious institutions. The South was

56. Harry S. Stout, "From Confederacy to Civil Rights: Continuity in Southern Pulpit Rhetoric." This unpublished article noted the continuity between the language during and after the Civil War.

the cornerstone that the world had rejected that would eventually form the foundation of a reborn nation. The South, like Christ, lived for others.

Polite white theology saw religious conservatism as an essential part of this Southern theology, and even liberal church leaders, such as the Poteats of North Carolina or W. O. Carver of Southern Baptist Theological Seminary, preferred to call themselves "conservatives." Although outsiders might wonder what "conservative" might mean in this context, Southerners instinctively understood.

Southern civil theology needed to affirm Southern unity even when a candid observer might have denied that such unity existed. Indeed, Southerners often masked from themselves the fact of their own diversity. Geographically and economically there were many different Souths: the rich coastal plains and river valleys, ideal for cotton and large-scale agriculture; the poor lands of the hill country; the natural manufacturing sites along the fall line that separates the Piedmont from the coast; the resource-rich areas of Alabama, Louisiana, and Texas; and the red clay farmlands. Despite the democratic rhetoric about white equality, economic class separated whites into different cultural and social strata with very different interests and religious commitments. But the prevalent Southern social theory insisted that all these diverse units be considered part of one entity, the "South," and that this South collectively had a special mission to the nation. The South was untouched by the various apostasies of the North — political, social, and economic — and thus only the South could save America to save the world. The South was Christian America's last best hope.

The tendency of Southerners to wear masks meant that theological issues and issues of social and political control were intertwined. The struggle that separated Vanderbilt University and its divinity school from the Methodist Episcopal Church, South, was presented as a struggle over control of the institution, an almost classic clash between businessmen and clerics, typical of the secularization of education in the second and third decades of the twentieth century.[57] As a result of this battle, new Methodist divinity schools were established at Emory in Atlanta and at Duke in North Carolina, and Southern Methodist University in Dallas was developed further. Interestingly, the theological issues — biblical criticism and evolution — that often angered Southern Methodists were kept beneath the table. The white establishment could fight about power, but not over the ideology that provided the mortar of sectional relationships.

The conservative quality of Southern religion was often more apparent than real. Although Southerners were suspicious of Republican forms of progressivism, both Bryan and Wilson were regional heroes. Further, Southern re-

57. See above, chap. 12, pp. 263-65.

ligious leaders welcomed parts of the progressive agenda. Most Southern clergy, for instance, embraced prohibition, despite their own professed distrust of any mixture of religion and politics, and such revivalists as Samuel "Golden Rule" Jones were always popular. Both Baptist and Methodist theological schools had teachers, such as the Baptist W. O. Carver and Charles Spurgeon Gardiner, who advocated social and political ideas similar to the teachings of the Northern social gospel. Women's training schools, a bearer of progressive thought in the North, were also popular in the South, although often with a mixture of gentility intersected into the missionary program. The great progressive campaigns against prostitution and gambling were also welcomed throughout Dixie, as the churches and their supporters went to war against these vices. Southern Methodist women's organizations were notably more liberal on race than their male counterparts or the church as a whole. The *Progressive Farmer* was among the region's most popular publications.

The Southern story also has to be told against the background of the region's rural character. The only denomination arguably more rooted in the urban South, the intellectually influential Southern Presbyterians, had only about 80,000 members across the South in 1920. The greatest period of Presbyterian growth would be from 1930 to 1960 when they grew at about 10 percent per year. Whatever the childhood roots of most Northern fundamentalists or, for that matter, liberals,[58] Northern fundamentalism and its institutions were centered in cities, and much of the fundamentalist battle in the North revolved around the control of the new denominational structures created by the organizational revolution.[59] In contrast, the organizational revolution was just beginning in the South, and many of the region's most influential seminaries would be established after 1920. As in the Old Northwest, seminaries tended to be linked to urban constituencies, and the development of seminaries in the South paralleled the larger development of urban institutions in the region.

The rural character of the South also meant that Southerners lived in a different economy than their Northern counterparts. For most of the North, once the brief postwar depression ended, the 1920s were a "second great barbeque" with relatively full employment and the rapid growth of such manufactures as automobiles, tractors, and radios. Not everybody got rich, and there was always more poverty than the nation wanted to admit, but those who

58. The most fundamental observation about most of Europe and North America in the period from 1880 to 1920 was the massive migration of people from rural to urban areas. Even cosmopolitan cities, such as Berlin, London, and Madrid, were primarily inhabited by people who had lived in the countryside for all or most of their youth.

59. Ferenc Morton Szasz, *The Divided Mind of Protestant America, 1880-1930* (University: University of Alabama Press, 1982), p. 85.

shaped public opinion prospered. People felt well-off, and that was what mattered. In contrast, the twenties were a decade of economic disillusion for the South. The Great War had raised agricultural prices to almost astronomical heights, and Southern and Midwest farmers had responded by putting more land into cultivation and by purchasing, often on credit, new machinery to further increase production. The boll weevil, which halted the development of cotton cultivation in Mexico, crossed into Texas around 1892 and advanced rapidly throughout the South, moving north, west, and east at about seventy miles a year. By the 1920s almost all the South was infested. Despite the bug, overproduction dropped cotton to ten cents a pound in 1921. For Southerners, this represented a serious crisis. Many Southerners felt as if they stood on Mount Nebo and looked into a promised land, only to have God tell them they had to wander for forty more years in the wilderness. The coming of the Great Depression and the Dust Bowl capped these hard times with an even more difficult economic reality.

IV. The Southern Baptist Crisis

Southern Baptists entered the 1920s in a spirit of jubilee. Their two seminaries, Southern and Southwestern, were under the leadership of two of the more capable presidents in those schools' history, E. Y. Mullins and Lee Scarborough, who were masters at making more with less. In many ways both schools were long shadows of their leaders. Both men were products of the new Texas that had been settled by Southerners fleeing the Black Belt after the Civil War. But there the similarity ended. Mullins was a highly sophisticated theologian who was influenced by Wilhelm Hermann, Borden Parker Bowne, Herman Lotze, William James, Lewis French Stearns, and Frank Hugh Foster.[60] Despite this intellectual pedigree, Mullins was a thoroughly conservative theologian who held to a high doctrine of inspiration, although not that of the Princeton theologians. In his systematic classes he replaced James Boyce's *Abstract of Systematic Theology,* a thinly disguised summary of Charles Hodge, with his own *Christianity in Its Doctrinal Expression.* The wording of the title was important; for Mullins, Christianity was an experience of grace and rebirth. Theology was derived from the experience, and not the experience from theology. While religious experience demanded an intellectual analysis, all doctrine, at least potentially, needed to be revised and corrected.

60. See E. Glenn Hinson, "Edgar Young Mullins," in *Makers of Christian Theology in America,* p. 348.

In contrast, Scarborough was the voice of a more boisterous Southwestern Baptist style. In his inaugural address in 1915 he declared his adherence to sound doctrine: "if we do (ignore doctrine), we will give out an emasculated Christianity, an enervated, effeminate religion. If you take the bone-food out of what you feed your child, you can't grow a strong body. If you take doctrines, basic fundamental truth out of what you feed his soul, you will not grow a strong Christian character. An invertebrate Christianity is not Christianity at all."[61] No one ever applied the dreaded epithet "invertebrate" to Scarborough or the young Texans he rallied to his cause.

The place of both seminaries in the fundamentalist controversy can be understood in part in terms of finances. Southern Seminary was by far the better financed, although its revenues did not equal those of the more prosperous Northern Baptist schools. Northern conservatives considered the school a model Baptist institution and appreciated its efficiency as well as its doctrinal standards. Southern managed to educate a large student body — perhaps the most diverse in educational background of any major seminary in the country — by using large classes and, despite its proud elective system, very little variation in academic program. Mullins continually struggled with the financial problems of the school, especially after he decided to move the seminary to a more suburban campus. Southern Seminary's style reflected the school's aspirations, its history, and its actual finances. Like much of the South between the Civil War and the Second World War, the school's values reflected those of a shabby gentility. After the move in 1926, the campus was dominated by colonial buildings, surrounded by magnolias and black servants. Like much of the South, its outward magnificence and grace barely hid the fact that it was deeply in debt.

Scarborough's Southwestern was even more poorly financed than Louisville. Until the establishment of the Cooperative Program, Southwestern was under the Texas Baptist Convention, from which it received most of its funding. There was never enough money, faculty were often underpaid, and there was little room for frills. Nonetheless, the school was expansive and expanding, establishing schools of Christian education and church music. But increased enrollment meant increased financial pressures.

Both presidents greeted the end of the First World War with relief. The war had reduced enrollments and contributions, and both schools were hurting. The crusading mentality that had fired the war seemed also to have spread

61. Lee Scarborough, "The Primal Test of Theological Education" (inaugural address, 1915), quoted in Lee Scarborough, *A Modern School of the Prophets* (Nashville: Broadman, 1939), p. 18. See Thomas Nettles, "J. L. R. Scarborough: Public Figure," *Southwestern Journal of Theology* 25, no. 2 (Spring 1983): 24-42.

to the denomination, creating hope for better times. Southern Baptists launched their $75 Million Campaign to raise money for various Baptist missions and schools. Miraculously the campaign received more than $92 million in pledges. However, pledges were more readily made than paid. By 1922 it was clear that the campaign would fall short of its goal by almost $15 million. It was the beginning of almost two decades of financial nightmares that would bring the convention and its agencies almost to formal bankruptcy and leave them unable to pay their debts.

The schools, lacking the large endowments of the older Northern Baptist schools or a large number of wealthy patrons, were thrown back on the denomination for support. For good or for ill, this meant that the question of seminary finance merged with angry conservatives wanting to use the power of the purse to keep the seminaries theologically pure. On Founders' Day in 1920, as the board met to approve the plans to relocate the campus:

> Dr. C. A. Stakely of Montgomery Ala followed Dr. McConnell in a marvelous address on the unique theme, "the Seminary and Darwinism." He called attention to the fact that the Seminary and Darwinism were both born in 1859, and then traced the life of the great Seminary and that of Darwinism through the changes these sixty eventful years, drawing the striking comparisons as to their past influences, their present status, and their future outlook. Darwinism, he said, has been abandoned by practically all of the leading scientists of the world, and is evidently near the end of its decline. The Seminary has grown with increasing usefulness, prestige, and power through all the years, until its influence now reaches around the world.[62]

Stakely's comments reflected a growing Southern concern about evolution. From 1920 to 1926 evolution dominated each successive Southern Baptist Convention. The controversy ended when the convention adopted the McDaniel resolution in 1926 that stated: "This convention accepts Genesis as teaching that man was the special creation of God and rejects every theory, evolution or other, which teaches that man originated in, or came by way of, a lower animal ancestry." This was accompanied by a resolution offered by S. E. Tull that all employees of the convention, including seminary faculties, should publicly agree with this affirmation.[63]

62. M. T. Andrews, account of the special meeting of the board of trustees called to vote on the relocation of the school to its new location. The board met on Founders' Day 1920. Southern Seminary Archives.

63. Cited in Robert Baker, *The Southern Baptist Convention and Its People, 1607-1972* (Nashville: Broadman, 1974), p. 398.

The debate about evolution peaked in the South in the early 1920s with over twenty state legislatures considering such legislation, and five — Florida, Arkansas, Tennessee, Mississippi, and Oklahoma — adopting laws that prohibited its teaching in the public schools. Even where the bills were defeated, the debate was often passionate. In a sense it was a classic progressive battle with the advocates of evolution relying on the idea that education should be directed by professional educators and scientists, while the opponents stressed the need of public schools to respond favorably to the values of those they served. This interpretation may help explain why the debate was more heated in the South than in the rest of the country. In the 1920s the South was just beginning to close the gap between its schools and those of the North and West. One sign of this was, of course, the growing number of high schools in the region as well as the generally increasing educational level of the population.[64] But the transformation to a more bureaucratic system was not as complete as it was in the North, and hence the schools were immediately subject to popular pressure and control. Pressures brought on local school boards, which often refused to hire evolutionists as teachers or avoided textbooks that featured the theory, were more often successful than more statewide efforts.[65]

The debates among Baptists tended to follow the larger debates in particular areas. In both Oklahoma and Arkansas anti-evolutionary forces were strong in the state legislature, and those two states contributed two of the Southern Baptist Convention's most eloquent advocates of prohibiting the teaching of evolution in the convention's schools, C. P. Stealey and S. E. Tull. Anti-evolution sentiment was generally weaker in the eastern South. In this region, where the long-established Baptist colleges had considerable influence, evolution was less of an issue among Baptists. Indeed, William Poteat, the president of Wake Forest College and one of the South's more prominent biologists, led the successful fight to defeat an anti-evolution bill in North Carolina.[66] The debate was not confined to the physical South. Members of the Southern dias-

64. The literature on the history of public education in the South is extensive.

65. Willard B. Gatewood, ed., *Controversy in the Twenties: Fundamentalism, Modernism, and Evolution* (Nashville: Vanderbilt University Press, 1969), pp. 37-38, notes that anti-evolutionary sentiment was very widespread throughout the country and that what was distinct about the South was that the campaign was so sharp and so effective.

66. Willard B. Gatewood, *Preachers, Pedagogues, and Politicians: The Evolution Controversy in North Carolina, 1920-1927* (Chapel Hill: University of North Carolina Press, 1966). Like all generalizations, this one must be nuanced. Clearly, Poteat was able to command a majority in the state convention, but that body, like most Baptist groups, was largely controlled by the larger and wealthier churches that often had Wake Forest graduates as pastors. Whether rank-and-file sentiment was in agreement is not as clear.

pora, even when they served churches in the North and did not have status in the various Southern bodies, retained considerable influence. These included John Roach Straton, William Bell Riley, A. C. Dixon, and J. C. Massee.

Lee Scarborough believed that the theory of evolution was both false and morally corrupting. During the debate over the Baptist Faith and Message, a 1920s rewrite of the New Hampshire Confession adopted by the convention in 1925, Scarborough repeatedly asked Mullins whether the statement was sufficiently strong on the subject.[67] After all, the Baptist Faith and Message affirmed that "man was created by the special act of God, as recorded in Genesis,"[68] and did not affirm the historicity of Adam and Eve. Mullins's position was less clear-cut. Apparently he had accepted some elements of the evolutionary hypothesis as a young pastor, but by 1922 he was warning the convention:

> We have been much concerned over modern rationalism, and the false assumptions of materialistic science. It seems to me three things are clear. First, we will not tolerate in our denominational schools any departure from the great fundamentals of the faith in the name of science false so called. Second, we will not be unjust to our teachers, nor curtail unduly their God-given right to investigate truth in the name of science. Firm faith and free research is our noble Baptist ideal. Third, we will be loyal to every fact which is established in any realm of research. Just as we are loyal to the supreme fact of Christ, His Virgin Birth, His sinless life, His atoning death, His resurrection and present reign.[69]

Whatever his own views, Mullins knew that some members of his faculty as well as many teachers in denominational colleges thought evolution was probably true. Somewhat like Robert Speer and the Northern moderates, he wanted to stand firm for the truth while permitting dissent and preserving unity.

Mullins's work as chair of the committee that prepared the 1925 Baptist Faith and Message was perhaps the best clue to his position on the disputed issues. Mullins supported the use of the New Hampshire Confession of Faith, with only slight modifications, but he inserted a strong preface to the document. The preface was a ringing reaffirmation of the right of private interpretation of the Bible, a restatement of Mullin's famed "Axioms of Religion,"[70] and a clear attempt to make the Baptist Faith and Message less of a creed. The document was

67. E. Y. Mullins, papers, Southern Baptist Theological Seminary, p. 98.

68. Quoted in Walter Shurden, *Not a Silent People* (Nashville: Broadman, 1972), p. 93.

69. Quoted in Shurden, *Not a Silent People,* p. 95.

70. The *Axioms of Religion,* frequently reprinted, was perhaps Mullins's most popular book. It has retained popularity with both moderate and conservative leaders in the convention.

to be clear enough to give guidance and open enough to permit some measure of freedom: almost a mirror image of Mullins's own Southern Seminary.

The Baptist Faith and Message did not end the dispute. S. E. Tull's resolution came after the Baptist Faith and Mission was approved, and the faculties had to be polled on the issue. Despite some dissent on the faculties, both seminaries and the Baptist Bible Institute (later New Orleans Seminary) reported their compliance.[71] As was true of various Northern Baptist investigatory commissions, the seminary's statements were probably not completely honest, but the compromise was that the conservatives would accept outward conformity while allowing the seminary presidents some freedom to keep less than orthodox faculty. At least on the surface, the compromise held until the 1960s when a new round of controversies over Genesis disrupted the Southern Baptist Convention.

One reason why both sides accepted this dubious deal was the absolute necessity of doing something about the convention's financial crisis. The failure of people to pay their pledges to the $75 Million Campaign left all the denominational agencies strapped for funds. Equally important, the "agent" system, whereby the convention bodies in the states and across the South appointed agents to travel from church to church preaching their cause, had become a scandal. Not only were there far too many agents roaming the territory, but they were expensive and difficult to control. Many were more noted for their emotional extremism than for their knowledge or advocacy of their cause. Convention causes acquired the vague aroma of the medicine man and traveling vaudevillian.

To respond to these problems, the convention leadership proposed the adoption of the Cooperative Program, which was essentially a series of unified budgets, similar to the arrangements that created the Northern Baptist Convention. Each congregation was to budget a certain amount for its total contribution. This amount would be divided between the state convention and the Southern Baptist Convention. In turn, those bodies would devise unified budgets for all their work that would be approved by the respective bodies. In exchange, the conventions had significant control of the various agencies that was exerted through the naming of the trustees and the annual review of the various agencies' reports. Under the provisions of this plan, both Southern and Southwestern were placed under convention control,[72] and many state Baptist

71. Robert A. Baker, *Tell the Generations Following: A History of Southwestern Baptist Theological Seminary, 1908-1983* (Nashville: Broadman, 1983), p. 262.

72. Whether Southern's trustees could refuse to seat new trustees elected by the convention was a major issue in the recent moderate-fundamentalist battle in the SBC. It seems to me that they could have done so, since the school's charter always retained the necessity of the board's election of its own members, but only at the cost of ending the financial agreement.

colleges accepted a similar arrangement with their own conventions.[73] Southern Baptist poverty kept the Cooperative Program from attaining its full potential until the post–World War II prosperity and the migration of population from the North changed the financial situation of the churches. However, once that occurred, Southern Baptist seminaries became the best-financed in the country. In the meantime, the convention languished as its financial problems, if anything, grew. The embezzlement of almost a million dollars from the Home Mission Board in 1928 was only part of the larger fiscal disaster.

Dollars were not the only reason the compromise was accepted. Convention loyalists had the good fortune to have J. Frank Norris as their most vocal opponent. Norris was a notoriously hard character to understand. He was a graduate of Southern Seminary, onetime editor of the *Baptist Standard,* uncompromising foe of alcohol and gambling, and master of homespun Southern rhetoric. His attacks on his foes knew no boundaries, and he specialized in the combination of personal and ecclesiastical issues. For instance, his adversary, George Truett, pastor of the First Baptist Church of Dallas, had killed a companion in a hunting accident as a boy. The incident preyed on his mind for years — and Norris marked every anniversary of the death with a telegram reminding Truett of his "sin." Norris found himself progressively excluded from various Baptist bodies: the Pastors' Conference in Fort Worth, 1914; the Tarrant County Baptist Association in 1922; the Texas Baptist Convention in 1924.

Norris's personal life was no more pleasant than his ministry. In a 1926 sermon he accused H. C. Meacham, Fort Worth's mayor and a Roman Catholic, of using city funds for Catholic charities. He also said the mayor had bribed a young woman to keep her from bringing serious charges against him. Meacham and his supporters were understandably upset, and they sent lumberman D. C. Chipps to talk with the preacher. Words were exchanged, shots were fired, and Chipps lay dead on the floor of Norris's study: the corpse was unarmed.[74] Nonetheless, an Austin jury later acquitted Norris of murder on the grounds of self-defense.

Other Southern fundamentalists also had unsavory characters. John R. Rice, for instance, an early follower of Norris and an extremist in his own right, was a well-known Southern fundamentalist. Rice left the convention in the 1920s in the midst of the debates over the new financial plans and went on to publish the *Sword of the Lord,* one of the nastiest fundamentalist journals. Al-

73. Many colleges, such as Baylor in Texas, went back to their original charters in the aftermath of the conservative takeover of the SBC and assumed something like their earlier relationship to their constituency.

74. C. Allyn Russell, *Voices of American Fundamentalism: Seven Autobiographical Studies* (Philadelphia: Westminster, 1976), p. 34.

though a Methodist, Robert R. "Bob" Jones, Sr., founder of the "World's Most Unusual University," was also a master of anger and vitriol. Taken together, it is hard to image a trio more opposite to the gentlemanly traditions that motivated men like Truett, Mullins, and Scarborough, not to mention the very cultured presidents of Southern Baptist colleges. If finances made them a shabby gentility, they were still gentility, and they still spoke softly.

In short, their own excesses defeated the more conservative Southerners. As theologically orthodox as many Southern Baptists were and as willing as they were to pass resolutions calling for uniformity on doctrinal issues, they were not, and would not embrace anyone who was, as ill mannered as Norris, Rice, and Jones. If race supported white unity in the South, social class also demanded a certain standard of manners. This was perhaps especially true as large numbers of white Southerners were migrating from the countryside to the cities. While they wanted — as is common with other ex–rural dwellers — to continue the comforting patterns of religion from home, they did not want their churches to look country or crude. Many contemporary black urban congregations, incidentally, also had the same dual expectations.[75]

V. The Southern Presbyterians

At first glance, the inclusion of the Southern Presbyterians in a section on the impact of fundamentalism seems almost out of place. As their historian Ernest Trice Thompson makes clear, there was little controversy in the General Assembly over the issues, and very few pastors were disciplined by local presbyteries. Further, the church was the smallest of the tribes of Zion, having only about 80,000 members in the 1920s. Its greatest period of growth came in the three decades from 1930 to 1960, as Southern Presbyterianism's blend of orthodox theology, social respectability, and urbane good manners lifted the church to more than one million members. Yet, even on the verge of the 1983 merger, the Southern Presbyterian Church continued to be a small pond with most of those at its assemblies and synods knowing each other personally.

Yet the denomination had an undercurrent of fundamentalism and conservative evangelicalism that ran from the 1920s through the 1970s that informed much of the church's life. Much of that stream flowed from the deep in-

75. The social defeat of the fundamentalists was most obvious in the South, where some of the cruder fundamentalists held court, but it was also a factor in the North. Many very cultivated Northern conservative leaders felt the sting of this aspect of their defeat, such as James Gray of Moody Bible Institute and William Bell Riley, and it hurt badly.

volvement of the Presbyterian Church, US, in the China mission. Most of the founders of the Bible Union of China, organized in 1920, were Southern Presbyterians, and this group was the source of much of the information that such conservatives as Griffith-Thomas used in their exposés of modernism in China. Further, the Chinese mission had a disproportionate number of dispensationalists who were appointed by the China Inland Mission and through other agencies. The Bible Institute of Los Angeles (BIOLA) had a China campus.

Liberals were also well represented in China. In 1911 Nanking Theological Seminary, originally a joint venture of the Northern and Southern Presbyterian Churches, became an interdenominational school with students and faculty from the Methodist and Disciples joining the Presbyterians. The only official inroad that liberalism made in the school, at least in the 1920s, was the occasional use of William Newton Clarke's *Outline of Theology* and *Hasting's Bible Dictionary.*[76] Yet textbook use is rarely an indication of what happens in a classroom or what is actually communicated to students. Lian Xi believes that many missionaries held "liberal and syncretic" ideals, and he speaks of "the predominance of liberalism in foreign missions" as a matter of fact.[77]

Two of the products of the Southern Presbyterian mission to China illustrate the tensions within it: L. Nelson Bell and Pearl Buck. Bell was a missionary physician who went to China to practice evangelistic medicine. By the 1920s he had become concerned with the drift toward modernism in the China mission, especially the proposal to construct a united American Protestant mission, the National Christian Council, and was actively building a base of American supporters to keep the mission, and by extension the Southern Presbyterian Church, free of heresy. Bell would influence his denomination and American religion more significantly after he returned from China in 1941 and founded the *Southern Presbyterian Journal,* served as an influential trustee of Columbia Theological Seminary, and cofounded *Christianity Today.*

Bell was one of those bothered by John Leighton Stuart, president of Peking University and a second-generation Southern Presbyterian missionary. As a child, Stuart had come to appreciate Chinese civilization and culture and believed that it offered much to the West. Stuart's problems with his conservative opponents revolved around the question whether Christianity represented a final religion or not, and he came to interpret Christ in distinctly Confucian

76. Ernest Trice Thompson, *Presbyterians in the South,* vol. 3, *1890-1972* (Richmond: John Knox, 1973), p. 320.

77. Lian Xi, *The Conversion of Missionaries: Liberalism in American Protestant Missions in China, 1907-1932* (University Park: Pennsylvania State University Press, 1997), p. 219.

78. Xi, *The Conversion of Missionaries,* p. 219.

ways.[78] Stuart went before his presbytery, East Hanover, twice, and was acquitted both times. Among his critics were J. Gresham Machen and William M. McPheeters of Columbia Theological Seminary. The fact that Stuart could not be held accountable, despite his obvious "modernism," infuriated Southern conservatives for years.[79]

The most famous China hand was Pearl Sydenstricker Buck.[80] Like Stuart, she was raised in China by missionary parents. While she received a Western education, her parents hired Chinese tutors who taught her something of Buddhism and Tao. Young Pearl also played and studied with Chinese children. After returning to America and graduating from Randolph-Macon, a Methodist college in Virginia, she applied to the Southern Presbyterians for a missionary appointment in China. While in China she married John Lossing Buck, a Northern Presbyterian, and transferred to that board. In 1921 she and her husband moved to Nanking, where she taught English at the university. Eleven years later she scored a major critical and financial triumph with the publication of *The Good Earth,* which won a Pulitzer Prize. But by this time the meaning of her own novel had sunk in to her consciousness. When the very controversial *Rethinking Missions: A Layman's Inquiry after One Hundred Years* appeared, she favorably reviewed it for the *Christian Century.* She found *Rethinking* to be "a great book" and said she agreed with its every conclusion.[81] In 1932 she delivered an address to 1,200 Presbyterian women at a luncheon that was printed in *Harper's Monthly* as "Is There a Case for Foreign Missions?" This essay was republished as a pamphlet. Her view of the case for missions, at least as Presbyterians had historically understood the term, was negative. "I am wearied unto death with this preaching. It deadens all through, it confuses all issues, it is producing, in China at least, a horde of hypocrites."[82] China did not need anyone seeking to make Christian converts, although there was work there for Westerners who would listen and learn from China and carry their learning back to the West. After a few months of debate, Buck resigned from the board.

Although Pearl Buck was with the Northern board at the time of her res-

79. See Yu Ming Shaw, *An American Missionary in China: John Leighton Stuart and Chinese-American Relations* (Cambridge: Harvard University Press, 1992), and *Fifty Years in China: The Memoirs of John Leighton Stuart, Missionary and Ambassador* (New York: Random House, 1954).

80. Pearl S. Buck, "Is There a Case for Foreign Missions?" *Harper's Monthly,* Jan. 1933, pp. 145-47. See also William Hutchison, "Modernism and Missions: The Liberal Search for an Exportable Christianity," in *The Missionary Enterprise in China and America,* ed. John K. Fairbanks (Cambridge: Harvard University Press, 1974).

81. Longfield, *The Presbyterian Controversy,* p. 201.

82. Quoted in Xi, *The Conversion of Missionaries,* p. 121.

ignation, she highlighted the conservative concerns in the Southern Presbyterian Church. Buck was, of course, a child of the church who had served as one of its missionaries, and she taught at Nanking University, a school supported by the church. While moderates and denominational loyalists might argue that she was unusual or even a sport, she did confirm many conservatives' fears. Support for such interdenominational activities as Nanking suffered, and conservative Southern Presbyterians, led by Bell, resisted union with the Northern church for more than fifty years.

CHAPTER NINETEEN

Reform in Many Places: The Beginning of AATS

In 1918 George Horr, the energetic liberal president of Newton, began to plan a conference of Baptist seminary leaders. While his announced purpose for the meeting was the need for Baptist seminaries to cooperate in planning for the emergency of the war, he was sure the war was only a hiatus in his denomination's accelerating theological conflict. When he presented this plan to Abbott Lowell of Harvard, Lowell was pleased to host a dinner for the assembled scholars. This was not the first conversation between the two presidents. Horr, determined to elevate the standards of his seminary, had worked hard to build bridges between his school and the distinguished university on the other side of the Charles. For his part Lowell had shown considerable interest in theological education, negotiating an agreement with Andover Seminary that brought the nation's oldest seminary to the Cambridge campus and that promised eventually to unite the two schools. Later Lowell would introduce Horr to Dr. Richard Cabot, one of the founders of the clinical movement, and a succession of Newton (later Andover-Newton) faculty, including Nels Ferré, would take their doctorates at Harvard. Prior to the Baptist meeting, Horr mentioned to Professor Henry Foote of Harvard the need for a larger meeting, a suggestion Foote relayed to Lowell. At the dinner for Baptist professors, President Lowell issued his personal invitation for the conference to meet in August of that year.

The Baptist meeting had dealt with many of the main issues before the schools. As President Clarence Barbour noted, the schools "are going to face some very lean years,"[1] but these practical problems were secondary to the

1. Clarence Barbour, *Conference of Baptist Theological Seminaries, Held at Boston and Newton Centre, Massachusetts March 12 and 13, 1918 at the Invitation of the Newton Theological Institute* (Boston: The Conference, privately printed, [1918]), p. 8.

larger questions before theological educators. E. Y. Mullins, the president of Louisville's Southern Baptist Seminary, believed that the schools would face a whole new postwar world that required changes in every area of seminary life. Mullins, like many Southerners, believed that Wilson, the first Southern president after Reconstruction, had grasped the truth about the new international order.

> This will be notably true regarding nationalism and internationalism. What is the Christian conception of the nation? What are the Christian principles governing the relationships between nations? On the one side will be the ideals of mutual respect, cooperation, and federation on terms of equality and justice; on the other, the ideal of brute domination, of the mere struggle between contending powers, and the ruthless trampling upon the weak. Questions of disarmament and permanent world-peace will become vital issues. The status of aliens under our government and the political status of women are questions which will undoubtedly assume new importance as a result of the war.[2]

As Baptists saw the matter, then, the war emergency was both an opportunity and a threat, the chance to turn toward the future and to make constructive theological and educational change.

The larger conference also took this broad approach, stressing both the problems posed by the war and the need for constructive change. President Lowell's keynote address, "The Social and Religious Problems Which the War Has Presented to the Minister," dealt with current events, but the other items on the agenda included the parish minister, religious education, professional teachers, social service and missions, the case method,[3] and aid for students. The opportunity the conference provided for such discussions was new. Although the Religious Education Association included a section on theological seminaries that routinely presented one or two papers a year, the first Conference of Theological Seminaries provided a much more focused opportunity to discuss a number of issues. And those discussions included the most influential leaders of the seminary community, senior faculty, successful presidents, and the deans of the university-related schools. Despite denominational differences, these discussions revealed what some theological educators had known for

2. E. Y. Mullins, in *Conference,* p. 8. Wilson's belief in the self-determination of nations was related to his Southern background as well as to general American experience.

3. The case method had largely replaced the lecture in the better law schools, and the new Harvard Business School had adopted it for their program. To some theological educators, case study offered a creative way to approach theological problems.

some time: the problems of theological education needed to be addressed on a broad, ecumenical basis. Consequently, the conference appointed a continuation committee to explore the possibility of a permanent organization. The group was to meet again in 1920.

W. Douglas Mackenzie of Hartford Seminary worked hard in the period between the two meetings to form the organization. Mackenzie was convinced that "If we are to establish the Conference of theological seminaries and colleges securely and on a broad basis, we must be very careful in our appointment of Committees and even of chairmen of Committees to see that the various institutions, and especially the various types of theological color, are duly represented."[4] In practical terms, this meant that the conference needed to fix its attention on those issues that were common to all schools and to avoid theological controversy.[5] These issues included fees, the preparation of students prior to seminary, the need for adequate financing, and the general problems of seminary administration. Above all, Mackenzie was interested in standards.

In a 1911 article, "The Standardization of Theological Education,"[6] Mackenzie had lamented the fact that the United States lacked either traditions or agencies strong enough to hold seminaries to a high view of their task. Perhaps equally significant, Mackenzie had rejected the idealistic view of nineteenth-century theological educators that high quality would necessarily produce imitation or that churches with scholarly ministers would grow faster, thus leading others to enroll in such schools. Mackenzie proposed no solution to the problem in this early essay, but the success of the first conference suggested a way to approach the problem.

Mackenzie's continuation committee did its work well. In 1920, with Mackenzie in the chair, the conference declared itself a permanent organization, complete with constitution, officers, and a growing list of supporting institutions. That Mackenzie had judged correctly was evident almost immediately. Perhaps the most encouraging sign of the promise of the new body was the quality of those who were at the annual sessions. With few exceptions, from the beginning, the conferences were attended by leaders from the best-endowed and most successful seminaries.

The conference began with a threat and opportunity on the horizon. Af-

4. W. Mackenzie to Henry Foote, Feb. 13, 1923, Hartford Archives.

5. The conference and, later, the AATS have by and large stayed within these limits. The one exception was when it invited Professor J. Gresham Machen to speak in 1924. Machen's speech caused an uproar, and threatened the organization's unity in its early period. The organization did not make that mistake again.

6. William Douglas Mackenzie, "The Standardization of Theological Education," *Journal of the Religious Education Association* 6, no. 3 (Aug. 1911).

ter the discontinuation of the Interchurch World Movement (IWM), the Institute of Social and Religious Research agreed to continue the IWM's survey of seminaries and hired Robert Kelly to complete this task. In an earlier chapter, we discussed the context and finding of this survey.[7] In the present context, it is important to notice that the Kelly report and its implications occupied the Conference of Theological Schools for its first decade. Before the report was published in 1924, they labored to control its results. With Mackenzie watching Kelly's every move, the seminary leaders on the advisory committee almost violated the integrity of the report through their demands for control over the findings and, more importantly, over the interpretation of those findings. Once the report actually appeared, the schools had to struggle with what they ought to do in the light of its findings.

Although Kelly wrote much of it between the lines, he had a vision of the future of Protestant theological education. Like John D. Rockefeller, Jr., who ultimately paid for the study, Kelly believed that denominationalism was the curse, not the blessing, of American religion. The denominations had filled the nation with small rural churches, barely able to pay an educated or semi-educated pastor, and their record in the cities was equally uninspiring. Hence, both seminaries and churches had to face reality and reduce the number of congregations, schools, and denominations. Not only did this conclusion apparently agree with the national passion for large-scale enterprises, it also was connected to the popular ecumenical movement that was already planning a Life and Work Conference for Stockholm in 1925 and a Faith and Order Conference for Lausanne in 1927. Further, this had been the medical community's response to the Flexner study of medical schools. Almost immediately after Flexner's conclusions became known, a number of medical schools closed and those schools not affiliated with a university sought such affiliation. Given the historical relationships between theological education and university study, Kelly implied that this was a logical road for the seminaries to follow as well.[8]

The question before the conference was, if not Kelly's solution, then what was the way forward? The facts Kelly had outlined, which were after all based on information provided by the schools themselves, were — aside from an occasional minor error — beyond reasonable dispute. At the 1920 meeting William Adams Brown, perhaps the most active American theological educator, had sug-

7. See chaps. 14–15 above.

8. Kelly was far from alone in this proposal. William Rainey Harper and his successors at the University of Chicago had argued for this approach on the grounds of "efficiency," and Charles Briggs, Union's noted heretic, had supported it for more scholarly reasons. See Charles Briggs, *History of the Study of Theology,* prepared for publication by his daughter Emilie Grace Briggs (London: Duckworth, 1916).

gested that the only way forward for the seminaries was to embrace their diversity.[9] This general approach was seconded by Mackenzie, who complained about Kelly's approach to Galen Fisher, the institute's director: "Sufficient attention is not given to the nature of the constituency which the seminaries serve, the different genius of the churches they represent, the character of the preparation which students bring with them to the seminary and the requirements which the churches actually make of the students who enter the ministry." There was much wisdom in this argument. Theological education was not medical education. Outside the various Lutheran denominations, whose ministers consistently were the best-schooled in America, seminary education had proved to be a hard sell to American churches. It is doubtful whether fewer, but less easily utilized, seminaries would fare better than the smaller localized schools. A string of university schools might easily be ignored by the various judicatories.

The first step was for the conference to propose a second survey to the Institute of Social and Religious Research. This was a hard sell. After all, the Kelly report had also been sponsored by the institute, and few material criticisms of that survey had been offered. One suspects that Galen Fisher was not completely convinced that the seminaries did not protest too much. Fisher, however, was a skilled member of the Rockefeller team who realized, as did other Rockefeller executives, that their money gave them entry into organizations that would have otherwise been closed to them. Using the funding of the new survey as bait, he gently pushed the Conference of Theological Seminaries to move toward greater standardization of theological schools.

The long discussions between the institute and the conference did result in a gradual improvement of the research plan for the survey. In part, this was a matter of making sure that the new study did not simply reproduce the Kelly survey. Perhaps the key moment in this process occurred in 1928 when the conference accepted in principle a research plan that had three emphases: a "personnel" study or the examination of the work of ministers in both rural and urban settings, an area study or the examination of the differences between urban and rural ministers, and the study of the seminaries themselves.[10] William Adams Brown was to supply a major interpretative essay that would provide a theological rationale for the survey's conclusions. The plan was later modified to include a special study of field education. Field education or supervised work in a ministry setting was becoming a significant innovation as the seminaries,

9. Published as William Adams Brown, "The Common Problems of Theological Schools," *Journal of Religion*, 1921, pp. 282-95.

10. Committee on the Study of Theological Education, report, *Bulletin 6*, 1928 biennial meeting of the Conference of Theological Seminaries, p. 14.

led by such schools as Union, Yale, and Chicago, wanted to find ways to use their students' employment in the churches educationally.

Fisher's policy of making haste slowly also allowed the conference to continue the vital discussions that were gradually shaping a consensus about the nature of theological education. In 1924, for example, Herbert Evans delivered an address on the standardization of theological education that suggested that accreditation might be a useful way forward. Other reports were heard on such matters as the nature of theological students, theological curriculum, the rural churches and their problems, the theology of crisis, classroom teaching, clinical pastoral education, and the ecumenical movement.

In 1930 Brown presented a key address on the aims of theological education. This address was an early but very clear statement of the "professional model" of ministry that would largely replace the older ideal of the learned pastor, at least among theological school administrators. The basic premise of this understanding of the seminary was that "the aim of the seminary as an educational institution must be determined by the purpose of the church for which it is to train ministers; by the nature of the ministry they are to render."[11] Whereas the earlier understandings of theological education had stressed what the minister needed to know, this understanding stressed teaching people what they needed to know to perform a certain ecclesiastical function. Like many ecumenical definitions of faith, this one was strengthened by the fact that each school was able to define what the church was for its own constituency. Brown himself offered only the briefest notes toward an ecclesiology: "The Christian church is the organized fellowship which has for its special function the cultivation of the religious life through the worship of God as revealed through Jesus Christ and the releasing and directing of energies which are to bear fruit not only in the development of Christian character in individuals, but in the creation of a Christian society."[12] In line with this interpretation, Brown saw a good seminary education as performing four functions: to clarify the nature of the God revealed by Jesus, to deepen students' loyalty to the cause for which Christ died, to provide them with the knowledge and skills needed for the task for which they are called, and to fit them to be effective ministers of the church, "which is the social agency through which the purposes of Christ are accomplished."[13] In advocating these goals, Brown made clear, nothing was said that weakened the seminaries' obligation to provide sound biblical, historical, and theological instruction.

11. Committee on the Aims of Theological Education, report, *Bulletin 10*, 1932 biennial meeting of the Conference of Theological Seminaries, William Adams Brown, chair.

12. Committee, *Bulletin 10*.

13. Committee, *Bulletin 10*.

What the committee's report did, however, was to separate the aims of theological education from the question of what was the proper theological encyclopedia. C. H. MacGregor, speaking for the older understanding, eloquently challenged the legitimacy of this approach: "Concerning seminary training as it may be conceived by some people, the objective to turn out an effective ministry may be a legitimate statement. But it seems to me irrational to talk about the objectives of theological education and then to rule out the theological sciences. It is as though we were to say that the objective of musical education is not to cultivate the musical sciences but to train men to fill the orchestra platform."[14] Although MacGregor's position continued to be supported by many members of seminary faculties,[15] especially during debates over curriculum or faculty additions, the appeal to a self-evident, or at least theologically self-evident, understanding of what students had to study was seriously out-of-date. By the 1930s it was clear that few schools (and perhaps no particular institution) could teach all the disciplines and subdivisions that had a right to be included in an ideal curriculum. While schools, including conservative Princeton, provided some room for electives, the yearly or biyearly catalogues of the better schools listed many courses and, occasionally, disciplines that probably would not be taught or would not be taught soon. In short, schools would, by the nature of the case, have to choose which areas they would emphasize and which areas they might neglect or exclude. The emphasis on the larger aims of theological education provided a place from which judgments, albeit not very precise ones, could be made and resources allocated. Different schools with very different academic programs could pursue the same goals without having to adopt the same program or hire identical faculties.

Brown's 1930 report prepared the way for the next two biennial meetings of the conference. The 1932 meeting reached tentative agreement on the vexing issue of theological degrees, settling on the bachelor of divinity, the master of sacred theology or master of theology, and the doctor of theology as the appropriate degrees for the schools.[16] In effect, this was a summary of what the schools were already doing. Despite the apparent diversity in nomenclature, the vast majority of schools issued these degrees, and they had become an unofficial but real standard. Yet it was clear that this recommendation would be de-

14. David Blaine Cable, "The Development of the Accrediting Function of the American Association of Theological Schools, 1918-1938" (Ph.D. diss., University of Pittsburgh, 1970), p. 73. I have relied on Dr. Cable's fine study throughout this chapter.

15. In the 1980s Edward Farley raised the question of theological encyclopedia in a new way in *Theologia: The Fragmentation and Unity of Theological Education* (Philadelphia: Fortress, 1983). For this important debate, see below.

16. Committee, *Bulletin 10.*

bated for some time. In particular, the problem of whether the basic degree should be another bachelor's degree or a master's degree continued to bother many, and there was considerable sentiment for a professional doctorate that a minister could earn, at least in part, through home study. The schools would revise this issue in 1940 with even more passion.

But 1930 was significant, or at least symbolic, in another sense. The leading seminary presidents and deans from approximately 1900 to 1930 had much of the character of the "captains of erudition" that had transformed the leading liberal arts colleges into universities. Almost by definition, these leaders had often transformed their institutions largely by force of their own personality and theological suavity. But such charismatic leadership could not and did not continue in most schools, although it would continue to appear from time to time at particular institutions. The newer generation of leaders were more administrators, experts in how to make structures and governance effective. This new leadership included people like Clarence Barbour, who negotiated the union of Colgate and Rochester; E. C. Herrick, who found ways to unite Andover and Newton; and Henry Sloane Coffin of Union. If the earlier generation of leaders were denizens of the older Protestant denominational establishments, these leaders were often most at home in the new structures of ecumenical Christianity.[17] They were masters at the art of getting along and behind-the-scenes negotiation.

The Conference of Theological Schools was fortunate to have this new breed take leadership during the period in which it was moving toward accreditation. The conference and to a lesser extent its successor, the American Association of Theological Schools (AATS), often disguised its leadership behind large committees that included representatives from many different schools and perspectives, while smaller working committees did the planning for the next session or prepared key reports. This pattern was common to ecumenical organizations, including the Federal Council of Churches, since these bodies had to model consensus as well as achieve it. In the conference's first decade, the strongest voices were W. Douglas Mackenzie of Hartford, William Adams Brown of Union, and Shailer Mathews of Chicago. In the second decade the strongest voices, in addition to Brown, were Luther Weigle of Yale, Lewis Sherrill of Louisville, and Edward Roberts of Princeton.

Luther Weigle personified the new style of seminary leadership. He had come to the divinity school at Yale in 1916 from Carleton College, and he became dean in 1925. Working closely with the Yale administration, Weigle's goal was to raise the academic standards of the divinity school and thereby establish

17. The ecumenical movement was an important school for Protestant leaders and theologians, particularly the emerging World Council of Churches.

it as an integral part of the university. The faculty under his leadership included Liston Pope, Roland Bainton, H. Richard Niebuhr, Robert Calhoun, and Kenneth Scott Latourette. Among his achievements were the construction of the new campus and the inclusion of women in the student body. Weigle, a Lutheran, was also an enthusiast for the ecumenical movement and a participant in its most important meetings. Interestingly enough, although his field was religious education, he served as the chair of the Standard Bible Commission that produced the Revised Version and worked closely with Catholics in the production of a Catholic version. Weigle was a member of the executive committee of the AATS for twenty years, and he was often decisive in its deliberations.

Edward Roberts was among the first seminary deans. A professional theologian with interests in apologetics, he was appointed by Princeton as instructor in systematics in 1930, and he became the school's registrar in 1932. He became dean of students in 1937 and dean of the seminary in 1945. As dean, he led the school through a successful postwar academic expansion. Almost from the beginning of his career he was active in the Conference of Theological Schools, serving first as the second (unpaid) executive secretary of the association and later as its president. He also served on the Commission on Accrediting and as one of the architects of the later Niebuhr survey of theological education.[18]

Lewis Sherrill, a soft-spoken Texan who served as the dean of Louisville Seminary, was another religious educator. He studied under Weigle at Yale, and the two men remained close friends. Perhaps befitting the dean of a school that served two Presbyterian denominations divided by a common confession, Sherrill was a master of negotiation and compromise, a person almost instinctively trusted by others. He served as the first executive director of the association from 1935 to 1938 and oversaw the first work on accreditation.

Brown was the leader who bridged the two generations. Brown, a prolific writer on theological subjects, was an early advocate of and participant in the ecumenical movement. Perhaps Brown's interest in the ecumenical dimensions of Christianity came from his own academic background. Although he taught and wrote in the area of systematic theology, he had worked with Harnack in Berlin and had a deep appreciation of classical ecclesiology. Throughout the twenties he wrote and published on theological education, and he had a good grasp of both the practical and historical factors that had shaped American schools. Like others with a Yale background (he held three Yale degrees: A.B., A.M., and Ph.D.), he was deeply concerned with how theological education re-

18. For Dean Roberts's life, see "In Memoriam: Edward Howell Roberts, Minute of the Board of Trustees," *Princeton Seminary Bulletin* 48 (1955): 30-32; and the faculty minute by Robert Rankin, *Princeton Seminary Bulletin* 49 (1955): 20-23.

lated to the emerging universities and how American universities, particularly state institutions, could responsibly teach "theology" in their programs.

Interestingly enough, another Yale man, Mark May, chosen in 1929 to conduct the survey, had little direct impact on the development of the association. The first choice apparently had been O. D. Foster, a Columbia University professor. May was an expert in "character education," an important subdivision of education in the 1930s. May's nontheological perspective provided important counterweight to that of the conference leadership. As someone outside of the guild, he was able to push the surveyors for a broader, more public perspective.

The completion of the Brown-May study in 1934 provided the final push for the transformation of the Conference of Theological Seminaries into an accrediting agency. This was in line with the usual development of associations of schools. Typically an association would begin as a gathering of institutions that faced similar problems. Among colleges, these problems were often related to the late nineteenth-century educational revolution. In the absence of the older classical education, for instance, what standards should colleges require for admission and for the various degrees, and how were such classical degrees as the bachelor of arts to be related to the new and very popular professional programs? The associations would debate these questions until, at a certain point, they resolved to replace their informal standards of membership with a more formal list of those members that met certain standards of membership. Philanthropy played a key role in this process. The associations often used the definitions earlier established by the Carnegie Foundation to differentiate between colleges and universities. The transformation of an association into a standard-setting body with an official list of institutions could be a very slow process. For instance, the North Central Association did not publish its first list until 1913; the Southern States Association until 1919; the Middle States Association until 1921. Interestingly, the Western States Association, dominated by large state universities, did not publish its official list until 1948. But New England, self-consciously the home of many of the nation's premier colleges and universities, was the last of the regions to formalize its procedures. The New England Association of Colleges and Schools did not publish an official list of those that met its standards until 1952.[19]

Accrediting associations never acquired a monopoly in the certification of schools. The basic right to grant degrees, for instance, was bestowed by the various state legislatures, which retained some rights of superintendence over institutions within their bounds. In New York, where the State Board of Re-

19. William K. Selden, *Accreditation: A Struggle over Standards in Higher Education* (New York: Harper and Brothers, 1960).

gents dated back to 1787, these rights included the right of periodic review, making the state the primary court of academic acceptability. In other states the various state departments of education and occasionally the state universities retained certain rights over chartered institutions as well. The formation of accrediting associations did not compromise prior governmental rights of superintendence, even after the federal government assumed some powers of regulation over the process in the 1940s.

Equally important, the churches maintained certain rights in many American theological schools. Presbyterians, for instance, demanded that the trustees of Presbyterian schools be elected by the General Assembly, and Episcopal bishops maintained the rights of ordinaries over the seminaries in their jurisdiction. The Methodist Church was even more careful, perhaps because of Methodism's close relationship with the university movement. From the 1890s the Methodist University Senate had ruled on the educational standards of Methodist schools, and in 1911 it took oversight of the seminaries and theological schools. In time this oversight extended to the right to evaluate non-Methodist schools that educated Methodist candidates for ministry. Since Methodists were often the largest minority group in non-Methodist seminaries, this imbued Methodist certification with considerable practical value. As time passed, some Protestant denominations came to list graduation from an AATS-accredited school as a criterion for ordination, but this requirement could be and often has been overruled by various judicatories that, for whatever reasons, favored certain nonaccredited or not-yet-accredited schools.

The 1936 meeting ratified the transformation of the conference into the American Association of Theological Schools by officially adopting the new name and new rules for membership. Henceforth the association was to have a list of accredited members that was kept separate from the list of those affiliated with the group. There were a number of reasons for this division of the house. There was the desire to avoid having a "grandfather" clause that made previous membership in the association prima facie evidence of accredited status. Although the association had turned down the application of a Bible school in 1932, the primary issue for many members was the establishment of theological education as graduate, professional study. This was especially important to such Baptist schools as Andover-Newton, Colgate Rochester, and Chicago whose enrollments were suffering from competition with conservative Baptist seminaries that offered the Th.B. degree, and even more pointedly from competition with Bible schools. But the two-list system was also important for other reasons. Much of the work of the conference had been the education of its members, particularly seminary administrators, in the contemporary problems of theological education. The second list would permit those schools that, for whatever reason, were not accredited by the association to continue their membership without embarrassment. Some schools, like Bangor Theological Seminary, which understood itself as having a special ministry to older students, elected not to apply for AATS membership until the 1960s. Bangor Seminary, however, did continue to be active in the association for much of this time.

The same meeting adopted the first standards for the accrediting of theological schools. The exact meaning of the standards was vague. The AATS explicitly stated:

> It is recognized that weaknesses in some of these facts may be compensated for by unusual strength in others. The Association does not treat its standards as definite rules and specifications to be applied in an exact and mechanical fashion. It does not suppose that the status of an institution can be satisfactorily determined by finding that it has met these standards one by one until all have been met. There is no desire to enforce these standards in arbitrary fashion; they are to be administered by the Commission on Accrediting Institutions by stimulus and development.[20]

Aside from a somewhat snide question of whether the gentlemen did not protest too much, the disclaimer pointed to the fact that many members of the association, not to mention the almost one hundred Protestant schools that were not members, would not be able to fulfill the letter of the law. In other words, the first standards were intended to be more guidelines than rules, more a future to be hoped for than a reality already grasped. The first Commission on Accrediting — Edward Roberts, Lewis Sherrill, Everett Herrick, Abdel Ross Wentz, Arthur McGiffert, Jr., Richard Davidson, Luther Weigle, Albert Breven, Lavens Thomas, and Sandford Fleming — would have to fill out their meaning. Like all early conference and association committees, this one was carefully balanced. Denominationally, the commission included American Baptists, Southern Methodists, Lutherans, Episcopalians, and Presbyterians; sectionally, it included members from the East, the West, Canada, and the Midwest; and theologically, members from conservative as well as liberal Protestantism.

The early standards were similar to those of other accrediting associations, although perhaps not as definite. They included the usual criteria: admission, degrees, length of course (residence), library, equipment, finances, and faculty. Taken together, these short statements provide a clear picture of what contemporaries felt was a good theological school: It was an institution that admitted college graduates to a three-year program of study that included bibli-

20. Quoted in American Association of Theological Schools (hereafter AATS), *The First Report of the Commission on Accrediting* (Louisville, 1938), p. 4.

cal, historical, practical, and theological courses. This curriculum should include courses in homiletics, religious education, pastoral theology, liturgics, church administration, and the application of Christianity to modern social problems. The curriculum should be taught by a competent faculty of at least four professors who, together with the administrative officer, have control over the curriculum and the granting of degrees. In keeping with the graduate character of the institutions, faculty members should not teach more than twelve hours a week. The institution itself was to provide adequate resources for the teaching of this curriculum, both in buildings and in endowments, and was to maintain a library that was "alive, adequate, well-distributed and professionally administered, with collections bearing especially upon the subjects taught."[21] Most interesting was the provision of a subjective element. Standard 8 defined what the association called "general tone": "In accrediting a Theological Seminary or College regard should be had for the quality of its instruction, the standing of its professors, the character of its administration, the efficiency of its offices of record and its proved ability to prepare students for efficient professional service or further scholarly pursuits."[22] In other words, did the school feel and act like a graduate seminary and did others, particularly the school's denomination, regard it as such? But within this language were important clues for the further standardization of theological education, including the importance of good record keeping.

The procedure for evaluation was relatively straightforward. A school that wanted to be accredited had to submit eighteen forms or schedules. These included forms for the school's history, its control or governance, its individuality, its enrollment, and its graduates. In addition, the school was called to report on its admission standard, graduation standard, curriculum, faculty, library, equipment, finances, administration, records, extension services (if any), and careers of graduates. Each faculty member, in addition, was to fill out a schedule that included the teacher's education and experience. As the commission noted, these required "no small amount of labor" and were "seldom completed in less than a month."[23] Once the chairman of the commission had analyzed the reports, a visitor was appointed who would spend at least a day on the campus. The commission charged a fee of twenty-five dollars for the visit. The visitor was to file a complete report.

In presenting its first list of forty-six schools, the Commission on Accrediting noted that it had received sixty-one applications. It did not act on three

21. AATS, *The First Report,* pp. 5-6; quotation on p. 6.
22. AATS, *The First Report,* p. 6.
23. AATS, *The First Report,* p. 8.

of these — Chicago Theological Seminary, Harvard Divinity School, and Queen's Theological College — and rejected twelve, the most common reason being that the school did not have four full-time faculty members. This was one area where the commission felt it could not make accommodations by allowing schools to add up the time contributed by part-time instructors. "[I]f exceptions should be made, through interpretations, to the requirement of four full-time professors as a minimum, there would be no stopping place until a point of absurdity had been reached."[24] But that answer may have concealed more than it revealed. The size of the faculty was the key to a number of less easily determined questions, including the stability of the curriculum, the spiritual and academic advice available to students, and the level of scholarship. Further, in a world in which the president and perhaps a part-time registrar were often the only administrative officers, the size of the faculty directly affected the school's ability to be effectively administered. Decisions on faculty size were, however, much more easily defended than these more complicated and value-laden judgments.

But if the commission held the line on faculty size, it was unable to do so on the other standards. Frankly admitting that "very few institutions met the standards in every particular," the commission had to come up with a system for dealing with schools that fell short of its minimum expectations. The solution was a many-headed hydra. Minor infractions were to be noted in three ways. Those deviations that had no impact on academic quality were to be reported to the school's administration but not to the association as a whole. The most common minor deviation was the use of a different nomenclature than bachelor of divinity for the first degree. More serious deviations — that is, those that did affect academic quality — were to be reported to the school as "significant deviations." Admission of students from nonaccredited colleges was the example given by the commission. Since many small church colleges were understood as "feeder schools" to their denominations' seminaries, particularly in the Midwest and South, this particular "deviation" was almost ecclesiastically mandated, or at least politically unavoidable. Significant deviations were also not matters of public record. The third category of minor infraction was "information." "Information" was where the commission, usually through its investigator, found something amiss that was not explicitly covered by a standard but did impact a specific standard. The example given was allowing students to simultaneously enroll for the bachelor of divinity and the master of arts.[25]

That still left areas where even the forty-six accredited schools fell short

24. AATS, *The First Report,* p. 11.

25. AATS, *The First Report,* pp. 11-12.

on issues the association felt were crucial. In effect, the association adopted a policy of public shaming. The schools would be included on the list of accredited schools, but there would be a notation or footnote to its accredited status that listed the nature of the offense. The only schools that had no notations were Augustana Lutheran Seminary, Colgate-Rochester, Drew Theological Seminary, Emmanuel College in Victoria University, Episcopal Theological School (Cambridge), Lutheran Theological Seminary (Gettysburg), Lutheran Theological Seminary (Mount Airy), Oberlin Theological Seminary, Princeton Seminary, Presbyterian Theological Seminary (McCormick), and Yale University Divinity School.

The vast majority of notations were related to violations of the association's rule that admission should be based on an accredited bachelor of arts degree. Indeed, notations 1 to 3 represented an ascending scale of noncompliance. Schools with between 10 and 24 percent of their student bodies comprising noncollege graduates received notation 1; schools with between 25 and 49 percent received notation 2; and schools with between 50 and 74 percent, notation 3.[26] Since no notation was given when noncollege graduates constituted less than 10 percent of the student body, this was the origin of the later "10 percent" rule that permitted schools to have 10 percent of their enrollment without college. One of these three notations was given to twenty-four of the forty-six schools initially accredited, or to more than half of the institutions listed as in compliance with the standards.

Equally important, a number of schools were cited for maintaining a system whereby the first year of seminary counted as the last year of college. These included some of the better schools in the association — Andover-Newton, Candler, Evangelical Seminary, Garrett Biblical Institute, and Union, New York. Since this pattern was common among university-related law colleges and medical colleges, its absence among theological schools — as well as the fact that it was worthy of censure — may have reflected the isolation of these schools from the larger university world as much as it did a lack of devotion to graduate professional education. Some seminary leaders would continue to advocate such arrangements until the postwar expansion of professional education rendered the issue mute for law and medicine as well as theology.

Perhaps the most disturbing of the common notations were notations 7-10, which dealt with the quality of the library and its administration. The schools that received one or more of these notations included Bonebrake, Evangelical School of Theology, Reading, Pennsylvania; Evangelical Theologi-

26. Only two schools fell into this category: the College of the Bible in Lexington, Ky., and Gammon Theological Seminary in Atlanta.

cal Seminary (Naperville, Ill.); Pittsburgh-Zenia; Presbyterian Theological College in Toronto; and Vanderbilt. But this was clearly the tip of the iceberg. In 1946 the association would help found the American Theological Library Association to work toward higher standards for seminary libraries. Even though each version of the AATS (ATS) standards would raise the bar for seminary libraries, especially for professional staff, seminary libraries have often remained small and poorly financed.

The 1940 meeting of the AATS expressed real satisfaction with the progress being made. Eleven new schools were added to the list of accredited schools, and the yearly statistics filed by member schools indicated that member schools were making substantial progress in meeting the standards. Perhaps ironically, the executive leadership of the association took this opportunity to praise the work of those institutions that, because of either the decisions of the committee or their own recognition that they did not meet the standards, were not accredited: "The Committee is aware that among the schools not able to qualify for accreditation, many are rendering a service to theological education which is valuable and in some cases distinctive. They are doing what the rest of us are not in position to do, and for that reason deserve our gratitude."[27] This awareness was coupled with a point, already emphatically made in the Brown-May study, that needed repetition. Seminaries depended on the churches for their health as well as for students and finances. As Lewis Sherrill reminded the group, the standards depended on churches that were strong enough and wealthy enough to hire the graduates of these institutions: "Once more, numerous small churches cannot now support a fully-trained minister at a salary which he reasonably expects; what is the implication of that fact when the need of a second set of standards is being considered?"[28] While this point would soon be all but forgotten in the religious boom that followed the Second World War, Sherrill had made an important observation. The type of minister produced by an AATS-accredited school expected and deserved more professional status and compensation that many American clergy in fact received. The later religious boom, which saw many small rural churches become large suburban congregations, hides the fact that most American Protestant churches remained too small to afford the type of pastor trained by the seminaries. When the number of such churches grows, the seminaries expand to train those pastors; but when the number of such churches declines, the number of students in basic seminary programs declines proportionately. The relationship between stan-

27. AATS, *Bulletin 14,* July 1940, Twelfth Biennial Meeting of the Association at the College of the Bible, p. 31.

28. AATS, *Bulletin 14,* Address of President Lewis Sherrill, p. 31.

dards of theological education and the financial strength of American Protestantism is a key part of the history.[29]

This sense of progress was reflected in the executive committee's report, which attempted to make recommendations about the ideal preseminary program, that is, to spell out in some detail which studies seminaries considered important for theological students. While this was a continuation of an earlier discussion in 1936, the report distinguished very clearly between seminary and collegiate work. "The emphasis is on a 'liberal arts' program rather than on the elements commonly known as 'pre-professional.' In the judgment of the Association the appropriate foundations for a minister's later professional studies lie in a broad and comprehensive college education, while the normal place for a minister's professional studies is the theological school."[30] The potential for some tension with the growing college and university departments of Bible in this statement was obvious. What was the proper study of religion as part of the intellectual equipment of an educated man, and what was the professional study of faith? The clash over this issue would come in the 1950s, but it was already implicit in the way the AATS had set the issue. Despite its assurances that its proposed program of preseminary studies was not compulsory on any school and its insistence that the list it provided was not exhaustive, the association did recommend that its members adopt the preseminary program as part of their admission requirements and that they print the list of courses in their catalogues to help students who might enroll in seminary plan their program.

Sherrill presented a report from the Committee on Theological Degrees. The gist of the matter was that the large majority of schools was satisfied with the existing nomenclature. Yet the dissatisfaction with the second bachelor's degree and with the lack of a professional doctorate continued to be noted, now in even sharper terms than earlier. In a sense, accreditation had already raised the standards and the aspirations of theological schools and their graduates. The pressure for new degrees and new nomenclature would expand as more schools actually met the association's standards.

The association, however, could not simply expand its standards. Much of Europe and Asia was already at war, and those with eyes to see and ears to hear

29. This problem has dogged theological education since disestablishment. Although some American ministers have done well financially, not all American ministers have. While poor pay and low prestige are not confined to the countryside, rural churches, subjected to the successive farm crises that had plagued rural areas since the 1890s, have suffered to a disproportionate degree. The popularity of the auto in the 1920s further complicated this problem by separating many part-time ministers' place of residence from their place of ministry.

30. AATS, *Bulletin 14*, Report of the Executive Committee.

realized that the United States would be involved in one or both of those conflicts within a short space of time. War could easily erode the standards the association had labored so hard to establish. After all, this had been the experience of seminaries in the last conflict. "Experience of twenty five years ago [i.e., the Great War] suggests that institutional pride, in keeping up a showing can temporarily justify measures for recruiting and standards of work in preparation for the ordinary parish ministry, which those same institutions are the first to repent of in later years."[31] The schools did not know it, of course, but the Second World War was to provide confirmation of their decision to adopt accreditation. The new executive director of the association, Edward Roberts of Princeton, had already begun negotiating with the government about standards for military chaplains. Arguing that graduates of AATS schools were parallel in their qualifications to graduates of accredited medical and legal institutions, he was able to secure a privileged place for them in the armed forces. Although the Protestant clergy never campaigned for a draft exemption for ministers and theological students, once this was granted, Roberts campaigned hard for preseminary students to be included in the deferments. Accreditation would play a major role in this decision as well. In that sense, although the war would disrupt the development of AATS and its member schools, it would also, paradoxically, establish the value of what they were doing. After the war it would be much harder for a seminary to stand outside the association than to participate in it.

But if the full effects of the war on American theological education were not clear, even in 1940, American theological educators knew they were on the verge of a new era for American theology. Even as Henry Pitney Van Dusen was exhorting them to offer positions to refugee European scholars, Sherrill was telling them that "it is impossible to avoid the assumption that as a group, theological scholars of the North American continent must take up responsibility for a much larger share of the world's total creative work of this nature, rather than has been the case in the past."[32] The schools had put their house in order just in time to take up the challenges of a nation destined to play a more important role in the political and intellectual history of the world.

In retrospect, the development of the Conference of Theological Seminaries into the American Association of Theological Schools was a key event in the development of twentieth-century theological education. Despite the small number of schools accredited in 1938 and 1940 and despite the large number of notations, these schools were the vanguard of much of the subsequent develop-

31. AATS, *Bulletin 14,* Address of President Lewis Sherrill, p. 18.

32. AATS, *Bulletin 14,* Address of President Lewis Sherrill, p. 19.

ment of theological education in the United States. The basic idea of accreditation is to make haste slowly. Standards are set, standards are met, standards are raised, and then the cycle begins again. Hopefully, the spiral is ever upward, although this is not inevitable, and improvement becomes an institutional habit. As early as 1940 the value of this approach was clear. The listed schools reported improved libraries and stronger faculties, and their general tone was beginning to improve. The war would only confirm the impression made by the 1940 figures. If the imperial presidents had proven that they could remake a school with charisma, the leaders of AATS proved they could remake schools a step at a time, gradually, transporting the whole into something better.

CHAPTER TWENTY

Brown-May

Beginning in the early twenties and continuing to the midthirties, American sociologists of religion, many of whom were connected with the Institute of Social and Religious Research, conducted a series of studies of Protestant Christianity. Perhaps because so many of these studies were coordinated by a single funding agency, they were comprehensive in their scope, dealing with the urban and the rural church, with African Americans and Native Americans, with large cities and small towns. The institute's studies provide us with the best available picture of American religion in the 1920s and 1930s. Despite their rigor, these studies provoked much debate when first published. The Lynds' classic studies of Middletown (Muncie, Ind.), for instance, revealed much about this small city that contemporaries found shocking. When this all-American town was closely examined, the data indicated that Muncie was almost devoured by the new consumerism, with automobiles being more important in some families than electric lights. Perhaps more important, Muncie was less churched than a visitor might suppose. Despite the churches' imposing buildings, the churches had little impact on daily life and were much less well-attended than their membership lists might suggest. There were hints of changes in sexual mores as well. These same secular trends were even more pronounced when the Lynds returned ten years later to see how the Depression had changed the city. The novelists of the 1920s pictured a secular America; the Lynds documented its existence.

When the cold eyes of the sociologists turned to the infrastructure of the Protestant churches, they found outward prosperity and inward rot.[1] Despite

1. Among the projects of the Institute of Social and Religious Research were: *Town and Country Church in the United States,* Edmund de S. Brunner, Herman Morse, Marjorie Patten, C. Luther Fry, Benson Landis, Helen Belknap, and Mrs. E. de S. Brunner, 1922, 1923; *Churches of Distinction in Town and Country,* Edmund de S. Brunner, 1923; *Tested Methods in Town and*

the impressive membership numbers that the churches continued to publish, their reality was much less rosy. In areas like New England, for instance, the rural church had declined precipitously, and attendance at services appeared to be half what it had been a generation earlier.[2] Religious services were often infrequent with many rural churches relying on part-time pastors, who often lived far from the church and conducted worship or Sunday school once or twice a month. Nor were urban churches, despite their wealth, much better off. The social fluidity of American cities meant that churches were perpetual migrants, at this location one year, and forced to follow their membership to another site the next. Whether in the countryside or on the urban frontier, too many churches existed, and these churches were often engaged in forms of competition and advertising that might make an ad man, such as Bruce Barton, blush with shame at his profession. Moreover, research increasingly indicated that the local congregations were not representative of their communities. In 1929 H. Richard Niebuhr, a theologian and ethicist with a very sharp eye, published his *Social Sources of Denominationalism.*[3] In this study Niebuhr reported that

Country Churches, Edmund de S. Brunner, 1923, 1924, 1928, 1930; *The Red Man in the United States,* C. E. E. Lindquest, 1923, 1924; *Diagnosing the Rural Church,* C. Luther Fry, 1924; *The St. Louis Church Survey,* H. Paul Douglass, 1924; *1,000 City Churches,* H. Paul Douglass, 1924; *United Churches,* Elizabeth R. Hooker, 1926, 1928; *The Springfield Church Survey,* H. Paul Douglass, 1926; *The Church in the Changing City,* H. Paul Douglass, 1927; *Home Mission Aid,* C. Luther Fry, 1928; *Minneapolis Churches and Their Comity Problems,* Wilbur Hallenbeck, 1929; *Church Comity,* H. Paul Douglass, 1929; *Protestant Cooperation in American Cities,* H. Paul Douglass, 1929; *Industrial Village Churches,* Edmund de S. Brunner, 1930; *The U.S. Looks at Its Churches,* C. Luther Fry, 1930; *The Strategy of City Church Planning,* Ross W. Sanderson, 1932; *Hinterlands of the Church,* Elizabeth R. Hooker, 1932; *The Negro's Church,* B. E. May and J. J. W. Nicholson, 1932; *Protestant Home Missions to Catholic Immigrants,* Theodore Adel, 1933; *Church Union in Canada,* Claris Edwin Silcox, 1933; *Larger Parishes,* Edmund de S. Brunner, 1934; *Church Unity Movements in the United States,* H. Paul Douglass, 1934.

Foreign Missions: *Christian Literature in Moslem Lands,* 1923; *World Missionary Atlas,* Harlan Beach and Charles H. Fahs, 1925; *Trends in Protestant Giving,* Charles H. Fahs, 1929.

Education: *Theological Education in America,* Robert L. Kelly, 1924; *The Education of Negro Ministers,* W. A. Daniel, 1925; *Indiana Survey of Religious Education,* 3 vols., Walter S. Athearn, 1923, 1924; *Undergraduates,* R. H. Edwards, J. M. Artman, and Galen Fisher, 1928; *The Education of American Ministers,* William Adams Brown and Mark May, 1934.

Institute of Social and Religious Research projects: *Race Relations: Tentative Findings of the Survey of Race Relations,* 1925; *Negro Problems in Cities,* Thomas Jack Woofter, Jr., 1928, 1929.

In addition, both Arthur E. Holt and Samuel Kincheloe published classical studies that were not connected to the institute.

2. Luther Fry, *Diagnosing the Rural Church* (New York: George H. Doran Co., Institute of Social and Religious Research, 1924), p. 186.

3. H. Richard Niebuhr, *The Social Sources of Denominationalism* (New York: Henry Holt, 1929).

local congregations most often contained members from the same social class, race, or ethnicity. These earthly ties, he argued, were often more fundamental to their identity than the theological categories imposed by their creed. In a world of voluntary societies, birds of a feather flock together.

Nor was this discouraging picture confined to the United States. When the Hocking Commission, or Laymen's Inquiry, composed of seven leading men in the American churches and chaired by the noted Harvard professor William Hocking, studied the much-promoted missionary work abroad, it found a similar situation. Rather than modern knights in shining faith, as church literature pictured the missionaries, the inquiry found that American missions were most often staffed by undertrained men and women who had little knowledge or appreciation of the people among whom they worked. Perhaps, as the commission suggested, in a world in which Africa and Asia were awakening, the presence of such inadequate representatives did the churches or those they hoped to serve little good.[4]

While much of the controversy over the report centered on Hocking's suggestion that the missions needed to move beyond proselytizing, the book's picture of exported mediocrity was much more damaging to Protestant self-consciousness than any amount of ideological deviation. If the missionary movement was in such trouble, the crisis in less glamorous and less popular areas of the church's life must be even more extensive. While the various denominations had their own polities, the missionary movement had provided the warp and woof of Protestant bureaucracies. Although generalizations are risky, the bureaucracies appear to have been the most socially aware and perhaps most theologically liberal component of American Protestantism.[5] The report indicated that the rot at the bottom was also found at the top.

A central theme in all these studies was the poverty of the ministry. While there were some rich churches, these were rare and far between. Most ministers were compensated at the level of working men. Paul Carter compared clerical compensation in the prosperous 1920s with that of other trades: "Discounting the parsonage rent of the one, and the bonuses and overtime for the other, a

4. Laymen's Foreign Missions Inquiry, Commission of Appraisal, *Re-thinking Missions: A Laymen's Inquiry after One Hundred Years,* William Hocking, chairman (New York: Harper and Brothers, 1932).

5. Donald K. Gorrell, *The Age of Social Responsibility: The Social Gospel in the Progressive Era, 1900-1920* (Macon, Ga.: Mercer University Press, 1988), notes the influence of the social gospel on the national bureaucracies. Varying forms of social and liberal Christianity were very important on the field, especially in the Christian colleges and schools in China. While Hocking's report applauded these directions in missionary work, it also called into question the leadership of the enterprise.

Baptist minister made a few cents less per week than did a boot and shoe worker; a Methodist minister made a dollar a week more than did a furniture maker and a Congregational minister's wages compared very favorably with those of an electrical worker or hod carrier and were only $3.62 a week short of those of an iron and steel worker. As for masons, plumbers, plasterers, and bricklayers, the clergy were hopelessly outclassed."[6] Similar figures could be found in almost all the studies. In an America that had never known or appreciated Saint Francis, such poverty was almost certain to be misinterpreted. Americans tended to judge a man's masculinity by his capacity to earn money and provide a high standard of living for his family. The minister obviously did not do this, and there was a widespread conviction that something perhaps more sinister was involved in this life of renunciation. Just as popular Protestant imagination was filled with stories about the sexual adventures of celibate priests, so the common Protestant snide remark was that ministers were in it "for the money" or because they could not get another job. Few Americans could understand loving Jesus for thirty dollars a week and change.

While the Kelly survey needed to be read against the background of the relative successes of progressive Protestantism, the Brown-May study needs to be read as part of the significant number of studies by the Institute of Social and Religious Research. As we noted earlier, the institute, a Rockefeller-funded think tank, was inclined to cast a very realistic eye at American religiosity and American religious institutions. Its leaders realized what few Protestant church officials would admit: the churches were in deep, systemic trouble. Many local congregations were dying, in debt, or ineffectual, and the national church bodies were in little better shape. Brown and May's classic study was part of this larger consensus about the condition of American religious institutions, and part of Brown and May's task was to show how theological education might renew or help renew the churches.

I. Professionalism as Reform

From the beginning William Adams Brown and his collaborator, Mark May, sought to communicate their sense of the need to reform the church's ministry.

6. Paul Allen Carter, *The Decline and Revival of the Social Gospel: Social and Political Liberalism in American Protestant Churches, 1920-1940* (Ithaca, N.Y.: Cornell University Press, 1954), p. 73. William Adams Brown and Mark May, *The Education of American Ministers,* vol. 4, *Appendices* (New York: Institute of Social and Religious Research, 1934), table VII, paints an even more depressing picture of the relative salaries of ministers compared to other employees in industry and government.

In discussing the goals of the study, Brown said "its primary purpose" was to provide theological educators with information "they now lack." But its goal was not only informational: "Its ultimate aim is to bring home to those who control the policy of the churches which supply the seminaries with their students the importance of creating conditions within the church that will attract to the ministry men of the highest intellectual and moral caliber and so supply to the nation and to the world the spiritual leadership it needs."[7] In short, Brown and May wanted their study to call for a twentieth-century reformation of the ministry. The clergy were the key to the church's future in a time when religion could no longer be assumed to be part of American public life.

The survey's focus on the ministry is evident from the beginning of the document to its end. The title of the study, for example, is *The Education of American Ministers,* and the summary volume, *Ministerial Education in America.* In the organization of the whole report, volume 2, the summary of the material on the ministry, is significantly placed before volume 3, the summary of the material on the seminaries. Further, from the beginning Brown is careful to place the study in the context not of the development of higher education in general, but of professional education. In this sense the report was parallel to the well-known Flexner study as well as Alfred Red's study of legal education and Charles Mann's noted study of training for engineering. For Brown and May the seminary is a professional school that follows similar procedures to other forms of professional education. It follows that the minister is a professional, a person educated to accomplish a specific task.

The definition of theological education as professional education pervades the study, even in places where it might not have been expected. Although Brown stresses the importance of advanced theological study as part of a seminary's task, he believes such advanced study is, like religious education or foreign missions, a specialized ministry. And specialization in ministry, like specialization in other professions, is a necessity set by the times. "That specialized training is necessary in the ministry as in all the professions, is not a question. It follows naturally from the development of specialized forms of service — educational, missionary, social, philanthropic — to which we have already called attention. The only question is when it shall be given and how. Shall it precede or parallel general professional training, or shall it follow it in the third year or in graduate course?"[8] Even

7. William Adams Brown and Mark May, *The Education of American Ministers,* 4 vols. (New York: Institute of Social and Religious Research, 1934), 1:5. The four volumes are: vol. 1, *Ministerial Education in America;* vol. 2, *The Profession of the Ministry;* vol. 3, *The Institutions That Train Ministers;* and vol. 4, *Appendices.* The study will be referenced as Brown-May, followed by the volume number, a colon, and the page reference.

8. Brown-May, 1:60.

the need for such advanced study highlights the differences between the seminary and the liberal arts college or the graduate school of arts and sciences.

What did Brown and his collaborator mean by the term "professional"? Despite their frequent comparisons of ministry with law and medicine, the answer is not easy to formulate. In some ways it might be easier to say what they believed a professional minister was not. Clearly, the professional minister was not the old-fashioned learned cleric who spent his time among books and papers. Nor was he the opportunist who learned a few tricks of the trade and performed them well. Nor was a professional minister someone who ignored the life of the mind. An anti-intellectual minister was as close to the antithesis of what Brown advocated as one could get. After all, as Brown explained, "Whether we define the minister's responsibility broadly or narrowly, he is above all else a teacher, and what he can do to influence others in their conduct will be conditioned in large part by the presuppositions which he finds them holding."[9] Given these caveats, professional ministry, like other professional work, was task oriented. A minister or the ministry as a whole could be or should be judged by how well the ministerial tasks or duties are performed. Brown and May listed five duties of the pastoral office — "teacher, evangelist, leader of worship, pastor, and administrator"[10] — that a minister needed to perform well. While they believed that ministers needed to be taught best practices, they did not see ministerial education as vocational education. Rather, good ministerial education involved a knowledge of the basic principles that inform good ministerial practice. Brown and May both believed that this included significant work in the social and natural sciences.

Why did the surveyors stress the importance of professional education? In part, it was an attempt to relate the ministry to the twentieth-century social order. The centrality of the professions, after all, is one of the marks of the modern industrial city that is organized more around the temple of "know-how" than around the classical temples of religion and scholarship.[11] As Burton Bledsoe so eloquently put it: "The culture of professionalism has been so basic to middle class habits of thought and action that a majority of twentieth cen-

9. Brown-May, 1:11.

10. Brown-May, 1:23.

11. This understanding of professionalism goes back to Max Weber's classical analysis of the concept of *Beruf*. For a contemporary statement of the thesis, see Thomas L. Haskell: *The Emergence of Professional Social Science: The American Social Science Association and the Nineteenth Century Crisis of Authority* (Urbana: University of Illinois Press, 1977), p. 26. Some of Weber's analysis is readily available in Max Weber: "Wissensachaft als Beruf," in *From Max Weber: Essays in Sociology*, trans. and ed. H. H. Garth and C. Wright Mills (New York: Oxford University Press, 1977), pp. 129-56.

tury Americans have taken for granted that all intelligent modern persons organize their behavior, both public and private, according to it."[12] Professions, above all, were worthy of a decent level of support that reflected their substantial knowledge and skill.

The appeal to professionalism was also an attempt to get beyond the denominational impasse that seemed, especially to those connected to the Institute of Social and Religious Research, to be choking American religious institutions to death. In many ways this was a difficult and dangerous argument to make and one that seemingly went against experience. All American religion on the local level was denominational. Further, each denomination had its own theological definition of ministry, and even among what were called the evangelical churches — current language would say ecumenical — church traditions suggested very different patterns of ministerial behavior and ministerial personality. The ideal Presbyterian pastor was a very different person from the ideal Methodist elder. If one looked beyond the evangelical denominations' boundaries, the differences were more substantial. What, for instance, were the marks of commonality between the Anglo-Catholic Episcopalian and the pietistic Church of the Brethren leader?[13]

The United States also had strong native religious traditions that weighed heavily against the ideal of a professional ministry. Part of the ethos of American piety was that religion, to be real and authentic, had to come from a heart that was unencumbered by worldly concerns. Both Baptists and Methodists had earlier stressed the necessity of a "free" ministry, and many Americans had a secret or not-so-secret anticlericalism. While this was sometimes expressed through denunciations of the clergy as enemies of progress or the like, disestablishment tended to focus on financial issues. The clergy were in it for the money or for a status they could not earn in the "real world." In adopting a professional understanding of ministry, Brown and May knew they were opposing this popular understanding. Part of the definition of a professional is that professionals are paid for what they know as well as what they do.

Brown and May were willing to oppose popular and ecclesiastical positions because they could not see any other solution to the financial and other problems of American Protestantism. The survey indicated that a minister needed an income of around three thousand dollars to live in middle-class

12. Burton Bledsoe, *The Culture of Professionalism* (New York: Norton, 1976), p. 1.

13. H. R. Niebuhr and Daniel Day Williams, eds., *Ministry in Historical Perspective* (San Francisco: Harper and Row, 1956, 1983), demonstrate much of the continuing power of the various traditions in American life. Written during the apogee of the post–Second World War revival, these essays are more inclined to feel that the persistence of these traditions was supportive of the gospel rather than a hindrance to it.

style. This was approximately equal to the salary of an associate professor in a college and above the salary of a clerk. The catch was that there were only about 18,000 churches in the country with sufficient membership (Brown and May estimated 350 members were needed) to raise this amount of money. This meant that 155,000 churches were unable to pay at that level.[14] Brown and May suspected, not without reason, that the home mission departments of the various denominations had been more concerned with establishing new congregations than with bringing the gospel to areas where it was unknown or applying it to social issues. But whether the culprit was in the bureaucracy or in the hidden recesses of American patterns of faith, the picture was bleak. Competent people were leaving the ministry for other professions, including schoolteaching, and they were hard to replace. As Brown noted: "Our study has shown that one of the most serious obstacles to the maintenance of a well-trained ministry is the over-churching which has been a by-product of the denominational system. In community after community of a thousand to fifteen hundred people we find anywhere from three to seven or eight churches. It is impossible to ask a self-respecting man to serve a church under such conditions."[15] Seminaries, Brown concluded, should not "embark on a program of even moderate expansion."[16]

II. The Schools and Their Students

Brown and May meticulously surveyed the standards that the various denominations had established for ordination and concluded, rightly, that they were almost universally high. Even the Northern Baptists and Methodists had adopted lists of qualifications that included college and seminary. Nonetheless, the percentage of ministers with both college and seminary remained under 40 percent, with only the Lutheran and Reformed churches passing the 80 percent

14. In 1919 the National Committee of the Home Mission Council set, as a desirable ratio for an effective rural church, 1 church per 1,000 people. According to this standard, it appears that in 1926, under the most favorable conditions of consolidation, there would not have been more than 52,800 effective rural churches, whereas the census of religious bodies reports a total of 167,664 rural churches. Brown-May, 2:114 (using 1,500 people per church as an urban standard). According to this standard, there could not have been more than 42,000 effective urban churches in 1926, whereas the census of religious bodies reports a total of 64,290. According to these figures, the country can support only about 94,800 churches, indicating an excess of at least 137,000 weak churches. Of this excess, about 30,000 are Negro churches and 105,000 are Protestant white churches.

15. Brown-May, 1:50.

16. Brown-May, 2:120.

mark.[17] Further, fewer ministers were being admitted each year who had only collegiate training. The conclusion that the standards were more important on paper than in fact was inescapable. In polite terms, Brown explained: "For wide latitude is open in practice to the interpretation of the church's rules, and with the powers granted them in the constitution, bishops and presbyteries admit to the ministry many candidates whose academic preparation is deficient."[18] Interestingly enough, another explanation was also offered. As many as one-fourth of American ministers changed denominations at least once in their ministry, and while it is difficult to prove, this may have been particularly commonplace in the wake of the fundamentalist-modernist controversy. Churches rarely demanded that new transfers meet their standards.

The formal denominational standards were also weakened by the very hierarchical structure of American religious institutions. In general, national bodies, perhaps because they are separated from the various local groups, tend to hold more liberal and more educated views than the people they represent. This is not surprising since national bodies tend to be heavily influenced by the church's bureaucratic leadership and by the pastors of "big-steeple" congregations. Generally speaking, these were the best-paid and best-educated leaders the denomination possessed. When it came to finding a pastor for Molly's Creek, however, localism ruled.[19] If a fully qualified person could not be found, then a less qualified pastor would be found. After all, the best pastor was the pastor who was present.

Seminary students reflected the economic and political strength of the churches. Most came from average families with limited cultural and financial resources. Almost half came from places with less than 1,000 population, and most of the remainder came from small towns and small cities. They tended to attend small denominational colleges, often also semirural, many of which were undistinguished. Only 54 percent of the colleges they attended were "fully accredited," and "sectionally accredited" bodies represented only another 24 percent. This was far from the standard of the law schools and medical schools, where 95.7 percent and 93.3 percent, respectively, came from accredited institutions. The more prestigious private colleges and universities were under-

17. Brown-May, 4:16-17. May believed the census data may have exaggerated the number of ministers with college and seminary since it never asked ministers for any evidence of their achievements.

18. Brown-May, 1:41.

19. American religious organizations, whatever the formal polity of a group, tend toward a de facto congregationalism that is rooted, in large measure, in the separation of church and state. Since the church exists only because people pay for it, they expect their contributions to meet their needs or they will go elsewhere.

represented, as were the state universities, which were rapidly increasing their enrollments.

Interestingly, seminary students tended to have interrupted their education more often than other students in graduate professional schools and to be older at the time of admission. Many were already serving nearby churches and taking advantage of the system of rails and roads to attend school. Like many people in the increasingly test-conscious 1930s, Brown and May turned to intelligence tests to compare ministers with other professionals. Since such tests were not widely available, May turned to a limited study of the relationship between IQ and when the decision to enter the ministry was made. The survey indicated that those who entered college planning to attend seminary scored lower than those who had decided for the other professions; a similar gap existed between those considering the ministry and those considering other professions, but that gap narrowed as time passed. When all the decisions were considered, however, the aggregate totals were almost the same for ministry as for other professions, 148 versus 150. In other words, those whose decisions came at the end of the collegiate process — a process that could be seen as a discernment process — raised the intellectual average of the ministry considerably.[20]

Like the Protestant churches in general, these students were largely based in the countryside, they came from families that were slightly above the educational average, and they were part of the younger cohort gradually moving toward the cities. In other words, ministers came from near the mean or the median of young men active in the Protestant movement. In the days of Dwight L. Moody, this same profile would have identified the "bright young men" who built the railroads, created much of American industry, established many of the great universities, and helped refound the American professions. Yet this may have been an underrated cohort. In the midst of the Depression, members of this cohort continued to advance their own educational programs and to position themselves in various ways for the end of hard times. When the Second World War began, many rose to leadership positions in the armed forces, and their younger brothers took advantage of the GI Bill in unprecedented numbers. Much of this cadre provided the denominational and high-steeple leadership for the postwar religious boom.[21]

Brown and May, like most of the religious community, worried about

20. Brown-May, 1:118-20.

21. Critics of the revival of the 1950s often commented on its theological vagueness and devotion to pragmatic goals, such as the building of new Sunday schools. This makes good sense when we think of the leaders as people who completed their theological education in a time when Brown and May's idea of the professional minister, who traveled somewhat intellectually light, was the most exciting vision of theological education available.

whether the separation of church and state was not excluding religion from the most important segments of American higher education.

Most interestingly, Brown and May discovered that seminaries were essentially regional institutions. This was as true of the great as of the small. Most seminary students were already serving nearby churches when they entered, and others came from nearby. These commuter students took advantage of the system of rails and roads to aid them in their commute.[22] Not surprisingly, students tended to minister in areas close to the schools they attended. The great age of the "residential" seminary was in fact in the future, after the GI Bill and national prosperity made it possible for students to pick up and go to school where they liked rather than where it was most convenient.

Given the problems of poorly financed congregations, denominations that were unable or unwilling to enforce their standards, and a generally uninspired body of candidates, the seminaries clearly had their work cut out for them. In fact, a cynic might ask whether the seminaries could reasonably hope to have a major impact on either the churches or the ministry, aside from the more prosperous pastorates. Brown does not struggle with this question, aside from a reference to a handful of studies that indicated that seminary-educated pastors tended to serve larger and more effective churches. Nor does he or May apply the same economic analysis to the seminaries and their place in the financial order of American Christianity. But the basic observation that the health of the church and the health of the seminaries were linked has been borne out in subsequent history. After the Second World War, both local churches and seminaries expanded rapidly, and the percentage of seminary-trained pastors in local churches rose dramatically. As the Protestant mainstream has waned, its theological schools have also experienced difficulties; during the same time, the evangelical schools, supported by growing churches, have expanded and improved their schools.[23]

What about the theological schools in general? How were they equipped to prepare professional leaders for the churches? As might be expected of an in-house study, Brown and May took a basically optimistic view of the schools and their future. There were several reasons for this optimism. Perhaps first and foremost was the professional model itself. They realized they were still in the early days of the reformulation of the American profes-

22. One of the jokes that made the rounds near several seminaries was that the milk train that came on Monday morning was bringing back the "empty" seminarians as well as the empty milk cans. Under the impact of the rails, most seminaries appear to have adopted schedules that began at noon on Mondays and ended at noon on Fridays to allow travel time.

23. See below, chap. 26. Notice that some of these problems have been concealed due to the decision of many schools to offer a much greater variety of academic programming.

sions, and that ministry, while perhaps behind medicine, was not far behind law or the newer professions.[24] Further, the authors were aware that seminaries had been in a process of fundamental change for the last twenty-five years or so.[25] What was needed, they believed, was the continuation and acceleration of certain aspects rather than a completely new start or the reestablishment of the institutions.

III. Optimism

The Brown and May study was conducted from a thoroughly realistic and comparative perspective. When compared to many other educational institutions, the seminaries did not necessarily fare badly. For example, when 71 seminaries were compared with 848 privately controlled institutions and 223 public institutes, the seminaries had on the average more books per student in the library — 268 to 52 to 32 — more productive funds per student — $6,739 to $1,818 to $318 — and more total receipts per student — $765 to $508 to $592.[26] Comparisons with more elite institutions somewhat modified these conclusions, but they still pictured institutions that, although clearly declining in comparison with them, were not greatly inferior to them.[27] In many cases these comparative advantages allowed theological schools to enroll students without charging tuition and to give many students subsidies for their living expenses. Both of these practices had been under fire since the 1890s. The opponents believed they supported indolence and less than "manly" habits of dependence, while proponents believed they enabled "poor but pious" young men to advance intellectually. From the perspective of the professional ideal, Brown could refer to the tendencies of subsidies as "evil."[28] While the debate raged furiously, neither side won the argument. The combination of rising costs and the availability of government funds, either as Veterans Administration benefits or college loans,

24. Law has had many of the same problems as ministry in attaining professional status. In part, this is because society has needed lawyers representing different social interests as well as lawyers representing the best civil and business practice. Hence, despite studies of legal education, proprietary law schools continued in many states even after World War II and admission requirements to the bar varied widely from state to state. Even in medicine, one must be careful not to see Flexner as the Newton who spoke and all was light. Even after Flexner, not all doctors had both a college degree and a medical degree, and disputes over the best premedical preparation continue even today.

25. See, for instance, Brown-May, 1:120.

26. Brown-May, 4:228, table 92.

27. Brown-May, 4:230, table 94.

28. Brown-May, 1:146.

ended the subsidy system and in most seminaries necessitated continually increasing tuition.[29]

The most important of the reforms that had been undertaken, Brown and May believed, were in the area of curriculum. Brown with his well-trained eye for theological nuance noted that the tradition of dividing theology into Scripture, history, theology, and practical theology was rooted in a classical understanding of revelation. In effect, the prospective preacher followed the implications of the theological presuppositions out to their logical conclusion. Hence, the old curriculum placed a heavy premium on the study of the Bible in the original languages and on learning to do exegesis correctly. While the program had a certain coherence, it neglected historical study and often placed its emphasis, whether intentionally or not, on the more intellectual sides of church teaching. Brown and May noted that a conservative understanding of the curriculum was still held by many contemporary faculty members.[30]

Yet the report emphasized that the curriculum had undergone considerable change in the last twenty-five years. It noted four areas of change: in scope, in the number of electives, in the provision for specialization, and in the insistence on some learning by doing. The result was an academic program that featured eight primary areas of study: English Bible, biblical Greek and Hebrew, theology and the philosophy of religion, church history, comparative religion and missions, religious education and the psychology of religion, practical theology, and Christian sociology and ethics. Studies of the various schools indicated that the largest number of courses was offered in biblical subjects, with practical courses next in popularity. Christian ethics, sociology, and comparative religions and missions were the least common offerings. Although the curricula of different schools varied, there were three types: a fixed curriculum in which all courses are elective, a mixed curriculum with some required and some elective courses, and all-elective programs. Several schools, including Boston's Episcopal, used a tutorial system, modeled on Cambridge and Oxford, where a student read with a professor. Within these broad classifications there were variations. Electives, for instance, might be confined to a department or area (any course in religious education), or they might be free electives that could come from any area of the curriculum. The system of majors and minors, used to bring some order to the undergraduate curriculum, was not widely used, although Drew used it very effectively. Yale, perhaps the most important

29. It is probable that seminary students are subsidized more than any other group of students except those in the training for commissions in the army and navy. Brown-May, 1:146.

30. Brown-May, 3:34. The fourfold curriculum has also been used as a basis for seminary organization, even in schools that do not share its intellectual presuppositions. The endowed chairs of many older schools, of course, often enshrined this understanding of the curriculum.

seminary of the period, ordered its curriculum around six ministry fields: preaching and pastoral service, foreign missionary service, religious education, community service, religious leadership in colleges and universities, and teaching and research in religion. Interestingly, Yale had a three-year program for students who were not carrying heavy fieldwork and a four-year program for those who were doing such preparation. Yet, when all is said and done, what is most remarkable about Brown and May's findings is that the schools had, by guess or divine guidance, reached a remarkable consensus about the formal shape of the curriculum, while differing significantly about the details. Outside of Yale and such adventurous schools as Episcopal Theological School, the schools agreed that something needed to be taken from each of the eight areas and that considerable focus should be placed on biblical studies.[31]

Despite its universality, this basic curricular scheme had some potentially serious flaws. Perhaps, at least from Brown and May's perspective, the most serious difficulty was that it was not sufficiently professional. At times there was a tendency for the curriculum to lose its professional focus and become merely vocational training. The practical fields could easily come to focus on the tasks the minister had to perform rather than the functions of ministry. Preparing a Sunday school lesson, for instance, was a different thing from understanding how Scripture and theology ought to inform religious education. Brown himself advocated the threefold division of the curriculum that the Conference of Theological Seminaries had suggested at Cleveland in 1931:

> I. A Division or Group of Fields dealing with religion, particularly the Christian religion, in its historical aspects. These would include the History of Religion, Old and New Testament, Church History and ecumenics.
>
> II. A Division or Group of Fields dealing with the interpretation of Christianity in the present. These would include the systematic interpretation of Christianity, theology and philosophy of Christianity, Christianity and human personality, and Christian and the social order.
>
> III. A Division or Group of Fields dealing with the work of Christianity in the present. These would include the work of the minister in preaching, pastoral, administrative, cooperation of ministers, the work of the church at home, including religious education, and the work of the church abroad.[32]

31. Brown-May, 3:58.
32. Brown-May, 1:122.

Hopefully, this type of organization would make the aims and objectives of the various studies more evident.

Brown and May's recommendations were in line with how students saw the value of their courses: "In the appraisal of the most helpful course, English Bible was mentioned by 78 per cent. of the students, practical theology by 57 per cent., theology and philosophy by 55 per cent., religious education and psychology of religion by 45 per cent., church history by 43 per cent., biblical Greek and Hebrew by 26 per cent." Students tended to give high ratings to courses that stressed social and psychological knowledge, and while religious education was not as strong as in the 1920s, Shailer Mathews's observation that it was the most popular field was probably still accurate.[33]

In part, seminary students shared in the widespread "vocationalism" of much of American education. Since the reason for going to school was to improve one's social and economic prospects, the content of education must be related to that goal as well. The importance of this belief for American higher education should not be downplayed or denigrated. In its various forms, it was one of the ideological foundations for a system of higher education that by the early 1930s was providing the United States with the highest proportion of people with advanced education in the world. Since students went to seminary to serve the church, there was nothing questionable about their natural interest in what enabled them to do that effectively.

The other problem with the curriculum was how it was taught. Although some teachers used discussion and seminar methods, the report found that seminary teachers overwhelmingly preferred the lecture method, followed by examinations and, occasionally, papers.[34] Thus the curriculum appeared to be primarily designed for the communication of knowledge that was pursued for its own sake. Little emphasis was placed on the integration of knowledge or its application.

Perhaps this was one reason for the heavy emphasis the report placed on field education. Another reason was that it was the clearest example of where seminaries abandoned their reliance on liberal arts methods of education and embraced a professional model more in line with schools of social work and education. Frank Foster, a graduate student at Union (New York) who was preparing a dissertation on the subject, did the basic research. Field education had developed from the seminaries' hope that they could find a way to use educationally the outside employment of their students. Graham Taylor had developed one of the earliest programs using sociological techniques at Hartford

33. Shailer Mathews, "Let Religious Education Beware," *Christian Century,* 1927, p. 362.
34. Brown-May, 3:124.

Seminary, and Union placed its first-year students in nearby missionary and ecclesiastical positions. But in most schools field education, student aid, and student part-time employment were different sides of the same reality. Foster naturally began by attempting to get some terminological clarity by defining "outside work" as all types of student employment. "Fieldwork" was "only those types in some measure educationally controlled by the seminaries."[35]

Foster quickly found that the practice of seminaries in regard to outside work was a jumble. While approximately a third of the institutions he studied closely regarded outside work as primarily educational, two-thirds saw it as either primarily or secondarily part of student aid. Even in those schools that had a strong fieldwork program, students were most often permitted to take outside work purely for remuneration after or before their fieldwork requirement was met. Almost 70 percent of all students were engaged in some type of outside employment, and those students spent a median of eighteen hours a week in their placement.

The most common placements were as student pastors and in religious education and club (youth) work. Not surprisingly, since few schools had housing for married students, schools tended to steer them toward student pastorates where they would have a parsonage. The greater financial needs of many married students also played a role in this decision. Such placement, of course, illustrated the basic problem. If the placements were for professional training, one would expect a statistical pattern that roughly corresponded to the general student population in each of the different opportunities provided. Foster emphatically did not find this to be the case. A similar point could and was made about the way the different opportunities were divided by classes.

Student pastorates were by far the most important form of field education. At Yale there were eighty-seven student pastors, for instance, and the school took some pains to see that the student's abilities corresponded to the church's need. The various practical courses attempted to use this experience in their teaching, and field trips to congregations using the most effective methods were frequently made. Yale faculty were charged with visiting the student pastorates and with having conferences with students about their work. The seminary sought to keep good records of employment and of the various churches served. Much was coordinated through the Interseminary Commission for the Rural Church, a cooperative group composed of the five New England seminaries. At Boston University students were required to put their outside work under seminary supervision and received academic credit for their experiences. The Duke endowment included considerable funds for summer

35. Brown-May, 3:193.

pastorates, and J. M. Ormond established a systematic way of making and supervising those appointments. At Virginia students worked directly under faculty members at various "missions" — noncanonical congregations — near the seminary, while at Auburn one of the faculty pastored three small churches, using his students as assistants.

Foster was also fascinated by the new clinical training movement[36] and by education experiences that promised to add a more practical component to the training of ministers. These included organized field trips — including some programs that were similar to later immersions — and work in social service agencies. In short, field education, as Foster conceived it, involved almost any activity not bound by the classroom and its limits. Field education ideally was to provide the type of training received by the "psychiatrist and the social worker" — the two main competitors of the clergy, according to Brown and May — and perhaps to gain similar expertise.[37] Clearly, field education was the cutting edge of much of 1930s theological education:

> This review of significant experiments in progress must indicate the vitality of the movement to make supervised field work a fully integrated aspect of theological education. Indeed the evidences of effective field work . . . might with reason lead to the conclusion that supervised, graded experience as the core around which curriculum courses are formed, will soon be considered as essential to an adequate training for the ministry as it is now considered necessary to an adequate training for engineering, for law, and for medicine.[38]

Although Foster cited examples of where this high ideal had been realized, including the programs at Union, Yale, and Chicago, the general practices of the seminaries were, at best, chaotic. Field education was a program that had all of contemporary educational thinking behind it, including Dewey's belief in the value of learning by doing, but at the same time it rarely functioned as the theory implied. In many ways finances weakened the best of the seminaries' intentions. Students' need for income, the lack of faculty and supervisory time, and the tendency to assign field education as part of church-seminary relations were all reasons cited for this obvious failure. Field education was also an academic stepchild, often administered by a faculty member part-time, and without academic standing. Consequently, institutions found it easy to let the program drift away from its academic moorings.

36. See below, chap. 25.

37. Brown-May, 1:9.

38. Brown-May, 3:251.

Further, field education lacked romance. Theological education is by nature concerned with the overarching world of theological theory. For most faculty and for many students, this is a grand adventure, a quest for the truth or at least for the truth that an individual can preach. The fundamentalist-modernist controversy made this aspect of theological education even more central. Hence, students are urged to understand cosmology, to delve deeply into the mystery of Christ, and to investigate "the Great Tradition." Very sophisticated methods of historical and literary analysis are used, even in the weakest of schools, to attain those goals.

In comparison, field education, like sociology and psychology of religion, forced the student to deal with the mundane world of local religion. The student had to move from dealing with the mystery of the composition of the Gospels to the everyday world in which people are struggling with more mundane matters in a local body that is often underfinanced and understaffed. Further, the prospective minister rarely dealt with those limit cases, such as death or disaster, where the personal depth acquired through long years of preparation was a major value. Field education, thus, exposed many of the contradictions that the seminaries had difficulty facing. It lay bare, in particular, the deep fear that ministry might turn out to be primarily administering a small local charity well and that seminaries did not prepare people well for the reality of living and working in a minor charity organization. Field education, in short, was a reality check for both students and faculty.

Neither the data nor the conclusions of Brown and May's study were original. We have refrained from repeating topics discussed in the earlier Kelly survey, for example, because Brown and May's data indicated that little change had taken place in the few years between the two reports. Brown's frequent first-volume references to the work of the Conference of Theological Schools as well as May's references to studies undertaken by others indicate how indebted the two authors were to the contemporary literature on theological education. Many of the proposals for change in theological education had been tucked into journals with limited circulation, and only a handful, such as William Rainey Harper's noted essay on the changes in theological curriculum, had provoked contemporary debate. Part of the problem in theological education was that the left hand did not know what the right hand was doing, and Brown and May, even more than Kelly a decade earlier, was a summary piece that exposed the often hidden debates of the last thirty years. In many ways the report was similar to Brown's other works. Brown was one of liberalism's great academic popularizers. He had the capacity to read and absorb massive amounts of theology and to suggest, often in very tentative ways, avenues that other theologians might take. Whereas many of his contemporaries, such as Douglas

Macintosh, were noted for their dialectical sharpness, Brown sought a catholicity of approach that allowed different voices to emerge. If Philip Schaff was America's first great ecumenical theologian, then William Adams Brown was its second.

The importance of Brown and May's report lay precisely in its irenic and ecumenical spirit. Like the association it helped to birth, the two authors were deeply concerned with finding a consensus that could help the schools and churches deal with the problems of an American Protestantism that had some resources but did not have the high cultural power and prestige it had enjoyed in the progressive period. The way it elected to do this was to self-consciously link Protestant leadership and the professional ideal that was so powerful in the America of its time. In many ways Brown and May's ideal minister is like the ideal Depression-era bureaucrat: a mixture of know-what and know-how. In a time of confusion and lack of direction, simple competence is a virtue. And this is finally what the Brown and May study wanted the schools to produce: men and women whose life and work were marked by competence and a high level of performance.

The ideal of simple professional competence formulated by Brown and May was the cleanest understanding of the seminary formulated between 1930 and 1960. In many ways it was an uninspiring ideal. Unlike the progressive ideal of the seminary that saw the educated minister as the tribune of reform, the professional model of theological education did not try to remove the ministry from its social location. The churches were in trouble, much of it of their own making, and they needed leadership that was able to do the basic tasks of ministry and do those tasks well in order to prosper. The surveyors were convinced that a competent, well-educated ministry could begin to address many of the problems that confronted American people of faith and do it without rancor and without the promotional extravaganzas of much contemporary religion. The minister should know how to be there in times of personal crisis, to speak with intelligence and sound sense on Christian topics, to organize an educational program, and to be able to address public issues.

The Brown-May study was of course deeply concerned with such issues as ministerial status and ministerial compensation. If there was a subtext to the study, it was that the economics of ministry needed reformation. A competent clergy was worthy of an adequate salary. Of course, and Brown and May knew this, the rampant denominationalism that populated the American countryside with too many churches was not easily changed. But they hoped to make a start in this direction by being honest about the problem. Perhaps because Brown was the consummate Protestant insider, he could say this more clearly than Kelly, whose voice was muted by his critics.

Brown and May's formulations were, despite fits and starts, reigning orthodoxy among theological administrators until the late 1960s. Faculties were constructed with the professional model in mind, and seminary curricula with few exceptions followed a professional model that looked toward a greater balance between academic and practical courses. If, as we noted above, the Brown-May study may have underestimated the quality of the students in the seminaries at the beginning of the 1930s, the value of its understanding of theological education may have also been underestimated. The period in which the professional model was the dominant understanding of theological education was, after all, one of the strongest periods in the history of the American Protestant churches.

CHAPTER TWENTY-ONE

Seminaries and the Second Righteous Empire

In 1944 the newly elected president of Union Seminary, Henry Pitney Van Dusen, mounted the dais at the meeting of the American Association of Theological Schools (AATS). It was no ordinary occasion. The patrician Van Dusen had been groomed for the position for years by Henry Sloane Coffin, and his works carried the authority of the leader of the liberal movement. Van Dusen confidently stated:

> More than these, there would seem to be suggested a far larger measure of collaboration among the seminaries in the united discharge of some of their major responsibilities, a cooperative surmounting of some of their most harassing problems — a united presentation of the claims of the ministry with good hope of claiming larger numbers of men of first-rate ability and promise; coordinated research with hope of far more significant contributions to Christian knowledge and strategy; cooperation in curricular experimentation, with good promise of heightened enrichment and sure advance; sharing of responses of libraries, faculties and other facilities; a solid front in relations with Government, Roman Catholicism, Secularism the great anti-Christian forces within society; united evangelism in tackling the employment of instruments of cooperation such as the Association through which in these latter years many of us have discovered such fruitful and serviceable fellowship in common problems and tasks.[1]

Van Dusen, who prided himself on his Christian realism, felt there were sound reasons for his optimistic mood. Just a year earlier he had published his *What Is*

1. Henry Pitney Van Dusen, "The Church Tomorrow: The Role of the Seminaries," Presidential Address, *American Association of Theological Schools Bulletin,* 1944, p. 29.

the Church Doing?[2] a carefully done survey of Christian life around the world in a time of war. Despite the horrors of the struggle, Van Dusen found much to inspire hope, including the resistance of many Christians to totalitarianism. But there were other exciting trends. Unlike World War I, when hostilities in Europe had also created warfare on the missionary front, not one Christian mission had been forced to close due to the political and economical situation.[3] Despite the confident statements from Japan that Christian missions would collapse once the power of European armies and the availability of Western wealth were withdrawn, the calamity did not happen. The younger churches were flourishing, creating and educating their own ministry, and producing leaders of prophetic imagination and power. He gushed: "A second major impression is the unexpected strength of the Younger Christian Churches, and even of those still more immature groups of Christians who had not yet taken their formal place among the Churches of Christ; their readiness for, and capacity to discharge, responsibilities for which they have had meager training and for which it was assumed that they were as yet incompetent."[4] The sense of standing on the edge of a new day was almost contagious.

Van Dusen saw two great movements coming together in the church of his day that were vital to the seminaries. In his AATS address he gave what was almost a classic interpretation of the status of the church in his time.

> I have elsewhere termed these two developments the movement of expansion and the movement of consolidation. The first aimed to extend the sweep of Christian allegiance to the farthest limits of the earth, so that Christianity might become in fact what it had always been in profession — a world religion. The other took as its ultimate goal the coordination and unification of the multitudinous and diverse branches and agencies of Christian influence into an effective organism, so that the Christian Church might become in truth what it had always been in ideal — a world community — the effort toward Christian Unity.[5]

The image is almost cosmic. The Christian church had exploded, like some supernova, across the world stage, and now, as the excitement cooled, it was discovering new solidity and new unity. While reason might have predicted that only a united church might inspire a great missionary effort, in fact it was the other way around. The great missionary effort was producing ecclesiastical unity.

2. Henry Pitney Van Dusen, *What Is the Church Doing?* (New York: Scribner, 1943).
3. Van Dusen, "The Church Tomorrow," p. 51.
4. Van Dusen, "The Church Tomorrow," p. 87.
5. Van Dusen, *What?* p. 20.

I. Seminaries and Missions

Van Dusen was right to call attention to the relationship between the seminaries and the missionary movement. From the beginning a large percentage of seminary graduates entered the foreign field, and some seminaries, such as Andover and Virginia, were strong centers of missionary outreach in their own right. From early on the various missionary agencies were one of the prime markets for seminary graduates. By the 1890s the Student Volunteer Movement had become a major source of seminary enrollment. The YMCA urged young men to consider missions as a career. Many of the most respected Christian voices of the 1920s and 1930s, including E. Stanley Jones, Sherwood Eddy, and John R. Mott, had their roots in the missionary effort. All three were popular and effective speakers at student missionary conferences, where they urged young men and women to get all the education possible for what they believed was the highest of Christian callings. Seminary leaders periodically held chapel services that urged young people to commit themselves to the work abroad. Furloughed missionaries were present at almost all schools, and they interacted with the students, preached in local churches, and served as general missionary advocates. These combined efforts paid off. While exact figures for all seminaries are not available, Princeton, Union, and Yale sent between 10 and 12 percent of each graduating class abroad for at least part of their careers.[6] In turn, the missionary boards and agencies supported, at least for male candidates, a full seminary and college course. Even in denominations where the general level of ministerial preparation was low, such as the Southern Baptist Convention, the Foreign Missions Board sought and recruited seminary graduates for their work abroad.

The symbiosis between seminaries and missionary agencies went deeper than this. American missionaries abroad tended to take the American seminaries they had attended as models for what theological education ought to be. Almost every denomination involved abroad established a network of schools that included elementary-, secondary-, collegiate-, and seminary-style institutions. American seminary graduates were prized as instructors in these institutions, and they often served as a place for bright young men, who had been excluded by the small number of teaching opportunities in the United States, to take up a satisfying theological career. When Princeton held its centennial celebration in 1911, the academic parade included representatives from every conti-

6. Robert Elliot Speer, "Princeton on the Mission Field," in *The Centennial Celebration of the Theological Seminary of the Presbyterian Church in the United States of America at Princeton, New Jersey* (n.p.: The Seminary, 1912).

nent. More than twenty-five such schools were represented, including Elat Theological School in West Africa; Union Theological School, Foochow, China; United Theological Seminary, Bangalore, South India; and Western Turkey Theological Seminary, Marsovan, Turkey. In 1909 Baptists owned almost as many schools abroad as at home, including Burman Theological Seminary, Ramapatnam Theological Seminary, Theological Seminary (China), Shanghai Baptist Seminary, Yokohama Theological Seminary, and Theological Seminary of the German Baptists (Hamburg). The missionary movement also promoted a "globalization" of the seminaries. The larger schools, such as Union, Yale, and Princeton, had the resources to support a large number of "foreign" students, but most schools had at least a few candidates from abroad. In the 1950s, for instance, Herbert Gezork, president of Andover-Newton and a graduate of the Baptist missionary seminary in Hamburg and Southern Baptist Seminary in Louisville, boasted that a growing number of students were at the school from "India, China, Japan, Hawaii, Jamaica, Turkey, Greece, and various countries of Europe." Rockefeller-sponsored "International Houses" were located near Union (New York) and the University of Chicago.

When Van Dusen said in 1947, "The theology of the world Christian mission is prevailingly that of liberal evangelicalism,"[7] he pointed to a shared understanding of religious and political life that united Americans with people around the world. In areas where American missionary influence was strong, such as China, the missions and the schools often shared theological and political values. Many Protestant Americans, for instance, idealized Christians Sun Yat-sen and his successor Chiang Kai-shek, who, like Sun, had married into the influential Methodist Soong family. Since approximately half of the American foreign service comprised children of missionary parents, this shared perspective helped shape American foreign policy in the 1930s and 1940s. Interestingly, Henry Luce, the founder of *Time,* was the son of an old China hand who shared many of these same values and saw that they were widely disseminated. L. Nelson Bell, one of the founders of the neo-evangelical movement, was also an old China hand who was disillusioned by the failure of the China mission to win that nation[8] and blamed the liberal consensus on missions for the halt of effective evangelization. In response, Bell began a crusade to return to an earlier understanding of the church's work abroad.

The liberal consensus that Van Dusen saw in the Christian world mission

7. Henry P. Van Dusen, *World Christianity* (New York: Abingdon-Cokesbury, 1947), p. 200.

8. John Charles Pollock, *A Foreign Devil in China: The Story of Dr. L. Nelson Bell, an American Surgeon in China* (Minneapolis: Published for the Billy Graham Association by World Wide Publications, 1971).

was the product of almost half a century of debate.[9] In 1900 William Newton Clarke, the liberal Baptist theologian at Hamilton, published *A Study of Christian Missions.* The book was a self-conscious attempt to apply what was then called the "new" theology to the popular missionary enterprise. As Clarke saw the matter, the Christian mission did not have to commend itself in terms of the traditional pattern of proclamation and conversion. Christian faith was destined to make its way gradually into the cultures of other nations. While Clarke did believe that Christianity would displace the other faiths, he had little doubt that the primary means of expansion would be through cultural assimilation. At much the same time, younger German theologians in the history-of-religions schools were questioning the absoluteness of Christianity. Led by the brilliant social philosopher Ernst Troeltsch, these theologians saw Christianity as a product of religious evolution that had absorbed elements from other faiths in its own development. As Christianity became a world religion, they reasoned, it would continue to learn from other faiths. This did not necessarily mean that all historians of religion were pessimistic about the worldwide Christian mission. Missionary Albert Schweitzer, after all, came from the same school of biblical interpretation. Schweitzer and Troeltsch, like other German academics of their age, assumed that Western culture's development of science, technology, and medicine gave it a privileged position. But, like Clarke, they suggested that missions be carried out on cultural, rather than theological, grounds.

Theologians were and are, of course, paid to be consistent. Most missionaries were not theologians, but they were deeply impressed by the transforming power of Western cultural institutions. Schools, colleges, and hospitals were the most popular missionary enterprises with both missionaries and the missionized. In China, India, and Japan, young Asians responded enthusiastically to Western cultural initiatives. The Christian movement was, in effect, a path into the new world that Western capitalism was creating, and particularly in its American forms, it did not seem to require the political subordination associated with European imperialism.[10]

E. Stanley Jones was perhaps the most popular American missionary of the 1920s and 1930s. Although he had begun his career working with lower-caste Indians, he turned to the newer philosophy of missions and established a

9. William R. Hutchison, *Errand to the World: American Protestant Thought and Foreign Missions* (Chicago: University of Chicago Press, 1987).

10. One must be careful, however, not to read later Western interpretations of missions into earlier periods. Many colonial churches were much stronger at the end of imperialism than their European sponsors had assumed they would be. This was particularly obvious in Indonesia and India.

series of ashrams. These featured his famous "roundtable" approach to missions explained in his best-selling *Christ of the Indian Road* (1925)[11] and his *Christ of the Round Table* (1928). In these works Jones argued that Christianity could make its way in Asia as the fulfillment of existing Asian faiths and that these faiths would find their highest truth in Christ. Jones's favorite image of the roundtable was designed to show that the dialogue took place with anyone sitting at the "head" of the table or serving as chair. Jones's popularity was such that when the Federal Council of Churches decided in 1938 to launch a series of preaching missions throughout the United States, they asked him to come home and serve as the headliner of the effort. Jones, who loved addressing large audiences, was glad to oblige, and he consistently outdrew other pulpit stars.

II. Early Missiology

American seminaries, like English universities, were slow to develop systematic teaching in the area of missions. A survey reported by W. A. Hill in 1938 revealed that of sixty-eight seminaries, only twenty-two had full-time professors of missions and that many relied on part-time instructors, often missionaries on furlough or in retirement. Yet some American missiologists were people of worldwide stature who made major contributions. Tennessee-born W. O. Carver, for instance, a brilliant student at Louisville's Southern Baptist Seminary, was asked to remain at the school after completing his doctorate in 1896. After substituting for a colleague in a missions class in 1897, he became deeply interested in the field. He began to design courses in missions and comparative religions, and in 1900 he was officially elected to the first full-time chair of missions in the United States. Thoroughly ecumenical and prodigiously learned, Carver served as his denomination's eyes and ears in missionary education and the emerging ecumenical movement. He was deeply impressed by Hartford's establishment of the Kennedy School of Missions, an American school modeled on the missions schools of Europe, and hoped his own Southern Baptist denomination would find the funds to establish such an institution. In a 1926 letter to E. Y. Mullins he wrote: "I wish to speak again of a matter that I have mentioned at other times. I am now sure that it will be but a short time till there will be a School of Missions somewhere in the South. The conditions are

11. The book sold more than 600,000 copies. Jones's Hindu dialogue colleagues may have recognized his hope that they would be converted, albeit with nontraditional means. Jones was well regarded through much of the world and was in demand as a speaker in areas as far apart as Brazil and London.

ripe for it and it will not long be delayed. I greatly wish that we might have the honor and the prestige of inaugurating it. They have had such schools for a hundred years in Great Britain, and there are already three or four in this country. All the missionary statesmen are now calling for this form of instruction."[12]

Harlan Beach was another influential early missiologist and the founder of the strong tradition of missionary study at Yale. A graduate of Yale and Andover, Beach served in China under the American Board of Commissioners until his wife's poor health forced him to return to the United States. He became active in the student movement, serving as educational secretary of the Student Volunteer Movement (SVM). In 1901-3 he published his comprehensive *A Geography and Atlas of Protestant Missions,* a classical study of the present prospects of the church. In 1906 he became professor of missions at Yale. Although the position was new, Yale had a long and distinguished history of involvement in the missionary movement. George Edward Day, dean of the divinity school from 1888 to 1895, had an intense interest in missions, and when he retired he donated his collection of books to the library. In addition to significant bequests by both Day and his wife, Day spent many of his remaining years collecting money and resources for the Day Missions Library.[13] In 1911 Beach became the librarian of this collection and spent much of his life making it, along with the Missionary Research Library established by John D. Rockefeller at Union,[14] one of the major research centers for world Christianity. Together with Dean Charles Brown, he devised a missionary track in the school's curriculum. An inveterate traveler, Beach attended all the great missionary meetings and continued to travel to various fields to update his knowledge of the actual situation of the missions.

The quality of Beach's work as a missionary librarian and pack rat should not be underestimated. His own studies were of course meticulously researched. But it was his successor, Kenneth Scott Latourette, who demonstrated the depth of the collection. Like Beach, Latourette was a product of the SVM who served two years in the "Yale in China" program. Upon his return, he published extensively on China and Japan while teaching at Baptist Dennison University. In 1921 he moved to Yale, where he began research for his monumental

12. The original letter is in the E. Y. Mullins collection at Southern Baptist Seminary, Louisville.

13. Stephen L. Peterson, *A Steady Aim towards Completeness: The Day Missions Library Centennial Volume* (New Haven: Yale University Library, 1993).

14. Ironically, Henry Pitney Van Dusen never recognized the great value of the Missionary Research Library, which never received adequate support during his presidency. See R. Pierce Beaver, "The Missionary Research Library: A Sketch of Its History," *Occasional Bulletin from the Missionary Research Library,* Feb. 1968, pp. 1-8.

seven-volume *History of the Expansion of Christianity* (1937-45). Latourette's thesis was that Christianity's expansion was irregular. Like other historical movements, Christianity went through periods of intense advance that were often followed by periods of stagnation or even geographical decline. With the harnessing of the power of Western capitalism in the nineteenth century, Christianity entered into its great century with the faith spreading from Europe to the whole world. While Latourette recognized that the twentieth century was a time of testing for these new churches and for the missionary movement that created them, he firmly believed that the churches had resources in the modern world that would enable them to meet the challenge. Prior to reading Latourette, few Americans, apart from professional missiologists, had a coherent picture of the extent of the church. After reading him, many stood in awe at what God was doing in their own time.[15]

Latourette's studies also pointed toward a different approach to the often chaotic history of modern Protestantism with its often confusing patchwork of denominations, agencies, personalities, unions, and schisms. Like his contemporary William Warren Sweet, who also had the ability to synthesize large quantities of information, he elected to treat Protestantism as a historical entity defined by its presence and activity in the world. In that sense Latourette wrote missionary history from an ecumenical perspective, even when many of the ecumenical agencies were in process of formation. His was an intellectual and theological achievement of the first order.

III. Missionary Education

Since missionary agencies were so important as employers of seminary graduates and as generators of interest in theological education, those agencies and their understanding of the seminaries were crucial to the schools' well-being. Unfortunately, many of those who looked critically at missionary education found that missionaries were poorly prepared.

In 1910 missionary agencies from the different sending countries and their churches met at Edinburgh to plan for what they believed, in common with popular Protestant belief, would be the great age of missions. Missionary education was a major item on the agenda. Commission V, chaired by

15. Such was apparently the experience of Union's Van Dusen, who referred to Latourette in his writings on the ecumenical movement and the world church, always with a sense of profound gratitude for Latourette's sense of the whole church. Other missionary-inclined presidents, such as Princeton's John Mackay, a noted missiologist in his own right and an expert on Protestantism in Latin America, also found Latourette's account inspiring.

W. Douglas Mackenzie of Hartford Seminary, took a critical look at the preparation of missionaries. As Dr. Campbell Gilson noted: "[W]e have worked too much upon the assumption that a missionary's work consists in the first place in doing some evangelistic preaching, and then gathering little groups of people to whom you give elementary Christian instructions. It may have been so in the earlier days of missions, and it may be so still in some of the fields where you are working among ruder races."[16] Missionary education, in other words, was directed toward a view of missions as they were and not toward preparing missionaries for the world in which they would actually serve. Wide agreement existed on the commission that missionary training had to be "different from that ordinarily given in our seminaries."[17] Although commissioners disagreed on specifics, as often happens in curricular discussions, they did agree on the outline of an effective program: "the science and history of missions, the religions of the world, sociology, pedagogy, and the science of language."

The question was how to implement the suggestions that Edinburgh made. In 1911 Mackenzie became chair of the Board of Missionary Preparation of the Conference of Foreign Boards, which attempted to use the Edinburgh report as a standard for future missionary appointments. As with ordination standards, however, it was easier to get agreement on the standards than uniformity in their application. The conference also disagreed over where and how missionary training should take place. Mackenzie's own school, which had been blessed by a substantial program in Islamic studies, was able to establish a "school of missions" that was able to offer all the specialized courses that Edinburgh suggested. Many seminaries believed that Hartford's concept of a theological university was the best answer. Both Southwestern and Eastern Baptist Seminaries, for instance, established their own schools of missions, and later Fuller Seminary in California would find the "theological university" the best way to provide the specialized training needed. Others saw the university as the ideal place for such education. John Clarke Archer could wax enthusiastic about the advantages of the university for those working on the foreign field.

> It is to the "university man" to which reference is made. The facilities and atmosphere of the university seem almost if not altogether indispensable — "the wide culture and the open air." The foreign missionary lives in a more diverse and a more exacting world than does the home minister, and is in greater need than he is of the sensitiveness to his environment. He

16. *The Preparation of Missionaries: The World Missionary Conference Report of Commission V; The Training of Teachers* (London and Edinburgh: Oliphant, Anderson and Ferrier; New York: Fleming H. Revell, 1910), p. 160.

17. Harlan Beach, in *The Preparation of Missionaries,* p. 160.

> should enter his field with the largest possible intellectual equipment, for, having entered, he is so engrossed in his task that [he] has little time to reconsider and revise the stock with which he came. If, for example, his training be originally inadequate, he is likely to be less concerned than he should be with the question of theological reconstruction demanded by the situation in which he works.[18]

The prospective missionary and furloughed missionary, viewed from this perspective, would take their specialized courses at the university while taking their more theological work in the divinity school. Yale Divinity School was the bellwether in the development of this understanding of the task.

As R. Pierce Beaver noted, one result of the Edinburgh conference was the expansion of the number of schools with a full-time professor of missions. There were only four such professors in the United States in 1910 — at Southern Baptist Theological Seminary, Omaha Presbyterian, Yale Divinity School, and Episcopal Theological School in Boston. This changed in the 1920s. Union Seminary appointed Daniel Fleming, for instance, to direct the school's department of foreign service and, later, to serve as the school's professor of missions.[19] Although fewer new appointments were made in the 1930s, in part due to the Depression, by 1938 twenty-two of the nation's leading seminaries had appointed someone to that position.[20] Scholars interested in missionary work met together regularly, and in 1952 the Society of American Professors of Mission (no *s*), a professional guild of missiologists, was formed. A larger and more comprehensive body, the American Society of Missiology, was created in 1972.

The new departments of missions did much to enrich the seminary curriculum, particularly through the teaching of the history of religions[21] and the history of missions. However, these departments were crucial in the larger dis-

18. John Clark Archer, "The Function of the Theological Seminary in the Enterprise of Missions," in *Education for Christian Service* (Members of the Faculty of the Divinity School of Yale University) (New Haven: Yale University, 1922), p. 286.

19. For Fleming's importance in the larger debate over missions, see Conrad Cherry, *Hurrying toward Zion: Universities, Divinity Schools, and American Protestantism* (Bloomington and Indianapolis: Indiana University Press, 1995), pp. 75-76.

20. W. A. Hill, "Missions in the Theological Seminaries of the United States," *International Review of Missions* 23 (1934).

21. At Harvard and the University of Chicago, the history of religions had been separate from missiology since the turn of the century. Union Seminary's Robert Ernest Hume was primarily a student of the world's faith, and the seminary maintained a separate professor of missions (for Hume's career see "Robert Ernest Hume, 1877-1948," *Union Seminary Quarterly Review* 3, no. 3 [Mar. 1948]: 28-29). This was not true in many other schools, including other university schools.

cussions in the churches about the nature of the missionary enterprise. Daniel Fleming's *Whither Bound in Mission,* published in 1925, was particularly evocative. Fleming believed that all religions reflected the cry of the human heart for God, and perhaps more important, all religions faced common enemies in such phenomena as racism, war, ignorance, and secularism. Christians needed to recognize the larger threat to human spiritual life and to learn to cooperate with leaders from other traditions in the pursuit of peace, progress, and social justice. Fleming was not alone in proposing such an alternative future for the missionary enterprise, and his ideas were widely discussed at the Jerusalem Missionary Conference in 1928.

In 1932 *Re-thinking Missions: A Laymen's Inquiry after One Hundred Years* was published.[22] Sponsored by the Institute of Social and Religious Research with the strong personal support of John D. Rockefeller, Jr., the Laymen's Inquiry was perhaps misnamed. The chair and principal author of the report, William Ernst Hocking, was arguably America's leading contemporary philosopher of religion,[23] whose thoughtful books were highly respected within both university and seminary circles. Further, many of the most able people in American religion were among his team of surveyors, including the missiologist Daniel Fleming and others who had been active at the Madras conference. But *Re-thinking Missions* was a radical document precisely because it shouted from the housetops what had been whispered among professional missionaries. For missions to be viable, it stated, they needed to surrender the idea of converting individuals, not to mention whole societies, and concentrate on meeting the human needs of the world. In other words, missions should concentrate on such institutions as schools, hospitals, and libraries. Ideally, Hocking and his committee argued, this should be done by cooperating with the leaders of other world religions and movements for human betterment, such as the one represented by Gandhi in India. The report's favorite metaphor for the missionary was the ambassador for Christ (Eph. 6:20) who represented what we have "learned through Jesus Christ" and could forge alliances with others.[24]

22. Many American Protestants felt blindsided by this report, but many of the basic ideas had been discussed for some time. See Grant Wacker, "Second Thoughts on the Great Commission: Liberal Protestantism and Foreign Missions, 1890-1940," in *Earthen Vessels: American Evangelicalism and Foreign Missions, 1880-1980,* ed. Joel A. Carpenter and Wilbert Shenk (Grand Rapids: Eerdmans, 1990).

23. Hocking would be better known today, perhaps, had he not occupied the uncomfortable historical place between William James and process theology. Like the Boston personalists, with whom he shared the Wesleyan tradition, Hocking was deeply concerned with how the self experienced the world and understood its environment.

24. Hutchison, *Errand to the World,* p. 159.

Debate occupied much of the 1930s. Robert Speer, for instance, was outraged by the report and saw it as a threat to the world missionary enterprise, and although the Congregationalists and Methodists promised to take account of its findings, other denominations and sending agencies went on record against it. Rockefeller's own Northern Baptist Convention, for instance, rejected the report's suggestions totally, despite his threat to discontinue his family's sizable annual contribution, a threat that he kept, causing a substantial reduction in the Baptist budget. And in 1938 Hendrik Kraemer, the reigning European missiologist, denounced the work as having no Christian content.[25]

Re-thinking Missions was a serious setback for the seminaries. The 1910 Edinburgh report had bitterly complained about the inadequacies of the graduates of Bible schools, and now *Re-thinking Missions* expanded that critique to include almost all the American Missionary Force abroad. The church was not producing the educated, forceful leaders demanded by a world in crisis. Despite the churches' heavy investment in social ministries, for instance, few trained social workers or sociologists were found among its foreign ambassadors. But even the core religious mission of the churches was seriously compromised. Hocking pointed to the seminaries abroad: "They (American missionary seminaries) are reproductions on a small scale of the American denominational seminaries of a former generation. There are some excellent scholars at work in the best of them, but these institutions have not been uniquely planned to meet the peculiar problems and tasks of the countries where they exist."[26] Serious consolidation would be needed if the younger churches were to receive a more adequate ministry.

Missions were also central to the development of American denominations. As the various Protestant denominations developed their national organizations, the missionary movement was the primary spark plug of national denominational growth. When a new denomination was created, the establishment of foreign missionary work was one of the first steps in the creation of a national body. In addition to the theological dimensions of these actions, the motive was also financial. Beginning with the first appeals of the voluntary societies in the decade from 1810 to 1819, the centrality of missionary giving to the churches' national work grew every decade. This was particularly true of the period from 1890 to 1920 when the churches constructed elaborate national bu-

25. Kraemer's work, *The Christian Message in a Non-Christian World* (London: Edinburgh House Press, for the International Missionary Council, 1938), reflected the influence of Karl Barth and Emil Brunner.

26. Laymen's Foreign Missions Inquiry, Commission of Appraisal, *Re-thinking Missions: A Laymen's Inquiry after One Hundred Years,* William Hocking, chairman (New York: Harper and Brothers, 1932), p. 109.

reaucracies. The process of financial growth during this period is easily illustrated. The SVM generated large numbers of volunteers — the "men" in the famous slogan of men and money — and to finance the new personnel the churches launched the Laymen's Missionary Movement, one of the most successful Protestant funding drives. Two of the twentieth century's great Protestant fund-raisers, John R. Mott and Sherwood Eddy, were members of the SVM and the Laymen's Missionary Movement. In turn, funds from this initiative as well as other intradenominational financial campaigns financed the construction of the national and international offices of the Protestant churches. The groundswell of missionary interest also shifted local church patterns. The integrated yearly budget with expenses and benevolences viewed together became an ideal, and the churches shifted from their traditional reliance on such financial measures as collections, subscription lists, and pew rents to a system largely based on pledges. If the result was not a cornucopia of ecclesiastical wealth, the missionary enterprise gave the national church organizations considerable financial resources.[27]

Perhaps the best example of the interaction was the Southern Baptist Convention and its affiliated congregations. By the midtwenties Southern Baptists were broke, embarrassingly broke. They owed substantial debt on the new suburban campus of Southern Baptist Theological Seminary, and the Foreign Mission Board had to admit that it lacked the funds to bring its workers home in the event of a national emergency. In an effort to pay off the debt and keep institutions afloat, various agencies had covered the South with agents who were almost as ubiquitous as the boll weevils that were consuming the South's largest cash crop. The crisis was so great that Southern Baptists paused, if only for a moment, in the midst of their long debate over evolution, and adopted the Cooperative Program. The Cooperative Program called for the churches to make one gift to the denomination that would be divided among state and national agencies. Local churches were to include this contribution in their annual budgets, and in turn the various agencies surrendered the right to appeal to churches for direct support. Despite the large number of agencies supported by the new fund, most Southern Baptists saw the Cooperative Program as missionary support.

The Cooperative Program had tremendous implications for Southern Baptist seminaries. The most important was that the trustees of the schools

27. For the growth of church bureaucracies, see James Moorhead, "Engineering the Millennium: Kingdom Building in American Protestantism," *Princeton Seminary Bulletin* 15 (1994): 104-28. Also, James Moorhead, "Presbyterians and the Cult of Organizational Efficiency, 1870-1936," in *Reimagining Denominationalism: Interpretative Essays,* ed. Russell Richie and Bruce Mullin (New York: Oxford University Press, 1994).

were now appointed by the convention. While some traces of the older self-governing boards remained, particularly at Southern Baptist Theological Seminary, the schools were "agencies" of the churches whose budgets, salaries, and leadership could be (and often were) reviewed by the convention itself. In time, this close financial relationship made the Southern Baptist schools among the best financed in the nation, but the price paid for this prosperity was that they became an addendum to the convention's larger missionary work.

The importance of missions, both at home and abroad, helps us to understand the importance of the period from 1945 to 1960. Christian expansion would continue around the world, but in the immediate post–World War II period, the mainstream churches faced a major missionary crisis. As colonialism and imperialism gradually receded, the churches faced demands that they withdraw their missionary forces and leave their considerable properties in the hands of the local churches. In many cases these demands were reinforced by the nationalization of church property, especially schools and universities, and strict laws prohibiting foreign missionaries. Both the churches and the seminaries had to devise means of dealing with this new world order and with the demands of formerly missionary churches to have their own voices heard. The end of imperialism also heralded the end of the West's intellectual monopoly on Christian teaching.

IV. Missions Become the Ecumenical Movement

American Protestants, at least in their better moments, were aware that their constant division into smaller and smaller organizations was somehow vaguely ridiculous. The American small town with churches of four different denominations precariously perched at the town's major intersection was a potent symbol of the inner divisions of the churches. H. Richard Niebuhr, in his insightful *Social Sources of Denominationalism* (1929), pointed out that American religious organizations often reflected the deeper divisions of the society: ethnicity, social class, and above all, race. But what looked strange in an American context looked even odder when exported abroad. In such areas as India the differences between Methodists, Congregationalists, Anglicans, and Lutherans were not only minor, but they also inhibited the work of the missionaries. Early on American missionaries began cooperating with each other in various ways: schools for missionary children, the maintenance of retreat centers for the missionaries, and support for such interdenominational agencies as the YMCA. And the success of these common ventures suggested that the process needed to be carried further. Sherwood Eddy, the popular YMCA secretary for Asia, helped to create the United Church of South India, a precursor to the Church of South India.

Missions also contributed indirectly to the rise of an ecumenical spirit at home. The professionalization of church leadership made possible by the increase in church revenues also pointed toward new patterns of unification. Henry Pitney Van Dusen, who became a major authority on cooperative Christianity, identified six expressions of the ecumenical spirit: consultations for fellowship and counsel, comity agreements to divide responsibility and avoid competition, cooperation in joint action, federation, union, and interdenominational institutions. Interestingly, although denominational participation in these different organizations often had to be ratified by the appropriate judicatories, all six were essentially created and staffed by the new bureaucrats. In many ways the new bureaucrats experienced the heady sense of freedom and accomplishment that was common to any emerging profession. By dint of their expertise and knowledge, they were able to make independent decisions about the good of the whole. Although these decisions were reviewed and were often controversial, both the executives' sense of themselves as experts and the tendency of their elected boards to accept them as such insulated both the decisions and their makers from review. Unfortunately, the mask of expertise often hid the theological and moral grounds on which decisions had actually been reached. Angry conservatives in almost all denominations felt themselves excluded from the table, leading many to create an alternative world of Protestant institutions.[28]

The network established among church bureaucrats is, in many ways, similar to the earlier "righteous empire" of benevolent societies and organizations. Like that earlier expression of Protestantism, this movement was characterized by the close personal relationships between the leaders. Many came from similar backgrounds. Almost all came from private colleges, whether denominationally related or simply Protestant, and they had often been participants in the YMCA or the SVM. As collegians and seminary students, they were socialized into their roles by participation in various youth organizations that debated the place of the church in the world. Not surprisingly, these organizations often focused on social issues that earnest young people considered of pressing significance. By the midtwenties, after the nation had been hit with the revelations of World War I profiteering and the full extent of Allied loans, the question of war was the subject of passionate discussion. Prospective leaders passed through these various stages early in their careers. Often beginning in the SVM or the YMCA, the prospective church bureaucrat was often noted for

28. See below, chap. 26. See also Joel Carpenter, *Revive Us Again: The Reawakening of American Fundamentalism* (New York: Oxford University Press, 1997).

his (and much more rarely her) capacity to move a crowd or to raise funds. In turn, this capacity as a Protestant advocate attracted the attention of those higher up in the organization. By the time of their appointment, the new bureaucrats were already part of an "old boys'" network that united upcoming "stars" with those long in the work. Interestingly, few of the new leaders began their rise to influence in the pastorate.

The habit of organization that church leaders acquired as youth continued as they reached professional maturity. On the national level, American Protestantism in the 1920s and 1930s consisted of a bewildering patchwork of committees, councils, and conferences. While the membership of these groups varied, they often shared the same denominational executives. The relationship of the executives to these agencies was never uniform. At times an agency might be composed exclusively of denominational leaders; at the other extreme, the executives might be present only as facilitators. However the executives participated, the significant thing was that they were talking together on a regular basis.

The executives' conversations convinced many of them that denominational issues were less important than many thought. Long before more formal ecumenical structures were formed, denominational executives had come to see many issues less denominationally and more bureaucratically.

In time, such conversations might yield results. In 1935 five denominational groups — Congregationalists, Northern Baptists, Northern Presbyterians, Reformed Church in America, and Protestant Episcopalians — reached a comity agreement. In this document they promised not to support with home mission funds churches in competition with each other in new areas. This modest proposal was ten years in the making and required the executives involved to draw on the good will they had established during this period to provide the cement that held the covenant together.

V. Church Unions

As important as comity agreements were, the more important fruits of these discussions were some denominational mergers. These mergers did not flow from a single cause. Clearly, the financial crisis of the 1920s and 1930s greatly encouraged denominational leaders to think about mergers. As moneys became harder to raise, the only way the church bureaucracies could continue their work was to find another way to organize themselves. Interestingly, a similar motive influenced many secular business leaders in the same period, as more and more businesses consolidated. But more was involved than money and zeitgeist, as important as they were. Church unions also grew out of the lived theological experience and convictions of many church leaders.

By 1920 many of the leaders of America's Protestant establishment had been educated in seminaries influenced by the new theological directions of the 1880s and 1890s. While some schools remained resolutely confessional — Princeton and the Lutheran Seminary at Philadelphia, for instance — many schools, liberal and conservative, had moved away from confessionally based education to curricula that stressed semiautonomous theological disciplines, ethics, and practical courses. Students often read the same textbooks in schools of similar orientation and often held similar ideas. Certain theological schools, often allied with universities, trained many of the nation's theological teachers. These influential schools include Union (New York), Yale, Boston University School of Theology, and Southern Baptist Theological Seminary. These same schools, incidentally, trained a disproportionate share of denominational and missionary officials. Perhaps most important, although the social gospel declined in public visibility, the movement's basic ideas had become part of the fabric of the mainstream Northern churches. In the light of the tremendous social issues confronting the nation, many denominational particularities seemed almost spiritual luxuries.

In the 1920s and 1930s a number of highly visible church unions were consummated. In Canada the United Church of Canada was formed from the Methodist, some of the Presbyterian, and the Congregational denominations. Other unions included the Evangelical Church, formed in 1922 from the Evangelical Association and the United Evangelical Church; the Congregational Christian Churches in 1931, formed by the Congregationalists and the Christian Churches; the merger of the Evangelical Church and the Church of the Brethren formed the Evangelical United Brethren in 1934; the union of the Evangelical Synod and the (German) Reformed Church in 1934 formed the Evangelical and Reformed Church; and most significant, the 1939 union of the Methodist Episcopal Church, the Methodist Protestant Church, and the Methodist Episcopal Church, South.

Lutheranism was particularly ripe for denominational unions. During the nineteenth century immigration changed the face of American Lutheranism. As immigrants arrived from Germany, Denmark, Sweden, and Norway, they established various denominations to serve their own ethnic groups. Interestingly enough, these new denominations often elected to use the term "synod" to describe themselves. The word comes from Greek roots that mean a "walking together," and that is a useful way to understand such denominations. In a real sense they were leagues of churches that had common theological and ethnic interests. Often these interests merged in the creation of small theological schools that were part of the synod's desire to preserve faith and heritage together.

Many factors led to comparatively rapid changes in the configuration of American Lutheran churches. Many of these were common to other churches of similar ethnic background. Perhaps the most important was the gradual decline of immigration from these countries. Although as northern Europeans, Lutherans were in an advantaged position under the 1924 immigration act, American conditions had changed. The vast expanses of cheap land, for example, that attracted many Lutheran immigrants filled up, and declining agricultural prices in the United States made new farms a more risky venture. Without new recruits from the old country, even such passionately ethnic bodies as the Augustana Synod, Swedish, found themselves facing a second and third generation interested in having services in English. These same young people wanted seminary classes in that language as well.

Immigrant Lutherans were also facing the increasing cost of denominational life. Although the Evangelical Lutheran Church in America had passed through the denominational process more or less in tandem with the other colonial denominations, the more recently established synods were now facing the problem of funding more elaborate organizations, just as second- and third-generation Lutherans were less ready to sacrifice for religion and culture.

Among the Lutheran mergers were the United Lutheran Church, formed in 1918 from the merger of the various "general synods" of the previous century and the United Synod, South, which subsequently attracted to itself the Slovak Zion Synod (1920), the Icelandic Synod (1940), the American Evangelical Lutheran Church, and in 1962 the Augustana Synod. The Ohio, Iowa, Buffalo, and Texas Synods combined in 1930 to form the American Lutheran Church. In 1962 this church was joined by the Evangelical Lutheran Church, a predominantly Lutheran body.[29] Continuing conversations among all Lutheran groups continued, and many denominations hoped they would grow into closer union.

Theologians and seminaries were particularly important in the negotiations for church unions, in part because they were the "experts" in the issues that divided the churches and were, consequently, able to help the participants in the discussions determine what was important and what was not. Perhaps more important, especially in the more ethnic denominations, the theological faculties were in close contact with the rising leadership of those bodies and were able to help the older leadership with the changes that had already taken place.

29. I have used the excellent chart in Daniel G. Reid, ed., *Dictionary of Christianity in America* (Downers Grove, Ill.: InterVarsity, 1990), p. 667, to keep track of the Lutheran consolidations.

VI. Councils

In addition to the drives for formal cooperation and church merger, the period from 1920 to 1950 saw an increase in the power and influence of councils of churches. Basically a council of churches was a place where differing Christian groups, especially different churches, could come together to discuss common problems and, occasionally, to take collective action. The advantage of councils of churches was almost the mirror image of church unions. If a church union forced a denomination to consider its theology before joining with another, a council of churches was explicitly nontheological in character, with only minimum theological requirements for membership.

Arguably, the most important of the councils was the Federal Council of Churches, established in 1908. Much of the excitement around this group came from its innovative system of governance. Like both the Baptists and the Congregationalists, the council was essentially a cooperative federation of autonomous bodies that agreed to work together for common purposes. While the idea had some theological roots — particularly in the understanding of association developed by Congregationalist theologians in the nineteenth century — part of its advantage was that the churches could cooperate without resolving their differences over such matters as the Lord's Supper or the proper petitions in the Lord's Prayer. While this made it an ideal forum for social Christianity, it also enabled it to serve as a model for agencies serving other, similarly common purposes, such as the International Council of Religious Education, one of the components of the later National Council of Churches and the sponsor of the Revised Standard Version of the Bible.

Although denominations were members of the council, its leaders tended to be denominational executives and closely related members of the elite. In many ways it was a continuation of the same old boys' network that controlled other areas of American Protestant life. The council was, consequently, close to such elite theological schools as Yale and Union (New York). Charles MacFarland and Samuel McCrae Cavert were common visitors to Union and influential in seminary life. The relationship at times amounted to almost unofficial faculty status, as when Van Dusen asked Cavert to serve as the editor of the Festschrift for William Adams Brown.

From the beginning the Federal Council was committed to social Christianity, and its comparative freedom allowed it to take positions that were more advanced than what the individual denominations adopted at their judicatory meetings. The council addressed, at least by resolution, such issues as the rights of labor to organize and strike, the importance and morality of birth control, the suppression of the Jews in Nazi Germany in the 1930s, the rights of African

American service personnel in the Second World War, and the need for a well-considered and ethical atomic policy.

In 1950 the Federal Council was superseded by the National Council of Churches, which was an attempt to find even broader patterns of cooperation. In addition to the denominations, the National Council included the Foreign Missions Conference of North America, the Home Missions Council of North America, the International Council of Religious Education, the United Council of Church Women, and similar agencies. As a way of symbolizing the unity that these represented, the council's offices were located in an impressive building, the Interchurch Center, only a few blocks from Union Theological Seminary and Riverside Church.

As important as the Federal and National Councils were, the real excitement was on the world stage. Beginning with the Edinburgh Missionary Conference in 1910, Protestant leaders from many different locations began meeting periodically for consultation, planning, and serious theological discussions. The customary way to trace the development of the World Council is to stress the gradual institutionalization of two streams of conversation: Life and Work and Faith and Order. Significantly, both were called "movements" in their earliest days. The word "movement" suggested spontaneous enthusiasm, grassroots excitement, and an almost irresistible direction of change. In many ways the language was secularized eschatology that suggested that the old order of the church was traveling through time to its future in the brave new world that God was creating.

Life and Work came from the gradual awakening of Christian social concerns on all continents. The growing antagonism between capital and labor was one source of such thought, but, particularly in Europe, the growing threat of war between 1900 and 1914 forced many concerned Christians to seek to work across increasingly fortified national boundaries. The creation in 1910 of the Associate Councils of Churches in the British and German Empires for Fostering Friendly Relations between the Two Peoples was one institutional sign of the depth of this concern. Charles MacFarland represented the American Federal Council in an effort to keep these dialogues going, and their importance was recognized by Andrew Carnegie, who gave two million dollars to establish the Church Peace Union in 1914, just as the world tottered on the brink of war. Ironically, the Constance Peace Conference, partly funded by this money, was held in August 1914, a classic example of too little, too late.[30] The conference did see the establishment of a perhaps presumptuously named World Alliance to

30. Ruth Rouse and Stephen Charles Neill, eds., *A History of the Ecumenical Movement*, vol. 1 (Philadelphia: Westminster, 1968).

Promote Peace and Wartime Charity. Archbishop Söderblom of Sweden became an international leader as Christians, particularly those in neutral countries, struggled to offer some leadership in a world apparently devoted to almost endless killing fields. In conjunction with the other Scandinavian prelates, a meeting was called for 1917 in Uppsala. While the major combatants did not take part, the meeting did begin significant discussion of the conditions for peace in postwar Europe. Söderblom and his fellow bishops nonetheless continued to try to marshal world Christian opinion around social issues.

These efforts often looked puny both to contemporaries and later observers. A few bishops, the handful of idealists from the World Alliance for Peace, and the radical Christians of the newly formed Fellowship of Reconciliation (England, 1914, with international chapters thereafter) were no match for the forces of nationalism and hate that had encompassed Europe. But in a world in which single battles involved armies of millions and death totals in those battles were almost incalculable, these efforts seemed to some contemporaries as prophetic deeds. Perhaps the best symbol for them was the poppy so beloved by American veterans. The significance of the poppy was that after all the carnage of battle, nature produced a small miracle of beauty that pointed to the renewal and regeneration of life. If the small red flower seemed so insignificant in the face of the rivers of red blood, many hoped that it, and not the armies, represented the future of Flanders.

But the churches' failed attempts to influence foreign affairs that led to war and the peace process that followed it also awakened the guilt of regret. What if the churches had been more united; what if they had taken joint action sooner; what if they had been clearer advocates of justice from the beginning? Sensitive national religious leaders, such as William Adams Brown, had struggled with such questions throughout the war, but as the various nations settled into peace, increasing numbers of dedicated souls wrestled with them. Would next time be different? Next time was unthinkable. No responsible person could think otherwise. But what could be done to ensure that?

One possible answer was suggested by the 1920 Geneva Conference, held in the same month as a similar conference to plan a meeting on Faith and Order. The dual scheduling encouraged churches to send representatives to both meetings. At the first session Nathan Söderblom unveiled his hopes for a truly ecumenical conference that could lead to the establishment of an ecumenical council of churches. As the proposal was discussed and modified, an arrangements committee established a Universal Christian Conference on Life and Work. The organizational need to accomplish the meeting evolved rapidly with separate sections established for Eastern Orthodox, European, British, and American committees. In 1925 the conference met in Stockholm.

In many ways the meeting was a personal triumph for the Swedish archbishop who worked hard to build consensus for the undertaking. But to focus too much on one individual would be to lose the importance of the Life and Work Conference for American theological education. Söderblom had been a member of the SVM and was active in the student movement in Europe. As a scholar, he had specialized in the history of religions, and he was in the midst of an able academic career when the king named him to head the Swedish church. Although deeply appreciative of such "high church" movements as liturgical renewal and acutely conscious of the challenges posed by Eastern Orthodoxy, he shared enough of the irenic spirit of such people as Brown to speak to the liberal constituency of the American churches. In short, Söderblom built excitement around the Life and Work Conference by energizing the leadership, which included many seminary leaders, around his project. Like the archbishop, they were acutely conscious of the need for the churches to help prevent another world catastrophe. The issue of war and peace was the number one issue debated on seminary campuses in the 1920s and 1930s, and for many people it dwarfed the more immediate set of issues posed by the fundamentalist crisis.[31] The *Christian Century* recognized the importance of the world war as a theological event when it ran a series of discussions in 1929 on how various religious leaders had been changed by their experience of the war, and we need to remember that of the various seminary news events of the 1930s, perhaps the most tragic was the government's refusal to give citizenship to Yale theologian Douglas Clyde Macintosh because he refused to promise to fight in any future American war. Macintosh had served in the Great War as a YMCA worker and as a chaplain.

From Stockholm 1925 to Oxford 1937, the Life and Work movement served as the school of international affairs for American seminary leaders. Strongly supported by liberal seminary leaders, such as Henry Sloane Coffin of Union, the movement facilitated contact between such important theological teachers as Reinhold Niebuhr and his more liberal ally, John C. Bennett, and European church officials. A list of important American theologians who contributed to the 1937 Oxford conference, either as participants or as authors of important documents, reads like a who's who of American ethics and theology. The list includes Reinhold Niebuhr, Edwin Aubrey, John C. Bennett, Robert L. Calhoun, Georgia Harkness, Walter Horton, Kenneth S. Latourette, Eugene Lyman, Paul Monroe, and Paul Tillich. Coffin was the chair of the education session of the meeting, and Bennett chaired the section on social ethics.

31. See Martin E. Marty, *Modern American Religion*, vol. 2, *The Noise of Conflict, 1919-1941* (Chicago: University of Chicago Press, 1991).

The Life and Work movement was an advanced seminar for American theologians. Coffin, one of the better developers of strong faculty in American theological history, convened interesting meetings of aspiring and established theologians to discuss contemporary events. These meetings, which were by invitation only, allowed for in-depth discussion of ideas and strategies, and such thinkers as Tillich often used them to explore new ideas, such as his interpretation of the demonic. The Life and Work movement in many ways was an extension of this same method. Coffin always found the money and the people he needed to produce the results he desired. Many longtime Coffin friends and allies, such as John Foster Dulles, also received some of their basic foreign experience through the Life and Work movement.

Samuel M. Cavert noted the importance of Oxford 1937 in changing the attitude of many influential Americans toward European affairs. He writes: "After Oxford it was clearly seen that an acceptance of the Ideals of Jesus and appeals to follow the way of love were not enough, and that there must be a realistic facing of the stubborn facts of man's selfishness and its manifestations in the power structures of society." Cavert recognized, perhaps because of his friendship with many of the participants, that this was also a theological event of tremendous importance. "At Oxford it became plain that differences in social policies are often rooted in what are essentially theological understandings of the nature of God and man. After Oxford the separation between those who were concerned with the Christian faith and those who were concerned with Christian practice was much less noticeable." Theological and philosophical criticism, in other words, was already social criticism. This was, of course, an implicit theme in the thought of Reinhold Niebuhr, but the ecumenical movement helped to crystallize it and to force further exploration of the theme. Other theologians found themselves talking similar language.

Ties to the parallel Faith and Order movement were equally important. The movement for a world meeting on faith and order had begun in the United States when Episcopal bishop Charles Brent, fresh from the 1910 Edinburgh meeting, made a motion at a joint meeting of convocation: "That a Joint Commission be appointed to bring about a Conference for the consideration of questions touching Faith and Order, and that all Christian Communions throughout the world which confess Our Lord Jesus Christ as God and Saviour be asked to unite with us in arranging for and conducting such a Conference."[32] Anglicanism had blown high and cold on movements for Christian unity. Despite its stress on the outward symbols of unity, Anglicanism was a deeply divided house with some Anglicans seeing themselves located in a broad, middle

32. Cited in Rouse and Neill, *A History,* p. 407.

type of Catholicism, similar to the Eastern churches, while others held to a much more Protestant view of faith. The Anglican churches' fourfold statement of principles for renewal, the so-called Lambeth Quadrilateral with its insistence on the Nicene Creed and the historic episcopate, had often served as much to halt or hamper movements toward reunion as to promote them. Many attempts at cooperation had failed because Anglicans insisted on full participation of the Eastern churches. The Anglican demand for the reordination of clergy by bishops in apostolic succession kept them out of such important church unions as the United Church of Canada. Many liberal Christians also felt uncomfortable and excluded by Anglican insistence on the Nicene Creed as a mark of orthodoxy. The movement toward Faith and Order, paid for in some measure, at least initially, by such American churchmen as J. P. Morgan, was the exception to this pattern.

In 1920 at Geneva, at the same time Life and Work was organizing, Faith and Order held a preliminary meeting to give the movement more permanent direction. Some seventy churches were represented, and like many ecumenical meetings, it did its most effective work when it established continuation and executive committees. After considerable haggle, the great meeting was held at Lausanne in August 1927. In many ways this initial meeting was less successful than that of the Life and Work movement, but it did achieve important unity on its statement "The Church's Message to the World — the Gospel," a document that made important contributions to various movements toward church union. But, as in Geneva, the most important act was the appointment of a continuation committee. As more formal responses to discussions were received, they were used as the basis for study groups in many of the participating churches. In 1937 the World Conference on Faith and Order reconvened at Edinburgh. The second meeting of the conference was, in one sense, as inconclusive as the first. Differences in style and content remained serious obstacles to the unity, not to mention the union, of the churches.

Yet, and this was a considerable gain, the representatives of the various churches had learned to feel comfortable with one another and to trust each other's basic instincts. When the proposal to form a World Council of Churches was received, it was endorsed by those at the Faith and Order Conference as well as those in Life and Work, and representatives were sent to Utrecht to help plan the new body. As the world raced headlong toward war, the World Council, although it never met, had some reality. When the conflict ended, John D. Rockefeller, Jr., made a grant of one million dollars to the new agency to plan its proposed meeting at Amsterdam in 1948.

One aspect of the new council that might easily be overlooked was its insistence that member churches confess faith in the divinity of Christ. The Federal Council of Churches had earlier struggled with whether to include the Unitarians and had concluded in the negative. The formulation also allowed the council to exclude such troublesome bodies as the Church of Jesus Christ of Latter day Saints that stood outside the traditional confessional boundaries. The decision, however, might have caused more serious problems for American Christians had it not been for a few considerations. First, the requirement applied to the official faith of denominations, not to either the actual faith of those bodies or to whether they enforced their confession or not. Hence, such churches as the Congregational Christian that may have had a large percentage, perhaps even a majority, of clergy who held and taught nontraditional Christologies could be included. Second, the liberal evangelicalism held by such American liberal leaders as Henry Sloane Coffin and Henry Pitney Van Dusen saw itself as reinterpreting, rather than replacing, traditional formations. The importance of this position is easy for twenty-first-century historians of theology to overlook. Like other carefully framed mediating positions, such as Boston personalism,[33] evangelical liberalism did not draw the sharp lines that the more consistent modernists, fundamentalists, and neoorthodox drew. Instead, like Bushnell, it was in the habit of comprehension, always bringing many points of view to bear on a particular issue. In a world where dialogue was increasingly influential, liberal evangelicalism was in an excellent place to speak to different positions and, perhaps, was ideally suited for those who would chair the meetings.

Almost as an aside, the historian needs to note that the liberal evangelicals had other advantages in the ecumenical movement. In many ways liberal evangelicalism was a scholarly position that was passed on at Union Theological Seminary in New York. Brown, Coffin, and Van Dusen were related as scholarly grandfathers and fathers to one another. Like any coherent theological school, they gained from several generations working away at the same problems from similar perspectives. But, and it is a significant "but," these three collaborators and their good friend and fellow internationalist Sherwood Eddy were also comparatively wealthy men who were able to finance their frequent trips — and occasionally, also those of their friends — to ecumenical meetings out of their own private funds. Likewise, they had important connections with other people of great wealth in America whose resources could be tapped for ecumenical purposes.

Van Dusen and other evangelical liberals had no doubt that they were

33. The distinction between Boston personalism and evangelical liberalism was not sharp. In general the personalists tended to have clearer philosophical roots for their position, while evangelical liberalism was more a hermeneutics of theology or even a metatheology.

called upon to recast the seminary tradition. In an address for the inauguration of Don Wendell Holter as president of the National Methodist Theological Seminary, "The Challenge to Theological Education: Today and Tomorrow," Van Dusen said:

> What is required is that theological education in its every aspect be recast within the enveloping reality of World Christianity, both as World Mission and as World organism. That implies a thorough-going reorientation both of the general philosophy and framework, and of every major theological discipline. It implies that every one of our theological colleges, whether denominational or inter-denominational or non-denominational in sponsorship, should regard itself, with new seriousness, as a training school for leadership, not of a particular communion, but of the One Universal Church of Christ.[34]

Union added two significant visiting professorships — the Luce Professorship in World Christianity and the Fosdick Visiting Professorship (1954) — and Princeton's John Mackay became the nation's first professor of ecumenics. Other schools added courses on the ecumenical movement or ecumenical theology. But such changes were not the heart of the matter. Van Dusen believed that seminaries had to shift their sense of responsibility and accountability from their particular confessional or theological tradition to the church as a whole. Union and Yale, of course, personified this ideal, but even those schools that were more confessional in character hurried to embrace this new idea as much as possible. Mackay very carefully stated: "It will be said, however, that any seminary which is church-related is bound to be sectarian. That I deny with all my soul. An institution can be confessional-related and be, nonetheless, ecumenically minded."[35]

Ecumenical-mindedness represented a shift in seminary accountability. For many schools that felt hassled by the modernist-fundamentalist battles in their denomination, the term represented a relocation of ecclesiastical responsibility from the present church to the coming church. Just as the Federal Council was free to deal with issues like birth control, still controversial in most of the denominations served by the council, in the name of the church, so the ecumenical seminary was free to deal with issues in the name of the whole church

34. Van Dusen, "The Challenge to Theological Education: Today and Tomorrow" (speech delivered for the inauguration of Don Wendell Holter as president of the National Methodist Theological Seminary, Kansas City, Mo.), p. 6.

35. John Mackay, "Some Questions regarding Theological Education with Special Reference to Princeton Seminary," *Princeton Seminary Bulletin* 49 (Jan. 1956): 7.

that might not reflect either their supporters or, for that matter, the clear needs of the ministry. In effect, the ecumenical movement became a substitute for church and confession. In the 1940s and 1950s, as this sense of responsibility to the ecumenical church was forming, its effects were not dramatic. Close ties between denominations and their schools, often reinforced financially, as well as the professional understanding of ministry tied the schools much to their constituencies. But, as the 1950s wore on and many creative people began to feel the full weight of expected ecclesiastical conformity, the more radical implications of the idea became more obvious. Many schools and scholars would be "of the church" but not "in the church."

There was another, less obvious, meaning to ecumenical-mindedness. As Walter Brueggemann argued, there was an ecumenism of scholarship that insisted that seminary teachers were essentially responsible to their guilds for the quality of their scholarship and the content of their classes.[36] This type of ecumenism was, in theory, separable even from explicitly Christian belief and was particularly strong in the biblical and historical areas. By the 1950s there was a remarkable uniformity in the texts used in classes that transcended denominational boundaries. The publication of a widely used text could significantly augment a professor's income as well as prestige. By the 1960s the better seminaries would institutionalize this type of ecumenism through such means as tenure and systems of peer review. Scholarly ecumenism, thus, also separated theological schools from their traditional lines of accountability.

The theological implications of ecumenical-mindedness for how seminaries conducted their work were profound, even revolutionary. The liberal seminary and to a large extent the neoorthodox seminary of the 1940s and 1950s had been built around the service of the empirical church. The essential justification of these schools was simple: their graduates could and did serve the church more effectively than pastors with less education. The ecumenical movement shifted the attention of the seminaries away from ecclesiastical realities just as the 1960s and 1970s saw the churches increasingly unable to underwrite the cost of theological education. The neoorthodox theology of the 1940s and 1950s had tended in this same direction, to be sure, but many proponents of neoorthodoxy, especially such vigorous theologians as H. Richard Niebuhr, remained concerned with the actual state of affairs, with history as it was actually lived. And some strong practical departments, including Yale's fine program in religious sociology that contained Kenneth Underwood and Liston Pope, refused to relinquish the social sciences.

36. Walter A. Brueggemann, "Ethos and Ecumenism: The History of Eden Theological Seminary, 1925-1970" (Ph.D. diss., St. Louis University, 1974), p. 142.

CHAPTER TWENTY-TWO

A Reborn Theological Discussion

Although seminaries are important as places where prospective ministers and other religious leaders are trained, they are equally — if not more — important as places where competent scholars debate and discuss the intellectual status of the Christian faith. Even when changes in theological orientation do not produce changes in curriculum, they quickly penetrate to both basic and advanced courses where they enliven the discussion and present students (and later the churches they serve) with creative options. Much of this volume has been concerned with the changes in theological education that were generated by the liberal or modernist movement in theology. These included the scholarly guilds, the development of a number of new disciplines, a deep and abiding interest in social issues, and finally, a sense that ministry was a profession, analogous to other professions. Although some conservatives contributed to its establishment, the creation of the American Association of Theological Schools was one of the greatest products of American liberalism. The new theologians of the 1930s and 1940s did not challenge these achievements. In fact, they treasured them and worked hard to perfect them. In general, they agreed with the greatest of their number, H. Richard Niebuhr, when he called these the "advancement of theological education." Perhaps equally significant, the forms created by and large by liberal church leaders were also adopted by the new religious conservatives of the 1950s and 1960s who created an impressive string of evangelical theological schools.

In short, the churches, along with much of Western civilization, had benefited from a remarkable time when such teachings as progress seemed to be sober appraisals of a world in which God and man cooperated for good. Like the Newtonian science that deeply influenced its leading thinkers, it was a world of bodies in regular motion through a largely undisturbed space, and even the biological sphere, despite Darwin's emphasis on the role of chance, seemed guided by these same continuities. The nineteenth-century world was — like the thirteenth-century world of Thomas Aquinas — confident in its intellectual synthesis, at home with its urbane surroundings, and trusting the productivity of its economic base. But there are other parallels between the two great seasons of theological progress. The Black Death shattered Thomas's intellectual world, and the most creative theologians moved toward the *via moderna* of Scotus and Occam and the idea of a God beyond human cleverness and understanding. While the university remained structurally similar to what it had been in Thomas's day, its ethos was transformed. Thomism lived on, of course, in the postplague university as one option among many, the *via antiqua,* but Thomism was, at best, part of a very complicated theological discussion.

Much the same happened to liberal theology and indeed to liberal Western culture with the coming of the world war. To be sure, the war changed no central idea of Western life. The Allies had fought, or so they claimed, for the deepest values of the West — reason, democracy, and self-determination — and the Central Powers were committed to liberal culture as well. The end of the war, consequently, should have brought about the victory of, or at least the advancement of, the deepest liberal values. But it did not turn out that way. Many believed that the highest values of the West died during the war, and ironically, many thinkers believed that the war was the natural outgrowth of a decadent Western civilization. Such arguments did not require sophisticated analysis. One need only open one's eyes. Especially in Europe, the war's aftereffect was a sense of moral sickness and confusion. The ideas of those who had been on the boundary of the age of progress, such as Nietzsche, were now on the front burner.

History often seems to follow its own uncanny logic. Just as the liberal world of the nineteenth century crumbled, its scientific basis in Newtonian physics also underwent a transformation. Einstein, Bohr, and Planck pictured a physical world in which predictability and regularity were increasingly conditioned by probabilities and discontinuity. The life sciences, whose development would be one of the great twentieth-century intellectual stories, were beginning to claim more and more territory as "life" filled more and more of the mental terrain. And for good or ill, Freud and his followers opened up the darker corners of the human soul. After more than a millennium of speculation about the will, thoughtful people realized anew that the question of why humans act as they do was a mystery, particularly to themselves. Despite the humanistic foundations of the new psychology, capitalists seized the new psychological insights and used them to sell everything from cigarettes to soap. Art moved steadily toward increasing abstraction and apparent disharmony. Even tonality, long considered the irreducible foundation of Western music, was challenged. Perhaps ironically, such liberal institutions as the university continued — and they were increasingly the genesis point of even more radical ideas — and liberals and liberal theologians continued to live in them, but they were no longer the only residents in the house. Like the late medieval world, the modern world had become a place of competing ideologies, and the faculty of theology, the house of competing ideas.

Some sense of this larger world of thought is essential if one is to understand the theologies of the 1930s and 1940s. The changes in theology are often traced to the 1919 publication of Karl Barth's *Epistle to the Romans.* Barth's own account of this epoch-making event pits the lonely pastor, unable to reach his congregation, reaching desperately for the Bible. This act of defiance of the academic establishment and its hermeneutics became the clarion call that awakened theology anew to its divine task of presenting the Word of God. But while this legend, like all legends, has some elements of truth, it is still more fiction than fact. A more realistic and hopefully more accurate statement is that Barth's manifesto was issued to a world where intellectual and theological change was imminent. In the wake of the world war, every area of Western experience was under examination and question. Theology would have required divine intervention to stay out of the whirlwind. Rather, Barth's work was an announcement, much as Niels Bohr's theory of the atom and Wittgenstein's analysis of language were announcements, that an important area of human discourse had to find new forms of expression. And it should be noted that all did not change. Not only did the reigning liberal theologians live out their tenure, but German theology responded, not by harkening to a new drummer, but by becoming a far more diverse discipline with different thinkers finding their own perspective.

Barth was, of course, far from the American shore. In general, Americans of the 1920s had only the vaguest awareness of European intellectual and artistic trends. Although some continued to study abroad, particularly in England and Scotland, the older tradition of scholars traveling to Germany for advanced training was in abeyance. In most disciplines American schools were considered as good as or better than their postwar European counterparts. This was particularly important in theology where American theologians and biblical scholars had served as conduits for ideas originally developed on the Continent. And this comparative isolation did provide some space for a few American theologians, such as Edgar Goodspeed and D. C. Macintosh, to hold center stage, and for American theological sciences, especially religious education, to flourish.

Some American theologians mourned the isolation. Reinhold Niebuhr, a theologian who read German easily, noted in 1928:

> For months, even years, we have been hearing of Barth and the Barthian movement in Germany. But the reports have been fragmentary. None of Barth's books was available to us in translation. It seems the fate of American theology, at least so far as it is developed in the pulpit rather than the theological school, that it must orient itself without any sense of cooperation with German theology. Perhaps that is not so much its fate as its punishment for the superficiality which creates a market for every casual book of sermons while translations of significant theological treatises are left on the shelves.[1]

For all of Niebuhr's yearnings, he and his brother, H. Richard, labored hard and long to Americanize their American denomination and to bring its schools into harmony with the dominant American style. German theological thinkers might still have something to say, but the German university was no longer a model.

The way the new European theology became known in America was important for understanding its impact on American theological education. In general, Barth became known to Americans very slowly, while Emil Brunner quickly captured the American theological imagination.

Although Barth was perhaps the most significant Christian thinker of the twentieth century, he long remained an enigma to American theologians. Douglas Horton, who translated Barth's *Word of God and Word of Man,* published in 1928, admitted that he had found Barth by accident while browsing the new-book display in the Harvard library. Barth's *Dogmatics in Outline* appeared in English in 1949, and it was 1956 before *Church Dogmatics,* volume 1, part 1, including the crucial and very rich "footnotes," became available in English. Was Barth concerned with the existence of a New World market for his studies? He avoided travel to the New World, making a brief American tour only in the 1960s, and he was often harshly critical of American theological activism.

In contrast, Emil Brunner, like Barth a Swiss theologian, seemed more aware of the vagaries of the American market. Jaroslav Pelikan noted the difference between Barth and Brunner:

> "Nach Amerikan gehen? Das ist fuer Brunner, aber nicht fuer mich!" Whether or not this declaration ascribed to Karl Barth a decade or so ago is apocryphal, it does express an accurate assessment of the relative prestige borne by "two bs" in the theology of American Protestantism in the 1940s and 1950s. Perhaps Bultmann and Bonhoeffer, like Brahms and Bruckner,

1. Reinhold Niebuhr, "Karl Barth Apostle of the Absolute," *Christian Century,* Dec. 13, 1928, p. 1523.

> may be said to complete the quartet. Thus, when some of us were seminarians or theological instructors, the trim volumes of Emil Brunner's theological monographs — *Revelation and Reason, Man in Revolt, The Mediator and the Divine Imperative* — stood on many more American shelves than did Barth's *The Epistle to the Romans* or *The Word of God and the Word of Man.*[2]

Brunner was in fact oriented toward America. Immediately after the war he spent a year at Union Seminary (New York), and he made his first American lecture tour in 1928, speaking at Princeton among other places. Likewise, he often visited England and was very interested and involved in the ecumenical and missionary movements. Japan fascinated him. Later he identified with Frank Buchman's Oxford Group, a renewal movement popular with middle-class American Presbyterians and English Free Church leaders. In the academic year 1938-39 Brunner served as a visiting professor at Princeton. Throughout his career he retained a sixth sense for the theological questions that middle-class people were asking, and busy pastors found it easy to move from his work to their weekly pulpit duties. Perhaps because he was personally known, Brunner's books were translated into English shortly after they appeared, and they were immediately reviewed in leading theological journals. Brunner published *The Theology of Crisis* in English translation in 1929 and *The Mediator* in 1934.[3] While many reasons can be given for Brunner's widespread popularity in America, his skill at making his ideas and his work available to an Anglo-American audience was a crucial element in his success.

Sydney Ahlstrom has correctly noted that Americans were interested in more new European theologians than Barth and Brunner.[4] Such Swedish theologians as Anders Nygren, Gustaf Aulén, and Yngve Brilioth became well-known in America. Aulén's classic *Christus Victor* appeared in an English translation in 1931, and Nygren's *Agape and Eros* was in a readily available translation in 1939. Student Christian Movement (SCM) published both. SCM often served as a distributor for European books in English-speaking countries.

We should not minimize the problems that Americans faced entering into the European debate. Walter Lowrie, the pastor of Saint Paul's American Church in Rome, read the early works of Barth while in Rome and was led by them to read Søren Kierkegaard in German translation. Determined to under-

2. Jaroslav Pelikan, "Karl Barth in America," *Christian Century* 79, no. 16 (Apr. 11, 1962): 451-52.

3. E. G. Homrighausen, "Brunner's *The Mediator,*" *Religion in Life,* 1935, pp. 296-304.

4. Sydney Ahlstrom, "Continental Influence on American Christian Thought Since World War I," *Church History* 27 (1958): 256-71.

stand the implications of Kierkegaard's thought, he taught himself Danish. His two-volume biography of Kierkegaard, however, did not appear until 1938, with the shorter life not appearing until 1940. Despite the apparent popularity of Kierkegaard, Lowrie was unable to locate a commercial or scholarly publisher in the 1930s and 1940s to help underwrite the cost of his volumes, and he was forced to foot the bill for their private printing.[5] The glacial pace of translation could also frustrate the spread of other works.

There was also an accidental quality to some of the transmission of European works. Wilhelm Pauck, for instance, who came to America in 1925 from Germany, was one of the first professors in America to recognize Barth's importance. His 1931 book, *Karl Barth: Prophet of a New Christianity,* was a thoughtful but critical contribution to the literature on European theology. But Pauck was perhaps more important for making Americans, particularly scholars, aware of the European "Luther Renaissance." The new Luther studies revealed a more theological Luther than nineteenth-century historiography had known. Pauck and later his close friend, Paul Tillich, also served as important conduits to other less well-known European intellectual developments, such as religious socialism. Tillich became a major American theologian in his own right in the 1950s.

During much of the 1920s, one has the feeling that the new thought from Europe was more seeping into the American discussion than an influential part of it. As we have seen, the twenties were a difficult decade for the Protestant churches, which were confronted with widespread criticism from those without and declining numbers of those within. Moreover, the great fundamentalist/modernist battle was being waged on all fronts. Yet there are some signs that the new theology was receiving a careful hearing. In 1928 three very thoughtful essays on Karl Barth appeared in the *Christian Century.* In the first, written by Douglas Horton, entitled "God Lets Loose Karl Barth," the author acknowledges that Barth's *Epistle to the Romans* is the "weirdest" of commentaries, but he insists the discerning reader would notice that Barth has two themes. The first is the sovereignty of God and God's right to reveal Godself as God would; the second is an important point about the relationship of Christ and human culture: here "Professor Barth is the embodiment of the continental reaction to associating christianity with a particular social movement, whether it be 'kultur,' pacifism, socialism or anything else."[6]

In a thoughtful essay with the surprising and very misleading title "German Fundamentalism," Boston University theologian Albert Knudson dis-

5. See "Walter Lowrie," in *Sons of the Prophets: Leaders in Protestantism from Princeton Seminary,* ed. H. T. Kerr (Princeton: Princeton University Press, 1963).

6. Douglas Horton, "God Lets Loose Karl Barth," *Christian Century,* Feb. 16, 1928, p. 204.

cussed Barth's basic position. Knudson was quite sure that Barth was no American fundamentalist. "Quite different is the attitude of Karl Barth and his friends. These men differentiate their position sharply from the orthodoxy of the past. Not only do they reject the traditional conception of the Bible, their whole theological method is different. They do not single out a number of specific doctrines such as the Virgin Birth, the bodily resurrection of Jesus, or the substitutionary theory of the atonement and make them tests of theological soundness."[7] The heart of the concern of the neoorthodox theologians, Knudson continued, was the modern world that had convinced humankind, erroneously, that "modern man . . . can save himself. He has no sense of sin, and no conscious need of a divine authority on which he may lean for guidance and for redemption."[8] This was not something new, however. In a very insightful statement, Knudson noted: "It is the modern world as a whole that has created for Barth his religious problem. The problem is not a new one. It is essentially the same as that which Schleiermacher, Troeltsch and Rudolf Otto have dealt [with] in significant ways, the problem namely of the uniqueness and absoluteness of religion and of Christianity."[9] The place where Knudson felt he had to dissent most clearly from this project was Barth's growing rejection of philosophy as part of theological discourse. In what sounds almost like a prophecy of the 1960s Death of God movement, Knudson asserted that "a theology that feeds on skepticism will eventually perish thereby."

Reinhold Niebuhr's reading in that same year was remarkably similar. With his characteristic ability to put much in sharp focus, Niebuhr asserted that the new theology "is, in fact, a revival of the theology of the reformation. Calvinistic in its conception of God and Lutheran in its emphasis upon the experience of justification by faith." The reformation note, Niebuhr felt, added an element of realism to Barth's critique, even a note of tragedy. "But the merit of this note of tragedy in religion is that it saves us from the easy optimisms into which we have been betrayed by our moral evolutionism. After all, there is something just as unreal in most modern dogmas of salvation through moral evolution as in the older doctrines of salvation."[10] This made Barth a welcome ally in Niebuhr's own struggle to find a faith that was honest about the human condition and yet offered a ray of hope that could prevent a person from falling

7. Albert C. Knudson, "German Fundamentalism," *Christian Century,* June 14, 1928, p. 762.

8. Knudson, "German Fundamentalism," p. 763.

9. Knudson, "German Fundamentalism," p. 764. Karl Barth reached a similar conclusion in his *Protestant Theology in the Nineteenth Century: Its Background and History* (London: SCM, 1972).

10. Reinhold Niebuhr, "Karl Barth," p. 1523.

into despair. In language that would echo through much of his later work, Niebuhr declared: "Is it not true that history is the sorry tale of new imperialisms supplanting old ones; of man's inhumanity to man, checked in one area or relationship expressing itself in new and more terrible forms in other areas and relationships. Is it not a monstrous egoism and foolish blindness which we betray when we imagine that this civilization in which commercialism has corrupted every ideal value is in some sense superior to the medieval ages or that the status of the industrial worker differs greatly from that of the feudal slave." But, like Knudson, Niebuhr knew he could not take Barth's route. In the last analysis, "The other question to be considered is whether Barth does not pay too high a price for the religious advantages of his theology, even if these are real. There is, to be sure, a note of moral realism in Barthian thought that is not found in quietistic theology. The peace which comes to the soul through the assurance of pardon, the inner harmony which is realized by overcoming the sense of moral frustration, does not absolve the sinner of his sins. We are all sinners still even after we have been saved."[11]

In retrospect, these three essays defined the American response to the theology of crisis. Americans, while they recognized the importance of the theocentric elements in Barth and his early allies, were more impressed with the perspective that the new theology offered on the problem of human culture. In simple, if not simplistic, terms, the question was how did the human world look when viewed from God downward rather than from humankind upward. Yet for Americans it was still largely a question of anthropology, not theology. But perhaps equally important, although some Americans, like Edwin Lewis, became more Barthian than Barth, most stated, with Horton, Knudson, and Niebuhr, that while they were impressed, they also had serious reservations.

From these 1928 essays to 1939, when the *Christian Century* published its famous series "How My Mind Has Changed," the question for most American theologians was how much emphasis they would put on the value of the new style of theology for understanding culture and humankind and how strongly they would state their reservations about the new perspective. Very few were willing either to reject out of hand or to affirm fully the new style of thought. In one sense the Americans tended to do what many of the most able European theologians had also done. Although Emil Brunner was clearly influenced by Barth, for example, he was never willing to renounce the philosophical task altogether. Rather, as he saw the issue, the question was which philosophical perspectives best illuminated the message of the gospel. In Brunner's case the I-Thou theology of the Jewish philosopher Martin Buber seemed most to fit

11. Reinhold Niebuhr, "Karl Barth," p. 1524.

those criteria. Rudolf Bultmann, the brilliant young biblical critic who had early supported Barth, took a more reified approach in investigating the value of Heideggerian existentialism for biblical interpretation.

Part of the significance of early neoorthodoxy for theological education was the way it contributed to a renewed theological discussion and exchange. Rarely in human history has there been so much fire under the pot. We can identify at least three crises that helped spark debate. First and foremost, the economic collapse could not be avoided. Just when things had been looking so good, especially in the United States, they turned bad, and not even all the king's men could put them right again. Even nature seemed involved, as dry winds raced across the plains, carrying much of the nation's premier topsoil with them. To this crisis was added a deep and lasting international crisis. In Europe dictatorships replaced democracies in Italy, Germany, and eventually Spain, and in Russia the Communist ideology that promised so much entered its Stalinist phase. Japan began its search for a place in the eastern sun by invading China, the center of American investment and missionary activity. And were this not enough, many felt that Western culture itself — the whole rich texture of traditions, literature, music, custom, and religion — had also reached an impasse. Thinking and talking may have been the only antidotes to despair and discouragement, and theological conversation provided a way to help clear some of the poison.

Reinhold Niebuhr was the ideal theologian for the 1930s and 1940s. Niebuhr, the son of a Missouri pastor, had studied at Eden Seminary (1913) and had gone from there to Yale Divinity School (B.D.) and Yale University (M.A.). Significantly, he never earned a doctoral degree, perhaps because his grades in the master of arts program were too low. At the time, he noted that his one advantage was "that although we are somewhat ostracized for not holding any academical degrees we have found this somewhat compensated for by the fact that we read and write German."[12] Niebuhr was to use this to his advantage throughout his career. While he was at Yale, the modernist D. C. Macintosh captured his imagination as Macintosh would later capture the imagination of his brother. While Niebuhr later went in a different direction from his teacher, he wrote, "I was subsequently to discover that Macintosh's challenge of the age-old alliance between the Christian faith and philosophical idealism was important."[13] His brother, H. Richard, also always recognized his debt to this beloved teacher. If there was one thing that characterized Niebuhr's thought, it was his thorough

12. William G. Chrystal, ed., *Young Reinhold Niebuhr: His Early Writings, 1911-1931* (St. Louis: Eden Publishing House, 1977; New York: Pilgrim Press, 1982), p. 53.

13. Reinhold Niebuhr, "Intellectual Autobiography," in *Reinhold Niebuhr: His Religious, Social, and Political Thought,* ed. Charles Kegley and Robert Bretall (New York: Macmillan, 1956), p. 4.

rejection of the idealistic position in ethics and theology. Whatever "Christian realism" meant, Niebuhr never wavered from the duty of the believing person to face things as they actually were. In retrospect he was aware of his deep affinities with the liberal tradition: "I have never thought of myself in that category [neoorthodoxy]. I think when it comes to the crux I belong to the liberal tradition more than to theirs. Whenever I read them or argue with them, Brunner for instance, I always feel that they are trying to fit life into a dogmatic mold and that they have hard and fast biblical presuppositions which I do not share. Further their indifference to and lack of understanding of political and social problems has always made them foreigners to me."[14]

The key to Niebuhr's prolific career lay in the fact that he was a public intellectual.[15] The period between 1920 and 1960 was the classic period of the pundit whose sharp essays or bright columns made an important contribution to the larger discussion. Such magazines as the *New Republic*, the *Atlantic Monthly*, *Harper's*, and the *New Yorker* brought people the best of current opinion and criticism, often in essays that read like a brilliant conversation. Among liberal Christians the *Christian Century* provided a similar place for serious discussion, as did Abingdon's successful serial *Religion in Life*.[16] In the 1920s Niebuhr established himself as the master of this genre, and published on average between ten and twenty articles a year throughout his career. After his 1928 appointment at Union Seminary, Niebuhr became a constantly featured speaker on the college and seminary lecture circuit. In addition to the meetings held by the larger YMCAs and the SCM, many colleges had active student ministries that often scheduled a week or more of special events, often called Religious Emphasis Week or something similar, that featured a well-known Christian speaker. Niebuhr was in high demand for all these events, and he was particularly gifted at the faculty discussions that were part of these occasions. He learned early to speak to believers and unbelievers. The ecumenical movement also provided him with a constant supply of opportunities for speaking and for conversation.

14. Richard Wightman Fox, *Reinhold Niebuhr: A Biography* (New York; Pantheon Books, 1985), p. 214.

15. Compare with Martin Marty, "Reinhold Niebuhr, Public Theology and the American Experience," in *The Legacy of Reinhold Niebuhr*, ed. Nathan Scott (Chicago: University of Chicago Press, 1974).

16. The *Century* was published biweekly and carried news of the churches and ethically significant materials along with its featured essays and editorials. *Religion in Life* was a quarterly magazine that featured articles that were generally one step up from the *Century* but were not necessarily scholarly essays. Many provocative pieces that would not have been published in the more guild-oriented *Journal of Religion* or *Journal of the Society of Biblical Literature* were published in this journal.

Niebuhr was aware that his work as a public intellectual made him something of a stranger to the more formal work of the academy. He was appointed to the faculty at Union Seminary in New York after a considerable battle among the school's mandarins. In the end, because Sherwood Eddy offered to pay half his salary provided he continue to comment on current affairs, he was hired. Niebuhr described his first years as a professor in these words:

> This (his appointment at Union) was a hazardous venture, since my reading in the parish had been somewhat undisciplined and I had no scholarly competence in my field, not to speak of the total field of Christian theology. My practical interests and the devoting of every weekend to college preaching prevented any rapid acquisition of competence in my ostensible specialty. It was therefore a full decade before I could stand before a class and answer the searching questions of the students at the end of a lecture without the sense of being a fraud who pretended to a larger and more comprehensive knowledge than I possessed.[17]

At the end of that training decade, Niebuhr produced his *Nature and Destiny of Man,* the Gifford Lectures for 1939 that were published two years later. The book has a legitimate claim to be one of the classics of twentieth-century theology, and in it Niebuhr explores the principal themes of his thought: the rejection of idealism, the importance of the concrete Hebrew understanding of humankind, the depths of insight in Augustine, and the continuing relevance of the doctrine of original sin. It is easy to misunderstand the work. Niebuhr is not saying, as James Thurber once mocked, that "we all have our flaws . . . and mine is being wicked."[18]

Rather, sin arises from the ontological condition of humankind that is caught between the demands of freedom on the one hand and the reality of finitude on the other. Hence, eschatology does not mean that a time will come when this dialectic will finally be overcome. Any such hope must focus on the "end of history." Niebuhr's "end" has many meanings, since end is both the goal as well as the terminus of thought. At times he speaks as if the end were God's vision of where human life ought to be going, hence the possible impossibility. Christ, at the center of history, shows that finally it is God's love that justifies the unrighteous.[19] In other words, traditional Christian ideas provide us with powerful, perhaps the most powerful, categories for understanding the human situation.

17. Reinhold Niebuhr, "Intellectual Autobiography," p. 8.
18. Cited in Marty, "Reinhold Niebuhr," p. 14.
19. Clearly, Niebuhr was influenced by his colleague Paul Tillich at a number of places.

Nature and Destiny revealed the distance between Niebuhr's thought and classical Christian orthodoxy. Conservative theologian Edward J. Carnell, who wrote his Harvard dissertation on Niebuhr, was acutely conscious of the distance between Niebuhr and biblical orthodoxy.

> This . . . is the grand irony of Christian realism. Reinhold Niebuhr can prove that man is a sinner; but man already knows that. Reinhold Niebuhr can develop the dialectical relationship between time and eternity, but this is beyond the tether of a dime store clerk or a hod carrier. When it comes to the acid test, therefore, Christian realism is not very realistic. Niebuhr does not speak about Christ's literal cross and resurrection at all. He speaks, at most, of the symbols of the cross and resurrection. But of what value are these symbols to an anxious New York cab driver.[20]

In some ways an analogy with Clement of Alexandria is apt. Clement believed that Christian theology provided the true gnosis in a world of competing gnosticisms; likewise, Niebuhr believed that Christianity provided the "true" ideology in a world of competing ideological claims. Christianity provided a clearer and more consistent interpretation of the world than any other system of thought; this was good news in a world in which Marxism, Nazism, and other systems claimed the right to provide the rationale for the jumbled nature of human affairs.

In many ways H. Richard Niebuhr had a more far-reaching and much more careful mind than his brother. If Reinhold's public theology was theology done in the public arena, H. Richard's public theology was done for a more university and seminary audience, perhaps because he had attained the professional credentials his brother lacked. In *The Meaning of Revelation* he spoke of the deep influence of two people on his own thought: Ernst Troeltsch and Karl Barth. Troeltsch, a member of the history-of-religion movement in Germany, saw the primary challenge for Christian faith in the relativism implicit in modern historical and social studies. This gave H. Richard a unique perspective on the general cultural crisis of his time, and it is no accident that his best-known work was *Christ and Culture,* in which he attempted to correlate different types of theology with their corresponding social and cultural visions. In the same way, his two investigations of American religion, *The Social Sources of Denominationalism* and *The Kingdom of God in America,* dealt with the ways churches interacted with their environment. In *Social Sources* the focus was on the impact of society, particularly social class and race, on the development of

20. Edward J. Carnell, quoted in Alister McGrath, *Evangelicalism and the Future of Christianity* (Downers Grove, Ill.: InterVarsity, 1995), p. 77.

American religion; in *The Kingdom of God in America* he was concerned with how the church had shaped and sustained American democratic institutions. Hans Frei suggested that Niebuhr saw the world in terms of a dialectic between natural-cultural religion, purely a human artifact, and the revelation in Christ.[21] The suggestion is particularly useful in interpreting the interplay in Niebuhr between an insistence that the Bible has to be read as a cultural entity and his equally strong insistence that it be read as revelation. Perhaps more important, H. Richard insisted that both be done together. Readers of Scripture, however, do not come to such a sacred text from a position of neutrality. Readers can only ask what it means for them to read the text from their faith perspective, for revelation comes to faith and not to humankind in general.[22]

In its broadest outlines, H. Richard's method opened up possibilities for a number of theological disciplines concerned with the religious meaning of culture. What was needed for a particular inquiry to become grist for the theologian's mill was for that inquiry to allow for both rigorous empirical analysis and sustained theological reflection. Both church history and biblical studies, for example, which were tied to empirical methods derived from secular historiography and philology, could now be seen again as authentic sources for theological reflection again. In a similar way the method suggested that other cultural artifacts, such as literature, had an essential theological core that could be examined in the light of Christian teaching and given a rigorous theological reading.

Such methodological sophistication, however, had important implications for theological schools. Much of liberal scholarship, although clearly a study of religion and religious responses, has no particular theological character. In effect, the history of theology, including biblical theology, had been substituted for the reality of theological thought. H. Richard Niebuhr suggested a fruitful way past this impasse — in effect, answering the question of what is theological about theological education — that other seminary teachers found both attractive and convincing. It was a compelling and subtle vision.

The new theological emphases found a place most quickly in such areas as systematic theology and ethics. In part, this was because of the nature of

21. For Frei's insightful interpretation, see Hans Frei, "The Theology of H. Richard Niebuhr," in *Faith and Ethics: The Theology of H. Richard Niebuhr,* ed. Paul Ramsey (New York: Harper Torchbooks, 1957).

22. H. Richard Niebuhr accepted much of Troeltsch's contention that each culture had its own central religious core that revealed itself in its most sacred artifacts and records. In theological language, God was not speaking to the world in God's Word; rather God was speaking to the church. Whether a member of another religion would discern the revelation in the midst of Hebrew history was another matter.

these disciplines. Of all the so-called classical disciplines, these were the least affected by the guild structure of the academy and the most closely related to the church. Indeed, the responsiveness to these fields led Schleiermacher to define them as part of practical theology. In contrast, church history and biblical studies were very much part of the modern university guild structure. Unlike systematic theology, these disciplines derived much of their theological character from the fact that the object of their investigation and study had been theological constructs or events relevant to theology. Perhaps most important to understanding the lag between the historical and the theoretical disciplines was the highly technical character of the disciplines that required a substantial apprenticeship in languages, archaeology, and other related studies before the young scholars could turn to their own work. The twenty years from 1930 to 1950 were a particularly rich period for new studies, as archaeological discoveries of tremendous significance were made throughout the Middle East.

Yet the crises of the 1930s and 1940s also affected the practitioners of these disciplines, particularly the younger scholars whose methodological directions were not yet clearly defined. In some ways the crisis was more pronounced in this area. Around 1900 German and Continental scholars began to move from the older liberal or mediating tradition of Ritschl and Harnack to the more radical type of scholarship represented by the history-of-religion school. The history-of-religion scholars assumed that the meaning of any document was to be determined by its relationship to its immediate situation and not to the questions the modern interpreter might formulate. Viewed from this perspective, the Bible — or at least the Bible as read by scholars — seemed distant from modern readers. There are, in effect, two questions about Scripture: What did it mean, and what does it mean? The more the answer to the first rooted the Bible in the ancient Near East, the more pressing the second question became. The question of relevance, always acute for biblical scholarship, became even more acute.

Yet the new approach to theology represented by neoorthodoxy was a gift. There were many components to the new biblical studies. First, there was an international interest in the discipline of biblical theology.[23] Walter Eichrodt's *Theology of the Old Testament* (1933-39) demonstrated that historical investigation could provide a theologically meaningful way to read the text, and Oscar Cullmann, initially a professor at the University of Strasbourg, had already begun to develop his insightful analysis of such classical theological terms as

23. James Smart is correct in saying that the phrase "biblical theology movement" is somewhat misleading. All but the most historicist biblical scholars had always had some interest in the theological teachings of the Bible, if for no other reason than to critique commonly held notions. Further, the American practitioners of biblical theology were a very diverse lot, ranging from Paul Minear to G. Ernest Wright, who drew from many sources.

Heilsgeschichte and the biblical use of such Greek terms as *kronos* and *kairos.* James Muilenberg, who came of age as a scholar during the late 1930s, believed that this was the most important single change in biblical studies: "The most striking of all the developments of the past half-century, and I suspect to many of us the most fruitful and significant, has been the revival of biblical theology. The domination of the historical approach to the Scriptures, ever since the publication of Gabler's famous monograph in 1787, is so strong that few scholars were tempted to undertake the task of rendering the faith of ancient Israel into orderly and systematic form that theology requires."[24] Closely related was the European interest in the nature of biblical language, reflected in such long-term projects as the *Theological Wordbook of the New Testament* and the more massive *Theological Wordbook of the Old Testament.*

The new interest in biblical theology also provided a rationale for the revival of the study of biblical languages in some seminaries.[25] Since it was biblical culture and history, rather than the biblical text, that was the bearer of revelation, biblical languages could be studied to provide a student with the needed exposure to that culture. In one sense the idea of a brief required exposure to the biblical languages simply accepted the common wisdom that few students learned enough in their divinity course to really understand the Bible in the original languages. James Barr noted: "It is notorious that the number of ministers within the Church of Scotland who can read a page of Hebrew, or who can control from their own knowledge a statement made about the Hebrew language, is extremely small. This is true not only of those who had great difficulty with Hebrew as students, but also of those who have in fact done quite well in it; and it is also true of a great majority of professional theologians outside the Biblical field."[26] The new standard was quite different. "The classic argument was, presumably, that Hebrew was needed primarily in order to be able to read the Biblical text with more accuracy; the new argument is, rather, that Hebrew is essential if we are to enter into the basic thought forms of the Bible. . . . Thus we reach the position that Hebrew language study is dogmatically necessary, because without it we should be cut from the 'Hebrew Mind.'"[27]

24. James Muilenberg, "Old Testament Scholarship: Fifty Years in Retrospect," *Journal of Biblical Research,* 1960, pp. 173-81.

25. University divinity schools and the more liberal seminaries in general were rarely as intrigued with this aspect of the biblical revival.

26. James Barr, "Position of Hebrew Language in Theological Education," *Princeton Seminary Bulletin* 55 (1962): 6-24, here p. 17.

27. Barr, "Position of Hebrew Language," p. 18. Barr was one of the leading critics of the idea of a Hebrew mind. But he stated the case that many were making so clearly that he is an excellent example of the common wisdom.

Since contact with the Hebrew and the Greek "minds" was now the goal, such programs as Princeton's intensive summer courses in the languages, begun in the 1950s, were an excellent way to achieve this level of knowledge. Southern Baptist Seminary's requirement of a semester in each biblical language was another approach to this same standard. Students could immerse themselves in the language for six to eight weeks, learn the rudiments of pronunciation and grammar — at least enough to read a commentary with comfort and to understand references to grammatical and lexicographic matters in class — and, above all, develop a sense of the cultural milieu of the biblical writers. This was felt to be particularly important for Hebrew because the verbal system and, consequently, the sense of time were so different from those of most Western languages.

The new language studies were not convincing to everyone. The more liberal seminaries continued to question whether it was worthwhile for students to invest the time needed to learn even such a modicum. While they often allowed their Bible departments to institute the intensive courses, more or less modeled on those at Princeton and Union, they resolutely resisted making those courses required. Perhaps more seriously, the university-related schools and the more conservative schools resisted the new emphasis on accelerated courses in the biblical languages. In part, this was because certain methods of instruction were enshrined in the large university, although universities have been remarkably open to changes in the teaching of language; but it was more because both the universities and the more conservative schools continued to believe that the purpose of learning the language was to acquire the ability to read the language easily. Perhaps, too, many university-oriented scholars wondered what such categories as "Hebrew" mind or "Greek" mind might mean historically or linguistically.

Second, while few biblical scholars were willing to abandon the older techniques of their guild, serious questions were being raised about whether the constant refinement of the various source theories had not reached an end. The form critics, both in Old and New Testament, had demonstrated that many passages had a long history before they were incorporated into the various sources used by the biblical authors. The fact that a story was in the "priestly" code, hence, did not mean that it was not much older than that.

Third, Americans had always been interested in the physical character of the Holy Land, and the period from 1940 to 1960 was a rich one for biblical archaeology. William Foxwell Albright, the son of Presbyterian missionaries, received his Ph.D. in Oriental studies from Johns Hopkins in 1916 and spent much of the decade from 1919 to 1929 in Jerusalem working with the American Schools of Oriental Research, which later named its Jerusalem institute after him. In 1929 he became professor of Semitic languages at Johns Hopkins. Albright early showed his genius for popularizing his work. In 1932 his University of Virginia lectures, *Archaeology of Palestine and the Bible,* were published,[28] and in 1940 his more theological *From the Stone Age to Christianity: Monotheism and the Historical Process* appeared.[29] Like Brunner and Niebuhr, Albright delighted in carrying his case to the academic elite and was constantly in demand for conferences and lectures.

The firstfruits of the new approach to the Bible was the production of the Revised Standard Version of the Bible (New Testament, 1946; Old Testament, 1952). Like the neoorthodoxy of many of the younger scholars, such as James Muilenberg, who did the "grunt work" of translation, the RSV combined both theological and critical suavity. Wherever possible, it sought to preserve as much of the language of the King James as possible. Despite some passionate debate, the RSV became the first new Bible to win widespread acceptance since the King James, eventually being adopted by even the American Catholic Church.

The new biblical scholars determined to be faithful to church and academy. In practical terms this meant an obligation to make the results of their studies available to as large a public as possible. Princeton Seminary's founding of *Theology Today* in 1944 and the establishment of *Interpretation* by Union Seminary (Richmond) in 1947 reflected this commitment. While both journals maintained high theological standards, they were marketed toward the serious pastor or college instructor who wanted to incorporate the best of current theological work into her or his ministry. In that sense they were designed to fill the space between such guild-oriented publications as the *Journal of Biblical Literature, Church History,* and the *Journal of Religion.* The closest parallel to them was *Religion in Life,* which focused more on theological and ethical issues.

Methodist Abingdon-Cokesbury Press financed the boldest attempt of the new biblical scholars to reach out to the church: the *Interpreter's Bible.*[30] This is a remarkable document in the history of theological education in that it brought together many of the leading biblical scholars and many people dis-

28. Albright, *The Archaeology of Palestine and the Bible* (New York: Fleming H. Revell, 1932). For Albright's developed views, see *History, Archaeology, and Christian Humanism* (Baltimore: Johns Hopkins University Press, 1966).

29. For the development of American archaeology, see Bruce Kuklick, *Puritans in Babylon: The Ancient Near East and American Intellectual Life, 1880-1930* (Princeton: Princeton University Press, 1996).

30. *The Interpreter's Bible: The Holy Scriptures in the King James and Revised Standard Versions with General Articles and Introduction, Exegesis, Exposition for Each Book of the Bible,* ed. George Arthur Buttrick and others, 12 vols. (New York: Abingdon-Cokesbury, 1951-57).

tinguished in other theological fields to produce a usual introduction to the twin arts of careful biblical study and ecclesiastical proclamation. The series proposed to do this by paralleling the more traditional exegetical study and a contemporary exposition of the text.[31] To sense the generational change in biblical studies from the liberal era, one can see both the *Interpreter's Bible* and the International Critical Commentary (ICC) as the testament of a generation of scholars. The ICC made no pretense at addressing the question of relevance or the question of the church. Its long and somewhat pedantic discussions were designed to exhaust, as far as contemporary research permitted, the critical issues in the text. In contrast, the hope was that the *Interpreter's Bible* would be used by average ministers in the preparation of their weekly sermons. Biblical studies were to be relevant as well as accurate. Scottish theologian and pastor William Barclay attempted something similar in his popular series of commentaries aimed at a lay audience interested in serious study of the Scriptures.

The new biblical understanding scored its greatest triumph in relating its message to the churches in the Northern Presbyterian Christian Faith and Life curriculum (1947)[32] and the later Southern Presbyterian Covenant Life Curriculum (1962).[33] Both of these curricula, of course, came into being in the midst of the postwar boom in religion, and this may help to explain the enthusiasm with which they were greeted. Under the shadow of the bomb, Americans were hungry for meaning and categories that could help them understand their destiny. But neither curriculum was a mere "period" piece. Both presented substantial biblical and theological categories in an educationally sophisticated manner, and perhaps more important, they allowed Presbyterianism to move beyond the liberal-modernist controversy. Once people became accustomed to seeing Israel's faith as a response to the mighty acts of God, it became easier — perhaps almost necessary — to place the great confessions of the Reformation in much the same light. Just as God had acted and Israel had responded with a new faith expressed in different sources, so perhaps God had also acted in the Reformation and the people of God had responded in diverse ways. G. Ernest

31. The New Interpreter's Bible, published in 1994, has replaced the ecclesiastical "expositions" with the more neutral "reflections."

32. William Allen Silva, "The Expression of Neo-Orthodoxy in American Protestantism, 1939-1960" (Ph.D. diss., Yale University, 1988), stresses the importance of this curriculum for both the Presbyterian church and the American theological community. Silva is particularly important for his delineation of the influential neoorthodox figures of the 1940s, a time when some of the best biblical scholars were just entering their prime.

33. W. Eugene Marsh, "Biblical Theology, Authority and the Presbyterians," *Journal of Presbyterian History* 59 (1981): 113-30.

Wright's work on the Pentateuch was the model for the two denominations' later books of confessions.[34]

In a sense the decisions of the two Presbyterian churches to adopt books of confession in the place of their historic reliance on the Westminster Confession were nonevents. Led by Princeton Seminary's John Mackay, one of the most able American seminary presidents, the more conservative Presbyterian schools had already moved from orthodoxy to neoorthodoxy. John Mulder and Lee Wyatt saw the transformation as primarily occurring in the theological classrooms: "In short, Old School Calvinism, its defenders, and its explication in the classical textbooks were gradually replaced with works by Barth and, especially, the more readable Brunner, as well as others by faculty members who propounded the new theology, and by a curriculum that supported the neoorthodox vision of Christian doctrine."[35] Yet, conservative Presbyterianism was always as much a biblicism as it was a confessionalism with many Presbyterians holding fast to the confession as a way of holding fast to the Scriptures. What enabled sincerely conservative Presbyterians to make their movement to a new theology was the conviction that the new theology honored Scripture as well as or in many cases better than the old. The heart of the new Presbyterianism was fidelity to God's self-revelation.[36] And it was the new emphases on biblical theology that made possible both a high view of Scripture and modern biblical

34. Whatever was true of the Bible, the Protestant confessions had a different historical origin in a world that believed, increasingly as time passed, that it was possible to state the main points of faith clearly and concisely. Their hope was nothing less than to summarize the faith once delivered to the saints in a series of statements that would be used as the basis for both legal and ecclesiastical discipline. Confessions in fact superseded and replaced each other. Not all confessional differences were sufficient to separate churches, of course, but this does not change their basic historical meaning.

35. John Mulder and Lee Wyatt, "The Predicament of Pluralism: The Study of Theology in Presbyterian Seminaries," in *The Pluralistic Vision: Presbyterians and Mainstream Protestant Education and Leadership*, ed. Milton J. Coalter, John M. Mulder, and Louis B. Weeks (Louisville: Westminster John Knox, 1992), pp. 37-70, 46.

36. John Mackay, perhaps the most influential neoorthodox Presbyterian, always traced his school's position back to God's self-disclosure. "Upon the basis of these presuppositions Christian theology makes certain affirmations. The first affirmation concerns the nature of theology itself. Christian theology is not the science of religion. Neither is it a philosophy of religion. It is not a branch or department of any of the disciplines that constitute human culture, whether it be philosophy, psychology, sociology, or history. Christian theology is an intellectual effort to interpret the meaning and apply the implications of God's self-disclosure of himself in history" (John Mackay, "Theology in Education," *Christian Century*, Apr. 25, 1951, p. 521). Although popular in the classroom at Princeton (also Union, Richmond; Louisville; and McCormick), Brunner never defined these schools in the way that adherence to God's self-disclosure as a theological norm did.

study. Not incidentally, many leading advocates of the new methods, including Floyd Filson, G. Ernest Wright, and Bernhard Anderson, were active Presbyterian ministers. Although neoorthodoxy, like the earlier liberalism, was not confined to one denomination, one could say that just as Baptists, Congregationalists, Methodists, and Disciples had been in the vanguard of American liberal theology, so neoorthodoxy was a period of Presbyterian and Lutheran theological leadership.

Biblical theology appealed to Presbyterians for two primary reasons.[37] The first was its thoroughly biblical character. Whatever was true of Protestantism in general, Presbyterians were a people of the book who aspired to take Scripture seriously. At the same time, Presbyterians were caught in a social and intellectual bind. Whatever they may have felt about fundamentalist theology, many conservative Presbyterians were uncomfortable with the social and intellectual isolation of the fundamentalist position. Emotionally, the Presbyterians were, like most descendants of European state churches, committed to a centrist mentality that held together extremes of thought as well as behavior. In that sense the new biblical studies were a godsend. They enabled Presbyterians to reclaim their place on the American religious landscape without losing their souls. Not all Presbyterians responded to the new biblical theology, of course, but enough did to change the major Presbyterian seminaries over to the new position well before confessional change was actually effected.

Yet, if the confessional change did not give Presbyterian seminaries permission to change, it was nonetheless very significant for their future development. Not only did the confessional change make it easier to build an ecumenical faculty, but as neoorthodoxy both in biblical studies and in theology declined rapidly after 1968, it allowed the schools to use more general academic standards to determine faculty membership. In that sense, what many of the founders of Presbyterian seminaries had seen as their distinctive reason for being was abandoned, quietly in some places, with rejoicing in others.[38]

The new theology did not have as dramatic an impact on other American denominations. Clearly, among Southern Baptists and Missouri Synod Lutherans the new theology was an element in the bitter divisions of the 1970s and 1980s, and in many ways the new theology, especially biblical theology, made a significant contribution to the increasing division between new and young evangelicals on the right. These stories will be told elsewhere. For the crucial

37. Lefferts Loetscher, *The Broadening Church: A Study of Theological Issues in the Presbyterian Church Since 1869* (Philadelphia: University of Pennsylvania Press, 1954).

38. The full significance of this for American religion will be discussed below. Part of the consequence of the end of neoorthodoxy for American religion as a whole was the gradual erosion of the center.

middle decades of the twentieth century, the theology of crisis was a true theological revolution that affected what many teachers and administrators said and did. If the only change in some schools was, as Mulder noted, that those schools adopted a "core" over an "elective" curriculum, then that was because the innovators had captured the citadel and made it their own.

CHAPTER TWENTY-THREE

The Rural Church

From 1910 until 1960 many seminaries saw part of their task as the specialized training of ministers for rural churches. While almost forgotten today, this work was often a seedbed for later innovations in seminary education, including specialized training for specific tasks, field education, and social scientific research. Arguably, it was the area where the social gospel made its deepest penetration into seminary life, and the rural church was almost a perpetual source of hope and, unfortunately, frustration for those who wanted to bring about the kingdom of God on earth. The work both benefited and suffered from the romantic agrarianism that has been so commonplace in the United States.

Until the last decade of the nineteenth century, Americans followed the sun to the West. Landownership was the dream of every peasant society, and the vastness of America promised that every peasant might become a freeholder, and every freeholder a yeoman or even a gentleman. Under the best of conditions farming was a difficult business that required a combination of skill, knowledge, and plain luck for success. In Europe, relatively stable peasant communities had transmitted the first of these from generation to generation. People knew how close to Saint John's Day[1] they should plan to pick berries, and when planting had to be complete for them to make the crop. Few Americans lived in such stable communities. While most who went west to farm had some experience, either in the East or, in the case of immigrants, in Europe, they did not know local conditions or the specific needs of American soils. Many a farm

1. June 24. Saint John's Day is one of the "quarter days" that introduces a season of the year. The others are Christmas, December 25, Annunciation or Lady Day, March 25, and Michaelmas, September 29. English leases traditionally dated from Lady Day, and many agricultural practices were timed around Saint John's Day or midsummer.

wore out before the farmer learned how much rotation to give tobacco or corn. By the time these rural communities became mature, however, American rural history was on another course. By the 1890s the railroads, centralized meatpacking, and the beginnings of agribusiness transformed traditional rural society, just as RFD (rural free delivery) transformed rural communications and helped create mail-order businesses. American politics almost immediately felt the effects of the new countryside. Both populism and the rural progressivism of William Jennings Bryan reflected political attempts to rectify the balance of power between farmers and those who bought and transported their crops.

I. The New Rural Order

The late nineteenth-century rural crisis was the natural result of modern economics. Like other producers of raw materials, farmers found themselves on the bottom of the order of production. Each successive processor of their product — whether mills or railroads or retailers — added value to what they created. Moreover, each successive processor had the right, almost the obligation, to further inflate the price of the product through such techniques as advertising and brand recognition that increased the demand side. Thus farmers sold their products at the bottom of the economic ladder and purchased their supplies and household necessities near the top of that ladder. To further complicate the rural plight, farmers suffered from an unregulated market. In this pure capitalist market, an increase in production often led to a decrease in price, unless it was accompanied by increasing demand.[2] While years of lesser production, in theory, should have offset the years of high production, prices never went up as far or as quickly as they went down. New farm machinery only made the problem worse. The new machines could only be purchased on time, and the new production they made possible further depressed the market. The farmer who had no control over the larger market experienced a world in which the more he worked the less he earned. By the time of Franklin Roosevelt, the 25 percent of Americans working on farms received less than 3 percent of the income,[3] and the percentage of the nation's goods and services — including such modern niceties as electric-

2. For the effects of the new economy on rural life, see William Cronon, *Nature's Metropolis: Chicago and the Great West* (New York: Norton, 1991), and Albro Martin, *Railroads Triumphant* (New York: Oxford University Press, 1992).

3. Jacob H. Dorn, "The Rural Ideal and the Agrarian Realities: Arthur Holt and the Vision of a Decentralized America in the 1930s," *Church History* 52 (Mar. 1983): 51. Dorn's figure may exaggerate rural income in that it also apparently contains the "second job" that many farmers held in a nearby town and factory.

ity and modern schooling — received by rural people was even less. A steady migration to the cities began, and many of the larger landowners, North and South, moved to town and had their farms worked by tenants.

Traditional rural society was not simply a village of farmers. Rather, it was a complex society that included farmers, their suppliers, blacksmiths, small merchants, market operators, lawyers, doctors, and ministers. As farming modernized, many of these people withdrew from the countryside. By the 1920s the automobile had come to play an important role in the delivery of services, encouraging professionals and merchants to move farther from their consumers. The tractor also contributed to the countryside's loss of population. Those labor-intensive tasks that had depended on the "hired hand" were now easily done by the owner-operator in less time. The hands migrated to the cities, perhaps to work in a factory, only to be replaced at picking time by swarms of migrants. The migrants left as soon as the harvest was completed.

The automobile also changed the lifestyle of the smaller farmers. They often used the car to get to a "second job" in a nearby factory — especially in the winter — that they needed to hold life together. As one author noted, "forces operating at least through the whole Anglo-Saxon race are driving the farmer from his farm."[4] The most full-time of jobs was becoming part-time.

Protestant churches were hit especially hard by the crisis in the countryside. Much of nineteenth-century American religious history was the story of the competition of the various denominations for a place in the American Eden. While never as glamorous as the foreign missionary movement, home missionary societies were established by the major American denominations to spread the gospel and their own ecclesiastical organizations. In addition to such formal efforts, Baptist farmer-preachers, Disciples elders, and Methodist circuit riders often battled for the same plot of land, cheek by jowl, with none willing to relinquish even the most meager toehold. Often the churches were stretched far beyond their human resources. Baptist John Mason Peck found that one-third of his churches' ministers were dangerous, one-third of minor usefulness, and one-third had promise.[5]

Immigrant Lutherans, who were often the best-organized newcomers to America, often planned how they would establish their churches before they left Germany, and the existing Lutheran bodies stood ready to help their countrymen create new structures.

4. Henry Wallace, "The Ideal Rural Civilization," in *Messages of the Men and Religion Movement*, vol. 6, *The Rural Church* (New York: Association Press, 1912), p. 46.

5. Colin Brummit Goodykoontz, *Home Missions on the American Frontier with Particular Reference to the American Home Missionary Society* (New York: Octagon Books, 1971).

Villages and small towns found themselves with an ecclesiastical establishment that might have served a small city equally well. "Church Street" was often lined with magnificent buildings, occupied by a handful of worshipers, separated by doctrines only vaguely understood. "[U]nder rural conditions, sectarianism found its richest soil."[6] In the best of times it was vaguely ridiculous — the appropriate butt of a Mark Twain satire — but when the best of times departed, the comic gave way to the tragic. Many churches were quarter- and half-time churches whose ministers migrated weekly from a nearby town, while others were strung along seemingly endless circuits and church fields that stretched over thirty and forty miles. The countryside was overchurched and, at the same time, underserved.

Nor was the countryside the location of unusually biblical or concerned laypeople. Memories of the extent of religious knowledge in the rural countryside should be discounted. The various forms of Christian education, such as the Sunday school, the youth group, and later the vacation Bible school, were more likely to flourish in urban areas, where hosts of volunteers were potentially available, than in the countryside where resources in people, denominationally published aids, and books were more limited. One of the major efforts of the Southern Baptist Convention in the 1920s was to encourage churches to construct "evergreen" Sunday schools that would function during the winter as well as the summer months, and other denominations had similar programs. Studies of the religious life of men drafted into the American army in the First World War, many from rural backgrounds, reflect a level of ignorance that would be remarkable even at the end of the twentieth century. Part of the rural church crisis was the failure of the church to find effective means to teach the faith in rural communities.

Rural church pastors often made American Protestantism sound rural, and it was not difficult for the pundits to turn Dayton, Tennessee, the site of the famed monkey trial, into a metaphor for the whole of Protestant Christianity. The progressive historians who were defining the nation's past at this point had no doubts on this score. For Parrington, Beard, and Turner, the Protestant mind was part of what the nation was leaving behind.[7] Even the Puritans, whose love of learning was so manifest, were part of this critique. And others shared the thesis that the triumph of the city was a victory over the rural, the backward, the ill informed, and the religious. Ironically, early liberal historians of fundamentalism identified that movement with rural life and missed the larger con-

6. Charles L. White, *A Century of Faith* (Philadelphia: Judson, 1932).

7. See Richard Hofstadter, *The Progressive Historians: Turner, Beard, and Parrington* (New York: Knopf, 1968).

text in which many educated Americans simply identified all Protestants with the nation's rural past.[8]

Ironically, the great expansion of knowledge and education in the early twentieth century highlighted the isolation of the rural church and its leadership. In one of the classic studies of the plight of the rural church, published in 1913, Charles Gill and Gifford Pinchot noted: "Long ago the leaders of modern religious thought began to apply the scientific method to their study of religion. The readjustment of religious doctrine in accordance with the scientific method calls for religious teachers of better equipment than we now have in this country. The lack of them leads at times to a striking discrepancy between what is taught in the country churches and what is taught in the colleges and seminaries."[9]

In other words, the ministry in rural areas had a serious cultural lag. In general, educational reform and expansion began in the cities and only gradually moved to the countryside. A city might have its high school many years before such an institution was established to serve the surrounding countryside. Despite rural free delivery, which made books and magazines more available, the number of cultural resources available to rural people was limited both by availability and by price.

Graham Taylor recalled that his first parish, located in the country, applied considerable pressure on him to preach the received wisdom, although this problem was not unique to the rural churches. Urban congregants, who were often the first generation to move into the cities, also pressured their ministers to give them that old-time religion. But one must be leery of overly identifying the countryside with ignorance and social conservatism.[10] What might be more accurate is that the cultural balance of power between urban and rural shifted decisively toward the cities long before the demographic balance changed, leaving the rural areas constantly behind. The intellectual coin of the realm was made in the cities, not the countryside.

The fact that so many Americans were only one generation from the farm

8. Stewart Grant Cole, *The History of Fundamentalism* (Hampden, Conn.: Archon Books, 1963; original 1931).

9. Charles Otis Gill and Gifford Pinchot, *The Country Church: The Decline of Its Influence and Its Remedy* (New York: Macmillan, 1913), p. 32.

10. There were many rural areas with very deep progressive traditions, such as Wisconsin and pre–World War I California. Nor were rural churches necessarily less open to modern social trends. See Wayne Flynt, *Alabama Baptists: Southern Baptists in the Heart of Dixie* (Tuscaloosa: University of Alabama Press, 1998). After all, both Roosevelt and Wilson carried rural states in their election campaigns, and Franklin Roosevelt was always a powerful vote getter in the rural South.

in the first few decades of the twentieth century meant that their memories of their childhood and its religion were often romanticized. Like mother, apple pie, and Currier and Ives prints, the experience grew richer with the telling. Rural nineteenth- and twentieth-century life often needs translation, especially when urban people remember their childhood. George Harris spoke for many when he noted about his rural childhood: "The parson was a commanding figure, or if not commanding, was regarded with veneration by reason of his office. The religious services of the Lord's Day were the great occasions. Everybody went to church except the sick and those who cared for them."[11] Like many childhood memories, Harris's "remembered" religious conditions were more like those of his grandparents and perhaps great-grandparents than of his parents. Few churches, even in pious New England, would have had such an experience after disestablishment.

The myth of the pious countryside, however, was potent, whatever truth claims might be made for those stories. For most Americans the countryside was more than a place. It was America, spelled in capital letters, and writ large on the walls of their hearts. Talk of its decline, consequently, reflected people's awareness that Protestantism, the religion of the countryside, was itself in deep distress. The comparative isolation of the rural pastor was perhaps a metaphor for the widespread sense of ennui and loss felt by Protestants in the 1920s.[12] In struggling with the church in the countryside, Protestant seminaries and theologians were also struggling with themselves.

II. Seminaries and the Countryside

Despite a statement often repeated in the literature about seminaries, few seminaries were founded to serve the rural and small-town church. Most either were located in or near major centers of population or elected to move there early in their history, usually after the town in which they were originally located failed to grow. The exceptions are important. Bangor Theological Seminary in Maine was deliberately located in the midst of a number of small churches to help pro-

11. George Harris, *A Century's Change in Religion* (Boston and New York: Houghton Mifflin, 1914), p. 13.

12. William Hutchison, ed., *Between the Times: The Travail of the Protestant Establishment in America, 1900-1960* (Cambridge, U.K., and New York: Cambridge University Press, 1989); Robert T. Handy, *A Christian America: Protestant Hopes and Historical Realities* (New York: Oxford University Press, 1971); Robert T. Handy, "The American Religious Depression, 1925-1935," *Church History* 29 (1960). See also Henry May, *The Loss of American Innocence* (Chicago: Quadrangle Books, 1964).

tect these churches from Jesse Lee and other Methodist exhorters. Omaha Presbyterian Seminary was originally intended to serve rural German immigrants, and Dubuque and Wartburg were also oriented in a rural direction. Hamilton, later Colgate, likewise had a special ministry to the smaller churches of upstate New York, so much so that the founders of Rochester self-consciously wanted their school pointed in an urban direction. In the twentieth century, one reason Southeastern Baptist Theological Seminary was located in then rural Wake County, North Carolina, was the desire to serve the small churches of southern Virginia, North Carolina, and South Carolina.

Such exceptions prove the rule. Rural seminaries, like rural schools of law and medicine, were unusual and often underfunded and underenrolled. Some, like Omaha, closed because of financial pressures; others, like Colgate, merged with other institutions; and a handful continued to hold to a small-town and rural mission. But those seminaries often faced intense competition from their better-financed urban cousins who saw rural churches as excellent "starter" churches for their graduates.

The coming of railroads and later the automobile tightened the relationship between seminaries and the countryside. By using the rails, student ministers could serve rural churches on weekends while earning their degrees on weekdays. Many schools adopted schedules that had no classes on Friday afternoons and Monday mornings to encourage this practice. When the automobile became more popular, particularly in the 1920s, the area a seminary could serve in this way expanded. Seminary administrators were aware of the importance of the shift from the rails to the auto, and if a school relocated, it tended to seek a place in the suburbs near the highways that had enough room for "parking." Both Louisville Presbyterian and Southern Baptist Theological Seminary, for example, planned their suburban campuses around the needs of the automobile. The case of Southern provides an almost perfect illustration of the process. The Baptist flagship seminary moved from a location near the train station to a large campus in what was then the deep suburbs. Perhaps not incidentally, the period of greatest seminary involvement with rural life, roughly from 1910 to 1950, was the period in which transportation opened up more of the countryside to seminaries as a source for student scholarships and experience. Just as cities had their hinterlands that provided them with resources, so seminaries served a hinterland that might be a circle with a fifty-, seventy-, or hundred-mile radius. This period ended when the newly prosperous post–World War II suburbs came to offer better access to remunerative employment. After 1950 students more often sought employment as assistant pastors or youth ministers in larger congregations than as rural pastors.

III. The Rural Church Movement

The rural church movement was a major influence on the seminaries in their relationship with rural churches. The movement began in the late 1880s, when many Americans became aware of the spreading discontent in the countryside,[13] and peaked during the depression years of the 1930s. James Madison characterized the movement in this way:

> The rural church movement drew on major currents in early twentieth-century life. Like other reform movements of the Progressive Era, it was fueled largely by men and women from strongly Protestant homes seeking careers that "offered the possibility of preaching without pulpits," as Robert M. Cruden has noted. The church reformers were unusual in their focus on rural, rather than urban problems, but their movement reflected the methods and orientations of urban reformers. Most of these spokesmen for rural church reform were professionals who believed in progress through rational study, efficient planning, and organized effort. They gloried especially in the new science of sociology. Most reflected also the teachings of the social gospel by combining liberal theology with the imperative of social action.[14]

While general Protestant awareness of the rural church movement ebbed and flowed, President Theodore Roosevelt's 1908 establishment of the Country Life Commission made many aware that the rural crisis had a spiritual and religious component. The commission found that the church was the primary social agency that survived in the countryside and the one most respected by rural people. Hence, it followed that if progress was to be made in solving rural social problems, the church "must take a larger leadership . . . in the social reorganization of rural life."[15] Of course, the church was not to work alone. A vital role

13. Edwin Earp, *The Rural Church Movement* (New York and Cincinnati: Methodist Book Concern, 1914), p. 84. Actually articles on the plight of the rural church began to appear in religious journals about the same time as the better-known pieces on the American cities. Of special note in this early literature, Samuel Dike, "The Religious Problem of the Country Town," *Andover Review,* 1884; Samuel Dike, "The Religious Problem of the Country Town II," *Andover Review,* 1884; William DeWitt Hyde, "Impending Paganism in New England," *Forum,* 1892; G. T. Nesmity, "The Problem of the Rural Community with Special Reference to the Rural Church," *American Journal of Sociology,* 1903.

14. James H. Madison, "Reformers and the Rural Church, 1900-1950," *Journal of American History* 73 (Dec. 1986): 3, 645-68, here p. 646.

15. Quoted in J. O. Ashenhurst, "The Rural Awakening," in *Messages of the Men and Religion Movement,* 6:56.

was projected for the state agricultural colleges, for the county agents, and for rural schools. The more radical hoped that such social experiments as the cooperative movement, where farmers banded together to bargain with suppliers, railroads, and purchasers, might give small farmers some of the power of the new agribusinesses.

The Men and Religion Forward Movement of 1912 was also important in building interest in the rural church. Men and Religion Forward represented an attempt to deal with one of the most serious Protestant crises: the progressively serious decline of male membership in the church.[16] The result was often a display of hyper-masculinity that suggested Teddy Roosevelt as much as Jesus.

> To counteract the feminine taint and attract the missing men, movement literature emphasized the masculine qualities of the church and churchmen, continually referring to "virile hymns," "Christian manliness," and most often, "strong men." Men who attended M&RFM activities were no pantywaists, but were "ready for the strongest utterances of the strongest men." These "strong men" found the "exciting masculine pages of their Bible" to be "worthy of the best time and mightiest effort of the manliest man." The "battalion of experts" who conducted the campaign, all "hearty meat eaters," engaged in strenuous physical exercise regularly on tour.[17]

While the movement stressed the basic Christianity of such masculine activities as business and sports, its real hook in reaching out to men was its emphasis on the social gospel. To be a man of faith was not to engage in the sentimental "surrender" so characteristic of female piety; it was to attack aggressively the world's problems efficiently and rationally. Walter Rauschenbusch, the best theologian of the social gospel, remarked that "The movement has probably done more than any other single agency to lodge the Social Gospel in the common mind of the Church. It has made social Christianity orthodox."[18] Incidentally, it also partially accomplished its purpose. The number of men involved in Protestant churches grew.

Given the movement's business focus, it is interesting that one-sixth of its published "messages" were devoted to the problems and opportunities of the

16. Gail Bederman, "The Women Have Had Charge of the Church Work Long Enough: The Men and Religion Forward Movement of 1911 and the Masculinization of Middle Class Protestantism," in *A Mighty Baptism: Race, Gender, and the Creation of American Protestantism*, ed. Susan Juster and Lisa MacFarlane (Ithaca, N.Y., and London: Cornell University Press, 1996); originally published in *American Quarterly* 41 (Sept. 1989): 432-65.

17. Bederman, "Women Have Had Charge," p. 119.

18. Walter Rauschenbusch, *Christianizing the Social Order* (New York: Macmillan, 1912), p. 20, quoted in Bederman, "Women Have Had Charge," p. 128.

rural church. The material on the rural church is remarkable, emblematic of American social Christianity at its best. The messages, of course, discuss the most visible problem of the rural church — the nonresidence of pastors — and correctly identify its economic cause as too many churches paying too-low salaries. Much of the rest of the argument rests on the ability of the various denominations to find a way to solve this problem. Kenyon Butterfield, the influential president of the Massachusetts Agricultural College in Amherst, had been a member of the original Roosevelt Commission and had a deep appreciation of the place of the church in rural life. His message to the Men and Religion Forward Movement was an influential sketch of what the churches should be doing about rural leadership.[19] His first proposal was that the churches needed to develop a "rural clergy as a professional group that tends to specialize itself and that tends to induce other men to make it their life's work." The ideal should be "permanent service," not in a particular parish, but in a type of ministry.[20] But if someone is considering permanent service in a rural church, then the question of how to prepare people for that profession becomes pressing. Butterfield was certain that "methods in the country church cannot be those of the city church," if for no other reason than that the "rural mind is not the urban mind."[21] Rural culture needed to be studied from a variety of perspectives. Butterfield, who knew the problems of farmers, believed that thorough training in rural economics was essential for someone who needed to understand "all the phases of the big problem which we call the rural question."[22] Other areas of needed study were rural sociology and rural life.[23]

Butterfield's complaints that rural ministers were disconnected from their parishes was supported by a plethora of rural church leaders. In part, it was the age-old complaint that ministers were too removed from real life to provide real leadership, and the gender stereotype of the time was that ministry was an effeminate occupation for those without manly and practical skills. Edwin Earp, a Methodist preacher, sounded like the perpetual American semi-

19. Butterfield had developed similar ideas in his *Church and the Rural Problem* (Chicago: University of Chicago Press, 1909). Butterfield was later a member of the International Missionary Council and an active supporter of the ecumenical movement.

20. Kenyon Butterfield, "The Supply of Leaders for the Country," in *Messages of the Men and Religion Movement,* 6:78.

21. Butterfield, "Supply of Leaders," p. 78. We would say "culture" and not "mind" today.

22. Butterfield, "Supply of Leaders," p. 79.

23. For similar arguments more than fifty years later, see Thomas Ford, "The Roles of the Rural Parish Minister, the Protestant Seminaries, and the Sciences of Social Behavior," in *The Sociology of Religion: An Anthology,* ed. Richard D. Knudten (New York: Appleton-Century-Crofts, 1967).

nary critic: "The old time theologically trained minister was unfitted by his training to meet the needs of country life. He deteriorated because he was unable to make use of the educational resources of the open country. He had been accustomed to draw his illustrations from literature and the church fathers. He had no mind to grasp, as did Jesus, the significance of the plant and animal life that crowned his pathway in the rural parish."[24]

He was not alone. In almost biblical terms, H. Paul Douglass wrote that unless theological seminaries repented and became rural-minded, they could not prepare people for rural service,[25] and Warren Wilson cited former Governor Beaver of Pennsylvania as saying: "The trouble with the country minister is that he does not know how to farm. The old style preachers could and did farm. They taught their people how to farm the land. The theological seminaries should so train the minister that he would know how to bore a hole in the ground and see whether that spot would do for the planting of a Baldwin apple tree."[26] Beaver was hopefully a better politician than a historian. At the time, most seminary students came from rural and small-town backgrounds, and there was never a period in which the American ministry had served as agricultural instructors.

While Butterfield was able to point to the large number of conferences and other informal means of instruction about the rural churches, many of which were offered by state universities, he believed that the "theological seminaries and other institutions from which clergymen graduate are . . . the natural centers at which training courses may be expected to be developed." Yet he knew that little was being done at these institutions, in part because the curriculum had become so crowded with elective courses. His hope was that "separate schools or highly specialized courses for country clergymen" would be developed to help meet the need.[27] Butterfield also maintained that seminaries and churches should avail themselves of the services of the state agricultural colleges that had already developed much expertise in this area.[28]

In a sense Butterfield, like Douglass, was asking the seminaries to become rural minded. H. N. Morse, director of the Interseminary Commission for

24. Edwin Earp, *The Rural Church Serving the Community* (Nashville: Abingdon, 1918), p. 89.

25. H. Paul Douglass, *The New Home Missions, an Account of Their Social Redirection* (New York: Missionary Education Movement, 1914).

26. Warren Wilson, *The Church of the Open Country* (New York: Missionary Education Movement, 1911), p. 163.

27. Butterfield, "Supply of Leaders," p. 81.

28. Texas A & M in College Station, Tex., maintained an active interest in the rural church over a number of years and provided valuable courses for rural church leaders.

Training the Rural Ministry[29] and 1930s rural church advocate, saw seven marks of such awareness:

1. The seminaries should recognize the need for specialization in this area.
2. Graduation from agricultural college should be accepted for admission to the seminary.
3. The course in rural ministry should include such classes as rural church methods, rural sociology and economics, and fieldwork in a rural setting.
4. Rural church studies must be conducted at a high intellectual level.
5. Materials related to the rural church should be included in every course.
6. Contact with the student should continue after graduation.
7. Special programs for non–college graduates should be included.[30]

In retrospect, the demands for "rural mindedness" are similar to later demands that seminaries be sensitive to the particular needs of women, African Americans, and other minorities. To respond to the needs of a special group is to formulate special courses, include materials about that group in the general courses, and help the student with placement.

Like most proposals for a more professional ministry, Butterfield's recognized the financial distress of many rural church leaders. Not only were salaries low, but these poor stipends were not always regularly paid.[31] Although churches attempt various ways to remedy this problem, including home missions supplements and the adoption of minimal wage scales, even today rural ministry is comparatively poorly compensated. Once a pastor has established his or her worth in a rural or small-town parish, the financial pressure to move upward has already become almost irresistible.[32] In that sense professional rural ministry has been caught in a cul-de-sac. The desperate needs of rural areas call for an extraordinarily well trained and sensitive pastor; the fiscal realities of church life tend, then as now, to drive such able people to the cities and suburbs.

The rural church movement, like other progressive movements, believed that effective action depended on an objective picture of social conditions. Warren Wilson, who was the Presbyterian executive in charge of rural life, was typical of progressive church leaders, before and after the First World War. A

29. See below, pp. 555-56.

30. H. N. Morse, *The Profession of the Ministry: Its Status and Problems* (New York: Interseminary Commission for Training the Rural Ministry, 1934), *Bulletin* 9.

31. F. M. Barton, "A Living Wage for Rural Pastors," in *Messages of the Men and Religion Movement,* 6:83-95.

32. In the 1990s, graduates of Bangor Seminary's highly successful Small Church Program, headed by Douglas Walrath, followed this same pattern.

graduate of Oberlin and Union (New York), he had earned his doctoral degree from Columbia University. He was active in meetings of other such denominational officials and a recognized authority in rural sociology. Wilson, who published the results of seventeen surveys during his tenure with the Presbyterian Church, described the value of such studies: "Survey is the name for a systematic study of a people, with a view to serving them as they have need. The people studied may be a parish or community or a city, county, or larger social population. The survey is orderly and systematic in method, comprehensive in the facts studied, so that nothing is left out of account."[33] There are some key elements in this definition that explain the passion for surveys among rural reformers. The first is that surveys were not dispassionate reports by impartial observers; rather, the essence of a survey was that, through questionnaires and interviews, it asked people to provide their own input. Surveys were undertaken "with a view to serving them as they have need." Equally important, surveys were not random observations. A good survey required discipline and planning. At a minimum, sociologists need to know what to ask and how to correlate the answers they receive with other significant data. At another place Wilson wrote: "To know a community sufficiently well to command a statesmanlike view of its conditions and betterment means scientific investigation, study, tabulation, and generalization. The facts need to be understood, the interrelations, bearings and determining influences of certain facts and experiences need investigation. Most important of all, these facts must be interpreted correctly and their meaning for the church clearly known."[34] The number of pitfalls awaiting the careless was legion.

Rural church leaders advocated something like later Congregational studies as part of rural church leadership. In an interesting observation, E. Fred Eastman noted that such outward signs of religious decline as falling congregational membership and an apparent lack of interest in religion were matters to be studied. "The modern minister is not content with assigning such causes as 'Worldliness,' 'Love of money,' 'Cooling of the Heart,' 'Grip of Sin,' etc., to this state of affairs. He knows that such phrases are descriptions of symptoms, not causes, and that the trouble lies deeper. He undertakes a survey and he makes . . . actual discoveries."[35] Eastman's passion for data furthered an interest in accurate maps, economic conditions, demographics, transportation, recreation,

33. Warren Wilson, *The Church at the Center* (New York: Missionary Education Movement, 1914), p. 9.

34. Quoted in Marvin Judy, *From Ivy Tower to Village Spire* (Dallas: Southern Methodist University Press, 1984), p. 41.

35. E. Fred Eastman, "The Minister's Use of the Survey," in *Messages of the Men and Religion Movement*, 6:167.

morals, educational and religious opportunities, and social agencies at work in an area. The final results, Eastman maintained, should be presented to the community in the form of a comprehensive report.

The Institute for Social and Religious Research made the study of the rural church a major priority. The goal was to follow the lead of church executives "as to what they needed to know about the rural church," and the plan of attack was global. In each state the institute appointed a full-time executive who had some experience with the rural churches in that state. In turn, this executive appointed county managers to conduct the actual survey. Over one thousand of these county supervisors were women. When all was said and done, some four-fifths of all American counties were surveyed.[36] It was one of the most comprehensive studies of rural life before Franklin Roosevelt's federally sponsored studies.

In many ways the larger survey confirmed what earlier rural church advocates had argued. The ministry was the key to the success of rural churches. As Morse and Brunner put it dryly: "From the point of view of business efficiency, the country church lacks adequate supervision and direction. There are few kinds of business which will run themselves without trained personal supervision; and the church is not one of these."[37] While the language of business efficiency may shock the modern reader, who is more inclined to separate economics and religion, it should not overshadow Morse and Brunner's point. In a complex world, everyone's business is no one's business. Rural people did not have large blocks of time to invest in their churches.

The rural church movement and its allies consistently advocated two changes in the countryside. The first was the need to consolidate smaller churches into larger religious bodies. Many different plans for doing this were common at the time.[38] Some advocated federated churches that would use a formula to adjudicate the differences in polity; others advocated undenominational or community churches, while some advocated "larger parish" programs that took advantage of newer forms of transportation.[39] The Methodists used their circuit system to some advantage in placing contiguous churches under common leadership, and other denominations intimated this with multiple-point charges.

36. H. N. Morse and Edmund de S. Brunner, *The Town and Country Church in the United States* (New York: George Doran Co., 1923).

37. Morse and Brunner, *Town and Country Church,* pp. xi-xii.

38. See Ralph A. Felton, *Local Church Cooperation in Rural Communities* (New York: Congregational and Christian Churches, n.d.); E. Tallmadge Root, *Church Federation* (1909), pamphlet.

39. For a discussion of such auto-based proposals, see Edmund de S. Brunner, *The Larger Parish, a Movement or Enthusiasm?* (New York: Institute of Social and Religious Research, 1934).

The other consistent argument was the need for something like the rural equivalent of the institutional church. Few rural church reformers shared the popular agrarian myths that stressed the purity of the countryside. They were aware that many of the social problems associated with the city — prostitution, alcoholism, family violence — were common in rural areas as well and that rural isolation might actually intensify them, rather than alleviate them. The churches had to be aggressive advocates of righteousness to combat such vices, and this meant providing recreation as well as religion, training as well as catechism.

In many ways the reformers' hopes for the churches were similar to educational reformers' hopes for rural schools. As the population of rural areas declined, many rural schools found themselves unable to offer graded instruction and lacking the resources, in libraries and equipment, to provide a modern education. Further, it was difficult to get the best graduates of the normal schools, later called teachers colleges, to settle in rural areas. The small size of these schools also made it difficult for them to offer the various extracurricular and other activities considered vital to modern schooling.

In a real sense the difference between the fate of rural school consolidation and rural church consolidation reflected the American separation of church and state. Although the battle was often prolonged, the state eventually prevailed in the battle over school consolidation. In part this was because many rural people supported the reforms, but it was also because the state had the power, especially the financial power, to force compliance. In contrast, the church was a voluntary agency. Church consolidations occurred only when all members of the churches, or at least a large majority of them, wanted the union to succeed. But a minority could block a rural church merger for any number of reasons, including particular individuals' commitment to the building as a sacred space, and there was little that denominational officials could do, other than ending home missionary aid, to move the project further along. A failed merger, after all, might replace two weak congregations with three, four, or more even weaker and less effective bodies.

One of the earliest programs to advocate rural church cooperation and federation was the Interdenominational Commission of Maine, which first met in 1891 in response to a call from William DeWitt Hyde of Bowdoin College. The commission brought together Baptists, Free Will Baptists, Christians, and Methodists. The churches agreed that they would no longer establish new congregations in rural areas where other churches already had a congregation and that they would work to strengthen existing work rather than establish new congregations. In 1899 Vermont established the Vermont Interdenominational Comity Committee for the same purpose. Significantly, H. Paul Douglass believed: "If the Baptist, Congregational, and Methodist religious forces of Vermont were reorganized into non-duplicatory churches of two hundred members each, with pastors receiving $1,000 salary each, not only would Vermont be more efficiently supplied with the gospel, but $65,000 would be released for use elsewhere."[40]

In the 1930s Hilda Libby Ives, ordained in Maine in 1926,[41] helped many Maine and Vermont churches federate.[42] For many years she taught rural church ministries at Andover-Newton.

How did the seminaries respond to the rural church movement? Courses in the rural church often entered seminary programs in much the same way as other courses on specialized ministry. First, a school would appoint a visiting instructor, and when and if enrollments or financial support grew, it would expand that area. Baptist and Methodist seminaries were particularly interested in rural church programs, and most of them offered courses in rural ministries. Even in these schools the amount of work varied. In 1944 J. Merle Davies, a home missionary expert, noted that "It is startling to find that out of the 246.09 course hours per week offered by the average seminary only 2.51 hours are given to the highly specialized field of the rural church — a field which includes one-half of the churches."[43] Many of these courses were in rural sociology and the special problems of small churches.

Dr. Jesse Ormond of Duke University pioneered one of the most creative approaches to the rural church. The Duke Endowment, established out of the profits from the electric power company, not tobacco, provided for a number of scholarships to the divinity school on the condition that those receiving the aid serve a rural church, either during the term or during the summer months. Dr. Ormond administered these funds on behalf of both the university and the endowment, aiding some 713 rural congregations, and assigning some 1,215 Duke students to these parishes during his tenure. Ormond used his rich contacts on Tobacco Road to become an expert on the churches and published a book, *The Country Church in North Carolina,* that was noted as a contribution to rural so-

40. Douglass, *The New Home Missions,* p. 57.

41. She may have been the first woman ordained in the state, at least the trustees of Bowdoin believed so, when they gave her the first honorary doctor of divinity degree awarded to a woman in 1948. Her base of operations was Portland, from which she was able to serve the whole state, a real task before the construction of I-95!

42. Her papers are at Andover-Newton Theological Seminary and provide a rich source for northern New England's religious and social history.

43. J. Merle Davies, "The Preparation of Missionaries for the Post-War Era," *International Review of Missions* 23 (1944): 241-53. This study was done in wartime when many schools had cut their programs to essentials. The average probably ran much higher.

ciology. When Ormond died in 1954, the North Carolina Conference established the Ormond Center for Research, Planning and Development of the Churches at Duke Divinity School.

Arthur Holt of Chicago Theological Seminary was perhaps the best known and most passionate of the seminary rural church advocates.[44] One of the first Americans to receive a Ph.D. in ethics, Holt had been a noted Congregational executive before coming to Chicago in 1924 as Graham Taylor's successor. A tireless activist, Holt quickly became the leader of the faculty at Chicago and turned the school in a consistently social activist direction. Early in his career he decided that the most important question before America was not the battle between labor and capital, but the question "whether we are to build our cities with a standard of life which cannot be matched on the farm."[45] Under his leadership, Chicago became noted for its work with rural churches and for its expertise on rural problems.

Among Holt's innovations was his yearly "hike" with his students to investigate particular areas. His field trips included visits to rural Louisiana, to the Tennessee Valley, to Berea College, and to Tuskegee and Talladega Colleges. Like other rural church advocates, Holt determined that his students would be able to do the social and religious research he felt was essential to efficient ministry. His classes became showcases of maps, graphs, charts, and other empirical studies. "Keep your facts ahead of your oratory" was his motto.[46] In all his work he reminded students that while capital, labor, and white-collar workers had their advocates, no one spoke for the farmers or other rural workers. Holt applauded the work of Henry Wallace and others in the Roosevelt administration who sought to improve rural conditions, and he approved of such radical experiments as the Tennessee Valley Authority that sought to eliminate a major center of rural poverty.

Holt's educational philosophy led him to establish the Merom Institute in 1936 on an abandoned college campus in Indiana. Merom was devoted to the renovation and strengthening of rural life, and it provided a base for conferences, continuing education, and field education for the seminary. In addition, Holt saw the Merom center as an intellectual resource for those struggling to keep country life human, and the institute provided books, drama, and instruction in rural crafts. In some ways he appears to have hoped that Merom would be the seed of a new type of theological seminary. In retrospect, the project is

44. Holt was a "regular" contributor to the *Christian Century,* both as an essayist and as an editorial writer. Most mainstream pastors would have had some familiarity with his work during the 1930s and 1940s.

45. Quoted in Dorn, "Rural Ideal," p. 55.

46. Quoted in Dorn, "Rural Ideal," p. 56.

difficult to evaluate. Jacob Dorn, who has done the most research into Holt's writings, sees Merom as an expression of Holt's almost limitless trust and admiration for rural people, and hence as part of the romanticism that lurked in the work of the hard-boiled sociologist. Yet, in retrospect, Merom had features that pointed to later developments in theological education, including the idea of an immersion experience, the need for seminaries to be true intellectual centers for the church, and the need for theological schools to have a distinctive ministry of advocacy. Perhaps romanticism and prophecy are not antithetical after all.

The need to address the training of rural ministers more adequately led to some important experiments in seminary cooperation. Perhaps the most important of these was the Interseminary Commission on Training the Rural Ministry, established in 1929 by Union (New York), Yale Divinity School, Andover-Newton, Boston University, and Bangor. The commission began when John D. Rockefeller, Jr., a major landholder on Maine's Mount Desert Island, wrote to the Congregational Church Extension Board for aid in staffing his summer church with the most capable person possible. The Congregationalists admitted that no one specialized in that type of preparation, and Rockefeller used his resources and contacts to bring about major discussions of why this was the case. The New England seminaries, in response to these probes, presented Rockefeller with a proposal for joint work in the area, and Rockefeller promised the schools $26,000 a year for three years with a possible renewal after an evaluation of their efforts. The result was a string of very able people in the New England area working on rural church problems. C. M. McConnell was appointed at Andover-Newton and Boston University, Malcolm Dana served both Yale and Hartford, and Ralph Adams served as director of research services and associate professor of rural church work at Bangor.[47]

The Interseminary Commission was particularly important in the history and development of field education. When the newly formed Association of Theological Schools wanted to study state-of-the-art supervision, it turned to the Interseminary Commission. What the commission accomplished in field education was not necessarily original — many of the basic ideas went back to Graham Taylor — but it implemented them over a large territory. Basically, the coordinated programs stressed the development of serious knowledge about local communities with careful supervision of the student's work. The commis-

47. Ironically, Bangor's isolation, which made it difficult to share a professor with a nearby school, worked to its advantage. The tendency to combine research and administrative positions in the commission with the Bangor professorship resulted in one of the premier library collections on rural church work.

sion also became the primary advocate of church federation in New England. Hilda Libby Ives, who, like most commission faculty, often served several seminaries at once, was the leading exponent of this approach, and she helped to create many of the federated churches in northern New England during the commission's heyday in the 1930s and 1940s.

The creative use of field education became the most important single impact of the rural church movement on seminaries as a whole. Part of the reality of seminary life in the 1930s and 1940s (and in some areas even to the present) was that students served small, rural churches while attending seminary. The rural church movement encouraged the seminaries to keep up with these students and their churches, to visit these churches periodically, and to take some responsibility for their health. Many seminary field educators became, in effect, rural bishops who were as important, if not more so, to many rural churches as their own denominational officials. The automobile made some of these professors modern Wesleys. Walter Cook of Bangor was one such traveler, always ready to visit one more rural stronghold of faith, complete with fishing pole and worldly wisdom. Garland Hendricks of Southeastern Baptist, toward the end of the period, was another.

The decision in the 1960s by the supporting seminaries to transform the Interseminary Commission for the Training of the Rural Ministry into the Interseminary Commission on Church and Community marked the beginning of a serious decline in seminary interest in the rural church. Although some rural church programs continued, the tendency was for funding to shift to church and community or to explicitly urban programs. Further, field education programs became less dependent on rural and small-church pastorates as a source of experience and scholarships.

The reasons for the decline of the rural church movement in seminaries were complex. In part, it had to do with the continuing decline of rural America. In crude terms, the rural market became less attractive. While the majority of Protestant churches remained small and rural — they still are — fewer of these churches were able to afford a highly trained minister or to appeal to graduates as a place where they could get important experience. The larger churches with their multiple staffs and important denominational connections were the best way to climb the ecclesiastical ladder.

It was also a matter of cultural context. The rural church did not seem to fit Kennedy's or Johnson's America, and sounded to many, more New Deal than Great Society. The decline in rural church programs was related to the theological and sociological trends. The seminaries were discovering the cities, and much of the pop theology of the 1960s was devoted to singing the praises of the urban experience or bemoaning the effects of the Protestant neglect of urban life. The seminaries turned from the rural churches to address the very serious crises in the cities, especially civil rights. Even the best seminaries found these problems daunting and expensive to address.

But if the problem were only a change in social context, the seminaries might have retained more of their rural programs. Theological change also played an important role in the decline of rural church studies. The ideal minister, according to rural church advocates, was an expert in the nitty-gritty of human social life, a combination of theologian, social worker, and advocate. By the 1960s this understanding was dated. Those seminarians attracted to the social sciences tended to envision a ministry in counseling, and those interested in social issues tended to define their work as social action. Mainstream theology was also austere and distant, and increasingly interested in locating theology on the cultural frontiers. Young clergy, steeped in the problems of the new hermeneutics of Heidegger and his successors, found the countryside less inviting than had their earlier liberal and neoorthodox counterparts. In other words, rural cultural lag was far greater when measured from a projected future than when calculated on a present baseline. Further, unlike evangelical Protestantism, which retained a lively relationship to American popular culture, mainstream Protestantism withdrew from it. Fosdick's radio programs had numerous rural listeners, but by the 1960s those expert in new media, including the very popular Billy Graham, were predominantly conservative.

The mainstream understanding of American religion also became less precise and more impressionistic. "Theology" came to be an easy synonym for religious talk about anything, and subsequently the value of the precise type of inquiry favored by the rural church movement had lesser, if any, value. Seminaries discontinued the "scientific study of religion" as soon as important retirements occurred. In this atmosphere it took almost twenty years for mainstream Protestant leaders to discover that they were losing members at an alarming rate.

One of the problems the descendants of giants face is that they never quite measure up to their predecessors. The theologians and ethicists of the late 1950s and 1960s lived in the shadow of the achievements of the Niebuhrs. Both Richard and Reinhold had a talent for combining the empirical and the theological into a coherent whole that has been and still is unfortunately unusual, a gift of God's most special providence. But their descendants did not recognize this talent as grace. Instead, they tried to do for their generation what they imagined that the Niebuhrs had done for theirs. Unlike the Niebuhrs, whose realism was rooted in the very concrete social realities of the 1930s and 1940s, their successors labored to bend theology to their situation. Theological and value-laden language became ever more common, and empirical language ever less so. The term "community" is a good example of this trend. Unlike "rural church" or "rural society," "community" meant everything from a circle of friends exchanging stories about the good old days, to people sharing a common vocation, to the traditional rural village. It could refer to everyone, and hence it referred to no one. The community in "church and community" was whatever group the theologian believed that he or she was addressing.

In short, the rural church movement in the seminaries burned out as theological and ecclesiastical fashions changed. From the time of Teddy Roosevelt to the 1960s, it was assumed that the Protestant churches were vital to rural America much as the African American churches were vital to people of color. The church carried rural culture, and its theology penetrated rural life. "Country" music, of course, continued to celebrate this close relationship in songs that mixed pathos and sentiment. But the Protestant churches, or at least their leaders and teachers, no longer heard the melody or provided the bass. The loss of expertise led to a loss of interest. Nashville did a better job of responding to the deepening rural crisis of the 1970s and 1980s than did the churches or their schools.

CHAPTER TWENTY-FOUR

Religious Education

In 1940 and 1941, two of America's most noted religious educators, H. Shelton Smith and Harrison Elliott, published books on the nature and future of their discipline. The two books were diametrically opposed. Smith's *Faith and Nurture,* polemical in tone and content, read like an exposé. Using his considerable historical and theological skills, Smith traced the failure of modern religious education back to its founders' untheological appropriation of what Smith called the "progressive" tradition, especially the pedagogy of American philosopher John Dewey. Although Smith maintained, both in this and later studies, that the religious educators' discovery of the importance of the psychology of religion was of permanent importance, he contended that the movement had substituted development and discovery for revelation. The Christian faith was about God's entry into history as much, if not more, than God's participation in natural processes.

In contrast, Harrison Elliott's misnamed *Can Religious Education Be Christian?* saw the type of neoorthodoxy favored by Smith as an incredible folly. With a historical sense that matched Smith's (and a personal knowledge of the field and of its pioneers that dated back to the early 1920s), Elliott found the origins of religious education in an attempt to apply what educators had learned from modern psychology and sociology to the church. As Elliott understood modernity, people had learned as much or more about human nature scientifically as they had learned about physical nature or biology. Although Elliott believed that reactionaries might try to turn back the clock, history was essentially unidirectional. While attempts to return to an earlier day might seem attractive to clergy fretful about their authority, all they could accomplish was to expose the church to the disdain of the educated people of the country. Despite the pessimism inspired by the Depression, scientific knowledge was here to stay.

The contemporary reader of these manifestos realizes that more was at stake than might first meet the eye. Both Smith and Elliott entered the combat firmly convinced that the future of the church, the seminary, and their shared intellectual discipline was at stake. Smith, of course, knew that he took the side that was growing in popularity. The Northern Presbyterian Church had already held the first official conversations that would lead to the Christian Faith and Life Curriculum, and other denominations were also anxiously reevaluating their church school programs. "Biblical theology," "ecclesiastical faith," and "let the church be the church" were part of the theological jargon that would dominate the discussion for the next two decades. Elliott recognized that he was on the defensive. Like his somewhat more philosophically idealistic near contemporary William E. Hocking, Harrison Elliott wrote as a representative of the moderate liberalism that was popular in the mainstream denominations. His book, originally a Yale doctoral thesis written under Luther Weigle and Hugh Hartshorne, was circulated before publication among the nation's leading liberal and realist theologians, including Union colleagues Reinhold Niebuhr, Henry Pitney Van Dusen, and Henry Sloane Coffin. Although no one could have spoken for such a theologically diverse group, Elliott wrote as much as their representative as in his own voice. He was proud of the solid liberal record of achievements, including the social gospel, the Federal Council of Churches, and the Layman's Report on Foreign Mission. Not the least of these achievements was the creation of a new style of religious education that an earlier generation had hailed as the "Saviour of the Churches."[1] A convinced modernist, Elliott appreciated this great tradition because its distinguished history suggested an even greater future.

As Elliott and Smith recognized, the debate cut to the very heart of American Protestant culture and its relationship to the increasingly secular world around it. For Smith the culture stood in perpetual danger of surrendering the gospel to a variety of pseudoreligions that threatened the human enterprise. No matter how remarkable the cultural achievement, the prophet had to stand opposed to these idolatrous elements. For Elliott, culture was the nutrient that supported the growth and development of human persons. While evil people and evil structures might corrupt parts of the human enterprise, they could not corrupt all of it.

If the positions they advocated seemed mutually exclusive, Smith and Elliott were right about the timely nature of the issues they were discussing. They stood at an important crossroads in the development of American reli-

1. Harrison Elliott, *Can Religious Education Be Christian?* (New York: Macmillan, 1940), p. 9.

gious education. By the 1950s many of the most important independent training schools for religious education professionals had merged with nearby seminaries or were in danger of closing. The position of religious education departments, highly regarded in the two earlier surveys of theological education, would likewise be altered. To theological faculties, newly in love with the apparent classicism of the neoorthodox movement, American religious education appeared to be an anomaly, strangely out of place in schools struggling to respond to the "strange new world within the Bible." Perhaps most ironically, many of the key ideas of earlier religious education, such as method, were reinterpreted by colleagues as "how to do it" tips and dismissed as somewhat less worthy of first-rate minds than exegesis, history, or theological speculation. In many congregations the larger debate over religious education was played out in local struggles between the pastor and the director of religious education. In these battles the pastor held almost all the important cards, especially sacral authority, and the result was that many directors of religious education became vagabonds or left the church. In many congregations the position itself was changed from a position in religious education to a more clerical assistant or associate pastor. Not surprisingly, religious educators responded by attempting to remake their discipline in a more "theological mode."

How had things come to this pass? What consequences were there for the larger development of theological education? Perhaps most important, what happened to the once fruitful dialogue between the social sciences and seminary leaders? Some perspective on these larger questions can be gathered from an overview of the development of the field of religious education and of its changing place in the larger ecology of American theological education.

I. An Aborted Beginning

When Horace Bushnell published his classical study *Christian Nurture* in the 1840s, he lived in a society that was numerically and culturally Protestant. Once one understands that, one can see that *Christian Nurture* was a Janus-like argument. Clearly, the book looked back romantically to Christendom and its institutions. Bushnell assumed that Christian ideals and practices had once penetrated every facet of life, and he hoped that the Victorian world's embrace of earlier patterns of virtue and social life might reproduce that earlier pattern. With its idealized picture of the middle-class household, presided over by a mother relatively free to nurture her children, *Christian Nurture* was an exercise in nostalgia and sentimentality, an example of the feminization of Victorian

Christianity.[2] Yet *Christian Nurture* was more than that. The book also looked toward a future. What was new was its rejection of the two leading theological understandings of how Christianity was transmitted: conversion and baptismal regeneration. For the advocates of both positions, the prospective believer was caught in the powerful grip of original sin that would eventually corrupt both mind and body. For the Puritans and their evangelical successors, one entered the faith through the narrow door of a conversion experience that broke down the boundary between human sin and divine righteousness. By its nature, even for the most passionate Wesleyan, this experience had a supernatural element that overcame the effects, if not the reality, of the original taint. Conversion was, consequently, a washing away or healing of sin. The other alternative was equally supernatural. For most Episcopalians and all Lutherans and Catholics, the sacrament of baptism was the means by which the grace of Christ was transmitted to the believer. The waters of baptism cleansed the infant of some of sin's power and penalty. In baptism the new Christian was thus regenerated and incorporated into the church.

Bushnell's problem with both of these was profound. Like his teacher Nathaniel Taylor, Bushnell did not accept the traditional doctrine of original sin. While sin was somewhat inevitable, given the limits of human life, it was not necessary, and a sacramental or ecclesiastical solution to the problem of sin was thus beside the point. But this left Bushnell with a serious problem. If sin and by extension grace and righteousness are not related to ontological or actual states, how can sin or grace enter human life? Bushnell's answer to this dilemma was through education. Bushnell suggested that a child, resident in a Christian culture, would absorb the faith through the interaction of all the cultural forces around the child. In short, the child would never know himself or herself to be anything but a Christian. Like other New Englanders, in love with the new belief in education as a primary means of social progress, Bushnell believed that the home, the school, the community, and the church formed a partnership that would direct the child in the right path. Since sin came from the failure of these institutions to properly provide for the child, educational progress was essential to the nation's moral growth.

2. Ann Douglas, *The Feminization of American Culture* (New York: Knopf, 1977), popularized this concept. Bushnell was one of her prime examples. Clearly, the book was also related to the cult of domesticity that was so important in upper middle-class life at the time.

II. Struggling with the Sunday School

Whether the idyllic world Bushnell described existed in his own day, it clearly did not exist after the Civil War. While remnants of the grand educational coalition envisioned by Bushnell continued, the moral link between schools, colleges, communities, and churches gradually weakened. Although the churches retained some influence in higher education, the new curricula being developed did not generally include courses in theology or Bible, and compulsory chapel was widely being abandoned.[3] Further, Protestant influence on the rapidly growing world of elementary and high school education waned. McGuffey's Readers, perhaps the best illustration of the pre–Civil War link between Protestant culture and education, were gradually replaced as American educators sought more secular alternatives.[4] Elements of Bushnell's world remained — especially the perceived link between education and moral progress — but that world was already more present in memory than in actual social structures.

In the post–Civil War world, Americans were already beginning to become aware of the consequences of their progressive abandonment of traditional European religious instruction. It was not clear what would take the place of catechism and confirmation. Conservative Episcopalians and Congregationalists, for instance, experimented with private schools that, like Arnold's Rugby, aimed at the formation of a social and economic elite. But, in the main, Protestants relied on the Sunday school and similar voluntary agencies. By the time of the Great War, the Sunday school was a visible symbol of Protestantism. Such noted leaders as Dwight L. Moody, Henry Jacobs, and John Vincent won their initial fame as Sunday school leaders. While the huge Sunday school parades attracted much attention, perhaps the most potent indicator of the cultural power of the Sunday school was the establishment of Chautauqua, the Sunday school "university."[5]

Among Disciples, Baptists, and Methodists, the Sunday school was occasionally a surrogate church. The popular denominations had covered the nation with a network of believers that was an inch deep and a mile wide. The ma-

3. This was not true at all schools, to be sure. Yale was noted for its chapel services, as were many women's colleges, including Wellesley.

4. For the history of the famous readers, see John H. Westerhoff, *McGuffey and His Readers: Piety, Morality, and Education in Nineteenth-Century America* (Nashville: Abingdon, 1978).

5. Robert W. Lynn and Elliot Wright, *The Big Little School: Sunday Child of American Protestantism* (New York: Harper and Row, 1971). Also see Anne M. Boylan, *Sunday School: The Formation of an American Institution* (New Haven: Yale University Press, 1988).

jority of their churches were small rural congregations, struggling from revival to revival, that were unable to pay even a poorly trained leader. With "preaching" held only every two, three, or four weeks, the Sunday school became the primary place where their members heard the gospel and offered prayer and praise.

Despite this outward success, all was not well in the Sunday school Zion. Like much of American Protestantism, the institution had acquired a strongly gendered character. The bulk of classes was taught by women, and even when Sunday school literature was written by males, it often breathed the bathos of late Victorian sentimentalism. At a time when women were generally less schooled than men, this meant that the Sunday school often functioned at a lower intellectual level than much of American public life. The schools, to be sure, benefited from the growth of education for women, especially the growth of the normal (teachers) schools, but the gap between the newspaper and Sunday school literature was evident to all.

Perhaps, more seriously, the heavily female character of the schools involved them and their teachers in the almost archetypical male drama of finding an identity beyond the home. To be a man was to enter the world on one's own terms, a drama that Mark Twain captured brilliantly in *Tom Sawyer.* For most males this process occurred in steps. First, the teenager acquired freedom from mother and the constraints of domestic life, and later, when he had acquired economic independence, he also became independent of his father. Finally, when he was able to support a household, he entered the domestic sphere. Leaving Sunday school behind was often the tentative first step in the drama of maturation, and the Sunday school was rarely able to shake off its place in this psychodrama. Given the needs of male adolescents to justify their actions, the schools themselves became the object of either demonization or sentimentalism; young men remembered them as intellectually sterile and morally vacuous or as part of an idealized childhood before they had to struggle with more adult matters.

This gendered drama had other repercussions throughout American Protestantism that influenced religious education. Such revivalists as Moody and Sankey unapologetically preached sermons to young men, often in their late twenties, urging them to "come home" to Jesus, mother, and the church. Other ministers counterbalanced the world of the feminized Sunday school with the "muscular Christianity" of Jesus, and the social gospel advocates urged men to discover that the gospel was intended for their world of business, politics, and society.

The Sunday school's gender crisis was accentuated by some related spiritual developments. Perhaps the most important of these was the declining place of the experience of conversion.[6] Despite Bushnell, American Sunday school leaders continued to argue that the Sunday school was not only the primary gate into church membership, but also an engine that drove many people to a conversion experience. This claim was clearly not always sustainable. First, significant numbers of American Protestants, including many of the brightest and best, did not have the expected experience. Some of the religious energy of the late Victorian period indeed may have come from an unconscious desire to substitute hours of frenzied activity for the "sweet hour of prayer" that had already become a sentimental memory. The failure of so many people to have the expected experience left a very hollow place in the hearts of many, and this was associated, for good or ill, with the Sunday school. At the same time, the new sciences of psychology and sociology were raising serious questions about the nature of conversion. Edwin Starbuck's *Psychology of Religion: An Empirical Study of the Growth of Religious Consciousness* (1899) — with an important preface by William James — demonstrated that many accounts of conversion could be best understood in terms of adolescent sexual guilt, especially over masturbation. In 1902 William James's Gifford Lectures identified conversion with the "twice-born soul's" self-healing of its sick soul. But if conversion was either not attainable by many or more a symbolic way of describing personal development, then the purposes of the Sunday school itself needed to be refined.

In short, by 1900 American Protestant educators were in a challenging position. Despite the outward prosperity of the churches, they saw their position in public education eroding and were aware of serious problems in their own congregational practices. In a more despairing or realistic age, they might have acquiesced in the situation or withdrawn into a Christian ghetto, but the 1890s were a flamboyant age, despite the fin de siècle atmosphere of decadence, and like the Student Volunteers, Protestant educators dreamed of the evangelization of the world in their generation, of growing prosperity, and of the continual progress generated by science and technology. It was not an age for regrets, apologies, or Jeremiahs.

III. James, Dewey, and Coe

These optimists had some very important resources ready at hand. For centuries philosophers and educators had struggled with the question of what and how human beings knew. Nineteenth-century theologians and educators

6. Anne Boylan, "The Role of Conversion in Nineteenth Century Sunday Schools," *American Studies* 20 (Spring 1975): 35-78.

tended toward either a Kantian understanding of the limited nature of human ideas or the more expansive idealism associated with Hegel. But, especially in English-speaking countries, the publication of Darwin's *Origin of Species* suggested to many another way forward.[7] Humans, like other living beings, lived and reproduced in a complex natural environment that taxed their capacity to survive its many dangers. In their struggle to live and reproduce, the human species discovered its ability to form ideas, theories, and patterns of cooperation. Over time the rich mental life engendered by these primitive struggles gave way to all the trappings of civilization and government that made human life more secure and enjoyable. The key elements in this equation were response, learning, and control.

Among the first to reflect on these implications for psychology was the talented American physician and philosopher William James. The scion of a talented and intellectually eclectic family, James published his two-volume *Principles of Psychology* in 1890, followed shortly thereafter by an abbreviated one-volume edition for classroom and general use. *The Principles of Psychology,* like many other epoch-making intellectual publications, was a creative summary of current thinking, put together by a first-rate mind.

James was quick to draw out many of the educational implications of modern psychology. To be sure, James was careful not to claim too much for his research. In his *Talks to Teachers,* James admitted freely — perhaps even disingenuously — that "Psychology is a science, and teaching is an art; and sciences never generate arts directly out of themselves. An intermediary inventive mind must make the application, by using its originality." Indeed, "the worst thing that can happen to a good teacher is to get a bad conscience about her profession because she feels herself hopeless as a psychologist."[8] But these reservations should not obscure James's enthusiasm for what psychology brought to the educational task. Since learning had a physical basis in the brain, teachers should be conscious of the contribution of activity and of health to the learning and developmental process. A good mind without a good breakfast produced a poor student, while a less able mind in a sound body might well master more complex materials than his better-endowed colleague. Batting a ball might not teach mathematics, but students who played ball might be more able to do

7. Perry Le Fevre, "Evolutionary Thought and American Religious Education," *Journal of Religion* 40 (1960): 296-308. The classic example of the impact of Darwinism is John Dewey's *The Influence of Darwin on Philosophy.* See John Dewey, *The Influence of Darwin on Philosophy, and Other Essays in Contemporary Thought* (Bloomington: Indiana University Press, 1965; original 1910).

8. William James, *Talks to Teachers on Psychology: And to Students on Some of Life's Ideals* (New York: H. Holt, 1907), chap. 1.

mathematics, because they had developed a strong sense of cause and effect and of the relative position of objects. Further, when one recognized that consciousness was not a constant state — that is, not identical with being awake — but a stream of thoughts, sensations, reactions, emotions, etc., one recognized that this stream has its high points and its low points. The teacher's task was to find ways, such as stories or effective blackboard use, to prepare the mind to learn by using all the senses. James recognized, as Dewey would also, that the priority of experience in shaping consciousness meant that education was not primarily the mastery of material. People learned as they experienced the world and used their prior learning to interpret their present experience. In effect, the purpose of learning was to equip the mind to learn from the next experience. Education was, consequently, a lifelong task. The old canard that the goal of modern education was more education was true. Learning was part of the nature of the human species and the key to its biological survival.

James's work was revolutionary in its implications. Perhaps one way to measure its import is to examine the intellectual development of two philosophers, John Dewey and George Albert Coe. In many ways Dewey, born just before the Civil War in 1859, was a young philosopher on the rise when he read James. After graduation from college and some experience as a high school teacher, he went to the new Johns Hopkins University where, although he did some work with G. Stanley Hall and Charles Peirce, he became a convinced idealist. A somewhat conventional Congregationalist who never had the expected conversion experience, Dewey was nonetheless moderately active in religious life, especially in those activities that involved youth and college students. His 1887 *Psychology* proposed a synthesis between Hegelian thought and the newer experimental thought of such contemporaries as Hall. Dewey struggled with the implications of psychology and, interestingly enough, with more theological issues through the 1890s. By the time he received an appointment at Harper's new University of Chicago in 1894, his direction was set: Dewey had accepted the new directions in psychology indicated by such thinkers as James, and he was ready to apply those insights to education. He established "the laboratory school" shortly after his arrival on his new campus to test his ideas. The school was, like much of the innovation around Chicago, not completely planned or adequately financed, but these shortcomings, as serious as they were, do not lessen the importance of this step. Education, already seen by many middle-class Americans as the future of the republic, was to become scientific and experimental. In 1899 Dewey published his famous *School and Society* in which he completed his theoretical formations by linking, as did much of American middle-class opinion, schooling with democracy and its values.

The parallels with the career of George Albert Coe are striking. Although

Coe was raised as a Methodist, he, like Dewey, did not have the expected conversion experience. Moreover, like Dewey, he had little difficulty accepting the theory of evolution. In his later years he noted, "I settled the question, as far as I was concerned, on a Sunday morning by solemnly espousing the scientific method, including it within my religion and resolving to follow it wherever it should lead."[9] While a student at Boston University, Coe recognized that the philosophy of Borden Parker Bowne contained a hidden apologetic, and he continued his studies at the University of Berlin. But Coe's interest in secular philosophy did not lessen his interest in religion. Like his contemporary William Hocking, with whom he shared so much spiritually, he had a passion for understanding religion and an appreciation of religion's ability to transform human life.[10] In 1900 Coe published his *Religion and the Spiritual Life,* a work that built on the work of such psychologists of religion as Edwin Starbuck, and in 1908 he published the essay "What Is Pragmatism?" in the *Methodist Quarterly Review* in which he announced his belief in a philosophy that dealt with the "rough and tumble of life." By this time Coe was already using his famous metaphors, "the Democracy of God" and "Salvation by Education."

IV. The Religious Education Association

Coe's thought was maturing in a crucial decade for the development of religious education. The period from 1900 to 1910 was crucial for the development of the new psychology as an academic discipline. In 1902 the International Sunday School Association voted not to develop a series of graded lessons but to retain the uniform lesson plan. To many, this seemed to fly in the face of all that contemporary educators and psychologists had learned about childhood religious development. Among those shocked by this decision was William Rainey Harper, president of the University of Chicago. Harper, whose keen mind realized that more was at stake than a method of curriculum development, persuaded the Council of Seventy, the leadership of the American Institute of Sacred Literature, an organization of biblical scholars, to call a meeting of all those interested in the current status of Christian education. As often was the case, Harper had read the Protestant psyche well. The meeting was enthusiastically attended and brought together people from all areas of Protestant edu-

9. H. Shelton Smith, "George Albert Coe: Revaluer of All Values," *Religion in Life* 22 (1952): 40-57, here p. 49.

10. Hocking was, of course, philosophically different from Coe. He was a convinced idealist while Coe was more of a pragmatist.

cational life, from college and university presidents to Sunday school teachers. The assembled group quickly organized itself as the Religious Education Association (REA) and adopted a statement of purpose: "To inspire the educational forces of our country with the religious ideal; to inspire the religious forces of our country with the educational ideal; and to keep before the public mind the ideal of religious education, and the sense of its need and value." A number of departments were formed, including special departments devoted to the public schools, to colleges, to seminaries, and of course, to the Sunday school. Not surprisingly, given its origins and leadership, the REA tended toward the more progressive position on these issues.

Like so much of Harper's empire, the REA had few resources other than the good will of what progressives called the "religious public," and it might have died shortly after its founder did in 1905 had not Henry Cope become executive secretary in 1906. Cope served until 1923. Cope, an energetic English Baptist, tackled the problems of the association with gusto and made its journal, *Religious Education,* first published in 1906, an indispensable publication for seminary libraries. Although he was not the only person to recognize the need for a new professionalism in religious education, he was a clear and consistent advocate of that step. Cope saw professionalism resting on four foundations: "first on a rational developed consciousness of a definite and specific social function; second, upon a growing body of scientifically ascertained knowledge which leads to certain specialized skills; third, upon group cooperation in research and experimentation, and fourth, upon social recognition of its function."[11] In other words, Cope believed that religious educators should receive a similar education to public school teachers and administrators.

The drive for professionalism affected religious education at all levels. At its most basic, it was a concern for the new ministry of religious education in local churches. As Protestant churches in cities and suburbs grew numerically and financially, some began to hire a second staff person in religious or Christian education. Among the first to serve were such people as William Boocock, the founder of the Association of Directors of Religious Education; Herbert Evans of Second Baptist, St. Louis; and Horace Greeley Smith, St. James Methodist Church, Chicago. From 1912, when perhaps 12 people served in such a capacity, to 1926, when over 800 served, the numbers of people serving in this specialized ministry steadily increased. Such persons, Cope believed, should be recognized as having their own specialty apart from that of the pastoral ministry. "The assistant-pastor-director plan will not work. This is the day of specialization:

11. Henry F. Cope, "The Professional Organization of Workers in Religious Education," *Religious Education* 16 (1921): 166.

the pastor is a specialist in his field and should not dishonour it by expecting that one trained in another field can lightly step in and do his particular work. The director is a specialist and the advantages of this special training should be conserved for his own field, a difficult and sufficiently important one, calling for all his powers."[12] Like Harper, Cope wanted professional religious educators employed at different levels. Like many members of the REA, he remained deeply concerned about religion in the public schools and in the nation's colleges and universities.

V. Yale and Union

The person who exemplified Cope's drive for professionalism was the Lutheran dean of Yale Divinity School, Luther Weigle. Weigle was a member of one of the earliest and best-equipped religious education departments of his day. Yale's department had followed a typical evolution. Dean Frank Sanders, a close friend and coworker of Harper, was the first president of the REA and took an active role in promoting the new discipline. Beginning with guest lecturers in Christian education, Sanders gradually expanded Yale's offerings until a full course was available in 1908. By 1910 Yale student demand had led to the creation of a full department. In 1915 that department had an impressive list of courses: "courses offered in general pedagogy cover principles of education and educational hygiene, educational psychology, methods and courses of study, and school organization. Under religious pedagogy, courses cover principles and methods in religious education, the history and materials of religious education, the psychology of adolescence, and the leadership of bible-study groups."[13] Charles Foster Kent, one of the pioneers in the development of college teaching in religion and a friend of Harper, was among the active members of this department. Yale's curriculum, one of the first to offer what would later be called vocational tracks, had two early programs in religious education: a one-year program for nonordained church workers and a bachelor of divinity in religious education for those entering the ministry.

In the 1920s Weigle expanded Yale's program. Reasoning that the key to religious education as a profession was the development of a competent body of advanced teachers and researchers, Weigle created a strong doctoral program

12. Quoted in Dorothy Jean Furnish, *DRE/DCE — the History of a Profession* (N.p.: Christian Education Fellowship, United Methodist Church, 1976), p. 21.

13. Frank Ward, "Religious Education in the Theological Seminaries," *Religious Education* 10 (1915): 436.

in religious education to train new faculty members. In addition, he began publication of the Yale Studies in Religious Education. While many volumes in the series were his students' dissertations, the series demonstrated that religious education could generate a literature comparable in quality to that produced in other academic disciplines.[14]

Weigle's Yale was not alone, of course, in this development. The close relationship between Union Theological Seminary and Columbia Teachers College permitted that seminary to accomplish similar goals. The Union–Teachers College alliance was a natural. Not only were the two institutions adjacent to one another after both moved uptown to Morningside Heights, but the two schools had other, more personal relationships. Teachers College developed from a vocational college for young women, originally established by Grace Hoadley Dodge, the daughter of Union trustee and benefactor William Dodge. As a trustee of the Kitchen Garden Association, Ms. Dodge realized that the needs of young women were changing, and in 1884 she transformed that association into the Industrial Education Association. She became a passionate advocate of vocational training in the schools and was appointed to the New York City School Board in 1887. In that same year, Nicholas Murray Butler became the salaried head of the Industrial Education Association, while retaining his position as a professor of philosophy at Columbia College, and they worked together to remake the association as the New York City College for the Training of Teachers. In 1891 the school became Teachers College and affiliated with Columbia. Perhaps because of the intense religious character of Ms. Dodge, Teachers College was interested in religious education before its affiliation with Union. The Sunday school that later became the Union School of Religion was originally an experimental Sunday school associated with Teachers College. George Coe, who became Union's professor of religious education in 1909, was particularly interested in the connection with Teachers College because of his belief that religious educators needed credentials, such as the M.A. and Ph.D., that had status in the secular world.

The Union School of Religion was an important part of the professionalization of religious education. Clearly drawing on Dewey's experimental school at Chicago, on the insights of the child study movement, and on the educational psychology of Teachers College's Edward Thorndyke, the school fashioned goals and objectives that were almost a meditation on the word "experimental." The school was unmatched in its devotion to the methods of observation, statistics, and record keeping. Hugh Hartshorne, Coe's associate at

14. See Robert Lynn, "The Uses of History: An Inquiry into the History of an American Religious Education," *Religious Education* 67 (Mar.-Apr. 1972): 83-97.

Union, was particularly interested in the creation of a body of data about how children learned religion and moral habits. In this sense the school was part of the larger interests of both Union and Teachers College. Coe himself saw the school as providing a place where students could test the psychology they had learned in college in the crucible of experience. Coe wrote: "[T]he laboratory method requires my students to sharpen their psychology far beyond the standards of the college course in psychology. It requires them to deal with some of their philosophical and theological concepts in a definite, analytical way that tests one's grasp as few things can test it."[15] The school was definitely on the side of what Coe called "transformative" education, using art, story, discussion, play, and other student activities as part of its program. In addition, the school experimented with curriculum, methods of teaching, and graded worship experiences. Finding substitutes for such ineffective practices as the "Sunday school assembly" was a major task of the school. Hartshorne's *Book of Worship for the Church School* and his very popular *Stories for Worship and How to Follow Them Up* were products of these attempts to find alternatives to the Sunday school assembly.[16] Perhaps the most important variation on the theme of experiment, at least for the history of theological education, was the school's determination to provide seminary students with hands-on experience in dealing with children and young people. Coe believed that such experience might enable the minister to "enter into the life of his Sunday school not as an outsider, but as its most vital and progressive member. He will be able to understand what he sees and learns."[17] Sarah Fahs stated the goals of the Union School in language that identified it with the educational methods of other professions: "This was a practice school. It was analogous to a hospital for doctors. . . . The purpose of the school was primarily to afford an opportunity for the theology students to become aware of the problems of religious education and to have some experience in developing skill in meeting those problems."[18]

The ultimate meaning of experiment in the Union School was more audacious. Coe saw himself as a religious and social reformer as well as an educator. In his *Religion of a Mature Mind* Coe spelled out his (and many other reli-

15. George A. Coe, quoted in Kim Younglae, *Broken Knowledge: The Sway of the Scientific and Scholarly Ideal at Union Theological Seminary in New York, 1887-1926* (Lanham, Md.: University Press of America, 1997), p. 152.

16. Hugh Hartshorne, *Book of Worship for the Church School* (New York: Scribner, 1915); *Stories for Worship and How to Follow Them Up* (New York: Scribner, 1921).

17. George Albert Coe, "The Theological Seminary: The Laboratory Method in the Department of Religious Education," *Religious Education Association Journal* 7 (1912): 423.

18. Quoted in Harris Parker, "The Union School of Religion, 1910-1929: Embers from the Fires of Progressivism," *Religious Education* 88, no. 4 (Fall 1991): 60.

gious educators') theological foundations: "salvation by education" and "the democracy of God." These concepts were the best resolution of the ancient debates over faith and works. "[Y]et one thing that Christianity can never do, it cannot let education alone. The debate over salvation by works and salvation by faith may seem to exhaust the alternatives, yet there always remains a back lying assumption that the world's salvation is to be accomplished partly by educating the young."[19] Unlike either works or faith, education dealt with the development of a whole person. Vital faith was not so much what one believed or what one did as who one was. Following his mentor at Boston, Coe believed that personality provided the foundation that united thinking and acting. In fact, the less theologically faith was expressed, the more authentic it was likely to be. In an interesting aside, Coe noted: "Bushnell saw that Religion goes deeper than the reason and the deliberate will, which develop relatively late in life, and that the spiritual life is strongest when it is most akin to habit and instinct. Further, he saw, as did Aristotle, that virtue need not always be a product of insight or conscious choice."[20] Education in the sense of providing the foundations of personality was the way in which God worked in the midst of human history: "Salvation by education is a possibility and a fact because education is not merely something that we do to and for the child, and not merely this united with the child's own efforts for himself. God is the central reality of the whole. He is the moving force, the giver of the inner law, and the goal of all human development. Through education he extends his saving grace to the child."[21] Ecclesiologically, this meant that the Christian movement, considered as an educational reality, was much broader than the Christian churches themselves and included all those organizations that shaped and molded human personality. Thus, Coe was as concerned about the ethos of a "Christian" college's football team as he was about the formal instruction the college provided in the Bible. If the team's ethos was victory at any price, it had stepped outside of its professed Christian commitment.

As Coe stated in his 1917 textbook, *A Social Theory of Religious Education,* the purpose of religious education was: "The . . . growth of the young toward and into mature and efficient devotion to the democracy of God, and happy self-realization therein." The two primary elements in this famous summary, the democracy of God and happy self-realization, pointed to the heart of Coe's understanding of education. Participation — the dialectic interaction of per-

19. George A. Coe, *The Religion of a Mature Mind* (Chicago and London: Fleming H. Revell and Co., 1902), p. 2.

20. Coe, *Religion,* p. 303.

21. Coe, *Religion,* p. 319.

sons with other persons and the world — was the key to learning. As the theory of evolution so clearly demonstrated, the human brain was an interactive organism that reached out to the world through the organs of sense and directed the person as the person acted in the world. Thus, Coe believed, one led students to religious experience by having them interact with people who had religious experiences. Harrison Elliott, Coe's often overlooked successor at Union, developed this into a consistent theory of the application of group dynamics to the practice of education.[22] Group participation was not the same as the academic seminar in which specialists or want-to-be specialists poured over each other's research, hunting for flaws in method, content, or — as a last resort — grammar. Rather, it was the class organized as a democracy in which each individual brought unique experiences to the table and shared those experiences with others. Hopefully, in the midst of this interaction, the persons involved would be changed by their encounter with each other and with other points of view. Like the good Methodists that both Coe and Elliott were, they hoped participation in such democratic experiences would produce more vital and lively believers. Religious education was more town meeting than the droll memorizations of the traditional Sunday school, and many religious educators followed Coe in both his stress on democracy and his confidence that democratic forms of religious education would increase, rather than decrease, the power of religious faith in individual lives.

Although Coe and Elliott were not metaphysical thinkers in the traditional sense of that term, they recognized that the idea of the democracy of God had theological implications. Both believed that God was a participant in the educational process and that whatever primacy might attach to the divine, the group as a whole determined its own course. Did this mean that God was also learning from God's experience of the world? Alfred North Whitehead, who developed his unique understandings of metaphysics in a series of books written in the 1920s, believed so. For Whitehead, God changed as a result of God's participation in the "actual occasions" of nature, a metaphysical idea similar to Coe's concept of the democracy of God. Similar ideas were also advanced by Charles Hartshorne, whose work also owed much to Charles Peirce and pragmatism.

22. Harrison Elliott, *The Why and How of Group Discussion* (New York: Association Press, 1920); Harrison Elliott, *The Process of Group Thinking* (New York: Association Press, 1928); Harrison Elliott, *Group Discussion in Religious Education* (New York: Association Press, 1939).

VI. Conservative Religious Educators

Perhaps the most interesting thing about religious education is the way it early impacted normally conservative institutions. Like Yale, Louisville's Southern Baptist Theological Seminary first established a lectureship in religious education and then moved toward a full professorship. What was different at Louisville was the role of the denomination in this process. President E. Y. Mullins entered into a financial partnership with the Southern Baptist Sunday School Board in which Southern Baptist Theological Seminary and the board shared the expenses and the control of the new discipline. Nor was the denominational input nominal. Mullins very much wanted to invite Henry Cope to lecture at the seminary, but the board felt that Cope's views were too liberal for it to endorse, and Cope was not invited. In 1906 Mullins created the first chair of religious education in a seminary (the earlier appointments at Hartford had been to a separate school within the Hartford Seminary Foundation), and appointed Byron DeMent, then of Furman University, to the position. The chair, which later became the Basil Manly Chair of Sunday School Pedagogy, attracted some prominent religious educators, including Gaines Dobbins and, after World War II, Findlay Edge.[23] Ironically, considering the intellectual quality of the religious education faculty, religious education was marginal at Southern Seminary, which regarded itself as "a school of the prophets" and was primarily involved in training preachers and teachers for Baptist colleges.

Another conservative institution that early invested heavily in religious education was Fort Worth's Southwestern Baptist Theological Seminary. Although many First Baptist churches in Southern cities tended to be large, Texas Baptist churches often had more than five hundred active members. While frequently theologically conservative, these churches tended to be very open to the various new forms of congregational life developed during the early twentieth century. Modeling themselves on the institutional churches of the North, particularly Chicago, these large congregations had all the trappings of big-city church life — multiple Sunday services, large robed choirs, spacious buildings, church parlors, and expansive Sunday schools. When such churches considered adding new staff members, their leaders' thoughts naturally turned to someone to work with the Sunday school. This decision may have been aided by the denomination's Sunday school board's resolute campaign to have the pastor, not the superintendent or later the director of religious education, seen as the ultimate super-

23. K. Stephen Combs, "The Course of Religious Education at the Southern Baptist Theological Seminary, 1902-1953: A Historical Study" (Ph.D. diss., Southern Baptist Theological Seminary, 1978), p. 96.

visor of the Sunday school. Such clearly hierarchical understandings of pastoral authority lessened the possibility of those conflicts between pastor and director and confirmed the pastor as the ultimate leader of the congregation.

Religious education grew rapidly in the Fort Worth seminary. The department was established in 1915, and its first professor, J. M. Price, expanded the program rapidly. In 1920 he stepped outside the pastoral curriculum and established a bachelor of religious education program; in 1921 he added a master of religious education and reorganized his department as a separate school with its own administration. In 1925 enough faculty had been hired to justify the division of this school into departments.[24]

Southwestern's development of a school of religious education made it the dominant force in Southern Baptist religious education for much of the twentieth century. Despite the prestige of Southern, Southwestern supplied the bulk of the ministers of religious education as well as many of the leaders of the Sunday school board.

With the exception of Princeton, Southern Baptist openness to religious education was mirrored across the more conservative side of the American religious spectrum. Philadelphia's Eastern Baptist Seminary developed its religious education program throughout the 1930s and 1940s and made it a major feature of the institution. Later, religious education would be a strongly featured part of the "neo-evangelical" movement. While it may not be possible to offer definitive reasons for the fascination of American conservatives with religious education, the question deserves serious examination.

Part of the answer lies in the capacity of modern people to compartmentalize life. Since the popular wisdom was that religious education was mainly about "how to do it," both students and faculty could disregard the considerable intellectual apparatus that supported the field. Gerald B. Smith of Chicago told the story of a young divinity student who found the lack of traditional content in his theological courses frustrating. The student's problem, however, was removed when he realized that "what is said in this class shocks me as theology until I remember that in religious education the same things seem all right." Since so many of the ideas in religious education, such as the need for lessons to be developmentally appropriate, were part of the common wisdom of educated people, few people asked for the warrants that made such ideas believable. Like the coins in their pockets, they assumed that others would accept them at face value.

Another reason conservatives were able to absorb so much of the reli-

24. See Ralph D. Churchill, "The History and Development of Southwestern's School of Religious Education to 1956" (Ph.D. diss., Southwestern Baptist Theological Seminary, 1956).

gious education movement was their tendency to live in intellectual ghettos. Southern Baptist religious educators, although they often attended the summer schools at Chicago and Union and occasionally even earned advanced degrees from those institutions, did not join the REA. While this may have been, in part, a reaction to the "modernism" of the leadership, it was also because Southern Baptists rejected almost all ecumenical activity, including the Federal Council of Churches. Accreditation, however, was one area where cooperation was possible and desirable, and Southern Baptists took leadership positions in the Association of Schools of Religious Education until it was absorbed by the American Association of Theological Schools in the 1960s. A similar pattern often obtained among Southern Baptist intellectuals who might be and often were avid readers in their disciplines but did not take active roles in such groups as the Society of Biblical Literature or the American Society of Church History. A similar pattern was found among other non-Princetonian conservatives.

In a sense, "progressivism" and "pragmatism" are very loose terms. Particularly in the South, many theological and racial conservatives were remarkably progressive when the issues did not touch Southern particularities. Woodrow Wilson was the most important Southern hero after the Civil War generation, and Roosevelt was almost as popular. Before the 1980s, many Southern theological conservatives were progressive democrats. All in all, social class was a more important predictor of early twentieth-century political activity than religious affiliation, liberal or conservative. Granted this, the ability of conservative religious ideals to dwell side by side with liberal ideas about church efficiency was no more striking than the ability of faith in the Tennessee Valley Authority to lie cheek by jowl with a distrust of evolution.

Further, while one does not want to discount the high quality of the abstract arguments of Peirce, James, Dewey, and others, pragmatism was an American theology that expressed the common wisdom of a nation built on the can-do principle. Americans took easily to systems of thought that were metaphysically lean and practically plump. If the functioning of an idea did not determine its truth or value, it did determine its usability. After all, advertisers made a fortune in the 1920s by applying various psychological theories to the hawking of goods.

But whether any or all of this reflection proves to be accurate, American conservative theologians and religious educators made an alliance in the 1920s and 1930s. This odd-couple marriage was the beginning of the reconciliation of evangelicalism and American culture that many associate with the World War II conservative movement. From religious education (always carefully referred to as Christian education by conservatives), it was only a short step for evangelicals and their institutions to make their peace with psychology, counseling, and other aspects of American middle-class culture.

VII. Decline

Just as it was on the verge of merging its accrediting functions with those of the American Association of Theological Schools, the Association of Schools of Religious Education heard this gloomy picture of the present state of its discipline:

> Any low ranking of Christian Education courses (as being the cute "how to" kind) in the eyes of faculty and others may cause a minister to low rate the educational work in his mind; this may make for difficulty working with a director, and for his own lack of communicating to his workers a respect of this task. Jesse Ziegler in his reporting his regional meetings for the AATS says "It is not easy to find a theological school where it is Christian education that the students are excited about and where the professor of that field carries the major influence with his faculty colleagues" — He points to the fault as the almost universal "degeneration of all 'how to'" subjects within the curriculum.[25]

Reading that statement after carefully reading the works of George A. Coe, Harrison Elliott, Lewis Sherrill, and J. M. Price raises serious questions. American religious educators were thoughtful intellectuals in dialogue with the best scientific and philosophical thinking of their time. About the results of the social sciences, for example, they were far ahead of their contemporaries in such departments as Bible and systematic theology that, with very few exceptions, were locked into literary and philosophical approaches to religion. Indeed, the statement — particularly the Ziegler quote — is almost perverse in its misunderstanding. For the religious educators, method was the careful application of psychological and social theory to the concrete tasks of teaching, ministering to youth or college students, and conducting an adult education class. If we know that a three-year-old child is not capable of grasping such an abstract theological idea as eternal damnation, then it is no more proper to introduce that idea than to expect the child to be able to write or draw with a narrow pencil that his or her tiny fingers cannot grasp. Like-

25. Wesner Fallaw, in American Association of Schools of Religious Education Records, assembled by Patrick Carmichael in 1966, p. 308. The interior Ziegler quotation is from "The Vocation of Theological Education," *Religious Education*, Nov.-Dec. 1961, pp. 400-401.

wise, if one knows that marriages tend to reach a crisis point in their fifth year, this knowledge may be far more useful in preserving marriage than all the exegesis of Matthew 5:32. What had happened to bring things to this pass? Had religious education deteriorated or had something else colored the opinions of many theological educators?

The 1930s were a very hard decade for religious education, and the discipline never completely recovered from the American religious depression. Some of the problems were internal to the discipline itself. The most important of these was the failure of the character education movement.

American Protestants have always had a nostalgia for McGuffey's Eclectic Readers. The readers, which sold 122 million copies, seemingly witnessed to an America in which community, school, and church worked together to educate good citizens. The yearning for that simpler America was particularly strong in the 1920s as American young people openly experimented with new styles of morality, and as rising incomes permitted more and more people the luxury of a four-year resident college education. The media, especially the radio and the movies, depicted this moral experimentation with glamour and excitement. Even the organized crime figures that profited from the sale of illegal alcohol became larger than life folk heroes engaged in a running battle with authority. To make matters worse, army tests of the religious knowledge and practice of young men entering into military service in England and the United States yielded a bleak picture. Few had even the most rudimentary knowledge of Christian faith as measured by such criteria as the ability to name biblical books, persons, or teachings. Many Americans had a deep sense that the foundations of personal character and morality were crumbling.

In response, both Christian and secular education took up "character education." The basic idea of character education was that the schools should find ways to inculcate moral training, at least around such common virtues as personal honesty, into their programs of study. Religious educators, who had long worried about the secularization of the public schools, were particularly intrigued by the possibilities that this offered for their discipline. Character education seemed to transcend religious particularity. This made it particularly attractive to religious educators who had moved in the same direction. By the mid-1920s the REA included Catholic and Jewish members, and the editors of *Religious Education* were careful to see that articles reflecting Jewish and Catholic emphases and concerns were regularly included. Further, American religious liberalism tended to see a moral life, especially the development of a Christlike character, as the goal of religious faith. Character education seemed a way to approach these larger goals.

According to Heather Warren, character education was the principal topic among 1920s religious educators.[26] While religious educators shared an apparent consensus about what they hoped schools would achieve, there was much debate about whether to have separate classes designed to promote character or to incorporate character education into the regular program. In addition, how the churches ought to be involved in the larger task was the subject of endless debate, and finally of court cases, as different stratagems were tried and found wanting. J. M. Artman, Cope's successor as executive secretary, pressed hard to rename the journal *Character Education,* and while this failed, he did succeed in having the association sponsor a second journal by that name.

Not all religious educators were impressed by the emphases. Such leaders as Boston University religious educator Walter Althern questioned the character education movement from the beginning, as did Coe, to a lesser extent. As criticism grew, Rockefeller's Institute of Social and Religious Research commissioned Hugh Hartshorne, recently dismissed from Union and hired by Yale, and Mark A. May, his Yale faculty colleague and a specialist in character education, to study the existing programs. In *Studies in the Nature of Character* — three volumes: *Studies in Deceit, Studies in Self-Control,* and *Studies in the Organization of Character* — Hartshorne and May presented massive empirical evidence that existing programs of character education were not improving the moral life of children and young people. As Harrison Elliott later summarized the findings: "Those who conducted the research came to the conclusion that the moral education which these children had received had resulted in no general moral standards which controlled their conduct. They concluded that their moral knowledge was unrelated to the situations in which it would be used and had as a result little or no effect upon conduct."[27] In retrospect, Hartshorne and May's intellectual honesty represented the moral triumph of the ideals of their discipline. Educators, including Christian educators, had claimed that education had to be rigorously evaluated using empirical methods. When the two researchers did that, they found that their own discipline had been measured and found wanting.

Hartshorne and May's conclusions were published just as the Depression began. By the early 1930s, religious educators were acknowledging that their field was in a crisis.[28] In part, what was happening was the old, old story in

26. Heather Warren, "Character, Public Schooling, and Religious Education, 1920-1934," *Religion and American Culture* 7 (Winter 1997): 61-80.

27. Elliott, *Can Religious Education?* p. 47.

28. For a sampling of the literature, see George A. Coe, "The Present Crisis in Religious Education," *Religious Education* 28 (Apr. 1933): 181-85; Hugh Hartshorne, "A Study of the Status of Religious Education," *Religious Education* 27 (Mar. 1932): 245-47; P. H. Hayward, M. N. English, et al., "What the Depression Is Doing to the Cause of Religious Education," *Religious Edu-*

American life: last hired were first fired. At a period when many local churches were overburdened by debts on their buildings, decreasing revenue made hard choices necessary. The natural decision in such conflicts was either to dismiss the director of Christian education, not to replace a director who left, or to greatly reduce the compensation offered for the position. By the time congregations, at least in the mainstream denominations, had recovered sufficiently to hire directors of religious education, the discipline had lost much of the excitement of its early days. In many theological schools, also, religious educators learned that the old adage, last hired, first fired, was still in play.

As a result of these pressures, religious education, especially in the parishes, underwent a transformation. Although religious education had attracted many women in the 1920s, the 1930s saw the profession become a "pink ghetto." Furnish estimates that in 1938, only 26 percent of the profession were men and 74 percent were women.[29] While the percentages of seminary teachers of religious education were not as gender-weighted, seminaries often appointed their first woman faculty member to the position in religious education. As with directors of religious education, this decision was at least partially economic. Women, especially single women, worked for considerably less than their male counterparts. Further, the few opportunities for women in religious vocations meant that many women faculty members, such as Georgia Harkness, who began her career in religious education, were extraordinarily skilled.[30] Nonetheless, the feminization of religious education in the 1930s, like the earlier feminization of elementary education, lowered the prestige both of practitioners and of theorists. In subtle ways feminization also eroded the political position of religious education professors on many faculties. If the professor was male, he was regarded as teaching in a "female" profession; if a woman, she was disregarded because of gender. Common gender stereotypes drifted from women in general to religious educators in particular.

Gender-related problems also dogged the profession in other ways. In 1950 Wesner Fallaw noted that religious educators tended to serve only two or three years in any given assignment and that tensions between pastors and religious ed-

---

cation 27 (Dec. 1932): 873-86; John K. Norton, "Education in the Depression," *Religious Education* 29 (Jan. 1934); Hugh Hartshorne, Helen R. Stearns, and W. Uphaus, *Standards and Trends in Religious Education* (New Haven: Yale University Press, 1933).

29. Furnish, *DRE/DCE*, p. 39.

30. Among the women graduates of the Boston University School of Religious Education were Georgia Harkness, who taught at Garrett and Pacific School of Religion; Hulda Niebuhr (New York University and McCormick Theological Seminary); Blanche Carrier of the University of Pittsburgh; Goldie McCue of Ohio Wesleyan; Ethel Tilley of Hastings and Meredith Colleges; Rhoda Edmeston of Scarritt; and Edna Baxter of Hartford Seminary Foundation.

ucators were frequently reported.[31] Outside of the Southern Baptist Convention, religious education programs in seminaries were marketed to female students, and some schools added or strengthened religious education programs to have a place for women students they had barred from, or at least discouraged from taking, the bachelor of divinity program. Partly to encourage men to study religious education, Southern Baptist Seminary, where religious education operated under the additional disadvantage of not fitting the school's self-understanding as a school for preachers, experimented in the 1950s with a religious education degree done in conjunction with the basic pastoral degree. The B.D. with Religious Education, later the M.Div. with Religious Education, combined two years of classical theological study with one year (thirty hours) of religious education.

Depression-era finances also greatly weakened the REA and changed its character. From its beginning, the REA was not the voice of the scholarly guild of religious educators. The Association of Professors and Researchers in Religious Education, established later, would be that type of organization. Rather, the REA was intended to be a broad coalition uniting all those interested in its mission. Hence, the organization had its own paid executive secretary, its serious (but not necessarily scholarly) journal, and a library. By 1935 the association was in debt $23,975.93. Skilled negotiations led the creditors to reduce that by 60 percent, with the debt committee agreeing to mount a vigorous fund-raising campaign. Despite generous gifts from members of the board, the association was unable to make its payments in 1938, and the creditors agreed on a onetime payment of $6,751.00 as meeting the obligation.[32] The result was a shift to voluntary leadership. Orville L. Davies described the change:

> REA was in a crisis. Artman's resignation was accepted, effective June 30, 1935. With income greatly reduced the program must be curtailed. What now? Discontinue? "No," said the Rochester Convention, because the historic function of the Association remained unchanged. Reorganized with Hugh H. Hartshorne as president, E. J. Chave as chairman of the Board and of the Executive Committee, H. S. Elliott as chairman of the Editorial Committee, the sails were set for voluntary leadership which helped the lightened vessel to weather the storm on a minimum budget and small office expenditure. Here was proof of the adhesive strength of a strong, determined pioneering fellowship.[33]

31. Wesner Fallaw, "The Roles of Ministers and Directors of Christian Education," *Religious Education* 9 (1950): 41-44.

32. *Religious Education,* no. 34 (1939): 115; Orville L. Davies, "A History of the Religious Education Association," *Religious Education* 44 (1949): 41-54.

33. Davies, "A History," p. 51.

Despite Davies' almost chipper description, the crisis had deep symbolic significance. Like social action, religious education was an intensely public enterprise that prided itself on its central position in American religious life. During the early years of the organization, its membership roles and annual meetings were almost a who's who in American educational and ecclesiastical life. By the midtwenties the leadership of the organization was shifting toward academic teachers of religious education, although valiant efforts were made to retain some of its lay character. After 1935, although the organization retained vitality, its marginal status was evident.

The 1930s decade was also a period of intense theological debate in which the religious educators found themselves on the losing side. In a sense these problems began at an improbable place, New York's Union Theological Seminary. In 1923, after a dispute between Coe and the new president, Henry Sloane Coffin, over the granting of tenure to Hugh Hartshorne and over Coe's radical proposals to reorganize the curriculum, Union's department of religious education recovered.[34] Harrison Elliott, although lacking Coe's creative brilliance, was a highly skilled theologian and educator in his own right with extensive experience in YMCA work. Elliott's coming did not mark a major transition in Union's program. Not only did he share many of Coe's ideas, but Coe was still on Morningside Heights as a professor at Teachers College, and Dewey's influence on New York education was felt everywhere.

The event that marked the new order at Union was the discontinuation of the experimental Union School. In 1928 a student named Spear Knebel conducted an Eastern worship service that compared the resurrection of Christ with the story of Attis Cybele (this story is related in more detail in chapter 18).[35] Coffin was genuinely outraged. Although he knew that such ideas were not uncommon in the then-reigning history-of-religions school of biblical interpretation, he did not feel that they were either proven sufficiently or faithful enough to the tradition to be featured at an Easter children's service. He immediately fired off a letter to Elliott stating his objections, and the school became the center of a protracted debate over the nature of academic freedom at Union. When the smoke cleared, Elliott had lost the battle, and in 1929 he "voluntarily" closed the school. His associate, Sarah Fahs, the principal of the experimental school, continued to teach at Union but, along with Union's other well-known "part-time" teacher, Harry E. Fosdick, retreated to the comparative safety of the new Riverside Church.

34. Brian A. Tippen, "A Historical Look at the Succession of Major Professors of Religious Education at Union Theological Seminary," *Religious Education* 88, no. 4 (1993): 503-22.

35. Parker, "Union School of Religion," p. 605.

Coffin's distaste for the more radical experiments of his colleagues came at the same time that Americans began to read and appreciate the new European theology associated with Barth, Brunner, Tillich, and, later, Bultmann. Over the next decade this theology would become more prominent and gain adherents at almost all American theological schools — Chicago was the glaring exception — with some schools, especially such formerly staunch outposts of orthodoxy as Princeton and McCormick, becoming almost solidly neoorthodox. There were three aspects of the new theology that almost guaranteed conflict with religious educators. First, neoorthodoxy drew heavily on European philosophical, literary, and theological sources. In contrast, religious education was profoundly American in its origins, goals, and purposes. In many ways religious educators had an almost Midwestern ebullience that was in sharp contrast to the mood of anxiety and despair common among their neoorthodox critics. Second, the new theology was not interested in the social sciences so beloved by religious educators. To many of them, especially those of the second rank, social science was part of the culture that the churches were called to critique. The best guide to the human condition, many neoorthodox theologians believed, was literature, especially the existentialist-leaning works of such writers as Dostoyevsky, Camus, and Kafka. The popularity of various existentialisms reinforced the tendency to understand human affairs from the perspective of the unusual, and authentic personality was often defined in terms of decisions rather than developments. The contrast with the working assumptions of the religious educators could not have been greater. Imagine a dialogue between Kierkegaard and John Dewey on human development. For Kierkegaard, individuals struggled until they were so overwhelmed by their moral and religious condition that they dared to jump to the next level.[36] For Dewey, moral maturation was a matter of individuals learning more about their world, especially other people, their bodies and minds, and naturally adopting developmentally appropriate behaviors. Third, the new theology was concerned with the Bible. Although it did not repudiate biblical criticism, neoorthodoxy desired to overcome the distance between the present and the biblical past, while to the religious educators that distance often provided an important zone of religious freedom. For them, especially the more liberal, the Bible was one guide to human faith, and one that was valuable insofar as it was confirmed by our experience.

The most vocal of the critics of traditional religious education was Elmer Homrighausen of Princeton. Homrighausen lacked the dialectical subtleties of

36. From the perspective of developmental psychology, Kierkegaard had provided a philosophical frame for the late adolescent, particularly male, search for identity.

Smith, and his views may have been, for that reason, more widely held. For Homrighausen the divide between the new theology and the progressive educators was vast.[37] In simple terms, "Christianity has doctrines, definite concepts of man, God, sin, salvation, history, society, creation, and the like. These are not chosen by us, but God chooses them for us."[38] If so, religious education is really theological education or, to be more specific, education in theology done in the context of a local congregation or church.

This understanding of religious education called into question the most fundamental assumption of most religious educators: the distinction between transmissive and transformative education. Transformative education implies that the student, the teacher, and the subject matter may be changed by the educational experience and that such change is educationally valuable. Indeed, the task of the teacher is to provide an environment where such changes occur. But, given Homrighausen's definition of religious education, the primary task is the transmission of accurate theological information. As Homrighausen understood religious education, it was primarily concerned with the transmission of the biblical message, albeit understood in neoorthodox terms, and not with the learner per se. In short, it was another way in which the Word was preached. Homrighausen recognized this: "Theology and educational philosophy and methodology have not been on good terms for some time. This breach has been due in some cases to the dogmatism of theology which runs counter to the creative and progressive spirit of education."[39] For those of liberal bent, that was precisely the problem of course, but whereas Homrighausen was willing to allow secular knowledge to fall by the wayside, they wanted to defend it. But as faculties tipped toward the new theology, this attitude made the position of the religious educators more perilous.

Religious educators tried to respond to the concerns of Homrighausen and his allies. In 1940 the International Council of Religious Education, which represented the directors (ministers) of religious education and Protestant denominational leaders, adopted *Christian Education Today,* a statement of goals for religious education. The document was important for two reasons. First, it demonstrated the continuing vitality of the older Progressive Party. Many, if not most, professors of religious education had been appointed during the discipline's days of wine and roses in the 1920s, and they were not ready to give up prized insights into such issues as developmentally appropriate lessons. Second,

37. E. G. Homrighausen, "The Salvation of Religious Education," *International Journal of Religious Education,* May 1939, pp. 12-13.

38. Quoted in Elliott, *Can Religious Education?* p. 69.

39. E. G. Homrighausen, "Theology and Christian Education," *Religious Education* 48 (1953), cited in Elliott, *Can Religious Education?* p. 69.

the International Council stressed the importance of the theological content of Christian education, especially the teaching of the Bible.

The International Council was also involved in one of the more popular projects associated with neoorthodoxy: the publication of the Revised Standard Version (RSV) of the Bible. The publishing company of Thomas Nelson, whose primary stock-in-trade was the Bible, was suffering from depressed sales. Although the company recognized that the American Revised Version, produced in the last century, was no longer popular, it also realized that a new version that met the needs of people for a Bible in a more contemporary idiom might be a best seller, as the American Revised Version was when it was first introduced. Consequently, the firm made a grant of $36,000 to the International Council for a revision of the American Standard Version. The work was put in the very capable hands of Luther Weigle, dean of Yale, who made the inspired decision to base the revision on the King James idiom and not on the aesthetically unpleasing American Standard Version. The project was badly underfunded, and the original grant did not provide sufficient funds for the extensive travel and office work needed. To stretch his resources Weigle decided to employ many younger biblical scholars in his team of translators, in effect trading the academic capital of working on a new Bible for much of the honorarium the work deserved. Although interrupted by the Second World War, the project was a success. Nelson's ten-year exclusive publishing rights paid off immediately, and the International Council, which became part of the National Council of Churches in 1950, acquired a copyright and earned significant financial rewards for many years.

VIII. A Neoorthodox Curriculum

The success of the RSV suggested that a new series of Sunday school lessons, based on recent biblical scholarship, might revitalize Christian education. Almost from the beginning of the discipline, religious educators had searched for a curriculum that could link the best of present-day biblical scholarship and the local churches. In the 1920s the mainstream denominations issued a series of graded Sunday school lessons designed to put some of the insights of the religious educators into practice.

Like earlier Sunday school curricula, the 1920s series were designed to be taught by laypeople. While this was unavoidable, given the finances of the churches, it did represent a retreat from the deepest convictions of some religious education experts. From the earliest days of the religious education movement, the discipline's leaders had urged churches to take steps to improve the quality of their teaching, either by hiring professional teachers or by instituting programs of teacher training.

The new curricula inadvertently illustrated the wisdom of the professionals' position. The Northern Presbyterian experience has been carefully examined by William Kennedy, whose study highlighted the negative responses and falling revenues that followed the introduction of the new curricula. Other Northern denominations had similar experiences. Not surprisingly, a typically American jeremiad often accompanied these criticisms. In the old days, the argument ran, the Sunday school had been easily taught and manifestly effective. In contrast, the new curriculum was "beyond" most teachers and had little biblical content. Neither criticism was completely accurate. One reason for the rise of interest in religious education originally was the excruciatingly low level of American religious instruction. Further, every survey, including those conducted by the armed forces, indicated that very few Americans possessed even minimal knowledge of the Bible, its teachings, or its characters. But such observations did not moderate the voices of discontent. The myth of the destruction of the people's church at the hands of experts became a commonplace.

Did such criticisms have roots in the fundamentalist movement? Perhaps. During the 1930s fundamentalist religious presses, including David C. Cook, sold as much Sunday school literature as the denominational presses, and they were quick to present their materials wherever there was a substantial conservative presence. Moreover, Cook's promotional literature skillfully highlighted the ease with which people could teach their materials. Many Presbyterian and other denominational leaders felt action was necessary to preserve an important denominational revenue source. The new curricula would have to be competitive with the increasingly popular conservative alternatives.[40]

Mindful of the declining prestige of religious education, Presbyterian leaders chose a young neoorthodox biblical scholar, James Smart, to serve as the overall editor and charged him to include more biblical content in the new curriculum. Like Weigle, Smart had to rely on younger scholars, such as Paul Minear, to write much of the text. But the older progressives were still very much part of the process. They pushed Smart and his coworkers to be sure that the material was developmentally appropriate to the proper age group, insisted on illustrations that were not too literal, and demanded developmentally appropriate themes for different age groups. The result was one of the better curricula

40. William Bean Kennedy, "The Genesis and Development of the Christian Faith and Life Series" (Ph.D. diss., Yale University, 1957); William Bean Kennedy, "Neo-orthodoxy Goes to Sunday School: The Christian Faith and Life Curriculum," *Journal of Presbyterian History* 58 (Winter 1980): 326-70.

adopted by American churches. While there were still complaints about "teachability," the new curriculum had the good fortune to be published at a time when the general educational level of Americans, especially Presbyterians, was rising, and in an era when many women — the primary pool for Sunday school teachers — were choosing to work primarily in the home. Its success was also aided by the fact that the postwar generation was intensely civilly minded and had a high proportion of joiners. In other words, the new curriculum was born into a world that had more and better-trained people available to teach it. The quality of volunteers had improved, but not through any ecclesiastical effort.

Ironically, Faith and Life did not rebound to support the reputation of religious education. The neoorthodox theologians had claimed that proper attention to Scripture would lead to a revitalization of all aspects of church life, and the new curriculum seemed to provide confirmation for that contention. The new orthodoxy appeared to have defeated the old liberalism on the liberals' favorite field of battle: relevance and effectiveness. The clear implication was that all aspects of the churches' and seminaries' lives had to be given a more theological bend. Not for the last time, theologians took credit for religious changes that were in fact not under their control.

IX. The Cost of Discipleship

As often is the case, ideological conviction and financial realities came together in the 1950s. Although seminaries and schools of religious education benefited from the post–World War II expansion and the GI Bill, that growth had been costly. Even schools that had historically prided themselves on their lack of tuition had to levy modest charges, sometimes hidden as fees, but it was almost impossible to keep pace with the accelerating cost of theological education. By the end of the religious revival in 1967, many schools would be hurting financially, and they would live on the financial edge during the lean decade of the 1970s.

One way to help control these rising costs was to incorporate religious education, including the training of directors of religious education/ministers of Christian education, directly into seminary programs. Many of the remaining independent schools of religious education were joined with nearby seminaries; for example, the Tennent School of Religious Education became part of Princeton Seminary, and the Presbyterian College of Christian Education part of McCormick. The Association of Schools of Religious Education, the accrediting agency for institutions preparing people for religious education careers, turned over its functions to the American Association of Theological Schools in 1965.

More significant for the whole of theological education, however, was what happened to religious education in the seminary. To ensure that young religious educators had the theological skills believed necessary, most seminaries required them to complete the core curriculum of some thirty hours of basic theological study. Those who earned the master of religious education degree completed this program by taking thirty hours of electives, usually including twenty hours in religious education. Programs of field education for religious education were merged with programs maintained primarily for the master of divinity program. Naturally, variations existed, both in where schools began the process and where they ended it, but the basic outline was common to many institutions. Among Southern Baptists, who already profited from large-scale educational institutions, the development of the bachelor of divinity degree with religious education at Southern and its spread to other Southern Baptist schools represented a similar development.

The effect of these changes was to place religious education at most seminaries under the control of the regular theological faculty. Looking back on this development, Wesner Fallaw stated in an address to the Association of Schools of Religious Education: "Eventually the curricula of schools of religious education and seminaries may well become more similar than dissimilar, hence, students looking toward filling church positions as teachers, preachers, and administrators will readily attend the same schools, studying together in many or most of the same classes, thereby, together learning to see the whole task of Christian leadership."[41] Fallaw hoped this integration would mark the end of some of the fruitful bickering that characterized the inner life of many church staffs, and he clearly hoped that religious education would become a "theological" discipline that was seen as important to the church and gospel as dogmatics. Perhaps most important, he believed that this was the dawning of a new age for religious education: "And now that most churches have won the struggle for an educated preaching ministry it is time to institute an educated teaching ministry."[42]

The complete incorporation of religious education into the seminary and theological system came at a high price. Religious education provided the gateway through which much of modern American social science, particularly psychology, entered the seminary system. With the increasing demand that religious education speak theologically, some of its value as a mediator of American worldly wisdom decreased. Religious educators were asked to do

41. Fallaw, in American Association of Schools of Religious Education Records; the Curriculum of Schools of Religious Education, p. 250.

42. Fallaw, in American Association of Schools of Religious Education Records; the Curriculum of Schools of Religious Education, p. 254.

what they did poorly and not encouraged to do what they did well. Not surprisingly, many of the discipline's most able people either changed fields or moved to administrative positions. Perhaps most painfully, as mainstream Protestantism entered into a period of visible decline in the 1970s and 1980s, the denominations' grip on religious education weakened, and many expensively produced curricula did not sell as well as expected. The massive entry of women into the workforce weakened religious education on the local level, and the end of the "pink ghetto" in the church encouraged many highly trained and very competent women religious educators to seek pastoral ministry or seminary appointments outside of their original discipline. In many schools, enrollments dropped. The "Saviour of the Churches" had become a potent indicator of their coming demise.

Perhaps the most serious aftereffect of the theologizing of religious education was the increase in theological muddle that accompanied the decline of the mainstream churches in the 1970s and 1980s. The conscious or unconscious lesson that people had learned from the travail of religious education was that theological language was the price of admission to the seminary faculty and seminary curriculum. So in a time of increasing secularity and social unrest, theological faculties were struggling to "think theologically" or to teach students "theological reflection." Much poorly done sociology and social analysis was, consequently, polished with a fine patina of God and religious language that contributed little to the larger discussion. More seriously, the church's outreach to children and youth, long a key to its prosperity in America, was seriously impaired, intensifying an already critical situation. On one point at least, Coe and Elliott had been correct: the churches ignored the new human sciences at their peril.

CHAPTER TWENTY-FIVE

Field Education and Clinical Training

When William Rainey Harper proposed the use of "theological clinics," he was attempting to align the preparation of ministers with the best in contemporary professional education.[1] In the new university, Harper saw a growing tendency to train professionals by combining classroom work with on-the-job experience. The pacesetter was medical education, where the better schools had all but abandoned the traditional large lecture rooms for the laboratory, the clinic, and the intern year. Legal educators did not apply the new model as consistently. The legal profession had shifted from its traditional focus on the solicitor and the barrister to a world in which legal training was also preparation for various positions in the new corporate America or in the expanding federal government. Few of these lawyers would ever draw up a will, argue a lawsuit, or enter a courtroom to defend a person accused of a crime. Yet the "case study method," moot courts, and clerkships with prestigious lawyers or judges were very much part of the process by which the young candidate moved ahead. Both education and social science relied on practical experience heavily, with practice teaching or clinical work an important part of the program.

I. Early Developments

Harper's proposal should have been a natural. Although ministers tended to be more schooled than contemporary lawyers and doctors,[2] many American pas-

1. William Rainey Harper, "Shall the Theological Curriculum Be Modified, and How?" *American Journal of Theology,* 1899, p. 61.

2. This would continue to be true until after World War II when the GI Bill made it pos-

tors had learned their basic pastoral skills in the school of hard knocks — Baptists, Methodists, and Disciples especially. The Methodists had formalized this as part of their Course of Study that provided among other things for a more experienced minister to mentor a younger candidate. Methodist practice was unusual only in that it was codified; other churches did much the same without rule or book. Moreover, although most seminaries did not charge tuition until the 1950s, most clergy came from the lower middle class, whether rural or urban, and were unable to afford school without outside employment. Married students, although not the majority until after World War II, were forced to find an outside source of funds, especially if they had children. Educationally, tradition and finances seemed to point to the wisdom of using student employment as part of the larger seminary program.

The religious and intellectual ethos of the late nineteenth and early twentieth century also supported such experiments. Not only did such revivalists as Dwight L. Moody argue for experience over doctrine, they also inspired hordes of active young Christians who wanted to be about the Lord's work. The various training and Bible schools that sprang up to meet these needs stressed experience in the field as part of their program, and some institutions, notably Moody Bible Institute, seemed to be almost a network of student-led ministries; Methodist Boston University encouraged its students to take to the streets of Boston with the message of free grace. Virginia Lieson Brereton has provided us with a picture of the sea of activity at such schools as the Bible Institute of Los Angeles:

> [Assignments] purposely rotated so that students would acquire a variety of experiences. As part of their practical work it was usual for Bible School students to lead church choirs, teach Sunday school and Bible classes, or organize and advise young people's groups. The focus for some, however, was not churches but rather religious and philanthropic institutions of other kinds: students worked in asylums, almshouses, old people's homes (as they were called), hospitals, prisons, industrial homes, rescue missions, settlement houses, and city missions. In these settings they sometimes did social service work, feeding and clothing the destitute.[3]

---

sible for legal and medical schools to make the B.A. followed by a three-year professional course more or less standard. Until then, many schools relied on programs that "counted" the first year of professional school as the senior year of college or required only two years of college for admission.

3. Virginia Lieson Brereton, *Training God's Army: The American Bible School, 1880-1940* (Bloomington and Indianapolis: Indiana University Press, 1990), p. 96.

Graham Taylor, one of the most energetic of educators, began his career at Hartford Seminary in Connecticut by devising a system of student placement and congregational study. The students were to report back to the seminary, having filled out fairly comprehensive schedules of their activities. These forms asked for such data as when and where they had held evangelistic meetings, the number and gender of those in attendance, and their own evaluation of the event. Taylor also had his students provide him with information oriented more toward sociology. After moving to Chicago Theological Seminary, Taylor continued to stress the importance of evaluated experience, as did Arthur Holt, his able successor. Both established a tradition of seeing field education as applied sociology.

Ironically, one of the earliest successful programs, at New York's Union Seminary, was based on another premise. With remarkable consistency throughout the seminary's history, Union placed itself at the center of the placement and evaluation process. In 1893, for example, Union worked through the City Missionary Society[4] and placed students at various churches and missionary stations where they conducted prayer meetings, ran Sunday schools, and occasionally helped with general pastoral work. At the time of the Brown-May report, Union — although it had few student pastorates — was still placing its first-year students throughout the city. Interestingly, Union used its first-year field education as part of its program of student aid, counting the income toward tuition, another early Union innovation.

In financing this program, turn-of-the-century Union — the nation's richest theological school — was flexing its economic muscle. The school provided placements and supervision because it could afford to do so. Few other seminaries had this luxury. Most seminary students depended on their church employment to provide them with income. Hence, students in more urban schools might work as assistants or associates or for the YMCA, while students in small-town and rural seminaries took "student churches." While it may be a slight exaggeration, most seminaries were as dependent on the aid these churches provided as they were on their endowments. Even in a largely tuition-free work (the university-related divinity schools and Union were exceptions), most students needed the informal scholarships provided by church work in order to attend. The availability of funds often determined the quality and duration of early field education programs. Duke Divinity School's excellent summer pastorate program was made possible by generous grants from the Duke Endowment.

4. See Evangelical Alliance, *Christianity Practically Applied* (New York: Baker and Taylor, 1893).

II. Clinical Training

As Grant Wacker observed, many in the late nineteenth century were deeply interested in the role of the Holy Spirit.[5] Part of this fascination was a renewed interest in physical healing. Hypnotism continued to have a following, especially as notable psychiatrists and psychologists studied its effects. New Thought and Christian Science proposed metaphysical systems, somewhat related to Emersonian idealism, that appealed to many, especially women. Elwood Worchester, pastor of Boston's Emmanuel Church (Episcopal), explored the relationship between healing and faith in his own church, a large institutional church that tried to meet a variety of human needs, including the need for recreation. The Emmanuel Movement spread to a number of other cities.[6] By 1908 Worchester, Samuel McComb, and Isadore Coriat had published their own examination of the new field of religion and health.[7] Part of the significance of the Emmanuel Movement is the number of people who influenced theological education, including Richard Cabot and Anton Boisen, who were associated with it in some way.

The fascination with the Spirit pointed to a partnership between medicine and ministry. Many diseases were, of course, psychosomatic disorders, and early twentieth-century therapeutics stressed long periods of bed rest. Moreover, many churches had substantial investments in hospitals and, particularly in the West, in TB sanitariums. Further, the churches had a long history of providing access to medical care for some of the indigent. At the same time, Freud and other psychoanalysts were receiving a respectful hearing in the United States. Whatever Americans might make of Freud's unconscious mind or Jung's collective unconscious, many were able to understand the new psychology in terms of the traditional American emphasis on the "good fellow" who was able to get along with others. The new psychotherapy suggested that people might take charge of their own lives and prevent the most serious personality and mental disorders. In 1909 the National Committee for Mental Hygiene was formed, and colleges and universities became interested in what could be done to prevent serious maladjustments.

The 1925 publication of Richard Cabot's "A Plea for a Clinical Year in the Course of Theological Study" was a pivotal event in the evolution of both field

5. Grant Wacker, "The Holy Spirit and the Spirit of the Age in American Protestantism, 1880-1910," *Journal of American History* 72 (June 1985): 45-62.

6. See John Gardiner Green, "The Emmanuel Movement, 1906-1919," *New England Quarterly* 7 (1934): 494-532.

7. Elwood Worchester, Samuel McComb, and Isadore Coriat, *Religion and Medicine, the Moral Control of Nervous Disorders* (New York: Moffat, Yard and Co., 1908).

education and clinical training.[8] Cabot saw that the intern year was the natural outgrowth of Christian theology: "When we urge a theological student to get 'clinical experience' outside his lecture rooms and his chapel, to visit the sick, the insane, the prisons and the almshouses, it is not because we want him to get away from his theology but because we want him to practice his theology where it is most needed, i.e. in personal contact with individuals in trouble."[9] Yet, the significance of this essay was not in its content. Cabot simply repeated ideas that had been commonplace since Harper, and he seemed unaware of the serious conversations that had taken place in the Conference of Theological Seminaries, beginning with the Baptist meeting in 1918.[10] Nor did he seem aware of the very important and creative work done by Elliott and Coe at Union and Teachers College. The responses to his essay were likewise ordinary, as critics suggested that perhaps social service sites might be as valuable as hospitals as the scene for such courses. Two things made the essay important.

First, there was Cabot himself. The scion of the bluest of blue-blooded families, Cabot had established a strong reputation as a teaching physician at the Harvard Medical School. In 1914 he published his first full-length ethical study, *What Men Live By*,[11] and he became increasingly interested in how the seemingly incompatible worlds of ethics, faith, and scientific medicine interacted. Eventually he became Harvard's professor of social ethics. His "Plea for a Clinical Year," hence, was an authoritative word from a person well qualified as a teacher and researcher. Second, Cabot had the personal connections to make his proposal a reality. He had established a close friendship with Anton Boisen, the chaplain at Worcester State Hospital, and they had already created a program at that hospital that put his ideas into practice. Cabot was also to be a close friend and ally of Russell Dicks, the chaplain at Massachusetts General Hospital who was an early student of Boisen at Worcester.

As envisioned by Cabot and his collaborators, the clinical program involved supervised experience at a site not under the control of the seminary. The student at Worcester State Hospital, Boston General, or Massachusetts

8. Richard Cabot, "A Plea for a Clinical Year in the Course of Theological Study," *Survey Graphic*, Sept. 1925; reprinted in Cabot, *Adventures on the Borderlands of Ethics* (New York and London: Harper and Brothers, 1926), pp. 1-22. All the standard histories of clinical training stress the importance of Cabot's work. See, for example, Edward Thornton, *Professional Education for Ministry: A History of Clinical Pastoral Education* (Nashville: Abingdon, 1970).

9. Quoted in Charles E. Hall, *Head and Heart: The Story of the Clinical Pastoral Education Movement* (Decatur, Ga.: Journal of Pastoral Care Publications, 1992), p. 6.

10. The Conference of Baptist Theological Seminaries, held at Boston and Newton Centre, Mass., Mar. 12 and 13, 1918, at the invitation of the Newton Theological Institute.

11. Richard Cabot, *What Men Live By* (Boston and New York: Houghton Mifflin, 1914).

General was in an environment controlled by the medical profession, and the chaplain supervisor mediated between the hospital authorities and the students receiving clinical training. Although some later clinical programs featured work in nonhospital settings, particularly prisons and other social agencies, the model remained the same. In effect, this permitted clinical training to develop parallel to the seminaries. Hence, those involved in clinical training were later able to determine who would serve as supervisors, to set the standards for those persons, and to determine what constituted a unit of training. Thus, even those schools that developed their own programs had to deal with teachers who were semi-independent of the seminaries and whose wishes had to be respected, if the seminaries were to utilize the opportunities provided by the various sites. Although not exactly identical, it was similar to the relationship between a teaching hospital and the local medical school.

From 1925 to 1935 clinical educators put together their most important pedagogical tools: the small group, the case study, and the verbatim. The use of small groups was an important part of religious education in the 1920s, and many clinical pioneers, including Boisen, Dicks, and Philip Guiles, first professor of clinical training at the newly united Andover Newton Theological School, had attended Union Seminary (New York) and studied with Harrison Elliott.[12] Small-group teaching placed its primary emphasis on the interaction among the students. Part of the problem for every group was the interaction between the "leader" and the "group." Since group education stressed the development of the person more than the mastery of a subject matter, groups could deal with such difficult issues as ministerial identity and transference. The group also made it possible to confront students with their own failings in a way that the supervisor, working alone, was less able to accomplish. A student whose peers agreed with the supervisor's reading of a particular visit or a particular incident had fewer defenses than if she or he had faced a lone critic.

Anton Boisen was particularly associated with case studies, which he called "living documents" in contrast to the books and articles favored in more traditional classrooms.[13] Boisen, a brilliant but deeply troubled individual, had become interested in the issues of religion and psychology after his first major

12. Harrison Elliott, *Group Discussion in Religious Education* (New York: Association Press, 1930); also, Harrison Elliott, *The Process of Group Thinking* (New York: Association Press, 1928). Carl Rogers and Rollo May also attended classes taught by Elliott.

13. Henri J. M. Nouwen, "Anton T. Boisen and Theology through Living Human Documents," *Pastoral Psychology* 19 (1968): 49-63; Robert Powell, *Fifty Years of Learning through Supervised Encounter with Living Human Documents* (New York: Association for Clinical Pastoral Education, 1975); Seward Hiltner, "The Heritage of Anton T. Boisen," *Pastoral Psychology* 16, no. 158 (Nov. 1965).

schizophrenic breakdown. Perhaps because it provided the best hope for dealing with his own situation, Boisen adopted a more psychotherapeutic understanding of mental illness. Mental illness, he believed, represented an acute moment in a person's spiritual development — the make-or-break point of the soul — and hence had immense spiritual significance. Carefully composed notes on the course and development of the illness consequently could provide the clinician with models for the development of sin and salvation within the soul. Educationally, the case study approach stressed the analysis of the "patient's" life as a whole and enabled the theological student to see how religious faith might impact the situation. Boisen lacked the theological and philosophical tools to develop the implications of this theory completely. In the 1940s a very influential group composed of Paul Tillich, Seward Hiltner, Gotthard Booth, Ruth Benedict, David Roberts, Rollo May, and Harrison Elliott met regularly to explore the implications of depth psychology for theology.

The third major pedagogic tool was the verbatim. In their 1936 *Art of Ministering to the Sick,* Dicks and Cabot asked for their readers' criticism of what they called "note writing as a creative art."[14] What they meant by this phrase was: "Note writing is the development on paper of one work with a given patient after that work is done. When we reproduce in writing . . . a contact, an interview, a working relationship, we do not merely record it, we rethink it and so develop its meaning, not while we are seeing a patient but as soon after as possible."[15] The verbatim, as it came to be called, had two parts. First, it was a record, as nearly as possible, of what was actually said and of the emotional temper of the conversation. As a written record, it could be shared with others without violating the patient's privacy.[16] The supervisor did not have to be present to review the student's work, and indeed, a skilled supervisor could tell from the verbatim when the student had made potentially significant omissions or had revealed her or his personal problems. Perhaps, equally important, the verbatim made possible the evaluation of the supervisor as well as the student.

14. Russell Dicks and Richard C. Cabot, *The Art of Ministering to the Sick* (New York: Macmillan, 1936; frequently reprinted), p. vi.

15. Dicks and Cabot, *Art of Ministering,* p. 24.

16. This was not Dicks's original intent. He originally saw the verbatim as essentially an individual educational tool that a minister could use to improve his or her own practice. See Dicks and Cabot, *Art of Ministering,* p. 254.

III. Sectarianism and Growth

Helen Flanders Dunbar's career made her a symbol of clinical training's new prominence. Perhaps because her career was inhibited by her gender, Dunbar collected a variety of degrees, including an M.D. from Yale and a B.D. from Union (New York) as well as a Ph.D. in medieval literature.[17] Interestingly enough, she was also among the first of Anton Boisen's students at Worcester. She also traveled to Europe where she underwent analysis and qualified as a therapist. Although she had considerable influence on theological education, she was noted as one of the founders of psychosomatic medicine. Her 1935 study *Emotions and Bodily Changes: A Survey of Literature on Psychosomatic Interrelationships* was based on her work at Presbyterian Hospital where she was on the psychiatric staff. Dunbar continued to be a pioneer in this field, and she was the first editor of *Psychosomatic Medicine,* a publication supported by the Macy Foundation. In 1930 she became the director of the Council for Clinical Training of Theological Students (after 1938, Council for Clinical Training) and served in that position until 1935, when she was succeeded by Seward Hiltner.

Although the Council for Clinical Training grew rapidly during her tenure, Dunbar's most important contribution to clinical training was her 1934 appearance before the American Association of Theological Schools (AATS). Her brief but effective presentation convinced many theological educators that clinical training could be an important part of ministerial preparation.[18] In concrete terms, this meant that the seminaries would, by and large, trust the various clinical centers to provide the on-site training and to determine the qualifications for supervisors, while the seminaries would provide the more theoretical training and in some cases offer academic credit for clinical courses.[19]

Many faculties resisted giving credit for clinical training. In part, this was because of the crowded condition of the theological curriculum; in part, it was an effort to preserve turf; and in part, it was the effect of the theological judgment that three years was little enough time for a person to develop a thoughtful understanding of the Christian message. Yet, interestingly enough, the demand for and interest in clinical training were only indirectly related to the

17. According to Robert Powell, from 1929 to 1939 she went under the name H. Flanders Dunbar and, thereafter, under the name Flanders Dunbar. Robert Powell, "The Helen Flanders Dunbar Memorial Lecture on Psychosomatic Medicine and Pastoral Care," Columbia Presbyterian Center, New York Presbyterian Hospital, 1999.

18. Edward Thornton, *Professional Education for Ministry: A History of Clinical Pastoral Education* (Nashville: Abingdon, 1970), pp. 84-88.

19. In effect, organizations such as the council took on the task of training the supervisors, while the seminaries jealously controlled the question of credit for the course.

issue of academic credit. A sufficient number of candidates for the ministry and ministers felt the need for this type of education to provide the centers with the number of candidates they needed, and in some cases more than they needed. When judicatories began mandating clinical training for their ministers, as they increasingly did in the 1960s, they did not require that the clinical component receive seminary credit. A student might elect to take clinical training anywhere and still meet the requirement. In effect, this meant that the pressure, at least from the students, was on the faculty to grant credit for what the denominations required for ordination. Most faculties eventually agreed and gave credit for work in recognized programs.

The clinical programs could maintain their independence from the seminary and credit system because they represented the growing edge of ministerial practice in the 1930s and 1940s. The most noted ministers, such as Harry Emerson Fosdick and Norman Vincent Peale in New York, and Theodore Adams in Richmond, Virginia, had adapted their ministries to the new psychology. The experience of Adams was typical. In 1930, while a young pastor in Toledo, Ohio, he attended a lecture at St. Luke's Hospital in New York in which Charles Rice convinced him that it was "more important to listen than to talk." After receiving a call to Richmond's prestigious and wealthy First Baptist Church, Adams appointed trained pastoral counselors to his staff and continued to study psychology on his own. His own preaching, like Fosdick's, increasingly dealt with how religion could enable people to live well-adjusted lives in the midst of human problems and predicaments.

The experience of the Second World War intensified ministers' sense of the need to be in touch with human problems. More than eight thousand clergy served in that struggle, and they returned aware of their own need for further training in counseling. Naturally, they communicated this need to new candidates for the ministry. Just as earlier ministers had told prospects that they needed to be able to win people for Christ, the new warning was the need to understand human life as it was lived. Major grants went to seminaries to support programs in psychology and religion.[20] In addition to this institutional growth, serious theologians began to study the relationship between theology and psychology. Paul Tillich was perhaps the best known of these. Tillich's "method of correlation" allowed theology and psychology to stand together as question and answer. Union's David Roberts published his *Psychotherapy and the Christian Understanding of Man* in 1950, followed a few years later by Albert Outler's *Psychother-*

20. Union received money from the Old Dominion Foundation; the National Mental Health Foundation funded programs at Harvard, Loyola, and Yeshiva; and the Lilly Endowment funded a program at the University of Chicago.

apy and the Christian Message (1954). In *Peanuts,* the archetypical comic strip of the 1950s, young Lucy plays at therapist in a stand, similar to the lemonade stands of the 1930s, that offers health and healing for a nickel. In this environment the clinical educators would have had to suffer a major disaster not to succeed.

The new field of pastoral counseling was closely related to the clinical movement, and many of the same people, such as Seward Hiltner, participated in its creation. Interestingly enough, it followed the same basic pattern of establishing its primary training centers apart from the seminaries. One of the most successful of these was located at Marble Collegiate Church in New York; another was at Baptist Hospital in Winston-Salem. Many of the same techniques of learning and education — the case study, the verbatim, the group — were used to educate counselors. As pastoral counselors more and more tended to establish independent practices apart from the churches they served, many insurance companies and a few states insisted on formal standards for those involved in such "for hire" activities. In turn, this moved pastoral counseling closer to the university standards for counselors.

The semi-independence of the clinical training centers provided them with useful protection against the rough-and-tumble politics of many seminaries. The supervisors received their credentials from one of the various Councils for Clinical Training, and these councils were free to set their own standards based on professional background and experience. By 1944 they were insisting that their supervisors be able to demonstrate that they (1) were ordained, (2) were well adjusted, (3) were interested in ministry, (4) possessed knowledge of other professions, (5) had administrative ability, (6) had a year of clinical training in two or more centers, (7) had served as an assistant supervisor for a period, and (8) possessed some teaching ability.[21] In 1944 the National Conference on Field Education, supported by the AATS, also established some minimum expectations for clinical programs: they were to be one day a week or twelve full weeks in length, to have ordained supervisors with clinical pastoral education experience, to provide access to human beings, to have a formal system of evaluation of student notes on meetings with their clients, and to be integrated, if possible, into the programs of the seminaries.[22]

Both the standards for the centers and the standards for supervisors presupposed relatively small operations that were at least semi-independent from each other. If a chaplain-supervisor left one institution, that person's clinical program often migrated with him or her to the next one. There were several attempts to make the programs less mobile.

21. Hall, *Head and Heart,* p. 40.
22. Hall, *Head and Heart,* p. 58.

One of the most important of these was the establishment of a network of seminaries and clinical centers in New England. Andover Newton Theological School, created by the union of Andover and Newton Seminaries in 1932, began its career as a united institution by calling A. Philip Guiles as its professor of clinical training.[23] Guiles brought many advantages to this position. He was a graduate of Union Seminary in New York and of the University of Edinburgh. Perhaps most important, especially for an institution with chronic financial problems, Guiles brought his own financing. His father-in-law's Earhard Foundation provided Andover Newton with Guiles's salary and support for his various undertakings. Guiles understood his work primarily as coordinating the various clinical centers in New England with the different seminaries, and he established a chain of schools and centers that covered the region from Bangor south. Guiles also began Andover Newton's highly successful master of theology program in pastoral care. For many would-be supervisors, this program provided both an opportunity to receive advanced clinical training and a sound theoretical knowledge of pastoral psychology. Guiles's successor, John Bellenski, by all accounts an acerbic individual, continued Guiles's strategy of networking centers and schools. The stability provided by this network enabled the programs at such institutions as Boston General, Massachusetts General, and Worcester State Hospital to become well-known nationally.

In 1955 five Texas seminaries — Austin Presbyterian, Brite College of the Bible (now Brite Divinity School), Episcopal Theological Seminary of the Southwest, Perkins School of Theology, and Southwestern Baptist — formed the Institute of Religion at the Texas Medical Center in Houston. The initial hope was that the center could provide all the clinical training needed for the bachelor of divinity (later, the master of divinity), the master of theology, and the doctor of theology degrees. Initially, the different schools' professors of pastoral care shared supervisory responsibilities with six chaplain supervisors and offered a variety of courses at the center. Interestingly enough, the center not only enrolled seminary students but also provided clinical education for medical and nursing students. H. Richard Niebuhr, Daniel Day Williams, and James Gustafson believed that this cooperative model would dominate the future,[24] but the institute, perhaps because of its distance from the participating schools, has become an independent educational entity. The School of Pastoral Care at Baptist Hospital in Winston-Salem, originally closely related to

23. Philip Guiles, "The Beginnings of Clinical Training in New England," *Andover Newton Theological School Bulletin* 40, no. 1 (Dec. 1947). Vaughan Dabney, "Austin Philip Guiles," *Andover Newton Bulletin*, Feb. 1954.

24. H. Richard Niebuhr, Daniel Day Williams, and James Gustafson, *The Advancement of Theological Education* (New York: Harper, [1957]), p. 75.

Southern and Southeastern Baptist Theological Seminaries, also became a freestanding organization.

The downside of the separation of the centers from the seminaries was an almost natural tendency toward sectarianism and competition. Much of the battle dated back to the complex battles between Anton Boisen, Richard Cabot, Philip Guiles, and Helen Dunbar. In retrospect, the battles had both an incidental and a material side. The incident that sparked some of the disagreement was Boisen's second hospitalization for schizophrenia in 1930 and his subsequent move to Chicago. Boisen interpreted this hospitalization as a deep spiritual crisis, and he understood his recovery in language drawn from both psychotherapy and religion. In his autobiography, *Out of the Depths,* Boisen wrote:

> A review of this record will show that I have passed through five psychotic episodes during which my thinking has been irrational in the extreme and my condition was such as to warrant the classification of "schizophrenic reaction, catatonic type." By that is meant that in sharp contrast to those forms of schizophrenia in which some adaptation to defeat and failure has been made and accepted, they were periods of seething emotion which tended to make or break, periods in the development of the personality in which fate hung in the balance and destiny was in large measure determined. Of these five psychotic episodes I believe I can say that, severe as they were, they have for me been problem-solving experiences. They have left me not worse but better.[25]

In simple terms, Guiles and Cabot were not convinced of this theological interpretation while Dunbar and Seward were. Beneath this battle over Boisen's mental health (or lack of it) was a deeper battle: Guiles and Cabot saw clinical training as largely ancillary to medicine. The purpose of clinical training was to enable the minister to be a part of the medical team that restored the patient to health. The other major focus of the New England group was mental hygiene. The minister was not to do therapy as much as help people practice preventive psychiatry by establishing healthy patterns of life and thought.[26] Dunbar, perhaps because of her work with psychosomatic illnesses, was not at home with the medical focus. She believed that clinical training was much more involved

25. Quoted in William L. Hiemstra, "A History of Clinical Pastoral Training in the United States," *Reformed Review* 16 (May 1963): 30-47, here p. 34.

26. Although the mental hygiene movement was important throughout the United States, the movement was particularly important in the East where it was in harmony with a new emphasis on parenting and child raising.

in psychotherapy: the cure of the minister and of his client. Boisen's perspective was similar, and Hiltner tended in the same direction.

The result of this battle was that Guiles and Cabot left the Council for Clinical Training, which Dunbar had moved to New York, and established their own Institute for Pastoral Care. The William Whitney Foundation continued to support the council, while the Earhard Foundation supported Guiles and his group. While there were minor differences between the two approaches, such as the New York group's tendency to use case studies and the New England group's tendency to use the verbatim, the two were more separated by attitude than by method. Yet, much of the history of clinical training in the 1940s and 1950s is an account of their battles and of the efforts of the AATS to negotiate at least a temporary peace.

In the 1950s both the Southern Baptists and the Lutherans formed their own clinical education associations. Although all American denominations experienced growth after the Second World War, the Southern Baptists and Lutherans were transformed. Lutherans found themselves less concerned with their traditional ethnic differences and moving rapidly from countryside to city. As a symbol of their new status, their new churches were often very modern in design, capturing in architecture such biblical themes as the ark, and occasionally experimenting with circular sanctuaries. The transformation of the Southern Baptists was equally dramatic. Always numerous, they had poured from their rural homelands into the cities of the South and the West in unprecedented numbers. Fired by a new, more urban evangelism, they won significant numbers of new believers, many from rural backgrounds, and developed an extensive bureaucracy. For the first time since the Civil War the denomination was out of debt and able to expand the services it provided its local churches. For both Lutherans and Baptists, their suburban/urban context meant they needed to struggle with problems, such as the pressures on family life, that had not been visible in their rural past. Wayne Oates, an energetic professor at Southern Baptist Theological Seminary, made the care of the family one of the principal tasks of the psychologically trained pastor.[27] The new clinical training association represented the arrival of both churches as major influences on the American scene.

The increasing diversity of the clinical movement made unification a pressing concern for both those leading clinical education and the leaders of

27. Wayne Oates, like many of the pioneers in pastoral counseling, began his work in religious education and moved from there into counseling. Along with Richard Young, he began clinical work among Southern Baptists at Winston-Salem's Baptist hospital. For more than twenty years, he was a regular summer school teacher at Union Seminary in New York.

the AATS. The association sponsored national meetings of clinical educators in the 1950s, and these meetings often involved many of the leaders of American theological education — both Paul Tillich and James Gustafson were present, for instance, in 1958 — and were important to the eventual unification of the various organizations. However, the association became even more deeply involved after Jesse Ziegler, a religious educator and psychologist, became its executive director in 1960. In many ways Ziegler was a man untimely born. His essential vision was shaped by the various drives for national unity that followed the Second World War. In these dreams the real America was coming into being through those forces and institutions that were able best to express the national ethos. For Ziegler this meant the consolidation of theological education. In a speech at Fort Worth, he candidly expressed his dream:

> For the most part, 144 member schools of AATS carry on their work with a minimum of relationship with and utilizing the resources of the other schools. It is quite conceivable that the work done in those schools could be done at a higher level of quality, be more realistically oriented to a uniting church, cost less money, permit sharper specialization of faculty if those 144 schools were brought into fifteen to twenty centers in the United States or Canada. Maybe it should be as high as twenty-five. At the current enrollment this would average about 1000 students and a few over 100 professors to such a center. There might be fewer faculty — there could certainly be a different distribution of roles for faculty. No more duplication of basic library works would be required. Library development could now be in depth. The richness of the potential could be enhanced if the various centers chose different specialties for their graduate studies.[28]

Ziegler was also committed to the idea of a "professional" ministry that would take its place in the professional world that he believed was shaping American life. The unification of clinical training was an important step toward the achievement of both of these goals.[29] W. Clarence Stone, an insurance executive, was recruited to finance further work toward the unification of the clinical programs.

The issues that separated the two clinical associations most deeply were related to questions about the certification of supervisors. This is not surprising. The associations were not "learned societies," analogous to the various

28. Jesse Ziegler, "Theological Education in a Changing Society," *Southwestern Journal of Theology* 9 (1967): 31-41.

29. See, for Ziegler's perspective, Seward Hiltner and Jesse H. Ziegler, "Clinical Pastoral Education and the Theological Schools," *Journal of Pastoral Care* 15, no. 3 (Fall 1961).

scholarly guilds, but professional associations whose primary functions involved determining who had the right to practice and who did not. In this situation small differences might mark major impediments to further cooperation. The same was also true of personalities. New England's John Bellenski had to be dragged every step along the way.[30] Finally, in 1965, an agreement was reached on the nature of clinical pastoral education: "Clinical pastoral Training is theological education on the experiential level. . . . It . . . confronts the student with the human predicament. It supplies the supportive milieu for him to understand himself as a person, to know himself as a pastor, to integrate his theology more meaningfully and to become more aware of human worth and potential."[31] The adopted definition explained why clinical pastoral education had been so effective. The clinical experience permitted both liberals and conservatives to struggle with theological questions using human experience as the central point of entry. The 1965 agreement sidestepped the vexing question of the relationship of clinical training to psychotherapy by insisting that the goal of all such programs was to promote the "growth" of both ministers and patients. In 1967 the consolidation was finally accomplished and the various associations merged.

Contemporaries believed that this was a great achievement and an important step toward the eventual unification of theological education itself. Yet, later observers cannot approach these events with the same sense of victory. In many ways the agreement came just as the social and religious order that supported it faced many challenges. Mainstream church membership, for example, peaked in that year and began a long and steady decline. Even more important, the post–World War II preoccupation with psychological health was also beginning to wind down. Like other students, seminary students were finding more of their inspiration in radical social action, particularly the antiwar protests, that was sweeping over colleges and universities. It became fashionable to speak about the minister as an agent of social change.

Unification also came at a time when Americans were becoming progressively less interested in national organizations or in the various ties that created national unity. Historians turned, for example, to the study of particular classes, regions, and groups and away from the emphasis on the creation of a national consensus; scholarly canons constructed over many years were gradually modified to include new areas of study, and many came to see diversity as a

30. Edward Thornton revealed to me in a converation after the publication of his history that he had never been able to get full access to the records of the Institute of Pastoral Care. I experienced similar difficulties getting access to original sources in the 1970s.

31. Hall, *Head and Heart,* p. 131.

national good. It was as if the clinical educators had finally got their act together just as management decided that a new play was needed to revive the theater. Clinical educators often seemed to be singing the Lord's song in a strange land.

IV. Beyond the Hospital

While clinical training was on the rise, other forms of supervised ministry were more or less in the doldrums. The problem was partially conceptual. The Brown-May survey noted that there were three current interpretations of fieldwork: it was a practical way of dealing with the student's economic needs, a form of service to the church and to the community, and an integral part of the seminary curriculum.[32] But having noted the diversity in the field, Frank Clifton Foster, whose 1932 dissertation provides the study with its information about field education practices,[33] offered a definition of fieldwork that might, with minor modifications, have been offered at any subsequent time: "Field Work is the guided experience of students, carried on under the supervision of those more skilled than they in its performance, and related to the curriculum through consideration in the classroom of the problems and difficulties encountered on the field."[34] Within this definition, some schools were doing remarkable work. Virginia Theological Seminary (Alexandria, Va.) had a chain of nearby student pastorates that were supervised by faculty members who served as periodic celebrants; Lane Seminary scheduled its academic programs in blocks of ten weeks to permit students to do their placements; and Union (New York) had its students participate in a study of poverty on the Upper West Side. Such programs, however, reached only a handful.

Taken as a whole, field education had serious problems. Despite the widespread agreement on its educational value, few schools gave credit for its completion, offered students a graded program, or gave their directors of field education faculty rank or status. Whatever the schools' official publications might say, most schools appeared to use fieldwork primarily as a source of student

32. William Adams Brown and Mark May, *The Education of American Ministers,* vol. 1, *Ministerial Education in America* (New York: Institute of Social and Religious Research, 1934), p. 137.

33. Frank Clifton Foster, "Field Work and Its Relation to the Curriculum of Theological Seminaries" (Ph.D. diss., Columbia University, 1932; independently printed).

34. William Adams Brown and Mark May, *The Education of American Ministers,* vol. 3, *The Institutions That Train Ministers* (New York: Institute of Social and Religious Research, 1934), p. 249.

revenue. The persistence of the Great Depression, further, meant that the schools were unlikely to have the financial means to change this situation in the foreseeable future. Serious work on field education was not possible for most schools until the post–World War II religious prosperity offered new financial opportunities.

Field education was in an anomalous position. Everyone knew what it, at least theoretically, could accomplish, and almost everyone found that he or she could not afford to do it.[35] The result was predictable. Field education fell to the bottom of the faculty ladder with many directors (if they were graced by that title) hired by the president more or less as administrators charged with maintaining good relationships with the various student placements. Such directors were almost constantly on the move, visiting with people in supporting parishes, and often serving as conflict managers whenever the newfangled ideas of seminaries ruffled old-fashioned feathers.

In many ways there was a tug-of-war between the congregations that hired the students and the teachers who taught them. Both ends of the rope wanted the bulk of the students' time, and students often found themselves drawn to the side that made the most demands. Although many schools continued to maintain that they were three-year schools in which the curriculum was appropriate to the students' academic location, many students took four, five, or more years to complete the program.

The advocates of field education also faced another, more serious problem: Exactly what were students expected to learn from this supervised experience? Over the course of years the traditional fourfold curriculum had divided into disciplines and subdisciplines. In no area was this more evident than in pastoral studies where separate courses and occasionally separate departments taught preaching and worship, religious education, and pastoral care. Most schools also had professors who taught church administration and polity. Further, almost all these courses had a "skills" component where the student "practiced" the various arts of ministry described by the professor's title.

A consistent supervisory approach to learning might have sought to teach all the pastoral arts through clinical or field experiences or to integrate them all in a supervisory experience. The appeal of this latter option did lead some schools, particularly Lutheran institutions, to develop intern-year programs in which the student ministered under supervision for at least a year. But intern programs were very expensive. Not only did some compensation have to be provided for the supervisors, but the students, who had to return to the seminary, were frequently unable to get sufficient remuneration to support themselves in

35. Only about twenty schools provided credit for field education.

the parish environment. If, as at Andover Newton, the internship was intended to be the fourth and last year of the seminary program, students found that their ecclesiastical status (and salaries) was limited by their lack of a seminary degree. Further, few schools had the resources or denominational support for an extensive internship program, and hence most schools continued to face the question of integrating sufficient experience into their programs.

In other words, during the key decades between 1925 and 1955 clinical training established clear methodological and institutional forms that would serve it well during its subsequent career. In contrast, the most that field education could muster in that same period was a continued assertion that field education needed to realize its educational potential. Field education seemed destined always to be a bridesmaid, never a bride.

V. The Return of Field Education: Suburbs and Ghettos

Daniel Aleshire, reflecting on what it felt like to be assigned to religious education at Southern Seminary, stated that at Southern the theological fields clearly saw themselves as the eagles whose thought and exegesis soared to the highest heavens. In contrast, Aleshire maintained, the practical fields often experienced themselves (and were treated by others) as though they were the turkeys of theological education, doomed to spend their lives in the lowlands.[36] While the experience of exclusion was common to many in the practical fields, field educators in 1945 had even more reason to see themselves in a negative light. Few had faculty status; most were seen by colleagues and administrators as essentially managers of an employment bureau; and they had not developed anything like the clinical educators' sophistication in supervision or in the training of supervisors.

Yet fieldwork or field education had many resources. As a rule, students had few complaints about their field assignments. In fact, the repeated complaints of teachers that students neglected their studies in favor of their field assignments may indicate that then, as now, many found their work outside class as important as their more formal studies. The dependence of the seminaries on field education financially should not be overlooked. Although the seminaries had received a boost from the GI Bill, the 1950s and 1960s witnessed continually rising administrative costs, the introduction or radical increase of tuition, and the proliferation of new responsibilities. While the general religious revival

36. Daniel Aleshire, "Finding Eagles in the Turkey's Nest: Pastoral Theology and Christian Education," *Review and Expositor* 85 (Fall 1988): 695-709.

provided some new revenues, much of this was marked for capital improvements. In this context, field education was an all but indispensable part of the seminaries' financial health.

The 1950s and 1960s also saw major shifts in American religious life that were crucial for the development of field education programs. Perhaps the most important was the rapid rise of the suburban church following the war. The seminaries, or at least those in or near large cities, had long used the larger urban churches, especially the institutional churches, as placements for students along with such organizations as the YMCA and other charities. But the mainstay of fieldwork had been the small rural church within traveling distance of the school. These small churches, some of which hosted generations of seminarians, may have provided a modicum of financial support, but they were almost by definition one-person ministries. The most that a school might hope to do in such a situation was to provide an occasional visit by the fieldwork director to the site or seminars on campus where the "problems" of the placements might be discussed.

Many American theological educators were suspicious of the new suburban churches and their influence, however. Complaints that the renewed interest in religion was superficial were heard on all sides, and these laments were frequently turned as much against theological education as against the churches.[37]

But the new suburban churches seemed to offer more educational promise. Unlike the small churches that had been the mainstay of earlier fieldwork efforts, these congregations provided an experienced pastor; significant programming for children, adults, and youth; and considerable financial resources. All the arts of ministry could be experienced in a single environment. The danger was, of course, that such churches would simply use students as cheap labor. Suburban pastors in the 1950s and 1960s were frequently on the verge of burnout, and few had sufficient time to supervise a student fieldworker. Nonetheless, these beehive churches seemed better equipped to provide students with a quality experience than the earlier teaching congregations. Field educators seized the new opportunity with gusto, and field education at many seminaries became synonymous with experience in a suburban setting.

In this, they were helped by some of the deeper trends of the 1950s. Despite the rash of books relating psychology and ministry, many theologians were suspicious of clinical training and pastoral psychology. Since Kant, Protestant theologians had tended to translate ancient religious categories into

37. Gibson Winter, *The Suburban Captivity of the Churches: An Analysis of Protestant Reponsibility in the Expanding Metropolis* (Garden City, N.Y.: Doubleday, 1961).

social imperatives and to see Christianity as a cultural force. Any form of theological education that stressed internal states and private experience, hence, was suspect almost from the beginning.

The mainstream churches were also in the midst of what was arguably their greatest triumph: their participation in the civil rights movement.[38] Following the Second World War, an increasing number of Americans of both races came to believe that the patterns of racial segregation and discrimination that had shaped American life for a century were wrong. Slowly at first and then more rapidly, ancient legal barriers to equality were removed. The 1964 Civil Rights Act capped almost fifteen years of steady advance. Mainstream Protestant churches had been active in these efforts. Not only did important Protestant theologians, such as Robert McAfee Brown, participate in many of the demonstrations, but many members of local churches joined letter-writing campaigns demanding that Congress pass more stringent laws.

The question for many socially concerned faculties was where could students receive the type of experience-oriented learning that this type of social activism demanded. The East Harlem Protestant Parish, founded in 1948 by three Union graduates, J. Archie Hargraves, George W. Webber, and Daniel L. Benedict, was one place. The parish was a radical ecclesiastical innovation that sought to develop new techniques of urban ministry. Drawing deeply on the American communal tradition, the leaders of the parish lived and worked together and sought to find creative solutions to social problems that had resisted a half-century of social work. More than five hundred Union students did their field placements in the parish, and many of them, such as Frederick Buechner, found their lives and faith revived by the experience.[39]

East Harlem was not alone. Sherman Eddy's 1930s' experimental Delta Cooperative Farm in Mississippi and Clarence Jordan's Koinonia Farms were likewise exciting models.[40] The postwar publication of Bonhoeffer's works, especially the account of his "seminary," *Life Together*, suggested that a further integration of theology and meaningful religious and political action was possi-

38. James F. Findlay, Jr., *Church People in the Struggle: The National Council of Churches and the Black Freedom Movement, 1950-1970* (New York and Oxford: Oxford University Press, 1993).

39. Robert Handy, *A History of Union Theological Seminary in New York* (New York: Columbia University Press, 1987), pp. 252-53.

40. For a description of the farm and its ministry, see Rick L. Nutt, *The Whole Gospel for the Whole World: Sherwood Eddy and the American Protestant Mission* (Macon, Ga.: Mercer University Press, 1997), pp. 272-74. On Clarence Jordan's project, see Tracy Elaine K'Meyer, *Interracialism and Christian Community in the Postwar South: The Story of Koinonia Farm* (Charlottesville: University Press of Virginia, 1997).

ble, as did the growth of the Urban Training Centers in the 1960s. In some ways it looked like the story of Cinderella might be repeated: the despised step-daughter, field education, might become the heir apparent to the kingdom.

Yet, despite these hopes, most fieldwork or, as it came to be called in the 1960s, field education was tied to the local church, in terms of both placements and intellectual justification. As Samuel Miller of Harvard put it graphically in 1950, no matter how hard candidates for the ministry studied or how competent their instructors, they needed to "take the plunge" into the real church and experience what it meant to have substantial responsibilities before they were professionally qualified.[41] Whatever else field education might be, at least part of its goal was to help ensure that seminary graduates had sufficient grasp of the real church to be able to function adequately. In that sense field education was the place where theological study, whether in the classical or theoretical fields, was hardened in the crucible of real life.

In short, field education in the 1950s and 1960s was strengthened and sustained by two understandings of its role in theological education, both based on the perceived need for students to experience the real world. On the one hand, field education was one place where the student might encounter the new frontiers of ministry, and thus it was often the focal point of hopes for the reform of theological education. On the other hand, field education was central to those who, like Jesse Ziegler and many leaders of the AATS, believed that the seminary was essentially a graduate professional school that had to train competent reflective practitioners of the art of ministry.

VI. Conversations and Organizations

The post–World War II development of fieldwork began with the biennial meetings of the Conference on Field Work in 1945. Like many other important developments in American religion, the conference had been proposed earlier, but the pressures of foreign affairs and the war forced its postponement. Like the similar conferences that led to the union of clinical training and to the establishment of the Association of Seminary Professors in the Practical Fields, these meetings were supported and encouraged by the AATS. In one sense the conferences provide almost a textbook example of the formation of a professional guild. The early meetings were largely devoted to developing members' awareness of their common plight and common professional problems. As

41. Samuel Miller, "The Future of Theological Training," *Harvard Divinity Bulletin* 24 (Apr. 1960): 1-8.

time passed, the meetings became occasions for the exchange of information about what was happening in field education. Finally, the conferences spawned a full-fledged professional body with its own standards for membership, its own journal, and an agenda for theological education.[42]

The professionalization process was accompanied by increasing attention to field education by theological educators. The field received a major boost in 1957 when Niebuhr, Williams, and Gustafson argued for the centrality of field education and urged that seminaries emphasize such learning in the future. While the Niebuhr report was not directly responsible for a series of new AATS initiatives, it did encourage them. In 1962 the AATS added to its standards its first formal statement on field education: "Educational field experience effectively related to instruction and under competent supervision should normally be required of all candidates for the B.D. degree and the degree in Christian Education."[43] At the same meeting, plans were unfolded for the AATS to sponsor a series of six national field education consultations, under the leadership of Dean Milton Froyd, that would provide guidance for schools as they sought to meet the new standard. In 1964 the AATS adopted notations that clarified its standard:

N3.2 In this school, field experience is not adequately related to instruction.
N3.3 In this school, field instruction is not under adequate supervision.
N3.5 In this school, educational field experience is not requirement for the B.D. degree or the degree in Christian education.[44]

The problems highlighted in the new standards were those that had been mentioned repeatedly in the literature.

The new standards came as Russell Becker's highly touted "In Parish" program at Yale Divinity School went into operation. Becker's program was historically important because it was one of the few programs to attempt to meet the critics of field education head-on and to show that field education could fulfill the potential that all agreed it had but that it had never realized. Essentially, Becker's approach rested on three foundations. First, he wanted to avoid the one-on-one type of supervision that had frequently left the student as an underpaid and underutilized assistant to the pastor: "[T]he student is not set in a one-to-one relation to the pastor at the parish. He is set as part of a clus-

42. See Maureen Egan, "The History of the Association for Theological Field Education and Its Contribution to Theological Education in the United States, 1946-1979" (Ph.D. diss., St. Louis University, 1987), for a detailed examination of this process.

43. Quoted in Egan, "History," p. 109.

44. Quoted in Egan, "History," p. 123.

ter of students. This means that, at points of question and challenge to the existing program, the student is strengthened by the support of peers who very likely have the same question. He is not apt to find himself all alone in striking at the root of some pastor's pet enterprise." Students were to be supervised in groups that provided a chance for interaction with each other as well as their supervisors. Second, supervisors were to receive substantial training for their positions. The lack of preparation was one of the historic flaws of field education, especially when compared to clinical training. The supervisors met for two hours of training every week during the academic year.[45] Third, the program was to strive for an integration of the practical and classical disciplines.[46]

Becker's program was not the only innovative approach. The Federated Faculty of Chicago, Andover Newton, and many of the Lutheran schools experimented with a formal intern year during which the student returned to campus periodically for reflection and discussion. In many ways the intern years were close to what medical educators called a residency. Unlike a medical intern, the theological intern was often functioning as a professional, even if not yet ordained, and reporting to others on work that had been accomplished. But the major advantage of the intern-year program was that students had to work in an environment similar to the one they would face for the rest of their ministry, while receiving some aid and guidance from the seminary during the crucial first year of ministry. Intern programs, however, were very expensive and often lacked the support of the classically trained members of the faculty, who saw the degree as leading either to ministry or to further academic study.[47]

By the 1960s an informal system of advanced pastoral training existed in most denominations. Promising young seminary graduates were carefully placed in prominent churches, often under pastors who had a good reputation as effective practitioners. Within three or four years those assistant pastors would move on to a medium-sized or large church and begin their formal rise in the clerical profession. These informal networks may have been among the

45. Becker admittedly never solved the problem of supervisors. When a minister moved, as often happens in American Protestantism, he had to begin the process of training a new supervisor all over again. And, unlike clinical training, the training a supervisor received at Yale did not necessarily translate to other programs.

46. Russell J. Becker, "The Place of the Parish in Theological Education," *Journal of Pastoral Care* 21 (1967): 163-70.

47. This is the most favorable reading of what was clearly a major behind-the-scenes battle at some theological schools. Whatever the truth of the matter, the prevailing wisdom at Andover Newton Theological School, for instance, is that the faculty did in the program and never gave it more than token support.

most important informal means of advanced pastoral training available. Unfortunately, the schools were never able to use these networks systematically or acknowledge their importance publicly. In some denominations, such as the Southern Baptists, these networks often united generations of ministers, including seminary professors and presidents, in a chain of service to powerful churches in the larger cities. In turn, these networks served to create or sustain the various ministerial networks — the "old boys" — that held the most important positions in the denomination.

The AATS commissioned Charles Fielding to do a reflective study of theological education that was published in 1966. Although Fielding stated that "nothing short of revolutionary reform is required in theological education,"[48] the gist of the report was that seminaries needed to perfect their use of the professional model of education. Naturally, fieldwork was one of the primary concerns of the report. Fielding, like earlier commentators, noted that the term "fieldwork" often referred to three very different activities: student employment for pay, student social service, and student work under supervision. The latter, which he called field education, was where seminaries should place their emphasis.

Fielding published his report just as the nation and the church were entering into a period of rapid social change. The ideas that he so clearly articulated, to be sure, had some momentum behind them. In 1972 the AATS again revised its standards for field education.

> The program shall make provisions for exercising various forms of ministry, subject to critical reflection with scholars of the religious heritage, behavior sciences, and other pertinent areas.
>
> Applicable criteria:
>
> a. Each student secures experience in at least one form of ministry under supervision.
>
> b. Supervisors are aware of and committed to the School's educational objectives.
>
> c. Supervising personnel are clearly part of the teaching and evaluative resources with opportunities to assist in the overall design of the curriculum.
>
> d. Professors in the academic disciplines are involved in the process of theological reflection on the ministries performed.
>
> e. Provision is made for growth in the competence of supervisory personnel.

48. Charles Fielding, *Education for Ministry* (Dayton, Ohio: AATS, 1966), p. xiii.

f. A significant part of the curriculum is taught in the context of ministry by teams of ministers and representatives of academic disciplines.

g. Procedures encourage classroom teachers and supervisory personnel to share new understandings on a regular basis.

h. There are written understandings of responsibilities of students, supervisors, and the institution.

These standards were the high point in the development of the discipline. In his criticism of Fielding, Thomas Oden pointed to the seminaries' need to go beyond the professional model proposed by Fielding and Ziegler:

> In this connection, the report completely ignores the idea of the theological [school] as a disciplined community in which prayer, study, and the sense of mission interact vitally. Perhaps it is because of this omission that the report fails to make the obvious criticism due the American seminary faculty: it is in no sense a disciplined, missioning community bound together by a common rule, a daily office or a common life; instead, it has followed in the comfortable and highly individualistic path of American education and business. Until seminary faculties become genuinely disciplined communities of commonly ordered life (perhaps using the Taize community or Bonhoeffer's Finkenwalde experiments as suggestive paradigms), their call for communities of commitment in local parishes and experimental ministries will have a rather phony and disingenuous ring.[49]

The dissatisfaction expressed by Oden was widely shared, especially among younger faculty members and students. There was a strong sense that the professional understanding of ministry, at least as expressed by such advocates as Fielding and Ziegler, was at the end of its tether. The wind was blowing in another direction.

The 1970s were a particularly rough decade for field educators. With the professional model increasingly tattered, they found themselves attempting to fulfill the dreams of those who believed that the seminaries could create a new, socially relevant church. The task was doomed to failure. America's Protestant churches were entering a period of numerical decline that would become increasingly evident as time passed. By the late 1980s talk about the churches as the vanguard of national revolution or as change communities seemed as dated as bell-bottom pants. But this removed the second major inspiration of the discipline. If neither the professional model nor the social change model was applicable, what was the role of field education in the curriculum? By 1980 two

49. Quoted in *Christian Century* 84 (1967): 536.

watchwords had emerged: thinking theologically and theological reflection. In many ways this was another cul-de-sac. While most field educators agreed that the goal of field education was "to develop self-conscious methodologies for perceiving and testing whatever it is that gives a theological dimension to a given situation,"[50] no one could give a clear definition of what such thinking might be or how it related to the theological thinking done in other parts of the curriculum. And how the other aspects of field education, such as supervision and performance on the job, related to this ideal was even less clear. Perhaps the problem comes down to the difficulty Protestant educators have had historically in admitting that ministry is both a job and a vocation and that the test of both job and vocation may be whether the task is performed well or poorly, competently or incompetently.[51]

50. Egan, "History," p. 144.

51. Joseph Hough and John B. Cobb, *Christian Identity and Theological Education* (Chico, Calif.: Scholars, 1985), suggest that the concept of the "reflective practitioner" might be useful for theological educators. This idea seems to have special relevance for field education.

PART III

Questions in the Midst of Triumph

CHAPTER TWENTY-SIX

American Conservative Protestantism Recovers

By 1930 both liberal and conservative American Protestantism were in the midst of a serious religious depression. Unlike earlier downturns in the religious marketplace, this one was structural. As Robert Handy noted, Protestantism was undergoing a second disestablishment as Protestant influence as well as Protestant power receded.[1] Pre–World War I American culture had been Protestant in a way that post–World War I America was not. America's religious conservatives felt the pain of this cultural shift acutely. They were, after all, the sons and daughters of those who had poured heart and soul into the missionary movement, the revival, and Christian higher education. Not only had the leadership of these national organizations passed into the hands of the liberal wing of the church or, to be more precise, those moderates who would work with modernists, but the sneering voices of H. L. Mencken and Clarence Darrow still rang in their ears. America's media had a field day with the events at Dayton, Tennessee, and much of the nation — that part that read newspapers and magazines, or listened to the newly popular radio — had a good laugh, at the conservatives' expense. Many liberal and modernist Christians joined in the fun, picturing their conservative opponents as buffoons who, however powerful ecclesiastically, were not to be taken with intellectual or moral seriousness.[2]

1. Robert Handy, *A Christian America: Protestant Hopes and Historical Realities* (New York: Oxford University Press, 1971); William Hutchison, ed., *Between the Times: The Travail of the Protestant Establishment in America, 1900-1960* (Cambridge, U.K., and New York: Cambridge University Press, 1989).

2. Such liberals as the *Christian Century*'s Morrison never seemed to realize that the humanists and others were poking fun at all Christians, not just the fundamentalists.

I. Outsiders and Insiders

Liberal rejoicing at the embarrassment of their conservative opponents demonstrated something else: the liberal wing was not ready to lead American Protestantism. While there was a harmonious and tolerant side to the thought of some American liberals, this was unfortunately often confined to their theology, where tolerance was part of the modernist mystique. The harsher side of modernist thought was shown in their aggressive church politics. By exploiting their alliance with denominational moderates, the liberals were able gradually to take over much of the organizational structure of Protestantism, its bureaucracy, and its ecumenical organizations. Only two moderately conservative schools — Princeton and Southern Baptist — were invited to participate in the American Association of Theological Schools (AATS). Ironically, among both liberals and conservatives, the word "ecumenical" was often a code word for liberal theology.[3] Liberal power rested on one of the ironies of American life: the further one was removed from local conditions and local prejudices, the easier it was for a small, elite group to acquire power and influence disproportionate to its numbers.

The liberal victory also permeated the writing of American religious history. Historians such as William Warren Sweet and Winthrop Hudson wrote Protestant history from the perspective of the eventual victory of liberal Christianity. Taking the "broadening church" as their model, these historians saw the future of Christianity as firmly in the hands of liberal and neoorthodox church leaders. If conservatives were mentioned, they were depicted as rural folk, destined to become part of the national urban consensus, or as representatives of ethnic traditions, doomed in advance by the melting pot. The coming Great Church was represented by the new National Council of Churches, established in 1950, and symbolically headquartered at 475 Riverside Drive, New York, close to Riverside Church and Union Seminary. Protestant historians were in line with the larger climate of American opinion. The period from 1932 to 1968 was the high point of American political liberalism and confidence in the capacity of national elites, whether the brain trust or atomic scientists, to solve the nation's ills. Like the earlier Puritans, the conservatives believed they were a righteous minority that had been excluded arbitrarily from their natural place in the nation's religious life.

In short, Protestant conservatives in the 1930s and 1940s were outsiders.[4]

3. This is not to say that the ecumenical organizations were necessarily as committed to theological liberalism as their liberal supporters.

4. See R. Laurence Moore, *Religious Outsiders and the Making of America* (New York: Oxford University Press, 1986).

While one might argue that a theological definition of conservatism is more useful, substantial reasons exist, it seems to me, to be cautious about such definitions. The most compelling of these is the differentiation of theological positions among right-of-center Christians. As befits people who take theology seriously, conservatives cannot be said to have a common creed. Moreover, the statements of faith that do unite conservative coalitions, such as fundamentalism or the parachurch movement, are very sketchy. Most often they spell out only a bare minimum for cooperation or what the framers felt must be defended at all cost. Classical fundamentalism, for example, drew four of its five points from classical Christology. Since the answer to the question of who was and is Jesus was, in fact, a central theological issue, the affirmations served to define an important difference. "Outsider," in contrast, deals with the conservative sense of living on the banks of the mainstream.

The outsider is a person who is recognized as such by those who hold the positions of power or authority and must be transformed by those inside those institutions to be accepted.[5] The outsider is not necessarily an enemy, since he or she can be converted or educated enough to change his or her status, but as long as the outsider retains his or her identity, the outsider will be kept at a distance. What is most important for a consideration of conservative education is what outsider status does to a religious community. Generally speaking, outsider religious groups become Janus-like in their attitude to the world around them. Looked at from one direction, they are deeply concerned with the issue of boundaries and with the coherence of their own group. This is often expressed as hostility toward those in power and the need for polemics against them as well as careful maintenance of their own internal standards. Lines are drawn and maintained, and outsiders are characteristically more willing to lose a lukewarm ally or member than risk the effects of the loss of identity.

Yet outsiders are not sectarians. They do not necessarily reject the surrounding society or seek to completely withdraw from it. Ironically, they are often almost fanatically loyal to aspects of the larger world and its symbols. Thus conservative Protestants, like Mormons and other outsiders, are often fervent nationalists, waving the flag and declaring their undying loyalty to the root myths, stories, and legends of the society. The power of American conservatives' devotion to these central myths can be seen in their behavior during the turbulent thirties when many European and American liberals turned to either authoritarianism or Marxism for guidance. By and large, few American reli-

5. It is not essential for this argument that insiders have a majority or even the support of a majority; what is essential is that those inside be seen, by themselves and others, as having the power and authority to determine the standards.

gious conservatives entertained such choices. American fascism, despite its leaders' claim to represent "fundamentalism," was unable to rally a significant body of religiously motivated adherents.

Outsiders often see themselves as prophets or reformers who have the answer to the larger world's problems, an answer that will not be heard by the current powers or principalities, and that in the normal course of events provokes opposition. Interestingly, two great historians of outsider groups, Catholic Tracy Ellis — the masterful exponent of the pre–Vatican II church — and evangelical Mark Noll, have noted that these groups form an "intellectual ghetto" that may make life more difficult for those among them who want to kick against the pricks of their status.

Within the group itself, however, life is not experienced as a continual warfare against the powers of darkness. Indeed, the various activities and lifestyle decisions made within the group are the reason for the boundaries in the first place, and members of the group want to enjoy these as much as possible. They are "precious memories," bought for a high price from the surrounding society.[6] Conservative Christians genuinely enjoy themselves in their prayer meetings, Bible studies, youth fellowships, missionary activities, and conferences. When conservative Christians move outside of their communities, it is often experienced as a deep and personal loss, almost an exile, and causes trauma similar to the cessation of an addiction.

From 1930 to 1960 all churches on the right were outsiders, and to a certain extent all conservative American Protestants shared some religious convictions, ideas, and practices. Missouri Synod Lutherans often found themselves singing "gospel" music; conservative Presbyterians and Baptists in the North were deeply influenced by Christian Reformed theology and eventually by some Christian Reformed practices. In turn, Christian Reformed young people faced the same restrictions on dancing, movies, and cigarettes as their holiness counterparts. The Scofield Bible was, like the body of Christ, ubiquitous, and found on the home altars of almost all conservative groups. David C. Cook's and Fleming Revell's books were advertised everywhere on the right and seem to have found readers among both Pentecostals and Presbyterians. Southern Baptists were numerous enough to found a regional empire of their own; yet, they were also deeply influenced by the various threads of conservative America.

6. Clearly speaking, I have found the rational-choice sociology of such thinkers as Rodney Stark very useful here. Basically, Stark argues that human beings relate through systems of exchange in which they both give something and receive something in return. See Rodney Stark and Roger Finke, *Acts of Faith: Explaining the Human Side of Religion* (Berkeley: University of California Press, 2000).

But these similarities also concealed deep differences. Southern Baptists distrusted and disliked the various Pentecostal and Holiness churches on both theological and social grounds. Missouri Synod Lutherans placed atypical stress on the sacramental life of the churches, and they and the Christian Reformed believed in a very highly educated clergy. Presbyterian conservatives were divided on issues ranging from the use of alcohol to the need for staying within a particular denomination to the necessity of strict subscription. Many conservatives formed independent Bible congregations that had few links with other believers. If casual observers had difficulty telling the difference between Southern and independent Baptists, the members of both churches would have little difficulty enlightening them.

The groups also differed in how they understood their outsider status. The dominant place of evangelical theology in the Protestant South, for example, made it difficult for the majority of Southerners to see liberalism as their principal religious enemy. The most brutal Southern Baptist battle, the Texas brawl between J. Frank Norris and his opponents in the state Baptist convention, pitted opponents with similar theological stances against one another. Both Truett and Norris could have subscribed with good faith to the five fundamentals and affirmed — in good Southern fashion — that the Bible was true in all its details and nuances. Instead of doctrine, the Southern Baptist sense of standing outside came from the marriage between the denomination and the Southern and agrarian way of life. Southern life in general was marked by a profound distrust of those forces, intellectual and social, that threatened the unique character of the South and, particularly, of Southern race relations. Both the Christian Reformed Church and the Lutheran Church–Missouri Synod inherited European polemics against the more accommodating and established wings of their own denominations. Northern fundamentalists, many of whom were the heirs of Moody's crusade to save the cities, burned with resentment against those who had marginalized them. The watchmen on the wall had issued their call, and Jerusalem not only slept but sent out soldiers to silence those who had tried to warn of the dangers.

If the 1930s are read from the perspective of the conservative attitude toward the larger society, stringent and militant voices are clearly audible. Many of the old warhorses of the 1920s were still charging their modernist opponents at full gallop, and they seemed angrier than ever. J. Frank Norris and William Bell Riley were as nasty as ever, and Norris may have reached new heights of invective. Even the mild-mannered Reformed Episcopalian James Gray, president of Moody Bible Institute, sharpened his tongue. They were not alone, to be sure. Such neoorthodox churchmen as Reinhold Niebuhr were also masters of invective, as were their more traditionally liberal critics. Battles between Marxists and other socialists were also conducted in high-rhetoric fashion. The Depression (a wonderfully expressive term for an economic downturn) was aptly named. Poverty made the nation's public and intellectual life just a little cruder and crustier than it had been in the nation's previous decade of wine and roses.

Where fundamentalism becomes interesting for the history of theological education is not in its polemics against liberalism. These were the backdrop for other developments, to be sure, but they had little impact on educational issues. The polemics that did influence conservative education (and all of conservative religious life) were those around the thorny issue of separation. Separation was not new. Almost every new religious sect and movement withdrew from another body, and churches historically enforced separation by excommunicating everyone who disagreed on significant points. What was different was that many fundamentalists argued that "true believers" would necessarily leave their denominational churches, while other fundamentalists believed they should stay to leaven the lump. Some, such as Robert McQuilkin, founder of Columbia Bible College,[7] argued for separation from those who refused to leave their denominations. The perennially angry Carl McIntyre, who withdrew first from the Presbyterian church and then from Machen's new church, expressed similar sentiments.

Such internal snippiness framed many issues for conservative educators. Although conservatives, particularly those in the newer denominations, continued to favor denominational forms, many conservative educators tried to sidestep the ecclesiastical issue altogether. Conservative educators had a workable model at hand. The first wave of dispensational excitement had encouraged the formation of a number of missionary organizations, both domestic and foreign, that were dedicated to the evangelization of the world without waiting for the denominations and their slow and deliberate policies. These parachurch organizations tended to have minimum formal confessions of faith, often as bare-boned as the fundamentals, and they were often not concerned with the nature of the churches to be formed abroad. Parachurch bodies had financial supporters and not members. The governance of these organizations was similar to that of other American charities. They were usually incorporated with their own boards of trustees and formal annual meetings, but the real power lay in the hands of the founder and president. If for any reason people became dissatisfied with the goal of the ministry, they could stop writing their

7. R. Arthur Mathews, *Towers Pointing Upward* (Columbia, S.C.: Columbia Bible College, 1973).

checks. In fact, the leadership of these ministries often struggled to replace those who disappeared from the mailing list.

Parachurch bodies were (and still are) self-consciously nondenominational. This is true in at least two primary senses. First, they deliberately stress their nonecclesiastical character. Their supporters are drawn from many different churches, and they are careful not to offend the denominational sensitivities of any of their supporters. Equally important, they profess to be above doctrinal debates. Their statements of faith usually contain a strong, but not well-defined, position on the Bible and on salvation through Christ alone. The rest is commentary. Like the World Council of Churches standard for membership — faith in Christ as Lord and God — they attempt to make sure that the tent is large.

Although the original excitement behind the parachurch groups was the missionary movement, the radio shaped its more recent forms. By the 1930s radio had penetrated American life, and the image of the family gathered around the large standing radio was an American icon. From the beginning, liberals and conservatives had followed divergent radio strategies. With few exceptions the liberals directed their primary efforts toward programs that stations would carry as part of their "public service" requirements for federal licensure. The Federal Council of Churches coordinated the liberal efforts and attempted to restrict airtime to members of its own denominations. As befitted representatives of the majority culture, these programs were often professionally produced and featured preachers, such as Harry Emerson Fosdick[8] and S. Parkes Cadman,[9] with substantial national reputations.

The conservative approach to the radio was different. Largely excluded from the free use of the airways, conservative preachers sought to purchase time and to raise money from their audiences to pay the fees. Initially, most conservative broadcasters were limited to local stations, but it was not long before the more enterprising, such as Aimee Semple McPherson, had developed extensive hookups for their programs and could be heard nationwide. Perhaps because of the pressures of the market, these radio preachers adopted the sounds of America's popular culture, adapting the old-fashioned gospel hymn to the new medium. But more important, they learned they could do as much with many small contributors as their more established competitors could do with a handful of well-heeled backers. Both Moody Bible College and BIOLA (Bible Institute of Los Angeles) established their own stations in the 1920s, and

8. Unlike many liberal churches, Riverside did have its own radio studio.

9. F. S. Hamlin, *S. Parkes Cadman, Pioneer Radio Minister* (New York: Harper and Brothers, 1930).

other large Bible schools developed their own programs. Howard Ferrin's Providence Bible College was supported almost entirely by radio contributions.[10]

Many conservative institutions were able to adopt the parachurch formula to their own purposes. Parachurch organizations were mission-driven, small contribution–financed organizations that were able to sustain themselves by constantly recruiting new supporters. Unlike churches or denominations, they were independent organizations that could continue their ministries despite the vagaries of the conservative theological marketplace. Moreover, their supporters could remain members of local churches and continue to make contributions to their own denominational efforts.

A. The Maturation of Bible School Education (1930-60)

The influence of the parachurch movements on the Bible schools is evident in the histories and catalogues of such schools as Moody, BIOLA, and Columbia in the 1930s and 1940s.[11] As new areas of ministry became more popular, the Bible institutes moved quickly to provide training for these new ministries. This was particularly true on the foreign field. In the 1930s and 1940s, conservatives were becoming the majority voice in American Protestant missions abroad, in part because the larger churches were having to cut back their operations for financial reasons. Since a popular interpretation of premillennial doctrine was that Christ would not return until all had heard the gospel, many conservative missions were to new areas with unique needs. The Wycliffe Bible Translators, founded by L. I. Legters and W. Cameron Townsend, for instance, saw the provision of the Scriptures in new languages as its goal, and many missions to such areas as the Amazon early came to depend on "missionary aviators" for transportation and supply.[12]

10. See Joel A. Carpenter, *Revive Us Again: The Reawakening of American Fundamentalism* (New York: Oxford University Press, 1997), p. 133. Providence Bible College became Barrington College.

11. Virginia Lieson Brereton, *Training God's Army: The American Bible School, 1880-1940* (Bloomington and Indianapolis: Indiana University Press, 1990), p. 65, notes that many training schools closed in this period and that these were the schools that did not become Bible schools.

12. See E. F. Wilis and M. A. Bennett, *Two Thousand Tongues to Go: The Story of the Wycliffe Bible Translators* (New York: Harper and Row, 1964), and George M. Cowan, *The Word That Kindles* (Chappaqua, N.Y.: Christian Herald Books, 1979). Gerard Colby, with Charlotte Dennett, *Thy Will Be Done: The Conquest of the Amazon; Nelson Rockefeller and Evangelism in the Age of Oil* (New York: HarperCollins, 1995); Hugh Steven, *Doorway to the World: The Mexico Years; The Memoirs of W. Cameron Townsend, 1934-1947* (Wheaton, Ill.: Harold Shaw, 1999); James C. Hefley and Marti Hefley, *Uncle Cam: The Story of William Cameron Townsend, Founder*

In fact, many Bible schools were parachurch organizations in their own right, often becoming quasi denominations. William Bell Riley, whose Bible schools helped him create a small empire in Minnesota, noted that seminary graduates were not doing a good job in small northwestern churches: "[Every year we had] an agent go east and search through the graduates of defunct theological seminaries to see if some could be had for Minnesota." Few wanted to come, and those who did "were actually the leftovers." Not surprisingly, "their success in Minnesota was never marked." Riley continued: "On the contrary, when two or three of them had come one after another for a few months to one of these little churches, the local constituency concluded that it [the church] could not be saved and were ready to vote on sell the property and turn in to the State Convention the result."[13] In response, Riley used his schools to find and train people who were willing to go into the countryside and find those who were lost. In turn, these ministers looked to Riley and his schools for leadership and for placement in new churches. Other Bible schools, such as Moody, had a more urban string of churches, but the school functioned in a similar way.[14]

The Bible school or college was also a remarkably exportable institution. The decline of Western imperialism after the Second World War threatened the elaborate structure of educational institutions constructed by the mainstream churches. Many of these schools were nationalized or otherwise transformed in the late 1940s through the early 1960s as Western military and administrative power retreated. Mainstream American churches surrendered control of institutions capable of generating much prestige, but they lacked the energy or theological motivation to establish a new network of educational institutions. But the evangelicals recognized, as they did in America, that Bible schools and institutes could be easily and, most importantly, inexpensively established. The various parachurch ministries and sending agencies have used their earlier experience in the United States to create a worldwide network of such institutions that have given conservative American Protestants, including Pentecostals, an advantage in the Third World.

---

of the Wycliffe Bible Translators and the Summer Institute of Linguistics (Waco, Tex.: Word, 1974); Alan Campbell Wares, comp., *Bibliography of the Wycliffe Bible Translators* (Santa Ana, Calif.: Wycliffe Bible Translators, 1970). Wycliffe had its own subsidiary, Jungle Aviation, that was charged with this task.

13. William Vance Trollinger, *God's Empire: William Bell Riley and Midwestern Fundamentalism* (Madison: University of Wisconsin Press, 1990), p. 92. Liberal rural church advocates shared Riley's dismay at the failure of seminary graduates to penetrate the countryside.

14. One must be careful not to make the Bible schools appear unique at this point. Both Union and the University of Chicago maintained a string of churches that were open to their own theological style and to whom they sent generations of graduates.

In *The Advancement of Theological Education,* H. Richard Niebuhr noted that "the growth of the Bible School movement in the United States is not always to be regarded as a phenomenon of the opposition of 'conservatives' to 'liberals'; it is an indication of the increased participation of certain groups to provide higher education of a Christian type for their young people and, particularly, for their ministers."[15] What Niebuhr observed might be called the maturation of the conservative evangelical community. His point could be seen, perhaps, most clearly in denominations like the Assemblies of God and the Church of God (Cleveland, Tennessee) that moved steadily up the educational ladder, founding first Bible schools, then Bible colleges, and finally seminaries.

Despite the Depression and world war, or perhaps because of them, Americans in general were moving toward a society in which formal credentials were increasingly important for employment and promotion. Much American economic opportunity moved from the small-town and city world in which people could make face-to-face evaluations of potential employees and business partners to a world in which both government and industry had to hire people essentially on the basis of their credentials and past experiences. Completion of college or university thus became an important achievement, whether the specific degree program had any immediate relevance to the "job" or not. Unlike previous wars, for example, much of the World War II officer corps was recruited from among college graduates, and during the war the government sponsored accelerated college and professional programs, including programs in theology and ministry.

Credentialing society was the positive side of the secularization of the American university so aptly described by George Marsden.[16] Part of the "ghost in the machine" left behind by Protestant America had been the belief that education rested on a harmonious understanding of the role of the various arts and sciences. As modern scientific and liberal religious views gained ascendancy, especially among educational administrators, conservative religionists found it more difficult to make peace with those institutions. Early plans by conservatives for a fundamentalist university and for the accreditation of Bible schools as a consequence were quietly dropped in the late 1920s.[17] But conservatives found it easier to accommodate to the emphasis on credentialing. As long as a person had the proper credentials, that person was eligible for entry into the right niche in the economic and perhaps the intellectual elite.

15. H. Richard Niebuhr, Daniel Day Williams, and James M. Gustafson, *The Advancement of Theological Education* (New York: Harper, 1957), p. 5.

16. George Marsden, *The Soul of the American University: From Protestant Establishment to Established Nonbelief* (New York: Oxford University Press, 1994).

17. Trollinger, *God's Empire,* p. 41.

One can see the impact of this new order almost immediately on the Bible schools. Initially they were primarily for adults who had clear vocational goals in mind. In that sense they were similar to the many business schools, law schools, and other semiprofessional schools that developed in turn-of-the-century America. As conservatives became more disenchanted with their denominational institutions, these schools went through a period in which students would come for a year of precollege inoculation against modernism before entering college.[18] By the 1940s these schools were seeing themselves as Christian alternatives to mainstream institutions and were offering the bachelor of arts degree.

Full admission to the charmed circle depended on the schools acquiring accreditation, that is, defining their graduates in a way that would make them acceptable to the larger culture. In 1947 representatives of fifty Bible schools met at Winona Lake, Indiana, a noted fundamentalist retreat, to begin work toward an accrediting association.[19] Twelve of these schools were Pentecostal. Pentecostal churches had difficulty during the war securing approval for their chaplains, although some had been granted that status, and they were very aware that the cold war buildup would continue those problems.[20] In 1949 the new Association of Bible Institutes and Bible Colleges established its own standards, many of them based on those of the AATS. These included minimal education attainments for faculty, a professional librarian, and the bachelor of Bible degree as the basic certification. For many of these schools formal accreditation was only a station on their way to becoming Christian colleges and occasionally Christian universities in their own right. In time many would, following AATS guidelines, separate their seminaries from their collegiate and undergraduate schools.

B. Unity, Expansion, and Loss

Conservative Christianity never completely relied on the Bible school to educate its leaders. The American Baptists had established a string of more conservative schools that were often as large or larger than their liberal counterparts. From 1930 to 1960 Gordon, Northern, and Eastern enrolled more Baptist students than Newton, the University of Chicago, and Colgate Rochester. The suc-

18. I am indebted to Joel Carpenter for this observation.

19. Frank E. Gaebelein, "Education," in *Contemporary Evangelical Thought*, ed. Carl F. H. Henry (Great Neck, N.Y.: Channel Press, 1957), p. 173.

20. Edith Blumhofer, *The Assemblies of God* (Springfield, Mo.: Gospel Publishing House, 1989), p. 115.

cess of these schools put the more liberal seminaries on the defensive. In the 1920s Newton — the denomination's flagship freestanding seminary — joined with Andover, for instance, for financial reasons, and the University of Chicago Divinity School became more ecumenical and for a season federated with Congregationalist Chicago Theological Seminary.

There were other strong conservative schools. Among Missouri Synod Lutherans, Concordia taught a strictly confessional Lutheran theology, and if time and declining immigration lessened the difference between Philadelphia and Gettysburg, Philadelphia was still markedly confessional. Both Southern Baptists and Southern Presbyterians maintained strong schools that taught a conservative evangelical position. In the Northern Presbyterian Church, most seminaries continued to teach some version of the older Princeton theology.[21]

Despite their still substantial place in American theological education, American conservatives harbored real unease. The new theology of Barth and particularly Brunner was making inroads in many traditionally conservative institutions, and many feared that Princeton's new president, John Mackay, would lead the school in a more neoorthodox direction. McCormick in Chicago had shifted in that direction. While the heyday of neoorthodoxy in Southern seminaries (Baptist and Presbyterian) would be after the Second World War, the seeds for that development had already been planted and needed only postwar prosperity to flourish.[22]

II. The National Association of Evangelicals

If the theological winds seemed to be growing colder, the angry divisions among conservatives made many responsible conservative leaders uneasy. The most radical conservative leaders, such as J. Frank Norris and John R. Rice, often sounded as demented as fundamentalism's critics claimed them to be. Further, the National Council's domination of free radio programming continued to be a serious matter of concern. At the same time, the nation's evangelicals felt there were real grounds for hope. Despite the religious depression of the 1930s, conservative congregations had grown in numbers and influence. Further, many conservatives hoped for a new awakening that might inspire America to

21. John Mulder and Lee Wyatt, "The Predicament of Pluralism: The Study of Theology in Presbyterian Seminaries," in *The Pluralistic Vision: Presbyterians and Mainstream Protestant Education and Leadership,* ed. Milton J. Coalter, John M. Mulder, and Louis B. Weeks (Louisville: Westminster John Knox, 1992), pp. 37-70.

22. Dale Moody of Southern and those who studied with him would be very important figures in this movement, as would Shirley Guthrie of Columbia.

return to its spiritual and religious roots. But to bring about a great revival, conservatives knew, they would have to forge a different relationship with American culture.

The person most influential in building a consensus among moderate conservatives was J. Elwin Wright, who headed up a parachurch movement, the Harvesters, that had Pentecostal leanings. After inheriting this ministry from his father, Wright traveled throughout New England and much of the nation conducting revival and renewal meetings. Joel Carpenter noted that Wright's direction as an evangelist was set in 1929 when he invited William Bell Riley and other leading fundamentalists to a ministers meeting in Boston. After this amazingly successful event, Wright renamed the Harvesters the New England Fellowship, and began to establish a number of new ministries, each of which was almost a textbook example of a successful parachurch program. His supporters came to include Baptists, Congregationalists, evangelical Episcopalians, and Holiness and Pentecostal people; he himself joined Park Street Congregational Church, where Ockenga was pastor. In the process of building his own empire, Wright came to know many of the most influential conservative leaders and to gain their respect.

Despite the formation of Carl McIntyre's American Council of Churches, largely intended to oppose the Federal Council, Wright and his allies, particularly Ralph Davis of the Africa Inland Mission, another parachurch organization, went ahead with plans to establish the National Association of Evangelicals (NAE). A preliminary call for a meeting went out in 1942, and in 1943 the association was officially formed in Chicago. By this time the nation was at war, and concerns about issues ranging from access to the radio to the appointment of evangelicals as chaplains were uppermost. During World War I, after all, the Federal Council of Churches and the YMCA, both under liberal leadership, had represented Protestantism before the government on these matters, and there were natural fears that a more liberal council would be no more respectful of evangelical claims for inclusion in the military than they had been of evangelical demands for a share of the free radio time.

Although the National Association faced a long and arduous battle with McIntyre and his American Council, the new organization was a remarkable body. Perhaps reflecting Wright's own background, the association brought together representatives of parachurch groups, denominations, and individuals interested in the cause. No earlier American religious organization had represented such a swatch of organizations involved in American religious life, although the later National Council of Churches would do so. If some of the larger groups, such as the Southern Baptists, did not join the cause, the NAE attracted important representatives from their ranks. Like American conservatism itself, it was a mosaic of different views. The organization's statement of faith reflected that breadth. Modeled on the statements used by many parachurch organizations, it avoided noticeable particularities or points of dispute, like inerrancy, and set forth concrete points of agreement that most evangelicals (and even many liberal Christians) could accept.

The organization also early proved its value as an advocate of evangelical causes. Within a year the NAE had created the National Association of Religious Broadcasters and launched a major campaign for access to the media. As Wright and his friends saw the issue: "Besides the Catholics and Jews, we have two great divisions of the church, probably approximately of equal strength. The first is represented by the Federal Council of Churches of Christ in America. This includes the so-called liberal or modernist groups. The second is the evangelical or conservative group, which, up to the present time, has been without cohesion and consequently without representation."[23] In short, there were ten to twenty million Christians who had been denied their equal share of the media's attention by what evangelicals felt was a self-appointed monopoly. Other parachurch bodies, including the Bible schools, also found themselves strongly supported by the new organization. By 1949 it had united evangelical theologians in the Evangelical Theological Society, a professional guild devoted to biblically based theology.

III. A New Apologetic

Formation of the NAE was not the only notable event in the 1940s. One important milestone was a shift in evangelical thought. As Marsden and others have noted, Scottish commonsense philosophy provided much of the intellectual background of the Princeton theology that had such an abiding influence on the right. Despite the continuing popularity of Warfield and Hodge, more for their doctrine of Scripture than for their overall system, this approach to modernity had serious flaws. The most obvious one was that it could not account for the persistence of liberalism. According to commonsense philosophy, human minds would tend, at least over time, to interpret similar data in the same way. Thus, Newton's physics was highly debated when it was formulated, but as observations and experiments were conducted, mature minds came to accept Newton's "laws." In theory, the same thing should have happened in theology, but there was little evidence that it had happened or might happen in the fu-

23. Arthur H. Matthew, *Standing Up, Standing Together: The Emergence of the National Association of Evangelicals* (Carol Stream, Ill.: National Association of Evangelicals, 1992), p. 40.

ture. If anything, the argument appeared to be going the other way. Short of following Machen and accusing one's opponents of having left the faith, there seemed to be little response to this problem. Evangelicalism, once called the apologetic religion by Warfield, was badly in need of an apologetic.

The very small, but very highly educated, Christian Reformed Church pointed the way out of this dilemma. In Holland, Abraham Kuyper united elements of traditional Calvinism, contemporary European theology, and his own thought in a comprehensive theory of culture. At the heart of this perspective Kuyper had put the idea of the worldview, or that set of assumptions and intellectual habits that gave our ideas much of their content. Kuyper, who retained much of traditional Dutch rationalism, believed that we could influence our worldview by our rational choices, especially when those apparently innate ideas were challenged by events or happenings that called them into question. Since common grace might establish an adequate worldview, the system pointed to the need to maintain Christian cultural institutions, such as colleges and seminaries. At the same time, it explained liberalism as an acculturated habit of mind that needed examination.[24] Kuyper's thought was picked up and developed by Cornelius Van Til, who in turn passed the baton to Gordon Clark of Wheaton College.

The reputations of Van Til and Clark have suffered because many who encountered them found them very unpleasant people. Despite his intellectual abilities, for instance, Clark was dismissed from Wheaton — in large measure over his too-consistent Calvinism — and spent years defending himself in his own Orthodox Presbyterian Church. But such observations should not obscure the fact that Clark was a first-rate mind whose classes roamed through Western philosophy. Perhaps more important, Clark convinced young conservatives that they were the legitimate heirs of the great tradition of Western philosophy and theology. Among those Clark deeply influenced were Carl F. H. Henry, Paul Jewett, and E. J. Carnell. His followers remained convinced that he had given them the Rosetta stone that would enable them to enter the modern world without compromising their faith.

The combination of the new emphasis on worldview and the credentialing society encouraged a number of bright young intellectuals to enter and complete graduate studies in the late 1940s. These include Harold Ockenga (Ph.D. Pittsburgh), Carl F. H. Henry (Ph.D. Boston), Bernard Ramm

24. James D. Bratt, ed., *Abraham Kuyper: A Centennial Reader* (Grand Rapids: Eerdmans; Carlisle: Paternoster, 1998); Peter Heslam, *Creating a Christian Worldview: Abraham Kuyper's Lectures on Calvinism* (Grand Rapids: Eerdmans; Carlisle: Paternoster, 1998). My explanation of Kuyper is, alas, somewhat oversimplified.

(Ph.D. University of California), Daniel Fuller (Th.D. Basel), E. J. Carnell (Th.D. Harvard), Kanneth Kantzer (Ph.D. Harvard), Merrill Tenney (Ph.D. Harvard), John Gerstner (Ph.D. Harvard), Harold Kuhn (Ph.D. Harvard), Glenn Barker (Harvard), George Ladd (Harvard), Roger Nicole (Harvard), Samuel Schultze (Th.D. Harvard), George Turner (Ph.D. 1946), J. Harold Greenlee (Ph.D. Harvard), Jack Lewis (Ph.D. Harvard), Lemoine Lewis (Ph.D. Harvard), and Harold Lindsell (Ph.D. New York University).[25] Many of their students would follow the same Ivy League pathway, seeking admission to the most prestigious American universities. For both these new evangelicals and their supporters, it was important that their teaching credentials come from secular universities. There were many reasons for this. The most important was the desire to show the world that evangelical scholars could compete at the highest rungs of American academic life. Harvard was as important as a symbol of academic attainment as it was for the quality of its intellectual training. But aside from the question of prestige, conservative scholars benefited from the secularity of the modern university. As long as doctoral students were able to establish their own special areas of research, secular universities did not demand that students step outside of their own disciplinary bounds.

Was there a "new evangelical" mind? Mark Noll in his jeremiad *The Scandal of the Evangelical Mind* maintained that evangelical scholars, particularly the new evangelical generation, had not made substantial intellectual gains.[26] The scandal of the evangelical mind, in effect, was that there was not much of an evangelical mind. Yet that judgment may have more polemic than descriptive value. The new evangelical scholars often read everything, amassing large personal libraries, and they passionately engaged their opponents on

25. They had come to Harvard Divinity School or, in the case of two of them, Boston University's School of Theology to learn their trade and earn their credentials as theologians. During the middle to late 1940s more than a dozen evangelical Protestants received Harvard doctorates: three from the Churches of Christ, one Pentecostal, and eleven from a fundamentalist background. Among the fundamentalists were Samuel Schultz and Kenneth Kantzer, both of whom would go on to teach at Wheaton College, where Merrill Tenney (Ph.D. Harvard, 1944) had preceded them; John Gerstner, who become the church historian at Pittsburgh Theological Seminary; Burton Goddard and Roger Nicole, who had begun what would turn into long careers at Gordon Divinity School; Terrelle Crum of the Providence Bible Institute; and five who would join the faculty of Fuller Theological Seminary: Edward John Carnell, Gleason Archer, George Alan Ladd, Paul King Jewett, and Glenn Barker. Carnell was also enrolled in the doctoral program in theology, where he was joined for several summers by Carl F. H. Henry, a fellow Wheaton graduate who was on the faculty of Northern Baptist Theological Seminary in Chicago. Carpenter, *Revive Us Again,* p. 191.

26. Mark Noll, *The Scandal of the Evangelical Mind* (Grand Rapids: Eerdmans; Leicester, England: Inter-Varsity Press, 1994).

the left and the right. The intellectual reach, for example, of an E. J. Carnell was extraordinary. In addition to a thorough knowledge of philosophy and conservative theology, Carnell was a careful, if critical, reader of Reinhold Niebuhr and Paul Tillich. Carl F. H. Henry is another example. Through a long and fruitful career, Henry read and commented on the major theologians of his generation, from Karl Barth to Hans Frei. Hence, it might be more accurate to say that the new evangelicals had an encyclopedic understanding of scholarship that involved them in the task of trying to keep up with as much of the discussion as possible. While this type of scholarship often produces a breadth of knowledge, it rarely produces those insightful and risky monographs that often make possible advance in the more technical fields of theology, such as biblical studies.[27] It was, however, ideally suited to the defense of an embattled minority.

The new evangelicals were seriously limited by their social location in the American educational landscape. Noll, commenting on post–World War II evangelical scholarship, noted that most evangelical scholars taught in colleges. He continued: "[C]olleges have a different goal from the research universities. Most important, they function under entirely different reward structures." Universities reward original and creative thinking, new research, and the production of scholarly literature. In contrast, liberal arts institutions "provide general guidance, general orientation, and general introduction." In other words, they are institutions of nurture and synthesis designed to prepare students for their future life as leaders. In many ways these general attributes are particularly intense at conservative Christian colleges that are as concerned with nurturing faith as with the growth of intellect.[28]

IV. The Evangelical University, the Neoorthodox Challenge, and Fuller Seminary

Since the late nineteenth century American Christians had struggled with the relationship of the new university to faith. However, most liberal Christians were confident that through departments of religion, campus ministries, and particularly the university-related divinity schools they would dominate the discussion for an indefinite future. Moreover, through the 1950s mainstream Protestants believed that the Christian scholar, the academic consecrated to

27. Mark Noll, *Between Faith and Criticism: Evangelicalism, Scholarship, and the Bible in America* (San Francisco: Harper and Row, 1986).

28. Noll, *Scandal*, pp. 16-17.

both learning and Christianity, would be a prominent part of any future university organization. From its inception to the 1960s, the National Council of Churches worked to keep alive a network of such teachers and to feature their work in its own publication, the *Christian Scholar.*

Conservative scholars were not so confident about the university. In the Netherlands Kuyper had established the Free University of Amsterdam to interpret the world according to the Christian worldview. Pre–Vatican II Catholic educators had a similar hope, based on the popularity of neo-Thomist thought. American evangelicals shared the hope that a university could be founded on very different principles or, perhaps better, worldviews. Conservative denominations had established a number of Christian colleges, although many of these, especially in the South, saw themselves more as part of general American education than of their church's historic mission. Indeed, many of the best of these schools, including Southern Baptist–controlled Wake Forest and Richmond, saw themselves as significantly more liberal than their sponsoring bodies. Further, many of these schools, even the most theologically conservative, experienced tensions with their sponsoring bodies, especially over evolution. Given declining conservative influence in many denominational colleges, the best example of their educational hopes that evangelicals had was Wheaton College.[29] Wheaton functioned as a West Point for the movement, educating the best of potential conservative leaders and providing a think tank for American conservatism.

Yet conservative evangelicals knew that Wheaton was not a university and wondered whether it had the energy or financial resources to become such. Throughout the 1940s and 1950s evangelicals continued to work for the establishment of such an institution. Plans and schemes multiplied, especially after the Graham revivals. It was not to be. The closest evangelicals came was in 1955 when plans were made to build such a school on the campus of Gordon College. This was to be the first of four such campuses, located in the principal regions of the country. Like other such plans, this one failed.[30] Ironically, the failure had nothing to do with conservative anti-intellectualism or any of the other plagues of the evangelical mind. Rather, the principal supporters of evangelical causes, especially Maxey Jarman and J. Howard Pew, were not convinced that

29. For Wheaton, see Michael S. Hamilton, "The Fundamentalist Harvard: Wheaton College and the Enduring Vitality of American Evangelicalism, 1919-1965" (Ph.D. diss., University of Notre Dame, 1994).

30. George Marsden, "Why No Major Evangelical University? The Loss and Recovery of Evangelical Advanced Scholarship," in *Making Higher Education Christian: The History and Mission of Evangelical Colleges in America,* ed. Joel Carpenter and Kenneth W. Shipps (St. Paul, Minn.: Christian University Press; Grand Rapids: Eerdmans, 1987).

such schools were economically possible.[31] As Jesus said, the children of darkness were often more wise in their generation than the children of light. With few exceptions, previous Christian colleges and universities had moved toward a more secular position, not only in obedience to ideology, but also because of their desperate need for more students and better financing. Only by casting the net over as large an area as possible were these schools able to garner the resources needed for a modern educational operation.

In retrospect, the failure to establish a national Christian university was a key nonevent in the history of conservative theological education. Although evangelicals were becoming more numerous and more prosperous, the pool of available resources was not extensive or deep enough to support so many institutions. Even Dallas Seminary, the dispensational flagship institution, was forced to abandon its traditional reliance on "faith giving" and move toward an active program of solicitation,[32] and Fuller would be very fortunate that David Weyerhaeuser became one of the school's most faithful contributors.[33] Clearly, for instance, Weyerhaeuser's wealth and institutional savvy sparked the expansion of that institution to include schools of psychology, missions, and education. Ockenga wrote to Fuller in 1961:

> Dave Weyerhaeuser certainly has the welfare of the Seminary in mind and is thinking aggressively. His idea of buying up the properties around that area when it can be done feasibly, has my full sanction. He also has a deep interest in a subsidiary school of psychology, which would have my support providing that it is set up that the tail does not wag the dog. It might be that we can project a school of Christian education, a school of missions, a school of music, a school of psychology, if and when funds are available. If the funds for the school of psychology become available, I do not think that we ought to turn them down.[34]

If small-scale institutions lived this close to the edge, how could evangelicals hope to bear the cost of a full university, not to mention four such institutions?

The financial realities exposed in the failure of evangelicals to establish a university highlight their most enduring contribution to conservative theologi-

31. David Lee Russell, "Coming to Grips with the Age of Reason: An Analysis of the New Evangelical Intellectual Agenda, 1942-1970" (Ph.D. diss., Michigan State University, 1993), p. 65.

32. See Michael S. Hamilton, "More Money, More Ministry: The Financing of American Evangelicalism Since 1945," in *More Money, More Ministry: Money and Evangelicals in Recent North American History,* ed. Larry Eskridge and Mark A. Noll (Grand Rapids: Eerdmans, 2000).

33. The letters of Harold John Ockenga while president reveal his increasing reliance on the Weyerhaeuser funds for the school.

34. Ockenga to Charles Fuller, Aug. 17, 1961.

cal education. Whether by design, by accident, or by the cunning of the market, conservative evangelicals came to support a comparatively small number of institutions that were strategically located around the country. This enabled them to concentrate their efforts and greatly multiply their influence.

There are two examples of this strategy. The first is denominational. Despite its numerical size, the Southern Baptist Convention almost went bankrupt in the 1920s. After negotiating some strategic loans, the convention's leadership launched an aggressive plan to pay off the indebtedness and to control expenses through the Cooperative Program. Theological education was the beneficiary of this system as the schools received a set amount from the convention for each candidate they educated as well as some funds for capital needs. The financial realities of Southern Baptist life, moreover, imposed some discipline on the establishment of new schools. So, when the denomination grew rapidly in the post–World War II period, the convention's leadership was able to exert considerable control over the establishment of new schools. The result was an effective system of six schools, widely dispersed through the area served by Southern Baptists, that all attained considerable size. This system lasted until the losers in the Baptist controversies of the 1980s established a string of new and much smaller institutions for the education of "moderate" clergy. The decision of the Missouri Synod to concentrate its graduate-level theological work at Concordia in St. Louis was another example of this careful use of resources.

The second example is the schools established or reestablished by descendants of Northern fundamentalism. These included Fuller, Dallas, Trinity, and Gordon. These seminaries were something new. Most earlier conservative schools had been founded to serve those parts of a mainstream church that had retained their loyalty to biblical truth. Thus, Austen De Blois of Eastern spoke for the founders of all these schools when he said: "The purpose of our Seminary is to compete triumphantly with the modernist theological seminaries. To do so we must meet them on their own level in the educational field. We must give just as virile an intellectual discipline. We must prepare just as accurate a scholarship, and a scholarship more sound. We must secure for our Baptist pastorates an ever-enlarging group of thoroughly trained men."[35] Such schools continue to be founded by those who feel excluded or withdraw from other denominations. Conservative Baptist Seminary's Vernon Grounds, for example, could have used De Blois's words when he founded his seminary in 1948.

35. Norman Maring, "Conservative but Progressive," in *What God Hath Wrought: Eastern's First Thirty-five Years,* ed. Gilbert Lee Guffin (Chicago: Judson, 1960), p. 43. See also Austen K. De Blois, *The Making of Ministers* ([Philadelphia]: Judson, 1936).

In contrast, the new or renewed institutions established after World War II did not represent a part within an existing denomination. They were intended to serve a much broader constituency of churches, parachurch organizations, and missions. In many ways these schools were the conservative attempt to build institutions similar to such liberal interdenominational schools as New York's Union Seminary.

Fuller was the pioneer and pacesetter for these seminaries. George Marsden, the historian of Fuller, has located the school in the new evangelicals' desire to reform fundamentalism. As Marsden sees the new evangelicals, they "repudiated both the doctrinal and the cultural implications of a thoroughgoing dispensationalism while they remained loyal to the fundamentals of fundamentalism." Like many other reformers in American history, Marsden's "new evangelicals" hoped to recover some of the dynamic of an early period. As he put it, "their version of fundamentalism was defined primarily by the culturally centrist tradition of nineteenth-century evangelicalism. Theologically, they stood for a moderate form of classic Calvinist Protestantism."[36] Marsden's view has the advantage of focusing attention on the intellectual motives of people who, after all, believed that orthodoxy was essential to Christian faith and were willing to act on their presupposition.

The "new evangelicals" did have a coherent intellectual agenda. In 1946 Carl F. H. Henry published *Remaking the Modern Mind.* He followed this a year later with *The Uneasy Conscience of Modern Fundamentalism.* Taken together, the two books constituted a manifesto that set forth the theological program that Henry would follow throughout his career. In *Remaking the Modern Mind,* significantly dedicated to Gordon Clark, William Harry Jellema, and Cornelius Van Til, Henry called for conservatives to seize the intellectual opportunities present in current intellectual life and to use the wealth of resources provided by the Christian tradition to answer the world's questions. *Remaking* was the first of a series of writings by younger evangelicals calling on fundamentalists to replace their defensive stance with a more engaging apologetic. Henry's second attack was on fundamentalism's tendency to withdraw from vital engagement with the issues of the day. Like many thoughtful Americans, Henry believed that the United States was at a vital crossroads in its history. The nation had won a great triumph over Nazism, but the fruits of that victory could not be enjoyed. America's erstwhile ally, Soviet Russia — long distrusted by evangelicals because of its ruthless persecution of Bible believers — had seized much of Europe, and the Communist Party was apparently on the verge of vic-

36. George Marsden, *Reforming Fundamentalism: Fuller Seminary and the New Evangelicalism* (Grand Rapids: Eerdmans, 1987), p. 3.

tories in Greece, Italy, and France.[37] Further, the United States itself faced serious social dislocations. Henry believed that it was time for action.[38] Many evangelicals would respond to his call, including Billy Graham, and both social advocacy and anticommunism would be part of the general evangelical agenda.

Yet we must be careful. Henry and his fellow younger evangelicals were only one component of the complex alliance that came together to found Fuller Seminary. Perhaps the most important leader was Harold Ockenga, the scholarly conservative who pastored Boston's Park Street Church. Although he had left Princeton to study at Westminster under Machen and Van Til, Ockenga was not intensely theological. He wore his conservative orthodoxy lightly, much as Henry Pitney Van Dusen of Union wore his liberalism. While few ever doubted his personal fidelity to the fundamentals, the fundamentals did not dominate his every thought. His great dream was evangelical unity. Ockenga, a highly trained philosopher in his own right, together with J. Elwin Wright, had been one of the architects of the National Association of Evangelicals, and while establishing that organization, he had created a large network that included Charles Fuller, C. Davis Weyerhaeuser, J. Howard Pew, and Wilbur Smith. More than any other national evangelical leader, Ockenga appreciated the power of the parachurch movement and its particular combination of missionary cooperation and independent action. The yearly Missions Fair at his congregation was a cornucopia of Christian initiatives at home and abroad. Ockenga shared Henry's desire for social and intellectual respectability. After all, Park Street was almost an exemplar of what a wealthy, socially acceptable church should be: ushers in morning coats, very well dressed parishioners, and an immaculately dressed staff. Much more than Henry, who saw the world in the type of sweeping generalizations favored by such contemporary intellectuals as Jacques Barzun and Reinhold Niebuhr, Ockenga was a man born to have influence in the boardroom and in conversations held with one or two people just beyond earshot of the other participants.[39]

Ockenga's passion was to expand inner evangelical cooperation and to forge an alliance with the numerous moderate conservatives, such as L. Nelson Bell, who remained in the mainstream denominations. Billy Graham was an

37. Anticommunism was, of course, a much broader movement than evangelicalism, but evangelicals were prominent in the movement and often identified strongly with political leaders, like Richard Nixon, who embraced that position.

38. One must be careful not to separate *The Uneasy Conscience* from its cold war environment. Like other new evangelicals, Henry was deeply worried about the power of Communism as an ideology that was opposed to God.

39. The standard study of Ockenga is Harold Lindsell, *Park Street Prophet: A Life of Harold John Ockenga* (Wheaton, Ill.: Van Kampen Press, 1951).

important part of this strategy. Graham first established himself as an evangelist in Youth for Christ, initially a loosely related series of rallies for high school students, and his style of evangelism, including the type of music favored by his music minister, George Beverly Shea, reflected the communication skills learned in that movement. Although liberal Christians, including Reinhold Niebuhr, saw Graham as a Billy Sunday reborn, Graham's ministry was much more multifaceted than that. Building on the experience of earlier radio evangelists, Graham built a media empire that included books, magazines, movies, radio, and television. He and his very well dressed team carefully mirrored middle America and its business community in their appearance and their language. If Wheaton-trained Graham retained any of his Southern country boy character, it was the measured accent of a young Southerner who went north after the war, determined to claim a place in the national sun. In him, Ockenga found the perfect ally and public voice. Graham would be a major figure in the creation of Fuller and the re-creation of Gordon.

Charles Fuller represented the evangelical cooperation so prized by Graham and Ockenga. Fuller was a remarkable man. In the 1920s he had come to experience a growing sense of Christian vocation and had been attracted to the new medium of radio. Fuller had both a sharp mind and a strong will, and he quickly became a master of the new medium. He left nothing to chance: each detail of each broadcast, whether held at his home studio or on the road, was as carefully planned as the Jack Benny show, and he labored to fit every element of his services into the rigorous time slots demanded by the new media. Whether as a result of study, experimentation, or insight, he came to know how long a hymn should be, which letter spoke to many in the audience, and how long a passage he should read from the Bible. He was very good at what he did, and his hard work earned him more money than he needed for himself or his ministry.

Fuller wanted to make a contribution to education, but he had difficulty in deciding whether he should establish a Bible school or a seminary. Ockenga had awakened in him a broader vision of "the central stream of Christianity which avoids many of the eddies of our modern sectarian life,"[40] and convinced him that the proper place for this tradition was a theological seminary or a university.[41] Fuller was also an opportunity for Ockenga. Ever practical, Ockenga knew how difficult it was to establish a first-rate institution from his own experience with the Gordon board. In a revealing letter to Fuller, he wrote: "We have

40. Ockenga to Fuller, Oct. 31, 1946, Fuller Archives.

41. Although Ockenga had graduated from Westminster, he does not seem to have seen the school as a model.

been trying to build a strong seminary here at Gordon College and are succeeding in part, but we lack the needed resources to make it the kind of school we would like it to be."[42] Ockenga would later, together with J. Howard Pew, return to that project. But for now, Fuller had sufficient money and land to launch an important institution.

With the question of financing apparently settled, Ockenga was able to plan the institution. His model was Princeton, which he believed to be the best-designed and best-supported seminary in the country, and he and Fuller sought the best conservative faculty available for the new institution.[43] To attract teachers at that level, of course, the new institution had to pay first-class wages and offer benefits commensurate with its expectations. Whatever else Fuller Seminary was to be, it was not to be second-rate. Evangelicals had enough of a struggle with Franciscan poverty at their other schools to satisfy their need for sacrifice. Further, this would be a faculty that could and would publish on the level of other faculties.

Clearly, Ockenga and Fuller believed that they had found a formula for success, and from its first class onward Fuller did attract many of the brighter and more able evangelical students. Many of its early graduates were religious entrepreneurs, like Bill Bright, the energetic founder of Campus Crusade for Christ, who believed that they had a world to win for Jesus. But spiritual victories often bring earthly crosses, and Fuller was true to this old evangelical insight. The founders had hoped that the school's graduates would be readily accepted into the Presbyterian ministry, but this was the occasion of a major battle that Fuller won only after many battles on various fronts. Too many mainstream Presbyterians remembered the pain and anguish of the Machen schism to give his spiritual grandchildren position in the church.

Fuller's search for full academic acceptability was also held up by a long, arduous struggle with the AATS. The primary issue was the fiscal relationship between the new school and the foundation established by Charles Fuller to help finance the operation. The association believed that the arrangement compromised the school's independence, and to receive the coveted prize Fuller accepted the association's position. Other evangelical schools, seeking full accreditation in the 1950s, were also forced to comply with the association's image of what a theological school ought to be. Baptist seminaries, for instance, surrendered their very effective (and very denominationally relevant) Th.B. degrees,

42. Ockenga to Fuller, Oct. 31, 1946, Fuller Archives.

43. "I have set up at present a form for the faculty based upon Princeton Seminary which I hold to be the best equipped culturally and educationally in America and which, of course, heightens the tragedy of its departure from the faith." Ockenga to Fuller, Mar. 12, 1947.

and both Eastern and Northern established separate liberal arts colleges to prepare people for full enrollment in their schools.

In retrospect, as important as accreditation was to the faculty and to many of those interested in the seminary's intellectual project, two other issues were perhaps more important to the school's future. The first was the pressing problem of finances. As Marsden makes clear, poor investments limited Charles Fuller's capacity to provide for the institution. What the founders had believed was a mother lode was a much narrower vein than anyone had suspected. Perhaps more seriously, Fuller Seminary cost more to operate than had been anticipated. As Fuller noted, the school's very prosperity was a curse in the tight market for evangelical income. "Satan has been busy spreading reports over the country that we have no need — that the Foundation is very large." In the 1950s most American theological schools were facing serious financial problems. By the 1960s the age-old debate over whether seminaries and divinity schools should raise part of their operating funds from tuition was resolved. Schools could, by and large, no longer operate without substantial tuition charges. In 1955 Fuller wrote to Ockenga that "We desperately need more general contributions — large and small — more will [bring] more giving friends of the school, and those who help spread the information that we HAVE PRESSING NEED of financial help."[44]

Fiscal necessity changed Fuller as it changed many American schools. Despite the school's partial origins in the parachurch movement, many of its first faculty and its early president E. J. Carnell had hoped for a school that would be a research and teaching institution, a university divinity school — so to speak — not related to a particular university. But money is a hard master. The seminary was forced to move closer to its constituency, especially that part of its constituency that was willing to give. Ockenga actively courted Pew as a potential giver, and he constantly scouted for other rich potential contributors. While the later expansion of the school to include schools of psychology, missions, and education was of course related to the church's mission, those enterprises were very popular with donors and supporters.[45]

The second problem was related to the nature of conservative theology itself: the need to defend the truth once delivered to the saints.[46] Theological conflict was a mark of the evangelical community from 1950 to 2000, as evangelicals, in common with other American Christians, tried to balance theological inclusiveness with the demand for theological integrity. In addition to serious battles at other

44. Fuller to Ockenga, Aug. 16, 1956: I have reversed the order of the two sentences.

45. Fuller has always had a large number of Baptist faculty members, and in general, Baptists and Methodists have been avid supporters of the practical fields.

46. I do not wish to imply that liberal theology somehow avoided nastiness. Liberals were often as exclusionary and empire building as their conservative counterparts.

evangelical schools, including Gordon-Conwell and Trinity, disruptive theological battles struck the Southern Baptist and Missouri Synod denominations and offset the favorable publicity conservatives received in the American press.

Fuller was the point guard in these battles. There were many reasons for the school's exposed position. The new evangelical position advocated by some early faculty advocated the reform of fundamentalism, to use Marsden's useful phrase, and reform movements always provoke defenders of the status quo. Equally serious were the hopes that many evangelicals, perhaps including Fuller's most determined enemies, had placed in the institution. Fuller was to be the evangelical lighthouse, the place where the brilliance of evangelical truth would shine forth into a modernist darkness. Like evangelist Billy Graham, the school was part of the long-expected revival that would return the nation to its religious roots and make America what God would have it be. Further, Fuller was the down payment or earnest on the great evangelical university that would point the way to a revival of Christian scholarship. No single institution or perhaps any combination of evangelical institutions could do what people hoped Fuller might do, and not surprisingly, Fuller failed to deliver on those hopes.

The first wave of controversy that swept over Fuller was the case of Hungarian theologian Béla Vassady, a Barthian, who was hired to teach at the school, beginning in 1949. American conservatives had a love-hate relationship with Barth.[47] Cornelius Van Til of Westminster was the most vocal anti-Barthian among American evangelicals,[48] but other evangelicals had similar concerns. In some ways Van Til's analysis was acute. Even in *Church Dogmatics* Barth retained the essential liberal belief that theology was a response to the historical situation of the church and, thus, open to continual revision. Theology was a task in progress, always awaiting another study, another formulation. The truth delivered to the ages became the truth expressed for the present time. Van Til and his evangelical allies, in short, feared that many Barthians would move from *Church Dogmatics* to a fully developed liberalism.[49] Many Death of God theologians, in fact, had begun their careers as Barthians.

47. Phillip R. Thorne, *Evangelicalism and Karl Barth: His Reception and Influence in North American Evangelical Theology* (Allison Park, Pa.: Pickwick, 1995), p. xiii; Richard Albert Mohler, "Evangelical Theology and Karl Barth: Representative Models of Response" (Ph.D. diss., Southern Baptist Theological Seminary, 1989).

48. Cornelius Van Til, *The New Modernism* (Philadelphia: Presbyterian and Reformed Press, 1946); Cornelius Van Til, *Karl Barth and Evangelicalism* (Philadelphia: Presbyterian and Reformed Press, 1964); Cornelius Van Til, *Barthianism and Christianity* (Philadelphia: Presbyterian and Reformed Press, 1962).

49. To be fair to Van Til, whose polemics were often bitter and shrill, neoorthodoxy outside of Southern institutions did collapse rather rapidly in the 1970s and 1980s.

Barth was, of course, the most orthodox of the current theologians. In studying Reinhold Niebuhr, E. J. Carnell, who greatly appreciated Niebuhr's ability to speak to intellectuals, finally had to conclude that "Niebuhr does not speak about Christ's literal cross and resurrection at all. He speaks, at most, of the symbols of the cross and resurrection."[50] The same point could of course be made about Emil Brunner, Oscar Cullmann, and others. In particular, many evangelicals were deeply suspicious of Brunner's and Cullmann's tendency to separate history into sacred history *(Heilsgeschichte)* and profane history *(Geschichte)*.[51] This formulation often made *Heilsgeschichte* into legend and myth.

Evangelicals were also aware of the institutional dangers implicit in neoorthodoxy. The "fall" of Princeton was a much more vivid memory for them than the fall of Adam, and clearly Brunner had been used to lead Princeton further from orthodoxy. Neoorthodoxy was also beginning to make significant inroads in Southern institutions where it became the "Brunner pass" that enabled people to cross from the old theology to a more ecumenical perspective.[52] There was enough grease on the slippery slope for these fears to be more than a chimera.

Given where American evangelicalism was at the time, Vassady's fate was sealed once the issue was raised. The faculty adopted a creed that explicitly affirmed inerrancy, and Vassady, who was nothing if not intellectually honest, admitted that he could not sign it. The time had come for him to move on. But the deeper issues were to plague Fuller for some time. Almost as soon as the smoke over Vassady cleared, the school was caught up in a debate over dispensationalism. In 1952 George Ladd, a graduate of Gordon and Harvard, published his *Critical Questions about the Kingdom of God,* followed four years later by his *The Blessed Hope* (1956). To the nonfundamentalist, these learned works seem almost fanatically biblical. Ladd supports almost every line of his argument

50. Quoted in Alister McGrath, *Evangelicalism and the Future of Christianity* (Downers Grove, Ill.: InterVarsity, 1995), p. 77. See also Edward John Carnell, *The Theology of Reinhold Niebuhr* (Grand Rapids: Eerdmans, 1951).

51. Jewett studied with Brunner in Zürich. Paul King Jewett, *Emil Brunner's Concept of Revelation* (London: James Clark, 1954). "If it be granted on the one hand that faith must have a broader historical foundation than Kierkegaard allowed and yet on the other hand that we can no longer define this base as coterminous with the Gospel tradition, how are we to determine what is essential and what is not? What constitutes the 'substance' of the Gospel tradition? If Brunner can delete the Virgin Birth, the empty tomb, the forty-day post resurrection ministry, and the bodily ascension, where are we to draw the line?"

52. Thorne, *Evangelicalism and Karl Barth,* p. 157; for the early impact on Southern Presbyterians, see Holmes Rolston, *A Conservative Looks to Barth and Brunner* (Nashville: Cokesbury Press, 1933).

with a careful and sustained argument from Scripture. Yet, despite the biblicism, the conclusion is clear: "Now, in the history of theology, dispensationalism is novel, and the modern refinements of it are novel. Dispensationalism has no place in the great classical stream of evangelical history."[53] After the death of Charles Fuller, statements implying dispensationalism were excised from the seminary's confessional norms. Ladd's position had moved the school further from classical fundamentalism and more toward the center of nonseparatist conservatism.

The next great debate to engulf Fuller was one that would eventually involve most neoconservative institutions: biblical inerrancy. In retrospect, the reason Fuller Seminary could deal with this issue as forthrightly as it did was the presence on the faculty of Daniel Fuller, the son of the founder, who had studied with Karl Barth. In some ways this was determinative for the discussion. While Daniel Fuller was not the only noninerrantist on the faculty — Paul Jewett had similar commitments — he had the advantage of family connections. Early in his academic career Harold Lindsell, Fuller's dean in the 1950s, and Harold J. Ockenga, chairman of the board and sometimes president, noted the direction that the younger Fuller's thought was going, only to have the elder Fuller assure them that the young man continued to affirm the basics of faith. By 1968 the Evangelical Theological Society actively debated Daniel Fuller's views, but the school stood behind him. In 1972 the school changed its confession of faith and removed both the premillennial and the inerrancy clauses.

The problems at Fuller had far-reaching implications. Billy Graham, Ockenga, and other conservative members of the new evangelical movement turned their attention to other schools. Gordon Seminary and College, long key evangelical institutions, were in the midst of a minor crisis. As it had with other schools in the Baptist tradition that had combined liberal studies and theology, the association of theological schools wanted a clear separation between the two institutions, but funding was scarce. Ockenga responded by putting together a financial coalition based on union with Conwell Seminary, one of the institutions that grew from the nineteenth-century evangelical empire of Russell Conwell, and the substantial fortunes of J. Howard Pew, whose foundation committed itself to support the seminary if it would set certain policies, including ending academic tenure. Gordon also benefited from gifts from Graham and his supporters. The new Gordon-Conwell, while it had its own traditions and character, was almost a second attempt at the creation of a "Fuller," and the bearer of many of the same dreams.

53. Address by George Alan Ladd given at the American Baptist Theological Seminary, Spring 1959, Mount Hermon Conference, typescript, Fuller Archives, p. 16.

The other important consequence of the theological changes at Fuller was a largely self-conscious theological layering of the other major evangelical schools. Trinity Evangelical Seminary, for instance, moved toward a much more consistent inerrantist position and saw itself, rightly or wrongly, as the new leader of the neo-evangelical forces. Whether consciously or not, Gordon-Conwell was midway between Fuller and Trinity, a self-consciously mediating voice. Dallas Seminary, long the bastion of scholarly dispensationalism, did not move toward a more conservative position, but the seminary did emphasize its place as the anchor of American fundamentalism. In less than thirty years, evangelicalism had moved from a relative theological unity to a considerable educational and theological diversity.

The historian may note an important parallel between Fuller and other evangelical institutions. Andover Seminary in the nineteenth century had likewise been born of the desire for evangelical respectability and the hope that a clear, consistent theological position could be maintained. As at Fuller, this determination barely survived the first generation of faculty before the school began to change. Many of the pressures for change came from the shifting world of academic fashion. To do theology at the level envisioned by Andover's founders was to be exposed to intellectual and religious issues of ever increasing complexity that competent scholars had to address. As at Fuller, when Andover made those changes, the debate sparked throughout American Calvinism resulted in other schools adopting positions abandoned at Andover or taking different intellectual directions altogether.

The laying of American evangelicalism was not necessarily bad. American conservative Protestants were (and still are) a remarkably varied group of people who have differing theological and institutional loyalties. From the fundamentalist-modernist controversy, however, American conservatives have been very good at covering up their differences. The five fundamentals, for example, were a conscious attempt, not to defend all of inherited orthodoxy, but to stand by the christological core of faith, and the cry of biblical inerrancy, although it became divisive, was originally a commonplace. The differences, however, cannot be forever concealed. Some evangelicals are confessionalist, contending for the truth once delivered to the saints in all its complexity; others are pietists, confident in their experience of God; and many are Pentecostal, sure of God's present power. As long as these diverse groups believe that "liberalism" or "neoorthodoxy" threatens the Bible, they will be able to form alliances, at least in the short run, but once that threat is removed or, as is apparently the case at present, liberalism is less culturally central, that diversity will emerge again.

CHAPTER TWENTY-SEVEN

The Second World War, Ideological Struggle, and the Advance of Theological Education

The role of war in human development has always fascinated historians. Clearly, the type of corporate effort required by war tests a people and, particularly, its younger generation, and modern warfare, perhaps more than past styles of armed conflict, has raised the ante. Not only must hastily trained officers and men run a sophisticated military organization that puts an almost unimaginable number of people and amount of material onto battlefields on sea and land, but the whole nation must respond to the crisis by increasing industrial productivity and sponsoring scientific and technological work whose value is not readily apparent. The Second World War raised these stakes even higher than the First. For Americans the war was a multifront struggle fought on land, on sea, and in the air against enemies who had little in common, ideologically or militarily, with an ally that many suspected would rather have been (and perhaps secretly was) an enemy. Once the war was over, the worst fears of many about this strange alliance seemingly were verified as Soviet tanks, perhaps the best engineered in the world, formed a mobile cordon sanitaire around middle Europe.

Since the Civil War, the American military had increasingly relied on technological advance to defeat its enemies. America's can-do trump card began with the Civil War generals' creative use of the railroads and development of the Gatling gun and continued through the effective use of steam transportation and fighter aircraft in the First World War. By 1941 the strategy was a given of American military planning. Drawing heavily on British advances in electronics, especially the development of radar and advanced radio communications, the Americans made lightning advances in almost all technical areas from the production of ships, airplanes, and tanks to advanced military electronics to the development of the atomic bomb. These technical advances were not purely homegrown. Despite the technical colossus represented by Cal Tech and MIT, the United States was not the technical leader of the world until after World War II. But the blindness of America's enemies played into the hands of American war planners. Enlisting many of the most able scientists from Nazi-occupied Europe, the United States constructed an arsenal of intellect unequaled in world history. While anti-Semitism was part of American culture, arguably it existed in a milder form than elsewhere. Refugee Jewish scientists, spit out by Hitler's Fortress Europe, made a major contribution to the war machine.[1]

Both the enlistment of whole populations and technological war raised serious ethical questions that tested the mettle of the churches and the seminaries. In addition to the great debate over pacifism that occupied so much time from the midtwenties until the outbreak of hostilities, blanket or saturation bombing, submarine warfare, the use of napalm against Japanese troops dug into island caves, and the atomic bomb posed the question of the appropriate limits of military action. Did the fact that German women and foreign slave labor were keeping German military production high justify the destruction of Dresden, its women, children, dogs and cats, in a fireball that rivaled Hiroshima? Does a national crisis mean that the state can imprison some people strictly because of their racial and ethnic background?[2] What does the nation owe to its African American citizens whose loyalty to and love for the country were displayed again and again?

The churches also faced practical problems. Although the First World War was a bloodbath for most of Europe, America entered late and took comparatively lighter casualties. Nonetheless, the losses were still heavy. How does the ministry cope with a seemingly endless parade of bodies, widowed parishioners, and weeping children? What do chaplains say to women and men under these circumstances? Are they morale officers, or does the ministerial and priestly role mean more than "say two prayers and call me in the morning"? How does one deal with the transformation of communities as the military and military-related industries transform the social and economic landscape of the

1. No form of prejudice is mild to those who experience it, and American anti-Semitism had its very sharp edges. Throughout the thirties, for instance, neither Roosevelt nor Congress was open to revising American immigration laws to permit permanent or even temporary residence to Jews escaping from Germany and, later, Europe. The official silence of the administration on the destruction of Jews in eastern Europe, despite creditable intelligence reports, was part of the price extracted by American prejudice.

2. Alas, concentration camps and the whole mechanism of security are products of modern technology and production.

nation? Ministry under these conditions, whether in the parish or as a chaplain, became a challenge. Whereas the Brown-May survey detected little interest in higher-educational standards among the rank and file of the ministry, the generation that fought the war hungered and thirsted for more training, more depth, and more answers.

Both the Second World War and the cold war that followed were periods of intense ideological struggle. Both the Nazis and the Communists constructed their own complicated ideologies that offered reasons for their programs of action. Moreover, both offered these as alternatives to Christianity, and their adherents believed and taught that their own creeds were destined to replace the Nazarene in the hearts of women and men. In what was almost a mummery of the religious past, both developed elaborate systems of ritual and education designed to replace the practices of the old religion. Both had a millennial fervor about the future. Both the good Nazi and the faithful Communist believed that their position was destined to be universally accepted. Although Japan was only marginally related to the battle over the future of Christian culture, the Japanese state was committed to a racial religion, enshrined in the rituals of state Shinto, that elevated the Japanese people above all others. Although Stalin moderated his persecution of the churches during the war, both Japan and Germany engaged in sporadic persecution during the conflict. The churches were part of the battle, whether they acknowledged that fact or not, and they had to respond to the challenge.

I. The Peace Movement

In retrospect, the churches' pathway to the second war was checkered. During the 1920s Americans became aware of many of their own mixed motives for entering World War I, and in particular they learned about the influence of large corporations and the media on the decision to fight. Shamefaced, the nation, or at least its most sensitive citizens, confronted the fact that their idealistic pronouncements about the war and its goals sharply contrasted with the "real" causes of the conflict. In a fit of almost Wesleyan conviction, many Americans repented and resolved that they would not support war again. The depth and persistence of this conversion were profound. Throughout the 1930s the churches received repeated confirmation of the current problems. This intelligence included reports of bloody religious persecutions in Stalin's Russia, the church struggle in Germany and the increasingly anti-Semitic quality of German laws, the destruction of Protestant churches in Franco's Spain, the Japanese attacks on the beloved China mission. Nonetheless, the churches did not turn bellicose.[3] As late as 1936, even Reinhold Niebuhr could not describe any actual conditions in which he would support armed conflict, and most Christian leaders, whether officially pacifist or not, would have agreed with him.

Seminary students, like other Protestant youth, were deeply affected by the peace movement, perhaps more so. In June 1942 Albert Beaven noted that "the attitude of distrust toward war as a method, which has been associated with the Christian idealistic efforts of the students for international peace during the last twenty years, has tended to concentrate on the theological campus more heavily than elsewhere."[4] Most seminary students had already begun to climb the ecclesiastical ranks by active participation in the various Christian youth and college movements, ranging from such interdenominational groups as the YMCA and Christian Endeavor to denominational youth unions. Following the lead of the Methodists, who were on this issue, as on prohibition, far in advance of other, less socially progressive churches, young American men proudly signed pledges, similar to the pledge cards promising sexual purity or abstinence from liquor, to refuse to participate in war. Evaluating the importance of these pledges is difficult, particularly since most of those who made them later served in the military. Some of these pledges may have been the result of peer pressure or of youthful idealism. But this could also be said of other ways that youth expressed their newly maturing faith, such as public commitments to "full-time Christian service." But just as the promise to enter full-time Christian service was crucial to the lives of many young people, including many of those in seminary, the peace pledge was an important rite of passage to many young men. The ritual marked their coming of age as Christians, and for some replaced the traditional conversions that were less in vogue. The peace demonstration at Union Seminary in New York in 1940, for example, was both a political demonstration and a profoundly religious act for those who took part.[5] Such a well of conviction must have made it difficult for other students to express a contrary point of view.

The 1940 decision of Reinhold Niebuhr and his Union Seminary colleagues Sherwood Eddy, John C. Bennett, Henry Sloane Coffin, and Henry Pit-

3. Martin E. Marty, *Modern American Religion,* vol. 2, *The Noise of Conflict, 1919-1941* (Chicago: University of Chicago Press, 1991), was probably being ironic when he said about this period that "in a superficial way, peace remained a popular cause." If there was one issue that united the churches, even those with a more promilitary heritage, it was the demand for peace. What was difficult was securing support for various ways to maintain peace, such as the World Court.

4. Albert W. Beaven, "Theological Schools in the Creative Tomorrow," *Bulletin* 15 (Thirteenth Biennial Meeting of the AATS) (1942): 19-25.

5. David E. Roberts, "The Case of the Union Students," *Christian Century,* Oct. 30, 1940, pp. 1340-42.

ney Van Dusen to renounce pacifism went against the stream of Christian and, especially, seminary opinion. In their new journal, *Christianity and Crisis,* as well as less frequently in such traditional liberal publications as *Christian Century,* Niebuhr and his allies argued that both political and religious reasoning supported intervention in Europe. The resulting intellectual battle pitted friend against friend and former friend, and even today the reader who studies the argument has a seat at a theological banquet. Theologically, neither side vanquished the other. Niebuhr and his realists were never able to counter effectively the pacifist reliance on the plain meaning of Jesus' language about nonresistance, and the pacifists were never able to refute Niebuhr's searching arguments about the need for humans to act to interdict the forces of evil.

Both Niebuhr and his critics were overtaken by events. During 1940 and 1941 many Americans realized that, whatever governments might say, a state of war existed between the United States and Germany and Japan. The nation had already been sharing intelligence with Great Britain, and began a rapid program of rearmament and acquired important military bases from England. On a more bellicose level, the American use of armed naval vessels to convoy British ships during the battle of the Atlantic was an act of war.

American public opinion, long shocked by the treatment of the Jews in Germany, kept pace with these developments. Given the passionate American debates over America's role in the conflict, the war began with an irony worthy of Niebuhr himself. Japan, which had everything to lose from American intervention in China, bombed Pearl Harbor, and Hitler, who believed that Germany had lost the First World War in part because of American intervention, declared war on the United States.

Despite the depth of religious feeling, pacifist piety had little public effect on the country in the short run. Passionate discussions about the war among official Protestant bodies continued, to be sure, and as late as 1944 the Methodists found themselves debating and passing a minority report that called on their churches to pray for an American victory.[6] Yet students and ministers volunteered for World War II in significant numbers, and although the various Protestant denominations and the federal government cooperated to ease the requirements for conscientious objector (CO) status, comparatively few of those who registered applied for this exemption.[7] Whether from conviction or

6. Gerald Sitzler, *A Cautious Patriotism: The American Churches and the Second World War* (Chapel Hill: University of North Carolina Press, 1997), p. 34.

7. All told, 42,973 received CO status out of 10,022,367 men called up, with another 6,073 denied that status. This was less than one-half of 1 percent of all required to register. See Martin E. Marty, *Modern American Religion,* vol. 3, *Under God, Indivisible, 1941-1960* (Chicago: University of Chicago Press, 1996), p. 22.

calculation, the government had learned the value of treating tender consciences with care. Such trials as the one where Yale theologian D. C. Macintosh was denied citizenship because he questioned war would not reoccur.[8] If World War II was the good war, World War II did not make war good. In the 1950s and 1960s those veterans of the prewar pacifist movement often became active in questioning American foreign policy, protesting the use of atomic force, and protesting the tragic adventure in Vietnam.

II. The War and the Draft

Wars disrupt educational institutions. Young men are either called to the colors or volunteer, faculty enlist or participate in other ways, and the government often casts covetous eyes on the physical and social capital that schools have accumulated. Colleges and universities have the laboratories and libraries that facilitate the applied science that is such a part of modern warfare. The atom, after all, was split at the University of Chicago, and part of the Manhattan Project was located at Bonebrake (today, United) Seminary. In Anglo-Saxon countries, the pressure on colleges and universities is particularly acute. Historically, colleges in English-speaking countries have prepared people to be leaders, and leadership is an important resource for war.

Almost from the beginning, the church-related colleges — the source of the majority of seminary students — were deeply involved in the conflict. The Christian colleges themselves were facing major challenges. First, the long-range shift from a system of higher education primarily based in private institutions to one based on large public institutions was already far advanced. Often a single state university enrolled more students than all the private colleges in the state. Second, as George Marsden demonstrated,[9] the climate of opinion that surrounded higher education was increasingly secular, despite arguments during the war for the unity of religion and civilization. Third, the church-related colleges were caught in a financial squeeze. Despite the recovery that the churches were making economically, many believed that these schools had to raise funds from a much broader public if they were to survive.

In the short run the war offered these colleges some added revenues and prestige. The A-12 (Army Officers Training Program) and the V-12 program allowed colleges to offer a special accelerated program to train military officers.

8. The case was decided in 1931.

9. George Marsden, *The Soul of the American University: From Protestant Establishment to Established Nonbelief* (New York: Oxford University Press, 1994).

While the colleges could, in theory, tailor the program to their own requirements, the military appears to have determined much of the actual program. The compulsory religious activities some colleges had required were of course out-of-bounds for this program. The intervention by the military was welcomed, despite the pacifist sentiments of many faculty members. The extra income cushioned the economic impact of the war and allowed the colleges to survive the war without substantial losses. Many church-related colleges also benefited from government-funded research, especially in the sciences. By war's end "upwards of half of the income supporting certain institutions came from the national government."[10] Perhaps more important, the program suggested that the colleges and the government form a permanent alliance after the war ended.

More immediately, the colleges were crucial to theological schools as a source of students, and one of the goals of the American Association of Theological Schools (AATS) was to keep the supply of qualified students flowing into the seminaries. Early in the war the churches, Protestant and Catholic, persuaded the government that ministers and active seminarians should be shielded from the draft. By the time of the biennial meeting of the AATS in 1942, the seminaries' attention had shifted to including college students committed to the ministry under this same umbrella.

The essential argument the AATS made was that, since the military required men to be graduates of both college and seminary to serve as chaplains, the 4-D for college students was needed to ensure a future supply of qualified religious officers. Seminary leaders were also concerned with what today would be called strategic planning. The original wording of the Selective Service Act protected men who entered seminary without college, and this probably would have encouraged some men to enter seminary as soon as possible. Instead, the AATS wanted the law to reflect the four-three pattern that it considered essential for effective ministry. The AATS appointed a committee to negotiate with the government that included Henry Pitney Van Dusen, Dr. Gould Wickey, Dr. Luther Weigle of Yale, and Dr. E. H. Roberts and A. W. Beaven of Colgate Rochester. Albert Palmer appraised the effects of the law:

> The changed situation forced upon us by the conscription of eighteen-year-old youth means that the church must begin choosing and enlisting its future ministers at the ages of fifteen, sixteen, or seventeen! Otherwise they will be drawn off into the army or started on a treadmill of training in the

10. Christopher J. Lucas, *American Higher Education* (New York: St. Martin's Press, 1994), p. 232.

> applied sciences in preparation for the army or war industries and none will be left for the churches to train as ministers except for the crippled, or, possibly, the conscientious objectors. Or will we enter upon an age of women ministers?[11]

They were partially successful in their mission. General Hershey, the administrator of the Selective Service, issued orders that protected candidates for the professions in college as part of a plan to continue the professions after the war, and the clergy benefited from their professional status. However, these deferments were scheduled to end in 1945.

Did the AATS and its representatives realize that they were creating a loophole in the law that could (and probably did) shelter many people from military service? In 1945 Ralph Douglas Hyslop, writing in *Religious Education,* piously declared, "Those who might be tempted to seek deferment for other than the right reasons can easily be discovered and weeded out if we make the right reasons clear, compelling and determinative."[12] Dean Luther Weigle made the same point even more pointedly: "The primary responsibility of the Divinity School in relation to the war, therefore, is to do its own distinctive work in the education of ministers, effectively, thoroughly, and as quickly as is consonant with sound educational procedures. It must exercise the utmost care in the selection of students, so that it may not become in any sense a refuge for those whose motive is the avoidance of military duty."[13] Yet, despite the rhetoric, no evidence exists that seminaries became more selective during the conflict. In the main, they remained open-admission institutions, as they had always been. If anything, as Stevenson noted so honestly in his history of Lexington Seminary, the draft laws encouraged Disciples college students to continue on to seminary.[14] Once the relatively popular world war ended and was followed by the cold war, Korea, and Vietnam, the conscription laws had an even more visible impact on enrollments.

The lodestar of the AATS relationship with the government during the war was federal support for the four-three pattern of ministerial preparation.

11. Albert Palmer, "The Threat to the Christian Ministry," *Christian Century,* 1943, p. 386. In Germany the draft of pastors, to be sure, resulted in many parishes being served by ministers' wives and other "necessary pastors." In that situation, this seems to have increased the church's prestige and not to have weakened it. Palmer's argument was perhaps a bugaboo.

12. Ralph Douglas Hyslop, "The Right Men for the Ministry," *Religious Education* 40 (1945): 3-7.

13. Luther Weigle, "The War Time Service of the Yale University Divinity School," *Christian Education* 26, (1935): 107-12.

14. Dwight Eshelman Stevenson, *Lexington Theological Seminary, 1865-1965: The College of the Bible Century* (St. Louis: Bethany Press, 1964), p. 271.

Using both the AATS committee and the Federal Council of Churches, Protestant seminary leaders labored to make such legislation a reality. Part of the leverage they had was the identification of the chaplain as a religious professional who needed similar credentials to those of other professionals, especially doctors and lawyers. While numerically powerful denominations, such as the Baptists, were able to secure appointment for some graduates of approved but not accredited seminaries, the pressure from students and graduates for degrees that needed no explanation was strong. Southwestern Baptist Seminary, the nation's largest seminary, applied for and received AATS accreditation in part because of these pressures, and Northern Baptist applied for regional accreditation in 1947.[15] Although there were many competent graduates of Bible colleges, they were excluded from serving as chaplains as well.

The most important benefit that seminaries received from their partnership with the government was inclusion in the Servicemen Readjustment Act of 1944 (the GI Bill) and Public Law 550 of 1952. Under these laws the government agreed to provide funding for both college and professional education, and when the war ended the seminaries, like the colleges, saw rapid increases in enrollments. In effect, the new money for undergraduate education was as important to the seminaries as the direct benefit they received, because it created a larger pool of candidates for the graduate program of the schools. Simply put, it made the most idealistic and persistent dream of American seminary educators financially conceivable.

The GI Bill also had an indirect influence that no one, including the government planners, appeared to have anticipated. By funding the education of men with wives and, in some cases, children, the government changed the character of seminary education. Schools anxiously sought to provide married students' housing, and they struggled to find ways to include wives and children in their common life. Some of these changes were superficial. Most schools appear to have adopted PHT (putting hubby through) ceremonies for those wives who survived the course, and some made it possible for wives to attend classes, either during the day or at night. Perhaps more important, the schools came to see themselves as places for both genders. The prewar seminary was a thoroughly masculine institution with only a handful of women, usually enrolled in religious education or missionary preparation courses. The standard advice to young men was not to marry until studies were completed and they were able to

15. Warren Cameron Young, *Commit What You Have Heard: A History of Northern Baptist Theological Seminary, 1913-1988* (Wheaton, Ill.: Harold Shaw, 1988), p. 45; Robert A. Baker, *Tell the Generations Following: A History of Southwestern Baptist Theological Seminary, 1908-1983* (Nashville: Broadman, 1983).

"support" a wife. Married students' families often lived in parsonages in the surrounding countryside, while the student lived on campus as a single man during the week and commuted to wife and church on weekends. Although some seminary leaders continued to urge students not to marry if they had not done so before entering seminary, students married both before and after matriculation.

III. The New Ecology

In a sense World War II created a new educational environment for the seminaries that changed their character as much as or more than any single factor in the post–World War II period. In addition to cementing the dominant place of the state university in American education, the war and the patterns of federal financing that followed created a new type of independent college that was partly private, partly public. Aside from a handful of Southern Baptist colleges that were theologically opposed to colleges receiving federal funds, almost all schools accepted the government's generous offers of research grants and financial aid for such projects as the construction of laboratories. As the church-related colleges expanded in numbers and in financial complexity, the proportion of funds from the churches and occasionally even the amount in absolute dollars declined. For college presidents anxious to tap every possible source of revenue, the churches appeared to be a drag on their campuses' development. The pressure of finances, more than any other factor, encouraged schools to call themselves first Christian colleges and then simply "private" colleges.

This radically changed the environment in which theological schools operated. The freestanding seminary became an unusual American institution. In the nineteenth century the seminaries had been one of many institutions that depended on the churches for financial and other support. Increasingly the seminaries, especially those in the mainstream, were the sole survivors of this network. At first glance this situation might have seemed advantageous. A more thorough analysis, however, is less sanguine. The seminaries were no longer part of a comprehensive network of institutions that shared financial support. Perhaps more important, long-established networks between seminaries and colleges that provided an easily recruited student body gradually declined. By the 1960s the system of feeder colleges was clearly disintegrating, and would disappear for many seminaries in the coming decades. Most seminaries had long been cut off from the universities; they were now isolated from the colleges as well.

The financial consequences of this isolation were also considerable. By and large the seminaries were cut off from direct federal financial aid. To be sure, many theological schools received considerable indirect benefits from the

GI Bill and the later system of government-guaranteed student loans. The loans permitted ministerial candidates to borrow at low interest rates, and since only a handful of students could afford seminary tuition without such help, the loans made it possible for seminaries to increase their tuition. Nonetheless, the new federal aid to education meant that theological schools were at a permanent economic disadvantage in the larger ecology.

The consequences of this economically marginal position were felt early in the postwar period. After the war ended the costs of higher education spiraled upward. With the aid of the federal government, universities and colleges increased the size of their administrations and greatly increased the compensation and benefits paid to their faculties. The new higher standards of education, in turn, pressed the seminaries to keep up with other educational institutions, and the accrediting agencies, both the AATS and the regional bodies, gradually upped the standards that seminaries had to meet to stay in business. Seminaries found themselves in what would be a chronic situation. Legally and professionally, they had to have many of the features of a small college or university, including a fuller administration, housing directors, student life coordinators, etc., but at the same time, all but the largest schools were about the size of a successful undergraduate department.

Seminaries entered into a period of financial difficulty almost immediately after the war ended. Even during the heyday of the postwar religious revival, the denominations did not have the money to pay the increasingly large costs of theological schooling. Since the 1880s, seminary leaders had debated whether the schools should charge tuition, and the university-related schools had done so. But the postwar financial situation made tuition a necessity for most seminaries.

IV. Chaplains

The military experience of chaplains was also of considerable importance for theological education. Chaplains served in a nondenominational setting in which the materials they used and the duties they performed were determined by a nonecclesiastical chain of command. The armed forces themselves were religiously diverse. The altar rail on a given Sunday brought Baptists, Methodists, Presbyterians, Episcopalians, and Pentecostals to a common cup, and the chaplain's personal ministry included spiritual advice to men and women whose personal moral convictions might differ substantially from his or her own. The more able chaplains searched for and found ways to make diversity less divisive than it might have been otherwise. At times this meant adopting positions that might have been questioned in a local church or on the mission field. Almost all chaplains found that the nonreligious aspects of their work required a tolerance not needed or desired in civilian life. At times they found themselves supervising gambling games, distributing beer chits, and advising on ways to avoid venereal disease.

In many ways the experience of chaplains in the Second World War was very different from that of religious workers in the First World War. In that earlier conflict many who provided religious services for the troops were short-timers, often appointed by the YMCA, who were sent abroad for a limited amount of time. Many pastors took a leave from their congregations to do this work. In contrast, chaplains in the Second World War, like other troops, were enlisted for the duration, and the war dragged on until 1945. Nor did the end of hostilities mean the end of the chaplaincy. After a few brief years of comparative disarmament, the United States adopted a "cold war" military policy that required the maintenance of a "hot"-war-sized armed services. Chaplaincy, consequently, became an important ministerial specialty, and the prestige of the military chaplaincy helped to legitimate chaplaincies in many other areas.

The educational needs of military chaplains were similar to the needs of the pastors of the new suburban congregations springing up around the country. After the war the nation entered into a sustained housing explosion as service personnel and their families took advantage of GI loans that permitted them to move into the suburbs. Both developers and denominational officials were, for differing reasons, committed to limiting the number of churches constructed in these new settlements, and various polity agreements, largely between mainstream churches, determined which denominations might receive (by purchase or grant) key real estate in a growing subdivision. The resultant congregations, while they continued to wear their ecclesiastical union labels, reflected much of the diversity of wartime Protestant chapels. As in the military, these congregations favored activity and organization and minimized theological and other differences between their members.

Although many theologians found the religion of chapel and suburb theologically bland, this style of piety was not new. In fact, the religion of chapel and suburb reflected one of the deeper tendencies in American Protestantism. Since the Puritans, many lay members understood churches as community-building entities that should be based on as broad a consensus as possible. The tendency to theology lite was a product not only of those revivalists who believed that the saving of souls was a nontheological business, but also of the broad American middle class. At least since the Victorians, many churches existed to provide life with some uplift, to help people have positive thoughts and live serene lives.

The religion of quiet uplift also impacted the media. Bishop Fulton Sheen, a European-trained Catholic philosopher and apologist, caught much of this mood in his very successful radio and television broadcasts that featured religious advice on daily life. For all his clerical garb, the good bishop was careful to avoid the thornier issues that separated the various people in his audience. For him Catholicism was practical Americanism, and Americanism, applied Catholicism. Although Billy Graham, perhaps the most visible and influential post–World War II media star, continued to preach his own version of American revivalism, he also stressed the importance of religion as a way to peace of mind. On a less sophisticated theological level, Norman Vincent Peale made "positive thinking" an American religious watchword.

The religion of chapel and suburb flourished during the 1950s. Americans joined churches in record numbers, and by 1956 some 62 percent of the nation claimed some religious affiliation.[16] Further, churches were investing large sums in new buildings, often dedicated to religious education, and hiring staff members to help with the increasing number of children coming for Sunday school.[17] Theologians were quick to note the problems connected with this explosion of faith. Henry Pitney Van Dusen, for instance, noted that the "revival of religion" had been paralleled by no corresponding resurgence or recovery of morality. For Van Dusen this was the most "disturbing, confronting contradiction." Following Jonathan Edwards's criterion of genuine faith, Union's president noted that the acid test of faith was moral growth. "[I]f one could plot the complex and illusive data on a graph, the curve of religious vitality and the curve of moral health would be seen to be moving in opposite directions."[18]

Martin E. Marty made a similar observation. Writing in 1958 in the *New Shape of American Religion,* Marty noted that certain aspects of the revival had crested at different times. The wave of political piety associated with the postwar anticommunist crusade, he believed, reached its height during the McCarthy years (1951-54). In contrast, the Graham phase of the revival appears to have crested with Graham's triumphant revival in New York City in 1957. Moreover, Marty noted, the cultural place of religion changed around the same time. Zen

16. Martin E. Marty, *The New Shape of American Religion* (New York: Harper and Row, 1958), p. 13.

17. See Dennison Nash, "A Little Child Shall Lead Them: A Statistical Test of the Hypothesis That Children Were the Source of the American Religious Revival," *Journal for the Scientific Study of Religion* 7 (1968): 238-40. The baby boom was at least partially responsible for the boom in religion. American parents, even if their own faith was shaky or almost nonexistent, wanted their children to have some religious or, at least, moral training.

18. Henry Pitney Van Dusen, "Theological Students Today," *Union Seminary Quarterly Review,* 1959, p. 31.

Buddhism began to acquire a following; skeptical writers such as Bertrand Russell were reintroduced to publishers' lists; and the mood, always difficult to read, shifted. The reputation of John Foster Dulles, long America's primary example of a Christian statesman, began to fall. In the new atmosphere he appeared more dated than profound.[19] Comedian Lenny Bruce was more funny than shocking. And although Marty did not notice it, life among serious college students was also changing rapidly. Antinuclear activism was attracting the allegiance of many, and interest in the civil rights movement was replacing campus ministry.

Another sign that the revival was ending was that seminaries began to face enrollment issues. The rush of men into religious vocations that followed the war appeared to be drying up, and schools had to recruit students avidly again. Although the Vietnam War would temporarily make seminaries and the ministry more attractive to young American males, the pattern of a declining interest in ministry among this traditional group was established in the late 1950s. Had Protestant seminaries not found new constituencies, particularly women, in the 1970s and 1980s, they would have had to retreat from their postwar expansion.

V. Scholarship and the Postwar Era

One of the more interesting by-products of the religious prosperity of the 1940s and 1950s was a widespread scholarly interest in revivals and revivalism. Beginning with his doctoral dissertation at Harvard,[20] William G. McLoughlin tirelessly argued that the ebbs and flows of religious revivals were important clues to what happened in American culture.[21] Other religious historians, including Edwin Scott Gaustad and Timothy L. Smith, took similar positions, and John E. Smith launched the very important Yale edition of the writings of Jonathan Edwards.[22] In many ways the new interest in revivalism was closely connected to

19. Marty, *New Shape*, p. 13. Marty is right in pointing to the reputation of Dulles as an indicator. Dulles was a close personal friend of Van Dusen — he had defended him in an ecclesiastical trial — and he had arranged for Union Seminary to provide cover for British intelligence operating in the United States during the war.

20. William G. McLoughlin, "Professional Evangelism: The Social Significance of Religious Revivals Since 1865" (Ph.D. diss., Harvard University, 1953).

21. Perhaps most persuasively in William G. McLoughlin, *Modern Revivalism: From Charles Grandison Finney to Billy Graham* (New York: Ronald Press, 1959).

22. Edwin Scott Gaustad, *The Great Awakening in New England* (New York: Harper and Row, 1957); Timothy Smith, *Revivalism and Social Reform in Mid-Nineteenth Century America* (Nashville: Abingdon, 1957). Marty discusses the significance of both of these works as well.

the more general interest among American historians in the ways America, a land apparently divided ethnically, geographically, and economically, had managed to find a national consensus about democratic values. The revival tradition with its progressive loss of doctrinal precision seemed an important clue to how religion had contributed to the nation's sense of community. In other words, like the 1950s themselves, the interest in revival was part of the larger tendency to see religion as a social glue that made an improbable nation work. Jewish philosopher Will Herberg's *Protestant, Catholic, and Jew* attempted much the same thing, although using the more neutral-sounding language of sociology.[23]

Ironically, the religious revival occurred at a time when American theology was flourishing; indeed, it was in the midst of a theological renaissance. Both Reinhold Niebuhr and Paul Tillich appeared on the cover of *Time* magazine, one of the most important voices of the American middle class, and other popular magazines, including *Look*, ran articles on American theology. The times were intellectually exciting. Biblical studies, largely inspired by the biblical theology movement and by widespread interest in archaeology, came alive, and at many schools Hebrew and Greek returned to central curricular positions. To be sure, these languages were now more often taught as ways into the Greek and Hebrew "minds" than as preparatory to a lifelong reading of the texts in the original languages, and often even the instructors claimed that the purpose of the courses was to enable a student to use a dictionary and to follow commentaries. Theologian Robert McAfee Brown captured some of the excitement of these new studies in his *The Bible Speaks to You.*[24]

Part of the reason for the sense of a theological renaissance in the late 1940s and 1950s was the expansion of the seminaries. There were more jobs available, and the schools tended to hire young professors, fresh from graduate school, who were determined to make a name for themselves. The new academic professionalism encouraged by war led the most ambitious of these to publish substantial works, and the popular interest in religion often provided them with readers, both among the general public and in the newly popular religion courses in colleges.

Creative theology, of course, requires more than a strong financial and institutional base. Despite the apparent blandness of chapel and suburb, 1950s theologians knew that the winds of doctrine were shifting. In part, this was because they were living in a generational shift. The big names that had dominated American Protestant thought, such as Reinhold and Richard Niebuhr

23. Will Herberg, *Protestant, Catholic, and Jew* (Garden City, N.Y.: Doubleday, 1955).

24. Robert McAfee Brown, *The Bible Speaks to You* (Philadelphia: Westminster, 1955).

and Paul Tillich, were approaching retirement, and various younger theologians both benefited and suffered from pundits designating them the heirs apparent to these soon-to-be-vacated thrones.

Beneath the surface, theology was bubbling with excitement. Rudolf Bultmann, whose star had been obscured in the American heavens by the great light of his contemporaries Barth and Brunner, was central to the larger discussion. For Bultmann modern world-consciousness separated present-day people from the mythic world of the New Testament writers. To recover the New Testament message, Bultmann believed, theologians had to find an equivalent language that could express the truth of these earlier teachings. Bultmann himself believed that existentialism, very popular in postwar Europe, with its emphasis on decision, provided the best way forward. At the same time, Tillich's mature theology became more widely known, and American theologians began to wrestle with the intellectual paradoxes of a God beyond God and symbols that pointed beyond themselves. The often disturbing works of Dietrich Bonhoeffer appeared in English translation for the first time during this period. These included *The Cost of Discipleship* (1948), *Letters and Papers from Prison* (1953), *Life Together* (1954), and *Ethics* (1955).[25] Although or perhaps because Bonhoeffer died before he had worked out all the implications of his thought, his works provided serious theologians with numerous hints and suggestions for further reflection. If few became his disciples, many became his students.

The 1940s and 1950s also saw the flourishing of a new American school of theology, process theology, that drew deeply on the insights of Alfred North Whitehead. Process theology was a natural outgrowth of the traditional American liberal interest in questions around science and religion, and it was particularly concerned with finding an intellectually respectable way to address the church's unfinished business with evolutionary science and genetics. The technical details of process theologians did not account for its popularity. Process theology offered a persuasive way to separate the question of the will of God from the question of the presence of God. The God of process did not actively participate in determining the direction of personal or national histories, and hence it was an improper understanding of God that saw God as causally involved in the death of this or that person from war or cancer (one of the greatest fears of this age of anxiety). Yet process enabled the pastor to speak of God's presence in this world in a comforting and helpful way.

Seminaries benefited from both the religious and the theological revivals. The religious revival attracted young men and women who wanted to find a

25. *The Cost of Discipleship* (London: SCM, 1948); *Letters and Papers from Prison* (London: SCM, 1953); *Life Together* (New York: Harper, 1954); *Ethics* (London: SCM, 1955).

culturally central position from which to address the personal and corporate problems of the nation. The ministry itself was a far more attractive and important profession than it had appeared to be in the 1930s, and this sense of importance offset the job's obvious disadvantages such as lower pay or less job security. For some, too, it was a place where the psychological wounds from World War II or Korea might be allowed to heal. Many felt they had done the unspeakable and the unthinkable and needed to do an extraordinary penance. Further, W. H. Auden referred to the postwar period as "the age of anxiety," and the seminaries obviously were a place where young men and women could deal with their personal insecurities. The very popular courses in clinical training provide some evidence for that,[26] as does the fascination with existentialism and other philosophies that stressed the act of will as the cure for anxiety and fear. But these various needs could produce a sense that the seminary was "a hospital without walls."

As with so many other aspects of the 1940s and 1950s, the indirect effects of the theological renaissance may have been more important than its direct consequences. At the end of the war, educators published two notable reports, *General Education in a Free Society* (the Harvard Report) and *Higher Education for American Democracy* (the President's Report). Both of these sharply questioned the vocation emphases of the 1930s and called upon colleges and universities to take up the teaching of values and meaning. In many ways the theology of the 1940s and 1950s was an exemplar of how this might be done. Biblical and historical studies in the seminaries seemed to be able to combine the most rigorous critical methods with a manifest openness to the values and ethical teachings of the texts themselves. For the first time in many years, theologians were at home in the Zion of American higher culture, and they could even dream, as did H. Richard Niebuhr in his classic *Christ and Culture,* of the renewal of a Protestantism that had a transformative effect on the whole of the human enterprise.

The intellectual excitement of postwar schools was also evident in two Rockefeller grants to the seminaries. As Krister Stendahl noted, "It is a fact and no overstatement, when we say that theological education as we know it in the 1950s, 1960s, and of now, is really inconceivable without the massive support that came from John D. Rockefeller, Jr. I do not speak just for Harvard, but for theological education in the land and beyond. And beyond is not general language, but refers to the theological education front in Asia, Africa, and Latin America."[27] As early as 1944 Rockefeller had felt a need to make a major gift to

26. See below, chap. 30.

27. Jerry Dean Weber, "To Strengthen and Develop Protestant Theological Education: John D. Rockefeller, Jr., and the Sealantic Fund" (Ph.D. diss., University of Chicago, 1997), p. 2.

theological education. He commissioned his staff in 1952 to prepare a study on the needs of theological education. His earlier gifts to theological schools included separate grants to Union Theological Seminary, Yale Divinity School, the University of Chicago Divinity School, Colgate Rochester, and Harvard. The staff report, written by Yorke Allen, "an interim report on trends in theological education," set the stage for his largest contribution, the Sealantic Fund that received $22 million between 1954 and 1960. Allen's report highlighted the need for aid to be given to the university divinity schools that were seen as the keystones of the liberal theological enterprise. In part, the emphasis on the university schools reflected Rockefeller's personal commitment to an undenominational form of Christianity in harmony with American culture. Graduates from university-related schools were the types of pastors he believed could provide the type of enlightened leadership that his own congregation, Riverside Church, had received from Harry Emerson Fosdick, but it was more than that. Both Allen and Rockefeller recognized that to transform the schools, it was essential to transform the institutions that educated teachers, and the university schools were clearly best equipped to do this. The first gifts reflected this commitment: Vanderbilt, $2.9 million; University of Chicago (Federated Faculty), $1.25 million plus $500,000 matching; Pacific School of Religion, $1 million plus $500,000 matching; Union Theological Seminary, $1 million plus $500,000 matching; Harvard University Divinity School, $500,000, $1 million given earlier; Yale, $1 million plus $500,000 matching.[28] As had been the case in the past, Rockefeller's staff had identified a problem and found a way to help solve it. For the next fifty years the Sealantic institutions educated a large majority of those who taught in mainstream Protestant seminaries or served as executives in ecumenical enterprises.

The other main beneficiary of the Sealantic gift was the AATS. Again, Rockefeller's staff targeted the association because it was a way to influence American Protestant theological education as a whole. The service of the association as the spokesman for the seminaries in World War II had given it added prestige and influence, and AATS seemed about to make the long-hoped-for standard of four years of college followed by three years of seminary a reality. The group had also proven its value to theological schools in other ways. Reform by accreditation is a laborious process that makes haste slowly through ten-year reports, carefully crafted recommendations, and the power of example. Looked at from this perspective, no doubt exists that the AATS procedures had made significant — if not the most — contributions to the schools. Even the problem of the libraries, long seen as almost intractable, had become al-

28. "Foundations, Fortunes and Federated Faculties," *Christian Century*, Jan. 4, 1956.

most manageable as the association had helped found a professional association for seminary librarians, the American Theological Library Association, and had steadily increased the standards for both collections and their caretakers. The association's role in legitimating the new practical fields had been an important one. The time had arrived for it to have a permanent, paid executive director and a staff if it was to realize its potential influence as a major shaper of theological education. The Rockefeller grant made that possible. The association was now even more clearly both an accrediting agency for seminary leaders and the professional organization for seminary presidents and, increasingly, deans.

The other major Rockefeller gift was the Rockefeller Brother's Fund, supported by the sons of John D. Rockefeller, Jr.[29] President Nathan Pusey of Harvard, who chaired the fund, had a deep appreciation for the intellectual and moral leadership of a well-educated and theologically alert ministry. As president of Harvard, Pusey was an eloquent advocate of liberal education and a major contributor to the renewed interest in general education that followed the war. He understood theology as part of this larger conversation and, in fact, as its heart and core. "Theology should not be thought of as a minor intellectual exercise among other intellectual exercises. . . . It is expected to carry an answer to deepest hungers and needs."[30] Pusey convinced the Harvard Corporation to strengthen the divinity school, which had fallen on hard times after the departure of Andover, and raised funds to support its growth. He believed it was necessary that theological studies "be given a fresh impetus and a new life within this University,"[31] and he made the reestablishment of a strong endowment for the school a major priority. With solid funding the faculty improved, and Harvard acquired a strong reputation as a center for the scholarly study of Christianity.

The basic idea behind the Rockefeller Brother's Fund was a combination of Pusey's dedication to the liberal arts and his interest in theological education. Each year the fund would select a number of very highly qualified graduates of the nation's better colleges — young men with real professional and academic promise — and give them a year at a major divinity school to consider the ministry as a possible place for their talents. If they decided not to enter the ministry, the experience of a year of disciplined study of faith would make them better believers and scholars; if they entered church service, they might

29. Robert Rankin, "Strengthening the Ministry," *Christian Century* 72, no. 11 (Apr. 27, 1955): 496-98.

30. Nathan Pusey, "A Faith for These Times," in *The Age of the Scholar,* by Nathan Pusey (Cambridge: Harvard University Press, 1963), p. 7.

31. Quoted in Weber, "To Strengthen," p. 150.

help raise the standards of the ministry. In explaining the program to the AATS, Pusey said:

> No church group has been attracting as much first-rate ability into its ministerial ranks in recent years as it could profitably use. On the other hand, there is also some reason to believe that the minister's career could be congenial and rewarding to more first-rate college graduates than have in recent generations been inclined to give it serious consideration. It is hoped that this program will do something to march at least a few more especially talented people against a persistent major shortage in our society and in so doing show them a way to constructive lives through the churches.[32]

Among those who received the first round of grants was a young novelist and Princeton graduate, Frederick Buechner, who fulfilled the fund's goals admirably.

The postwar prosperity of church and theology hid many of the deep fissures in Protestant life that followed the end of the war. American Protestants had been generous to a fault in supporting the expansion of Christianity to the non-Western world, and they had established a major string of colleges, universities, and seminaries around the globe. As the Western empires receded, first in Asia and then in Africa, these institutions often were nationalized and placed under government control. Where this did not happen, the mainstream churches, which had the largest investments abroad, often had to turn these institutions over to newly independent churches. These churches frequently had a deep sense of mission and potential, and some of the most creative ecumenical work took place in such areas as India, where newly enfranchised believers constructed churches with creative forms of government and liturgy. In time, most of these churches prospered.

But there was a widespread uneasiness. The "fall" of China to Communism, which American political conservatives used as a major exhibit in their anticommunist crusade, was a disaster for American Christians. China was the largest and best-financed American field, the one place where it appeared that the American missionary strategy might actually win the emerging middle class. Something died in the Protestant soul as Protestants, liberal and conservative, mourned the loss of close friends, of institutions carefully constructed, and of prayers faithfully shared.

The mainstream retreat from the foreign field deeply affected the seminaries. Missions had been one of the great causes of seminary life, and annually most seminary presidents had mounted the rostrum and called for a symbolic

32. Quoted in Robert Rankin, "The Rockefeller Brothers Theological Fellowship Program," *American Association of Theological Schools Bulletin* 21 (1954): 111.

tenth of the student body to go abroad. Many had, including many who were excellent teachers and theologians, and the missionary field was an attractive career option for young pastors. Moreover, seminaries had invested, often substantially, in homes for returning missionaries, in programs of missionary education, and in missionary faculty. These investments had, to be sure, not been in vain. American pastors were perhaps the best-informed American professionals, outside of those in the foreign service, about the larger world and world events.

More important, there was also an uneasiness about American culture. Many Americans had believed that the end of the war would bring a renewal of the Great Depression, but a variety of factors, including military spending at almost wartime levels, had prevented the worst of these prophecies from coming true. The United States was a land of apparently endless prosperity. Yet something was wrong, deeply wrong, with the picture. The suburban life that had promised so much had become a grind, and many people would have agreed with Union theologian David Roberts that American corporate life had generated a religion that was "not even a worthy form of humanism,"[33] and Gibson Winter was already writing articles protesting the suburban captivity of the churches. Martin E. Marty saw theology as offering some salvation, and perhaps it might have done so.[34] But there too the energy had begun to fag. Despite all the candidates nominated as the next Niebuhr or the new Tillich, no one would arise with the strength to wrestle that Excalibur from the stone. What Marty thought was the sound of a rising tide was really the sound of the ebb.

Not surprisingly, seminary enrollments dipped. There was trouble in Zion that would rock American Protestantism repeatedly in the next decades. But at the time, most saw the world as bright with promise. The Second World War and the prosperity that followed seemed to prepare a place for America's ever struggling seminaries to rest, grow, and enjoy some of the fruits of their labors. But history would prove this to be an oasis and not the promised land. But at the time, few saw that possible future. The rest invited H. Richard Niebuhr to prepare a report on how far they had come.

33. Cited in Marty, *New Shape*, p. 62. David Roberts, "The Organization and the Individual," *Christianity and Crisis*, June 24, 1957, p. 83.

34. Marty, *New Shape*, chap. 6, "Signpost to Theological Resources," pp. 110-21.

CHAPTER TWENTY-EIGHT

Mr. Niebuhr Speaks: Seminaries Advance

When World War II ended, the United States was economically dominant. The formerly strong economies of Germany, Japan, and England had been exhausted by the conflict, as were the secondary economic powers of eastern Europe. In many fields Americans had almost a monopoly. After a brief slowdown the American economy boomed as the nation's businesses took advantage of the new prosperity. Such programs as the Marshall Plan to aid Europe, while idealistic in their origins, also enabled American companies to conquer new markets.

I. A Question of Standards

Education was among the new growth industries. Christopher Lucas observed the way this expansion was system-wide. A higher percentage of the population completed high school, and in turn a higher percentage completed college, and so on up the ladder to professional and doctoral programs.[1] The pressure of numbers, in turn, led colleges and particularly universities to adopt a more corporate model of leadership. Multiversities stood in the forefront of this organizational revolution. The multiversity was a large institution whose budgets and complexity were roughly comparable to those of a leading corporation. Many states further gathered their various educational enterprises into state university systems. This process was aided by a pattern of institutional growth that enabled such institutions as teachers colleges to become colleges and then universities in their own right.

1. Christopher J. Lucas, *American Higher Education* (New York: St. Martin's Press, 1994).

Prosperity also encouraged American educators to think critically about their enterprise. Between the end of the war and the launching of Sputnik (1957), much of this thought centered on the question of the aims and purposes of higher education. During the Depression American education had often oriented itself toward the vocational aspirations of its students, but educators were ready to critically examine that link. The Western intellectual tradition had historically placed heavy emphasis on the transmission of culture. At a time when many believed Communism to be a major threat to civilization itself, educators argued that society's leaders needed a strong cultural foundation to withstand the onslaught. The liberal arts, often referred to as "general education" in the literature, came into new prominence. Whole fields of inquiry were transformed by this interest. The American historians of the 1920s and 1930s were fascinated by the economic problems of the nation. The leading historians of the 1950s and 1960s, in contrast, were interested in the cultural consensus that supported American democracy, despite internal and external challenge. American Protestant church historians, following this trend, wrote confidently of the "great tradition" of the separation of church and state.

The educational boom promoted serious consideration of academic standards. With most schools having sufficient applicants to fill their available places, schools could ask serious questions about requirements for admission, the ability of libraries to sustain serious research, and the work expected of students for a degree. Seminaries were very much players on this field of dreams. Flush with record enrollments and with a cadre of young, ambitious new faculty members, the seminaries seemed to have finally found their place in the sun. The literature of theological education sparkled with proposals for a fourth year of study; for core curricula;[2] for the upgrade of the degree to a full, recognized master's; for the creation of a professional doctorate; and for standardized psychological and achievement tests. A few ambitious schools experimented with intern years, modeled on medicine's very successful postacademic experience-oriented programs, that might enable students to make the transition from classroom to parish. Much time, however, separated proposals from their final enactments. Many of the dreams of the 1950s and early 1960s were not realized until the 1970s. By that time the prosperity and optimism that had generated the original proposals had faded, and the schools were caught in chronic financial problems. When the highly praised Curriculum for the Sev-

2. Theological education as graduate professional education was a mantra for the AATS under Charles Taylor and Jesse Ziegler. See Jesse Ziegler, *ATS through Two Decades: Reflections on Theological Education, 1960-1980* (Vandalia, Ohio, 1984).

enties — an AATS program that reflected the best thinking of the 1950s and 1960s — was completed, however, the carefully drawn proposals were no longer contemporary.

The AATS was, naturally enough, at the center of thought about renewed standards for theological schools, particularly after Rockefeller's grants gave the organization a full-time staff. Part of the association's stake in the postwar discussion was the evolution of its own accrediting standards. While the standards had changed, particularly in the area of libraries, many people believed that a more thorough revision was essential. That major revision was in fact made in the 1960s. Interest in a new survey of theological education was naturally part of the preparation for more sweeping changes, and the topic was discussed throughout the late 1940s. In 1952 the association made serious plans for the study, approached the Carnegie Foundation for funding, and assembled a team to do the study and, more important, the interpretation. H. Richard Niebuhr was a natural choice to head the study. He was arguably America's most able theologian and ethicist and at the very peak of his powers. Unlike his better-known brother, Reinhold, H. Richard was not involved in the discussion of contemporary politics, and hence devoted more of his efforts to theological questions. Niebuhr's thought was a rich harvest of insights derived from thinkers as diverse as Jonathan Edwards, Ernst Troeltsch, and D. C. Macintosh that dealt with the question of how religion, culture, and revelation intersected. Niebuhr chose two younger colleagues to work with him. Daniel Day Williams, then of the Federated Faculty at the University of Chicago, had received his doctorate from Columbia in 1940 and was one of the most important midcareer theologians. Williams, who called himself a chastened liberal,[3] was far from repentant about his commitment to the American liberal tradition. He believed that liberalism, especially as modified by the philosophies of Hartshorne and Whitefield, had understood the essential religious questions of contemporary people. Hence, he believed, theologians had to struggle with the metaphysical questions posed by science. The third member of the team was James Gustafson, a recent Yale Ph.D., who was looking for his initial scholarly appointment. Unlike Niebuhr and Williams, who were both established scholars, Gustafson's point of view was evolving at that time.

The report of the survey team was divided in two parts and a codicil. The two parts were to be a theological reflection by Niebuhr on theological education. This was published first under the title of *The Purpose of the Church and*

3. Dr. Williams frequently used this term and similar ones when I was a student at Union in the 1960s to describe his position.

Its Ministry;[4] the second part, the results of the survey itself, appeared as *The Advancement of Theological Education* in 1957.[5] The codicil was a collection of essays on the ministry in different periods, edited by Niebuhr and Williams, entitled *The Ministry in Historical Perspective*.[6]

Although each volume was self-contained, the three together reflected a panoramic view of theological education. *Advancement* dealt with the human — all too human — shape of actual theological schools in the mid-1950s. In it the three authors attempted to give an accurate snapshot of theological education as actually practiced and to make concrete suggestions for its improvement. But the reader was to read this report in its context. As Niebuhr never tired of saying, human life takes place in a concrete historical situation that conditions all human thought, actions, and feelings. Theological education in America, thus, was the heir of previous attempts to create a faithful ministry as well as a response to contemporary conditions. In a real sense the whole revolved around the first slim volume. Unlike for secular institutions, the description of the historical situation was not sufficient. Theologians professed to know and teach about God, and they had to be held accountable before God as well as before humankind. The divine reality, as much as human circumstance, shaped existing theological institutions and claimed those institutions' future.

Niebuhr assumed the relativity of certain theological arguments, and all three volumes assumed this on almost every page. Lovingly but firmly, Niebuhr and his coworkers deconstructed the commonplaces of theological educators. Although both liberal and fundamentalist biblical scholarship, for instance, claimed to report on the Bible as it was intended to be read, Niebuhr and allies suggested that both were historical responses appropriate to a certain period in the church's development. Hence, both had to be judged by revelation. *The Ministry in Historical Perspective* was particularly effective in deflating unwarranted claims. Despite the rhetoric about the tradition of the "learned ministry," *Ministry* suggested that the American churches had been served by a rich variety of ministerial types and that each of these had made a contribution to the churches' struggle to be faithful.

4. H. Richard Niebuhr, Daniel Day Williams, and James Gustafson, *The Purpose of the Church and Its Ministry* (New York: Harper and Row, 1956).

5. H. Richard Niebuhr, Daniel Day Williams, and James Gustafson, *The Advancement of Theological Education* (New York: Harper, 1957).

6. H. Richard Niebuhr and Daniel Day Williams, eds., *The Ministry in Historical Perspective* (New York: Harper and Row, 1956).

II. In the Sight of God: Niebuhr on Theological Education

The Purpose of the Church and Its Ministry appeared first and remains one of only a handful of quality discussions of the "theology" of theological education. Unlike William Adams Brown, Niebuhr's predecessor as a theologian of theological education, or David Kelsey, his successor, Niebuhr did not approach theological education in terms of questions of theological epistemology, his own academic specialty. Nor did he follow the theological encyclopedist practice of deriving the nature of theological thinking from the intellectual demands of the creed or confessional. Theological education was not a cook's tour of theological disciplines that were a sine qua non, given in the very structure of Christian faith itself. A person could study, for example, both the classical and the practical disciplines offered in theological schools and not necessarily receive a theological education. What, then, was distinctive about theological study? To answer that question, Niebuhr turned to first principles. Since most people attended theological school to enter the ministry, he believed the prior question had to be: What is the purpose of the church and its ministry? Only after a clear answer to that fundamental question was formulated should one consider what schools and churches were actually doing to meet that goal.

Niebuhr had deliberately asked a question that had multiple dimensions. The very word "purpose" suggests it is a question about culture. Cultures do two things. First, a culture is a system or structure of meaningful actions that provides people with a sense of boundaries and of personal and corporate value. In other words, culture is the larger context in which people can act to accomplish some aim or goal. Second, cultures are always communal, always involving many people, and always involve past and present. When one asks about purposes, the question focuses not on the various means employed or the various maze ways taken, but on the context that makes that purpose meaningful. One cannot understand the purposes that motivate people without some reference to their cultural situation. Purposes are, consequently, immanent parts of the societies in which those formulating them live, and since purposes often intend a change or a transformation of the state of affairs, they transcend their context. As Niebuhr said, "[T]he approach cannot be from one direction only. No simple inductive or deductive procedure is sufficiently fruitful." Hence the very sharp warning against attempting to "reduce the larger inquiry to one inquiry with one method."[7]

7. Niebuhr, Williams, and Gustafson, *Purpose*, p. 7. Parenthetical page numbers placed in the following text are to *The Purpose of the Church and Its Ministry.*

The tension in Niebuhr's discussion between purpose as a cultural ideal and purpose as a cultural product is essential for understanding *The Purpose of the Church and Its Ministry.*[8] One cannot abstract the purpose of the church from the work of a single congregation with its own location and history, nor can one derive an understanding of the church apart from such specific incidences. Communities must have institutions, and institutions must have communities. The schools that "serve in the Church and serve for the church cannot abstract community from institution or institution from community" (p. 8). Hence the person discussing theological education is always involved in polarities, especially the tensions between unity and plurality, between locality and universality, between Protestant and Catholic, and between church and world (pp. 24-26). These tensions set the stage for any meaningful discussion of church experience. To be in this community means that one or the other pole of these dynamic pairs is always drawing people from one aspect of their culture to another aspect of that same culture. Thus, while church life is the number of specific actions and beliefs that help individual churches and ministers find their way to a faithful life, it is also the way these interact with other aspects of human experience.

Niebuhr's turn to the almost Ritschlian identification of the purpose of the church as the increase of the love of God and the love of neighbor is part of this emphasis on particularity. He is very aware of the many goals and objectives that affect every Christian body: the teaching of trinitarian faith, the preaching of the Word and the administration of the sacraments, the religious education of the young. These are valid and valuable parts of church life. But "the question is whether there is one end beyond the many objectives as there is one Church in the many churches" (p. 28). This does imply, as Niebuhr is quick to affirm, that the various things the church does are only means to a greater end. Religious actions are valuable in and for themselves. One administers communion, for instance, because it is "fit and proper so to do" — and the meaning of the sacrament is, so to speak, in people's own participation. Rather, Niebuhr is proposing that this underlying formation makes more sense of how Christians move through the maze ways of their contemporary religious life than other categories, such as the increase of biblical knowledge, the salvation of souls, or the creation of a redeemed community. Each of these alternatives

8. Dr. Niebuhr may have had in mind Jonathan Edwards's seminal essay "The End for Which God Created the World." In that essay Edwards argues that God's final purpose, his own glory, can be realized only by God's own love for God and, hence, by the movement of all being back to its primal home in Being Itself. Everything else that God proposes — the history of redemption — participated in this final goal both in terms of movement toward that end and as the present realization of that end.

expresses a distinctive view of faith, to be sure, but they tend to be too partial to provide the goal of the Christian quest. The best way forward, Niebuhr believes, lies in his formulation. Niebuhr's argument should be stated fully:

> Is not the result of all these debates and the content of the confessions and commandments of all these authorities this: that no substitute can be found for the definition of the goal of the Church as the increase among men of the love of God and neighbor? The terms vary: now the symbolic phrase is reconciliation to God and man, now increase of gratitude for the forgiveness of sins, now the realization of the kingdom or the coming of the Spirit, now the acceptance of the Gospel. But the simple language of Jesus Christ himself furnishes to most Christians the more intelligible key to his own purpose and to that of the community gathered around him. (p. 29)

The increase of the love of God and humankind is not so much a matter of cause and effect as of the final destiny of a series of actions. When a stone is thrown into a lake, we expect to see concentric circles form in the water. But when the church acts, it acts in hope that some movement might occur toward the increase of the love of God and neighbor. Another way of putting the same insight is to say that the increase of the love of God and neighbor is the ultimate rationale that makes sense of how Christians live within their culture, including their religious culture, and of where that culture should be heading. When the increase of the love of God and neighbor is the goal or purpose of the church, the church participates in the ultimate end of the church's ministry and moves toward that goal.

The increase of the love of God and humankind is intended to be relational language. When we speak of God, we must speak of the human creatures that God loves and that love God in turn and who must therefore love those that God loves. For Niebuhr, "love" is an extremely rich term that can be described only in language that is almost poetry. Love is rejoicing in the presence of the beloved, gratitude, happiness in the thought of the other, desire that the other be rather than not be, happy acceptance of what the other might give, deep respect for the otherness of the beloved, and above all, loyalty to the other's cause. And for humans, love to God is always love to the ultimate, the One on whom we are absolutely dependent, reconciliation with the One who gives life and death, and whose demands are too great to bear. In words that suggest the argument in *Monotheism and Western Culture,* Niebuhr writes:

> Reconciliation to God is reconciliation to life itself; love to the Creator is love of being, rejoicing in existence, in its source, totality and particularity.

> Love to God is more than that, however great this demand and promise are. It is loyalty to the idea of God when the actuality of God is mystery; it is the affirmation of a universe and the devoted will of maintaining a universal connection at whatever cost to the self. It is the patriotism of the universal commonwealth. The Kingdom of God, as a commonwealth of justice and love, the reality of which is sure to become evident. (p. 37)

Niebuhr's understanding of the neighbor is as broad as his understanding of God. The neighbor is the one who is near and far, the one who has shown compassion to me, and the one who has sought my life. The neighbor is "not humanity in its totality but rather in its articulation, the community of individuals and individuals in community" (p. 38). In other words, the neighbor is the human world as it confronts the self or the church and is confronted by it.

Niebuhr admits that his analysis "has removed us a long way from the actuality of schools, churches, and ministry in the churches in the United States and Canada" (p. 39). Yet this removal, this distance, is for the good. Since all schools follow proximate and limited goals, a deeper understanding of the ultimate purpose of the schools allows us to put those proximate goals in some perspective. In good Reformed fashion, in other words, Niebuhr is suggesting that such a critical principle is needed to do things "decently and in good order." Thus Niebuhr reminded theological schools: "It is one thing to be reconciled to God and man and to conceive some love for the neighbor and hence to participate in the community of which Jesus Christ is the pioneer and founder; it is another thing to take for granted that if one is brought into membership with the historical society called the Church love of God and neighbor will automatically ensue" (p. 42). Niebuhr gave many examples of how this ecclesiastical fallacy might work. The Protestant love of the Bible, divorced from God's ultimate goal, may become idolatry, just as an overemphasis on the historical-critical approach to the Bible may lead people away from the God of the Bible. Denominationalism, divorced from the love of God and neighbor, may become a nasty sectarianism, and even the very popular tendency in the 1950s to confuse Christology with theology, divorced from its larger goal, may become a Unitarianism of the second person. In effect, the concept of increase of the love of God and neighbor is a critical or regulative principle that allows particularities to be seen in a new light.

Theological schools live in and through particularity. They, like their churches, exist in a certain place, at a certain time, and have their own clear identity. All of this is necessary and good. But this partiality is also a temptation for the seminaries and their supporters to confuse the part with the whole, to mistake their immediate cause with the ultimate purposes of God. The principle of the increase of the love of God and neighbor is strong enough not only to condemn obvious evils, but also to lead theological schools in a collective examination of conscience. Like all examinations, the increase of the love of God and neighbor exposes those subtle violations of the first commandment that are the special temptation of religious folk. Hence, careful attention to this purpose is essential for the health of any seminary. As Niebuhr says, "Unless the forms in which idolatries appear at any particular time are illuminated and criticized there is no prospect for ultimate health" (p. 47).

Niebuhr was aware of the difficulty people might have evaluating theological education from this perspective. Much of the seminary life of Niebuhr's time (and ours) is concerned with particularities. In a sense seminaries, like local congregations, are easily corrupted. At all small institutions, individuals have disproportionate influence over the future of the institution. In Niebuhr's time, as in ours, administrators, faculty members, and occasionally trustees often invested intense loyalty in one or another partial good. Naturally the advocates of these partial goals, each wanting to control the whole, have clashed with one another, with the stronger side politically carrying the day. While a transcendent goal might be easily applied to these continual disagreements, such a sense of purpose might condition the discussion and allow the participants to view their work "before God."

Niebuhr's analysis of purpose suggested that the most serious problems of theological schools were not those that were readily visible. The pursuit of limited and partial goals by institutions tends to corrupt the very talk about God that the schools are designed to encourage. In subtle ways the love of self replaces the love of God as the center of the school and its mission.

In other words, before Niebuhr and his colleagues turned to the actual analysis of theological schools — and *Purpose* appeared one year before the summary volume — Niebuhr was calling the seminaries to ask whether their most serious problem was not "bad faith" rather than finances, faculty salaries, or the quality of students. The first question a school's leaders must ask is not how many FTEs (full-time equivalents) a school may have; it is whether that school has striven to be loyal to the ultimate purpose of the church. Was an institution shaped around the demands of the kingdom, or did it live from some lesser good? Thus, for a denominational seminary the question was not whether it served a particular denomination or not. That was given in its history and basic documents. The more substantial question was whether, in so doing, it served to increase the love of God and the love of neighbor or made denominational loyalty the goal of its educational life. The same question could of course be put to those seminaries that saw themselves as heroic advocates of a theological perspective. Was a school's passionate liberalism or conservatism part of its attempt to increase the love of God and neighbor or a cause undertaken for its own sake?

III. Servants of the Servants of God

Understanding the contemporary ministry, Niebuhr admitted, was a difficult and often vexing task. That the role of the minister was confused in the modern world seemed to Niebuhr, as it did to others, almost self-evident. This confusion was naturally reflected in the work of the theological schools, "where a frankly pluralistic approach to the work of the ministry" was widespread and "where men are prepared for the varieties of ministerial work" without any reference to a common function that all ministers had to undertake (p. 53). As a result, the schools were unclear about their "precise objectives" and spoke about ministry in generalities. Contemporaries gave reasons for this vocational confusion, and Niebuhr, ever faithful as a scholar, listed them, but he saw the problem as theological: "the problem of [the church's] ministers is always how to remain faithful servants of the Church in the midst of cultural change and yet to change culturally so as to be true to the Church's purpose." Hence, Niebuhr was not interested in any proposals that might turn ministry "into something else" (p. 57).

The good news was that a consensus appeared to be emerging. The building blocks of this newer understanding were the traditional loci theologians used to understand ecclesiastical office: the work of the ministry, the purpose of that work, the nature of the call, the source of ecclesiastical authority, and the people the minister served (p. 58). These core concerns were key to the whole argument. Niebuhr is clear that whatever else we may think about ministry, these theological loci must be continued and respected. Thus, for instance, ministers continue to do the many functions tradition prescribed: they must offer the sacraments, preach the Word, exercise oversight over the congregation, and give pastoral care to needy souls.

Historically, Niebuhr believed that the tendency had been for the church to make one or another of these tasks primary and to ignore or downplay the other. The result of this selectivity was to subject the church to a particular reading of its chief goal or purpose. Thus medieval Catholics concentrated on directing "needy souls that they might escape from the snares of sin and achieve everlasting life; in contrast, reformation clergy saw the purpose behind these tasks as the proclamation of the forgiveness of sins" (p. 59). Every action for the Reformed or evangelical pastor was preaching, whether it was public or private discourse, catechetical instruction, sacramental administration, or the like. In a similar way, Wesleyans and other evangelicals had adopted the work of the ministry to their chief purpose, "the rescue of women and men from hell." In other words, "the Unity is given . . . by directing each function to a chief, though still proximate, end. Now that end is the salvation of souls from eternal punishment, now the cure of guilty souls . . . , now the reconciliation of God and man through sacrifice and sacrament and works of expiation."

Niebuhr was correct in noting that the seminaries of his day were seeking ways out of this impasse. The twentieth century's diverse theological curricula, for all their determination by local faculty politics, reflected an awareness that all the ministers' multiple tasks were valid and had to be considered in a responsible program of ministerial formation. He was also correct about the way tradition had honored one function of ministry over another. Clearly, the nineteenth-century Protestant curricula were based on the belief that preaching, especially biblical preaching, was the core task of the minister.

Niebuhr noted that the belief in a call to the ministry shaped much of the modern understanding of the ministry. As he saw it, the call to the ministry had certain common elements: (1) the call to be a Christian, (2) the secret call or inner conviction, and (3) the ecclesiastical call or public confirmation. As was true of the various tasks of the ministry, the churches had placed more emphasis on one or another of these elements. Thus the medieval church had been concerned, above all else, with the ecclesiastical confirmation of pastoral authority, while such evangelists as Wesley were almost ready to abandon the public call in order to have godly people proclaim the message to sinners. The most important question for modern ministers, however, was how these diverse considerations could be kept in proper balance.

Even greater vagueness imbued the question of authority. The problem was not that of official authorization, but the deeper question of the rationale behind the minister's work. Niebuhr was convinced that this could not be prophetic authority: "though the minister in all times is 'man of God,' he does not as minister undertake to prophesy with a 'Thus says the Lord' and to claim that his words are the Word of God." The minister's teaching is more similar to the testimony of a witness in court whose words, like those of any witness, need to be weighed, criticized, and at times not believed, for "the ambassador of Christ is no plenipotentiary" (p. 68).

Niebuhr's idea of call is related to this vision of the ministry. As he saw his contemporaries, the heavy emphasis on the "secret call" that had dominated American Protestantism for one hundred years was being replaced by a more providential view that understood the call of the ministry in much the same way that people were called to a variety of vocations. It was not "first of all, a mystic matter" that takes place in solitude. Rather, the call comes from the dynamics of social relationships, the church as the "called and calling Church." The challenge is for young people to consider whether they are not called of God: "ask them to reflect especially on the requirements that he laid upon them by his watchful providence over the whole course of their lives" (p. 85).

Niebuhr believed that the ministers of his own time had successfully redefined call in terms of contemporary biblical scholarship. Just as scholars had shown that the Old and New Testament were products of the community rather than works of religious genius, so contemporary ministers recognized that they came from the church community and were tied to it by service.

Having said this, Niebuhr noted, as he did in the case of the call, that there are certain common elements in the doctrine of ministerial authority: institutional authorization, scriptural and theological learning, and personal authenticity. Each age rearranges these to fit its own understanding of the purpose of the church. Niebuhr believed that his own time had some special problems in this area. Outside of the Roman Church, few people accepted the authority of institutions, and while the Bible continued to have weight among church members, many ministers were no longer confident of its authority. With the erosion of these foundations of ministerial authority, one naturally saw that authority diminish or almost disappear.

Niebuhr was not sanguine about the recovery of Protestant ministerial authority. "The question is not whether the ministry will reflect the institutional forms of leadership in the world but whether it will reflect these with the difference that Christian faith and church life require; whether, in short, the minister will remain 'man of God' despite the fact that he is now a director instead of a ruler" (p. 90). As Niebuhr knew, democracy had ended for many, if not most, Protestants the possibility of any finite human being assuming power over another's soul. Everyone had to believe, to act, and to live for himself or herself. But this recognition of autonomy, so long in coming, did not necessarily mean the end of common purpose and common action. It was Niebuhr's hope that the idea of the spiritual director could bridge the gap between the older concept of an authoritative and often authoritarian ministry and the new American order.[9]

The easiest of the four contributors to an understanding of the ministry was the question, to whom was the minister sent? Here again the tension was historically conditioned. Every minister was sent both to a specific congregation of believers and to those outside that fellowship. But the problems come as

9. Niebuhr explored the religious dynamics of democracy in two studies: *The Social Sources of Denominationalism* and *The Kingdom of God in America*. The two books are almost twins: *Social Sources* deals with the American churches' loss of social integrity, while *The Kingdom of God in America* deals with the churches as creators of a democratic community.

people try to balance these two pressures. "Today there is uncertainty about the ministry in Church and world partly because it is not clear whether the Church is fundamentally inclusive or exclusive, whether therefore the minister's concern is to extend to all in his reach or only to a faithful elite." In concrete terms, is the minister "a parish person or a builder of a separated community" (p. 75)? But this tension was also ultimately theological. Niebuhr noted that many ministers easily replaced the theological anthropology with the understanding of humanity taught by natural and social science. But those who refused to do this ran the risk of becoming irrelevant. "Often," Niebuhr wrote, "the ministry seems to be divided between those who sought to make the gospel relevant by allegorizing it so as to meet the needs of modern men and those who regarded its earlier translations as so literal that any new translation" betrayed its deeper meaning (p. 78). Instead, Niebuhr suggested ministers were sent to people understood as existing before God and not as autonomous individuals or groups.

Niebuhr's belief that the purpose of the church and ministry was to increase the love of God and humankind dictated his solution to the question of whom the ministry should serve. If the church was true to its ultimate purpose, its ministry would naturally flow beyond itself and into the world. After all, if the church increases the love of humankind, it must be as comprehensive in its service as it is in its devotion. But it was more than this. Niebuhr believed that despite the different forms that religious questions had taken, they still reflected the same human dilemmas. If one age asks what I must do to be saved and another, what I must do to escape my addictions, the church is obliged to point the way to a religious resolution of these very real human needs. Human beings badly need rebirth and deliverance. There is a human cry of freedom from "heteronomy of existence, from the life of mass man" (p. 94).

Niebuhr's treatment of these four classic loci of thought about the ministry was key to the concept of ministry that he saw emerging in his own time: the pastoral director. From the beginning Niebuhr wants to make it clear that he is dealing not with a pastoral job description, but with a way of locating the purpose or goal of ministry. Ministers will continue to do the classical functions of ministry, to be called persons, to have authority, and to serve humankind, but the question is, what provides a center or core of all these diverse elements for our own time? Niebuhr is saying this core must be theologically conceived.

Niebuhr argued for his conception of the pastoral director from an observation about church architecture. The modern church building has its own center.

> The focal point of the complex building is a room for which no name yet has been found. To call it either auditorium or sanctuary seems false. It is

> the place of worship and instruction. The prominence given to Holy Table or altar, to cross and candles, does not indicate so much that this is the place where the sacraments are celebrated as that it is the place of prayer. The pulpit, however, has not been related to a secondary place as though preaching were not now important. Another architectural feature is symptomatic. The minister now has an office from which he directs the activities of the Church, where also he studies and does some of his pastoral counseling. (p. 81)

The work of the pastoral director reflects this architecture. The minister is the one who moves from office to worship center and back again. He or she is not the "big operator," the ecclesiastical executive who is able to get things done; rather the minister is the overseer of the church. The best example Niebuhr can find is Augustine of Hippo, who combined his work of pastoral oversight with a deep theological understanding of the faith (p. 82). Preaching that calls "into being a people of God who as Church will serve the purpose of the Church in a local community" is vital to this concept. But it is not only preaching. Niebuhr believes that the contemporary pastoral director would be more vital as a worship leader because his goal is not only to save sinful humanity but "to demonstrate [the churches'] love of God, whose love of man is proclaimed in the Gospel" (p. 83). Above all, the pastoral director is the "teacher of teachers," a master Christian educator who directs the learning of the church toward "the increase among men of the love of God and neighbor" (p. 84).

Unfortunately, the phrase "pastoral director," which Niebuhr hoped would remind people of the great bishops of the church, could too easily be read as "pastoral manager" and define the minister as the executive in charge of a small charity. Such misinterpretations obscure the theological dimensions of the concept. In a world in which the laity have both ultimate control over the congregation and spiritual autonomy, Niebuhr believed that the minister's essential task was to keep an increasingly diverse company of believers on a true course. The proper work of the pastoral director is not to resolve, for instance, the petty disputes among Sunday school teachers — although he or she may spend much time doing that — but to see that the Sunday school, whatever happens in a particular situation, does "increase the love of God and neighbor."

The best translation of "pastoral director" is bishop. The ancient bishop was theologian and overseer, celebrant and preacher, friend and counselor. In other words, Niebuhr is advocating a ministry that applies the deepest possible understanding of faith to everyday church life; that is, a resident practical theologian. This term can be taken literally. Niebuhr believed that the minister's work was to enable people to "practice" their faith in ways that helped them to participate in the church's purposes. Although this might involve the minister in transmitting some theological content, the practical theologian was not someone who popularized the various theologies current at the time. The pastoral director coordinated and interpreted the actual experiences of the congregation while the congregation struggled to be the church in a particular place.

Niebuhr was concerned, as many people were in the 1950s, that the sheer pace of activity in the suburban church might contribute to the "burnout" of many of the best ministers. His attempt to define the work of the ministry theologically was an attempt to define the minister's task more as an interpreter of Christian life than as its instigator or manager. Ultimately the concept reflected confidence in the laity's capacity to be the church and to achieve the church's ultimate purposes.

IV. The House of Theology

What, then, of the theological schools that were, after all, the occasion for the writing of the essay? Again, Niebuhr is careful to point out that the problems of theological schools are essentially theological problems first and foremost. In an important passage, he writes: "If Biblical study has become a specialty or series of specialties today the reason is not to be sought in the development of specialization among teachers of theology but in the loss of a controlling idea in theological education — an idea able to give unity to many partial inquiries" (p. 97). The schools suffered from the "uncertainty of aim" (p. 98). Hence the curriculum appears to be more "a collection of studies" than a "course of study," and the schools are characterized by "hidden and open conflicts" between people who think themselves "self-sufficient" (p. 99). Perhaps the greatest symbol of the underlying discord in Niebuhr's mind was the conflict between the "content" or "classical" teachers and those who advocated "practical training." Thus, Niebuhr said, almost brutally: "Such is the first, superficial impression: our schools, like our churches and our ministers, have no clear conception of what they are doing but are carrying on traditional actions, making separate responses to various pressures exerted by the churches and society, contriving uneasy compromises among many values, engaging in little quarrels symptomatic of undefined issues, trying to improve their work by adjusting minor parts of the academic machine or by changing the specifications of the new material to be treated" (p. 101). In short, the seminaries were guilty of an almost damnable muddle. Trying to raise church towers, they had built new Babels.

Although Niebuhr admitted that he saw no new theological understanding on the horizon that might end this confusion, he was not without hope. The theological renaissance of the 1950s seemed to him (at least at this time) to be generating "a sense of renewal and promise, a feeling of excitement about the theological task" that "is accompanied by invigoration of intellectual inquiry and of religious devotion" (p. 103). The best example he could give of this was the renewal of Old Testament studies. At one time they had the excitement of a "high school recitation" at "two o'clock" on a May day (p. 104). But in his day they were making vital contributions to the larger discussion. Much the same could be said about New Testament studies, church history, and theology. The discussion was moving to include all aspects of human life, including art, literature, and philosophy. There was also a "robust" sense of the church developing among students and faculty members, and even an increased liveliness in the chapel services (p. 105).

Niebuhr's sense of theological renewal influenced his vision of the seminary as "the intellectual center of the church." In a poetic passage he describes the nature of the seminaries' relationship to the church: "To speak in Aristotelian language, the efficient, material, formal and final cause of the theological cause are identical with those of the Church. Its motivation is that of the Church — the love of God and neighbor implanted in human nature by creation, redeemed, redirected and invigorated by the acceptance of the good. Its membership consists of churchmen: existing and historic individuals, gathered together in a common life of faith which among other things seeks understanding of itself, the Church, and neighbor" (p. 107). Since the seminary was never the whole church, its special character came from its responsibility to think about God and humanity before God. But this very act places the theological school in a difficult, almost paradoxical position. Like other sciences, theology must be "disinterested as all pure science is disinterested." Consequently, theology must concentrate on its "objects" for their own sake only, while maintaining a true love of Being (p. 108). But what are the objects of theological reflection? The answer is not simple. For Niebuhr the answer is, as it was for Calvin, the knowledge of God and of ourselves. He, however, prefers to make this a threefold formula: the knowledge of God, companions, and ourselves (p. 113). Such knowledge is always relational in the sense that it is defined by the relationship between the three — we know God only in relationship to companions and ourselves, and we have theological knowledge of ourselves only in relationship to God and companions. But it is also relational knowledge in the sense that it cannot be separated from our participation in the divine reality. In this latter sense, theological knowledge is similar to our knowledge of the human sciences since that knowledge is always bound up with our humanness.

Niebuhr's belief in the seminary as the intellectual center of the church was compatible with the popular idea of theological education as professional education. Theological schools, Niebuhr argued, reflect on two aspects of the church's intellectual life. On the one hand, a seminary is the "place or occasion" where the church exercises its intellectual love of God; on the other, the seminary is the place where the church reflects critically on its practices of worship, preaching, teaching, and the care of souls. This means that the seminary is like any other intellectual center "where both 'pure science' and 'applied science' are pursued" (p. 111).

The Purpose of the Church and Its Ministry was published in the midst of the postwar religious boom. While many Christian leaders knew that many denominational colleges were becoming ecumenical or, perhaps better, generic Christian, they did not have a strong sense that they were moving toward secularity. More than a half-century later, Niebuhr's concept is more prophetic. Seminaries and divinity schools are virtually the only place where serious thinking about God takes place. In our context the phrase "intellectual center" implies much more than it did to Niebuhr and his generation. The seminary is the intellectual center of the church because it is the only place with the resources in people and materials for serious reflection on the objective and subjective dimensions of Christian faith.

V. Advancement

The Advancement of Theological Education was an evaluation, a report, and a program. One could read the title of the work with different emphases. On the one hand, it was about the growth of theological education. It was written in the midst of an educational and religious revival that had surrounded the most extensive expansion of theological education in the nation's history. The experience of these twenty-five years called into question the widespread belief that theological education had declined after its triumphant beginning in Puritan New England.

> Historians are pointing out increasingly that the matrix of American religious life as we now know it is not to be found in the seventeenth century but in the nineteenth, not in New England only but also on the frontier; that the origins of those denominations which exercise a large influence in the twentieth century are to be found in the revivals of the eighteenth and nineteenth centuries more than in the Puritan movement; that all of the churches, including those which originated in the Reformation, have been deeply influenced by the experiential religion of the revival period; that

American college and theological systems had their effective beginnings in the nineteenth century.[10]

While Niebuhr appreciated the energy and native ability of the Baptists, Methodists, and Disciples who had spread Christianity across the great West,[11] he had no illusions about the intellectual content of frontier faith. Their theology had been "experimental and highly practical" and closely tied to the democratic traditions of the nation.[12] If anything, Niebuhr believed the popularity of these churches had encouraged the traditional confessional churches to adopt many of their emphases. In turn, advancement meant the spread of the higher educational standards to the popular denominations.

Less than a generation earlier the Brown-May study had indicated that seminaries were not educating a majority of the nation's ministers, but *Advancement* noted that the graduate theological seminary was becoming the mainstream Protestant norm. Even the continued growth of the Bible colleges and schools reflected an increased interest in providing higher education. The conclusion was obvious: "Theological Schools are being founded and are growing, not only because American Protestants desire a well-educated ministry, but also because ministers want theology."[13] While this was probably an optimistic reading of the desire of many clergy for a credential that would reflect their professional standing, the post–World War II generation of clergy does seem to have had an unusually strong interest in theology.[14]

The second meaning of "advancement" was statistical. The long-established schools had grown by an average of 151 percent.[15] The number of graduate seminaries had increased fourfold in the period, and at least 80 percent of the students were college graduates.[16] With more than 25,000 seminarians, 1 theological student was enrolled for every 2,375 Protestant church mem-

10. Niebuhr, Williams, and Gustafson, *Advancement,* p. 2.

11. See H. Richard Niebuhr, *The Kingdom of God in America* (Chicago and New York: Willett, Clark and Co., 1937) and *The Social Sources of Denominationalism* (New York: Henry Holt, 1929).

12. Niebuhr, Williams, and Gustafson, *Advancement,* pp. 2-3.

13. Niebuhr, Williams, and Gustafson, *Advancement,* p. 5. There was clear evidence to support Niebuhr's final point. Theological publishing, directed toward the general public, was at a high level, and Niebuhr himself had been featured in *Life.*

14. Estimating clergy interest in theology is very difficult. The 1950s saw the new summer pastoral institutes growing, and the demand for a professional doctorate might indicate more scholarly interests. Clearly, many clergy were also contemplating shifting into teaching in the increasingly popular religion departments.

15. Niebuhr, Williams, and Gustafson, *Advancement,* p. 10.

16. Niebuhr, Williams, and Gustafson, *Advancement,* p. 8.

bers in the United States. The teachers who taught these students had a generally higher level of education than their predecessors. Many were young teachers just beginning their careers.[17] Although the perceptive might note a cloud the size of a man's fist that prophesied the economic crises of the 1960s and 1970s, seminaries appeared to be financially healthy institutions. On a per student basis, their endowments were among the largest in American higher education, and the amount contributed by the denominations was slowly increasing. Hence seminaries were able to maintain a very favorable student-faculty ratio and correspondingly small classes. In the denominational worlds in which seminaries lived, the schools were elite institutions that stood head and shoulders above the small collegiate institutions sponsored by their churches, the capstone of a still extensive system of Protestant education.[18]

The third meaning of "advancement" pointed to the schools' futures. Jon Diefenthaler noted that Niebuhr saw the survey as "an opportunity to actually reform the church" and that he "relished the opportunity that the entire project afforded him to address the administration of so many schools."[19] Niebuhr admitted that he found the task of reviewing the data presented to him by the staff "exhilarating."[20] The excitement did not lie in the numbers themselves, but rather in the possibilities those numbers disclosed. American and Canadian theological schools had the potential to become much better institutions, and Niebuhr could see in the reams of information presented to him some hope for a way out of the doldrums of the past. Niebuhr and his colleagues were not alone in feeling they were at a *kairos* moment. This was the age, after all, of the core curriculum, of the dream of a four-year basic program, and of the expansion of physical resources.[21] Niebuhr's vision was more elusive than the prag-

17. Niebuhr, Williams, and Gustafson, *Advancement*, p. 20. Niebuhr did note that in a considerable number of schools these advancements had not been made.

18. This led to serious cases of hubris among some seminary professors and administrators who tended to undervalue the work of their collegiate counterparts. The very success of the seminaries in the 1950s may have marked the beginning of the end of the various "feeder" networks that had sustained the schools.

19. Jon Diefenthaler, *H. Richard Niebuhr: A Lifetime of Reflections on the Church and the World* (Macon, Ga.: Mercer University Press, 1986), pp. 86-87.

20. Diefenthaler, *H. Richard Niebuhr*, p. 87.

21. See above, chap. 20. The almost breathless excitement of Merrimon Cuninggim's prose conveys much of the feeling of the time. "The New Currriculum at Perkins," *Christian Century*, Apr. 18, 1954, pp. 574-75. We list some things the faculty believed this approach called for: emphasis on the wholeness of the minister's task, and thus on the curriculum as a total experience; integration of the various parts of the curriculum, that the subjects be not marbles in a jar but slices off the same loaf; proper sequence of studies; and federation of classroom and fieldwork, viewed as laboratory, that the necessary association of the two aspects of the minis-

matic dreams of many seminary administrators, and thus both more and less achievable. He wanted to renew the inner core of the institutions, the men and handful of women charged with the task of teaching. Since his time as president of Elmhurst College, he had dreamed of an American theology, watered by the best of world Christian thinking, that would equal the technical and doctrinal studies produced abroad. If presidents and deans dreamed of new buildings, new programs, and new hires, Niebuhr dreamed of renewed faculties.

The actual writing of *Advancement* was divided among the three project directors. Niebuhr was to edit the whole and to take primary responsibility for chapters 1, 2, 3, and 9. These chapters bore the titles "Some Recent Trends in Theological Education," "Trends in the Economics of Theological Education," "Problems of Government," and "The Line of Advance." Daniel Day Williams was to do 4, 5, and 6: "The Theological Faculties," "The Course of Study," and "Theological Teaching in Classroom, Field, and Library." James Gustafson was responsible for 7 and 8: "Theological Students: Varieties of Types and Experience" and "The School as Community."

VI. Trends, Economics, and Government

This chapter has already alluded to the two most important trends that Niebuhr found: the number of schools and the number of theological students were constantly rising. Twenty-seven new seminaries had been founded over the last thirty years, most of them in denominations without a strong tradition of theological training for their pastors. The graduate theological seminary, long on the edge of American religious and educational experience, had captured a place near the center of the Protestant enterprise. Although seminaries had been traditionally "open admission" institutions, there was a new emphasis on the quality of the student body. Seminaries were sending recruiters to ministerial associations and colleges; the Rockefeller Brother's Fund was seeking the best and the brightest for a look-see year in theological school; and standardized testing was now part of the process in many schools. Although faculties were not growing at the same rate as the student bodies, growth in the size of faculties had been consistent.[22] The percentage with earned doctorates had likewise grown.

ter's life, contemplation and activity, be started in the seminary years. Recognition was given to two other factors: that individual differences suggest the provision of electives even as the common dimensions of the minister's task suggest a large common core of study; and that successful communication of the gospel calls for training in certain techniques.

22. Niebuhr, Williams, and Gustafson, *Advancement*, p. 17.

So far as *effectiveness* in teaching is concerned, there may have been retrogression. That retrogression is due to five factors: the increased student load per teacher; the increase of administrative duties of a large number of the teachers; the difficulties offered by the curriculum dilemmas; the demands made on the theological faculties by increasingly active denominations, local churches, and other agencies; and connected with all these, the financial difficulties under which the schools labored. These financial difficulties are sharply reflected in faculty salaries, in stipends for students preparing for theological education, and in the practice of professors supplementing their incomes by professional work activities outside the school.[23]

In terms of curriculum, two tendencies almost diverged. On the one hand, the course of study in many schools was becoming more complex as new disciplines, especially in the practical area, were added and forays into secular disciplines, such as sociology and psychology, were made. But what was most dramatic was the decline of the elective system, one of the favorite liberal reforms, and its replacement by a more traditional curriculum. In simple terms, "biblical, church-historical and theological studies have been re-established or re-emphasized as the stable but not static basis of the curriculum."[24] But the new curricula posed a major dilemma: at almost all schools the curriculum was a solid phalanx of required courses that allowed little room for innovation. The demand for a fourth year of study was directly related to this curricular overcrowding.

The economics of the seminaries was directly related to their growth. A full two-thirds of the schools had done some major construction project, with married student dormitories the most common addition and libraries the next most common.[25] Niebuhr noted that the churches (and individual members of them) had generally responded to the demand for new facilities. What concerned him in the financial picture was a shift in the percentage of funds devoted to administration and library and to faculty. The figures indicated that the cost of administration had increased from 3.5 percent in the Brown-May survey to almost 15 percent. At the same time, the percentage spent on instruction had declined a similar amount, from 44 percent to 33 percent.

Niebuhr pointed to low faculty salaries as one consequence of this pattern of allocation. He was aware that salaries in higher education were generally low, compared with the compensation received in other professions, in-

23. Niebuhr, Williams, and Gustafson, *Advancement,* p. 20.

24. Niebuhr, Williams, and Gustafson, *Advancement,* p. 21.

25. Many schools had ambitious plans for their physical plants, although few completed them.

cluding the ministry. This highlighted one of the major themes of the report: "It has been the period (1928 to 1953) in which the seminaries have been challenged to make their greatest advances in centuries, when the need for a well-educated ministry has been most widely recognized, when the requirement that teachers of theology be highly prepared professionally has been accepted. And this has also been the period in which the teaching profession in the seminaries as well as elsewhere suffered a decline in compensation in terms of the purchasing power of the salaries paid."[26] In the highly compensated period after World War II, teachers were among the few who did not benefit from the massive increase in gross national product. "Catching up" was to be the task of the 1960s and 1970s.

No one can be faulted for failing to be a prophet. In his analysis of the financial situation of theological schools, Niebuhr noticed that the schools were largely dependent on endowments and church contributions. Despite passionate debates during the 1920s and 1930s, seminaries were still essentially low-cost institutions. Outside of the university schools, tuition was nonexistent or minimal and not a major factor in determining seminary budgets. Even in university-related divinity schools, the endowment was frequently able to provide substantial scholarship aid for students who lacked their own source of funding. The report assumed that there should be a parallel between church support for seminaries and state support for higher education, and complained that "taking Protestant theological education as a whole, it is clear that the churches as organized denominations do not support the seminaries to the same extent that state and federal governments support other types of professional education."[27] The prosperity of the mainstream churches in the 1950s made this complaint sound far more reasonable than it would a decade later when many schools entered a period of rising tuition and fees in the attempt to find stability in the midst of the rapid fluctuations of the American economy.[28] Perhaps it is only an incidental irony, but 1957 — the year the report was published — marked the beginning of a series of articles announcing the end of the religious boom.[29]

However, Niebuhr and his colleagues may have missed important signs of impending crisis. As they noted, not all schools published detailed financial re-

26. Niebuhr, Williams, and Gustafson, *Advancement,* p. 40.

27. Niebuhr, Williams, and Gustafson, *Advancement,* p. 34.

28. James McCord, "Financial Theological Education," *Christian Century* 88 (Jan. 27, 1971): 106-7.

29. See, for example, Seymour Lipset, "What Religious Revival?" *Columbia University Forum,* Winter 1958, pp. 17-21. These articles were different from earlier theological criticisms of the revival by such theologians as Niebuhr.

ports, and many of the poorer schools were very weak financially.[30] But even at the top, serious problems existed. Princeton Seminary was running a substantial deficit in the last years of Mackay's presidency.[31] Despite massive financial campaigns by the university-related schools, their financial balance was precarious.[32] Further, the expansion of the number of seminaries was a mixed blessing financially. Since the primary source of new endowment for the schools was a relatively small number of wealthy people in each denomination, each new school added to the competition for limited resources. Southern Baptists, who founded some of the largest of the new seminaries in this period, escaped this problem by underwriting seminary budgets out of the denomination's Cooperative Program.

The survey was, however, much more insightful in identifying government as a major problem for theological schools. Niebuhr and colleagues were acutely aware that the governance of seminaries had developed on an ad hoc basis and had little relationship to the polity or ecclesiology of the sponsoring denomination. Niebuhr was deeply concerned about the continuing power of required statements of faith and their tendency to suppress creative teaching. Not only were boards involved in these heresy hunts, but also students. In words that almost describe later problems at Concordia and at the various Southern Baptist seminaries, Niebuhr wrote: "Its pressures are exerted through the classroom visitations of official — but more frequently unofficial — guardians of faith, through students who listen to their instructors' lectures with ears attuned to departures from the sound forms of words or the well-established train of ideas. Such students, it has been reported, have on occasion used tape recording machines for the purpose of gathering sure evidence against suspected heretics." While the battle for academic freedom might have been won at the university-related and interdenominational schools, it clearly had not been won everywhere. A "governmental arrangement" was needed to protect the proper exercise of "Christian liberty."[33]

"One-man rule" was a serious by-product of the ad hoc history of semi-

30. Niebuhr, Williams, and Gustafson, *Advancement,* p. 29.

31. William K. Selden, *Princeton Theological Seminary: A Narrative History, 1812-1992* (Princeton: Princeton University Press, 1992), p. 150. When James McCord arrived, the cumulative deficit was $800,000.

32. This appears to have been true of Van Dusen's Union as well. Despite its role as the nation's seminary of record and its distinguished faculty, its pool of potential givers appears to have been shrinking. By the 1970s Union's financial problems would become one of the most important sagas in American theological education as the nation's former theological flagship gradually slipped further and further behind in the search for new funding.

33. Niebuhr, Williams, and Gustafson, *Advancement,* p. 45.

nary governance. Although Niebuhr did not name specific presidents, theological schools in the fifties provided myriad examples of the problem. The autocratic rule of Henry Pitney Van Dusen at Union was legendary, and *Advancement* appeared in the same year that Duke McCall of Southern Baptist Theological Seminary secured the dismissal of thirteen faculty members for questioning his executive authority at the institution.[34] The problem was not solved, however, by discussion or reason. The turmoil of the 1960s made "one-man rule" a dated concept in most institutions.

The survey also identified another problem: muddle. The governmental structures of some schools were so complicated as to be almost unchartable. These included Andover-Newton and the Federated Theological Faculty,[35] whose confusions were products of their history, but they were not alone. Such complicated arrangements, as many at the time recognized, tended to concentrate power in the hands of one person, since only the president had access to all the various levels. Equally important, they tended to dissipate the energies of the school, as much effort was expended in simply keeping the school functioning. A rash of denominational mergers threatened to make the number of improbable arrangements even larger as places on seminary boards became markers in the endless game of denominational politics.

The question of the relationship of seminaries to colleges and universities was a key governance issue. Niebuhr and his colleagues found at least six patterns of affiliation between seminaries and other forms of higher education that ranged from divinity schools in nondenominational universities, such as Harvard or Yale, through divinity schools in denominational-related universities, to seminaries that had either been part of a college, perhaps as a department, or were on the same campus. Interestingly, Niebuhr recognized the Southern Baptist and Southern Presbyterian pattern in which the seminaries prepared the teachers for the colleges and, in turn, received many, if not most, of their students from other institutions in their denominational system. In many ways the issue could be divided into parts: the relationship of seminaries or divinity schools to universities and the relationship of seminaries to colleges.

For Niebuhr the affiliation of a seminary with a university was a high value. He and his colleagues believed that the university connection prevented seminaries from neglecting their functions as intellectual centers of the

34. McCall's action dispersed a number of very capable faculty members to the new Southern Baptist institution, Southeastern Baptist Theological Seminary, at Wake Forest, N.C. The new school both continued Southern Baptist Theological Seminary's tradition of sound theological study and represented a more faculty-centered approach to theological education.

35. Niebuhr did not name these institutions, but the knowledgeable reader had no problem identifying them.

church,[36] and created an atmosphere that encouraged, but did not guarantee, a fruitful conversation between church and culture.[37] Interestingly enough, the School of Theology at the University of Southern California, originally a Methodist school, separated from its sponsoring institution in 1957 and moved to Claremont, California, where it joined with other seminaries in establishing a theological center.

Yet, if relations with a university were good, relations with colleges were more risky. The movement that the surveyors observed was for seminaries to become independent of their college affiliations and to subsequently develop some type of relationship with a university. The AATS likewise encouraged seminaries closely related to colleges to become independent institutions.

VII. Doctor Williams Speaks

Daniel Day Williams was charged with the central sections on faculty, academic programs, and teaching. Williams wrote at a time when the seminaries had difficulty acquiring and keeping strong faculties. Part of the reason was that the schools were in a period of expansion in which "a considerable shuffling of faculties takes place as men are called from one school to another."[38] Yet, this was not the only reason. Although the better seminaries had sought highly trained specialists since the Civil War, the higher standard for seminary faculties was now widespread. Schools wanted teachers who had been through the various academic ranks.[39] Unfortunately, few educational centers had programs that were able to produce the type of teacher that was desired. The survey was taken just as such schools were expanding in size and geographical location,[40] although many biblical scholars continued to do some work in Germany.

Williams identified many of the problems of the seminary faculty in the dual character of the vocation or office. Like the schools they served, seminary

36. Niebuhr, Williams, and Gustafson, *Advancement,* p. 53.

37. Niebuhr did note, almost as an aside, that there was a danger of the loss of confessional integrity from the university connection, but this was not a developed concern. Niebuhr, Williams, and Gustafson, *Advancement,* p. 53.

38. Niebuhr, Williams, and Gustafson, *Advancement,* p. 54.

39. Like colleges, seminaries were seeking younger instructors who had come of age in the new professional world of the 1950s.

40. That the expansion may have been too swift was indicated by Claude Welch's *Graduate Education in Religion: A Critical Appraisal* (Missoula: University of Montana Press, 1971). Welch's conclusions were very controversial at the time, and he perhaps judged many programs too harshly. Nonetheless, his general conclusion that the field had expanded too hastily was justified.

teachers were responsible both to the academy and to the church. "There is first the double responsibility of the theological teachers for scholarship and for the churchmanship. He is a faculty member in a school and responsible first to the school. But he is usually also a minister of the church and his denomination. He frequently serves on denominational boards in addition to his activities in a local church. He is often called upon for special services in the churches as lecturer, writer, or consultant, and sometimes for positions of denominational leadership."[41] The report affirmed the value of the various extra tasks that seminary teachers did for the churches. Clearly, these tasks were important, but they had serious consequences. When combined with the large amount of seminary teaching that dealt with basic subjects that allowed their students to do ministry, seminary professors had little time for that basic research that "may produce results only after many years."[42] In regard to publication and research, Williams stressed the existence of two sets of standards. In the university-related or research-oriented seminaries, faculties were subject to the usual academic tensions of publish or perish as well as the endless debate over whether good teaching or sound scholarship was more important for promotion and tenure. Many denominational schools, however, operated on a different basis. Faculties were largely undifferentiated. Most faculty members were full professors, and there was less competition between faculty members for scarce resources or higher salaries.

Yet the distinction between university-style seminaries and other schools did not answer the basic vocational questions. Williams listed a number of ideal types the researchers had encountered in writing the report: "For some the intellectual task has a high place; whereas for others the calling is to prepare men for the ministry through sound teaching but there is no special concern to work at the frontiers of intellectual problems. For still others the theological position is an opportunity to instruct, advise, and encourage theological students on the basis of the teacher's experience in the church. Here the teaching position is conceived primarily as an opportunity for personal inspiration and practical counsel." These differences in style, however, in many ways mask the basic question about the nature of theological instruction. "What is the relation of the intellect and its critical inquiries to the progress of the Christian faith?"[43]

What then made for a good faculty? Williams and his colleagues were not afraid to address this issue. Clearly, one area was "balance." The question often came down to full appointments in the practical fields. Many schools, for exam-

41. Niebuhr, Williams, and Gustafson, *Advancement,* p. 54.

42. Niebuhr, Williams, and Gustafson, *Advancement,* p. 57.

43. Niebuhr, Williams, and Gustafson, *Advancement,* p. 58.

ple, were seeking their first full-time homiletics professor, since the additional administrative burden now prevented the president or dean from also filling this position. There were clear needs for more psychologists, sociologists, and ethicists. In a sense, Williams was asking the schools to return to the visions of the 1920s, which had been put on hold during the Depression years, and use their new prosperity to bring them into compliance with their own theological visions.

Williams noted that seminary faculties had an almost impossible workload. Much time was spent counseling students with personal and academic problems,[44] fulfilling committee responsibilities, and performing other tasks. As a practicing educator, he was aware that these common tasks were rarely equally shared. The schools were cursed with a full measure of individualism. Every school had the popular professor who spent his time gathering his own tribe of followers and ignored common responsibilities, and every school had the "brilliant professor whose lectures and work are so important to the school . . . that the school must be to some extent built around him."[45] Individualism created other problems for faculties. Perhaps the most serious of these was that it inhibited the dialogue that might vitalize teaching in many disciplines.

The suggestions for the improvement of teaching were largely for the improvement of the status of the faculty: higher salaries, more money for learned societies, protection of faculties from too much outside work, and the use of tutors to handle much of the routine academic counseling. Above all, much of what was needed for improvement was financial. Money, or rather the lack of it, was the single most important factor preventing "good schools from being great ones, and fair schools from becoming good ones."[46] Yet, even when the financial needs were fully acknowledged, a faculty member still had to develop a "clarity for himself as to what is needed from him as teacher, as preacher, as member of the school, and representative of the church."[47] In other words, faculties had to answer the question: What did it mean to be a Christian scholar in the middle of the twentieth century?

The closely related problem of the curriculum suffered from a similar theological muddle. The curriculum at most schools had developed as much by accident as by design, and often new required courses had been added whenever the school appointed a new faculty member. The clear tendency was for curricula to become unwieldy. In an aside that said much more than Williams's

44. Niebuhr noted that a disproportionate amount of time was spent on students with serious personal problems, resulting in little time being spent on students who were well adjusted.

45. Niebuhr, Williams, and Gustafson, *Advancement,* p. 67.

46. Niebuhr, Williams, and Gustafson, *Advancement,* p. 73.

47. Niebuhr, Williams, and Gustafson, *Advancement,* p. 74.

statistics, he said, "if theological schools could teach everything that they regard as a desirable part of the curriculum and could give as much time to each subject as seems desirable the present period of theological study would need to be more than doubled."[48] At a minimum, the proposal for a fourth year of theological study needed to be implemented. As it was, four-fifths of a student's efforts went into required work.

Williams and his colleagues were convinced that the task of constructing a theological curriculum was a profoundly theological task. In contrast to past experiences with fixed curricula and with elective systems, they hoped to find a way to capture the dynamics of a religion that "has as its center a personal response to the reality of the creative, redeeming, and inspiring God," a curriculum that captured "the integrity of the Christian way of life as it binds God and man, past and present, together."[49] There were several suggestions for how this might be done. One proposal was that a curriculum be constructed that rested on students meeting with strong academic and religious counselors who help them make creative choices in their professional growth. Yale had a program that worked on this basis. Another suggestion was to form "core" curricula that could permit students to build on common assumptions. The Perkins program with its division of the curriculum into four areas: life and work of the local church, Christianity and culture, the Christian heritage, and the Bible, was one of the most evocative of these. But these were only suggestions. In the last analysis the survey could only recommend that the classical disciplines be included in some form and that the curriculum as a whole promote dialogue between the sacred and secular worlds. If implemented, these principles pointed toward a different style of theological training. For example, how does modern psychology impact our understanding of the biblical text? Williams believed that answering that question was as important to the biblical fields as answering historical or literary questions.

The proposal for integrative teaching went against the trend of most educational practice at the time. In general, seminaries were becoming more open to the various academic guilds and their demands than they were to the larger work of theological construction or theological hermeneutics, although both would be debated extensively in the 1960s and 1970s. In a sense the talent required for this was very much like the talent required for good preaching. A faculty member would need to be able to show the theological dimension of a scholarly development and in turn discipline his or her teaching by the use of a theological norm.

48. Niebuhr, Williams, and Gustafson, *Advancement,* p. 81.

49. Niebuhr, Williams, and Gustafson, *Advancement,* p. 82.

Williams then attempted to survey the various fields of study. In many ways this section illustrated the problems of trying to examine theological education too minutely. The survey had included meetings of representatives of the various theological disciplines, and these reports were largely the result of those meetings. The section, consequently, reads like the transcript of an endless faculty meeting as Williams rehearses subject by subject the problems of curriculum building in specific areas. The almost eternal debate, for example, between those who believed that the biblical languages should be required and those who disagreed was rehearsed in some depth.[50] Almost nothing was added to earlier debates, although Williams, ever the sharp-eyed logician, pointed out that the argument that the biblical languages were needed to appreciate the untranslatable words and concepts of Scripture was fatally flawed. After all, the illustrations of the "untranslatable" words were all in English! The one major advance in the discipline, and one that would have warmed William Rainey Harper's heart, was the use of summer intensives to teach the languages to free the regular year for more theologically oriented study. Unfortunately, the interest in biblical theology that the surveyors saw as one of the great advances in the discipline was already beginning to decline.

Likewise, most of the comments about the teaching of church history could have been made at any time during the previous fifty years. There were too much material, too little time, and too much resistance to history among the students.[51] Interestingly, only a few schools required a course in history of theology or history of doctrine, leaving the history professors with the task of providing the background to many of the crucial issues of theology. Much the same was true of the discussion of systematic theology that focused on whether students had sufficient philosophical background to appreciate many of the issues under discussion. Minimal time was devoted to the more practical fields and to specialized ministry.

Perhaps the most important part of Williams's section was the prominence it gave to nonclassroom theological education, especially field education, clinical training, and the library. The transformation of student employment

50. This is perhaps the most unrewarding of all the long-running debates in theological education. In many ways, no new insights have been added to the debate since the first dissenters left the Church of England and insisted on ordaining "unlearned" or, at least, unlettered men to the ministry. Those who believe in the languages believe they so improve understanding of the Bible that they must be maintained at all cost. Those who disagree argue that this improvement is not empirically verifiable, and indeed, that the evidence is that few graduates ever use the languages or the insights gained from their study after leaving the seminary.

51. One senses that the conference of representatives of the historical discipline that the surveyors held as part of their research was not particularly fruitful.

into meaningful employment was an abiding goal of progressive educators. One learned how to do something by doing it in the presence and with the help of someone who did it well. To the progressive mind, ministry seemed suited to such an approach, and such denominations as the Methodists had long had extensive mentoring programs, and Lutherans had followed German precedent in their use of the "vicar" year, usually inserted between the middler and the senior terms. The internship would enable a student to leave the seminary and to return prepared to ask more pertinent questions. While field education and clinical training would have probably grown, at least at the better schools, without the push given by the survey, the survey gave those approaches a new legitimacy. Field education would have an important role in subsequent reformulations of the Association of Theological Schools standards.

At their most profound level, field education, intern years, and clinical training contributed to the "scientific" character of theology as Niebuhr had defined it in *The Purpose of the Church and Its Ministry.* In that volume[52] Niebuhr had argued that the scientific character of an academic discipline was related to the presence of the object of investigation to both students and learners. Thus, "scientific" history depended on access to primary as well as secondary materials about the past. Like history, theology's access to its object was indirect. One studied God by studying human beings in relation to God. Given this understanding, the various ministry-based programs of theological education were a laboratory that provided the prospective minister with the needed exposure to living faith that would enable him or her to enter into other studies.

Williams was also prophetic in his understanding of the educational role of the library and the librarian. Although he believed that the formation of the American Association of Theological Libraries (1946) was an important step forward, he and his colleagues were aware of how much needed to be done in this area. In part, it was a matter of securing competent, well-compensated leadership for the library, and this rested in large measure in changing attitudes toward the work of the librarian and the library. *The Advancement of Theological Education,* consequently, strongly affirmed the educational role of the librarian and argued that the librarian needed to be a full partner in the educational task and a member of the faculty. By granting faculty status, the librarian's salary, often significantly below that of the teaching faculty, would have to be increased if anything was to be accomplished.[53]

The surveyors realized that the "tremendous flood of book publishing" meant that the cost of maintaining a good library was going to continue to in-

52. See below, chap. 30.

53. Niebuhr, Williams, and Gustafson, *Advancement,* p. 132.

crease — it was already increasing at the better universities. Since *Advancement* believed that seminaries needed to be in dialogue with the larger intellectual life of the time, including the most important discoveries in the social sciences, the projected increase in costs was astronomical. The sheer mass of material needed would force seminaries into "cooperative strategies" for the future. Part of such cooperation was for libraries to develop special collections that might serve the needs of a region or a denomination.

The surveyors were deeply concerned with what made for effective teaching and turned to their theological stance as a way of trying to make sense of the complex problem of teaching and learning. As they saw it, seminary instruction primarily suffered from the adoption of a didactic stance. Basically, a didactic stance was one that, whatever method of instruction was employed, served to make students passive receptors of truth. Such an approach to education was not confined to any one party or any particular; rather, it often occurred when faculty passionately tried to include "everything" in their courses or were overly concerned with meeting denominational or other requirements. In contrast, theological teaching is concerned "with fidelity to the demands imposed upon his [the teacher's] mind and spirit by the task at hand." This means the examination of presuppositions, keeping theology close to concrete human problems, and a movement "back and forth from the structure of the Christian faith to concrete experience," and which keeps the vocational goal of the students clearly in view.[54] In other words, good seminary teaching took seriously the fact that the classes were theological classes that were part of the continuing unfolding of revelation. The best classroom was one that was continually open to this possibility.

VIII. Gustafson Speaks

Gustafson's report on who went to seminary was more somber than contemporaries realized. Read carefully, Gustafson was pointing toward a coming crisis of enrollment, at least among white males, that would become more evident after the Vietnam War.[55] Part of the problem lay in the types of students attending seminary. Gustafson noted ten varieties:

54. Niebuhr, Williams, and Gustafson, *Advancement*, p. 142.

55. There is no doubt that the Vietnam War kept seminary enrollments artificially high from the mid-1960s to the early 1970s. Enrollments actually had begun to decline in the late 1950s and early 1960s until the war pushed them to artificial levels.

1. There is the student who is in seminary because his parents, pastor, and home congregation have decided for him that he will make a good pastor.
2. A man may be suffering from deep wounds in himself and seek through theological education to limit his own disturbed mind and spirit.
3. A student who functions well in interpersonal relations and anticipates the prestige and success that will be forthcoming from a ministerial career will find his way to seminary.
4. A person who has prematurely tasted the fruits of success in a church career as a boy evangelist, dynamic youth leader, or student movement executive must complete what are to him often only *pro forma* requirements for ministerial status.
5. The man who has decided for the ministry at an early age, frequently out of a sense of alienation in the world, and who enjoyed the protection of the preministerial group in college will find his way to seminary.
6. A zealous spirit characterizes the student who has found a gospel and knows its saving power. He wishes to share his good news with the world.
7. Religion and theology present themselves as objective intellectual problems to a searching mind, and the theological school seems to be the place to pursue a study of these problems.
8. An experience of a tragically disorganized society, or of disordered minds, often leads a student to study for the ministry. He sees the church as an institution out of which flow healing processes for the social and personal evils of our time.
9. Frequently found in the present generation is the man seeking for a faith adequate to bring order into the intellectual and moral confusions that have characterized his previous personal and academic experience.
10. Finally, there is the rare student of mature faith who lives in the knowledge that it is God who saves and justifies. He is seeking to become an adequate servant of his Lord.[56]

Like others who studied under H. Richard Niebuhr, Gustafson knew that ideal types were abstract and that many of the attributes he described separately might be found in complex arrays in particular cases. In other words, while the number of seminary students continued to be high, the reasons for their enrollment were complex and not always encouraging.

Gustafson noted that nondenominational seminaries — by which he meant large university-related schools — often attracted troubled students. As he saw it, the "heterogeneity of nondenominational schools" meant that many

56. Niebuhr, Williams, and Gustafson, *Advancement*, p. 147.

of their students had "no structure of theological tradition or church-relatedness"; therefore they came to seminary obsessed with their own problems. Gustafson was equally concerned with the number of students who had come to seminary from an intellectually protected environment. As he saw these students, they attended small denominational colleges where they had primarily associated with other preministerial students. They often had been ill at ease with bawdy stories or with the common speech of workers and farmers.[57] Other specific problems included a shift in interest among those most concerned with the church's public ministry from social problems to individual care.[58]

Part of the reason for the diversity of students was the seminaries' lack of admission standards. With surprising candor Gustafson noted that seminaries had to cast a wide net because they lacked "insight into the qualities and characteristics that make for effective ministry."[59] Hence, both churches and schools "tend to draw the outside boundaries beyond which a person is found not acceptable."[60] Thus, most seminaries tended to admit students with a C average, and some admitted "selected" students who had not reached this standard. Only a handful required a B or better. While the use of standardized tests was becoming more common, it was far from normative, and most psychological tests were administered after admission, more as a matter of advisement than selection. Interestingly, students were not expected to have religious or vocational certainty; the University of Chicago required only an "interest in religion." In part, this was because theological education was a process of intellectual and moral change, but Gustafson was aware that this could erode the mission of the schools and leave them primarily teaching people about the Christian religion and not teaching those devoted to its practice.

The real significance of Gustafson's findings about the type of student entering seminary and eventually the ministry did not become evident until the late 1970s and 1980s when students trained in the late 1950s and early 1960s reached their professional maturity. As these graduates entered into positions of leadership, they were confronted with the reality of a steady decline in membership and resources among the Protestant mainline churches. The leadership crisis was compounded by the fact that the late 1960s and 1970s saw significant numbers of seminary graduates adopt a socially relevant understanding of ministry as their primary self-identification. When the Protestant mainstream

57. Niebuhr, Williams, and Gustafson, *Advancement*, p. 148.
58. Niebuhr, Williams, and Gustafson, *Advancement*, p. 156.
59. Niebuhr, Williams, and Gustafson, *Advancement*, p. 176.
60. Niebuhr, Williams, and Gustafson, *Advancement*, p. 177.

went to the well, there was little water left to draw that might have refreshed its parched spirits.

Gustafson's discussion of the dynamics of theological education, as experienced by the student, was another ideal type. As he saw theological education, it involved "the whole man" and was as concerned with the students' maturation as with the communication of information. Above all, the transformation sought was that theological education "become increasingly theonomous" and put all aspects of the student's and the world's life in the "service of the Lord God."[61] In other words, God and the church had to become the student's center of meaning and purpose. In a real sense the task of theological professor was to induce a crisis, a *kairos*, a tension in the life of the student that made this radical growth possible. Of course, no common crisis point existed for all students. For some the crisis was in biblical studies, for others in theology, and for yet others in the task of communicating the gospel. Naturally, although Gustafson did not use the term, the residential character of theological education contributed to this atmosphere as students hashed the key ideas over and over again in "bull sessions" and "cell groups." The issues were, so to speak, visualized as inescapable. In any event, the key moment was when a student "came alive" and made the dynamic of faith his own personal dynamic.

In retrospect, Gustafson's description of how theological education was ideally experienced sounds very much like Eric Erikson's description of an identity crisis, mixed with some elements of Rollo May[62] and Paul Tillich. In effect, an old identity had to be surrendered and a new identity formed in dialogue with the new community. Contemporary clinical training also tended toward a belief in crisis as a useful, if not essential, element in the training of ministers. Crisis was, of course, a major theme in contemporary psychology and theology. Reading Gustafson, one almost has the feeling of a theologically induced neurosis. But one wonders about what was behind the rhetoric and the ruminations. Was it only that language formed in the 1930s and 1940s, when the nation faced depression and war, carried over in a time of prosperity or even that the teachers of that era remembered the excitement of their own voyages of self-discovery in the midst of those crises? Or was it the result of having student bodies composed almost entirely of males between the ages of twenty-one and twenty-eight? After all, this age and gender cohort often faces a variety of crises as they find their way through the thickets of employment, military service, and

61. Niebuhr, Williams, and Gustafson, *Advancement*, p. 160.

62. May, a New York psychiatrist, had received theological training at New York's Union Seminary. He and Tillich were members of a group that met frequently on Friday evenings in May's apartment to discuss the relationship between modern depth psychology and theology.

marriage. What these challenges have in common is the need for young males to find a role in society that enables them to participate meaningfully in the adult world. But another possibility exists that the historian cannot overlook. The dialectic may not have been primarily from teacher and institution to student but the other way around. Perhaps the perpetual crisis of late adolescence influenced the way teachers shaped their own understanding of their subject matter. If so, then the situation, especially in the nondenominational schools, may have been a ticking bomb that needed only a larger crisis, such as Vietnam, to create a series of institutional crises, such as the one that affected New York's Union Seminary. In that case, world and national events only mirrored the widespread sense of angst that fueled the seminary life of the time.

Gustafson noted some other matters that were closely related to the seminary's character as a small society of young males. Traditional social events, such as teas, were attended only under duress, for example, and the real social life of students took place in small groups. Not surprisingly, the schools exerted considerable pressure on students to conform to school-established patterns. Liberal schools tended to force students into their own shape, while conservative schools did likewise. Political liberalism was the "tie that binds"[63] at other schools. Despite the requirement of college for admission, many students were anti-intellectuals who wanted only the surface of things. Schools had even witnessed the formation of "neoorthodox" and "liberal" parties that struggled for influence over such matters as the chapel and other areas that students believed they could influence.

IX. H. Richard Summarizes

After as long and detailed a report as *Advancement,* someone needed to highlight the various conclusions and recommend changes in seminary life. This task fell, naturally enough, to H. Richard Niebuhr. The greatest need, as the report had made clear from the beginning, was for "gifted, concerned, thoughtful, and experienced scholars and teachers."[64] And this meant, Niebuhr believed, that the schools and the AATS needed to shift their emphasis to the development of excellent doctoral programs in theology. This required additional funding, since doctoral education was so expensive. Further, the schools had real work to do in meeting their obligations to those who were already involved in teaching: higher salaries were needed, especially for senior professors

63. Not a quote from Gustafson.

64. Niebuhr, Williams, and Gustafson, *Advancement,* p. 202.

whose salaries lagged behind younger teachers, and larger faculties were needed to lighten the workload and permit more varied teaching.

The practical needs of the faculties led Niebuhr to question the popular proposal of a fourth year of theological study. The implementation of this proposal, he believed, would require the expansion of the regular faculty by at least one-fourth as well as the proportional increase in other expenses. The only other choice would be to lower the total number of students admitted by one-fourth to make room for the needed expansion! Niebuhr did, however, applaud the idea of an intern year as a way to improve the standards of the ministry. In a similar vein, he believed that training for specialized ministries should be separate from the regular program of the schools. "In-service training" — the surveyors' term for continuing education — was, as it had been for some time, a confused and confusing mix of short classes, conferences, and the like that had little form or content.

As so often was the case, Niebuhr and his colleagues knew that real reform could come only from serious changes in the financing of theological education. Living in a time when the churches were flush with income, they hoped to see the churches bear more of the cost, but they realized that the nondenominational schools would have to rely on individual philanthropy. Little did they realize that within twenty years, almost all seminaries would be in that boat!

X. The Mountains

The reader of *Advancement* feels, correctly, that he or she has come to the climax of a story, and that is in fact the case. The transformation of theological education that the early liberal theologians had foreseen had largely taken place, and seminaries had reorganized themselves around a very new understanding of theological education. What had been prophecy was now commonplace, and the most important remaining question was where to find the people and the money to fill in the various holes that still remained. But, as Niebuhr and his colleagues made clear, the practical issue was the question of an alternative to the present system, as well as strategic additions to it. The atmosphere was electric with possibilities. The 1960s, as we shall see, will call much of their optimism into question.

The Niebuhr report, however, was more than a victory party for the American seminary. Particularly in *The Purpose of the Church and Its Ministry,* Niebuhr raised the most difficult question about theological education: What made it *theological* education and not merely education in a variety of theological disciplines? It was the right question. Clearly, seminaries were called to be not simply schools, but part of the history of the work of redemption that played an important role in the establishment of God's reign and rule. But the nature of that role was not clear. Seminaries were not parish churches nor judicatories; yet the work they did was fundamental to the functioning of the church at all levels. Niebuhr cut this Gordian knot by defining all Christian life in terms of Jesus' teachings. Churches, ministers, seminaries — all existed to increase the love of God and neighbor. In this way they moved existence steadily onward toward its telos. Over two hundred years earlier Jonathan Edwards had defined missionary work in much the same way in *The History of the Work of Redemption.* Every step the missionary took was one step closer to the realization of God's ultimate purpose. Niebuhr's reading of the seminary was part of this same sweep of human history. Seminaries were moving toward God's greater future.

CHAPTER TWENTY-NINE

Transformation:
The Birth of Religion Departments

The 1911 report *For the Advancement of Teaching,* issued by the Carnegie Foundation, spoke for many when it said many colleges "have inaugurated simple and wholesome courses of religious instruction, and a still larger number of such institutions are asking themselves the question: Why is it not possible to teach religion in a college in such a manner as to deal with its fundamental truths without offending the specific and special views of any body of men?"[1] The report's evident frustration reflected a concern that had simmered among the nation's educators for some time. In a nation deeply religious and overwhelmingly Protestant, why was it so difficult to examine the Bible in the public space of an institution of higher learning?

The question had a long and involved history before the Carnegie Foundation issued its report. The Carnegie investigators wrote toward the end of a season of change that had totally transformed American higher education. A person entering college in the years immediately following the War between the States would have enrolled in a program of studies that, despite the addition of a little advanced mathematics and a modicum of natural science, had deep roots in the ancient and Renaissance understanding of the learned gentleman. Basically, the student was expected to master certain basic texts, appropriately called the classics, in the original languages. While variations admittedly existed from school to school, Seneca, Augustine, and Erasmus would have recognized and approved of the core of the antebellum curriculum.

In retrospect, this cultural tradition fell like Jericho's walls. Led by such innovators as Harvard's Charles Eliot, first those colleges that were becoming uni-

1. Carnegie Foundation for the Advancement of Teaching, *For the Advancement of Teaching,* Sixth Carnegie Report on Teaching, 1911 (New York, 1912), p. 94.

versities and then the smaller colleges adopted programs that stressed the knowledge of modern culture. The student would study English, modern languages, natural and social science, and mathematics. At a certain point the student would elect, out of his or her own understanding, a concentration or major. And while some educators wanted to preserve the gentlemanly tone of higher education, the schools themselves became de facto oriented toward a modern economy. Professional schools of all kinds found their home in the universities, often as graduate departments, and the schools of arts and sciences themselves became professional institutions, preparing teachers for the expanding world of American education, including both high school and college. As the schools became more practical, higher education began a long period of expansion that still continues.

Many of America's Protestants saw the fall of the older pagan curriculum as an opportunity to find a new and more vital place in American education. Despite the popular image of traditional education as somehow overclerical, religion had been an extracurricular activity. The course in moral philosophy, usually taught by the president in the senior year, was basically Scottish philosophy hashed up with practical moral admonitions. The new curricula promised to change that. In theory the new courses of study offered the opportunity for religion to receive the same serious academic attention as other areas of human life. In an America already half-secular, the elective curriculum provided a way for the churches to enter into public life in a way consistent with society's increasingly scientific and democratic character. A student could choose to take a biblical course, a historical course, or whatever else the student believed was educationally sound. In church-related colleges, the Bible course early became a popular "liberal arts" elective.

I. Pioneers

The Methodists were among the first to realize the potential of this new approach. In planning their new central university, Vanderbilt, the conference stated: "Not a college belonging to the Church ought at any time to have been without a Chair of Biblical Literature; and no young man should at anytime have left its walls without having been taught, in connection with the study of the Bible, the doctrines and usages of the Methodist Church. We should be glad if arrangements were made whereby every student should attend upon the instructions of the Biblical Chair. As a mere literary production, the Bible cannot be ignored by any one pretending to a liberal education."[2] Henry Fowle Durant (d. 1881), a highly successful Boston lawyer and lay evangelist, had an equal pas-

2. Methodist Episcopal Church, South, "Report on the Committee on Education," *Journal of the General Conference*, 1870, p. 237.

sion for Bible as part of the curriculum. In establishing Wellesley College, a pioneer school for women, he insisted on four full years of biblical study.[3]

Perhaps the greatest nineteenth-century advocate of collegiate Bible study — or at least the noisiest — was the Baptist William Rainey Harper.[4] Harper, a Semitics scholar, was among the first to receive a doctor of philosophy degree from Yale, and he never shared much of his contemporaries' fascination with European scholarship. In 1888-89 he launched his first course in English Bible at Yale. An energetic and engaging lecturer, Harper filled the lecture hall. This confirmed his belief that the college could and should be a center of effective biblical instruction. Harper did not neglect more advanced studies. At the same time as his popular Old Testament introduction, he offered courses in Assyrian, Ethiopian, Arabic, comparative Semitic grammar, and the Hebrew text of the prophets. Yet the English Old Testament course was an important element in Harper's vision of the place of the Bible in higher education, because it indicated that serious scriptural study could and should begin in the undergraduate program and move by stages to coursework needed by the most advanced students in the field.

Early in his career Harper launched a program popularizing serious biblical study that envisioned a hierarchy of biblical scholars that reached from the Sunday school to the university. Harper established summer schools of Hebrew in different areas of the country — many of which he taught — that used an inductive method that he believed enabled a student to begin to read after only a few months. In addition, he taught classes at Chautauqua and other Christian camps. Both as a professor at Yale and as president of the University of Chicago, he kept a sharp eye out for promising young biblical scholars and worked hard at placing them in college and university teaching positions. Interestingly, although the faculty was often the same, Harper insisted that the college and graduate schools at Chicago have their own departments of Semitic languages. Harper's biblical empire was fed by a series of journals that ranged from the *Old Testament Student,* later the *Biblical World,* designed for the less advanced student, to such scholarly publications as *Hebraica* and the American *Journal of Semitic Languages.* Harper was also influential in the establishment of the Society of Biblical Literature and Exegesis, one of the nation's first scholarly guilds, and he often shepherded his advanced students to its annual meetings, both for personal growth and, hopefully, for professional placement or advancement.

3. Florence Morse Kingley, *The Life of Henry Fowle Durant, Founder of Wellesley College* (New York: Century, 1924).

4. James P. Wind, *The Bible and the University: The Messianic Vision of William Rainey Harper* (Atlanta: Scholars, 1987).

Part of the rationale for Harper's expanded emphasis on the Bible in higher education was his deep conviction that modern biblical scholars had broken the wax that had kept the Bible sealed over the generations. Biblical study, like other branches of human learning, had passed through a scientific revolution that made it worthy of a place in the schools. The study of biblical history and literature had been elevated to a level, scientifically considered, with that of other history and literature. "We may frankly acknowledge that the methods employed almost universally twenty-five years ago in connection with the study of Scriptures — methods still in vogue in many quarters — were unworthy, not only of the subject itself, but of any place in an institution of higher learning."[5] But this scientific revolution was not isolated. Harper knew that religion was being studied everywhere with new eyes, and he noted "the work . . . which has in recent years been accomplished by eminent psychologists, along lines related to the religious life." Like many others, he was deeply moved by the World's Parliament of Religions, held in Chicago in 1893.

Harper's enthusiasms were contagious. The Religious Education Association, which he helped found in 1903, was particularly interested in college teaching, and its journal regularly reported on the progress of college religion departments.[6] In 1911 *Religious Education* conducted an important study of the preparation of those teachers and called for their full integration into college faculties. Harper also inspired former student Charles Foster Kent to take up the cause of collegiate biblical instruction.

Kent, who graduated from Yale in 1889, became the exemplar of the pre–World War II religion professor. Although one might not include Kent in a list of the most creative biblical scholars of his time, he was indefatigable in his devotion to contemporary scholarship. His writings, including such solid pieces as his three-volume history of Israel and his historical geography of Palestine, were widely read, and went through several editions.[7] In addition, he wrote for Sunday schools and for the general public.

As impressive as Kent's scholarship was, his real passion was the teaching

5. George Marsden, *The Soul of the American University: From Protestant Establishment to Established Nonbelief* (New York: Oxford University Press, 1994), p. 243.

6. "Report of the Committee Appointed in 1911 to Investigate the Preparation of Religious Education Teachers in Colleges and Universities," *Religious Education* 7 (Oct. 1912): 332.

7. Charles Foster Kent, *Biblical Geography and History* (New York: Scribner, 1911); Charles Foster Kent, *The Founders and Rulers of United Israel: From the Death of Moses to the Division of the Hebrew Kingdom* (New York: Scribner, 1908); Charles Foster Kent, *A History of the Hebrew People from the Division of the Kingdom to the Fall of Jerusalem in 586 B.C.*, 6th ed. (New York: Scribner, 1897); Charles Foster Kent, *A History of the Jewish People during the Babylonian, Persian, and Greek Periods*, 3rd ed. (New York: Scribner, 1899).

of Bible literature. He believed that the Bible was essential to the maintenance of both Protestantism and democracy, and equally important, he believed that the only way it could be made accessible to present-day Americans was through the critical method. Like Harper, he worked to popularize his vision. Kent was among the founders in 1909 of the National Association of Biblical Instructors (NABI), later the American Academy of Religion, and he was instrumental in the movement to establish schools of religion in conjunction with American state universities. In 1922 he established the National Council of Schools of Religion, which became the National Council on Religion and Higher Education in 1924. For this work he enlisted the support of America's leading Protestant laymen, including John D. Rockefeller, Jr., and the backing of the Edward W. Hazen Foundation, established in 1925 and centered in New Haven.

Kent's own study of state universities indicated that less than 30 percent of them, and an even smaller percentage of state teachers colleges, offered courses in religion.[8] He found that those who favored such teaching tried several expedients to allow them to work under the separation of church and state. Although the schools of religion, largely sponsored by the Presbyterians and Congregationalists, and the Disciples' Bible colleges were very different, the idea behind them was simple. Since the constitution apparently prohibited the teaching of religion at public expense, the churches should assume the cost of providing high-quality religious instruction in conjunction with state schools. Hopefully, the state universities would recognize the academic value of the courses offered and legitimate the work by granting credit. While some schools succeeded — such as the Iowa School of Religion, organized with instructors from the state's three largest religious traditions, Protestant, Catholic, and Jewish — many others did not survive the 1920s. In some cases the Depression dried up funding, and in others the universities themselves moved to establish control, financial and academic, over the ventures.[9]

Outside of the state universities, however, the reformers had largely attained their goals. By 1930 the vast majority of denominational and private colleges had established able departments of religion, and those that lagged behind, such as Baptist University of Richmond, had appointed part-time instructors.[10] In this same year the Conference of Church Workers in Univer-

8. Charles Foster Kent, "The Undergraduate Courses in Religion at Tax Supported Colleges and Universities of America," *Bulletin of the National Council on Religion and Education,* 1924, pp. 1-34.

9. Marsden, *Soul,* p. 337.

10. Willard E. Uphaus and M. Teacue Hipps, "Undergraduate Courses in Religion at Denominational and Independent Colleges and Universities of America," *Bulletin of the National Council on Religion and Higher Education* 6 (1924).

sities and Colleges, meeting in Chicago, proposed that most schools press onward and develop a concentration or major in Bible or religion.

Kent was also involved in the very difficult task of recruiting qualified instructors for these programs. Under his leadership the National Council established a program of "Council Fellows" that helped meet the need. By 1941 the program had produced 202 fellows, including 31 women, 5 African Americans, 3 Catholics, and 2 Jews.[11] Yet, despite the efforts of Kent and others, many believed that the quality of instruction in religion and Bible courses was low. An article in *Collier's* in 1941 stated: "Bible was taught by a loveable old gentleman who delivered lofty lectures and never bothered his sleeping classes with details like questions or examinations."[12] This perception unfortunately continued, in both academic and popular opinion, until the 1970s.[13] There was no substantial evidence to support this stereotype. Religion and Bible teachers tended to teach at the level prevailing in their institutions.

II. The Thirties and Beyond

Although the number of qualified instructors and departments seemed substantial in the 1930s, the evident prosperity masked some real difficulties. Whether because of the fundamentalist crisis or secularization or both, many people engaged in the field felt the ground moving under them. Chester Warren Quimby, president of NABI, noted in 1933: "That all is not well with the teaching of the English Bible is a well-known and all too human axiom. The early hope that we might become an influential national society has failed. The Southern section — the very core of the Bible Belt — was stillborn. The Central and Western sections have become vague societies of religion. The Bible departments of our own section are fast changing to Departments of religion, so that now although we only are left, they are seeking our life to take it away."[14] Quimby need not have feared. The strange world of the Bible that had seemed so distant to the undergraduate of the 1920s was about to become more contemporary. As depression deepened and militarism and racism triumphed in Germany and Japan, many saw the sec-

11. Marsden, *Soul,* p. 338.

12. Marsden, *Soul,* p. 338.

13. See Ray Hart, "Religious and Theological Studies in American Higher Education: A Pilot Study," *Journal of the American Academy of Religion* 59 (1991): 715-827, and Claude Welch, *Graduate Education in Religion: A Critical Appraisal* (Missoula: University of Montana Press, 1971).

14. Quoted in Jonathan Z. Smith, "Connections," *Journal of the American Academy of Religion* 56 (1990): 1.

ular, prosperous world of the 1920s as an opium dream or a delusion. Questions about meaning of life, of politics, of Western civilization, and the like quickly came to the fore. People felt that strange quiet that often precedes a catastrophe and watched and waited as world war became first a nasty dream in the night, then a possible outcome of far-off events, and finally part of their current experience. And this dread did not end with the advent of peace. The atomic bomb changed international relations, and two — and soon more — nuclear powers faced each other like strangers in the night.

By 1936, what Robert Handy called an American religious depression had begun to lift.[15] Although the fundamentalist-modernist battles had left the churches badly scarred, both mainstream and conservative churches experienced an increase in membership that continued in fits and starts until 1967. At almost the same time, American theology and biblical studies entered a "golden age." Partly inspired by newer trends abroad, theologians demonstrated that the Christian tradition contained valuable resources for dealing with the social and existential crises of the time. The biblical theology movement, remarkably free of traditional biblical criticism's pedantry, rediscovered the contemporary prophetic power of the Scriptures. To further enrich the feast, the psychology of religion, earlier primarily interested in more scientific issues, ripened into an interest in counseling. Just as faith spoke to the depths of social and political malaise, so it also spoke to the hidden places in the human psyche. Appropriately, *Time* magazine, the voice of the informed American middle class, published cover pictures of Reinhold Niebuhr and Paul Tillich, the nation's best-known religious thinkers.

The religious recovery was accompanied by a rapid expansion of higher education. Faced with unemployment, many young people elected to extend their education, perhaps hoping to gain a "white-collar" skill that would provide some protection against the vagaries of the economic order or even to win the security of a government appointment. The experience of war and the GI Bill would spur further growth in higher education. At the same time, colleges and universities were rethinking their educational priorities. Although Robert Hutchins's proposal of a great books curriculum never won universal favor, colleges and universities were aware that education had to be equal to the national challenge. The Harvard Report of 1945 and the President's Commission report of 1947 stressed the need for higher education to pay attention to the core values of Western civilization.[16] The President's Commission further suggested that

15. Robert T. Handy, "The American Religious Depression, 1925-1935," *Church History* 29 (1960).

16. *General Education in a Free Society: Report of the Harvard Committee* (Cambridge:

higher education had overemphasized the purely intellectual at the cost of the moral and the spiritual.

The combination of the post-1937 revival in church membership, the theological renaissance, and the new emphasis on the humanities made religion and Bible departments growth industries in postwar higher education. In effect, departments of religion had three sources of students. Church-related colleges, whose leaders were often fighting a losing battle on such issues as college chapel, found that a required religion course satisfied their ecclesiastical sponsors and was stimulating enough to students not to be burdensome. Further, religion professors, like professors of French, were relatively numerous and inexpensive. Second, those students who participated in the religious renewal were attracted to serious study of the faith. The Protestant campus ministers, who occasionally taught courses in religion departments, encouraged students to enroll in a religion course. Young people planning a career in "full-time Christian service" found the concentration in religion to be a useful leg up on a seminary curriculum that was progressively more complex and more difficult to navigate. Third, religion courses provided important "general education" credits. Religion departments were particularly crucial for students with an interest in the Middle East, Asia, and to a lesser extent Africa. Returning military personnel were an important component in this cadre. Having served in Asia in the Second World War and the Korean conflict, many service personnel had an appreciation of and interest in the culture and the religions of that region. Courses in the history of religion were among the few course offerings in the 1940s and 1950s that touched on life outside western Europe and America. Lawrence Little, in his 1950 survey of Methodist religion departments, found that the most commonly offered course was comparative religion, and one suspects that it was also the most popular with other religion departments.[17]

III. The Impact of Seminaries on the Teaching of Religion

The way religion professors were trained reflected the threefold source of students. Most religion professors began with a sense of call to the ministry during their undergraduate careers. During seminary they discovered a deep interest and passion for scholarship. In some cases this interest in study was related to a

---

Harvard University Press, 1945); President's Commission on Higher Education, *Higher Education for American Democracy* (Washington, D.C.: Government Printing Office, 1947).

17. Lawrence Little, "Religion Courses in Methodist Colleges," *Religious Education* 45 (1950): 25-30.

deep awareness of the limits of the church, both as a social organization and as an employer, or even a personal loss of faith, although most saw their scholarship as part of their vocation. The prospective teacher would then enroll in a graduate school,[18] often at the same institution where he received his bachelor of divinity. Upon completion of that program, the prospective teacher would either gravitate toward a seminary position, which was considered more prestigious because it offered a chance to concentrate in one's field, or toward college work. The colleges did however attract many first-rate scholars, such as Paul Ramsey of Princeton or Clyde Holbrook of Oberlin, who found the call to the university more satisfying than other alternatives and who refused entreaties to enter the seminary world.

Seminaries and religion departments were thus deeply intertwined. Almost all religion professors were seminary graduates, and many of the courses they taught were undergraduate versions of the standard theological curriculum. Although some religion departments in state universities had started, the older pattern continued, with few state universities and even fewer state educational colleges offering courses in Bible or religion. Since most of the schools hiring religion faculty were denominationally related, they tended to turn for teachers either to their own denomination's seminaries or to the university divinity schools. With its program in religion and higher education, close relationships with the Hazen Foundation, and distinguished faculty, Yale early had a dominant position.

IV. Troubled Waters

In the late fifties and sixties the relationship between religion departments, seminaries, and churches began to disintegrate. Religion professors became conscious of themselves as members of a separate academic guild, and mounted an increasingly successful campaign to establish undergraduate and occasionally graduate departments of religion in state universities and to define the study of religion as either a humanistic or a social scientific field.

In his evocative *The University Gets Religion,* D. G. Hart adapts the secularization thesis to the development of college and university departments of religion. According to Hart, these departments begin in liberal Protestantism's concern to preserve the moral and spiritual qualities of the establishment. As higher education itself became less concerned with religion or with Western

18. Lawrence DeBoer, "Seminary and University: Two Approaches to Theology and Religion," *Journal of Bible and Religion* 32 (1964): 343.

civilization, religion departments naturally moved in the same way. George Marsden summarized an earlier version of Hart's thesis:

> During the 1960s, however, the predominant outlook in the field changed rapidly. Most important was the impulse to professionalize religious studies. Because of its ties to the residual Protestant establishment, its staffing by seminary graduates, and its associations with Bible requirements at a church-related school, the academic study of religion was often regarded as a second-class discipline and seldom taken seriously among the humanities. The response was to define the field increasingly in scientific terms. Thus religious studies would have a methodology more like the social sciences. The new trend was to study religion "phenomenologically," so that the object of study was the abstraction "religion," the common traits of which could be exemplified by looking at particular religious traditions.[19]

Hart was not optimistic about the long-ranged viability of this watered-down version of religious teaching. Students are interested in religion courses, he believes, because they have the very religious concerns that the university's secularity rules out of court. Hence, they will not long be content with a merely academic study. Hart considers this a positive good:

> Ironically, then, by excluding religion as a field of academic study, the university may be paying religion great respect. . . . Some still might wonder whether the secular character of the university puts too heavy a burden on the religious. The nature of modern intellectual life as the university has come to define it does, indeed, require believing scholars to make choices that are difficult. They may have to live in an apparently schizophrenic manner, separating what they do in the classroom or publish from what they do at home or as part of a community of faith. It may be time for faithful academics to stop trying to secure a religion-friendly university while paying deference to the academic standards of the modern university. If the old religions are right, in the new heavens and new earth there should be plenty of enduring rewards that will make tenure, promotion, and endowed chairs look like so much hay and stubble.[20]

The Hart-Marsden thesis has much appeal. Clearly, there is a strong tendency for religion departments to move toward a secular definition of religious studies, such as that advocated by Samuel Preuss or the Santa Barbara "Religion

19. Marsden, *Soul,* p. 414.

20. D. G. Hart, *The University Gets Religion: Religious Studies in American Higher Education* (Baltimore: Johns Hopkins University Press, 1999), p. 251.

within the Boundary of Reason Alone" conference.[21] Further, some people prominent in the study of religion sound much like the militant secularists of the eighteenth-century Enlightenment. The report of the Jesus Seminar, for instance, was dedicated to Galileo, Jefferson, and Strauss, and somewhat sophomorically declared: "The Christ of creed and dogma can no longer command the assent of those who have seen the heavens through Galileo's telescope."[22] Many American Academy of Religion programs and papers are also worthy of satire. Yet we must be careful not to exaggerate either the impact of new methods of study, rationalism, or postmodernism. Much teaching of religion still takes place in church-related colleges or colleges that were recently church-related; many of the faculty are still graduates of Yale, Harvard, the University of Chicago, and Union Seminary–Columbia University; and biblical studies still have an important place in the curriculum. Indeed, as Ray Hart discovered in his 1991 survey, neither most of those who taught Bible nor most of those who taught church history saw themselves as teaching religion courses, since their methods were similar to methods used in the university divinity schools.[23] He did notice, however, that many members of religion departments, especially younger scholars, tended not to identify with theology as a designation for their work.

V. The Grounds for Divorce

Without, I hope, quibbling over language, I would like to suggest that the separation of religious studies or religion from theological studies was more a divorce than it was a smooth development and that, like many divorces, it left both partners battling over the children and the property.

This separation between religious studies and theology revolved around two central events. The most important of these was not chronologically prior. From the 1920s to the 1950s Protestant religious leaders had struggled with the question of how to introduce religion into the general state university curriculum. Despite some small gains at some state universities, few had heeded this advice. The Supreme Court, in fact, was apparently distancing religion from contact with American public life, including outlawing prayers and Bible reading in the public schools. Yet there was another strain in American church-state

21. Santa Barbara Colloquy, "Religion within the Limits of Reason Alone," *Soundings* 71 (1988).

22. Robert Funk, Roy W. Hoover, and the Jesus Seminar, *The Five Gospels* (New York: Macmillan, 1993), v. 2.

23. Ray Hart, "Religious and Theological Studies," p. 744.

law. The great expansion of higher education following the Second World War would not have been possible without federal aid to higher education, and many church-related colleges had received generous grants from the government for varied purposes, including the construction of needed buildings and, especially, laboratories. This had already begun to change the relationship between the seminaries and the colleges. Although many colleges had rejected denomination control earlier in response to the 1906 offer of the Carnegie Foundation to fund pensions, those that had remained church-related (and that employed many religion professors) were poor compared to their denomination's theological schools. Federal aid, as well as more sophisticated fundraising, changed that. Previously financially strapped colleges found themselves comparatively prosperous, and many of these would eventually find their way into the ranks of private colleges as they sought to broaden their constituencies.

In line with this tendency, the Supreme Court made it clear in 1963 in *School District v. Schempp* that objective teaching about religion was acceptable in all public schools. As Justice Brennan noted, "Nothing we have said here indicates that such study of the Bible or of religion, when presented objectively as part of a secular program of education, may not be effected consistent with the First Amendment." In other words, teaching about religion, if done objectively, was part of the study of what it meant to be human. Departments of religion in state universities, not surprisingly, entered into a period of expansion that lasted until the 1980s when their growth, along with other humanities, slowed.[24] Perhaps equally important, the court decision strengthened the position of all departments of religion. Whatever suspicion might have remained that they were covert campus ministries, religion departments were now legally recognized as part of a liberal education.

The decision could not have come at a better time. Religion departments had been on the defensive since 1956 when the AATS had issued its (voluntary) guidelines for preseminary study. Basically, the guidelines reflected a conservative version of the bachelor of arts that stressed the knowledge of English, foreign languages, literature, and history, while downplaying the importance of natural and social science. What was striking, however, was that the guidelines recommended only three hours of religion — far fewer than most church-related colleges required — and did not list religion as a possible major. The leaders of the National Association of Bible Instructors (NABI) felt that they had been unjustly attacked, and subsequent statements by theological educa-

24. Dorothy Bass, "The Independent Sector and the Educational Strategies of Mainstream Protestantism," in *Religion, the Independent Sector, and American Culture*, ed. Conrad Cherry and Rowland A. Sherrill (Atlanta: Scholars, 1992), p. 70.

tors only fanned their resentment. At a time when they knew they were growing in numbers, programs, and quality, their elder brothers, the seminary faculties, had sat them down hard.

In retrospect, the AATS guidelines were as arrogant as they were unwise. Theological schools were coming off the best season in their history. In 1934 theological schools had educated only about 43 percent of all mainstream ministers; in 1956 the figure had grown to around 80 percent. Both the Baptists and the Methodists, historically resistant to making seminary training a norm for service, were on the verge of moving in that direction, and the Southern Baptists were engaged in a significant expansion of their system. Many leaders were talking openly about the need to expand the program to include a fourth year of study, either in the classroom or in the field. As the accreditation agency for theological schools recognized by the government, the AATS had acquired real power. Its leaders were moving aggressively to eliminate the popular bachelor of theology degree that mixed two years of liberal arts with three years of theological study.

The decision on preseminary study was in line with this larger use of association muscle. Charles Taylor added salt to the wound when he said: "The plain fact of the matter is, that taking the country by and large, courses in religion are not offered 'according to the best academic standards.' Even in some of our universities they are not on a par with studies in other fields."[25]

Religion faculties reacted quickly to the insult. The NABI appointed a distinguished committee to study the issue, composed of L. J. Arthur Baird, John L. Creek, Earl Cranston, J. Allen Easley, Edward C. Hobbs, Walter G. Williams, and A. Roy Eckardt. This committee carefully drafted a response, "Preseminary Preparation and Study in Religion," that was adopted by the NABI in 1958 and published in the April 1959 number of the *Journal of Bible and Religion*.[26]

"Preseminary Preparation and Study in Religion" assumed that religion departments "ought to assume responsibility for a guided pre-theological program which seeks to integrate, as perhaps no other program can, the whole of liberal learning." In common with other liberal arts, religion courses "develop the student's ability to think clearly and to understand the world of human affairs and ideas."[27] Further, undergraduate study in religion helped the seminaries "to reduce some of the pressures within an already overburdened theologi-

25. See William A. Beardsley, "The Background of the Lilly Endowment Study of Preseminary Education," *Journal of Bible and Religion* 34 (1966): 100.

26. National Association of Biblical Instructors (hereafter NABI), "Preseminary Preparation and Study in Religion," *Journal of Bible and Religion* 27 (1959): 139-42.

27. NABI, "Preseminary Preparation," p. 139.

cal curriculum."[28] In other words, religion and the Bible functioned much as theology departments had in the medieval universities, teaching the "queen of the sciences" and recruiting and nurturing leaders for the churches.

Granted these presuppositions, the NABI proposed a compromise. If the term "religion major" suggested too narrow a preparation, perhaps another way could be found for the colleges to define their work in ministerial preparation. "If the term 'religion major' seems objectionable for one or another reason, it may be wise to substitute some such terms as 'pre-theological major.' Furthermore, as an alternative to this form of major, the student should — provided, of course, that appropriate course offerings are at hand — pursue a minor in religion so as to afford a sound preliminary foundation for graduate and professional preparation in the seminary."[29] The report ended with a call for the AATS and the NABI to work together. The call recognized that "it is high time" that the NABI take "positive steps on its side to secure for the ministerial student optimum value from his seven or more years of undergraduate, graduate, and professional preparation."[30]

The result of this call was extensive negotiation between the AATS and the NABI over a comprehensive study of preseminary preparation. With the aid of the Lilly Endowment, an agreement was reached in 1960 to establish a committee to conduct the research. Conducting the actual research were Keith R. Bridston, an ethicist, and Dwight Culver, a sociologist. The hope was that the dialogue between the two scholars would enrich the final product. Perhaps because of the politically heated atmosphere, the researchers were charged with conducting a comprehensive survey that would include seminary and college administrators, teachers, students, and pastors. The basic study was finished in 1963, and the report appeared two years later in 1965.[31]

Although both the AATS and the by-now American Academy of Religion devoted an entire issue of their respective journals to the report, the study was a disappointment. Despite the interaction between the two authors, the document seemed composed of largely underinterpreted statistics, on the one hand, and overcontextualized theology, on the other. Perhaps the most useful aspect of the study was the frank recognition that the preparation of ministers for their work included the periods before and after seminary and that seminary education needed to be understood as the keystone supporting the sides of the arch.

28. NABI, "Preseminary Preparation," p. 140.

29. NABI, "Preseminary Preparation," p. 141.

30. NABI, "Preseminary Preparation," p. 142.

31. Keith R. Bridston and Dwight W. Culver, *Preseminary Education: Report of the Lilly Endowment Study* (Minneapolis: Augsburg, 1965).

While many at the time believed that the report slanted toward the seminaries, the present-day reader might be more impressed by the growing uneasiness about what actually constituted theological education and, in particular, the question of how theological schools fit into the larger ecology of American learning. For one thing, as the collegiate professors gleefully pointed out: "This brings us back to a matter of entrance standards for the seminary. The Directors rightly criticize the seminaries for lack of authoritative requirements of those entering their classes. The seminaries tend rather to say, 'this is desirable,' and 'this is recommended,' but not so often to say, 'Without this you do not enter at all.'" Perhaps what the seminaries needed was an examination, perhaps modeled on that required for college admission, that could be administered to all candidates.[32]

The college and university teachers were also very nervous about the report's emphasis on colleges as "secularizing" students. To them the report seemed almost deliberately wrongheaded. Harry Adams said the thesis of the report was: "to become educated is to become cultured and to become cultured means being secularized."[33] In other words, what the college did was shake students out of the various religious ghettos of their childhood and introduce them to the "real" world. Religion departments stood accused of hindering this process by providing students with a religious ghetto. To college teachers, who struggled every day with the secularity of their students, this argument seemed incredible. Indeed, Van Harvey, a noted theologian who moved easily between college and university, observed that many seminary teachers yearned for the comparative freedom of the colleges.[34]

There was also a sense of frustration with the report's easy assumption that the seminaries were the intellectual leaders of American religious studies. Clyde Holbrook, the Danforth Professor of Religion at Oberlin and a noted authority on the teaching of religion, chided the authors for not paying attention to "ideas which have been developed in the colleges and universities. The interests in the relation of theology and literature, in existentialism, analytical philosophy, and the sociology of religion, first developed in the undergraduate and graduate sectors of higher education before their incorporation into seminary programs."[35] In fact, college teachers sensed that their seminary colleagues were

32. Arthur Moore, "The Lilly Study and the Theological Curriculum," in "Theological Education," special issue, *Journal of Bible and Religion* 34 (1966): 149.

33. Harry Adams, "Major Issues in the Lilly Study," in "Theological Education," special issue, *Journal of Bible and Religion* 34 (1966): 131.

34. Van A. Harvey, "Reflections on the Teaching of Religion in America," *Journal of the American Academy of Religion* 38 (Mar. 1970).

35. Clyde Holbrook, "The Lilly Study: Challenge to College and Seminary," in "Theological Education," special issue, *Journal of Bible and Religion* 34 (1966): 163.

somewhat isolated from the vital currents of contemporary intellectual life. Edmund Perry noted that "religion is becoming a respected field of inquiry for sociologists, anthropologists, political scientists, and paleontologists."[36] Equally significant, Perry noted that religion departments were no longer content to be auxiliaries to the theological schools: "The undergraduate department of religion is not what it used to be. This fact is more important than anything disclosed in Pre-Seminary Education. The implications of this fact are legion, but two, by way of recapitulation, will suffice: (1) The content of the undergraduate curriculum in religion will not be determined by considerations of the service it can render to Protestant seminaries; and (2) this content will be inclusive of convictional traditions, faithfully represented, other than the Judaeo-Christian tradition."[37] Perry's observation was accurate. The teaching of religion was rapidly becoming an academic guild with its own standards and system of professional rewards. Perhaps the most important sign of the change was the change in nomenclature from the National Association of Bible Teachers to the American Academy of Religion (AAR) in 1964. Holbrook, president of the newly renamed body, delivered the key address, "Why an Academy of Religion?"[38] Holbrook had recently published *Religion: A Humanistic Field,* a work commissioned by Princeton University and the Ford Foundation.[39] In it he had made it clear that the scholar of religion had to accept the same rules that were followed in the university as a whole and did not need or want any special favors. The address made the same point in more graphic terms as Holbrook exegeted each term in the new name. The term "academy" expressed the intent of the body to be fully part of American higher education. It was an "American" academy, for instance, because it reflected the high quality of scholarship actually done in the United States and Canada. This was more than the jingoism of young writers determined to write the "Great American Novel." Reading between the lines, one could see it as a swipe at the seminaries' notorious tendency to prefer German scholarship to more native materials. But at a minimum, it was a promise to develop a recognizably American approach to scholarly issues. The most important word was "religion." Holbrook was clear that the study of religion was a professional field in its own right: "What I want to affirm is that the broadening of the spectrum of interests of this association

36. Edmund Perry, "The Lilly Study: Challenge to College and Seminary," in "Theological Education," special issue, *Journal of Bible and Religion* 34 (1966): 113.

37. Perry, "The Lilly Study," p. 114.

38. Clyde Holbrook, "Why an Academy of Religion?" *Journal of Bible and Religion* 32 (1964); republished in *Journal of the American Academy of Religion* 39 (1991).

39. Clyde Holbrook, *Religion: A Humanistic Field* (Englewood Cliffs, N.J.: Prentice-Hall, 1963).

may assist in a fundamental way to excite, especially among undergraduate professors in religion but also among those who work anywhere in the field, an enthusiasm for scholarship which can be sustained across a broad front of diverse methodologies."[40]

It wasn't the Fourth of July; there were no rockets, no fireworks, and no picnics. Nonetheless, Holbrook had declared the religionists independent. Two years later the *Journal of Bible and Religion* was rechristened the *Journal of the American Academy of Religion*. And a more meaningful change was also in the offing. Although the National Association of Bible Teachers had usually met at a seminary — most often, Union in New York — during the Christmas holidays, the new association discontinued that pattern. Through its joint meeting with the Society of Biblical Literature (SBL), considered the most academic of the seminary guilds, the renamed body made its claim to scholarly equality with the seminaries. In 1979 the Council of Learned Societies recognized the AAR, further emphasizing its equality with the SBL and the American Society of Church History, which were long-term members. By the early 1980s this recognition was more than a formality. University and college religion professors were outpublishing their competitors by a significant amount in quantity, and no one doubted that they were publishing the most seminal religious research.

VI. The Welch Report

An important step in the development of religion as an independent discipline was the publication of Claude Welch's *Graduate Education in Religion: A Critical Appraisal*.[41] The Welch study saw itself as part of a long series of influential reports on education, beginning with Abraham Flexner's *Medical Education in the United States and Canada*. By this time the genre had certain features: a survey of institutions in a particular area, the measuring of those institutions against their own highest ideals, and the presentation of radical suggestions for the future, including the reduction in the number of institutions. Welch fit the Flexner pattern to a tee. His survey provided a comprehensive picture of the fifty-two graduate schools in religion, and he noted that twenty of these dated from the 1960s. Clearly, religion was a growing field. But the popularity of the field suggested that quality might be thinner than quantity. Welch provided a

40. Holbrook, "Why?" 39 (1991): 383.

41. Claude Welch, *Graduate Education in Religion: A Critical Appraisal* (Missoula: University of Montana Press, 1971).

list of twenty-four programs that he felt were either marginal or inadequate. The list included such well-known schools as Chicago Theological Seminary, Concordia Seminary, University of California at Santa Barbara, University of Southern California, Union Theological Seminary (Va.), and Baylor University. Naturally, these schools cried foul. While they claimed they did not know that Welch would rate the schools,[42] more likely most of them had expected to make the cut.

The *Christian Century*'s February 2, 1972, issue, "Welch Report Weighed in the Balance," was devoted to the matter. The Welch report's clear advocacy of religion as an independent academic discipline committed to a worldwide perspective took the editors by apparent surprise. Noting, as many would in subsequent years, that the universities offer abundant opportunities to study religions as part of culture, the editors argued that students enrolled in religion courses "because that is where they frequently encounter an exciting mixture of intellectual and (veiled) existential, academic and (disguised) spiritual pursuits. They come because they were programmed to do so by families, Sunday schools, parochial schools, synagogues, and churches which compulsorily miseducated but still educated them to ask these values-and-meanings questions."[43] Further, the *Century* continued, the Welch report had an animus against seminaries and much of the actual teaching of religion because it concentrated on the "local kitchen" rather than the world scene.[44]

Methodist theologian F. Thomas Trotter, then dean at Claremont, had a clearer understanding of the import of the Welch report. As a matter of fact, Trotter asserted, many university teachers in programs of religion simply did not care for the theological tasks of the church, and the seminaries needed to recognize that their proper task was to be the "church's school, holding the church accountable for the faithfulness that new occasions may demand in the life of obedience in the Gospel."[45] Trotter believed this task was imperiled. Seminaries were the second most expensive professional schools, with only the medical schools spending more on each student. Further, they were facing a major crisis. Admitting that the bulge in seminary enrollments from 1968 to 1971 had resulted from young men evading the draft, Trotter foresaw hard times ahead. Just as the colleges and universities had been forced to define themselves apart from the seminaries, so, Trotter suggested, did the Welch report call the seminaries to do likewise.

42. Martin E. Marty, "Rating Welch's Ratings," *Christian Century*, Feb. 2, 1972, p. 5.
43. *Christian Century*, Feb. 2, 1972, p. 111.
44. *Christian Century*, Feb. 2, 1972, p. 112.
45. *Christian Century*, Feb. 2, 1972, p. 112.

The Welch report had noted that the newly independent university and college departments of religion suffered from an "identity crisis," a point Welch made even clearer in his 1972 *Religion in the Undergraduate Curriculum.* Religion departments had already entered the curriculum cafeteria that became popular in the wake of the Vietnam War. As the growth of religion departments slowed in the 1980s and 1990s, the awareness of this "identity crisis" became part of the life of the AAR as it, and particularly its leaders, struggled with the question of what was religion as an academic discipline. It was a daunting task, for if religion was, as many apologists for the new religion departments claimed, part of culture, there was no reason to study it apart from other cultural manifestations. And indeed, the very identification of religion with culture suggests that such study is inappropriate. After all, what postmodern historian would study politics, for instance, apart from such issues as gender, economics, and geography? Much of the literature of the 1980s and 1990s, including the Santa Barbara Conference, "Religion within the Limits of Reason Alone," represented attempts to square this circle.

VII. Final Papers

In 1991 Ray Hart published his "Religious and Theological Studies in American Higher Education: A Pilot Study." The study had four goals: "(1) those matters pertaining to and connecting with the intellectual coherence (or perhaps, of equal importance, the incoherence) of the field; (2) the quality of teaching and the quality of graduate preparation for teaching in the field; (3) the forces and counter forces affecting the 'globalization' or the 'internationalization' of the field; and (4) the perceived relations (if any, and if any, of what nature) between the study and practice of religion." Hart was realistic about the crisis in the study of religion that he believed, I think correctly, was part of a general crisis in the study of humanities, characterized by "enrollment declines, fiscal constraints, retrenchment." The results of this crisis were evident: "the first budget cuts are in the college of liberal arts, with that sector, the humanities, within that segment, religious studies."[46] Perhaps most discouraging, his figures indicated that religion departments had become, along with foreign languages, one of the less appreciated and less well-paid academic specialties: "On the evidence of our probe, the study of religion unquestionably is most tenuous, and has the least security of any of the institutional types, in the public sector. Salaries in the teaching of religion tend to be lower than in other fields in the university.

46. Ray Hart, "Religious and Theological Studies," p. 722.

Graduate programs are judged not to 'model' much less offer instruction in, good teaching."[47] In his opinion, this religious studies crisis was complicated by the fact that the post–World War II generation of scholars who had midwived modern religion departments was retiring.

The most interesting thing was that Hart's study indicated that the divorce decree between religion departments and seminaries was final. Although most religion teachers (75 percent) continued to have at least one seminary degree, the younger faculty in the area clearly favored an independent understanding of their discipline. The clear implication was that this segment of religion faculties would continue to expand and the departments would become more integrated into the larger fabric of their institutions.

The separation of religion departments from seminaries, implicit in the formation of the AAR, was the most significant event in the post–World War II history of American theological education. If nothing else, the separation of the two fields placed a major strain on the work of those graduate faculties that continued to prepare teachers for both. Were such faculties primarily to consider themselves as producing religion scholars or theologians? But the separation had other consequences. The most important was that the seminaries lost, apparently for good, their predominant place in American religious and theological scholarship. Aside from the more ecclesiastically rooted practical fields, colleges and universities were well suited to serious research into religious history. After 1960 religionists wrote many of the most important works of scholarship in theology, and encouraged by strict publish-or-perish rules, produced volumes of erudition. Seminaries were no longer king of the hill.

In time the seminaries would suffer financially from this separation. In the 1960s, with enrollments bloated by war and revival, seminary leaders were able to ignore the loss of their infrastructure. The religion departments had been crucial parts of the networks that fed students to the seminaries, and religion, especially Bible, teachers were important recruiters of future ministers. The increasing lack of "feeder schools" would plague seminaries, especially schools like Union, New York, for the rest of the century and apparently beyond. In a world in which "one hand washes the other," seminary leaders failed at a crucial point to strengthen their collegiate colleagues. In turn, the colleges and universities became more distant from the seminaries.

47. Ray Hart, "Religious and Theological Studies," p. 757.

CHAPTER THIRTY

The Sixties: The Dawn of a New Age

John F. Kennedy's election symbolized, perhaps far more than he or his contemporaries realized, a major shift in American life. Kennedy was young, among the youngest men ever elected president, and his election marked the passing of the torch of leadership in America to the younger generation that had fought the world war. Youth was good, inherently good, inherently noble, and Kennedy filled his cabinet with wunderkinder whose dreams were remaking America. Perhaps the greatest example of this newly minted confidence in youth was Kennedy's Peace Corps, which sent many young idealists, often immediately out of the universities, around the world to take up the civilizing mission that the nation had historically entrusted to its churches. To be sure, the rapid expansion of higher education in America might have been enough by itself to give higher education a youthful tinge. The number of professors more than doubled between 1950 and 1960, as more and more young Americans saw college followed by graduate school as the normal route to middle-class life.[1] As so often happens, the material changes in human life were reflected in the ideology of the age, and the ideology of the age was carefully tailored to the nation's social and material foundations. American higher education, thus, found itself entering a crucial decade with many teachers almost contemporaries of their students, and all believing that youth and vitality provided an edge over wisdom and experience.

More than ever, theological education was part and parcel of American higher education. The work of the AATS had paid handsome dividends as the schools set and reached higher academic standards. The expansion of higher

1. Lewis Perry, *Intellectual Life in America: A History* (New York: F. Watts, 1984), p. 434. Perry noted that by 1960 the number of professors began to approach the number of ministers.

education provided the schools with a potential corps of new teachers, often unseasoned by pastoral experience, ready to take the reins. Ironically, this generation's way to influence was paved by the previous generation. The restrictions on faculty and administrative hiring imposed by the Depression and the Second World War created a pent-up demand for new faculty and administrative personnel. And this new generation was to have very long legs. Often appointed from the mid-1950s to the mid-1960s, this postwar generation retained its position and power until the 1990s and in some cases beyond.

To speak of the generation of theological educators coming into influence and power from 1960 to 1965 is also to describe a generation that was mindful of living in the shadow of greatness. The 1930s, 1940s, and 1950s had seen a "theological renaissance" dominated by such thinkers as Barth, Brunner, Tillich, Bultmann, and Reinhold and H. Richard Niebuhr. The sky around these great luminaries had been studded with many thinkers of a lesser order, but these able theologians and scholars were of more than ordinary ability. The leaders of the new generation anxiously wondered who would be the "next Niebuhr," and many instructors, not normally given to hubris, secretly yearned for that position and the recognition that would come with it. With an irony that Reinhold Niebuhr might have appreciated, just as teachers yearned for his soon-to-be-vacant throne, his style of informed public discussion of religious issues passed out of vogue. The new style was modeled on university research standards. Often a single post-1960 theological monograph would have more footnotes than both Niebuhrs had used in all their works put together!

The theological students these instructors taught were also young. After the first flush of the returning soldiers had passed, students tended to move directly from college to theological school. This trend was accelerated by improvements in birth control. Although the practice of a newly married couple, fresh out of college, arriving at seminary with plans for her to work while he studied reached back to the 1950s, the introduction of the birth control pill in the 1960s strongly reinforced it.[2] The PHT degree (putting hubby through) seemed to be a secure part of the folklore and an informal practice of most seminaries, as was the custom of providing some preparation for pastors' wives. But like so much of the age of Camelot, this new freedom had many implications, many of them ironic. Seminaries could afford, for example, to insist that fieldwork be more educational, knowing that the income was not as necessary to family support as it once had been, and many schools took the opportunity to discourage the student pastorates that had provided much of the support for married couples earlier.

2. The ethics of sex were to become a hot topic later in the decade. See below.

I. The Community of the Alienated

More important, the prevalence of young and young-married seminarians without children tended to make seminary almost an extension of undergraduate school and to invite the carryover of late adolescent practices into what had traditionally been young adulthood in America. In effect, two of the marks that middle-class American culture used to measure the onslaught of adult responsibilities — graduation from college and marriage — were nullified by the seminary.[3] In more than a figurative sense, the seminaries "adolescentized" students by encouraging them to identify with those in college and perhaps even in high school.

Although the decade had begun with a drop in enrollment, events quickly turned things around. Even before the Vietnam War heated up, the 4-D deferment was one of the most secure tickets out of the draft. Those not attracted to traditional parish ministry, further, had a choice of many new or renewed forms of ministry, including college and university teaching and campus ministry, that offered exciting alternative careers. After the war intensified and dragged on and on, seminary was the one safe haven from the crisis of a generation. A young man might go to seminary and be a protestor, or he might go to seminary and ignore the conflict, simply waiting it out. In any case, he had a unique opportunity not to participate in the events that were shaping his age cohort. While the number of students in seminary because of Vietnam was disputed at the time, F. Thomas Trotter was right when he claimed in 1972 that a high percentage were avoiding military service.[4]

Seminary observers often commented on the changed character of the student body. Noted New Testament scholar Norman Pittinger was typical. "The first thing that strikes one," he observed, "about the modern theological student is that he hates the church."[5] Pittinger's observation was more than wartime hyperbole. In a study of ten years of graduates at North Carolina's Duke Divinity School and Southeastern Baptist Theological Seminary, O. Kelly Ingram and Robert M. Colver noted:

> Another disturbing fact is that there are mounting numbers who are going into parish ministries and are expressing dissatisfaction within the ranks.

3. It is important to realize that most seminarians were the contemporaries of young adults who were officers in the military.

4. T. Thomas Trotter, "The Church's Stake in the Seminaries," *Christian Century* 89 (Feb. 2, 1972): 112-14, here p. 114.

5. Norman Pittinger, "Theological Students Today," *Christian Century* 84 (Apr. 26, 1967): 527.

> Their negativity toward parish ministry is seconded by the drop-outs from ministry and those in non-parish ministry. Duke, in contrast to Southeastern, demonstrates a ten year trend toward increasing alienation from parish ministry, but, strangely enough, the generation gap is more evident at Southeastern than at Duke. At Southeastern, "dropping out" is characteristic of an age group. While at Duke it correlates with both age and year of graduation.[6]

The widespread student alienation from the church and — by extension — from traditional theology was an important component of almost everything that happened in the decade: the fascination with alternative forms of ministry, the search for new and more exciting curricula, and of course, the host of new plans of governance that followed the student disturbances in 1967.

Theological faculties were not simply led along the path of alienation by noisy students. There was a deep change in the piety of the faculties. Frederick Ferré fondly remembered his father's life of personal prayer and biblical study. Nels, as he remembered him, had "a glow of spirituality" that was marked by long hours of prayer and personal biblical study. His father's theology and life expressed his love for the church and sincere desire for its improvement. In a very revealing confession, he went on to say, commenting on the mystical passages in his father's writings: "I found such passages embarrassing and unprofessional. They threatened my sense of control over the argument: they derailed the careful train of thought; they sometimes left threads dangling that frustrated my demand for order. Most of all, perhaps, they exposed the poverty of my own spiritual life and the thinness of my commitment to the church. He chose the seminary to be the forum for almost all his life's work; I chose the academy."[7] If the elder Ferré was more spiritually alive than many of his contemporary theologians, he was far from alone. Many liberal and neoorthodox theologians had vibrant spiritual lives marked by deep ecclesiastical commitments. Their successors in the 1960s were often less churched, more professional, and less important as role models. Not surprisingly, many students in the sixties and seventies complained bitterly about the lack of spiritual life on campus.

In short, the sixties were marked by a deep dissatisfaction with the traditional church and its ministry. In such works as Peter Berger's *Noise of Solemn Assemblies* and Gibson Winter's *Suburban Captivity of the Churches*, sociologists probed the failures of the American Protestant congregations to deal cre-

6. O. Kelly Ingram and Robert M. Colver, "Notes on the Graduating Classes of 1958-1967 of Duke Divinity School and Southeastern Baptist Theological Seminary," *Duke Divinity Review* 36, no. 2 (1971): 100-111, here p. 101.

7. Frederick Ferré, "Towards Transformational Theology: A Dialogue with My Father," *Religion in Life* 47 (1978): 6-22, here 13.

atively with the new explosive world of the American urban landscape. Harvey Cox put many of these conclusions and others into his immensely popular *The Secular City,* a work that, ironically, seemed to celebrate the decline of religious influence in the cities as part of the human quest for autonomy and freedom. The authors of these works noted that the mainstream churches had largely isolated themselves from the most dynamic aspects of their culture. In many ways these works revealed the often hidden but usually present gender anxiety of America's male clergy. The church seemed destined to spend its time in the world of women and children, while the real men, those on Kennedy's New Frontier, struggled in the brave new world of the American cities and their often oppressive economies.[8] The vague sense that there was trouble in Zion, never far beneath the surface of the 1950s, was now in full view.

II. Civil Rights and Unfinished Business

The treatment of African Americans was America's longest-standing and least-acknowledged social question, and the issue was nowhere as festering as in theological education. To be sure, the handful of African American seminaries had managed by the 1950s to secure African American leadership, but they were significantly more underfunded and undercapitalized than other theological institutions. In fact, as H. Richard Niebuhr had noted in *The Advancement of Theological Education,* the number of students in the best African American schools actually declined during the 1945-1955 decade.[9] The best estimate was that fewer than 100 African American students received the bachelor of divinity degree in one year. Nor were African American students welcome in predominately white institutions. The two leading African American religious thinkers of the 1950s, Benjamin Mays and Howard Thurman, had been turned down by white seminaries before they were finally accepted at the University of Chicago and Colgate Rochester, respectively.

The Second World War marked the beginning of a rise in the curve of Af-

8. Harvey Gallagher Cox, *The Secular City: Secularization and Urbanization in Theological Perspective* (New York: Macmillan, 1965); Peter L. Berger, *The Noise of Solemn Assemblies: Christian Commitment and the Religious Establishment in America* (Garden City, N.Y.: Doubleday, 1961); Gibson Winter, *The Suburban Captivity of the Churches: An Analysis of Protestant Responsibility in the Expanding Metropolis* (Garden City, N.Y.: Doubleday, 1961). For a general treatment see Diamond Etan, *Souls of the City: Religion and the Search for Community in Postwar America* (Bloomington: Indiana University Press, 2003).

9. H. Richard Niebuhr, Daniel Day Williams, and James Gustafson, *The Advancement of Theological Education* (New York: Harper, 1957), p. 234.

rican American expectations and achievements. African American troops had served with distinction during the conflict. Although many of their military positions had involved clearly second-class tasks that others did not want, such as emptying garbage and general maintenance, many of their other tasks, including loading and unloading munitions, were dangerous as well as physically challenging. Moreover, some had served on the front lines. In 1944 thirteen African Americans were commissioned as naval officers, and black volunteers were part of the army that battled to recover territory lost in the Battle of the Bulge. The Tuskegee Airmen, the 332nd Fighter Group, received a collective citation for their bravery over Berlin in 1945. If few of these achievements were as celebrated as they should have been, the experience of war and military decoration made these returning soldiers less willing than ever to accept their legally and socially mandated second-class status.

Equally important, African Americans had been engaged in a major movement of self-liberation since the First World War. With the decline of immigration during the First World War and its virtual abolition afterward, cities and factories in the North had an almost insatiable demand for cheap labor. Ambitious African Americans from the South poured into the nation's largest cities, often occupying housing that had previously been reserved for whites, and establishing their own churches, businesses, and social organizations. A sociologist with a map of the churches in a city could chart the progress of the "black invasion" by noting when a particular white congregation elected to move "farther out" to the edges of the city or to the suburbs. Blockbusting — selling one house in a neighborhood to African Americans and causing, thereby, a shift in the color of the area — became a persistent white nightmare. Suburban flight began long before the desegregation of the urban schools. "Inner city" became a code word for African American neighborhoods that attempted to shift attention from racial to urban sociology. Yet, if the schools and other social services they experienced in the inner city were not on par with those of the white majority, they were several steps above what Southern blacks had received earlier. Fast trains and cheap cars made escape from peonage far easier than it once had been.

Government was also nervously moving toward more integration. Harry Truman, an unlikely racial reformer, steadily integrated the armed forces. His strategy was that of a classic slugger in boxing. First he would hit at one area and then, after the excitement over that step had died down, he would hit at another. By 1948 he committed to a racially integrated military. Meanwhile, sports, an area crucial to the economic and social advance of other minorities, gradually opened its doors to African American participants. Boxing was the first to be integrated, but it was the integration of baseball in 1947 with the naming of Jackie Robinson to the Dodgers that marked the most significant breakthrough.

African Americans were also making theological progress. Morehouse College in Atlanta was the focus of many of these intellectual transformations. Benjamin E. Mays (1894-1984) was the most prominent African American religious and educational leader before Martin Luther King, Jr.[10] Elected president of Morehouse College in 1940, he was determined that the school would become a prestigious institution, and he labored hard at faculty development and recruitment. The establishment of a Phi Beta Kappa chapter was one mark of his leadership. Mays was a graduate of the University of Chicago, and his exposure to the scholarly precision of the Chicago school stood him in good stead throughout his life. In his most influential book, *The Negro's God,* he used the historical-critical assumptions of his teachers to dig under the surface of African American religious expressions. What he found was remarkable. While much African American religion gave people hope for the living of their lives and had great value for their survival, strains in the spirituals and elsewhere called for liberation in the here and now. Mays, needless to say, was fascinated by this type of this-worldly faith and made it an integral part of his own spirituality. But Mays's work was also suggestive of a new direction in theological method. Like H. Richard Niebuhr, Mays combined the results of the scholarly study of religion with the normative interests of theology and ethics. In other words, Mays treated African American religious life as though it were an independent and valuable source of revelation, especially when considered critically. While traveling to India in 1937 to attend an ecumenical conference, Mays met Gandhi and recognized the spiritual and political power of his ideal of nonviolence. He was careful to introduce his students at Morehouse to Gandhi's religious vision.

One of Mays's most important contributions to African American theological education was his role in the establishment of the International Theological Center (ITC) in Atlanta in 1958, a new institution composed of four Atlanta seminaries: Morehouse, Johnson C. Smith, Charles H. Mason, and Phillips. All four schools faced serious challenges, and as their parent colleges moved toward Southern States accreditation, they were in real danger of being sacrificed for the greater good of the larger institution. With substantial aid from the Rockefeller-established General Education Board and the Sealantic Fund, the ITC provided Atlanta and African American theological education with a new lease on life.

10. This material is based on Benjamin E. Mays, *Born to Rebel: An Autobiography* (New York: Scribner, 1971); Benjamin E. Mays and Joseph William Nicholson, *The Negro's Church* (1933; reprint, New York: Arno Press, 1968); Benjamin E. Mays, *Seeking to Be Christian in Race Relations* (New York: Friendship Press, 1957); Benjamin E. Mays, *The Negro's God as Reflected in His Literature* (Boston: Chapman and Grimes, 1938).

Howard Thurmond (1899-1981) was only slightly younger than Benjamin Mays, one of his teachers at Morehouse, and was of a different theological cast. Whereas Mays made his career as an institution builder and spokesman for African American people in the ecumenical movement, Thurmond was more a mystic and spiritual adviser. Early in his career he was deeply influenced by Rufus Jones and his studies of the mystical tradition, and he sought to incorporate the best of the mystical tradition into his interpretation of life. His Church of Fellowship for All Peoples was an early and important experiment in interracial church life, and he was the first African American to hold a full faculty position at Boston University School of Theology.

Like Mays, Thurmond wanted to push the theological envelope. He was convinced that the experience of race and oppression was important for contemporary thinking about religion, and his *Jesus and the Disinherited* explored the ways Jesus' life touched upon the contemporary issue of racial exclusion. Religious faith with its unique powers to inspire, to overcome, and to heal was the only source of strength that was equal to the challenge of finding justice in the current situation. In short, religious faith was the source of a new humanity and new possibilities. Interestingly enough, Martin Luther King read *Jesus and the Disinherited* and was said to carry a copy with him on his travels.

The civil rights movement accelerated with the *Brown v. Board of Education* decision in 1954 and the subsequent slow march of desegregation across the nation. A good argument can be made that the revolution was spearheaded by the courts and its subsequent success assured by the willingness of the federal authorities to use force to enforce those court decisions. Martin Luther King, however, was able to capture its inner spiritual dynamic, and his influence was a major factor in shaping theological education in the 1960s and beyond.

In retrospect, King was ideally suited to influence theological educators. Unlike many African American pastors, King was a trained theologian. He had graduated from Crozer Theological Seminary with a bachelor of divinity and later earned a doctorate from Boston University. He spoke the language of white liberalism easily and convincingly, and he knew the types of appeals that would make his message compelling to that audience. At the same time, King was the son of a successful African American pastor who had served as his father's associate when only eighteen. The language of the African American church was instinctive with him, and his sermons had the capacity to involve his congregations in Montgomery and Atlanta. In other words, King was culturally bilingual.

White seminary instructors and students responded to King's call to participate in the struggle in large numbers. Together with African American religious leaders, this white participation helped give King's demonstrations and marches a deeply religious tone. At the 1963 March on Washington, for example, as many as forty thousand white church members, including many clergy and seminarians, may have been in attendance, although numbers are necessarily imprecise.[11] The demonstrations fed a hunger deep in the souls of seminary teachers and their students, and many felt a sense of renewal and rebirth. Perhaps for the first time these leaders experienced the socially transforming power that Walter Rauschenbusch and H. Richard Niebuhr had seen in the Christian tradition. Perhaps to their surprise, when President Lyndon Johnson, an improbable racial reformer, took up and extended the civil rights program of his slain predecessor, John Kennedy, the churches played a major role in the write-in campaign that convinced many Congressional representatives that the nation wanted the controversial Civil Rights Act of 1964.[12] Critics, including both Niebuhrs, had questioned the tendency of American neoorthodox theologians to downplay the role of the social gospel in the nation's history: the civil rights movement suggested that new power lay in what by American standards were ancient truths.

In addition to its contribution to the seminaries' sense of élan, the civil rights movement sparked three important responses: an interest in ending racial discrimination in theological education, some important new initiatives in field and continuing education, and a new and potent form of liberal theology.

First, many seminaries committed themselves to becoming multiracial institutions in both faculty and staff. In the South the university-related divinity schools took the institutional lead in moving away from segregated practices. Perkins began its desegregation program, for example, in 1950, and Duke's divinity schools began petitioning the university for permission to admit African American students in the late 1940s, although the university did not finally approve the practice until 1961. Emory admitted African Americans for the first time in 1961.[13]

Southern Baptist seminaries lagged behind their Methodist counterparts, in part because their institutions were directly responsible to Southern public opinion. But the schools were affected. Students at Louisville's Southern Baptist

11. The figure comes from Glenn R. Bucher and L. Gordon Tait, "Social Reform Since the Great Depression," in *Encyclopedia of the American Religious Experience,* ed. Charles H. Lippy and Peter W. Williams (New York: Scribner, 1988), 3:1467.

12. See James M. Findlay, Jr., *Church People in the Struggle: The National Council of Churches and the Black Freedom Movement, 1950-1970* (New York and Oxford: Oxford University Press, 1993), especially pp. 48-65.

13. See Conrad Cherry, *Hurrying toward Zion: Universities, Divinity Schools, and American Protestantism* (Bloomington and Indianapolis: Indiana University Press, 1995).

Theological Seminary petitioned for the admission of African American students in 1950, as soon as Kentucky's Day Law requiring segregation was officially repealed, and the seminary began its gradual program of desegregation a year later. The strongest pressure on Southern Baptist institutions, however, did not come from within the schools. Southern Baptist churches were deeply committed to missions, and their missionaries had labored for almost a century in Nigeria and other African countries. Southern Baptists did not participate in the general retreat from foreign missions that was common among mainstream denominations, and they retained a strong sense of obligation for their mission churches abroad. When leaders from those churches applied to attend Southern Baptist schools, the schools felt they had to admit them and provide them with support.

As experience was to show, the seminaries' commitment to African Americans proved difficult to achieve. Sunday morning was (and still is) America's most segregated hour, and many African American denominations distrusted the idea of a learned minister. This distrust was not primarily racial. Their white counterparts in the same ecclesiastical family often shared similar feelings.

Many white Southerners, as well as their African American counterparts, had long distrusted an educated ministry. For Euro-American and African American Baptists in the South, a seminary-trained clergy was directly related to the social status of individual congregations. In the 1950s and 1960s, as white Southerners moved to the cities and joined the middle classes, the social situation was ripe for a change, and this change happened with almost bewildering speed. During this period the number of seminary graduates serving Southern pulpits grew, and Southern denominations founded new seminaries to increase the supply. Southern Baptists, the largest Southern denomination, are an important example of this larger trend. In 1940 the denomination had two seminaries, Southern and Southwestern, both of which were in serious financial trouble. In 1970 the denomination sponsored six seminaries that collectively enrolled almost half the Protestant seminarians in the United States, and if the six schools were not rich, they were prosperous and well financed. Likewise, African American seminary enrollments, both in historically African American and Euro-American seminaries, have tended to rise as more and more African Americans have entered the American middle class.[14]

14. One of the difficulties in discussing African American religion is that the religion of African Americans shares many social, theological, and historical connections to the Euro-American religious movements. One is never sure where to place the emphasis in a phrase like "African American Baptist," and one cannot tell the story without attention to both the African American component and the Baptist component.

Secondly, the civil rights movement inspired a number of new experience-centered forms of field and continuing education. If the civil rights revolution had done nothing else, it clearly exposed the difficulty that Euro-American churches had in dealing with the problems of the cities, reaching the poor, and acting as agents of racial and class reconciliation. To many, the times seemed to demand that the clergy enter into a brave new world. In simple terms, the question was how could a ministry largely raised in the white suburbs and educated in de facto or legally segregated institutions enter meaningfully into the religious and ethical life of a racially diverse and tense environment. If the ancient church father Tertullian mused over what Jerusalem might have to do with Athens and the church with the academy, his modern successors were equally mystified by what Scarsdale had to do with Harlem, the seminary with the world.

There were some important precedents. The East Harlem Protestant Parish, founded by George Webber, Archie Hargraves, and Donald Benedict in 1948, was based on the idea that students could learn to cope with the experience of urban poverty only by living and working in the area.[15] The parish inspired similar experiments in Cleveland and in Chicago. Other examples of this immersion-type educational experiment predated the 1960s as well. Sherwood Eddy and Reinhold Niebuhr had sponsored Providence Farms in Mississippi as an interracial and socialist experiment, and Clarence Jordan's Koinonia Farms, located in Georgia, had long been almost an obligatory stop for socially conscious Southern seminarians. The need was to find some way to combine what had been learned from these experiments with the contemporary situation. The result was the establishment of a series of Urban Training Centers, also known as UTCs. A proposal sent to the National Council of Churches in 1961 listed four possible constituencies for these organizations: seminarians, working pastors, inner-city laity, and Peace Corps volunteers. Part of their charm was that, like the clinical education movement, they were to operate parallel to the seminaries but not be part of the larger educational bureaucracy. Like other 1960s organizations, they wanted to travel light, but there was also some concern that they not be seen as alternatives to the established institutions but as their partners.

The movement to create such centers moved rapidly. The Chicago UTC, established in 1962, served by such able leaders as Gibson Winter of the University of Chicago, provided much leadership for the new initiative. It pioneered

15. This was based in part on the experience of the French worker-priest movement. The best study of the East Harlem Protestant Parish is Alicia Benjamin, "Christian Urban Colonizers: A History of the East Harlem Protestant Parish in New York City, 1948-1968" (Ph.D. diss., Union Theological Seminary, 1988). The dissertation is particularly interested in the events that eventually led to the termination of the experiment.

the famed "urban plunge," in which a student was given a few dollars and told to survive for a week or more in the city. In many ways the idealism of the "plunge" highlighted the need of the churches for more operational knowledge of the urban scene. Unlike these financially strapped white seminarians, African Americans and other urban immigrants tended to move to neighborhoods where they had family or friends. Even the most homogeneous urban area was in fact a sequence of little Jacksons or little Memphises where familiar faces helped newcomers find a place. What appeared to Euro-American observers to be a community-less mass of humanity fighting for survival was more aptly described in terms of its many centers of social loyalty.[16] The Chicago UTC was soon joined by other similar organizations, with MUST (Metropolitan Urban Service Training) in New York and MTC (Metropolitan Training Center) leading the parade. A national organization was formed in 1968 when more than thirty such centers existed, each with its own carefully constructed string of initials. The highly stylized names were supposed to convey both the urgency and the need for the mission, but they also reflected the early popularity of President Johnson's War on Poverty that promised to raise the living standards of the nation's poorest.

The high point of the Urban Training Movement came when MTC in Washington resolved to sponsor its own form of theological education, the Theological Education Demonstration Project, or Intermet. John Fletcher of Virginia Episcopal Seminary was chosen to head the project, and he planned the new venture during a 1970 leave. Like many theological educators in the 1960s, Fletcher was convinced that the traditional seminary with its emphasis on professionalism had failed. "What is the problem?" he wrote. "One definition, supported by considerable research, is that the seminary pattern isolates students from significant learning experiences with groups to whom they must relate as clergymen. Among these groups are: laity in a congregation, his ecumenical peers in the ministry, community learners and conflict groups, denomination boards and officials, and other professionals like physicians, lawyers, administrations, etc. These groups send the clergyman signals in his day to day work about what it means to be competent."[17] The center of the program was to be a careful encounter between the student and the structures of the community in which the student was working. From these experiences the student was to learn to ask theological questions in a new way.

16. The trips "home," celebrated in much African American literature, had many purposes. On the one hand, they renewed and reinforced old ties, but they also recruited new people for the migration north. African American churches were a vital part of this network.

17. For Fletcher's understanding of Intermet, see John C. Fletcher and Tilden Edwards, Jr., "Inter-met: On the Job Theological Education," *Pastoral Psychology* 22 (Mar. 1971): 21-30.

By 1974 the Urban Training Movement and Intermet had largely passed from the scene. The reasons for their demise were complex. The new militancy of the civil rights movement after Martin Luther King's murder contributed to it, but it was not the only cause. A jaundiced observer might argue that the movement collapsed from the weight of its overblown rhetoric and naive understanding of the human condition, but such observations prove both too much and too little. They prove too much in that such judgments are true of almost all the movements of the early 1960s, from the hippies to the middle-class audiences that pushed and shoved to attend *Hair.* Just as the idealism of Emerson and the Transcendentalists looked dated on the battlefields of the Civil War, so the early 1960s looked dated after 1968, and even more dated after Kent State. But too little also is said in those judgments. Institutions tend to be created in stages. First, a movement discovers a need; second, some more practical visionaries create new institutional structures to meet that need; and finally the movement takes on the trappings of permanence. The Urban Training Movement failed somewhere between the second and third steps. The centers were very expensive to maintain, and as seminaries and churches began to awaken to the financial crisis before them in the 1970s and beyond, it was easy to let them die a natural death.

Yet the Urban Training Movement was not fated to be one of the many relics of the Age of Aquarius. The sense that theological students could not be made acquainted with other cultures except by immersion in them has remained part of theological education. The AATS's program on globalization was built on a similar understanding, although without as extensive an immersion, and the belief that relevant theology may emerge from exposure to social structures became a theological commonplace.

Third, the civil rights movement, and Martin Luther King in particular, changed the way many theologians, in the United States, Latin America, and Europe, understood theology.[18] King always understood himself to be a Baptist

18. The literature on King is vast. Among those who have stressed the theological importance of his work are: Jarl Sheppard and Thomas Mikelson, "The Negro's God in the Theology of Martin Luther King, Jr.: Social Community and Theological Discourse" (Th.D. diss., Harvard University, 1988); Drew W. Hansen, *The Dream: Martin Luther King, Jr., and the Speech That Inspired a Nation* (New York: Ecco, 2003); Valentino Lassiter, *Martin Luther King in the African American Preaching Tradition* (Cleveland: Pilgrim Press, 2001); Keith D. Miller, *Voice of Deliverance: The Language of Martin Luther King, Jr., and Its Sources* (New York: Free Press/Macmillan, 1992); Luther D. Ivory, *Toward a Theology of Radical Involvement: The Theological Legacy of Martin Luther King, Jr.* (Nashville: Abingdon, 1997); William M. Ramsay, *Four Modern Prophets: Walter Rauschenbusch, Martin Luther King, Jr., Gustavo Gutiérrez, Rosemary Radford Ruether* (Atlanta: John Knox, 1986); James H. Cone, "The Theology of Martin Luther King, Jr." (unbound manuscript, Harvard University, 1985).

minister and preacher whose task was the building up of the "beloved community." The sources he had at his disposal for this task were rich and complex. Clearly, he inherited the creative African American theologies of Mays and Thurmond, and his interest in the thought and practice of Gandhi is well-known. King's sources, however, went beyond these influences. His studies at Crozer and at Boston University included the full range of the American liberal tradition, including Walter Rauschenbusch and Paul Tillich. King's theological achievement was to bring these together in compact rhetorical statements that often penetrated to the depths of the biblical message and its metaphors.

What King discovered was the method and power of a theology of particularity. When approached in a sympathetic and pastoral way, the traditions of a particular people became a gold mine of metaphors and symbols that they could use to effect their own liberation. Earlier religious nationalists had followed a similar pathway, but King carried the argument one step deeper. As he understood his work, the ultimate goal of theology and his social action was the liberation of the oppressor as well as of the oppressed. Once the task was completed, the dream was that a new community might replace the communities that had been divided by culture and race. Ultimately, King looked forward to the redemption of all people.

The links he established between particularity and redemption formed an important paradigm for the various theologies of particularity that followed him. Latin American liberation theologians were inspired by King's work in the United States, as were later feminist and gay theologians. His influence was also felt in the theologies of such South African leaders as Desmond Tutu, who articulated their own theological particularities in creative ways. As Robert McAfee Brown said, theology was being done in "a new key."

The close relationship between liberal Protestants and the civil rights movement changed after the long hot summer of 1968 saw violence erupt in 125 cities in response to the death of Martin Luther King. One year later James Forman further separated the civil rights movement from the churches when he presented the Black Manifesto, a demand for reparations from the American churches for centuries of African American suffering. Much of the controversy over Forman centered in the "holy triangle" formed by Union Seminary, the Interchurch Center — 475 Riverside Drive — and Riverside Church, where Forman initially presented his demands. In many ways Forman had chosen a soft target. Few other institutions in the nation would have given him a hearing.

Forman's demands created a full crisis at Union. Students seized the administrative offices of the school and formed a chorus supporting Forman's demands. In the confusion of the times, it was difficult to gauge the support that the protesting students actually enjoyed, although it was probably less than the press or the administration supposed.[19] The faculty and trustees acted moderately by promising to raise funds for African American economic development, a response that was largely copied by the various white denominations. In total funds, the grants were modest and more symbolic than actual, but they were powerful symbols. To many white Americans, those symbols were negative. The sense that white churchmen had followed their conscience to support African American liberation was replaced by a sense that white liberal churchmen did not understand the harsh world of violence and anger that the civil rights movement had created. The strong ties of affection that had bound the Northern churches to the civil rights struggle and to the National Council of Churches (NCC) were strained to the breaking point. In some individuals and congregations the experience marked a deep and permanent alienation between members. On a national level, opposition to the NCC, for example, moved from the evangelical movement into the mainstream. Raising money became far more difficult.

The civil rights movement provided the model or precedent for how other demands for inclusion in society and in the church would be handled by the seminaries. The movement for women's liberation provides a good example. The issue of the place of women in the economy and in American public life had been more or less put on hold from 1930 to 1960. During the Great Depression, for instance, the very high levels of female employment in the 1920s sagged, and many displaced women workers simply returned to their households to wait out the crisis. Despite a brief rise during the Second World War, the same trend continued as the nation struggled to right itself in a nuclear world. By 1960 things were changing. Rising divorce rates fueled by progressively easier divorces made the household an insecure place, and the end of the postwar economy meant that fewer families could attain a middle-class standard of living on one salary alone. The pill accelerated this same trend as women had more security in family planning, which was essential for career development. For a variety of reasons, including the widespread Southern belief that the inclusion of discrimination based on sex would scuttle the bill, the Civil Rights Acts of 1964 prohibited discrimination based on gender. A lively secular feminist literature developed that attracted and repelled some Christian women who shared the larger aspirations of the women's movement.

The position of women in the church was perhaps more retrograde than

19. I was a graduate student at Union at the time, and my memory was that support for Forman and other radical issues was more or less like the earlier support for the American Revolution: one-third supported, one-third opposed, and one-third were neutral. The percentage of those who were vocal was even smaller.

in any other area of American life. Only a handful of women were enrolled in bachelor of divinity programs, and women were encouraged to study "religious education," which unfortunately had become a women's ghetto. Outside of religious education and the library, women faculty members were even more unusual. Although the mainstream churches were slowly removing the formal bars to ordination, many denominations retained those barriers. Mary Daly's *The Church and the Second Sex*, published in 1968, was an important critique of the underlying social, religious, and theological issues involved in the exclusion of women. Other, more radical works would follow. As in the case of African Americans, some seminaries moved to establish women's studies departments, and many began to search actively for women faculty members.

In many ways the interest of women in church vocations and in Christian theology came at a very important time in the history of theological schools. As Vietnam wound down and the draft was replaced by the lottery, the number of male ministerial candidates in the mainstream churches began a decline that, with fits and starts, continued for the rest of the century. Hence, the seminaries had many extra places for women, and the churches, already struggling to find ways to staff rural and declining urban churches, had places for their employment.

III. The Decline of Neoorthodoxy

Intellectually, the 1960s were the end of an era. Since the 1930s the new theologies associated with Barth, Brunner, and the two Niebuhrs had served as a focus for American theology, and almost every theological discipline had been renewed through their contact with this larger movement. Equally important, the "theological renaissance" and the ecumenical movement had inspired a new interest in the church, its standards, and its worship. But despite its apparent dominance, this movement quickly ebbed in the 1960s, and its ebbing left behind eddies and currents that seemed to threaten to carry much away in a powerful undertow.

Whether neoorthodoxy ebbed or not is of course a matter of judgment and perspective. Yale theologians Hans W. Frei and George Lindbeck sought to continue the work of H. R. Niebuhr at Yale, and were important educators of younger theologians. Since Yale remained among the most important educators of young theologians, this is a not inconsiderable exemption. Yale stood firmly in the American center.

Seen from the perspective of the American South, neoorthodoxy flourished through much of the remaining century. Among Southern Baptists, Dale

Moody, the influential professor of theology at Louisville's Southern Baptist Seminary, was deeply interested in Emil Brunner's theology. Moody was the leading Southern Baptist systematic theologian during the key period from 1950 to 1970 when the denomination's seminary system expanded at a rapid rate. Consequently, his students were strategically placed where they exerted major influence over the system as a whole. Although often more circumspect in his language, Southwestern Baptist Seminary's John Newport was also deeply influenced by neoorthodoxy, especially the work of Paul Tillich, and his students helped spread that perspective throughout the Southwest. Interestingly, both Moody and Newport were part of a handful of creative Southern Baptist intellectuals who studied for a season at New York's Union Seminary. Whether the neoorthodox understanding of Scripture was adequate for the modern church was one of the substantial issues in the theological controversy that racked Southern Baptists in the 1970s and 1980s.

Albert Outler at Perkins, although more mainstream than his Southern Baptist counterparts, created a neo-Wesleyanism that was an important counterpart to other forms of neoorthodoxy and that has served the United Methodist Church well as a beacon in its subsequent search for identity. A similar argument could be made about the course of theology among Southern Presbyterians. As among Baptists and Methodists in the South, neoorthodoxy was an important intellectual bridge between traditional Southern theology and twentieth-century perspectives.

Further, traditional neoorthodoxy had a deep, if hard to document, influence on American evangelicalism. Part of the difficulty lies, of course, in the fact that the word "neoorthodoxy" was often used loosely to describe any type of theology that took modern biblical studies seriously. The Southern Baptist debate over Ralph Elliot's 1961 *Meaning of Genesis* may have started a twenty-year struggle over the role of "inerrancy" in the denomination, but the question of the value of neoorthodox biblical studies was never far from the surface of that impassioned debate. Many of those accused in Harold Lindsell's *Battle for the Bible* were not "liberals" in any classic understanding of the word, but conservative neoorthodox-leaning evangelicals struggling with critical understandings of the Bible. Even today, to associate an evangelical thinker with neoorthodoxy may be to question that thinker's credentials with some people in his or her constituency. Yet the influence seems evident. Paul King Jewett studied with Emil Brunner in Switzerland, and Daniel Fuller — who was at the center of a protracted evangelical battle in the 1960s — studied with Karl Barth. Other ties were less obvious, but perhaps just as real. E. J. Carnell, a leading evangelical apologist who served for a season as president of Fuller, wrote his Harvard dissertation on the thought of Reinhold Niebuhr, and throughout his career continued to be in dialogue with neoorthodox thinkers. The translator of Barth's *Church Dogmatics*, Geoffrey Bromiley, made his career at Fuller.[20]

Yet the generalization that neoorthodoxy ebbed in the 1960s still has meaning. Although its decline appears precipitous, its antecedents must be carefully noted. The Presbyterian Church, USA, and its successor, the United Presbyterian Church, were arguably the denominations most deeply influenced by neoorthodoxy. Under its auspices they revised their Sunday school literature and, perhaps equally importantly, their confessional documents. The Confession of 1967 is of course liberally salted with neoorthodox language about the Bible, but the decision to adopt the *Book of Confessions* in place of one normative confession also reflects neoorthodox influence. What was important was that the church confessed its faith on the basis of Scripture and not in any of the historically conditioned forms in which that profession was enshrined. Yet Presbyterianism had a liberal wing that was only half convinced by the new theology and often saw it as the lesser of two evils over against fundamentalism. Likewise, both American Baptists and Methodists had strong liberal wings. Among Baptist schools, neither the University of Chicago nor Colgate Rochester had more than a handful of neoorthodox teachers, and Methodist Boston continued to have a very influential personalist contingent.

IV. The Second Wave of the Theological Renaissance: Doubts, Affirmations, and Interpretations

Although it is somewhat artificial, one can interpret much of the theological life of the 1950s as the "Second Wave of the Theological Renaissance." Unlike the first wave in the 1930s and 1940s, the second wave was no longer as captivated by the power of traditional theology to provide a useful heuristic. While maintaining some of the insights of the earlier movement, the dominant theological voices of the 1950s were deeply aware that the intellectual programs posed by the modern world were still problems for theology. With passion and with precision many American theologians turned to the writings of Bultmann, Bonhoeffer, and Tillich for clues on how to address an increasingly complex theological situation.

20. See for some documentation of this thesis Richard Albert Mohler, "Evangelical Theology and Karl Barth: Representative Models of Response" (Ph.D. diss., Southern Baptist Theological Seminary, 1989); Phillip R. Thorne, *Evangelicalism and Karl Barth: His Reception and Influence in North American Evangelical Theology* (Allison Park, Pa.: Pickwick, 1995); Gregory Bolich, *Karl Barth and Evangelicalism* (Downers Grove, Ill.: InterVarsity, 1980); Donald McKim, ed., *How Karl Barth Changed My Mind* (Grand Rapids: Eerdmans, 1986).

The turn to Bultmann, Bonhoeffer, and Tillich in the 1950s also eroded much of the neoorthodox position. Although many saw them as neoorthodox, their theologies raised questions that eroded confidence in the conclusions of theological renaissance. During the Second World War, Bultmann elected to continue to do theology as usual with minimum political and social commitments. Although his form of existential theology seemed to have affinities with the early Barth, he was essentially a critical New Testament scholar who had reached radical conclusions about the historicity and interpretation of the text. Such works as his *Jesus and the Word, A Commentary on the Gospel of John,* and *Theology of the New Testament* made important contributions to the biblical discussion. As a historian, Bultmann reached an even more radical conclusion: the worldview of the New Testament was substantially different from the worldview of modern humanity. Consequently, modern people often read the New Testament with wonderment, confused over what it said, and not convinced that it had any meaning for the present. A major part of the problem, Bultmann contended, was the mythology that provided the framework for the New Testament message itself. This methodology included such myths as the story of the cosmic redeemer, a belief in heaven and hell, and the existence of angels and demons. For modern readers, consequently, it made little sense to speak of an act of God in Christ or of his death as atonement for the forgiveness of sins. Although some theologians argued that "myth" was used differently in theological studies than in ordinary discourse, this was clearly not true of Bultmann. Bultmann meant by myth the same as most modern readers: a myth was a story about the supernatural that we knew, on its face, not to be the case. Bultmann was not the first to see myth in the New Testament, of course, but what set him apart from others was his contention that myth so penetrated the New Testament that the myth could not be removed without destroying the meaning of the whole. Hence, the task for theology was essentially hermeneutical. The New Testament had to be interpreted in the language of modern existential philosophy.

Paul Tillich was a richly systematic thinker. Much of his later thought was contained in his earlier writings, which had a religious sparkle to them that often enabled people to see things in a new light. *The Courage to Be, The Protestant Era,* and similar essays were rich with suggestive reinterpretations of Christianity. For example, Tillich argued that the demonic was a religious way of describing the forces of evil that threatened human personhood and that justification by faith meant that the individual was accepted. The more radical implications of Tillich's thought did not become clear (at least to nontheologians) until the publication of his later works, particularly his *Systematic Theology,* published between 1951 and 1963. In these studies Tillich struggled with the brokenness of Western religious symbols. Even (or particularly) the symbol of God had been damaged almost beyond repair. Humankind needed to realize that God was not personal and not active in the ordinary sense of those words but was "being itself" in its relationship to the finitude of our particular being. But this use of a traditional Platonic image for God did not solve the problem. "Being itself" was only another symbol that had to be transcended.

In many ways Tillich and Bultmann ended their songs on the same note. Unlike earlier liberals, they realized that they could not weed the garden of orthodox theology and remove all the traces of premodern myth and symbolism. Biblical message and Christian faith were too closely related for anyone to remove the weeds without uprooting the surrounding growth. The only way forward was to embrace this seemingly impossible situation. Interestingly, H. Richard Niebuhr came to a similar impasse. Throughout his career Niebuhr struggled with the implications of Ernst Troeltsch's thought for theology. Troeltsch had applied the insights of the history-of-religions school of biblical study to the whole of the Christian tradition that he saw as one religious expression among many. In his early works Troeltsch, a good friend of Max Weber, developed a comprehensive religious sociology that stressed the different ways in which churches and sects related to the social order. But, as his thought matured, Troeltsch returned repeatedly to the question of the "absoluteness of Christianity" or, to use a less wooden translation, to the question of Christianity's claim to possess a universal truth. By this time his studies of world religions had convinced him that all religions reflected their cultural milieu and that none had the right to instruct or replace the others. Troeltsch's argument for Christianity was thus provisional. Protestant Christianity provided strong social and cultural leadership for the German nation and enabled that nation to express its deepest ethical insights creatively. Niebuhr's two studies of the American churches, *The Social Sources of Denominationalism* and *The Kingdom of God in America,* embraced much of Troeltsch's sociological analysis. By the end of his life, like Troeltsch, Niebuhr was exploring the theoretical implications of his sociological method self-consciously. Like Troeltsch, although with less rancor, he was no longer convinced of the "absoluteness" of the Christ event. In an important article, "Reformation: A Continuing Imperative," that appeared in the *Christian Century,* he wrote simply: "I do not have the evidence which allows me to say that the miracle of faith in God is worked only by Jesus Christ and that it is never given to men outside that sphere of his working, though I may say that where I note its presence I posit the presence also of something like Jesus Christ."[21]

21. H. Richard Niebuhr, "Reformation: A Continuing Imperative," *Christian Century* 77 (Mar. 2, 1960): 249.

Niebuhr also pled with his fellow theologians not to allow the insights of the liberal period in theology to be lost. His last two works, *Radical Monotheism and Western Culture* (1960) and *The Responsible Self* (1963), heralded the change of the theological scene. *Radical Monotheism* remains one of his most difficult works. Both works were more programmatic than completed essays, and one can only wonder how Niebuhr might have connected the dots had he not died in late 1960. In them he suggested that theology needed to return to a reexamination of first principles, including the complex relationship between monotheism and Western culture, and see how those first principles functioned philosophically and culturally. He was also convinced that Christian ethics, which was his field of instruction, needed to take seriously the nature of the self that was capable of responding to new situations in multiple ways.

The place of the brilliant German theologian Dietrich Bonhoeffer in the theology of the 1950s and 1960s is undeniable, sparked by the publication of his *Ethics* and his *Letters and Papers from Prison*. Bonhoeffer seemed almost to have prophesied current theological trends from his Nazi jail. His martyr's death in a world that often seemed tragically short of heroes gave his words additional moral authority, and the fact that no one knew precisely what he meant (including Bonhoeffer) gave other theologians license to use his ideas as they would. Despite the cautions of such Bonhoeffer scholars as Union's Paul Lehmann, popular theological writing often pictured Bonhoeffer in a series of slogans, including "the world come of age," "religionless Christianity," and "the man for others." Hence, Bonhoeffer was widely understood as teaching that the church needed to travel light theologically and jettison much of its unwieldy dogmatic baggage from the past.

In the long run, Bonhoeffer's *Ethics* was his important contribution to Christian thought. His experiences in Nazi Germany raised hard questions about how one acted ethically in the midst of a thoroughly immoral situation. What does it mean, for example, to tell the truth when so doing may mean that another person is condemned to death or a concentration camp? If the only way to oppose a regime was by duplicity, might not such behavior be more faithful to the gospel than the internal righteousness traditionally required of believers? In other words, ethical behavior was always conditioned by the context in which that behavior took place and not necessarily by the church's traditional standards of behavior. Where Bonhoeffer might have taken this discussion, had he lived, is not clear.

Bonhoeffer raised the one question that all theologians had to discuss as they struggled with the role of the church in the post–World War II world. In a world of systemic violence in which governments and corporations work together to oppress the poor, what do the traditional commands to honor the

King mean? Clearly, if those commands are not contextualized, the church would become an ideological supporter of evil governments. Consequently, revolution with all its violence and destruction of property had to be a permitted option. But the issues were not only political. Did the context of a decision about, for example, sexual ethics change the character of that decision, and if so, how could some level of responsibility be maintained? Bonhoeffer had opened Pandora's box.

V. God's Death

In many ways the Death of God theologians of the 1960s were the heirs of the discussions of the 1950s. Although many later commentators noted that the so-called Death of God movement did not last long as a theological movement, the movement summarized the theological uneasiness of the decade. Perhaps more than anything else, the Death of God theologians expressed a growing frustration with the way theological problems were defined. After them, few wanted to explore the older ways or the older issues.

Despite articles in the popular newsmagazines and the popularity of several theological best sellers, including J. A. T. Robinson's *Honest to God* (English edition, 1963; American edition, 1964), Christian atheism, if that is what was advocated, was not an easily defined movement. Death of God theology was not a theological school, as that term is usually used. In fact, those associated with it argued many different theological positions that had little in common. Gabriel Vahanian, the coiner of the phrase, was primarily reflecting on secularization, and the angry ex-Barthian William Hamilton, who sounded like a middler theological student who had lost his faith, was many intellectual miles from the philosophical Paul M. Van Buren. Thomas Altizer, in contrast to the rest, was interested in the fate of God after God's radical decision to become finite in Jesus Christ! And Richard Rubenstein's deep anguish over the Holocaust was without parallel in the others associated with the position.

The Death of God theologians were correct that the symbol of God no longer held the central place in modern life it once did. As Gabriel Vahanian, the first and most sociologically oriented advocate of the position, never tired of saying, the death of God was a cultural fact, a happening, for people in the West that the church needed to recognize and accept. Perhaps the best evidence for the truth of his position was the failure of American theologians in the midst of the Vietnam War to identify that "civil religion" that sociological theory had posited as necessary for premodern and modern cultures. Indeed, the record from Lincoln to Kennedy was of the decreasing frequency and persuasiveness of religious rhetoric in the public square. The Supreme Court recognized this when it ended such traditional pious practices as prayer and Bible reading in the schools and employed the right of privacy as a counterweight to such religiously inspired laws as those prohibiting birth control and abortion.

The decline of the mainstream churches pointed in the same direction. Despite record church memberships, the mainstream churches had begun a steady decline in membership and influence that would continue for the remainder of the century and beyond. In one sense the situation was simple. The prosperity of the mainstream churches was based on their ability to stand at the nation's cultural center and to struggle, no matter how imperfectly, with the intellectual and religious issues that arose in that space. When that center no longer needed, or felt it needed, religious language, the churches lost influence.

VI. American Theology Comes of Age

Ironically, at the very time American theologians faced this profound crisis, the nation's seminaries found themselves increasingly responsible for the development of their own theology. The great fountain of German academic theology that had watered American religious thought for over a century, from 1860 to 1969, did not go completely dry of course, but German theology and biblical studies suffered from their own crisis. Many of the most Protestant German regions were in eastern Germany or in areas ceded to other countries, and the new rulers in the East were not interested in strengthening either the Protestant churches or their intellectual life. Moreover, despite the important work of the Confessing Church and its successors in wartime and postwar Germany, the secularization of German life continued at a rapid pace. Church attendance fell rapidly, and, as fast as the German economic miracle permitted, the weekend became a time for rest and recreation. Despite the power of the Christian Democratic Party, the German churches — like their American counterparts — had progressively less impact on public life.

The most creative new German voice, Jürgen Moltmann, struck some interest with his "theology of hope," but despite his prolific production, his theological leadership did not match that of his better-known predecessors. Most of the energy of Moltmann's early followers turned toward the new theologies of liberation emerging in the Third World. Wolfhart Pannenberg, the other major candidate for intellectual leadership, was much more of a technical theologian than his more widely read rival, and his works quickly became a matter for specialists. Needless to say, neither replaced Barth, Brunner, or Bultmann in the hearts of American theological teachers. Although some interest remained in German biblical and historical studies, Germany's predominance in these areas was no longer assured. In the 1950s a young American biblical scholar who wanted to rise to the top of his profession needed to spend some time in Germany; by 1970 this was optional; by 1980 rare. If anything, the tide began to run the other way, as German theologians read American black and feminist theologians.

The ebbing of the tide of German scholarship was of course a reflection of the changing role of Europe. America was now the largest economic and military power, and the nation's institutions of higher education took the place of the German and English universities as the primary nodes of international scholarship and science. Learning follows money as carnivores follow game. But this commonsense observation does not deal completely with the impact of the new situation on American schools. Faced with the serious competition mounted by the university religion departments for intellectual leadership and by the need to maintain their institutions despite declining interest in the ministry, American seminaries did not have the resources, either in energy or in finances, to take responsible theological leadership.

VII. 1967 and Kent State

The 1967 student protest rocked even the most conservative theological schools and had almost catastrophic impact on the mainstream theological schools. Contemporaries felt that the earth had shaken and that theological education would never be the same again. The historian, rereading the documents of that time, is impressed again and again with the almost apocalyptic sense that gripped seminary faculties and administrators as they tried to turn, if not regain control of, the rudder, as institutions seemed headed toward either utopia or ruin and wreck. And some things have never been the same: the imperial presidencies, characterized by such talented leaders as Union's Henry Pitney Van Dusen or Andover's Herbert Gezork, were largely extinct. All schools adopted some form of "shared governance."

Curriculum was a major focus of the post-1967 seminaries. In part, this new interest was student inspired. Many students were not interested in the traditional or the neoorthodox programs of theological study, and they wanted programs that would allow them more room for individuality and election. Most seminaries followed the common college and university pattern of expanding the number of electives, weakening or even replacing their grading systems, and adding courses or even departments in such areas as women's or feminist studies, African American studies, and peace studies. There was a clear openness to interpretations of academic life that downplayed the idea of a normative "canon" of studies, and faculty members scrambled to find new readings that would fit student expectations. A predominantly elective institution operates as a small free market in which individual faculty members offer their own abilities and expertise to students whose attendance and tuition support the enterprise, and those teachers whose offerings made no bow to the common expectations found their enrollment diminished.

The market logic also helps to explain why the better-known and more ecumenical seminaries were the most affected. These schools depended for their prosperity on their ability to recruit students from across a broad band of churches and religious agencies. In many ways they were more the children of movements than of ecclesiastical structures. But this broad ability, which protected them from control by the denominations, also exposed them to the harsh discipline of the marketplace. After all, more denominationally inclined students could always go to their denominational seminaries. Whether they expressed it or not, the leaders of such seminaries had to follow their clientele.

However, the historian must be very careful not to offer too easy an interpretation of the situation. In traditional language, the student riots were part of the *causa sine qua non* of the curricular changes. Without massive student unrest, nothing would have happened. But this does not mean that they were the material cause of those changes. I would suggest that the new curricula were part of the same theological crisis that was dogging the seminaries in other areas. The theology of the early 1960s left the leaders of the nation's elite seminaries without needed guidance in formulating a theological curriculum, and, like the restless students, they were searching for light in what had become a great dark. In this atmosphere of crisis they were unable to give persuasive reasons why things should be done in certain ways or to give a persuasive account of the enterprise as a whole. Nor did the end of the period of student unrest bring new answers to these larger questions. In the 1980s and 1990s such talented theologians as Edward Farley and David Kelsey were still pondering what made theological education "theological." The question in its simplest form was stark: How did theological education differ from either general cultural studies or bondage to an all-too-temporary understanding of church leadership?[22]

22. Edward Farley, "The Reform of Theological Education as a Theological Task," *Theological Education* 17 (Spring 1981): 93-117. See also Edward Farley, *Theologia: The Fragmentation and Unity of Theological Education* (Philadelphia: Fortress, 1983); and David Kelsey, *To Understand God Truly: What's Theological about a Theological School* (Louisville: Westminster John Knox, 1992).

VIII. Other Dimensions of the Crisis

Another way to describe the crisis is to notice that student unrest marked a hiatus in the transmission of a series of practices. Philosopher Alasdair MacIntyre noted that human activities are often practices in which one generation passes on to the next a set of skills that the next can then develop further.[23] The links in the chain of experience are thus crucial to the enterprise, as they insure that the practice does not have to begin again from the beginning point. While the chain of practices in theological education was not completely disrupted in the 1960s, it was weakened. Theological educators in the 1970s and 1980s may have had a less well-developed skill base than might otherwise have been the case.

Many of the reforms proposed in the Niebuhr-Williams-Gustafson report were delayed. Much of the rhetoric of the Association of Theological Schools at the time revolved around the concept of "professional" education.[24] The use of the word "professional" to describe education for ministry was not new. It reached back to the medieval division of the university into three professional faculties, law, medicine, and theology, and each generation of theological educators had given "professional" their own interpretation. The classical liberal educators, such as Shailer Mathews, used the term to denote someone who got the job done effectively and efficiently, and the neoorthodox theologians had seen "professional" as the ability to use theological ideas to interpret human life or existence. H. Richard Niebuhr, for example, wrote about the "pastoral director" who used the knowledge of faith to guide a congregation toward a richer fulfillment of its mission.

In the literature of the AATS, "professional" had an additional meaning. From its beginnings the association was among the most inclusive American ecumenical agencies, and in the fifties and sixties it broadened its membership to include both evangelical and Roman Catholic schools. By its nature the association needed language that could encompass its diverse membership without offending any of its members' theological understanding of their clergy. "Profession" and "professionalism" seemed to provide just that Olympian point of view. By talking of ministerial education as professional education, the association could differentiate its members from liberal arts colleges and graduate schools, use models of how people were prepared for other occupations, and avoid limiting controversial theological language. In other words, as the associ-

23. Alasdair C. MacIntyre, *After Virtue: A Study in Moral Theory* (Notre Dame, Ind.: University of Notre Dame Press, 1981).

24. For an excellent example of this language, see Jesse H. Ziegler, ed., "Theological Education as Professional Education" (topic of a conference at Episcopal Theological School, Cambridge, Mass., 1967), *Theological Education* 5 (Spring 1969): 139-302.

ation's leaders used the term, the emphasis was on education that would enable ministerial candidates to do a good job in the terms of the standards of the denomination in which they served and the communities in which they lived. The reservation was essential to the association's work and self-understanding. The association did not want to homogenize American religion by establishing a single standard for ministry, and its leaders were more aware of the need to preserve those distinctions than many of the seminaries it served.

There were four parts of the association's commitment to a professional understanding of seminary education: the Curriculum for the Seventies project; the Readiness for Ministry project; the use of the term "master's degree" for the first theological degree; and the development of the doctor of ministry. Of these, the most popular was the 1970 change in the degree nomenclature from bachelor of divinity to master of divinity. The bachelor of divinity language, based in a long academic tradition, had been adopted in the early twentieth century when seminaries began to offer degrees on a regular basis. At first the better seminaries had awarded the bachelor of divinity to distinguish those among their graduates who had both college and seminary, although some schools also required an academic thesis or comprehensive examination. In line with this understanding, the Association of Theological Schools sponsored the bachelor of divinity nomenclature as part of its drive for a four-three (college plus seminary) pattern of education, and some conservative academics wanted to continue to honor this tradition. However, American public opinion did not associate a second bachelor's degree with advanced academic or professional preparation, and ministers, who often spent as long (or longer) preparing for their work as did lawyers, social workers, or educators, found their preparation undervalued. The master of divinity also had the possible value of opening up opportunities for an increasing number of seminary students who were seeking nonparish positions as social workers, teachers in community colleges, and similar vocations. The new master of arts programs had the same goal.[25]

Both the Curriculum for the Seventies and Readiness for Ministry were implemented at an inauspicious time. Although there were some complaints, especially about the supposed lack of theological content of both programs, the more common response was indifference. In other words, the proposals fell on deaf ears.

The Curriculum for the Seventies stressed the importance of field education and the development of partnerships with universities and other seminaries in the traditional academic areas.[26] Much of the instruction in the classic

25. Ziegler, "Theological Education as Professional Education."

26. See *Theological Education* 6: 3.

disciplines was to take place in ecumenical clusters that would actively promote an ecumenical understanding of the traditional foundations of theology. Ideally, seminaries develop internships, practica, and other means of providing students with evaluated experiences that would enable them to participate actively in the real world of the church. Although it was not stated, the curriculum implied that those theological disciplines most similar to the various disciplines in university schools of arts and sciences should be taught there.

Readiness for Ministry followed a similar course. Seminary leaders knew there was a basic disconnect between seminary and congregational ministry. Graduates and laypeople reported that the first years in the ministry were an often painful period of professional learning in which the new minister had to learn to cope with a very complicated profession. This sense of disconnection had also informed much of the thinking that went into the Curriculum for the Seventies. If this assumption is accurate, and there is almost no evidence to suggest it is not, then it ought to be possible by carefully constructed interviews, discussions, and advisement to determine what the churches were seeking in their pastoral leadership, to help the students evaluate what they were learning, and to provide grounds for judgment on when and how students ought to enter professional life. As the various testing documents evolved, Readiness for Ministry increasingly took account of those styles of leadership and character most valued by the laity.

Although some theological educators complained about the amount of time needed to administer the instrument, the most alarming problem in Readiness for Ministry was not the process. It was what the surveyors found. In general, American Protestant Christians were less interested in their pastors' theological competence than in their spirituality and leadership ability. Despite the persistence of much traditional theological language, especially in liturgy and hymns, American church members did not see themselves primarily as participants in a tradition. Readiness for Ministry revealed, even before the sociologists took notice, that denominational loyalty was not a primary motive for church attendance. By the 1980s the fact that America was a spiritual marketplace in which prospective members shopped for a congregation that felt right to them was almost indisputable.[27]

The doctor of ministry program was part of the same search for a competent, professional ministry. Almost from the beginnings of American theologi-

27. In a very perceptive essay, Amanda Porterfield noted the way the various religious currents of the 1960s, supported by deep roots in the work of such American thinkers as Ralph Waldo Emerson, had focused on personal spirituality. See Amanda Porterfield, *The Transformation of American Religion: The Story of a Late Twentieth Century Awakening* (New York: Oxford University Press, 2001).

cal education, many educators believed that the three-year period was too short to accomplish what the schools needed to do. This criticism had two different origins. First, the amount of material available in the classical theological disciplines, especially biblical studies, grew with the expansion of the disciplines. As more and more schools adopted university standards for tenure and promotion, this increase would become exponential. Theology was literally awash in a sea of its own products, and almost every course was hard-pressed by the question of depth or breadth. The perennial debate over the place of the biblical languages and how much time should be devoted to their study further complicated this question. At the same time, experience had made it evident, at least to many people, that the three-year program did not allow enough time for students to learn adequately the nuts and bolts of professional ministry. Theological schools needed something like the intern year in medicine or the period as a law clerk to help students develop as competent religious leaders.

After almost three decades of intense debate over a professional doctorate, some of the leading seminaries decided to act on their own. In 1962 Claremont created its doctor of religion, and it was quickly followed by the University of Chicago's doctor of ministry in 1964. Other schools announced that they were contemplating programs, including San Francisco's proposed part-time doctor of the science of theology. These actions cut short the interminable debate. The Association of Theological Schools had to act to establish standards, and appointed a committee headed by Seward Hiltner to make recommendations. In 1968 this committee proposed a comprehensive degree that included field examinations and languages; in effect, an academic degree in the practical disciplines. This was rejected by the association, and in 1970 schools were authorized to offer the doctor of ministry degree either as part of a four-year program or as a program that ministers could use to upgrade their existing degrees.[28] The latter was to prove more lasting. In almost all schools the requirement for the doctor of ministry tended to be a master of divinity, three years of experience, a year of residence (twenty-four to thirty academic credits), and a project in ministry.

In many ways the doctor of ministry was born out of season. Had it been born in the heyday of liberal theology, especially as developed at the University of Chicago, it might have pioneered another way of seriously thinking about the place of the church in the modern world. Had it been born in the late 1940s and 1950s when neoorthodoxy and the ecumenical movement were providing a renewed appreciation of the church and its work, it might have served as the

28. For an excellent summary of this history, see Jackson Carroll and Barbara Wheeler, "Doctor of Ministry Program: History, Summary of Findings and Recommendations," *Theological Education*, Spring 1987.

valuable bridge between the church's best thinking and its best practices. As it was, the degree was born in the midst of a serious and sustained theological crisis. There existed no models in this environment for the sustained reflection on pastoral practice envisioned by those who proposed the degree.

Further, the D.Min. came into being just as disciplinary understandings of the various theological fields were becoming normative. The trappings of university life — tenure, compulsory publication, specialization — had passed from the university divinity schools to almost all seminaries. As Edward Farley and others later pointed out, this division of the theological sciences provided little foundation for theological education as traditionally conceived as a reflective habitus. In short, the problems of the degree were not rooted, as many critics supposed, in its lack of theological content. On the contrary, the most serious problems of the doctor of ministry were directly related to the failure of theology, broadly conceived, to provide models for effective and sustained theological reflection.

Equally seriously, the degree did not speak to some real deficiencies in the theological preparation that most ministers received. Entering seminary with almost no biblical studies, for example, ministers left the schools with less sustained biblical study than many undergraduate religion majors. Similar observations could be made about the other classical theological disciplines. Once the various branches of theological study were seen as academic disciplines in their own right, the best that seminaries could hope to do was to provide an "introduction" and a few "electives" in each of those areas. Seminaries, consequently, often appeared to be offering a program that was often at the level of junior or senior year in college.

Why did the degree spread to most ATS schools within a few years of its approval? In part, its popularity was because the doctor of ministry offered an incentive for continuing education. The seminaries had long labored to interest ministers in continuing education, and some programs, such as the College of Preachers in Washington, D.C., attracted strong support. The Alban Institute, one of the survivors from the Intermet experiment, also enjoyed considerable popularity. But most continuing education programs strained to build enrollments; their expenditures also far exceeded their revenues. The doctor of ministry offered a way to tempt ministers to return to campus and reengage serious thought about their ministries: a small but valuable achievement. Perhaps more important, the seminaries faced a decline in enrollment just as their costs were increasing. The doctor of ministry was a possible solution to both emergencies, and the slight increase in prestige that the degree provided, especially in the South and West and among ethnic communities, such as Korean Christians, made it marketable.

IX. A Roman Revolution

People were astonished when the new pope, John XXIII, announced plans in 1959 to call an ecumenical council to deal with persistent tensions between the church and the modern world. In the United States, at least, Catholicism was flourishing as it never had before. Catholics moved up the social ladder rapidly after the Second World War, and the church's most powerful prelates, the archbishops of Boston, Philadelphia, New York, and Chicago, were major players on the national religious and political scenes. Catholic organizations also remained strong. The Catholic Church was clearly part of the postwar religious boom, and the election of John Kennedy in 1960 indicated how far the church had come in the decades since the anti-Catholicism of the Al Smith campaign.

The pontiff, however, was not primarily looking at his American children. In Europe the Catholic Church had been one of the losers of the Second World War. Staking much of its reputation on the various authoritarian dictatorships of the 1920s and 1930s, the church found itself saddled with concordats with Italy, Germany, Spain, and Portugal at the end of the war. The struggle against modernity and democracy that began with post-Napoleonic Europe had ended with the defeat of the conservative forces. If that were not enough, those areas of Europe that were most solidly Catholic were now in Communist hands, and the church faced both persecution and sustained anti-Catholic propaganda. In Italy and France, challenges from strong Communist parties and from a general atmosphere of secularism made the future seem insecure. Even in Latin America, where the church still enjoyed remnants of power and privilege, Protestantism was growing rapidly among the urban middle classes, as was Communism among the lower classes. For a number of years Catholic theologians in Holland and Germany had publicly worried about the church's position in the modern world, and Pope John realized that these problems had to be addressed. Aggiornamento was more than a slogan; it was a necessity.

Although many thought the council would be carefully managed from behind stage by the curia, this did not happen. The council began by rejecting early drafts of resolutions proposed by curial conservatives, and then proceeded to formulate and adopt carefully drawn statements on religious liberty, on the liturgy, and on the nature of the church as the people of God. These often had to be rewritten several times before the bishops were willing to accept them. Vatican II was among the most participatory councils in Christian history.

The various documents produced by the council, including *Lumen Gentium*, had considerable significance in their own right. The rigid top-down Catholicism that had characterized much modern Catholic life was replaced by a vision of the church based on the people of God. The new openness to Protestants and others marked a reversal of past Catholic positions and promised that the church might become an influential dialogue partner in many pluralist contexts. Yet, as significant as these formulations were, the new sense of a church on the move that did not face many predetermined limits was more important for what happened subsequently than the actual documents themselves.

This was true for the impact of the council on American Catholic theological education. Within a few short years the church moved away from a program of priestly formation that began with the minor or high school seminary and toward a pattern similar to the Protestant college and seminary. Changes inside seminary life were equally dramatic. The older pattern of theological study that stressed the mastery (and often memorization) of dogmatic manuals and canon law was replaced by lectures and seminars that required research and personal reflection. Seminary chapels were renovated to permit new, more experimental liturgical celebrations. Even small matters shifted. The wearing of clerical clothing, for example, became optional, except during special events, such as episcopal visitations. In some schools Protestant faculty members were hired to provide students with another understanding of theology, and many schools instituted lay training programs. Some Catholic sisters were also hired to teach in what had been a rigidly male preserve. Schools applied for and were granted Association of Theological School membership. In an interesting but ultimately unsuccessful experiment, Woodstock Seminary, one of the oldest and most prestigious Jesuit institutions, moved from its traditional Maryland campus to join Union Seminary (New York) on Morningside Heights. Rarely have institutions changed this much, this quickly. After less than a decade, few would have recognized Catholic theological education.

Protestants were not sure what these changes meant, but they found themselves applauding them and influenced by them. Catholic faculty members often joined Protestant faculties, and some Catholic theological language, especially words like "formation," became ubiquitous. Catholic theologians and biblical scholars were assigned in classes. Perhaps the most important set of changes had to do with the renovation of Protestant teaching in worship. Watered by the deep Catholic studies of the patristic era, Protestant theologians set out to create more traditional and, at the same, more modern forms of corporate worship. Over time these resulted in new orders of worship that replaced the sixteenth-century Reformation's one-sided emphasis on grace and forgiveness as the heart of the gospel with a more patristic concept of participation in the divine mysteries. American Protestants worshiped in a fuller and more corporate manner as a result of the council. For many years to come, liturgics would be one of the most exciting areas in the seminary curriculum.

Vatican II had a downside. Many priests and religious women and men left formal ministry behind them, many in order to marry. Initially many Catholic leaders reasoned that the ending of compulsory celibacy would be the next reform, and these hopes continued to be vivid into the 1980s.

Celibacy was only one reason for precipitous decline in the number of Catholic seminarians. Moreover, it was no longer as clear what it meant to be Catholic. In 1968 Pope Paul issued *Humanae Vitae,* condemning the use of artificial birth control. American post–Vatican II priests and people disobeyed the pronouncement, often after long struggles of conscience, and gradually came to a position indistinguishable from that of their Protestant and secular neighbors. Another reason for the declining numbers was the refusal of the church to consider ordaining women priests. Although not as dramatic, Protestants had faced a similar decline in the number of male candidates for ministry and had used women ministers to staff their pulpits.

Facing rapid declines in enrollment, Catholic seminaries were unable to keep pace with the need for replacements. Just as they were instituting reforms that greatly increased their economic costs, their resources in both students and financial support declined rapidly. Like their Protestant counterparts, they became involved in a constant quest for new revenues, including development programs, student recruiters, lay programs, ecumenical doctor of ministry programs, and other such experiments.

Historians can easily miss the importance of what did not happen in Catholic theological education in the 1960s. In the 1950s Catholic theology was poised for a major advance, and given Catholic numbers and wealth, one might have predicted a "Catholic" age in American theology. The expected theological renaissance did not happen, although much credible work was completed. Despite the expansion of theology departments in Catholic colleges, the decline in vocations weakened the financial and institutional base that could have supported a thorough renewal of American Catholic thought.

X. The World Is Too Much with Us

Student demonstrations and riots are the best-known events in the educational history of the 1960s. As the Vietnam War accelerated, colleges, universities, and seminaries were struck by a series of student demonstrations that seemed to rock those institutions to their foundations (see above, p. 749). The schools most affected were schools whose faculty and administration had long-standing reputations as defenders of liberal causes and much of whose leadership was already publicly committed to opposition to the war. Thus, New York's Union Seminary and nearby Columbia University were among the schools most impacted by the wave of protests. The high point of the student revolts occurred in 1970, when the invasion of Cambodia set off a nationwide wave of protests. This time, however, the unthinkable happened: students were killed at Kent State in Ohio and Jackson State in Mississippi. The wave of incidents then gradually receded until they became less commonplace. By 1976 student protests were rare events. Not surprising given the penchant of academics for self-examination and analysis, book after book appeared attempting to explain what had happened and what had gone wrong with the American educational enterprise. The sheer mass of paper suggested that American education might be preparing for a series of reforms comparable to those of the post–Civil War era.

A general sense of bad conscience around issues of war and peace permeated the seminaries. During the 1920s and 1930s the vast majority of Protestant church leaders supported some version of Christian pacifism, and the internal battle over support of a war against the Axis Powers had continued up until the bombing of Pearl Harbor. Although many continued to rally to the flag after the end of hostilities, deep discomfort remained, especially around the question of the use of nuclear weapons. Most American Christians, further, had applauded the decline of Western imperialism in Asia and Africa. At best, they were reluctant players in contemporary realpolitik.

Students in the late 1960s could, consequently, mine a rich vein of guilt on the part of the Protestant establishment. Even before the publication of the Pentagon Papers, a collection of official government documents that highlighted the decisions that had led to the conflict, many seminary teachers felt pangs of guilt over American foreign policy in Asia. Thus, while they disagreed with the student techniques in making their voices heard, they were very much in harmony with the message they had believed in the 1930s.[29] Many were further emboldened by the relative success of the churches in their support of civil rights laws.

Next to the issue of war and peace, no set of issues was more perplexing for the church than the questions raised by the sexual revolution. Studies of sexual behavior in America had long identified a gap between the nation's public professions and its private practices, and this gap apparently widened even further after the pill became readily available. The signs of a massive shift in national mores were everywhere to be seen: rising divorce rates, young people living together before marriage, the public availability of sexually explicit materials, and subtle shifts in the amount of sexual material that was available through the mainstream media. Manuals of sexual instruction, previously

29. Many seminary leaders had been members of the various Protestant youth organizations that were central to the pacifism of the 1930s.

available only under the counter of "certain" bookstores, were now on the best-seller list.

The sexual revolution largely found the seminaries unprepared, despite their heavy investments in counseling and religious psychology. Like the popular Catholic rejection of papal pronouncements on birth control, the change in mores happened more or less independent of ecclesiastical teaching or contemporary ethical theory. It just happened. Even in the 1960s it was clear that the issues raised by the new patterns of sexual behavior would be divisive. A series of court decisions, beginning with *Griswold v. Connecticut* (1965), struck down laws prohibiting the sale and distribution of contraceptives, and in 1973 *Roe v. Wade* ended most restrictions on abortion. In these decisions the courts effectively removed government from much of the regulation of private behavior that American law had long proscribed, and other restrictive laws, such as those prohibiting sodomy, were clearly marked for judicial repeal.

Although American conservative theology and institutions had been growing for some time, issues of sexual morality and the church's public stance toward them helped to spark an unprecedented growth of American conservatives. They also contributed to the rise of a new American religious conservatism that was deeply concerned with issues around the family.

American evangelical seminaries clearly benefited from this controversy. During the 1950s these schools had begun to win a significant place in American theological education. Fuller Seminary, for instance, demonstrated that evangelicals could win both accreditation and respect for one of their flagship institutions, and Gordon and Trinity had already begun to develop into major conservative centers. The excitement and verve of conservative evangelical institutions would have remade the American Protestant map in any event. Billy Graham and Bill Bright, for instance, had already devised effective means to use the American media society for Christian ends, just as such thinkers as Edward J. Carnell and Carl F. H. Henry had proved that they could participate meaningfully in the larger debate. If *Christianity Today* had not yet become a conservative equivalent of the *Christian Century,* it was well on its way. Yet the conclusion that conservative seminaries were aided and influenced by the debate over "lifestyle" issues has much warrant. Even more than Vietnam and other such political issues, sexual ethics and the protection of the morals of the coming generation touched evangelicals deeply and affected their everyday lives. And conservatives were afraid they no longer represented a majority on such questions. This had many consequences for evangelical life. Evangelicals quickly abandoned the apolitical stance that had characterized them in the past. Someone had to say something and say it effectively and earnestly. Perhaps because so many evangelicals had roots in the Baptist and Methodist traditions, both historically more open to social sciences than their Reformed counterparts, these departments in conservative seminaries began to flourish. Conservative seminaries and churches also began to discover a need for "Christian psychology and counseling" that could provide biblically based answers for those facing sexual and family-related issues. Fuller Seminary's accredited School of Psychology took leadership in this area and was followed by similar, if smaller, initiatives at other schools.

Liberal schools were likewise affected. The basic liberal stance approved of culture and often treated cultural life as a source of revelation. Somehow profound truths had to be at hand in the changes that were taking place. Vast cultural shifts, consequently, could not be ignored or combated. Liberals wanted to understand those changes and hopefully influence them. Liberals had used this basic strategy in dealing with such intellectual revolutions as Darwinism, social science, and race, and they had no ready alternative approach to the society at hand.

Part of the problem liberals faced was that Christian Scripture and church tradition were solidly against the moral changes taking place in the society. The New Testament, written in the very sexually lax world of the first-century Roman Empire, exhorted Christians to distinguish themselves from the world by exercising sexual self-control, and whatever social practices might or might not have existed, the church continued through its history to hold a very high standard of sexual restraint. Luther and Calvin, although strong advocates of sex in marriage, were equally strong advocates of sexual discipline. Part of the aftermath of the Reformation, for instance, had been the closing of many houses of ill repute and the keeping of careful parish registers of marriages, births, and deaths. Modern Catholicism had been, if anything, even more rigid in its formal teaching. In past times of moral laxity, the church had always insisted that Christians needed to stand apart from the moral corruptions of the age. In addition, American Protestants had a long and historic fascination with the public control of sexual behavior.[30] In short, few responses lay at hand to handle the questions.

The basic approach to the changed situation was to follow suggestions in Bonhoeffer's *Ethics* and in H. Richard Niebuhr's *Responsible Self*, and to stress the importance of acting ethically within a situation or context. Paul Lehmann's *Ethics in a Christian Context* (1963) was a careful attempt to define how Christians might use their own location as believing and moral persons within a Christian community to make moral decisions. But the work that at-

30. See James Morone, *Hellfire Nation* (New Haven and London: Yale University Press, 2003).

tracted the most attention was Joseph Fletcher's *Situation Ethics* (1963). In this volume Fletcher, an Episcopal theologian, posited that what was right and wrong in a particular situation depended on the presence or absence of self-giving love. Thus, loveless sex in marriage might be ethically irresponsible, and sex in a loving relationship outside of marriage, even an adulterous one, ethically acceptable. To many, this seemed like no ethical guidance at all, especially when compared with the certainties of the Ten Commandments.

For good or for ill, both liberal and conservative seminaries were deeply immersed in various social issues by 1970. It was hardly a good omen for their future. The mainstream schools had often seen themselves as comprehensive institutions, but the new climate of opinion did not encourage comprehensiveness. The questions were often binary, and if particular academic thinkers wanted to stress the subtleties in their positions, outsiders and even colleagues understood them as standing on one side or the other of the question. In this case "horns of the dilemma" was more than a figure of speech. Many people on both sides lay in wait for a theologian or ethicist to step over their imaginary lines.

XI. The Wolf at the Door

The sixties were crisis enough for most educational institutions, and even in the most comfortable schools they caused serious thought and examination. But they were even more serious for seminaries. When James McCord replaced the popular and able John Mackay at Princeton in 1961, the Presbyterian flagship institution was running a serious deficit. His institution was not alone. Princeton's rival across the Hudson, Union, was also facing hidden but growing financial deficits that would total almost $500,000 a year by the end of the decade.[31] Other schools faced similar problems. Costs were rising at a rate of 12 to 14 percent a year, and few schools had new sources of income in sight. Seminary education had passed legal education in costs and was among the most expensive forms of professional education in America. The best projection was that costs would double in the next decade, and many popular proposals for reform would increase that by four or five times. Further, some historic patterns of injustice needed correction. Faculty salaries, for instance, were often as much as 41 percent lower than that of their secular counterparts. Even had the sixties been as placid as the fifties are popularly believed to have been, the end of the

31. Linda Marie Delloff, "Union Theological Seminary," *Christianity and Crisis*, Apr. 9, 1990, p. 119.

decade would have found many of the nation's seminaries in crisis. Many were predicting that some seminaries might have to close their doors, and others believed that only a thorough reorganization of the whole seminary system could save the enterprise.

In response to the financial crisis, the American Association of Theological Schools appointed the Resource Commission, a blue-ribbon panel composed of Arthur Mackay (McCormick), John Dillenberger (Graduate Theological Union), Paul Harrison (University of Pennsylvania), Lynn Leavenworth (American Baptist Convention), Edward Malone (Maryknoll Missioner of Maryknoll Seminary), and Henry Pitney Van Dusen (president emeritus of Union Seminary). They were joined by the association staff, led by Jesse Ziegler, David Schuller, and Charlotte Thompson. Warren Deem of Arthur D. Little, a leading accounting firm, provided the commission with needed expertise. The commission optimistically stated that "while the number of seminaries experiencing operating deficits has increased, seminaries generally seem to have been able to increase income at a rate commensurate with consistent operating costs."[32] But that was the only comforting conclusion. More threateningly, the commission noted a pattern of rising costs for administration, faculty, and facilities at a time when "no significant new sources of funding for theological education have emerged," and national church bodies paid only a small portion of the cost of educating their candidates.[33]

One of the most distressing findings of the Resource Commission was that, despite all the talk about new forms of theological education, the seminaries were not engaging in serious financial planning and modern cost-oriented bookkeeping. In striking language the commission asserted: "Few seminaries appear to have attempted the unglamorous job of calculating, even in very preliminary ways, cost consequences and income requirements of the educational goals which they hold for their institutions for the years ahead." Hence, planning was often little more than acknowledging the need for new faculty or for improvements in facilities. Basically, schools assumed financially that the world would always continue much as it always had.[34] This, however, led to the commission's most pointed and accurate charge. Many schools were in de facto bankruptcy. In other words, they had entered into a survival mode that made it difficult for them to make any significant changes. At best they could rearrange their intellectual and financial furniture.

The commission strongly believed that the way forward lay through in-

32. "Resource Commission Report," *Theological Education,* Summer 1968, p. 39.

33. "Resource Commission Report," p. 40.

34. "Resource Commission Report," p. 56.

creasing patterns of cooperation, ranging from the merger of several institutions, to the banding together of various schools for specific purposes, to informal patterns of mutual help and support. They had good examples of the power of such cooperation in the International Theological Center in Atlanta, the Graduate Theological Union in Berkeley, and the Boston Theological Institute. The potential savings from cooperation were significant. Sharing a president, for example, permitted two institutions to save on the costs of the central administration, but, if anything, the potential gains from sharing such underutilized resources as faculty, library, and buildings were even greater. These savings might finance the changes that so many believed were so desperately needed.

If nothing else, the Resource Commission exposed what many had suspected about American theological education: it remained a largely mom-and-pop operation in an America that increasingly demanded administrative expertise. Indeed, it was vital that seminaries move toward more modern accounting and planning processes and that they project out their costs over several years. Indeed, the high percentage of seminary expense that went to salaries made this a relatively simple step that should have been self-evident to those guiding the enterprise. The report also made it brutally clear how much American theological education paid for its dispersion into a number of small schools that often duplicated and reduplicated each other's efforts, even within the same locality. In a world of ecumenical theology in which few people understood or appreciated the differences between denominations, this seemed a high price to pay for distinctives that were more a matter of history than of present reality. It was a soulful refrain of too many schools for the market to bear.

There was another response to the same situation. James McCord, Princeton's new president, understood himself as a professional seminary leader, and he set out to make Princeton a model of financial respectability and strength. McCord's understanding of his place at Princeton was similar to that of the presidents of Southern Baptist seminaries, especially Duke McCall of Southern, and, like them, he was determined to graft a modern educational management team on the traditional tangle of seminary government, and also like them, he was willing to override faculty and even denominational opinion to achieve his goals. As a result, Princeton largely escaped the tensions and experiments that had such effect at its sister school across the Hudson. But above all, McCord believed that the president had to head up a continual fund-raising effort. Under his leadership, Princeton became the best-endowed theological seminary in the country.

McCord paid a price for his success, as did the more entrepreneurial presidents that followed his example. Seminary presidents had traditionally served as public theologians for their denominations, speaking and writing on the issues confronting the denomination. At their best they had given direction and shape to theological change in their churches, and sometimes in larger contexts. Such leadership was simply not possible for someone with McCord's understanding of his office. Despite his almost unlimited energy and theological appetite, only so many hours existed in his day.

XII. A Time of Crisis

As the sixties flowed into the seventies, American Protestant theological education came to an important crossroads in its history. A sense of crisis and confusion seemed everywhere. Many of these crises were not the results of fads or momentary excitements. The theological crisis had been building for a decade or more; the racial crisis was America's longest-standing public disgrace; and the administrative and financial crisis had deep roots in the very nature of the seminary as a small institution. The decline of the Protestant mainstream, already well under way by 1970, would complicate these problems, and the vocational crisis among Catholic and Protestant males would continue to the present. It was a time for wise people to stop and reflect seriously on what the future might bring.

Conclusion

Given the diversity of American Protestantism, theological educators had reached a remarkable degree of consensus about the nature of their task. Good theological education was graduate professional education, conducted in schools that were either independent or semiautonomous parts of a university. Part of the measure of their success would be that the Association of Theological Schools (ATS) in the United States and Canada became the principal spokesman for those who educated religious leaders. After 1970 the association entered a period of unprecedented prosperity. Many evangelical and Roman Catholic schools petitioned for and received membership and accreditation. Deep divisions ran through American Christianity, but the ATS was an ecumenical organization that in time of ecclesiastical peace and ecclesiastical war found a deeper unity. The ATS continued to evolve its standards, and its increasingly numerous and well-supported programs of education and leadership training provided the leaders of theological schools with a common set of "best practices" they could use to guide their institutions. At a time when various cultural wars engulfed American denominations and local congregations, this unity was no mean achievement. Not surprisingly, the ATS would receive strong financial support from the Lilly Endowment under the leadership of both Robert Lynn and Craig Dykstra.

The success of the ATS rested on the achievements of Protestant theological educators in the period from 1870 to 1970. Although theological education remained diverse, the seminaries had come to a common understanding of theological education that saw it as a combination of the scholarly study of Christianity and the transmission of the skills and insights needed in contemporary pastoral ministry. Although Protestant and later Catholic and evangelical theological educators tried to find a measure of unity in this larger picture, the plain truth may be that none existed. The theological schools did not, for example, offer a program that united theory and practice, nor did they develop a program based solely on the "best practices" in the profession. Rather, in the face of the challenges of modernity, the schools attempted to bring together many semiautonomous or autonomous university disciplines with the best they knew about the contemporary church and its practices. In a sense, the unity was in the challenge: both the so-called classical and the new practical disciplines worked at relating the faith to an ever changing modern world. Yet the intellectual and practical means of meeting that challenge varied greatly. They rarely, if ever, spoke with a common voice. Attempts to square the circle by making all seminary study advanced theological research or by making seminaries schools for ministry were unsuccessful. The genius of the institutions was that they were both unflinchingly graduate and unreservedly practical.

The intellectual achievements of Protestant theological educators from 1870 to 1970 were considerable. The challenges to meaningful Christian faith in that difficult century cut to the very core of inherited belief and practice. Biblical criticism and evolution, to name only two, called for a major rethinking of Christian theology and for the introduction of new modes of theological analysis. If the seminaries did nothing else, they provided a place where men and women of good will and intellectual ability could discuss those questions with a high degree of personal and intellectual integrity. The result was a rich harvest of American theologies, ranging from early progressive orthodoxy to later process theology that dug deep beneath the inherited beliefs of many believers and ecclesiastical leaders. Like the theologians of the late Middle Ages, who faced the challenge of a new Aristotelian philosophy, American theological liberals had much on their plates. If all of what they wrote did not become part of a library of Christian classics, it is in part because the issues were too large to be solved in a generation or even two or three. That so much was accomplished was miracle enough.

Equally important, the new currents of thought generated new forms of theological orthodoxy. Part of the irony of church history is that innovation and change often occur before the orthodox faith is settled or sometimes even known. After all, ancient orthodoxy was a response to the growth of Gnosticism, not Gnosticism to ancient orthodoxy. Throughout much of the period that we have studied, conservative theology was in the shadow of its liberal cousin. The liberals held the most prestigious seminaries and benefited from the support of the most active philanthropists, and the combination of status and money seemed to make them the clear winners. But human events are much more complicated than deconstruction would allow. Thoughtful conservatives, ranging from Machen to Carnell, continued to find in biblical orthodoxy eternal truths, and this theological creativity naturally led to the establishment of new seminaries. Like their liberal counterparts, conservative American theologians were willing to take new directions, to formulate new teachings, and to explore new ecclesiastical practices, including the creative use of radio and television. American conservatism was not simply the older Protestant faith republished for a new audience; it was a unique product of the same spiritual and intellectual voices that created the liberal tradition.

The seeming polarization of progressive and conservative theology is of course partly a historian's useful fiction. One outcome of the new theological situation was that theologians discovered, for good or ill, that theology was always done in a particular voice and for a particular time. Just as in the Middle Ages, when dragons could be fought only by knights brave of heart and true of spirit, so the dragon of modernity summoned the best that the churches could provide. But modernity was not any old beast. Like shifting chimeras, each new decade between 1870 and 1970 seemed to cast the modern in a new form and to give it new weapons. Its opponents and proponents likewise changed. Often, much like a great painter, an American theologian would pass through several periods in his or her intellectual and religious development. In citing the multitalented Reinhold Niebuhr, for example, the historian needs to put a date with each observation and carefully identify the context of every quotation. Niebuhr had enough theologies for a whole generation of thinkers! Likewise, the late 1940s Carl F. H. Henry was very different from the 1970s model. Such changes of direction were perhaps most evident in theology and in ethics, but they were also found in all the theological disciplines.

In discussing the intellectual achievement of the modern seminary, the expanded knowledge of the Bible must be highlighted. Although a handful of universities before 1970 sponsored biblical studies, the bulk of biblical work was produced by seminary professors, often working with limited library and research facilities, who kept to their work like a dog at a bone. Gradually the nature of Israel's language and its place in the complex cultural world of the ancient Near East became clearer, as did the nature of the language and context of the New Testament. No matter how often particular conclusions have been replaced by later, more adequate studies, the foundations of basic methods established in this period have remained.

The biblical fields pioneered the division of theology into a number of separate intellectual disciplines. An intellectual discipline was as much a matter of mind as of social organization. Basically, scholars constituted a discipline when they taught a specific subject, researched the issues involved in that subject, and limited admission to their own ranks by formal and/or informal means. From the beginning, a discipline was a network of people, publications, and places that enabled human knowledge to advance. To extend the metaphor, it was a nationwide seminar in which new ideas could be tested and approved. Disciplinary study was not the same as genius. The disciplinary approach permitted scholars of average abilities and attainments to participate in the onward development of knowledge by providing them with a secure root to new knowledge. Each disciplinary generation, in effect, began where the previous one had left off. By the turn of the century, the seminary was the home to a number of disciplines and, like other educational institutions, was capable of generating new disciplines as they were needed. Some of these new disciplines were subdivisions of older disciplines, but some also represented genuine new beginnings.

The creation of the theological disciplines underlay the intellectual excitement of much of the last century. If the talented amateur might still find a place on some faculties, the goal of most seminary administrators was to attract as many bright practitioners of the theological disciplines as possible. In part, the hope was that these scholars would attract new students, but this was not the only motivation. The schools were devoted to the premise that learning was of fundamental value, that discovery was in and of itself good, and they wanted people who could meet the current benchmarks of scholarly achievement.

The creation of the disciplinary seminary was one of the gifts of this century to its post-1970s successors. For all the problems of the disciplinary seminary, the school was able to examine the Christian faith from a significant number of methodologically different perspectives. And seminaries were able to claim with real justification that they were part of the larger scholarly community, the modern equivalent of the Renaissance republic of letters.

The seminaries in this period also confronted a major change in the social location and understanding of Christian ministry. Like many changes that slowly occur over a long time, this one is maddeningly difficult to date, but it is all too evident at its beginning and end. In the early nineteenth century, despite the rise of the belief that the pastor should be primarily an evangelist, especially among many Baptists and Methodists, the ideal pastor was a resident intellectual and was expected to be primarily a teacher of religious and moral truth, and seminary education was designed (even among Baptists and Methodists) to produce a person skilled in thought, speech, and pen. The better clergy were often active in the larger intellectual life of their cities and villages, and it was not unusual for someone to move easily from ministry to the equally congenial task of being a public intellectual or a college president or professor. People assumed that the skills necessary to the one sphere were also suited to the other.

By 1900 this understanding was in tatters. If no one was completely sure what the pastor needed to be in the modern world, an uncertainty that continues today, thoughtful people no longer regarded the pastor as primarily a teacher or intellectual leader. In many ways the princes of the pulpit reflected this change. Such pastors as Phillips Brooks were more masters of inspiration than masters of doctrine, and other ministers, such as Washington Gladden, saw themselves, at least in part, as agents of social change. Churches were also more complex. No longer simply communities of Word and sacrament, congregations were also the site of many different organizations, including the Sunday school, various missionary organizations, and occasionally even young men's and young women's clubs. Every successful minister was the administrator of a small charity. Interestingly enough, by 1900 the link between service in colleges and in the ministry had begun to break. Few ministers moved from pulpit to desk, and even in religiously related colleges, the ministerial president was becoming a rarity. Ministry was its own profession.

What is remarkable about how the seminaries responded to this change is not that they squared the circle and made everything come out right. They did not do so, and perhaps could not have done so. But from an early period they did begin to develop courses and strategies to enable pastors to cope with these changing conditions. Room was made in the curriculum, usually by reducing the long hours of language drills, for courses in religious education, counseling, hospital visitation, sociology, psychology, missions, evangelism, and church leadership. Further, a significant place was found for social ethics, often called "applied Christianity," and efforts were made to keep ministers open to the broader world in which they would serve. Interestingly, many of these new subjects were pioneered in the Bible schools and in the various women's missionary training institutes.

Perhaps the most important new innovation was field education. Nothing like this had ever existed in the traditional forms of theological education. In the colonial period, to be sure, a young man lived with an older pastor, but the older pastor was expected to keep the young candidate at the books and at the desk. Reading divinity was essentially directed study. In contrast, field education was the recognition that many of the skills and sensitivities needed in modern ministry were best learned from those who had those skills. Clinical education, which developed from a similar insight, became a crucial part of this search for a relevant and useful preparation for ministry.

The practical fields also opened up new dialogues for the seminaries with modern sociology and psychology. These modern intellectual disciplines — and the various professions, such as social work, that they helped spawn — had much in common with theology and, perhaps more importantly, with modern ministerial practice. Even those theological educators who wanted to preserve the tradition pure and undefiled found that these disciplines offered perspectives and techniques that could be avoided only at a minister's peril. And this peril was real. American attitudes toward sex, divorce, alcohol, and entertainment shifted at almost breakneck speed, and well-equipped churchmen needed the perspective of the social sciences and helping professions to stay in the game.

Theological educators also succeeded in finding a place for themselves in the whirling system of American higher education. During the last part of the nineteenth century, American education began to assume the form it has retained to the present. Basically, the older system of elementary education in the home or private school followed by academy and occasionally college was replaced by a more open-ended system that began with state-sponsored elementary education. This was followed by a high school program that included many of the sciences and skills needed by the new expanding industrial economy as well as some traditional college preparatory classes, including Latin, and some of the new disciplines, such as English and history, that were replacing the traditional classical program of the colleges. Despite much debate, American educators retained the college, but they completely transformed it. Rather than the traditional classical program, the new college was a transitional institution that provided both a general educational degree, generally called the bachelor of arts, and the more practical bachelor of science. In both programs the emphasis was primarily on a broad education combined with a concentration or major. Interestingly, some professional programs, especially in such fields as education and social work, made their basic training part of the bachelor's degree, often building their professional work on the first two years of general study. This pattern was common in all professions. Medical and law schools often allowed students to begin their professional work after the second or third year; a full degree became the standard requirement only after the Second World War. Interestingly, the traditional master of arts program was retained, and until the great expansion of Ph.D. programs after the Second World War, it served to train many collegiate instructors as well as the most advanced high school instructors.

Where did theological education fit into this complex thicket? Early seminaries had not granted degrees although they required college before entry, and the functional standard was the ability to read Latin and understand some Greek. To this foundation the seminary added a program of Hebrew, biblical studies, and theology, with various schools adding courses in preaching and pastoral practice. There was an organic link between the work of the traditional college and that of the traditional seminary. No one needed to puzzle over questions like why college was seen as preparatory or which skills were needed for study.

The new situation was undefined. As the classical component of the bachelor of arts declined — a decline that was matched by the decline of the use of Greek and Hebrew in theological classes — the intellectual justification for the graduate status of theology became more suspect. Many felt that theological study ought to begin at the conclusion of the college general education program, basically after two years of study, and the bachelor of theology degree remained popular until the 1950s. Others, especially the leaders of the more prestigious and wealthier schools, believed that the bachelor of arts was essential preparation. They popularized the bachelor of divinity degree as the appropriate symbol of this understanding of the seminary. Before 1930, almost all schools admitted nondegree candidates, who often outnumbered the degree candidates by a wide margin.

Accreditation and, ironically, given the American separation of church and state, the actions of the federal government settled the issue at the time. The mark of a good seminary became the bachelor of divinity degree (later the master of divinity degree), which was understood to rest on a solid bachelor of arts degree. It was a high mark, and the postwar revival of religion brought the schools and the churches enough money to put it in reach. While some schools, particularly such Baptist citadels as Eastern Baptist, suffered from the new standards, most basked in it. To their faculties and graduates, the triumph of the college-seminary pattern reflected the coming of age of American theological education. The degree itself would soon proudly become a master of divinity. And for a season, seminaries were able not only to insist on graduates from a bachelor's program but to define some of the elements of a good preparatory bachelor's degree, much as medical schools insisted on some courses in a premed degree.

The postwar religious boom, at least in retrospect, was a bump in the history of American Protestantism. While it filled American Protestants with a sense of pride and achievement — they could even see themselves as the soul of the nation — it was not destined to last. By the 1970s, theological schools — faced with a new round of increasing costs in higher education as a whole and a declining ecclesiastical base — would be again facing financial difficulties. In turn, these would lead some increasingly to question the four-three pattern and the whole degree structure. The idea of certain courses as part of necessary preparation for seminary went quickly by the board. But the dominance of the M.Div. and its implicit four-three pattern has continued for fifty years and promises to continue for some time.

One of the fractures in this system, barely perceived in 1970, was that it reflected an ecology of Protestant institutions. The seminary was closely related to the denominational college; the college recruited many of its students from the local church's youth group and its state and local pyramid organizations;

the youth groups recruited from Christian camp; and the Christian camp, in turn, was stocked by the Sunday school. This ecology nurtured a person's decision to enter "full-time Christian service" over several decades. While obviously not every young person who was involved in this organizational structure entered the ministry, it was impossible for a young person to escape the "claim of Christ" on his or her life. After the postwar revival faded and these organizations declined in numbers and influence, the seminaries found it increasingly difficult to recruit new students, especially young males.

The "feeder schools" were particularly important to the pre-1970s seminary. In addition to a steady supply of students, these institutions formed a vertical intellectual community. Scholarly seminary graduates were often recruited to teach in their departments of Bible and religion, and seminaries often sought replacements for their own faculties from the faculties of these schools. The seminary, consequently, was always related to the collegiate world. After 1960 many denominational colleges in the North became secular institutions, a pattern later repeated in the South.

A historian does not have to be a postmodernist or particularly given to deconstruction to note that the seminary circa 1970 was a thoroughly middle-class institution that, despite its departments of social ethics and occasional student radicals, represented the values of middle-class America. Just as the Protestant churches were at home on the nation's Main Streets, so the seminary was at home in the post–World War II world of expanding professional opportunities and middle-class expectations. In a sense this had always been so. Baptists and Methodists, who began with a lower-class and lower middle-class membership, joined the club of denominations with theological schools as they developed middle-class congregations, just as other churches of the dispossessed, such as the Assemblies of God, would follow the same path. Indeed, one of the great strengths of the seminary in this period was its capacity to take a variety of candidates for the ministry and provide them with the status and education that enabled them to mingle easily with an increasingly educated and prosperous constituency.

The unspoken alliance with the white middle classes was also the seminaries' greatest liability. By 1970 the seminary's friends and critics were equally aware that the schools had not served African Americans, women, or other minority groups. In this sense, corporately and institutionally, the seminary was part of the American tragedy of racism.

The historian studying African American theological education in this period must self-consciously note the story of both a racial and a cognitive minority. On the one hand, the story of African American religion can be seen as a creative response to the realities of exclusion. As in the antebellum period, African Americans found new ways to make do with what they had at hand, using elementary schools, a few high schools, and a handful of seminaries and universities to educate their pastors. In retrospect, one is amazed at their accomplishments. Despite many problems, all of which were noted by sociologists at the time, African American churches often attracted some of the group's most able leaders, and to a remarkable degree these men and women maintained and at times deepened the religious and theological traditions they shared with their white coreligionists. As African American colleges passed slowly under African American leadership, they produced some of the most able religious leaders of the twentieth century, including such powerful figures as Martin Luther King and Howard Thurman.

Moreover, the isolation of the African American community functioned, as did other forms of ethnic separation, to enable African American churches and their ministers to continue religious traditions over a comparatively long period of time. The characteristic African American combination of inherited elements of religious worship, especially in music and preaching, with various American evangelical theologies made for a powerful and unique theological and religious tradition. Many elements of this remarkable religious movement passed into the Pentecostal and charismatic movement that shaped so much of twentieth-century American Christianity. Less directly, African Americans influenced American evangelicals, who found themselves singing gospel music in their churches and listening to it on the radio.

On the other hand, the historian must also acknowledge the sad truth that "poverty sucks." In excluding African Americans from advanced theological education, the mainstream Protestant churches, North and South, condemned the African American pastor to cultural marginality. No matter how large the church or how brilliant the sermons, the African American pastor was still by and large seen as ignorant and was not taken seriously by his white contemporaries. Few had the tools or the sophistication to analyze and critique the traditions they had inherited. Perhaps even more tragic, few had the means to address the white majority on the depth of their people's plight in a hostile promised land. If discrimination and segregation were the manure that fertilized African American religion, manure, no matter how beneficial, still smells.

Perhaps the highest price seminary educators paid for their discrimination against African Americans was intellectual. Both liberal and conservative theologians agree about the seriousness of the intellectual crisis that confronted and still confronts the churches as they seek to find their place in a scientific and secular world. In not finding ways to include African Americans in advanced theological study, theological educators did more than deprive the emerging black middle classes of needed sophisticated leadership. They robbed themselves and their churches of the intellectual abilities and cultural heritage of a large percentage of the nation's Protestants.

The women's issue was similar, but more complicated. Although the standards of most American denominations prohibited the ordination of women, women gradually entered ecclesiastical employment. The missionary movement of the late nineteenth century employed women in increasing numbers in various nonparochial ministries at home and abroad, and American congregations quickly followed suit, hiring women for such positions as directors of religious education. Although the education for these positions was often referred to as "training," it provided women with a natural entry into theological education. As some of these newer ministries matured, they increasingly demanded a program of professional education that met particular standards. The master of religious education was the most common designation for these programs. Although many of those teaching religious education in theological schools were male, the position was one of the few available to women on pre-1970 theological faculties. The library was the other. While these positions could enable a handful of women, such as the talented Georgia Harkness, to enter into other, almost all-male, domains, religious education was often a "pink ghetto" in both seminary and church. The real movement of women into the seminaries and into the pastoral office took place after 1970.

Particularly after the Second World War, women entered seminaries indirectly as the wives of male seminary students. In many ways their presence on campus transformed the schools from semimonastic communities to communities that more closely resembled the world in which ministry would take place. The wives were also a seemingly endless source of financing as they often worked to pay for their husbands' education. The schools celebrated this in mock fashion when they awarded the wives the PHT degree (putting hubby through) during graduation week. The indirect, but real, subsidy provided by the spouses' labor enabled the seminaries of the 1950s and 1960s to attract the youngest seminary population in history and permitted the practice of charging tuition to spread from the elite schools to more modest institutions.

The losses from the virtual exclusion of women from the master of divinity program and the professoriate are difficult to calculate. The churches were predominately women's organizations, and the contribution of the Protestant minister's wife had long been essential, or nearly so, to the ministry. Most churches were in fact hiring two for the price of one, and the tendency of post-1960s ministers' wives to work outside the home often brought a painful adjustment to many congregations. The women's revolution that began in the 1960s, consequently, was not about women's presence in theological education or the church, but about women's power and influence in the churches and the schools. Working out the implications of this would be among the major tasks of the seminary after 1970.

The failure to incorporate African Americans and women into the Protestant seminary was evident to many, if not most, Protestant theological educators in 1970. The civil rights and women's movements were, after all, regularly discussed in countless newspapers and in such magazines as *Time* and *Newsweek*. If the situation has any surprising element, it is that theological educators were, by and large, convinced that they would be able to handle these issues with few, if any, real structural or ideological changes. The challenges would prove greater than anyone anticipated.

What seminary leaders did not anticipate was their changed place in the intellectual and educational world. The 1960s seminary had been based on a certain understanding of the place of theological education. Although seminaries had long been small fish in a large pond, the educational changes that followed the Second World War and that accelerated after 1970 turned the world upside down. In simple terms, the educational world became increasingly democratic as the number of people with either a bachelor's degree or a bachelor's degree plus graduate study soared. At the same time, the number of colleges, universities, professional schools, and junior colleges likewise increased, as higher education became a major component in the American economy. As the relative position of the seminary declined, so did the seminaries' capacity to raise money and attract executive leadership. With the exception of a handful of schools, including Princeton — soon to be the best-endowed seminary in the world — the seminaries became country cousins, often underfunded and underappreciated.

By 1970 many seminaries were just beginning to struggle with the implications of their changed location in the American educational world. With the exception of such university-related schools as Harvard, Yale, and Union, most seminaries had managed to avoid all but nominal tuition charges. This practice reached back deep into the nineteenth century when seminaries were founded for the education of "poor but pious" youth for the ministry, and beyond that to the English tradition of appointing scholarship students to church positions. But this was changing, along with other aspects of seminary finance. As American higher education grew, the costs connected with schools increased as well. The seminaries were in the same position as America's mom-and-pop stores. Retailing had come to rely on marketers, advertisers, skilled accountants, and other professional leaders. Likewise, education had come to require deans, registrars, development officers, and admissions specialists. During the two decades after the Second World War, the better seminaries had taken steps toward a more complex bureaucratic structure; after 1970, the pressures on all schools to follow their lead would increase.

The new complexity encouraged the end of the imperial presidencies of the seminary past. The story of theological education from 1870 to 1970 was largely the story of great presidents, such as William Rainey Harper and Henry Pitney Van Dusen, who were able to articulate strong visions for their schools and to implement them. The American Association of Theological Schools was a presidents' club where strong leaders met to set the standards for the schools and to exchange ideas about theological education's future. The post-1970s president would have to share power with other administrators, including the dean, and faculties would increasingly demand and get a larger role in the appointment of new colleagues. The president was on the way to becoming the chief fund-raiser and public voice of an institution, while others directed the everyday operation of the schools.

This volume carried the discussion of the academic study of religion well beyond 1970. In part, this was because history is rarely neat. Some parts of a larger story do not end with the neat chronological precision that the historian hopes exists in the sources that he or she has examined. But, in this case, the reason for the elongated treatment is, I hope, more profound. With the success of the American Academy of Religion (AAR) and, more important, the various college and university departments supporting it, the seminaries lost the virtual monopoly they had possessed on American religious scholarship. From the 1870s onward, the seminaries had been the primary interpreters of such intellectual phenomena as biblical criticism, the changing position of religion in the national culture, and the impact of science on religious faith. With the success of the AAR, this ended. Gradually the center of American religious scholarship shifted toward the college and the university. While creditable research continued to be done in seminaries, theological schools were no longer dominant in the one area where they proved their larger cultural value.

One of life's ironies is that the pie maker rarely gets to eat the pie. Part of the American definition of theological education was rigorous biblical studies, and the seminaries saw the nurturing of the biblical guild as one of their functions. Despite numerous studies that indicated that the study of the biblical languages had little, if any, carryover into the ministry, the seminaries retained the teaching of Greek and Hebrew and some schools required them for the degree. The schools' leaders believed that such investments would provide the next generation of biblical scholars and translators with the gold and silver of Scripture, and they, in turn, would be able to pass that on to future generations. Biblical departments had been kept strong with seminaries often having more scholars in this area than any other. And the work of the seminaries had paid rich dividends. By 1970 the German dominance of biblical studies had ended. Fewer German books were translated into English, and although some Americans continued to make the traditional scholarly hajj to Germany, the United States was now the epicenter of serious biblical study. Earlier American biblical pioneers had dreamed of such a reversal of fortunes, but their institutions were not to be its beneficiaries. While seminaries continued to house significant biblical scholars, American biblical scholarship largely passed into the hands of the universities and the divinity schools related to them.

Theological education in 1970 represented a mixed bag of real achievements and faced some substantial challenges. While the most visible of these, such as gender and race, were important, the hidden problems of finances and the changing character of religious scholarship were equally significant. Protestantism has always been a religion of teaching, of doctrine, and of scriptural interpretation. Remove these from Protestant experience, and the resultant religion would have little cultural or moral power. Protestant theological education from 1870 to 1970 developed a way of balancing these essential religious components with the more recently felt need for informed and skillful practice. The resultant understanding of theological education and ministerial preparation had long legs. Roman Catholics and conservative Protestants accepted its basic outlines and enriched them with elements of their own religious traditions, and even schools devoted to the education of Jewish rabbis adapted many of its features. This pattern of imitation continues even today as Pentecostal Christians and representatives of non-Christian traditions, including Buddhism, are adopting similar understandings of how religious leaders should be prepared. Like the clinical system in medical education and the case system in law, schools training religious leaders developed a common way of thinking about their task.

What happened to this understanding and the schools that embodied it after 1970? While I have had to continue some aspects of the story beyond that date, the story of this volume comes to its conclusion at that time. My understanding of the next forty years is far less historical than my understanding of earlier periods. During those years I worked as a theological educator, and my understanding is colored by own experiences. If time and health permit, I hope to produce a short history of that period, perhaps modeled on Gaius Glenn Atkins's *Religion in Our Times*, that will tell the rest of the story, combining my research and my reflections. In any event, that is my hope.

Bibliography

Abbott, Lyman. *The Theology of an Evolutionist.* Boston and New York: Houghton Mifflin, 1897.

Adams, Harry. "Major Issues in the Lilly Study." In "Theological Education." Special issue, *Journal of Bible and Religion* 34 (1966).

Ahlstrom, Sydney. "Continental Influence on American Christian Thought Since World War I." *Church History* 27 (1958): 256-71.

Albright, William Foxwell. *The Archaeology of Palestine and the Bible.* New York: Fleming H. Revell, 1932.

———. *History, Archaeology, and Christian Humanism.* Baltimore: Johns Hopkins University Press, 1966.

Aleshire, Daniel. "Finding Eagles in the Turkey's Nest: Pastoral Theology and Christian Education." *Review and Expositor* 85 (1988): 695-709.

Allyn, Russell C. *Voices of American Fundamentalism: Seven Autobiographical Studies.* Philadelphia: Westminster, 1976.

American Association of Theological Schools. *The First Report of the Commission on Accrediting.* Louisville, 1938.

———. *Bulletin 14.* July 1940. Twelfth Biennial Meeting of the Association at the College of the Bible.

Anderson, George. "Challenge and Change within German Protestant Theological Education during the Nineteenth Century." *Church History,* Mar. 1970.

Anderson, James. *The Education of Blacks in the South, 1860-1935.* Chapel Hill: University of North Carolina Press, 1988.

Archer, John Clark. "The Function of the Theological Seminary in the Enterprise of Missions." In *Education for Christian Service* (Members of the Faculty of the Divinity School of Yale University). New Haven: Yale University, 1922.

Armstrong, Anthony. *The Church of England, the Methodists and Society, 1700-1850.* London: University of London Press, 1973.

Army and Religion, The. New York: Association Press, 1920.

Arnold, Harvey. "The Death of God: George Burman Foster and the Impact of Modernity." *Foundations* 10 (1967): 331-53.

Ashenhurst, J. O. "The Rural Awakening." In *Messages of the Men and Religion Movement,* vol. 6, *The Rural Church.* New York: Association Press, 1912.

Atkins, Gaius Glenn. *Religion in Our Times.* New York: Round Table Press, 1932.

Bacon, B. W. "Enter the Higher Criticism." In *Contemporary American Theology,* by Vergilius Ferm. New York: Round Table Press, 1932-33.

Bailey, Warner M. "William Robertson Smith and American Biblical Studies." *Journal of Presbyterian History* 51 (Fall 1973): 285-308.

Bainton, Roland. *Yale and the Ministry: A History of Education at Yale for the Ministry from the Founding in 1701.* New York: Harper and Brothers, 1957.

Baker, Robert. *The Southern Baptist Convention and Its People, 1607-1972.* Nashville: Broadman, 1974.

———. *Tell the Generations Following: A History of Southwestern Baptist Theological Seminary, 1908-1983.* Nashville: Broadman, 1983.

Barr, James. "Position of Hebrew Language in Theological Education." *Princeton Seminary Bulletin* 55 (1962): 6-24.

Barth, Karl. *Protestant Theology in the Nineteenth Century: Its Background and History.* London: SCM, 1972.

Barton, F. M. "A Living Wage for Rural Pastors." In *Messages of the Men and Religion Movement,* vol. 6, *The Rural Church.* New York: Association Press, 1912.

Bass, Dorothy. "The Independent Sector and the Educational Strategies of Mainstream Protestantism." In *Religion, the Independent Sector, and American Culture,* edited by Conrad Cherry and Rowland A. Sherrill. Atlanta: Scholars, 1992.

Beardsley, William A. "The Background of the Lilly Endowment Study of Preseminary Education." *Journal of Bible and Religion* 34 (1966).

Beaven, Albert W. "Theological Schools in the Creative Tomorrow." *Bulletin* 15 (Thirteenth Biennial Meeting of the AATS) (1942).

Beaver, R. Pierce. "The Missionary Research Library: A Sketch of Its History." *Occasional Bulletin from the Missionary Research Library,* Feb. 1968, pp. 1-8.

———. *All Loves Excelling: American Protestant Women in World Mission; A History of the First Feminist Movement in North America.* Rev. ed. Grand Rapids: Eerdmans, 1980.

Beck, Rosalie. "The Whitsitt Controversy: A Denomination in Crisis." Ph.D. diss., Baylor University, 1985.

Becker, Russell J. "The Place of the Parish in Theological Education." *Journal of Pastoral Care* 21 (1967): 163-70.

Bederman, Gail. *Manhood and Civilization: A Cultural History of Gender and Race in the United States, 1880-1917.* Chicago and London: University of Chicago Press, 1995.

———. "The Women Have Had Charge of the Church Work Long Enough: The Men and Religion Forward Movement of 1911 and the Masculinization of Middle Class Protestantism." In *A Mighty Baptism: Race, Gender, and the Creation of American Protestantism,* edited by Susan Juster and Lisa MacFarlane. Ithaca, N.Y., and London: Cornell University Press, 1996. Originally published in *American Quarterly* 41 (Sept. 1989): 432-65.

Bendroth, Margaret. *Fundamentalism and Gender, 1885 to the Present.* New Haven: Yale University Press, 1993.

Benjamin, Alicia. "Christian Urban Colonizers: A History of the East Harlem Protestant Parish in New York City, 1948-1968." Ph.D. diss., Union Theological Seminary, 1988.

Berger, Peter L. *The Noise of Solemn Assemblies: Christian Commitment and the Religious Establishment in America.* Garden City, N.Y.: Doubleday, 1961.

"Bible as a Theme for the Pulpit, The." *Andover Review* 5 (Apr.-June 1886).

Bledsoe, Burton. *The Culture of Professionalism.* New York: Norton, 1976.

Bloch, R. H. *God's Plagiarist: Being an Account of the Fabulous Industry and Irregular Commerce of the Abbé Migne.* Chicago and London: University of Chicago Press, 1994.

Blumhofer, Edith. *The Assemblies of God.* Springfield, Mo.: Gospel Publishing House, 1989.

Bolich, Gregory. *Karl Barth and Evangelicalism.* Downers Grove, Ill.: InterVarsity, 1980.

Bomberger, J. H. A. *The Protestant Theological and Ecclesiastical Encyclopedia: Being a Condensed Translation of Herzog's Real-Enzyklopädie.* Philadelphia: Lindsay and Blakiston, 1858; New York: Harper, 1869-80.

Bonhoeffer, Dietrich. *The Cost of Discipleship.* London: SCM, 1948.

———. *Letters and Papers from Prison.* London: SCM, 1953.

———. *Life Together.* New York: Harper, 1954.

———. *Ethics.* London: SCM, 1955.

Bowden, Henry Warner. "The First Century: Institutional Development and Ideas about the Profession." In *A Century of Church History,* edited by Henry Warner Bowden. Carbondale and Edwardsville: Southern Illinois University Press, 1988.

Bowser, Beth Adams. *Living the Vision: The University Senate of the Methodist Episcopal Church, the Methodist Church, and the United Methodist Church.* Nashville: Board of Higher Education and Ministry of the United Methodist Church, 1992.

Boylan, Anne M. "The Role of Conversion in Nineteenth Century Sunday Schools." *American Studies* 20 (Spring 1975): 35-78.

———. *Sunday School: The Formation of an American Institution.* New Haven: Yale University Press, 1988.

Bratt, James D., ed. *Abraham Kuyper: A Centennial Reader.* Grand Rapids: Eerdmans; Carlisle: Paternoster, 1998.

Brereton, Virginia Lieson. "Preparing Women for the Lord's Work." In *Women in New Worlds: Historical Perspectives on the Wesleyan Tradition,* edited by Hilah F. Thomas and Rosemary Skinner Keller. Nashville: Abingdon, 1981.

———. *Training God's Army: The American Bible School, 1880-1940.* Bloomington and Indianapolis: Indiana University Press, 1990.

Bridston, Keith R., and Dwight W. Culver. *Preseminary Education: Report of the Lilly Endowment Study.* Minneapolis: Augsburg, 1965.

Briggs, Charles. "The Scientific Study of Holy Scripture." *Independent,* Nov. 30, 1899.

———. *History of the Study of Theology.* Prepared for publication by his daughter Emilie Grace Briggs. London: Duckworth, 1916.

Brook, Charles H. *A Brief Historical Review of the First African Baptist Church* [*of Philadelphia*], *Certain Other Interesting Information and the Official Program of the Centennial Anniversary Celebration.* Philadelphia: The Church, 1909.

Brown, Ira V. "The Higher Criticism Comes to America, 1880-1900." *Journal of Presbyterian History* 38, no. 4 (Dec. 1960): 193-212.

Brown, Jerry Wayne. *The Rise of Biblical Criticism in America, 1800-1870: The New England Scholars.* Middletown, Conn.: Wesleyan University Press, 1969.

Brown, Robert McAfee. *The Bible Speaks to You.* Philadelphia: Westminster, 1955.

Brown, William Adams. "Theological Education." In *A Cyclopedia of Education*, edited by Paul Monroe. 5 vols. New York: Macmillan, 1914.

———. "The Responsibility of the University for the Teaching of Theology." *Yale Divinity School Quarterly* 16, no. 4 (June 1920).

———. "The Common Problems of Theological Schools." *Journal of Religion*, 1921, pp. 282-95.

———. *Beliefs That Matter: A Theology for Laymen*. New York: Scribner, 1928.

———. *The Case for Theology in the University*. Chicago: University of Chicago Press, 1938.

Brown, William Adams, and Mark May. *The Education of American Ministers*. 4 vols. New York: Institute of Social and Religious Research, 1934. Vol. 1, *Ministerial Education in America*. Vol. 2, *The Profession of the Ministry*. Vol. 3, *The Institutions That Train Ministers*. Vol. 4, *Appendices*.

Bruce, F. F. *The English Bible: A History of Translations*. London: Lutterworth, 1961.

Brueggemann, Walter A. "Ethos and Ecumenism: The History of Eden Theological Seminary, 1925-1970." Ph.D. diss., St. Louis University, 1974.

Brunner, Edmund de S. *The Larger Parish, a Movement or Enthusiasm?* New York: Institute of Social and Religious Research, 1934.

Bucher, Glenn R., and L. Gordon Tait. "Social Reform Since the Great Depression." In *Encyclopedia of the American Religious Experience*, edited by Charles H. Lippy and Peter W. Williams. New York: Scribner, 1988.

Buck, Pearl S. "Is There a Case for Foreign Missions?" *Harper's Monthly*, Jan. 1933.

Butterfield, Kenyon. "The Supply of Leaders for the Country." In *Messages of the Men and Religion Movement*, vol. 6, *The Rural Church*. New York: Association Press, 1912.

———. *Church and the Rural Problem*. Chicago: University of Chicago Press, 1913.

Buttrick, George Arthur, ed. *The Interpreter's Bible: The Holy Scriptures in the King James and Revised Standard Versions with General Articles and Introduction, Exegesis, Exposition for Each Book of the Bible*. New York: Abingdon-Cokesbury, 1951-57.

Cable, David Blaine. "The Development of the Accrediting Function of the American Association of Theological Schools, 1918-1938." Ph.D. diss., University of Pittsburgh, 1970.

Cabot, Richard. *What Men Live By*. Boston and New York: Houghton Mifflin, 1914.

———. "A Plea for a Clinical Year in the Course of Theological Study." *Survey Graphic*, Sept. 1925; reprinted in Cabot, *Adventures on the Borderlands of Ethics* (New York and London: Harper and Brothers, 1926).

Calhoun, David. *Princeton Theological Seminary: Faith and Learning, 1812-1868*. Edinburgh: Banner of Truth Trust, 1994.

———. *Princeton Seminary: The Majestic Testimony, 1869-1929*. Edinburgh: Banner of Truth Trust, 1996.

Callen, Barry L. *Guide of Body and Mind: The Story of Anderson University*. Anderson, Ind.: Anderson University and Warner Press, 1992.

Cameron, Richard. *Methodism and Society in Historical Perspective*. Methodism and Society, vol. 1. New York and Nashville: Abingdon, 1961.

———. *Boston University School of Theology: 1839-1968*. Boston: Boston University School of Theology, 1968.

Canfield, Norman Jay. "Study the Most Approved Authors: The Role of the Seminary Library in Nineteenth-Century American Protestant Ministerial Education." Ph.D. diss., University of Chicago, 1981.

Carnegie Foundation for the Advancement of Teaching. *For the Advancement of Teaching.* Sixth Carnegie Report on Teaching, 1911. New York, 1912.

Carnell, Edward John. *The Theology of Reinhold Niebuhr.* Grand Rapids: Eerdmans, 1951.

Carnes, Mark C., and Clyde Griffen, eds. *Meanings for Masculinity.* Chicago: University of Chicago Press, 1990.

Carpenter, Joel A. *Revive Us Again: The Reawakening of American Fundamentalism.* New York: Oxford University Press, 1997.

Carpenter, Joel A., and Wilbert Shenk, eds. *Earthen Vessels: American Evangelicals and Foreign Missions, 1880-1980.* Grand Rapids: Eerdmans, 1990.

Carroll, Jackson, and Barbara Wheeler. "Doctor of Ministry Program: History, Summary of Findings and Recommendations." *Theological Education,* Spring 1987.

Carter, Paul A. *The Decline and Revival of the Social Gospel: Social and Political Liberalism in American Protestant Churches, 1920-1940.* Ithaca, N.Y.: Cornell University Press, 1954.

———. *The Decline and Renewal of the Social Gospel: Social and Political Liberalism in American Protestant Churches, 1920-1940.* Ithaca, N.Y.: Cornell University Press, 1956.

———. *The Spiritual Crisis of the Gilded Age.* De Kalb: Northern Illinois University Press, 1971.

———. *Another Part of the Twenties.* New York: Columbia University Press, 1977.

Cauthen, Kenneth. *The Impact of American Religious Liberalism.* New York: Harper and Row, 1962.

Centennial Celebration of the Theological Seminary of the Presbyterian Church in the United States of America at Princeton, New Jersey, The. N.p.: The Seminary, 1912.

Chernow, Ron. *Titan: The Life of John D. Rockefeller, Sr.* New York: Random House, 1998.

Cherry, Conrad. *Hurrying toward Zion: Universities, Divinity Schools, and American Protestantism.* Bloomington and Indianapolis: Indiana University Press, 1995.

Chiles, Robert. *Theological Transition in American Methodism.* New York and Nashville: Abingdon, 1963.

———. *Theological Transition in Methodism.* New York: Abingdon, 1965.

Churchill, Ralph D. "The History and Development of Southwestern's School of Religious Education to 1956." Ph.D. diss., Southwestern Baptist Theological Seminary, 1956.

Clark, Calvin Montague. *History of Bangor Theological Seminary.* Boston: Pilgrim Press, 1916.

Clutter, Ronald. "The Reorganization of Princeton Theological Seminary Reconsidered." *Grace Theological Journal* 7, no. 2 (1986): 179-201.

Coe, George A. *Salvation by Education.* Chicago and London: Fleming Revell, 1902.

———. "The Theological Seminary: The Laboratory Method in the Department of Religious Education." *Religous Education Association Journal* 7 (1912).

———. "The Religious Breakdown of the Ministry." *Journal of Religion* 1 (Jan. 1921): 18-29.

———. "The Present Crisis in Religious Education." *Religious Education* 28 (Apr. 1933): 181-85.

Coffin, Henry Sloane. "Criticism and Queries." *Journal of Religion* 1 (Mar. 1921): 189.

Colby, Gerard, with Charlotte Dennett. *Thy Will Be Done: The Conquest of the Amazon; Nelson Rockefeller and Evangelism in the Age of Oil.* New York: HarperCollins, 1995.

Cole, Stewart Grant. *The History of Fundamentalism.* Hampden, Conn.: Archon Books, 1963; original 1931.

Collins, Mary F. "Hartford's Training of Women." *Hartford Seminary Record* 20 (1910): 293-97.

Colwell, Ernest Cadman. "Toward Better Theological Education." *Journal of Religion* 20, no. 2 (Apr. 1940): 109-23.

Combs, K. Stephen. "The Course of Religious Education at the Southern Baptist Theological Seminary, 1902-1953: A Historical Study." Ph.D. diss., Southern Baptist Theological Seminary, 1978.

Committee on the Aims of Theological Education. Report. *Bulletin 10.* 1932 biennial meeting of the Conference of Theological Seminaries. William Adams Brown, chair.

Committee on the Study of Theological Education. Report. *Bulletin 6.* 1928 biennial meeting of the Conference of Theological Seminaries. P. 14.

Cone, James H. "The Theology of Martin Luther King, Jr." Unbound manuscript, Harvard University, 1985.

Conforti, Joseph. *Jonathan Edwards: Religious Tradition and American Culture.* Chapel Hill: University of North Carolina Press, 1982.

Conser, Walter H. *Church and Confession: Conservative Theologians in Germany, England, and America, 1815-1866.* Atlanta: Mercer University Press, 1984.

Cope, Henry F. "The Professional Organization of Workers in Religious Education." *Religious Education* 16 (1921): 166.

Cowan, George M. *The Word That Kindles.* Chappaqua, N.Y.: Christian Herald Books, [1979].

Cox, Harvey Gallagher. *The Secular City: Secularization and Urbanization in Theological Perspective.* New York: Macmillan, 1965.

Cremin, Lawrence A. *Traditions of American Education.* New York: Basic Books, 1976.

———. *American Education: The Metropolitan Experience.* New York: Harper and Row, 1988.

Cronon, William. *Nature's Metropolis: Chicago and the Great West.* New York: Norton, 1991.

Crunden, Robert. *Ministers of Reform: The Progressives' Achievement in American Civilization, 1889-1920.* New York: Basic Books, 1982.

Cuninggim, Merrimon. "The New Currriculum at Perkins." *Christian Century,* Apr. 18, 1954, pp. 574-75.

Cunningham, John. *University in the Forest: The Story of Drew University.* Andover, N.J.: Afton Publishing Co., 1972.

Curti, Merle, et al. "Anatomy of Giving: Millionaires in the Late Nineteenth Century." *American Quarterly* 15 (1963): 416-35.

Cutshall, Elmer Guy. "The Doctrinal Training of the Traveling Ministry of the Methodist Episcopal Church." Ph.D. diss., University of Chicago, 1922.

Dabney, Robert. *A Defense of Virginia and through Her, of the South.* New York: E. J. Hale and Son, 1867.

———. "The Influence of the German University upon Theological Literature." *Southern Presbyterian Review,* Apr. 1881, pp. 440-65.

Dabney, Vaughan. "Austin Philip Guiles." *Andover Newton Bulletin,* Feb. 1954.

Daniel, W. A., and Robert Kelly. *The Education of Negro Ministers.* New York: George Doran Co., 1925; New York: Negro Universities Press, 1969.

Dates and Data. N.p.: Trustees of Andover Seminary, 1926.

Davies, J. Merle. "The Preparation of Missionaries for the Post-War Era." *International Review of Missions* 23 (1944): 241-53.

Davies, Orville L. "A History of the Religious Education Association." *Religious Education* 44 (1949): 41-54.

Dayton, Donald. *Discovering an Evangelical Heritage.* New York: Harper and Row, 1976.

"Death of Johns Hopkins." *Sun,* Thursday morning, Dec. 25, 1873; reprinted on the Web pages of Johns Hopkins University, visited July 27, 1997.

DeBerg, Beth. *Ungodly Women: Gender and the First Wave of American Fundamentalism.* Minneapolis: Fortress, 1990.

DeBoer, Lawrence. "Seminary and University: Two Approaches to Theology and Religion." *Journal of Bible and Religion* 32 (1964): 343.

Dennison, Charles G., and Richard C. Gamble, eds. *Pressing toward the Mark: Essays Commemorating Fifty Years of the Orthodox Presbyterian Church.* Philadelphia: Committee for the Historian of the Orthodox Presbyterian Church, 1986.

Dewey, John. *The Influence of Darwin on Philosophy, and Other Essays in Contemporary Thought.* Bloomington: Indiana University Press, 1965; original 1910.

Diamond, Etan. *Souls of the City: Religion and the Search for Community in Postwar America.* Bloomington: Indiana University Press, 2003.

Dicks, Russell, and Richard C. Cabot. *The Art of Ministering to the Sick.* New York: Macmillan, 1936. Frequently reprinted.

Diefenthaler, Jon. *H. Richard Niebuhr: A Lifetime of Reflections on the Church and the World.* Macon, Ga.: Mercer University Press, 1986.

Dike, Samuel. "The Religious Problem of the Country Town." *Andover Review,* 1884.

———. "The Religious Problem of the Country Town II." *Andover Review,* 1884.

———. "Shall Churches Increase Their Efficiency by Scientific Methods?" *American Journal of Theology* 16, no. 1 (Jan. 1912): 20-30.

Dillenberger, John. *Protestant Thought and Natural Science.* Garden City, N.Y.: Doubleday, 1960.

Doggett, Laurence Locke. *A Man and a School: Pioneering in Higher Education at Springfield College.* New York: Association Press, 1943.

Dorn, Jacob H. "The Rural Ideal and the Agrarian Realities: Arthur Holt and the Vision of a Decentralized America in the 1930s." *Church History* 52 (Mar. 1983).

———. "The Social Gospel and Socialism: A Comparison of the Thought of Francis Greenwood Peabody, Washington Gladden, and Walter Rauschenbusch." *Church History* 62 (Mar. 1993): 82-100.

Dorrien, Gary. *The Making of American Liberal Theology.* Vol. 1, *Imagining Progressive Religion, 1805-1900.* Louisville: Westminster John Knox, 2001.

———. *The Making of American Liberal Theology.* Vol. 2, *Idealism, Realism, and Modernity, 1900-1950.* Louisville: Westminster John Knox, 2003.

Dougherty, Mary Agnes Theresa. "The Methodist Deaconess, 1885-1919: A Study in Religious Feminism." Ph.D. diss., University of California, Davis, 1979.

———. "The Social Gospel according to Phoebe." In *Women in New Worlds: Historical*

Perspectives on the Wesleyan Tradition, edited by Hilah F. Thomas and Rosemary Skinner Keller. Nashville: Abingdon, 1981.

Douglas, Ann. *The Feminization of American Culture.* New York: Knopf, 1977.

Douglas, Horton. "God Lets Loose Karl Barth." *Christian Century,* 1928.

Douglass, H. Paul. *The New Home Missions, an Account of Their Social Redirection.* New York: Missionary Education Movement, 1914.

Du Bois, W. E. B. *The Souls of Black Folks.* Boulder, Colo.: Paradigm, 2004.

Durant, John, ed. *Darwinism and Divinity: Essays on Evolution and Religious Belief.* Oxford: Basil Blackwell, 1985.

Earp, Edwin. *The Rural Church Movement.* New York and Cincinnati: Methodist Book Concern, 1914.

———. *The Rural Church Serving the Community.* Nashville: Abingdon, 1918.

Eastman, E. Fred. "The Minister's Use of the Survey." In *Messages of the Men and Religion Movement,* vol. 6, *The Rural Church.* New York: Association Press, 1912.

Egan, Maureen. "The History of the Association for Theological Field Education and Its Contribution to Theological Education in the United States, 1946-1979." Ph.D. diss., St. Louis University, 1987.

Eisenstein, Elizabeth L. *The Printing Press as an Agent of Change: Communications and Cultural Transformations in Early Modern Europe.* Cambridge and New York: Cambridge University Press, 1979.

Eliot, Charles. "On the Education of Ministers." *Princeton Review,* May 1883, pp. 340-56.

———. *University Administration.* Boston and New York: Houghton Mifflin, 1908.

Elliott, Harrison. *The Why and How of Group Discussion.* New York: Association Press, 1920.

———. *The Process of Group Thinking.* New York: Association Press, 1928.

———. *Group Discussion in Religious Education.* New York: Association Press, 1930, 1939.

———. *Can Religious Education Be Christian?* New York: Macmillan, 1940.

Encyclopaedia Britannica: A Dictionary of Arts, Sciences, and General Literature. 9th ed. New York: Samuel L. Hall, 1878-95.

Erickson, Millard J. *A Basic Guide to Eschatology: Making Sense of the Millennium.* Grand Rapids: Baker, 1998. Reprint of *Contemporary Options in Eschatology: A Study of the Millennium* (1977).

Ernst, Eldon. *Moment of Truth for Protestant America: Interchurch Campaigns Following World War One.* Missoula, Mont.: American Academy of Religion, 1972.

Evangelical Alliance. *Christianity Practically Applied.* New York: Baker and Taylor, 1893.

Fallaw, Wesner. "The Roles of Ministers and Directors of Christian Education." *Religious Education* 9 (1950): 41-44.

Fallon, Daniel. *The German University: A Heroic Ideal in Conflict with the Modern World.* Boulder, Colo.: Associated University Press, 1980.

Farish, Hunter Dickenson. *The Circuit Rider Dismounts.* New York: De Capo Press, 1969.

Farley, Edward. "The Reform of Theological Education as a Theological Task." *Theological Education* 17 (Spring 1981): 93-117.

———. *Theologia: The Fragmentation and Unity of Theological Education.* Philadelphia: Fortress, 1983.

Felton, Ralph A. *Local Church Cooperation in Rural Communities.* New York: Congregational and Christian Churches, n.d.

Fevre, Perry Le. "Evolutionary Thought and American Religious Education." *Journal of Religion* 40 (1960): 296-308.

Fielding, Charles. *Education for Ministry.* Dayton, Ohio: AATS, 1966.

Findlay, James. "Moody, Gapmen, and the Gospel: The Early Days of Moody Bible Institute." *Church History* 31 (Sept. 1962): 322-25.

Findlay, James F., Jr. *Church People in the Struggle: The National Council of Churches and the Black Freedom Movement, 1950-1970.* New York and Oxford: Oxford University Press, 1993.

Fleming, Sandford. "Board of Education and Theological Education, 1911-1963." *Foundations* 8 (Jan. 1965): 3-25.

Fletcher, John C., and Tilden Edwards, Jr. "Inter-met: On the Job Theological Education." *Pastoral Psychology* 22 (Mar. 1971): 21-30.

Flexner, Abraham. *Medical Education in the United States and Canada: A Report to the Carnegie Foundation for the Advancement of Teaching.* New York: Carnegie Foundation, 1910.

———. *Universities: American, German, English.* New York: Oxford University Press, 1930.

Flynt, Wayne. *Alabama Baptists: Southern Baptists in the Heart of Dixie.* Tuscaloosa: University of Alabama Press, 1998.

Ford, Thomas. "The Roles of the Rural Parish Minister, the Protestant Seminaries, and the Sciences of Social Behavior." In *The Sociology of Religion: An Anthology,* edited by Richard D. Knudten. New York: Appleton-Century-Crofts, 1967.

Fosdick, Harry E. *The Modern Use of the Bible.* New York: Macmillan, 1924.

———. *The Living of These Days: An Autobiography.* New York: Harper and Brothers, 1956.

Foster, Frank Clifton. "Field Work and Its Relation to the Curriculum of Theological Seminaries." Ph.D. diss., Columbia University, 1932. Independently printed.

Foster, Frank Hugh. *The Life of Edwards Amasa Park.* New York: Fleming H. Revell, 1936.

Foster, George Burman. "Concerning the Religious Basis of Ethics." *American Journal of Theology* 12 (1908).

———. "The Contribution of Critical Scholarship to Ministerial Efficiency." *American Journal of Theology* 20 (1916).

"Foundations, Fortunes and Federated Faculties." *Christian Century,* Jan. 4, 1956.

Fox, Richard Wightman. *Reinhold Niebuhr: A Biography.* New York: Pantheon Books, 1985.

Fox, Richard Wightman, and T. J. Jackson Lears, eds. *The Culture of Consumption: Critical Essays in American History, 1880-1980.* New York: Pantheon Books, 1983.

Freeman, Maria. *Pursuing the Higher Criticism: New Testament Collections at the University of Chicago.* Chicago: University of Chicago Press, 1993.

Frei, Hans. "The Theology of H. Richard Niebuhr." In *Faith and Ethics: The Theology of H. Richard Niebuhr,* edited by Paul Ramsey. New York: Harper Torchbooks, 1957.

Fry, Luther. *Diagnosing the Rural Church.* New York: George H. Doran Co., Institute of Social and Religious Research, 1924.

Funk, Robert W. "Watershed of the American Biblical Tradition: The Chicago School, First Phase, 1892-1920." *Journal of Biblical Literature* 95 (1976): 4-22.

Funk, Robert, Roy W. Hoover, and the Jesus Seminar. *The Five Gospels.* New York: Macmillan, 1993.

Furnish, Dorothy Jean. *DRE/DCE — the History of a Profession.* N.p.: Christian Education Fellowship, United Methodist Church, 1976.

Gaebelein, Frank E. "Education." In *Contemporary Evangelical Thought,* edited by Carl F. H. Henry. Great Neck, N.Y.: Channel Press, 1957.

Gatewood, Willard B. *Preachers, Pedagogues, and Politicians: The Evolution Controversy in North Carolina, 1920-1927.* Chapel Hill: University of North Carolina Press, 1966.

———, ed. *Controversy in the Twenties: Fundamentalism, Modernism, and Evolution.* Nashville: Vanderbilt University Press, 1969.

Gaustad, Edwin Scott. *The Great Awakening in New England.* New York: Harper and Row, 1957.

Geer, Curtis Manning. *The Hartford Theological Seminary, 1834-1934.* Hartford: Case, Lockwood, and Brainard Co., 1934.

Geiger, Roger. *To Advance Knowledge: The Growth of American Research Universities, 1900-1940.* New York and Oxford: Oxford University Press, 1986.

General Education in a Free Society: Report of the Harvard Committee. Cambridge: Harvard University Press, 1945.

Getz, Gene. *MBI: The Story of Moody Bible Institute.* Chicago: Moody Press, 1969.

Gilbert, James. *Redeeming Culture: American Religion in an Age of Science.* Chicago: University of Chicago Press, 1997.

Gill, Charles Otis, and Gifford Pinchot. *The Country Church: The Decline of Its Influence and Its Remedy.* New York: Macmillan, 1913.

Gilpin, W. Clark. *Preface to Theology.* Chicago: University of Chicago Press, 1996.

Gladden, Washington. *Who Wrote the Bible? A Book for the People.* Boston and New York: Houghton Mifflin, 1891.

Glick, Thomas, ed. *The Comparative Reception of Darwinism.* Chicago: University of Chicago Press, 1988.

Goldberg, David. *Discontented America: The United States in the 1920s.* Baltimore: Johns Hopkins University Press, 1999.

Goodspeed, Edgar J. *As I Remember.* New York: Harper and Brothers, 1953.

Goodspeed, Thomas Wakefield. *A History of the University of Chicago: The First Quarter Century.* Chicago: University of Chicago Press, 1916.

Goodykoontz, Colin Brummit. *Home Missions on the American Frontier with Particular Reference to the American Home Missionary Society.* New York: Octagon Books, 1971.

Gorrell, Donald K. *The Age of Social Responsibility: The Social Gospel in the Progressive Era, 1900-1920.* Macon, Ga.: Mercer University Press, 1988.

Green, John Gardiner. "The Emmanuel Movement, 1906-1919." *New England Quarterly* 7 (1934): 494-532.

Greene, John. *The Death of Adam.* Ames: Iowa State University Press, 1959.

Griffin, Paul R. "Black Founders of Reconstruction Era Methodist Colleges: Daniel A. Payne, Joseph C. Price, and Isaac Lane, 1863-1890." Ph.D. diss., Emory University, 1983.

Griffith-Thomas, W. H. "Modernism in China." *Princeton Theological Review,* Oct. 1921.

Guiles, Philip. "The Beginnings of Clinical Training in New England." *Andover Newton Theological School Bulletin* 40, no. 1 (Dec. 1947).

Gustafson, Robert K. *James Woodrow (1828-1907): Scientist, Theologian, Intellectual Leader.* Lewiston, N.Y.: E. Mellen Press, 1995.

Gutjahr, Paul C. *An American Bible: A History of the Good Book in the United States, 1777-1880.* Stanford: Stanford University Press, 1999.

Hagenbach, K. R. *Encyclopaedie und Methodologie der theologischen Wissenschaften.* Leipzig: Weidmann'sche Buchhandlung, 1833. American ed., New York, Phillips and Hunt; Cincinnati, Walden and Stowe, 1884.

Haines, George Lamar. "The Princeton Theological Seminary, 1925-1960." Ph.D. diss., New York University, School of Education, 1966.

Hall, Charles E. *Head and Heart: The Story of the Clinical Pastoral Education Movement.* Decatur, Ga.: Journal of Pastoral Care Publications, 1992.

Hall, Peter. *Cities in Civilization.* New York: Pantheon Books, 1998.

Hamilton, Michael S. "The Fundamentalist Harvard: Wheaton College and the Enduring Vitality of American Evangelicalism, 1919-1965." Ph.D. diss., University of Notre Dame, 1994.

———. "More Money, More Ministry: The Financing of American Evangelicalism Since 1945." In *More Money, More Ministry: Money and Evangelicals in Recent North American History,* edited by Larry Eskridge and Mark A. Noll. Grand Rapids: Eerdmans, 2000.

Hamlin, F. S. *S. Parkes Cadman, Pioneer Radio Minister.* New York: Harper and Brothers, 1930.

Handy, Robert T. "The American Religious Depression, 1925-1935." *Church History* 29 (1960).

———. *The Social Gospel.* New York: Oxford University Press, 1966.

———. *A Christian America: Protestant Hopes and Historical Realities.* New York: Oxford University Press, 1971.

———. *A History of Union Theological Seminary in New York.* New York: Columbia University Press, 1987.

———. *Undermined Establishment: Church-State Relations in America, 1880-1920.* Princeton: Princeton University Press, 1991.

Hansen, Drew W. *The Dream: Martin Luther King, Jr., and the Speech That Inspired a Nation.* New York: Ecco, 2003.

Harper, William Rainey. "Bible Study in the Pastorate: Facts and Figures." *Old Testament Student* 6 (1881).

———. "The Teaching of the Old Testament." *Old Testament Student,* Mar. 1888.

———. "Ideals of Educational Work." *Proceedings of the National Educational Association* 34 (1895).

Harr, John Ensor, and Peter J. Johnson. *The Rockefeller Century.* New York: Scribner, 1988.

Harris, George. *A Century's Change in Religion.* Boston and New York: Houghton Mifflin, 1914.

———, et al. "Modifications in the Theological Curriculum." *American Journal of Theology* 3 (1899): 46.

Hart, D. G. "Doctor Fundamentalis: An Intellectual Biography of J. Gresham Machen, 1881-1937." Ph.D. diss., Johns Hopkins University, 1988. Revised as *Defending the Faith: J. Gresham Machen and the Crisis of Conservative Protestantism in Modern America* (Baltimore: Johns Hopkins University Press, 1994).

———. "J. Gresham Machen, Karl Barth and 'The Theology of Crisis.'" *Westminster Theological Journal,* 1991, pp. 197ff.

———. "Machen on Barth." *Westminster Theological Journal,* 1991, pp. 189-96.

———. *The University Gets Religion: Religious Studies in American Higher Education.* Baltimore: Johns Hopkins University Press, 1999.

Hart, Darryl. "The Princeton Mind in the Modern World and the Common Sense of J. Gresham Machen." *Westminster Theological Journal* 46, no. 1 (Spring 1984): 8-9.

Hart, Ray. "Religious and Theological Studies in American Higher Education: A Pilot Study." *Journal of the American Academy of Religion* 59 (1991): 715-27.

Hartranft, C. D. *The Aims of a Theological Seminary: An Address Delivered Before the Alumni Association of the Theological Seminary, New Brunswick, NJ.* New York: Board of Publication of the Reformed Church in America, 1878.

Hartshorne, Hugh. *Book of Worship for the Church School.* New York: Scribner, 1915.

———. *Stories for Worship and How to Follow Them Up.* New York: Scribner, 1921.

———. "A Study of the Status of Religious Education." *Religious Education* 27 (Mar. 1932): 245-47.

Hartshorne, Hugh, and M. C. Froyd. *Theological Education in the Northern Baptist Convention.* Philadelphia: Judson, 1945.

Hartshorne, Hugh, Helen R. Stearns, and W. Uphaus. *Standards and Trends in Religious Education.* New Haven: Yale University Press, 1933.

Harvey, Charles E. "John D. Rockefeller, Jr., and the Interchurch World Movement of 1919-1920: A Different Angle on the Ecumenical Movement." *Church History* 51 (1982): 198-209.

———. "Speer versus Rockefeller and Mott, 1910-1935." *Journal of Presbyterian History* 60 (Winter 1982): 283-99.

Harvey, Van A. "Reflections on the Teaching of Religion in America." *Journal of the American Academy of Religion* 38 (Mar. 1970).

Haskell, Thomas L. *The Emergence of Professional Social Science: The American Social Science Association and the Nineteenth Century Crisis of Authority.* Urbana: University of Illinois Press, 1977.

Hatch, Carl E. *The Charles A. Briggs Heresy Trial: Prologue to Twentieth-Century Liberal Protestantism.* New York: Exposition Press, 1969.

Hayes, Samuel. *The Response to Industrialism, 1885-1914.* Chicago: University of Chicago Press, 1957; rev. ed., 1995.

Hayward, P. H., M. N. English, et al. "What the Depression Is Doing to the Cause of Religious Education." *Religious Education* 27 (Dec. 1932): 873-86.

Hefley, James C., and Marti Hefley. *Uncle Cam: The Story of William Cameron Townsend, Founder of the Wycliffe Bible Translators and the Summer Institute of Linguistics.* Waco, Tex.: Word, 1974.

Heim, S. Mark. "The Path of a Liberal Pilgrim: A Theological Biography of Douglas Clyde Macintosh" (parts 1 and 2). *American Baptist Quarterly* 2 (1983): 236-55, and (1985): 300-320.

Hempton, David. *Methodism and People in British Society.* Stanford: Stanford University Press, 1984.

Herberg, Will. *Protestant, Catholic, and Jew.* Garden City, N.Y.: Doubleday, 1955.

Heslam, Peter. *Creating a Christian Worldview: Abraham Kuyper's Lectures on Calvinism.* Grand Rapids: Eerdmans; Carlisle: Paternoster, 1998.

Hiemstra, William L. "A History of Clinical Pastoral Training in the United States." *Reformed Review* 16 (May 1963): 30-47.

Hill, W. A. "Missions in the Theological Seminaries of the United States." *International Review of Missions* 23 (1934).

Hiltner, Seward. "The Heritage of Anton T. Boisen." *Pastoral Psychology* 16, no. 158 (Nov. 1965).

Hiltner, Seward, and Jesse H. Ziegler. "Clinical Pastoral Education and the Theological Schools." *Journal of Pastoral Care* 15, no. 3 (Fall 1961).

Himmelfarb, Gertrude. *Darwin and the Darwinian Revolution.* Chicago: Ivan Dee, 1996.

Hiscox, Edward Thurston. *The Standard Manual for Baptist Churches.* Philadelphia: American Baptist Publication Society, 1890.

Hoffecker, W. Andrew. *Piety and the Princeton Theologians — Archibald Alexander, Charles Hodge, and Benjamin Warfield.* Grand Rapids: Baker, 1981.

Hofstadter, Richard. *The Progressive Historians: Turner, Beard, and Parrington.* New York: Knopf, 1968.

Hogg, W. Richey. "Sixty-five Years in the Seminaries: A History of the Interseminary Movement." Privately published, 1945.

Holbrook, Clyde. *Religion: A Humanistic Field.* Englewood Cliffs, N.J.: Prentice-Hall, 1963.

———. "Why an Academy of Religion?" *Journal of Bible and Religion* 32 (1964); republished in *Journal of the American Academy of Religion* 39 (1991).

———. "The Lilly Study Challenge to College and Seminary." In "Theological Education." Special issue, *Journal of Bible and Religion* 34 (1966).

Homrighausen, E. G. "Brunner's *The Mediator.*" *Religion in Life,* 1935, pp. 296-304.

———. "The Salvation of Religious Education." *International Journal of Religious Education,* May 1939, pp. 12-13.

Hopkins, Charles Howard. *The Rise of the Social Gospel in American Protestantism.* New Haven: Yale University Press; London: Oxford University Press, H. Milford, 1940.

———. *History of the YMCA in North America.* New York: Association Press, 1951.

Horton, Isabelle. *High Adventure Life of Lucy Rider Meyer.* New York: Methodist Book Concern, 1928.

Hough, Joseph, and John B. Cobb. *Christian Identity and Theological Education.* Chico, Calif.: Scholars, 1985.

Hovey, G. R. *Alvah Hovey.* Philadelphia: Judson, 1928.

Howell, Mabel Katherine. *Women and the Kingdom: Fifty Years of Kingdom Building by the Women of the Methodist Episcopal Church, South, 1878-1928.* Nashville: Cokesbury Press, 1928.

Hudson, Winthrop. "Methodist Age in America." *Methodist History* 12 (1974): 2-15.

Hurst, John. *A Select and Classified Bibliography of Theology and General Religious Literature.* New York: Scribner, 1853.

Hutchison, William. "Modernism and Missions: The Liberal Search for an Exportable Christianity." In *The Missionary Enterprise in China and America,* edited by John K. Fairbanks. Cambridge: Harvard University Press, 1974.

———. *The Modernist Impulse in American Protestantism.* Cambridge: Harvard University Press, 1976.

———. *Errand to the World: American Protestant Thought and Foreign Missions.* Chicago: University of Chicago Press, 1987.

———, ed. *Between the Times: The Travail of the Protestant Establishment in America, 1900-1960.* Cambridge, U.K., and New York: Cambridge University Press, 1989.

Hyde, William DeWitt. "Impending Paganism in New England." *Forum,* 1892.

Hyland, Jack. *Evangelism's First Modern Media Star: The Life of Reverend Bill Stidger.* New York: Cooper Square Press, 2002.

Hyslop, Ralph Douglas. "The Right Men for the Ministry." *Religious Education* 40 (1945): 3-7.

Illick, Joseph E., III. "The Reception of Darwinism at the Theological Seminary and the College at Princeton, New Jersey." *Journal of the Presbyterian Historical Society* 38 (1960): 152-65, 234-43.

Inauguration of Don Wendell Holter as President of the National Methodist Theological Seminary, The. Kansas City, Mo., n.d.

Ingram, O. Kelly, and Robert M. Colver. "Notes on the Graduating Classes of 1958-1967 of Duke Divinity School and Southeastern Baptist Theological Seminary." *Duke Divinity Review* 36, no. 2 (1971): 100-111.

"In Memoriam: Edward Howell Roberts, Minute of the Board of Trustees." *Princeton Seminary Bulletin* 48 (1955): 30-32.

Interchurch World Movement of North America. *World Survey.* New York: Interchurch Press, 1920.

Ivory, Luther D. *Toward a Theology of Radical Involvement: The Theological Legacy of Martin Luther King, Jr.* Nashville: Abingdon, 1997.

Jackson, Kenneth T. *Crabgrass Frontier: The Suburbanization of the United States.* New York and Oxford: Oxford University Press, 1985.

James, William. *Talks to Teachers on Psychology: And to Students on Some of Life's Ideals.* New York: H. Holt, 1907.

Jewett, Paul King. *Emil Brunner's Concept of Revelation.* London: James Clark, 1954.

Jones, Howard Mumford. *The Age of Energy: Varieties of American Experience, 1865-1915.* New York: Viking Press, 1971.

Jones, Thomas Jesse. *Negro Education: A Study of the Private and Higher Schools for Colored People in the United States.* U.S. Bureau of Education Bulletin 1916, no. 38-39. Washington, 1917.

Judy, Marvin. *From Ivy Tower to Village Spire.* Dallas: Southern Methodist University Press, 1984.

Juster, Susan, and Lisa MacFarlane. *A Mighty Baptism: Race, Gender, and the Creation of American Protestantism.* Ithaca, N.Y., and London: Cornell University Press, 1996.

Kegley, Charles, and Robert Bretall, eds. *Reinhold Niebuhr: His Religious, Social, and Political Thought.* New York: Macmillan, 1956.

Kelly, Balmer. "No Ism but Biblicism: Biblical Studies at Union Theological Seminary." *American Presbyterianism* 66 (1988).

Kelly, Robert L. *Theological Education in America: A Study of One Hundred Sixty-One Theological Schools in the United States and Canada.* Foreword by Rt. Rev. Charles Henry Brent. New York: George H. Duran, 1924.

Kelsey, David. *To Understand God Truly: What's Theological about a Theological School.* Louisville: Westminster John Knox, 1992.

Kennedy, William Bean. "The Genesis and Development of the Christian Faith and Life Series." Ph.D. diss., Yale University, 1957.

———. "Neo-orthodoxy Goes to Sunday School: The Christian Faith and Life Curriculum." *Journal of Presbyterian History* 58 (Winter 1980): 326-70.

Kent, Charles Foster. *A History of the Hebrew People from the Division of the Kingdom to the Fall of Jerusalem in 586 B.C.* 6th ed. New York: Scribner, 1897.

———. *A History of the Jewish People during the Babylonian, Persian, and Greek Periods.* 3rd ed. New York: Scribner, 1899.

———. *The Founders and Rulers of United Israel: From the Death of Moses to the Division of the Hebrew Kingdom.* New York: Scribner, 1908.

———. *Biblical Geography and History.* New York: Scribner, 1911.

———. "The Undergraduate Courses in Religion at Tax Supported Colleges and Universities of America." *Bulletin of the National Council on Religion and Education*, 1924, pp. 1-34.

Kerr, Hugh, ed. *Sons of the Prophets: Leaders in Protestantism from Princeton Seminary.* Princeton: Princeton University Press, 1963.

Kim, Younglae. *Broken Knowledge: The Sway of the Scientific and Scholarly Ideal at Union Theological Seminary in New York, 1887-1926.* Lanham, Md.: University Press of America, 1997.

Kimmel, Michael. *Manhood in America: A Cultural History.* New York: Free Press, 1996.

Kingley, Florence Morse. *The Life of Henry Fowle Durant, Founder of Wellesley College.* New York: Century, 1924.

Kling, David. "Newman Smyth." In *Dictionary of Heresy Trials in American Christianity*, edited by George H. Shriver. Westport, Conn.: Greenwood Press, 1997.

Klotz, John W. *Light for Our World: Essays Commemorating the 150th Anniversary of Concordia Seminary.* St. Louis: Concordia, 1965.

K'Meyer, Tracy Elaine. *Interracialism and Christian Community in the Postwar South: The Story of Koinonia Farm.* Charlottesville: University Press of Virginia, 1997.

Knudson, Albert C. "German Fundamentalism." *Christian Century*, June 14, 1928, p. 762.

Kraemer, H. *The Christian Message in a Non-Christian World.* London: Edinburgh House Press, for the International Missionary Council, 1938.

Krivoshey, Robert Martin. "Going through the Eye of the Needle: The Life of Oilman Fundamentalist, Lyman Steward, 1840-1923." Ph.D. diss., University of Chicago, 1973.

Kuklick, Bruce. *The Rise of American Philosophy: Cambridge, Massachusetts, 1860-1930.* New Haven and London: Yale University Press, 1977.

———. *Puritans in Babylon: The Ancient Near East and American Intellectual Life, 1880-1930.* Princeton: Princeton University Press, 1996.

———. *A History of Philosophy in America, 1700-2000.* Oxford: Clarendon, 2001.

Langford, Thomas A. *Practical Divinity: Theology in the Wesleyan Tradition.* Nashville: Abingdon, 1963.

———. *Wesleyan Theology: A Sourcebook.* Durham, N.C.: Labyrinth, 1994.

Lassiter, Valentino. *Martin Luther King in the African American Preaching Tradition.* Cleveland: Pilgrim Press, 2001.

Latourette, Kenneth Scott. *A History of the Expansion of Christianity.* New York: Harper, 1937-45.

———. *Beyond the Ranges: An Autobiography.* Grand Rapids: Eerdmans, 1967.

Lawrence, William. *Memories of a Happy Life.* Boston and New York: Houghton Mifflin, 1926.

Laymen's Foreign Missions Inquiry, Commission of Appraisal. *Re-thinking Missions: A*

Laymen's Inquiry after One Hundred Years. William Hocking, chairman. New York: Harper and Brothers, 1932.

Levine, David O. *The American College and the Culture of Aspiration, 1915-1940.* Ithaca, N.Y.: Cornell University Press, 1986.

Lincoln, C. Eric, ed. *The Negro Church in America* [by] E. Franklin Frazier; *The Black Church since Frazier* [by] C. Eric Lincoln. New York: Schocken, 1974.

Lindsell, Harold. *Park Street Prophet: A Life of Harold John Ockenga.* Wheaton, Ill.: Van Kampen Press, 1951.

Lipset, Seymour. "What Religious Revival?" *Columbia University Forum,* Winter 1958, pp. 17-21.

Little, Lawrence. "Religion Courses in Methodist Colleges." *Religious Education* 45 (1950): 25-30.

Livingston, David. *Darwin's Forgotten Defenders: The Encounter between Evangelical Theology and Evolutionary Thought.* Grand Rapids: Eerdmans, 1987.

Loetscher, Lefferts. *The Broadening Church: A Study of Theological Issues in the Presbyterian Church Since 1869.* Philadelphia: University of Pennsylvania Press, 1954.

Longfield, Bradley J. *The Presbyterian Controversy: Fundamentalists, Modernists, and Moderates.* New York: Oxford University Press, 1991.

Lucas, Christopher J. *American Higher Education.* New York: St. Martin's Press, 1994.

Lynd, Robert S., and Helen Merrell Lynd. *Middletown: A Study in Modern American Culture.* 1929. Reprint, New York: Harcourt Brace, 1957.

Lynn, Robert Wood. "The Harper Legacy: An Appreciation of Joseph Kitagawa." *Criterion* 24, no. 3 (1985).

Lynn, Robert Wood, and Elliot Wright. *The Big Little School: Sunday Child of American Protestantism.* New York: Harper and Row, 1971.

MacDonough, Giles. *Berlin: A Portrait of Its History, Politics, Architecture, and Society.* New York: St. Martin's Press, 1997.

Machen, J. Gresham. *Christianity and Liberalism.* New York: Macmillan, 1923; Grand Rapids: Eerdmans, 1946.

MacIntyre, Alasdair C. *After Virtue: A Study in Moral Theory.* Notre Dame, Ind.: University of Notre Dame Press, 1981.

Mackay, John. "Theology in Education." *Christian Century,* Apr. 25, 1951.

———. "Some Questions regarding Theological Education with Special Reference to Princeton Seminary." *Princeton Seminary Bulletin* 49 (Jan. 1956): 3-12.

Mackenzie, W. Douglas. *Christianity and the Progress of Man as Illustrated by Modern Missions.* London and Edinburgh: Oliphant Anderson and Ferrier, 1898.

———. *The Final Faith: A Statement of the Nature and Authority of Christianity as the Religion of the World.* New York: Macmillan, 1910.

———. "The Standardization of Theological Education." *Journal of the Religious Education Association* 6, no. 3 (Aug. 1911).

———. *Fundamental Qualifications of the Foreign Missionary: Being a Report Presented by President Mackenzie at the Second Annual Meeting of the Board of Missionary Preparation, Held in New York City, Dec. 16, 1912, and Issued in Pamphlet Form by Authority of the Board.* New York, n.d.

———. *The Kingdom of God and the League of Nations.* Hartford: Hartford Seminary Press, 1919.

———. "Letter from W. Mackenzie to Henry Foote." Feb. 13, 1923. Hartford Archives.

Macquery, Howard. *The Evolution of Man and of Christianity.* New ed. New York: D. Appleton and Co., 1891.

Madison, James H. "Reformers and the Rural Church, 1900-1950." *Journal of American History* 73 (Dec. 1986): 3, 645-68.

Maring, Norman. "Conservative but Progressive." In *What God Hath Wrought: Eastern's First Thirty-five Years,* edited by Gilbert Lee Guffin. Chicago: Judson, 1960.

Marsden, George M. *The Evangelical Mind and the New School Presbyterian Experience: A Case Study of Thought and Theology in Nineteenth-Century America.* New Haven: Yale University Press, 1970.

———. *Fundamentalism and American Culture: The Shaping of Twentieth Century Evangelicalism, 1870-1925.* New York: Oxford University Press, 1980.

———. *Reforming Fundamentalism: Fuller Seminary and the New Evangelicalism.* Grand Rapids: Eerdmans, 1987.

———. "Why No Major Evangelical University? The Loss and Recovery of Evangelical Advanced Scholarship." In *Making Higher Education Christian: The History and Mission of Evangelical Colleges in America,* edited by Joel Carpenter and Kenneth W. Shipps. St. Paul, Minn.: Christian University Press; Grand Rapids: Eerdmans, 1987.

———. *The Soul of the American University: From Protestant Establishment to Established Nonbelief.* New York: Oxford University Press, 1994.

Marsh, W. Eugene. "Biblical Theology, Authority and the Presbyterians." *Journal of Presbyterian History* 59 (1981): 113-30.

Martin, Albro. *Railroads Triumphant.* New York: Oxford University Press, 1992.

Marty, Martin E. *The New Shape of American Religion.* New York: Harper and Row, 1958.

———. "Rating Welch's Ratings." *Christian Century,* Feb. 2, 1972, p. 5.

———. "Reinhold Niebuhr, Public Theology and the American Experience." In *The Legacy of Reinhold Niebuhr,* edited by Nathan Scott. Chicago: University of Chicago Press, 1974.

———. "Joseph Kitagawa, the Harper Tradition, and the Divinity School." *Criterion* 24 (1985): 12.

———. *Modern American Religion.* Vol. 1, *The Irony of It All, 1893-1919.* Chicago: University of Chicago Press, 1986.

———. *Modern American Religion.* Vol. 2, *The Noise of Conflict, 1919-1941.* Chicago: University of Chicago Press, 1991.

———. *Modern American Religion.* Vol. 3, *Under God, Indivisible, 1941-1960.* Chicago: University of Chicago Press, 1996.

Massa, Mark Stephen. *Charles Augustus Briggs and the Crisis of Historical Criticism.* Minneapolis: Fortress, 1990.

Mathews, R. Arthur. *Towers Pointing Upward.* Columbia, S.C.: Columbia Bible College, 1973.

Mathews, Shailer. *Scientific Management in the Churches.* Chicago: University of Chicago Press, 1912.

———. *Patriotism and Religion.* New York: Macmillan, 1918.

———. *The Faith of Modernism.* New York: Macmillan, 1924.

———. *New Faith for Old: An Autobiography.* New York: Macmillan, 1936.

Matthew, Arthur H. *Standing Up, Standing Together: The Emergence of the National Association of Evangelicals.* Carol Stream, Ill.: National Association of Evangelicals, 1992.

Matthews, Merrill, Jr. "Robert Lewis Dabney and Conservative Thought in the Nineteenth Century South: A Study in the History of Ideas." Ph.D. diss., University of Texas, Dallas, 1989.

May, Henry. *The Loss of American Innocence.* Chicago: Quadrangle Books, 1964.

Mays, Benjamin E. *Seeking to Be Christian in Race Relations.* New York: Friendship Press, 1957.

———. *The Negro's God as Reflected in His Literature.* Boston: Chapman and Grimes, 1938; New York: Russell and Russell, 1968.

———. *Born to Rebel: An Autobiography.* New York: Scribner, 1971.

Mays, Benjamin E., and Joseph Nicholson. *The Negro's Church.* New York: Institute of Social and Religious Research, 1933.

McAllister, J. Gray. *The Life and Letters of Walter Moore.* Richmond: Union Theological Seminary, 1939.

McBeth, Leon. *Women in Baptist Life.* Nashville: Broadman, 1979.

McClelland, Charles E. *State, Society, and University in Germany, 1700 to 1914.* Cambridge and New York: Cambridge University Press, 1980.

McCord, James. "Financing Theological Education." *Christian Century* 88 (Jan 27, 1971): 106-7.

McCulloh, Gerald O. *Ministerial Education in the Methodist Movement.* Nashville: United Methodist Board of Higher Education and Ministry, Division of Ordained Ministry, 1980.

McDowell, Paul Patrick. *The Social Gospel in the South: The Woman's Home Mission Movement in the Methodist Episcopal Church, South, 1886-1939.* Baton Rouge: Louisiana State University Press, 1982.

McFarland, John T., Benjamin S. Winchester, R. Douglas Fraser, and James Williams Butcher. *The Encyclopedia of Sunday Schools and Religious Education: Giving a World-Wide View of the History and Progress of the Sunday School and the Development of Religious Education Complete in Three Royal Octavo Volumes.* New York: Thomas Nelson and Sons, 1915.

McGiffert, A. C., Jr. *No Ivory Tower: The Story of the Chicago Theological Seminary.* Chicago: Chicago Theological Seminary, 1965.

McGrath, Alister. *Evangelicalism and the Future of Christianity.* Downers Grove, Ill.: InterVarsity, 1995.

McKim, Donald, ed. *How Karl Barth Changed My Mind.* Grand Rapids: Eerdmans, 1986.

McLean, J. L. "The Presidency of Theological Seminaries." *Bibliotheca Sacra* 58 (1901): 314-37.

McLoughlin, William G. "Professional Evangelism: The Social Significance of Religious Revivals Since 1865." Ph.D. diss., Harvard University, 1953.

———. *Modern Revivalism: From Charles Grandison Finney to Billy Graham.* New York: Ronald Press, 1959.

Meland, Bernard. "A Long Look at the Divinity School and Its Present Crisis." *Criterion* 1 (Summer 1962): 21-30.

Methodist Episcopal Church, South. "Report on the Committee on Education." *Journal of the General Conference,* 1870.

Methodist Episcopal Church, South, Minority Report. Committee on Education. 1870.

Meyer, Carl S. *Log Cabin to Luther Tower.* St. Louis: Concordia, 1965.

Mikelson, Thomas Jarl Sheppard. "The Negro's God in the Theology of Martin Luther King, Jr.: Social Community and Theological Discourse." Th.D. diss., Harvard University, 1988.

Miller, Keith D. *Voice of Deliverance: The Language of Martin Luther King and Its Sources.* New York: Free Press/Macmillan, 1992.

Miller, Samuel. "The Future of Theological Training." *Harvard Divinity Bulletin* 24 (Apr. 1960): 1-8.

Mills, Frederick V., Sr. "Alexander Winchell." In *Dictionary of Heresy Trials in American Christianity,* edited by George H. Shriver. Westport, Conn.: Greenwood Press, 1997.

Milton, C. Sernet. *Afro-American Religious History: A Documentary Witness.* Durham, N.C.: Duke University Press, 1985.

Mitchell, Hinckley. *For the Benefit of My Creditors.* Boston: Beacon Press, [1922].

Moehman, Conrad Henry. "How the Baptist University Planned for New York Was Built for Chicago." *Colgate Rochester Divinity School Bulletin* 9 (Feb. 1939): 119-34.

Mohler, Richard Albert. "Evangelical Theology and Karl Barth: Representative Models of Response." Ph.D. diss., Southern Baptist Theological Seminary, 1989.

Moore, Arthur. "The Lilly Study and the Theological Curriculum." In "Theological Education." Special issue, *Journal of Bible and Religion* 34 (1966).

Moore, George. "An Appreciation of Professor Toy." *American Journal of Semitic Languages and Literatures* 34 (Oct. 1919): 6-7.

———. "The Training of the Modern Minister: Address before the National Congregational Council." Hartford Seminary Record, 1907, p. 37.

Moore, James R. *The Post-Darwinian Controversies.* Cambridge: Cambridge University Press, 1979.

———. "Herbert Spencer's Henchmen: The Evolution of Protestant Liberals in Late Nineteenth Century America." In *Darwinism and Divinity,* edited by John Durant. Oxford: Basil Blackwell, 1985.

Moore, LeRoy, Jr. "The Rise of Theological Liberalism at the Rochester Theological Seminary, 1872-1928." Ph.D. diss., Claremont Graduate Schools, 1966.

Moore, R. Laurence. *Religious Outsiders and the Making of America.* New York: Oxford University Press, 1986.

Moore, Walter William. "The Preparation of the Modern Minister." In *Opportunities of the Christian Minister,* edited by John R. Mott. New York: YMCA, 1911.

Moorhead, James. *American Apocalypse: Yankee Protestants and the Civil War, 1860-1869.* New Haven: Yale University Press, 1978.

———. "Presbyterians and the Cult of Organizational Efficiency, 1870-1936." In *Reimagining Denominationalism: Interpretative Essays,* edited by Russell Richie and Bruce Mullin. New York: Oxford University Press, 1994.

———. *World without End: Mainstream American Protestant Visions of the Last Things, 1880-1925.* Bloomington: Indiana University Press, 1999.

———. "Engineering the Millennium: Kingdom Building in American Protestantism." *Princeton Seminary Bulletin* 15 (1994): 104-28.

Morone, James. *Hellfire Nation.* New Haven and London: Yale University Press, 2003.

Morse, H. N. *The Profession of the Ministry: Its Status and Problems.* New York: Interseminary Commission for Training the Rural Ministry. *Bulletin* 9, 1934.

Morse, H. N., and Edmund de S. Brunner. *The Town and Country Church in the United States.* New York: George Doran Co., 1923.

Moss, Arthur Bruce. "Something Old — Something New: The First Fifty Years of Northern Baptist Theological Seminary." *Foundations* 8 (Jan. 1965): 26-48.

Mueller, William. *A History of Southern Baptist Theological Seminary.* Nashville: Broadman, 1959.

Muilenberg, James. "Old Testament Scholarship: Fifty Years in Retrospect." *Journal of Biblical Research,* 1960, pp. 173-81.

Mulder, John, and Lee Wyatt. "The Predicament of Pluralism: The Study of Theology in Presbyterian Seminaries." In *The Pluralistic Vision: Presbyterians and Mainstream Protestant Education and Leadership,* edited by Milton J. Coalter, John M. Mulder, and Louis B. Weeks. Louisville: Westminster John Knox, 1992.

Myer, S. Reed, Jr. "After the Alliance: The Sociology of Religion in the United States from 1925-1949." *Sociological Analysis,* Fall 1982, pp. 189-204.

Nash, Dennison. "A Little Child Shall Lead Them: A Statistical Test of the Hypothesis That Children Were the Source of the American Religious Revival." *Journal for the Scientific Study of Religion* 7 (1968).

National Association of Biblical Instructors. "Preseminary Preparation and Study in Religion." *Journal of Bible and Religion* 27 (1959).

Nearing, Scott. *Social Religion: An Interpretation of Christianity in Terms of Modern Life.* New York: Macmillan, 1913.

Neely, Dixon McCater. *The President as Educator: A Study of the Seminary Presidency.* Atlanta: Scholars, 1996.

Nelson, Ronald. "Higher Criticism and the Westminster Confession: The Case of William Robertson Smith." *Christian Scholar's Review* 1 (1970): 5-18.

Nesmity, G. T. "The Problem of the Rural Community with Special Reference to the Rural Church." *American Journal of Sociology,* 1903.

Nettles, Thomas. "J. L. R. Scarborough: Public Figure." *Southwestern Journal of Theology* 25, no. 2 (Spring 1983): 24-42.

Niebuhr, H. Richard. *The Social Sources of Denominationalism.* New York: Henry Holt, 1929.

———. "Reformation: A Continuing Imperative." *Christian Century* 77 (Mar. 2, 1960).

Niebuhr, H. Richard, and Daniel Day Williams, eds. *Ministry in Historical Perspective.* San Francisco: Harper and Row, 1956, 1983.

Niebuhr, H. Richard, Daniel Day Williams, and James Gustafson. *The Purpose of the Church and Its Ministry.* New York: Harper and Row, 1956.

———. *The Advancement of Theological Education.* New York: Harper, 1957.

Niebuhr, Reinhold. "Karl Barth Apostle of the Absolute." *Christian Century,* Dec. 13, 1928.

Noll, Mark A. *The Princeton Theology, 1812-1921 — Scripture, Science, and Theological Method from Archibald Alexander to Benjamin Breckinridge Warfield.* Grand Rapids: Baker, 1983.

———. *Between Faith and Criticism: Evangelicalism, Scholarship, and the Bible in America.* San Francisco: Harper and Row, 1986.

———. *The Princeton Defense of Plenary Verbal Inspiration.* New York: Garland Press, 1988.

———. *The Scandal of the Evangelical Mind.* Grand Rapids: Eerdmans; Leicester, England: Inter-Varsity Press, 1994.

Norton, John K. "Education in the Depression." *Religious Education* 29 (Jan. 1934).

Norwood, Frederick A. *From Dawn to Midday at Garrett.* Evanston: Garrett Theological Seminary, 1978.

Nutt, Rick L. *The Whole Gospel for the Whole World: Sherwood Eddy and the American Protestant Mission.* Macon, Ga.: Mercer University Press, 1997.

———. *Many Lamps, One Light: Louisville Presbyterian Seminary; A 150th Anniversary History.* Grand Rapids and Cambridge: Eerdmans, 2002.

Palmer, Albert. "The Threat to the Christian Ministry." *Christian Century,* 1943.

Park, R. E. "Education in Its Relation to the Conflict and Fusion of Cultures: With Special Attention to the Problems of the Immigrant, the Negro, and Missions." *Publications of the American Sociological Society* 8 (1918).

Parker, Harris H. "The Union School of Religion, 1910-1929: Embers from the Fires of Progressivism." *Religious Education* 88, no. 4 (Fall 1991).

Patten, Simon N. *The Social Basis of Religion.* New York: Macmillan, 1911.

Paulsen, Friedrich. *The German Universities and University Study.* New York: Scribner, 1906.

Payne, Daniel A. *Recollections of Seventy Years.* New York: Arno Press, 1968.

———. *Annual Conference, 1853.* New York: Arno Press, 1972.

———. "The Christian Ministry: Its Moral and Intellectual Character." In *Sermons and Addresses, 1853-1891.* New York: Arno Press, 1972.

Peabody, Francis. "Social Reforms as Subjects of University Study." *Independent,* Jan. 14, 1887.

Pelikan, Jaroslav. "Karl Barth in America." *Christian Century* 79, no. 16 (Apr. 11, 1962): 451-52.

Perry, Edmund. "The Lilly Study: Challenge to College and Seminary." In "Theological Education." Special issue, *Journal of Bible and Religion* 34 (1966).

Perry, Lewis. *Intellectual Life in America: A History.* New York: F. Watts, 1984.

Peterson, George E. *The New England College in the Age of the University.* Amherst, Mass.: Amherst College Press, 1964.

Peterson, Stephen L. *A Steady Aim towards Completeness: The Day Missions Library Centennial Volume.* New Haven: Yale University Library, 1993.

Pierce, Richard D. "The Legal Aspects of the Andover Creed." *Church History* 15 (1946): 28-47.

Pierson, George Wilson. *Yale College: An Educational History, 1871-1921.* New Haven: Yale University Press, 1952.

Pinnock, Clark H. "Baptists and Biblical Authority." *Journal of the Evangelical Theological Society* 17 (Fall 1974): 193-205.

Piper, John F. *The American Churches in World War I.* Athens: Ohio University Press, 1985.

Pittinger, Norman. "Theological Students Today." *Christian Century* 84 (Apr. 26, 1967).

Pollock, John Charles. *A Foreign Devil in China: The Story of Dr. L. Nelson Bell, an American Surgeon in China.* Minneapolis: Published for the Billy Graham Association by World Wide Publications, 1971.

Porter, E. W. *Trinity and Duke, 1892-1926*. Durham, N.C.: Duke University Press, 1964.

Porterfield, Amanda. *The Transformation of American Religion: The Story of a Late Twentieth Century Awakening*. New York: Oxford University Press, 2001.

Potts, David B. "Social Ethics at Harvard, 1881-1931: A Study in Academic Activism." In *Social Sciences at Harvard, 1860-1920*, edited by Paul Buck. Cambridge: Harvard University Press, 1965.

Powell, Robert. *Fifty Years of Learning through Supervised Encounter with Living Human Documents*. New York: Association for Clinical Pastoral Education, 1975.

———. "The Helen Flanders Dunbar Memorial Lecture on Psychosomatic Medicine and Pastoral Care." Columbia Presbyterian Center, New York Presbyterian Hospital, 1999.

Preparation of Missionaries, The: The World Missionary Conference Report of Commission V; The Training of Teachers. London and Edinburgh: Oliphant, Anderson and Ferrier; New York: Fleming H. Revell, 1910. P. 160.

President's Commission on Higher Education. *Higher Education for American Democracy*. Washington, D.C.: Government Printing Office, 1947.

Primer, Ben. *Protestants and American Business Methods*. [Ann Arbor]: UMI Research Press, 1979.

Princeton Theological Seminary. *Semi-centennial Catalogue of the Theological Seminary, Princeton, New Jersey: from 1812-1862*. New York: John F. Trow, printer, 1862.

Proceedings Connected with the Semi-centennial Commemoration of the Professorship of Rev. Charles Hodge, D.D., LL.D.: in the Theological Seminary at Princeton, N.J., April 24, 1872. New York: A. D. F. Randolph and Co., 1872.

Pusey, Nathan. "A Faith for These Times." In *The Age of the Scholar*, by Nathan Pusey. Cambridge: Harvard University Press, 1963.

Putnam, Robert. "Bowling Alone: America's Declining Social Capital." *Journal of Democracy* 6 (Jan. 1995).

Ramsay, William M. *Four Modern Prophets: Walter Rauschenbusch, Martin Luther King, Jr., Gustavo Gutiérrez, Rosemary Radford Ruether*. Atlanta: John Knox, 1986.

Rankin, Robert. "Strengthening the Ministry." *Christian Century* 72, no. 11 (Apr. 27, 1955): 496-98.

Rauschenbusch, Walter. *Christianizing the Social Order*. New York: Macmillan, 1912.

———. "The Conservation of the Social Service Message." In *Messages of the Men and Religion Movement*, vol. 2, *Social Service*. New York: Association Press, 1912.

———. *A Theology for the Social Gospel*. 1917. Reprint, New York: Abingdon, 1960.

Reid, Daniel G., ed. *Dictionary of Christianity in America*. Downers Grove, Ill.: InterVarsity, 1990.

Reid, Ira De A. "The Church and Education for Negroes." In *Divine White Right: A Study of Race Segregation and Interracial Cooperation in Religious Organizations and Institutions in the United States*, by Trevor Bowen. New York and London: Harper and Brothers, published for the Institute of Social and Religious Research, 1934.

Religion among American Men. New York: Association Press, 1920.

"Report of the Committee Appointed in 1911 to Investigate the Preparation of Religious Education Teachers in Colleges and Universities." *Religious Education* 7 (Oct. 1912).

"Report of the Committee of Ninety-Seven." In *Messages of the Men and Religion Movement*, vol. 1, *Congress Addresses*. New York: Association Press, 1912.

Richardson, Harry V. *Dark Salvation: The Story of Methodism as It Developed among Blacks in America.* C. Eric Lincoln Series in Black Religion. Garden City, N.Y.: Doubleday, Anchor Press, 1976.

Richardson, Joe M. *Christian Reconstruction: The American Missionary Association and Southern Blacks, 1861-1890.* Athens: University of Georgia Press, 1986.

Ritchie, Russell, ed. *Reimagining Denominationalism.* Oxford: Oxford University Press, 1994.

Robbins, Jerry. "Robert Dabney: Old Princeton and Fundamentalism." Ph.D. diss., Florida State University, 1991.

Roberts, David E. "The Case of the Union Students." *Christian Century,* Oct. 30, 1940, pp. 1340-42.

———. "The Organization and the Individual." *Christianity and Crisis,* June 24, 1957.

Rogers, Jack B., and Donald K. McKim. *The Authority and Interpretation of the Bible: An Historical Approach.* San Francisco: Harper and Row, 1979.

Rogers, Max. "Charles Augustus Briggs: Conservative Heretic." Ph.D. diss., Columbia University, 1964.

Rogerson, John William. *Old Testament Criticism in the Nineteenth Century.* Philadelphia: Fortress, 1985.

———. *W. M. L. de Wette, Founder of Modern Biblical Criticism: An Intellectual Biography.* Sheffield: JSOT Press, 1992.

Rohr, John von. *The Shaping of American Congregationalism, 1620-1957.* Cleveland: Pilgrim Press, 1992.

Rolston, Holmes. *A Conservative Looks to Barth and Brunner.* Nashville: Cokesbury Press, 1933.

Romanowski, William D. "John Calvin Meets the Creature from the Black Lagoon: The Christian Reformed Church and the Movies, 1928-1966." *Christian Scholar's Review* 25 (Sept. 1967).

Root, E. Tallmadge. *State Federations.* Pamphlet. 1909.

Rosell, Garth M. "Finney's Contribution to Higher Education." *Fides et Historia* 25, no. 2 (Summer 1993).

Rotundo, Anthony. *American Manhood: Transformations in Masculinity from the Revolution to the Modern Era.* New York: Basic Books, 1993.

Rouse, Ruth, and Stephen Charles Neill, eds. *A History of the Ecumenical Movement.* Philadelphia: Westminster, 1968.

Rowe, Henry. *History of Andover Theological Seminary.* Newton, Mass.: [Andover-Newton Theological School?], 1933.

Rudnick, Milton H. *Fundamentalism and the Missouri Synod: A Historical Study of the Missouri Synod.* St. Louis: Concordia, 1966.

Rudolph, Frederick. *Curriculum: A History of the American Undergraduate Course of Study.* San Francisco: Jossey-Bass, 1977.

Runyan, William A. *Dr. Gray at Moody Bible Institute.* New York: Oxford University Press, 1935.

Russell, David Lee. "Coming to Grips with the Age of Reason: An Analysis of the New Evangelical Intellectual Agenda, 1942-1970." Ph.D. diss., Michigan State University, 1993.

Ryan, W. Carson. *Studies in Early Graduate Education: The Johns Hopkins, Clark University, the University of Chicago.* New York: Carnegie Foundation for the Advancement of Teaching, 1939.

Sandeen, Ernest Robert. *The Roots of Fundamentalism: British and American Millenarianism, 1800-1930.* Chicago: University of Chicago Press, 1970.

Santa Barbara Colloquy. "Religion within the Limits of Reason Alone." *Soundings* 71 (1988).

Saunders, Ernest W. "A Century of Service to American Biblical Scholarship." *Council on the Study of Religion* 11, no. 3 (June 1980): 69.

Scales, T. Laine. "All That Befits a Woman: The Education of Southern Baptist Women for Missions and Social Service at the Women's Missionary Union Training School, 1907-1926." Ph.D. diss., University of Kentucky, 1994.

Scarborough, Lee R. *A Modern School of the Prophets.* Nashville: Broadman, 1939.

Schaff, Philip. *A Companion to the Greek New Testament and the English Version.* New York: Harper and Brothers, 1885.

———. *A Documentary History of the American Committee on Bible Revision.* New York: The Committee, 1885.

———. *Theological Propaedeutic: A General Introduction to the Study of Theology, Exegetical, Historical, Systematic, and Practical, Including Encyclopaedia, Methodology, and Bibliography; A Manual for Students.* New York: Scribner, 1892-93.

———. *The Creeds of Christendom.* New York and London: Harper and Brothers [1919].

Schleiermacher, Friedrich. *Brief Outline.* Translated by William Farr. Reprint, American Theological Library, 1963.

Schlereth, Thomas J. *Victorian America: Transformations in Everyday Life.* New York: HarperCollins, 1991.

Schlesinger, Arthur. "A Crucial Period in American Religion." *Massachusetts History Society Proceedings* 64 (Oct. 1930–June 1932): 523-46.

Selden, William K. *Accreditation: A Struggle over Standards in Higher Education.* New York: Harper and Brothers, 1960.

———. *Princeton Theological Seminary: A Narrative History, 1812-1992.* Princeton: Princeton University Press, 1992.

Semmel, Bernard. *The Methodist Revolution.* New York: Basic Books, 1973.

Shaw, Yu Ming. *An American Missionary in China: John Leighton Stuart and Chinese-American Relations.* Cambridge: Harvard University Press, 1992.

Shirley, Timothy Wade. "J. P. Boyce and B. H. Carroll: Two Approaches to Baptist Theological Education." Th.M. thesis, Southern Baptist Theological Seminary, 1987.

Shriver, George H. *Philip Schaff: Christian Scholar and Ecumenical Prophet; Centennial Biography for the American Society of Church History.* Macon, Ga.: Mercer University Press, 1987.

Shurden, Walter. *Not a Silent People.* Nashville: Broadman, 1972.

Silva, William. "The Expression of Neo-Orthodoxy in American Protestantism, 1939-1960." Ph.D. diss., Yale University, 1988.

Sitzler, Gerald. *A Cautious Patriotism: The American Churches and the Second World War.* Chapel Hill: University of North Carolina Press, 1997.

Smith, Charles Spencer. *A History of the African Methodist Episcopal Church Being a Volume Supplemental to a History of the African Methodist Episcopal Church by Daniel Alexander Payne, DD, LLD, Late One of Its Bishops, Chronicling the Principal Events* in the Advance of the African Methodist Episcopal Church from 1856 to 1922.* Philadelphia: Book Concern of the AME Church, 1922.

Smith, Gary Scott. "Presbyterian and Methodist Education." In *Theological Education in the Evangelical Tradition,* edited by D. G. Hart and R. Albert Mohler, Jr. Grand Rapids: Baker, 1996.

Smith, H. Shelton. "George Albert Coe: Revaluer of All Values." *Religion in Life* 22 (1952): 40-57.

Smith, Jonathan Z. "Connections." *Journal of the American Academy of Religion* 56 (1990).

Smith, Timothy. *Revivalism and Social Reform in Mid-Nineteenth Century America.* Nashville: Abingdon, 1957.

Smyth, Newman. *Old Faiths in a New Light.* New York: Scribner, 1887.

———. *The Place of Death in Evolution.* New York: Scribner, 1897.

———. *Through Science to Faith.* New York: Scribner, 1902.

Soares, Theodore. "Practical Theology and Ministerial Efficiency." *American Journal of Theology* 16, no. 3 (July 1912): 426-43.

Stanley, J. Taylor. *A History of Black Congregational Christian Churches of the South.* New York: United Church Press, 1978.

Stark, Rodney, and Roger Finke. *Acts of Faith: Explaining the Human Side of Religion.* Berkeley: University of California Press, 2000.

Steven, Hugh. *Doorway to the World: The Mexico Years; The Memoirs of W. Cameron Townsend, 1934-1947.* Wheaton, Ill.: Harold Shaw, 1999.

Stevens, Abel. *History of American Methodism.* New York and Cincinnati: Methodist Book Concern, n.d.

Stevenson, Dwight Eshelman. *Lexington Theological Seminary, 1865-1965: The College of the Bible Century.* St. Louis: Bethany Press, 1964.

Stevenson, Louise. *Scholarly Means to Evangelical Ends: The New Haven Scholars and the Transformation of Higher Education in America, 1830-1890.* Baltimore: Johns Hopkins University Press, 1986.

Stilgoe, John. *Metropolitan Corridor: Railroads and the American Scene.* New Haven: Yale University Press, 1983.

Stimson, A. B. "Missionary Training Colleges." *Christian Alliance* 1 (May 1888).

Stout, Harry S. "From Confederacy to Civil Rights: Continuity in Southern Pulpit Rhetoric." This unpublished article noted the continuity between the language during and after the Civil War.

Stover, John. *American Railroads.* Chicago: University of Chicago Press, 1961; new ed., 1997.

Strauss, William, and Neil Howe. *Generations: The History of America's Future, 1584 to 2069.* New York: Morrow, 1991.

Strong, Josiah. *Our Country.* In *The Social Gospel: Religion and Reform in Changing America,* by Ronald C. White and C. Howard Hopkins. Philadelphia: Temple University Press, 1976.

Stuart, John Leighton. *Fifty Years in China: The Memoirs of John Leighton Stuart, Missionary and Ambassador.* New York: Random House, 1954.

Susman, Warren. *Culture as History: The Transformation of American Society in the Twentieth Century.* New York: Pantheon Books, 1984.

Sweet, Leonard. "The University of Chicago Revisited: The Modernization of Theology, 1890-1940." *Foundations* 22 (1979): 324-51.

Sweet, William Warren. *Methodism in American History.* New York and Cincinnati: Methodist Book Concern, 1938.

———. *Revivalism in America: Its Origin, Growth, and Decline.* New York: Scribner, 1944; Gloucester, Mass.: P. Smith, 1965.

Szasz, Ferenc Morton. *The Divided Mind of Protestant America, 1880-1930.* University: University of Alabama Press, 1982.

Tappan, Richard E. "The Dominance of Men in the Domain of Woman: The History of Four Protestant Church Training Schools, 1880-1918." Ed.D. diss., Temple University, 1979.

Taylor, Graham. "Sociological Training of the Ministry." In *Christianity Practically Applied,* vol. 2. New York: Barker and Taylor, 1894.

Taylor, Marion Ann. "The Old Testament in the Princeton School." Ph.D. diss., Yale University, 1988.

Templin, J. Alton. *An Intellectual History of the Iliff School of Theology: A Centennial Tribute, 1892-1992.* Denver: Iliff School of Theology, 1992.

Terry, Milton. *Biblical Hermeneutics: A Treatise on the Interpretation of the Old and New Testaments.* New York: Phillips and Hunt; Cincinnati: Cranston and Stowe, 1883.

Theological Training of Women, The. Hartford: Hartford Theological Seminary, 1892.

Tholuck, August. *Theological Encyclopaedia and Methodology.* [Andover, Mass.]: [Allen, Morrill, and Wardwell], 1844.

Thompson, Earl. "The Andover Liberals as Theological Educators." *Andover-Newton Quarterly* 8, no. 4 (1968).

Thompson, Ernest Trice. *Presbyterians in the South.* 3 vols. Richmond: John Knox, 1973.

Thorne, Phillip R. *Evangelicalism and Karl Barth: His Reception and Influence in North American Evangelical Theology.* Allison Park, Pa.: Pickwick, 1995.

Thornton, Edward. *Professional Education for Ministry: A History of Clinical Pastoral Education.* Nashville: Abingdon, 1970.

Tippen, Brian A. "A Historical Look at the Succession of Major Professors of Religious Education at Union Theological Seminary." *Religious Education* 88, no. 4 (1993): 503-22.

Toulouse, Mark G., and James O. Duke, eds. *Makers of Christian Theology in America.* Nashville: Abingdon, 1997.

Towne, Edgar. "A Single Minded Theologian: George Burman Foster." *Foundations* 20 (1977): 367-79.

Trachtenberg, Alan. *The Incorporation of America: Culture and Society in the Gilded Age.* New York: Hill and Wang, 1982.

Trollinger, William Vance. *God's Empire: William Bell Riley and Midwestern Fundamentalism.* Madison: University of Wisconsin Press, 1990.

Trotter, T. Thomas. "The Church's Stake in the Seminaries." *Christian Century* 89 (Feb. 2, 1972): 112-14.

Tucker, Ruth A., and Walter Liefeld. *Daughters of the Church.* Grand Rapids: Zondervan, 1987.

Tucker, William J. *My Generation: An Autobiographical Interpretation.* Boston: Houghton Mifflin, 1919.

Turner, Frank. *Victorian Faith in Crisis: Essays on Continuity and Change in Nineteenth Century Religious Belief.* New York and Palo Alto: Stanford University Press, 1990.

Uphaus, Willard E., and M. Teacue Hipps. "Undergraduate Courses in Religion at Denominational and Independent Colleges and Universities of America." *Bulletin of the National Council on Religion and Higher Education* 6 (1924).

Van Dusen, Henry Pitney. *What Is the Church Doing?* New York: Scribner, 1943.

———. "The Church Tomorrow: The Role of the Seminaries." Presidential Address. *American Association of Theological Schools Bulletin,* 1944, p. 29.

———. "Theological Students Today." *Union Seminary Quarterly Review,* 1959.

Van Til, Cornelius. *The New Modernism.* Philadelphia: Presbyterian and Reformed Press, 1946.

———. *Barthianism and Christianity.* Philadelphia: Presbyterian and Reformed Press, 1962.

———. *Karl Barth and Evangelicalism.* Philadelphia: Presbyterian and Reformed Press, 1964.

Veblen, Thorstein. *The Higher Education in America: A Memorandum on the Conduct of Universities by Business Men.* New York: Huebsch, 1918.

Veysey, Laurence. *The Emergence of the American University.* Chicago: University of Chicago Press, 1965.

Wacker, Grant. "The Holy Spirit and the Spirit of the Age in American Protestantism, 1880-1910." *Journal of American History* 72 (June 1985): 45-62.

———. "In the Beginning Was Finney . . . or Was It Bushnell? The Holy Spirit and the Spirit of the Age in American Protestantism, 1880-1901." Notre Dame Seminar in American Religion, Center for Continuing Education.

Wade, Louise. *Graham Taylor: Pioneer for Social Justice, 1851-1938.* Chicago: University of Chicago Press, 1964.

Walker, Clarence. *A Rock in a Weary Land: The African Methodist Episcopal Church during the Civil War and Reconstruction.* Baton Rouge: Louisiana State University Press, 1982.

Walker, Williston. *The Creeds and Platforms of Congregationalism.* Introduction by Elizabeth Nordbeck. New York: Pilgrim Press, 1991.

Wallace, Henry. "The Ideal Rural Civilization." In *Messages of the Men and Religion Movement,* vol. 6, *The Rural Church.* New York: Association Press, 1912.

Wallis, Ethel Emily, and Mary Angela Bennett. *Two Thousand Tongues to Go: The Story of the Wycliffe Bible Translators.* New York: Harper and Row, 1964.

Walsh, Andrew Harold. "For Our City's Welfare: Building a Protestant Establishment in Late Nineteenth Century Hartford." Ph.D. diss., Harvard University, 1996.

Walther, James Authur, ed. *Ever a Frontier: The Bicentennial History of the Pittsburgh Theological Seminary.* Grand Rapids: Eerdmans, 1994.

Ward, Frank G. "Religious Education in the Theological Seminaries." *Religious Education* 10 (1915): 278.

Wares, Alan Campbell, comp. *Bibliography of the Wycliffe Bible Translators.* Santa Ana, Calif.: Wycliffe Bible Translators, 1970.

Warfield, B. B. "The Improvement of Our Theological Seminaries." *Independent,* June 20, 1895.

———. "Our Seminary Curriculum." In B. B. Warfield, *Selected Shorter Writings,* edited by J. E. Mercer. Philadelphia: Presbyterian and Reformed Press, 1970.

Warner, Sam Bass. *Streetcar Suburbs: The Process of Growth in Boston.* Cambridge: Harvard University Press, 1978.

Warren, Heather A. *Reinhold Niebuhr and the Christian Realists.* Chicago: University of Chicago Press, 1997.

Warren, Palmer Behand. "An Introductory Survey of the Lay Training School Field." *Religious Education* 11 (1916).

Weaver, Rufus. "Life and Times of William Heth Whitsitt." *Review and Expositor* 37 (Apr. 1912): 159-84.

Weber, Jerry Dean. "To Strengthen and Develop Protestant Theological Education: John D. Rockefeller, Jr., and the Sealantic Fund." Ph.D. diss., University of Chicago, 1997.

Weber, Max. "Wissenschaft als Beruf." In *From Max Weber: Essays in Sociology,* translated and edited by H. H. Garth and C. Wright Mills. New York: Oxford University Press, 1977.

Weber, Timothy P. *Living in the Shadow of the Second Coming: American Premillennialism, 1875-1982.* Chicago: University of Chicago Press, 1987.

Weigle, Luther. "The War Time Service of the Yale University Divinity School." *Christian Education* 26 (1935): 107-12.

Welch, Claude. *Graduate Education in Religion: A Critical Appraisal.* Missoula: University of Montana Press, 1971.

Wells, Jonathan. *Charles Hodge's Critique of Darwinism: An Historical-Critical Analysis of Concepts Basic to the Nineteenth Century Debate.* Lewiston, N.Y.: Edwin Mellen Press, 1988.

Wentz, A. R. "A New Strategy for Theological Education." *Christian Education,* Apr. 1937.

Westerhoff, John H. *McGuffey and His Readers: Piety, Morality, and Education in Nineteenth-Century America.* Nashville: Abingdon, 1978.

White, Andrew Dickson. *A History of the Warfare of Science with Theology in Christendom.* 2 vols. New York: D. Appleton and Co., 1919.

White, Charles L. *A Century of Faith.* Philadelphia: Judson, 1932.

Whitsitt, William. *A Question in Baptist History.* Louisville: Charles A. Dearing, 1896.

Wiebe, Robert. *The Search for Order, 1877-1920.* New York: Hill and Wang, 1967.

Wigger, John H. *Taking Heaven by Storm: Methodism and the Rise of Popular Christianity in America.* New York: Oxford University Press, 1998.

Williams, Daniel Day. *The Andover Liberals: A Study in American Theology.* New York: Octagon Books, 1970.

Williamson, Harold, and Payton Wild. *Northwestern University: A History.* Evanston, Ill.: Northwestern University, 1975.

Wilson, Charles Reagan. *Baptized in Blood: The Religion of the Lost Cause.* Athens: University of Georgia Press, 1980.

Wilson, H. L. McGill. "On the Buildings of the Theological Seminary of the Presbyterian Church in the United States of America, 1817-1950." *Princeton Theological Seminary Bulletin* 43 (Winter 1950): 24-27.

Wilson, Warren. *The Church of the Open Country.* New York: Missionary Education Movement, 1911.

———. *The Church at the Center.* New York: Missionary Education Movement, 1914.

Wind, James P. *The Bible and the University: The Messianic Vision of William Rainey Harper.* Atlanta: Scholars, 1987.

Winter, Gibson. *The Suburban Captivity of the Churches: An Analysis of Protestant Responsibility in the Expanding Metropolis.* 1st ed. Garden City, N.Y.: Doubleday, 1961.

Worchester, Elwood, Samuel McComb, and Isadore H. Coriat. *Religion and Medicine, the Moral Control of Nervous Disorders.* New York: Moffat, Yard and Co., 1908.

World Missionary Conference. *The Report of Commission V: The Training of Teachers.* London and Edinburgh: Oliphant, Anderson and Ferrier; New York, Chicago, and Toronto: Fleming H. Revell Co., 1910.

Wright, G. E. "The Study of the Old Testament." In *Protestant Thought in the Twentieth Century,* edited by Arnold Nash. New York: Macmillan, 1951.

Xi, Lian. *The Conversion of Missionaries: Liberalism in American Protestant Missions in China, 1907-1932.* University Park: Pennsylvania State University Press, 1997.

Young, Warren Cameron. *Commit What You Have Heard: A History of Northern Baptist Theological Seminary, 1913-1988.* Wheaton, Ill.: Harold Shaw, 1988.

Younglae, Kim. *Broken Knowledge: The Sway of the Scientific and Scholarly Ideal at Union Theological Seminary in New York, 1887-1926.* Lanham, Md.: University Press of America, 1997.

Ziegler, Jesse. "Theological Education in a Changing Society." *Southwestern Journal of Theology* 9 (1967): 31-41.

———. "Theological Education as Professional Education." *Theological Education* 5 (Spring 1969): 139-302.

———. *ATS through Two Decades: Reflections on Theological Education, 1960-1980.* Vandalia, Ohio, 1984.

Index